21967

P9-DWT-490

EDITORIAL STAFF

G. MICHAEL McGINLEY, *MANAGING EDITOR*

JONATHAN ARETAKIS, *Editorial Assistant*

ELIZABETH ELSTON, *Assistant Editor*

JOHN F. FITZPATRICK, *Associate Editor*

SANDRA D. KNIGHT, *Editorial Secretary*

W. KIRK REYNOLDS, *Associate Editor*

STEVEN A. SAYRE, *Assistant Editor*

JOEL HONIG, *Associate Editor*

ELIZABETH I. WILSON, *Associate Editor*

HELEN CHUMBLEY, *Copyeditor*

WILLIAM H. FARICY, *Copyeditor*

NORMA FRANKEL, *Copyeditor*

EMILY GARLIN, *Proofreader*

WILLIAM M. HOFFMAN, *Copyeditor*

CAROL HOLMES, *Proofreader*

ELIZABETH C. HULICK, *Copyeditor*

MARCIA MERRYMAN-MEANS, *Copyeditor*

ANJU MAKHIJANI, *Production Manager*

NANCY NIEVES, *Production Assistant*

LIST OF SUBJECTS

Volume 5

vi

EUROPEAN WRITERS
The Romantic Century

JACQUES BARZUN
EDITOR

GEORGE STADE
EDITOR IN CHIEF

Volume 6

VICTOR HUGO

TO

THEODOR FONTANE

LIBRARY-MEDIA CENTER
SOUTH PUGET SOUND COMMUNITY COLLEGE
2011 MOTTMAN ROAD, S.W.
OLYMPIA, WA 98502

CHARLES SCRIBNER'S SONS / NEW YORK

Copyright © 1985 Charles Scribner's Sons

Library of Congress Cataloging in Publication Data
(Revised for volumes 5, 6, and 7)
Main entry under title:

European writers.

Vols. 5– . Jacques Barzun, editor; George Stade,
editor in chief.
Includes bibliographies.
Contents: v. 1–2. The Middle Ages and the
Renaissance: Prudentius to Medieval Drama. Petrarch to
Renaissance Short Fiction—v. 3–4. The Age of Reason
and the Enlightenment: René Descartes to Montesquieu.
Voltaire to André Chénier—v. 5–7. The Romantic
Century: Johann Wolfgang von Goethe to Alexander
Pushkin. Victor Hugo to Theodor Fontane. Charles
Baudelaire to The Well Made Play.
1. European literature—History and criticism—
Addresses, essays, lectures.   I. Jackson, W. T. H.
(William Thomas Hobdell), 1915– .   II. Stade, George.
III. Barzun, Jacques, 1907–
PN501.E9   1983   809′.894   83–16333
ISBN 0–684–16594–5 (v. 1–2)
ISBN 0–684–17914–8 (v. 3–4)
ISBN 0–684–17915–6 (v. 5–7)

Published simultaneously in Canada
by Collier Macmillan Canada, Inc.
Copyright under the Berne Convention.

All rights reserved. No part of this book
may be reproduced in any form without the
permission of Charles Scribner's Sons.

1 3 5 7 9 11 13 15 17 19   V/C   20 18 16 14 12 10 8 6 4 2

PRINTED IN THE UNITED STATES OF AMERICA

"Ivan Goncharov": Quotations from *Oblomov and His Creator: The Life and Art
of Ivan Goncharov* by Milton Ehre. Copyright © 1973 by Princeton University
Press. Material adapted by permission of Princeton University Press.

"Ivan Turgenev": The publisher gratefully acknowledges the permission
granted by Columbia University Press to reprint with editions *Ivan Turgenev*
by Charles Moser. Copyright © 1972 Columbia University Press. Originally
published as number 60 of the Columbia Essays on Modern Writers series.

The paper in this book meets the guidelines for permanence and durability of
the Committee on Production Guidelines for Book Longevity of the Council
on Library Resources.

LIST OF SUBJECTS

Volume 6

LIST OF SUBJECTS

Volume 7

LIST OF SUBJECTS

VICTOR HUGO
(1802–1885)

MANY WRITERS LEAD quiet, dull lives, at least as they appear to outside observers. Day after day they sit at their desks in a struggle to forge beauty out of the raw material of language. But there are others whose colorful careers make them the delight of their biographers. Among nineteenth-century French writers Victor Hugo stands out as one who was genuinely dedicated to creating enduring works of art and yet who was so active, in both his private life and the political arena, that he managed to remain constantly in the public eye. Indeed he became so famous and revered that when he died, more than a million people watched the funeral procession as it wound through the streets of Paris.

Victor Marie Hugo was born on 26 February 1802 in Besançon. As a child Hugo led an active and varied life. His father, Léopold-Sigisbert Hugo, who became a general in Bonaparte's army, was constantly on the move, and his family often traveled with him. When Victor was five, there was a brief stay in Naples, and in 1811 Victor found himself in Madrid, where he attended school with children of the Spanish nobility. In Madrid he first experienced the phenomenon of exile. For not only was he far from his native France, but he also became aware that the Spaniards, living under the puppet regime of Napoleon's brother Joseph, were in a sense exiles in their own land. This experience was to be more than just a childhood memory; nearly half a century later Hugo was destined to become a political exile as a protest against the regime of Napoleon III, who had seized power by means of a coup d'etat.

The stay in Spain lasted less than a year. By 1812 Hugo's mother (née Sophie Trébuchet) had separated from General Hugo and returned to Paris. Here she tried to bring order and stability to the lives of her three children (the two older sons, Abel and Eugène, were born in 1798 and 1800). Like the others, Victor received a middle-class education, and his mother hoped that he would go on to study law, the standard dream of nineteenth-century French bourgeois parents. General Hugo sent Victor and Eugène money so they could attend the university, but Victor was in no mood for such a placid existence. The story goes that at the age of fourteen he had declared, somewhat grandiloquently, "I want to be Chateaubriand or nothing," referring to France's greatest author of the time. Instead of attending law classes, he and his brothers founded the literary review *Conservateur littéraire* (Literary Conservative; 1819–1821). Victor worked hard to develop his ability as a poet, and his efforts were rewarded in 1819 when he won two prizes offered by the Academy of Toulouse. In those early years his political allegiance, thanks to his mother's influence, was to the restored monarchy, and so his prize-winning odes celebrated the return of the Bourbons after the downfall of Napoleon Bonaparte.

In that same year, 1819, Victor fell in love with a young woman named Adèle Foucher, but his ambitious mother forbade the match on the grounds that the Fouchers could not offer a sufficient dowry. When Sophie Hugo died in 1821, Hugo was left poor but also free of maternal restraint. He resumed courting Adèle and continued to write odes. There was nothing romantic about this verse, which was written in a neoclassical style full of shopworn rhetorical devices and archaic vocabulary. But these odes pleased Louis XVIII because of their royalist fervor, and the king granted his young supporter an annuity of twelve hundred francs. Now Hugo was in a position to support a wife, and in October 1822 he and Adèle were married. The young couple had five children, but only four of them survived infancy: Léopoldine (1824), Charles (1826), Francois-Victor (1828), and Adèle (1830).

Although Hugo was still quite young, his literary reputation developed rapidly, partly because he continued to produce works, both prose and poetry, that kept his name before the public, but even more because of the magic of his flamboyant personality. It was, and still is, the custom of France for writers to form *cénacles*, or literary coteries. As early as 1820 the authors who contributed to the *Conservateur littéraire* began meeting together. Other groups were formed in 1821, 1823, and 1824. Each time Hugo emerged as the leader. By 1827 the best of the young romantic artists and writers had gathered around him. Among them were the painters Louis Boulanger, the Deveria brothers (Achille and Eugène), and Eugène Delacroix; the poets Alfred de Musset and Alfred de Vigny; the prose writers Alexandre Dumas *père* and Prosper Mérimée; the musician Hector Berlioz; and the man who was destined to become one of France's foremost literary critics, Charles-Augustin Sainte-Beuve.

As leader of the young romantics, Hugo had by now abandoned the stilted neoclassicism of his early odes and was eager to transform French poetry, which had grown rather pale and sterile during the preceding century. He was not the first poet of his century to feel the need for change. Alphonse de Lamartine had already begun the process, developing the personal, melancholy side of French romanticism with his *Méditations poétiques* in 1820. But further innovation was needed. In 1826 Hugo wrote a series of ballads in which he experimented with more supple forms of versification. Instead of relying exclusively on the traditional six-, eight-, and twelve-syllable lines, he composed poems with lines of three and seven syllables, and in one ballad he even alternated and rhymed lines of eight and of one syllable. As for the content of these ballads, he showed no interest in repeating the quiet, intimate lyricism of Lamartine. Instead he turned to the colorful pageantry of the Middle Ages and celebrated an era when, at least as the romantics saw it, religious faith and personal honor were so strong that men were not afraid to die for their God or king.

Three years later Hugo published *Les orientales* (Poems of the Orient). The setting, North Africa and the Near East, and much of the subject matter, for example the Greek war of independence (which had begun in 1821), were different from that of the *Odes et ballades* of 1826; the inspiration, though, was similar. Again there were experiments in versification, and as in the *Ballades*, the subject matter was designed in the best romantic tradition to appeal to those who longed for cultures that scorned the cautious bourgeois attitudes of modern France. To the average Frenchman, the Near East conjured up visions of lands where no one was forced to shiver through a Parisian winter, where women were both innocent and ardent, and where passions could find their natural expression unhampered by prudence or restrictive laws. Even violent death appeared as an attractive fantasy in such a setting because, like passionate love, it could serve as a protest against the practicality of Western society. *Les orientales* exploited these fantasies of violent passions and sudden death in exotic cultures, and as a result the volume was avidly read and widely acclaimed.

Like poetry, the French theater of the early nineteenth century was in great need of renovation. Tragedies were still being written and produced in imitation of the seventeenth-century dramatists Pierre Corneille and Jean Racine, and especially of the neoclassical eighteenth-century theater of Voltaire. These plays were written in the traditional alexandrine, or twelve-syllable, verse, had five acts, and usually dealt with heroic figures from classical antiquity. They observed the unities of time (the action should take place within twenty-four hours) and place (within the same city if not the same place). Decorum was essential. Because the tone of the plays had to remain elevated, no mixture of lofty tragedy and ignoble farce was allowed, and it was considered improper for anyone to die onstage. But the dullness of this old-style theater inspired Hugo to proclaim the need for change. In 1827 he wrote *Cromwell* (a play so lengthy that it is rarely staged), in which he violated as many of the traditional rules of the French classical theater as possible. More important than the play, however, was its preface. In it he formally urged abolishing the sacrosanct unities of time and place, and he urged as well the mixing of the sublime and the grotesque, because, as he pointed out, a steady dose of the noble and elevated simply does not reflect the reality of human experience and, besides, it is very boring. This preface became a bible for the new romantic generation. As the poet Théophile Gautier wrote in *Histoire du romantisme* many years later: "It shone before us like the Tablets of the Law on Sinai."

If Hugo was already the leader of the romantic school, his dominance became absolute after the tumultuous success of his play *Hernani*, presented at the Théâtre Francais on 25 February 1830. *Hernani* practices what the preface to *Cromwell* preaches. The action spans a period of many months, and the setting moves from Saragossa in Spain to the mountains of Aragon to Aix-la-Chapelle in the Rhineland and back again to Spain. Hugo also mixed the soaring idealism and elevated language of the tragic mode with bits of low comedy (for example, the king of Spain, bent on seducing the heroine, hides in a closet to escape detection). Not even the unity of action is fully respected. On one level *Hernani* is a political drama in which Charles I, king of Spain, is elected Charles V of the Holy Roman Empire and learns that the best way to govern is by exercising clemency rather than by indulging in repression. On another level it is a tale of jealousy and love. The political outcast Hernani adores Doña Sol, betrothed to the aged Don Ruy Gómez de Silva. Their love ends tragically when, in order to save his honor, the hero must give up his life to the jealous old man; Doña Sol, refusing to live on after Hernani's death, commits suicide with him onstage in the final act. Other deviations from the classical norms of the theater lay in the use of less abstract vocabulary, in the intermingling of ordinary language with flights of lyricism, and in the frequent use of enjambment, or run-on lines. The conservative neoclassicists, alarmed by such radical ideas, banded together on the night of the play's first performance, intending to hiss *Hernani* off the stage. In this way, they reasoned, the upstart romantic drama—which they saw as hardly better than the melodramas played for the rabble in less prestigious theaters—might be crushed once and for all. But Hugo arranged to have his own troops planted in the audience, so that the premiere was a noisy and disputatious occasion. The romantics emerged victorious from the battle and went on to rule the Paris stage for another decade.

By 1830, then, Victor Hugo had become an enormously active and successful man of letters. To those around him he appeared strong, self-confident, and able to dominate any situation. But there was another side to Hugo, one that must be understood if we are to have any true knowledge of the man and any real appreciation of the depth and richness of his art. Under his impressive exterior Hugo was a man tortured by feelings of guilt, feelings so strong that they forced him to look inward, down into the dark world of his own unconscious. There he discovered a mysterious and menacing universe, inhabited by forces that threatened to erupt and overwhelm his outer or conscious personality. In a desperate effort to communicate to himself and to his readers something of the nature of this shadowy inner world, Hugo adopted the technique of concretizing these inner terrors through imagery. As an adolescent he had already stumbled on the metaphor he would use to dramatize the dangers that live hidden within the psyche. Translating a section of Vergil's *Aeneid* into French verse at the age of fifteen, he had written:

Là, dans un antre immense, au jour inaccessible,
Vivait l'affreux Cacus, noir géant, monstre
   horrible.

           (*Oeuvres poétiques*, 1.83)

There, in an immense cave, inaccessible to the
   light of day,
Lived dreadful Cacus, a black giant, a horrible
   monster.

As will become evident in the course of this essay, Hugo was to develop over the years many variations of this basic image of a monster hiding in the darkness, ready to leap upon any unsuspecting passerby.

What were Hugo's inner monsters? The first stemmed from his relationship with his father. When his parents separated, Hugo took his mother's side in the bitter dispute and rejected his father, only to learn later that General Hugo was not the ogre that he had believed him to be. By 1828, when his father died, Hugo had reestablished a friendly relationship with him. But the guilt over the earlier repudiation remained and appeared in

later years in works that dramatize an angry father taking vengeance on his son. This pattern manifests itself even at the theological level in *La fin de Satan* (*Satan Redeemed,* 1886), which begins with God—the ultimate father archetype—throwing Lucifer out of heaven and into hell for having rebelled.

Just as serious was the fact that Hugo felt responsible for his brother's insanity. By the age of seventeen Eugène had begun to show signs of emotional instability. When Victor proved to be a better poet in the days of the *Conservateur littéraire,* Eugène became irritable and jealous. More serious was their rivalry in love: both fell in love with Adèle Foucher. On the day Victor married Adèle, Eugène lost his reason completely; he soon had to be put in an institution, where he died in 1837. Hugo's sense of guilt was enormous, as shown by the recurring theme in his work of one brother being responsible for the death of another. In *Bug-Jargal* (1826), one of Hugo's early works of fiction, we find two men (one white, one black) who call each other "brother"; inadvertently the former is responsible for the death of the latter. The theme reappears in Hugo's dramas of the 1830's and 1840's, but it is nowhere more obvious than in the unfinished play *Les jumeaux* (The Twins) of 1837, which is based on the story of the Man in the Iron Mask: one royal brother has the other imprisoned in order to usurp his place on the throne. Nor was this theme limited to Hugo's playwriting. In his prose romance *Notre-Dame de Paris* (1831; normally translated as *The Hunchback of Notre Dame*), as well as in many later poetical works, there are numerous references to Cain's murdering his brother and his feeling enormous guilt.

As powerful as these two guilt complexes were, they were matched by yet another. Hugo's wife was an ordinary middle-class woman, but with the ardor of first love, young Victor had idolized her in the most extravagant terms, writing her letters full of such phrases as: "Adèle, who am I in comparison with you? Oh . . . I wish you were present because I'd kneel down before you as if you were a divinity." Victor refused to believe that she did not appreciate poetry (which she did not), because he seems to have felt that if one has a beautiful soul, then one *must* appreciate poetry. Inevitably Adèle's placid bourgeois temperament clashed with Hugo's soaring idealism, and her physical strength, weakened by numerous pregnancies, could not cope with Hugo's ardent sexuality. After some hesitation she found solace with a more gentle and less demanding friend of the family, Sainte-Beuve. In his turn, Hugo was unfaithful. In 1833 a beautiful young actress, Juliette Drouet, responded quickly to the poet's love, and they began a relationship that was to last until her death fifty years later. But Juliette alone could not satisfy Hugo's desires. In 1845 he was surprised—and embarrassed—when the police and an irate husband caught him in flagrante delicto. Later, in exile on the British Channel Islands, he seemed unable to keep away from the servant women of his establishment. For one who had preached the purity and transcendence of ideal love between man and woman, this intense carnality was frightening, particularly since, as he saw it, women had a power over him that he could not resist. In *Les travailleurs de la mer* (1866; usually translated as *The Toilers of the Sea*), Hugo's narrator concluded: "When a girl reaches sexual maturity, the angel in her vanishes," and she can be redeemed only by motherhood, which resanctifies her.

Hugo suffered intensely from three powerful and enduring sources of guilt, and reason and will alone could not, of course, remove them. Many years later he had even more reason to ponder the spectacle of consciousness and reason overpowered by the forces of the unconscious, because during the exile years his daughter Adèle went insane. Hugo summed up his concern in 1863 when he wrote a brief prose work entitled *Promontorium somnii*, whose very title reveals that we live on a "promontory" that looks out into the vast, unknown world of dreams. In this essay he creates a dramatic metaphor to warn of the dangers lurking in the inner darkness of the imagination:

> Who has not seen this horrible drama taking place in the tall grass? A junebug has flown around, buzzed, . . . bumped into walls, trees, and people. He has nibbled on branches where bits of greenery are to be found. . . . Suddenly from around a blade of grass, a monster rushes toward him. It is . . . an agile and splendid scarab beetle, all green and crimson, flame and gold, an armed jewel . . . with claws. . . . He pounces on the passerby . . . who has no chance to escape. The ferocious beetle opens the bug's belly, plunges his head then his upper body inside him, and devours him on the spot, eating him alive. His prey struggles, fights, strains with despair; he clutches at the blade of grass, pulls himself along, tries to flee, dragging the monster who is devouring him. In this way is a man seized by madness. There are dreamers who are this poor insect. . . . Their dream, dazzling and frightful, grabs them and destroys them.

And Hugo went on to comment: "A dreamer must be stronger than his dream" if he is to escape destruction. Hugo was no doubt thinking specifically of his brother and his daughter when he wrote this passage, but he knew that he too was far from immune. Perhaps his ability to exteriorize his guilt through writing saved him from the onslaught of his inner monsters.

Hugo was not alone among the romantics to have an intuitive awareness of the power of the unconscious. As Mary Wollstonecraft Shelley wrote of Mrs. Radcliffe in 1797 when reviewing her most recent Gothic romance, *The Italian*, the romantics as a whole had "an uncommon talent for exhibiting . . . the vague and horrid shapes which imagination bodies forth." In France, Charles Nodier had already written works exploring the world of nightmare and fantasy: *Smarra ou les démons de la nuit* (Smarra; or, The Demons of the Night, 1821) and *Trilby ou le lutin d'Argail* (Trilby; or, The Imp of Argail, 1822). In 1828 Hugo discovered the startling *Caprichos* (*Caprices*, 1799) of Francisco Goya, in which the Spanish artist dramatized with unforgettable vividness the monsters that appear when reason sleeps at night.

These and other artists and writers exercised some influence on the direction that Hugo's vision was taking, but Hugo's intense and enduring obsession with the "horrid shapes which imagination bodies forth" was more than just a case of literary influence. Faced with the need to deal with his unconscious, Hugo searched for an artistic medium that would be effective for exploring this hidden world. Although he believed that one could use prose, he decided that lyric poetry, closer to the seat of the emotions, was the ideal vehicle. As early as the preface to his first book of odes (1822) he had remarked: "The domain of poetry is unlimited. Under the real world, there exists an ideal world that reveals itself . . . to those who have been accustomed to see in things more than the things themselves." One of the *Orientales* develops this same idea that the poet is a seer, someone whose gaze can plunge beyond the limits of the "real" world: "Mes yeux plongeaient plus loin que le monde réel" ("Extase" ["Ecstasy"]).

Any encounter with the deepest inner mysteries of life is very likely to be a formidable experience. Hugo was very much aware of this fact, and in a poem of 1831, "La pente de la rêverie" ("Descent into Reverie"), he warned:

Amis, ne creusez pas vos chères rêveries;
Ne fouillez pas le sol de vos plaines fleuries;
Et, quand s'offre à vos yeux un océan qui dort,
Nagez à la surface ou jouez sur le bord,
Car la pensée est sombre! Une pente insensible
Va du monde réel à la sphère invisible;
La spirale est profonde, et quand on y descend,
Sans cesse se prolonge et va s'élargissant,
Et pour avoir touché quelque énigme fatale,
De ce voyage obscur souvent on revient pâle!

(1.1–10)

Friends, do not dig down into your most
  cherished reveries;
Do not go down beneath the flower-covered fields;
And when a tranquil ocean appears before your
  eyes,
Swim on the surface or play along the water's
  edge;
Because thought is dark! An imperceptible slope
Goes down from the real world to the invisible
  sphere;
The spiral goes deep, and when one goes down
  into it,
It keeps going on and widening out,
And because one has touched some deadly
  enigma,
One often returns pale from that dark voyage.

It was in the *Ballades* of 1826 that Hugo first began to develop the idea that the invisible world could be made concrete and visible through the magic of poetry. As he explained in his preface, he turned to the ballad form because it was a *capricieux* (whimsical) genre that lent itself to the telling of popular traditions, superstitions, and legends, a form that Hugo believed could capture the world of dreams. His technique, which developed and went beyond that of his precedessors François Réne de Chateaubriand and Lamartine, was to project the shapes of the inner world onto exterior nature, where they would assume the form of objects, vegetation, animals, and humans. These inner forces, concretized through metaphor, would then act out in the narrative sequence of the ballad the drama of the inner psyche.

One of the *Ballades*, a poem entitled "Les deux archers" ("The Two Archers"), is not considered one of Hugo's important creations, but it does provide an excellent example of Hugo's technique. The story has a vaguely medieval setting. One night two bowmen, who fear neither God nor man and who spend their lives carousing and blaspheming, are seized by Satan as they travel through a dark forest and killed. But their souls find no rest, and they are forced to "live" a demonic life each night until finally the stone statue of a saint comes to life and exorcises the demon. The next day the two men are found lying dead on the ground and are given proper burial. At the end the poet announces that he will not yield to the normal practice of our "vain age of science" and supply some abstract moral to the tale. He simply asks us to bow down before the miraculous. Since no obvious meaning is attached to the narrative, the ballad might appear to be no more than one of those apparently trivial pseudomedieval pieces frequently encountered in romantic literature. Nonetheless a meaning emerges, not from any conscious statement, but from the archetypal symbolism of setting, characters, and action. Night and the forest are age-old symbols of the unconscious, and in this dark world the conscious ego (the two bowmen) is powerless. The two archers represent Hugo's own consciousness, and like Hugo, who had repudiated his father, they have turned their backs on the ultimate father archetype, God. As a result they are tortured by the demon—that is, their guilt—until the father himself in his mercy—as represented by the statue of the saint—comes to their rescue and cleanses their souls.

Other good examples of this procedure can be found in *Les orientales*. We recall that overtly this poetry dealt with the Greek war of independence and the exoticism of the East. But if viewed in the light of the struggle between the rational and irrational forces of the psyche, many of these poems take on a richer meaning. A prime example is the well-known anthology piece "Les djinns" ("The Genies"). Set in some vague "Oriental" seacoast town, it tells of an Arab trembling before the aerial onslaught of a swarm of malevolent genies. Making use of the freer versification with which he had experimented in his *Ballades* (the poem opens with two-syllable lines, then rises, stanza by stanza, to a length of ten syllables, and then falls back to a final stanza whose lines are once again only two syllables), Hugo

describes the quiet town in the gray light of predawn. Then the evil genies come out of the semidarkness and attack the narrator's home. His dwelling is shaken but does not collapse, perhaps thanks to a prayer that the man offers up to the Prophet. Finally the genies fly away, leaving the man alone and the town once again peaceful. The pattern is one of initial order, followed by dangerous chaos, with order returning at the end. It is not too much to say that the poem reflects a man's consciousness and reason being assaulted by some evil that surges apparently out of nowhere. In this poem Hugo did not link the action specifically to his own life. There is nothing to indicate that the genies represent Eugène's insane jealousy attacking him or the poet's remorse over his brother's madness. But one can conclude that the poem does show an intense awareness of how the ego, symbolized by the man's house, can be threatened by destructive forces that lurk within.

The technique of fusing the inner and outer worlds by projecting psychic forces into concrete imagery found its most magnificent expression at this time in one of the world's literary masterpieces, *Notre-Dame de Paris*, whose title celebrates the famous cathedral in Paris. On the surface this lengthy prose romance appears purely exterior and far removed from the unconscious, as it treats the reader to a dazzling evocation of Paris in the late Middle Ages as the romantic generation imagined it. Hugo brought to life the wit and effervescence of students in the Latin Quarter, the pageantry of officialdom, and the sinister lair of the thieves and cutthroats who infested the city. Religion and politics play an important role, as is appropriate in a city dominated by the twin edifices of the Cathedral of Notre-Dame and the fortress-prison of the Bastille. Increasingly anticlerical and liberal, Hugo presents the Catholicism of the Middle Ages as superstition, condemning the power of a fanatical priesthood that could arrange to torture and sentence innocent people to death as witches. Equally hard on the monarchy, he attacks Louis XI for keeping political prisoners locked in cages for years in the Bastille; and with the knowledge of hindsight Hugo even has one of his characters anticipate the day in 1789 when the people will rebel against this oppressive system. Hugo was also trying to make an aesthetic point. In choosing to celebrate the grandeur of the medieval Gothic cathedrals, he was trying to mobilize public opinion in the hope that many ancient churches, abbeys, and abandoned castles could be saved from the builders, who were demolishing these old edifices in order to obtain cheap materials for their modern structures.

The story of *Notre-Dame* is as follows: Claude Frollo, the archdeacon of the Cathedral of Notre-Dame, is a solitary man who spends his time seeking to make gold by alchemy. His only family is a younger brother, Jehan, who is a happy-go-lucky adolescent, and the grotesque hunchback bell ringer of the cathedral, Quasimodo, whom Frollo had found years earlier abandoned as an infant near Notre-Dame and whom he had adopted as his son. The plot is set in motion when Claude Frollo becomes obsessed with a pretty gypsy, Esmeralda, who dances in the public square with a pet goat that performs "magic" tricks for the crowd in return for a few coins. To rid himself of her presence and his obsessive desire for her, and persuaded moreover that she is a witch, Frollo decides to have her tried for sorcery and executed. She is duly imprisoned and tortured until she "confesses" her guilt. But before she can be killed, she is saved by Quasimodo, who grabs her on the very steps of Notre-Dame and whisks her inside to sanctuary. His motive is that she had once befriended him when no one else would, so that now he adores her. Esmeralda, though herself virtuous and virginal, was brought up among the thieves of the city; in an effort to save her, they attack the cathedral one night. Unaware of their beneficent purpose, the hunchback fights them off (killing Frollo's younger

brother in the process) until the priest escapes with her. Still obsessed with her beauty, Frollo asks her to choose between him and the gallows. Esmeralda chooses the latter and is hanged. When Quasimodo learns of her fate, he finally turns on his master and pushes him off an upper walkway of Notre-Dame to his death. Quasimodo then dies in the charnel house, embracing Esmeralda's body.

When the book was published, some critics were fascinated by Hugo's knowledge of history and medieval customs. The reviewer for *La revue des deux mondes*, for instance, went so far as to exclaim that four men could have spent their entire lives researching the material and just barely managed to acquire it all. (Actually, Hugo used only a few secondary sources, to good advantage.) But it is a mistake to judge *Notre-Dame de Paris* from the standpoint of its historical erudition. Generally speaking, the details of history in romantic fiction do not constitute a goal in themselves; they are in fact a means to a different end. Unlike the later realistic novelists, who placed their characters in a very precise historical moment and forced them to face the social realities of their culture, French romantic writers, paradoxically, used history only in order to transcend it. They had no patience with the average person, who, they believed, lived only for three meals a day and a comfortable home, whereas they, a more sensitive and imaginative elite, sought a loftier ideal. Theirs was a quest for transcendence, and it led them to search for some absolute, whether in the form of God (among those romantics who retained their religious faith), or of a perfect love, or—among artists—of art. Even death became an absolute because it, like other absolutes, offered freedom from the tyranny of history and time. Time was the great enemy, because it reminded them that they were, after all, only finite human beings, and so could never really achieve the ultimate for which they longed. Thus if the romantics gloried in their differences—real or imagined— from most people, they also suffered because of them. They wondered why it was they who were singled out for the exquisite torment of seeing the ideal without being able to attain it. The only answer that seemed plausible was that some blind fate was at work in the universe and had chosen them as victims. At one time or another most of the major poets of the day dramatized in their work the power of fate.

Hugo too was preoccupied with the theme of fate. He believed that fate had selected him to bear painful personal burdens—the feelings of guilt discussed above—and that there was nothing he could do to avoid suffering. The feeling that there was no escape had appeared in certain earlier works, especially *Hernani,* in which a sense of doom hovers over the hero. Hernani feels accursed *(maudit);* no matter what course of action he chooses, disaster ultimately overtakes him. In *Notre-Dame de Paris* this theme is even more insistent. In the preface Hugo imagines that he has seen the Greek word for fatality *(Ananke)* carved into the wall on one of the inner stairways of the cathedral, and he concludes: "It is around this word that this book has been written." Fatality is not an abstract term here; rather it is closely linked to sexual obsession, a fact that no doubt determined Hugo's use of the image of the spider as his central organizing image.

Many cultures have used this image and given it varying interpretations, but because of the arachnid's ability to ensnare its unwary prey, it is frequently a symbol of the trapping power of female sexuality. The spider lies passively in wait until the victim comes within reach; then it pounces and envelops its prey, sucking out its vital fluids and leaving only an empty husk. Given Hugo's feeling that he could not escape the destructive lure of the female (and by 1831 he was already tempted to be unfaithful), it was not surprising that he would use the spider image to dramatize how easily a man can be ensnared by sexual desire. Of course the spider image cannot become dynamic if it stands alone: a predator needs a victim. Thus Hugo doubled his image by add- ing the figure of the hapless fly caught in the spider's web. The symbolism is further complicated by the fact that Hugo enriched the dual spider-fly motif by having it stand for any sexual obsession, regardless of whether the character is male or female. Ultimately, like the scarab beetle of *Promontorium somnii,* the motif becomes a symbol of fatality without sexual overtones. The present analysis includes only the two main characters, Esmeralda and Claude Frollo (for a detailed study, see my *Perilous Quest,* ch. 3).

Hugo first presents the central image and its interpretation when in a room up in the cathedral Claude Frollo gazes at the

big spider's web that stretched in front of the window. At that moment a foolish fly seeking the sunlight . . . flew into it and was caught. With the quivering of the web, the huge spider leaped from its central cell, bounded over to the fly, which it bent in two, while its hideous sucking tube burrowed into the fly's head. "Poor fly," said the king's attorney of the ecclesiastic court, and he reached forward to save it. The archdeacon, as if suddenly awakened, seized his arm violently: "Master Jacques, let fate alone!"

The symbolism is clear enough. As the fly, a symbol of the vulnerable human ego, heads toward the sunlight, its absolute, it is overpowered by the sudden appearance of the monstrous creature that has been lurking in the darkness, that is, in the depths of the unconscious.

The image is then directly applied to the characters. The archdeacon muses: "It flies, is happy . . . and seeks the springtime and the open air, but should it fly into the deadly rose window of the web, the spider appears. Poor dancing girl! Poor predestined fly! . . . It's fate. Alas, Claude, you are the spider." The appropriateness of the image is reinforced by the fact that the sunshine toward which Esmeralda flies is a dazzlingly handsome Captain Phoebus (who represents Apollo, the sun) and that the priest, like an arachnid, is always in black. In psychological terms, one might say that although Esmeralda appears on the surface to be innocence personified (she is often compared to the Virgin), she is very much subject to her unconscious drives. Although Captain Phoebus is stupid and insensitive and unworthy of her adulation, she loves him passionately and is quite prepared to let him make love to her with no thought of marriage; and at the end of the tale, her passion for him leads to her death. She can no more escape desire than can the priest.

But as Frollo is quick to realize, the spider-fly motif is reversible. He too is a fly seeking the sun, only his idea is the alchemist's gold: "You were flying toward knowledge, to the light, to the sun . . . in the broad daylight of eternal truth, and as you hastened toward the dazzling window that opens up onto another world . . . you did not see the spider web stretched out for you by destiny." Because Esmeralda is pretty, Hugo could not describe her as an ugly spider, but she acts out the role of a figure that suddenly emerges to torment its victim. She taunts Frollo until he screams, saying over and over to him: "It's Phoebus I love!" It is even possible to take Esmeralda's role in this scene one step farther and view her as a symbol not only of the fatality of sexual attraction but also of Frollo's inner feminine nature (or anima, to use the terminology of Jungian psychology). Frollo, who has spent all his time with books and chemicals, is a man given over to the worship of the intellect, and he is therefore completely out of touch with his own inner feminine. When a man's feminine side has been repressed and denied too long, it can turn destructive and lead him to his downfall, an outcome represented literally by Frollo's fall from the balcony of the cathedral at the story's end.

One of the most powerful episodes in the book goes beyond the spider-fly motif and dramatizes Hugo's awareness of the power—and the danger—of the entire unconscious. It appears early in the story, when a secondary character, Pierre Gringoire, a pleasant, rather sensible writer of dull allegorical dramas, is wandering alone in Paris after nightfall. Seeing Esmeralda, he follows her for no particular reason except that she is pretty, only to be led into a labyrinthine tangle of alleys in which he soon loses his bearings. Soon, vague shapes begin to take form around him. He becomes conscious of beggars of all kinds, many apparently blind and crippled, lurking in the darkness and asking for alms. They begin to swarm around him, "howling, yelping, all going every which way," and Gringoire, surrounded by these shapes, cannot turn back. They push him inexorably toward some dimly illuminated central point. He finds himself prisoner in the infamous Court of Miracles, the thieves' lair of fifteenth-century Paris, where he is quickly condemned to be hanged as an outsider. But suddenly the crowd gives way before the "pure and dazzling" Esmeralda, whose charm and beauty have always captivated the cutthroats among whom she lives. Although motivated only by pity, she agrees to marry Gringoire according to the customs of the thieves in order to save his life. Technically no longer an outsider, he is spared his life and the story continues.

Although this Court of Miracles actually existed and can be viewed in the novel as an excellent example of romantic "local color," it is of greater interest if understood in psychological terms. The episode in the court describes the process by which an overly rational man (or his mind) can be led little by little by the feminine part of his personality down into the labyrinth of his own unconscious, a world inhabited by all the shadowy aspects of his being that have been repressed. In this unfamiliar and even frightening world, the swarms of creatures whom Gringoire encounters are less people than nightmare shapes. One notes immediately that the thieves who lunge at him are greedy for gold and eager to kill just for the fun of it and that their vicious traits are precisely the opposite of those that the easygoing and likeable Gringoire shows in his conscious, or "daytime," life. They represent his own repressed, or "shadow," side—although pretending he can live happily in poverty, he would like money (he is flat broke) and would like to have the power to take vengeance on those who had made fun of a play that he had produced. In addition to these hidden aspects of his own personality, Gringoire comes up against a formidable father figure. These thieves have their own king, and he is the one who condemns the poet to death, just as Hugo imagined that his own father had condemned him. The Court of Miracles is truly a metaphor—almost an allegory—for the *under*-world where we keep hidden our worst desires and fears.

But it would be a mistake to assume that the unconscious is only a place of danger and that whatever has been repressed needs to be kept hidden. Modern depth psychology recognizes that the West has also repressed useful and even necessary traits of personality. This is especially true for people so given over to the rule of reason and logic ("masculine" traits) that they have ignored the riches that their inner feminine can provide. Of course, as we saw in the case of Frollo, the feminine can and will turn destructive if ignored too completely or for too long, but Gringoire has a less repressed personality than Frollo, and he enjoys the feminine when he finally meets it in the person of Esmeralda. After all, if Gringoire is saved in the Court of Miracles, it is because the very figure that led him into this hidden world, his elusive feminine, is also a presence and a power that can rescue him.

Esmeralda is not the first beneficent or consoling feminine figure to appear in Hugo's work. In one of the earlier *Ballades*, "Une fée" ("A Fairy"), he had written:

> J'aime, en un rêve sans effroi,
> Qu'une fée, au corps diaphane,
> Ainsi qu'une fleur qui se fane,
> Vienne pencher son front sur moi.
>
> (1.2–5)

I enjoy it when in a dream in which I have no sense of fear,
A fairy, with a diaphanous body,
Like a fading flower,
Comes and leans her forehead against me.

Like Esmeralda, who appears in the dreamlike world of the Court of Miracles, this fairy, too, appears in a dream, and her task is also to comfort and console. In addition to serving to counterbalance an excess of "masculine" reason, this ideal feminine figure in Hugo's works acts to offset the negative feminine (as symbolized by spiders and later, as we shall see, by an octopus). The luminous, angelic feminine figure will continue to make an appearance on occasion throughout the rest of the poet's work, and her function will remain the same: to lead, comfort, console, and at times rescue the beleaguered hero.

After *Notre-Dame de Paris* Hugo wrote a number of plays: *Le roi s'amuse* (*The King at Play*) in 1832, *Marie Tudor* and *Lucrèce Borgia* in 1833, and *Angélo, tyran de Padoue* (*Angelo, the Tyrant of Padua*) in 1835. Of these efforts, only *Le roi s'amuse* has survived, because Giuseppe Verdi borrowed its plot for his opera *Rigoletto* (1851). Otherwise it is fair to conclude that these are inferior works and need not detain us further. Of greater importance during the 1830's was Hugo's lyric poetry. In 1831 were published *Les feuilles d'automne* (*Autumn Leaves*), in 1835 *Les chants du crépuscule* (*Twilight Songs*), in 1837 *Les voix intérieures* (*Inner Voices*), and in 1840 *Les rayons et les ombres* (*Lights and Shadows*). These volumes are of very diverse inspiration, but they are dominated by the great romantic themes of nature, love, and death. To mention only two frequently anthologized poems, in "Passé" ("The Past," in *Les voix intérieures*) and "Tristesse d'Olympio" ("Olympio's Sorrow," in *Les rayons et les ombres*) the poet compares the idyllic past, with its passionate love affairs, to the sad present, in which nothing remains of a love that was once so beautiful. Only memory, the poet concludes sadly in the latter poem, rescues love from the inexorable passage of time.

Only a few of the poems in these four collections deal directly with the world of the unconscious. In addition to "La pente de la rêverie," mentioned earlier, another that has attracted the attention of modern critics is "A Albert Dürer" (from *Les voix intérieures*). In this poem the unconscious is symbolized neither by the labyrinthine streets of Paris nor by the ocean of "La pente de la rêverie" but by another traditional image, the one that he had used for "Les deux archers": the forest. Paying homage to the German artist, Hugo wrote:

Une forêt pour toi, c'est un monde hideux.
Le songe et le réel s'y mêlent tous les deux.
Là se penchent rêveurs les vieux pins, les grands
ormes
Dont les rameaux tordus font cent coudes
difformes,
Et dans ce groupe sombre agité par le vent,
Rien n'est tout à fait mort ni tout à fait vivant.

(1.13–18)

For you a forest is a hideous world
Where dream and reality intermingle.
There the old pines and the huge elms,
Whose twisted branches bend into a hundred
grotesque angles, lean over as they dream,
And in this dark group stirred by the wind,
Nothing is completely dead or completely alive.

The vision then becomes surrealistic as the dark roots of the trees slowly contract under the creeping brambles and the eyes of nightmare figures gleam from the depths of a cave. That this eerie forest of "A Albert Dürer" represents the human unconscious is suggested by another of the poems of *Les voix intérieures*, "Après une lecture de Dante" ("After a Reading of Dante"):

Quand le poète peint l'enfer, il peint sa vie.
Sa vie, ombre qui fuit de spectres poursuivie;
Forêt mystérieuse où ses pas effrayés
S'égarent à tâtons hors des chemins frayés;

Noir voyage obstrué de rencontres difformes;
Spirale aux bords douteux, aux profondeurs
énormes. . . .

(11.1–6)

When the poet paints hell, he paints his life;
His life, a shadow fleeing before pursuing
specters;
A mysterious forest where his frightened steps
Go astray as he gropes his way far from the beaten
path;
A dark, stormy struggle blocked by grotesque
encounters,
A spiral of uncertain contour and of enormous
depth.

The language at the end of the above quotation is similar to that of "La pente de la rêverie." It is perhaps no coincidence that these two poems were published the same year in which Hugo's brother Eugène died.

"Après une lecture de Dante" closes in surprising fashion, however. Hugo does not deny the dark reality of the unconscious, but he does warn Dante—that is, himself (as well as his reader)—not to become so obsessed with it that he loses contact with the rest of his life. He urges Dante to fix his gaze on the "serene" figure of his guide, Vergil, whose eyes are "full of light." Because light is a traditional symbol of reason, consciousness, and the outer world of day, the meaning becomes clear: Hugo is announcing his decision to turn away from the dangers of the inner depths and become active in the outer world.

Part of this outward-directed energy turned once again to the theater. In 1838 he wrote a very successful play, *Ruy Blas*, and in 1843 a much less successful one, *Les burgraves*. In fact the failure of the latter on the Paris stage (due to its implausible plot and overblown pseudoepic tone) has led historians of literature to designate 1843 as the close of the French romantic period. But Hugo's main activity in the exterior world after 1840 was social and political. He was elected to the French Academy in 1841 and elevated to the peerage four years later. One of his most cherished dreams was to play a role as a key political adviser to the constitutional monarchy. He linked his own political future with that of the liberal duke of Orléans (1810–1842), who would, he supposed, assume the throne upon the death of the reigning monarch, Louis Philippe. This hope was dashed when the duke died in a carriage accident, but Hugo continued to support the house of Orléans. Even after Louis Philippe's regime collapsed with the Revolution of 1848, Hugo still clung to his hope, proposing that the duchess of Orléans be declared regent. But the country was eager for real change and chose to establish the Second Republic. Because Hugo realized there was no future in supporting the house of Orléans, he presented himself as a candidate to the National Assembly and was elected as a deputy in June of that tumultuous year.

It may seem surprising to find Hugo interested in exercising political influence. After all, the French romantics as a group had generally considered themselves above the concerns of ordinary people. But during the 1830's and 1840's Hugo and many of the other romantics began to feel that as an elite they were in a position to do more than proclaim their suffering and their superior sensitivity. They came to believe that they had a responsibility to become leaders who could help France achieve a more noble destiny. Lamartine had already been elected to the Chamber of Deputies in 1833, and in 1848 he became for a few months the head of the provisional revolutionary government. George Sand, the champion of romantic love in her earlier novels, was busy in 1848 issuing socialist proclamations in favor of the new government. Even Vigny, by temperament something of a loner, ran for election during that year.

Hugo was more cautious in his revolutionary fervor than were some of his fellow writers, and in the months that followed the inauguration of the Second Republic, he steered a somewhat zigzag course down the middle of the political road. On the one hand he supported liberal measures that abolished imprisonment for debt, slavery in the colonies, and the death penalty for political offenses. But his liberalism had its limits. The new government created national workshops in an effort to give all who needed to work the opportunity to do so. To Hugo such a measure smacked too strongly of socialism, and he opposed it. At first Hugo had hoped that the new president of the republic, Louis Napoleon Bonaparte, elected in December 1848, would be a champion of moderate republicanism; and as he had done in the case of the house of Orléans, he tried to move near the president in order to play an influential role as an adviser. But soon this dream had to be abandoned. In July 1849 Hugo moved more to the left and broke with the new president and with the conservative majority in the Assembly over two issues. The first was public assistance to the poor. In a ringing speech to the Assembly, Hugo expressed his belief that poverty could be eliminated, that there was no need for those who could not help themselves to suffer needlessly. A second and equally serious matter was the Roman expedition. In 1848 Italian patriots had rebelled against the political power of the papacy. When a republic was declared, the French government sent a military expedition to Rome, ostensibly to keep the Austrians from interfering. But the expedition did not go there to defend political freedom. General Nicolas Charles Oudinot besieged Rome, defeated Giuseppe Garibaldi, occupied the Eternal City, and restored the temporal power of the papacy. By the time Louis Napoleon finally abandoned any pretense of democratic government and seized power in a coup d'etat on 2 December 1851, Hugo had become an outspoken member of the liberal opposition. Faced with imprisonment, he fled to Brussels. The Belgian authorities, eager to maintain cordial relations with Paris, soon urged the troublesome Hugo to leave, and so on 1 August 1852 he departed for the British Channel

Island of Jersey. He lived in Saint Helier until 1855, at which time he moved to the smaller island of Guernsey, where he resided with members of his family, the faithful Juliette housed nearby. (It was not until 1870, when the Second Empire was overthrown following the disaster of the Franco-Prussian War, that Hugo was willing to return to France, where he was triumphantly hailed as a living symbol of the republic.)

It first appeared that political protest would be Hugo's dominant activity in exile. In 1852 he published two violent attacks against the regime of the man who had assumed the title Napoleon III. The first was a brochure, *Napoléon-le-Petit* (*Napoleon the Little*, 1852), whose title recalls a famous remark that Hugo made in July 1851 on the floor of the Assembly: "What! because we have had a Napoleon the Great must we now have a Napoleon the Little?" The other volume was a book of satirical, even vituperative, poetry aimed at the new emperor and his cohorts. Entitled *Châtiments* (*Punishments*, 1853), it was naturally greatly admired by opponents of the Second Empire. But today, more than a century later, it only rarely captures the imagination of the reader, for whom such figures as Charles Morny, Eugène Rouher, Raymond Troplong, and a host of others in the imperial entourage are at best only vague names gathering dust in the archives of history. Nor does the modern reader, after Hitler and Stalin, find Napoleon III to be the epitome of evil in the world.

Fortunately for the twentieth century most of the literature that Hugo wrote in exile had a different inspiration, one that brought Hugo back to contemplating the unknown. By now he was no longer content to look inward. He had always been curious about that other unknown universe, the one that reaches out beyond the clouds into the depths of space. In "Soleils couchants" ("Sunsets") of 1831, the poet-narrator, meditating on clouds lit up by the setting sun, wondered whether there might be some ultimate secret hidden behind their beauty, and he urged anyone of sensitivity to try to peer behind the veils of nature ("Regardez à travers ses voiles"). During the years of exile this earlier passing thought became a compelling interest. Hugo now sought to become a visionary who could see beyond the limitations of life itself in order to penetrate the mysteries of the universe. As he put it, there were "two infinities," the ocean here below ("l'océan d'en bas"), by which he meant the real ocean (and which he also used as a metaphor for humanity's inner universe), and the ocean above ("l'océan d'en haut"), the sky, which if explored with visionary eyes might possibly yield the secrets of God.

The constant presence of the ocean surrounding the Channel Islands was without question a powerful stimulus to Hugo's imagination, but it was not the only one. Two major events in the poet's life played a vital role in forming his more cosmic orientation. In 1843 Hugo had been traveling on a vacation in the Pyrenees. On the return trip he happened to read in a newspaper that his daughter Léopoldine, recently married, and her husband, Charles Vacquerie, had drowned in a boating accident on the Seine. This tragedy was a terrible shock to Hugo: Léopoldine was his favorite child. In fact Hugo says—and we have no reason not to believe him—he almost lost his sanity as a result.

The other event was set in motion by the visit of an old friend, Delphine de Girardin. She arrived on Jersey in September 1853, bringing with her the new craze from Paris, table tipping. These séances seemed at first no more than a parlor game, and Hugo initially refused to participate. But when the table tapped out the information that his dead daughter was present (one tap for *A*, two for *B*, and so on), Hugo quickly became convinced that he could enter into contact with the mystery that lies beyond human life, and he became committed to the phenomenon. During these sessions he was able to communicate fleetingly with Léopoldine, and he held more

21967

extended discussions with great figures of the past, including Shakespeare, Dante, and the spirit of Christ.

The truth of what really transpired during these extraordinary sessions will never be known for certain, even though we possess transcipts of them. We may dismiss at once any thought of an elaborate hoax, although it is difficult to accept that there were genuine conversations with the supernatural. All the figures interrogated spoke perfect French, and more significantly, when Shakespeare spoke in verse, his style was identical with Hugo's own. Because Hugo was never the medium himself—his son Charles usually assumed that task—critics conjecture that by some telepathic means Hugo's deepest thoughts unconsciously influenced his son's handling of the table. Yet there remain aspects of the affair that are difficult to explain. It was during this period (1853–1855), for instance, that a local ghost called the White Lady ("la Dame blanche"), a woman who according to legend had murdered her child and was condemned to haunt the area, entered Hugo's life. Her spirit announced one evening through the table that she would visit Hugo at three o'clock in the morning, and at the precise hour the doorbell rang without any visible cause. On other occasions she made her presence felt with strange cries, and one night Hugo's two sons reported that she filled the living room with light, without the use of lamps.

Whatever may have been the substance of all this spiritualist activity, Hugo and the members of his family became so involved with table tipping that Madame Hugo, remembering the fate of Eugène, began to fear for the sanity of her daughter Adèle; she could also see that her husband was so preoccupied with the table that he seemed to be losing his interest in the everyday world. And later, when one of the participants in these sessions, a friend of the family named Jules Allix, lost his reason during a séance, everyone became frightened, and the sessions were perma-

nently suspended. But the impact of Léopoldine's death and of the spiritualist experience on Jersey, including the visitations of the White Lady, gave renewed impetus to Hugo's desire "to plunge beyond the limits of the real world."

The result was the publication in 1856 of a remarkable book of poetry, *Les contemplations.* Using the events of everyday life as a springboard, Hugo began his volume with poems celebrating the simple pleasures of life; but he quickly expanded this vision to explore those mysteries that lie outside the range of human consciousness. The opening poempreface indicates that he had not forgotten "La pente de la rêverie" of 1831. Once again taking the image of the ocean with its hidden marine life as a symbol of the unknown and what lurks within it, Hugo imagined that a voice, presumably that of God, was encouraging him to persevere on his visionary path:

> *Poète, tu fais bien! Poète au triste front,*
> *Tu rêves près des ondes,*
> *Et tu tires des mers bien des choses qui sont*
> *Sous les vagues profondes!*
>
> (11.9–12)

Poet, you are doing the right thing! Poet with the
  sad brow,
    By dreaming near the ocean,
You draw up from the sea many things that are to
  be found
    Beneath the deep waves!

Hugo was not one to be afraid to venture out from the water's edge and plunge beneath the surface. But the poem makes clear that the sea is not only a symbol of the individual unconscious. Hugo proceeds to equate it with God himself: "La mer, c'est le Seigneur" (The sea is the Lord), he concludes, a concept that leads to Hugo's intuition that the way "down" into the ocean and the way "up" into the heavens (that is, the way down into the unconscious and up to God) are in the last anal-

SOUTH PUGET SOUND LIBRARY

ysis identical quests. With this realization that the "ocean below" and the "ocean above" are no longer opposites, psychology and theology, the immanent and the transcendent, fuse into a single unitive vision that anticipates the insights of the depth psychologist Carl Jung and the theologian Paul Tillich in the twentieth century.

The work is carefully structured, being divided into two parts, "Autrefois" ("Formerly") and "Aujourd'hui" ("Today"), which are separated by the death of Léopoldine. The first part is itself subdivided into three books: "Aurore" ("Dawn"), "L'Âme en fleur" ("The Soul in Bloom"), and "Les luttes et les rêves" ("Struggles and Dreams"). As the titles of the first two books indicate, the emphasis in the earlier part is on the charm and innocence of youth and love. "Mes deux filles" ("My Two Daughters"), book 1, number 3, a brief portrait of Léopoldine and Adèle when they were eighteen and twelve respectively, is a good example:

> L'une pareille au cygne et l'autre à la colombe,
> Belles, et toutes deux joyeuses. . . .

> One like a swan and the other like a dove,
> Beautiful and both happy. . . .

Another early poem, book 2, number 10, inspired by Hugo's own amorous recollections of life as a younger man, begins:

> Mon bras pressait ta taille frêle
> Et souple comme le roseau;
> Ton sein palpitait comme l'aile
> D'un jeune oiseau.

> With my arm around your delicate waist,
> Supple as a reed;
> Your breast fluttered like the wing
> Of a young bird.

But even in these early books there are intimations that life has more depth than is immediately apparent. In "La fête chez Thérèse" ("The Party at Teresa's"), book 1, number 22, the reader is treated to the description of an elegant costume party, with the guests strolling through a charmingly maintained garden and then watching a play in an outdoor theater. But when day ends and night falls, couples leave the artificial world of manicured garden and theatrical stage and take refuge in the woods:

> Chacun se dispersa sous les profonds feuillages;
> Les folles en riant entraînèrent les sages;
> L'amante s'en alla dans l'ombre avec l'amant;
> Et, troublés comme on l'est en songe, vaguement,
> Ils sentaient par degrés se mêler à leur âme,
> À leurs discours secrets, à leurs regards de flamme,
> À leur coeur, à leurs sens, à leur molle raison,
> Le clair de lune bleu qui baignait l'horizon.
>
> (11.81–88)

Each went off under the heavy foliage;
The wild girls laughingly dragged off the more serious men,
Taking their lovers with them into the shadows;
And, disturbed as one is in a dream, vaguely,
They seemed little by little to take into their souls,
Into their private conversations and their passionate glances,
Into their hearts, their senses, and their weakened reason,
The blue moonlight that bathed the horizon.

Beyond the world of daylight, with its artifice and social conventions, lies the world of instinct, a place where nature's power reveals itself in its glory and without which life would be sterile indeed. And yet, as we have seen so often before in Hugo's work, this shadowy world is a place of danger. If in "La fête chez Thérèse" instincts and desire are presented as life-giving, Hugo is quick to remind his reader that evil is never very far away. After describing the glories of God's creation at night (book 1, number 4) the poet announces at the end: "Et, pendant ce temps-là, Satan, l'envieux, rêve'' (And meanwhile, Satan in his envy ponders).

In part 2—"Aujourd'hui"—the vision expands more fully, as Hugo, stunned by the death of his daugher, not only reveals his personal anguish in a poem like "A Villequier" (the name of the village where she was buried), but also seeks to reach out beyond the limitations of this world. The three divisions of this second section, "Pauca meae" ("A Few Songs," meaning some poems dedicated to his dead daughter), "En marche" ("On the Way"), and finally, "Au bord de l'infini" ("On the Edge of the Infinite"), reflect this progression from the personal to the cosmic by their very titles. One poem in *En marche*, "Pasteurs et troupeaux" ("Shepherds and Flocks"), is a perfect example of Hugo's desire to expand outward toward the infinite. It begins with deceptive simplicity: "Le vallon où je vais tous les jours est charmant" (The valley where I go every day is charming). In this idyllic setting complete with birds, flowers, and even a little pond, the poet sometimes meets a young shepherdess, who smiles at him. It is almost as if one were back among the idyllic poems of books 1 and 2. But daylight fades away, night falls, and "le pâtre promontoire" (the promontory shepherd), that is, the headland standing guard over the ocean, begins to dream as it listens to the endless noises of the night. It admires the beauty of the night, but if it sees in the moon rising over the sea a symbol of triumphant ascension, it is well aware that down below all is darkness as the "shadows tremble" and

> . . . l'âpre rafale
> Disperse à tous les vents avec son souffle amer
> La laine des moutons sinistres de la mer.

> . . . the harsh squalls
> Disperse with their bitter breath
> The wool of the sinister whitecaps [also "sheep,"
> a pun in French] of the sea.

The poem reveals a constant pattern of expansion from the finite to the infinite: from valley to headland, from pond to ocean, from day to night, and behind these images from the limited world of consciousness to the larger universe of dream and mystery.

The vision expands still further in "A la fenêtre, pendant la nuit" ("At the Window During the Night"), book 6, number 9. Here the ordinary world is barely mentioned as the poet meditates on the stars and what lies behind them. Musing on humanity's smalless and its ignorance of ultimate things, Hugo comes to no peaceful resolution of his cosmic anxiety. He warns the reader that the Creator is possibly a terrifying force, who may even now be changing the natural order that we think is so stable. He imagines that there is no reason to assume that God is not at this moment sending oceans of new constellations toward us, which will petrify us with fear and shake our very souls:

> Peut-être en ce moment, du fond des nuits
>   funèbres,
> Montant vers nous, gonflant ses vagues de
>   ténèbres
>   Et ses flots de rayons,
> Le muet Infini, sombre mer ignorée,
> Roule vers notre ciel une grande marée
>   De constellations!
>   (11.103–108)

> Perhaps at this moment, from the depths of the
>   funereal night,
> Coming up toward us, swelling its waves with
>   darkness and with light,
> Mute Infinity, a dark and unknown sea,
> Is rolling toward our own sky a huge tidal wave
>   Of constellations!

Except for an epilogue dedicated to his dead daughter, *Les contemplations* closes with a lengthy (786 lines) philosophical poem: "Ce que dit la bouche d'ombre" ("What the Mouth of Darkness Says"). In this poem-treatise Hugo repeats his warning that the universe is not only incomprehensible but dangerous; he even uses a cosmic variant of his spider image to communicate his feelings, describing "l'hydre Univers tordant son corps écaillé d'astres" (the hydra Universe twisting its body bespangled with stars). But if the universe is unfathomable in some ways, Hugo believes that it is comprehensible in moral terms. Accepting the idea that people undergo repeated incarnations in which the soul either rises to more celestial forms or sinks to even baser ones, Hugo announces that we have a choice in life and that to choose evil is to bring punishment upon oneself. Hugo hopes (11.781–782) that evil will ultimately disappear, that there will be no more tears, no more shackles, and no more mourning, but he has no intention of offering the reader easy comfort. The role of the poet is not to assure the average person that all is well; in fact in the very first book (number 28) he had made it clear that the poet must be like those beautiful green forests, full of love and the songs of birds, where one suddenly encounters a lion. Just as the poet had to face the fear of the unknown and his own inner darkness, so must the reader. As Hugo states in his prose preface: "Alas, when I speak to you about myself, I am speaking to you about yourself. Why can't you sense that? You are a fool if you think that I am not you."

The majestic achievement of *Les contemplations* would have been enough to crown a literary career, but Hugo scarcely paused in his labors. Many years earlier, when he first began to be directly concerned with the injustices that society inflicts upon the helpless, Hugo had written works of social protest. In 1829 had appeared *Le dernier jour d'un condamné (The Last Day of a Condemned Man)*, which attacked the death penalty; in 1834 *Claude Gueux*, which protested against inhuman prison conditions. These early efforts became the germ of a vast social novel, whose first version, *Les misères*, was written between 1845 and 1848, but which was later expanded and given greater depth and scope in 1861. Published in 1862 with the definitive title *Les misérables*, it quickly became world famous.

At the social level *Les misérables* inveighs against the cruelty of the penal system, society's refusal to treat ex-convicts with compassion, and the plight of unwed mothers. Jean Valjean, imprisoned for years first for having stolen a loaf of bread and again for trying to escape, is finally released from prison, only to be confronted by a hostile world. He becomes even more bitter than he had been before. But his negative attitude is changed by a worthy bishop, Monseigneur Myriel, from whom he steals valuable silver candlesticks and dishes. Arrested by the police, Jean Valjean is freed by the testimony of the prelate, who pretends that he had in fact given the silver to his overnight guest. After this episode Jean is a transformed. Although he breaks parole and disappears, he emerges as the compassionate Monsieur Madeleine and becomes the mayor of the town of Montreuil-sur-mer. He brings prosperity to the town and befriends the poor as best he can, but in order to save the life of an innocent man believed to be himself, he has to reveal his identity in court. Before he can be arrested for parole violation, he once again drops out of sight, tracked by an inflexible and fanatical policeman, Javert. Jean adopts a little girl, Cosette, daughter of an unwed mother who died in poverty, and the two find refuge in Paris, hiding out for a time in a convent. The years pass, and Cosette falls in love with Marius, who occupies the central role in the latter half of the novel. The son of a noble officer in Napoleon's army who had died at Waterloo, Marius is at first an ardent champion of Bonapartism. But he evolves politically until he is willing to risk his life for democracy during the Paris insurrection of 1832. Wounded at the barricades and facing certain death, he is saved by Jean Valjean, who carries him to safety through the sewers of Paris. At the end of the story Marius and Cosette marry, and Jean, now an old man, dies, his destiny fulfilled.

The story is far richer than a brief summary suggests. One section is devoted to the battle of Waterloo, and Hugo also explores the role of convents in the modern world, the dynamics of student political groups, and the jargon of hardened underworld thieves. These and other apparent digressions are not irrelevancies but are integral to the liberal political and social views expounded in *Les misérables*. Important as they are, they should not cause one to lose sight of the central theme. Jean Valjean's life and struggle for salvation are at the heart of the novel, and his battle is in a sense everyman's. Just as Valjean had hidden his true self and adopted a false identity, all human beings don masks, or personas, when faced with the difficulty of coping with the outer world. A persona is necessary if one is not to be overly vulnerable; but if one confuses the persona with the real self, growth is impossible and in time one becomes fixed and rigid. This is what happens to Javert, the policeman whose dedication to the word of the law ultimately dehumanizes him by making him inflexible. But in the case of Jean Valjean, it is a blessing that he is moved by events so that he cannot settle for the comfortable but limited life of a respected mayor but must set out to complete his own destiny.

Not coincidentally, Jean's quest for salvation involves him with the unconscious and its familiar symbols: a mysterious forest and a watery underworld. He meets Cosette by a well in a dark wood at night—his first encounter with the feminine. She brings a gentle, humanizing touch to his life that he had not known before. But as is true of any archetypal figure, she also represents a danger. As Cosette grows into womanhood, Jean develops a latent incestuous desire for her, and when she falls in love with Marius, Jean becomes violently jealous. But when he later saves Marius for Cosette by going down into the watery, excrement-filled sewers of Paris (that is, by showing a willingness to face the negative aspects of his own being), the episode becomes a metaphor dramatizing the idea that a descent into hell to confront one's own inner excrement is a necessary prelude to resurrection to a greater psychic wholeness.

Once again Hugo makes it clear that the descent into the waters is not without risk. In an extended metaphor he describes the horror experienced by a man who falls overboard at sea during a storm and who cries out in vain for help as he drowns. Hugo had not forgotten Eugène, Adèle, or Léopoldine. Despite the dangers of the quest, however, Jean proves to be a true hero by accepting the challenge and overcoming the perils. At one point he even permits himself to be buried alive in a coffin and then later unearthed so that he and Cosette can escape the stifling convent where they are safe but stagnating. In this episode of burial Hugo stresses intensely the idea that we must die to one life before emerging to the light of a new one. As Jean dies, in a section entitled "Nuit derrière laquelle il y a du jour" ("Ultimate Darkness, Ultimate Dawn"), he has fulfilled the mission reflected in the symbolism of his name. He is the Jean who had to go down into the valley of darkness (*val*, or valley) in order to become the true Jean that he was meant to be: Jean-Val-Jean. And as in *Les contemplations*, Hugo is not satisfied to let the readers be casual bystanders; he hopes that we will recognize ourselves in the anguish of his protagonist, yet he also hopes that we may in our own ways achieve our true identities.

During this same period Hugo continued to write poetry, and in 1859 he published the first series of another remarkable work. Entitled *La légende des siècles* (*Legends and Chronicles of the Ages*), it was amplified and filled out by two more series in 1877 and 1883. Hugo intended the work to be the epic of humanity, "the development of the human race over the centuries, mankind rising out of the shadows on its way to the ideal, the paradisiacal transfiguration of earthly hell, the slow, perfect coming to full bloom of freedom." *La légende* begins with a poem celebrating the earth and the tranquility of nature prior to humanity's appearance ("Hymne"); then in "Le sacre de la femme" ("The Consecration of Woman") it describes Eve's oneness with nature as she awaits the birth of her first child in Eden. However, humanity cannot exist in an atemporal paradise. History, with all its evil, comes into being, according to Hugo's "La conscience," not through Adam and Eve's disobedience but in Cain's act of killing his brother Abel.

Once evil has appeared, it expands and takes root everywhere. With the exception of a poem like "Booz endormi" ("Boaz Asleep"), most of the episodes (which describe the decline of the Roman Empire, the viciousness of Oriental potentates, and the barbarism of the Dark Ages) suggest that there may not be much hope for humanity. Evildoers loot and kill and would be entirely free from retribution were it not for some isolated noble patriarch or knight errant who rises to denounce their evil. Behind these men stands the austere figure of God himself, who reveals that in his good time evil will be conquered. Hugo's vision of future justice is based on the idea that evil is perpetuated by kings and priests and despots who have claimed to represent the divine and have succeeded in convincing credulous humanity that they are above mortal men. But the true Godhead knows that they are false gods and is eager for humanity to rebel against these petty figures who have usurped God's prerogatives and kept people in bondage on earth. This is the message of the key poem, "Le satyre," in which a satyr is summoned before the gods of Olympus and ordered to entertain them with his songs. The Olympian deities stand for all the cruel tyrants of the world, and the satyr is a symbol of humanity in its still partially bestial form ("made of slime and azure sky"). But as the beast sings, he becomes another of those divinely inspired figures who denounce the evil of those who oppress people. He prophesies that humanity will one day shed that part of its nature that is too earthy and, like a caterpillar transformed into a butterfly, take wing and become pure soul. Then false gods will no longer exist. As the satyr sings he grows in size and by the poem's end he has swelled to cosmic proportions. Then he orders Jupiter to get down on his knees before him.

Hugo's idealistic vision of the elimination of social evils is in accord with the eighteenth-century doctrine of progress, retained and developed further by many thinkers and writers of the nineteenth century. It was a belief that affirmed that people could eradicate evil and darkness both in themselves and in society, thus ushering in a twentieth century of peace and prosperity. As to how this might be accomplished, Hugo often expressed the faith, one that he shared with such other contemporary figures as the novelist George Sand and the historian Jules Michelet, that if anyone could lead France into a more beautiful future it was the common people ("le peuple"). Unlike the now irrelevant aristocracy and the greedy bourgeoisie, the common people, they believed, being closer to nature, had the energy and the good instincts that might well make them the hope of the world. In another poem of *La legende*, "Les pauvres gens" ("Poor Folks"), Hugo dramatized the paradox that those living on the edge of poverty are most likely to have compassion on the helpless and needy.

Yet Hugo remained uneasy about the people. If he idealized "le peuple," he also knew they could easily degenerate into a vicious rabble. The horrors of 1793 and 1794 were never far from his mind, and from time to time (both in *Notre-Dame de Paris* and in *Les misérables*) he included very unflattering portraits of the lowest classes. Because he never really felt fully secure about the enduring virtue of the poor, he never went so far as to confuse humanity's limited or relative virtue with God's ultimate righteousness. God would have the last say, Hugo believed, and would sound the trumpet on Judgment Day and separate the wicked from the just. At the very end of this enormous work (over seven hundred pages in some editions), God reminds all creation that he would only have to blow out the lights for everything to revert to primordial darkness ("abîme" [abyss]).

At the same time that Hugo was working on *La légende des siècles*, he had another major project underway: *La fin de Satan* (most meaningfully translated as *Satan Redeemed*). Hugo worked on this theological epic poem between 1854 and 1860, and although he never completed it (the text was published posthumously in 1886), it was well enough advanced so that the poet's thought emerges clearly. At the metaphysical level Hugo was wrestling with the age-old questions of good and evil and universal salvation. Does God desire to keep evil (Satan) in existence, even if relegated to hell? Is God powerless to redeem the wicked or merely unwilling to do so? Hugo's conclusion is optimistic. The angel Liberty (daughter of God and Lucifer) descends into hell, where she destroys with her dazzling light Satan's sole companion, Isis-Lilith, a ghoul left over from an older, pre-adamite creation, whom Hugo uses as a symbol of fatality. Liberty brings peace to Satan's tortured soul, so that by the end of the poem the fallen angel is prepared to accept God's offer to return to heaven and once again be first among the angels.

The optimism of the poem has its political dimension as well. Hugo imagines that Cain, in slaying his brother, had used a bronze nail, a wooden club, and a rock, and that these objects survived the Flood and became the bronze sword of war, the wooden gallows, and the stone prison. But with Isis-Lilith's destruction, fatality will no longer reign in human affairs, and Hugo looks forward to the time when war, executions, and prisons will be abolished.

But the primary level of this poem is psychological. Recent critics have been unanimous in seeing *La fin de Satan* as an attempt by Hugo to free himself from the sense of guilt that had haunted him for so many years. Once again, the importance given to Cain's murder of Abel underscores Hugo's sense of responsibility for his brother's madness, and God's initial repudiation of Satan provides more evidence—if any more were needed—of how seriously Hugo took his father's real or imagined disapproval. But this time the angel, who represents God's grace on the theological plane and in psychological terms, is Satan's own positive feminine side (positive, because she was born from one of Lucifer's white feathers before he became evil and turned into Satan); she permits Satan to overcome feelings of guilt and hate and to develop the emotion of love. To his great joy, he discovers that he will not be damned forever but will be reborn as the celestial Lucifer.

If Hugo decreed in *La fin de Satan* that fatality could be overcome, he was less optimistic about another area of human life. Hugo's next major work of fiction was *Les travailleurs de la mer.* In its preface he comments that in *Notre-Dame de Paris* he had wanted to show the "fatality of [church] dogma" that condemned innocent people as witches, and in *Les misérables* "the fatality of laws" that condemned a hungry man to the galleys for years just for stealing a loaf of bread. And now it is his idea to expose "the fatality of things"; that is, how objects can at times become so important that they determine the course of a person's life. But none of these three "fatalities" can be considered ultimate, Hugo concludes. Dogma may be rejected, laws can be changed, even objects are rendered harmless if one's attitude toward them changes. The ultimate fatality, which no one can escape, is that of the "human heart." This idea was not new for Hugo. In *Notre-Dame* he had shown Esmeralda throwing away her life because of an inexplicable passion for the unworthy Captain Phoebus, and in *Les misérables* Jean Valjean is tortured by jealousy when Cosette falls in love with Marius, because his love is something more than paternal (there is a clear parallel here with Hugo and his daughter Léopoldine). In *Les travailleurs de la mer* one finds once more the inexplicable operation of the human heart. The action of the story is set on the Channel Island of Guernsey. A young man, Gilliatt, sees a girl whom he knows only slightly write his name in the snow one wintry day, and he falls in love with her from afar. The plot is set in motion when Mess Lethierry, the girl's uncle, with whom she lives, loses the small steamer that has been the source of his wealth. Clubin, an associate, has arranged for the ship to be wrecked on some reefs and plans to flee the country with a large sum of money that he has stolen. Swimming to escape from the wreck, Clubin is seized by a huge octopus and drowned. The boat thus becomes the object that will exert its fatal influence upon the hero's life. In order to win the girl's hand, Gilliatt goes out alone to the wreck in a small boat to retrieve the engine so that Lethierry can rebuild his ship and his fortune. In addition to performing the Herculean task of removing an engine from the hull of a steamer and placing it on a much smaller craft, Gilliatt must also battle a hurricane and the giant octopus that had killed Clubin. Beyond all probability he succeeds, only to find when he returns to land that the girl is in love with another man. Unable to conquer "the fatality of the human heart," he commits suicide by letting himself drown.

The "fatality of the human heart" is a phrase whose meaning becomes clear only when one remembers that much of humanity's emotional behavior springs from the depths of the unconscious; to the conscious ego, which cannot see its origin, this behavior is as mysterious as if fatality were controlling one's life. Gilliatt has no sisters (like Hugo) and lives alone with his mother. His father is never mentioned. He has no male figure to guide him as he grows up and no experience with young women. As he is also a solitary, meditative individual who spends entire days alone dreaming, his desire for women builds up inside him with such intensity that he does not hesitate to risk his life for a girl he scarcely knows. His eroticism is all inner fantasy. In fact he has so little contact with reality that it is almost as if he sees the stranded ship as the girl herself. The text explains that the ship's name, Durande, and the girl's, Déruchette, are actually two forms of the same

word, and that "a man who knows how to handle a ship knows how to handle a woman. Both respond to the moon and the wind."

The desperate quest for women has its frightening aspects for Gilliatt as it did for Hugo. When the hero had on one occasion come across some naked women bathing in the sea, he discovered that "the sight of a naked woman horrified him." But the battle with the octopus shows Gilliatt's fear of female sexuality much more graphically. The octopus, the marine equivalent of the spider of *Notre-Dame,* lives under the reef in a beautiful grotto hollowed out by the action of the waves. Looking for food, Gilliatt squeezes through a narrow opening into this cave. It seems to him like a palace inhabited by some naked goddess, where beneath the water one can see a dazzling arch flanked by "'dark legs." The symbolism is clear; like the octopus's cave sex appears at first beautiful and enticing, but it is in reality as ugly and as deadly as the octopus itself. Suddenly the creature emerges and clamps its tentacles on the hero, who becomes "the fly of this spider" and is about to be "drunk alive" and emptied into "this horrible sack." Gilliatt manages to kill the beast with a knife, whose traditional phallic nature cannot escape even the most inattentive reader. (It may seem paradoxical to have a phallus destroying the fear of sexuality, but the text is clear on this point.) This act of metaphorically destroying the danger of the female seems to free the hero from his sexual obsession, but this new freedom does not liberate him from the most fundamental manifestation of the feminine: the maternal. At the end, he reverts to passivity, choosing to let himself be reabsorbed into the womb of the maternal sea.

Beyond the sexual and psychological implications of the narrative, *Les travailleurs de la mer* raises metaphysical and religious questions as it opens out onto the mystery of the universe. One good example of Hugo's desire to communicate the idea that something exists beyond what we can measure can be found in the description of an old abandoned house.

Perched on a promontory overlooking the sea, this mysterious dwelling becomes invested in the moonlight with an aura of "sacred horror," as if it had been transformed into "an enormous altar of the darkness"; and Hugo wonders whether some extraterrestrial presence manifests itself in such places "surrounded by the sea." He answers his question affirmatively when Gilliatt, having apparently succeeded in his quest to save the engine only to realize that his little boat is leaking and may sink, stuffs his remaining clothing into the leak, and, naked in the middle of the night before the immensity of sea and sky, prays desperately for help. "Prayer," writes Hugo, "is addressed to the mercy of the darkness . . . and before the powerful fixed gaze of the supplicant, one feels that it is possible for the Unknown to be disarmed." By allowing Gilliatt's prayer to be answered—the leak is stopped and the sea becomes calm—Hugo seems to suggest that an incomprehensible presence can enter human life, forcing us to accept that we are not the ultimate measure of existence. In this case, however, God's mercy serves only to prepare the ironic conclusion: heroic efforts cannot control the "fatality of the human heart."

By the end of his life, though, Hugo had largely shaken free from the feeling that fatality was omnipotent; in his last two novels he celebrates a more optimistic vision, both in the political domain and in the realm of human emotions. *L'Homme qui rit* (*The Laughing Man*, 1869) is set in the early eighteenth century and deals on the political level with the British aristocracy, which Hugo admired up to a point because it had performed the valuable service of limiting the power of the king. But because the aristocracy had in its turn degenerated into an arrogant elite, Hugo believed, it would be replaced by a more popular form of government. On the personal, psychological level, the hero, Gwynplaine, finds himself between two opposing female figures. One, Duchess Josiane, represents female carnality that ensnares men sexually.

Like the fly caught by the spider in *Notre-Dame* and like Gilliatt in the lair of the octopus, the hero wanders through unknown passageways only to find himself in a chamber, and behind the "transparent, silver web" (of a curtain), at the center of which "one usually finds the spider," Gwynplaine sees "that formidable object, a naked woman." The hero is saved from the clutches of the spider by still another incarnation of Hugo's positive feminine figure. In the Manichaean dualism of the work, the heroine, Déa (Goddess), represents spiritual values, in contrast with Josiane, who stands for flesh and matter. Déa is blind, and because Gwynplaine's face has been grotesquely disfigured since childhood, her blindness has the obvious function of permitting her not to judge him physically. More significantly, as a symbol of the feminine—even of the soul—Déa is keenly attuned to the values of the inner world. She is responsible for turning the hero away from the exterior world with its temptations of political power and carnal lust; at the end they unite happily in death, passing over to a paradise of transcendent light.

Political considerations dominate Hugo's last novel, *Quatrevingt-treize* (*Ninety-Three*), based on the year 1793 of the French Revolution. Published in 1874, this novel rejects the old feudal monarchy because it was based on hereditary privilege and created massive social injustice. But it also repudiates revolutionary Jacobinism because of its inflexibility and its unwillingness to move beyond a strict concept of justice to a more human and loving ideal. The protagonist, Gauvain, pleads for a third way, a simple world of both justice and love, a world that will permit people to climb "the rungs of the ladder that reaches up to God." Then God opens the door, as the text puts it, "and we have only to enter."

If Hugo's optimism seems a little facile at this point, another work (incomplete and published posthumously in 1891) serves as a corrective. Entitled *Dieu (God)*, this lengthy theological poem puts Hugo himself in the role of the questing hero. Led by an angel in a dream through various stages of world religious thought, he discovers that although he and humanity make progress on the road to an understanding of the divine, there always seems to be the same distance to travel before one arrives. Since the work was left incomplete, it has not been altogether possible to ascertain the exact order of the text, but the poem apparently ends with a phrase summing up Hugo's belief that no matter how much spiritual progress is made by an individual or by humanity as a whole, God, that is, perfection, cannot be fully understood or reached in this life. The only way to move beyond our human limitations and enter into union with God is to die: "Il [Dieu] me toucha le front du doigt. Et je mourus" (He [God] touched my brow with his finger. And I died).

For a writer to endure as a dynamic presence over the centuries, he must first possess verbal brilliance. In this respect Hugo was particularly gifted. He could manipulate French verse with an ease that no other poet of his day could match. But in addition, an artist must have such a fundamental view of human life that his vision is not limited to the transitory values of his generation or century. Here, too, Hugo was fortunate. If he usually shared the prevailing nineteenth-century belief that humanity was destined to make uninterrupted progress toward moral as well as technological perfection, it was also his belief that there was some deep center to the human soul that escaped the scrutiny of rational thinking. Fortunately, Hugo never tried to "explain" the soul or the deepest center of the unconscious in logical terms. Had he done so, he would have had to use the scientific language of his day, which inevitably would have become outdated. By giving his readers only images and stories, he avoided limiting himself to his own era, thus making his insights accessible to future generations. Similarly, he was careful never to reduce God to a size that the human mind could grasp. Again, this

would have linked him too closely to the theology of the day, which, like all intellectual theologies, would have become outmoded. Although on such matters as ethics, politics, and social institutions, Hugo was not afraid to take definite positions, he was careful to leave the deepest mysteries of life shrouded in uncertainty. In this manner he transcended his own age; and because since his death our world has become a place where easy answers are less and less acceptable and where people see the future as more uncertain than they did over a century ago, Victor Hugo has been increasingly recognized as a writer for our time as well as for his own.

Selected Bibliography

FIRST EDITIONS

POETRY

Odes et poésies diverses. Paris, 1822.
Odes. Paris, 1823.
Nouvelles odes. Paris, 1824.
Odes et ballades. Paris, 1826.
Les orientales. Paris, 1829.
Les feuilles d'automne. Paris, 1831.
Les chants du crépuscule. Paris, 1835.
Les voix intérieures. Paris, 1837.
Les rayons et les ombres. Paris, 1840.
Châtiments. Brussels, 1853.
Les contemplations. Brussels and Paris, 1856.
La légende des siècles. Brussels and Paris, 1859. Second series, 1877; third series, 1883.
Les chansons des rues et des bois. Paris, 1865.
L'Année terrible. Paris, 1872.
L'Art d'être grand'père. Paris, 1877.
Le pape. Paris, 1878.
La pitié suprême. Paris, 1879.
L'Âne. Paris, 1880.
Religions et religion. Paris, 1880.
Les quatre vents de l'esprit. Paris, 1881.
La fin de Satan. Paris, 1886.
Dieu. Paris, 1891.
Toute la lyre. Paris, 1888–1898.
Les années funestes. Paris, 1898.
Dernière gerbe. Paris, 1902.

VICTOR HUGO

PLAYS

Cromwell. Paris, 1827.
Hernani. Paris, 1830.
Marion de Lorme. Paris, 1831.
Le roi s'amuse. Paris, 1832.
Lucrèce Borgia. Paris, 1833.
Marie Tudor. Paris, 1833.
Angélo, tyran de Padoue. Paris, 1835.
Ruy Blas. Paris 1838.
Les burgraves. Paris, 1843.
Torquemade. Paris, 1882.
Le théâtre en liberté. Paris, 1886.
Amy Robsart. Les jumeaux. Paris, 1889.

PROSE FICTION

Han d'islande. Paris, 1823.
Bug-Jargal. Paris, 1826.
Le dernier jour d'un condamné. Paris, 1829.
Notre-Dame de Paris. Paris, 1831.
Claude Gueux. Paris, 1834.
Les misérables. Brussels, 1862.
Les travailleurs de la mer. Brussels and Paris, 1866.
L'Homme qui rit. Brussels and Paris, 1869.
Quatrevingt-treize. Paris, 1874.

MISCELLANEOUS WORKS

Littérature et philosophie mêlées. Paris, 1834.
Le Rhin. Paris, 1842.
Napoléon-le-petit. London, 1852.
William Shakespeare. Brussels, 1864.
Actes et paroles. Paris, 1875–1876.
Histoire d'un crime. Paris, 1877–1878.
Choses vues. Paris, 1887–1900.
Promontorium somnii. Paris, 1901.

MODERN EDITIONS

There are far too many modern editions to permit a complete listing. A few of the more useful and available are listed below.

INDIVIDUAL WORKS

Les contemplations. Edited by Léon Cellier. Paris, 1969. Classiques Garnier.
La légende des siècles. Edited by A. Dumas. Paris, 1964. Classiques Garnier.
La légende des siècles. La fin de Satan. Dieu. Edited by Jacques Truchet. Paris, 1950. Bibliothèque de la Pléiade.

Les misérables. Edited by M.-F. Guyard. 2 vols. Paris, 1957. Classiques Garnier.
Notre-Dame de Paris. Edited by M.-F. Guyard. Paris, 1961. Classiques Garnier.
Notre-Dame de Paris. Les travailleurs de la mer. Edited by J. Seebacher and Yves Gohin. Paris, 1975. Bibliothèque de la Pléiade.

COLLECTED WORKS

Oeuvres complètes de Victor Hugo. Edited by Paul Meurice, Gustave Simon, Cécile Daubray. 45 vols. Paris, 1904–1952.
Oeuvres complètes. Edited by F. Bouvet. 4 vols. Paris, 1961–1964.
————. Edited by Jean Massin. 18 vols. Paris, 1967–1970.
Oeuvres poétiques. Edited by Pierre Albouy. 3 vols. Paris, 1964–1974. Bibliothèque de la Pléiade.
Théâtre complet. Edited by J.-J. Thierry and Josette Mélèze. 2 vols. Paris, 1963. Bibliothèque de la Pléiade.

TRANSLATIONS

Hans of Iceland. London, 1888.
Hernani. In *Laurel Masterpieces of Continental Drama.* Vol. 2: *The Romantic Influence.* New York, 1963. Pp. 281–379.
The Last Day of a Condemned Man. London, 1931.
The Laughing Man. London, 1887.
Les misérables. Translated by Norman Denny. 1 vol., New York, 1980. 2 vols., 1982.
Ninety-Three. New York, 1962.
Notre-Dame of Paris. Translated by John Sturrock. New York, 1978.
The Novels and Poems of Victor Hugo. 16 vols. New York, 1887–1896.
The Novels Complete and Unabridged of Victor Hugo. 28 vols. Philadelphia, 1892–1894.
Poems. New York, 1901.
Songs of Twilight. Translated by George W. M. Reynolds. Paris, 1836.
Things Seen. London, 1964.
The Toilers of the Sea. New York, 1961.
Translations from the Poems of Victor Hugo. New York, 1887.
Works. Philadelphia, 1892–1897.

VICTOR HUGO

BIOGRAPHICAL AND CRITICAL STUDIES

Albouy, Pierre. *La création mythologique chez Victor Hugo.* Paris, 1963.

Barrère, Jean-Bertrand. *Hugo: L'Homme et l'oeuvre.* Paris, 1952.

Baudouin, Charles. *Psychanalyse de Victor Hugo.* Geneva, 1943. New ed., Paris, 1972.

Brombert, Victor. "Hugo's *Condemned Man:* Laughter of Revolution." *Romanic Review* 70:119–132 (1979).

————. "Victor Hugo, la prison et l'espace." *Revue des sciences humaines* 117:59–79 (1965). Translated as "Victor Hugo's Spaceless Prison," in Brombert's *The Romantic Prison.* Princeton, N.J., 1978. Pp. 88–119.

Gaudon, Jean. *Le temps de la contemplation: L'Oeuvre poétique de Victor Hugo des "Misères" au "Seuil du gouffre" (1845–1856).* Paris, 1969.

————. *Victor Hugo, dramaturge.* Paris, 1955.

Glauser, Alfred. *Victor Hugo et la poésie pure.* Geneva, 1957.

Grant, Elliott M. *The Career of Victor Hugo.* Cambridge, Mass., 1945.

Grant, Richard B. *The Perilous Quest: Image, Myth, and Prophecy in the Narratives of Victor Hugo.* Durham, N.C., 1968.

————. "Sequence and Theme in Victor Hugo's *Les orientales.*" *PMLA* 94: 894–908 (1979).

Houston, John P. *Victor Hugo.* New York, 1974.

Josephson, Matthew. *Victor Hugo: A Realistic Biography of the Great Romantic.* Garden City, N.Y., 1942.

Levaillant, Maurice. *La crise mystique de Victor Hugo (1843–1856) d'apres des documents inédits.* Paris, 1954.

Maurois, André. *Olympio; ou, La vie de Victor Hugo.* 2 vols. Paris, 1954. Translated by Gerald Hopkins as *Olympio; or, The Life of Victor Hugo.* New York, 1956.

Nash, Suzanne. *"Les Contemplations" of Victor Hugo: An Allegory of the Creative Process.* Princeton, N.J., 1976.

Petrey, Sandy. "History in the Text: *Quatrevingt-treize* and the French Revolution." Purdue University Monographs in Romance Languages, 3. Amsterdam, 1980.

Peyre, Henri. *Hugo, sa vie, son oeuvre.* Paris, 1972. Translated by Rhoda P. Roberts as *Victor Hugo: Philosophy and Poetry.* University, Ala., 1980.

Riffaterre, Michael. "Victor Hugo's Poetics." *American Society of the Legion of Honor Magazine* 32: 181–196 (1961).

————. "La vision hallucinatoire chez Victor Hugo." *MLN* 78: 225–241 (1963).

Van Tieghem, Philippe. *Dictionnaire de Victor Hugo.* Paris, 1969.

Ward, Patricia A. *The Medievalism of Victor Hugo.* University Park, Pa., 1975.

Zumthor, Paul. *Victor Hugo, poète de Satan.* Paris, 1946.

RICHARD B. GRANT

ALEXANDRE DUMAS PÈRE

(1802–1870)

PLAYWRIGHT

EARLY IN FEBRUARY 1829 the posters placarded in front of the Théâtre Français, the building in the rue Richelieu that housed the Comédie Française, invited patrons to the production of a new play, *Henri III et sa cour* (Henry III and His Court), by Alexandre Dumas. The author, not yet twenty-seven years old, had an obscure and low-paying job as copy clerk in the secretariat of the duc d'Orléans. He had arrived in Paris seven years previously, determined to make a name for himself by writing for the stage, and had indeed collaborated in the confection of two short vaudevilles (sketches interlarded with songs) that had been produced at different boulevard theaters as makeweights for the evening's entertainment. But one night when he was a boy in his teens he had been introduced to François Joseph Talma in the great actor's dressing room in the Théâtre Français. On that memorable occasion Talma had solemnly laid his hand on Dumas's head, declaiming: "Alexandre Dumas, I baptize you poet in the name of Shakespeare, Corneille, and Schiller." Ever since then Dumas had been fired with the ambition to write a play for Talma's theater that would cause him, if possible, to be acclaimed the French Shakespeare, or at least the French Schiller.

In the intervening years, Talma, the last of the great tragic actors, had died, leaving the first national theater of France in disarray. Its audiences were thin, composed chiefly of the dwindling remnant of those who retained a taste for the neoclassical tragedies that had held the stage during the First Empire (1804–1815). The Parisians by and large greatly preferred as entertainment the spectacular melodramas, gay vaudevilles, and amusing farces they could see at the Gymnase, the Variétés, the Porte-Saint-Martin, and other commercial theaters. But in 1825 there had been a hopeful development: the Brussels-born Baron Isidore Taylor was appointed to the directorship of the Comédie Française. He had had a checkered career: he had served in the army, having been commissioned in 1815, the year of Waterloo, had written and produced five plays, had been stage manager at the Panorama-Dramatique, and was known to be keenly interested in archaeology. For Taylor it was clear that the Comédie Française could only recover its former status and popularity if it were prepared to venture beyond the tradition of the five-act tragedy set in ancient Rome and played by actors in sandals and togas before conventionally drab sets; paying audiences needed something more exciting and appealing to the eye. He scented romanticism in the air, and he felt that unless the senior actors of the Comédie Française were cajoled into risking a new type of drama, their theater would continue its slide into obsolescence.

ALEXANDRE DUMAS PÈRE

Alexandre Dumas's father, Thomas-Alexandre Davy or Dumas, was born in Haiti in 1762. His own father (Alexandre's grandfather) was a nobleman of ancient lineage, Alexandre-Antoine Davy de la Pailleterie, and his mother (Alexandre's grandmother) was a black slave called Marie-Cessette Dumas. When he returned to France to claim his inheritance, Alexandre-Antoine arranged for his son to accompany him; the boy, though illegitimate, had every expectation of being made his heir. This never happened: as a result of a violent quarrel with his father, Thomas joined the army as a ranker, assuming the name Dumas out of loyalty to his mother whom the old man had abandoned in Haiti. Only three years later, in 1789, the French Revolution broke out; in 1792 France declared war on Austria and in the succeeding campaigns the young Dumas rose rapidly through the ranks and was ultimately promoted to general. Although fighting with distinction in Italy and Egypt under Napoleon, he eventually became a prisoner of war, and as the result of ill treatment emerged broken in health and was retired from the army, dying eventually in 1806. His widow, whom he had married in 1792, brought up their son, Alexandre, as best she could, for she was left in very straitened circumstances. By the time Alexandre came to Paris, a fresh turn of events had swept Napoleon from power, which explains why the young man, who had been educated in the provinces, had so few contacts of any importance in the capital, either in the political or in the literary world. He had no means of introducing himself to the young romantics, though his literary allegiance lay with them. But he did succeed in interesting Taylor in his first full-length play, based on the life of Queen Christina of Sweden. In spite of Taylor's backing, Dumas's *Christine,* though accepted and put into rehearsal, was never actually produced by the Comédie Française; it was eventually seen, however, at the Odéon, where it had its first night on 30 March 1830.

This disappointment, far from discouraging the young author, seems to have spurred him on to fresh efforts, and in the summer of 1828 he set to work on *Henri III et sa cour.* The theme had occurred to him in the course of a chance reading of certain court memoirs of the sixteenth century; he learned how the duc de Guise, the notorious "Scarface," having got wind of an intrigue between his wife and the comte de Saint-Mégrin, one of the king's favorites, gave her the choice of dying by either cold steel or poison. She chose poison, whereupon the duke, who had merely wanted to frighten her, made her drink a harmless bowl of soup. Elsewhere, in Pierre de l'Estoile's memoirs, he read of the assassination of Saint-Mégrin outside the Louvre by a band of armed men in the pay of the duc de Guise. Finally, the dramatic link between these two stories was provided by an incident that did not concern Saint-Mégrin at all, but that many years later Dumas was to incorporate in his novel *La dame de Monsoreau* (1846; translated as *Chicot the Jester*): another jealous husband forces his wife to send her lover, Bussy d'Amboise, a note asking for an assignation, and then stations a gang of cutthroats to dispatch him outside her window.

Dumas's previous dealings with members of the Comédie Française over *Christine* had taught him a few useful lessons. They were professionals with years of experience of the stage behind them; also they were for the most part middle-aged and did not take kindly to direction from striplings in their twenties, however gifted the young men might be. For, in accordance with regulations drawn up in the seventeenth century, the company was a self-regulating body, and Taylor's functions were little more than advisory. When it came to putting on a new play, there was no direction in the modern sense, though it was understood that the author could attend rehearsals and make comments. Dumas took these duties very lightly; according to one of the actors, Joseph-Isidore Samson, when a particular point caused dissension during a rehearsal, Dumas refused to intervene, saying that they understood such matters better than he and that whatever they decided was, he was sure, the best. In any case he had written the play with parts deliberately fashioned to suit particular members of the cast: Mademoiselle Mars, the leading actress of the period, was to take the part of the duchesse de Guise, and Firmin, the one friend Dumas had in the company, that of Saint-Mégrin. A considerable sum of money— over eight thousand francs—was set aside by Taylor for the production. Four sets were specially designed, and the costumes made for the lead parts were considered remarkable for their historical accuracy. This policy paid off, for the costumes worn by Mademoiselle Mars, Firmin, and Michelot (who played the part of Henri III) provoked a ripple of applause on the opening night.

This first night was in the end a great success. The curtain went up at the start on a scene that might have come straight from a novel by Sir Walter Scott: the laboratory of the astrologer Ruggieri. This first act, and the succeeding one, set in the king's court, were received with polite applause, but the third act drew shrieks of pleasurable terror from the audience. In France at that period overt violence on the stage was a rarity, even in the melodrama. In 1827 Parisian audiences had been overwhelmed when a British company had crossed the Channel to present a season of Shakespeare at the Odéon Theater; for the first time they had been able to witness from their seats the spectacle of Hamlet dueling with Laertes, Othello smothering Desdemona, and Lady Macbeth snatching the dagger still dripping with Duncan's blood from her husband's nerveless grasp. All this was regarded as utterly barbaric by the traditionalists but by the majority of spectators as an exciting innovation. So when the duc de Guise, in Dumas's play, ordered his wife to write to Saint-Mégrin giving him an appointment for that night, and on her indignant refusal squeezed her arm with his mail gauntlet until she cried out in agony, the habitués of the Comédie Française were divided between those who wanted to hiss and those who insisted on clapping—but the latter, mostly the young, were in the majority.

If the first performance of Hugo's *Hernani*, a year later, has come to be regarded as the true turning point by which romanticism replaced classicism, this is because classical tragedy had always been written in verse; *Hernani* was a verse play and therefore, according to the conventions of the time, deserved more serious consideration than *Henri III et sa cour*, which was written in prose. In addition, Hugo was a well-known figure, the acknowledged leader of the romantic school, while *Henri III*, by an unknown author, an outsider claimed by no particular literary movement, took the critics by surprise. Before they could formulate any reservations, the loud applause from the auditorium had decided the issue. By the time Hugo's play was ready for production at the same theater, the forces of reaction had regrouped, and battle was joined.

Dumas's next important play, *Antony* (1831), was written after the "battle of *Hernani*." It was intended again for the Comédie Française, which accepted it, though without enthusiasm. In his *Souvenirs dramatiques* (1868) Dumas suggests that there were three reasons the theater did not turn the play down flat: first, the earlier success of *Henri III*, which meant that a new play by the same author would be bound to arouse interest; second, the fact that this production, unlike that of *Henri III*, would not involve the Comédie in any major expense, since it was not a costume drama; and finally, Dumas hints that the actors were secretly counting on the censors to refuse the play a license. In this last respect they were disappointed, and Dumas was served, by the historical accident of the July Revolution of 1830. After every revolution in France, from that of 1789 on, the machinery of dramatic censorship came to a halt. It was invariably brought into operation again a little later, but *Antony* benefited from the temporary intermission; Dumas himself admitted, with hindsight, that it was unlikely the play would have been permitted on the stage under normal circumstances.

At any event, the Comédie Française was slow in putting it into rehearsal, and during rehearsal insisted on one modification after another, until finally Dumas lost patience altogether and took the play to the Porte-Saint-Martin, a theater that specialized in melodrama. That company included one brilliant actress, Marie Dorval, who proved far better suited to the part of the heroine than the more coldhearted Mademoiselle Mars could ever have been, while the actor Bocage made a lasting reputation as Antony, the misanthropic lover in revolt against all social conventions, whose name became a byword for a certain type of romantic hero.

Antony was set in contemporary Paris and based in certain recognizable particulars on an affair Dumas was currently engaged in with Mélanie Waldor, the wife of an army officer. But there is little resemblance between Antony, brooding over his bastardy, and Dumas, whose birth was legitimate and who was of all the romantics perhaps the least given to melancholy and unsatisfied ambition. The situation at the outset of the play is that Adèle has contracted a loveless marriage with an army colonel stationed away from Paris, and has one daughter—exactly Mélanie's situation. After a long absence Antony, who had known Adèle before her marriage, returns from his travels; in order to escape his importunate lovemaking she sets off to join her husband in Strasbourg. Antony, however, overtakes her on the way and seduces her in the inn where she is spending the night. Back in Paris, at a fashionable gathering, the two lovers realize their secret is now public property, and also learn that the husband is returning to settle accounts. In the fifth act Antony and Adèle are shown wrestling with a moral dilemma that would have been quite understandable to audiences in 1831, however farfetched it might seem today: should the lovers flee together or should they die together? In either case Adèle's honor would still be lost; her little

daughter would bear all her life the stigma of her mother's unchastity. The one escape from this situation is that Adèle should die at Antony's hands and that he should pretend to have killed her in exasperation at her rejection of his love. The last line of the play, "the most celebrated curtain-line in France," as Robert Baldick has called it, was spoken by Antony to the irate husband who bursts into the room and stands aghast at the sight of his wife's corpse: "She was resisting me, and so I murdered her."

Why this totally improbable denouement should have stirred audiences of the time to such a pitch of frenzied excitement—Dumas was mobbed in the theater at the end of the first performance by a crowd of young fans who tore his coat to pieces so as to be able to carry off some fragment of it as a relic—remains something of a mystery. But there was a certain primitive male brutality about Dumas's theater that may have had a special appeal for the generation of 1830: his heroes, Richard Darlington in the play of that name (1831), Alfred d'Alvimar in *Angèle* (1833), are young men who use women as the means to the achievement of their social ambitions and then abandon them or get rid of them by some violently criminal act. Dumas in private life never went to this extreme, but his dealings with Catherine Labay, the mother of his first child, with Mélanie Waldor, and with her successor, Belle Krelsamer, who bore him a second child, were all marked by a certain swashbuckling ruthlessness that he needed to exaggerate only slightly to create the villainous but irresistible protagonists of his dramas.

In addition Dumas possessed to a far greater degree than any other of the French romantics a sense of the theater, which meant that he intuitively felt what the audience wanted and gave it to them, occasionally anticipating their longings and forcing their tastes. Arsène Houssaye, who was in charge of the fortunes of the Comédie Française from 1849 to 1856, called him "l'homme-théâtre," meaning that he incarnated as none other did the spirit of the theater; but it was the theater of his time, not of all time. With one exception—*La tour de Nesle* (1832), a melodrama that has proved suitable for film and for television—his plays, some of them enormously successful when first produced, have proved impossible to revive. They incarnate brilliantly certain stereotypes of the romantic age: the tortured, antisocial Antony; later the ruthless, power-hungry Richard Darlington; and especially Edmund Kean, a faithful representation of the notorious Shakespearean actor of the Regency period in England. Dumas clearly enjoyed depicting the last, a violent, eminently theatrical man, a Don Juan riddled with debt, taunting the critics and the aristocrats, a man of the people who chanced to be a genius. *Kean* was written in 1836 for the actor Frédéric Lemaître, who had such an affinity with Kean that he hardly needed to act the part. This is perhaps one other reason why Dumas's plays, even when highly successful in their day, have not survived: they were written for certain actors and actresses, *Richard Darlington* for Lemaître, *Angèle* for Bocage, *Mademoiselle de Belle-Isle* (1839) for Mademoiselle Mars. For this last play, a comedy with tragic overtones, Dumas returned at last to the Comédie Française, giving its senior actress the chance to show how, even at the age of sixty, no one could better play the part of an eighteen-year-old ingenue.

La tour de Nesle is of all Dumas's plays the one that comes nearest, both in subject matter and in characterization, to the historical novels that he had not at the time even thought of. Set in Paris at the beginning of the fourteenth century, the novel concerns the lascivious orgies in which Marguerite of Burgundy, queen of France, and her two sisters indulge night after night in a gloomy tower overlooking the Seine. The young men who are decoyed there to pleasure the ladies are never permitted to talk of their adventures subsequently; their usual fate is to have their throats cut by hired ruffians who then fling their bodies into the river. One young man,

Buridan, escapes. He then blackmails the queen into having him appointed minister. They pursue their criminal careers together for some time, until in the end they fall out, denouncing each other. André Maurois has called *La tour de Nesle* "a classic of theatrical excess," and other critics have speculated on the play's appeal. What has perhaps not been properly noticed is that this appeal must be the same as that of the novels, for Buridan is a less developed forerunner of all Dumas's impetuous young heroes whose fate it is to love great queens: from La Mole who loves Marguerite de Navarre, to Charny who loves Marie Antoinette. Such attachments are bound to end tragically, for if love implies mastery, as Dumas undoubtedly believed, how can a queen submit to being mastered by a vassal?

HISTORY AND FICTION

Although Dumas built his reputation on his plays, by themselves they could not have given him the wide appeal he still enjoys today. Stage fashions changed rapidly in the first half of the nineteenth century, and before that century was midway through, the romantic drama that Hugo and he had spearheaded no longer drew the eagerly attentive audiences it had in the 1830's. Dumas's son, Alexandre *fils*, in his first play, *La dame aux camélias* (The Lady of the Camellias, 1852; later translated as *Camille*), lit the way to a different kind of theater, one that dealt with difficult questions of domestic morality confronting the smug and self-satisfied bourgeois society of the Second Empire (1852–1870). A new generation demanded a new type of play, essentially modern, serious, sermonizing, calling into question all the by now old-fashioned romantic shibboleths.

Dumas *père* could afford to yield the stage to this new wave of dramatists, for by 1852, as the result of a bare eight years of prodigious and unremitting labor, he had firmly established himself as master in a totally new field.

723

The period between the publication of *Les trois mousquetaires* (*The Three Musketeers,* 1844) and *Ange Pitou* (1851) saw the appearance of perhaps a dozen full-length historical novels, together with what is usually regarded as his masterpiece, *Le comte de Monte-Cristo* (*The Count of Monte Cristo,* 1844–1845), which is set in contemporary times. Some of these works are dauntingly long: *Joseph Balsamo* (1846–1848) runs into five volumes in the standard edition, *Le vicomte de Brage-lonne* (1848–1850; part of which was translated as *The Man in the Iron Mask*) into six. Even taking into account Dumas's amazing constitution and his ability to work eighteen hours out of the twenty-four, and after making due allowance for whatever help he may have received from his collaborators, Auguste Maquet in particular, the feat is still astounding.

The historical novel had been popularized in France by Sir Walter Scott, whose entire works were translated in the 1820's almost as soon as they came out. Thinking to cash in on the current "Scottomania," some of the leading French romantics had brought out imitations, using incidents from the history of their own country as the framework of their romances: Alfred de Vigny in *Cinq-Mars* (1826) had dealt with a conspiracy against Cardinal Richelieu; Prosper Mérimée had written his *Chronique du règne de Charles IX* (Chronicles of the Reign of Charles IX, 1829) around the massacre of Saint Bartholomew's Day (a bloody episode also figuring at the beginning of Dumas's *La reine Margot* [1845; translated as *Marguerite de Valois*]); and Hugo had produced, in 1831, his *Notre-Dame de Paris* (*Hunchback of Notre-Dame*), set in fifteenth-century Paris. These early examples of the genre were appreciated more for their historical content than for their merits as novels, though, in spite of its pedantic displays of erudition, Hugo's first venture into the field still finds plenty of admirers for the vividness of imagination shown in certain outstanding episodes. But it is significant that at the time each of these works was for the author an isolated venture (though Hugo did write a novel about the French Revolution toward the end of his life). Clearly the reception had not been such as to encourage any of these authors to follow Scott's example and write a series of novels about a particular period.

How was it that, a dozen years later, Dumas was able to revive this formula with such outstanding success? The starting point was his friendship with Auguste Maquet, already mentioned. Maquet was a teacher of history at one of the great Paris schools. He had literary ambitions and had written *Le bonhomme Buvat* (Bumbling Old Buvat), a short story about the Cellamare conspiracy against the regent of France in 1718; it was based on the memoirs of the bibliophile Jean Buvat. Unable to find a publisher, Maquet took the manuscript to Dumas, who read it and offered to buy it from him if Maquet granted him the right to rework it. This was the origin of *Le chevalier d'Har-mental,* which was published in installments in the newspaper *Le siècle* before appearing in volume form in 1842.

The serialization of popular fiction in the daily press was a fairly new development in France, though it had started some time earlier in England. In 1836 the newspaper proprietor Émile de Girardin, with his eye on the English precedent, launched *La presse* as a cut-price daily. He hoped that he would gain a wide circulation by publishing *feuilletons,* novels that appeared chapter by chapter, in each issue. The fashion caught on, and by the 1840's most newspaper editors had several fiction writers on their payroll and were prepared to pay very highly for the products of their pens if these seemed likely to attract new readers and keep old ones. Dumas's talents were precisely suited to this form of fiction, which depended heavily on the ability to tantalize the public with a plot involving frequent and exciting twists and turns. His fluency helped, as did even the historical pretensions of the fiction, which seemed to engage the readers' attention, giving them the illusion that they were not merely following an enthralling story but also learning something about their country's past at the same time. The sudden flowering of the *roman-feuilleton,* the serial novel, explains why most of Dumas's historical fiction was written over a relatively short period of time. With the advent of the Second Empire and the more rigorous control of the press that the new administration decided was necessary, the *roman-feuilleton,* particularly in the form of the historical novel, was dealt its deathblow, for although it was not an overtly political form of art, it was vulnerable to the new controls. Any fiction that dealt with the crimes, conspiracies, and revolutions of the past could be regarded as having certain political implications for the present that the censors preferred not to risk.

Dumas had no illusions about the historical value of his novels. "We lay no claim to being a historian," he remarked in an aside in *Les quarante-cinq* (*The Forty-Five,* 1848); "if occasionally we become one, it is when by chance history sinks to the level of the novel, or better still, when the novel rises to the height of history" (2.31). This somewhat cryptic utterance is akin to what he once said to Lamartine, when the poet-statesman professed himself astonished at the immense popular acclaim he had achieved with his *Histoire des Girondins* (1847): "The reason, my dear Lamartine," he explained, "is that you have raised yourself to the level of fiction" (*Causeries,* 1860). Dumas was not, of course, implying that fiction was simply a higher form of history, but that a good historian should be able to interest his reader as much by the historical account as by first-rate imaginative writing. For there is nothing dry as dust in history as such; only the dullness of pedantry makes it seem lifeless. Dumas was highly responsive to the fascination of the past. He even tried his hand at writing works of "straight" history: *Gaule et France* (1833), *Isabelle de Bavière* (1836), *Les Stuarts* (1840).

History formed the backcloth to many of his plays and intruded to a marked degree in his travel books; there was nothing he loved more than to visit spots "steeped in history."

But there is one marked difference between the historian and the historical novelist. The former deals with all events that he reckons, with hindsight, were important; the latter introduces into his fiction only such historical events as he wishes to, and is governed in his decision to do so by broadly aesthetic considerations. Thus Dumas gives the massacre of the Huguenots on Saint Bartholomew's Day pride of place in *La reine Margot,* mainly because it is illustrative of certain tendencies in his characters: brutality, cowardice, and the readiness to change one's religious allegiances if political ends require it. In *Vingt ans après* (*Twenty Years After,* 1845) he recounts the return of Charles I as a prisoner from Newcastle to London, his trial, and his execution, not for what these events signified in the broadest sense but in order to emphasize certain traits of character in his heroes: D'Artagnan's daring plotting, Athos's devotion to lost causes. But he is just as content to skirt such major issues and concentrate instead on the nine days' wonders, a flood in Paris, a fireworks display that went wrong and caused the waiting crowd to stampede with much loss of life and limb. As for the big events of history, they are for the novelist, as he remarked in *Joseph Balsamo* (ch. 64), "what huge mountains are for the traveller. He observes them, travels round them, salutes them in passing, but he does not cross over them."

History, as Dumas understood it, was far more circumscribed than we would regard it today, being still largely a matter of recording the doings of kings and queens and their ministers. Who will succeed Charles IX when he lies ill and likely to die? Will it be his brother, who already sits on the throne of Poland, or will Henri de Navarre make good his claim? The Valois give way to the Bourbons, but to the men of the sixteenth century it was scarcely conceivable that any country in Europe should not have a monarch at its head. This is Athos's viewpoint in *Vingt ans après*: the king dies, but not the monarchy. "The king is but a man, royalty is the spirit of God" (ch. 24). But Athos was a gentleman of the old school; even before Louis XIV reached his majority, the historical process was whittling away the old feudalism and the monarchy no longer seemed so sacred. Dumas shows Anne, queen and regent, faced with a popular rising because she has ordered the arrest of Broussel, a councillor beloved of the people. Can the rabble tell her what she may or may not do? "Good God," she reflects, "what has become of the monarchy?" What indeed? "The commoners had not spoken up for the princes, but they rose up in arms for Broussel; this was because Broussel was a plebeian, and in defending Broussel they instinctively felt they were defending themselves" (ch. 60).

The history of France of the three centuries preceding the French Revolution, as Dumas covers it in his historical novels, debouches on to that revolution; this is the cataract to which all the currents flow, faster and faster as the brink is approached. Afterward there will be no more kings and queens, or they will be shadows of themselves, mere puppets seated on fragile thrones. "France resembles a centuries-old hourglass," Dumas wrote in *Le collier de la reine* (*The Queen's Necklace*, 1849–1850), "for nine hundred years it marked the hour of the monarchy; then the powerful right hand of the Lord God grasped it and turned it over; for centuries to come it will mark the era of the common people" (ch. 16). And in the new era, as Honoré de Balzac saw, true royalty is to be found incarnated not in any king but in the silver coin that bears the royal effigy, the *pièce de cent sous*, the five-franc piece; autocracy has been succeeded by plutocracy, and the most powerful man in France is neither Charles X nor Louis Philippe, but the mysterious count of Monte-Cristo, whose fabulous wealth sets him higher

than the king and gives him more power than any of the king's ministers.

The royal figures that strut through the pages of the historical romances belong to history, and Dumas portrays them much as chroniclers of their own period described them: weak, covetous, lecherous, dilatory, but not entirely cowardly; with flashes of nobility, capable of arousing strong affection and a loyalty too seldom rewarded. We see Charles IX living in terror of his mother, keeping in check her fierce hatred of Henri de Navarre, dying finally of the poison she had destined for the future King Henri IV of France but keeping the secret of her guilt locked in his breast till the end so that no stain should be cast on the honor of the royal house. Then we are shown his successor, Henri III, a sybarite, superstitious, passionately attached to the young men who form his band of "minions," and mourning their deaths with genuine affection at the end of *La dame de Monsoreau*. The queens too are portrayed with their strengths and weaknesses: Louise, the pallid, neglected wife of Henri III; Anne, consort of Louis XIII, proud, petulant, ungrateful, yet inspiring the love of two cardinals and of the duke of Buckingham; the luckless Henrietta of England, living in penurious exile, cheated and swindled by Cardinal Mazarin, but full of dignity, a fond mother and a devoted wife; and above all Marie Antoinette, a tragic figure somewhat idealized by Dumas, who traces her career through five novels (*Joseph Balsamo, Le collier de la reine, Ange Pitou, La comtesse de Charny* [1852–1855], and *Le chevalier de Maison-Rouge* [1845]). Imprudent and capricious at the start, she is shown her final fate—death on the scaffold—in Balsamo's crystal glass, and in the end meets it transfigured by her sufferings, no longer arrogant yet not crushed, bearing herself with a quiet dignity. "Madame Veto," "Veuve Capet," to use the insulting names bestowed on her by the revolutionaries, she is still queen of France, and signs herself so in the prison register.

The historical characters in Dumas's novels

are not invariably kings, queens, princes of the blood royal, powerful ministers. Many of those who play the most important roles, including D'Artagnan himself, Bussy d'Amboise, Chicot the jester, and Cagliostro, are based on real people mentioned in the memoirs he consulted, but in such cases he permitted himself considerable liberties, giving the soldier of fortune greater chivalry, the charlatan greater dignity, all of them much more complexity than the historical record showed. No one would have it otherwise, for this is where the creative writer must be allowed his head. But occasionally he introduces others whose names history has preserved not because they were men of power, but because they were men of influence. In the twenty-third chapter of *Vingt ans après*, Raoul is taken by his father to visit Paul Scarron, a noted wit of the period and the author of a novel on the adventures of a group of strolling players. All the literary lions are in Scarron's chambers: Gilles Ménage, the philologist, whom Molière is supposed to have caricatured as Vadius in his comedy on the bluestockings; Georges de Scudéry, whom Raoul salutes as the author of *Clélie* (1654–1660) and *Artamène, ou le grand Cyrus* (1649–1653)— showing great prescience, for they were not written at the time (Dumas can make mistakes); and Françoise d'Aubigné, the future Madame de Maintenon, whom Scarron was to marry in 1652. The purpose of this catalog of beaux esprits is clear: in that age of battles, conspiracies, and sudden deaths, the arts of society are beginning to be cultivated. "Do gentlemen write verses?" asks Raoul naively; "I thought they would scorn to." Athos laughs. "Only when they are bad verses; when they are good, it is an additional luster."

This chapter in *Vingt ans après* is not an isolated tour de force. Molière and the poet Jean de La Fontaine appear episodically in *Le vicomte de Bragelonne*, while in *Joseph Balsamo* the quirky figure of Jean Jacques Rousseau is given a fairly important part to play, though one still marginal to the main action.

Gilbert, the young hero of this long and intricate novel, is introduced at the start of the book reading *The Social Contract*; Rousseau is his god. Later Gilbert meets the great man. At first he does not realize who he is; Rousseau is engaged in his harmless hobby, botanizing, and Gilbert, who is starving, is glad to share the older man's frugal meal when the offer is made to him. After that the philosopher takes the boy home, introduces him to his companion Thérèse, and in spite of querulous protests on her part, insists on letting him sleep in the attic. The following day, he shows him how he earns his living: not by writing immortal works, but by copying music, a task at which Gilbert shows himself unexpectedly apt.

All these details are based on well-attested fact, and the portrait of Rousseau, with his self-pity, his suspicion of his fellow philosophers, his misanthropy, his vanity, is excellently drawn in the teasing scene in which Gilbert talks in glowing terms about the author of the *Discourse on the Origin of Inequality* without realizing that the stranger he is addressing actually wrote the treatise. In a later episode Rousseau is invited to the Trianon to superintend a rehearsal of his early work, the light opera *Le devin de village*. He refuses the offer of a private carriage to take him to Versailles and arrives instead in a public conveyance, dressed in his usual clothes, to be received by the master of ceremonies with ill-concealed astonishment. But he passes unnoticed at the court; only the dauphine, Marie Antoinette, asks to see him, and when he is eventually presented to Louis XV he stands tongue-tied and abashed, while the monarch converses with him politely about trivialities. Apart from the fact that Dumas seems not to have realized that both the *Confessions* (1781) and the *Rêveries d'un promeneur solitaire* (Meditations of a Solitary Wayfarer, 1782) were published posthumously, he does not appear to have done any great violence to the historical record; but there is an obvious risk in mixing real characters with fictitious ones. Rousseau and his cross-grained housekeeper Thérèse actually lived; Gilbert lived only in Dumas's imagination. Goethe could associate *Dichtung* with *Wahrheit,* but in Dumas, too often the truth sits uneasily with the poetry.

ORESTES AND PYLADES

Among the books that Dumas mentions in his memoirs as having impressed him deeply in his childhood is Charles-Albert Demoustier's *Lettres à Émilie sur la mythologie* (Letters to Emily on Mythology, 1786–1798), and it was probably here that he first came across the story of Orestes and Pylades. After the murder of Agamemnon by his wife's lover Aegisthus, the child Orestes, Agamemnon's son, was taken away by his uncle Strophius and brought up in the same household as Strophius' son, Pylades. The two cousins became fast friends, and when they had grown to manhood it was Pylades who helped Orestes in his plan to kill both his stepfather Aegisthus and his mother Clytemnestra. The union between them was finally sealed when Pylades married Orestes' sister Electra.

This legend provides the basis for a persistent motif that recurs in one after another of the historical novels, although often with an odd variant: two young men, predestined to be inseparable friends, may start by being sworn enemies. Thus in *La reine Margot,* on the evening of 24 August 1572 two young cavaliers arrive in Paris, the one from Piedmont, the other from Provence. They both stop in front of an inn bearing the sign La Belle Étoile, and after a few words of conversation, they tell each other who they are: Annibal de Coconnas, Boniface de La Mole. Coconnas is well built and jovial, La Mole slender and melancholic. What is more to the point, this being the eve of Saint Bartholomew, Coconnas is a Catholic, La Mole a Protestant; the one has business with the duc de Guise, leader of the Catholic league, the other with Henri de Navarre, the head of the Huguenot faction. So,

having first booked rooms in the inn, they both make their way to the Louvre to report to their respective patrons.

They meet again at supper that night and afterward fall to playing cards. La Mole then goes to bed, and the innkeeper has a private word with Coconnas. Every Protestant is to be put to death that night; this includes La Mole. Coconnas objects: "'M. de La Mole is my companion, M. de La Mole has supped with me, M. de La Mole has played a game of cards with me.' 'Yes, but M. de La Mole is a heretic, M. de La Mole is condemned, and if we do not kill him, others will.'" Coconnas yields reluctantly to these arguments, but La Mole, forewarned, makes his escape over the rooftops.

In the subsequent fighting, the two young men encounter and wound one another, are nursed back to health, fight a duel and again wound one another, this time more seriously. Conconnas is the slower to recover, but La Mole nurses him devotedly, and when they are both on their feet again they are blood brothers for life; or as Dumas puts it:

> The friendship of the two gentlemen, which began in the inn of La Belle Étoile and was violently interrupted by the events of the night of Saint Bartholomew, was resumed henceforth with a new impetus, and soon outstripped that of Orestes and Pylades to the tune of five sword-thrusts and one pistol-shot distributed about their persons.
>
> (ch. 17)

The one falls in love with Marguerite de Navarre, the other with the duchesse de Nevers, but these highborn ladies cannot save them from a cruel and shameful end: both are arrested, tortured, and finally beheaded in public, Coconnas supporting his friend, whose bones have been broken by the executioner.

The formula that served Dumas so well in *La reine Margot* was used, whether consciously or unconsciously, fairly regularly in his historical fiction and can be said to constitute a key myth, one he found strangely irresistible. Essentially the myth requires an encounter between two young men from opposite camps who start by quarreling and then come to appreciate one another's qualities, after which they become bosom friends and sworn allies. In *La dame de Monsoreau,* in some respects a sequel to *La reine Margot,* the two are called Saint-Luc and Bussy d'Amboise. The fact that they serve different masters does not prevent them from espousing each other's interests throughout the book, and at the end, in the fatal ambush that is laid for Bussy, Saint-Luc is by his side to rescue Bussy's mistress Diane, though he cannot save his friend. In *Le collier de la reine* it is Philippe de Taverney and Olivier de Charny who represent the derivatives of this myth: both are young, both are aristocrats, both are new to the court—and both are passionately devoted to Marie Antoinette. Their rivalry is the source of the quarrel between them, finally resolved when the queen, to extricate herself from a compromising situation, arranges a marriage between Charny and Philippe's sister Andrée de Taverney. This union corresponds, of course, to one of the vicissitudes of the original legend, when Pylades marries Orestes' sister Electra.

But it is in *Le chevalier de Maison-Rouge* that the Orestes and Pylades legend is most obviously employed, in the story of the friendship between Maurice Lindey, the republican officer, and Lorin, the Anacreontic poet. It seems that Dumas took deliberate precautions lest it should ever cross his reader's mind that the strong affection that binds the young men together might be due to some more passionate tenderness that in his day was regarded as depraved. He could not altogether conceal the fact of Henri III's homosexuality, but he was careful to provide both La Mole and Coconnas with mistresses who exchange confidences about the prowess of their lovers. In *Le chevalier de Maison-Rouge* Maurice is jealously devoted to Geneviève Dixmer, and Lorin has his own mistress, Artémise, a girl shapely enough to compete for the honor of representing the Goddess of Reason in a kind of revolutionary

forerunner of the Miss World competitions of our day.

Both the young men are dedicated republicans, though Maurice's love for the royalist Geneviève puts this friendship to a severe test. As Lorin complains, before matters have gone very far: "You are forcing me to sacrifice my duty to my friendship, or my friend to my duty. And I am very much afraid, Maurice, that it is my duty I shall sacrifice." Later, Lorin remonstrates with him more seriously, warning him he is on a slippery slope: "I am not blaming you, I am arguing with you. Remember the altercations Pylades and Orestes used to have every day, proving beyond question that friendship is a mere paradox, since these model friends were forever quarrelling" (ch. 32). In the end both Lorin and Maurice are arrested, together with Geneviève, and all three are guillotined.

Les trois mousquetaires, Dumas's most famous historical novel, shows not two friends, but four; we may regard this situation as a simple reduplication of the original pattern. The opening chapters show the same initial hostility of the characters, springing this time from trivial causes: D'Artagnan, in his impetuous chase after Rochefort, succeeds in provoking the anger of each of the musketeers in turn and agrees to meet them on the dueling ground at half-hourly intervals to settle the quarrel. D'Artagnan is about to cross swords with Athos—Porthos and Aramis are waiting their turn—when a detachment of the cardinal's guardsmen arrives on the scene to arrest them, dueling, under a recent edict, having been prohibited by law. The musketeers refuse to yield their swords and prepare to resist. D'Artagnan, seeing they are three against five, does not hesitate to join the minority. The result of this battle, which Dumas, himself a practiced swordsman, describes in great detail, is the defeat and rout of the cardinal's men. Later, in chapter 9, having buried their quarrel, the musketeers swear their celebrated oath at D'Artagnan's invitation: "All for one, and one for all!"

Of the three musketeers, Porthos may well be the one for whom D'Artagnan feels most affection: Porthos, the gentle, stupid giant, the Obélix to D'Artagnan's Astérix, always astonished at his friend's perspicacity and foresight. Porthos represents brute strength and vanity, two qualities that should hardly commend him to the reader; but in addition he has a certain childlike innocence that one cannot but find endearing; when Dumas eventually killed him off in *Le vicomte de Bragelonne,* his son saw him wipe a tear from his eye. Athos has a nobility of soul that in *Les trois mousquetaires* is obscured by his strange taciturnity and his occasional bouts of heavy drinking; but in *Vingt ans après,* the immediate sequel, this addiction to wine has been conquered, thanks to the need to set an example for his son Raoul. And Athos has at all times *moral* courage (physical courage, needless to say, is something all four possess in equal measure); Athos is the only one who is not overawed by Richelieu. Aramis is, as Dumas calls him, a hieroglyph: he yearns to enter the church when a soldier, but hankers after a life of soldierly activity when in his monastery; and at all times he is a man of mysteries and secrets jealously guarded. But D'Artagnan is the man of good counsel, the planner, and the others realize this and let him organize every strategy. Although the youngest of them all, D'Artagnan is judged by Athos to be the soundest reasoner, "la plus forte tête," of the quartet.

It has been said that *Les trois mousquetaires* is a novel imbued with the spirit of the early morning. It has a juvenile charm and brio, which in *Vingt ans après* has been lost, to be replaced by the lengthening shadows of the afternoon. It is in *Vingt ans après* that the Orestes and Pylades myth can be seen reasserting itself, with the musketeers split into two groups, at first hostile to each other and later joining forces.

Les trois mousquetaires had ended on a melancholy note. After all the adventure of the road, after "all quality, pride, pomp, and circumstance of glorious wars," the four friends disperse, and D'Artagnan is left mourning his lost youth. Over the next twenty years, nothing happens to him but to grow into middle age. *Vingt ans après* shows him still awaiting promotion, serving Cardinal Mazarin instead of Cardinal Richelieu and aware of the sad difference. Mazarin has few supporters on whom he can rely, and he has heard of the exploits of the four musketeers in former times. He would feel safer with them as a bodyguard. So he asks D'Artagnan to trace his old friends and bring them together once more, a task that takes him all over France and is only half successful. Porthos alone is willing to join him, on promise of a barony. But Athos and Aramis are not prepared to serve Mazarin, being members of the Fronde, the party of disaffected gentlemen pledged to the overthrow of the cardinal. The discovery that they are on different sides is made when the four clash in a midnight encounter. D'Artagnan and Porthos are outnumbered and forced to retire, but they agree to meet the other two in the Place Royale the following day. Talking over the situation with Porthos beforehand, D'Artagnan makes the point that none of them is so wedded to the cause they serve that they should think their new loyalties outweigh the old one: "No, it is not the civil wars that separate us, it is the fact that none of us is twenty any longer, that the generous impulses of youth have given way to the murmurings of self-interest, the whisper of ambition and the counsels of egoism" (ch. 29). Nevertheless, at the actual meeting there is distrust on both sides until Athos symbolically breaks his sword across his knee and urges Aramis to do the same, swearing he will never again turn his weapon against either Porthos or D'Artagnan. The others are carried away by this effusion of manly sentiment and repeat after him, on Aramis's crucifix, the oath "to be united in spite of all and forever."

And so the "band of brothers" is reconstituted, free to follow the call of adventure. Shortly afterward they all find themselves in England, D'Artagnan and Porthos as Mazarin's ambassadors to Oliver Cromwell, Athos and Aramis obedient to the request of the unfortunate Queen Henrietta, who wants at least two intrepid friends near her husband, Charles I, in his hour of need. It is D'Artagnan, subsequently, who devises successive plans to deliver the king, with as much ingenuity and as little success as the chevalier de Maison-Rouge has trying to save Marie Antoinette from the ferocious Jacobins. Then the musketeers return to France and this time join forces against Mazarin, whose treachery releases D'Artagnan from his duty to him. Everyone is satisfied in the end—the villains all dead, and Louis XIV in the wings, ready to take over when he reaches his majority in a year's time. *Vingt ans après* concludes much as does *Les trois mousquetaires:* Porthos returns to his estate to enjoy his new dignity, Aramis to his monastery; and D'Artagnan agrees to keep an eye on Raoul for Athos: "The four friends embraced with tears in their eyes. Then they separated without knowing whether they would ever meet again." But at least, more fortunate than Coconnas or La Mole, than Lorin and Lindey, they do not meet on the scaffold.

PRISONERS AND ESCAPEES

In *The Romantic Prison* (1978) Victor Brombert establishes the theme of imprisonment as both fundamental and widespread in all romantic literatures in Europe. No author was so preoccupied with the subject as Dumas, and there is scarcely one of his novels in which it is not introduced somewhere or other. In his first successful attempt at a work of fiction, *Le chevalier d'Harmental*, the hero is sent to the Bastille by the prince regent for his part in a conspiracy that miscarried; the book ends with his release, his captor unexpectedly relenting. *La tulipe noire* (*The Black Tulip*, 1850), a historical novel set exceptionally in Holland, opens with a description of the mob bursting into the Buytenhoff prison,

in order to drag Cornelius de Witt from his cell and lynch him. Later in the same book the harmless tulip grower Cornelius van Baerle is imprisoned at Dordrecht on a trumped-up charge and is released only with the help of the jailer's daughter.

In France there was one prison above all whose destruction was still regarded as symbolizing the beginning of a new era; this was the Bastille. In *Ange Pitou* Dumas describes at length and in detail its storming and the butchery of its garrison. At the start of the account, he reminds us that "there was not just one bastille in France; there were a score of bastilles, called Fort-l'Évêque, Saint-Lazare, le Châtelet, la Conciergerie, Vincennes, le château de la Roche, le château d'If . . ." (ch. 13). For readers of *Le comte de Monte-Cristo*, a novel set in Dumas's own time, the château d'If is the most celebrated of all, the island prison in the Mediterranean that lies no more than a short boat ride from Marseilles.

On the point of marrying his chosen bride, Mercédès, Dantès falls victim to the machinations of Fernand, his rival in love, and Danglars, a fellow seaman who bears him a grudge. They denounce Dantès to the authorities as a Bonapartist agent, and it falls to a certain Villefort to investigate the case. Unluckily Villefort, a magistrate loyal to the monarchy, happens to be the son of an ardent Bonapartist, and Dantès was the bearer of a highly compromising letter addressed to Villefort's father. Villefort has Dantès brought before him, convinces himself that the young man knows nothing of the contents of the letter, and destroys it in front of his eyes; but to make assurance doubly sure, he signs the order for Dantès's indefinite imprisonment in the château d'If. The lettres de cachet of the ancien régime have been legally abolished, but administrative action can achieve the same ends, sending a man to prison without trial, without his ever knowing the reasons, and with no hope of any revision of the sentence; for he has not been formally sentenced.

Dantès remains in prison for fourteen

years. After the first seventeen months he is visited by a prison inspector, whom he implores to bring him to trial. He waits patiently for a fortnight, three months, ten months, until he begins to wonder whether the inspector's visit has not been a dream. He asks for a glimpse of the sun, the chance to take exercise, books to occupy his mind; all these are refused him, and he is denied even conversation, for the warders have orders not to speak to him. It would be an inhuman punishment for one guilty of the worst crime, and for a man who knows himself guiltless of any crime it is a pointless torture. Dantès realizes he has had the misfortune to cross the path of unscrupulous enemies. He does not know who they are, but he condemns them in imagination to the worst of torments and finds even the worst is too good for them. Then he makes up his mind to die by refusing food; he is near to achieving his purpose when he hears a scratching at the wall near his bed.

It is his neighbor, the abbé Faria, who has been in prison four years longer than he has. Faria has occupied his time tunneling, but in the wrong direction, since he ended in Dantès's cell when he thought he was working his way to the sea. Faria is his salvation; he teaches Dantès everything, for Dantès, a poor sailor, knows nothing but his trade. But Faria gives him little hope of escape:

> I have but rarely seen escapes succeed. Lucky escapes, escapes crowned with complete success, are escapes that have been carefully planned, prepared step by step. That is how the duc de Beaufort escaped from the château de Vincennes, the abbé Dubuquoi from Fort-l'Évêque, and Latude from the Bastille. There are also those that chance may offer; these are the best; let us wait our opportunity, and if it presents itself, let us profit from it.

(ch. 16)

The opportunity arises, not for Faria but for Dantès. Faria dies and is sewn into a sack; Dantès has the courage to reenter the dead man's cell, remove the corpse and put it in his own bed, then hide inside Faria's sack. He expects to be buried somewhere on the island, but the prison officers toss him into the sea, for "the sea is the cemetery of the château d'If." And so at last Dantès, having cut himself out of his sack, swims to freedom.

The escape of the duc de Beaufort, to which Faria made reference, forms a substantial part of Dumas's narrative in *Vingt ans après*. The episode is related in the comic vein as much as Dantès's imprisonment is presented in the tragic. In the social scale the two prisoners are a world apart: Beaufort, a prince of the blood, one of the grandsons of Henri IV; Dantès, an insignificant member of the French merchant navy. The duke is allowed all the amusements, exercise, and delicate fare of which Dantès is cruelly deprived. Beaufort, who is brave, popular, but rather stupid, spends his time breathing fire and slaughter against Mazarin, to whom he owes his imprisonment. One of his pastimes is to draw caricatures of the cardinal, using charcoal from the fire, until Monsieur de Chavigny, governor of the château de Vincennes, forbids the fire to be lit and lets Beaufort shiver. He then spends months training a dog to carry out various tricks highly disrespectful of the cardinal; the dog is poisoned. And so the petty war goes on, the prisoner being treated with all the respect due to his rank, but in fact thwarted at every turn.

Eventually the duke's escape is organized by his friends outside, among whom is Athos, who contrives that his own servant, Grimaud, should be given employment in the prison; Grimaud smuggles in a silk cord under the crust of a venison pasty. The cord allows Beaufort to climb down the outside walls to where three friends wait with horses:

> "Gentlemen," said the prince, "I will thank you all later; but at this moment, there is no time to be lost, we must be on our way. Let him who loves me, follow me!" And he leapt on to his horse and sped off at a gallop, filling his lungs

with air and shouting out with an expression of joy impossible to convey: "Free! . . . free! . . . free!"

(ch. 15)

One other unforgettable escape, which has catastrophic consequences, is that of Milady in *Les trois mousquetaires* after she has been decoyed by De Winter to his castle near Portsmouth. She has only a few days to break out if she is to fulfill Richelieu's order and prevent the departure of Buckingham with his fleet to the relief of the embattled Huguenots at La Rochelle. Felton, the warder De Winter has found for her, appears incorruptible, until she discovers him to be a religious enthusiast, which gives her a hold over him. She pretends to be a co-religionary and, further, invents such convincing tales about Buckingham's wickedness that Felton not only agrees to arrange her escape, but having done so seeks audience with the admiral and stabs him. The assassination is historical fact, though what the real Felton's motives may have been is a matter for conjecture; Dumas's explanation, if farfetched, is at least dramatically effective as well as psychologically plausible.

Not all imprisonments end with the escape of the prisoner. The Man in the Iron Mask, whose story dominates the last part of *Le vicomte de Bragelonne,* is never released, and La Mole and Coconnas only leave their prison cells for the torture chamber and, some weeks later, for the place of execution. We have seen how, in spite of the efforts of the musketeers, nothing can be done to save Charles I from the ax. Seen from the vantage point of posterity, the fate of Marie Antoinette has a similar inevitability. The imprisonment of the royal family in the Tour du Temple, part of the medieval fortress that used to belong to the Knights Templars in Paris, took place on 13 August 1792. On 5 December the trial of Louis XVI opened before the Convention and on 21 January 1793 he was executed. So much belongs to the history of France; Dumas's *Le chevalier de Maison-Rouge,* the action of which starts on 10 March 1793, follows the developing story quite closely, down to the queen's trial and execution on 16 October. The royal family, or what was left of it—the queen, her fourteen-year-old daughter, and her young son—are at first shown sharing a room in the Temple. But on the refusal of all three to answer questions concerning an attempt the previous night to spirit them away, the boy, the uncrowned heir to the throne, who was always known to royalists as Louis XVII or the Orphan of the Temple, is removed from his mother's care and given into the custody of the brutal shoemaker Simón. After a further attempt by her would-be deliverers that again unluckily fails, the queen is removed to the Conciergerie, the most ancient prison in Paris, destined to hold many other victims of the Terror, including in the last batch Maximilien Robespierre, hoist with his own petard, since he was the man principally responsible for the use of the guillotine as an instrument of policy. Dumas's portrayal of Marie Antoinette at this stage shows her to be no longer the same haughty queen we see in *Le collier de la reine* and in *Ange Pitou;* she is humble, eager to notice signs of compassion in the tone of voice of her warders, however rudely they may address her. One final plot is hatched to set her free, which she refuses to allow since it involves killing two guards, whose deaths she does not want on her conscience. An alternative scheme is devised, in which she is asked to saw through one of the bars of her cell. But there are by now two agents working to rescue the queen, each in ignorance of the other's plans, and their efforts in effect cancel one another out. History, or destiny, did not intend that Marie Antoinette should escape the guillotine.

PROVIDENCE: THE GRAND DESIGN

We have noted how Marie Antoinette had been shown the manner of her death when she first crossed the frontier into France, arriving as the dauphin's bride in 1770. At the start of the long novel cycle that bears his name, the mysterious Joseph Balsamo, an unwelcome guest at the château de Taverney, mentions that the future queen of France will be arriving the following day and will honor the old baron de Taverney by visiting his tumbledown house. The prediction is duly fulfilled and Balsamo's reputation as a sorcerer confirmed. The princess thereupon asks him to tell her fortune, which at first he declines to do, saying it is better she should remain in ignorance of the future. But she insists, and taking a glass of clear water, he places it in a dark corner and tells the princess to look at it kneeling, "so that you will be in the posture needed to pray God to spare you the terrible end that you are about to see" (ch. 15).

Balsamo's injunction raises by implication the whole question of human freedom and predestination, for if the end that is already determined for Marie Antoinette can be averted by her prayers, then it is clearly not immutably fixed; and if it cannot be averted, then why does Balsamo invite her to pray?

Curiously, although the breath of freedom is part of the very atmosphere of Dumas's world, so that no worse fate can befall any of his characters than to be trapped in a prison, in a larger sense his characters often give the impression of being the helpless prisoners of a chain of circumstance variously called Providence, destiny, chance, or God: "chance, or rather God, whom we see at the bottom of everything," he writes in *La tulipe noire* (ch. 14), using the authorial *we*. In an unusual passage of metaphysical argument almost apologetically introduced into *Les quarante-cinq* as one of Chicot's "ingenious theories" (3.19), Dumas develops the idea that chance events are God's "reserve forces," using the term in the military sense. When it seems that men have everything under control and are guiding events in the direction that suits them best, then God "brings up his reserve" and casts in front of the wheels the chance pebble that alters the course of events, causing them

to run as he wishes, not as men have calculated they should run. Dumas is saying a little more here than that "the best laid schemes of mice an' men/Gang aft a-gley"; for the best laid schemes ought not to go astray, Dumas reasons, and there is no accounting for the fact that they do unless one allows for the intervention of an intelligent power beyond men's reckoning.

A striking illustration of the working of this power is to be found in the Musketeers saga. In *Les trois mousquetaires* we learn how Athos in his youth met and fell in love with the talented, beautiful, but perversely wicked woman spoken of in the book simply as Milady. He married her, then discovered she had been branded by the hangman on the shoulder, proof that she had been found guilty of some unspeakable crime, sacrilege at the least. He ordered his servants to hang her on the nearest tree, but, as so often is the case in Dumas, the dead have a habit of coming back to life again. Much of *Les trois mousquetaires* is concerned with the attempt by Athos, seconded by his friends, to complete this piece of unfinished business; eventually Milady is captured and, in full view of the four musketeers and of De Winter, her head is struck off by the public executioner. It is a private act of justice. But Athos is never entirely satisfied that he had the right to take the law into his own hands; when he learns that Milady had a son, and that the son, known as Mordaunt, has come of age and is seeking revenge on his mother's murderers, he is thrown into turmoil, seeing the young man as nemesis made flesh, sacred, inviolable. When Aramis aims a musket at Mordaunt, Athos strikes it down, murmuring, "It was quite enough to have killed the mother. . . . The son has done us no harm." Even when Athos learns that Mordaunt had been Charles Stuart's executioner and later came within an ace of blowing up all the musketeers in the ship that was to take them back to France, Athos is still unwilling to let Mordaunt die. In one of the most memorable scenes of *Vingt ans après* Mordaunt is swimming in the open sea, begging them to have pity on him and take him aboard, pleading that a son is always bound to try and avenge his mother's death. Athos, in agony of spirit, stretches out a rescuing hand. But Mordaunt will be avenged even at the cost of his own life and drags Athos off the boat and down into the depths of the sea with him. The others watch in horror, but after an interval the lifeless body of Mordaunt, with a dagger in his chest, floats to the surface, and a little later Athos, exhausted, rises to the surface and clutches the side of the boat. "It was not I who killed him," he whispers, "it was destiny" (ch. 77). Was it destiny that allowed Mordaunt to escape Aramis's musket and D'Artagnan's sword only to die at the hand of the man who least wanted to kill him?

For the novelist, who predetermines the novel's denouement, what can pass as the work of Providence or of destiny is simply the slow achievement of the denouement, and his art consists in persuading the reader that what appears fortuitous is actually foreordained and can take on the semblance of a pattern working itself out. But it is different when the novelist is dealing with large movements of history, where the eventual outcome is known to all. For Dumas, as we have seen, history was largely transacted in the courts and palaces of kings. He deals with the decline of two dynasties, that of the Valois and that of the Bourbons. He seems to have subscribed to the theory that all dynasties degenerate in time. In the case of the Bourbons, he was provided with a majestic instance, stretching over two centuries, of this slow but irreversible decadence. The Bourbons were brought to the throne in the person of the "good" king Henri IV and achieved unparalleled greatness under his grandson Louis XIV. They declined in the person of the voluptuary Louis XV, during whose long reign the storms gathered, and finally collapsed with Louis XVI, a worthy man but a weak monarch, incapable of controlling or combating the revolutionary march of events. The portrait Dumas draws of Louis

XVI in *Ange Pitou* testifies amply to the final abjection:

> This short, stout body, with no spring and no majesty, these blurred features devoid of expression, this pallid juvenility wrestling with premature senescence, this unequal struggle of a powerful physique and a mediocre intelligence, to which the pride of rank alone gave intermittent flashes of value . . . all that signified degeneration, debasement, impotence, ruin.
>
> (ch. 22)

Yet Louis XVI was the direct descendant, five generations removed, of Henri IV, the intelligent, ambitious, farsighted king who seems, in the Valois novels, to have no chance at all of succeeding to the throne but who works steadily toward that end. He is secretive, watchful, ready to change his religion back and forth as occasion demands, forcing himself to face dangers boldly when he cannot face them fearlessly, constantly opposed by that most redoubtable of adversaries, the all-powerful queen mother Catherine de Médicis, who is totally unscrupulous, who threatens his life time and again, but who confesses herself in the end beaten: "The hand of God is stretched over this man. He will reign, he will reign!" (*La reine Margot*, ch. 34).

Catherine has her own soothsayer, the perfumer René, whose shop on the Pont Saint-Michel is shunned by the superstitious townsfolk, particularly at night. The scene in the nineteenth chapter of *La reine Margot* is to all intents and purposes a repeat of the first act of *Henri III et sa cour*, written sixteen years before. Catherine is visiting René to watch him read the future in the entrails of chickens that she herself kills and disembowels. The omens are always the same: the chicken squawks three times and its liver is seen hanging on the left; this betokens three deaths followed by the extinction of the line. The deaths are those of her three sons: first Charles, the present king; then François, who will never reign; and finally Henri III, the last of the line, who will be assassinated by Jacques Clément. Inspection of the chicken's brain shows the letter *h* repeated four times; so Henri de Navarre will reign over France as Henri IV.

Given that Catherine clearly believes her interpretation of the omens, it seems illogical that she should strive to prove them false by making a series of attempts on her son-in-law's life: "This hateful Henri, forever eluding her ambushes which would be fatal to others, seemed to walk under the protection of some invincible power that Catherine insisted on calling chance, though at the bottom of her heart a voice told her the true name of this power was destiny" (ch. 37); and destiny controls and provokes the chance event. Her last plot miscarries disastrously. Catherine borrows a rare book on falconry belonging to René and treats each page with a poison she has used before; it is slightly sticky and causes the leaves to adhere. She tells François d'Alençon, her youngest son, to leave the book in Henri's chamber, but it is Charles IX who finds it there and who starts reading it, licking his fingers to turn the pages. François, watching him helplessly and knowing that his brother has already absorbed a mortal dose of the poison, "bethought himself that there was a God in heaven who was perhaps not chance" (ch. 40). Catherine's efforts to defeat destiny are thus turned to her own confusion, for she has no control over chance, the chance that took the king to Henri's chamber in his absence, the chance that always works to turn to predestined ends even the most ingenious of her plans.

Chance, fate, the will of God: to Dumas these bring about the fall of the Valois, in part because the last kings of this dynasty are particularly weak, in part because their ultimate successor is particularly cunning. But it is chance that works as the instrument of destiny: the chance that Charles IX read the work on falconry, the chance that Henri III is a homosexual and has no heir, and the chance that his natural heir, his younger brother François, has incurred the deadly hatred of Diane de Monsoreau and that her faithful follower, Rémy le Haudouin, has discovered the secret of the *aqua tofana*, the poison the Médicis perfected. It is the Valois's own sins and follies that bring destruction on them; in this way Dumas succeeds in equating chance with fate and fate with the will of God without ever wearying the reader with a triumphant demonstration of these equivalences; events are allowed to speak for themselves.

The omens are a different matter, and it is possible that divination by the inspection of animals' entrails (haruspication) was introduced into *La reine Margot* simply to provide the local color of an age when superstition and barbarous cruelty were still rife and men's lives were held almost as cheap as hens'. There is some evidence that Dumas did believe events could be foretold by guesswork based on intelligent interpretation of current trends; but forecasting of this kind is very different from René's precise predictions of the manner in which the line of the Valois will become extinct and very different again from Balsamo's accurate and detailed prophecies, notably in the prologue to *Le collier de la reine*. Here Cagliostro (Balsamo under an adopted name) is attending a dinner party hosted by Cardinal Richelieu in April 1784. Using once more his glass of clear water, Cagliostro is able to predict the violent ends of most of the other guests, beginning with La Pérouse, the explorer. La Pérouse is about to leave on his last, ill-fated expedition, in the course of which he will be killed by the natives of one of the South Pacific islands. This disastrous outcome is predicted by the seer after La Pérouse has left the house. Why did Cagliostro not warn him? ask the others in alarm. "Any warning would be useless," he replies; "the man who sees where destiny is leading cannot change that destiny" (ch. 2). This observation confirms what Dumas wrote in *La tulipe noire*:

When fate starts ordering some disaster, it seldom happens that it fails to warn its victim in charity, just as a swordsman warns his adversary, so as to give him time to put up his guard. Almost always, these warnings come from the instinct of self-preservation in man or from the complicity of inanimate objects, often less inanimate than is generally supposed; almost always these warnings are ignored. The blow whistles through the air and falls on the head of the man whom the noise should have warned and who, on receiving the warning, should have taken cover.

(ch. 17)

This is the law by which Dumas meets the objection that a knowledge of the future that should enable men to avoid disaster seldom does; the god speaks through Cassandra, but her prophecies are always mocked.

A historical figure, today Cagliostro is usually accounted a clever charlatan. The question historians have never resolved is how he managed to win the following he did in such a skeptical age as his, when doubt was thrown on all oracles, portents, and soothsaying. Dumas chose to regard him as a man with occult powers, not just a prophet of the future but a man who had virtually conquered death and discovered the secret of seeing what was happening at great distances by sending a suitable medium into a trance and instructing her spirit where to go and what to look for. Two such mediums figure in *Joseph Balsamo:* the first is Balsamo's own wife, Lorenza, with whom he abstains from sexual relations for fear she should lose her powers; and the second is Andrée de Taverney, the future comtesse de Charny.

The belief, prevalent in the romantic age, that certain mystic powers were vested in virginity, may account for the fact that both Lorenza and Andrée need to remain undefiled if they are to be of any use to Balsamo. But he is eventually unable to resist the temptation to make love to Lorenza, and Andrée, inadvertently left by him in a mesmeric trance, is found by Gilbert, who rapes her. Knowing nothing of what has happened, she is horrified to find herself pregnant, until Balsamo reveals the true facts to her brother Philippe. Gilbert offers to marry Andrée, who contemptuously refuses, so he arranges to steal the child shortly after his birth and have him brought up by a foster mother in a remote village.

It is hard to be certain what Dumas meant us to think of Gilbert. His behavior toward Andrée is atrocious. She is presented as innocent, a dutiful daughter and an affectionate sister, and if she refuses to encourage or even countenance the love of the lowborn Gilbert, she surely has the right to give her heart to which man she chooses. In fact she later falls in love with Olivier de Charny and marries him. In killing Gilbert at the end of *Joseph Balsamo*, Philippe is doing no more than any brother should according to the prevailing convention, especially since he had offered Gilbert fair combat beforehand. Yet Gilbert is not entirely unworthy: he is proud though poor, he is not lacking in courage (there is an occasion when he risks his own life to save Andrée's), and he thinks for himself. He has absorbed the basic philosophy of the Enlightenment: "that all men are brothers, that societies are ill-organized where some are serfs and slaves, that one day all individuals will be equal" (ch. 4). If he is on occasion cruel, if he takes advantage of helpless innocence, he can be said in such instances to foreshadow the cruelties and injustices of the French Revolution. When Dumas resurrects Gilbert in *Ange Pitou,* he gives his previous conduct a certain symbolic value and thereby to some extent excuses it. As Marie Antoinette reflects:

This under-gardener, this Gilbert, was he not a living symbol of what is happening at this time, a man of the people who can rise above the baseness of his birth to concern himself with the politics of a great kingdom, a strange actor who seems to personify in himself, thanks to the evil genius that is hovering over France, both the insult offered to the aristocracy and the attack made on the monarchy by the plebs?

(ch. 31)

Having violated a daughter of the aristocracy in times past, Gilbert has returned to flout the royal authority by helping to sack the Bastille; it is all of a piece.

The problems of personal power, free will, and the workings of Providence are nowhere dealt with so fully as in *Le comte de Monte-Cristo*. After he has regained his freedom, Dantès remembers how Faria had led him to discover the identity of the secret enemies who had condemned him to perpetual imprisonment. Faria had asked him who could have profited from the crime. Three names were mentioned: Danglars, in whose interest it was that Dantès should not become captain of his ship; Fernand, who envied Dantès his bride, Mercédès, whom he himself wished to marry; and Villefort, to whose father Dantès was carrying the incriminating letter. Once Dantès secures the fabulous treasure that Faria had bequeathed him, he devotes himself single-mindedly to exacting terrible retribution from these three men. He soon discovers that they are still alive and prosperous, never thinking for one moment of the poor sailor they left moldering in the underground dungeons of the château d'If.

A modern Monte-Cristo, in possession of great wealth and desiring vengeance, might have hired an assassin and disposed of the three in short order. But Dantès has noticed that this is not how God works; He moves slowly, along tortuous paths, and Dantès/Monte-Cristo wants to imitate him. He has an important conversation at an early stage with Villefort (who of course has no idea who this multimillionaire really is) in which the count explains his intentions by means of a parable. He relates how Satan once tempted him, as he had tempted the Savior before, offering to give him whatever he wanted if he agreed to bow down and worship him. After long reflection, Monte-Cristo had said to Satan: "Listen, I have always heard tell of Providence, and yet I have never seen it, nor anything that resembles it, which makes me think it does not exist; I wish to be that Providence, for I know

nothing finer, more splendid, more sublime in the world than to dispense rewards and punishments." Satan sighed. "You are mistaken," he said. "Providence exists; only you cannot see her, because as a daughter of God, she is invisible as he is. You have seen nothing that resembles her, since she works by hidden devices and walks along obscure ways. All I can do for you is to make you one of the agents of Providence" (ch. 48). So Monte-Cristo accepted the bargain, and declares now that even if it meant consigning his soul to perdition, he would if required strike the same bargain a second time.

As the agent of Providence Monte-Cristo has simply to observe the working of cause and effect and occasionally to intervene actively to smooth its path. But on the whole the criminals bring about their own downfall. What is curious is that they are never brought to book for callously causing an innocent man to spend fourteen years cut off from the light of day, but for other crimes they have committed since, which they had thought so well hidden as to be undiscoverable. The count needs merely to bring these to light for the criminals to suffer their due punishment. It is thus no personal vendetta that he is pursuing; he is the servant of a higher justice. Mercédès tells him that her son blames him for the misfortunes that have befallen his father, but Monte-Cristo replies that they are not misfortunes but the chastisement of the Almighty: "It is not I who strike down M. de Morcerf [Fernand], it is Providence that is punishing him." "And who are you to substitute yourself for Providence?" she asks, and he shows her the letter of denunciation that Fernand wrote those many years ago. It was thanks to this act of treachery that Fernand was able to marry her; but another act, just as treacherous, won him his vast fortune, and Monte-Cristo, who has brought this last one to public knowledge, is having him punished for it: "Betrayed, assassinated, cast into a tomb, I have emerged from this tomb by God's grace, and I owe it to God to avenge myself. He has sent me to accomplish this vengeance, and this I will do" (ch. 39).

Monte-Cristo remains implacable almost to the very end, until he realizes that he had taken on himself more than a man should. When Villefort shows him the dead bodies of his wife and son, "he realized he had overstepped the rightful bounds of revenge; he realized he could no longer say: God is with me and for me" (ch. 111). For the first time he doubts whether he is justified in doing what he has done. For "the gods commit no evil, the gods can stay their hands when they wish; chance is not their master, they on the contrary are the lords of chance" (ch. 112). Monte-Cristo, superman though he is, cannot foresee every consequence of his actions, and so he cannot avoid staining the integrity of his purpose by committing incidental evil. Is he not being punished for blasphemy when he thought to substitute himself for Providence? This uncertainty, this ambiguity, hangs like a dark cloud over the concluding pages of *Le comte de Monte-Cristo*.

REMEMBRANCE OF THINGS PAST

Although it was widely accepted in the nineteenth century that playwrights were free to enlist collaborators (and well over half the plays staged in Paris during this period were the work of two or three writers), it was just as generally understood that a novel could only have one author. The exceptions to this rule—the Goncourt brothers, Erckmann and Chatrian—were regarded as allowable since they signed their works together; there was therefore no deception. Dumas was a different case. It was known that he had several collaborators, among them Auguste Maquet, whose name he never allowed to appear on the cover of any of his novels. As far as is known, Maquet never wished to have credit and was quite content to let Dumas use the discoveries he made in his reading without expecting anything more than the handsome fee the great

man paid him. But the arrangement that worked so well for many years broke down around 1851. Dumas, as we have seen, relied on the appetite of the newspapers for serial stories to provide him with the large income he needed for foreign travel, for building himself a palatial house outside Paris, for financing his own theater, and of course for paying Maquet for his research work. Once that source of income dried up, Dumas, always generous to a fault and recklessly improvident, suddenly found himself insolvent; he broke abruptly with Maquet and left Paris for Brussels in full flight from his creditors.

The long succession of historical novels came to an end, the last being *La comtesse de Charny,* in which, as Craig Bell has said, "instead of history being embedded in romance, romance is embedded in history." Much of it reads like raw Maquet, without the leaven that Dumas's imagination and style normally gave to his friend's scenarios. Dumas busied himself instead with his memoirs, a project he had conceived around 1874. Even though he recounts the story of his life only to 1832, the point at which he left France for a tour of Switzerland, they turned out to be the longest single work he ever wrote. In fact the enormously popular *Impressions de voyage en Suisse* (*Travels in Switzerland,* 1833–1837), though written and published long before *Mes mémoires* (*My Memoirs,* 1852–1855) were even started, can be regarded as a kind of continuation of them.

If personal preferences go for anything, the first part of *Mes mémoires* can be recommended as the best; it covers Dumas's boyhood in Villers-Cotterêts and in the surrounding forests, before he left for Paris. At the age of fifty, Dumas could still recall with evident relish and total accuracy the household as it existed before his father's death. In particular he depicts such delightful characters as the black servant Hippolyte, who—with disastrous results—tended to take too literally the orders he was given, and the gardener Pierre, whom Dumas recalls cutting open a live snake before his eyes to free the frog it had swallowed. Dumas remembers his father taking him to see Marie Pauline Borghese, Napoleon's younger sister; on another occasion the child was frightened out of his wits at the sight of what he took to be a witch—it was Madame de Genlis, the illustrious author. After his father's death the family fell on hard times, but the little boy did not experience this change of circumstance as a change for the worse. The forest of Compiègne became a limitless playground; the birds and beasts that were its denizens became his companions and at times his victims; the poachers became his friends, and the gamekeepers his natural enemies. He writes with especial affection of a certain ill-favored, pockmarked villain called Boudoux, whose great talent was his ability to imitate the calls of birds and attract them onto limed twigs; on one occasion the boy spent three days and nights in the woods with him and reappeared only when his mother had given him up for lost. Dumas remembered Boudoux's talent later and attributed it to Ange Pitou, a composite of all the clever poachers he had known in his boyhood.

Compelled to dwell on the distant past to write these opening chapters of his autobiography, in middle age Dumas found the memories returning to him with a sort of magic vividness. Between 1827 and 1847, as he says in the prologue to *Le meneur de loups* (The Wolf Man, 1857), he had scarcely ever thought of the little villages lost in the forest where his boyhood was spent; he was always eagerly pressing on into the future, which seemed to hold so much promise. But once all his literary and worldly ambitions were achieved, he found himself dwelling with nostalgia on the past.

On the verge of entering the sandy deserts, one is quite astonished to see gradually emerge beside the path one has already trodden, marvellous oases of shadow and greenery, alongside which one had passed not only without stopping, but almost without seeing them. One was in such a hurry those days, pressing on to reach the goal that is never reached—happiness! It is at that moment that one realizes how blind and ungrateful one has been; it is then that one resolves that if ever again one should encounter on one's path one of those leafy groves, one will stop there for the rest of one's life, and plant one's tent to end one's days in that spot.

But, as he goes on to say, these oases never reappear, except in memory.

Memory, that brilliant will-o-the-wisp, dances above the receding track; memory alone is sure not to lose her way. Then, every time she revisits an oasis, every time she recaptures some past incident, memory returns to the tired traveller and, like a humming of bees, like the song of a bird, like a murmur of spring water, she tells him what she has seen.

So, while Dumas was still writing his memoirs, he also began writing a series of short novels set in the countryside around Villers-Cotterêts, much as George Sand, who counted as one of his most ardent admirers, had written in her forties the stories set in her native Berry that today remain the most widely read part of her oeuvre: *La mare au diable* (*The Devil's Pool*, 1846), *La petite Fadette* (*Little Fadette*, 1848), *François le champi* (*François the Foundling*, 1850). The stories that draw on Dumas's past are set in a different part of France but have the same strongly marked regional flavor, the same tinge of folklore and legend. *Conscience l'innocent* (*Conscience the Innocent*, 1852), *Catherine Blum* (1854), and *Le meneur de loups* are three very different works; the first the tale of a simpleminded village boy, regarded nonetheless with affection and even admiration by the countryfolk; the second an idyll between the son and the niece of an honest gamekeeper in which the course of true love is threatened by rivals and by a villainous vagrant called Mathieu; and the third a weird legend of a wolf man, with overtones of the Faust myth.

From 1853, when he returned to Paris, until 1857, Dumas was busy running his own newspaper, *Le mousquetaire*. In 1858 he set off on a long trip through czarist Russia, starting in St. Petersburg and going as far south as the Caspian Sea and the Caucasus mountains. Then came his celebrated adventure with Garibaldi in Sicily and Naples. When he finally returned to Paris, in 1864, the decline was beginning to set in; he had put on weight, he was no longer as active as before, nor as adventurous, and when an invitation came to visit the United States, he wriggled out of it. He was still writing until the very end: *Les blancs et les bleus* (*The Whites and the Blues*, 1867–1868), a historical novel of the revolutionary wars; two collections of retrospective essays, the *Souvenirs dramatiques* (*Memoirs of the Stage*, 1868) and *Histoire de mes bêtes* (*The Story of My Pet Animals*, 1868), and yet another novel, *Création et rédemption* (*Creation and Redemption*, 1872), not published until after his death. The title is possibly more suggestive than the plot, which concerns the long efforts, ultimately successful, of a doctor to instill intelligence into the mind of an idiot girl.

It is almost an axiom of nineteenth-century French literary history that those writers who were idolized during their lifetime—Dumas, Hugo—should suffer neglect after their death and never totally recover the status they enjoyed, while those who were neglected and misprized while they were alive—Stendhal, Baudelaire—should benefit from rehabilitation and even apotheosis in the twentieth century. Dumas was a highly popular writer among his contemporaries and for perhaps fifty years after his death, but popularity is a somewhat suspect quality in the eyes of posterity. He had infinite powers of invention, both of plot and of character, but this counts for little in an age that looks more for depth of

analysis than for fertility of imagination: one Emma Bovary counts for more than any number of Margots, Dianes, or Andrées. He had too little to say, at least in his novels, about his own age (this was almost the exclusive concern of Balzac), and what he had to say about earlier centuries cannot be taken very seriously today when historians are more interested in such questions as the growth of industrialism and the economic causes and consequences of wars than in the struggles of monarchs to keep their thrones. Even when Dumas deals with ideological issues—the wars of religion or the pressure of the Enlightenment on the rigidities of the ancien régime—his treatment is bound to seem superficial. But he was after all a novelist who merely found his subjects in history, and as a novelist he still casts his spell, for he had that supreme politeness of the professional writer, he never forgot his reader, he never treated the reader's demands as unimportant or unworthy. He had the gift of juggling with half a dozen subplots without ever losing the thread, of building slowly up to a dramatic climax so that the excitement rises steadily by carefully graduated steps, of inventing passages of dialogue that can amuse or enthrall but are never tedious. Admittedly the sophisticated will dismiss these gifts as minor ones. Dumas was no intellectual, but he provides a healthy relief from intellectuality. It cannot be said that we ever learn any deep lessons from Dumas, for he offers little to reflect on and few insights. But, as Robert Louis Stevenson asks about *Vingt ans après:*

What other novel has such epic variety and nobility of incident? often, if you will, impossible; often of the order of an Arabian story; and yet all based in human nature. For if you come to that, what novel has more human nature? not studied with the microscope, but seen largely, in plain daylight, with the natural eye? What novel has more good sense, and gaiety, and wit, and unflagging, admirable literary skill?

(*Memories and Portraits*, pp. 145–146)

Selected Bibliography

EDITIONS

The complete works of Alexandre Dumas, excluding the plays, run to 286 volumes in the Collection Michel Lévy (Paris, 1848–1900). Which works should really form part of the canon—that is, those written wholly or largely by Dumas—is a complicated question. F. W. Reed's *Bibliography of Alexandre Dumas Père* (London, 1933) is an attempt to guide the reader through the thickets; other useful bibliographical tools are Douglas Munro's *Alexandre Dumas Père: A Bibliography of Works Translated into English to 1910* (New York, 1970) and his *Alexandre Dumas Père: A Bibliography of Works Published in French, 1825–1900* (New York, 1981).

PLAYS

Fifteen volumes were published in the Michel Lévy edition (Paris, 1863–1874). None of Dumas's plays has been translated into English. A start has been made in producing an excellent annotated edition of the plays in French: *Théâtre complet*, edited by Fernande Bassan (Paris, 1974–). The following are the best-known plays, listed with the dates of first performance, which are also the dates of first publication, unless indicated otherwise. For all plays Paris is the city of publication.

Henri III et sa cour. 1829.

Christine. 1830.

Antony. 1831.

Richard Darlington. 1831 (published 1832).

La tour de Nesle. 1832.

Angèle. 1833 (published 1834).

Kena. 1836.

Mademoiselle de Belle-Isle. 1839.

Les demoiselles de Saint-Cyr. 1843.

FICTION

Time has made its own selection in the enormous output under this head. The following list includes all those novels that have deserved to survive. They were published in Paris, and those titles with asterisks are the ones included in the handsome Swiss edition, with prefaces by Gilbert Sigaux on the historical sources of each work (Lausanne, 1962–1967). Scholarly reeditions of these works include *Le comte de Monte-Cristo*, edited by J.-H. Bornecque (Paris, 1962), and *Les trois mousquetaires* and *Vingt ans après* in one volume, edited by G. Sigaux (Paris, 1966).

Le chevalier d'Harmental. 1842.

Georges. 1843.

* *Les trois mousquetaires.* 1844.

* *Le comte de Monte-Cristo.* 1844–1846.

* *La reine Margot.* 1845.

* *Vingt ans après.* 1845.

* *Le chevalier de Maison-Rouge,* 1845.

* *La dame de Monsoreau.* 1846.

* *Joseph Balsamo (Mémoires d'un médecin).* 1846–1848.

* *Les quarante-cinq.* 1848.

* *Le vicomte de Bragelonne.* 1848–1850.

* *Le collier de la reine.* 1849–1850.

La tulipe noire. 1850.

* *Ange Pitou.* 1851.

Olympe de Clèves. 1851–1852.

Conscience l'innocent. 1852.

* *La comtesse de Charny.* 1852–1858.

Catherine Blum. 1854.

Les Mohicans de Paris. 1854–1859.

Le meneur de loups. 1857.

* *Les compagnons de Jéhu.* 1857.

* *Les blancs et les bleus.* 1867–1868.

Création et rédemption (posthumous). 1872.

NONFICTION

AUTOBIOGRAPHICAL

Mes mémoires, 1852–1855. Best consulted in the edition by P. Josserand. 5 vols. Paris, 1954–1968.

Causeries. Paris, 1860.

Histoires de mes bêtes. Paris, 1868.

Souvenirs dramatiques. Paris, 1868.

TRAVEL BOOKS

Impressions de voyage en Suisse. 1833–1837. Modern reprint in two volumes. Paris, 1982.

De Paris à Cadiz. 1848. *Le véloce.* 1851. These two volumes contain an account of his travels in Spain and North Africa in 1846–1847.

De Paris à Astrakhan. 1859. *Le Caucase.* 1860. An account of his travels through Russia. The first volume has been edited by Jacques Suffel under the title *Voyage en Russie.* Paris, 1960.

TRANSLATIONS

The early translations listed in Douglas Munro's bibliographies are not particularly reliable, and the later ones are too often mere abridgments. Those currently available, including some abridgments, are:

Adventures in Caucasia. Translated by A. E. Murch. Philadelphia, 1962. Abridged.

Adventures in Czarist Russia. Translated by A. E. Murch. London, 1960. Abridged.

The Black Tulip. New York, 1951.

Chicot the Jester. New York, 1968. Translation of *La dame de Monsoreau.*

The Companions of Jehu. New York, 1903.

The Count of Monte Cristo. New York, 1941.

The Forty-Five. Boston, 1900.

From Paris to Cadiz. Translated by A. E. Murch. London, 1958. Abridged.

The Man in the Iron Mask. New York, 1965. Translation of part of *Le vicomte de Bragelonne.*

Marguerite de Valois. New York, 1969. Translation of *La reine Margot.*

My Memoirs. Abridged by A. Craig Bell. London, 1961. Limited to events in which Dumas himself engaged.

On Board the "Emma": Adventures with Garibaldi's "Thousand" in Sicily. Edited by R. S. Garnett. New York, 1929. Contains considerably more material than is to be found in the book Dumas published in 1861, *Les Garibaldiens.*

The Queen's Necklace. London, 1957.

The Road to Monte-Cristo. Abridged edition of *Mes mémoires* by Jules Eckert Goodman. New York, 1956.

Tangier to Tunis. Translated by A. E. Murch. London, 1959. Abridged.

The Three Musketeers. New York, 1960.

Travels in Switzerland. Translated by R. W. Plummer and A. Craig Bell. London, 1958. Abridged.

Twenty Years After. New York, 1960.

CORRESPONDENCE

Lettres d'Alexandre Dumas à Mélanie Waldor. Edited by Claude Schopp. Paris, 1982. Apart from this volume, no serious attempt has been made to collect and publish Dumas's extant letters, of which there must be hundreds in libraries and private collections.

CRITICAL STUDIES

Adler, Alfred. *Dumas und die böse Mutter: Über zehn historische Romane von Alexandre Dumas d.Ä.* Berlin, 1979.

Almeras, Henri d'. *Alexandre Dumas et les trois mousquetaires.* Paris, 1929.

Audebrande, Philibert. *Alexandre Dumas à la maison d'or: Souvenirs de la vie littéraire.* Paris, 1888.

Baldick, Robert. *The Life and Times of Frédérick Lemaître.* London, 1959.

Bassan, Fernande. *Alexandre Dumas père et la Comédie-Française.* Paris, 1972.

Bell, A. Craig. *Alexandre Dumas: A Biography and Study.* Folcroft, Pa., 1979.

Blaze de Bury, Henri. *Mes études et mes souvenirs: Alexandre Dumas, sa vie, son temps, son oeuvre.* Paris, 1885.

Bouvier-Ajam, Maurice. *Alexandre Dumas ou cent ans après.* Paris, 1973.

Charpentier, John. *Alexandre Dumas.* Paris, 1947.

Chincholle, Charles. *Alexandre Dumas aujourd'-hui.* Paris, 1867.

Clouard, Henri. *Alexandre Dumas.* Paris, 1955.

Ferry, Gabriel. *Les dernières années d'Alexandre Dumas, 1864–1870.* Paris, 1883.

Gaillard, Robert. *Alexandre Dumas.* Paris, 1953.

Glinel, Charles. *Alexandre Dumas et son oeuvre: Notes biographiques et bibliographiques.* Reims, 1884.

Hemmings, F. W. J. *Alexandre Dumas: The King of Romance.* New York, 1979.

Jan, Isabelle. *Alexandre Dumas, romancier.* Paris, 1973.

Janin, Jules, *Alexandre Dumas, mars 1871.* Paris, 1871.

LeComte, L. Henry. *Alexandre Dumas (1802–1870): Sa vie intime, ses oeuvres.* Paris, 1902.

Maurois, André. *Les trois Dumas.* Paris, 1957. Translated by Gerard Hopkins as *The Titans: A Three-Generation Biography of the Dumas.* New York, 1957.

Neuschaefer, Hans Jörg. *Populärromane im 19. Jahrhundert.* Munich, 1976.

Parigot, Hippolyte. *Alexandre Dumas père.* Paris, 1901.

Pifteau, Benjamin. *Alexandre Dumas en manches de chemises.* Paris, 1884.

Ross, David. *Alexandre Dumas.* Newton Abbot, 1981.

Stowe, Richard S. *Dumas.* Boston, 1976.

Tadie, Jean-Yves. *Le roman d'aventures.* Paris, 1982.

F. W. J. HEMMINGS

PROSPER MÉRIMÉE

(1803–1870)

P ROSPER MÉRIMÉE DID not consider himself a professional writer. His literary efforts were always diversions he fitted into an active social life and, after his first appointment to a government post, an exceptionally busy career. For twenty-five years he served as inspector general of historic monuments, concurrently serving as secretary to as many as nine government committees. Especially after the age of thirty, he engaged regularly in historical research—a lifelong interest that he considered to be his true calling. He was elected to both the Académie des Inscriptions et des Belles-Lettres and the Académie Française. Napoleon III appointed him senator in 1853. Made a chevalier of the Legion of Honor at the age of twenty-eight, he ultimately achieved the rank of grand officer under the Second Empire.

As a writer Mérimée belongs to the romantic generation that came to maturity in the 1820's. Four years younger than Honoré de Balzac, two younger than Victor Hugo and Alexandre Dumas *père*, he was one year older than George Sand and seven older than Alfred de Musset. His first works enjoyed considerable success in romantic literary circles; his best and most enduring ones began with *Chronique du règne de Charles IX (Chronicle of the Reign of Charles IX)* in 1829. His only historical novel, this was also his first venture into prose fiction, the genre in which he excelled

and in which—especially in the development of the modern short story—his greatest influence on later writers can be seen.

The most persistent characteristics of Mérimée's writing are clarity and intelligence; rapid action; intense, often violent emotions described dispassionately; an abiding fascination with local color; and a narrative technique marked by understatement, irony, and detachment. His style is natural, conversational, and terse. Because both his nature and his taste led him to avoid the overblown rhetoric and excessive lyricism to which his fellow romantics so easily fell victim, he has often been praised for his classicism. Whatever it may be called, his unaffected, direct, and sober style makes him today one of the most readable of his contemporaries.

As a man Mérimée seemed to reflect the qualities found in his writing. His public image was that of a dandy. His distant and supercilious manner, his enigmatic personality, and his disconcerting penchant for irony and sarcasm offended many. The testimony of his close friends, however, a few unguarded self-revelations in his stories, and particularly his vast correspondence give a very different picture. Beneath his often unpleasant exterior he emerges as a sensitive man who struggled all his life to contain his emotions and to disguise his feelings. Skeptical, complex, and contradictory, he emerges also as a man capable of great generosity, of the most devoted friend-ship with both men and women, and of un-flagging loyalty.

Mérimée was born in Paris on 28 September 1803, the only child of Jean François Léonor and Anne Moreau Mérimée. Both his parents were artists. His father, a moderately success-ful academic painter, served for nearly thirty years as secretary of the École des Beaux-Arts; his mother was a teacher of painting and a tal-ented portraitist of children. Like many only children, young Prosper was spoiled and pre-cocious, though as a student at the Lycée Na-poléon he excelled only in Latin. He was taught to draw and paint, first at home and then by other teachers. Though neither he nor his parents had any illusions about the extent of his artistic gifts, his skill at sketching proved to be of great use during his years as inspector general of historic monuments; and painting was always, especially toward the end of his life, an enjoyable and satisfying hobby. He learned English at home as a child, and he gave his father credit for teaching him what Italian he knew. At school he began to read Spanish on his own; later, while a law student, he continued his explorations of English and Spanish literature and still found time to pursue interests in Greek, philology, and numismatics.

Despite his family's predilection for things intellectual and artistic, their home life was never bohemian, and no doubt it was in the home that Prosper developed the practical side of his nature and his respect for order, comfort, and security. Very early, too, he re-vealed his extreme emotional sensitivity and began to build his defenses. Though loving and generous, his parents were down-to-earth and unsentimental. His mother especially was dry and outspoken, with a keen sense of the ridiculous and a cutting wit (Stendhal once described her as "capable of experiencing emotion once a year"). She was apparently the source of an anecdote repeated by all Mérimée biographers, in which the boy, cut to the quick by his parents' laughter at his tearful apology for some minor wrongdoing, vowed never again to let others see his true feelings. This determination was subsequently reinforced by the teasing to which he was subjected at school because of the English-style clothes in which his mother outfitted him. Interestingly, it was the stereotype of the dandified, aloof Englishman that he chose to cultivate in both dress and manner for the rest of his life.

In an important way Mérimée's upbringing also reflected his parents' eighteenth-century values. Both his parents were atheists (his mother more aggressively so) and he was raised in an atmosphere not of mere indiffer-ence to religion but of active skepticism and anticlericalism. Mérimée often alluded to the fact that he had never been baptized, and all his life he resisted the attempts of others (most frequently women) to convert him, sometimes flippantly but sometimes with sur-prising seriousness and sincerity, as in a letter to Madame de La Rochejaquelein: "I have the misfortune of being a skeptic, but it's not my fault. I have tried to believe, but simply have no faith. Though I am not insensitive to po-etry, I have never been able to write verse either. I am too much a 'matter-of-fact man.'" At the same time he found himself strongly at-tracted to the supernatural and the occult. This interest was first evidenced by his study of magic when he was about sixteen; and though he laughed at himself for it, all his life he readily admitted to being superstitious. The critic Charles Augustin Sainte-Beuve, who knew him well, once observed that Mér-imée did not believe that God existed, but on the other hand was not altogether sure that the devil did not.

As he neared the end of his law studies, Mérimée was encouraged by his father to fre-quent the romantic salons. There he encoun-tered most of the young writers and artists prominent in the new movement, and he al-lied himself particularly with the liberal group that gathered around the painter

Étienne Delécluze. At one such gathering, when he was nineteen, he met Stendhal, whose theories on the drama—soon to be set forth in *Racine et Shakespeare* (1823; 1825)—Mérimée was the first to convert into practice in an unpublished and now lost tragedy, *Cromwell,* and in the *Théâtre de Clara Gazul* (*The Plays of Clara Gazul,* 1825). Despite twenty years' difference in age, the two men were inseparable for a number of years and always remained excellent friends. In a tribute to Stendhal some time after his death, Mérimée stressed their dissimilarity, stating that except for a few shared likes and dislikes in literature, he and Stendhal had "not a single idea in common" and indeed spent most of their time together arguing. Yet the same essay (*H.B.,* 1850), as well as their correspondence, reveals temperamental affinities, common tastes, and a mutual respect and appreciation that resolve the seeming paradox of their friendship. Both professed atheism and anticlericalism, and both delighted in mystifying and disconcerting others. They were much preoccupied with their sexual prowess and shared a taste for obscene humor. They were able to criticize each other's work with startling bluntness, but apparently without personal offense.

There is no doubt that Stendhal's friendship exerted an important influence on Mérimée, but its exact nature, like its extent, is difficult to assess precisely. At the very least, Mérimée's ideas and attitudes were strongly colored by his friend's. From Stendhal, quite probably, Mérimée drew the general view that authentic expression of one's true nature was impossible amid the conventions and hypocrisy of nineteenth-century society. Mérimée's interest in sixteenth-century France and in the study of primitive, unfettered passions may also have come from Stendhal, along with his admiration for individuals whose energy and singleness of purpose let them ignore or reject all restraints of morality or civilization. But consideration of these resemblances calls

attention also to an important difference: unlike Stendhal, Mérimée could never commit himself wholeheartedly to such beliefs or values.

Reluctance to subject oneself to the intellectual domination of another can indicate an uncompromising independence of mind. In the case of Mérimée it may also, as suggested by A. W. Raitt, reflect a kind of prudence. Whatever contempt he might have felt for contemporary society, by nature Mérimée was too practical, even too cautious, to be willing to risk total repudiation of the values of modern civilization. This hesitation, consciously self-imposed or innate, determined the limits of Stendhal's influence on his younger friend. At the deepest level, it also underlies the pervasive irony, the moral detachment, and the avoidance of definite answers that characterize almost all of Mérimée's writing.

Mérimée's first published literary works were two elaborately planned and executed hoaxes. *The Plays of Clara Gazul* purported to be a group of plays by a Spanish actress, translated and edited by one Joseph L'Estrange. *La guzla,* which appeared two years later, was ostensibly a collection of prose translations of Illyrian ballads. Both volumes enjoyed early critical success, especially the former, but neither attracted a wide audience of readers, and the only attempts to stage any of these plays during the nineteenth century failed. About Mérimée's reasons for concealing his identity as author we can only speculate. They probably included his fondness for practical jokes, the influence of Stendhal's obsession for pseudonyms and mystification, and some shrewd self-protection should his works be badly received. Further, all his life Mérimée was intrigued by instances of deception and false appearances. But he leaves no doubt about his intentions in writing "Clara's" plays. There he is openly topical, iconoclastic, and provocative. He is topical in his choice of subjects and themes related to recent social and political issues and in his desire to demonstrate the workability of new ideas about the theater. He is iconoclastic in his attitudes toward the institutions and the conservative sociopolitical climate of France under Charles X. And he is provocative in the aggressiveness with which he sets out to discredit what he disapproves of.

The first edition of *Clara Gazul* was composed of six plays: *Les espagnols en Danemarck (The Spanish in Denmark); Une femme est un diable, ou la tentation de Saint Antoine (A Woman Is a Devil, or the Temptation of Saint Anthony); L'Amour africain (African Love); Inès Mendo, ou le préjugé vaincu (Inez Mendo, or Prejudice Overcome); Inès Mendo, ou le triomphe du préjugé (Prejudice Triumphant);* and *Le ciel et l'enfer (Heaven and Hell).* To the second edition Mérimée added two more plays that he wrote in 1829: *L'Occasion (The Opportunity)* and *Le carrosse du Saint-Sacrement (The Carriage of the Holy Sacrament).*

The Spanish in Denmark is based on an episode from the Napoleonic Wars. A Spanish division stationed on the Danish island of Fyn was spirited back to Spain by the English fleet in order to fight against the French, who were at that time trying to establish Joseph Napoleon as king of Spain. Mérimée's plot consists primarily of the schemes of the French authorities to prevent the Spaniards' escape. The French are the villains of the piece, except for Madame de Coulanges—a young woman engaged with her mother, Madame de Tourville, in spying for the French. Madame de Coulanges falls in love with a heroic young Spanish colonel, Don Juan Díaz, confesses her shameful past and present to him, is forgiven, and escapes with him to Spain after her mother—sensing where her best financial prospects lie—turns against the French. Madame de Tourville's perfidy foils a planned massacre of the Spanish officers, and she is handsomely paid off by Don Juan for her help and for her promise to stay out of her daughter's life henceforth.

A Woman Is a Devil is about a young in-quisitor named Antonio who falls in love with a dark-eyed beauty named Mariquita. Unable to conquer his lust, Antonio finds himself "in an hour a fornicator, a perjurer, and an assassin." Mariquita observes at the end that the spectators will surely agree with the title of the play when they consider the consequences of the passion she has aroused. *African Love,* set in Moorish Córdoba, is also a bloody little drama of passion and jealousy. Two Arabs, sworn brothers, find themselves in love with the same woman, Mojana, whom they force to choose between them. The rejected suitor strikes the other, who then kills his rival and stabs Mojana to avenge the loss of his friend.

The prejudice overcome in the first *Inès Mendo* play is that of caste. Don Esteban, a young nobleman of seventeenth-century Galicia, defies convention to marry for love, even after he learns that his beloved Inès is the executioner's daughter. Esteban kills a would-be seducer of Inès and is condemned to death for his crime. As he mounts the scaffold to be beheaded by Inès' father, the latter chops off his own right hand instead, proclaiming that he is no longer the executioner. The king arrives providentially, pardons Esteban, and dubs Mendo a gentleman. In the second play the original prejudice triumphs. The marriage of Don Esteban and his peasant bride founders on the rocks of boredom and Esteban's second thoughts about his misalliance. A former love of his, the duchess of Montalvan, arrives, fleeing from Spain for political reasons. Esteban leaves Inès and escorts the duchess to Portugal. His infidelity to Inès is repaid by the duchess, who promptly leaves him for another man. Repentant, Esteban finds Inès dying in a convent in Badajoz just in time to receive her forgiveness. But Mendo, convinced now that saving Esteban's life had been a mistake, shoots him.

Heaven and Hell, the last of the plays in the first edition, is a short, bitter melodrama of jealousy and religious hypocrisy, more subtle than *A Woman Is a Devil* but no less strongly anticlerical. Its characters are a young noblewoman, Doña Urraca, her lover, and her confessor. The wily priest worms a secret from Doña Urraca that leads to her lover's condemnation by the Inquisition. Unable to persuade her lover to kill the priest, Doña Urraca does so herself and leads her lover from prison to freedom.

The verve and subjects of these plays satisfied the French romantic craze for Spanish, or at least foreign and exotic, flavor; some scholars find more influence here from Lord Byron and the English Gothic school than true Spanish color. At the same time, Mérimée uses every opportunity to exploit current liberal ideas, attacking the church and challenging both the domestic and foreign policies of the reactionary French government of the 1820's. The historic basis of *The Spanish in Denmark*, for example, presented from the Spanish viewpoint of its nominal author, could easily be seen to make a strong comment on France's intervention in 1823 in the continuing civil strife in Spain. Even more immediately apparent is Mérimée's adherence to the tenets of the new romantic drama, at least as conceived by Stendhal: use of prose instead of verse, depiction of violence and death on the stage, and rejection of the classical unities of time, place, and action as well as the separation of genres. And, as though to make sure that the apparent was recognized for what it was, in the prologue to *The Spanish in Denmark* and in various explanatory prefaces and notes by the "translator," Mérimée wittily dismisses some of the most hallowed classical principles and calls attention to those aspects of form, content, and style that were intended to please contemporary audiences.

Though of unequal length, the plays are all short and to the point. The dialogue is in brisk, colloquial prose that is devoid of any trace of lyricism. Action and passion, both relentlessly violent, dominate. The breakneck speed of events leaves little opportunity for psychological development, but the characters nonetheless often attain a vivid reality. Settings and action, unhampered by the unities, move through space and time at the author's whim; mood and genre shift and mingle with even greater ease.

But for all his apparent acceptance of the new spirit and school, Mérimée does not swear full allegiance to either romantics or classicists. The fictitious biography of Clara Gazul, for one thing, is too patently tongue in cheek to be taken at face value even if her identity as the author is believed. In the plays themselves, Mérimée by no means directs his mockery only at the classicists. He has replaced the stately, declamatory movement of tragedy by rapid, eventful action that is often so melodramatic as to verge on—if not actually fall into—parody. Comic details in dramatic or tragic scenes combine genres, but sometimes break the mood too effectively to let the reader take the surrounding action with full seriousness. When at the end of *African Love* the fatally stabbed Mojana rises and addresses the audience—"Mesdames, Messieurs, that is the way the comedy *African Love* ends—or rather, the tragedy, as they say now"—Mérimée's irony is clearly aimed in all directions. All these plays end in the same way. An actor abruptly steps out of character, turns to the audience to say that the play is over, and asks the public's indulgence for any mistakes the author has made. The effect varies from piquant to disconcerting, but the ultimate impression is that Mérimée takes romantic drama no more seriously than the pseudoclassical tragedy of the eighteenth century.

The two plays added later to his *Clara Gazul* enhance the impression of Mérimée's independence from the romantic movement. *The Opportunity* depicts a student in a Havana convent who has fallen in love with the young priest who serves as father confessor. After declaring her love in a letter, she learns that one of her friends also loves Fray Eugenio and is loved by him. Planning to commit suicide, she is overcome by jealousy and impulsively poisons her friend instead, then runs off to drown herself. The plot of *The Carriage of the Holy*

Sacrament, like that of *The Spanish in Denmark,* is based on a historical incident. Camila Périchole, an actress and the mistress of the viceroy of Peru, persuades her lover to give her the new golden coach he has just received from Spain so she may impress her rivals. She then gives it to the bishop of Lima to be used for carrying the sacraments to the dying with dispatch and appropriate pomp, assured by a canon that this carriage will be the "Elijah's chariot that will carry [her] straight to Heaven."

Though the plot of *The Opportunity* sounds, in outline, not unlike those of the earlier plays, the characters and the action are developed more subtly, and the tone is much more consistent. The final disclaimer (Fray Eugenio asks the audience not to think too harshly of him for causing the deaths of the two girls) is distinctly less jarring than the others, and the priest is presented with relative sympathy throughout. There is also a simple lyricism in the atmosphere and language of *The Opportunity* that was totally absent before. Similarly, in *The Carriage of the Holy Sacrament* Mérimée avoids the violence and tension of the earlier plays, this time, as befits a comedy, with less action and slyer wit. He pokes fun at the viceroy of Peru and the bishop of Lima, but they are not caricatures like the priests in *A Woman Is a Devil* and *Heaven and Hell;* in the tradition of Molière, Mérimée mocks them more for their human foolishness than for their roles as representatives of church and throne. Whereas the dialogue of *The Opportunity* achieved a suitable pathos, here it sparkles with verve and humor; and in both plays interest is focused at least as much on characters as on plot. Finally, behind the exoticism of the New World settings and the discreet local color, both these plays are classical in form. The unities of time, place, and action are strictly, if unobtrusively, observed, and neither play strays from the tone appropriate to its genre. The resultant absence of excess and greater naturalness of characterization

have doubtless contributed much to making these the only plays by Mérimée to achieve some degree of success on the stage. *The Carriage of the Holy Sacrament* also served as the basis of Jean Renoir's 1952 film *The Golden Coach.*

As a hoax, *La guzla* was much more successful than *Clara Gazul.* This time Mérimée maintained secrecy even to the extent of having the book published in Strasbourg instead of in Paris. The twenty-eight ballads (four were added later), with their impressive "documentation," were apparently most convincing; only Victor Hugo seems not to have been taken in by the trick. Though few copies were sold in France, the work was praised by critics, and enjoyed much acclaim outside of France. A few months after it appeared, a German poet included his translations from Mérimée in an anthology of Serbian folk songs he published in Germany. English critics too were impressed, and a British scholar wrote to ask for the Serbian originals. But perhaps the greatest tribute to Mérimée's artfulness came when Alexander Pushkin and the Polish poet Adam Mickiewicz translated several of the ballads "back" into Slavic tongues. The secret of the authorship was revealed by Johann Wolfgang von Goethe, to whom Mérimée had sent a copy signed "from the author of *The Plays of Clara Gazul,*" but not before Mérimée had been able to savor fully the success of his hoax.

La guzla, after a preface, opens with a biography of Hyacinthe Maglanovitch, principal among the Illyrian guslars, or bards, from whom the anonymous translator supposedly secured the ballads in his collection. (The gusla is a single-stringed instrument on which the bards accompanied themselves.) The ballads treat conventional folk subjects: bandit life, tribal wars, patriotism, friendship, love, and the supernatural. In the latter category Mérimée includes some that deal with vampires and the evil eye and that draw again as much on the English Gothic novel as on his nominal sources. Typical of these is "Maxime et Zoé," in which the mysterious lover woos his beloved only at night so that his face cannot be seen. When they prepare to elope Maxime appears veiled, but during the journey Zoé pleads with him to remove his veil so that they may embrace. Finally he gives in and shows that he has two eyeballs in one eye. At this sight Zoé falls dead, and Maxime tears out his eyes. Only in the grave are they eventually reunited.

Perhaps to enhance the air of authenticity, Mérimée included one genuine Serbian ballad already familiar to the romantics through many translations: "Ballade de la noble épouse d'Asan-Aga" ("The Ballad of Asan-Aga's Noble Bride"). But the quality of Mérimée's pastiches is attested to by their acceptance as real and by the feeling for primitive poetry that they reveal. Such poems were the only kind of poetry that, by his own admission, Mérimée appreciated. Their attraction for him can be readily understood: their primitive simplicity, intense emotion, local color, and terse narration anticipate precisely the characteristics of much of his later prose fiction. In a preface to the second edition of *La guzla* Mérimée dismisses the entire work as an exercise in local color, but the obvious care that he lavished on these prose poems and his continued interest both in the genre and in many of its themes argue against taking his assertion too literally.

After writing these works filled with the color of distant, exotic places, Mérimée turned for the background of his next two works to the color of remote historical periods. The vogue for Sir Walter Scott's novels had been growing steadily in France for a decade or more. A troupe of English actors had increased the Parisian public's taste for historical drama in the mid-1820's by memorable performances of, among other things, Shakespeare's chronicle plays. Both these influences are evident in *La Jaquerie* (1828) and the *Chronicle of the Reign of Charles IX*. Though by the time he wrote the latter Mérimée was already react-

ing against Scott, he was no less absorbed in history, and literary fashion again coincided neatly with Mérimée's own interests.

The subject of *La Jaquerie* (more commonly spelled *Jacquerie*) is the fourteenth-century peasants' revolt known by that name. Composed entirely in dialogue and divided into thirty-six scenes, *La Jaquerie* is not a drama despite its form. It has no hero, no central group of characters, no unifying plot; and it is clearly unperformable. As a work of history it is equally open to criticism. Its subtitle best explains what it is: *Scènes féodales* (Feudal Scenes). Rather than a narrative or dramatic representation of the events of the *Jacquerie*, it is an attempt to evoke varied aspects of life and society in France during that calamitous period.

In the preface Mérimée points out his concern with historical verisimilitude as opposed to factual accuracy, and asserts that in this work he has tried "to give an idea of the atrocious mores of the fourteenth century." For the depiction of those atrocious customs, he has chosen to invent all his characters and situations so he can more readily, and less obviously, control what both convey to the reader. Without distorting known fact he can select those specific traits of character or details of behavior that give insight into the period and its mentality; they are no less valid observations for being attributed to nonhistorical personages. He gives us then, instead of portraits of well-known historical figures, a broad sampling of imagined individuals from all levels of society in situations that are not inconsistent with historical reality. Individually simple, together they form a rich and convincing picture of a society in a state of upheaval. The means of presentation—dialogue and dramatic action—bring to the whole the greatest degree of immediacy and concreteness.

La Jaquerie has probably been more severely and more universally criticized than any of Mérimée's works; the harshest of the criticisms, however, stem from judging it as drama or as history. But even if, in fairness to Mérimée, La Jaquerie is not evaluated in terms of what it was not intended to be, it still cannot be viewed as a complete success. The local color is sometimes heavy-handed (more than one critic has commented on the excessive use of medieval oaths), and the action frequently verges on melodrama. The absence of a focal character or clear plot line does lead to some confusion and a lack of unity, though the work is not formless, as a comparison of the first and last scenes alone will demonstrate.

The image that Mérimée gives of the Middle Ages is almost unrelievedly brutal and ugly; indeed one critic has observed that the few instances of goodness or nobility to be found in La Jaquerie are there simply because a minimum of contrast is indispensable. But if Mérimée is guilty of exaggeration in this respect, he is not guilty of partiality. The oppressed are shown to be no better than the oppressors morally or otherwise, and Mérimée in no way attenuates his depiction of their bestiality, selfishness, and stupidity. The ultimate collapse of the rebellion appears to be as much a consequence of their shortcomings as it is of the power of the upper classes. Mérimée reveals here his deep pessimism about human nature. Yet black as it is, his picture of the Middle Ages brings a realistic corrective to the idealized view held by most of the romantics.

The first edition of La Jaquerie also included a play entitled La famille de Carvajal (The Carvajal Family, 1828). Based on the story of Beatrice Cenci, which also inspired Percy Bysshe Shelley's verse drama The Cenci (1819), it is set in the Spanish colony of New Granada in the seventeenth century. It is a strange work, akin in setting though not in tone to the last two Clara Gazul plays. The plot is wildly melodramatic, and the horrors are piled on each other in such profusion that most critics feel Mérimée must have intended it to be a parody. That view is supported by the obviously fake letters quoted in the preface to explain why Mérimée wrote the play, but his real intent remains as elusive as his reasons for appending the play to La Jaquerie.

Over the years La Jaquerie has been little read and severely judged, but Mérimée's next work has from the start been one of his most popular. Set during the Wars of Religion in the second half of the sixteenth century, the Chronicle of the Reign of Charles IX, like its predecessor, depicts a struggle against tyranny. In this respect both subjects were daring choices under the repressive regime of Charles X, the second one all the more so because of the added element of religious fanaticism. As in La Jaquerie, however, Mérimée's doubts about the degree of virtue on either side prevent him from turning his book into a justification of one or the other. The slight bias he shows in favor of the Protestants exists possibly because they, like the peasants in La Jaquerie, are victims.

The plot of the Chronicle is slight, barely enough to unify a series of loosely related episodes. Bernard de Mergy, a young Protestant from the provinces, comes to Paris in the summer of 1572 hoping to serve his religion by joining Admiral Gaspard de Coligny. He finds his elder brother, George, an agnostic though nominally a Catholic; falls in love with Diane de Turgis, a pious and beautiful Catholic countess; and, thanks to his regular assignation with her, survives the Saint Bartholomew's Day massacre. Escaping later from Paris, Bernard joins the Protestant forces at La Rochelle. On a sortie against the besiegers he orders his men to fire on an advancing line of Catholics, realizing too late that they are led by his brother, who is fatally wounded. After George's death, Mérimée abruptly ends his narrative and tells the reader that he may decide for himself what eventually happened to Bernard and Diane.

In form the Chronicle resembles a picaresque novel, in which a naive young hero provides the main link between diverse episodes that gradually teach him the ways of the world. The important difference is that Mérimée is visibly less interested in his hero's education than he is in the background tableaux of sixteenth-century life and the massacre. He remarks at the beginning of his preface to the novel:

> In history I like only anecdotes, and among anecdotes I prefer those in which I believe I find a true picture of the customs and characters of a given era. This taste is not very elevated; but, I admit to my shame, I would willingly give all of Thucydides for authentic memoirs of Aspasia or a slave of Pericles; for only memoirs, which are intimate chats between the writer and his reader, provide the portraits of *people* that entertain and interest me.

In rapid succession Mérimée shows a group of German mercenary soldiers making merry in a French inn, the life of fashionable young Catholic courtiers, Coligny in his hôtel de Châtillon, the court at the château de Madrid, a royal hunt, a duel on the Pré-aux-Clercs, and a romantic midnight rendezvous with a masked lady. Bernard and his brother find themselves naturally, if not inevitably, in these situations, which Mérimée evokes through picturesque, revealing detail, lively dialogue, and crisp narration. In contrast to his practice in *La Jaquerie,* he introduces historical figures into the *Chronicle,* but he follows Scott in keeping them in the background. Their brief appearances augment the general sense of reality through sudden, memorable images, such as Charles IX sniping from his window in the Louvre, or such individualizing quirks of behavior as Coligny's use of toothpicks. That he refuses to follow Scott further, however, Mérimée makes clear in chapter 8: entitled "Dialogue Between the Reader and the Author," it boldly interrupts the narrative to announce that Mérimée rejects lengthy descriptions and has no intention of giving a general overview or interpretation of the period.

The narrative throughout is in Mérimée's most typical, matter-of-fact style, which evokes a heightened emotional response by the contrast between the bare directness of the writing and what is being related. In his account of the massacre Mérimée uses another simple device, also to increase the impact of this central episode: he tells it twice. First Bernard and Diane, closeted in her house, reached only by the sounds of fighting, the reflected glow of fire, the smell of smoke and burning pitch, imagine with mounting horror the bloody activity outside. After the arrival of George at the end of the chapter, the narrative leaps back in time to trace. his progress through the streets and show, as he saw it, the carnage only suggested before. In both versions Mérimée's precise description, firm control of viewpoint, and unerring choice of vivid detail account for the realism and emotional intensity. And a typical irony envelopes the whole episode when we recall Bernard's observation as he waited outside Diane's house earlier that evening: "The night was beautiful. A gentle breeze had tempered the heat, and the moon appeared and disappeared among thin, pale clouds. It was a night made for love." In these pages the qualities and strengths of Mérimée's mature art are already apparent. His characteristic limitation also is evident: his refusal, or inability, to work on the broad scale required for a comprehensive view of the period or for the creation of a more powerfully unified work.

The main characters are not greatly developed, but they are individual enough to hold the reader's interest and sympathy. Bernard is sincere, enthusiastic, and brave as well as naive. Diane offers an amusing mixture of piety, sensuality, and romanticism. George's friend Béville is stylish and gallant, yet human beneath his flippancy. Only George displays any real complexity, and the centrality of his role in the novel is soon apparent. His profound skepticism and hatred of fanaticism reflect Mérimée's own. Early in the book he tells Bernard, "I could not and I cannot believe. Belief is a precious gift which has been denied me, but for nothing in the world would I try to take it away from others.'' And he adds, ''Wouldn't the atrocities of our civil wars be enough to uproot the most robust faith?'' The counterpart of this conversation is found in George's death scene. There he struggles desperately to affirm his moral and intellectual independence, first when a priest and a minister quarrel at his bedside about which faith George will die in, then as he argues with Béville, whose atheism succumbs to fear of the unknown as he dies. By closing his novel with George's death rather than continuing the story of Bernard and Diane, Mérimée confirms the importance he attaches to George in comparison with his brother and his mistress. The fictional lovers are lightly dismissed, but George remains unseparated from the historical events that were Mérimée's real story.

One further aspect of the *Chronicle* is noteworthy: humor. By far the majority of Mérimée's writings contain some humor, even if only the bitter humor of irony. This novel contains more humor than any other single work of his. It is present in detail, such as George's concealment of a copy of Rabelais inside the cover of his missal; in situations, such as Diane's attempts to convert Bernard in bed; in characters like the witty priest, Father Lubin; and in fully developed comic episodes such as the one in which Bernard and the German soldier Hornstein, both disguised as priests, are compelled to play out their assumed roles and baptize a pair of chickens ''perch'' and ''carp'' so some Catholic soldiers can eat them on Friday. The humor serves both to relieve and at times to underscore the grimness of the action and adds a subtle touch of realism, reminding us that the century of religious wars also produced a François Rabelais.

In the eight months between publication of the *Chronicle of the Reign of Charles IX* and the end of 1829 Mérimée published more than he did in any other comparable period: the two plays that completed *Clara Gazul*, three more ballad imitations eventually added to *La guzla*, and five of the tales later collected in

Mosaïque (*Mosaic*, 1833). The next year, partly to recover from a disappointment in love, he made his first trip to Spain, where he traveled for more than five months. Soon after his return to Paris, Mérimée received the first of three successive civil service appointments, this one as head of the secretariat of the navy. Boredom with his work—which he nonetheless performed with distinction—and further frustrations in love contributed to sending him into a period of frenzied dissipation. In 1834 the minister of the interior appointed Mérimée to the newly created post of inspector general of historic monuments. This post, which he was to hold for twenty-six years, significantly altered the pattern of Mérimée's life. It confirmed the end of his youthful ''literary'' period and what he called his ''good-for-nothing years,'' redirected his intellectual concerns to history and archaeology, and committed him to a life of constant travel.

Women were always important to Mérimée. He was deeply attached to his mother and made his home with her from the time of his father's death until hers in 1852. There are stories of childhood crushes on some of his mother's attractive pupils, and one of them, a quiet English girl named Fanny Lagden, was probably his first mistress. Fanny remained an obscure presence on the periphery of Mérimée's life, gradually assuming, with her married sister Emma Ewer, a more active role in caring for him and seeing to his needs as his health declined. It was to Fanny that Mérimée left the bulk of his substantial estate; her grave is beside his in the Protestant cemetery at Cannes.

Émilie Lacoste, with whom Mérimée had a tempestuous liaison during his middle twenties, appears to have been the first of his mistresses to exercise a direct influence on his literary career. Challenged to a duel by her husband, Mérimée quixotically refused to fire and was wounded in the left arm and shoulder. His wounds permitted him to write, however, and during his convalescence he produced the *Chronicle*. Madame Lacoste was the model for Diane de Turgis, recognizable both from physical description and from her unusual combination of sensuality and militant piety. She appears in the story "Le vase étrusque" ("The Etruscan Vase," 1830) as Madame de Coursy, whose lover, like Mérimée, experiences agonies of retrospective jealousy upon discovering that he is not the first to have enjoyed his lady's favors.

Mérimée's brief, unhappy affair with George Sand in 1833 has attracted far more attention and speculation than its importance to either partner would seem to merit. A liaison soon after with a dancer at the Paris opera provided him with the model for the heroine of his tale "Arsène Guillot" (1844). But the three most significant and lasting of Mérimée's relationships with women all began in the first two years of the 1830's.

Before his trip to Spain, Mérimée had met and fallen in love with Valentine Delessert, the young, intelligent, and attractive wife of a wealthy Protestant banker twenty years her senior. Mérimée's other amorous entanglements did not prevent him from paying court simultaneously to Madame Delessert, who did not finally yield and become his mistress until six years had passed. Valentine was the love of Mérimée's life, and his devotion to her far outlived their actual liaison. To her he showed all his work before it was published, accepting changes that she suggested for "La Vénus d'Ille" ("The Venus of Ille," 1841) and Colomba (1841). He soon became a regular visitor at her salon and an "adopted uncle" to her two children. As Valentine's ardor cooled and she was drawn to other men—she subsequently became the mistress of Charles de Rémusat and later of Maxime du Camp—Mérimée's emotional dependence on her grew still more evident. Deprived of their former intimacy, he lost all motivation for imaginative writing.

Some time after the final break with Valentine, which came in 1855, Mérimée wrote, regretfully, to Madame de La Rochejaquelein: "I would like to write and I cannot. . . . I never

in my life wrote anything for the public, always for someone." In another letter he asserted, "I no longer write novels since I am no longer in love." And ten years after the break he confided to Ivan Turgenev, "When I was writing, it was for the entertainment of a beautiful lady. When I no longer entertained her, I stopped doing anything." Valentine's influence on Mérimée was thus prolonged negatively.

After Carmen appeared in book form in 1846 he published two plays and one short story but no other imaginative works. The story was "Le manuscrit du professeur Wittembach" ("Professor Wittembach's Manuscript," 1869), later retitled "Lokis." The plays were Les deux héritages and Débuts d'un aventurier (The Two Inheritances and An Adventurer's Beginnings, both 1853). The first is a slight domestic comedy; the second, a loosely connected series of historical scenes, has as its subject the career of one of the impostors who claimed the throne of Russia as Dmitri, son of Ivan the Terrible.

On a stagecoach journey during his trip to Spain in 1830 Mérimée met the count de Teba, a former officer in Napoleon's army who had only recently returned from exile. Immediate mutual sympathy led the count to invite Mérimée to his home, where he presented his new acquaintance to his wife and two little daughters, Francisca and Eugenia. Upon the death of the count's elder brother, he and his wife became the count and countess de Montijo; their younger daughter was destined to become empress of France. Again Mérimée was cast in the role of "bachelor uncle," entertaining the girls with stories and games and giving them their first French lessons.

Though the count de Montijo died in 1839, Mérimée remained a devoted and much loved friend of both the girls and the countess. The countess in turn became perhaps Mérimée's closest confidante, one with whom he shared concerns and feelings he would reveal to no one else. During his first stay in Spain the countess told him a tale that later became the basis of *Carmen*, and she encouraged his interest in the people and history of Spain. They were never lovers, but they were on close enough terms for him to advise her on family matters. When Eugénie was being courted by Louis-Napoleon, Mérimée expressed his opposition to the match unequivocally; but with characteristic grace and loyalty, when the marriage was settled upon, he gave his whole-hearted support to the decision his friends had made. One of the very few times that Mérimée was known to break down in tears was when he said farewell to the empress Eugénie before she left for exile in England at the close of the Franco-Prussian War.

Jeanne-Françoise Dacquin, known to her family as Jenny, also occupied a unique place in Mérimée's life. The daughter of a Boulogne lawyer, she first wrote to Mérimée to compliment him on the *Chronicle of the Reign of Charles IX*. She wrote in English and signed herself "Lady Algernon Seymour." A correspondence ensued and, a little more than a year later, she consented to a meeting at which he learned her identity. Much impressed by her intelligence, wit, and physical charm, Mérimée prolonged the correspondence—he only too interested in seducing her, Jenny firmly determined on either marriage or friendship, but nothing in between. Their correspondence continued—a mixture of affection, irritation, intellectual exchange, and good-natured camaraderie—for the rest of Mérimée's life. Whether they ever became lovers remains an open question, but their friendship meant too much to both of them for either to wish to break it off. Jenny never married, and the last letter that Mérimée wrote, just two hours before he died, was a note to her. A few years after his death Jenny published Mérimée's letters, with some omissions and deletions, as *Lettres à une inconnue* (*Letters to an Unknown Woman*, 1874). Her identity as the *inconnue* remained secret until 1892, and the original letters were burned at her death three years later.

Mosaic, as the title implies, is composed of varied short pieces, though they are too disparate to form a pattern. All of them had been published before in two magazines, the *Revue de Paris* and the *Revue française*. In addition to the six stories that have constituted most editions of *Mosaic* since 1842, the first edition included one more tale, "Fédérigo"; three pseudo-Illyrian ballads; a "Spanish" romance in the same vein, "La perle de Tolède" ("The Pearl of Toledo"); a one-act comedy, "Les mécontents" ("The Malcontents"); and three "Lettres adressées d'Espagne" ("Letters from Spain"). The ballads, including "The Pearl of Toledo," are in every way comparable to those in *La guzla*. "The Malcontents" is perhaps the weakest of Mérimée's works. A comedy evoking royalist conspiracies against Napoleon, its characters fail to come alive, and the intended satire of contemporary aristocrats lacks force and point. The "Letters from Spain," on the other hand, are travel writing at its most colorful. Mérimée's precise observation and terse narration combine to create an impression at once picturesque and realistic. The second letter, which describes an execution, is particularly remarkable for the way in which Mérimée's unemotional, objective narration conveys the strong feelings implicit in the event. The third letter, about highwaymen, includes a portrait of the bandit José-María and other details that reappear in *Carmen*.

The tales in *Mosaic* were Mérimée's first short stories, and they rank among his best. They represent more than simply another facet of his art, however; the modern short story may be said to begin with them. Most strikingly in the first three—"Mateo Falcone," "Vision de Charles XI" ("Charles XI's Vision"), and "L'Enlèvement de la redoute" ("The Storming of the Redoubt")—but no less genuinely in the others, Mérimée established a new form and approach for short fiction. In contrast to such contemporary writers of short stories as Charles Nodier, Stendhal, and Balzac, Mérimée gave primacy to brevity, concentration, and singleness of focus. In contrast to fables, exempla, fairy tales, and philosophical tales—all traditionally moralistic or didactic in intent—Mérimée's stories are objective, impartial, and free of both moral commentary and extraliterary purpose.

Since Mérimée did no theorizing about fiction until his own creative years were past or nearly so, we do not know to what extent his achievement was the result of conscious planning or a natural consequence of his particular talent and temperament. He was too intelligent and too serious an artist, however, not to realize when he began writing short fiction that he had found his medium. Short stories suited him because, as Sainte-Beuve observed in an article in 1831, "the broad view doesn't suit him . . . he believes in clearly defined, concrete facts, each carried to the limits of its special kind of passion and its expression in physical reality."

Although no two stories in *Mosaic* are alike, they share those general characteristics and—a constant in all Mérimée's writing—narrative interest. Together they also demonstrate impressively the range of Mérimée's technical skill. A narrator is present in each of the first four stories, for example, yet his presence and function are felt differently in each case. In "Mateo Falcone" he steps into the opening paragraphs to "authenticate" what he is about to tell, then to remove those events in time as well as space. In "Charles XI's Vision" he speaks directly to the reader before the central anecdote to affirm its documented veracity, and again afterward to lend the confirmation of later historical events to the prophetic vision. In "The Storming of the Redoubt" Mérimée briefly states his source for the tale, then lets the central character relate in first person the experiences and feelings that constituted his baptism of fire. In "Tamango," though the narrator does not interject himself directly into the story until the very end, his viewpoint is felt continuously in the savage, unrelieved irony that bathes the entire story.

In all the stories Mérimée's gift for stripping away nonessentials is evident, as is his sureness in choosing memorable details. The bloodstain on Charles XI's slipper after the vision has faded, though invented by Mérimée, gives more convincing evidence of the intervention of the supernatural than do the documents Mérimée summarizes. Mateo Falcone's son reveals all his peasant shrewdness when he puts his cat and her kittens on the haystack that conceals the wounded fugitive Gianetto; and he displays his cupidity even before the fatal temptation of the watch by asking what Gianetto will give him before he agrees to help, though he knows full well the code of hospitality to outlaws that his father respects. In "The Etruscan Vase" the vase becomes a tangible symbol of the jealousy that gnaws at Saint-Clair. Such concrete details eliminate the need for lengthy description or explanation and heighten credibility. Mérimée does not try to conceal his presence as narrator; on the contrary he frequently interposes remarks addressed to the reader or to some imaginary listener. In this he follows the accepted practice of his time; Stendhal and, even more, Balzac allowed themselves the same privilege. But Mérimée never suggests what the reader should think of his story or characters. His objectivity is composed of this restraint, the detachment imposed by his persistent irony, and especially his vivid realism.

The subjects of these stories are as varied as their forms. Originally subtitled "Moeurs de la Corse" ("Corsican Customs"), "Mateo Falcone" is the grim account of a father who kills his only son because the son has violated his code of honor by betraying a fugitive from the law. "Charles XI's Vision" evokes a bloody, prophetic vision of the downfall of the Swedish house of Vasa. The terse "The Storming of the Redoubt" is an episode from Napoleon's Russian campaign, recounted by an officer on the front lines fresh from military school. "Tamango," considerably longer than the preceding, is also more complex. It is a tale of treachery and catastrophe in the West African slave trade, told with Mérimée's most relentless narrative impulse and an irony that spares neither primitive nor civilized societies. In "Fédérigo" Mérimée retells a Neapolitan legend about a clever rogue who outwits both Satan and Jesus in order to lengthen his life and eventually find a place in paradise. Mérimée comments on the story's mixture of pagan Greek and Christian elements, but the crux of the plot is a version of the legend of the three wishes.

"The Etruscan Vase" and "La partie de trictrac" ("The Game of Backgammon") signal a new direction for Mérimée, as in them he shifts the interest from action to the exploration of the feelings and thoughts of his characters. Heretofore Mérimée had conveyed emotions through carefully noted outward manifestations. Now, looking into his characters also, he adds a new dimension to his writing.

He begins "The Etruscan Vase" with a portrait of his hero, Saint-Clair, that is an excellent example of his new technique, and that has the added interest of being a vivid self-portrait as well:

> He was born with a tender and loving heart; but, at an age when impressions that last a lifetime are too easily formed, his excessive sensitivity had attracted the teasing of his friends. He was proud and ambitious; he cared, as children do, about the opinions of others. Henceforth he strove to conceal all outward evidence of what he considered a dishonorable weakness. He attained his goal, but success cost him dearly. He was able to conceal from others the emotions of his oversensitive heart, but by locking them up in himself he made them a hundred times more cruel. In society he earned an unfortunate reputation for insensitivity and indifference; and when he was alone his troubled imagination created torments for him that were all the more frightful because he would never have dreamed of revealing them to anyone.

Though Mérimée alters details of the events and characters that inspired this story, its emotional truth is real and personal throughout. "The Game of Backgammon" is not based on personal experience, but is only slightly less successful in depicting the effects of an overpowering emotion, in this case the remorse of a sailor whose life collapsed as a consequence of the one time he cheated at gambling.

The subjects Mérimée chose for these stories were, for the most part, not original with him. His originality lay in the way he handled and arranged his materials, and he is now far from the pastiches of *Clara Gazul* and *La guzla*, clever as they may have been. The local color is better integrated into the stories, as in "Mateo Falcone," where characterizations and credibility depend on it; or in "Tamango," where the precise, detailed descriptions of the slave ship and the primitive customs reinforce the irony by pointing up resemblances between primitive and civilized societies.

If no discernible pattern emerges from this mosaic, the tales are nonetheless related by a certain consistency in their views of people and life. Whether looking at a code of honor, a war, or the slave trade, Mérimée seems to see first of all human cruelty. Even the superficial glitter of Parisian life only half conceals the cruelty that lurks there too. All people are subject to destructive passions and to forces that exceed their control or defy rational explanation. The consistent pessimism that colors all the tales except "Fédérigo" is made bearable only by the distance and detachment that come from Mérimée's objective narration and irony. And finally, several endings, like those of "Clara Gazul's" plays and the *Chronicle*, seem to depreciate the tales just told. But where the earlier works thus questioned the value of the fictions, the endings of "Mateo Falcone," "Tamango," "The Etruscan Vase," and "The Game of Backgammon" suggest the ultimate indifference of the world to the suffering and defeat of their heroes, an indifference all the more devastating to the reader because the heroes are so unaware of it.

Because of his period of dissipation, and later because of his travels and the demands of his work, Mérimée's writings over the next decade and a half are quite widely spaced. Interestingly though, each of them in some way looks back to *Mosaic*. *La double méprise* (*The Double Misunderstanding*, 1833) and "Arsène Guillot" (1844) follow in the psychological vein of "The Etruscan Vase," even to the extent of having heroes modeled on Mérimée. "Les âmes du purgatoire" ("Souls in Purgatory," 1834), like "Fédérigo," is the straightforward retelling of a popular legend. "The Venus of Ille" picks up the supernatural and mythological elements of "Charles XI's Vision" and "Fédérigo." *Colomba* recalls the Corsican setting of "Mateo Falcone," whereas *Carmen* can be traced back to the "Letters from Spain"; and both of these tales are concerned on a deeper level, as was "Tamango," with the contrast between civilization and primitivism.

The Double Misunderstanding is about a young woman, Julie de Chaverny, who finds after six years of marriage that not only does she not love her husband, but she cannot even bear to be in his company. She takes pride, however, in having retained her virtue and in appearing to be a model of resignation. After a public insult at the hands of her boorish husband, she decides to seek a formal separation but first wants to talk the whole matter over with Madame Lambert, a friend who lives a short way out of Paris. To Julie's annoyance, when she arrives at Madame Lambert's she finds other guests, but she is persuaded to remain for dinner. At this point Darcy, an old acquaintance of Julie's who has just returned from six years in the Near East, enters. At the end of the evening Julie sets out alone, but is stranded when her carriage breaks down in a violent storm. Darcy, en route home, finds her and offers to drive her the rest of the way. A surge of confused feelings—relief at her rescue, distress about her husband, uncertainty about herself—leads Julie to yield to Darcy's advances in the carriage; almost immediately afterward she is appalled at what she has done. Mortified, distraught, and suffering from a severe cold brought on by the rainstorm, she leaves the next day to go to her mother in Nice. Forced to stop at a country inn because she is too ill to travel, Julie dies there alone two days later. Her husband comes to see her grave and order a stone; a few months later Darcy contracts an advantageous marriage.

One of the most criticized aspects of *The Double Misunderstanding* is its structure. The first twelve chapters, through the seduction, are spacious, and Julie's feelings are analyzed with great subtlety. From that point on, leisurely analysis is supplanted by headlong action. The events of the first twelve chapters cover a period of two or three days and occupy fifty-four pages; the last five chapters contain more action and skim rapidly over three or four months in the space of eight pages. Some readers admire the subtle psychological analysis, others find it prolonged to the point of tedium, but all are bothered by the disproportion between the two parts. The imbalance is indeed awkward, but it can perhaps be explained by considering a tendency Mérimée shows elsewhere. In the *Chronicle*, when he had said what he wanted to say, he simply stopped. Similarly, in "The Game of Backgammon" the narrator is interrupted and breaks off his story just before the end, but not before Mérimée has told what he was most concerned to tell. *The Double Misunderstanding* is built upon the same psychological premise as "The Game of Backgammon" (and "The Etruscan Vase"): that a single unforeseen and uncharacteristic act or emotion can destroy a life. In each case, the single act or emotion that interests Mérimée forms the center of the story and determines its shape; everything else is reduced as far as possible. In "The Etruscan Vase" Mérimée has most successfully solved the problems posed by this approach; in *The Double Misunderstanding* he compensates for its weaker structure with a depth and richness of psychological analysis that he surpasses in none of his other works.

PROSPER MÉRIMÉE

Anticipations of Flaubert's *Madame Bovary* (1857) in *The Double Misunderstanding* have also been pointed out frequently—the languishing young wife, unhappy in marriage and given to viewing herself as a heroine of romance; the boring husband; even the seduction in a carriage. Looked at this way, *The Double Misunderstanding* may be seen as an ironic commentary on the romantic perspective. All Julie's fantasies turn out to be something quite different when they are realized, and Mérimée's irony is directed against her unrealistic view of life rather than against Julie herself. Even the famous final line, "Those two hearts, for all their mutual misunderstandings, were perhaps made for each other," can be taken as a romantic cliché gone wrong. This idea is explored with perceptivity and skill by two British scholars, Robert Lethbridge and Michael Tilby, who call attention to Mérimée's constant pricking of romantic bubbles in this story. A. J. George also sees Julie as a romantic heroine adrift in a real world. Comparing her with Mateo Falcone, the "noble savage" whose unquestioning acceptance of his code of honor makes him ignore a more universal human code, Professor George finds both to be striking examples of Mérimée's ability to take conventional literary types and present them "out of focus."

In the opening paragraphs of "Souls in Purgatory" Mérimée points out the existence of two bodies of legends about two distinct Don Juans—Don Juan Tenorio, the hero of Tirso de Molina, Molière, and Wolfgang Amadeus Mozart; and Don Juan de Mañara, whose name Mérimée changes to Maraña. Both natives of Seville, according to legend, the two men had somewhat parallel lives but significantly different deaths, the former being dragged off to hell by a statue, the latter experiencing a conversion and dying in grace after founding the Hospital de la Caridad in Seville. Mérimée saw the tomb of Don Juan de Mañara there in 1830, and it is his story that he relates.

"Souls in Purgatory" remains something of an oddity and a puzzle for Mérimée scholars: an oddity because it is so unlike everything else he wrote, a puzzle because his reasons for writing it are obscure. Most probably he decided to capitalize on the new interest in the legends aroused by two recent revivals in Paris of Mozart's *Don Giovanni* (1787) and the continuing popularity of Byron's *Don Juan* (1819–1824). Typically, however, Mérimée chose to examine the lesser-known Don Juan. The Spanish setting and story were consistent with his interests, but the story itself is different from Mérimée's other tales. It is unusually long, and though there is action, there is virtually no dialogue. Except in the rarest flashes, Mérimée's habitual irony and humor are totally absent. The dramatic episode in which Don Juan witnesses his own funeral and his subsequent conversion are treated with the utmost seriousness. Some critics, noting the lack of irony even in the handling of the religious elements, suggest a link between the conversion of Don Juan and Mérimée's feelings, at the time he wrote this tale, about his own dissipations. However, any such connection seems remote, if only because there was no conversion, dramatic or otherwise, in Mérimée's life. But more than one reader has been struck by parallels between the friendship of Don Juan and his comrade-in-sin Don García Navarro and that of Mérimée and Stendhal. Taken as a whole, "Souls in Purgatory," like "Fédérigo" and "The Storming of the Redoubt," is an entertaining story, narrated with style and great technical skill, but one that leaves little further to be said about it.

Three years after "Souls in Purgatory" Mérimée published "The Venus of Ille," which he considered his best work. Based on an ancient legend, it is a story of the supernatural in the most realistic of settings. Mérimée puts himself in the story as narrator, drawing details from his own travels and archaeological studies for both characterizations and elements of plot. Having visited Mount Canigou in the province of Roussillon, the narrator is on his way to visit an antiquary in the village of Ille. His guide tells him about the recent discovery in Ille of a Roman statue of Venus, and mentions that his host's son is to be married on the next Friday. Already stories are about of the malevolence of the statue, which, in falling, had broken the leg of one of the men trying to dislodge it from the ground and set it up.

Monsieur de Peyrehorade, the antiquary, welcomes the narrator effusively but will not show him the celebrated statue until the next day. The narrator is unfavorably impressed by Alphonse, the antiquary's son, whose passion for pelota is so great that he joins a game against a group of visiting Spaniards on the morning of his wedding. Finding the large ring he is to give his bride an encumbrance, he takes it off and slips it on the statue's finger. In his hasty departure for the ceremony, Alphonse forgets the ring and uses another. Back in Ille that night, he confesses to the narrator that he cannot retrieve the original ring; the statue's finger has closed on it. The next morning Alphonse is found dead in the nuptial chamber, his body marked as by an iron band around his chest. A Spaniard who had threatened Alphonse after the game is questioned and exonerated. When the hysterical bride is finally restored to her senses, she says the statue killed her husband. A few months later Monsieur de Peyrehorade dies, and his widow has the statue melted down and made into a church bell. But twice since the bell has been in use the grape vines have frozen, which the villagers perceive as the continuing evil influence of the Venus.

In contrast to another of his fantastic tales, "Charles XI's Vision," "The Venus of Ille" is both more developed and more complex. Here a whole series of mysterious incidents leads to the climax. The first that the narrator hears of the Venus is a description of the fear accompanying her discovery, the menacing look on the statue's face, the accident that occurred as they tried to stand it up. The narrator's first

glimpse of the statue, from his room by moonlight, is marked by another strange happening: as a pair of village youths pass by, one of them throws a stone at the statue and it ricochets off and strikes him on the head. And at the narrator's first close look he too notices the expression on the statue's face: "maliciousness to the point of spitefulness. . . . Disdain, irony, cruelty showed on this face which was yet of an incredible beauty." Superstitions and feelings of menace intensify the atmosphere of fear. At the same time, the solid realism of the depiction of preparations for a provincial wedding; the authority of the narrator, whose knowledge of archaeology is constantly compared to the half-knowledge of Monsieur de Peyrehorade; and all the concrete details of local color make the ominous intrusions of the supernatural seem as real as the people and the landscape.

By the end of the story, though Mérimée has suggested a rational solution to the murder, few readers will choose it over the convincing fantastic explanation. The double solution satisfies Mérimée's skepticism, of course, but it also indicates the hold that the irrational continued to exercise over this most rational of men. Mérimée was also fascinated by mythology, and throughout the story he discreetly underscores mythological dimensions. The destructiveness of unrestrained passion is embodied in the statue of Venus; on this level the story aligns itself with Mérimée's other tales of consuming passion.

In 1839 Mérimée visited Corsica for the first time, ten years after he had written "Mateo Falcone." In April the following year he published his *Notes d'un voyage en Corse (Notes on a Trip to Corsica)*, another of the lengthy reports that regularly followed his official journeys of inspection; three months later *Colomba* appeared in the *Revue des deux mondes*. After the *Chronicle*, *Colomba* is the longest of Mérimée's works, and, with *Carmen*, it ranks among his most popular. It is unique in Mérimée's output in being a love story with a happy ending; that, along with the picturesqueness of the locale and most of the characters, probably accounts for much of its appeal. The theme of the work, however, is the contrast between the primitive and the civilized; this contrast becomes the personal dilemma of the hero, Orso della Rebbia, a young lieutenant returning home after having been educated abroad and serving under Napoleon. It appears in the internal conflict that Orso experiences because he has grown away from his Corsican heritage, and it is also embodied in the two women in his life: the young Englishwoman Lydia Nevil, whom he meets on the boat back to Corsica; and his sister, Colomba, who has waited two years for Orso to return and avenge the murder of their father.

In spite of the admiration the book has aroused, it has been criticized on two counts. First, some readers find the local color excessive. The obvious response to this objection is that Mérimée was entranced by his visit to Corsica, the people he met there, and their customs. He deliberately included as many authentic details and personal recollections as he could—this was one of his purposes in writing *Colomba*—but he carefully maintained narrative tension as well. Mérimée even pokes fun at his preoccupation with local color when he describes Lydia's unceasing quest for things new and exotic.

The other criticism is that Mérimée does not really come to grips with the issue of civilized versus primitive cultures, nor does he force Orso to do so. He has Orso kill the two Barricini brothers in self-defense, thereby satisfying both Colomba's demand for vengeance and Orso's revulsion at the idea of the vendetta. Though this solution is perhaps too neatly contrived, it is not inconsistent with Mérimée's familiar reluctance to choose primitive passion at the expense of civilization, however much the primitive and passionate may intrigue him.

Though Orso is the focal character, and the gradual breakdown of the veneer of civilization that covers his native instincts is skill-fully traced, he never achieves the force of Colomba herself, and the book is appropriately named for her. She does not enter the story until chapter 6, but once there she dominates it completely. Her every action and reaction are directed by her obsession with vengeance, causing her sometimes to be compared with Electra. Any appearance of civilization in Colomba, too, is only that; her unforgiving cruelty in the final scene with old Barricini, who mourns his dead sons, leaves no doubt on that score. Orso may have compromised with his heritage, but Colomba affirms hers to the end, and it is Colomba we remember.

"Arsène Guillot," like *Colomba*, occupies a unique place among Mérimée's works. Its heroine is presented with complete and obvious sympathy. Though the story was written for Valentine Delessert—she is the "Madame" addressed several times by the narrator—Arsène was based on Céline Cayot, a dancer in the opera ballet with whom Mérimée had had an affair just prior to his liaison with Madame Delessert. Mérimée was probably motivated to write this story when he did because of the Catholic revival of the early 1840's, which aroused all his anticlerical feelings. He found the new piety hypocritical and pretentious, and in his story he contrasts the honest superstition of the grisette Arsène with the conventional religiosity of the wealthy and proper Madame de Piennes.

Madame de Piennes first sees Arsène buying a votive candle for Saint Roch in the church of that name. When Madame de Piennes learns later that Arsène has attempted to commit suicide, she determines to help her and also to lead her to repentance and salvation. A surprise visit from Max de Salligny, a former friend and admirer who announces that he is giving up his life of dissipation, gives Madame de Piennes another soul to save. She learns by accident that Max is the lover for whom Arsène still grieves, and then only gradually does she recognize that her own motives have gone far beyond the purely religious. After Arsène's death Mérimée ends the story without resolving the situation between Madame de Piennes and Max.

As a tale of psychological analysis "Arsène Guillot" ranks high. Though Arsène is a simple character, depicted even with a trace of sentimentality, she is believable as well as appealing. As with Julie de Chaverny, Mérimée reveals Madame de Piennes's complexity and explores her contradictory feelings sensitively and convincingly. By keeping interest focused on her specific feelings rather than trying to generalize, Mérimée avoids any hint of a polemical tone, though his stance is implicit in the contrast between the two women. Max too, though more sketchily presented, is delineated with exceptional sensitivity.

With *Carmen,* which appeared in the *Revue des deux mondes* in October 1845, we come to Mérimée's last major literary work. As we have seen, Mérimée heard the story on which he based *Carmen* during his first visit to Spain in 1830. Details recorded in the "Letters from Spain," including the name he chose for his heroine, also subsequently found their way into his tale. Later visits to Spain and later studies—for example, work he did on gypsies in the early 1840's—all made their contributions too. The superb integration of these diverse elements is doubtless owed to the long gestation period of the tale and the full array of technical resources Mérimée had developed over twenty years of writing.

The story opens with a first-person account of an archaeological expedition in Spain, during which the narrator meets the bandit Don José and later Carmen herself. This opening section is reminiscent of the beginning of "The Venus of Ille" in its pedantic tone and in its functions. As in the earlier work, Mérimée carefully builds the authority of the narrator and a convincing realistic framework for the events that are to follow. The main body of the story begins when the narrator visits Don José in prison, where he is awaiting execution for murder. At this point Don José becomes the narrator and relates in his own words the story of his meeting with Carmen, his desertion from the army, and his becoming a bandit for love of her. As helpless in the grip of his passion for Carmen as Alphonse de Peyrehorade was in the arms of Venus, Don José twice kills other men out of jealousy. When he finally realizes that Carmen will never be his alone, Don José murders her, buries her in a wood as she had wished, and surrenders to the police.

By having Don José tell his own story, Mérimée for the first time lets his readers see the effects of passion from the inside. When Don José speaks, we see Carmen exactly as he saw her, and we experience his feelings with a greater immediacy and impact than would otherwise be possible. One of Mérimée's finest achievements, in this story or elsewhere, is the convincing language he puts in Don José's mouth; vivid yet spare, colorful yet always natural in its choice of metaphor and image, it faultlessly reveals the man who speaks as he recounts his tragic story.

Though Carmen is seen only from the outside, she is a no less compelling presence. Her hypnotic beauty and animal sensuality, her fierce independence and childish petulance, her stoical fatalism are all projected with the greatest intensity and the most economical of means. And though, like the Venus of Ille, she stands for forces too elemental and mysterious to be defined, Carmen is never less than real and individual.

It is hardly possible to speak of local color in *Carmen* as one speaks of it elsewhere in Mérimée. Here it is neither gratuitous nor an added exotic flavor. It is an integral part of the specific reality within which this drama of passion is played. Mérimée's control of detail is at its most assured. Secondary characters, settings, evocation of milieux all fit tellingly but naturally into the total scheme. The perfectly unified whole that results attains a monumentality far beyond its actual modest dimensions.

The enormous and continuing popularity of Georges Bizet's opera has made *Carmen* far better known today in that form than in the original. When adapting Mérimée's story, Bizet and his librettists, Henri Meilhac and Ludovic Halévy, naturally changed a great deal, and much has been made of their "whitewashing" of the more sordid aspects of story and characters. But virtually all the changes can be justified on dramatic and musical grounds alone, and they are frequently less fundamental than they seem at first glance.

For the opera, Carmen's series of lovers was reduced to one—the *picador* Lucas, whose role was expanded into that of the *toreador* Escamillo. A dramatic and musical foil for Carmen was created in Micaëla, Don José's innocent country sweetheart, who was suggested by a passing reference in the story to the modest, blue-skirted girls of Navarre with their braided hair. Some secondary characters disappear from the opera, like old Dorothée, in whose house Carmen and Don José have their rendezvous; but others, like Carmen's gypsy friends Frasquita and Mercedes, are added. For clarity and force, the action is simplified and broken down into four basic episodes: the meeting of Don José and Carmen at the cigarette factory in Seville and his freeing of Carmen instead of escorting her to jail; their reunion at Lillas Pastia's tavern after José's release from prison and the armed challenge of an officer, which forces José to desert; a gathering of the gypsy smugglers at their mountain camp, where Carmen tells José she no longer loves him; and the final quarrel and murder of Carmen outside the bull ring in Seville (rather than in a wood near Córdoba).

Yet all but the most drastic changes remain superficial. Bizet does not alter Mérimée's conception of either Carmen or Don José, and the drama still springs from their characters and the fatal passion that links them. A surprising amount of detail from the story is retained in both text and action, and at several points—most notably in acts 1 and 2 and in the opera's final scene—the dialogue follows Mérimée almost word for word. Even the rich variety of mood and atmosphere created by Bizet's music, though seeming to be in such sharp contrast to the vivid but persistently dark colors of Mérimée's narrative, is drawn from it; the brighter moments, the songs, and the dances are all present or implicit in the story. By thus adhering as closely as possible to his source and basing changes or additions on ideas found in the story, Bizet has preserved the essence of Mérimée's tale and imbued his own masterpiece with a large share of its emotional power.

The year after *Carmen*, Mérimée wrote two more stories, "L'Abbé Aubain" ("Abbot Aubain") and "Il vicolo di Madama Lucrezia" ("Madame Lucrezia Lane"). The former is an amusing tale told in letters about a provincial matron who fancies that a handsome young priest has fallen victim to her charms. "Madame Lucrezia Lane," not published until 1873, is a mildly entertaining story of apparently supernatural happenings in Rome that turn out to have a thoroughly natural explanation. Then, in late 1846, came the publication of *Carmen* in book form. To the three original chapters Mérimée now added a fourth, devoted entirely to remarks on the life and language of European gypsies. He ended this addition as follows: "That is quite enough to give the readers of *Carmen* a favorable notion of my studies on the Romany language. I shall close with an appropriate proverb: *En retudi panda nasti abela macha.* If you keep your mouth closed, flies won't get in." This passage is most often read, and no doubt justly so, as Mérimée's final judgment on fiction. He had questioned the value of fiction for a long time; from now until almost the end of his life, history was to be his chief concern, and flights of imagination were to be replaced by the study of verifiable fact.

Beginning in the late 1830's, history occupied a larger place in Mérimée's life and work. His travels as inspector general of historic monuments led to lengthy published accounts of his journeys of inspection and to essays on art and archaeology. The possibility of election to the Académie des Inscriptions et des Belles-Lettres and to the Académie Française—both possibilities were realized within six months in 1843–1844—gave impetus to his research in ancient history and to publication of two volumes of an unfinished life of Julius Caesar: *Essai sur la guerre sociale* (Essay on the Social [Marsic] War) and *Conjuration de Catalina* (Cataline's Conspiracy), the two works then being published jointly as *Études sur l'histoire romaine* (Studies in Roman History, 1844). Early in the 1840's, encouraged by Madame de Montijo, Mérimée began a biography of King Pedro I of Castile; not surprisingly, because of the Revolution of 1848, it attracted little attention when it was published that year. It was well received in other countries, however, and was soon translated into Spanish and later into German and English. It remains his most original and important historical work.

Mérimée's approach to history was essentially the same as his approach to literature. In both he was drawn to the unique glimpse into human behavior, the exceptional individual, the mores of an era and its particular color. The narrative vigor, the realism, and the sense of drama found in his fiction are present also in his historical writing, along with insistence on precision of facts and scrupulous discrimination between fact and conjecture. The reluctance to generalize that is typical of Mérimée's fiction characterizes his historical writing also; for that reason his historical works are almost all biographical in orientation.

At about the age of forty-five Mérimée began to study Russian, and though he never achieved the fluency he had in Spanish and English, he knew it well enough to do, with some help, a number of translations. His first, in 1849, was Pushkin's *La dame de pique* (*The Queen of Spades*, 1834). His reading in Pushkin, whom he regarded as the greatest of Russian writers, led him by way of *Boris Godunov* (1831) to the study of Russian history. Again it was the striking individuals that attracted him: the false Dmitris, the Cossack heroes Bogdan Chmielnicki and Stenka Razin, Peter the Great, and the false Elizabeth II. As history, none of his essays on Russian subjects equaled the *Histoire de Don Pèdre Ier, roi de Castille* (1848), to a considerable extent because of the unavailability of primary sources. Some of his essays are little more than adaptations or abridged translations of Russian works, and some reveal minor inadequacies in his command of the language. Whatever their limitations, however, the best have the strengths of Mérimée's dramatic sense, incisiveness, and narrative skill. They also played an important role in making Russian history accessible to French readers, something Mérimée almost alone was trying to do in the 1850's.

His translations and essays on Russian literature similarly helped prepare for the great surge of interest in Russian writers that developed in France during the last quarter of the century. Though he was less a pioneer here than in his historical writings—all the works he translated had been translated before—his reputation as a writer and public figure enabled him to make a particularly influential contribution to the cause of Russian literature. In addition to *The Queen of Spades*, Mérimée translated five poems by Pushkin and his short story *Le coup de pistolet* (*The Pistol Shot*); the latter is generally regarded as the best of his Pushkin translations. Since he neither appreciated nor understood Nikolay Gogol, it is surprising that in 1853 he translated his play *The Inspector-General* (1836) but perhaps not surprising that it is his least successful translation from Russian.

Mérimée met Turgenev in 1857, and the two men were close friends until Mérimée's death. Turgenev helped Mérimée with his translations and historical research, and Mérimée assisted Turgenev in various ways with the publication of the latter's novels in France. Mérimée also translated five of Turgenev's stories and wrote three essays, of unequal value, on his works. His respect and admiration for Turgenev as a writer were equaled by his sincere affection for the man; their correspondence shows that his feelings were reciprocated.

Since Mérimée had always remained sufficiently aloof from politics, his career was not seriously endangered by the collapse of the Orléanist government in 1848. He was greatly distressed, however, by the violence and rioting of the "June Days," the workers' revolt that followed dissolution of the national workshops on June 22; and he was deeply pessimistic about the new republic, believing that the country was falling into barbarism and that only an authoritarian government could restore order. He developed a particular fear of the socialists, a fear that was to revive with greater strength at the end of his life. Yet despite his professed disdain for French society and his skepticism about the French character, Mérimée was deeply patriotic. His concern for his country in 1848 was genuine, as was his later conviction that Louis Napoleon alone was capable of maintaining political and social stability in France. It was for this reason that Mérimée was able to support the Second Empire. His appointment as a senator was at the empress Eugénie's insistence, as was his acceptance of it. It is entirely to Mérimée's credit that he never sought personal advantage or political influence because of his closeness to the empress and emperor.

Despite his welcome at the imperial court, during his last two decades life became ever bleaker for Mérimée. His mother had died in 1852, and the final break with Valentine Delessert came a few years later, with devastating effect. Other friends near and far died also as the years passed, and with each loss Mérimée sank deeper into gloom. His depression was exacerbated by declining health. He eventually spent the winters in Cannes, where his

asthma and emphysema were relieved by the climate; there he again took up painting and began to study botany. In these years of illness Mérimée grew increasingly dependent on Fanny Lagden and her sister for their unobtrusive supervision of his household and for regularly going ahead to prepare his quarters in the south. Gradually, in the 1860's, his life again stabilized into a routine, but he still had to struggle mightily to fight off what he called his "blue devils," a task he found no easier now than it had been when he was twenty-five.

During these years Mérimée continued to be present at the imperial court when he was able and to serve there as "the empress's jester," telling stories or writing and performing in little comedies and charades. It was for the empress that Mérimée again took up his pen to write a new story, "La chambre bleue" ("The Blue Room," 1866). More broadly comic than anything else Mérimée wrote, it is a light, and to some readers banal, tale of a couple going off for an illicit weekend at a country hotel. They find themselves lodged in the hotel's "blue room" between a party of celebrating hussars and a solitary Englishman. After a series of farcical interruptions of the lovers' night together, suspense develops when mysterious noises are heard from the Englishman's room and a red liquid seeps under the connecting door. The lovers' fears of involvement in a criminal investigation are relieved the next morning when the mystery is solved: the drunken gentleman had upset his bottle of port.

"Lokis," which alone of Mérimée's last three tales was published during his lifetime, is both much longer and very different, though it too was written to entertain the empress's circle. Like "The Venus of Ille," it is based on an ancient legend, and Mérimée lavished much care on its writing. The story, set by Mérimée in Lithuania, tells of a count whose mother had been attacked and raped by a bear. Her son consequently has ursine traits in appearance and nature, which reach their peak in the murder of his bride on their wedding night. In its form too "Lokis" resembles "The Venus of Ille." The story is framed in visits by the narrator, a pedantic philologist, to the count's castle. A series of strange occurrences lead up to a wedding, and the next morning one of the newlyweds is found mysteriously killed. The underlying theme of the story is made explicit in a conversation between the narrator, the count, and a doctor when the count asks why passions can lead a man to commit acts that rationally he cannot accept. Here Mérimée touches on a problem that runs as a leitmotif through his works: the destructive force of passion. But he approaches it from an angle new to him.

The psychological implications and eroticism evident in "Lokis" are found also in "Djoumâne" (1869), which relates a series of bizarre happenings that befall an Arab soldier and only at the end are revealed to be a dream. Like "Lokis," "Djoumâne" offers rich opportunities for Freudian interpretation, but despite Mérimée's skillful narration it cannot justifiably be counted among his strongest works.

In his final years Mérimée endured a great deal of physical suffering. He continued to travel between Paris and Cannes regularly, but in July 1870 he knew that his end was near. The empress Eugénie offered to visit him, but he declined on grounds that it would be unseemly for his sovereign to climb the stairs to his apartment. When the disastrous French defeats began early in September, Mérimée managed to pay her a last visit at the Tuileries. After the capitulation at Sedan, the overthrow of the empire, and Eugénie's flight to England, Mérimée returned to Cannes. He died there just five days before his sixty-seventh birthday, and at his request was buried by a Protestant pastor. During the Paris Commune in 1871 all Mérimée's books, papers, and personal belongings were destroyed when the building in the rue de Lille where he had lived burned to the ground. The fire had been set by *pétroleuses*—communist women arsonists. It was an irony that Mérimée would have appreciated.

Selected Bibliography

EDITIONS

INDIVIDUAL WORKS

Almost all of Mérimée's works appeared first in periodicals; dates given here are those of first publication in book form.

Théâtre de Clara Gazul, comédienne espagnole. Paris, 1825. Drama.

La guzla, ou choix de poésies illyriques, recueillies dans la Dalmatie, la Bosnie, la Croatie et l'Herzégowine. Strasbourg, 1827. Poetry.

La Jaquerie, scènes féodales, suivie de La famille de Carvajal, drame. Paris, 1828. Drama.

1572. Chronique du temps de Charles IX, par l'auteur du Théâtre de Clara Gazul. Paris, 1829. Novel.

Théâtre de Clara Gazul. Paris, 1830. Drama. First edition to contain *L'Occasion* and *Le carrosse du Saint-Sacrement.*

1572. Chronique du règne de Charles IX. 2nd ed. Paris, 1832. Novel. First edition with definitive title.

Mosaïque. Paris, 1833. Stories.

La double méprise. Paris, 1833. Novel.

Notes d'un voyage dans le Midi de la France. Paris, 1835.

Notes d'un voyage dans l'ouest de la France. Paris, 1836.

Notes d'un voyage en Auvergne. Paris, 1838.

Notes d'un voyage en Corse. Paris, 1840. Art and archaeology. The official reports of Mérimée's tours of inspection of historical monuments.

Colomba. Paris, 1841. Novel. This volume also contains "La Vénus d'Ille" and "Les âmes du purgatoire."

Études sur l'histoire romaine. 2 vols. Vol. 1: *Guerre sociale.* Vol. 2: *Conjuration de Catalina.* Paris, 1844. History.

Carmen. Paris, 1846. This volume also contains "Arsène Guillot" and "L'Abbé Aubain."

Histoire de Don Pèdre Ier, roi de Castille. Paris, 1848. History.

H.B. par un des Quarante. Paris, 1850. Privately printed anonymous pamphlet on Stendhal.

Nouvelles de Prosper Mérimée. Paris, 1852. In addition to the second printing of *Carmen,* "Arsène Guillot," and "L'Abbé Aubain" the volume contains three translations from Pushkin ("La dame de Pique," "Les bohémiens" ["The Gypsies"], "Le Hussard" ["The Hussar"]) and a critical essay, "Nicolas Gogol."

Les deux héritages, suivis de l'Inspecteur général et des Débuts d'un aventurier. Paris, 1853. Drama. First publication of translation of Gogol's *Inspector-General.*

Dernières nouvelles de Prosper Mérimée. Paris, 1873. Stories. "Il vicolo di Madama Lucrezia" is here published for the first time and "Djoumâne" for the first time in book form. Other tales included are "Lokis," "La chambre bleue," "Le coup de pistolet" (translated from Pushkin), "Fédérigo," and "Les sorcières espagnoles."

Études sur les arts au moyen âge. Paris, 1875. History and art.

COLLECTED WORKS

Les âmes du purgatoire. Carmen. Edited by Jean Decottignies. Paris, 1973.

Colomba. Edited by Pierre Salomon. Paris, 1964.

Histoire de Don Pèdre Ier, roi de Castille. Edited by Gabriel Laplane. Paris, 1961.

Notes de voyages. Edited by Pierre-Marie Auzas. Paris, 1971.

Oeuvres complètes. The following volumes in this unfinished series were published by the Librairie Champion, Paris, under the direction of Pierre Trahard and Édouard Champion:

Carmen. Arsène Guillot. L'Abbé Aubain. Edited by Auguste Dupouy. 1927.

Dernières nouvelles. Edited by Léon Lemonnier. 1929.

Études anglo-américaines. Edited by Georges Connes. 1930.

Études de littérature russe. 2 vols. Edited by Henri Mongault. 1931–1932. Mérimée's translations from Russian are included here.

La Jaquerie, suivie de La famille de Carvajal. Edited by Pierre Jourda. 1931.

Lettres à Francisque Michel (1848–1870). Journal de Prosper Mérimée (1860–1868). Edited by Pierre Trahard. 1930.

Lettres à Viollet-le-Duc (1839–1870). Articles du Moniteur universel (1854–1860). Edited by Pierre Trahard. 1927.

Mosaïque. Edited by Maurice Levaillant. 1933.

Portraits historiques et littéraires. Edited by Pierre Jourda. 1928. Mérimée's pamphlet on Stendhal, *H.B.,* is included in this volume.

Théâtre de Clara Gazul (1825–1830). Edited by Pierre Trahard. 1927.

Romans et nouvelles. Edited by Henri Martineau. Paris, 1951.

————. 2 vols. Edited by Maurice Parturier. Paris, 1967. Most authoritative modern edition.

Théâtre de Clara Gazul. Edited by Pierre Salomon. Paris, 1968.

La Vénus d'Ille et autres nouvelles. Introduction and notes by Antonia Fonyi. Chronology by Pierre Salomon. Paris, 1982.

TRANSLATIONS

Carmen. Translated, with introduction and notes, by W. F. C. Ade. Woodbury, N.Y., 1979.

Carmen and Colomba. Translated and introduced by Edward Marielle. Baltimore, 1965.

Carmen, Colomba, and Selected Stories. Translated by W. J. Cobb. Foreword by George Steiner. New York, 1963.

Chronicle of the Reign of Charles IX. Translated by George Saintsbury. New York, 1975.

A Slight Misunderstanding (La Double Méprise). Translated by Douglas Parmée. London, 1959.

The Venus of Ille and Other Stories. Translated by Jean Kimber. Introduction by A. W. Raitt. Oxford, 1966.

The Writings of Prosper Mérimée. 8 vols. Edited by George Saintsbury (various translators). New York, 1905. The standard translation, now somewhat dated, of the novels, tales, and *Letters to an Unknown.*

CORRESPONDENCE

Une amitié littéraire: Prosper Mérimée et Ivan Tourguéniev. Edited by Maurice Parturier. Paris, 1952.

Correspondance générale. 17 vols. Edited by Maurice Parturier. Paris and Toulouse, 1955–1964.

PROSPER MÉRIMÉE

Lettres à une inconnue, précédées d'une étude sur Mérimée par H. Taine. 2 vols. Paris, 1874.

BIOGRAPHICAL AND CRITICAL STUDIES

Baschet, Robert. *Du romantisme au Second Empire: Mérimée (1803–1870).* Paris, 1958.

Bowman, F. P. *Prosper Mérimée: Heroism, Pessimism, and Irony.* Berkeley and Los Angeles, 1962.

Dale, R. C. *The Poetics of Prosper Mérimée.* The Hague, 1966.

Filon, Augustin. *Mérimée.* Paris, 1898. First biography of Mérimée.

George, A. J. *Short Fiction in France, 1800–1850.* Syracuse, N.Y., 1964.

Gobert, D. L. "Mérimée Revisited." *Symposium* 26:128–146 (1972).

Grover, P. R. "Mérimée's Influence on Henry James." *Modern Language Review* 63:810–817 (1968).

Léon, Paul. *Mérimée et son temps.* Paris, 1962.

Lethbridge, Robert, and Michael Tilby. "Reading Mérimée's *La Double Méprise.*" *Modern Language Review* 68:767–785 (1973).

Raitt, A. W. *Prosper Mérimée.* London and New York, 1970. The most up-to-date and authoritative study.

Sainte-Beuve, C. A. de. *Portraits contemporains.* Vols. 2 and 3. Paris, 1846.

————. *Causeries du lundi.* Vol. 7. Paris, n.d.

Smith, M. A. *Prosper Mérimée.* New York, 1972.

Trahard, Pierre. *La jeunesse de Prosper Mérimée (1803–1834).* 2 vols. Paris, 1925. These two volumes by Trahard and the two below are basic and indispensable.

————. *Prosper Mérimée de 1834 à 1853.* Paris, 1928.

————. *La vieillesse de Prosper Mérimée (1854–1870).* Paris, 1930.

BIBLIOGRAPHIES

Dickenson, L. D. "A Half-Century of Mérimée Studies: An Annotated Bibliography of Criticism in French and English 1928–1976." Ph.D. diss., Vanderbilt University, 1976.

Trahard, Pierre, and Pierre Josserand. *Bibliographie des oeuvres de Prosper Mérimée.* Paris, 1929.

RICHARD S. STOWE

HECTOR BERLIOZ

(1803–1869)

WHEN HECTOR BERLIOZ, Victor Hugo, and Eugène Delacroix were celebrated by Théophile Gautier as the great trinity of French romanticism, Gautier was naturally speaking of Berlioz the composer, Hugo the writer, and Delacroix the painter. But it tells us something about the stature of these three figures, and the scope of their imaginative powers, that he might conceivably have referred to Hugo as a graphic artist and to Berlioz and Delacroix as writers. It tells us something too about the artistic climate of the age. Renaissance man was never more at home than in the nineteenth century. He had gone out of favor during the rationalist centuries, which preferred to keep their arts well-classified in separate—and unequal—channels. A suspiciously irrational art, music ranked lowest in the classical hierarchy. Musicians counted as artisans rather than as artists and were regarded with disdain by literary critics and philosophers, who took it upon themselves to do the writing about the art. As Voltaire once quipped to the composer André Grétry: "How's this—You're a musician and you have a wit?"

Musicians have the romantics to thank for dispelling such prejudices, for setting music on an equal footing with literature and philosophy, and for bringing to an end the social servitude that Johann Sebastian Bach, Franz Joseph Haydn, and even the young Ludwig van Beethoven had to endure. They have Berlioz to thank, finally, for supplying a proper retort to Voltaire. "The art of music does not enfeeble the mind as much as writers have long wished us to believe," the composer once remarked slyly; "in fact the past century has seen—so they say—nearly as many musicians of wit as it has dim-witted writers."

Born on 11 December 1803 (in the twelfth year of the French revolutionary calendar) and named in keeping with the heroic, anticlerical fashion of the time, Louis Hector Berlioz was bred to independence from the start. He grew up to tales of Napoleonic battles and to the Napoleonic promise—and example—of a society open to talent. If, after Waterloo, glory could no longer be found on the battlefield, it could still be sought in art, a field then undergoing a revolution of its own. By the time Berlioz took his music to the courts of Germany and Russia, in the 1840's, romanticism had done its work: he was received with deference by sovereigns who were themselves schooled in the new ideology, and who recognized genius as the noblest of titles, art as the highest of callings, and music as the greatest of the arts.

Though Berlioz's own writings played a part in the teaching, such a radical shift of opinion was the work of more than one man or one generation. Composers such as Carl Maria von Weber and Ludwig Spohr had, before Berlioz, spoken for their art with articulate pride; among his younger contemporaries Robert Schumann, Franz Liszt, Felix Mendelssohn, and Richard Wagner had made the composer-writer a familiar figure. Yet even in such gifted company Berlioz's achievement as a writer stands out. Not everyone, perhaps, will agree with W. H. Auden, who set Berlioz's *Mémoires* (*Memoirs*, 1870) on a par with those of Saint Augustine and Jean Jacques Rousseau; or with Jacques Barzun, Berlioz's eminent biographer, who compares the *Traité d'instrumentation et d'orchestration moderne* (Treatise on Instrumentation and Orchestration, 1843) with the timeless excellence of William James's *Principles of Psychology* (1890); or with Gustave Flaubert, who said of Berlioz's correspondence, ''It outdoes Balzac''; or with Baron Isidore Taylor, the nineteenth-century arts administrator, promoter, and connoisseur, who pronounced the libretto of *Les Troyens* (*The Trojans*, 1856–1858) the finest in French since Philippe Quinault's *Armide* (1686). But such estimates convey the idea of an exceptionally strong and versatile literary ability. They call to mind not so much the artist-critic of modern times as the poet-artist, such as Michelangelo, or the poet-musician, such as Guillaume de Machaut, of an age before music and poetry had gone their separate ways.

Berlioz himself disavowed all pretensions to literary fame. This was not from false modesty, but from a lucid awareness of the relative worth of his twin artistic gifts. We may speculate, if we like, that if he had not become a composer he would surely have become a poet, novelist, or playwright. The fact remains that, unlike E. T. A. Hoffmann, Schumann, or Wagner, he never experienced the slightest uncertainty about his artistic vocation. Very early he determined to be a composer; his writing came second and almost always in a musical cause. In following his literary career we pursue only the shadow, as it were, of his existence. But it is a captivating shadow, always bounding off in unexpected directions; and like a shadow in the course of the day, it grows in importance with his later years until it ends up transcending its utilitarian purpose and taking on an artistic life of its own.

Most of what we know of Berlioz's childhood and adolescence comes from his own testimony in the first four chapters of his *Memoirs*. Compared with the lengthy childhood accounts of his great predecessors François René de Chateaubriand and Rousseau, this is scanty matter indeed. Yet Berlioz omits nothing essential to the only story he was interested in telling: that of his life as an artist. The economy of these opening chapters, their balance of humor and nostalgia, lightness and density—quick pacing and rapid shifts of tone, on the one hand, and intricate cross-weavings of thematic material, on the other—are indicative of the artistry of the work as a whole.

Artistry is not, of course, the best assurance of veracity. But in Berlioz's case the effort to mold his past into literary shape captures more of the elusive inner life of childhood—or so many of his readers have felt—than have many accounts far richer in anecdotal detail. His very choice of literary mode argues self-awareness: echoes of drama, pastoral, and romance in the *Memoirs* are all tinged with irony, making the dominant literary character that of the mock-epic. Thus Berlioz opens by feigning surprise that his mother should not have known herself the bearer of one predestined for glory. At the same time he succeeds in giving a heroic cast to his tale, which is that of a child from a small town in Dauphiné, named (with or without foreknowledge) after the hero of Troy, and destined to fulfill the promise of that name in a life of turbulence and drama across the breadth of Europe.

The drama, as Berlioz tells it, begins as a pastoral. It is with a sense of happy destiny, against a background of surpassing natural beauty, that Berlioz gives the primary (and related) revelations of his youth: music, literature, and love. He mentions also his early passion for the sea and exotic lands, an early sign of the spirit that would drive him beyond the encircling mountains of his native countryside to explore the unknown in his chosen fields of imagination.

Music, he informs us at once, entered his life through a decisive experience at his first communion. On a sunny spring morning, an expressive melody sung by a choir of young girls awakened in him a "mystical, passionate unrest," a religious ecstasy that he later recognized and attempted to analyze as the genuine, ultimate "musical effect." Though Berlioz makes light of his childhood religion ("so attractive since it gave up burning people") and his pious confessions as a boy ("Father, I have done nothing"), it is clear from his description that the religious setting had a direct bearing on his emotional response to the music. The ceremony he witnessed as a child, in which music performed its age-old liturgical function as dramatic interpreter of the faith, not only inspired his lifelong ideal as a composer but made him, despite his early loss of faith, one of the foremost composers of religious music in the nineteenth century.

The second chapter of the *Memoirs* offers a clue to this discord between childhood piety and adult unbelief in the portrait of Berlioz's father. A doctor by profession, erudite, inquiring, liberal (that is, unbelieving, but tolerant in the best tradition of the French Enlightenment), Louis Berlioz exerted a profound influence on his son's intellectual development. Sensing perhaps the boy's unusual promise, Dr. Berlioz decided to take over his son's schooling himself. Under his father's teaching, Berlioz enjoyed a rare combination of sympathetic discipline and undogmatic guidance—the ideal "negative" education advocated by Rousseau. The result for both teacher and student was a profound and abiding mutual affection, reinforced by a shared intellectual curiosity, love of classical antiquity, and delight in experiment and innovation (the elder Berlioz published what seems to be the first practical account of acupuncture in the West). His father's careful instruction, similar to that of John Stuart Mill by his father at about the same time, deserves much of the credit for the uncommon range of Berlioz's intellect, both as a composer and as a writer.

Like any other schoolboy of his time, Berlioz chafed at the daily task of memorizing long passages from Horace or Vergil. But Vergil's poetry came to affect him intensely—so intensely as to magnify his infatuation with Estelle Duboeuf, a local girl six years older, into the torments of forsaken Dido in *The Aeneid.* In the *Memoirs* he tells the story of his childhood love from an amused distance, parodying the classic love clichés ("Jealousy plagued me, pale companion of all true lovers . . ."). But the love and the suffering went deep, as we learn at once from a glance ahead to an encounter with Estelle seventeen years later. Berlioz called her his *stella montis* (star of the mountain) and never forgot her shining beauty.

This first love set the pattern for the working of an imagination that colored life with art (he associated Estelle not only with Vergil, but also with *Estelle et Némorin* [1788], a pastoral poem by Jean-Pierre de Florian), in an illustration before the fact of Oscar Wilde's dictum that life imitates art. Inordinately sensitive to the tragic in life, and endowed with an unrelenting memory for emotional experience, he found in music the one effective outlet for his powerful feelings. As a young man defending his vocation to his family, he argued that he had "experienced emotions strong enough to recognize their accents whenever I shall be called upon to make them speak." He had felt the call since boyhood; in fact the theme of the introduction to the *Symphonie fantastique (Fantastic Symphony, 1830)* is a melody he composed in his early teens, to a stanza from Florian's poem.

Berlioz was intended to succeed his father as country doctor and manager of the family property. The romantic message about the sanctity of genius having not yet reached the provinces, art did not figure among the professional choices open to a young man of good family, especially an eldest son. With Berlioz's parents, music in particular came up against a double prejudice—philosophical on the part of his rationalist father, religious on the part of his devout, conventional mother, for whom any connection with the theater (music, in France, meant theater) was tantamount to perdition. From the time Berlioz's inclinations made themselves felt, conflict was unavoidable; and in the end it made him despise the provinces whose quiet beauty had first nurtured his talent.

Berlioz's natural gifts in music count among the most exceptional in the history of the art. In his early years they developed virtually unaided, the product of imagination and instinct, on the one hand, and primitive encounters with music, on the other. Though he was taught both the flute and the guitar, his creative awakening owed more to church litany, folksong, military bands, and hunting calls—along with snatches of opéra comique, amateur renditions of classical string quartets, and a few pages of Christoph Gluck discovered in his father's library. Through his own efforts he learned enough harmony to compose a number of songs, which he attempted to publish, and two flute quintets, which he tried out on his local amateurs.

We do not know whether he made any such attempts in poetry or prose. The earliest of his writings to have survived are letters he wrote at the age of sixteen to a music publisher. The most we can say is that for him music and poetry were entwined from the start. The music that fired his imagination was music destined to express the passions of which he read. Well before he had ever heard an opera he knew, like Hugo's wishing to be "Chateaubriand or nothing," that his own ambition was to be "Gluck or nothing." When he heard his first opera, in Paris, "it was as if a young man possessing all the instincts of a sailor, but knowing only the boats on the lakes of his native mountains, were suddenly to find himself on board a three-decker on the open sea" (*Memoirs*, D. Cairns trans., ch. 5).

Sent to Paris in the fall of 1821 to study medicine, Berlioz at once discovered the principal musical offering of the capital—opera;

and though for over a year he dutifully followed the prescribed course of medical study, a letter home only one month after his arrival already spells out the inevitable. This letter is remarkable in foretelling not only his musical but also his literary future; for in describing a performance of Gluck's *Iphigénie en Tauride* (*Iphigenia in Tauris*, 1779), Berlioz finds expressions that foreshadow his analytic criticism of the 1830's. Already he observes the scenery, the lighting, the timing of the spectacle with the eye of a connoisseur; he explains the intentions of the characters as portrayed by the music; and he attempts to convey by analogy the expressiveness of the orchestra ("just as in winter, when you're alone, and you hear the wind blow—that's it exactly"). In another letter several months later, speaking this time of an opéra comique by the late-eighteenth-century composer Nicolas Dalayrac, Berlioz says he "absorbed" the music. The word (which recurs in a similar context in chapter 5 of the *Memoirs*) precisely conveys the emotional readiness of a mind thirsty for music and in the full impressionability of youth.

Meanwhile the scientific studies he was forced to pursue had their compensations. Though repelled by the practical side of medicine, he could not help being fascinated by the theory. He took a keen interest in the lectures he attended by the great men of science of the day—Joseph Gay-Lussac in physics, Louis Thénard in chemistry, Jean Amussat in anatomy. That interest proved valuable for his writings. As a practicing critic and musician, he remained alert to every kind of technical development in his art; as a writer, he repeatedly drew on science for imagery, with a range of allusion and a vividness of detail that recall Honoré de Balzac. Even the more gruesome aspects of dissection, which so revolted Berlioz as a student, came in handy later when he wanted to emphasize his abomination of certain facets of current musical practice. In protesting an inept, unauthorized piano arrangement of his *Francs-Juges* overture (The

Fehmic Court, 1828), for example, he condemned the perpetrator for "amputating" without considering the "internal and external anatomy," like an executioner who "cuts off some poor fellow's wrist, without taking into account the joints, the muscular attachments, the nerve endings and the blood vessels; he does it with one brutal stroke of the axe, and the patient's head falls soon after" (letter of 8 May 1836).

As a budding dramatist, Berlioz found even more appealing the courses in history and literature. His early letter on Gluck relates a history lecture so vividly as to inspire his sister to read the published text. He took special pleasure in hearing François Andrieux, a witty writer of the old school—so much so that he asked Andrieux to write the libretto for his first opera. The request (politely declined) betrays the conventional nature of Berlioz's tastes at this stage. His favorite literary works were still *Estelle et Némorin* and Bernardin de Saint Pierre's *Paul et Virginie* (1788). On the former he did in fact base his first opera, which he later destroyed; for the latter he retained special affection all his life.

Within a year after his arrival in Paris, Berlioz was studying music in earnest. For a time he worked on his own at the Paris Conservatory library, where he copied out entire scores of Gluck operas and where a dispute with the famous director of the conservatory, the irascible Luigi Cherubini, provided the material for an episode of slapstick comedy in the ninth chapter of the *Memoirs*. But it is far from true, as used to be supposed, that Berlioz was largely self-taught and, in consequence, poorly trained. By the end of 1822 he had become a student of the most illustrious composition teacher of the day, Jean Francois Lesueur.

A member of the Institute, honored by Napoleon for his opera *Les bardes* (*The Bards*, 1804), noted for his ceremonial music during the Revolution, a prolific writer and pamphleteer, and an erudite student of ancient Greek music, Lesueur set Berlioz an example of a composer of broad culture and high-minded artistic aims. Teacher and student immediately found common ground in their love of Gluck and Vergil and their admiration for Napoleon. Berlioz studied privately at first, then as a member of Lesueur's composition class at the conservatory. By the time he officially enrolled in August 1826, he was well on his way to maturity as a composer. He had written a mass, and it had been performed; and he had almost completed his first opera, *Les Francs-Juges* (the libretto by a young poet and law student, Humbert Ferrand, who was to become his closest and lifelong friend). At the end of his first year of courses at the conservatory he was ready to compete for the Prix de Rome, the first step on the ladder to official success in France.

It might seem as though little time were left, during these intense years of musical training, for Berlioz to learn the craft of writing as well. In fact the two apprenticeships went hand in hand. For the future polemicist, practice came first in those letters to his family in which he was forced to defend his calling. However punishing the experience, the years of family debate forced him to articulate his thoughts and so formed in him early the habit of writing strong prose. His classical education stood him in good stead, ironically, in confronting his former teacher. To his family's accusations of depravity, idiocy, and madness he opposed lucid, dignified arguments in carefully structured sentences. To an uncle he wrote:

> It seems to me that with the arts we can pay the debt society expects of us; . . . music elevates the mind by increasing its sensibility, and that quality being at the root of all the emotions, the cultivation of the fine arts cannot be a source of depravity to man.
>
> (August or September 1824)

To his father he wrote a ringing declaration, as convincing by its rhythm as by its maturity of thought:

I am involuntarily driven toward a magnificent career (no lesser epithet will do for that of the arts) and not toward my doom. I believe I will succeed; yes, I believe it, this is no time for modesty. . . . All outward signs point to it; and within me the voice of nature speaks louder than the most rigorous conclusions of rational thought.

(31 August 1824)

It does not speak well for Berlioz's father, however great his wisdom in other respects, that such reasoned eloquence left him unmoved. Even Lesueur's intervention and assurances ("music streams out of him from every pore") were of no avail. Each step of the young composer in trying his wings, each attempt to have a new work performed, heard, and understood, was treated by Dr. Berlioz as the final test of his son's talent, and any failure was liable to punishment by the ultimate weapon: the cutting off of funds. This strategy succeeded only in forcing the renegade to survive conditions of great hardship. Berlioz subsisted by teaching the guitar, solfège, and composition, by singing for a time in the chorus of a boulevard theater, finally by sheer physical deprivation. Yet in the *Memoirs*, his recollections of those years are neither bitter nor melodramatic. His musical fervor carried him through the most difficult times, and it is with sadness, rather than anger, that he speaks of the philistine obtuseness of his family.

In another time and place Berlioz's literary gifts might have remained hidden in his correspondence, like Wolfgang Amadeus Mozart's, or in a private journal, like Delacroix's. But Berlioz came to Paris during a period of great musical ferment. In the early 1820's he witnessed the "invasion" of the musical world by Gioacchino Rossini, the composer Stendhal hailed as another Napoleon. An aesthetic battle ensued, of the sort the French are famous for, that pitted the enthusiasts of Rossini against the defenders of Gluck. To Berlioz, as an ardent "Gluckist," the new Napoleon was an impostor whose dazzling melodies and orchestral effects were just that—effects; applied indiscriminately to both tragic and comic texts, they violated the fundamental Gluckian principle of expressive fitness. But there was an even deeper conviction that Rossini offended in Berlioz: that of art as a sacred calling. Even when the heat of polemics faded enough to allow Berlioz an unreserved admiration for some of Rossini's comic operas, he continued to oppose the philosophy that Rossini's music (and Italian opera in general) had come to embody, namely that music is no more than a pleasant sensual entertainment.

The Rossinian controversy brought out all Berlioz's combative instincts. Between 1823 and 1825 he entered the fray—and for the first time ventured into print, as far as we know—with three letters to the *Corsaire*, a small daily specializing in the arts. The *Memoirs* mention another piece so extreme in language that he found no editor to publish it. We can gauge the boldness of that article from the published ones, which are spirited to the point of impertinence. "Who could deny," ends one of them, "that all the operas of Rossini taken together cannot compare with a single line of one of Gluck's recitatives, three bars of a melody by Mozart or Spontini, or the least chorus by Lesueur!" Another lashes out with cutting irony at the most powerful music critic of the day, Castil-Blaze. But these early pieces are not only proof of a fighting spirit, they also demonstrate impressive authority on a wide range of artistic matters, including many of the central issues of the later criticism. Add to this the verve of the prose, and it is evident that Castil-Blaze had a potential rival.

During his early years in Paris Berlioz made progress in another literary domain as well. His exclusive concern with the dramatic genres of opera and oratorio, as his French training dictated, imposed a constant need for poems to set to music. Partly for that reason, no doubt, he cultivated friendships with writers (the habit stayed with him), to whom he continually appealed for texts. Often in his letters he would suggest poetic subjects. But one revealing set of letters shows him going further still. As he corresponds with one aspiring librettist about an opera based on Walter Scott's *Talisman* (1825), Berlioz sketches the outline of various scenes, formulates lines of verse, and mercilessly corrects his collaborator for lapses in French verse construction. This was in 1826. Twenty years would pass before he took the step, but already it is clear that eventually he would do without collaborators altogether.

The years 1827–1830 brought momentous changes both in Berlioz's life and in French art generally. Revolution was afoot, in art as well as politics, and Berlioz was poised for change. In the summer of 1827 his first cantata for the Prix de Rome completely disconcerted his academic judges. "Unplayable," they declared publicly; and in private: "Whatever possessed you to try so many new effects? Don't you know there's nothing new in the arts? The great masters have settled the forms; our job is merely to copy them." As an established critic in the following decade, Berlioz had a field day attacking this sort of professorial pedantry. For the time being he was frustrated by the need to "copy" in order to win the indispensable prize as against the urges of his own emerging musical personality. He won second prize the following year; but the first prize eluded him until his fourth try in 1830, when he took the precaution of curbing his dramatic instincts and supplying a "good little bourgeois accompaniment" to his cantata. His judges were fortunately unaware that by that time he had already composed one of the most revolutionary works in musical history, and his own first masterpiece: the *Symphonie fantastique.* The occasion of its premiere, on 5 December 1830, before an audience that included Liszt, was the musical equivalent of Hugo's play *Hernani,* eight months before, and a fitting end to the year of the July Revolution.

Not the rigid teachings of the conservatory, certainly, nor even the brilliance of native intuition alone, can account for a work of such daring and magnitude, which still seems modern after a century and a half. Berlioz's first symphony bears the marks of the powerful "thunderbolts," as he calls them in the *Memoirs,* that struck in rapid succession during the season of 1827–1828—first Shakespeare, then Beethoven. In the face of these giants even Gluck and Vergil were temporarily eclipsed. The music of Beethoven brought a revolution on two fronts. By demonstrating the powers of the symphony as a genre and of the orchestra as a medium, Beethoven upset in one blow the assumptions of classical training: that instrumental music was inferior to vocal; that the orchestra's role was merely to accompany the voice. Moreover the orchestra that played Beethoven in 1828, the Conservatory Concert Society, was itself a revelation. Composed of the best players from the opera and the conservatory, it was the first modern virtuoso orchestra, as dazzling to Wagner ten years later as to Berlioz at its founding. With Beethoven's symphonies before him and the conservatory orchestra to perform them, Berlioz now had his proof that there was indeed something new to be done in music, all academicians to the contrary.

Six months earlier, triumphal performances in Paris of *Hamlet* and *Romeo and Juliet* by a visiting English troupe had already shaken the old order in French art and jolted the romantic movement into battle order. But Shakespeare's influence on Berlioz went beyond a passing incitement to rebellion. The pessimistic realism of the tragedies, the structural freedom of the histories, the many-sided humor of the comedies, all touched in him an immediate sense of recognition and taught him crucial lessons in artistic freedom and scope. Few Frenchmen have ever taken in the breadth of Shakespeare as Berlioz did. He came to know almost all the plays intimately, finding them an unlimited source of musical inspiration and quoting from them continually in his writings. More often than not he quoted in English; he had begun to study the language in 1827 and persisted until he could speak it with relative ease and read Shakespeare in the original.

But when the Charles Kemble troupe brought Shakespeare to the Théâtre Odéon in September 1827, neither Berlioz nor most of the audience understood English. They responded, with the help of translations, to the rapid flow of scenes, to the novel English style of acting, and especially to one actress, whose imaginative, improvisatory renderings of Ophelia and Juliet at these performances made acting history. Her name was Harriet Smithson, and Berlioz fell head over heels in love with her. It was a literary passion, once again; this time for a goddess more brilliant and still more distant than Estelle. But his Shakespearean passion eclipsed the first in violence as much as a Shakespeare tragedy does a pastoral by Florian. Berlioz fell prey to a lover's extremes of hope and despair, energy and paralysis. And he had the imprudence, from the standpoint of his later reputation, to confide some of these extremes to his letters.

These are the letters invariably quoted by those seeking to portray Berlioz as a wild eccentric, a "romantic"—these and the account of this same period in the *Memoirs*, the very reticence of which seems only to irritate the sensation seekers. A word of caution is therefore in order about those passages in Berlioz's writings that strike modern readers as exaggerated, shocking, or embarrassing. If one takes into account the linguistic explosion of the years around 1830, on the one hand, with the epithets and emphasis and expansive tone typical of the contemporary style and the exuberance of youth, on the other, little remains of Berlioz's supposed eccentricity—unless it is a certain tendency of the imagination, extreme even for the time, to project himself into art, and a resulting incapacity to separate art from life. One often-quoted passage from the *Memoirs* illustrates this mental pattern: the episode in which he follows the funeral procession of an unknown woman in Flor-

ence, enters the morgue, and kneels beside her in homage to her ephemeral youth and beauty. Whatever the Freudian implications here, the obvious literary allusion is to the grave scenes of Ophelia and Juliet in Shakespeare. And given Berlioz's mentality, the scene is the more likely to have occurred for its reenactment of a poetic commonplace—the mourning of untimely death. He was to treat that theme himself in one of the most haunting pieces he ever wrote, the funeral procession of his *Roméo et Juliette* symphony (*Romeo and Juliet*, 1839).

Overwhelmed by the double impact of Shakespeare and Beethoven, Berlioz was temporarily unable to compose. Then a further discovery came to his aid: Goethe's *Faust I* (1808), which he read in the 1828 translation by Gérard de Nerval. Like many of his contemporaries, Berlioz found Goethe's insatiable, restless hero even better suited than Hamlet to render the sensibilities of a time when inertia itself hit the senses with unprecedented force. "I consume more boredom in an hour than I used to in a day," Berlioz wrote to a friend. But such boredom was the counterpart to a vitality that translated itself in an aggressive imagery of exploration and conquest: "There is a musical America," Berlioz declared exuberantly a few years later; "Beethoven was its Columbus, I will be Cortez or Pizarro." At the point of beginning his symphony, he wrote: "When I've drawn the first brace of my score, where my instruments of different ranks are lined up for battle; when I think of the field of harmonies that academic prejudice has kept virgin territory to this day . . . I lunge forward in a kind of frenzy to explore it" (30 January 1830). In the *Memoirs*, Berlioz links Goethe's *Faust* with the genesis of his *Fantastic Symphony*. Although in the end he did not produce the Faust symphony he had originally envisioned, it seems clear that the Faustian myth, by reminding him of his own creed of action, helped pull him out of the numbing shocks of the previous season and set him once more on his creative course. Late in 1828 he composed his extraordinary *Huit scènes de Faust (Eight Scenes from Faust),* the musical parallel to Delacroix's *Faust* lithographs. With uncharacteristic haste he rushed the new work to the publisher under the label "opus 1" and sent a copy, with a well-turned letter, to Goethe.

Further confirmation that he had regained his equilibrium comes to us by way of another "opus 1": his first real exercise in music criticism. Toward the end of 1828 he began actively seeking a journalistic platform to air his views. By the following spring he had gained a double foothold in the press: he was the Paris correspondent for the *Berliner allgemeine musikalische Zeitung* and the music critic of a new conservative paper, the *Correspondant.* For the specialized music journal he provided detailed, analytic commentaries, complete with musical examples, of *Fidelio* (1805, 1814) and *Der Freischütz* (1821), both recently performed by a visiting German opera company, and one notable report on the newly formed conservatory orchestra. In this last article, Berlioz takes the reader into the orchestra rehearsals and tells how the players, usually so bored, so contemptuous of the trivialities they perform daily at the opera, work tirelessly and with reverent attention to master the "labyrinth" of a Beethoven symphony. Their attitude exactly prefigures that of the coterie of artists he depicts twenty-five years later in *Les soirées de l'orchestre (Evenings with the Orchestra,* 1852).

To the *Correspondant* Berlioz contributed three major essays: a cogent argument for expressiveness in religious music; a long biography of Beethoven, the first of consequence to appear in France; and, shortly before the premiere of the *Fantastic Symphony,* what amounts to a manifesto on music akin to Hugo's manifestos on poetry and drama. This third article, "On the Notions of 'Classic' and 'Romantic' in Music," is of special importance because it shows Berlioz coming to grips with the logical problem of reconciling Gluck and Beethoven, opera and symphony, old art and new. Like Hugo, he argues for the new by casting back to "origins," giving first a definition of music and its basic elements. Of those elements the crucial one for romantic music— and the key to Berlioz's logical dilemma—is expression. As the first great master of expression in music Gluck, in Berlioz's view, is not a classic but the first romantic. Nevertheless the supreme romantic is Beethoven, who created a new type of music—Berlioz dubs it "the instrumental expressive genre"—that is dramatic and expressive *in itself,* without the help of words. Given in the name of Beethoven, this explanation also served for the path Berlioz himself had begun to pursue in his first symphony.

Unlike so much of his later breadwinning journalism, these were utterances dictated by choice, not financial need. Or rather, they reflect another need equally compelling: that of educating his public. Berlioz discovered early that if he was to find listeners for his music, he would have to teach them how to listen to it. His essays for the *Correspondant* set the pattern of his future instruction. They are not doctrinaire, for Berlioz abhorred dogma; nor do they so much as mention a work of his own. To the end, he chose to argue his principles through his admiration (or execration) of the works of others.

In one sense he would have preferred to disregard the audience entirely. The imagery with which, from 1829 on, he describes Beethoven's most rarefied music (his hearing of the C-sharp Minor Quartet op. 131 in March 1829 marks a turning point) implicitly condemns, indeed ignores, the public. Borrowing from the poetic myths of the day, Berlioz pictures Beethoven as an eagle soaring in the heavens, meditating in solitary oblivion of the crowded world below. The sublimities of a Beethoven piano sonata, he wrote, only made it more painful to

> come down out of my palace in the clouds, in order to slosh about in the big, dirty bazaar of Paris with rogues or idiots, artmongers who call themselves artists, mindless wretches who pro-

nounce smugly upon Mozart, Beethoven, Spontini, Weber . . . and I think of those bleary-eyed capons who sometimes look up from their dunghill and cluck stupidly, as though to greet the sun.

(28 December 1829)

Such animal images, and food images to similar effect, now begin to pervade Berlioz's writing, their pungency increasing with the years. A distinctive stylistic device makes its appearance too—a sudden drop from lyric enthusiasm to sardonic irony, from "poetry" to "prose." What might be called the ironic fall can always be counted on to rescue Berlioz's prose from sentimentality, often with an almost perverse suddenness. Even in the *Memoirs*, both at the end of the narrative proper and at the close of the final epilogue, the same reflex intrudes, cutting short a lyrical envoi with purposely jarring invective against the animal-like enemies of art.

From his point of view Berlioz's long-overdue Prix de Rome could not have come at a worse time. The stipulations for the prize obliged him to leave for Italy at the point when his career in Paris was getting off the ground. Worse, he was being sent into artistic exile: Italian music was at its lowest ebb, whereas Paris was then the center of every important happening in modern art. Then, too, Paris held him for more private reasons. Slanderous reports about Harriet Smithson had led him to address his affections elsewhere, with better success. Just before leaving for Italy, Berlioz had become formally engaged to a bewitching but volatile young pianist by the name of Camille Moke, later the famous Marie Pleyel. His parents approved the match, but his own uneasiness proved well founded. Several months after his departure, Camille married the wealthy piano manufacturer Camille Pleyel. As Berlioz relates in one of the most famous and colorful episodes of his *Memoirs*, the news of this betrayal very nearly drove him back to Paris to wreak a dramatic revenge—the idea being to kill Camille, her

husband, her mother, and himself. Obviously the plan aborted, and in the *Memoirs* Berlioz makes the most out of the comic potential of what was clearly one of the great crises of his life. The crisis resolved itself in Nice, where he experienced a "return to life" that inspired a composition by that title later in the year. As for the revenge on Camille, it came later in two stories he wrote at her expense on faithless, superficial women artists.

He managed to cut the two-year required stay in Italy to something over a year, from March 1831 to May 1832. Musical conditions south of the Alps proved even more wretched than he had imagined, as he reported to the *Revue européenne* in the satirically entitled "Letter of an Enthusiast on the Present State of Music in Italy." In Rome he found the eternally blue skies oppressive and inhibiting. Unable to compose, he succumbed to repeated attacks of "spleen," the romantic malady of isolation, boredom, irritability, and inertia that he describes with scientific precision in the *Memoirs*. The only cure, he discovered, was to leave the French Academy in Rome and head for the mountains.

As it turned out, those excursions brought much more than temporary relief from his ailment. The wild Italian country south of Rome plunged him back into the primitive sources of his creative energies, revived his thrill in the outdoors and his love of antiquity, and invigorated him with a sense of physical freedom parallel to the freedom he had recently won in his art. Like the hero of his later *Damnation de Faust* (*Damnation of Faust*, 1846) he drew fresh strength from "Nature, vast, unfathomable, and proud"; he relived the Vergilian ecstasies of his childhood on a soil alive with memories of Roman glory. An indefatigable walker, he came upon remote villages and monasteries and frequented their colorful inhabitants: learned monks, simple villagers, and the folk musicians (*pifferari*), vagabonds (*lazzaroni*), and bandits who were part of the reality as well as the Byronic legend of the

780

times. He endeared himself to the people of the mountain villages close to Rome by improvising guitar accompaniments to their dances. In his *Memoirs*, at the midpoint of the Italian travel section, Berlioz pays eloquent tribute to the "great, strong Italy, wild Italy" of the Abruzzi mountains. No amount of distaste for Italian opera was ever able to blot out the vividness of these impressions, which fed his creative life to the end. His next two symphonies and three operas owe their atmosphere to memories of the Mediterranean, the Italian mountains, the Roman carnival, the Napoleonic campaigns on Italian soil, and the wars and loves in Vergil. None of his subsequent major scores is without some debt to the wealth of inspiration of this crucial year.

But the immediate benefit from the stay in Italy was literary. Nearly twice as many letters have survived, understandably, from this year of exile as from any previous year, and they mark a clear leap forward in both mastery of expression and maturity of thought. A new verbal confidence, a greater intellectual openness, a more literary self-consciousness characterize the letters of this period. To his sister he sketches an amusing portrait of Horace Vernet, the director of the French Academy in Rome. To Madame Lesueur, wife of his former teacher, he composes a gallant letter full of painstaking travel descriptions in the manner of Chateaubriand or Madame de Staël. To Hugo, writing to express his admiration for *Notre-Dame de Paris* (*The Hunchback of Notre Dame*, 1831), he spins out long accumulative sentences in Hugo's manner. (It is instructive to compare this letter, a dithyramb without self-abasement, with the bathos of an early letter to the composer Rodolphe Kreutzer in 1823 or 1824.)

In the letters to his friends he mixes description, dialogue, anecdote, musical projects, and reflections about life, art, and politics. Sometimes an especially "fine" passage gets repeated in letters to more than one correspondent. This practice of reusing literary bits marks a new phase in Berlioz's writings.

From then on his letters serve as a kind of writer's notebook in which he tries out ideas for later publication. During his wanderings in Italy he indeed kept a real notebook, jotting down music and prose and even an occasional stanza of verse. Finally, he brought back from Italy one complete work, *Le retour à la vie* (*The Return to Life,* 1831), better known by its later title, *Lélio*. This was a venturesome species of drama, a "melologue" consisting of a speaking role and six musical numbers. It was created with previously written music as a sequel to the *Fantastic Symphony.*

Berlioz announced his new work to his friends with some pride as his first literary effort. Strictly speaking, that honor should go to the literary program he had appended to the companion symphony. Neither that program nor the melologue can, in fact, claim any great independent merit. In his effort to be literary, Berlioz lapses into the heavy, pathos-ridden diction of the period, imitating but—without equaling the genius—the manner of Hugo's *Dernier jour d'un condamné* (1829). Only where his text deals with music, in the satiric pangs of *Lélio*, does it "return to life" for us today.

But the text must be judged according to its aim: in both the symphony and melologue, the words serve to provide occasions for the music. In this they conform to a longstanding tradition, though in 1830 a rather outmoded one. By writing a program for his symphony, Berlioz may have intended to pay tribute to his old-fashioned teacher, Lesueur, who still believed in the eighteenth-century way of justifying music intellectually. The result, at all events, is a text as archaic in function as it was novel in content. For the theme of the artist expressing his feelings could not have been more timely. Berlioz's program, full of literary allusions to Chateaubriand, Thomas De Quincey, Hugo, and Hoffmann (whose *Contes fantastiques*, or *Tales of the Fantastic*, as the French translator called them, supplied the "fantastic" label for the symphony), amounts in itself to a romantic manifesto.

In the program for the symphony, the artist is described as passing through various stages of an unhappy passion, finally succumbing to nightmarish dreams brought on by opium. His elusive beloved (originally associated with Harriet Smithson) figures throughout in the guise of the famous idée fixe. The "reverie" theme that begins the work is incidentally in itself something of an idée fixe in Berlioz: though identified in the *Fantastic Symphony* with Chateaubriand's *vague des passions* (a state of unfixed, "floating" emotions), it shows a typically Berliozian combination of unrest, wistfulness, and predisposition to love that recurs in his later creations of Romeo, Faust, and Dido.

In *Lélio* the artist is pictured awakening from his nightmares, purged of his fateful passion, and pondering his fate. Now given a speaking role, he expresses his thoughts in a series of monologues on death and the after-life, on the position of the artist in society, and on the crimes perpetrated against genius by critics and arrangers. In a climax of indignation, he declares his wish to escape the coils of civilization by turning outlaw, through love, and finally through art (this last, a modern touch, since the work ends up implicitly reflecting on itself). Each successive state of mind gives rise to an appropriate musical number, the last of which, a choral and orchestral fantasy on Shakespeare's *Tempest,* completes the artist's "return to life."

The form of *Lélio* has often been dismissed as haphazard, disjointed, utterly mad. Actually it shows a skillful hand at contrast and balance, even dramatic suspense. In 1832, moreover, it was readily followed and understood by the audience, perhaps because it illustrated a still familiar genre, the monodrama or melodrama, as it was variously called (Berlioz later changed the designation to *monodrame lyrique*). It was a genre made famous by Rousseau's *Pygmalion* and popular for decades thereafter throughout Europe, especially in Germany and England. Its chief characteristic as a form is exactly what we find in *Lélio,* and to a lesser extent in the symphony program: the successive depiction of changing passions in the mind of one person. As a technique, the monodrama combined in various measures speech, music, and pantomime. Berlioz's immediate model was Thomas Moore, who coined the term *melologue* from *melodrama* and *monologue.* But he also had before him Beethoven's *Egmont* (1810), the melodramatic sections of *Fidelio* and *Der Freischütz,* and Goethe's *Werther* (1774) and (in parts) *Faust,* both of which have been considered masterpieces of mono-dramatic form. Today we can see in such works the forerunners of stream-of-consciousness fiction, and in *Lélio* a precursor of such attempts at loosening dramatic conventions as Igor Stravinsky's *Oedipus Rex* (1927) and Arnold Schoenberg's *Glückliche Hand* (1924), or more recently Michel Butor and Henri Pousseur's *Votre Faust* (1969).

Back in Paris from Italy in the fall of 1832 with his two-part *Episode de la vie d'un artiste (Episode in the Life of an Artist),* as the symphony and its sequel were jointly entitled, Berlioz carried off the first great triumph of his career. His two concerts were attended by every artist of note in the French capital, and he emerged famous, even notorious. As with its stars today, the public was quick to seize upon personal associations in the drama. In the interests of publicity, Berlioz himself encouraged the confusion, to his later regret: in the end he became a prisoner of the "fantastic" image he had helped create. It fixed him in the public mind as an eccentric, flamboyant extremist, with the consequence that his music was prejudged and its frenzied movements remembered at the expense of the delicate, atmospheric, religious ones. For the time being the public was delighted, especially with the daring attack on those "enemies of art" who defile masterpieces with arrogant "corrections" (one famous offender, the musicologist François Joseph Fétis, was in the audience and never forgot—or forgave—this public insult). The audience apparently

HECTOR BERLIOZ

paid little attention to a less obvious revolutionary feature of the work: the use of prose rather than verse for two of the songs. Another innovation was the ominous-sounding "unknown tongue" by which Berlioz rendered the speech of the dead in the *Choeur des ombres* (Chorus of Shades). Earlier uses of nonsense verse in opera had been for comic effect; here on the contrary the strange syllables contribute to the eerie, "terrible" atmosphere of the piece.

His *Lélio* brought one tribute so unexpected and fateful that in recalling it Berlioz could only exclaim repeatedly at the "strange novel" of his life. Among the notables attending his concert the first night was the original heroine of his drama, Harriet Smithson. The former darling of Paris, her beauty and fame both somewhat dimmed, had embarked on a venture in theater management that had brought her to the verge of financial ruin. This time it was she who was dazzled. She was introduced to the composer and a stormy courtship ensued, full of complications, disasters, and violent opposition by both families. Something of the stubbornness and sense of fatality with which Berlioz clung to his former idol may be gleaned from the chapter heading that summarizes these events in the *Memoirs:* "I am introduced to Miss Smithson. She is bankrupt. She breaks her leg. I marry her." The marriage nonetheless began happily, resulting a year later in the birth of a son. But the auspices were hardly favorable. Miss Smithson's career was over, Berlioz's just beginning; and he began it with his wife's debts to pay, family responsibilities to shoulder, and no income except one more year's stipend from the Prix de Rome.

To judge merely by the artistic results, the 1830's were years of glory for France and for Berlioz. Not since the 1660's, under Louis XIV, had French culture known such a golden age. Alone to uphold the balance in music against such writers as Lamartine, Vigny, Musset, Nerval, Gautier, Hugo, Stendhal, Bal-

zac, and Dumas, Berlioz brought forth one masterpiece after another. Three symphonies, each unique in scope and conception: *Harold en Italie* (*Harold in Italy*, 1834), *Romeo and Juliet*, the *Symphonie funèbre et triomphale* (*Funeral and Triumphal Symphony*, 1840); an opera, *Benvenuto Cellini* (1838); and his great *Requiem* (1837) add up to five major scores between 1834 and 1840—as many as in the remaining three decades of his life. Outwardly his success equaled his achievement. With the single exception of the opera, each score was acclaimed by a limited but vocal public and press.

Increasing his prominence as a composer was his visible presence as a conductor. In 1835 he took over the conducting of his concerts, and he soon gained recognition as the foremost conductor of his day. He was in fact the first professional, virtuoso conductor in our sense, that is, a glamorous baton-wielding performer whose sole instrument is the orchestra. Less visible but equally remarkable was his role as concert-manager and organizer. The composer himself hired the players, the soloists, the hall; saw to the tickets, the publicity, the dealings with authorities, the copying of parts, the construction of risers, the rehearsal schedule—and took the financial risks upon himself.

In a roundabout way even his opera brought its measure of glory: it fell under circumstances so scandalously unjust (sabotage by directors and performers, rowdy, organized opposition in the audience) that much of the press took Berlioz's part. Hugo wrote a letter of admiration and encouragement such as only he could write ("Sing, you who are made to sing, and let them shout who are made to shout"). Liszt wrote an article hailing Berlioz as a second Cellini, destined to a glory all the greater for the obstacles he had to overcome. Niccolò Paganini said publicly that if he were director of the Paris Opéra, he would at once commission three more operas from Berlioz and pay him royally in advance. In the event, only Paganini himself exercised such munificence. His gesture has become legendary: at a concert Berlioz gave shortly after the premiere of his opera, Paganini knelt before the composer-conductor, declared him Beethoven's only heir, and the following day sent him a gift of twenty thousand francs. (Two of Berlioz's greatest works we thus owe to Paganini: the *Harold* symphony for solo viola and orchestra, which he commissioned, and the *Romeo and Juliet* symphony, for which his gift supplied the leisure.)

The reverse side of this picture of glory and success is that Berlioz was desperately in need of such a windfall. Far from increasing his income, his ambitious concerts only forced him deeper into debt (part of the problem being a poor-relief tax that claimed up to a quarter of gross concert receipts). In such circumstances it was small consolation that he had become, during this same period, the leading music critic of the capital. He had no choice. In order to provide regular support for his family he was obliged to write, each year, an average of fifty articles. The necessity was the more galling because writing prose kept him from writing music and because in these early years he still had every confidence that his music would soon earn him a living as well as fame. But in France, as he gradually discovered, only opera could ensure both. In this postrevolutionary golden age there was no Sun King to bestow rewards, and the failure of *Benvenuto Cellini* was ominous.

Barring success as an opera composer, a professorship at the conservatory or a conductorship at the Opéra would have afforded Berlioz a steady income and an honorable, influential place in French musical life. He presented himself for every vacancy, but time after time the positions went to others. Obviously qualified but feared for his iconoclastic temper, Berlioz was to remain an outsider to the institutions of French musical power. The only post he ever obtained from the French government was a small sinecure as librarian at the conservatory in 1840, to which was added, three years before his death, that of curator of the instrument collection. Other false hopes of the 1830's included two chances for theater directorships, either of which would have made him into a full-scale entrepreneur. That his business skills were equal to the task no one could doubt who had seen him at work producing his concerts. Those who still incline to think of the romantics as ineffectual dreamers might be invited to read (perhaps along with Nerval's impressively argued petition for an assignment as a political correspondent in Germany) Berlioz's detailed plan of 1838 for rebuilding and profitably managing the recently destroyed Théâtre Italien.

Journalism was thus a last resort. The conventions of the trade forced Berlioz to review an endless string of insignificant operas, opéras comiques, ballets, and virtuoso pieces by composers who, as Ernest Newman said, were not fit to black his boots. It was a kind of slavery, and no amount of pleasure we can now take in his lively prose should make us doubt the torment that such forced labors inflicted. And yet there is no question that this hated chore brought its own relief. Berlioz's ability to turn his troubles and his violent dislikes into entertaining prose gave him not only distance from his plight but also a voice in helping alter it. His writing provided a weapon for "defending the beautiful and attacking its opposite," as he recorded with some pride in the *Memoirs*. Sometimes it gave him a chance to retaliate, as when the government reneged on its contract to have the *Requiem* performed and he concocted an imaginary sweet revenge in his story "The First Opera" (reprinted in *Evenings with the Orchestra*).

But such a weapon was double-edged. From the start Berlioz found himself incapable of compromising his principles for his own political advantage. He came down hard and courageously on any and all who violated them, whether performers, composers, managers, government, or the public itself. His caustic pen became famous and feared, with the result that after using it for attack he could no longer do without it for defense. His journalism soon became as indispensable to his musical position as to his livelihood.

Fortunately his critical chores were not all equally burdensome. In smaller journals he was usually free to choose his subject and speak his mind, though for especially trenchant satires he sometimes hid behind a transparent anonymity. Of these journals the most notable was the *Gazette musicale,* a counterpart both to Schumann's *Neue Zeitschrift für Musik* (founded in the same year, 1834) and to the elegant literary journal *L'Artiste.* The *Gazette* combined the scholarly aims of Fétis's *Revue musicale,* with which it merged in 1835, and the partisan purposes of Schumann's journal: it became the organ of a group of progressive writers, artists, and musicians who banded together in an idealistic attempt to uphold the nobility of art against the encroachments of the philistines. Berlioz played a leading role in these efforts from the first, turning out every kind of review, essay, and story (the *Gazette* often played host to the popular new genre of the musical novella), and even taking over the editorship for a time in 1837.

It was clearly a comfort, in these early years of battle, to have this forum and its sympathetic phalanx of fellow artists behind him. For at the *Journal des débats,* where he became critic in 1835 (inheriting the post from Castil-Blaze, whom he had so brashly attacked ten years before), his position was more powerful but also more constrained. There he was expected to produce feuilletons, that is to say informal, witty essays of high literary quality but aimed at a much broader public than that of the *Gazette.* Since each artistic genre or type of theater had its titular expert, Berlioz had to stay carefully within his assigned domain. He was assigned to review only concerts at first, then operas, but was not to deal with ballet or the Italian operas performed at the Théâtre Italien. His very power as an opera reviewer

held him in check, since his word could mean success or costly failure for lavish new productions at the Opéra, where he himself hoped to be admitted.

In form, his opera reviews were expected to follow certain conventions. Each began with a detailed summary of the action, a plot "analysis" that must above all entertain, even when the plot had nothing much to recommend it by way of entertainment. For this task Berlioz had before him the example of his colleague Jules Janin, called the "prince of critics" in his day, who had shown how to transform the required analysis into a piece of virtuoso prose capable of demolishing a work before the music ever came into question. Berlioz soon became as adept at the technique as Janin himself. Eventually he went so far as to perfect what he called the *feuilleton du silence,* a comic fantasia that blatantly avoids saying anything about the work in question—but thereby says it all. (Chapter 18 of *Evenings with the Orchestra* contains several amusing examples.)

Writing to entertain, often dealing with works of no intrinsic value or interest, does little to encourage immortal prose. Of Janin's once famous displays of wit, most have long since lost their glitter. If so many of Berlioz's have escaped the same fate, it is largely because he later took the trouble to extract the best passages from his often amorphous chronicles and set them carefully in his masterly volumes. One would never suspect, for instance, that the inspiring first toast in the epilogue of *Evenings with the Orchestra* had served in 1839 to introduce the review of an opéra comique. But in addition, Berlioz had one decisive advantage over Janin: he was a practicing artist, with convictions all the stronger for their direct bearing on his own work. As a result nearly everything he wrote, even the most light-handed review of the most frivolous opéra comique, sheds light on his basic principles. Like a good teacher, he knew how to keep his fundamental message constantly in mind, even as he varied its form to help drive home its contents.

In his serious criticism, as opposed to what he called his "feuilletonizing," Berlioz argues his principles directly. This criticism takes many forms: short biographies of old and modern masters, book reviews, studies of musical issues—of a genre, for example, such as opéra comique; of the elements of music, such as rhythm; of historical matters, such as the history of religious music; of the problem of musical expression; of matters of performance and acoustics; of musical education; of the role of music in society. Beyond all these, the core of his instructional program lies in what he called *la critique admirative* (admiring criticism).

The phrase is revealing, for it marks a new phase in the history of criticism: where classical criticism presupposes a godlike authority and judgment on the part of the critic, romantic criticism no longer judges ("criticizes" in the ordinary sense) but simply admires—and, so as not to fall into silence, attempts to convey that admiration to the reader. Such a criticism is in fact a form of worship, obviously suited only to the gods of art. Thus Berlioz performs his new critical rites chiefly for his idols—Gluck, Weber, Beethoven, Spontini—and only very occasionally for a popular contemporary: Rossini's *William Tell* (1829) and Giacomo Meyerbeer's *Les Huguenots* (1836) both have the honor, though neither work is spared numerous old-fashioned criticisms. But the works he returned to again and again throughout the 1830's were the symphonies of Beethoven.

It hardly exaggerates to say that, in the history of music criticism, these symphonies created the genre of the musical analysis—since analysis was the tangible result of the ambition to serve rather than judge the masterpieces of art. The meaning of the word derives from its use in the earlier "plot analysis": in essence, the musical analysis attempts to describe in words the "plot" of a musical work.

Its aim is to guide the listener to a perceptive hearing of the work itself, not by a literal program but by analogy, description, and technical illustration. Two decades before Berlioz, Hoffmann had devised a method, later adopted by Schumann, that separated the "poetic" from the "technical" analysis—the "hymn" from the "critique."

Berlioz fused the two, adapting the form of his commentary to the demands of each piece. At its best his method succeeds in capturing something of the rhythm and atmosphere of the music, as in the following one-sentence evocation of the terse and sinewy first movement of Beethoven's Fifth Symphony:

> Écoutez ces hoquets de l'orchestre, ces accords dialogués entre les instruments à vent et les instruments à cordes, qui vont et viennent en s'affaiblissant toujours, comme la respiration pénible d'un mourant; puis font place à une phrase pleine de violence, où l'orchestre semble se relever, ranimé par un éclair de fureur; voyez cette masse frémissante hésiter un instant et se précipiter ensuite tout entière, divisée en deux unissons ardents comme deux ruisseaux de lave; et dites si ce style passionné n'est pas en dehors et au-dessus de tout ce qu'on avait produit auparavant en musique instrumentale.
> (*Gazette musicale*, 29 April 1838. Reprinted in *À Travers chants*, p. 51)

> Listen to those orchestral hiccups, those chords in dialogue between the winds and strings that come and go, weakening like the painful gasps of a dying man, then give way to a phrase full of violence in which the orchestra seems to rise up, galvanized as if by fury; behold that seething mass hesitate a moment and then rush ahead, divided into two glowing unisons that resemble two rivers of lava; then say if this passionate style doesn't surpass and exceed anything ever produced before in the way of orchestral music.

Among his other instructional writings, the famous *Treatise on Instrumentation and Orchestration* occupies a special place. Published in 1843, it originally appeared in

1841–1842 as a series of articles in the *Gazette musicale.* Berlioz considered this text a manual for composers and did not count it among his literary works. Even more than the Beethoven essays, the *Treatise* is still used and quoted—together with its later companion piece, the essay "L'Art du chef d'orchestre" (The Art of the Conductor). This is not so much for its technical information, valid though it largely remains; what attracts the wider public is its wealth of general observations about art and musicianship and its verbal felicities in describing the expressive qualities of instruments. Its illustrative commentaries contain some of the finest of Berlioz's *critique admirative.* It has helped to train countless musicians, inspired many composers (by their own admission) to further creation, and fascinated readers in general. One of Émile Zola's heroes, in *L'Oeuvre* (*The Masterpiece,* 1886), goes into raptures over the description of the clarinets in a military band as "the warriors' beloved companions, proud-eyed, passionate women, whom the sound of arms exalts." The musicologist Jules Combarieu especially admires an allusion to the "chaste and reserved" voice of the French horn.

But to take such phrases out of context is misleading. Berlioz's imagery applies not to an instrument in the abstract, as baroque theory does, but to that instrument used within a specific range and dynamic level, under given dramatic circumstances, and in precise, ever-varying combinations with others. In the chapter on the flute, notice how carefully he distinguishes that instrument's expressive qualities from those of the other winds, as he explains its appropriateness to the "grief, humility, and resignation" of the scene in the Elysian fields from Gluck's *Orpheus:*

An oboe would have sounded too childlike and its voice would not have been pure enough; the English horn is pitched too low; a clarinet might have done better, but certain notes would have been too loud, and none of the softer notes could have approached the hushed, self-effacing, veiled sonority of the flute's low F natural and high B flat, both of which give such a melancholy character to the flute in the key of D minor where they recur. Finally, neither the violin, the viola, nor the cello, either individually or in groups, was suitable for expressing this infinitely sublime plaint of a desperate, suffering shade. Nothing else would have done but the very instrument chosen by the author. And Gluck's melody is so conceived that the flute lends itself to each anxious movement of this unending grief, still colored as it is by accents of earthly passion. It begins as a barely audible voice that seems afraid of being heard; then it moans softly, rising to a fever of reproach, to a cry of deep pain, the cry of a heart rent by incurable wounds; then it gradually subsides into the plaint, the moan, the sorrowing murmur of a soul resigned to grief—what a poet!

As much as the poetry, a strong vein of polemic enlivens this work, making it a compendium of Berliozian satire at its best. In his articles of the previous decade, Berlioz had lashed out repeatedly at the excessive use of brass and percussion—in works of contemporary French and Italian composers. Accordingly, his *Treatise* aims not only at exploiting the orchestra but also at protecting it from abuse. In the text, enthusiasm for special instrumental effects is always liable to veer off into outrage over current musical offenses. His own stake in a much-abused resource may be felt in the concluding tirade of the chapter on the trombone:

Some few composers [Gluck, Beethoven, Mozart, Weber, Spontini] knew how to use this noble instrument's various expressive qualities with intelligent reserve, . . . completely preserving its power, dignity, and poetry. But to compel it, in the manner of most composers today, to blare out in the credo of a mass brutal phrases more fit for the tavern than the temple; to resound as for Alexander's entry into Babylon when nothing more is at stake than a dancer's pirouettes; to stomp out a tonic and dominant oom-pah-pah under a ditty that a guitar would do to accompany; to mingle its Olympian voice with the trivial duet of a musical comedy or the vulgar noise of a contredanse; to prepare the triumphal entrance of an oboe or a flute in the tutti of a concerto—such uses impoverish and degrade a magnificent individuality. They turn a hero into a slave and a buffoon, rob the orchestra of all color, render ineffectual and meaningless any calculated gradation of orchestral forces; they demolish the art, past, present, and future; they are voluntary acts of vandalism—or else they show so egregious a lack of expressive sense as to verge on stupidity.

The volume is provocative by the very premises of its structure. It begins with one of those Berliozian cymbal-strokes that still reverberates today: "Any sounding body," comes the bold claim, "is a musical instrument when used as such by a composer." As a result of such radical empiricism, Berlioz can build up the orchestra from scratch rather than from tradition, treat any of the known instruments, no matter how rare, archaic, or novel, and associate or dissociate them according to their expressive affinities or differences. So logically does he manage his complex task that the work is as compelling in form as it is solid in philosophic substance. The essays on the various instruments, grouped according to the methods of sound-production (the voice takes its place among the winds) work their way up by inevitable progression to the grand finale: a chapter on the full orchestra. Poetry and polemic merge in a climactic Hugo-like vision detailing the potentially infinite uses of a great festival orchestra, the sum of all the sound-producing groups, colossal or delicate according to need, as flexible and powerful as nature itself, and capable of "making the most recalcitrant spirits tremble as its crescendo mounts, roaring like an immense, sublime conflagration!"

In December 1842, exactly ten years after he had returned from Italy to conquer Paris

with *Lélio*, Berlioz set out on his first musical campaign in Germany. He himself used the military analogy in deliberate allusion to the Napoleonic campaigns; along the way he dispatched to the Parisian newspapers what he jokingly called his "bulletins from the Grand Army." But joke or not, the military analogy aptly conveys the vast amounts of planning, persistence, and courage that such a venture required. Unlike earlier traveling composers who had invariably been performing virtuosos as well, Berlioz set out to succeed on the strength of his music alone. For his concerts abroad he had to transport his own music, gather together the available forces on the spot, and train the musicians to play works far more difficult than any they had ever encountered. Performers, critics, and public were alike unprepared for Berlioz's daring rhythms, novel orchestral sonorities, and unpredictable melodies. Even Germany, the "land of the symphony" as Liszt called it, was dismayed at first by this revolutionary Frenchman who, as the critic Edouard Hanslick testified, everywhere stirred up heated controversy over the very principles of music and art. Where Rossini's engaging, easily digestible music had conquered Europe without resistance, Berlioz's required all his strategy and persistence to succeed. But succeed it did, if one measures success by influence: in this sense Berlioz's victory, as both conductor and composer, was ultimately by far the more profound.

This first concert tour altered the pattern of Berlioz's existence in several important ways. From then on his foreign travels became a way of life, interrupted only by more or less extended sojourns in Paris. In his private life too the trip marked a turning point: it took him away from intolerable circumstances at home. His unfortunate Harriet, suffering all at once from the loss of her career, her looks, and her native surroundings, and from neglect by reason of her husband's consuming activities, had become insanely jealous, given to violent scenes and to drink. Berlioz ended up taking refuge with a singer of mediocre talent, Marie Recio, who accompanied him on the first concert tour and who eventually became his second wife. After his final separation from Harriet in the mid-1840's until her death in 1854, he supported two households.

The German campaign brought about a change in his literary stature as well. Upon his return he related his adventures in a series of ten travel letters for the *Journal des débats*. Their success, both in French and in German translation, provoked some jealousy in Janin, who went about saying that Berlioz had been born to write feuilletons (by implication: not music). What these letters in fact proved was that as a writer Berlioz was something more than an ordinary journalist. This became the more evident when he collected the letters, together with the narrative of his travels in Italy (first published in article form in 1836) and a selection of his best criticism and short stories, to make a book: the *Voyage musical en Allemagne et en Italie* (*Musical Travels in Germany and Italy*, 1844). The two-volume set sold out within a few years. Since Berlioz never had it reissued, choosing instead to reorganize its contents in later volumes, the work has remained obscure. It deserves a second look nonetheless, especially for what it shows of Berlioz's ability as a literary craftsman.

The two volumes unfold symmetrically, with just enough difference in the arrangement to ensure variety. Each begins with the travels, in Germany and Italy respectively; as a kind of postscript, the Italian travelogue includes the "Italian" short story "The First Opera." Then comes a section of critical writings, with an essay on general theory preceding essays on specific musical works; then a piece of imaginative writing on a theme of musical idealism; finally, in a kind of ironic fall, a satire on current realities of French musical life.

The epistolary genre that Berlioz hit upon to narrate his travels in Germany was conge-

nial both to him and to the public of the day. Among his recent models were Hugo's *Le Rhin* (*The Rhine*, 1841), Heinrich Heine's famous *Reisebilder* (*Travel Pictures*, 1827; French translation, 1835), and—for the fiction of the correspondence in particular—George Sand's essay-like *Lettres d'un voyageur* (*Letters of a Traveler*, 1834–1836); Liszt's more pedantic *Lettres d'un bachelier de musique* (*Letters of a Bachelor of Music*, 1837–1839) provided a more specifically musical precedent. After these varied examples Berlioz created a genre of his own: the travel letter about music and its social conditions. Stylistically it had most in common with Heine's blend of humor, poetry, and nostalgia, set off by abrupt shifts of mood. Berlioz instinctively shied away from Hugo's high descriptive manner, although he was as much removed as Hugo from formalistic descriptions in the eighteenth-century tradition; and he evoked scenery rather as a jog to the memory or an inducement to the imagination than for its own sake. (At the sight of the bleak, snowy plains of Russia, a few years later, Berlioz could think only of the miseries of the French retreat of 1812.)

In the letter form he could be at ease, combining the discursive freedom of the essay with the informality of direct address. He could make use of his flair for dialogue, drama, and storytelling, as in this excerpt in which he tells of the curiosity aroused by his concert in Brunswick:

Even the man in the street began to take an interest in the preparations for this concert, and the players and privileged listeners were plied with questions. "What happened this morning?—Is he pleased?—Is he really French?—Surely the French write only comic operas.—I hear the chorus finds him awful.—He said the women sang like dancers.—Then he knows the sopranos come from the corps de ballet?—Is it true he stopped in the middle of a movement to congratulate the trombones?—The orchestra attendant is positive that at yesterday's rehearsal he drank two jugs of water, a bottle of white wine, and three glasses of brandy.—Why does he keep saying to the leader, "César! César!"? (C'est ça, c'est ça!)," etcetera.

(*Memoirs*, p. 312)

And he could show off his gift for adapting his style to the temper of his correspondent. The letters to Liszt and Heine are particularly well "adapted," the latter sporting a witty imitation of Heine's characteristic ironies.

One leading theme of Berlioz's writings stands out sharply in these letters: that of Paris as the city of extremes, alternatively glorious and barbaric. The first letter begins with a retrospective contrast between the dreariness of artistic Paris and his memories of Germany, "where enthusiasm still exists." It continues with a wistful enumeration of the musical resources of Paris, which are superior to any in the world and, if properly organized and animated, could turn Paris into a musical mecca. The tenth letter takes up the Paris reflections once again but in a more somber vein, leading to a melancholy digression on the "industrialism of art" currently sweeping over Europe. In this way the Paris theme binds the ten letters together in a kind of cyclical form. The same is true of the Italian travelogue: though the departing composer curses his exile from the "center of civilization," the joy he feels upon his return is mixed with "a sudden pain . . . I fancied I heard the distant roar of Paris."

In all its ambivalence, the Paris theme informs Berlioz's writings as it did his life. His travels permitted an escape from the city that treated him so badly; increasingly, indeed, they supported him. Yet Paris always drew him back, and his travels abroad only made him more acutely aware of his attachment to his native culture, centered in the ungrateful French capital. When he came to compose his *Memoirs*, incorporating all the travel letters and narratives, the Paris theme supplied ready-made one of the unifying devices of the work.

Rendering fervent thanks to Germany in the tenth and last of his travel letters, Berlioz asks what hymn he could sing that would be worthy of that "noble second mother to all sons of harmony." By the end of 1845, as he left for a tour of central Europe (Vienna, Budapest, Prague, Breslau), an answer as to the "hymn" was in the making: a vast musical drama based on Goethe's *Faust*. Now a complete master of his art, fortified by two decades of progressively ambitious achievements, Berlioz could take up once again the *Eight Scenes from Faust* he had impetuously published (and quickly withdrawn) in 1829, to face in full the implications of their early daring. Part of the daring had consisted in the very notion of treating the Faust drama in a series of self-contained musical scenes, asking the listener's imagination to supply the links. In the mature *Faust* that method remains at work: he had attempted not to imitate or reproduce Goethe's poem (so the *Memoirs* explain) but to "extract" what the poem contains by way of "musical substance."

What the early work had not yet solved was the problem of creating, out of the disparate pieces of "musical substance," a dramatically convincing form. The intervening years had brought not one but many solutions; for the result of working with substance rather than with a preordained mold was in each case a new form, uniquely appropriate to its object, and superbly indifferent to accepted generic norms. In his *Romeo and Juliet* symphony Berlioz had taken bold liberties with traditional symphonic form by including a prologue (after Shakespeare) and an operatic finale, and in general freely dispensing vocal and instrumental forces according to the demands of the drama. In the *Damnation of Faust* he carried this organic freedom to an extreme he himself would never surpass. Drawing upon opera, symphony, and oratorio, he created a dramatic "legend," in the Latin sense of a work to be read or imagined rather than viewed onstage. It was his ultimate exercise in the formal liberty he had learned both from Goethe and from their common master, Shakespeare.

In retrospect we can see that the *Damnation* marks a watershed in Berlioz's career, in his two careers. At the time, he seems to have felt it more as a conclusion: in reaching back to his "opus 1," as the *Eight Scenes* had once been labeled, he may have thought to close the circle. As it turned out, the dramatic legend merely crowned the first half of his oeuvre. It also launched him in a role crucial to the second half: that of poet to his own music.

A French librettist normally had two distinct functions: he had to be both dramatist and versifier. Although Berlioz had tried his hand at an occasional line of verse, he had never yet trusted himself to present his poetry to the public. But he had never been reticent about assuming the dramatic portion of the writer's task. Looking over his major works, we may reasonably conclude that he never actually relinquished the dramatic conception to anyone. Even the libretto of *Benvenuto Cellini,* for which he had two official librettists (Auguste Barbier and Léon de Wailly) and the unofficial advice of Vigny, bears his stamp as unmistakably as the music. As Barbier testified when he published the libretto, it was the composer himself who had chosen the scenes from Cellini's *Life* and sketched the original plan. Who indeed but Berlioz, Roman memories in mind, could have conceived the dazzling carnival finale in which "for the first time in music," as Liszt said, "the mob speaks with its great raging voice" and in which part of the fun consists of a satiric musical contest? Cellini's yearning for the simple life of the shepherd belongs in the lineage of Lélio's brigand tirade, of Faust's envy of the peasants, and of Herod's envy of the goatherd's life in *L'Enfance du Christ (The Childhood of Christ,* 1854). The prayer intoned by the white monks

outside, while Teresa, Cellini's beloved, and Aseaius, his apprentice, sing a duet within, not only uses a chant familiar to Berlioz from his childhood in Dauphiné, but applies it in typical Berliozian fashion for a psychological juxtaposing of moods. The composer undoubtedly continued to supervise the work of his collaborators and even to suggest lines of verse, borrowings from Shakespeare and La Fontaine in the final scenes being likely results of his intervention.

Berlioz tells in the *Memoirs* of supplying his librettist for *Romeo and Juliet* with a prose sketch needing only to be set to verse. But he neglects to take credit for another accomplishment equally noteworthy: the arrangement of the Latin text of his *Requiem.* With a sense of drama unmatched by any requiem composer before or since, Berlioz dismantled and rearranged the liturgical text in such a way as to create (as Edward Cone has demonstrated) a veritable "divine comedy," guiding the listener on an inexorable progress through hell, purgatory, and heaven. After a feat of this order, Berlioz was ready for the much more complex demands of his Faust drama, whose construction he unquestionably took in hand from the start.

The wonder of his achievement there is that he was able to capture so much on such a small canvas. He retained only the three central figures of Goethe's *Faust I,* cut out much of the secondary action, inverted scenes, and combined or displaced others. In the process he managed to create a drama as powerful and as psychologically profound in its way as Goethe's. This he did by making every detail, every scene tell, each piece being, as Barzun has said, "both an object and an embodied criticism upon it." He places the peasant's chorus, for instance, so as to intrude from afar on Faust's springtime reverie and serve as an abrupt and bitter reminder of the unreflective joys Faust will never know. He instantly captures Mephisto's "spirit of denial" by having him appear at the most ironic possible moment, just after the Easter hymn has restored Faust to the bliss of heavenly faith. He reinforces the desolation of Gretchen's lament with snatches of the soldiers' and students' choruses, to the accompaniment of whose boisterous revelry (as she recalls) Faust had first entered her life.

Though Goethe's text triggered almost every detail of Berlioz's script, the Faust and Mephisto of the *Damnation* are unmistakably Berliozian creations. The Mephisto is even more bitingly sarcastic than Goethe's, the complex musical satire heightening the chill of his words. The Faust is more purely noble perhaps than Goethe's, more disdainful of the devil's lures, and also more believably human in his final fits of pity and fear. He is arguably more pessimistic in his views of unfeeling nature, whose destructive and creative sides he shares equally. He is also the one who of all Berlioz's dramatic heroes comes closest to being a self-portrait.

To put his scenario into verse, Berlioz addressed himself to an obscure journalist, Almire Gandonnière, now remembered solely for his part in Berlioz's work. The very choice (he might, for example, have asked Nerval) suggests a desire to keep a tight rein on the proceedings. Then circumstances came into play: Berlioz was traveling abroad and musical inspiration kept flooding in, outstripping the supply of verses. Of necessity he began to take over the literary task himself. To his surprise he discovered an unexpected facility in writing verse. To us the greater surprise lies rather in the generally conservative nature of the results. Why indeed use verse at all, when he had dared use prose in *Lélio?* One answer is that a drama as vast and varied as *Faust* demanded as wide a range of resources—those of rhyme and rhythm were not to be discarded out of hand; another is that he no longer felt the need to brandish his iconoclasm. In the early *Lélio* and in his *Elégie* (*Elegy*, 1829), from Thomas Moore, Berlioz had taken great delight in proving that music could exist perfectly well without the strict, measured verse

considered indispensable under classical rules. In the *Damnation* he by no means denied himself this freedom, but he balanced prose with verse, taking both Goethe and Shakespeare as warrants for running the gamut from the lofty alexandrines of Faust's soliloquies to the Latin prose of the students and the weird language of the demons (Berlioz devised both these last two himself).

For the bulk of the text, he used the classical French type of free verse; that is, rhymed verse freely disposed in lines of unequal length. Preferring, for music, short lines to long (his alexandrines are always carefully divided at midpoint), Berlioz found that vers libre gave him exactly the flexibility he needed. It is tempting to think that he learned to manipulate its difficult technique from one of its greatest masters, his favorite French poet, La Fontaine.

Gandonnière's part in the text dwindles, finally, to very little. Berlioz gives him credit for portions of four early scenes (1, 4, 6, and 7), but so jumbled are the scenic indications in the early editions that it is by no means clear which scenes are meant, nor, within individual scenes, which parts ought to be assigned to whom. It seems plausible to assume that Gandonnière began by drafting the monologues of Faust that open each of the first three sections of the drama. Yet within these the ear detects Berlioz's voice in the fine alexandrine couplet ending the first section ("Oh! qu'il est doux de vivre au fond des solitudes/ Loin de la lutte humaine et loin des multitudes" [Oh! how sweet it is to live in solitude/ Far from human strife and from the multitude]), and in the phrase echoing the idea of that couplet ("Que j'aime ce silence" [How I love this silence]) of the third section. One would like to spare him the blame for the artificiality of much of the rest. (An early Berlioz scholar, Julien Tiersot, did in fact assign the third monologue to Gandonnière, though the numbers would seem to indicate otherwise.)

As for the second monologue, we might reasonably argue Berlioz's predominating hand on the basis of sonorities of rhyme and rhythm typical of his verse. This piece distinguishes itself from the two others by its general harmoniousness of diction, the result of an abundance of dark, nasal vowels and frequent inner rhymes, or approximate rhymes, at points of stress (for example, "regrets," "quitté," "cité"; "trouver," "trembler," "illuminer," "tuer"). At the opposite extreme, many of Mephisto's lines and most of the scene in hell eschew rhyme altogether—an opposition perhaps between Christian rhyme and pagan prose. On occasion Berlioz achieves notably expressive effects in his verse: the wailing feminine endings in *ée* throughout "Ride to the Abyss" and the preceding recitative evoke at once Faust's desperation, Gretchen's plight, and Mephisto's mockery of both; the three successive enjambments at the end of the "Invocation to Nature," reminiscent of some of Hugo's effects, suggest the unending aspirations of Faust's restless spirit. Berlioz was justifiably proud of this last piece and of the final apotheosis, which in its simplicity looks forward to the limpid verse of *The Childhood of Christ*.

Although the *Damnation of Faust* was to become, after Berlioz's death, his most popular score in France (and—contrary to his intentions—his work most often staged), the Parisians paid little attention to its premiere in December 1846. Concertgoers stayed home, indifferent to the theme that had most stirred the romantics of 1830. By the 1840's most of the romantics had themselves given up serious drama: Dumas was busy turning out his famous serialized novels, then in their heyday; Hugo ventured one more ambitious play (*Les burgraves*) in 1843, which by its failure signaled the end of an era. In the musical theater even Meyerbeer's grand operatic spectacles were now too heavy for a middle-class public seeking in art only a pleasant distraction from the worries of the marketplace. No one caught the mood of the day better than Eugène Scribe, whose librettos and plays, lively and well-crafted though they are, embody a dreary, materialistic "common sense" totally at odds with the generous spirit of the romantics.

In such a climate Berlioz's two performances at the Théâtre Italien produced a succès d'estime with his faithful supporters, but at the same time a financial disaster. Taking no time to nurse his wounds (the neglect of his *Faust* hurt him deeply) nor even to wait for spring, Berlioz set off at once for Russia. Three chapters of his *Memoirs* relate this arduous trip, which recouped both his losses and his spirits. Unlike the Parisians, the Russians greeted his *Faust* with enthusiasm, prompting him to turn westward with a silent cry of triumph and reproach: "Alas—dear Parisians!" From this time on a note of increasing bitterness creeps into his references to France, and this cry, recurring like a leitmotiv in his later travel narratives, sums up in three words his mixed feelings toward his homeland.

Returning to Paris only long enough to plan his next escape, Berlioz headed for England, lured by what looked to be a permanent conductorship with a new opera company at Drury Lane. He took to London and the Londoners immediately, enjoyed trying out his English, and looked forward to his first settled position. But again things worked out contrary to plan. Before the end of the first season the opera manager went bankrupt. Berlioz rallied by giving several concerts of his music. Then revolution broke out in France, leaving him stranded in England and in danger of losing all he possessed at home.

At this point Berlioz, surrounded by political and economic chaos and in an altogether gloomy frame of mind, began to compose his *Memoirs*. Dated London, 21 March 1848, the preface is colored by the prevailing atmosphere of catastrophe. His life as a musician seemed over: "The art of music, long since dying, is now quite dead." Once again he looked to his writing as a means of keeping afloat. Moreover Chateaubriand's *Mémoires d'outre-tombe* (*Memoirs from Beyond the*

Grave, 1849–1850) had just appeared, setting a lofty example of literary style and autobiographical purpose. Their elegiac manner finds a direct echo in the last sentence of Berlioz's preface:

> Let us therefore make use of the time that is left, even though I may have to emulate the stoicism of those Indians of the Niagara who, after striving valiantly against the stream, recognize that their efforts are useless and, abandoning themselves finally to the current, contemplate with steadfast eye the short distance between them and the abyss, and sing, till the very moment that the cataract seizes them and whirls them to infinity.

Although Berlioz's childhood memories immediately lighten the tone, the dismal present keeps intruding in the narrative, breaking up the pastoral mood. In chapters 4 and 8, an intermittent counterpoint to the main narrative tells of the depressing conditions he found on his return to Paris in the summer of 1848. At that time a private grief turned his mind from general woes and summoned him home to Dauphiné: the death of his revered father. The familiar surroundings broke in on his mood of reckoning and recollection and aroused an unexpected feeling of renewal. A pilgrimage to the site of his childhood love stirred up the old emotions, and this time he went so far as to ask about Estelle's whereabouts and to write her a letter. There was no reply, but one gain directly followed: he had found a close for the *Memoirs.* The narrative of his rejuvenating excursion and the text of the letter to Estelle in chapter 58 constitute the real end to the work, closing the cycle of love and memory set in motion at the beginning. Both were written shortly after the visit and therefore within months of the opening chapters. Chapter 59, numerically the last, is dated six years later; its perspective is already that of an epilogue, looking back over his two great loves and describing the new barbarism of Paris that effectively blocked his future as a composer. Ac-

tually his creative life was far from over. But all that we learn from the *Memoirs* about the second half of his career comes in brief summaries added in successive codas: a postscript, a postface, finally a "Voyage en Dauphiné" (Trip to Dauphiné).

This last piece gives the Estelle theme one final twist. It consists chiefly of a moving exchange of letters between Berlioz and the now aged Estelle, whom he did meet once more in 1864. Such a close is especially satisfying because it unites both structural axes of the volume—the themes of love and of travel—in a final echo of the childhood pastoral. The wanderer comes home, as it were, to a resting point in both time and space. Berlioz himself memorably underlines his main themes just before the end:

> Love or music—which power can uplift man to the sublimest heights? It is a large question; yet it seems to me that one should answer it in this way: Love cannot give an idea of music; music can give an idea of love. But why separate them? They are the two wings of the soul.

The chronological distortion within the volume helps account for the sense of drama that, along with the humor and the frequent leavenings of dialogue, makes these *Memoirs* so uniquely vivid. But the drama results not merely from a deliberate effort to condense and arrange, nor from the persistence of the love theme, nor even from the turbulent action, graphically figured in the travel sections, which are more extensive than true-to-life chronology would allow. The very nature of the story that Berlioz tells is dramatic: "the relentless struggle," as he puts it, "that I have not ceased to carry on against men, ideas, and things." It is a struggle between an intractable reality and a tragic protagonist who is driven by an indomitable faith in music, art, and life. The all-conquering love for Estelle merely reflects even as it grows out of this larger faith. And though Berlioz speaks of resignation and despair, he relates the story of a battle still in progress: "I have not ceased to carry on." Nothing is conceded either at the time of writing or after.

A self-portrayal that so perfectly incarnates a myth—that of the romantic artist-hero—naturally gives rise to some skepticism, and critics who have pointed out distortions of fact in the *Memoirs* have sometimes thought to impugn the whole. Berlioz's contemporary admirers knew better: this artist actually lived his myth. Liszt was right to predict in 1839 that were Berlioz ever to write his memoirs, "we will be sadly surprised to learn how such a superior intelligence, so noble a heart, provoked such base emotions; we will refuse to believe that instead of sympathy, support, or at least impartiality, he should have found among many of his countrymen only opposition, injustice, or cowardly indifference" *(Letters of a Bachelor of Music).*

Four years of revolutions after the French upheaval of 1848 continued to fulfill Berlioz's doomsday prophecies about the death of art in Europe. His concern extended beyond art: his caustic remarks about republicanism during this time convey both horror at the ceaseless carnage and scorn for the philistinism that accompanied it. As though to allay these feelings, he turned to composing with a new vigor. In the aftermath of his father's death he completed the three-part *Tristia* (composed in 1831, 1844, and 1848; published in 1849), based on texts from Shakespeare and Moore. He then began a Te Deum as vast in scale and conception as his *Requiem.* As he worked he persuaded himself that this "outbreak of musical fury" was but a last flaring-up of creative energy, similar to "the last chapter of a novel that one writes with all the more pleasure that one is firmly resolved never to start up again." But the work itself, and the great vitality of the letters of the period, belie any such premature retirement. For in one sense a Te Deum—religious, military, and above all "popular"—

would seem the least likely work for Berlioz to attempt when his scorn for the mob was at its height and when the most mediocre kind of popular culture seemed to be stamping out music itself. In another sense it represented precisely the right response to current conditions: it made a dramatic statement about genuine, as opposed to decadent, popular culture.

A composer who in 1830 had orchestrated the *Marseillaise* with choral instructions addressing "everyone with a voice, a soul, and blood in his veins," and who in 1846 had roused the patriots of Budapest to a frenzy with his arrangement of the *Rákóczy* march, obviously had revolutionary blood in his veins. At the same time he never had much use for politics or political systems as such; a brief adherence to the Saint-Simonian cause in the early 1830's reflected only his intellectual sympathy for a doctrine coinciding with his deep-seated revulsion against social injustice. But like most of his fellow artists he had become increasingly disillusioned with the democratic promises of Louis-Philippe's constitutional monarchy. Alexis de Tocqueville's analysis of democracy as tending to foster mediocrity rather than the development of individual talent confirms what the composer observed during the same period.

There is no contradiction, then, between his disdain for democracy as a political system and his obsession with the idea of music for the masses. Fired since childhood by Chateaubriand's evocations of the great festivals of antiquity and by tales of the still recent festivals of the French Revolution, Berlioz dreamed a persistent dream of public ceremonies at which music would dignify itself and the nation by performing an integral part. The music he envisioned would be popular in the highest sense—fundamentally universal and nonsectarian, as in the ideology of the French Revolution. Given the superior modern means of the art, it would enable a composer to surpass even the grandest musical achievements of the past.

In his writings Berlioz evokes past and future musical splendors (as in the culminating vision of the *Treatise*) in a manner reminiscent of the apocalyptic frescoes of John Martin or Victor Hugo. What was utopian about Berlioz's conceptions, however, was neither their scale nor their material demands. Choruses and orchestras of thousands had existed before and could exist again; Berlioz proved as much during the 1840's when he gathered together large groups of performers at several festivals he organized in Paris during the intervals of his trips abroad.

His vision of the festival's role in society is most fully developed in a mythical short story, "Euphonia," written in the year of the Festival of Industry (1844) and later given pride of place in the last chapter of *Evenings with the Orchestra*. In this story he imagines an ideal musical city that serves as a gigantic conservatory designed to produce monumental music for national occasions. On such days, the audiences are "mass" audiences, but carefully chosen to include only those in some way qualified to listen. Realizing a perfect union of artist, audience, and nation, the festivals of Euphonia constitute the ultimate sign of a great civilization. They are religious celebrations for the worship of art as the expression of spirit, uniting all those present in the kind of privileged moments of musical ecstasy that Berlioz first experienced as a child.

Two new projects absorbed Berlioz in the aftermath of his *Te Deum:* a collection of his short stories and the founding of a philharmonic society. This last, a courageous attempt to free art from dependence on government and artists from financial risk, survived for a little over eighteen months, chiefly on the strength of Berlioz's energy and single-handed organizational prowess. During its brief existence it gave Paris the model for later, more successful ventures of the kind, and it brought to audiences contemporary and classical works outside the regular repertoire. Several of Berlioz's works were performed, including the *Requiem.* As for the literary project, it had to be shelved for lack of a publisher. But it lost nothing by delay. In a much expanded form, it turned into what many consider Berlioz's literary masterpiece, *Evenings with the Orchestra.*

We hear of this work as such when Berlioz is in London on a third visit in the spring of 1852. The previous year he had been sent to judge musical instruments at the Great Exhibition. This time he was leading the New Philharmonic Orchestra in a brilliant series of concerts that included epoch-making performances of Beethoven's Ninth Symphony and parts of his own *Romeo and Juliet* and *The Damnation of Faust.* So it was in an expansive mood that he announced to a friend the completion of a sizable book, "very amusing, caustic, and varied, called *Tales of the Orchestra.*" This Hoffmannian title was short-lived, perhaps because the new book contained not only tales of every description, from brief anecdotes to extensively developed dramas, but also histories, biographies, studies, discussions, dialogues—a generous selection from two decades of feuilletons.

Though Berlioz reworked all his varied materials, he was unable to prevent a certain unevennesss of texture—the high emphatic style of the 1830's clashing, for instance, with the pithy, mature prose of the late 1840's. Nevertheless the book is formally a masterpiece. Part of its success is due to the arrangement, the devices used for continuity, and the epithets that classify the stories and histories. But what first catches the reader is the imaginative framework, consisting of a prologue, an epilogue, and a cast of characters who appear throughout in well-defined, picturesque attitudes.

This framework rests upon the novel idea of "evenings." Berlioz presents a fictional narrator, named "the Author," who spends his evenings with the orchestral musicians of an opera company situated in a mythical "civilized town" of northern Germany. Together, the musicians and their visitor form a circle of storytellers in the tradition of Boccaccio's *Decameron* (1348–1353). But Berlioz's version of the setting is pointedly satiric: the Author and his friends the musicians carry on their discussions and storytelling in the orchestra pit and during the performances of bad operas—always nameless. When a masterpiece (carefully named) is played, they are on the contrary religiously silent and perform with reverence. Of the twenty-five evenings, seven are thus silent or musical, the rest are evenings of conversation and narration. The musical evenings occur with increasing frequency toward the end: a sign of progress, perhaps?—a slow victory of music over speech, of good music over bad?

What encourages such a reading is the infectious gaiety that animates the whole and the optimistic tone that inevitably results. Not that the substance of the stories and discussions is usually cheering—nothing could be more grim than the reviews of the state of music in Europe following the 1848 revolutions or of the deplorable standards of performance in the Paris and London theaters. Generally the humor tends to function as an outlet for the most depressing thoughts:

> With rare exceptions one may say that today a singing teacher is a man who imparts the ways of murdering good music while giving an appearance of life to bad. . . .
>
> The Opéra is madly in love with mediocrity. . . . It works itself up to ecstasy over platitude, shows a raging appetite for the insipid, and burns with the fever of love for what is lukewarm.[1]

And yet the presence of the coterie of artist-musicians gives this book a markedly different tone from that of the *Memoirs*, where the autobiographer appears most often in isolated

conflict with the world. In the *Evenings* each speaker benefits from an audience of sympathizers. "One can express such ideas and such deep emotions only before an audience that shares them," the Author-narrator remarks gratefully after his eulogistic biography of Spontini. Even though these men are, as one of them says, the "Catos of the lost cause," they nonetheless stand together in their worship of art, reminding one another of their privilege in knowing joys unsuspected by the majority of mankind. They do, after all, resemble in a moral sense the aristocratic circle of the *Decameron*, sheltered by their tenacious ideals from the surrounding plague.

If this many-sided volume may be said to have one dominant theme, it would be that of enthusiasm, taken in Madame de Staël's broad sense as the emotion at the root of all genius, imaginative power, and idealism. Like everything that Berlioz wrote, this book exhibits the tension between ideal and real; but in none of his other works are the problems of artist and audience, and more generally of artist and society, so thoroughly explored and exposed. These questions occupy the book's three most important stories, strategically placed in the first, twelfth, and last evenings. In all of them the heroes are idealistic musicians, enthusiasts of the purest kind, whose passion for art clashes with various kinds of incomprehension and abuse in the prosaic world around them. One of the heroes takes his Balzac-like "pursuit of the absolute" to the point of a "Suicide from Enthusiasm," as the story is called. This and the final story, the science fiction tale of Euphonia, are incidentally the "revenge" aimed at Camille Moke (Marie Pleyel). In each the hero uncovers and properly punishes the base nature of the heroine, who "prostitutes" both art and love. Both stories are told by the fiery Corsino, who acts as the double of the Author and who plays throughout a role similar to the protagonists of the exemplary tales.

Despite its cavalier habits, the select group

---

[1]All quotations from *Evenings with the Orchestra* are taken from the translation by Jacques Barzun.

in the pit clearly represents the model audience, discerning in both its enthusiasm and disdain. Even here, to be sure, the enemy intrudes, in the guise of the one musician who refuses to indulge in the jokes and the storytelling:

> Indefatigable, his eye glued to his notes and his arm in perpetual motion, he would feel dishonored if he were to miss an eighth note or incur censure for his tone quality. By the end of each act he is flushed, perspiring, exhausted; he can hardly breathe, yet he does not dare take advantage of the respite afforded by the cessation of musical hostilities to go for a glass of beer at the nearest bar. The fear of missing the first measures of the next act keeps him rooted at his post. . . . The reader will have guessed that I am speaking of the man who plays the bass drum.
>
> (prologue)

From other anecdotes and descriptions we learn about audience manipulation, for example in the spoof on the "enthusiasm business," the quite historical institution of the Opéra claque; in the recital of P. T. Barnum's management of Jenny Lind's American tour; and in other exposés of how art is turned into industry. Many of these satires still hit home. Try for example Berlioz's method of calculating the exorbitant earnings of famous singers by the number of syllables in each role: "in *William Tell:* My (1 fr.) presence (2 frs.) may well seem to you an outrage (8 frs.)/ Mathilda (3 frs.), my indiscreet steps (5 frs.)/ Have dared to find their way as far as this, your dwelling (13 frs.). Total, thirty-two francs."

Some essays take up these and related matters in the form of more general philosophical questions: What are the conditions of success for a work of art, especially an unfamiliar one? What is an artist to make of the inescapable truth that no work of art necessarily affects any two people alike? The relative nature of beauty haunted Berlioz. In the *Evenings* he faces it on the one hand with stoic resignation: such works as Beethoven's late string quartets, he reflects, are perhaps destined to remain the province of the few. On the other hand, he returns continually to his dream of universal music festivals. Thus he gives spirited accounts of the international "Beethoven Festival" held in Bonn in 1845 and of the stupendous chorus of charity children, sixty-five hundred strong, that he heard in London in 1851. In the "Letter to Spontini," he envisions a music theater dedicated to ideal performances of the great masters, a Bayreuth not restricted to one composer or nation; and again, in *Euphonia,* he describes a festival in honor of Gluck. There, utopia is realized in the coming together of performers ideally prepared to render great music and an audience ideally prepared to receive it.

To emphasize these ideas is not to turn the volume into a treatise on morality, aesthetics, sociology, or anything else. Whatever lessons it contains come as by-products of its exuberant, spontaneous drama, its humor, its darting glances at life in all directions: these have made its appeal even to readers unconcerned with music. But any reader must feel the strong guiding hand behind the brilliance: Berlioz's personality comes through on every page, and not less in the widely differing characters laughing and chatting in the pit than in the persona of the Author-narrator. Because of its conversational form, moreover, the work enables us to appreciate Berlioz as a conversationalist. His reputation in that improvisatory art resembles Denis Diderot's, whose manner Berlioz's early reviewers found akin to that of *Evenings.* All in all, the book is one of the happiest achievements in nineteenth-century French prose, one that alone would ensure Berlioz a claim to literary genius.

The immediate popularity of *Evenings with the Orchestra* heralded a time of general prosperity in Berlioz's life. Everywhere—outside of France—his works and his conducting were in demand. In Germany the efforts of the 1840's were paying off. A cult had grown up around his name in such towns as Hannover and Brunswick; there was talk of a musical directorship in Dresden; at the Weimar Opera, Liszt resurrected *Benvenuto Cellini* and rallied the best young musical minds of Germany in the closest approximation Berlioz ever had to a school of followers. In August 1853 Berlioz began what was to become a yearly series of concerts in Baden, where the enlightened director of the casino, Edouard Bénazet, gave him full powers and adequate means—a tantalizing foretaste of conditions in the imagined Euphonia.

Still Berlioz was wary of undertaking any new musical works. On the domestic side, back in Paris, things were far from heartening. Harriet had become a complete invalid, requiring costly, full-time care. His son, Louis, who took after him in his love of the sea, had embarked on a naval career and needed to be supported during his training. Much more than the finances, the young sailor's distant assignments caused his father constant worry. In chapter 57 of the *Memoirs*, written at the outset of the Crimean War (1853–1856), Berlioz twice interrupts the narrative with alarmed imaginings of the naval battles into which Louis's ship had been sent. Never one to sacrifice human concerns to artistic ones, Berlioz held his creative urges in check. The *Memoirs* tell of the sobering incident, dating from those years, of a symphony whose plan obsessed him for a week but that he forced himself to suppress, fearing that the expenses of composing and producing another large-scale work would jeopardize his wife's health.

And yet another score came into being during this period, almost without his knowing it. One day at a party he wrote out in a friend's album a little piece for organ. Detecting in his jotting a certain "rustic, naive charm," he set to it words of a corresponding nature, resulting in a four-part choral "Shepherd's Farewell to the Holy Family." This he later expanded into a medieval "mystery," the "Flight into Egypt," whose success encouraged him to add

a sequel, "The Arrival of the Holy Family at Saïs." After Harriet's death in 1854, he added a third, introductory part, "Herod's Dream," thereby completing his trilogy, *The Childhood of Christ.* For the first time the poetic text was entirely his own.

When the work was first performed, in Paris for Christmas 1854, the public exclaimed at this gentle, melodic composition from the legendary composer of fire-and-brimstone, and they gave it the warmest reception of any of his works since *Lélio* in 1832. He was only half pleased: such a reception for a "minor" work, he complained, was insulting to the greater ones. But he was wrong to belittle the score, even in favor of *The Damnation of Faust*, just as the Parisians were wrong to think he had changed his manner. The subject had naturally brought forth a chamber work in comparison with the symphonic scale of the *Damnation;* but its scope and variety, if not its pace, were equally as great.

Two arresting dramas surround a central oasis encompassing "The Flight into Egypt" and the preceding manger scene: the plight of Herod in the first part, that of the holy family in the third. As in *Romeo and Juliet*, a prologue sets the stage. Its slightly archaic mode and its focus on the simplest of scenes transport us to the sphere of folk legend, at once remote and familiar: "Dans la crèche, en ce temps, Jésus venait de naître" (In the manger, long ago, Jesus had just been born). We next perceive Herod by way of a Shakespearean close-up—the remarks of two guards on their night watch. Their impatience toward Herod's obsessive fears, together with the obsessional quality of the night-round music itself, prepare us for Herod and his nightmares in the next scenes. That is to say, we are prepared to ridicule Herod, at most to pity him, for his fear of the mysterious child; then the brutality of the massacres, prefigured in the frenzied whirling of the soothsayers, erases all compassion. Yet in Herod's soliloquy we are forced to sympathize with the world-weariness and solitude of any leader, be he king, priest, or artist. Indeed Herod's words call to mind Berlioz's own experience of the artist's lot: "O misère des rois! Régner et ne pas vivre!/ À tous donner des lois/ Et désirer de suivre/ Le chevrier au fond des bois!" (O the misery of kings!/ To rule and not to live!/ To be to all the lawgiver/ And only wish to dwell/ Like the goatherd in the woods!).

The third part of the trilogy balances the tremblings of the strong with the sufferings of the weak. The narrator describes the journey of the Holy Family in a gripping piece of epic narration in which the lines shorten progressively as the travelers weaken. Then comes the drama's high point: the appeals for shelter in the proud Roman city of Saïs and the cruel rebuffs ("Go away, dirty Jews!"), then the rescue by good Samaritans that brings about a shift of scene to a warm interior recalling the manger. The dialogue between the two families is of exquisite simplicity ("We call the child/ Jesus"). An epilogue then pulls us away once again to an epic distance, briefly recalling the central miracle of the Christian faith, the word made flesh—by a miracle of Berlioz's skill the text avoids sentimentality, even in the final chorus. It is a worthy prelude to Berlioz's most ambitious literary venture, the libretto of his next and grandest work.

The year 1855 saw another Parisian triumph for Berlioz, this time on a large scale: the belated premiere of his *Te Deum*, given as part of the Great Exhibition. Throughout the year, in Belgium, Germany, and England, he continued to reap laurels. A "Berlioz Week" in Weimar holds special significance because there, at the urgings of Liszt and his companion, Princess Carolyne Sayn-Wittgenstein, Berlioz summoned his courage for a work he both wished and feared to undertake: a grand opera based on his first poetic love, the *Aeneid*. He knew well the obstacles he would face in attempting to impose such a work on Parisian operagoers. But in April 1856 he took the plunge. (In June, as though by way of encouragement, he was elected to the Institute.) He began with the libretto; two years later he had completed *Les Troyens*, both words and music.

A remarkable series of letters to Princess Carolyne records his moods and thoughts during that time. In general the mood was one of exhilaration; as during the composition of *Romeo and Juliet*, he barely noticed his journalistic burden. Only when the work was complete did everyday reality once again obtrude. He was as much at a loss, he wrote, as Robinson Crusoe wanting to launch his canoe and finding it too heavy to carry to the water. Besides, Berlioz asks, "What if the sea is only a shipbuilder's dream?"

As he had feared, the sea indeed proved a mirage. His masterpiece in its entirety never reached the stage during his life. More shocking, though hardly more tragic, was the score's fate after his death: the publisher disregarded the contract to publish. Not until 1969, the centenary of the composer's death, did the complete score finally appear. No single factor has so warped Berlioz's general reputation as the long neglect of this tremendous work. Until it became widely known it was possible (and customary) to suppose a decline of his creative faculties and to picture his career as something like Beethoven's without the Ninth Symphony.

More than any other of Berlioz's works, *Les Troyens* defies quick summary. The achievement is monumental, the culmination of a life's work as musician, poet, and dramatist. To those who have come to know it well, it stands as the greatest French opera of the century and among the greatest of all time. In the judgment of the musicologist Donald Grout, it is the one opera in which an epic is successfully dramatized, and remains an epic. It is moreover the one true heir to the *tragédie lyrique* of Jean Baptiste Lully, Jean Philippe Rameau, and Gluck even as it incorporates the Shakespearean breadth and freedom of the romantic ideal. (This standard French term for tragic opera reflects the French emphasis on speech and drama: such a work is a tragedy in words that happen to be set to music—*lyrique;* in keeping with this tradition, Berlioz calls his work a *poème lyrique.*) Berlioz was not turning classic, his choice of subject notwithstanding; the French romantics in any case considered Vergil one of their own. In adapting his source Berlioz was guided by the same dramatic and poetic principles as in his previous scores, and his independence and daring are as great as ever.

He composed his epic in two distinct dramas, linked by the character and destiny of Aeneas, but also related through an intricate web of contrasts and parallels. For the main action he chose a classic operatic subject, the love of Dido and Aeneas. But his treatment of that tragedy draws much of its power, as it does in Vergil, from the psychological backdrop of the fall of Troy. This we are given to see, in the first two acts, primarily through the eyes of Cassandra, the daughter of Priam, beloved of Prince Corebus. She is developed from a sparse few lines in Vergil into a strong and touching heroine whose individual downfall incarnates that of a great city and its people. Her tragically useless gift of prophecy makes her a chorus as well as a party to the action: throughout the first act, her ominous warnings weave an ironic counterpoint to the Trojans' heedless joy at the apparent departure of the Greeks. Her horror as the wooden horse approaches, then passes in its fateful procession into the city, turns this scene into the most overwhelming of Berlioz's processions.

But it is when disaster has struck in the second act that Cassandra rises to her full stature as a "heroine of love and of honor." In a climactic scene wholly of Berlioz's invention, she teaches the Trojan women to die a noble death rather than submit to their conquerors. The advancing Greeks stop short in admiration and amazement at the sight of her, lyre in hand, "Bacchante à l'oeil d'azur s'enivrant d'harmonie" (A blue-eyed bacchante drunk with harmony). Defying the victors she stabs herself, exclaiming "Tiens! la douleur n'est rien!" (Here! pain is a trifle!) as she hands her dagger to another woman.

Cassandra's death prefigures Dido's in the final act of the opera but is both starker and more exalted, as befits a virgin princess. Chastity and freedom are the heroic themes of this finale; there is no freedom, no glory, no consolation in Dido's unspeakably desolate end. The love of Cassandra and Corebus likewise prefigures that of Dido and Aeneas, but the young lovers, impetuous, chaste, mutual, and absolute in their resolve to die together, contrast sharply with the noble queen and epic hero (it is as if Shakespeare were to include Romeo and Juliet and Antony and Cleopatra in one work). The mature love is more voluptuous from the start, issuing forth in a seemingly endless outpouring of sensuous lyrics after the love has been consummated symbolically, in the instrumental *Chasse royale et orage* (Royal Hunt and Storm) at the beginning of act 4.

Surrounding the action of the principal characters, three themes, or presences, deserve to be singled out as contributing to the epic breadth of the work: nature, the gods, and the people. In both parts of the opera Berlioz's love of popular festivals finds ample expression, most notably in the opening ceremonies at Dido's court and in the celebrational processions of builders, sailors, and farmers. He has been lavish in the creation of noble popular chants, that of the Trojans serving as one of the unifying links between the parts. He also brings out the less exalted side of the people, in a Shakespearean technique that heightens the nobility of the main characters. There is the comic bravado and terror of the populace in the opening scene at Achilles' grave; the small group of Trojan women who shrink from death; the pair of sentinels who see no reason to give up the good life in Carthage for the unknown perils of Italy. We also catch brief glimpses of the private, human sides of the noble characters in Aeneas' farewell to his son, in the intimate exchanges between Dido and her sister, Anna, and in a moving pantomime of Hector's widow, Andromache, and her son. The unexpected appearance of the latter pair injects a poignant reminder of the tragedies of war into the Trojan festivities, now shown as doubly heedless.

Though the people of Troy and Carthage give thanks as nations to the gods, and show a common fear of divine wrath, especially at the horrible death of Laocoon, only the elect are given to see and hear divine apparitions ("I heard nothing," says one of the sentinels when the Trojan chiefs start at the ghostly command: "Italie!"). Rather than bring the gods themselves on stage, as in the *tragédie lyrique* or in Vergil, Berlioz uses the specters of the human dead as his divine messengers (Mercury, who appears briefly, is a messenger in function rather than one of the all-powerful). There is less of Vergil than of Shakespeare, finally, in Hector's haunting of the battlements, even though the scene in which he appears to Aeneas is a superb translation of Vergil (Berlioz as translator merits a special study). Like the ghosts who appear to Shakespeare's Richard III, the shades of Cassandra, Corebus, Priam, and Hector perform a moral function more effective and imperious than any divine decree: we have witnessed their suffering and can understand their right to revenge. Drama is thereby sustained and sympathy spared for Vergil's fickle hero, who abandons both Troy and Dido. For although Aeneas acts by the gods' command, the absent gods of Berlioz's conception inspire no heartfelt allegiance. They are remote and cruel in their indifferent playing with mankind, and Cassandra's ironic reproach ("O noble exercise of omnipotence, to lead a people blindly to its doom!") echoes King Lear's "As flies to wanton boys are we to the gods;/ they kill us for their sport."

In the portents and storms of the second drama it is nature that chiefly acts the part of the gods; but at the same time it is nature's simple calm and beauty, and the joy men take in the sunshine, the sky, the fields, and the sea, that color Berlioz's conception from beginning to end. The Mediterranean images he had stored up from his months in Italy, long ago, now surface in some of the loveliest nature poetry ever to grace a libretto. Hear for example the play of vowel sounds in the famous septet: "Tout n'est que paix et charme autour de nous!" (All around in calm and rapture reign); the languorous consonants of "la mer endormie / Murmure en sommeillant" (The slumbering sea murmurs in its sleep); and the internal rhyme "nuit/ endormie" that introduces the dominant sound of the ensuing duet, "Nuit d'ivresse et d'extase infinie!" (Night of joy and unending ecstasy), which borrows ingeniously from the "duet" between Jessica and Lorenzo ("In such a night as this . . .") in the fifth act of Shakespeare's *Merchant of Venice*.

As opening to act 5, the song of Hylas, a young sailor homesick for his Trojan countryside, is a little gem: "Vallon sonore,/ Où dès l'aurore/ Je m'en allais chantant, hélas!/ Sous tes grands bois chantera-t-il encore,/ Le pauvre Hylas? . . ." (Echoing vale/Where from break of day/I used to sing, alas!/Will your great woods hear the song again/of poor Hylas?) The two opening words epitomize the various images of the mother-land evoked in the stanzas, while in the refrain, the "echoing vale" merges with the sound of the sea that, like a new mother, lulls the boy to sleep. What seems at first an hors d'oeuvre—a gentle berceuse opening the final act of catastrophe, desolation, and death—turns out in retrospect to foretell Dido's own heartrending nostalgia for past "nights of joy and unending ecstasy," for her "proud city," and (an echo of Shakespeare's *Othello*) for her "occupation gone." In the Vergilian context Hylas is himself a figure of doom. He recalls "sinless Palinurus" of the *Aeneid* who, rocked to sleep by the calm of the sea, falls overboard and drowns.

From the pastoral poems in short lines to the convulsed recitatives of Dido abandoned, from the popular hymns to the jocular exchanges of the sentinels, the range of genres and the mastery of the verse everywhere compel admiration. To be fully appreciated, the text would need to be printed separately, with a proper regard for the rhyme and metric schemes. It would then be possible to see with what virtuosity and care Berlioz worked as a poet within the limits he set for himself. His rhyme schemes are strict without rigidity, his line lengths the standard even-numbered ones (generally 6, 8, 10, or 12 syllables) but alternating flexibly. An exception to both is Aeneas' anguished cry at the thought of leaving Dido: "Mais je le dois . . . il le faut!" (But I must . . . it has to be!)—seven monosyllables, no rhyme.

Given the weight of convention hanging over his chosen subject and medium, the surprise is not that there are blemishes but that there are so few, and that Berlioz should so often manage to turn his formal limitations to expressive advantage. Nothing can seem more tiresome and artificial than neoclassical inversion coupled with euphemistic paraphrase (Aeneas to the ghost of Priam: "De la sombre demeure,/ Messager menaçant, qui t'a donc fait sortir?" (From the dark abode,/ Dire messenger, who has made you emerge?); but notice how powerfully—and simply—inversion underscores one of Dido's passionate cries of love and reproach to the departing Aeneas: "Ah! je connais l'amour, et si Jupiter même/ M'eût défendu d'aimer, mon amour insensé/ De Jupiter braverait l'anathème." (Ah! I know what love is, and if Jupiter himself/ Had forbidden me to love, my reckless love/ Of Jupiter himself would brave the interdict.) It might even be argued that the stiffness of Aeneas' initial response to the ghost is not inappropriate for his cowed and wavering state of mind. But if that scene begins tentatively it

evolves into one of the most vivid and direct of the entire work, as each menacing shade hammers in more strongly the command of his predecessor: "il faut vivre et partir! . . . Il faut partir et vaincre! . . . Il faut vaincre et fonder!" (You must live and depart! . . . You must depart and conquer! . . . You must conquer and found!)

All told, this libretto, studded with memorable lines both singable and dramatic, comes off as one of the strongest, leanest, and least artificial ever written. It is regrettable that Berlioz, from a compunction Wagner did not share, resisted urgings to have the libretto printed separately. Rich and varied in itself, the text could only have led to similar expectations of the music. Acquaintance with the text would have squelched the absurd legends that gossip had fostered about the work; it might have led to an earlier publication of the music; at the least it would have added to the corpus of nineteenth-century French literature a poem worthy, in parts, of Hugo, Baudelaire, and Verlaine, each of whom it occasionally suggests.

As after many of his greater musical efforts, in the years immediately following the completion of *The Trojans* Berlioz was much before the public as a writer. He gave private readings of his new libretto that sparked favorable reports in Paris society and press. In 1858 he published portions of the *Memoirs;* the next year he brought out a new volume of collected criticism entitled *Les grotesques de la musique* (Musical Grotesques).

So successful a volume as *Evenings with the Orchestra* called for a sequel, and the new work took up the challenge in a witty prologue: a fictitious letter to "the Author" from the chorus members of the Paris Opéra protests against the earlier volume's dedication to an opera orchestra in a "civilized" town of central Europe. Berlioz obligingly dedicates his new volume to "my good friends the choral artists of the opera in Paris, a barbaric town." Lacking the narrative framework of *Evenings* and consisting mainly of brief chapters, many no more than half-page anecdotes, the sequel is much slighter than its predecessor in substance and length. But this lightness brings its own perfection, yielding up one comic vignette after another. The travel letters that are included rank among Berlioz's most imaginative. In style, moreover, this work is more sustained and homogeneous than *Evenings*, a result of its deriving almost exclusively from writings of the mid-1850's.

Unlike Gautier's *Grotesques* (1844), which championed the long-defamed poets of the French baroque, Berlioz's volume depicts a gallery of ordinary and extraordinary figures from the musical world who give rise to a stream of discordant effects. Macabre jokes at each end sound notes of black humor: the work closes with the musical quotation of a "jolly refrain," the Dies Irae. In between comes a parade of musical amateurs, singers, instrumentalists, composers, arrangers, dancers, authors, critics, audiences (especially opéra comique audiences), all of whom Berlioz brings alive in scenes both comic and telling. Nor does he spare himself among the caricatures. We catch a glimpse of his terrifying deportment as a choral conductor in the prologue and later as a critic confronting a trembling young soprano about to make her debut. The tone ranges from light Voltairean irony to hard-hitting satire; it also affords, on occasion, a large dose of sympathy. Berlioz turns abruptly elegiac as he deplores a great singer's death in the tropics or muses over a wretched lot of streetsweepers in a painting by Nicolas Charlet. And in a continuing undertone, allusions to the surrounding decadence, a pervasive complaint of ennui, and the persistent dream of escape to exotic lands remind us that these writings are contemporary with Baudelaire's *Les fleurs du mal* (1857) and Flaubert's *Madame Bovary* (1856).

The *Grotesques* are the most literary of Berlioz's prose works in that they, more than any of the others, put the musical message second to sheer verbal sport. What stands out here is Berlioz's fascination with language, both speech and writing, sound and thought. His musician's ear catches his "grotesques" in the characteristic forms of speech: the dialect of a peasant woman in the Vosges mountains, the patter of a friendly coachman in Marseilles, the honeyed insinuations of an instrument maker trying to bribe a jury member at the Exhibition, the grandiloquent metaphors of dancers or pretentious writers, above all the pompous phraseology of the bourgeois (for example, the wealthy tradesman who wishes to make his son "either an army colonel or a great composer," or the Sunday stroller who would have liked to have been "a famous geologist—or is it geologer?" but not in any case "a famous grammarian"). The result of these varieties of discourse is a human comedy worthy, if not of Balzac, at least of Henri Monnier or Honoré Daumier.

Literary men attempting to write about music without knowledge of the art head the procession of grotesque figures. But repeatedly Berlioz proves his deep appreciation of literature, both in itself and in conjunction with music. One of the serious pieces in the volume deals with matters of prosody and discusses the aptness of verse or prose for music; another embroiders on the ancient theme of the writer's power to bestow (or by silence withhold) immortality. Berlioz turns his own literary culture to virtuoso purposes as he parodies literary styles, recasts proverbs in a manner anticipating Paul Éluard, or weaves quotations from the French classics (these too usually deformed) into his prose. He alludes to a well-known fable of La Fontaine, for example, in the following bit of whimsy about the Parisians' love of long operas, a sentence that also shows him indulging in rhyme, alliteration, and imitative effects of sound and rhythm:

On aime à y dormir, on aime à y pâtir, on aime à y bâtir des châteaux en Espagne, bercé par le bruit incessant de la cascade de cavatines, jus-

qu'à ce qu'un accident fasse que l'on rentre en soi-même, que la claque oublie d'applaudir, par exemple: alors on s'éveille en sursaut.

They love to suffer, to sleep, perchance to dream at these operas, lulled by the din of the endlessly cascading cavatinas, until something unexpected brings them back to earth, such as the claque forgetting to applaud: then they wake up with a jolt.

Whereas Berlioz's skill in satirizing comic types recalls Molière, who is himself evoked in one of the wittiest of the portraits, the mischievous elegance in the choice of terms, the economy and wit of the dialogue take after La Fontaine, whose spirit seems to infuse the volume from beginning to end. Several chapter titles directly parody the fable writer: "Orange Groves, the Acorn, and the Pumpkin"; "The Dilettantes of High Society"; "The Poet and the Cook."

So broad is the range of subject and allusion that the musical connection often seems to come in by afterthought. Berlioz pursues quick, far-flung chains of association: a piece on future air travel by "mail balloon," one on the sparrows of Paris, another on Admiral Nelson's bravery at Trafalgar—all wind up lambasting one or another opéra comique. The leaps of thought often work through sound, making their ultimate prototype the puns for which Berlioz had such a predilection. Through these intellectual high jinks, the "quality of unexpectedness" that Berlioz listed as one of the chief qualities of his music may be found as well in his prose.

Such linguistic tomfoolery has not always been held to his credit in France, where conventions die hard and where prose has traditionally been supposed to conform to common standards of order, clarity, balance, and reason. But in fact Berlioz is capable of turning out classical prose with the best of them. Janin, who aimed at many of the same effects, recognized and envied Berlioz's technical mastery and marveled at his "unbelievable"

care in polishing his prose. The *Grotesques* therefore supply the perfect answer to those who object to Berlioz's style (as if there were only one) for its unevenness of tone and texture, its stock epithets, its freedom bordering on casualness at times—standard criticism once applied, as Zola pointed out, to some of the most powerful writers in the French language. In Berlioz's late prose, we may conclude, the remaining blemishes were left to stand because he was after something other than a bogus perfection. Rather, as he once said, he aimed for the best word to render his feelings, without concerning himself if the result "lurched like the walk of a drunken man."

While *The Grotesques* reaped immediate success, *The Trojans* moved no closer to performance at the Opéra. In the meantime Berlioz was called into action, in 1859, to direct a revival of Gluck's *Orpheus* (1762) at the Théâtre Lyrique. His production, carried out according to stylistic traditions he was virtually alone in recalling, created such a sensation that, two years later, he was engaged to direct *Alceste* (1767) at the Opéra. Both tasks buoyed his spirits and inspired, moreover, a series of penetrating articles on these masterpieces. This analytical effort was timely. Not only were the philistines invading the theaters in record numbers; other invaders were sweeping into Paris, campaigning for the acceptance of *Tannhäuser* (1843–1844) at the Opéra, and proclaiming a musical doctrine—Wagnerism—that to Berlioz seemed as regressive as Rossini's had thirty years before.

Wagner has so long been accepted as the fountainhead of the musical revolution of our century that it takes historical imagination to understand how Berlioz could have viewed him as reactionary in his own time. To begin with, Wagner had a system, and Berlioz despised systems; they seemed to him a turn back toward an eighteenth-century mania that the romantics had disposed of in the name of artistic freedom. More importantly, several elements of Wagner's system as it was then formulated—in *Opera and Drama* (1851) and *The Artwork of the Future* (1849)—struck Berlioz as ominous threats to the ideal of musical independence he had so long defended. The chief of these, as he was the first to acknowledge, was none other than Gluck's own principle (Berlioz said ''impious doctrine'') that music must be subordinate to the text. Berlioz had fought for the Gluckian principle of expressiveness ever since Rossini had flouted it three decades earlier. But expression is not subordination, and here was a challenge from the opposite direction: Wagner went so far as to maintain that music was forever incomplete without a dramatic text and that, in his phrase, music needed to be ''saved'' by the word. Indeed Wagner had once offered to ''save'' Berlioz—whose symphonies were only minimally ''completed'' with words—by serving as his librettist.

Even more objectionable to Berlioz than Wagner's doctrine of music's dependency was the implied consequence of that doctrine: that Wagner's *Gesamtkunstwerk* (total artwork) would supersede all previous forms of art, and Wagner himself, by implication, all previous composers. Such an impoverishment of music and such an insult to his gods (not to mention himself) were more than even Berlioz's stoicism could bear. He revived with a new vigor his early declarations of musical freedom. He unleashed a barrage of satiric articles, or rather satirical comments embedded in articles never directly mentioning Wagner, all culminating in his final volume of collected criticism, *À travers chants* (Across the Fields of Song, 1862). That Wagner's efforts to be received at the Opéra succeeded where his own failed did not help matters, of course. But no personal animus can be detected in the famous article Berlioz wrote on Wagner's music—a highly sympathetic review, on the whole, reprinted in *À travers chants*, of Wagner's concerts of 1860—nor in his refusal to review and exploit the failure of *Tannhäuser* at the Opéra in 1861. He expressed a number of reservations about Wagner's music, but he attacked only the system. In reviewing *À travers chants*, one of Berlioz's fellow critics stressed the difference between jealousy and defense of principle:

> [Berlioz's] talent, his strength of conviction, his abhorrence of the commonplace, even his violence and bitterness enchant me; they come from his veneration of the great masters and from an impassioned, fanatical love of art—and not, as has been alleged, from the wounded pride or petty jealousies of a disturbed mind.
>
> (appendix to *À travers chants*)

Curiously enough most of the early reviewers of *À travers chants*, looking perhaps for a sequel to *The Grotesques*, dwelt primarily on the humorous bits, of which there are relatively few. They may have been distracted by the word play in the title, which evokes at once the usual expression *à travers champs* (across country) and the word *chants* (songs). Like many Berliozian puns, this one is poetically suggestive. All his life, Berlioz himself shunned the common road, blazing trails with the courage of his beloved explorers and adventurers. The title is especially appropriate for this volume dedicated to his musical gods, the great explorers in music.

Berlioz put into this last volume of collected criticism the essence of his musical philosophy. As usual he varied the form of his message, including in his selection (as the subtitle announces) ''Musical Studies, Adorations, Sallies, and Reviews,'' and he arranged his materials with his usual eye to logic and effect. Harking back to his artistic manifesto of 1830, he opens with a panoramic survey of the history of music, complete with a definition of music and its basic elements. Then Beethoven heads a section of ''adorations.'' The analyses of the symphonies are incorporated here, together with articles on the chamber music and *Fidelio*—this last having moved Wagner, on its first appearance, to write Berlioz an enthusiastic letter. Wagner may have seen himself in the following picture of the fate of Beethoven's opera, a variation on the theme of the unrecognized artist:

It belongs to that strong race of maligned works that have had heaped upon them the most inconceivable prejudices, the most blatant lies, but whose vitality is so intense that nothing can prevail against them—like those vigorous beech trees sprung from rocks and among ruins, which end up splitting the stones, breaking through walls, and finally rising up proud and green, the more solidly implanted in the soil that they have had more obstacles to overcome in working their way out of it; whereas the willows that grew trouble-free on a riverbank fall into the mud, where they rot away, forgotten. . . . Who knows but that light may dawn sooner then we think even for those whose spirit is now closed to this beautiful work of Beethoven's, just as it is closed to the marvels of the Ninth Symphony, the last quartets, and the great piano sonatas of that same great inspired one? At times a thick veil seems to cover *the mind's eye*, when it fixes on one part of the artistic heavens, and prevents it from seeing the great stars that radiate there. Then all of a sudden, without apparent cause, the veil is torn away, one sees, and blushes at having so long been blind.

The recent articles on Gluck's *Orpheus* and *Alceste* and a group of articles on Weber complete this look at the past. Separated by a leavening of humorous articles and essays on performance practices, these ''adorations'' take up well over half the book.

The final section moves on to matters of current interest. The essay on Wagner is flanked by brief laments on the wave of musical ''insanity'' sweeping across Europe. A review of a book on religious music—doubtless prompted in part by Liszt's recent, and in Berlioz's view misguided, attempts to ''purify'' sacred music of expressiveness—goes back to the issues of the critical articles of 1829. A review of several new symphonies brings a defense of the symphonic genre itself, threatened with extinction by Wagner's theory of musical progress.

Finally, as if to show that a defense of the symphony did not imply a rejection of opera, Berlioz includes a historical survey of five traditional operas on the Romeo and Juliet story, all measured against that model of genuine drama, the *Romeo and Juliet* of Shakespeare. To a sustained aesthetic manifesto this would have made a suitable ending. With predictable unpredictability, Berlioz closes instead with three light sallies, including a parody of Hamlet's ''To be or not to be'' soliloquy. At the very end, a half-page spoof on ''the lapdog school of singing'' is there to remind us, perhaps, to take all aesthetic schools with a grain of salt. Like every ''ironic fall,'' this one brings us back to the reality that anchors all systems and ideals in the conditions of imperfect life.

Preferring action to theory, Berlioz kept his real response to Wagner for his own music. By good fortune, a commission for an opera to inaugurate a new theater in Baden gave him the chance to act out his philosophy once again. The result was *Béatrice et Bénédict* (*Beatrice and Benedict,* 1862), a two-act opéra comique of fifteen musical numbers linked by spoken dialogue—a lesson in what could still be done with modest means and traditional, self-contained musical forms. The new opera was a happy affair for Berlioz from the start. For once he had no worries about performance or payment: Bénazet, the theater director, was liberal on both counts, and the new work received its first performance in Baden, to great acclaim, in August 1862. It is the last and lightest of Berlioz's major works, ''a caprice written with the point of a needle,'' by his own description; very Mozartian in the judgment of many, by virtue of its wit, lyricism, and effervescent charm.

Berlioz wrote the libretto himself, returning to a project of the 1830's based on Shakespeare's *Much Ado About Nothing*. A comparison of the final work with the early version, which survives as a sketch, provides a striking picture of his progress as a poet-dramatist over the course of thirty years. Originally the plan for the action included nothing more from Shakespeare than the two title characters, who mock each other and love itself, plus the intrigue to make them fall in love. The setting imitated the *Decameron,* with lords and ladies playing games and telling stories while the cholera raged all around. The plot called for a gardener, "grotesquely in love with love" and mortally afraid of the cholera, who marries in the first act but becomes disillusioned in the second in proportion as Beatrice and Benedict's love grows; a count and a countess who pretend to court the two protagonists in order to provoke their jealousy; and several other inventions that remind one of the opéra comique imbroglios Berlioz so often satirized in his own reviews.

The complications have all disappeared in the ultimate version, which is both simpler and wittier. Berlioz remains remarkably close to Shakespeare in developing both his action and his characters. The dialogue is often directly taken over from the source; the expertly polished verse makes clever use of rhyme and repartee to create character through wit. Berlioz reintroduces the lovers Hero and Claudio, the main characters of *Much Ado,* to serve as foils to the refractory pair and to establish the nuptial atmosphere that envelops the entire plot. That atmosphere reaches a peak of enchantment at the close of the first act, in an ethereal nocturne sung by Hero and her attendant maid on a poem of Verlainian delicacy. None of the darker elements of the plot remain—neither the villainous plotting in Shakespeare against Hero and Claudio, nor the jealousies of Berlioz's early version, nor even the comic fears of the gardener. What is left is pure froth.

Or froth, at least, on the surface. What makes Beatrice and Benedict so much more interesting than their sentimental counterparts, of course, is their unconventional skepticism about romantic love and their cuttingly worded insight into the inconsistencies of human life and character. The men's trio in the first act and the women's trio in the second both exploit these underlying conflicts. And when the hero and heroine succumb to their love, they become vulnerable to apprehensions and jealousies no less painful for their imaginary origins. Beatrice's tormented confession of love, taking off from the merest hint in Shakespeare ("She hath often dreamt of unhappiness and wak'd herself with laughing"), develops into a dramatic and moving piece of character revelation.

For comedy, musically expressed, Berlioz invented a ridiculous but lovable *Kapellmeister* named Somarone ("great ass," the name no doubt suggested by the insult to Dogberry in *Much Ado*). His contribution to the wedding is an epithalamium as grotesquely inappropriate in music as in words ("Die, die, tender lovers!"), which he rehearses with fatuous instructions to the players—instructions that parody both Hamlet's instructions to the players and Berlioz's own *Lélio.* In the second act Somarone contributes an "improvised" drinking song (his rhymes give out in the second stanza), a sunny counterpart to the drinking scene from the *Damnation of Faust.* The act winds to a close with a scherzo that captures, in its mixture of sentiment and mockery, the characteristic mood of the entire work.

With this Shakespearean fantasy, Berlioz took his leave of composing. Not his creative faculties but his will to do battle with music and theater managers finally gave out. The score itself he wrote at a peak of creative energy, the ideas pouring out so fast at times that he barely had time to jot them down. He continued to be tempted by subjects such as *Antony and Cleopatra, Othello,* and Flaubert's *Salammbô* (1863), but he remained steadfast in his resolve to compose no more: his life's work was as complete as circumstances would allow. He was moreover periodically incapacitated, sometimes for weeks on end, from an extremely painful disease diagnosed some years earlier as an incurable neuralgia. At the premiere of *Beatrice and Benedict* he was in such pain he could barely hold the conductor's baton.

His one remaining task, after *Beatrice and Benedict*, was the staging of *The Trojans*. For years the Opéra had kept him dangling, making promises and then retracting them. His hope that Napoleon III would order the work produced as Napoleon I had once done for Spontini's *La vestale* proved vain. In 1863 Berlioz finally broke with the Opéra altogether and signed a contract with the theater where he had directed Gluck's *Orpheus*. Compared with his letters, the postscript of the *Memoirs* gives only a feeble idea of the torments he endured as his work was shorn of the first two acts—and then further of some ten sections, in deference to an insufficient orchestra and chorus. During the performances the additional blight of an inept stage crew made the scene changes last nearly an hour. Despite all, the work was well received. It ran for twenty-two performances, proved a financial blessing for the theater, and brought the composer reams of complimentary letters and reviews. Further, it brought him royalties sufficient to liberate him, after thirty years, from his post of critic at the *Journal des débats*. His journalistic career ended with a warm review of Georges Bizet's first opera, *Les pêcheurs de perles* (*The Pearl Fishers*, 1863), the last of many utterances in the press in support of young composers. After that, as he wrote to a friend, he sometimes walked past the theaters simply for the pleasure of not having to go in.

No longer a producing composer, Berlioz no longer required his critical shield. But he continued active in many ways, both musical and literary. Indeed the artistic tasks that came his way—reading *Hamlet, Coriolanus,* and *Othello* to private circles of friends, directing *Alceste* at the Opéra in 1866, conducting the *Damnation of Faust* in Vienna that same year—provided his sole defense against increasing physical torment. In 1865 he completed his *Memoirs* and sent them to the printer, where he went to correct the proofs with his usual meticulous care (the copies

were ready by July 1865 but released only in 1870, after his death). He continued to attend sessions at the Institute, working to see justice done to young composers such as Georges Bizet, Camille Saint-Saëns, and Jules Massenet. He kept up his worldwide correspondence, discussing Latin prosody with a scholar; commending a young Danish composer on his idealistic fervor and his mastery of French; encouraging a boy prodigy in the study of Gluck and Beethoven; advising his old friend Humbert Ferrand, who wished to fit some new verses to a chorus by Gluck. His letters to family and friends are wittier, more spontaneous, more inventive than ever. Even his complaints of pain manage to be witty, as do his ever more frequent allusions to death.

The late correspondence brings Berlioz's literary career to a brilliant close. It confirms what so many quotations here have implied: that Berlioz was among the world's great letter writers. Over two thousand of his letters have survived, reflecting in their ensemble the bewildering activity of an artistic life spanning half a century. His correspondents cover every walk of life, from artists to royalty, government officials, businessmen, journalists, admirers famous and obscure, and friends. Not the least impressive aspect of these letters is their continual proof of his capacity for friendship, with any person great or small in whom he sensed the least bit of sympathy with his ideals. Despite his strong convictions he readily tolerated different points of view in others, and he remained steadfastly loyal to friends (Chopin, Mendelssohn, and Liszt all being good examples), from whom he differed greatly in opinions and style of life. It was the quality of these friendships that made life bearable for him in France, even as his gift for making new friends lightened the hardships of his travels.

Of the late letters, those to his childhood love, Estelle, are the most extraordinary in every sense of the word. Berlioz's second wife having died in 1862, he turned in his loneliness and reawakened passion to this dignified, white-haired widow—her name was now Madame Fornier—in whom he still saw the radiant "star" of his youth. The relationship remained at a proper distance, for she responded to his ardor at first with no more than surprise, then with an affectionate sympathy. But she allowed him to write and to visit her, and these occasions brought him great joy. In truth many of his letters rise to such a pitch of lyricism as to overstep the bounds of strictest decorum. It seems only fitting for one who lived so much by the imagination that these are the only love letters of his to have survived.

The most tender and private of Berlioz's letters remain those to his cherished son, Louis. Reared under difficult circumstances, slow to mature, Louis caused his father endless worry, even in the late years. But the two loved each other with a common Berliozian depth of feeling and suffered equally from the long separations imposed by the young man's seafaring career. In the last years their attachment grew. Louis became more expansive in his confidences and expressions of affection, and Berlioz felt that his own life hung on this thread: "Dear Louis—what would I do if I didn't have you?" It was almost as though he foresaw the ultimate catastrophe. In the summer of 1867, as he was on the way to a party in his honor, an acquaintance abruptly broke the news that Louis had died of yellow fever in Havana.

Berlioz never recovered from the blow. He lived on for another two years, often in excruciating pain, which doses of laudanum (opium) did little to relieve. In Paris and abroad he still cut an imposing figure, famous in name, aristocratic and distinguished in appearance, but giving the impression of a ghost from another age. He continued to receive invitations to conduct from as far away as the United States. The invitation that he accepted, in a final surge of energy, came from the opposite direction, from the empress of Russia. In November 1867 he set out, a dying man, on his second Russian expedition. Temporarily recovering his strength on the podium, he conducted Gluck, Beethoven, Mozart, and a number of his own works at six tumultuously successful concerts in Saint Petersburg. Among the most avid listeners were the composers known as the Five—Balakirev, Cui, Borodin, Mussorgsky, and Rimsky-Korsakov—upon whom Berlioz's influence was decisive. In Moscow he gave a monumental concert for an audience of ten thousand, producing with the offertory of his *Requiem* the kind of popular emotion he had always dreamed of. So well remunerated were these efforts that he commented wryly: "Despite my incessant suffering, I would rather not die now: I have enough to live on."

But from then on his decline was rapid, in morale as in health. He died on 8 March 1869, in the apparent belief that his life's work had been in vain. Yet even at the end we are entitled to see him as he described himself in the final chapter of the *Memoirs:* "burned out, but still burning" from an unquenchable "worship [of] Art in all its forms." His bitter remark that in France he was considered fit only to write feuilletons has not been borne out. In his music he has come to be more and more universally regarded, even in France, as the true heir of Beethoven that Paganini and Liszt once proclaimed him. In his writings he has shown himself to posterity as far more than a feuilletonist. Though it is his music that places him at the very summit of the romantic pantheon, his writings are in their way as unique and genuine as his music. Art in general would be the poorer without them, if only because they form, despite their pessimism, one of the most inspiring statements ever penned of the power of art and the human mind to withstand the adversities of existence.

Selected Bibliography

INDIVIDUAL WORKS

FIRST EDITIONS
Episode de la vie d'un artiste. Le retour à la vie. Paris, 1832.

HECTOR BERLIOZ

Grand traité d'instrumentation et d'orchestration modernes. Paris, 1843.

Voyage musical en Allemagne et en Italie. 2 vols. Paris, 1844.

La damnation de Faust (libretto). Paris, 1846. Written in collaboration with Almire Gandonnière.

Les soirées de l'orchestre. Paris, 1852.

L'Enfance du Christ (libretto). 1855.

Les Troyens (libretto). Composed 1855–1858.

Les grotesques de la musique. Paris, 1859.

À travers chants. Paris, 1862.

Béatrice et Bénédict (libretto). Paris, 1863.

Mémoires. Paris, 1870. Printed but not released in 1865.

MODERN EDITIONS

Berlioz. Fantastic Symphony: An Authoritative Score; Historical Background; Analysis; Views and Comments. New York, 1971. Contains the famous program of the symphony.

Hector Berlioz. Mémoires. Edited by Pierre Citron. 2 vols. Paris, 1969. Excellent introduction.

COLLECTED WORKS

Briefe von Hector Berlioz an die Fürstin Carolyne Sayn-Wittgenstein. Edited by La Mara [Marie Lipsius]. Leipzig, 1903. French text, German commentary.

Hector Berlioz. Cauchemars et passions. Edited by Gérard Condé. Paris, 1981. Selection of feuilletons.

Hector Berlioz. Lettres intimes. Paris, 1882. Letters to Humbert Ferrand. Preface by Charles Gounod.

Hector Berlioz. New Edition of the Complete Works. Directed by the Berlioz Centenary Committee of London under Hugh Macdonald. London, 1967–. The musical works with their texts. For list of volumes published and numeration scheme see Macdonald, *Berlioz*, appendix.

Les musiciens et la musique. Edited by André Hallays. Paris, 1903. Selection of feuilletons with a fine introduction on Berlioz as writer.

Oeuvres littéraires. Directed by the Berlioz Centenary Committee of France under Henry Barraud. Paris, 1968–. The following volumes have been published:

Vol. 1: *Les soirées de l'orchestre,* edited by Léon Guichard. 1968.

Vol. 2: *Les grotesques de la musique,* edited by Léon Guichard. 1969.

Vol. 3: *À travers chants,* edited by Léon Guichard. 1971.

Vols. 4–7: *Correspondance générale* (to 1854), edited by Pierre Citron et al. 1972–1983.

TRANSLATIONS

À travers chants. The following three volumes encompass the entire work, in a (dated) translation by Edwin Evans:

A Critical Study of Beethoven's Nine Symphonies. . . . New York and London, 1913. Reprinted London, 1958.

Gluck and His Operas. London, 1914. Reprinted 1972.

Mozart, Weber, and Wagner, with Various Essays on Musical Subjects by Hector Berlioz. New York, 1918.

Beethoven: A Critical Appreciation of Beethoven's Nine Symphonies and . . . "Fidelio." Translated by Ralph De Sola. Boston, 1975.

Barzun, Jacques. *Pleasures of Music.* New York, 1951, 1961. Abridged ed. Chicago, 1977. Anthology containing several of Berlioz's essays.

"The Conductor: The Theory of His Art." Translated by John Broadhouse. London, 1917. Reprinted St. Clair Shores, Mich., 1970.

Evenings with the Orchestra. Translated and with an introduction by Jacques Barzun. New York, 1956. Reprinted Chicago, 1973. Best of several translations.

Hector Berlioz: A Selection from His Letters. Translated and edited by Humphrey Searle. London, 1966.

Hector Berlioz: Selections from His Letters, and Aesthetic, Humorous, and Satirical Writings. Translated and with an introduction by W. F. Apthorp. London, 1879. Reprinted Portland, Me., 1976.

Hector Berlioz: Treatise on Modern Instrumentation and Orchestration. Translated by M. C. Clarke. London, 1882.

The Memoirs of Hector Berlioz. Translated, annotated, and with an introduction by David Cairns. New York, 1969, 1975. A scholarly edition, the best of several translations.

New Letters of Berlioz, 1830–1868. Translated and with an introduction and notes by Jacques Barzun. New York, 1954. 2nd ed. Westport, Conn., 1974.

"Sixty-one Letters by Berlioz." *Adam* 34:48–87 (1969). Special issue on Berlioz and Baudelaire.

Source Readings in Music History. Edited by W. O. Strunk. New York, 1950, 1965. Anthology containing Berlioz's analysis of Rossini's *William Tell.*

Note: The librettos appear in the original and in translation with various recordings of Berlioz's musical works, notably the Berlioz cycle issued by Philips with expert commentaries by David Cairns. See also translations of articles and reviews in issues of the *Berlioz Society Bulletin.*

BIOGRAPHICAL AND CRITICAL STUDIES

Bailbé, Joseph-Marc. *Berlioz, artiste et écrivain dans les "Mémoires."* Paris, 1972. A useful repertory of stylistic devices.

—————. *Berlioz et l'art lyrique: Essai d'interprétation à l'usage de notre temps.* Bern and Frankfurt, 1981.

Ballif, Claude. *Berlioz.* Paris, 1968.

Barraud, Henry. *Berlioz.* Paris, 1955; 2nd ed. 1979.

—————. "Un écrivain de race." *Le monde* (9–10 March 1969), p. 12.

Barzun, Jacques. *Berlioz and the Romantic Century.* Boston, 1950; reprinted New York, 1969. Abridged ed. Chicago, 1982. Most comprehensive and penetrating study to date.

Bloom, Peter A. "Une lecture de *Lélio ou le retour à la vie." Revue de Musicologie* 63:89–106 (1977). Special Berlioz issue.

Cairns, David. "*Les Troyens* and the *Aeneid.*" In *Responses: Musical Essays and Reviews.* New York, 1980. Pp. 88–110.

Cone, E. T. "Berlioz's Divine Comedy: The *Grande Messe des morts." Nineteenth-Century Music* 4:3–16 (1980).

—————. "Inside the Saint's Head: The Music of Berlioz." *Musical Newsletter* 1(3):3–12 and 1(4):16–20 (1971); 2(1):19–22 (1972). Reprinted in *Berlioz Society Bulletin,* nos. 86–88 (1975).

Culler, A. D. "Monodrama and the Dramatic Monologue." *Publication of the Modern Language Association* 90:366–385 (1975). Deals with *Lélio.*

Didier, Béatrice. "Berlioz conteur et écrivain." *Revue de Paris* 66:88–93 (1970).

—————. "Hector Berlioz et l'art de la nouvelle." *Romantisme* 6:19–26 (1976). Special Berlioz issue.

Elliot, J. H. "Berlioz the Critic." *Adam* 34:88–92 (1969).

—————. "The Composer as Journalist." *Times Literary Supplement* (18 February 1972).

Lebois, André. "Hommage à Berlioz écrivain." *Le Bayou* 18:52–65 (1954). One of the best studies on the subject.

Macdonald, Hugh. *Berlioz.* London, 1982.

Newman, Ernest. *Berlioz, Romantic and Classic: Writings by Ernest Newman.* Selected and edited by Peter Heyworth. London, 1972. Perceptive though not always reliable essays dating from 1905 to 1958.

Piatier, François. *Benvenuto Cellini de Berlioz ou le mythe de l'artiste.* Paris, 1979. Contains reprint of the libretto of *Benvenuto Cellini.*

Primmer, Brian. *The Berlioz Style.* New York and London, 1973. A study of the music, worthwhile even for nonmusicians.

Reeve, Katherine K. "The Poetics of the Orchestra in the Writings of Hector Berlioz." Ph.D. diss. Yale University, 1978.

Rolland, Romain. *Musiciens d'aujourd'hui.* Paris, 1908. Translated as *Musicians of Today.* Freeport, N. Y., 1915, 1969. Contains a classic essay on Berlioz.

Saint-Saëns, Camille. *Portraits et souvenirs.* Paris, 1900. Contains a classic essay by a close friend of Berlioz.

Smith, Patrick J. *The Tenth Muse: A Historical Study of the Opera Libretto.* New York, 1970, 1975. Pp. 305–311.

BIBLIOGRAPHIES

Holoman, D. Kern. *Catalogue of the Works of Berlioz.* New Berlioz Edition, vol. 24. London, 1985.

Hopkinson, Cecil. *Bibliography of the Musical and Literary Works of Hector Berlioz.* Edinburgh, 1951. 2nd ed. edited by Richard Macnutt. Tunbridge Wells, 1980.

KATHERINE KOLB REEVE

GEORGE SAND

(1804–1876)

INTRODUCTION

To THOSE WHO have been brought up in a French environment, George Sand is generally associated with such pastoral novels as *La petite Fadette*, (*Little Fadette*, 1848–1849) and *François le champi* (*François the Waif*, 1847–1848). Marcel Proust's case, in this respect, is typical. George Sand's rustic novels, which Proust received as gifts from his mother and grandmother, enriched and brightened his boyhood; and he always spoke of their author with affection and admiration.

Despite her controversial reputation, George Sand was greatly respected and admired by writers, painters, and composers, who did not hesitate to turn to her for advice and moral support. One of the few dissenting voices in this chorus of praise was that of Charles Baudelaire, whose animosity toward her was not without envy of her literary success and abundant creativity. While Proust saw in George Sand's prose the very essence of human generosity and moral goodness, Baudelaire regarded her as a dangerous and seductive apologist for romantic socialism. To be sure, he himself had flirted with revolutionary politics in 1848, a heady but brief escapade he later bitterly disavowed. For Baudelaire, George Sand became the living embodiment of the kind of romantic utopianism he had originally enthusiastically endorsed and eventually repudiated. That works poured forth from her pen with extraordinary ease while he labored painfully over every line of prose or poetry only heightened his hostility toward what he viewed as her facile sincerity, her gushing sentimentality, and her naive and idealized notion of human nature.

George Sand's position among French romantics is crucial by virtue of several factors: her life span embraced an era marked by momentous changes; she welcomed, indeed thrived on, conflict and strife; in both her fictional and nonfictional works she showed a keen awareness of the importance of the historical context in the life of every individual. History, as she saw it, is determined both by events of a cataclysmic nature—such as wars and revolutions—and by the slow, sometimes imperceptible impact of ideas. She recognized that the interrelation between these two sets of events is at once crucial and immensely complex. Events of an immediately portentous nature certainly played a decisive role in shaping George Sand's political and social attitudes and beliefs, as her autobiography, *Histoire de ma vie* (*Story of My Life*, 1854–1855), makes clear.

George Sand dealt more boldly than any of her female predecessors (including Madame de Staël) with such themes as passion, marriage, and the painful conflicts between love and duty. That she flouted social conventions openly in her own life, and lived her romances fully and intensively, added to her notoriety, but also obscured the seriousness of her commitment as a writer. Furthermore, her generous, compassionate nature caused her to identify with the weak, the poor, and the oppressed; she maintained strong ideological ties with the ideals of the Enlightenment and the French Revolution and remained a steadfast admirer and disciple of Jean Jacques Rousseau.

An uncommonly prolific output—owing partly to her longevity and partly to her industriousness—may well have contributed to a basic misunderstanding of George Sand's rightful place among great writers of the nineteenth century. The general reproach has been that she was too facile and unselfconscious to be ranked with such giants as Stendhal, Balzac, and Flaubert. She could not be a true artist because her easy, flowing style showed no obvious traces of self-torment or self-doubt. While far from unaware of this criticism, George Sand remained convinced that as an author she had the right, indeed the duty, to give free rein to her thoughts and feelings without undue concern for formal niceties. Hence her espousal of a direct, unambiguous, even improvisatory style of writing. Yet in spite of, or perhaps precisely because of, this absence of lengthy premeditation or painful revision, George Sand's style retains a freshness and richness that are only now being fully appreciated.

Not content to cultivate and nurture her own exceptional talents, George Sand did everything she could to encourage those she loved or admired: Alfred de Musset, Franz Liszt, Frédéric Chopin, Alexandre Dumas *fils*, Flaubert. She was, moreover, at the center of the cultural, artistic, and political life of her age. She regularly contributed to some of the most popular and influential periodicals of her time: the *Revue des deux mondes*, the *Revue de Paris*, and the *Figaro*, among others. She founded two reviews of her own, the *Revue indépendante* and the *Cause du peuple*. She not only enjoyed close friendships with such great

French writers, artists, and composers as Chateaubriand, Balzac, Musset, Hugo, Sainte-Beuve, Flaubert (whose talent she was among the first to recognize), Delacroix, Berlioz, Chopin, and Liszt; her renown extended beyond France, and among her foreign admirers were such diverse personalities as Mickiewicz, Turgenev, Dostoevsky, Heine, George Eliot, Henry James, and Whitman.

She was also a passionate pacifist and a writer with a profound sense of political commitment; she took an active part in the Revolution of 1848 and untiringly fought against social injustice and, of course, inequality of the sexes. In a society hostile to independent women with literary or artistic ambitions, she managed to gain the respect of the men who dominated the cultural scene as writers and as publishers. And in her own works, she expressed her rich and often painful experience as a woman who, against all odds, had determined to realize her full potential as a human being and as an artist.

George Sand in a mannish outfit and with a man's name created a titillating legend of assumed masculinity. But these idiosyncrasies were only the outward manifestations of a deep-seated uneasiness. Insinuations were made about her sexual identity and about lesbian tendencies. Her complex and at times contradictory personality, and of course her numerous love affairs, have continued to intrigue biographers and literary critics.

There was a high price to pay for the boldness with which George Sand transgressed the rules of society. Because she refused to accept the role expected of her, because she openly proclaimed equality of the sexes—at the very least in such social institutions as marriage— she was widely vilified and calumniated. Her social radicalism, and especially her novels with political messages, hardly helped to make her a ''respectable'' figure among the conservatives of her time. In effect, she was a woman and writer who came to embody all the liberal causes and struggles of her age.

GEORGE SAND

A CHILD OF TWO WORLDS

On the evening of 16 September 1808, a horseman returning home in the small town of La Châtre, in central France, was suddenly thrown and his neck broken as his mount unexpectedly reared at a pile of stones. Thus died, at the age of thirty, Maurice Dupin, a handsome officer in the French army who had distinguished himself on the battlefield. He bore the name of his famed grandfather, Maurice, count of Saxe and, under Louis XV, marshal of France, who had been equally renowned for his military and amorous conquests. The Dupins were also descendants of King Augustus II of Poland, one of the most notorious womanizers of his time.

In 1800 Maurice Dupin, serving as first lieutenant in Milan under Napoleon, had met and fallen in love with the vivacious Sophie-Victoire Delaborde, mistress of General Claude-Antoine Collin. That Sophie was the daughter of a bird-seller on the quai de la Mégisserie in Paris, that she had led a most irregular life and given birth to two illegitimate children of different fathers, did not deter him from marrying her in a civil ceremony on 5 June 1804. Hardly a month later, on 1 July, a daughter, named Amantine-Aurore-Lucile Dupin, the future George Sand, was born in Paris. The father was twenty-six, the mother thirty-one, at the time. Whether Maurice Dupin contracted these marriage vows out of passion or a sense of compassion and duty will never be known. What is certain is that his doting mother, the aristocratic and highly cultured Marie-Aurore Dupin de Francueil, chatelaine of the handsome country estate of Nohant, in Berry, where George Sand was to spend her childhood and many years of her life, was profoundly dismayed by this "misalliance." In her eyes the woman selected by her son would always remain little more than a camp follower.

In her compelling autobiography, *Story of My Life,* George Sand makes much of the fact that in her veins coursed the blood of both kings and paupers, patricians and plebeians:

> My ancestry, for which I have been so frequently and curiously reproached on both sides of my family, is indeed a rather curious fact, which has caused me to devote some thought to the question of genetics. I especially suspect my foreign biographers of being rather aristocratic, for they have all granted me an illustrious origin without taking into consideration (well-informed though they must have been) a rather glaring stain on my coat of arms. One is not only the child of the father, one is also a bit, I think, the child of the mother. It seems to me even more so, for we are connected to the womb that has carried us by the most direct, the most powerful, the most sacred bond. Thus while my father was a great grandson of Augustus II, King of Poland, and I am indeed a near if illegitimate relative of Charles X and Louis XVIII, it is no less true that I am just as intimately and directly related to ordinary people; moreover, there is no bastardy on that side of my bloodline.
>
> (*Histoire de ma vie,* G. Lubin ed., 1.15–16)

The premature death of her father left Sand, at an early age, in the care of two women, her mother and grandmother, who heartily disliked each other and who could not have been more dissimilar in upbringing, social background, and temperament. Poles apart in nature and rank, they had reluctantly accepted each other. Grief drew them together, but not for long.

High-born, cultivated, and well-read, Madame Dupin de Francueil was a disciple of the Encyclopedists, and wholeheartedly subscribed to their intellectual and moral principles. She was also talented and could sing beautifully, even in old age, the principal parts of the operas of Modeste Grétry as well as the part of Colette in Rousseau's *Devin du village* (*The Village Soothsayer,* 1752). Rousseau was an author she especially admired, and a charming anecdote related in Sand's autobiography tells how her grandmother had been so deeply moved by Rousseau's novel *La nouvelle Héloïse* (1761) and had wept so bitterly over the tragic fate of its heroine, Julie, that her sympathetic husband had managed to get the misanthropic Rousseau, then living in Paris, to dine at their home. The actual encounter turned out to be both embarrassing and touching for the shy, wary author and his worshiping disciple:

> Having completed my toilette, and with my eyes still red and swollen [from reading *La nouvelle Héloïse*], I go to the salon; I see a small man rather badly dressed and with a sullen expression. He rises rather heavily and mumbles a few unintelligible words. I look at him, and guessing who he is I want to speak and break into sobs. Stunned by this reception, Jean Jacques wants to thank me and breaks into sobs. . . . Rousseau shook my hand without saying a word to me. We tried to dine to put an end to all this sobbing. But I was unable to eat anything . . . and Rousseau sneaked out after dinner without having said a word.
>
> (*Histoire de ma vie* 1.49)

Madame Dupin de Francueil had also corresponded with Voltaire, and Buffon was another famous man she had known personally. At the age of thirty, she had married the sixty-two-year-old Dupin de Francueil, a cultured, worldly tax collector, in a marriage of reason that turned out to be a good one for the ten years before she was widowed. She then discovered, to her dismay, that her husband had left his financial affairs in disarray. The Revolution was to make further inroads into the estate. As an admirer of the Enlightenment, she had greeted the Revolution with enthusiastic approval; but she found herself imprisoned as an "ex-noble" and was released only after the fall of Robespierre.

On the other hand, George Sand's mother, in the writer's own words, was "a poor child of the old streets of Paris" about whose ancestry she knew next to nothing. Yet she managed to dig up whatever information she could about this branch of her family, for she took great pride in being the offspring not only of aristocrats but also of ordinary folk. For three years after the premature death of her husband, Sophie (Sand's mother) stayed at Nohant as her mother-in-law's guest. Madame Dupin de Francueil, however, was determined to become the guardian of her granddaughter and to take charge of her education. Sophie for her part loved her daughter dearly, but was too much of a realist not to see the clear advantages of this arrangement for the child's future. Thus in 1809 she reluctantly agreed to entrust Aurore to Madame Dupin. If Sophie was not a formally educated women, she was far from stupid and had artistic talents, notably for singing, embroidery, and drawing.

Young Aurore found herself torn between two women she loved for different reasons. Her natural affection for her mother had been considerably heightened by the latter's profound despair and loneliness upon her father's untimely death. Her grandmother never displayed her emotions, for she was a rational person who especially appreciated wit, good manners, graciousness, and self-possession. She was fair-haired, white-skinned, with delicate features, and she was unfailingly dignified and courteous in demeanor. Her mother, for her part, was a tempestuous, dark-skinned brunette, with an unpredictable streak in her nature and given to great outbursts of affection or rage. To be sure, the tragic death of the man both women adored brought about a rapprochement; but it could be only temporary. As for Aurore, she fondly loved her grandmother but worshiped her mother with a fierce passion that separation made even more intense.

Madame Dupin maintained an attractive apartment in Paris, where she settled with her granddaughter so that she could closely supervise her upbringing. But Aurore lived only for her mother's visits and hardly appreciated the elegant amenities and refined style of life that graced her new home. She obeyed her mother blindly, never questioning her most arbitrary or capricious demands, and eagerly shared her likes, dislikes, and prejudices. For example,

Sophie, like most people of her class, fervently admired Napoleon. Madame Dupin, on the other hand, regarded the emperor as an ambitious, ruthless, unscrupulous individual who had caused untold suffering through his wars of conquest. Aurore, like her mother, looked on Napoleon as a hero and great leader. Madame Dupin socialized with elderly men and women who nostalgically clung to the refined ways of the Old Regime, and young Aurore observed this circle with bemused curiosity.

In preparation for a suitable marriage, Aurore was duly tutored in the customary subjects: a smattering of history, Latin, mathematics, literature, music, and dancing. Madame Dupin and her charge divided their time between Paris and Nohant. In the spring of 1813 came the news of the disastrous Russian campaign, of the burning of Moscow, and of the retreat of Napoleon's legendary Grand Army. Sophie had in the meantime sparingly spaced her visits to her daughter, realizing that these only caused greater suffering and aggravated her own conflicts with her mother-in-law. In her loneliness, Aurore developed a passion for music and reading. She was not content, however, to play the piano and to read voraciously; she also composed musical pieces and tirelessly invented stories.

Madame Dupin found her charge increasingly difficult to handle, for the young girl had turned into a defiant, sullen rebel. That Aurore had in the meantime become deeply religious convinced Madame Dupin, against her own eighteenth-century anticlerical notions, that a convent would be the best solution to the problem. Thus Aurore spent two years in the convent of the Dames Augustines Anglaises, an English establishment in Paris, from 1818 to 1820. The summer of 1819 was a period of particularly intense devotion. Aurore eagerly welcomed the quietude and tranquillity of the convent, for she was weary, as she tells us in her autobiography, of being the perpetual "apple of discord" between her mother and grandmother. The rigors of claustral life held no terrors for her. Her grandmother became more alarmed by the extent of her religious fervor than she had been by her mutinous behavior as a temperamental child.

MARRIAGE

After leaving the convent Aurore was besieged with marriage proposals and projects. Her greatest fear at this time was that she would have to submit to an arranged marriage. In early 1821 her grandmother was stricken by apoplexy, and Aurore became her devoted nursemaid, staying up nights and helplessly observing the ineluctable progress of the malady. After many ups and downs, Madame Dupin de Francueil died on 26 December 1821.

Aurore was then seventeen years of age. She had inherited from her mother her dark hair and olive complexion. With her lively features, expressive eyes, and lithesome figure, she was an attractive if not beautiful young woman. She was also an accomplished one, for she had read widely, could play on the piano and harp as well as sing, knew how to draw, and was an excellent dancer and good horsewoman. A not inconsiderable fortune, including the Nohant estate in Berry and a sizable dowry inherited from her grandmother, would under normal circumstances have made her a most desirable match for a well-born young man. But her near-illegitimate birth and, more importantly, her mother's obscure origins and less than irreproachable past cast a shadow on her pedigree. Most of the suitors who presented themselves were therefore men well past their prime. Against repeated attempts at matchmaking on the part of well-meaning relatives and friends, Aurore fortified herself by reading Montaigne, Rousseau, and Chateaubriand. And since her grandmother's death, her relationship with her mother had been sorely tested by the latter's volatile, unpredictable temperament.

On 19 April 1822, Aurore was introduced to a tall young sublieutenant, Casimir-François

Dudevant. He was a worldly twenty-six to her innocent eighteen. He was the illegitimate but acknowledged son of a baron of the empire and a servant girl, Augustine Soulès. His family owned an estate at Guillery, in the Gascon country, and was financially independent.

Although Aurore had read many books, she had very little experience of the realities of life. She quickly succumbed to Casimir's easy charm and warm camaraderie. When he formally proposed on 2 June 1822, she gave her consent, and on 17 September the marriage took place in Paris. Soon thereafter the couple left for Nohant. At first Aurore was very happy, and on 30 June 1823 she gave birth to a son, Maurice. Her bliss, however, was short-lived. She had tried very hard to find fulfillment in domesticity; but she soon had to admit that, in her eagerness to escape from her mother's temperamental and overbearing ways and to assert her independence, she had succeeded only in exchanging masters. Casimir shared none of her intellectual interests, and he was an inept manager of the family estate. Hunting, drinking, and womanizing were his main passions. No wonder, therefore, that in 1825, Aurore, during a stay in the Pyrenees, should have fallen in love with Aurélien de Sèze, a young gentleman from Bordeaux with handsome, dark good looks and aristocratic bearing. On 15 November 1825, Aurore wrote her husband a long confessional letter. To be sure, her liaison with Aurélien had remained on a lofty, chaste, idealized level. A reconciliation of some sort took place.

Aurore's first real lover was Stéphane de Grandsagne, the impecunious tenth child of an aristocratic family. A student of medicine and natural history, he greatly impressed her with his scholarship and serious demeanor, and she saw much of him in the fall of 1827. She had known him since 1820, for she had been his pupil, and it was he who first encouraged her to wear men's outfits when riding so as not to be hampered by the tight-fitting women's clothes then in fashion.

When Aurore gave birth to a daughter, So-lange, on 13 September 1828, it was rumored that Stéphane was her father, a matter that has never been fully clarified. Casimir Dudevant, however, kept up a brave front, not only out of apathy and passivity, but also because he too had been unfaithful, and his taste in such matters was of a rather coarse nature.

THE METAMORPHOSIS OF J. SANDEAU INTO GEORGE SAND

Out of the disappointments she had encountered in life, Aurore began sketching plots of novels. She had always had a powerful need to express her thoughts and feelings in writing, and thus far had found her main outlet in long, effusive letters to friends and confidantes, as well as in novelettes, such as *Le voyage en Auvergne* (Travels in Auvergne) and *Le voyage en Espagne* (Travels in Spain) both penned in 1829 but published posthumously.

On 30 July 1830, Aurore met in Paris Jules Sandeau, a young lawyer of modest origins turned journalist and playwright. The events of the July Revolution had profoundly stirred her and coincided with her dreams of freedom and independence. She enthusiastically sided with the republican cause, and felt that the revolution had been betrayed when Louis-Philippe and the citizen-king's bourgeois monarchy gained the upper hand. She refused to keep her love affair with Sandeau secret in order to conform to the hypocritical dictates of respectability. In November 1830, Aurore, finding her relationship with her husband no longer tolerable, decided to make a clean break. She would spend half of the year in Paris and the other half in Nohant. She would have custody of Solange, and Maurice would stay in Nohant; and she would have an annual allowance of three thousand francs.

Aurore left Nohant for Paris in January 1831. She was then twenty-seven. She found herself the sole woman in a circle of young writers and artists. In order to move about more freely, especially in the evening, she donned a man's trousers, long frock coat, and hat. In such garb she could frequent restaurants and theaters, and circulate freely in the streets. What gave her special pleasure was that this outfit enabled her to flout bourgeois conventions regarding the proper role of woman in society.

Aurore's allowance from her estranged husband did not suffice for her financial needs. She decided to try to support herself with her pen. Sandeau, for his part, also had literary ambitions. They therefore agreed to join efforts, signing their productions, mostly short stories, J. Sandeau. Most noteworthy from this collaboration is the long novel *Rose et Blanche* (1831), the melodramatic story of an actress and a nun, which was quite favorably received by the public and critics.

Indiana appeared in 1832, under the pseudonym "G. Sand." Under the guise of a masculine narrator, *Indiana* tells the story, set during the last years of the Restoration and the 1830 Revolution, of a Spanish creole, Indiana, unhappily married to an elderly, unfeeling officer, Colonel Delmare. When she eventually escapes the bonds of matrimony in order to rejoin her lover, Raymon de Ramière, an egotistical nobleman who is also a self-indulgent womanizer and a political conservative, he rejects her in favor of a socially advantageous marriage. In her humiliation and despair, Indiana contemplates suicide; but fortunately she finds happiness with her loyal cousin, Sir Ralph Brown, a calm, noble Englishman. The main impact of the book lies in its eloquent and bold treatment of the "woman question." In her preface Sand clearly states the novel's intentions:

> Indiana is a type. She stands for *Woman*, a weak creature representing those passions that have been compressed, or, if you will, suppressed by human laws. She is Choice at odds with Necessity; she is Love blindly butting its head against all the obstacles set in its path by civilization.

Indiana is artistically transposed autobiography, and its heroine, like George Sand herself, finds disappointment in both marriage and passionate love. The artificially happy ending lacks plausibility but hardly detracts from the main thrust of the novel, which powerfully contrasts woman's quest for fulfillment in an authentic and passionate relationship with man's selfish vanity and sensuality.

Just as Aurore Dudevant had wished to escape from the narrowness of a woman's life by wearing male apparel, George Sand deliberately assumed a male identity as a writer, thereby setting an example followed by George Eliot, among others. The obstacles to her career as a novelist continued to be formidable. She submitted the manuscript of a novelette, *Aimée*, to an established author, Auguste de Kératry; he advised her to produce children rather than books. She was luckier with Hyacinthe de Latouche, a successful novelist and publisher of the *Figaro*, at that time a satirical journal with an antimonarchical viewpoint. Latouche perceived literary promise in the young woman's novel, and while sternly criticizing its weaknesses, he also invited her to join his team of journalists. Her debut proved an immediate success, albeit of a controversial nature, when one of her first articles, a sharp satirical piece directed against Louis-Philippe, caused the *Figaro* to be closed. She introduced Sandeau to Latouche, and the latter enlisted his services for the paper.

Although intoxicated with her newfound independence, Aurore needed to escape from the frantic pace of Parisian life. Since she had maintained cordial relations with her estranged husband, the latter, who lived at Nohant, easily accommodated himself to her presence whenever she felt the urge to breathe fresh air, replenish her strength, and write in the tranquillity of the country.

In the meantime her love for Sandeau had considerably cooled. With her active, energetic nature, she had found it increasingly irritating and disconcerting to put up with

Jules's indolence and bouts of depression, and she carried the main burden of their collaboration. For some years, however, she would continue to help him financially. Her own literary success, confirmed with the publication of *Indiana*, warmly praised by the most influential critics and admired by Balzac, only deepened the crisis in their relationship, for Jules greatly resented being relegated to a secondary position. A break became inevitable; it took place in March 1833.

By now George Sand had gained the admiration and interest not only of Balzac, but also of the critic Sainte-Beuve. Famous for the sharpness of his literary judgments, he had written a laudatory review of *Indiana* in the weekly *National* and soon became a trusted personal confidant and literary counselor. In 1832 George Sand published *Valentine*, another story of an unhappy woman torn between her husband and her lover. The denouement is excessively melodramatic in the most morbidly romantic tradition: the lover dies, impaled by the jealous husband on a pitchfork. But the novel is redeemed by its idyllic and rustic setting and its lively portraits of peasant types. In this respect it prefigures Sand's rural novels.

Lélia, published in 1833, is George Sand's boldest and most confessional novel. It owed a great deal to Balzac's recently published *Peau de chagrin* (*The Magic Skin*, 1831), which features a gifted but penniless young writer, Raphaël de Valentin, who throws himself into reckless orgies after being rejected by the beautiful but unfeeling countess with whom he has fallen in love. *Lélia*, on the other hand, depicts a young poet, Sténio, who is driven to despair and a life of debauchery after being repulsed by a seductive but unmerciful woman named Lélia. Lélia is a woman who, not unlike George Sand, finds disappointment in love and pursues her ideal of perfect, all-consuming passion by going from man to man. She might thus be looked on as a female counterpart of the romantic conception of Don Juan. The novel's bold, erotic scenes of phys-

ical passion made a tremendous impact on the contemporary reading public. No wonder, therefore, that *Lélia* should have been characterized by Curtis Cate as a "pre-Freudian novel."

Among George Sand's new friendships was that with Marie Dorval, the famous actress whose fiery performances had done so much to gain acceptance for such romantic playwrights as Hugo, Alfred de Vigny, and Dumas *père*. The intense, emotional nature of their intimacy gave rise to rumors of a lesbian relationship. In general, however, Sand, as she herself readily admitted, preferred the company of men to that of women, not because she considered herself superior to most members of her sex, but rather because, aside from sexual attraction, she felt that each gender is complementary to the other. She herself was volatile and high-strung; she therefore derived little pleasure or solace from women whose eagerness to confide in her their problems, insecurities, and frustrations only heightened her own disquietude and restlessness. Marie Dorval, despite her passionate, nervous temperament, remained the exception to that rule.

It was also in early 1833 that George Sand met and became fascinated by Prosper Mérimée, a great friend of Stendhal, Musset, Sainte-Beuve, and Delacroix. At that time Mérimée was primarily known for his plays in the tradition of the Spanish drama. A young, handsome, scholarly, and cynical dandy, Mérimée nevertheless soon became greatly intrigued by George Sand. They had a brief and unsatisfactory affair, the details of which she naturally confided to Marie Dorval.

ALFRED DE MUSSET

In June 1833, at a dinner for the contributors of the *Revue des deux mondes*, George Sand and Alfred de Musset found themselves seated next to each other. Musset was then twenty-three, six years younger than George

Sand. She was at first reserved toward this dangerously seductive, Byronic dandy with a notorious reputation for dissoluteness and debauchery. For his part, however, Musset was immediately conquered, and he soon declared his passion. Sand was touched by the ardent yet respectful courtship of this dazzling young poet. They exchanged letters, as well as elaborate compliments on each other's works. Musset wrote a poem inspired by *Indiana,* and also expressed enthusiastic admiration for *Lélia.*

George Sand was all the more sensitive to Musset's charm and flattering attentions since her recent amorous disappointments had left her in a depressed frame of mind. In the company of Musset she regained her natural cheerfulness and joie de vivre. He brought into her life enthusiasm, mischievousness, poetic imagination; she felt renewed and rejuvenated. By the end of July 1833 they were lovers, Musset was settled in her apartment on the quai Malaquais, and they were excitedly devising a plan to spend the winter in Italy.

On 12 December 1833 the couple set off on their journey, proceeding by steamship down the Rhône river in the company of Stendhal, who was reluctantly returning to Civitavecchia in order to resume his duties as French consul. At Marseilles, they went their separate ways. Two humorous sketches of the portly Stendhal by Musset record this encounter. One of the drawings shows a jolly Stendhal dancing a jig in his ample winter overcoat, top hat, and boots while George Sand observes him with a bemused smile.

The myth of the romantic couple had of course enormous appeal for the popular imagination, and it was fed in great part by the glamorous vision of the lovers in Venice, silently gliding in a gondola in the moonlight. Reality, despite ecstatic moments, never quite lived up to this exalted legend. The two temperamental travelers quarreled, and Musset ran after other women. He drank heavily and fell gravely ill. The stress of dealing with Musset's infidelities and sickness affected Sand's own health, and she soon had bouts of fever. They were attended by a young physician, Dr. Pietro Pagello, who had literary aspirations and promptly fell in love with George Sand. By the end of February 1834, she had yielded to his pressing advances, perhaps partly to get back at Musset for his philandering. Musset and George Sand returned to France separately. To be sure, there was to be a reconciliation in January 1835, but continuous quarrels prompted a final break in March 1835.

This stormy relationship lasted less than two years but was to have endless literary repercussions in George Sand's writings, notably in her correspondence, in her *Journal intime* (*Intimate Journal,* published posthumously), in her *Lettres d'un voyageur* (*Letters of a Voyager,* 1834–1836), and in her novel *Elle et lui* (*She and He*), published two years after Musset's death in 1857.

In this thinly disguised fiction Musset is easily recognizable in the portrayal of the painter Laurent, with his unpredictable moodiness, his erratic ways, and his fits of rage. Thérèse, on the other hand, is given an idealized treatment; she becomes Laurent's mistress more out of maternal compassion than sexual attraction. The parallel with George Sand is inescapable. As for Musset, his fictionalized autobiography, *Confession d'un enfant du siècle* (*Confessions of a Child of the Century,* 1836), presents his own highly colored version of their notorious affair. Musset's power and skill as a narrator are a good match for George Sand's passionate prose, and in his *Confession* one finds all the major romantic themes: melancholy and restlessness, generosity and suspiciousness, enthusiasm and nihilism, and above all else the pervasive ailment of the soul characterized as *mal du siècle.*

Mutual recriminations, allegations, and justifications between George Sand and Musset were plentiful. Even interested third parties did not hesitate to offer their say on the subject, among others Musset's brother, Paul, and Dr. Pagello. In this contest, however,

George Sand was bound to gain the upper hand, thanks to both her prolific pen and her longevity.

After Musset's early death, George Sand went on giving her side of the relationship. That her intimate revelations served only to fuel the accusations and denunciations directed at her unconventional behavior and "immorality" did not deter her from telling all, either directly in her works of a personal nature (letters, journals, autobiography), or in barely transposed form in her novels. It is probably in the correspondence between the two lovers that one can find the most authentic and moving expression of their passion, happiness, and eventual estrangement. A letter to Musset dated November 1834, written at night following a quarrel, will perhaps give an idea of George Sand's anguished frame of mind at that time:

> You do not love me. You do not love me any more. I cannot blind myself to the truth. Last evening while we were together I was feeling very ill. As soon as you noticed it you went away. No doubt it was right to leave me, because you were tired last night. But today, not one word. You have not even sent to inquire about me. I hoped for you, waited for you, minute by minute, from eleven in the morning until midnight. What a day! Every ring of the bell made me leap to my feet. . . . I wrote to you early this evening. You have not answered my note. They told my messenger you had gone out; yet you did not come to see me for even five minutes. You must have returned very late. Great heavens! Where were you all evening? Alas, all is over between us. You no longer love me at all.
>
> (*The Intimate Journal of George Sand*, Howe trans., p. 19)

Whenever powerful emotions upset her inner equilibrium, George Sand turned to letter writing or the diary form to seek an outlet for her spiritual turmoil. She was also fully aware that a woman, especially a famous one, is vulnerable to calumny. She had paid an excessively high price for her legal separation from her husband and for her freedom and independence. She had therefore learned that to love and forgive is not enough. She met slander and criticism with her usual fearless honesty and frankness. She had learned by now that her best therapy and cure for suffering and loneliness was to take refuge in writing. The written word somehow exorcised her inner demons.

During her stay in Venice, George Sand finished the novel *Jacques* (1834), which may not rank among her best but created a sensation. It is another story of adultery in which a married woman leaves her husband for a young dandy. She also completed the first four letters of the *Lettres d'un voyageur*. The letters, of which there would be twelve, enabled her to express her views on a wide range of topics in an informal manner that mingles observations on customs, manners, politics, and the arts with more introspective reflections on love and friendship. Unlike *Jacques*, which received unfavorable criticism from such connoisseurs as Balzac and Stendhal, the *Lettres d'un voyageur* were widely admired and contributed to the vogue of the personal kind of travel literature favored by the romantics.

What is it that attracted George Sand and the romantics to the travel journal or travel account as a literary genre? Their personal restlessness and love of travel, the delight they took in comparing cultures and civilizations, and the pleasure they derived from discovering new places and customs certainly had a great deal to do with this fascination. But traveling for the romantics was no mere search for novel sensations and pleasurable impressions. Their quest was of a more profound nature. They sensed intuitively that one of the deepest yearnings of the human spirit is for the unknown, the strange, the exotic.

It was also while in Venice, partly in order to seek escape from her emotional turmoil, that George Sand dashed off in a week *Leone Leoni* (1834), a novel inspired by the abbé Prévost's famous *Manon Lescaut* (1732), the last book she had read before leaving Paris.

She transposed the characters and reversed the situation by endowing the man, Leoni, with Manon's fatal seductiveness and amorality. Like Manon, Leoni is eventually redeemed through love for his adoring, forgiving mistress, Juliette, who like Prévost's Des Grieux yearns for a quiet existence in some rustic retreat, yet succumbs to passion and adventure. In both novels the story is recounted in the first person, and the main protagonist remains mysteriously elusive. As was the case with *Manon Lescaut* a century earlier, *Leone Leoni* was denounced as a dangerous, immoral work by conservative critics. And that Leoni should have been identified with Musset is no mere coincidence. He is a figure of larger-than-life dimensions, and he embodies at once the highest virtues as well as the basest vices of human nature. The personal tone of the narrative has led commentators to regard *Leone Leoni* as a barely disguised fictionalized autobiography.

George Sand's disastrous Venetian experience also found expression in such tales of passion and mystery as *La dernière Aldini* (*The Last Aldini*, 1838), the dramatic story of a patrician Venetian woman enamored of a gondolier; *L'Orco* (1838), a symbolic novella with fantastic overtones; and *L'Uscoque* (1838), a romance with Byronic strains greatly admired by Dostoevsky.

THE HUMANITARIAN AND SOCIAL REFORMER

George Sand's return to France in October 1834 inaugurated a difficult period of readjustment. As always when she needed to restore her inner equilibrium, she spent some time in Nohant. In November she posed for the painter Delacroix, whom she had long admired, and the resulting powerfully expressive portrait shows a youthful-looking woman mannishly dressed in a frock coat, with a kerchief around her neck and short hair framing her face. Her melancholy, serious demeanor is heightened by large, dark, expressive eyes, a longish nose, and sensitive yet unsmiling lips.

George Sand's concern for the poor and for political and social reform, as well as her passionate preoccupation with the cause of women's rights, took on new importance at this time. Musset's indifference to such issues could only contribute to her estrangement from him. She was ready to invest her enormous energies in activities that would have a broader scope than the dream of finding happiness through perfect love.

To assert her independence and freedom was now uppermost in George Sand's mind. She therefore wished to legally finalize her separation from her husband. Divorce, approved in 1792 during the Revolution, had been abrogated in 1816 under the Restoration. The only recourse for a woman in George Sand's position was legal separation of person and property. This she was able to obtain in July 1836, but not without much wrangling and a court trial, which she had tried in vain to avoid. She was at least able to remain sole mistress of her beloved Nohant, although Casimir got, for his part, the Hôtel de Narbonne on the rue de la Harpe, with its handsome annual revenue in rent. Sand gained custody of Solange, and Casimir of Maurice; but in fact she was able to keep both children.

The lawyer recommended to George Sand during her legal struggle with her husband was Michel de Bourges, a political activist in the cause of republicanism. Unlike the aristocratic Musset, he was of peasant stock and passionately committed to the social betterment of the downtrodden. George Sand herself was deeply preoccupied with social issues, and she and Bourges became more than partners during the legal entanglements with Casimir.

More than his personal attractiveness, Bourges's fiery speeches against an unjust society appealed to George Sand and reinforced her desire to revoke her conjugal vows. Through him she met a number of republican, revolutionary, and radical thinkers and familiarized herself more directly with socialist doctrines. Their relationship came to an end in July 1837, for he was not only a married man but also one who had a far greater understanding of social inequality than of the inequality of the sexes.

In 1835 George Sand met Robert Lamennais, the fiery and controversial French cleric whose *Paroles d'un croyant (Words of a Believer)* had appeared in 1834, and she turned to him for guidance and inspiration. She was profoundly affected by his socially minded zeal, which had alienated him from the ecclesiastical hierarchy. Herself estranged from Catholicism, she nevertheless retained strong religious feelings, and therefore thought at first that Lamennais's reforming fervor offered the best solution to her own dilemma.

For his part, Lamennais remained wary of this notorious woman who so insistently wished to become his disciple, and he kept her at arm's length. Her initial enthusiasm for him cooled considerably when she realized that he was not willing to endorse her bold ideas on marriage and divorce, as set forth in the "Lettres à Marcie" (Letters to Marcy), which appeared in 1837 in the *Monde,* Lamennais's own newspaper. Lamennais himself suspended these letters after the appearance of the sixth in the series—clear proof of his misgivings on this explosive subject.

It was Pierre Leroux, whose books and journalistic writings eloquently denounced social inequities, who had the most powerful impact on George Sand's political orientation. Introduced to him by Sainte-Beuve, she did not hesitate to hail him as an authentic speaker for the oppressed and to place his political theories alongside Rousseau's. Leroux, a widower in his forties with several children to support, eked out a meager living as a printer and compositor. As a brilliant young student, he had to give up scholarly aspirations and a promising career in order to go to work, for he came from a poor family.

Leroux's experience as a typesetter led him to become one of the founders of the *Globe,* a periodical that advocated Saint-Simonianism, which called for public control of the means of production and a more equal distribution of wealth; it was through the *Globe* that he met Sainte-Beuve, who in the early 1830's contributed to the publication. Leroux was also involved in the enormous enterprise of publishing a *Nouvelle encyclopédie* (New Encyclopedia), which was to follow the example of Diderot's famous compendium in making knowledge serve an ideology of general enlightenment and social betterment. Unlike the Encyclopedists, however, Leroux was a fervent if unorthodox Christian. But what especially appealed to Sand was that Leroux propounded emancipation of women and equality of the sexes. Immensely impressed by his idealism, yet aware of the utopian nature of many of his theories, she helped him in every way she could, making valiant efforts to spread his political doctrines as well as his Christian brand of socialism.

In her *Story of My Life*, George Sand describes her religious evolution in some detail. Under the influence of her grandmother's Voltairean deism, she chafed at having to learn her catechism by rote "like a parrot, without seeking to understand it" (1.840). She found herself facing a dilemma, for while her grandmother's example had led her to question the basic articles of Catholic faith, the same grandmother insisted on the importance of her making first communion. And when the day arrived, on 23 March 1817, Madame Dupin made it a point to be present at the ceremony, although "she had not set foot in a church since my father's marriage" (1.842).

This early skepticism gave way to a period of profound mysticism that corresponded with George Sand's two-year stay at the convent of the Dames Augustines Anglaises, from 1818 to 1820. Everything in the convent conspired to enhance the young girl's religious fervor, and she even became convinced that she was destined to be a nun. After leaving the convent, however, she found herself once more in a state of painful uncertainty; and she was a

Catholic in name only when, after reading widely and voraciously philosophers, moralists, and poets, she at last came upon Rousseau:

> While continuing to practice this religion, I had abandoned, without quite realizing it, the narrow path of its doctrine. . . . The spirit of the Church was no longer in me.
>
> (1.1053)

It was through Rousseau that George Sand had the revelation of a natural religion, freed from doctrine and dogma. She rejected the doctrines of original sin and eternal punishment for one's sins in the afterlife, and she argued against celibacy for priests. But she would never waver from her Rousseauistic faith in a benevolent God, and she continued to believe in the immortality of the soul. This religious faith based on individual feeling suited her temperament, for she was, as she proudly proclaims, "a being of sentiment," for whom sentiment alone settled the most portentous problems. This personal creed would coincide perfectly with her later militant political and social activism.

The Profession of Faith of the Savoyard Vicar in Rousseau's *Émile* (1762) became George Sand's own creed. Evoking this crucial revelation, she says: "As for religion, he seemed to me the most Christian of the writers of his time" (1.1061). And like Rousseau, she would always disapprove strongly of atheism and materialism while disdaining ontological and theological arguments. Her religious faith remained founded on a spontaneous impulse of the heart, a communion with God through social humanitarianism. She therefore had no difficulty endorsing Lamennais's unorthodox Catholicism and especially Leroux's messianic socialism. At the same time she never repudiated her anticlerical stance; on the contrary, she was especially hostile to the French clergy of her time. With increasing vigor and boldness she openly opposed the temporal power of the church, for she was convinced that it had failed in its mission to protect the poor and the powerless.

Some of the novels George Sand wrote after her association with Lamennais and Leroux—notably the mystical allegory *Spiridion* (1838–1839), the philosophically ambitious *Les sept cordes de la lyre* (*The Seven Strings of the Lyre*, 1839), the religio-socialist *Le compagnon du tour de France* (*Journeyman-Joiner*, rejected by the *Revue des deux mondes* in 1840), and the sweeping *Consuelo* (1842–1843), with its sequel, *La comtesse de Rudolstadt* (*Countess Rudolstadt*, 1843–1844), reflect her spiritual quest and evolution from orthodox Catholicism to Christian socialism. Her publisher, François Buloz, was not too happy with these metaphysical and ideological works and preferred, for obvious reasons, her best-selling novels of amorous conflicts and unhappy marriages. Sainte-Beuve also expressed strong reservations, and among more modern critics André Maurois has harshly characterized *The Seven Strings of the Lyre* as a "detestable pastiche of Goethe's *Faust*." On the other hand Ernest Renan, the religious historian and author of the famous *Vie de Jésus* (*Life of Jesus*, 1861), was a great admirer of *Spiridion*, and *Consuelo* was the favorite novel by George Sand of Dostoevsky and Whitman. Henry James considered *Consuelo* her masterpiece and the philosopher Alain ranked it with Goethe's *Wilhelm Meister.*

Consuelo is a novel of great sweep and scope, what the French call a *roman-fleuve*, and one for which George Sand did extensive research. Her heroine, Consuelo, is a Spanish-born singer and adventurous female Don Juan in quest of perfect love. More significantly, however, she is the artist searching for truthful self-expression. In many ways she is reminiscent of Madame de Staël's touching heroine Corinne, in the novel by the same name (1807). Her wanderings take Consuelo from Venice to the courts of Maria Theresa in Vienna and Frederick the Great in Potsdam; they also bring her into contact with the great composers of her day, for music plays an important part in the novel. In *Consuelo* George Sand expressed all her personal and artistic aspirations; with *Countess Rudolstadt*, it constitutes her most ambitious work. Above all else, the life of the heroine, a singer-composer like Madame de Staël's Corinne, represents, through her many trials and tribulations, a woman's odyssey, a female quest for creativity and spiritual transcendence. Unlike Madame de Staël, who had given *Corinne* a tragic ending by making her heroine the lonely victim of society's prejudices and her timorous lover's pusillanimity, George Sand ends *Consuelo* on a hopeful note. The heroine not only survives misfortunes and persecutions—she even manages to find happiness and serenity. Electing to live among simple, ordinary people, she offers them music in exchange for their hospitality, according to a communal system reminiscent of Leroux's philosophy of a propertyless society that resorts to barter rather than money as a means for the exchange of goods.

Having broken with Buloz as a result of his reluctance to publish her more ideologically oriented writings, George Sand founded the *Revue indépendante* with her friend Leroux (1841). To this journal she contributed articles and such works of fiction as *Horace* (1841–1842), a novel with strong socialist tendencies and an equivocal young hero, the charming but unpredictable Horace. Drawing on her own experience following her initial arrival in Paris and her introduction to a bohemian milieu, she gives a vivid and sympathetic depiction of rebellious young intellectuals and students. Horace is a kind of antihero whose personal seductiveness is a mixture of narcissistic affectation and lackadaisical languor. That he shares many traits with Jules Sandeau, George Sand's lover and first literary collaborator, is no mere coincidence. Sandeau, for his part, had recently published a fictionalized account of his liaison with George Sand, entitled *Marianna* (1839), which lacked gentlemanly discretion. No doubt a desire, conscious or unconscious, to

even the score had something to do with the creation of the charming but feckless and unpredictable Horace. But Horace is also reminiscent of some of George Sand's other lovers, notably Musset, with his ambiguity toward women and his violent outbursts of rage. *Horace* is one of George Sand's most colorful and engrossing works, and it deserves more attention than it has received thus far from critics and commentators.

After her return from Venice, George Sand managed, despite her absorbing activities and preoccupations, to make a number of new friends. In addition to Lamennais and Leroux, she singled out two intimates, Heinrich Heine, the German poet and journalist, who had been living in Paris since 1831, and Franz Liszt, the keyboard virtuoso. That both men had a strong concern for social justice could only endear them to her. Heine playfully called George Sand his cousin, and she in turn was very fond of him. Music had always been one of her great passions, so it was no wonder that she should be especially drawn to Liszt, an attraction that was mutual. But Liszt already had a romantic mate in the person of the countess Marie d'Agoult, who like George Sand had forsaken respectability for personal freedom. At the end of August 1836, George Sand with her two children joined Liszt and Marie d'Agoult in Geneva, where she pleasantly vacationed until October; in February and May 1837 she was in turn their hostess at Nohant, where one of her great joys was to listen to Liszt playing passages of his own composition on the piano.

Following her break with Musset, George Sand had been working on a new novel, *Mauprat*, which was published in 1837. Despite the cool reception accorded to it by such influential critics as Sainte-Beuve, it was one of her best works and continues to be highly readable to this day. Similarities between this novel and Emily Brontë's *Wuthering Heights*, which appeared ten years later, have been noted by subsequent critics. In both cases, love transforms and ennobles a rough-hewn, primitive man. But whereas Brontë's story ends in tragedy, George Sand's concludes on a note of hope and affirmation of the redeeming value of marriage.

Mauprat is set in the period immediately preceding the French Revolution. In the orphaned, mistreated young hero, Bernard de Mauprat, George Sand presents a compelling picture of an illiterate, brutish youth, all instinctual impulsiveness, who like Heathcliff rises above his stormy, unrestrained nature through suffering and a great love. Just as in *Wuthering Heights*, the brooding, somber atmosphere of an untamed natural setting blends with the violent emotions that rule Mauprat's life.

It is also worth noting that *Mauprat* is reminiscent of the eighteenth-century memoir novel, since Bernard is both protagonist and narrator. In this respect, the confessional tale of the old Mauprat follows a model that had already been well established in various guises by the great novelists of the preceding era. From his rich human experience the aging hero has acquired wisdom and a clear understanding of his flaws and limitations of character, and it is with unflinching honesty and forthrightness that he looks back on his life. *Mauprat* is a novel of experience, a bildungsroman with a strong didactic component. Its main attraction for the modern reader, however, lies in its mysterious, Gothic-like setting and its romantic duel between the near-savage young Bernard and Edmée, the exceptional young woman who will lead him toward greater spiritual and moral self-awareness and sensitivity. It is hardly surprising that, once more, George Sand should have endowed her female protagonist with a nobler character than her imperfect lover.

Marriage plays an important role in Bernard de Mauprat's redemption; as George Sand points out in the preface to her novel, it was precisely while suing for final separation from her husband that she felt the greatest need to extol the sanctity of this bond and its irreplaceable value as a social institution:

> While writing a novel as an occupation and distraction for my mind, I conceived the idea of portraying an exclusive and undying love, before, during, and after marriage. Thus I drew the hero of my book proclaiming, at the age of eighty, his fidelity to the one woman he had ever loved.

George Sand had written *Mauprat* laboriously and without deriving pleasure from the effort; yet it remains one of her most absorbing and original fictional creations.

FRÉDÉRIC CHOPIN

It was through Liszt that George Sand met Frédéric Chopin in the autumn of 1836. Chopin had been living in Paris since 1831. On their first meeting, impressions were mutually unfavorable. At twenty-six, Chopin found the thirty-two-year-old writer overly assertive and mannish, whereas she was struck by his frailty and almost girlish looks and demeanor. Despite his professed aversion to the controversial author, Chopin invited her to a soirée in his apartment in November 1836. In December he gave a musicale attended by such notables as Delacroix, Liszt and d'Agoult, Eugène Sue, Mickiewicz, and George Sand, who brought along Heine. Liszt and Chopin each played the piano. Seated in an armchair and smoking a cigar, George Sand was enraptured.

But it was not until June 1838 that the liaison between George Sand and Chopin began in earnest. In the meantime the composer had had an unhappy love affair with a young Polish compatriot, Maria Wodzinska. The year 1837 had also been a difficult one for George Sand, for it marked the final illness and death of her mother, as well as renewed legal difficulties with her estranged husband. During the winter of 1837–1838 her health suffered as a result of all these stresses, and she had severe attacks of rheumatism. By the end of February 1838, however, she was well enough to have Balzac as a guest at Nohant.

The spring of 1838 found George Sand again in Paris, where her lawsuit with Casimir Dudevant required her presence. She had sufficiently recovered from her ailment to appear at brilliant soirées attended by the leading writers and artists of the day. Listening to Chopin's piano improvisations at one such concert-dinner she was again enthralled. As in the case of Musset, her amorous feelings were inextricably intertwined with a maternal desire to protect and nurture a fragile, child-like genius.

Because of Chopin's weak lungs and her own recent bouts with rheumatism, George Sand was determined to spend the winter in a warm climate, and she persuaded him to disregard scandalmongers and escape Paris with her. In October 1838 the lovers departed for Majorca, taking with them George Sand's two children, the fifteen-year-old Maurice and the ten-year-old Solange.

After some searching they rented a sparsely furnished villa a short distance from Palma. The house, named *Son Vent* (House of Wind in the Majorcan dialect), lived up to its designation only too well. George Sand also made arrangements to rent several rooms in an abandoned monastery, the charterhouse of Valdemosa, a village farther to the north of Palma.

At first George Sand and Chopin were ecstatic and duly admired the beauties of the surrounding countryside. But they could not long remain oblivious to the total absence of the most elementary physical comforts in their picturesque but hardly livable dwellings. To attempt to either write or compose in such circumstances was a frustrating task, especially in the fall season, with its torrential rains and incessant gales, followed by even more trying winter storms.

Chopin fell ill, and George Sand had to cope with an invalid and two children. In February 1839, they slowly made their way back to France. By the time they reached Marseilles, Chopin's alarming condition had considerably improved. At the end of May they were back in Nohant, where Chopin could complete his recuperation.

The winter in Majorca had been a sobering experience, especially for George Sand. Devotedly nursing the ailing and frequently moody Chopin, she had come to regard him as a son rather than a lover. But her admiration for his genius and fondness for him remained undiminished. In the *Story of My Life* she paid him this homage:

> Chopin's genius is the most profound and the richest in feelings and emotions that ever existed. He has made a single instrument speak the language of infinitude; he was able to summarize, in ten lines that a child could play, poems of an immense elevation, dramas of an unequaled energy. He never needed great material means in order to give full expression to his genius. . . . His individuality is even more exquisite than that of Sebastian Bach, more powerful than that of Beethoven, more dramatic than that of Weber. . . . Only Mozart is superior to him.
>
> (2.421)

On returning from Majorca, George Sand settled down to a more tranquil routine. Realizing that Chopin needed a quiet, orderly life to survive and compose, she spent the summer months in Nohant and the winters in Paris. Chopin became a permanent host and fixture in Nohant, but he found country life rather monotonous and dull. George Sand did her best to distract him by inviting her Berry friends as well as Parisian luminaries. Disregarding his fastidiousness and bouts of temper and melancholy, she continued to assume responsibility for his health and well-being until 1847 (two years before his death), when in a bitter quarrel with her daughter, Solange, and the latter's husband, she discovered to her dismay that Chopin had sided against her. After the many years of loving solicitude, she felt deeply hurt and betrayed. That Chopin had been able, despite his precarious health and frequent bouts of depression, to write some of his finest compositions is in no small measure due to George Sand's attentiveness to his physical and spiritual needs.

THE FAILED REVOLUTION (1848)

After the Majorca disaster, George Sand came to the realization that she was past the age for passionate love affairs. She now threw her considerable energies into her work as a novelist and assumed, more then ever, the militant activist role of speaker for the downtrodden and the oppressed. Chopin, however, had this much in common with Musset: the plight of the poor was of only slight interest to him.

While eagerly pursuing her political activities, George Sand took a lively interest in popular poetry, for she came to look upon this generally neglected form of expression as a harbinger of the liberation and enlightenment of the masses. Hence her "Dialogues familiers sur la poésie des prolétaires" ("Familiar Dialogues on the Poetry of the Proletarians"), published in 1842 in the *Revue indépendante*. Parallel to her growing involvement in social issues was her heightened interest in the life and concerns of the peasants of her hamlet of Nohant and the Berry region. She eagerly took part in rustic weddings, feasts, and celebrations. She studied the local dialect and traditions, realizing that industrialization and the railways would soon do away with a provincial culture dear to her heart. And in the wintertime, when she was in Paris, she sorely missed the sounds and smells of Nohant.

No wonder, therefore, that she should have turned to the life of country folk as a theme for novels as well as crusading journalism. Hence

a cycle of works with rustic settings and characters, such as *Jeanne* (1844), which incorporates Berry legends and speech patterns : *Le meunier d'Angibault* (*The Miller of Angibault*, 1845), the story of a simple peasant girl (a novel admired by Balzac); *La mare au diable* (*The Devil's Pool*, 1846), dedicated to Chopin, a rural love story that was to become one of her most popular novels; *François the Waif*, which treats the theme of bastardy in provincial France and out of which Sand constructed a highly successful play (1849); *Little Fadette*, the touching story of a persecuted and eventually vindicated peasant girl; and *Les maîtres sonneurs* (*The Master Bellringers*, also translated as *The Bagpipers*, 1853), her most ambitious tale of rustic life.

George Sand's preface to *The Master Bellringers* is indicative of what she tried to achieve in her cycle of rural novels:

> The peasantry guess or comprehend much more than we believe them capable of understanding.... Therefore it is not, as some have reproachfully pointed out, for the mere pleasure of reproducing a style hitherto unused in literature ... that I have assumed the humble task of preserving the local color of Étienne Depardieu's tale [Depardieu is the narrator and hero of the novel]. If, in spite of the care and conscientiousness which I bring to my task, you find that my narrator sometimes sees too clearly or too deeply into his subject matter, you must blame my faulty presentation.

George Sand was intent on reproducing in these novels the manners, mores, and speech of the countryfolk of the Berry region that she knew so well from personal experience. But while she was fascinated by the traditions, values, and even superstitions of the local peasantry, she wanted to combine this local color with her political and humanitarian ideology. And she eminently succeeded in depicting the suffering and aspirations of the most humble rustics in these Vergilian idylls, for she had learned to respect their good sense and dignity in her frequent dealings with them. Her strong empathy for the plight of the French peasantry led her to make such revolutionary statements as this one, which highlights her preface to *The Devil's Pool:* "These riches that cover the soil are the property of the few and the cause of enslavement and exhaustion of the largest number."

In these folk tales with a rustic setting George Sand inaugurated a novelistic tradition that continues to thrive to this day. To be sure, to depict French peasantry with authenticity and truthfulness also tempted such nineteenth-century masters of the novel as Balzac, in *Les paysans* (*The Peasants,* 1844), and Émile Zola, in *La terre* (*The Earth,* 1887); and vivid glimpses of peasant mentality and mores are afforded in Flaubert's *Madame Bovary* (1857) and "Un coeur simple" ("A Simple Heart," 1877). But unlike Balzac, Flaubert, and Zola, who presented their peasant characters in a relentlessly harsh, even at times odious, light, and insistently underscored the ugliness, meanness, and quasi-bestiality of peasant life, George Sand put her talent as a writer in the service of her crusading humanitarian cause by elaborating a poetic, lyrical conception of this genre.

George Sand's uncommon capacity to identify with others enabled her to endow the most primitive and simpleminded peasant types with considerable nobility and dignity. Her romantic utopianism offers us an idealized and sentimentalized panorama of country manners and mores. Yet she knows how to spin a tale, set a scene, present believable and appealing characters, incorporate authentic-sounding dialogues into her narration, and create suspense. Her intense involvement with country men and women, their daily cares and preoccupations, their prejudices and superstitions, are apparent throughout these engrossing tales. It is therefore hardly surprising that their popularity should have been so enduring and that they should have delighted generations of French children and young adults. Proust's experience in this respect is eminently representative of that of his compatriots.

The year 1847 was a painful one for George Sand; she quarreled with her daughter, Solange, and broke with Chopin. Solange had married the sculptor Auguste Clésinger that year. Clésinger, as things turned out, was heavily in debt, and George Sand, deeply worried by her daughter's financial plight, tried her best to salvage her dowry. As always, however, she found her best revenge against the realities of existence in her creative work; she embarked on the ambitious enterprise *The Story of My Life.*

As a loyal disciple of Rousseau, George Sand endeavored to be fearlessly frank and truthful in recounting the main events of her life. But she differed from her master on some essential points. While truthfulness was her goal, she remained wary of the compulsion to tell all in the name of veracity. Her concept of autobiography, unlike that of Rousseau, was that a personal memoir need not be confessional. As a woman with a highly controversial reputation, she was determined not to feed the public's morbid curiosity for sensational revelations, and she was convinced that to dwell on one's failings and shortcomings would be both counterproductive and masochistic. One does not disarm one's readers through total and indiscriminate self-revelation. George Sand was of course keenly aware of the exigencies of the autobiographer and of the dangers that lurk in the writer's natural tendency to dramatize and color facts. In the opening pages of *The Story of My Life,* she gently takes Rousseau to task for being guilty of this kind of self-indulgence: "He accuses himself in order to have the opportunity of exonerating himself; he reveals secret misdeeds in order to have the right to reject public calumnies." And again: "I am deeply mortified when I see the great Rousseau humiliate himself in this manner."

George Sand's strategy as an autobiographer combines both revelation and reticence. A great deal of space is devoted to her ancestors and especially to the relationship between her father and mother before her birth. Having reached the fourteenth chapter before making her own appearance on the scene, George Sand realized her reader might be justified in becoming somewhat impatient at the slowness of her pace:

> If I pursue the story of my father, I will probably be told that I greatly delay keeping my promise of telling my own story. Must I repeat here what I said in the beginning of my book? . . . All human lives are interdependent, and the person who would present his story in isolation without relating it to that of his fellow man would only end up with an undecipherable enigma. This interdependence is even more evident when it is immediate and involves parents and children.
>
> (1.307)

George Sand also knew that many of her readers would be disappointed by her cautious reserve regarding intimate details of her love affairs, but she was willing to take this risk:

> The sorrows I would have to relate about purely personal events would have no general application. I will only deal with those that may have meaning for all humankind. Once more, therefore, scandalmongers, shut my book after reading the first page; it was not written for you.
>
> (1.15)

For George Sand autobiography becomes truly meaningful only if it is closely related to the broad historical context. Each individual destiny is significant insofar as it is part of the vast panorama of human events. The collective experience is what matters. George Sand's autobiography ranks among her most original and powerful works. Besides offering a sweeping and lively tableau of French society from the last decades of the Old Regime until the middle of the nineteenth century, she recounts her own saga with great gusto and unflinching honesty, and without any kind of self-pity.

When the Revolution of 1848 broke out, Sand was well prepared for it. Her political involvement in this momentous event was enthusiastic and from the outset she eagerly put her talents as a writer in its service. In addition to founding the journal *La cause du peuple*, she wrote political articles and exulted in the triumph of the republic. Her joy, however, was of short duration. While she wholeheartedly sympathized with the most radical elements of the revolution, she shied away from the use of force and illegal coercion as a means to achieving success for the right cause. The precedent of 1793 was too vivid in her mind to follow that radical course. To institute another Reign of Terror was not what she wanted, and she tried her best to combat the intransigence of her most uncompromising friends. Yet she also realistically anticipated the results of the elections. And, to be sure, her pessimistic expectations were entirely fulfilled.

When it was all over, George Sand was left with a feeling of profound disappointment. She had committed herself wholeheartedly to the revolution, notwithstanding the risks involved. Yet she did not regret her political involvement; far from it. That her ideal of a successful and bloodless revolution had not come about in her lifetime did not dishearten her for very long. A romantic in matters of the heart, she tended to be more pragmatic and realistic in her politics.

The 1848 disaster enabled George Sand to fortify and renew her sense of social commitment. More than ever she subscribed to such simple virtues as goodness, friendship, and generosity. Her last years were increasingly marked by an attempt to reconcile her political involvement with her personal need for retirement, and more and more she identified with the aging Rousseau of the *Rêveries du promeneur solitaire* (1782).

George Sand remained steadfast in her beliefs through the double tragedy of the war of 1870 and the Commune. By then, however, she had learned the hard lessons of serenity and detachment. Yet this newly acquired tranquillity was linked with a sense of sadness and melancholy, best reflected in her novel *Monsieur Sylvestre* (1865). She was now increasingly preoccupied with illness, old age, and death. But while she sought peace and repose, she was not yet quite prepared to renounce entirely the pleasures and challenges of human relationships. Her friendship and correspondence with Flaubert are perhaps the best case of a relationship based on opposites rather than affinities in character and literary inspiration.

THE GOOD LADY OF NOHANT

More than ever George Sand found renewed sources of energy and inspiration in her beloved Nohant, where she came to be known as "la bonne dame de Nohant" (the good lady of Nohant) because of her personal involvement in the well-being of the farmers of the locality. Her benevolence extended to animals and birds, and botany became one of her favorite hobbies. By now, thanks to her considerable productivity as a writer, her activism as a social propagandist, and her controversial personal reputation, she had become something of a living legend. Visitors from all corners of Europe flocked to Nohant.

Yet the conservative climate under the Second Empire hardly favored George Sand's political views, and some of the most noteworthy writers of the new generation, notably Baudelaire, the Goncourt brothers, and even Flaubert, had ambivalent attitudes toward women in general and little fellow feeling for women authors in particular. George Sand tried her best to adapt herself to the new aesthetic credo of realism. Her novel *Le dernier amour* (*The Last Love*, 1866) is dedicated to Flaubert and obviously influenced by *Madame Bovary*. Flaubert was one of George Sand's privileged houseguests at Nohant, and she in turn visited Croisset, Flaubert's home near Rouen. They delighted in corresponding with each other, and in his uninhibited letters to her Flaubert revealed his innermost thoughts and feelings. Their friendship had begun in 1863, when George Sand wrote an appreciative review of his novel *Salammbô*, and endured until her death. Flaubert, whose sexuality and relationships with women had always been fraught with torment and contradictions, was willing to make an exception to his general condescension toward women in favor of George Sand. He especially admired her courage and serenity as she faced the ailments and disabilities of old age.

George Sand worked hard and lived fully until her death, and as ever enjoyed gathering at Nohant old friends and their families. She also welcomed newer associates, such as the Russian novelist Ivan Turgenev, who visited in the spring of 1873. And she traveled quite extensively, visiting different parts of France. She was about to celebrate her seventy-second birthday when she began feeling constant and acute abdominal pain. When death came on 8 June 1876, despite the ministrations of hastily summoned doctors, she met it without fear or regret, with her children at her bedside.

The simple funeral service took place in the church of Nohant, and afterward the peasants carried the coffin to the small cemetery adjoining George Sand's estate, where she was buried next to her grandmother and her parents. There was a Catholic service, and Flaubert, who attended, noted that the country folk kneeling on the grass wept a great deal during the ceremony. He too, for that matter, shed copious tears, as he confided to Turgenev in a letter dated 25 June 1876:

> The death of poor old Sand has caused me infinite pain. I wept like a babe at her funeral, and twice: the first time when I kissed her granddaughter Aurore (whose eyes that day so closely resembled hers that it was as though she had risen from the grave), and the second time when the coffin was borne past me.

832

Flaubert was not the only friend who made the trip to Nohant to pay his last respects to George Sand. The score of mourners who stood at the graveside included the historian and critic Ernest Renan, the dramatist and novelist Dumas *fils,* the publisher Calmann Lévy, and the actor Paul Meurice, who had appeared in her plays and who read the funeral oration, which was written by Victor Hugo. Flaubert also noted in his letter to Turgenev that a gentle rain kept falling throughout the service. The rustic burial scene—a small country graveyard under an overcast sky and a steady drizzle, with an old priest muttering the prayer for the dead and peasant women with rosaries hanging from their gnarled fingers, the somber group of intimates forlornly huddling against the wind and rain—would not have displeased George Sand, for it might have fitted quite easily in a chapter from one of her novels.

CONCLUSION

George Sand's reputation has been greatly enhanced by the feminist movement. She has by now fully earned her niche in the pantheon of women of exceptional talent and generous commitment to the betterment of humankind. That she did not merely touch upon the popular chords of her time is now fully attested by the numerous editions of her works, translations into English and other languages, international societies and symposia in her honor.

George Sand's works do not easily lend themselves to classification. She was a romantic, but this classification hardly suffices to characterize the vast corpus of her works. Her novels are in turn historical, autobiographical, rustic. Her ideology, on the other hand, reflects her innermost political preoccupations. Yet her own rich and variegated personality is at the core of all of her writing. Her willingness to take chances with new forms and especially to renovate older genres is one of the keys to her great success as a writer. Granted, her faith in improvisation and spontaneity was sometimes greater than her technical ability. But it is this faith in renewal that endows her work, to a great extent, with a unique aura of freshness and authenticity. Familiar though she was with literary traditions, George Sand preferred to rely on her own inspiration. And in this she was not mistaken. Among her considerable talents was that of the accomplished storyteller. And her descriptive powers are far from negligible. On the other hand, her political involvement, culminating in the active role she played during the Revolution of 1848, should not be overlooked in assessing her contribution to French letters.

From the outset and in her own lifetime, George Sand has had her passionate apologists and vociferous detractors. As a result she has been excessively idealized by some and violently denounced by others. The feminist movement, however, has not only rekindled interest in George Sand; it has also vigorously fostered a serious reexamination of each of her works. Recent critical editions of her novels as well as of her autobiography and correspondence amply testify to this resurgence of interest. But in view of her voluminous output, much work remains to be done. Assessments of her writing and her personality are now being revised. She is a far more complex author and personality than had for long been believed. Above all, the diversity of her work attests to an exuberant affirmation of the values of generosity, courage, and love of life.

Selected Bibliography

FIRST EDITIONS

INDIVIDUAL WORKS
Rose et Blanche. Paris, 1831.
Indiana. Paris, 1832.
Valentine. Paris, 1832.

Lélia. Paris, 1833.

Jacques. Paris, 1834.

Leone Leoni. Paris, 1834.

Lettres d'un voyageur. Paris, 1834–1836.

Mauprat. Paris, 1837.

L'Uscoque. Paris, 1838.

L'Orco. Paris, 1838.

Spiridion. Paris, 1838–1839.

Les sept cordes de la lyre. Paris, 1839.

Le compagnon du tour de France. Paris, 1840.

Horace. Paris, 1841–1842.

"Dialogues familiers sur la poésie de prolétaires." In *Questions d'art et de littérature.* Paris, 1842.

Un hiver à Majorque. Paris, 1842.

Consuelo. Paris, 1842–1843.

La comtesse de Rudolstadt. Paris, 1843–1844.

Jeanne. Paris, 1844.

Le meunier d'Angibault. Paris, 1845.

La mare au diable. Paris, 1846.

François le champi. Paris, 1847–1848.

La petite Fadette. Paris, 1848–1849.

Les maîtres sonneurs. Paris, 1853.

Histoire de ma vie. Paris, 1854–1855.

Elle et lui. Paris, 1859.

La ville noire. Paris, 1860.

Monsieur Sylvestre. Paris, 1865.

Le dernier amour. Paris, 1866.

Journal intime. Edited by Aurore Sand. Paris, 1926.

COLLECTED WORKS

Oeuvres de George Sand. 16 vols. Paris, 1842–1844.

Oeuvres choisies de George Sand. 3 vols. Brussels, 1851.

Oeuvres illustrées de George Sand. 9 vols. Paris, 1851–1856.

Oeuvres complètes de George Sand. 115 vols. Paris, 1852–1926.

Théâtre complète de George Sand. 4 vols. Paris, 1866–1867.

Correspondance de George Sand et d'Alfred Musset. Edited by F. Decori. Brussels, 1904.

George Sand–Marie Dorval: Correspondance inédite. Edited by Simone André-Maurois. Paris, 1953.

Correspondance. 16 vols. Edited by Georges Lubin. Paris, 1964–1981.

Les lettres de George Sand à Sainte-Beuve. Edited by Osten Södergard. Geneva, 1964.

Lettres de George Sand à Alfred de Musset et Gustave Flaubert. Edited by Jean-Luc Benoziglio. Paris, 1970.

Oeuvres autobiographiques. Edited by Georges Lubin. 2 vols. Paris, 1970–1971.

MODERN EDITIONS

La comtesse de Rudolstadt. Edited by L. Cellier and L. Guichard. Paris, 1959.

Consuelo. Edited by L. Cellier and L. Guichard. 3 vols. Paris, 1959.

Elle et lui. Edited by M. Guillemin. Neuchâtel, 1963.

François le champi. Edited by P. Salomon and J. Mallion. Paris, 1962.

Indiana. Edited by Georges Lubin. Paris, 1976.

Un hiver à Majorque. Edited by B. Didier. Paris, 1984.

Lélia. Edited by P. Reboul. Paris, 1960.

Les maîtres sonneurs. Edited by P. Salomon and J. Mallion. Paris, 1968.

La mare au diable. Edited by P. Salomon and J. Mallion. Paris, 1962.

Mauprat. Edited by C. Sicard. Paris, 1969.

La petite Fadette. Edited by P. Salomon and J. Mallion. Paris, 1958.

Les sept cordes de la lyre. Edited by R. Bourgois. Paris, 1973.

Spiridion. Edited by Georges Lubin. Paris, 1976.

La ville noire. Edited by J. Courrier. Echirolles, 1978.

TRANSLATIONS

The Bagpipers. Chicago, 1977.

The Compagnon of the Tour of France. Translated by Francis Shaw. New York, 1976.

Consuelo: A Romance of Venice. New York, 1979.

The Country Waif. Translated by Eirene Collis. Lincoln, Neb., 1977.

The Devil's Pool. Translated by Hamish Miles. London, 1929.

Fanchon the Cricket. Chicago, 1977.

François the Waif. Translated by Jane M. Sedgwick. New York, 1894.

George Sand in Her Own Words. Translated by Joseph Barry. New York, 1979.

The George Sand–Gustave Flaubert Letters. Translated by Aimée L. McKenzie. Chicago, 1979.

Indiana. Translated by G. Burnham Ives. Chicago, 1978.

The Intimate Journal of George Sand. Translated by Marie Jenney Howe. Chicago, 1978.

Lélia. Translated by Maria Espinosa, with foreword by Ellen Moers. Bloomington, Ind., 1978.

Leon Leoni. Translated by G. Burnham Ives. Chicago, 1978.

Little Fadette. Translated by Hamish Miles. London, 1928.

The Masterpieces of George Sand. Translated by G. Burnham Ives. 18 vols. Philadelphia, 1900.

Mauprat. Translated by Stanley Young. New York, 1902. Republished Chicago, 1977.

My Convent Life. Translated by Maria Ellery McKay. Chicago, 1977. From the first book of Sand's *Histoire de ma vie.*

My Life. Translated and adapted by Dan Hofstadter. New York, 1979.

She and He. Translated by G. Burnham Ives. Chicago, 1978.

Valentine. Translated by G. Burnham Ives. Chicago, 1978.

Winter in Majorca. Translated by Robert Graves. Chicago, 1978.

BIOGRAPHICAL AND CRITICAL STUDIES

Atwood, William G. *The Lioness and the Little One: The Liaison of George Sand and Frédéric Chopin.* New York, 1980.

Barry, Joseph. *Infamous Woman: The Life of George Sand.* New York, 1977.

Blount, Paul G. *George Sand and the Victorian World.* Athens, Ga., 1979.

Brée, Germaine. "George Sand: The Fictions of Autobiography." *Nineteenth-Century French Studies* 4:438–449 (1976).

Carrère, Casimir. *George Sand amoureuse.* Paris, 1967.

Cate, Curtis. *George Sand: A Biography.* New York, 1976.

Cellier, Léon, ed. *Hommage à George Sand.* Paris, 1969.

Chonez, Claudine. *George Sand.* Paris, 1973.

Didier, Beatrice. "l'Image de Voltaire et de Rousseau chez George Sand." *Revue d'histoire littéraire de la France* 79:251–264 (1979).

————. "Femme/Identité/Écriture: À propos de l'*Histoire de ma vie* de George Sand." *Revue des sciences humaines* 168:577–588 (1977).

————. "Le souvenir musical dans *Histoire de ma vie.*" *Présence de George Sand* 8:48–52 (1980).

Doumic, René. *George Sand.* Paris, 1909.

————. *George Sand.* Translated by Álys Hallard. New York, 1910.

Dussault, Louis. *George Sand: Étude d'une éducation.* Montreal, 1970.

Greene, Tatiana. "De J. Sand à George Sand: *Rose et Blanche* de Sand et Sandeau et leur descendance." *Nineteenth-Century French Studies* 4:169–182 (1976).

Hovey, Tamara. *A Mind of Her Own: A Life of the Writer George Sand.* New York, 1977.

Howe, Marie Jenney. *George Sand: The Search for Love.* Garden City, N.Y., 1929.

Jordan, Ruth. *George Sand: A Biography.* London, 1976.

Larnac, Jean. *George Sand Révolutionnaire.* Paris, 1947.

Lubin, Georges. *Album Sand.* Paris, 1973.

————. *George Sand en Berry.* Paris, 1967.

————. "George Sand et l'éducation." *Nineteenth-Century French Studies* 4:450–468 (1976).

Mallet, Francine. *George Sand.* Paris, 1976.

Maurois, André. *Lélia ou la vie de George Sand.* Paris, 1952.

————. *Lélia: The Life of George Sand.* Translated by Gerard Hopkins. New York, 1953.

Maurras, Charles. *Les amants de Venise.* Paris, 1903.

May, Gita. "Des *Confessions* à l'*Histoire de ma vie*: Deux auteurs à la recherche de leur moi." *Présence de George Sand* 8:40–47 (1980).

Moers, Ellen. *Literary Women.* New York, 1973.

Paillou, Paul. *La vie émouvante de George Sand.* Paris, 1946.

Poli, Annarosa. *L'Italie dans la vie et dans l'oeuvre de George Sand.* Paris, 1960.

————. *George Sand et les années terribles.* Paris, 1975.

Salomon, Pierre. *George Sand.* Paris, 1953.

Séché, Alphonse, and Jules Bertaut. *George Sand.* Paris, 1909.

Seilliere, Ernest. *George Sand, mystique de la passion, de la politique et de l'art.* Paris, 1920.

Seyd, Felizia. *Romantic Rebel: The Life and Times of George Sand.* New York, 1940.

Thomas, Edith. *George Sand.* Paris, 1959.

Thomson, Patricia. *George Sand and the Victorians.* New York, 1977.

Waddington, Patrick. *Turgenev and George Sand: An Improbable Entente.* Wellington, N.Z., 1980.

Winegarten, Renée. *The Double Life of George Sand: Woman and Writer.* New York, 1978.

Winwar, Frances. *The Life of the Heart: George Sand and Her Times.* London, 1946.

GITA MAY

CHARLES-AUGUSTIN SAINTE-BEUVE

(1804–1869)

CHARLES-AUGUSTIN SAINTE-BEUVE was born on 23 December 1804 at Boulogne-sur-Mer, France. His father died some six months before his birth, and he was raised by his mother and his aunt. Although his family was not particularly well off, he managed to receive a fairly good education and by the age of thirteen was fluent in Latin. At the age of fourteen he was sent to Paris, where he completed his undergraduate studies in literature. He also attended an evening lecture series on philosophy, at which he heard speak and was introduced to the great Ideologue philosopher Destutt de Tracy.

Although groomed for a literary career, Sainte-Beuve cautiously chose to go into medicine instead, enrolling at the École de Médecine in 1823. The next year, however, his former rhetoric teacher, Paul Dubois, founded the *Globe,* a literary review with liberal political leanings, and invited his ex-student to submit articles. By 1827, when Sainte-Beuve met Victor Hugo after having favorably reviewed the young poet's *Odes et ballades* (1826), he had all but given up his medical career to become a professional literary journalist.

Sainte-Beuve quickly became close friends with Hugo and his wife, Adèle, and championed Hugo's romantic poetry in a series of articles over the next ten years. In 1828 he published his first book, *Tableau historique et critique de la poésie française et du théâtre*

français au XVIème siècle (Historic Tableau of French Poetry and the French Theater in the Sixteenth Century), a study of Pierre de Ronsard and the Pléiade poets that in part was intended to provide a poetic genealogy for Hugo: "the new school in France has continued the school of the sixteenth century with regard to technique and rhythm" (*Tableau,* p. 34). But even in this early work Sainte-Beuve was wary about describing this link through technique alone as a real tradition: "Apart from a certain common allure of style and verse form," he warned, "it is hard to see in what way our literary epoch could be linked to the one whose tableau has just been described." The problem of defining a cultural continuity, as opposed to a merely stylistic one, was to occupy him for the rest of his life.

Sainte-Beuve had literary as well as critical ambitions, however, and in 1829 he published *Vie, poésies et pensées de Joseph Delorme* (The Life, Poetry, and Thoughts of Joseph Delorme), a compendium of autobiographical lyrics and meditations loosely organized around a thinly fictionalized persona. Joseph Delorme, an alienated poet who dies of tuberculosis, is cast in the same mold as the other doomed heroes of romanticism, Goethe's Werther and Chateaubriand's René: but Sainte-Beuve provided a strange new twist to the figure by giving him no majestic moments, only "a long trail of revulsions and ennuis" culminating in premature aging and death, and by placing his antihero in an urban setting. This kind of persona, so different from the sublime egoist made popular by Hugo at the time, opened up new poetic possibilities that were to be exploited a generation later by Charles Baudelaire and his circle.

Unfortunately Sainte-Beuve never managed to develop the voice he had explored in his first work. Once admitted into Hugo's literary group, the Cénacle, around 1830, his poetry became stilted and conventional. In 1830, when his friendship with Victor and Adèle Hugo was blossoming, he wrote *Les consolations* (*Consolations*, 1830), whose theme is friendship as a means of salvation. In retrospect, it is clear that the friendship in question was that between Sainte-Beuve and Adèle, which became a full-fledged love affair sometime in late 1830 and ended in 1837. This liaison, whose details are rather pathetic, stimulated Sainte-Beuve to write a mediocre novel, *Volupté* (1834), as well as his final book of poetry, *Pensées d'août* (*Thoughts of August*, 1837). After Adèle ended the relationship, Sainte-Beuve satisfied his bitterness by composing and privately circulating a scurrilous account, in verse, of the affair (published in 1843 as the *Livre d'amour* [*The Book of Love*]).

Sainte-Beuve's failure as a poet during the 1830's was somewhat compensated for by his growing success as a critic during that period. As Matthew Arnold put it, "The critic in him grew more and more and pushed out the poet." By 1834, when Sainte-Beuve's friendship with Hugo had been strained to the breaking point because of his continuing affair with the poet's wife, he had become a sought-after reviewer and had already published his first collection of essays, *Critiques et portraits littéraires* (Critical and Literary Portraits, 1832). During this period Sainte-Beuve was also becoming a fixture in French literary society, particularly in the salon of Madame Récamier, whom he was to honor many years later with an essay.

The most important critical development for Sainte-Beuve in the 1830's, however, resulted from an invitation he accepted in 1837 to give a course at the Lausanne Academy on Port-Royal, the seventeenth-century convent and intellectual center. Out of the research he began while teaching the course emerged, over the twenty-year period 1840–1859, the five-volume *Port-Royal*, Sainte-Beuve's masterpiece. It is a stunningly supple blend of the literary analysis and biographical portraiture already perfected in Sainte-Beuve's earlier work, combined with a new, broader historical perspective to form a panoramic view of seventeenth-century French culture.

The 1840's were good years for Sainte-Beuve, at least until the revolution of 1848. At the beginning of 1840, in two major articles, "La Rochefoucauld" and "Dix ans après en littérature" (Ten Years After in Literature), he declared his independence from the romantic movement he had been backing with growing reluctance during the thirties. In the same year he finally became financially secure, being appointed assistant librarian at the Mazarine Library, a post that entailed both a salary and an apartment. The security seems to have paid off in increased production: over the next eight years Sainte-Beuve published three volumes of *Port-Royal*, as well as collections of articles under the titles *Portraits de femmes* (Portraits of Women, 1845), *Portraits littéraires* (Literary Portraits, 1844), and *Portraits contemporains* (Contemporary Portraits, 1846). In 1844 he was elected to the prestigious French Academy, and his reputation and future seemed assured.

But the outbreak of revolution in 1848 interrupted Sainte-Beuve's career, fundamentally altering his political and critical outlook. In the 1830 revolution, he had supported liberal causes, and in the early thirties had dabbled with Saint-Simonianism, an early French version of socialism. But he was shocked by the radicalism of the 1848 revolutionaries and fearful of what he viewed as mob rule. More seriously, his name had been mistakenly placed on a list of those secretly receiving money from the now-deposed monarchy, and in March 1848 the list was published. Stung by the ensuing false charges that he had been a government spy and unwilling to go through the public ordeal necessary to clear his name, Sainte-Beuve resigned his position, accepting a temporary lectureship at the University of Liège. These lectures, published as *Chateaubriand et son groupe littéraire* (Chateaubriand and His Literary Group, 1861), show a new concern for the political implications of both culture and criticism. For the first time Sainte-Beuve stresses the need for critical judgment as a counterbalance to the aesthetic sympathy he had shown so much of in earlier writings. It is hard not to see this change as prompted at least in part by Sainte-Beuve's own political misfortunes during this period.

After finishing his lectureship at Liège, Sainte-Beuve returned to Paris, where he began publishing in a Bonapartist newspaper, the *Moniteur,* the series of articles that would come to be known as the *Causeries du lundi* (*Monday Chats,* 1855–1869). Although his livelihood was now ensured, he still coveted an academic post, and his good standing with the conservative government of Napoleon III helped him to receive an appointment as professor of Latin poetry at the Collège de France in 1854. His course turned into a fiasco, with students booing and shouting him down, mainly because of his unpopular political opinions, but also because he was a very poor speaker. Only two of the lectures, later published as *Étude sur Virgile* (*Studies of Vergil,* 1857), were ever delivered. Sainte-Beuve offered his resignation, but instead was appointed in 1857 senior lecturer at the less politicized École Normale Supérieure, a post he held until 1861.

By the early 1860's Sainte-Beuve had become the single most powerful voice on the French literary scene. His reviews could make or break a young writer's career. As a result, even though many writers, such as Gustave Flaubert and the Goncourt brothers, privately despised him, he was much in demand as a

dinner guest, frequenting the famous literary gatherings at the Restaurant Magny. Sainte-Beuve's health was deteriorating, however, and when he was appointed to the Senate by Napoleon III in 1865 he was only rarely able to attend sessions. Most of his energy went into the weekly articles he was now writing for the *Constitutionnel.* In 1867, as the government was turning more repressive, Sainte-Beuve astonished his conservative friends and delighted his old liberal colleagues by attacking censorship, educational restrictions, and clericalism in a series of speeches on the Senate floor. The students now cheered him in the streets, but it was to be his last hurrah. In the two years remaining him he suffered continually from an obstructed bladder. Despite the extreme pain from his condition, which made it impossible for him to sit normally, he heroically continued to publish articles until the last weeks of his life.

When Sainte-Beuve died in 1869, after dominating the cultural arena for nearly a half-century, his importance to literary criticism was unquestioned. The English reviewer Robert Morley, writing in the *Fortnightly Review* in 1876, described him as "the most eminent man of letters in France in our generation." Nor was this praise simply a eulogistic formality; Sainte-Beuve's reputation remained extremely high among critics in the generation that followed. Matthew Arnold, who freely acknowledged his debt to the older critic, considered him "perfect, so far as a poor mortal critic can be perfect, in knowledge of his subject, in tact, in tone." Even at the turn of the century, it was still possible for Anatole France to extol Sainte-Beuve as "the saint of criticism."

By the mid-1950's, however, Sainte-Beuve had suffered a fall from grace, to the extent that William Wimsatt and Cleanth Brooks devoted only five pages to him in their standard reference work on the history of criticism. Today his name is seldom mentioned, his ideas rarely discussed, his articles and books hardly ever taught, even in graduate seminars in French literature. In short, Sainte-Beuve has become a persona non grata in contemporary critical discourse. This loss of status is even more astounding when one notes the continuing critical interest in his protegé Arnold, whose *Culture and Anarchy* (1869) has become a classic and an important landmark in the history of criticism. Why has Sainte-Beuve's reputation fallen so low?

One reason is that the genre in which he presents most of his ideas—the journalistic essay—is by nature transitory, tending to focus on topical figures and issues. As time goes by and the level of his subjects' achievement or significance becomes clear, many are forgotten. For example, Sainte-Beuve devotes hundreds of pages to such figures as Kirke White and Barbara de Krüdner, names that mean little or nothing to the modern reader. As the relevance of his subject matter fades, so in general does the relevance of the critic.

A second, but related, problem with journalistic criticism is that it forces the critic to produce an extraordinarily large volume of prose. In Sainte-Beuve's case the sheer mass of his output is staggering. He wrote a weekly column for more than twenty years, from 1849 to 1869; the collections of his reviews, called *Les lundis* because they greeted the Parisian reading public nearly every Monday during this period, comprise some twenty-eight volumes, or, as one critic calculates, about two and a quarter million words. And this is only a part of Sainte-Beuve's complete work. Needles of critical insight may be scattered in this haystack, but few students have the patience to search for them.

The third obstacle to immortality inherent in the journalistic essay is the formal constraint it places on thought. As Georg Lukacs has pointed out, the essay is by nature fragmentary and unsystematic, unamenable to the kind of extended theoretical explorations that are currently valued in literary criticism, especially French criticism. Very few of Sainte-Beuve's essays can be considered "metacritical," speculations about criticism per se; in

fact he complains about the growing tendency in reviews of his time

> to give almost no idea of the book which is the occasion of the article, but to look upon it only as a pretext for developing new considerations, more or less relevant, and for new essays. The author of the book disappears; it is the critic who becomes the principal and true author. What we have is books inspired by the appearance of other books.
>
> (*Selected Essays*, F. Steegmuller trans., pp. 179–180)

What Sainte-Beuve deplores—the disappearance of the author and the generation of a self-sustaining critical discourse—is now celebrated, another indication of the distance between his critical values and our own.

Part of the reason we value theoretical and formalist criticism today is that we are children of the modernist revolution in literature that took place in the years after Sainte-Beuve's death. Modernism, whose values are incorporated in much of today's critical dogma, claimed Proust, Baudelaire, Flaubert, and Stendhal as its forefathers. These writers, as well as their followers, had good reason to hold a literary grudge against Sainte-Beuve, either because he explicitly denied their importance or because as a totem of the nineteenth-century literary establishment he was an obvious target for the younger generation. The academic triumph of modernism entailed the discrediting of its enemies or rivals, and Sainte-Beuve was cast as one.

I do not wish to imply, however, that the modernist rejection of Sainte-Beuve was simply the result of an oedipal conflict. Proust's *Contre Sainte-Beuve* (first published in 1954; in English, *On Art and Literature, 1896–1919*), the best-known refutation of the critic, shows that the conflict was philosophical as well as personal, involving major disagreements about the definition of literature, the status of the author, and the nature of literary meaning.

Proust's personal disagreement with

CHARLES-AUGUSTIN SAINTE-BEUVE

Sainte-Beuve's evaluation of the founding figures of modernism leads him to charge the critic with bad judgment. Having set up judgment as the primary task of the critic, Sainte-Beuve fails to exercise it properly himself, according to Proust. Indeed, Proust says:

> if all nineteenth century literature bar *Les Lundis* had been destroyed by fire, so that it was from the *Lundis* that we had to assess the relative importance of nineteenth century writers, we should see Stendhal ranked below Charles de Bernard, below Vinet, below Molé, below Mme. de Verdelin.
>
> (*On Art and Literature*, S. T. Warner trans., p. 102)

How just is this criticism of Sainte-Beuve? For the most part, very just. Few readers today would even recognize the names of Bernard, Vinet, et al., while Stendhal has been canonized. In Stendhal's case, Sainte-Beuve was unable to appreciate the novelist's innovative methods of characterization, his extraordinary plot structures, or his unique ironic tone. He found Stendhal's characters lacking in depth: "They are not living beings," he complains, "but cleverly constructed automatons; almost at every move they make, we hear the machinery grinding and realize the author is outside them, turning the crank" (*Selected Essays*, p. 243); he failed to notice how, as Michael Wood has put it, "the mechanical motions work like Pascal's prayer, and . . . simulated love becomes the real, the sincere thing" (*Stendhal*, p. 17).

Sainte-Beuve must also be faulted for having underrated Balzac, although here the critic's judgment was tainted by a personal feud that developed between him and the great realist in the mid-1830's. Although he praised *Eugénie Grandet* (1833) in his first article on Balzac, Sainte-Beuve devoted most of his energy in that review to attacking the novelist. The author of *Physiologie du mariage, par un jeune celibataire* (*The Physiology of Marriage*, 1829) was accused of pandering to a feminine reading public by filling his books with lurid and melodramatic scenes. Sainte-Beuve's more serious charge against Balzac, however, was that of stylistic incompetence. With what was for him a rare attention to specific details, he exposed Balzac's rhetorical infelicities and pointed out his tendency to overidealize virtuous characters. Balzac returned the disfavor, unmercifully parodying and ridiculing Sainte-Beuve's preciosity in the latter's fictionalized autobiography, *Joseph Delorme*. But after Balzac's death, Sainte-Beuve wrote an obituary essay that, although not entirely eulogistic, recognized the novelist as "perhaps the most original, the most capable, and most penetrating" of the writers of the age (*Selected Essays*, p. 257).

Sainte-Beuve's attitude toward the younger generation of Flaubert and Baudelaire is less clearly wrongheaded. His famous review of *Madame Bovary* (1857) is marred by lapses into a rather mawkish sentimentalism, as when he suggests an alternative plot in which a provincial woman similar to Emma Bovary escapes Emma's fate by devoting her life to virtuous works. But at the same time, Sainte-Beuve is among the first to recognize Flaubert's astonishing technical virtuosity and its grounding in a scientific, or at least medical, appreciation of reality: "Son and brother of distinguished doctors, M. Gustave Flaubert wields the pen as others wield the scalpel." Although he was to remain uncomfortable with this form of literary perception, Sainte-Beuve certainly did not misjudge it, granting its "extraordinary power" (*Selected Essays*, pp. 290, 277).

In his relations with Baudelaire, Sainte-Beuve must be said to have been somewhat two-faced. The younger poet revered Sainte-Beuve both as a critic and as the author of "Les rayons jaunes" (Yellow Sunbeams), a poem whose antiheroic narrator and technique of free association heavily influenced Baudelaire as well as Théophile Gautier and Paul Verlaine. Baudelaire went so far as to honor *Joseph Delorme*, in which "Les rayons jaunes"

841

was published, as "the *Fleurs du mal* of an earlier time," and in private correspondence Sainte-Beuve accepted this as a compliment. In public, however, he was less than enthusiastic, failing to endorse his supposed protegé for admission into the French Academy and dismissing Baudelaire's *Fleurs du mal* (1857) as a novelty item:

> M. Baudelaire has managed to build for himself, out at the very farthest point of a neck of land reputed uninhabitable and beyond the frontiers of known romanticism, a bizarre kiosk of his own, ornate and contorted, but at the same time dainty and mysterious . . . I call it *la folie Baudelaire.*
>
> (*Selected Essays*, p. 267)

Sainte-Beuve's ability to evaluate literature, we may conclude, is neither as perfect as it might be nor as poor as Proust claims it to be. But Proust's critique of Sainte-Beuve's judgment is of only secondary importance in *Contre Sainte-Beuve;* the major objection is to what Proust takes to be Sainte-Beuve's method:

> To have devised the Natural History of Intellectuals, to have elicited from the biography of the man, from his family history, and from all his peculiarities, the sense of his work and the nature of his genius—this is what we all recognize as Sainte-Beuve's special achievement, he recognized it as such himself, and was right about it.
>
> (*On Art and Literature*, p. 95)

At the heart of this biographical method, Proust points out, is the assumption that by understanding the author as he appears in public one can understand the author as he appears in his work. But this assumption is false, says Proust, because "a book is the product of a different *self* from the self we manifest in our habits, in our social life, in our vices." Having distinguished between the two selves of the writer, the public and the private, he goes a step further, declaring that these two selves occupy completely different worlds, having no relation to each other:

> Sainte-Beuve remained unable to understand that world apart, shuttered and sealed against all traffic with the outer world, the poet's soul. He believed that it could be counseled, stimulated, repressed, by other people . . . failing to see the gulf that separates the writer from the man of the world, . . . failing to understand that the writer's true self is manifested in his books alone.
>
> (p. 106)

For Proust, Sainte-Beuve's method cannot touch the writer's true self; "if we would try to understand that particular self, it is by searching our own bosoms, and trying to reconstruct it there, that we may arrive at it." Although Proust remains vague about how we are to perform the kind of introspection necessary to understand the writer properly, his insistence on the absolute autonomy of the literary work points toward the development of a formalist method stringently indifferent to cultural and biographical factors, warning would-be critics against committing the biographical fallacy.

Most recently, however, there are signs that this dogmatic exclusion of social considerations from literary criticism may be coming to an end. A new critical historicism seems to be on the rise, represented in different ways by the reader-response school of Hans Jauss and Wolfgang Iser, and by the vogue for "discursive analyses" of the kind popularized by Michel Foucault. Foucault has also been partly responsible for leading what has been called a "return to the author," even if "the author" is now no more than a hypothetical construction on the part of the critic. Finally, there has been a revival of interest in the definition of culture and in the relation of the writer to culture and society.

In this emerging critical climate, Sainte-Beuve's ideas—literary historicism, the nature of the author, and the role of culture—may take on a renewed importance. To grasp these ideas clearly we must first examine the crisis within the philosophy of history to which they are a response: the crisis of historical relativism.

HISTORICAL RELATIVISM, POSITIVISM, AND NATURALISM

Our understanding of Sainte-Beuve's attitude toward the past tends to be obscured by our preconceptions of the nineteenth century's brand of historical consciousness. We are taught that even the greatest historians of Sainte-Beuve's era espoused "objective" historicism, a view of history that (naively) assumes that the past is transparent to the present, like an open book from which the truth can be read without difficulty. In reality, the best early historicists, among whom Sainte-Beuve should be included (Irving Babbitt, for one, considers him the greatest French historicist), were acutely aware of the gap that separated their age from previous ones, and of the problem of historical reconstruction. The great historian Leopold von Ranke may have claimed that every age was immediate to God, but this did not mean that every age was immediately accessible to the historian.

Sainte-Beuve's awareness of historical difference is very strong, as shown by his persistent stressing of the relativity of tastes, values, and even words. The same activity (for example, daydreaming) may mean something completely different to one age than it does to another: a history of reverie would be possible, and Sainte-Beuve almost casually sketches its outline:

[Although Mme. de Sévigné was given to solitary musings] this is not to say that she indulged in melancholy reveries, strolling along somber paths in the woods. . . . That kind of reverie had not yet been invented; it was not until 1793 that Mme. de Staël wrote her admirable book, *L'Influence des passions sur le bonheur*. Until then daydreaming had been more natural and more personal, and at the same time less self-centered.

(*Selected Essays*, p. 127)

Such a recognition that the past differs essentially from the present may simply confirm the historian in a belief in his own superiority to the past if he fails to recognize that his own values are relative, and that his own past differs from his present. This is the charge made by modern historicists against their nineteenth-century predecessors. But Sainte-Beuve is far from complacent about his own historicity; he notes that

every day I change, the years follow the years; my tastes of a former season are no longer my tastes of today; my friendships themselves wither up and are renewed. Before the final death of the mobile being that bears my name, how many men have already died within me!

(*Portraits littéraires* 3.544)

And he goes on to force home his sense of existential relativism on the reader as well: "You think that I am speaking of myself personally, reader: but reflect a moment and see if the same is not true of you."

His sense of historical relativism sometimes leads Sainte-Beuve to adopt an attitude of extreme skepticism about our ability to retrieve the past or even to gain knowledge about the present. "The diverse and changing aspects of incomprehensible reality" can make a mockery of our feeble attempts to impose order and discover truth in history. The patterns we deduce may be chimerical:

The century passes quickly; it hastens on; I don't know if it will soon arrive at one of those immense valleys, one of those broad plateaus, where society rests and installs itself for a long halt. I don't even know if society ever rests, ever really stops and pauses, or if all the stations that we believe we have discovered in the historical past are not the more or less illusory effects of perspective, mirages that form and play before our eyes in the distance.

(*Oeuvres*, M. Leroy ed., 1.491)

Although Sainte-Beuve would probably not go so far as to agree with Nietzsche that "there is *only* a perspective 'knowing,'" his skepticism at times stymies any effort at historical understanding: "We only know our own times well," he ruefully comments in his *Cahier vert* (*Green Notebook*, 1834–1847), "and in our own times only our own generation."

The real problem is that what seems true for one age is considered dogma by the next. When Sainte-Beuve exclaims, "Who am I to decide in the name of absolute truth?" he is not simply being modest but is voicing a common concern of his century. The absolute truth that had been grounded in religious faith can no longer be justified; relativism and skepticism are symptomatic of this loss of certitude. A new, more self-conscious theory of knowledge, a revised epistemology, is needed, one supple enough to allow for provisional truths but not so loose as to permit a subjectivism where all judgments would have the same value.

Positivism provides the theory of knowledge and naturalism provides the analytic tools to cope with the problems raised by postreligious historicism. A scientifically based philosophy developed in France during the early years of the nineteenth century, positivism is guided by one simple but powerful axiom: true knowledge can only be gained from experience of particulars, never from a priori principles. In positivism, as Foucault has put it, "the truth of the object determines the truth of the discourse that describes its formation"; the search for knowledge requires the patient accumulation of empirical data until patterns and meanings emerge from the mass of particulars. The coalescence of observed details into meaningful patterns of information thus becomes a crucial process, a process that must be regulated by a new methodology—that of naturalism. With its emphasis on categories and classification, naturalism guides the positivist toward order.

Sainte-Beuve is one of the first literary critics to look to natural science, and in particular to positivism and naturalism, for solutions to the dilemmas of relativism and skepticism raised in the historical or human sciences by historicism. It is interesting to speculate about the factors that led Sainte-Beuve to science. Clearly one important condition was the lack, in France, of the sharp German distinction between *Naturwissenschaften* (the study of nature) and *Geisteswissenschaften* (the study of the human spirit); another was probably Sainte-Beuve's training in medical school. Whatever the reasons, he did seek to "arrive at the truth, as we do in the study of nature." The critic, he proclaims, must be governed by the positivist ethos of impartial observation; his duty is to

> see the things and the men as they are, and to express them as he sees them, describe in the round, as a servant of science, the varieties of the species, the diverse forms of human organization, strangely modified morally in society and in the artificial labyrinth of doctrines.
>
> (Conclusion to *Port-Royal*)

Sainte-Beuve's scientistic tendencies led Arnold to characterize him as "a *naturalist*, carrying into letters, so often the mere domain of rhetoric and futile amusement, the ideas and methods of scientific natural inquiry." And in his only extended exposition of his method ("Chateaubriand jugé par un ami intime en 1803," *Causeries du lundi* 21 and 22 July 1862), Sainte-Beuve declares himself a naturalist working in the vast domain of the human spirit, and foresees "a time when a science of human nature will be constituted, and the great orders and species of minds will be sorted out." It is primarily from this one article, taken as representing Sainte-Beuve's actual method and reprinted in many anthologies of criticism, that we receive our modern image of him as the founder of a literary naturalism that fully flowers in the work of Ernest Renan and Hippolyte Taine.

It would be wrong, however, to take Sainte-Beuve's claims at face value as indicating his actual practice of criticism. In fact the article quoted above reveals as much about Sainte-

Beuve's alliance in his later years with Taine as it does about his own critical procedure. In practice he remains suspicious of all categories and systems. Although positivist in orientation, he is unwilling to sacrifice the individual and specific for the sake of a generalization. Thus, as René Wellek has put it, Sainte-Beuve

> is not a naturalist of the new kind. Rather, he should be described as the greatest representative of the historical spirit in France.... True historicism is not simply the recognition of historical conditioning, but a recognition of individuality along with and through historical change.
>
> (*A History of Modern Criticism, 1750–1950: The Age of Transition*, p. 37)

The overhasty categorization of individual phenomena, Sainte-Beuve argues, destroys the rich complexity of reality. His resolute antireductionism becomes clear when he inveighs against the use of the word "type" to describe a writer because it takes no account of changes over time or of nuances in the writer's personality. Similarly in the analysis of historical processes, the number of variables is so great that any systematic analogy between events must be tenuous at best. Commenting on the comparisons being bandied about between the French Revolution of 1830 and the English one of 1688, Sainte-Beuve warns that

> one would surely be mistaken if one were to speak of these external similarities—some necessary and essential to all comparable revolutions, others purely capricious and accidental— in order to draw political conclusions from the English situation in 1688 that would be applicable to the French situation in 1830.... We believe it useful to warn certain minds attracted by resemblance against this.
>
> (*Oeuvres* 1.335)

Even more dangerous than the erection of categories based on "superficial" resemblance is the systematizer's tendency to impose his own categories on the past instead of letting the past speak for itself in all its real confusion. Sainte-Beuve sees this happening in Jules Michelet's attempt to prove that Rabelais was actually an antimedieval humanist; Sainte-Beuve denigrates Michelet's

> allegorical thirst for a new explanation of which commentators have not yet thought. Every age has its hobby; and his, which does not jest, has the humanitarian craze, and thinks to do great honour to Rabelais by attributing it to him.... I fancy when we try to explain Rabelais according to our own ideas, he permits it merely to have a laugh over it.
>
> (*Essays*, E. Lee trans., p. 60)

THE ART OF BIOGRAPHY AND THE IDEA OF THE LITERARY CAREER

It should be clear from the preceding remarks that Sainte-Beuve's criticism is not strictly modeled on the methods of naturalism, nor does it seriously aspire to the certitude of the pure sciences. Even in his naturalistically inflected essay on method, he insists that criticism, in spite of its progress,

> will remain an *art* requiring a skillful artist, just as medicine requires medical tact in the man who practices it, as philosophy should require philosophical tact in those who call themselves philosophers, as poetry is accessible only to poets. Analysis involves a kind of emotion, too; indeed one might say that it has an eloquence of its own and even a poetic quality.
>
> (*Selected Essays*, p. 283)

The key to this sensitive, tactful criticism lies in the critic's ability to immerse himself emotionally and intellectually in the particulars of the object he is studying. In a kind of heuristic faith, Sainte-Beuve assumes that, as Irving Babbitt puts it, "almost any subject, when studied relatively, that is, as the outgrowth of something else, ramifies in every direction'' so that particulars lead to synthesis. Like the critic Erich Auerbach, who assumes that ''selecting characteristic particulars and following up their implications'' will ''open up a knowledge of a broader context and cast a light on entire historical landscapes,'' Sainte-Beuve believes that ''if you live in a subject even a short time you are, as it were, in a city filled with friends. You can scarcely take a step in the main street without being instantly accosted right and left and invited to enter'' (*Port-Royal* 1.412).

As Sainte-Beuve's view on this issue suggests, a humanistic gamble is involved here, the belief that behind or within the data there is a synthetic human essence to be found or restored. At some unforeseeable moment in the process of assimilating information about an author, ''analysis vanishes in creation, the portrait speaks and lives, you have found the man.'' Similarly, in the opening pages of his masterpiece, *Port-Royal*, Sainte-Beuve compares his critical undertaking to a walk through a church that starts in the darkness of a nave but in which

> very soon, to the right and left, chapels open: from their tombs, shrines, or confessionals, various holy persons will invite us in; we will encounter them and hear talk about them more than once before we end our tour; and we will await the opportunity to get closer to them in their own precincts, to come to the central meeting-place where they all join together.
>
> (*Port-Royal* 1.3–4)

This kind of revivification of the object of criticism requires, according to Sainte-Beuve, that one study the object as if it were a living person, even if it is an institution or an entire period. In fact, the development of an individual provides a paradigm for the critic's synthesis of evidence into a coherent whole. Just as studying a living creature's evolving relations with its environment allows the scientist to understand an entire ecology, so studying an individual's evolving relations to his society allows Sainte-Beuve ''to traverse an epoch'':

> In a word, I will proceed with Port-Royal as with a unique individual whose biography I would like to write: when he is not yet formed, and each day brings something essential for him, I will not leave him at all, but will follow him step by step through the decisive series of events; once he is grown up, I will act more liberally toward him, and in his interplay with things, I will sometimes consider them in themselves. . . . Literature, moral theory, the theological climate, all this will constitute a vast field where, after a certain moment in our story, we will constantly be roaming; Port-Royal, having become a full-fledged adult, will lead us there frequently.
>
> (*Port-Royal* 1.3–4)

Biography, by a calculated digression, shades into cultural history.

Biographical criticism, which Sainte-Beuve in effect invented, is today widely discredited among literary critics for having tried to explain the story by talking about the teller. In its debased form, of course, the literary biography does fall into the error of slighting literature while overemphasizing biography. But Sainte-Beuve would reply that an effective use of biographical material enriches our understanding of the human problems that literature grapples with: ''None of these [biographical] questions is immaterial when it comes to judging the author of a book or the book itself (unless it is a treatise of pure geometry)—above all, if it is a literary work, for no aspect of human life is alien to literature'' (*Selected Essays*, p. 290).

This is not to say that Sainte-Beuve simply goes about reducing artistic form to the content of the writer's life, as Proust would have us think he does. In fact Sainte-Beuve emphasizes that the relationship between biographical and literary fact cannot be determined in advance, but must be conceived anew for each writer. Sometimes, he admits, one may not find any meaningful link at all:

The references to Molière's own life . . . come down to rather vague general similarities or details: in actual fact, none of Molière's characters is *himself*. In most cases, these references must be regarded merely as a superior actor's artifices and byplays, or else as momentary identifications between the actor and the character, such as are familiar to comedians of all times and are intended to provoke laughter. In short, Molière's characters are not copies, but creations.

(*Selected Essays*, p. 118)

Elsewhere, the naturalist Taine is criticized for having dwelled on the poet Alexander Pope's physical characteristics instead of "literary truth."

Given that the relation between text and life is not simply one of copy to reality or one that is always important, what is the most common function of biographical information in Sainte-Beuve's criticism? The best way to describe it would be as a propaedeutic, a means of preparing the reader for a more nuanced appreciation of literature by introducing the psychological and social forces that may have impinged on the writer and affected his work. For example, after a discussion of the playwright Jean Racine's life, Sainte-Beuve comments that "on the basis of the foregoing brief remarks on Racine's character, way of life, and intellectual habits, it is easy to infer the essential qualities and defects of his work—to foresee, as it were, both his strong and weak points" (*Selected Essays*, p. 86). A successful biographer will discover in the artist's life the seeds that in the act of creation grow into the work.

For Sainte-Beuve the seminal moment in any artist's life is that time when the direction of his career first takes shape. Like Friedrich Schleiermacher, who believed that every writer acts upon a "germinal decision" that the critic must try to understand, Sainte-Beuve is obsessed with the origins of literary sensibility within the individual—"that ineffable moment from which everything dates."

Indeed, the evaluation of a writer at the beginning of his career is just as much a test for the critic as is the critic's judgment of the mature writer:

to judge a beginning author correctly and tactfully, without exaggerating his importance, to foresee his development when he himself is still incompletely aware of his powers, still experimenting, still growing, and to sense his limitations, as well as to formulate intelligent criticisms of an author who is at the height of his popularity—all this is the hallmark of the born critic.

(*Selected Essays*, p. 180)

It is important to note here that the origin of the literary career for Sainte-Beuve does not necessarily consist, as it does for such modernist authors as Proust and Oscar Wilde, of an "antagonism between more or less 'naturally' living and writing," to use Edward Said's words (*Beginnings*, p. 237). Rather, the origin marks a point of convergence at which the writer's career becomes feasible for him and conceivable to us.

Sainte-Beuve's incomparable literary portraits are most often acclaimed for the subtlety of his psychological insight into this initial phase of the writer's career. Although his psychology remains theoretically crude (he would never imagine doing the kind of analysis that Freud does of Goethe's "screen memories" in "A Childhood Recollection from *Dichtung und Wahrheit*"), he possesses a gift for transforming mere anecdote into illumination. This is an important quality in Sainte-Beuve's prose, but one that unfortunately can be appreciated only in an extended reading of his *Portraits littéraires*, especially those of the abbé Prevost, Jean de La Fontaine, and Racine.

In addition to pioneering the psychological approach to the understanding of a writer's origins, Sainte-Beuve is also one of the first critics to emphasize the importance of literary rivalry among the beginning conditions for a literary career. Anticipating Harold Bloom and W. J. Bate, he remarks that "nothing gives us as good an idea of a man's range and elevation as to see what antagonist, what rival, he chose at an early date." Of course, Sainte-Beuve never elaborates any theory of purely literary influence; although he recognizes that for great talents one could study intraliterary relations, he is always hesitant to isolate the literary from life as a whole.

For most writers, the literary career entails both an original formation of a psychological, intellectual, and sometimes purely literary motivation, and a second phase in which the writer participates as a writer in society. The critic must trace the writer's social trajectory if he wishes to understand the changes in style and content that occur during a career:

> Very great individuals dispense with groups: they serve as centers themselves, people gather around them. But it is the group, the association or alliance, with its active exchange of ideas and spirit of perpetual emulation in the presence of one's equals, that provides a man of talent with his outward setting, all his development, and all his value. There are talents who belong to several groups, who never stop traveling through successive milieus, perfecting themselves, being transformed, or being deformed. In such cases of shifting affiliations, of slow or sudden conversions, it is important to note the hidden and constant spring, the persistent motive force.
>
> (*Selected Essays*, pp. 286–287)

It is not surprising that Sainte-Beuve uses the word "milieu" here to describe the system of ideas and institutions to which the writer adapts in the course of his career. As Leo Spitzer has brilliantly shown, literary naturalists were just beginning to take over the term from its earlier biological context when Sainte-Beuve wrote these lines in 1862. But even if the word was newfangled, in practice Sainte-Beuve had long been studying the literary affiliations and influences that constitute, in part, the writer's environment. In fact his most important contribution to modern criticism is probably his conceptualization of this dynamic complex of values, concepts, relationships, and organizations—in short, his idea of *culture*.

CULTURE AND SOCIETY IN SAINTE-BEUVE

No one who reads Sainte-Beuve can fail to notice his intense and abiding interest in issues of literary and artistic culture. Unfortunately he never formalized his insights about the elements, conditions, and social role of culture, nor did he ever produce a full-length work taking the problem of culture as its central theme. There is no *Culture and Anarchy* in Sainte-Beuve's oeuvre. Because of this, and perhaps also because he did not write in English, he has been a much less popular totem figure than Matthew Arnold in English-language histories of the idea of culture. In fact, the most important of these histories, Raymond Williams' *Culture and Society, 1780–1950*, ignores Sainte-Beuve completely.

This is a shortcoming, for what emerges from a perusal of Sainte-Beuve's work as a whole is a surprisingly sophisticated view of culture as both a conditioning medium for artistic expression and a disseminator of values in society. Sainte-Beuve's double perspective allows him to study culture as a relatively autonomous set of artistic interests and institutions while at the same time recognizing its links to the political and social order.

To analyze culture in the first sense, as a matrix for art, is to assume that literature is primarily a historical product, rather than an aesthetic or intuitive one. According to this historicist premise, which pervades Sainte-Beuve's work, certain modes of writing, certain styles, must be considered culturally permissible (that is, acceptable) only at certain times and places. The writer is constrained not simply by his own imagination, but also by the aesthetic values of his audience. Thus one finds Sainte-Beuve debating whether Racine, writing in the seventeenth century, could have adapted himself to the nineteenth century's taste for verisimilitude and historical implications:

> In an epoch like ours . . . would he have been capable of that realism in portrayal of character and mores, which always prevails in postrevolutionary periods? . . . Could he have aimed at profound philosophical truths in interpreting historical episodes? Did he possess the strength and temperament to take all these elements into account, to harmonize them, to join and link them into an indissoluble and living form, to fuse them all in the fire of passions?
>
> (*Selected Essays*, pp. 81–82)

The answer would appear to be no. Like the twentieth-century historicist philosopher Hans-Georg Gadamer, Sainte-Beuve sees culture as consisting, in part, of a historically determinate set of generic preferences, a "horizon of expectations" circumscribing both writer and readers, which only the strongest writer can transcend.

But unlike Gadamer and the reader-response school of Jauss, Sainte-Beuve does not grant autonomy to the aesthetic demands of readers. Whatever the specific generic expectations the writer must fulfill, such aesthetic pre-understanding cannot exist per se but must be grounded in other kinds of expectations. Sainte-Beuve points out that Pierre Corneille's readers, for example, would be guided in their rejection of realism by philosophical expectations:

> [Seventeenth-century Frenchmen] looked for neither realism nor colorfulness in tragedy. They were more or less of the school of Descartes: "I think, therefore I am; I think, therefore I feel." The whole drama is confined to and takes place in the "inner substance . . . whose entire essence or nature consists in thought, and which needs no place in order to exist and depends on no material thing." Those are Descartes' words, and Corneille followed them out pretty much to the letter.
>
> (*Selected Essays*, p. 50)

This type of analysis, perhaps best represented in Sainte-Beuve's work by his digressions on Blaise Pascal in *Port-Royal*, has since blossomed into an entire discipline devoted to the study of the effects of philosophy on literary expression.

A second kind of underlying factor in aesthetic preferences, Sainte-Beuve argues, is what Hippolyte Taine refers to as "national temperament," those emotional proclivities and prejudices typical of a people. In order to be successful, literature must respond to this nonphilosophical element of culture. Thus the differences between French and Spanish versions of *El Cid*, to take one example, can be said to result from differences between French and Spanish sensibilities:

> Every nation endows its theater with just that degree of harshness or sensitivity which reflects its characteristic temperament, and which can be seen in its favorite games. The English would have to be a people fond of boxing in order to accept all of Shakespeare; Spain has its bullfights; France, in the years before *Le Cid*, had only its duels in the Place Royale.
>
> (*Selected Essays*, p. 40)

Here as elsewhere Sainte-Beuve, unlike his naturalist compatriot Taine, only uses a term like "temperament" as an ad hoc vehicle for presenting concrete examples, in this case examples of what Johan Huizinga later studied as "the play-element in culture." In the hands of some of Taine's followers, of course, the formalized idea of a characteristic national temperament, which Taine designates as "race," tends to degenerate into a mystical racialism in which innate qualities are thought to dominate all possible cultural influences on the individual. But for Sainte-Beuve, as indeed for Taine, race remains only one of many conditioning forces. Sainte-Beuve, in his review of Taine's *Histoire de la littérature anglaise* (*History of English Literature*, 1864) is careful not to weigh the scales in the nature/nurture measurement:

Whatever man desires to do, to think, or, since it is here a question of literature, to write, depends in a more or less intimate manner on the *race* from which he springs, whence he derives his natural attributes: not less does it depend on the kind of society and civilization in which he was educated and also on the time, and individual circumstances and events which occur daily in the course of life.

(*Essays*, pp. 228–229)

While philosophical ideas and unconsciously held ethnic ("racial") prejudices affect the artist both indirectly and in a purely ideological manner, there is a third element of culture that impinges directly and measurably on the typical literary career. This third element is composed of the various cultural organs—literary salons, intellectual groups, artistic schools, families of minds—with which a writer must associate in order to develop: forms of affiliation in the proper sense of the word. One of Sainte-Beuve's most important contributions to the study of culture is his delineation of such affiliative institutions. He insists that a central task of criticism is to reconstitute "the succession and the interaction of schools and groups, the names and characteristics of the true leaders of such groups, and to mark the kinds and degrees of their principal talents" (*Nouveaux lundis* 4.296), in a kind of sociological analysis.

Sainte-Beuve distinguishes between two general kinds of artistic associations, the first basically informal, the second more clearly hierarchical and bounded. In the first category fall what Sainte-Beuve calls groups and families. These are alliances between writers formed in a partisan spirit, the only difference between the two being that "groups" (like Chateaubriand's in Sainte-Beuve's *Chateaubriand et son groupe littéraire*) are usually seen from the outside, as fighting units engaging in cultural battles out of self-interest, whereas "families" (as in *Port-Royal*) usually appear as sharing common moral precepts.

Such informal organizations, if they existed in isolation from each other, would at best remain ineffectual and at worst would split culture into a multitude of constantly feuding factions. In *Chateaubriand*, Sainte-Beuve warns that only a more formal institution can prevent cultural disintegration and allow the writer a chance to develop and to pursue a career:

In order for literature to have a whole and consistent life, there must be a certain stability that is not stagnant; there must be, for the competition, a circle of competent and elite judges, something or someone who organizes, regularizes, moderates, and sets limits, who the writer keeps in mind and wishes to satisfy; without which he is completely unrestrained, dissipates his efforts, and loses his essence. . . . The great literary ages have thus always had a judge, a tribunal dispensing judgment, which the writer feels some dependence on, some balcony . . . from which honors and rewards are handed down.

(*Chateaubriand*, 1.52–53)

The most important of these tribunals of taste are the literary salons and the academies, both institutions that Sainte-Beuve simultaneously participated in and criticized. His ideas about the role of academies as regulating authorities within culture are commonly acknowledged to have influenced the two major nineteenth-century treatments of the subject, Renan's essay on the French Academy and Arnold's "The Literary Influence of Academies" (1865). But his most sustained work on literary associations focuses on the peculiarly French institution of the salon. Like his contemporary Victor Cousin, Sainte-Beuve calls attention to the cultural power of such figures as Madame Marie-Thérèse Geoffrin, whose literary salon stands out as "the great center and meeting place of the eighteenth century." Providing a clearly defined place within society where intellectuals can exchange ideas, the salon acts as a kind of womb where culture is engendered.

CHARLES-AUGUSTIN SAINTE-BEUVE

The importance of the salon for Sainte-Beuve, however, goes beyond its purely generative and mediating role within culture. As he defines it, the salon is a "complex mechanism" that brings together "not only men of letters in the strict sense, but also artists, sculptors and painters, establishing contact between those two groups and between them and people of society" (*Selected Essays*, p. 158). This is to say that in addition to encouraging the cross-disciplinary affiliation essential for a strong, broad-based culture, the salon in Sainte-Beuve's view serves as a liaison between culture and society.

The word "society," as Sainte-Beuve uses it in the quotation above, means something both more specific and less taken for granted than it does for us today. In a French context it connotes the class of people possessing *les moeurs*, a basically untranslatable term that Lionel Trilling renders as "manners and morals." As Williams has shown, society in this sense is a relatively modern development; in England, as a matter of fact, the first usage of the term recorded in the *Oxford English Dictionary* occurs in 1823. But Sainte-Beuve places the origin of cultured society in France more than a hundred and fifty years earlier, seeing evidence of it in the correspondence of Madame de Sévigné. In her letters, he argues,

> we find ourselves in a world very different from that of the Fronde and the Regency; we realize that what is called French society was at last constituted . . . the proprieties were observed; opinion began to stigmatize what was unsavory and ignoble. Moreover, as disorder and brutality became less conspicuous, decency and wit were gaining in simplicity.
>
> (*Selected Essays*, p. 123)

Culture, then, is linked to the proprieties and moral style of a society. But the nature of this relation for Sainte-Beuve needs to be specified. A strong culture does more than simply reflect society's existing mores—it can also exert an extraordinary influence on those mores. Indeed Sainte-Beuve believes that culture is as vital in directing the course of society as are the political and legal systems. He makes this point in an otherwise laudatory essay on the eighteenth-century critic Frédéric-Melchior Grimm, gently rebuking the older critic for underestimating the moral power of literature: "Grimm is mistaken; in attributing all public morality to a nation's institutions and laws, he forgets that during peaceful intervals books have a great influence" (*Selected Essays*, p. 187). Grimm, it must be remembered, was writing at a time when the idea of society had been born but before the idea of culture had been created during the nineteenth century. It is a measure of Sainte-Beuve's seminal role in this creation that he distinguishes himself from Grimm precisely on the question of culture's power over society.

To follow the comparison between politics and culture still further, the leaders of culture are for Sainte-Beuve like political leaders; thus Madame Geoffrin is "a kind of skillful administrator, almost a prime minister of society" (*Selected Essays*, p. 158). But if this is the case, then culture has its own politics, the stakes being control over the taste and morals of society. As compared with the continuing literary squabbles among various groups, this struggle for cultural hegemony is both total and cyclical in Sainte-Beuve's view. He argues that such struggle is essentially generational:

> Fifteen years, Tacitus once said, is a long time in human life. . . . That is the amount of time necessary for a generation to produce itself, to be born, to flower and to reign, then to find itself face to face with another new generation already grown, which in its turn disputes the empire with it.
>
> (*Chateaubriand* 1.44–45)

As the word "empire" implies, what at times may seem to be mere literary bickering can at certain critical moments become part of a broad struggle involving culture as a whole.

At such moments, Sainte-Beuve argues, it becomes possible not simply to make a power grab within culture—a domination that will be short-lived, ending when the next generation comes into control—but to seize the opportunity to forge a true cultural empire, an empire in the universalistic, Latin sense postulated by Vergil, Dante, and T. S. Eliot.

For Sainte-Beuve, the essence of empire is its simultaneous unity in diversity, its order consisting in a metropolitan center surrounded and fed by healthy cultural provinces. Against the danger of what he termed "provincialism," Sainte-Beuve insists on the need for an integrated, whole culture, exemplified for him in the Vergilian Rome he celebrates in his *Étude sur Virgile*.

Frank Kermode has pointed out how Sainte-Beuve, in his lectures on Vergil, emphasizes the importance of a common language and institutional center in overcoming provincialism. But the *Étude*, although it projects the ideal of a harmonious cultural empire, is at heart nostalgic in tone, fighting a rearguard action against the philistines (Sainte-Beuve was booed unmercifully when he tried to deliver his lectures), rather than presenting a strategy to act upon. For this we must turn to "Dix ans après en littérature," the well-known article of 1840 in which Sainte-Beuve definitively breaks with the romantic school of Hugo.

He begins by asserting that Hugo's celebrated "generation of 1830" has come full circle and is now facing something comparable to a mid-life crisis in an individual. The symptoms of this crisis Sainte-Beuve finds in the literary soirées of his time, with their collections of talent that appear to an outsider as unified groups, but which in reality are simply aggregates of self-promoting individuals. A lack of unity is not always bad: "No group exists, no doctrinal center, as it were, and in some respects I don't complain about this: variety and liberty are something to aim for." But the danger is that only "feudal chiefs"

will remain, and that as a result the culture will yield only "individual phenomena, more or less brilliant, but without any unifying force, without a goal—even a secondary one; without agreement—even a spurious one for the sake of appearances" (*Portraits contemporains* 1.518–519).

This prospect, to Sainte-Beuve, makes an accord among writers both possible and urgent. It has now become possible for them to work in "community and concert" for two reasons. First, because there is no overbearing leader but only "notable and distinguished individuals," they "can think of themselves as equals" and form a kind of republican cultural empire: "Let each of them follow his line for individual works and consent to coexist in certain relations of community and limits in judgment; let each one practice true equality and independence, based on mutual esteem with the allowance of some reservations" (*Oeuvres* 1.530).

The second enabling condition for cultural unification now present, Sainte-Beuve points out, is the shared threat to culture itself from industrialism and commercialism. Against the common enemy it should be easy to close ranks, especially since culture has already been isolated:

industrialism, greed, and pride have reached extravagant degrees, forcing all moderate minds . . . into a large camp apart. We are more than a group, we are close to becoming a city as a result of these excesses and plunderings that have rendered the rest of the literary countryside uninhabitable and that have forced together and reconciled all honest thinkers.

(*Portraits contemporains* 1.529)

If cultural unity were based only on this kind of defensive and negative posture of resistance, it would be temporary at best. What is needed, according to Sainte-Beuve, is "a common goal of recomposition and health." That moral and social end for culture, he continues, is to be supplied not by the writers themselves, but by criticism. As a form of "progressive conservatism," criticism "gains from our more proud or naive qualities, our errors, our successes and our failures, when they are well understood," and uses this knowledge to increase cultural harmony. Considering the importance of culture to society, the critic's social responsibility in this project is indeed great: "Linking criticism to literature, and building it on positive historical examples, linking it to a decent, healthy morality, would be to render a public, indeed a social service." (*Portraits contemporains* 1.568).

Criticism thus has a primary role to play, under certain social conditions, in providing culture with a moral foundation and thereby making cultural empire achievable. The ideal state of affairs for Sainte-Beuve would be one in which the orders of culture and society correspond perfectly, each reinforcing the other. But as his attitude toward industrialism and commercialism suggests, he recognizes that such a conserving (and conservative) union, although now possible within culture, is "far from us politically." As in literary life, so in politics, he sees a movement "toward a miserable fragmentation of intrigues, a diminution without end of all powers and functions." This degeneration may be averted in culture by a strong critical hand, but in political life Sainte-Beuve sees little hope, at least at that moment.

Political and social conditions, if bleak enough, may force a culture to unify in order to survive, as Sainte-Beuve sees happening in 1840; or, under happier circumstances, political order and cultural empire may help each other to expand and prosper. In other cases, however, the order of culture may be neither opposed to nor synergistic with the political order, but rather subordinated to it. In such cases the struggle for cultural hegemony appears nakedly as part of a political struggle, and there is no pretense of reconciliation between contending groups. In his earlier years,

Sainte-Beuve acknowledges the necessity for such cultural division during periods of social and political transformation:

> Modern society, when it comes to be better established and settled, must have its calm, its cool mysterious niches, its sanctuaries where sentiment may be perfected, its share of ancient woodland and yet uncharted springs. In its seemingly uniform setting, it must find room for a thousand distinctions of thought and many rare forms of inner life; failing which it will fall far below the previous civilization and scarcely satisfy a whole range of minds. At moments of change or of incoherent and confused organization, at moments such as the present [1834], it is natural that the most important tasks should come first, the heavy work take precedence, and that on all sides, even in literature, habits should be formed of hitting hard, aiming high, and announcing oneself with trumpet or megaphone. Perhaps in the end the discreeter graces will come back, with expressions suitable to their new surroundings. I would like to believe it: but while hoping for the best, we cannot expect to see their sentiment and their language taking shape overnight.
>
> (*Portraits littéraires* 2.105)

If culture is to develop that unity in diversity characteristic of empire, Sainte-Beuve seems to be saying here, it must speak the language of politics during revolutionary periods. This willingness to see culture become a political instrument probably derives from his Saint-Simonian optimism of the early 1830's. At this time, Sainte-Beuve went so far as to proclaim that "the people and the poets are going to march together . . . art is from this time forward on a common footing, in the arena with everyone, side by side with untiring humanity" (*Oeuvres* 1.377). Not only must art join the battle, he goes on, but its role must be to support the progressive elements of the revolution: "the mission, the task of art today . . . is to translate . . . to reflect and to shine forth in a thousand shades the sentiment of progressive humanity" (1.377).

CHARLES-AUGUSTIN SAINTE-BEUVE

In his later years Sainte-Beuve becomes less sanguine about the progressiveness of social upheaval, and he tends to see culture as a sort of superstructure that is more affected by changes in the political and economic base than vice versa:

> In every great political and social revolution, art . . . changes, modifies itself, and undergoes in its turn a revolution, not in its interior and proper principle (which is eternal) but in its conditions of existence and its means of expression, in its relations with objects and surrounding phenomena, in the diverse kinds of ideas and sentiments that it is tinged with, and in the inspiration that it draws upon.
>
> (*Oeuvres* 1.369–370)

Thus, although culture and society are in a dialectical relation with each other in which culture can dominate and influence society if well organized, both culture and society in turn depend on political and economic conditions.

The economic developments of his age are of great concern to Sainte-Beuve. Although not an extreme anticapitalist, he sees a danger to culture in the modern business world, where time is of the essence, specialization is the rule, and even conversation becomes a commodity. Discussing Madame de Sévigné, he contrasts her period with his own on these counts:

> In 1829, our utilitarian concerns make it hard for us to imagine what this life of leisure and conversation was really like. The world moves so fast in our day, so many things are by turns brought on the stage, that we scarcely have the time to observe and grasp them all. Our days are spent in studies, our evenings in serious discussions; as for friendly conversations, *causeries*, there are few or none at all. . . . In the period under consideration, this leisurely mode of life was not incompatible with interest in literary, religious, and political events. . . . Moreover, conversation had not yet become, as it was to become in the eighteenth century, in the open sa-

lons presided over by Fontenelle, an occupation, a business, a social requirement.

> (*Selected Essays*, pp. 123–124)

The condition Sainte-Beuve laments here is defined more precisely by Lukacs in the term "reification." Unlike Lukacs, however, Sainte-Beuve sees no dialectical necessity that such a distressing state of affairs should be a prelude to a Marxist revolution. Instead, when he takes economic realities into account, he tends to become nostalgic for an age when society, and, hence, culture, was viable, but before commercialism had invaded every aspect of life.

The privileged period seems to be the eighteenth century, one of those

> fortunate, favored ages when talented men could propose to form such associations [as that between Pope, Swift, and Bolingbroke] . . . such ages are the only truly classical ones in the broader sense of the word, the only ones which provided superior talents with a propitious climate and shelter. We know this only too well, living as we do in an age without inner unity, when talents, possibly equal to those of other ages, have been lost or frittered away because of the uncertainties and inclemencies of the times.
>
> (*Selected Essays*, p. 6)

The inclemencies of the times, as we have seen earlier, may be political as well as economic. For Sainte-Beuve as for Arnold, the primary political condition for culture is therefore order. Anarchy—which for both critics finally is synonymous with any political revolution—impinges in a fatal way on the precious peace of the cultural enclave. In the opening paragraphs of "Qu'est-ce qu'un classique?" ("What Is a Classic?"), written in the midst of the revolutionary period of 1848–1851, Sainte-Beuve explains how his words have been drowned out in the din and clamor around him:

> In order to treat such subjects, which are always somewhat abstract and moral, one must speak in

an atmosphere of calm, one must be sure of one's own and the reader's interest: one must, in short, take advantage of one of those brief moments of silence, moderation and leisure which are rarely the lot of lovely France—which indeed, her brilliant genius bears with impatience, even during periods when she is trying to behave herself and is not engaged in making revolutions.

(Selected Essays, p. 1)

Political order, insofar as it implies being "sure of one's own and the reader's interest," is closely related to a second political prerequisite for culture: a unified reading public. In modern society, Sainte-Beuve complains, no such public exists any longer, with disastrous results: "Criticism is more and more difficult and almost nonexistent . . . the principal cause of this decadence appears to be that criticism is not addressed to a public that has already more or less formed its detailed judgment and verifies it: nothing of all that." Culture alone cannot cope with this fragmentation, so characteristic of the modern public. One must look back to a Rousseauistic, primitive society to find the kind of relation between public and poetry that Sainte-Beuve considers truly healthy:

In ancient times, or even in all times, at a particular formative stage of society, poetry, far from being the kind of strange reverie and noble disease found in advanced communities, has been a purely human, general, popular faculty, as unindividualistic as possible, a product accessible to all, sung by all, invented no doubt by some, but inspired in the first place and very quickly claimed and reshaped by the bulk of the tribe or nation.

(Portraits contemporains: "Vigny," October 1835)

In the best of all possible worlds, culture would simply purify the language of the tribe.

Unfortunately we do not live in the best of all possible worlds, and culture, in the form imagined by Sainte-Beuve, must remain a ten-uous and difficult achievement, requiring an almost constant struggle against conditions that invite fragmentation, dissipation, provincialism, and cynicism. Such a struggle would be too much to bear were there not some paradigm or touchstone that could ensure the possibility of attaining ideal culture. For Sainte-Beuve that paradigm is provided by the classic.

THE CLASSIC AND THE MORAL DILEMMA OF CLASSIC STYLE

Sainte-Beuve's idea of the classic owes much to Goethe's earlier idea of a *Weltliteratur* (world literature). Goethe conceived of all the great books of the world as forming an order among themselves, a kind of symposium in which the national individuality of each work would be at once preserved and transcended. While maintaining Goethe's stress on the multinational character of the classical canon, Sainte-Beuve places his primary emphasis on the universalizing and unifying potential both of the canon as a whole and of individual classics. By admitting that other nations and cultures have produced great works, we learn to appreciate them and overcome provincialism; by reading the individual classics, we gain an understanding of our common tradition and overcome both relativism and political division.

Sainte-Beuve's catholicity of taste and aesthetic openness to other cultures is particularly evident in "What Is a Classic?" In that essay he chides those moderns who wish to revise the canon by substituting newer classics for the older ones. Sainte-Beuve agrees that "the Temple of Taste needs to be remodeled," but adds that

in rebuilding it our task is merely to enlarge it, to make it the Pantheon of all noble men, of all who have notably and durably increased the sum total of the human spirit, the enjoyments and conquests of the mind . . . every nation would have a corner of its own, but no one would feel constrained to remain within it.

(*Selected Essays*, p. 8)

The classical canon would thus be something like a United Nations of world culture, including the great Persian poet Firdusi as well as the French poet Racine. As in the orders of culture and politics, so in the order of the classic Sainte-Beuve favors a centralized empire made up of contributing yet independent parts.

To be considered a classic in the sense implied above, an author must not simply write well but must also represent his culture and nation as potentially universal entities, as Vergil represents Rome in the *Aeneid*. Every national classic does this to some extent, and the lucky reader will savor all these ideal possibilities. The danger of this kind of ecumenical approach to the classic, however, is that the reader may lose touch with his own cultural roots if he becomes too eclectic in his taste.

Two things in Sainte-Beuve's approach prevent this loss of identity from happening to his readers. First, they are warned that once one understands how the classics form a whole, "one must choose." This choice, he continues, should be made not at random, but rather "on the basis of our instincts," instincts deriving from our own culture:

Speaking our own language and governed by the conditions of the age in which we find ourselves, from which we derive our strengths as well as our shortcomings, let us ask ourselves from time to time, our heads lifted up to the peaks, our eyes on the group of mortals we most revere: "What would they say of us?"

(*Selected Essays*, p. 10)

The second thing preventing us from becoming what Sainte-Beuve calls "Wandering Jews" is the fact—not mentioned in "What Is a Classic?"—that in practice the literary peaks we look up to usually rise from a European landscape, standing as the supreme products of languages stemming from a common Latin civilization. Our classical canon tends to exclude non-European and non-Latin writers, leaving our own tradition, our own selection (governed by our language and our history) of what Arnold describes as "the best that has been thought or felt." Whatever freedom may have been granted the reader in the idea of an open Temple of Taste is thus tempered for Sainte-Beuve by the consolidating power of tradition: "The idea of the classical implies continuity and consistency, a tradition that forms a whole, is handed down, and endures."

The continuity provided by the classic is twofold. First, it is national: the greatest classics present both a venerable past and a world-historical destiny for their culture. The paradigm for this kind of temporal continuity is, of course, Vergil's *Aeneid*. Kermode has pointed out how, in Sainte-Beuve's comments about Vergil's ability to choose an ancient subject suitable for his own historical moment, "we sense not only Latin solidarity, but an admiration for a power that can preserve history as an integrated whole, include it in one enormous thought" (*The Classic*, p. 18). Second, it is stylistic:

A true classic, as I should like the term to be defined, is an author . . . who speaks to all in a style of his own, which happens also to be that of common speech, a style new but without neologisms, new and old at the same time, easily acceptable to any epoch.

(*Selected Essays*, p. 4)

Insofar as both forms of continuity, the temporal and the aesthetic or stylistic, draw together the old and the new, they make the classic into an essentially conservative creation:

A classic author . . . might well be revolutionary for a time, or at least seem so. But in truth, if he was violent at first and overthrew what stood in his way, he did so only in order quickly to right the scales in favor of order and beauty.

(*Selected Essays*, p. 4)

These words reveal the conservative bent at the heart of Sainte-Beuve's classical ideal. But they also raise an insoluble dilemma for the writer and the critic who seek to create a classic in their own time. How is one to gauge whether a style is simply destructive or will in fact restore order and beauty?

Sainte-Beuve struggles with this question throughout his career, particularly with regard to Hugo, whose forceful style is at first seen by Sainte-Beuve as foreshadowing a new classicism, but who is later denied classic status because his stylistic excesses do not subside into order.

One stopgap solution to the problem of defining a classic style is to distinguish, as Sainte-Beuve does, between two opposing kinds: on the one hand, a sublime, spontaneous, and personal style; on the other, a crafted and public one, which provides what Kermode defines as an "index of civility." This is a common romantic distinction, but unlike a typical romantic, Sainte-Beuve is very sympathetic to the second style, although he grants the superiority of the first:

> The great poets, the poets of genius, independent of the genre they practice, regardless of whether their temperament is lyric, epic, or dramatic, fall into two glorious families . . . the primitive poets, the founders, the pure archetypes, born of themselves and sons of their own works . . . contrasted with studious, polished, docile writers whose talents were developed by hard work . . . this secondary family, justly reputed inferior to its elder, but as a rule more understood by all, more accessible, and more cherished.
>
> (*Selected Essays*, p. 63)

Examples of this kind of distinction pepper Sainte-Beuve's work, particularly when he is

dealing with classic writers who live in the same period. In some cases, like this one in which Sainte-Beuve compares Corneille to Racine, the opposition is developed at great length:

> [Corneille] cannot learn anything, he cannot develop, unlike Racine who did learn and develop and achieved complete perfection. Racine's talent is one that allows him to accomplish all he sets out to accomplish—and besides, he had leisure and the habit of reflection. Corneille, on the other hand, owed everything to inspiration. What he could not do right off, he could not learn to do later. Racine's gift was that of art: he always gives us pure pleasure, even in his moments of weakness. Corneille's is the gift of spontaneous sublimity of thought and feeling— a firm grasp of his theme and of his language— but he also has his lapses.
>
> (*Selected Essays*, p. 43)

Such a mechanical application of categories is rare in Sainte-Beuve, but the trick of gauging a writer's style by setting up a series of comparisons is one that he employs frequently. The French philosophical school known as the Ideologues invented this technique of definition, which Sainte-Beuve probably learned from his early teacher, the Ideologue Pierre-Claude-François Daunou. Whatever its source, he at times erects it into a rule for doing any stylistic analysis: "A writer, as I see it, is only properly defined when one has named and distinguished in relation to him both those similar and contrary to him" (*Lundis* 4.44).

Stylistic analysis of this kind can be done without reference to the content or moral implications of the author's work. Sainte-Beuve, who is often accused of being incapable of perceiving the purely literary aspect of style apart from content, is in reality perfectly able to distinguish the stylistic from the moral. Indeed some of his most remarkable insights occur when he does this, particularly in the cases of writers favored by modernists, like Flaubert, Rousseau, and Montaigne.

In all three of these authors, Sainte-Beuve notes an extraordinary stylistic power, unaccompanied by any comparable moral discrimination. Flaubert, for example, is praised for his superb technique, but Sainte-Beuve points out that Flaubert's concern to handle the pen as others handle the scalpel means that he must ignore the moral issues implicit in his subject. Of Emma Bovary's terrible fate, Sainte-Beuve asks: "Is this moral? Is this comforting? The question does not seem to have occurred to the author. All he asked himself was one thing: Is it true?" (*Selected Essays*, p. 261). Rousseau's stylistic innovation, on the other hand, is seen by Sainte-Beuve as a phenomenon totally divorced from moral considerations. In an article on Rousseau written in the tense period just before the coup d'etat of 1851, a time when Rousseau's name would be sure to inflame political passions, Sainte-Beuve's opening lines deliberately turn away from questions about the content of Rousseau's work: "The writer who brought about the greatest single change in the French language since Pascal, and who ushered in, linguistically speaking, the nineteenth century, is Rousseau." Finally, with Montaigne, whom Sainte-Beuve fears as a skeptic, he admits an admiration for the way his "magical style" operates "within individual sentences and in the articulations of the ideas" to create "one continuous metaphor."

These kinds of insights can only be gained by setting questions of moral value to one side. But for Sainte-Beuve, stylistic power in itself, no matter how great, does not make an author a classic. He demands that the author take responsibility for his style: "No matter how true to life your characters may be," he reminds Flaubert, "they reflect the author's choice." Only those writers who use the power of their style in a moral way can truly be called classic. Thus Vergil, who is able to embed the Roman moral tradition in the *Aeneid* while maintaining a fine style, is a classic; Flaubert, in contrast, is incapable of writing such a classic, even when he attempts to do so in his historical novel *Salammbô* (1863), because he remains unfamiliar with the moral tradition that would link the world he describes to his own.

Although Flaubert's failure to achieve classic status results from a necessary trade-off between style and content and is thus acceptable to Sainte-Beuve, the sin of Rousseau and Montaigne in failing to put their superior styles to good use is inexcusable. Rousseau is accused of irresponsibly spreading a kind of moral epidemic, that of political romanticism:

> [In analyzing his own weaknesses in his books, Rousseau] did not realize that he was like a doctor who might set out to describe to ignorant laymen, in an intelligible, attractive way, some specific mental infirmity or illness; such a doctor would be partly to blame for the maniacs and madmen his book would produce by imitation or contagion.
>
> (*Selected Essays*, p. 196)

Fortunately Sainte-Beuve remains immune to this contagion. But he senses his susceptibility to infection from Montaigne, whom he considers the most dangerous of writers because his "magical style" lures readers into "universal doubt," a skepticism that culture and the classic should be fighting against. Montaigne's stylistic magic, Sainte-Beuve warns prospective readers, is exercised by "a kind of sorcerer, an evil genius who takes us by the hand, and who, guiding us through the labyrinth of opinion . . . blows out the light and leaves you utterly in the dark." If culture and the classic "conduce to sweetness and light," in Arnold's phrase, then Montaigne is an anticlassic.

Sainte-Beuve, then, sees three ways in which a writer may fall short of the classic style despite his stylistic excellence. First, he may intentionally avoid facing moral questions in order to refine his own style, as Flaubert does. Second, he may unintentionally transmit the wrong moral imperatives even though his style is exceptional, as with Rousseau. Finally, like Montaigne, he may join his stylistic power to evil ends. In denying such writers of genius the status of classics, Sainte-Beuve is clearly troubled, for their styles, taken in themselves, do "right the scales in favor of order and beauty," as the classic should. If their texts are morally destructive, at least their styles are constructive.

The only kind of writer Sainte-Beuve cannot abide at all is one who values energy over order, even in his style. This is his ultimate criticism of Hugo:

> When all is said, Hugo sets store by force alone; and on these grounds he admits Dumas, Balzac, almost as his *peers*, or at least endowed with a *power of talent* which seems to him the principal virtue. For him delicacy comes a long way behind, and only when these market porters have been found places. I too readily admire *power*, but I must be sure it is true intellectual power, not some purely physical strength of health and temperament. I admire power, not brawn.— Which is better: Ghengis Khan trailing all the hordes of Asia after him, or M. de Turenne at the head of 30,000 men?
>
> (from *Poisons*, quoted in Lehmann, p. 260)

As this metaphor implies, the classic style, which combines both power and organization toward a civilizing mission, is for Sainte-Beuve the style of Western empire itself. If in the end his ideal of the classic and culture is of limited usefulness to the modern reader, it is because it is tied to a Eurocentric and imperialist world view we can no longer accept so easily. But at its best, Sainte-Beuve's ideal provides the writer with a moral imperative to excellence, above and beyond any specific political goals:

> And after all, whatever the future and its cost, surely it is true that in art as in the moral life one must *do one's best?* That is not even a compari-

son, it is an identity I am stating: art for the artist is a part of his conscience and of his moral life.

> (*Portraits contemporains* 1.365)

Sainte-Beuve's specific contributions to modern criticism—the historicist approach to literature, the invention of literary biography, and the notions of culture and the classic—all, in the final analysis, grow out of this assumption about the identity of morals and aesthetics. We may accept or reject such an assumption and its critical consequences as we wish. But if we do reject it, we must also reject something we may wish to keep: Sainte-Beuve's own prose style, a style that effortlessly fuses moral or social judgments with an extraordinary aesthetic sensitivity. His style was lauded by Arnold as "incomparable," and was envied by Henry James; even his enemy Proust grudgingly acknowledged its beauty. Neither his style nor his ideas in themselves make Sainte-Beuve the exemplary critic he is; rather, it is the consistency of his style with his ideas, the undeniable integrity of his critical enterprise, that stands out, and that compels our admiration and respect today.

Selected Bibliography

EDITIONS

INDIVIDUAL WORKS

Tableau historique et critique de la poésie française et du théâtre français au XVIème siècle. Paris, 1828. Edited by Jules Troubat. 2 vols. Paris, 1876.

Vie, poésies et pensées de Joseph Delorme. Paris, 1829. Edited by Gerald Antoine. Paris, 1956.

Les consolations. Paris, 1830.

Volupté. Paris, 1834. Edited by Raphael Molho. Paris, 1969.

Pensées d'août. Paris, 1837.

Port-Royal. 5 vols. Paris, 1840–1859. Edited by Jules Troubat. Paris, 1888.

Livre d'amour. Paris, 1843. Edited by Jules Troubat. Paris, 1906.

Étude sur Virgile. Paris, 1857. 2nd ed. Paris, 1870.

Chateaubriand et son groupe littéraire sous l'empire. Paris, 1861. New ed. Paris, 1889.

Mes poisons, cahiers intimes inédits. Paris, 1926.

COLLECTED WORKS

Cahiers. Vol. 1: Le cahier vert (1834–1847). Edited by Raphael Molho. Paris, 1973.

Causeries du lundi. 15 vols. Paris, 1851–1862. Collected articles.

————. Paris, 1855–1869. 3rd and first complete edition.

————. Paris, 1943(?)–1949(?). Best modern edition.

Critiques et portraits littéraires. Paris, 1832.

Correspondance générale. Edited by Jean Bonnerot and Alain Bonnerot. 17 vols. Paris and Toulouse, 1935–1975.

Nouveaux lundis. 13 vols. Paris, 1878. Calmann-Lévy edition.

Oeuvres. Edited by Maxime Leroy. 2 vols. Paris, 1949–1951.

Portraits contemporains. 3 vols. Paris, 1846.

Portraits de femmes. Paris, 1845.

Portraits littéraires. Paris, 1844, 1862. Citations in text are to the latter, 3-vol. edition.

TRANSLATIONS

Essays by Sainte-Beuve. Translated by Elizabeth Lee. London, 1892.

Literary Criticism of Sainte-Beuve. Translated by E. R. Marks. Lincoln, Neb., 1971.

Portraits of the Eighteenth Century. Translated by Katharine Wormeley. 2 vols. New York, 1905, 1964.

Portraits of the Seventeenth Century. Translated by Katharine Wormeley. 2 vols. New York, 1905, 1964.

Selected Essays of Sainte-Beuve. Translated and edited by Francis Steegmuller and Norbert Guterman. Garden City, N.Y., 1963.

BIOGRAPHICAL AND CRITICAL STUDIES

Antoine, Gérald. "'Groupe,' 'École,' 'Famille,' 'Génération' dans la critique de Sainte-Beuve." *Revue de la littérature de la France* 80:737–748 (1978).

————, and Claude Pichois. "Sainte-Beuve juge de Stendhal et de Baudelaire." *Revue des sciences humaines* 85:7–34 (January–March 1957).

Arnold, Matthew. "Sainte-Beuve." In *The Complete Prose Works of Matthew Arnold,* edited by R. H. Super. Ann Arbor, Mich., 1965. Vol. 5, pp. 304–309.

————. "Sainte-Beuve." In *Encyclopaedia Britannica,* 9th ed., 1886. Also in *Five Uncollected Essays of Matthew Arnold,* edited by Kenneth Allott. Liverpool, 1953.

Auerbach, Erich. *Literary Language and Its Public in Late Antiquity and in the Middle Ages.* Translated by Ralph Mannheim. New York, 1965.

Babbitt, Irving. "Sainte-Beuve." In *Masters of Modern French Criticism.* Boston, 1912.

Baudelaire, Charles. *Correspondance générale.* Edited by Jacques Crepet. 6 vols. Paris, 1947.

Billy, André. *Sainte-Beuve, sa vie et son temps.* 2 vols. Paris, 1952.

Chadbourne, R. M. *Sainte-Beuve.* Boston, 1977.

Fayolle, Roger. *Sainte-Beuve et le 17ème siècle; ou, Comment les révolutions arrivent.* Paris, 1972.

James, Henry. "Sainte-Beuve's Portraits." In *Literary Reviews and Essays,* edited by Albert Mordell. New York, 1957.

Kermode, Frank. *The Classic.* New York, 1975.

Lehmann, A. G. *Sainte-Beuve, A Portrait of the Critic, 1804–1842.* Oxford, 1962.

Leroy, Maxime. *La pensée de Sainte-Beuve.* Paris, 1940.

Lukacs, Georg. *Soul and Form.* Translated by Ann Bostock. Cambridge, 1974.

Michaut, Gustave. *Sainte-Beuve avant les Lundis; Essai sur la formation de son esprit et de sa méthode de critique.* Fribourg, 1903.

Molho, Raphaël. *L'Ordre et les ténèbres; ou, La naissance d'un mythe de 17ème siècle chez Sainte-Beuve.* Paris, 1972.

Morley, J. M. *Nineteenth-Century Essays.* Chicago, 1970.

Nietzsche, Friedrich. *On the Genealogy of Morals.* Translated by Walter Kauffman. New York, 1969.

Proust, Marcel. *On Art and Literature, 1896–1919.* Translated by S. Townsend Warner. New York, 1958.

Richard, Jean-Pierre. "Sainte-Beuve et l'objet littéraire." In *Études sur le romantisme français.* Paris, 1970.

Said, Edward. *Beginnings.* Baltimore, 1975.

Spitzer, Leo. "'Milieu' and 'Ambiance.'" *Philosophy and Phenomenological Research* 3:1–42 (1942).

Wellek, René. "Sainte-Beuve." In *A History of Modern Criticism, 1750–1950.* Vol. 2: *The Age of Transition.* New Haven, 1965.

Williams, Raymond. *Culture and Society, 1780–1950.* New York, 1958.

Wimsatt, William, and Cleanth Brooks. *Literary Criticism: A Short History.* Chicago, 1978.

Wood, Michael. *Stendhal.* Ithaca, N.Y., 1971.

LAWRENCE ROTHFIELD

HANS CHRISTIAN ANDERSEN

(1805–1875)

LIFE

HANS CHRISTIAN ANDERSEN spent his life pursuing fame. In this respect the famous fairy-tale writer was a crazed lover. At a very early age he declared himself willing to suffer all kinds of humiliation and denigration to fulfill what he felt to be his divine destiny, to be a writer. Egocentric to the core, persistent and patient, he denied himself so that destiny would not be denied.

Andersen's perseverance was astounding. Yet his narcissistic striving to succeed as a great writer was also profoundly sad. The strain he placed himself under to produce was so great that he often succumbed to bouts of hypochondria, melancholy, and depression. His nerves became like volatile wires, frayed and tattered. By the time he finally forced fame to turn and smile on him, he was a desperate man. Not only did he question whether he was worthy of fame, but he demanded even more admiration and applause than he had already gained. He licked the boots of the aristocracy to obtain support, and he complained when the Danish nation did not continually crown his head with laurels. He perfected his dress and manners to conceal his desperation. He undertook numerous trips abroad to seek peace of mind. But he could not escape the fact that his life had become an aborted fairy tale and that fame had a Medusa's head.

Whenever he took pen in hand, it was to shield himself from his fears and to vent his anger. His fairy tales were the life he did not lead, what he wanted to say publicly but did not dare. His writings were majestic acts of self-affirmation and self-deception. They did indeed bring him fame, and he did indeed become one of the most famous writers of his day, as he had hoped; but they also prevented the world from knowing him. Even today the world-famous Hans Christian Andersen is really unknown.

The public image of Hans Christian Andersen still prevalent is one fed by the lies and myths he created. For instance, most of the photographs and portraits of Andersen reveal a man at ease with himself, a gentle, composed man often telling stories benevolently to children. He is always well dressed and appears in poses of perfect propriety. He is tall, gaunt, and not particularly handsome. Like the photographers and painters, most biographers have contributed to the deception of the public by emphasizing the quaint and gentle composure of the imaginative writer. They have associated him with the ugly duckling and sketched his life as the poor, gifted son of a cobbler who transformed himself into a successful, "beautiful" writer through his magical, innate talents: Hans Christian Andersen as fairy tale. His name has become virtually synonymous with the genre.

Yet to see him and his work as fairy tale is to do him an injustice. Andersen wrote over thirty plays, six novels, three autobiographies, and several travel books and volumes of poetry, aside from numerous essays, tales, and stories. He was respected and revered during his lifetime as an avant-garde writer. He was a gifted orator and performer, at home in all social classes, one of the most widely traveled men of letters in Europe, and personally acquainted with most of the prominent authors of the nineteenth century. These features of his life and work tend to be forgotten or neglected. The fame of the fairy tales has dwarfed both his total artistic achievement and his pathetic personal history.

One of the difficulties in writing about Andersen as Denmark's most versatile and famous writer is that he himself wrote three autobiographies, all of which tend to distort facts. His first attempt to document his life was *H. C. Andersens Levnedsbog 1805–1831*, written in 1832. It was not discovered until 1926, when it was published in Danish. His second endeavor, *Märchen meines Lebens ohne Dichtung*, completed in 1847 and revised in 1871, was translated into English as *The True Story of My Life*. The third account, *Mit Livs Eventyr* (1855), was translated as *The Fairy Tale of My Life*; this title indicates how Andersen continually sought to portray himself in all his autobiographical writings as a type of romantic hero, a poor swineherd turned into a prince. For instance, the 1847 version begins as follows:

> My life is a beautiful fairy tale, rich and glorious. If I had gone out into the world as a poor and lonely boy and had met a powerful fairy, and if she had said, "Choose your own course and goal in life, then I shall protect and lead you according to the development of your mind and the way things must reasonably happen in this world," then my destiny could not have been happier, nor more cleverly or better guided than the case has been. The story of my life will tell the world what it has told me: there is a loving God who directs everything for the best.

In 1805 there was a newly married couple, a cobbler and his wife, who lived in a small impoverished room in Odense. They loved each other dearly and deeply. He had just turned twenty-two, a remarkably talented man with a genuine poetic nature. She was somewhat older, ignorant about things concerning the world and life, but kind and generous. The man had recently become a guild master and had built his own shoemaker shop and wedding bed. For this purpose he had used the wooden frame on which the coffin of the dead Count Trampe had recently rested. The shreds of the black sheet, which were always to be found on the bed frame later, were souvenirs of this event. Then, on April 2, 1805, instead of the count's corpse, there was a live, crying child on this bed surrounded by flowers and candelabras. That was me, Hans Christian Andersen.

About the only thing true here is the date of Andersen's birth. The fact is that nobody knows exactly where Andersen was born. His parents had been married only two months before his birth and had no permanent residence. His father, Hans Andersen, who was born in 1782, became a journeyman shoemaker. In other words, he belonged to the lowest class of artisans and barely made enough to support himself and his family. He liked to read, take walks in the countryside, and make toys for his son. This was his talented or poetic side. Otherwise he was known to be a skeptical thinker, inclined to doubt the tenets of traditional Christianity. He died in 1816 after a desperate attempt to make money for the family by enlisting as a soldier in Napoleon's army.

Andersen's mother, Anne Marie Andersdatter, was born in 1775 and worked as a servant in various houses in Odense. In 1799 she gave birth to an illegitimate daughter. Later, after Andersen was born, she worked as a laundress and took other menial jobs. Far from being ignorant of the world, she knew real social conditions only too well. When Andersen refers to her as "ignorant," he means that she was illiterate, coarse, and superstitious. Such were Andersen's parents, and the noted Andersen biographer Elias Bredsdorff paints a more accurate picture of the writer's beginnings than the writer himself when he notes:

> Andersen's background was, from a social point of view, the lowest of the low: grinding poverty, slums, immorality and promiscuity. His grandmother was a pathological liar, his grandfather insane, his mother ended by becoming an alcoholic, his aunt ran a brothel in Copenhagen, and for years he was aware that somewhere a half-sister existed who might suddenly turn up and embarrass him in his new milieu—a thought which haunted his life and dreams.
>
> (*Hans Christian Andersen*, p. 16)

Thus Andersen's life was anything but a fairy tale. Though his parents doted on him, there was little they could offer him. Overly sensitive about his family's poverty and his own homely appearance, Andersen kept to himself. He had few friends and preferred to stay at home, where he would play with pictures, puppets, and dolls. By the time he was five, he was sent to school. His memories of his youth reveal a special fascination with the Odense jail and insane asylum, which were joined under a single roof. Given the history of insanity and immorality in his family, he feared going insane and being confined. At the same time he was also intrigued and attracted by the strange people in the jail and asylum. But more important than this attraction was his budding love for the theater.

Odense, a tiny city of eight thousand inhabitants, boasted a municipal theater that produced comic operas, operettas, and plays. When he was seven, his parents took Andersen to the theater, and a new, fantastic world exploded before his eyes: from this point on theater life came to represent a glorious realm of freedom from the misery of his life, and he hoped to become a great writer involved with the stage. At home, he began dressing up in costumes, acting out roles, and writing plays. As soon as he was able he read Shakespeare, and he gave recitals of his own plays to anyone he could attract. His mother became upset by

her son's theater mania, but her threats of punishment had no effect. And after the death of her husband in 1816, she was rarely at home to keep an eye on him. In fact she had become so poor that she sent her eleven-year-old son to work against his will. Engaged as an apprentice in a cloth mill, Andersen did not last long there. He could not bear the obscenity and rough treatment of the journeymen, and he left after he was ridiculed and manhandled during a recitation of songs for his fellow workers. His next job was in a tobacco factory, where he worked until his lungs became slightly damaged. His mother then had no choice but to allow him to remain at home, where he devoted himself once again to books and playacting.

In July 1818 Andersen's mother remarried. Her new husband was another journeyman cobbler, but the financial situation of the family improved. Andersen could now attend the local church school, where he was expected to forget theater and poetry and submit to rigorous religious training. Yet Andersen's obsession with the theater was stronger than the school's discipline. Upon his confirmation, in 1819, he was willing to risk anything for a chance to pursue his calling as an artist, although his mother tried to convince him to learn a trade. Finally, knowing how superstitious his mother was, Anderson persuaded her to visit a fortuneteller, who predicted that her son would achieve fame in Copenhagen. And in the fall of 1819 the fourteen-year-old Andersen set out for the city.

Copenhagen destroyed many of his illusions, and the period 1819–1822 was one of trial and hardship. At that time the capital was a relatively small port city of 120,000 inhabitants, and Danish society, dominated by the aristocracy and upper-middle classes, was highly stratified. Though there were increasing signs of liberalism and possibilities for social advancement as Denmark underwent a transition from late-feudal absolutism to a form of constitutional monarchy, the king and his close advisers played an enormous role in all decisions pertaining to government, economy, and the arts. Most of the leading writers of the day, such as Adam Oehlenschläger and Johan Ludvig Heiberg, were dependent on patronage. Almost all the major cultural institutions, such as the theater, ballet, opera, and symphony, benefited from royal subsidies and private contributions. It was practically impossible for a member of the lower classes to establish himself socially, for success did not require "genius" as much as manners, breeding, formal training, and connections. Andersen had none of these. Instead he was helped by the fact that he was naive and foolhardy, entirely unaware that he was pursuing the impossible.

Certainly he was not prepared for the Copenhagen he encountered in 1819. He arrived during vicious anti-Semitic riots that raged for more than ten days, and rented a tiny room in a poor district of the city. He then experienced a series of setbacks that almost caused him to return to Odense. Armed with a letter of introduction to a famous solo dancer at the Royal Theater, he made the first of numerous attempts to impress important people with his talent. During his first interview he took off his shoes to demonstrate how well he could dance. Given his awkwardness, this was a catastrophic sally, and he was obliged to leave as soon as he could find his shoes. Similar catastrophes followed; soon he began to feel that he would find neither employers nor patrons to back his artistic career. Yet Andersen's determination and unusual capacity for improvisation eventually did make an impression on various philanthropic gentlemen, who collected money for him to attend ballet school and later to take singing lessons. He even appeared in some small roles at the Royal Theater. Nevertheless, despite such training and experience, Andersen was never able to cut a gracious figure onstage; and the plays and poems that he began producing were either imitative or pretentious.

This pretentiousness was evident in the way he signed his first book, *Ungdoms-Forsøg*

(*Youthful Attempts*, 1822). He chose the nom de plume Villiam Christian Walter out of admiration for William Shakespeare and Sir Walter Scott, and he filled the book with stereotypes, stilted verse, and melodramatic scenes copied from his masters. Indeed, it became evident to all concerned (even to himself) that Andersen needed more formal schooling if he was to attain a measure of success as a writer or performer. Fortunately for him, the board of directors at the Royal Theater decided to offer him a three-year scholarship to attend a private school in Slagelse, a town fifty-six miles west of Copenhagen. Even more important was the choice of Jonas Collin, director of the board and a prominent legal administrator, as Andersen's prime adviser. A sober, highly intelligent, and sensitive man, Collin became Andersen's major benefactor and acted as his father for most of the writer's life. But Andersen had to endure five years of strict schooling before he was entirely accepted into the Collin home as an "adopted" son.

Although Andersen was seventeen when he entered the school at Slagelse, he had to be placed among the eleven-year-olds. This situation was humiliating for him, but he knew practically no Latin, Greek, geometry, geography, or history. Though he read voraciously, his grammar and style were faulty, and he remained an atrocious speller to the end of his life. Bothered by his deficiencies, Andersen pursued his studies with a vengeance. Despite his zeal, however, there were problems. The headmaster, Dr. Simon Meisling, was a moody, dissatisfied person who was apt to belittle the young man when he least expected it. For the next five years Andersen had to contend with Meisling's disparaging treatment in addition to the attempts of Meisling's wife to seduce him. Since he had few friends at school, he was often despondent, depending on letters and contacts from outside to encourage him in his studies. Andersen felt plagued by self-doubt and regarded the regimentation of school as stifling to a prospective writer with great imaginative powers. Meisling discouraged him from following his artistic leanings, and even Collin forbade him to write poetry for some time. Nevertheless, he was not to be deterred from pursuing his chosen destiny. In the spring of 1823 he wrote in a letter: "If anyone can become a poet [*Digter*] through the events of his childhood, then I will become one. Not a minor one, however, there are plenty of those. If I cannot become a great one, I shall strive to become a useful citizen in the community" (Bredsdorff, p. 54).

All or nothing—this was typical of Andersen. His use of the Danish word *Digter* is significant. Like the German term *Dichter*, it implies more than just "poet": it is often used to designate a great writer. And as Andersen's diary entries testify, he yearned to be nothing more and nothing less than a *Digter:*

What can become of me, and what shall I become? My strong imagination may now land me in an insane asylum. My turbulent feelings may turn me into a suicide. In early days, these two drives both united would have made me into a *Digter.* Oh Lord, are these really your ways here on earth?—Forgive me, Lord, for my shamelessness toward You, You who have done so unspeakably much good for me. Oh, forgive me, Lord, and continue to help me.

(20 September 1825)

Everything is guided by God. There is destiny. Man is free like the horse on a rocky island who can roam freely, but there are certain limits: it cannot go beyond them! You want the best for yourself by obtaining faith in yourself. So I seek my destiny, all bountiful God!—May the Lord arrange things so that good fortune accompanies me! If it is Your will that I become a *Digter,* You will not weaken my courage and rob me of my talents. My soul lives only for poetry. I believe to have felt Your hand as destiny has taken its course. Do not rob me of Your faith, my Lord, my Father, my one and only. Hear your weak child!

(27 September 1825)

It was not God who came to the rescue, though he would have liked to have believed this. Rather it was Jonas Collin, who interceded on Andersen's behalf whenever he had disputes with Meisling. By 1826, after the headmaster and Andersen had both been transferred to a school in Helsingör, it became clear to Collin that his sensitive ward could no longer endure Meisling's harshness. So he gave Andersen permission to move to Copenhagen to prepare for his final examinations, which he passed in 1828. The next year Andersen recorded another success when he took his university admission tests. However, he had no intention of attending the university, for he had already drawn attention to himself as writer. His second book, *Journey on Foot from Holmens Canal to the East Point of Amager*, written in imitation of E. T. A. Hoffmann, his literary idol at that time, was published in 1829; and his first play, *Love on St. Nicholas Tower*, was produced that same year at the Royal Theater. In 1830 a volume of poetry, *Digte (Poems)* appeared containing "You My Thought" ("Min Tankes Tanke ene Du er vorden"), which Edvard Grieg later set to music. Ten years after Andersen had arrived in Copenhagen, he began to be noticed by society.

From 1830 to 1835 Andersen sought to establish himself as one of the most promising writers, if not the most promising writer, in Denmark. He wrote plays, poems, travel books, and stories. He took trips outside Denmark to seek fresh impulses for his writing. In 1831 he journeyed to Germany, Bohemia, and Switzerland, and in each country he tried to advance his career by making the acquaintance of prominent people and leading writers of the time. In particular he was drawn to the German romantics Ludwig Tieck in Dresden and Adalbert von Chamisso in Berlin, who was the first translator of his poems into German. In 1833 Andersen received a two-year travel grant from King Friedrich VI, and he used it to visit the major cities of France, Italy, Switzerland, and Germany. In Paris he met Victor Hugo and Heinrich Heine. In Italy he spent most of his time with the sculptor Bertel Thorvaldsen, the writer Henrik Hertz, and other Scandinavian artists. During these trips he completed another volume of poetry and the long dramatic poem *Agnete and the Merman.* He also kept a personal diary in which he often complained about sickness and melancholy, and described people, cities, and landscapes as though he were writing for posterity.

When one reads Andersen's diaries and letters, it is evident that he felt most at home after he left Denmark. His constant journeys gave him a sense of freedom and an opportunity to mix with extraordinary and influential people. He rarely referred to his family background, and visited his mother only two or three times after leaving Odense. At the time of her death, in 1833, he was in Rome and wrote in his diary:

> A letter arrived from old Collin. My mother is dead, he reported. Thank God! These were my first words. Her sufferings, which I could not relieve, have now come to an end. But I cannot accustom myself to the thought that I am now so completely alone, without one single person who must love me because of blood ties!
>
> (16 December 1833)

These remarks reveal key features of narcissism and self-deception in Andersen's thinking. His diaries and letters show that he was inclined to pity himself, and it appears that his egoism prevented him from realizing a deep filial love and from experiencing either a fulfilling heterosexual or homosexual love. His chronic psychological problems stemmed largely from his incapacity to fulfill his sexual fantasies and erotic wishes, to assert himself as he wished to be understood. Andersen never married and never had sexual intercourse. For a long time literary historians and psychologists speculated that he was homosexual, but recent scholarship suggests that he was heterosexually inclined. The question of his sexual preference, however, is a side issue. He appears to have been an emotional

cripple who failed to satisfy his desires and needs in intimate relationships of any kind.

During the 1830's Andersen was attracted to three women: Riborg Voigt, the sister of a friend; Mathilde Örsted, the daughter of the prominent physicist H. C. Örsted; and Louise Collin, the youngest daughter of Jonas Collin. In all three instances he avoided making a firm proposal of marriage, because he feared commitment and was uncertain about his "manliness." His letters and diaries reveal that he felt socially and psychologically inferior to women. Lack of money, low social origins, ugliness, repressed hatred of his mother, the need for privacy—these were some of the factors that drove him to reject himself before he could be rejected by women. There was a strong element of masochism in his relations with women, which also manifested itself in his relations with men. But despite his suffering, Andersen enjoyed the "romantic" role of the rejected lover, a role that was to figure prominently in almost all of his novels and many of his tales.

Aside from the tentative relationships with Riborg, Mathilde, and Louise, Andersen developed a close friendship with Henriette (Jette) Wulff, with whom he shared his most intimate thoughts. A forthright, intelligent woman and champion of revolutionary causes, Jette Wulff was the daughter of the Danish admiral Peter Wulff, who had made Andersen a welcome guest in his home during the 1820's. A semi-invalid, Jette Wulff was one of the few women who did not threaten him sexually. Andersen took her criticism and concern to heart because he felt she supported him in his endeavors and rarely flattered him without good cause. If not for her tragic death off the coast of America in 1853, Andersen might have come to the United States. It had been her dream to settle in America, and she had encouraged her friend, who often made disparaging remarks about Denmark, to think about emigration.

The only other woman who figured prominently in Andersen's life as an "amour" was the famous singer Jenny Lind, who was known as the "Swedish Nightingale." He met her in 1840 and actually courted her for a short period, until it became apparent that she was not interested in marriage, only in a romantic affair. For Andersen, who shunned illicit relationships and brothels, an amorous relationship could be sanctified only through marriage. That he repressed his sexual drive so severely may have led to psychosomatic disturbances and account for his extraordinary vanity. Andersen sought outlets for his repressed sexuality in masturbation (as he records in his journals) and in performing his works (perhaps subconsciously an act of public masturbation). Moreover, his writings were part of a complex process of sublimation. His creative efforts became a necessity; what he referred to as his calling was his compulsive and therapeutic need to contend with neurosis. The more Andersen denied himself, his social background, and his sexual drives, the more he felt called upon by "God" to express his "genius."

As was customary in those days, Andersen formed close male friendships that were marked by homoeroticism. He studied with boys, was looked after by men, traveled exclusively with male peers, moved in male-ordained social circles, and explored realms open primarily to men. It is thus no wonder that Andersen placed men on a pedestal and glorified the male condition in a traditional, chauvinist manner. For instance, at the beginning of his novel *O. T.* (1836) he states:

> There is a condition of happiness which no poet has yet properly sung, which no lady-reader, let her be ever so amiable, has experienced or ever will experience in this world. This is a condition of happiness which alone belongs to the male sex, and even then alone to the elect. . . .
>
> Happy moment, which no woman, let her be ever so good, so beautiful, or intellectual, can experience—that of becoming a student, or, to describe it by a more usual term, the passing of the first examination!
>
> The cadet who becomes an officer, the scholar who becomes an academic burgher, the apprentice who becomes a journeyman, all know, in a greater or less degree, this loosening of the wings, this bounding over the limits of maturity into the lists of philosophy.

Whereas he feared women and gave voice to his fear by rejecting them or getting them to reject him, he felt more free to express his love for men—albeit a masochistic love—in letters and in conversation. His lifelong friendship with Edvard Collin is perhaps the best example of the kind of amorous relationship he had with men. The oldest son of Jonas Collin, somewhat younger than Andersen, Edvard Collin became the legal administrator who managed Andersen's literary and business affairs. Though Collin, like Jette Wulff, was critical of Andersen's melodramatic, egocentric tendencies and fierce ambition, he remained a devoted friend and adviser.

At one time he hurt Andersen deeply by refusing to address him with the familiar "you," or *du* in Danish, and he reprimanded him often because of the writer's excessive public displays—which went against the Calvinist grain of this prudent Danish bureaucrat. But Andersen desired and actually needed to establish a master-servant relationship with Collin. Generally speaking, Andersen placed himself in Collin's control by seeking his approval for everything he wrote and putting his business affairs in his hands. Whenever Collin became severe or critical, Andersen would play the role of the spurned servant-lover, feeling comfortable and productive in this situation. He re-created it time and again in other male relationships. Whether in quest of male or female love, Andersen generally adopted the obsequious attitude that suited his neurotic temperament. It was through portraying this dubious social and psychological situation in his writings that he achieved a measure of stability.

By the early 1830's, Andersen had drawn attention to himself in Copenhagen as a gifted writer, but not until 1835 did he achieve a major breakthrough and taste fame. On returning from Italy he published his novel *Improvisatoren* (*The Improvisatore,* 1835), the first Danish experimental novel of social realism. At the same time he collected five stories for children in his first volume of fairy tales, and with each successive volume his reputation spread throughout Europe. Actually fame came to Andersen more slowly in Denmark than in Germany, England, and France, and he continually complained about the devastating attacks on his works by leading Danish writers. Sören Kierkegaard wrote an entire book ridiculing *The Improvisatore,* and other writers were no less cruel, especially in their reviews of his sentimental plays. Andersen, however, was not singled out for unusual treatment; it had become fashionable for Danish critics to write with a barbed pen. Moreover, he had his fair share of a good press. After publishing the novels *O.T.* and *Kun en Spillemand* (*Only a Fiddler,* 1837), two additional collections of fairy tales, and several plays, Andersen had no cause to complain, especially after King Friedrich VI granted him an annual poet's pension of 400 rixdollars for the rest of his life, a sum augmented at different times later in his career. Thus by 1838 Andersen could feel financially secure, and he was recognized by Danish royalty as one of the kingdom's finest artists.

Unfortunately, he never felt emotionally secure. In Copenhagen his vanity was so well known that he became an easy target for criticism, some of it justified, some of it malicious. Andersen was like a child who cannot control his urge to be the center of attraction. He continually baffled himself and others because he could not restrain his urge to act out his eccentricities in public. For example, he seized every opportunity to recite his poems and stories. Once, in Rome, he intruded on a dinner party in a small restaurant and insisted on reading "The Ugly Duckling" to a group of

people he barely knew. When they politely suggested that he might enjoy himself more by sightseeing than by reading stories in a restaurant, he answered that he would prefer to entertain them in this way. Then without further ado he pulled a manuscript from his pocket and read.

This does not mean he was always overbearing. On the contrary, he tried to conceal his ambitious and competitive nature with his will to please and his desire to perform. Georg Brandes, the renowned Danish literary critic and a close friend of Andersen's, remarked astutely of the writer:

> Indeed, he did become a great man. But he did not become a man. There was not the slightest glimmer of manliness in the soul of this child, son of the common people. Much later he developed self-confidence. He developed it from the praise he received abroad but never manly vigor and courage. He lacked an aggressive spirit entirely, nor did he have the means to take the offensive. Never in his life did it occur to him to attack a powerful person for a good cause. He himself had been a poor devil much too long and needed love, kindness, goodwill, and especially recognition. If he used a weapon, then it was for self-defense and always in poetic form: his pen had a blunted point.
>
> (*Skandinavische Persönlichkeiten,*
> pp. 104–105)

Heinrich Teschner recorded Heinrich Heine's perceptive appraisal of Andersen's character:

> He seemed to me like a tailor. This is the way he really looks. He is a haggard man with a hollow, sunken face, and his demeanor betrays an anxious, devout type of behavior that kings love. This is also why they give Andersen such a brilliant reception. He is the perfect representation of all poets just the way kings want them to be.

Andersen as child and tailor. This childlike "tailor" was to impress the Western world with his talents from 1840 to 1875, and it should be stressed that he was like a *wander-*

ing tailor who put his skills to use making fine ornaments and clothes for "emperors." Characteristic of Andersen is the fact that even though he eventually could have afforded to establish a permanent residence in Copenhagen, he never did so. He traveled extensively every year and generally left Denmark whenever he could. Soon after the success of his play *Mulatten* (*The Mulatto*) in 1840, he embarked for Germany and Italy on his first train ride, and he wrote enthusiastically about the railroad, which added a new dimension to his view of people and the countryside. He knew he was always welcome in foreign countries, where he was wined, dined, and feted by the aristocracy, and received with honor in the best of the bourgeois homes and literary salons. In Denmark he was also given generous invitations to visit the estates of friends. Of course it was expected that Andersen would perform for his hosts, display his genius; and he did, often without their asking.

Andersen's rate of artistic production was astounding. Between 1840 and 1850 he finished several plays, wrote the travel book *En Digters Bazar* (*A Poet's Bazaar*, 1842), published poetry, and edited a new volume of fairy tales practically every year. The revolutionary upheavals of 1848–1850 were reflected in some of his stories, but Andersen, who basically supported the cause of enlightened monarchy, avoided direct involvement in political affairs. By 1850 he himself had become a kind of Danish institution.

During the 1850's and 1860's Andersen concentrated more and more on his fairy tales, which were no longer written exclusively for children. He also published the second version of his autobiography and made a trip to Zurich, where he met Richard Wagner. Andersen appreciated Wagner's imaginative use of folklore and was one of the first writers to recognize the composer's radical attempt to transform opera into a total artwork for all classes. By 1860 Andersen's annual pension had been raised to one thousand rixdollars, and he could afford extended journeys, such as

the one he took to France, Spain, and North Africa, recorded in travel books such as *In Spain* (1863). When the war between Denmark and Prussia broke out in 1864, he was deeply torn, especially since he had numerous friends in Germany, where he had always been prized as a great *Dichter.* In fact the king of Prussia had presented him with his first royal medal in 1846. However, Andersen's loyalties were clearly with Denmark; he remained in Copenhagen and devoted himself to writing new plays and fairy tales. In 1866, after the war, he resumed his travels and took the opportunity to visit Paris, where he received a special decoration. In 1869 he was honored with the Commander Cross in Copenhagen.

Sensing he was coming to the end of his career, Andersen wrote another autobiographical novel, *Lykke-Peer* (*Lucky Peter*), in 1870. Even in old age the desire to transform his youth into a fairy tale did not abate, and he remained as active as ever during the last five years of his life. By the summer of 1875 it became apparent that Andersen had cancer of the liver, yet he did not give up hope that a miracle would bring about a complete recovery. Indeed, after recuperating from an attack that had kept him bedridden, he made plans for another trip abroad. But his hopes for recovery were illusory, and he died on 4 August 1875.

WORKS

In the English-speaking world, the critical evaluation and general reception of Andersen's creative works have been confined to his fairy tales. Yet, as we have seen, such exclusive focus on the tales has contributed to a misunderstanding of the man and a neglect of his full literary achievement. To grasp the total significance of this remarkable man— "the tailor as romantic"—he must be viewed in the context of Danish culture and the changing literary scene in Europe.

Denmark experienced a major cultural shift at the beginning of the nineteenth century, from the universality of classicism to the romantic cult of genius and individualism. In part this was brought about by the lectures of Henrik Steffens. He introduced the German romantic writers and philosophers to the Danish intelligentsia, in particular to Oehlenschläger and N. F. S. Grundtvig, who in turn forged new paths in the arts and education for further generations of Danish writers.

An impressionable and voracious reader, Andersen benefited from the exciting cultural changes. He was particularly fond of German fairy-tale writers such as Tieck, Novalis, Hoffmann, Friedrich de La Motte-Fouqué, and Chamisso. In addition, he was attracted to the writings of Jean Paul Richter, Friedrich von Schiller, and Johann Wolfgang von Goethe, and was influenced by Shakespeare, Scott, and Washington Irving. But most important for his development was the peculiar form assumed by the Danish romantic movement, which was, as W. Glyn Jones notes,

> accompanied by what is known as the Aladdin motif, after the idea which Oehlenschläger expresses in his play *Aladdin*. This deals with the theory that certain people are chosen by nature, or God, or the gods, to achieve greatness, and that nothing can succeed in stopping them, however weak and ill-suited they may otherwise seem. . . . The twin themes of former national greatness and of the possibility of being chosen to be great, despite all appearances, assumed a special significance for Denmark after 1814.
>
> (*Denmark*, pp. 66–67)

It was Oehlenschläger who signaled the coming of the golden age of Danish literature with his poem *The Golden Horns* (1802), written after a famous encounter with Steffens. This work celebrates Denmark's pagan past and recounts how the gods took back their great gift to the Danes because greed had made them unworthy of their heritage. This national ballad, Oehlenschläger's other

poems, and his drama *Aladdin* (1805) instilled a new sense of hope and confidence in Danish social leaders, who had lost political and economic power during the Napoleonic wars. In order to regain national pride after 1814, the aristocracy and the prosperous middle classes were more willing than ever to encourage and support creative and scientific experimentation: tiny Denmark was to show its greatness.

Aside from Oehlenschläger, numerous other talented writers and artists began to make names for themselves. Grundtvig produced significant works in the fields of theology, history, politics, and education. B. S. Ingemann glorified the Danish Middle Ages in his epic poems and novels. H. C. Örsted became one of the founders of electromagnetics and espoused a philosophy of the immortality of the soul that was to influence Andersen. Thorvaldsen became one of the leading sculptors in Europe. C. W. Eckersberg established himself as one of the finest romantic painters in Denmark, and Steen Steensen Blicher had a major impact on the theater as a writer of poetic tragedies. Not only did Andersen absorb and learn from the works of these Danish writers, artists, and intellectuals, but he also came in contact with them: they served as both inspiration and point of departure for his writing.

Of all the Danish writers, the great dramatist and literary critic Johan Ludvig Heiberg played an immense role in Andersen's development. Heiberg was the pioneer of vaudeville in Danish theater. More important, the caustic criticism and sharp wit of the *Kjøbenhavns flyvende Post* (Copenhagen Flying Post), the literary journal he edited, elevated him to the position of cultural arbiter in Copenhagen. Some of Andersen's early poems and stories were printed by Heiberg, who first encouraged and later demoralized him. With his modern ironic sensibility and training in Hegelian dialectics, Heiberg influenced and judged almost all the prominent young Danish intellectuals of his time: Kierkegaard, who began writing his great philosophical works in the 1830's and 1840's; Hertz, who became one of the leading dramatists of this period; and Hans Peter Holst, who was active as a novelist, poet, and dramatist. These three writers and others competed with Andersen for Denmark's laurels and patronage. In an era of growing individualism, when the middle classes were seeking more power in central and northern Europe; when industrialism and urbanization were bringing rapid changes in cultural life and social mobility; when revolutions were changing the maps, mentalities, and hegemonies of European nations; when Denmark was forced to open its tight-knit society slightly to outside influences, it is not surprising that Andersen felt there was also a possibility for a talented young man to establish his claim to genius. The challenge was there. Andersen was imaginative, enterprising, and ingratiating.

Andersen's versatility as a writer needs to be addressed before we examine his fairy tales and consider how and why they have so completely overshadowed his other works in the twentieth century. Here we must bear in mind that Andersen desired to make a name for himself first as a dramatist, novelist, poet, and travel writer, not as a writer of fairy tales, and especially not as a writer for children. Although from the beginning of his career he worked with fairy-tale motifs, and saw his own life as a type of fairy tale, short narrative form was not at first his favorite means of embodying his ideas and dreams.

Andersen's greatest love was unquestionably the theater. Ever since his first visit to the Odense theater in 1812, he had dreamed of performing and writing plays. In the course of his life he composed over thirty dramatic works, and twenty-five of his original pieces, consisting of vaudevilles, opera librettos, romantic dramas, and comedies, were given more than a thousand performances. Today these works are largely forgotten, both in Denmark and abroad; but in Scandinavian theater history Andersen is significant for introducing

many foreign styles, such as the French opéra comique and the Austrian folk play, into the Danish theater. Moreover, his experience with the theater influenced the way he shaped many of his stories and fairy tales, for it was through an appreciation of the stage that he developed his keen senses of observation and drama.

Frederick Marker states that Andersen

belonged among the younger exponents of romanticism but at the same time points ahead toward the realism which eventually triumphed in the 1870's. The production history of his plays provides a microcosm of the exotic, historical, idyllic, and topical elements that were the popular components of the colorful, romantic stage picture.

(*Hans Christian Andersen and the Romantic Theater*, p. 31)

Though it was through the theater that Andersen wished to claim ultimate recognition for his genius, the theater occasioned his most disastrous failures and the most bitter attacks against him. In turn, these caused him to react vociferously against the entire Danish nation, albeit in letters, journals, and private conversations, rarely in public.

Andersen's early notable plays were in the style of vaudeville, which he, along with Heiberg, helped make respectable in Denmark. Most of these light dramas feature plots about love and intrigue, often written in verse and incorporating well-known songs and music. Andersen tended to blend folk figures with situations typical of serious drama to poke fun at the foibles of high and low characters. His first production, *Love on St. Nicholas Tower*, parodied the romantic tragedy of the times by having a tailor and a watchman speak high verse and fight over the hand of a sweet maid of the lower classes. Though Andersen became less satirical in his vaudevilles over the years, most of his other successful plays, such as *The Invisible Man on Sprogø* (1839) and *The Bird in the Pear Tree* (1842), as well as his adaptations of Johann Nestroy's and Ferdinand Raimund's Austrian folk plays, follow the same pattern of parodying social customs of Danes involved in a scandal or delicate love affair.

During the 1830's and 1840's Andersen also wrote librettos. His themes were often taken from romantic novels such as *The Festival at Kenilworth* (1836), based on a work by Scott. When he adapted his own dramatic poem *Agnete and the Merman* for the opera in 1843, it was a monumental flop, and the negative reaction by the public prompted a typically violent response by Andersen, who was in Paris at the time and wrote the following to Jette Wulff:

> This evening I learned—not from my friends since I didn't receive a letter, but from Berling's paper—that *Agnete* was performed and hissed off the stage. That had to happen. At the next performance there will be booing! But my work doesn't deserve this. It is the creation of a poet!—May my eyes never lay rest on this house that has only eyes for my mistakes, but no heart for that gift that enables me to create great things! I hate whatever hates me. I curse whatever curses me! As always, a cold draft of wind comes from Denmark that will turn me into stone abroad! They spit at me, trample me in mud! However, I'm a poet by nature, and God has granted them only one like me. But when I die, I shall ask the Lord never again to grant them such a poet!
>
> (29 April 1843)

The hurt and conceit expressed here were reiterated time and again in Andersen's letters and journals. Andersen was unwilling to recognize that he was capable of writing poor works, and he expected to be flattered as he flattered others. Though he repeatedly asserted that he hated Denmark and the cultivated Danish society, he slavishly sought to shine in his countrymen's eyes. Nor did he accept defeat. In 1846 he composed the libretto for J. P. E. Hartmann's *Liden Kirsten* (*Little Christina*, 1846), based on the true story of a

princess who became a nun, and this "comeback" was a resounding success.

His most renowned play, however, was not an opera but a melodrama, *The Mulatto,* which showed the strong influence of French romantic drama, especially that of Hugo. Based on the story *Les épaves* (The Waifs, 1838), by Fanny Reybaud, the drama concerns a young, sophisticated mulatto named Horatio who writes poetry and runs his own plantation in Martinique. He rescues Cecille, the ward of a white plantation owner named La Rebellière, and La Rebellière's wife. Both women are captivated by Horatio's noble nature, and their esteem for the mulatto infuriates La Rebellière. So he contrives to have Horatio declared a slave and sold at auction. But Cecille comes of age at this point, declares her independence, and rescues Horatio by offering to marry him. The mulatto is thus vindicated in the eyes of society. As in the best of Andersen's plays and other works, this compelling social drama emphasizes his favorite fairy-tale themes, or what might be called his Aladdin-and-Cinderella syndrome: the gifted pariah, a neglected genius, shunned and persecuted by society, manages to overcome adversity and shine in the eyes of the world. This theme of emancipation appealed to the rising middle and lower classes in Denmark and reflected the dreams of glory shared by the people in this tiny nation as a whole. To this extent, Andersen often acted as the spokesman of Denmark, even though he was criticized for being inept.

The attacks on Andersen as a playwright ultimately drove him to assume a pseudonym in the 1840's. By producing his plays pseudonymously he hoped to avoid the vitriolic barbs of his critics. From 1845 until his death in 1875 he wrote for the Royal Theater and the Casino Theater, where vaudevilles were staged. It was during this period that he turned more toward fairy-tale dramas and comedies. For example, he wrote *The Blossom of Happiness* (1845), about a forester who wishes to become a great person, such as a prince or a poet. This wish is granted by an elf, but the forester learns that the prince and the poet lead extremely difficult lives because of the responsibilities of their positions. So he is overjoyed when given the chance to return to his former, humble occupation. Another play, *Pearls and Gold* (1849), was an adaptation of Raimund's *Der Diamant des Geisterkönigs* (The Diamond of the King of Spirits, 1824). Here a young man is promised a statue of diamonds if he can find a young woman who has never lied. But once he finds her, he no longer wants to have the statue: she alone is worth more to him than all the riches in the world.

Andersen failed as a dramatist but, to his credit, he did stimulate many of his contemporaries to employ folk motifs, vernacular idioms, and fantasy in their plays. He may have had an influence even on Henrik Ibsen, whom he met. Whether this is the case or not, Andersen was clearly a forerunner in the Scandinavian movement that produced both Ibsen and August Strindberg. Throughout his life he occupied himself with the fantastic "other world" of the stage, but his plays never matched the artistry and luster of his fairy tales.

Nor did his novels, although he was at first recognized as one of Denmark's most promising novelists. When *The Improvisatore* appeared, it was an immediate success at home and highly praised thereafter in Germany and England. The impetus for the novel was Andersen's trip to Italy, where the action takes place. Antonio, a poor orphan with an amazingly poetic nature, has the good fortune to come under the patronage of a rich patrician family in Rome. He is sent to a Jesuit school, where he excels as a student and makes the acquaintance of the handsome and wild Bernardo, who leaves the school to become an officer. In the meantime, despite the severe discipline of the school and the criticism of his benefactors, Antonio develops his artistic skill as an improvisator. After a reunion with Bernardo, he makes the acquaintance of Annunziata, a great Spanish-Italian singer. Both Bernardo and Antonio fall in love with her, and naturally they fight a duel over her. After the first shot Antonio thinks mistakenly that he has killed his friend. He flees to the south of Italy, joins a band of robbers, leaves the robbers, and continues to have many adventures until he establishes a name for himself as an improvisator in the theater. Eventually he learns that Bernardo is alive, and he can return to the patrician society of Rome as a success. Indeed he even marries an ethereal young woman named Maria, whom he had once believed to be blind.

This autobiographical romance is based on the structure of the German *Künstlerroman*, in which a young man rebels against society to develop his skills independently as an artist. The artist remains a rebel, and often he makes his way to a type of paradise or dies in the attempt. This is the pattern in Tieck's *Franz Sternbalds Wanderungen* (*Franz Sternbald's Wanderings*, 1798), Novalis' *Heinrich von Ofterdingen* (1802), and Hoffmann's *Der goldene Topf* (*The Golden Pot*, 1814). Andersen broke with the general romantic pattern somewhat by having his artist return to the fold of society, where he obliges his benefactors to recognize his particular greatness as artist. Obviously, Andersen's work was a thinly veiled depiction of his own life and problems. In fact, he had once been criticized by Heiberg for being too much of a lyrical improvisator, and there is no doubt but that Andersen was clearly bent on responding to Heiberg by showing the positive aspects of versatility and improvisation. Though he impressed his contemporary readers by blending romance and adventure with surrealistic descriptions of the Italian landscape, the melodrama and bombastic language make the book difficult to read today. Like all his longer prose narratives, the novel is pretentious and derivative. By endeavoring to resemble the great German novelists he admired, Andersen became nothing but their pale shadow.

However, he did have success in his own day, and this success moved him to write other romances. He followed *The Improvisatore* with *O.T.* and *Only a Fiddler*, both set in Denmark. Again he mixed obvious autobiographical elements with fictional projections to illustrate his philosophy of genius. Andersen was intrigued by the character of the moody Byronic hero and thought of himself in these terms. In *O.T.*, his protagonist, Otto Thostrup, a brooding, mysterious character, has his initials tattooed on his shoulder. They stand for his name and for the Odense jail, in which his mother had been imprisoned. Otto and a twin sister were born in the Odense jail. When his mother died, he was adopted by a rich baron while his unknown sister was left to drift among the dregs of society. Haunted by this past, Otto seeks to clear his mother's name and find his sister. All this is accomplished with the help of his close friend Wilhelm. In the end Otto is no longer sullen and strange, and he looks forward to marriage with one of Wilhelm's sisters.

In *Only a Fiddler* the ending is not so happy. Here Andersen depicts the tragicomic lives of a poor boy named Christian and a rich Jewish girl named Naomi. They are drawn to each other as children but are separated by events. Naomi is raised in Copenhagen, becomes spoiled, snubs Christian, runs away with a Polish riding master, and eventually marries a French count, with whom she is unhappy. Christian does not lead such an adventurous life. Though a gifted musician, he plods along, never receiving the help he needs to realize his genius. He dies as a village musician in humble circumstances.

In both novels Andersen portrays the mores and manners of Danish society and shows how young men of genius from the lower classes must overcome obstacles to gain recognition. Though Christian never realizes his genius, it is clear that he is gifted, and that if he were helped in the right way by the upper classes he might achieve greatness and happiness. Otto's case in *O.T.* is different because he is aided by influential people, and success is guaranteed.

The social mobility and immobility of talented people intrigued Andersen, and he turned to this theme again in *De to Baronesser* (*The Two Baronesses*, 1848). This novel, filled with one incredible event after another, demonstrates that honest Hermann, the grandson of an eccentric old baroness who has worked her way up from the lower classes, deserves to marry a poor girl who has braved misfortune to keep her virtue. Both young people display the diligence necessary for success; theirs is a marriage of noble minds.

In later years Andersen attempted to write a philosophical novel about genius triumphing over agnosticism and despair. In *To Be or Not to Be?* (1857) Niels Bryde, the moody protagonist, succumbs to the temptation of evolutionary and materialist theories based on the ideas of the German philosophers David Friedrich Strauss and Ludwig Feuerbach. He loses his Christian faith, only to recover it when he realizes there is an immortality of the soul that manifests itself in every particle of life.

In *Lucky Peter*, Andersen's last novel, he returns to the structure of the *Künstlerroman* to reflect on his own life and genius. Again we have the rise to fame of the chosen son of common people. Peter, the poor but talented son of a coachman, is born in the same house as Felix, a rich merchant's son, and their lives are contrasted. Felix amounts to nothing more than a mediocre but rich merchant; Peter achieves greatness because he pursues his destiny with unerring zeal. When he is only a boy, his musical talent is recognized and he is given schooling that enables him to enjoy a meteoric career. Eventually he writes an opera appropriately entitled *Aladdin*, and after receiving a thunderous ovation for singing the title role at the premiere, he collapses and dies. This melodramatic novel appears to be based on Wilhelm Wackenroder's story "Der Tonkünstler Joseph Berglinger" ("The Musical Artist Joseph Berglinger," 1796), in which the hero dies at the greatest moment of his career. Andersen tries to enhance this familiar success story with colorful portraits of Danish social life, but the novel suffers from a contrived plot and didactic commentary. The more he repeats the same plot and ideas, the more trite and unconvincing they become.

Andersen was never really able to master long narrative prose. He was overly conscious of his models in Tieck, Jean Paul, Goethe, Hoffmann, and Scott, and he lacked their humor, subtlety of thought, and variety of theme. At times there are remarkable passages in his novels, especially passages describing country life and customs, but they are generally undercut by an insistent moralistic tone. Only when he forgets that he must follow a prescribed form to justify his life and ideas or to match the work of a famous novelist is he capable of introducing extraordinary chapters that come alive through closeness of observation and penetrating insights.

Andersen's poetry and travel books are similarly uneven. His initial book of poetry, *Digte,* was followed quickly by *Phantasier og Skizzer (Fantasies and Sketches)* in 1831. The first contains humorous poems for the most part; the second, melancholy love poems and occasional verse. Andersen could write all types of poetry with great facility. He composed most of his plays and librettos in verse and continued to publish volumes of poetry throughout his life, but he failed to break new ground as a poet because of his derivative styles. His best poems by far are the personal love lyrics; these are deeply felt expressions of longing and despair. In his other lyrical endeavors, he covers a broad range of topics, from folklore and national history to subjects pertaining to children. But though he always satisfies formal requirements of meter and rhythm, he brings nothing new to the themes and forms he employs.

Andersen was at his best when he could experiment with personal experience in his own idiom. This is evident in his first travel book, *Journey on Foot from Holmens Canal to the East Point of Amager,* a humorous and fantastic depiction of a journey, similar to Hoffmann's *The Golden Pot.* Andersen weaves together dream elements, literary references to Tieck, Jean Paul, A. W. Iffland, August Kotzebue, Chamisso, and Goethe, and vivid depictions of landscape to create an intoxicating effect. In his other travel books, such as *A Poet's Bazaar, In Sweden* (1851), *In Spain* (1863), and *A Visit in Portugal* (1866), Andersen mixes impressions, anecdotes, observations, stories, and literary topics with descriptions of the countries and peoples he visited. In addition he includes comments on the changing times. As he was perhaps the most widely traveled author in the nineteenth century, Andersen's notes on customs, portraits of prominent people, and depictions of his own experiences were illuminating for readers of his own time and are still fascinating today. In particular, *In Sweden* contains a highly significant chapter entitled "Poetry's California," in which he argues that literature must keep pace with modern technological developments. If the future belongs to the sciences, then literature must adjust and reflect the new inventions in order to point out the miraculous aspects of life:

> The sunlight of science must penetrate the poet; he must perceive truth and harmony in very tiny things as well as in the immensely great with a clear eye. This perception will purify and enrich his understanding and imagination and show him new forms that will make his words even more alive. Even individual discoveries will inspire us to new heights. . . . Our world is the time of discoveries—poetry, too, has its California.

Certainly Andersen thought of himself as a poetic harbinger of truth and wisdom, a prophet whose versatility should be acclaimed and respected. He sought to stamp his times with his plays, novels, and travel books, and to a certain extent he succeeded. But he made his lasting contribution to art in a form in which he least expected to achieve immortality.

HANS CHRISTIAN ANDERSEN

THE TALES

Although Andersen knew he was a simple "tailor" of humble origin, he pretended to be a "romantic" fairy-tale hero, a misunderstood genius or Aladdin. He suspected, however, that audiences and critics saw him differently and might even despise him. The more he tried to dismiss his suspicions and fears, the more he was troubled by nervous disorders and psychic disturbances. To contend with and perhaps rationalize his existence, he eventually made use of Örsted's ideas in *The Soul in Nature* (1850) and combined them with his own animistic belief in Christianity. An early mentor as well as substitute father for Andersen, Örsted argues that the laws of nature are the thoughts of God, and, as the spirit of nature becomes projected, reality assumes the form of miracle. Such views were readily accepted and adopted by Andersen, who felt that if life was divinely miraculous, then God also protected his "elect" and provided help when they needed it. Power is located in the hands of God, and only before Him does one have to bow. In truth, however, Andersen submitted more to a temporal, social system based on aristocratic-bourgeois hegemony than to God, and he had to rationalize the social relations of domination so that he could live with himself. As we know, he tried to deny his class origins and repress his rebellious feelings in order to gain money, comfort, praise, and freedom to exercise his occupation as writer. And as aspiring *Digter* he endeavored both to imitate great poets and to find his own voice and style to depict the social contradictions he had difficulty resolving for himself. Such a situation meant a life of self-doubt and anxiety.

It was not, therefore, from joy and exuberance that Andersen wrote his fairy tales; it was more from a sense of profound suffering, disappointment, chagrin, and resentment. Obviously he also derived great pleasure in composing these stories, and he retained a naive appreciation of his immediate surroundings and experiences that served to inspire his writing. Yet he was fundamentally driven to write most of his tales to quell the anguish he felt as he made his daily compromises to become a great *Digter*.

Altogether he wrote 156 tales. The first collection, *Eventyr fortalte for Børn (Fairy Tales Told for Children*, 1835), consisted of "The Tinder Box," "The Princess and the Pea," "Little Claus and Big Claus," "Little Ida's Flowers," and "Thumbelina." For the most part these were adaptations of folk tales expressly designed for a young audience. In 1837 he added "The Little Mermaid," "The Naughty Boy," "The Traveling Companion," and "The Emperor's New Clothes," and in each subsequent edition until 1843 he dedicated the tales to children. Thereafter the title of his fairy-tale anthologies was changed to *Nye Eventyr (New Fairy Tales)*, a more accurate indication of the direction Andersen was taking: he no longer wrote exclusively for young audiences (if he ever had), and many of his compositions even broke away from the fairy-tale genre.

Andersen wrote fables, allegories, anecdotes, legends, satires, farces, philosophical commentaries, and didactic stories. In general he developed and revitalized the German genre of the *Kunstmärchen*, or literary as opposed to oral tales, which had become popular in Europe by the beginning of the nineteenth century. Such various writers as Tieck, Wackenroder, Novalis, Clemens Brentano, Achim von Arnim, Joseph von Eichendorff, La Motte-Fouqué, Chamisso, Hoffmann, and Wilhelm Hauff had reworked folklore and introduced fantastic events and characters, together with complex ideas and subtle styles, into their tales. Their compositions were conceived to meet the tastes and needs of a middle-class reading public, whereas the oral folk tales catered to the taste of the lower classes and peasantry. Stimulated by the German romantics, Andersen gradually developed his own peculiar themes, a refreshing, humorous style, and lively colloquial dialogue. Many critics in his day frowned on his idiosyncratic use of Danish as vulgar, but it was just this unconventional colloquial quality that made his appeal unique. Moreover, like the German romantics, Andersen demonstrated how fantastic literature could be devastatingly realistic in its symbolic allusion to social contradictions.

In his autobiography, Andersen remarks that

the fairy tales became reading matter for children and adults. . . . They found open doors and open hearts in Denmark. Everyone read them. Then I eliminated the phrase "told for children" and followed this with three books of "new tales," which I created myself, and which were highly praised. I could not have wished for anything better. I felt anxious, afraid that I could not justify so much honor in my time. My heart was invigorated by the rays of sunshine. I gained courage and was greatly motivated to develop myself more in this direction and to pay more attention to the rich source from which I had to create. There is definitely progress to be found when one follows the order in which I wrote my fairy tales. One can notice my ideas taking clearer shape, a greater restraint in the use of my medium, and, if I may say, more healthy qualities and a natural freshness.

(*Märchen meines Lebens ohne Dichtung*, pp. 145–146)

It is difficult to know exactly what the "healthy qualities" in his tales are. If for Andersen "healthy" meant greater control over disquieting feelings, masterly sublimation, greater adaptation to frustrating conditions, and artful self-deception, then the tales do reflect "healthy qualities." Yet these same qualities conceal often-overlooked "unhealthy" ideas about social conditions and personal problems that were woven into his narratives. Too many readers regard Andersen's works unhistorically and universalize the symbolic formations of his tales as though the author and his social context were insignificant. They lose sight of the artist, his struggles, and his contribution to the evolution of the fairy-

tale genre. In Andersen's case, a critical, historical approach to his tales raises some interesting questions about their contradictory features and their reception in English-speaking countries.

Elias Bredsdorff has noted that only thirty of Andersen's 156 tales have been reprinted—in many translations, some accurate, many not. The tales that have been printed and circulated most in the United States and Great Britain are: "The Tinder Box," "Little Claus and Big Claus," "The Princess and the Pea," "Little Ida's Flowers," "Thumbelina," "The Traveling Companion" (1835); "The Little Mermaid," "The Emperor's New Clothes" (1837); "The Steadfast Tin Soldier," "The Wild Swans" (1838); "The Garden of Eden," "The Flying Trunk," "The Storks" (1839); "Willie Winkie," "The Swineherd," "The Buckwheat" (1841); "The Nightingale," "The Top and the Ball," "The Ugly Duckling" (1843); "The Fir Tree," "The Snow Queen" (1844); "The Darning Needle," "The Elf Hill," "The Red Shoes," "The Shepherdess and the Chimney Sweep," "The Little Match Girl" (1845); "The Shadow" (1847); "The Old House," "The Happy Family," "The Shirt Collar" (1848). Given the fact that these are the "classic" Andersen tales in English, it is worth commenting on their general features before evaluating other tales.

Although Andersen's tales have suffered from the clumsy hands of censors and poor translators up through the 1940's, two fairly reliable editions of his complete short prose narratives have made his entire canon accessible to the English-reading public, one translated by Jean Hersholt, the other by Erik Christian Haugaard. Despite these fine translations, it must be admitted that the full flavor of Andersen's unusual use of the Danish language is difficult to capture. Folk rhythms and colloquialisms, childlike humor and startling puns, topical and historical references, local color and cultural associations—all these have given him a special reception in Denmark, where he is considered distinctively

Danish, the spokesman of the common people, the representative of a vigorous nineteenth-century cultural force. But he is also one of the key figures in the development of the literary fairy tale in the world at large, primarily as the genre has been cultivated for children in the West.

Andersen's tales were among the first considered suitable and proper enough for the nurseries and households of respectable nineteenth-century middle-class families. It must be remembered that in both Great Britain and the United States the fairy tale had been stamped as subversive and suspect from the eighteenth century to the middle of the nineteenth century. It was not regarded as moral and instructive enough for the emerging bourgeois sensibility, which stressed utilitarian values, obedience, sexual abstinence, and Christian virtues. This is not to say that fairy tales for children were banned. Rather there was a limited market for them, since most educators, religious writers, and publishers waged a war against the pagan, superstitious, and irrational features of folk and fairy tales. Such a campaign made middle-class families wary of purchasing the tales. Yet by the 1840's there was a successful counter-campaign in England and America. First the romantics, and later such major Victorian writers as John Ruskin, Charles Dickens, William Makepeace Thackeray, George Macdonald, and Lewis Carroll, wrote fantastic tales for children and spoke out in defense of this imaginative literature.

It was exactly at this point that Andersen himself, influenced by the German romantics, Dickens, and the Danish romantic movement, began to insert himself into the debate. His participation in the literary discourse on fairy tales was not a deliberate critical act, but rather the outcome of his naive interest and predilection. Andersen had always been captivated by fairy tales as stories and dramas, and in 1834–1835 he began to concoct a recipe for the fairy tales that were to bear his imprint: he rewrote folk tales, added a dose of Christian moralism mixed with bourgeois individualism, stirred the ingredients with folk humor, and ladled everything out in a vernacular style. His aim was to please and, at times, to provoke children and adults of all classes.

If we look at those tales that made Andersen famous in England and America (and are still the most popular), it is striking that they are the ones written primarily from 1835 to 1848, the tales Andersen composed mainly for children. These thirty tales are serious and colorful variations on a few personal themes. The major ideas concern the recognition of artistic genius, nobility of mind versus nobility of blood, the exposure of class injustice and hypocrisy, the master-servant relationship, the immortality of the soul, and the omnipotence and omnipresence of God. Almost all the tales touched on Andersen's private desires and functioned psychologically to provide him with secret revenge or to justify his dubious actions to himself. The focus in this necessarily limited discussion will be on the hidden, ambivalent features of "The Tinder Box," "The Princess and the Pea," "The Emperor's New Clothes," "The Nightingale," "The Ugly Duckling," and "The Red Shoes."

"The Tinder Box" reveals how closely Andersen at first adhered to the patterns of the folk-tale tradition when he began writing fairy tales. Characteristic in a number of the magic folk tales (*Zaubermärchen*) is the rise of an adventurous hero who depends on his own talents and gifts from strangers to attain wealth and happiness. Generally speaking the protagonist is downtrodden, oppressed, the youngest member of a family, or a small person; but he is always clever and knows how to make use of his abilities. Once the protagonist is assigned a task or cast into the world, he usually has three encounters with gift-bearing creatures (giants, dwarfs, animals, fairies) and it appears that he will triumph easily. At the peak of his first rise in fortunes, however, there is a sudden fall, or peripetia, and the hero must call on friends and his own resources to renew his rise to power and riches.

HANS CHRISTIAN ANDERSEN

As oral stories, the magic folk tales were transcribed in simple, blunt language by Jacob and Wilhelm Grimm and other collectors at the beginning of the nineteenth century. Description and characterization were kept to a minimum. The paratactic sentences were built up with careful transitions so that clearly defined binary oppositions of good and evil could be immediately observed. From the outset the reader or listener of a folk tale knows that the narrative perspective is partial to the hero, who is bound to succeed; the question is always how. The magic of the oral tale depends not so much on the miraculous in the tale itself as on the ingenuity of the narrator in using the arsenal of folk motifs to vary well-known schemes so that they will touch on the dreams and needs of the audience.

In writing "The Tinderbox," Andersen employs the folk motif of the disgruntled soldier who, after years of loyal service, is discharged without due compensation by an ungrateful king. This lowly soldier seeks revenge and wins the hand of a princess. Andersen transforms this plot into a tale that mirrored the wishes of many maltreated, smart young men of the lower and middle classes. The rags-to-riches theme is central to his witty narrative about a young soldier, who by chance meets a disgusting witch whose lower lip hangs all the way down to her chest. He agrees to help her haul money and a tinderbox from a hole in the ground but then chops off her head when she will not tell him why she wants the tinderbox. He goes to town, takes quarters at an inn, lives sumptuously and merrily. He attends the theater, goes for drives in the king's park, and gives money to the poor because he remembers what it felt like not to have a penny in his pocket. When his "luck" runs out, however, he falls as quickly as he had risen in social esteem, and his fair-weather friends abandon him. A type of Aladdin figure, he accidentally discovers the magic of the tinderbox and the power of the three dogs who can provide him with anything he needs. Here Andersen subconsciously concocts a sociopolitical formula that was the keystone of bourgeois progress and success in the nineteenth century: use talents to acquire money and perhaps a wife, establish a system of continual recapitalization (tinderbox and three dogs) to guarantee income and power, and employ money and power to maintain social and political hegemony. The soldier is justified in his use of power and money because he is *essentially* better than anyone else—chosen to rule. The king and queen are dethroned, and the soldier rises to assume control of society through the application of his innate talents and good fortune.

The ironic tone of Andersen's writing, the melodious rhythms, the terse, delightful descriptions, and the dramatic sequences transform an oral folk tale into a colorful literary fairy tale that glimmers with hope. Instead of "once upon a time," Andersen begins the tale on an unusual note: "A soldier came marching down the road: . . . right! Left . . . right! He had a pack on his back and a sword at his side. He had been in the war and he was on his way home."[1] The witch admires his sword and knapsack and, convinced that he is a *real* soldier, willingly gives him all the money he wants. On a psychological level, the killing of the witch followed by the dethronement of the king and queen and the soldier's triumph as "true prince" are the sublimated artistic means Andersen uses to gain revenge on his mother, benefactors, and critics. All this is done with humor throughout the narrative, and there is a delightful picture of Andersen's wish fulfillment at the end of the tale once the king and queen are sent flying into the air:

> The royal guards got frightened; and the people began to shout: "Little soldier, you shall be our king and marry the princess."
>
> The soldier rode in the king's golden carriage; and the three dogs danced in front of it and barked: "Hurrah!"
>
> The little boys whistled and the royal guards

1. All quotations from the fairy tales are from the Haugaard translation.

881

presented arms. The princess came out of her copper castle and became queen, which she liked very much. The wedding feast lasted a week; and the three dogs sat at the table and made eyes at everyone.

Andersen must have derived immense personal satisfaction in writing this "radical" tale of role reversals, for underneath the humor is dead seriousness, an urge to express his social hostility and to prove himself at all costs. On another level, the tale can be read by children (and adults, of course) as a tale of the sexual and social maturation of a young person in a "dog-eat-dog" world. The soldier has a knapsack (mind, talents) and sword (power, phallus), and in confrontation with the outer world he learns not to waste his sexual and mental powers but to control and direct them to gain happiness. The psychological impulse of the tale is connected to Andersen's obvious criticism of the hypocrisy and injustice of the aristocracy. Throughout the tale, he depicts their artificiality, which is supplanted by the "true nobility" of his young, lower-class soldier.

"The Princess and the Pea" is also a tale about "true nobility," but told with tongue in cheek. A princess proves to be genuine when she feels a pea placed under twenty mattresses. This pea is then exhibited in the royal museum after her happy marriage with the prince, who had been seeking an authentic princess. Obviously Andersen was poking fun at the curious and ridiculous measures taken by the nobility to establish the value of bloodlines. On the other hand, he makes an argument for sensitivity as the decisive factor in determining the authenticity of royalty.

Andersen never tired of glorifying the sensitive nature of an elite class of people. This sensitivity is spelled out in different ways in other tales of 1835, such as "Little Ida's Flowers," "Thumbelina," and "The Traveling Companion." In all these stories "small" or oppressed people cultivate their special talents and struggle to realize their goals despite the forces of adversity. Ida retains and fulfills her dreams of flowers by resisting a crass professor's vicious attacks. Thumbelina survives many hazardous adventures to marry the king of the angels. Johannes, a poor orphan, promises to be good so that God will protect him, and indeed his charitable deeds lead to a marriage with a princess. All the gifted but disadvantaged characters, who are God-fearing, come into their own in Andersen's tales. In contrast, the rich and privileged are either ridiculed or exposed as insensitive, cruel, and unjust.

Perhaps the most amusing and famous of Andersen's tales about "false nobility," a story that has been adapted for film, television, and the radio many times, is "The Emperor's New Clothes." Here a king is literally robbed and denuded in front of our eyes because he wasted his time and money on beautiful new clothes instead of carrying out his responsibilities. Andersen quickly sets the tone of the narrative by taking his readers into his confidence and relating how two swindlers plan to trick the king and the parasites at court. We laugh at the foolish king as the plot develops, and then Andersen aptly introduces the courageous small child who cries: "But he doesn't have anything on!" By having a child speak the truth, Andersen emphasizes a learning process that relies on common sense and a perception of the contradictions in society. Seeing is depicted in this tale as the courage of one's convictions, and this depiction may be a major reason for the narrative's appeal for young readers, who are too often told "to see with your eyes and not with your mouth." For Andersen, sight must become insight, which in turn demands action.

Yet Andersen cannot be considered an anti-authoritarian writer, a champion of emancipatory children's literature. The courageous acts of his heroes are often undercut by their self-denial, humility, and willingness to sacrifice themselves in the service of a benevolent king. One of the classic examples of this type of tale is "The Little Mermaid," which harks back to the folk stories of a water urchin desirous of obtaining a soul so she can marry the human being she loves. Andersen also knew Goethe's "Die neue Melusine" (1819) and Fouqué's *Undine* (1811), stories of the ennobled aspirations of pagan water sprites. However, his tale about the self-sacrificing mermaid is distinctly different from the narratives by Goethe and Fouqué, who, perhaps out of their own sense of guilt for the tendency of upper-class men to seduce and abandon lower-class women, punished their noblemen for forgetting their Christian manners.

Andersen's perspective focuses on the torture and suffering that a member of the "lower species" must undergo to gain a soul. Characteristically he allows the mermaid to rise out of the water and move in the air of royal circles only after her tongue is removed and her tail transformed into legs, described as "sword-like" when she walks or dances. Voiceless and tortured, the mermaid serves a prince who never fully appreciates her worth. Twice she saves his life. The second time is most significant: instead of killing him to regain her identity and rejoin her sisters and grandmother, the mermaid forfeits her own life and becomes an ethereal figure blessed by God. If she does good deeds for the next three hundred years, she will be endowed with an immortal soul. Her divine mission consists of flying through homes of human beings as an invisible spirit. If she finds a good child who makes his parents happy and deserves their love, her sentence will be shortened. A naughty and mean child can lengthen the three hundred years she must serve in God's name.

But the question remains whether or not the mermaid is really acting in God's name. Her falling in love with royalty and all her subsequent actions involve self-denial and rationalization. The mermaid's sense of herself becomes divided and diminished because she is attracted to a class of people who will never accept her on her own terms. To join her supposed superiors she must practically slit her

own throat, and though she realizes that she can never truthfully express who she is and what she wants, she is unwilling to return to her own species. Thus she must somehow justify her existence to herself through abstinence and self-abnegation—a behavior preached by the bourgeoisie of the time and certainly not characteristically practiced by the nobility and upper classes.

Paradoxically Andersen seems to be arguing that true virtue and self-realization can be obtained through self-denial. The artistic conception of this paradox emanated from his own experience as a gangly, lower-class youngster who sought to cultivate himself through constant compromise and subjugation to external laws. By becoming voiceless, walking with legs like knives, and denying one's own needs, one will allegedly gain divine recognition for one's essential genius, a metaphor for the educated nod of approval from the dominant class. Nobility is indeed of the mind, but it also needs connections with nobility of the blood to succeed in the real world.

Andersen consistently defended notions of self-abandonment and self-deprivation in the name of aristocratic-bourgeois laws and standards designed to make members of the lower classes into tractable, obedient citizens. Such conformist thinking stemmed from the obsequious, "tailor" side of his personality. As eager as he was for his genius to shine, he was just as eager to please, and just as ready to humiliate himself before wealthy, powerful patrons. Both "The Nightingale" and "The Ugly Duckling," two of Andersen's most finely wrought tales, reveal how he sought to master his dilemma by turning it into a type of success story.

"The Nightingale" can be considered a metaphorical treatise about art, genius, and the role of the artist. It involves a series of transformations in power relations and service. First, the Chinese emperor, a benevolent patriarch, requests that a nightingale be brought to his court because he has heard so much about the bird's priceless art. When the chief courtier finds the nightingale, he exclaims: "I had not imagined it would look like that. It looks so common! I think it has lost its color from shyness and out of embarrassment at seeing so many noble people at one time." Because the common-looking bird (an obvious reference to Andersen himself) possesses an inimitable artistic genius, he is engaged to serve the emperor. Yet when the emperor is given a jeweled mechanical bird that never tires of singing, the nightingale is neglected. So he escapes from the artificial court society and returns to the forest. Later, when the mechanical bird breaks down and the emperor is on the verge of dying, the nightingale returns to serve the autocrat loyally as a natural genius with innate healing powers:

> "And my song shall make you happy and make you thoughtful. I shall sing not only of those who are happy but also of those who suffer. I shall sing of the good and of the evil that happen around you, and yet are hidden from you. For a little songbird flies far. I visit the poor fishermen's cottages and the peasant's hut, far away from your palace and your court. I love your heart more than your crown, and I feel that the crown has a fragrance of something holy about it. I will come! I will sing for you!"
>
> (p. 215)

Though Andersen intended to show in this tale how the health of an emperor—that is, the spirit of an empire—is dependent on true art, he also made it clear that art *wants* to be the devoted servant of an autocrat. Such was Andersen's private resolution of the artist's dilemma. He proclaimed the cult of genius and yet relegated the artist to the humble role of servant because he feared the loss of patronage and social prestige.

In "The Ugly Duckling" genius again assumes an admirable shape, but unlike the nightingale, the swan cannot fly on its own. This tale has generally been interpreted as a parable of Andersen's own success story, be-cause the naturally gifted underdog survives a period of "ugliness" to reveal its innate beauty. But more attention should be placed on Andersen's thesis about the servility of genius. The clumsy young swan, who is chased by coarse, lower-class animals from the hen-yard, must experience various arduous ordeals before he realizes his essential greatness. This self-realization is ambivalent, for just before he perceives his true nature he is ready to kill himself:

> I shall fly over to them, those royal birds! And they can hack me to death because I, who am so ugly, dare to approach them! What difference does it make? It is better to be killed by them than to be bitten by the other ducks, and pecked by the hens, and kicked by the girl who tends the henyard; or to suffer through the winter.
>
> (pp. 223–224)

These are not the words of an independent genius who can stand on his own. On the contrary, Andersen conveys his secret disdain for the masses and his longing to be accepted by court society. The young swan does not return "home" but lands in a beautiful garden where he is admired by children and adults. Beauty for the swan is measured by the "royal" swans and by the well-behaved children and people in the garden. In the end the swan's growth and flight become an apology for Andersen's escapist and elitist thinking.

Still, the tale has positive psychological features. As a fairy tale for children, the narrative suggests that each child has the potential to liberate himself from oedipal ties, to overcome social obstacles, to gain recognition. The transformation of the ugly duckling into a beautiful swan can thus be interpreted as the confirmation of dreams experienced by numerous children, regardless of class. Yet the swan, like the nightingale, becomes a tame bird—Andersen, who loved to travel and wander like a bird, constantly used this metaphor for himself. It is also interesting that, unlike most folk tales in which the hero becomes independent and omnipotent, Andersen's bird-like geniuses soar high only to return to earth.

Although docile and kind on the surface, Andersen was often merciless in his tales, especially when it came to curbing the pride of rebellious figures who need to be taught a lesson. In "The Red Shoes," Karen, a poor orphan, mistakenly believes she is adopted by a generous old woman because she wears red shoes (a symbol of vanity and sin). Although Karen tries to abandon the shoes, she cannot resist their allure. So she must be taken to task by a stern angel, who pronounces sentence on her:

> You shall dance . . . dance in your red shoes until you become pale and thin. Dance till the skin on your face turns yellow and clings to your bones as if you were a skeleton. Dance you shall from door to door, and when you pass a house where proud and vain children live, there you shall knock on the door so that they will see you and fear your fate.
>
> (p. 292)

The only way Karen can overcome the angel's curse is by requesting the municipal executioner to cut off her feet. Thereafter she does charitable work for the local minister. Upon her death, Karen's soul "flew on a sunbeam up to God." This ghastly tale—reminiscent of the gory, pedagogical best-seller of Andersen's time and later, the German Heinrich Hoffmann's *Struwwelpeter* (1845)—is a detailed description of the punishment that awaits anyone who dares to oppose authority. Andersen stressed that acceptance into God's kingdom depends on obedience, service, and self-restraint. In actuality he spoke not for God but for the standards of discipline and punishment instituted in Danish society. Pedagogically, the themes of Andersen's fairy tales for children comply with the norms and values of traditional Christian education. Needless to say, his classical status today is based on his acceptance of norms that still prevail in the realms of children's literature.

Yet Andersen's fame in English-speaking countries does not rest solely on his fairy tales for children. Such an intriguing, subtle story as "The Shadow" reveals Andersen as a significant precursor of surrealist and existentialist literature. As many critics have noted, this haunting narrative is highly autobiographical; it stems from the humiliation Andersen suffered when Edvard Collin adamantly rejected his proposal to use the familiar "you" (du) in their discourse—and there was more than one such rejection. By retaining the formal "you" (De), Collin was undoubtedly asserting his class superiority, and this was meant to remind Andersen of the social distance that separated them. Though they had come to regard each other as brothers during their youth, Collin held firmly to propriety. He controlled a certain portion of Andersen's life—something that the writer actually desired, but also resented.

In "The Shadow," Andersen clearly sought to avenge himself through his tale about a philosopher's shadow that separates itself from its owner and becomes immensely rich and successful. When it becomes a person in its own right and returns to visit the scholar, the shadow/Andersen puts the philosopher/Collin in his place by refusing to use the familiar du, and then he explains that it was poetry that made a human being out of him. Not only does the shadow become humanlike, but he gains power over other people through his ability to see evil. Ironically, the shadow's sinister talents allow him to improve his fortunes, whereas the philosopher, who can only write about the beautiful and the good, becomes poor and neglected. Eventually the philosopher is obliged to travel with his former shadow—the shadow now as master, and the master as shadow. When the shadow deceives a princess to win her hand in marriage, the philosopher threatens to reveal the truth about him. The crafty shadow, however, convinces the princess that the philosopher himself is a deranged shadow, and she decides to have him killed to end his misery.

The reversal of fortunes and power relations is not a process of liberation but one of revenge. Andersen's wish fulfillment was directed not only at Collin but at all his superiors, whether they were benefactors or enemies. Yet to see "The Shadow" merely as the product of a personal grudge is to do it an injustice. Andersen ingeniously reworks the folk motif of Chamisso's *Peter Schlemihls wundersame Geschichte* (1814), in which a young man sells his shadow to the devil to become rich; and he also explores the Hegelian notion of master-servant in a fascinating way. The shadow-servant, who is closer to the material conditions of life than the intellectual owner of his services, is able to take advantage of what he sees and experiences—the basic conditions of social life—to overthrow his master; whereas the master, who has been able to experience reality only through the mediation of his shadow, is too idealistic to defend himself.

From a philosophical viewpoint Andersen questions the idea of autonomous identity; from a psychological viewpoint he studies the manifestations of a split personality, a version of the doppelgänger motif common in nineteenth-century literature. The ironic reversal of roles appears at first to be a harmless joke, but Andersen convincingly depicts how the subconscious can subdue both conscience and consciousness. The final effect is a chilling picture of those dark and irrational undercurrents in human experience that continue to surface no matter how people try to repress them.

Written in 1847, "The Shadow" shows Andersen at the height of his powers as a fairytale writer. By now mature in his art, he no longer confined himself to writing stories just for children, and he exploited all types of sources and material for his tales, not just folklore. The length and style of the tales vary considerably. Some are a few pages in length, others are over thirty pages. Some are overly didactic and sentimental; others are ironic, complex, and bitter.

In "A Drop of Water" (1848) Andersen creates a philosophical allegory based on social Darwinism to convey a sardonic view of the cutthroat life and class struggles in Copenhagen. "The Story of a Mother" (1848) is a slightly veiled rendition of his mother's life and the trials and tribulations she endured. "There Is a Difference" (1855) concerns a haughty apple tree and a common dandelion, Andersen's point being that both are children of beauty blessed by God. "Everything in Its Right Place" (1853) and "The Pixy at the Grocer's" (1853) are political fantasy narratives that illustrate the influence of the 1848–1850 revolutionary years on Andersen. In the first story he depicts the rise to power of diligent, hardworking peasants and middle-class people over the aristocracy. In the other he pokes fun at a pixy who cannot make up his mind whether to fight for his ideals or to make a compromise with a grocer so he can have bread and security. Such is Andersen's metaphorical comment on people as reluctant revolutionaries.

Lovely (1859) is a brilliant satire on sentimental love and the false appreciation of art. Here a young sculptor is deceived by the outward appearance of a beautiful woman, marries her, and leads a banal life until her death frees him to pursue true art. *On the Last Day* (1852) is a short religious tract about the immortality of the soul. In *The Two Maidens* (1861) Andersen plays superbly with a change in the Danish language concerning gender to comment on the prospects of female emancipation. "The Puppeteer" (1861) is a fantasy story in which the dream of a puppeteer becomes a nightmare when he must contend with conceited actors in a theater instead of with his dolls.

In "The Dung Beetle" (1861) Andersen uses the fable form to write a humorous self-parody. A conceited beetle rises from a dung heap, travels around the world, and mistakenly believes he is honored everywhere without realizing how foolish and pompous he is. "In the Duckyard" (1861) is also a satirical

886

parable, but here Andersen is concerned with attacking the pettiness and arrogance of Danish critics.

His more positive ideas about literature are elaborated in the philosophical piece "The Muse of the Twentieth Century" (1861), in which he argues that poetry can benefit from the inventions of the modern industrial world—ideas that correspond to his essay "Poetry's California." Such optimism is modified in "The Snail and the Rosebush" (1861), a Socratic dialogue in which cynicism is matched against creative naiveté. In an amusing realistic anecdote, "Auntie" (1866), Andersen portrays an eccentric spinster obsessed with the theater, and he uses the occasion to reflect on the fanatic nature of theatergoers and practitioners.

"The Rags" (1868) is another of Andersen's amusing allegorical dialogues; two rags, one Norwegian and one Danish, assert the virtues of their respective cultures. When they are made into paper, their claims to greatness are gently mocked. The Norwegian rag becomes a piece of stationery on which a young Norwegian writes a love letter to a Danish girl, while the Danish rag becomes a sheet of paper on which a Danish poet composes an ode in praise of the loveliness and strength of Norway. "The Cripple" (1872), one of Andersen's final commentaries on art, is a fairy tale within a fairy tale about the social and moral value of the genre. A bedridden cripple named Hans reads tales to his parents, who reject them as worthless. Gradually, however, the adults learn to broaden their horizons and appreciate life through the stories. Hans himself makes a miraculous recovery because of them. Aided by the book of tales and the patronage of the rich family that has given it to him, he makes his way through life as one of Andersen's typical Aladdin figures.

The foregoing summary of Andersen's late and neglected tales can only indicate the broad spectrum of his interests. Many of these stories and others fall flat because they are obvious diatribes or homilies, blunt or too

quaint. But the best fuse the tensions of his personal experience with folklore and literary motifs to create vivid symbolic narratives that can be appreciated and interpreted in manifold ways. Two examples of his late period worth discussing in more detail are "The Ice Maiden" (1861) and "The Gardener and His Master" (1871); they represent major tendencies in his work as a whole.

"The Ice Maiden" comes from a legend that inspired Johann Peter Hebel to write *Unverhofftes Wiedersehen* (The Unanticipated Reencounter, 1811) and E. T. A. Hoffmann to create *Die Bergwerke zu Falun* (*The Mines of Falun*, 1819). Based on an actual event, the original story concerns a man who disappears on his wedding day and is found petrified in stone many years later. Hebel retold the story as a short, vividly realistic anecdote. Hoffmann expanded and transformed it into a mysterious, romantic fairy tale about a young man who must decide whether he will serve the queen of crystals in the underworld—which represents erotic and seductive art—or whether he will marry the wholesome daughter of a miner—who represents solid and virtuous middle-class life. Torn between two worlds, the young man ultimately disappears and dies in the mines. Many years later he is found and reunited with his wife in death. This theme is also touched on by Tieck in *Der Runenberg* (1802), and since Andersen was drawn to the German romantics, it is no wonder that he, too, was captivated by this story.

Composed in fifteen chapters, "The Ice Maiden" is one of Andersen's longer tales directed at both children and adults. The setting is Switzerland, which Andersen had recently visited. His hero is a young, talented orphan named Rudy who escapes the clutches of the "Ice Maiden" after she kills his mother. But she threatens to catch him too:

Mine is the power! . . . I crush anything that comes within my grasp and never let it go! A lovely boy was stolen from me. I had kissed him but not so hard that he died from it. Now he is again among human beings. He herds goats in the mountains. Upward, ever upward, he climbs, away from everyone else, but not from me. He is mine and I claim him.

(p. 739)

While the Ice Maiden pursues Rudy single-mindedly, he pursues his destiny and becomes the most skilled hunter and mountain climber in the region. Moreover, his noble character and perseverance enable him to win the hand of Babette, the daughter of a rich miller. On the day before their wedding, however, Rudy drowns while trying to retrieve a rowboat that has drifted from the island where he and Babette have been spending a quiet afternoon. The Ice Maiden was waiting for him and pulled him under. Babette, who had previously had a warning vision of their married life and of a sin committed against Rudy and God, is relieved by his death since it will prevent her from committing this sin. She spends the rest of her life alone, and Andersen ends his bittersweet tale by describing her situation as follows: "The snow on the mountainside has a rose luster, and so does the heart who believes that 'God wills the best for us all.' But few are so fortunate as Babette, who had it revealed to her in a dream."

Unlike the romantics, Andersen is not concerned with the problem of art and the artist in this story. Nor does he argue that society is too philistine and destructive for the creative artist, who must either devote himself to art or die. Andersen takes a more conservative position. He portrays the struggles of a poor, gifted boy who prospers because he is receptive to the natural wonders of divine creation. Such was Andersen's customary self-depiction in fictional form. Genius can be found in the lower classes, and given the proper conditions, it can flourish. Rudy's "nobility" is glorified, but Andersen also added a melodramatic ending that reflected his attitude toward unobtainable women, unrequited love, and Christian salvation.

Through careful description of the Swiss lo-cale and humorous sketches of the miller's household, Andersen transforms the common events and everyday routine of country people into a miraculous adventure story. Despite the unhappy ending, Andersen sought to convince his readers that everyone is actually fortunate because God's intentions are good. The religious and utopian elements of his thinking endow the tale with its powerful social appeal. Miracles can occur. The rise from rags to riches in accord with God's will is possible. Even though evil lurks in the world in the form of the Ice Maiden, spiritual happiness cannot be denied if one is true to one's God-given gifts.

This was Andersen's optimistic outlook. Yet he was also somewhat skeptical as to whether true genius could receive its just reward or be entirely happy, especially in Denmark. In one of his most scintillatingly critical tales, "The Gardener and His Master," written toward the end of his life, this skepticism is given full expression—as usual in a succinct, brilliantly ambivalent manner. The plot is familiar in its broad outlines. A haughty aristocrat possesses an excellent, humble gardener named Larsen, who tends his estate outside of Copenhagen. But the master never trusts the advice of the gardener, nor does he appreciate what his servant produces. He and his wife believe that the fruit and flowers grown by other gardeners are better. When they constantly discover, to their chagrin, that their very own gardener's work is considered the best by the noble families in the region, they hope he will not think too much of himself. Then Andersen comments:

He didn't; but the fame was a spur, he wanted to be one of the best gardeners in the country. Every year he tried to improve some of the vegetables and fruits, and often he was successful. It was not always appreciated. He would be told that the pears and apples were good but not as good as the ones last year. The melons were excellent but not quite up to the standard of the first ones he had grown.

(p. 1018)

The gardener must constantly prove himself, and one of his great achievements is his use of an area to plant "all the typical common plants of Denmark, gathered from forests and fields," which flourish because of his nursing care and devotion. So, in the end, the owners of the castle must be proud of the gardener because the whole world beat the drums for his success: "But they weren't really proud of it. They felt that they were the owners and that they could dismiss Larsen if they wanted to. They didn't, for they were decent people, and there are lots of their kind, which is fortunate for the Larsens."

In other words, Andersen himself had been fortunate, or, at least this was the way he ironically viewed his career at the end of his life. Yet there is something pathetic about the story. The gardener Larsen is obviously the storyteller Andersen, and the garden with all its produce is the collection of literary works he cultivated and improved throughout his life. The owners of the garden are Andersen's patrons and may be associated with the Danish royalty, the Collin family, and other upper-class readers in Denmark. We must remember that the Collin family and other aristocrats never came to recognize Andersen as *Digter* but thought of him as a fine, gifted popular writer. Andersen, whose vanity was unquenchable, petulantly complained that he was unappreciated in Denmark although other European countries recognized his genius. Such treatment at home, whether real or imagined, he symbolized in this tale.

The reference to the "common plants" that the gardener cultivates pertains to the folklore he adapted and enriched so that it would bloom aesthetically on Danish soil. Andersen boasts that he, the gardener, has made Denmark famous; pictures are taken of this garden and circulated throughout the world. Yet the gardener works within the confines of servitude and patronage, and the voice of the narrator Andersen, even though ironic, rationalizes the humiliating ways in which his masters treat Larsen: they are "decent" peo-ple. But we must wonder—and the tension of the narrative compels us to do so—why, if the gardener is superb and brilliant, he does not rebel and quit his job. Why does the gardener suffer such humiliation and domination?

Andersen pondered these questions time and again and presented them in different symbolic forms, as though he hoped his private problems as a "common" artist blessed with genius might be resolved through his different approaches. The result is an immense, rich canon of fairy tales that reflects the social situation of art and the artist as well as social injustices in the nineteenth century. Andersen tried desperately to give his life the form and content of a fairy tale, precisely because he was a troubled, lonely, and highly neurotic artist who sublimated in literary creation his failure to fulfill his wishes and dreams in reality. His literary fame rests on this failure, for what he was unable to achieve for himself he created for millions of readers, young and old, with the hope that their lives might be different from his. Ironically, to read the fairy tales of Andersen today and gain hope means that we must understand the despair of the writer, that we no longer neglect the disquieting features in his life and work.

Selected Bibliography

INDIVIDUAL WORKS

Note: In all instances place of publication is Copenhagen.

AUTOBIOGRAPHY
H. C. Andersens Levnedsbog, 1805–1831. 1832.
Märchen meines Lebens ohne Dichtung (The True Story of My Life). 1847.
Mit Livs Eventyr (The Fairy Tale of My Life). 1855.

DRAMA
Ungdoms-Forsøg (Youthful Attempts). 1822. Includes prose pieces.
Kjaerlighed paa Nicolai Taarn (Love on St. Nicholas Tower). 1829.

Den Unsynglige paa Sprogø (The Invisible Man on Sprogø). 1839.

Mulatten (The Mulatto). 1840.

Fugelen i Paeretraeet (The Bird in the Pear Tree). 1842.

Lykkens Blomst (The Blossom of Happiness). 1845.

Meer end Perler og Guld (Pearls and Gold). 1849.

LIBRETTOS

Festen paa Kenilworth (The Festival at Kenilworth). 1836.

Agnete og Havmanden (Agnete and the Merman). 1843. First published in 1833 as a dramatic poem.

Liden Kirsten (Little Christina). 1846.

POETRY

Digte (Poems). 1830.

Phantasier og Skizzer (Fantasies and Sketches). 1831.

NOVELS

Improvisatoren (The Improvisatore). 1835.

O.T. 1836.

Kun en Spillemand (Only a Fiddler). 1837.

De to Baronesser (The Two Baronesses). 1848.

At være eller ikke være (To Be or Not To Be?). 1857.

Lykke-Peer (Lucky Peter). 1870.

STORIES

Eventyr fortalte for Børn (Fairy Tales Told for Children). 1835.

Billedbog uden Billeder (Picture Book Without Pictures). 1839.

"Den grimme Aelling" ("The Ugly Duckling"). 1843.

Nye Eventyr (New Fairy Tales). 1843.

"Vanddrabben" ("A Drop of Water"). 1848.

"Historien om en Toder" ("The Story of a Mother"). 1848.

Paa den yderste Dag (On the Last Day). 1852.

"Alt paa sin rette Plads!" ("Everything in Its Right Place!"). 1853.

"Nissen has Spekhokeren" (The Pixy at the Grocer's"). 1853.

"Der er Forskjel" ("There Is a Difference"). 1855.

Deilig (Lovely). 1859.

To Jomfruer (The Two Maidens). 1861.

"Marionetspilleren" ("The Puppeteer"). 1861.

"Karnbassen" ("The Dung Beetle"). 1861.

"I Andegaarden" ("In the Duckyard") 1861.

"Det nye aarhundredes Musa" ("The Muse of the Twentieth Century"). 1861.

"Snglen og Rosenhaekken" ("The Snail and the Rosebush"). 1861.

"Isjomfruen" ("The Ice Maiden"). 1861.

"Moster" ("Auntie"). 1866.

"Laserne" ("The Rags"). 1868.

"Garneren og Herskabet" ("The Gardener and His Master"). 1871.

"Kroblingen" ("The Cripple"). 1872.

TRAVEL

Fodrejse fra Holmens Kanal til Østpynten of Amager i aarene 1828 og 1829 (Journey on Foot from Holmens Canal to the East Point of Amager). 1829.

En Digters Bazar (A Poet's Bazaar). 1842.

I Sverige (In Sweden). 1851.

I Spanien (In Spain). 1863.

Et besøg i Portugal (A Visit in Portugal). 1868.

TRANSLATIONS

Andersen's Works. 10 vols. Boston, 1869–1871. Author's edition.

The Andersen-Scudder Letters. Edited and translated by Waldemar Westergaard. Introduced by Jean Hersholt. Essay by Helge Topsoi-Jensen. Berkeley, Calif., 1949.

The Complete Fairy Tales and Stories. Translated by Erik Christian Haugaard. New York, 1974.

The Complete Stories of Hans Christian Andersen. Translated by Jean Hersholt. 3 vols. New York, 1949.

The Fairy Tale of My Life. Translated by W. Glyn Jones. New York, 1954.

Hans Christian Andersen's Fairy Tales. Translated by R. P. Keigwin. Introduced by Elias Bredsdorff. New York, 1950.

The Improvisatore; or, Life in Italy. Translated by Mary Howitt. London, 1847.

Lucky Peter. Translated by Horace E. Scudder. *Scribner's Monthly* (March and April 1871).

Only a Fiddler. Translated by Mary Howitt. London, 1845.

Pictures of Sweden. Translated by Charles Beckwith. London, 1851.

A Poet's Bazaar. Translated by Charles Beckwith. 3 vols. London, 1846.

Rambles in the Romantic Regions of the Hartz Mountains. Translated by Charles Beckwith. London, 1848.

In Spain. Translated by Mrs. Bushby. London, 1864.

The Story of My Life. Translated by Horace E. Scudder. Boston, 1871.

To Be or Not to Be? Translated by Mrs. Bushby. London, 1857.

The True Story of My Life. Translated by Mary Howitt. London, 1847.

The Two Baronesses. Translated by Charles Beckwith. 2 vols. London, 1848.

Wonderful Stories for Children. Translated by Mary Howitt. London, 1846.

BIOGRAPHICAL AND CRITICAL STUDIES

Atkins, A. M. "The Triumph of Criticism: Levels of Meaning in Hans Christian Andersen's *The Steadfast Tin Soldier.*" *Scholia Satyrica* 1: 25–28 (1975).

Bain, R. N. *Hans Christian Andersen.* London, 1895.

Barüske, Heinz. "Hans Christian Andersen—Der Mensch und seine Zeit." In *Aus Andersens Tagebüchern.* Vol. 1. Frankfurt, 1980. Pp. 9–29.

Berendsohn, W. A. *Phantasie und Wirklichkeit in den "Marchen und Geschichten" Hans Christian Andersens: Struktur- und Stilstudien.* Wiesbaden, 1973.

Böök, Fredrik. *Hans Christian Andersen: A Biography.* Translated by C. Schoolfield. Norman, Okla., 1962.

Born, Ann. "Hans Christian Andersen: An Infectious Genius." *Anderseniana* 2:248–260 (1976).

Brandes, Georg. "Hans Christian Andersen." In *Eminent Authors of the Nineteenth Century.* Translated by R. B. Anderson. New York, 1886.

Braude, L. Y. "Hans Christian Andersen and Russia." *Scandinavica* 14:1–15 (1975).

Bredsdorff, Elias. *Hans Andersen and Charles Dickens: A Friendship and Its Dissolution.* Copenhagen, 1956.

————. *Hans Christian Andersen: The Story of His Life and Work, 1805–75.* London, 1975.

Browning, George. *A Few Personal Recollections of Hans Christian Andersen.* London, 1875.

Burnett, C. B. *The Shoemaker's Son: The Life of Hans Christian Andersen.* London, 1941.

Dal, Erik. "Hans Christian Andersen's Tales and America." *Scandinavian Studies* 40:1–25 (1968).

Duffy, Maureen. "The Brothers Grimm and Sister Andersen." In *The Erotic World of Faery.* London, 1972. Pp. 263–284.

Grønbech, Bo. *Hans Christian Andersen.* Boston, 1980.

Haugaard, Erik C. "Hans Christian Andersen: A Twentieth-Century View." *Scandinavian Review* 14:1–15 (1975).

Heltoft, Kjeld. *Hans Christian Andersen as an Artist.* Translated by Reginald Spink. Copenhagen, 1977.

Jan, Isabelle. *Andersen et ses contes: Essai.* Paris, 1977.

Johnson, Spencer. *The Value of Fantasy: The Story of Hans Christian Andersen.* La Jolla, Calif., 1979.

Jones, W. Glyn. *Denmark.* New York, 1970.

Manning-Sanders, Ruth. *Swan of Denmark: The Story of Hans Christian Andersen.* London, 1949; New York, 1950.

Marker, J. *Hans Christian Andersen and the Romantic Theater: A Study of Stage Practices in the Prenaturalistic Scandinavian Theater.* Toronto, 1971.

Meynell, Esther. *The Story of Hans Andersen.* New York, 1950.

Mishler, William, "H. C. Andersen's 'Tin Soldier' in a Freudian Perspective." *Scandinavian Studies* 50: 389–395 (1978).

Mitchell, P. M. *A History of Danish Literature.* Copenhagen, 1957. Pp. 150–160.

Nielsen, Erling. *Hans Christian Andersen in Selbstzeugnissen und Bilddokumenten.* Hamburg, 1958.

Reumert, Elith. *Hans Christian Andersen the Man.* Translated by Jessie Bröchner. London, 1927.

Robb, N. A. "Hans Christian Andersen." In *Four in Exile.* New York and London, 1948; Port Washington, N.Y., 1968. Pp. 120–151.

Spink, Reginald. *Hans Christian Andersen and His World.* London, 1972.

Stirling, Monica. *The Wild Swan: The Life and Times of Hans Christian Andersen.* New York and London, 1965.

Svendsen, H. M., and Werner. *Geschichte der danischen Literatur.* Neumünster, 1964.

Teschner, Heinrich. *Hans Christian Andersen und Heinrich Heine: Ihre literarischen und persönlichen Beziehungen.* Münster, 1914. Ph.D. dissertation.

Toksvig, Signe. *The Life of Hans Christian Andersen.* London, 1933.

JACK ZIPES

ALEXIS DE TOCQUEVILLE

(1805–1859)

I

ALEXIS DE TOCQUEVILLE was one of the greatest, perhaps the greatest, of the political thinkers and historical writers of the nineteenth century. The principal support of such a claim is the lasting power of his writing. Often during the twentieth century, in different places and on different occasions, the few books that Tocqueville wrote have been rediscovered by people who thereafter became his respectful admirers. His reputation survives not only because of the excellence of his work but because the history of the last hundred and fifty years confirms the impression, again and again, that when we read him we are in the presence of a great mind whose judgment is virtually unerring, whose insight is often profound, and whose vision is startlingly applicable to our own times. That his vision has been much more accurate than that of Karl Marx or other nineteenth-century radicals has been recognized on occasion; such comparisons have been increasingly easy to prove. It is less often recognized that Tocqueville gains in comparison not only with utopians and radicals but with the great conservatives such as Edmund Burke, Joseph de Maistre, and Juan Donoso Cortés, as well as with the great liberals such as John Stuart Mill, Thomas Macaulay, and Lord Acton.

Tocqueville is the premier thinker of the democratic age. One of his admirers in the nineteenth century, the German philosopher Wilhelm Dilthey, ranked him among the three greatest political thinkers of all time, with Aristotle and Machiavelli. Yet Tocqueville is not very widely known.[1] In France historians and political thinkers devoted relatively little attention to him for almost a century after his death. The reason for this neglect was the customary prevalence of certain climates of opinion and intellectual fashions; but there is another condition that, even at this time of writing, has been an obstacle to the universal recognition of Tocqueville's importance. This condition is the unclassifiable nature of Tocqueville's ideology and achievement. Was Tocqueville a historian or a sociologist? Was he a conservative or a liberal? Was he an aristocratic skeptic or a believing Catholic? These are secondary questions about which there exists no intellectual or academic consensus to this day.

Tocqueville was an aristocrat who came to believe that democracy was inevitable; but the purpose of this belief was neither opportunism nor an accommodation to what seemed to him obvious. He saw his own aristocratic past and the unfolding democratic present with detachment, denying neither the former nor the latter. He was not the kind of aristocrat who

[1]His very name, especially in the English-speaking world, is often erroneously written: when not preceded by his first name it should be Tocqueville, not "De Tocqueville."

chooses to become a democrat; and he saw in the coming of democracy more than a social or economic development: he thought he detected in it the hand of God. "I cannot believe," he once wrote,

> that God has for several centuries been pushing two or three hundred men toward equality just to make them wind up under a Tiberian despotism. Verily, that wouldn't be worth the trouble. Why He is drawing us toward democracy, I do not know; but embarked on a vessel that I did not build, I am at least trying to use it to gain the nearest port.

This passage contains the essence of his historical vision. Tocqueville believed that the movement toward democracy—which, in his view, had begun earlier than historians and people in general were accustomed to think—was the great overriding theme of the historical evolution of the West, perhaps even of the entire world. The structure of Tocqueville's thought and his view of human nature differed entirely from those of the materialists and of Marx. Yet Tocqueville did not share the prevalent liberal view of history either, the one espoused and expressed by the historian Lord Acton, to the effect that the history of mankind is the essential unfolding of the history of liberty. Tocqueville's view of democratic evolution was clear, but he was fully aware of its complex nature, the main element of its complexity being the relation between its often contradictory elements of equality and liberty. His concentration on this subject would alone justify the recognition of Tocqueville as a latter-day Aristotle; yet Tocqueville, even more than his famous predecessor Montesquieu, knew that modern mass democracy is not comparable to the democracy of the Athenian city-state, that it is a new historical phenomenon. Tocqueville's political thinking was realistic and existential, not abstract and theoretical.

II

Tocqueville was born in 1805 of an ancient noble family of Normandy, whose title and land dated from the eleventh century. His parents had barely escaped the guillotine; his maternal great-grandfather, the famous political and legal thinker Malesherbes, had not. Perhaps in consequence of these harrowing experiences (the hair of Tocqueville's father had turned white at the age of twenty-two) the family life of the Tocquevilles had none of the airy worldliness of the French aristocracy of the eighteenth century; it was closely knit, religious, and affectionate, as well as protective of an only child who maintained his love and respect for his parents throughout his life. This respect was not only filial but also intellectual. His understanding and appreciation of the royalist and traditionalist convictions of his father went hand in hand with his understanding and defense of the democratic evolution of the world.

When the July Revolution of 1830 put an end to the rule of the last Bourbon king of France, Tocqueville was twenty-five years old; indeed, his twenty-fifth birthday came on the day when Charles X left Versailles forever. At dawn on the next day Tocqueville saw a melancholy historical scene that moved him to tears: the cortege carrying the king and his family into exile.

His father had been an important official in the last Bourbon regime. Most of his friends were convinced legitimists; Tocqueville was not. He had no illusions about the bourgeois regime of Louis-Philippe, but he had no illusions about the possibility of a Bourbon restoration either. After some soul-searching he took the oath of allegiance to the new government. But his restless mind was already looking ahead. Less than a month after the upheaval in July, and less than two months before he took the oath, he wrote to a friend: "I have long had the greatest desire to visit North America: I shall go there to see what a great republic is like; my only fear is lest, during that time, they establish one in France." He and his close friend Gustave de Beaumont managed, not without difficulty, an assignment from the government to study the American prison system; but the scope of their interest was rather more spacious than that.

They left in early April 1831, landed in the United States by mid-May, and returned to France nine months later. The product of their extensive (and at times dangerous) travels was three separate works: a study of the American penitentiary system; a romantic novel by Beaumont about slavery in America; and Tocqueville's own *Democracy in America,* of which the first volume was published in 1835 and the second in 1840.

Democracy in America is the great outstanding book about the United States in particular and about democracy in general. Its immediate success was due both to its inherent qualities and, perhaps even more, to the contemporary state of affairs: in the 1830's the United States was the only well-established democratic republic in the world. This kind of uniqueness was alone sufficient to stimulate interest in its description and analysis. The unequaled merit of *Democracy in America* appears when we consider that Tocqueville's work remains interesting, valuable, enduring, and thought-provoking long after the United States has ceased to be the solitary example of a democracy. *Democracy in America* has stood the test of time, which is astonishing when we bear in mind the changes in the institutions and population of the United States from what they were some hundred and fifty years ago.

In this encyclopedic and philosophical work, which covers nearly all of the institutions and characteristics of the American government and the American people, some of Tocqueville's observations and conclusions should have inevitably become outdated. Yet such instances are remarkably few. Perhaps the only one worth noting is Tocqueville's description of the power of the presidency and,

indirectly, of the federal government. These at that time seemed weaker than the powers of Congress and the states. What is remarkable is that this youthful foreign aristocrat should have had such an acute and profound comprehension of the American character. True, he had prepared himself well for his American journey by extensive reading; he knew English, and had had for some time a particular interest in the laws and institutions of England; yet it remains a rare occurrence that the best and most enduring book about a nation should be written by a foreigner.

The reason for this exceptional feat lies in Tocqueville's singular genius. This singularity can be seen in the method, style, and philosophy of *Democracy in America;* but the unity of this method, style, and philosophy does not derive solely from the subject of this first work. It reappears in Tocqueville's other books, written fifteen or twenty years later and dealing with different subjects.

The first volume of *Democracy in America* consists of two parts: the first and shorter one is a description of American self-government and political institutions; the second is a description and analysis of democratic government and majority rule in the United States. The first part is composed of eight chapters, the second of ten: but most of these chapters, especially the most important ones, are divided into numerous subchapters, and it is within these subchapters that Tocqueville's method—or, more precisely, the structure of his thought—is apparent. These subchapters are short, often hardly more than a page each. They consist of paragraphs that seldom run to more than a few lines. This kind of composition reflects the author's personality: Tocqueville's mind was quick, restless, and impatient. Yet the working of these qualities enhances, rather than diminishes, the value of what he has to say, for the compressed wisdom of his generalizations and the quiet profundity of his insights make them memorable. Here are a few examples:

[On the freedom of the press] I admit that I do not feel toward freedom of the press that complete and instantaneous love which one accords to things by their nature supremely good. I love it more from considering the evils it prevents than on account of the good it does.

(1.11)

[On democracy and envy] One must not blind oneself to the fact that democratic institutions most successfully develop sentiments of envy in the human heart. This is not because they provide the means for everybody to rise to the level of everybody else but because these means are constantly proving inadequate in the hands of those using them. Democratic institutions awaken and flatter the passion for equality without ever being able to satisfy it entirely.

(1.13)

[On universal suffrage] Those who consider universal suffrage a guarantee of the excellence of the resulting choice suffer under a complete delusion. Universal suffrage has other advantages, but not that one.

(1.13)

[On the budget and the costs of democratic government] There is in democratic societies a stirring without precise aim; some sort of prevailing feverish excitement finds expression in innovations of all sorts, and innovations are almost always expensive.

(1.13)

[On the enduring benefits of democracy] The vices and weaknesses of democratic government are easy to see; they can be proved by obvious facts, whereas its salutary influence is exercised in an imperceptible and almost secret way. Its defects strike one at first glance, but its good qualities are revealed only in the long run.

(1.16)

[On the danger of majority rule] My greatest complaint against democratic government as organized in the United States is not, as many Europeans think, its weakness, but rather its irresistible strength. . . . I am not asserting that at the present time in America there are frequent acts of tyranny. I do say that one can find no guarantee against it there and that the reasons for the government's moderation must be sought in circumstances and in mores rather than in the laws.

(1.16)

[On the races in the United States] When they have abolished slavery, the moderns still have to eradicate three much more intangible and tenacious prejudices: the prejudice of the master, the prejudice of the race, and the prejudice of the white.

(1.18)

The most famous and most often quoted passage in *Democracy in America* is at the conclusion of the first volume:

There are at the present time two great nations in the world, which started from different points, but seem to tend towards the same end. . . .

All other nations seem to have nearly reached their natural limits, and they have only to maintain their power; but these are still in the act of growth. All the others have stopped, or continue to advance with extreme difficulty; these alone are proceeding with ease and celerity along a path to which no limit can be perceived. The American struggles against the obstacles that nature opposes to him; the adversaries of the Russian are men. The former combats the wilderness and savage life; the latter, civilization with all its arms. The conquests of the American are therefore gained by the plowshare; those of the Russian by the sword. The Anglo-American relies upon personal interest to accomplish his ends and gives free scope to the unguided strength and common sense of the people; the Russian centers all the authority of society in a single arm. The principal instrument of the former is freedom; of the latter, servitude. Their starting-point is different and their courses are not the same; yet each of them seems marked out by the will of Heaven to sway the destinies of half the globe.

(Reeve-Bowen trans., 1.18)

What is the principal theme of *Democracy in America*? It is that American society is a living illustration of the possibility of a more or less orderly democracy, and that consequently both the conservative and the radical European views of democracy ought to be revised. Tocqueville's conservative contemporaries were wrong in believing that democracy inevitably leads to anarchy and chaos; the opposite is rather true: the universal acceptance of majority rule leads to slowness in the movements of thought, to conformity, and to the danger not of anarchy but of tyranny exercised by the majority. On the other side, the radicals were wrong in believing that the establishment of majority rule would suffice to ensure the freedom and happiness of people; these depend far more on the workings of certain laws, habits, and beliefs, including religion: in short, the character of a people influences its political institutions rather than the reverse. In the first volume of *Democracy in America* Tocqueville gradually rises to this theme, as the book advances from a description of American institutions to an analysis of American democratic society and its problems.

The first volume was published in 1835 in Paris. Despite the skepticism of its publisher, it was an instant success. Tocqueville became famous overnight: his work and his wisdom were praised in many quarters, primarily among the conservative liberals who formed what was perhaps the last great generation of French political thinkers in the 1820's and 1830's. Because of their judicious acclaim Tocqueville was then, and has been often since, classed among this group, known by the somewhat misleading adjective *doctrinaires.* Let me repeat, however, that he transcended such categories for many reasons, one of them being his awareness that the world was facing a new development of such scope and extent that the existing political categories were no longer sufficient; as he himself wrote, "a new science of politics was necessary for a new world."

The composition of the second volume of *Democracy in America* took twice as long as the first. Published in 1840, it was less of a success. Unlike the first, it received a number of severely critical reviews. Today we can see that the second volume is even more important than the first, more timely in its details and richer in its contents.

We note, first of all, that the title of the entire work is as accurate as it is honest. *De la démocratie en Amérique* (About Democracy in America) is not, as most people assume, a book principally about America; it is a book principally about democracy. And in this respect there is a subtle but significant difference in emphasis between the two volumes. Whereas it may be said that the main direction of Tocqueville's interest in the first volume is America even more than it is democracy, in the second volume it is democracy even more than it is America. The connection between the two volumes is nonetheless organic. Already, toward the end of the first volume, Tocqueville had written:

> Those who, having read this book, should imagine that in writing it I am urging all nations with a democratic social state to imitate the laws and mores of the Anglo-Americans would be making a great mistake; they must have paid more attention to the form than to the substance of my thought. My aim has been to show, by the American example, that laws, and more especially mores, can allow a democratic people to remain free. But I am very far from thinking that we should follow the example of American democracy and imitate the means that it has used to attain this end, for I am well aware of the influence of the nature of a country and of antecedent events on political institutions, and I should regard it as a great misfortune for mankind if liberty were bound always and in all places to have the same features.
>
> (1.17)

The second volume of *Democracy in America* has no subchapters. The volume has four parts, each consisting of twenty or more short chapters, except for part 4, a kind of conclusion, which has only eight. Throughout, however, all the terse, lucid, and aphoristic characteristics of the first volume appear again. The titles alone of some of these chapters suggest the form of Tocqueville's thought: "Why the Americans Show More Aptitude and Taste for General Ideas than Their English Forefathers"; "How Religion in the United States Makes Use of Democratic Instincts"; "How American Democracy Has Modified the English Language"; "Some Characteristics of Historians in Democratic Times"; "Why Some Americans Display Enthusiastic Forms of Spirituality"; "How an Aristocracy May Be Created by Industry"; "Why Great Revolutions Will Become Rare"; "Why the Ideas of Democratic Peoples About Government Naturally Favor the Concentration of Political Power"; "What Sort of Despotism Democratic Nations Have to Fear."

The succinctness in the second volume of *Democracy in America* is even more pronounced than in the first. The chapter "Some Characteristics of Historians in Democratic Times," for example, consists of forty-eight sentences in fifteen paragraphs; yet many of these paragraphs contain a particular argument so condensed and profound that it would be sufficient for an entire book, indeed, for the kind of book that could establish the reputation of a thinker. "I am very well convinced," Tocqueville writes,

> that even among democratic nations the genius, the vices, or the virtues of certain individuals retard or accelerate the natural current of a people's history; but causes of this secondary and fortuitous nature are infinitely more various, more concealed, more complex, less powerful, and consequently less easy to trace, in periods of equality than in ages of aristocracy, when the task of the historian is simply to detach from the mass of general events the particular influence of one man or of a few men. . . .
>
> M. de Lafayette says somewhere in his *Memoirs* that the exaggerated system of general causes affords surprising consolations to second-

rate statesmen. I will add that its effects are not less consolatory to second-rate historians; it can always furnish a few mighty reasons to extricate them from the most difficult part of their work, and it indulges the indolence or incapacity of their minds while it confers upon them the honors of deep thinking. . . .

> Those who write in democratic ages have another more dangerous tendency. . . . To their minds it is not enough to show what events have occurred: they wish to show that events could not have occurred otherwise. They take a nation arrived at a certain stage of its history and affirm that it could not but follow the track that brought it thither. It is easier to make such an assertion than to show how the nation might have adopted a better course. . . .
>
> If this doctrine of necessity, which is so attractive to those who write history in democratic ages, passes from authors to their readers till it infects the whole mass of the community and gets possession of the public mind, it will soon paralyze the activity of modern society and reduce Christians to the level of the Turks.
>
> Moreover, I would observe that such doctrines are peculiarly dangerous at the period at which we have arrived. Our contemporaries are only too prone to doubt of human free-will.

> (Reeve-Bowen trans., 2.1.20)

Probably the most important part of the second volume of *Democracy in America* is its concluding chapters. Tocqueville's argument here rises to its highest level; and these chapters also reveal a subtle and important change in his mind. In "What Sort of Despotism Democratic Nations Have to Fear" Tocqueville begins by saying that during his travels in the United States he became aware of the relatively novel danger of democratic despotism; "a more accurate examination of the subject, and five years of further meditation, have not diminished my fears, but have changed their object." He no longer dwells on the relative weakness of the central power in a democracy; rather the contrary. "If despotism were to be established among the democratic nations of our days," it would be wholly different from despotism in the past:

"It would be more extensive and more mild; it would degrade men without tormenting them. . . . [The] same principle of equality which facilitates despotism tempers its rigor.

I think, then, that the species of oppression by which democratic nations are menaced is unlike anything else that ever before existed in the world; our contemporaries will find no prototype of it in their memories. . . . The old words *despotism* and *tyranny* are inappropriate. . . . The first thing that strikes the observer is an endeavoring to procure the petty and paltry pleasures with which they glut their lives. . . .

Above this race of men stands an immense and tutelary power, which takes upon itself alone to secure their gratifications and to watch over their fate. That power is absolute, minute, regular, provident, and mild. It would be like the authority of a parent if, like that authority, its object was to prepare men for manhood; but it seeks, on the contrary, to keep them in perpetual childhood: it is well content that the people should rejoice, provided they think of nothing but rejoicing. For their happiness such a government willingly labors, but it chooses to be the sole agent and the only arbiter of that happiness; it provides for their security, foresees and supplies their necessities, facilitates their pleasures, manages their principal concerns, directs their industry, regulates the descent of property, and subdivides their inheritances: what remains, but to spare them all the care of thinking and all the trouble of living? . . .

I have always thought that servitude of the regular, quiet, and gentle kind which I have just described might be combined more easily than is commonly believed with some of the outward forms of freedom, and that it might even establish itself under the wing of the sovereignty of the people.

(Reeve-Bowen trans., 2.4.6)

It appears from the above that Tocqueville foresaw the tendency that many social and political thinkers a century later were still unwilling to recognize: the possibility that the age of aristocratic society and government would be succeeded by bureaucratic society and government rather than by a true democracy, even though Tocqueville did not use the term "bureaucracy." In any event, the last sentence of the magisterial work sums up his historical and political vision: "The nations of our time cannot prevent the conditions of men from becoming equal, but it depends upon themselves whether the principle of equality is to lead to servitude or freedom, to knowledge or barbarism, to prosperity or misery."

III

We have seen that the publication of the first volume of *Democracy in America* suddenly made the young Tocqueville a public figure. What followed were thirteen superficially uneventful years, the middle period of Tocqueville's life. I write "superficially," because beneath the external signs of an honorably progressing career there were evidences of frequent disillusionments, depressions, and torment.

Between 1835 and 1848, the thirtieth and the forty-third years of his life, Tocqueville was elected to the Chamber of Deputies and to the French Academy. He traveled in England, Ireland, Algeria, Switzerland, and Germany. He published the second volume of *Democracy in America* and a number of minor writings; the *Democracy* was being published in many translations across Europe and in the Americas. He married a middle-class Englishwoman from a respectable family who had served as a governess in France for years; Marie Mottley was several years older and several inches taller than her husband, an earnest and intelligent woman with a difficult temperament who bore him no children.

Tocqueville suffered from a weak chest; the progressive disease of his lungs grew worse through the years. He was now a respected public personage, but not a very successful political figure. He took part in the political life of France out of a sense of duty rather than out of ambition. He wanted to help channel the democratic tide in the direction of decency and order. Many people disliked the serious

899

and Olympian tone of his utterances; he seemed like Aristides the Just in the heedless democracy of Athens. On the evidence of his contemporaries we may add that his speeches in the Chamber were unduly learned, sometimes lengthy, and delivered without much oratorical talent. Yet at least one of Tocqueville's speeches became famous. On 29 January 1848 he spoke in the Chamber, accurately predicting that a revolution was brewing. "Gentlemen," he said,

> my profound conviction is that we are lulling ourselves to sleep over an active volcano. . . . When I consider what has been, at different times and epochs of history among different peoples, the effective reason why ruling classes have been ruined, I note the various events and men and accidental or superficial causes, but believe me, the real cause, the effective one, that makes men lose power is that they have become unworthy to exercise it. Consider the old monarchy, gentlemen. It was stronger than you, stronger because of its origin; it was better supported than you are by ancient customs, old mores, and old beliefs; it was stronger than you, and yet it has fallen into dust. Why did it fall? Do you think it was because of some particular accident? Do you think it was due to one particular man, the deficit, the Oath of the Tennis Court, La Fayette, or Mirabeau? No, gentlemen, there is another cause: the class that was ruling then had, through its indifference, selfishness, and vice, become incapable and unworthy of ruling.
>
> (*Recollections*, Lawrence trans., pp. 14–15)

He implored his colleagues in the Chamber to change the spirit of the government, because another great revolution was around the corner. His prophetic speech was received with apathy and ridicule. What Tocqueville had foretold came about less than a month later.

The memory of this speech, together with the reputation of Tocqueville's intelligent advocacy of an orderly democracy, led naturally to his leadership of the committee that was to write the constitution of the Second French Republic. During the deliberations a short but bloody second insurrection, in June 1848, turned the tide of sentiment and opinion more conservative. In December 1848 Louis-Napoleon was elected president of France. For the next two years he governed with the support of the Assembly, and in 1849 he appointed Tocqueville foreign minister. Tocqueville performed his duties with much energy and intelligence during a difficult and eventful period of French and European history. The fires of the 1848 revolutions had not yet died out: there was a war of independence in Hungary, a war in northern Italy; French troops were sent to Rome to crush the republican rebellion there and to restore the pope to his see. In October 1849 Louis-Napoleon dismissed the conservative-liberal cabinet of which Tocqueville was a prominent member. Tocqueville did not return to political life.

There was worse to come. Tocqueville accurately foresaw the political future: Louis-Napoleon would be supported as dictator by the majority of the people; his regime would be a new kind of democratic Caesarism. Tocqueville had only contempt for the Left radicals who in June 1848 had attempted the first socialist revolution in France; but he immediately realized that the fear-ridden reaction against the Left, equally contemptible, was a new phenomenon consonant with the development of democracy. It meant the appearance of a new radical Right, supported by masses of people out of fear of revolution and out of their sentiments of nationalism and respectability. "The insane fear of socialism," Tocqueville, this opponent of socialism, wrote in a letter, "throws the bourgeois headlong into the arms of despotism. . . . The democrats have served the cause of the absolutists. But now that the weakness of the Red party has been proved, people will regret the price at which their enemy has been put down."

It would be wrong to think that during the political phase of Tocqueville's career he wrote little. His literary dedication was exceptionally strong. But the largest part of his writings was unpublished on his death, and a good part remains unpublished even today. His friend Beaumont later said that "for one volume he published he wrote ten; and the notes he cast aside as intended only for himself would have served many writers as copy for the printer." Apart from his shorter writings and speeches in the 1840's, he kept up a very large correspondence. To put down his thoughts on paper, whether in letters to friends or only for himself, remained a necessity for Tocqueville throughout his life. Between 1849 and 1852, while the devolution of the French parliamentary democracy to the imperial regime of Napoleon III was progressing, Tocqueville's mind and body were racked with suffering. The cold and damp winters in the Tocqueville château in Normandy were bad for his lungs; and he complained that his state of mind was painfully agitated and depressed. In 1850 his doctors advised him to spend a winter further south; they also said that he ought to occupy his mind with other than political concerns. In Italy, at Sorrento, he began to write his recollections of the turbulence of the revolutionary years 1848–1849. He did so for his eye alone, one of the reasons for this discretion being his reluctance to make public the often caustic portraits of some of his friends and political associates. His manuscript, entitled *Souvenirs*, was eventually published by his great-nephew in 1893, thirty-four years after Tocqueville's death.

The *Souvenirs* (later translated as *The Recollections of Alexis de Tocqueville*) are perhaps the best of all possible introductions to Tocqueville's mind. They are obviously the most personal of his published books. Again we are in the presence of an extraordinary work, because of the character and the genius of its author. Again its contents demonstrate the unique and uncategorizable character of Tocqueville's achievement. The *Souvenirs* transcend the limits of what is called a memoir or a history. They are a kind of autohistory, a history written in the first-person singular, but not because of their author's dominant preoccupation with himself. The book is a participant's history, springing from the realization that history is participant knowledge par excellence. In this book, as also in some of his other writings, Tocqueville demonstrates—without, however, arguing the philosophical point—the inadequacy of the Cartesian and scientific separation of the universe into object and subject, the separation of the observer from the matter observed.

Tocqueville's purpose was to describe some of the things and some of the people he saw in 1848 and 1849—or, rather, some of the things he saw that he saw. He begins the book with an avowal:

Now that I am out of the stream of public life and the uncertain state of my health does not even allow me to follow any consecutive study, I have for some time in my retreat turned my thoughts to myself, or rather to those events of the recent past in which I played a part or stood as witness. The best use for my leisure seems to be to go back over those events, to describe the men I saw taking part in them, and, if I can, to catch in this way and engrave on my memory those confused features that make up the uncertain physiognomy of my time.

Along with this decision of mine goes another to which I shall be equally faithful: these recollections are to be a mental relaxation for myself and not a work of literature. They are written for myself alone. These pages are to be a mirror, in which I can enjoy seeing my contemporaries and myself, not a painting for the public to view. My best friends are not to know about them, for I wish to keep my freedom to describe myself and them without flattery. I want to uncover the secret motives that made us act, them and myself as well as other men; and when I have understood these, to state them. In a word, I want to express myself honestly in these memoirs, and it is therefore necessary that they be completely secret.

(*Recollections*, p. 3)

He returns to this theme later in the work: "I do not want to write a history of the 1848 Revolution. I am merely trying to retrace my own actions, thoughts, and impressions during that time." And again, after meditating on the difficulty of describing human motives and purposes: "Nevertheless I want to try to discover myself in the midst of this labyrinth. For it is only right that I should take the same liberties with myself as I have taken, and will often take again, with so many others."

These "liberties" are essentials in his gallery of portraits. Here are a few examples:

[His friend Dufaure, who did not come to the Chamber of Deputies on 24 February 1848, the first day of the revolution] Weakness was certainly not the reason, for I have subsequently seen him very calm and unmoved in much more dangerous circumstances. I think that in his concern for his family he must have wanted to put them in safety outside Paris first. His private and his public virtues, for he had both in great measure, did not march in step, for the former always came first; we saw things go that way more than once. In any case, I cannot count that as a great crime. Virtues of any sort are rare enough, and we can ill afford to quibble about their type and relative importance.

(pp. 38–39)

[Jean Pierre Sauzet, the president of the Chamber] He got easily excited over the smallest matter, so you can imagine what state he was in then. I found this excellent man—for such he was in spite of well-meaning bits of trickery, pious fibs, and all the other petty sins that a timid heart and vacillating mind could suggest to an honest soul—I found him, I say, walking about in his room, a prey to strong emotions. M. Sauzet had handsome but undistinguished features, the dignity of a cathedral verger and a large fat body with very short arms. When he was restless or upset, as he nearly always was, he would waggle his little arms convulsively in all directions like a drowning man. His manner, while we talked, was strange; he walked about, stopped and then sat down with one foot tucked under his fat buttocks, as he usually did in mo-

ments of great agitation; then he got up and sat down again without coming to any conclusion. It was a great misfortune for the House of Orleans to have a respectable man of that sort in charge of the Chamber on such a day; a bold rogue would have been more use.

(pp. 45–46)

[In the midst of the upheaval the two sons of Louis-Philippe appeared in the Chamber.] The count of Paris had a boy's thoughtlessness combined with a prince's precocious impassivity. Beside them stood the duke of Nemours, buttoned up in his uniform, erect, stiff, cold and silent: a post painted to look like a lieutenant-general. In my view he was the only man in real danger that day. All the time that I watched him exposed to this peril, his courage remained the same: taciturn, sterile, and uninspired. Courage of that nature was more likely to discourage and dishearten his friends than to impress the enemy; its only use would be to enable him to die honorably, if die he must.

(p. 48)

[Ledru-Rollin, the leader of the radical party] At that time, the nation saw Ledru-Rollin as the bloody image of the Terror. They regarded him as the evil and Lamartine as the good genius, mistakenly in both cases. Ledru was nothing but a great sensual sanguine boy, with no principles and hardly any ideas; he had no true courage of mind or heart, but he was also free of malice, for by nature he wished all the world well and was incapable of cutting an enemy's throat, except perhaps as an historical reminiscence or to please his friends.

(p. 110)

[On 24 June 1848 a committee of the Assembly appointed Tocqueville as a commissioner, one of a group including the deputies Cormenin, Crémieux, and Goudchaux; their job was to move from barricade to barricade, to encourage the National Guards fighting the battle of Paris. Tocqueville's portraits of his colleagues, too long to cite here, are full of acute but good-natured insights. Here is his summary.] I have always found it interesting to follow the involuntary effects of fear in the minds of men of intelligence. Fools show their fear grossly in all its nakedness, but the others know how to cover it with a veil of such fine and delicately woven, small, convincing deceits that there is a pleasure in contemplating this ingenious labor of the intelligence.

(p. 150)

[Toward the end of the uprising Thiers meets General Lamoricière, who won the battle of Paris.] M. Thiers came up and threw his arms round Lamoricière's neck, telling him he was a hero. I could not help smiling at that sight, for they did not love each other at all, but danger is like wine in making all men sentimental.

(p. 161)

[About the Assembly near the end of the uprising] The President called the Assembly together only at long intervals for short periods; and he was right to do so, for Assemblies are like children in that idleness never fails to make them do or say a lot of silly things. Each time the sitting was resumed, he himself told us all that had been learned for certain, during the adjournment. This President, as we know, was Sénard, a well-known lawyer from Rouen, and a courageous man; however, the daily comedy of the bar had from his youth led him to contract such an inveterate habit of acting that he had lost the faculty of truthfully expressing his real impressions, if by chance he had any. Inevitably he would add some turgid phrases of his own to the acts of courage he was narrating, and when he expressed the emotion which he, I think, really felt, in sepulchral tones, with a trembling voice and a sort of tragedian's hiccup, he even then seemed to be acting. Never were the ridiculous and the sublime so close, for the deeds were sublime and the narrator ridiculous.

(pp. 153–154)

Space does not permit my adding Tocqueville's two or three portraits of Louis-Philippe, masterpieces of historical and psychological description though they are. Like those just quoted, they show their author's talent for depicting human beings and their characters. This ability rarely comes out in *Democracy in America*, where Tocqueville deals principally with institutions and society as a whole, rather than with individuals. A second feature worth observing is that each of Tocqueville's portraits ends with, indeed is summed up by, an epigram about human nature itself. This is not only the result of intelligent artistry or the French style. The *Souvenirs* embody Tocqueville's deep understanding of human nature— the main requirement of a great historian. Thus it is not only the subject matter of the *Souvenirs* but the very substance of their author's thought that is historical.

Here is how Tocqueville saw the first days of the Revolution of 1848:

As I left my bedroom . . . the 24th of February, I met the cook who had been out; the good woman was quite beside herself and poured out a sorrowful rigmarole from which I could understand nothing but that the government was having the poor people massacred. I went down at once, and as soon as I had set foot in the street I could for the first time scent revolution in the air; the middle of the street was empty; the shops were not open; there were no carriages, or people walking; one heard none of the usual street vendors' cries; little frightened groups of neighbors talked by the doors in lowered voices; anxiety or anger disfigured every face. I met one of the National Guard hurrying, rifle in hand, with an air of tragedy. I spoke to him but could learn nothing save that the government was massacring the people (to which he added that the National Guard would know how to put that right). It was always the same refrain, which, of course, explained nothing to me. I knew the vices of the July government all too well, and cruelty was not among them. I consider it to have been one of the most corrupt, but least bloodthirsty, that has ever existed, and I repeat the rumor only to show how such rumors help revolutions along.

(p. 36)

The *Souvenirs* are more than a historical account. They contain the principles of Tocqueville's historical philosophy. We have seen that Tocqueville had predicted the coming of the Revolution of 1848. He had made an even more trenchant prediction in October 1847, which he decided to quote in the beginning of his *Souvenirs*. "The time is coming," he states,

> when the country will again be divided between two great parties. The French Revolution, which abolished all privileges and destroyed all exclusive rights, did leave one, that of property. Property holders must not delude themselves about the strength of their position, or suppose that, because it has so far nowhere been surmounted, the right to property is an insurmountable barrier; for our age is not like any other. . . . Soon the political struggle will be between the Haves and the Have-nots; property will be the great battlefield; and the main political questions will turn on the more or less profound modifications of the rights of property owners that are to be made.
>
> (p. 12)

In this respect, as in so many others, Tocqueville was ahead of Marx and of the socialist thinkers after him. Unlike them, however, Tocqueville did not for a moment believe that the struggle between the haves and have-nots would be the culmination of the history of mankind. He did not believe in economic man. Tocqueville did not think that the coming revolution would be anything but another act in the intermittent drama of violent shocks whereby the cause of equality was advanced in France by different people at different times. Already in the second volume of *Democracy in America* Tocqueville made the startling proposition that great revolutions were bound to become rare. In 1848, in the midst of the fighting, he remarked how there was something flashy and make-believe in this revolution:

> . . . there was absolutely no grandeur in this one, for there was no touch of the truth about it. We French, Parisians especially, gladly mingle literary and theatrical reminiscences with our most serious demonstrations. This often creates the impression that our feelings are false,
> whereas in fact they are only clumsily tricked out. In this case the quality of imitation was obvious. . . . It was a time when everybody's imagination had been colored by the crude pigments with which Lamartine daubed his *Girondins.* The men of the first revolution were still alive in everybody's mind, their deeds and their words fresh in the memory. And everything I saw . . . was plainly stamped with the imprint of such memories; the whole time I had the feeling that we had staged a play about the French Revolution, rather than that we were continuing it.
>
> (pp. 52–53)

Before that riotous day he wrote: "Nowhere did I see the seething unrest I had witnessed in 1830, when the whole city reminded me of one vast boiling cauldron. This time it was not a matter of overthrowing the government, but simply letting it fall." Throughout the *Souvenirs* Tocqueville insists on the marked differences among the revolutions of 1789, 1830, and 1848; and at the same time, on the frequently misleading and falsifying influence of the memories of these revolutions on the minds of all kinds of people, including Louis-Philippe and himself. More remarkable still, on occasion Tocqueville is able to distinguish—and he is driven by his honesty to describe—the difference between his impression of certain events when he first experienced them and the sometimes dissimilar impressions that came to his mind later and the conclusions he drew from them. One of the most engaging passages in the *Souvenirs* is Tocqueville's recollection of his argument with his friend J.-J. Ampère during the early days of the revolution:

> All the indignation, grief and anger that had been piling up in my heart since the morning suddenly erupted against Ampère; and I addressed him with a violence of language which makes me a little ashamed whenever I think of it and which only such a true friend as he would have excused. [He then reconstructs his own diatribe, and ends:] After a lot of shouting, we both

agreed to leave the verdict to the future, that enlightened and just judge who, unfortunately, always arrives too late.

(p. 68)

In sum, the *Souvenirs* are not only an incomparable account of the revolutionary year
1848–1849 in France and a set of clues to
Tocqueville's character; they are not only excellent illustrations of his historical talent;
but they also give us his view of history:

> For my part, I hate all those absolute systems
> that make the events of history depend on great
> first causes linked together by the chain of fate
> and thus succeed, so to speak, in banishing men
> from the history of the human race. Their
> boasted breadth seems to me narrow, and their
> mathematical exactness false. I believe, *pace* the
> writers who find these sublime theories to feed
> their vanity and lighten their labors, that many
> important historical facts can be explained only
> by accidental circumstances, while many others
> are inexplicable; and lastly, that chance, or
> rather the concatenation of secondary causes,
> which we call by that name because we can't
> sort them all out, is a very important element in
> all that we see taking place on the world's stage.
> But I am firmly convinced that chance can do
> nothing unless the ground has been prepared in
> advance. Antecedent facts, the nature of institu-
> tions, turns of mind and the state of mores are
> the materials from which chance composes
> those unexpected events that surprise and terrify
> us.

(p. 62)

IV

While he was writing his *Souvenirs,* during
the winter of 1850–1851 in Sorrento, the idea
of a book on Napoleon arose in Tocqueville's
restless mind. He began to compose his first
notes even though he was ill and weighted
down by the gloomiest thoughts about the future of France. By December 1852 his mind
had seized upon a different plan. He would
write a book describing the main features of
the French Revolution and include Napoleon.
Because of his illness he was again advised to
move away from Normandy, at least for a time.
He and Madame de Tocqueville found a country house near Tours. A fortunate circumstance attended him there: he was able to
search through the provincial archives in
Tours, where he was assisted by the excellent
archivist Charles de Grandmaison. Tocqueville now extended further the scope of his
projected work. He would deal not only with
the French Revolution and Napoleon but with
the origins of the Revolution. He immersed
himself more and more in that subject, which
became the first volume of a projected two-volume work. Again the title was precise: *L'Ancien régime et la révolution (The Old Régime
and the French Revolution).* Published in June
1856, it received a critical acclaim not dissimilar from that of the first volume of *Democracy
in America* twenty-one years before.

The Old Régime and the French Revolution
is the most conspicuous example of Tocqueville's powers as a historian. The writing is of
the same high quality as that of his earlier
works, and his philosophy is of course unchanged. Yet two new features are worth noting. One is the evidence of Tocqueville's talent for archival research—that is, his knack
for finding what is significant, illustrative,
vivid, and telling in all kinds of materials. The
other is his individual style of historiography.
In *The Old Régime and the French Revolution*
Tocqueville's method is more topical than
chronological. He is interested in why as well
as in how things happened; and the why is
often wrapped up in the how. As we found apt
illustrations in his chapter titles before, so we
may learn about the cast of his thought from
these:

> How the chief and ultimate aim of the Revolu-
> tion was not, as used to be thought, to overthrow
> religious and to weaken political authority in
> France.

(Gilbert trans., 1.2)

Why feudalism had come to be more detested in France than in any other country.

(2.1)

How administrative centralization was an institution of the old régime and not, as is often thought, a creation of the Revolution or of the Napoleonic period.

(2.2)

How the desire for reforms took precedence of the desire for freedom.

(3.3)

How certain practices of the central power completed the revolutionary education of the masses.

(3.6)

And so on. The main theme of the book is that many of the practices of the old regime, foremost among them administrative centralization, were responsible for the actual ills as well as the restlessness that plagued France and the French people before 1789. The emphasis on these origins of the French Revolution was something very new at the time. Yet *The Old Régime* is not a thesis-history; Tocqueville knew very well that great events are seldom the results of a single string of causes.

One of the main achievements of Tocqueville the historian is his revision of many standard notions about the origins of the Revolution. It is not true that the Revolution brought about a radically new kind of government: the vice of modern democratic rule, excessive centralization, had begun under the old regime. It is not true that royal abuses provoked the outbreak of the revolt: violence broke out where royal power proved the mildest, and counterrevolution was to rise in the west of France, where the feudal rules had lingered on longest. It could not be denied that in 1788–1789 there was a noble, generous, virile spirit in the air; on the other hand there was much pretense, vanity, and opportunism. "Une règle rigide, une pratique molle": rigid

rules and weak enforcement marked the character of the old regime. The clergy was neither ther weak nor corrupt: "I began to study the old society with many prejudices against the clergy; I finished full of respect." The revolutionary government adopted the worst administrative habits of the old regime, without recognizing that in this matter, as well as in many others, continuity proved to be even stronger than change.

"It is not my purpose," Tocqueville wrote in his foreword, "to write a history of the French Revolution; that has been done already, and so ably that it would be folly on my part to think of covering the ground again. In this book I shall study, rather, the background and nature of the Revolution."

We saw earlier that Tocqueville transcends ideological and academic categories; as is the wont of genius, his spirit also transcended his times. Tocqueville, who is all too often described as an admirable nineteenth-century thinker, a conservative liberal of a time and place now hopelessly remote, possessed a mind that had both eighteenth- and twentieth-century characteristics. His writings—if only by the fine clarity of his prose—bear many of the marks of the eighteenth century, when history was part and parcel of literature, in the broad and honorific sense. The lucidity, the economy, the aphoristic quality, and the symmetrical structure of many of his chapters put Tocqueville in the company of Montesquieu, Voltaire, and Gibbon. In these respects he has more in common with them than with the professional historians of the nineteenth century. Nor does his view of the nature of history accord with that of the nineteenth century. To him history is not a science possessing an ascertainable method. His view of history, based on his understanding of human nature, is akin, rather, to that of the few independent thinkers of the twentieth century who regard the application of scientific method to human affairs as unworkable and unduly restrictive of meaning.

A generation after Tocqueville's death the

French critic Émile Faguet wrote that the task Tocqueville "set for himself was to penetrate beneath accidental history to solid history, or beneath history to the physiology of peoples." From this correct analysis Faguet, however, came to the wrong conclusion: that Tocqueville was a sociologist rather than a historian. Yet Faguet missed the key to Tocqueville's historiographical talents. When Faguet wrote, more than eighty years ago, the texture of history had not yet changed. At that time it seemed still reasonable to concentrate on the history of the politically conscious classes; history was past politics and politics present history. Since then, it has become obvious that given the social and democratic character of our age the requirements of history writing must change; it is no longer reasonable to concentrate exclusively on the actions of the leading protagonists of the politically active classes and separate what Faguet called "surface" history from what lies "beneath" it. This Tocqueville already knew. The importance of *The Old Régime and the French Revolution* is not only that it is an extraordinarily enlightening and instructive interpretation of the French Revolution; it is also an extraordinarily instructive new type of history.

Tocqueville implicitly and, at times, explicitly refutes many of the dogmas of modern professional history writing. He is not only among the earliest to note that political history is no longer enough; he sees that the politically active classes may become powerless, and that their abdication of leadership is a development often more decisive than the alleged demands and decisions of the people. Revolutions are seldom made by the conscious dynamism of the people; yet Tocqueville rejects both the fatalistic notion that accidents govern history and the deterministic notion that people are moved by predetermined material motives. History is made by men, to whom God has given free will. He saw the historian's task as being moral as well as artistic. In his notes he often wrote: "What I am going to paint," "what I am trying to portray." He wished to paint rather than to chronicle, and he sought to detect the latent tendencies of the human heart and mind rather than to ascertain and explain regularities. His purpose was description rather than definition, comprehension rather than narration.

While Tocqueville was writing the first volume of *The Old Régime and the French Revolution* he was thinking more in terms of a European revolution. He considered that what had happened in France in 1789 was but the first phase of an epoch of European revolutions that, sixty years after the storming of the Bastille, was still going on. The European revolution, in turn, was but part and parcel of a greater movement toward social democracy, at the core of which stood the fundamental problem of the relation of liberty to equality, as well as that of democracy to Christianity. By the time the first volume was published he was well on his way through the second. Of the second volume we have his outline: it was to consist of five books, of which two (books 1 and 3) were almost completed; the rest consists of half-completed passages and notes to himself.

That Tocqueville died before he could finish this work was, and remains, a tragedy. As in the case of *Democracy in America*, the second volume might have been even more impressive than the first. The portions we have suggest this judgment. Book 1 deals with France immediately before the Revolution, book 3 with the coming of Bonaparte. In book 1 Tocqueville draws attention to the history of the *parlements*, those aristocratic assemblies that in 1788 initiated the attack on the old regime. The title of the fourth chapter reads: "How, Just When They Thought Themselves Masters of the Nation, the *Parlements* Suddenly Discovered That They Amounted to Nothing."

Perhaps the most brilliant completed portion of the volume (quoted in *The European Revolution and Correspondence with Gobineau*) is book 3, which treats France before the Consulate:

Between fear of the royalists and of the Jacobins, the majority of the nation sought an escape. The Revolution was dear, but the Republic was feared lest it should result in the return of one or the other. One might even say that each of these passions nourished the other; it was because the French found precious certain benefits ensured them by the Revolution that they feared all the more keenly a government which might interfere with these benefits. Of all the privileges that they had won or obtained during the previous ten years, the only one that they were disposed to surrender was liberty. They were ready to give up the liberty which the Revolution had merely promised, in order to finally enjoy the benefits that it had brought.

("How the Republic Was Ready to Accept a
Master")

The parties themselves, decimated, apathetic, and weary, longed to rest for a time during a dictatorship of any kind, provided only that it was exercised by an outsider and that it weighed upon their rivals as much as on themselves. This feature completes the picture. When great political parties begin to cool in their attachments without softening their hatreds, and at last reach the point of wishing less to succeed than to prevent the success of their opponents, one should prepare for servitude—the master is near.

It was easy to see that this master could rise only from the army.

("How the Nation, Though Ceasing to Be
Republican, Remained Revolutionary")

What a portrait of Napoleon Tocqueville could have given us. We have some of its features in the notes he left behind; they startle us with his many insights.

The last of Tocqueville's notes sums up his view of the Revolution:

Generally speaking, people are not very ardent or indomitable or energetic in their affairs when their personal passions are not engaged. Yet their personal passions, however vivid they may be, do not propel them either very far or very high unless these passions keep growing before their own eyes, unless they seem to justify themselves by being related to some greater cause for the service of mankind.

It is because of our human sense of honor that we are in need of this stimulant. Add to passions born of self-interest the aim to change the face of the world and to regenerate the human race: only then will you see what men are really capable of.

That is the history of the French Revolution.

Its narrowminded and selfish nature led to violence and darkness; its generous and selfless elements made its impulse powerful and great.

Tocqueville's books about the French Revolution are the clearest evidence that he was a modern historian. And yet, because of the deplorable habit of thinking in intellectual compartments, it is seldom that he is recognized as such. An interesting list could be compiled from the names of those who have asserted that Tocqueville was a conservative, a liberal, a historian, a sociologist, an aristocrat, a democrat, a Christian, an agnostic. In quite a few instances the commentators contradict themselves; at times Tocqueville is assigned to contradictory categories within the same monograph, essay, or review. Yet his books about the Revolution are crystal clear. They show, for instance, that while he did not believe that the voice of the people is the voice of God, neither did he believe that it was the voice of the devil. He was not one of those who thought that a nation has the right to go beyond its natural interests to impose ideas on others and arrogate to itself the role of teaching the world; yet he did not believe in a narrow concept of national interests either. He was not a French nationalist or a European imperialist; yet he did not assume that the achievements and the ideals of every nation and every civilization are of the same worth. He condemned the old regime as well as the Revolution and found virtues in both.

The Revolution, therefore, is hortatory history. I have suggested that it is hardly possible to comprehend Tocqueville's writings without considering the moral purposes of their author. In turn, it is only with these moral purposes in mind that one can avoid some of the mistaken conceptions of Tocqueville and his work. If the main concern of *Democracy in America* was the future of democracy, that book also reveals Tocqueville as more than a conservative democrat or a liberal aristocrat. If the main concern of the *The Revolution* included the future of France and of Europe, it also reveals Tocqueville as more than an old-fashioned historian or a forerunner of sociology. His preoccupation with the evolving relationship of Christianity and democracy, revealed in his letters and later writings, shows that he was neither a "progressive" Catholic nor an aristocratic skeptic, but a great Christian thinker and a magnanimous spirit.

V

During the summer of 1858 Tocqueville's physical condition worsened. He had to give up work on his book. In June he suffered a hemorrhage in one lung. His wife was also ill. In October his doctor in Paris recommended that they go south again. The next month they arrived in Cannes, completely exhausted. By February his health had improved a little. As always, he devoted considerable time and effort to correspondence with his friends. His last letters were dictated a week before he died, on 16 April 1859.

Next to his health, the most important development during Tocqueville's last months concerned his religion. Soon after they had arrived in Cannes the Tocquevilles began to look for a nursing sister. Since his illness prevented him from going to church, he asked one of the sisters to read him the prayers of the mass. The bishop of Orléans came to visit; he and another priest said mass in Tocqueville's rooms. He made his confession, took communion, and died at peace with himself and with his church.

These events were contested during the century that passed after Tocqueville's death. Certain people, especially certain intellectuals, claimed that Tocqueville's last religious acts were questionable, since they had been undertaken out of respect for the wishes of his wife. The support of their claim rests on a statement by Beaumont, as well as on an earlier phrase written by Tocqueville himself: "Je crois mais je ne puis pratiquer"—"I believe but I cannot practice"—a phrase that attests to Tocqueville's intellectual and moral scrupulosity, rather than to disbelief. He had been brought up by an admirable tutor, the abbé Lesueur; around the age of sixteen, Tocqueville said, he had recognized that his Christian beliefs were no longer unconditional.

The evidence for his private religious practices during the middle phase of his life remains fragmentary; the evidence for his religious practices during the last phase of his life is not. It is not only that the statement by Beaumont is contradicted by many other accounts and letters by Tocqueville's friends and members of his family. In 1962 this writer found three separate accounts by the nursing sisters in the archives of their congregation; published in the July 1964 issue of the *Catholic Historical Review*, they confirm the facts and attest to the sincerity of Tocqueville's religious acts.

Why lay stress on these private matters? For two reasons. First, they may help to answer the third among the series of questions previously posed: Was Tocqueville a historian or a sociologist? a liberal or a conservative? a skeptic or a believing Catholic? Second, his concern with religion appears with increasing frequency in Tocqueville's correspondence during the last decade of his life when, together with self-questioning about his own faith, the problem of the compatibility of religion with democracy became one of his deepest preoccupations. There are evidences of this already in his *Democracy in America* in the 1830's.

Tocqueville's correspondence was voluminous. Of the twenty-one volumes planned for the still uncompleted edition of his collected works, eleven or twelve will consist of letters. They are still being discovered in French family archives and in the stocks of manuscript dealers. The scope of his correspondence is amazing. It deals with innumerable topics of lasting interest. The letters about England, Germany, and Russia deserve minute attention. The quality of the writing is as high as that of his finished books. Tocqueville had often thought that he was solitary, but he put great value on his friendships. He was driven by a need to express his thoughts to his friends. His letters served him as a diary would another thinker. In them we find the germ of ideas Tocqueville would later develop in a book. For example, Tocqueville to Pierre Freslon, 10 August 1853:

> In reading the correspondence of the ministers of Louis XV with their subordinates, you see a crowd of little embryo professors of imperial administrative law. So true is this that the better one is acquainted with the old regime the more one finds that the Revolution was far from doing either all the good or all the harm that is supposed; it may be said rather to have disturbed than to have altered society. This truth springs up in all directions as soon as one ploughs the ancient soil.

Among the most important of these letters are those that Tocqueville wrote to Arthur de Gobineau. Gobineau met Tocqueville in the early 1840's. In 1849 he served as Tocqueville's secretary. During the 1850's they saw each other relatively seldom; but Gobineau tried out some of his theories in his letters to Tocqueville, whose reactions to Gobineau's ideas—and later to Gobineau's book *The Inequality of the Human Races*—are trenchant and extremely important. They are summary statements of the beliefs of the Catholic Tocqueville; and they are principal arguments for the incompatibility of Christianity with a philosophy of history dependent on conceptions of race. They also illustrate the idealism

of Tocqueville, who wrote his friend Louis de Kergorlay in 1835, twenty years before the development of his dialogue with Gobineau:

> Do what you will, you can't change the fact that men have bodies as well as souls—that the angel is enclosed in the beast. . . . Any philosophy, any religion which tries to leave entirely out of account one of these two things may produce a few extraordinary exemplars, but it will never influence humanity as a whole. This is what I believe, and it troubles me, for you know that, no more detached from the beast than anyone else, I adore the angel and want at all costs to see him predominate.

This passage, by no means an isolated one, shows the Pascalian element in Tocqueville's thought. Like his temperament and his faith, his views of human nature and of human knowledge were not Cartesian.

Tocqueville had little appetite for methodical philosophy, though on occasion he did not hesitate to criticize certain passages in Aristotle or Plato. Yet the processes of Tocqueville's thought were exquisitely philosophical. He saw, for example, that in human beings the relations of cause and effect are far more complex than in other organisms, let alone in the physical world. This perception is manifested in Tocqueville's discovery that revolutions often break out not when the pressure on people is the greatest, but when that pressure has recognizably begun to lessen. In short, the mechanical laws of the physical universe do not automatically apply to the human universe. As Tocqueville wrote in one of his last letters to Gobineau, in 1858: "A hypothesis which permits the prediction of certain effects that always recur under the same conditions does, in a way, amount to a demonstrable truth. [But] even the Newtonian system has no more than such a foundation." In this respect, too, Tocqueville's mind ran ahead of the nineteenth century. His ideas accord with those of some of the greatest twentieth-century thinkers, such as the Spanish philosopher José Ortega y Gasset, the French radical Christian humanist Georges Bernanos, and the German physicist-philosopher Werner Heisenberg.

We have seen that the recognition of Tocqueville has been far from universal and often inadequate, even though his literary legacy is unusually rich in scope and extent. We know much about his ideas, about the inclinations of his mind, and even about his religious and other beliefs. We know less about his private life. Many of his contemporaries resented Tocqueville's detached intelligence; they imputed to him an air of self-conscious superiority. Yet Tocqueville was a warmhearted human being, often to the point of excitability. His physical appearance was unprepossessing: he was small, thin, and nervous. The true nature of his nobility resided in his soul. In one of his notes he wrote: "Life is neither a pleasure nor a pain, but a serious spiritual business which it is our duty to carry through and to terminate with honor."

Selected Bibliography

EDITIONS

INDIVIDUAL WORKS

De la démocratie en Amérique. Vol. 1. Paris, 1840.
————. Vol. 2. Paris, 1860.
L'Ancien régime et la révolution. Paris, 1856.
Souvenirs. Paris, 1893.

COLLECTED WORKS

Oeuvres complètes. Edited by Gustave de Beaumont. 9 vols. Paris, 1860–1866.
Oeuvres complètes. Edited by J. P. Mayer et al. Paris, 1951– . Of the projected twenty-one volumes, sixteen had been published as of 1985, including two double volumes of *De la démocratie en Amérique.*

TRANSLATIONS

Alexis de Tocqueville: Recollections. Translated by George Lawrence and edited by J. P. Mayer and A. P. Kerr. Garden City, N.Y., 1970.
Democracy in America. Translated by Henry Reeve. New York, 1862. Revised by F. Bowen and Phillips Bradley. New York, 1945, 1961. Includes bibliography.
The European Revolution and Correspondence with Gobineau. Translated with introduction by John Lukacs. New York, 1959. Contains unfinished portions of Tocqueville's projected second volume of *The Old Régime* . . . as well as the Gobineau correspondence.
Journeys to England and Ireland. Translated by George Lawrence and J. P. Mayer. New Haven, Conn., 1958. Paperback edition, Garden City, N.Y., 1968.
Memoir, Letters, and Remains of Alexis de Tocqueville. Translated by Henry Reeve and edited by Gustave de Beaumont. New York, 1862.
The Old Régime and the Revolution. Translated by Stuart Gilbert. New York, 1955.
The Recollections of Alexis de Tocqueville. Translated by Alexander Taxeira de Mattos. New York, 1896.

BIOGRAPHICAL AND CRITICAL STUDIES

Alexis de Tocqueville: Livre du centenaire 1859–1959. Paris, 1960.
Corral, Luis Diez del. *La mentalidad política de Tocqueville con especial referencia a Pascal.* Madrid, 1965.
Drescher, Seymour. *Tocqueville and England.* Cambridge, Mass., 1964.
Lamberti, Jean Claude. *La notion d'individualisme chez Tocqueville.* Paris, 1970.
Marcel, R. P. *Essai politique sur Alexis de Tocqueville avec un grand nombre de documents inédits.* Paris, 1910.
Mayer, J. P. *Alexis de Tocqueville: A Biographical Essay in Political Science.* New York, 1940. Revised ed. with additional essay, New York, 1960.
Pierson, G. W., ed. *Tocqueville and Beaumont in America.* New York, 1938.
Redier, Antoine. *Comme diasit M. de Tocqueville.* Paris, 1925.
Zetterbaum, Marvin. *Tocqueville and the Problem of Democracy.* Stanford, Calif., 1967.

JOHN LUKACS

POETIC REALISM:
THEODOR STORM
(1817–1888)
GOTTFRIED KELLER
(1819–1890)
CONRAD FERDINAND MEYER
(1825–1898)

INTRODUCTION

IN THE GERMAN tradition, the term "poetic realism" refers to the literary mode predominant between approximately 1848 and 1890. The differences between poetic realism and social realism, the major literary movement in most other European countries in the mid-nineteenth century, have much to do with Germany's unusual sociopolitical status. Until 1871, when the German empire was founded with Otto von Bismarck as its chancellor, Germany consisted not of a single nation but of a number of provincial monarchies. Liberal efforts throughout the first half of the century to establish a national state culminated in revolutionary uprisings, in 1848, against local monarchs in several German cities; in March of that year an assembly of liberals called a national parliament in Frankfurt to draft a constitution for a united Germany. Although the uprisings were suppressed and the parliament soon collapsed, the year 1848 marks a watershed in the history of German literature. There arose a sense among intellectuals that culture could no longer be the same after politics had been brought to the forefront of daily life.

Julian Schmidt, who became coeditor of the literary and political journal *Die Grenzboten* in 1848, spoke for critics of the day in calling for a new kind of literature. In essays written in the 1850's he maintains that, in contrast both to the supernatural, fantastic quality of much of romanticism and to the utopian orientation of classicism, literature should now take real life as its point of departure. Yet Schmidt also criticizes the tendentiousness of *Vormärz* (pre-March, or prerevolutionary) political poetry and insists that the writer should not simply reproduce reality as it is but should infuse his works with a degree of idealism in order to elevate and move his reader. It is Schmidt's follower Otto Ludwig, however, who actually coined the term "poetic realism" for the synthetic literary mode Schmidt was prescribing. In a piece from the late 1850's entitled "Poetischer Realismus" Ludwig envisions a realism that will avoid both the monotony of idealism, epitomized in his opinion by Friedrich von Schiller's works, and the random multiplicity of detail characteristic of naturalism, by which he means the political literature of the 1830's. According to Ludwig, poetic or "artful" realism should distill a heightened, self-enclosed totality from the multitudinous and coincidental phenomena of external reality, a middle realm between the "objective truth of things" and the subjectivity of the shaping mind.

Subsequent practice bears out this theory to a considerable extent. The literature of the period can in fact be seen to span a charged field between the extremes of realism and poeticism. As far as the realistic aspects are concerned, writers in the German-speaking world (present-day Germany, Switzerland, and Austria) as elsewhere were affected by developments in nineteenth-century philosophy and science, notably positivism and Darwinism, both of which contributed to a progressive erosion of religious faith and a corresponding emphasis on the things of this world. Literature became vivid and precise in describing individuals, places, and eras. That the nineteenth century was a period of transition is nowhere truer than in Germany, which witnessed the supplanting of feudalism by capitalism and, following the establishment of Bismarck's empire, a belated industrial revolution. The work of the poetic realists registered these changes and their concomitant ills, such as increasing materialism, class inequities, and familial tensions. Yet in contrast to the social realism of novelists such as Stendhal, Balzac, Dickens, Thackeray, or Tolstoy, who depict individuals confronting social institutions against a panoramic background of history-making contemporary events, the literature of poetic realism, reflecting Germany's different conditions, tended to focus on the private activities of small groups of people in provincial regions (usually the writer's homeland), and

much of it was set in the distant past. In general, poetic realism was more effective in portraying the dramas of single lives than in depicting the individual's relation to society at large. Moreover, its realism was offset by an inclination to poeticize reality that manifested itself in markedly sentimental or idyllic aspects. These further distinguish poetic realism from social realism.

Because of its comparatively narrow focus, unlike social realism poetic realism was ill suited to the novel, except for the bildungsroman, or novel of development, which concentrates on the inner life of its protagonist rather than on his dealings with society. The chief genres of poetic realism are lyric poetry and, above all, the novella. The novella originated in Italy with Boccaccio's *Decameron* (1349–1351), a cycle of one hundred tales told by a group of well-to-do Florentines to divert themselves from thoughts about the plague. The literal meaning of the Italian word *novella*—"news" or "news item"—indicates the dualism between novelty and believability that continued to characterize the genre for centuries. This dichotomy is intrinsic to Johann Wolfgang von Goethe's famous definition, formulated in a conversation with Johann Eckermann in 1827, of the novella as an "event that is unheard of but has taken place." Maintaining the convention begun by Boccaccio and upheld in Goethe's *Unterhaltungen deutscher Ausgewanderten* (*The Recreations of the German Emigrants*, 1795), many novellas of poetic realism are set within a narrative frame in order to substantiate the illusion of veracity; yet they typically treat not ordinary but exceptional, striking events and personages. In contrast to the novel, the novella tends to revolve around a single conflict affecting a small number of characters who are already developed. Often a "thing-symbol" is crucial in bringing cohesion to the novella's plot. Because of its relative brevity the novella frequently contains sudden turning points or reversals, a feature that links it to the drama. Indeed the novella's concentration on a single conflict, its streamlined shape, and, in the nineteenth century, its concern with serious human problems inspired Theodor Storm to refer to it in an unpublished preface of 1881 as the "sister of the drama."

In addition to Storm, the most representative poetic realists are Gottfried Keller and Conrad Ferdinand Meyer. With all three writers, motifs from the poetry recur in the novellas, notably the element of nature, which plays a much greater role in poetic realism than in social realism. The fact that both Keller and Meyer were Swiss by no means excludes them from the tradition of German poetic realism. Although Switzerland was an independent sovereign state, Swiss authors were part of German literary life in the same way as writers from the provinces of what became the empire: they were joined by a common language, and all saw themselves as heirs of the tradition that had reached a zenith in Goethe. In the early 1890's, when Storm and Keller were dead and Meyer was no longer writing, poetic realism came to an end. It gave way, on the one hand, to naturalism and the belated arrival of social realism and, on the other, to aestheticism and symbolism. As we shall see, roots of all these modes may be found in the works of the poetic realists.

THEODOR STORM

Nowhere is the importance of the homeland for the writers of poetic realism more evident than in the work of Theodor Storm. Again and again his literary settings evoke the marshes and moors, the islands and dikes characteristic of the North Sea landscape around the small port city of Husum in Schleswig, where he was born on 14 September 1817. In later years he suggested that his strong sense of attachment to his native region was connected with the fact that his ancestors on both sides had lived in Husum or its environs for centuries and that many of their descendants had occupied prominent positions in the town

while he was growing up. A number of his early novellas are indebted to his idealized memories of this extended family.

Because the duchy of Schleswig belonged to Denmark until 1864, Storm was a Danish citizen by birth. But he was raised speaking German, and after graduating from the Latin School in Husum he spent a year and a half at a notable German high school in Lübeck. Here friends kindled his enthusiasm for modern German writers such as Goethe, Joseph von Eichendorff, and Heinrich Heine, whose works became formative influences on his own. Largely because of his father's insistence and example, Storm went on to study law, alternating between the universities of Kiel and Berlin. These pursuits failed to stifle his literary inclinations, which were particularly fostered by his activities in the "Clique" in Kiel, a literary and political circle dominated by Theodor and Tycho Mommsen. Together with the two brothers, Storm collected legends, fairy tales, and songs of the Schleswig-Holstein region and wrote poetry, much of which was published jointly in their *Liederbuch dreier Freunde* (Songbook of Three Friends) in 1843. In the same year Storm opened a law office in Husum, and three years later he married his cousin Constanze Esmarch.

Even while laying the foundations of career and family, Storm continued to write poetry. The first edition of his own poetry appeared in 1852. Though the last edition was published in 1885, the heyday of his lyric production was in the late 1840's and early 1850's, and the edition of 1852 contains most of his best-known pieces. The major themes of the collection are politics, nature, transience, death, and love. His political poetry was shaped by the revolution of 1848, which because of his special situation as a German in a Danish duchy affected Storm more directly than the other poetic realists. Inspired by the uprisings in favor of national unity that had recently broken out in a number of large towns in Germany, a group of Schleswig's German inhabitants began a war of independence from Denmark in March 1848. Several of Storm's poems express his dismayed reactions to the subsequent bloody battles between Danish royalist troops and the insurgents, who were finally put down in 1850. Even the early poem "Ostern" (Easter, 1846–1848; dates given after the titles of poems indicate the time of composition) reveals Storm's pro-German and anti-aristocratic feelings; it ends with the fervent line "Das Land ist unser, unser soll es bleiben!" (This land is ours, and ours it will remain!). The events of this period did much to turn Storm away from contemporary Danish literature, still given over to fantasy, and toward an interest in matters of everyday life. His increasing appreciation of the created world is especially evident in the poem "Oktoberlied" (October Song, 1848), which includes the following stanza:

> *Und geht es draussen noch so toll,*
> *Unchristlich oder christlich,*
> *Ist doch die Welt, die schöne Welt,*
> *So gänzlich unverwüstlich!*

No matter how wild things are out there, Christian or unchristian, nevertheless the world, the lovely world, is totally indestructible!

The second line of this stanza intimates another important characteristic of Storm's thought, one that was to grow steadily more pronounced: his antipathy to organized religion.

The somewhat devil-may-care tone of this stanza of "Oktoberlied" suggests that despite his pro-German sympathies Storm was by no means a political poet. Even his patriotic poems differ markedly in temper from the polemical, tendentious work of the *Vormärz* poets of the 1830's and 1840's. For instance, Storm's "Gräber an der Küste" (Graves on the Coast, 1850), a response to the final crushing of the German rebels near Husum, is deeply elegiac, and its haunting evocation of the seaside landscape adds much to its expression of

feeling for the dead. The novelist Theodor Fontane, a contemporary of Storm, considered him the greatest lyric poet Germany had produced since Goethe, and the opinion of a later novelist, Thomas Mann, was similarly enthusiastic. Storm continued the tradition of the *Lied* (poem intended to be sung) so prominent in the Storm and Stress and romantic periods in German literature. Such poetry is characterized by the unmediated expression of emotion, a strong appeal to the senses, and a formal simplicity and regularity that enable it to be set to music easily. As a poet Storm is best known for his atmospheric depictions of his native region. Pieces such as "Abseits" ("The Heath," 1847), "Die Stadt" ("The City," 1851), and his own favorite, "Meeresstrand" ("The Seashore," 1854), capture the local images so familiar to him—the breakers, gulls, mists, and lonely heaths of the "gray city by the sea." The permanence of the sea is often contrasted with the transience of human life, possibly the dominant theme of Storm's entire oeuvre. Ticking clocks appear frequently in his poems as reminders of the evanescence of existence, and much of his work treats death and dying. Finally, a sizable portion of his lyric writing is love poetry. Much of it was inspired by his passionate affair with Dorothea Jensen, the daughter of a Husum senator, during the first year of his marriage.

Perhaps in direct response to this love affair, many of Storm's poems and early novellas also show a commitment to the institutions of marriage and the family and an attention to domesticity, both of which are strongly reminiscent of the Biedermeier period in German literature (1815–1848), particularly the work of Adalbert Stifter. An example unusual in Storm for its humor is the poem "Von Katzen" (Of Cats, 1849), which describes a feline population explosion that fills the narrator's house from basement to gable with kittens. A more somber treatment of domestic life is found in the early novella *Marthe und ihre Uhr* (Marthe and Her Clock, 1848; dates of prose works signify the year of first publication); the unmarried and aging protagonist of this story exhibits the typically Biedermeier traits of moral seriousness, resigned contentment with her solitary life, and a preoccupation with the care of flowers and furniture.

The family plays a crucial role in the novella *Im Saal* (*In the Great Hall,* 1849), where a christening brings together members of several generations. This situation serves as a frame for the great-grandmother's narration, prompted by remarks about the hall, of her own childhood and subsequent wedding to the patriarch of the clan now gathered some eighty years later. Another novella, *Späte Rosen* (Late Roses, 1860), celebrates the mature love and appreciation of a man for his aging wife. But these stories too are imbued with a sense of the changes brought by the passage of time: Marthe's old clock ticks forth memories of the days before her mother died, leaving her alone; the rococo era of the great-grandmother's childhood in *In the Great Hall* is clearly idealized in contrast with the upheavals of the present day; and an awareness of the inevitable fading of youth and beauty pervades *Späte Rosen.*

These novellas demonstrate a phenomenon one encounters repeatedly in the works of poetic realism, a pattern that may be termed the subversion of the idyllic moment. This pattern reflects the period in which these writers were living, an era of transition from a feudal to an industrialized society. Having one foot in each world, they tended to think nostalgically of earlier ways of life as being simpler and more innocent, as they saw them gradually being eroded by the forces of progress. The resulting sense of loss surfaces in a variety of guises in their works; childhood or adolescence, for example, is often depicted as a time of love between individuals whom social or economic constrictions later drive apart.

This is precisely the pattern traced by Storm's *Immensee* (1850), the novella that made him famous and has since remained one of his most popular. Like *In the Great Hall* and

many later tales, *Immensee* consists of reminiscences triggered by a concrete object the narrator or main character perceives in the present. Here, a picture of his childhood love, Elisabeth, sends the solitary, elderly Reinhard off into dreams of his youth, conveyed in a series of vignettes. We are told of the idyllic days the two spent together as schoolchildren, playing hand in hand in the meadows; of Reinhard's budding poetic inclinations, shown in the adventure stories he tells Elisabeth and in the poems he writes for her; and of their separation when he leaves home to continue his studies elsewhere. Returning for Easter, he is struck by a strange coolness in Elisabeth. The nature of the change in her is intimated by the fact that the linnet he had given her has died and been replaced by the gift of a canary in a gilded cage from her new friend, Erich. Two years later Reinhard learns of Elisabeth's marriage to Erich. But what Storm tells here is not simply the old, hackneyed story of a lover forgotten in his absence. Visiting Immensee, Erich's estate, some years afterward, Reinhard notices the "sisterly" glances Elisabeth casts at her husband; and her emotional reaction to the folk song "Elisabeth" (beginning "Meine Mutter hat's gewollt" [My mother willed it]) makes the situation clear: Elisabeth has repressed her love for Reinhard and married the financially successful Erich at her mother's insistence.

Immensee thus dramatizes a theme that is particularly prominent in German literature and finds its most extensive treatment in the work of Thomas Mann: the conflict between the sensitive artist and the ordinary bourgeois. Indeed, Storm's keen awareness of this conflict, which he acutely experienced in his double life as a lawyer and writer, was one of the things that made his work so appealing to Mann. Mann said that his own novella *Tonio Kröger* (1903) was simply a modern version of *Immensee;* and in reflecting on the differences between himself and the unartistic personality that enjoys life unproblematically, the writer Tonio is reminded of a line from

Storm's poem "Hyazinthen" (Hyacinths, 1851): "Ich möchte schlafen; aber du musst tanzen" (I would like to sleep; but you must dance). The appearance of this theme in *Immensee* anticipates its very different treatment in Storm's *Pole Poppenspäler* (1874), where a family of puppet makers is treated with suspicion by the middle-class residents of the town in which they perform.

The element of social criticism in both *Pole Poppenspäler* and *Immensee* is unmistakable. *Immensee* makes an implicit negative comment not only on the materialistic aspirations of Elisabeth's mother but also on the social misery that resulted from the class system of Storm's day: at two significant points in the novella Reinhard meets girls begging. To the first girl, encountered when he is feeling homesick on his first Christmas away from home, he gives half the cake he has just received from Elisabeth; he meets the second girl after his last conversation with Elisabeth. The ragged condition of both girls heightens the reader's sense of Reinhard's own unhappy state, especially since the second of the two is the same gypsy girl whose vivacious sensuality had attracted him during his early student years, when she had worked as a singer in his local tavern. The song she had sung then, lamenting the transience of beauty, togetherness, and life in general, can be seen in retrospect as a melancholy foreshadowing of both the loss of Reinhard's happiness and her ultimate decline. The theme of unfulfilled love was one to which Storm returned in the novella *Im Sonnenschein* (*In the Sunlight*, 1854). Its opening vignette depicts an encounter between a young girl and a soldier during the rococo era; in a second vignette, occurring over sixty years later, we learn that the attraction came to nothing because the girl's father was against the military. Now the only tangible remnant of the affair is the girl's medallion containing a lock of her beloved's hair—a poignant reminder of disappointed dreams and frustrated hopes.

Merely to outline the plot of these early novellas does not do justice to their lyrical quality. *Marthe und ihre Uhr, In the Great Hall, In the Sunlight,* and above all *Immensee* are less stories in the conventional sense than they are atmospheric mood pictures, or impressions; Storm himself called them "situations." In these works characters are not fully drawn and images predominate over action, many of them echoing motifs in the poetry. In fact a number of Storm's poems, such as "Elisabeth," are incorporated into *Immensee*, which in the manner of the earlier romantic novel aims to integrate song or poem with narrative. As in lyric poetry, the effect of this novella is produced by suggestion and symbolism rather than explicit narration. For example the bird symbolism, whereby the tame canary in its gilded cage replaces the relatively undomesticated linnet, externalizes the supplanting of the somewhat unconventional Reinhard by the civilized, socially successful Erich. And the water lily that Reinhard swims after in Lake Immen seems to symbolize the happiness he might have had with Elisabeth, a happiness that appeared near but, like the lily, repeatedly eluded his grasp.

Yet the narrative structure, in which Reinhard's story is told in the third person and framed by glimpses of his present life as an old man, gives a degree of objectivity and distance to what might otherwise have become an excessively sentimental work. This technique may reflect the influence of Storm's memories of his love for Bertha von Buchan, whom he had met when she was a child and to whom he unsuccessfully proposed marriage in 1842. The narrative structure of *Immensee* helped him distance himself from this disturbing experience. More broadly, the use of the third person lends a universality to one of Storm's subtlest and most moving portrayals of the evanescence of youth and happiness.

Storm's life took a major turn with the definitive reoccupation of Schleswig by Denmark. Because of his sympathies with the German insurgents, his license to practice law in Husum was revoked by the Danish authorities in 1852, and the following year he went into exile with his family in Potsdam, near Berlin. Here he took a position as an assistant judge that was at first unpaid and then very poorly paid, so that he was forced, as a man in his mid-thirties, to rely on financial assistance from his parents and in-laws. His distress was compounded by homesickness and an antipathy toward Prussian officialdom as well as by an unusually big workload; it is no wonder that his literary output during these years was small. His stay in Potsdam did, however, bring him into contact with a number of important contemporary German writers, such as Eichendorff, Fontane, and others, many of whom Storm met after joining two prominent Berlin literary societies of the day, the Tunnel über der Spree and the Rütli. His professional position improved somewhat with his move in 1856 to the small Prussian town of Heiligenstadt in Thuringia, where he became district court judge. Yet as a freethinker in religious matters Storm could not help but feel ill at ease in this provincial Catholic town. In March 1864, during the war of liberation in which the Prussian and Austrian armies were to free Schleswig from Danish rule some months later, Storm returned at last to his native town, where he became district judge and chief of police.

Even back home, however, Storm's life did not remain free of upheavals. He suffered a severe blow in 1865, when his wife Constanze died after giving birth to their seventh child. This loss inspired some of his most compelling poems, such as "Tiefe Schatten" (Dark Shadows, 1865) and "Begrabe nur dein Liebstes!" (Do Bury Your Love!, 1865). Just over a year after Constanze's death Storm married Dorothea Jensen, who had refused all offers since her affair with him in 1847. But the early years of their marriage were by no means idyllic, since Storm maintained a virtual cult to the memory of his dead wife; for example,

he refused to allow his children to address Dorothea as "mother." He fictionalizes this touchy situation and its eventual resolution in the novella *Viola tricolor* (*Viola Tricolor: The Little Stepmother*, 1874). Two of his subsequent novellas are strongly autobiographical as well, dealing with his own children. *Ein stiller Musikant* (A Quiet Musician, 1875) reflects Storm's disappointment over the failure of his son Karl to become an accomplished musician; and the figure of Heinrich in *Carsten Curator* (*Curator Carsten*, 1878) is based on his son Hans, an unstable alcoholic who died young.

A knowledge of the autobiographical elements in these works is not necessary in order to appreciate them as representative of a new, protonaturalist phase in Storm's oeuvre. Like the naturalist writers Émile Zola and Gerhart Hauptmann after him, Storm was led by new developments in nineteenth-century science to take an interest in the role played by heredity and environment in human lives. In contrast to his early lyrical novellas, where it appears as a bastion of security and tradition, the family (as in later naturalist literature) now comes to be depicted in Storm's works as a kind of prison; individual traits are genetically predetermined and characters are pitted against each other because of social or psychological forces they cannot control. These inexorable forces assume a role comparable to that of fate in Greek tragedy, this feature being only one of those that link Storm's fiction to what he saw as the novella's "sister" genre, the drama.

The father-child relation is of particular interest to Storm. Both *Ein stiller Musikant* and *Curator Carsten*, for instance, reflect his sense of having contributed, biologically or through acts of omission, to the fates of the two sons on whom the stories are modeled. *Curator Carsten* suggests that Heinrich, who is totally unreliable, unable to manage money, and given to heavy drinking, is largely conditioned by the marriage of his solidly dependable father,

Carsten, to a passionate, flighty woman to whom he is ill suited. In a most dramatic portrayal of Storm's native landscape, Heinrich, on the edge of bankruptcy, goes to his father for financial help during a raging North Sea storm that threatens to flood the town. Knowing that Heinrich is drunk, Carsten locks him out, and the boy is later assumed to have drowned. Carsten's feelings of guilt and Storm's sense of the inescapability of heredity and upbringing are intimated by the narrator in the penultimate sentence of the story: "No one thinks about the fact that with each morsel of food he simultaneously gives his child a piece of his own life, which soon becomes a part of him forever."

Both the father-son conflict and the sea milieu recur in *Hans und Heinz Kirch* (Hans and Heinz Kirch, 1882), where the criticism of contemporary society is more pronounced than in earlier works. Storm attacks middle-class greed, provincial pettiness, and the influence of class differences by showing how these things increasingly alienate the seaman Heinz Kirch from his father, Hans, a prosperous, ambitious shipowner. Before embarking on a long voyage to the China seas, Heinz takes a moonlit boat ride with Wieb, a lower-class girl whose mother's reputation is questionable. After Hans's sister implies that the gossip provoked by this "scandal" is the reason Hans was not elected to the town council, he writes an enraged letter to his son that significantly widens the rift between them. When Heinz finally writes his father back, Hans refuses to accept the letter because it arrives with postage due, and he wants nothing to do with a son in financial difficulties. The narrator's description of the next fifteen years, which go by without a word from Heinz Kirch, is unusual in Storm in its references to larger contemporary events, such as the appearance of telegraph wires and railroads and the founding of the German empire. These historical details are counterbalanced by a number of sentimental scenes and contrived plot developments. When Heinz at last returns home, only to leave again for good, he is so changed that the townspeople and even his own family doubt his identity, though Wieb has proof that it is he. The story offers a striking example of Storm's treatment of the theme of familial alienation.

Among the most markedly naturalistic works by Storm is the late novella *Ein Doppelgänger* (A Double, 1886). The narrator recalls having met some years before a forester whose wife, Christine, turned out to be from his hometown. The bulk of the remaining narrative recounts his memories of Christine's father, John Hansen, the double of the title. Driven to steal by financial necessity, John served time in prison before meeting and falling in love with Hanna, a young field hand. Poverty and the stigma of being a former convict put strains on his marriage. He takes to battering his wife and daughter, and in a moment of rage accidentally kills Hanna. The murder is covered up, and John becomes a devoted father to Christine. The title refers to these two sides of John: the violent criminal and the loving father attempting to do penance for his past. With its picture of individuals controlled by economic circumstances, the household as a battleground, and the inescapability of the past, the story represents a naturalistic transformation of the romantic theme of the doppelgänger. But here again, the novella's realism is offset by poetic elements, such as the scenes between John and the child Christine after his reformation and the idyllic relationship between the adult Christine and the forester. Most notably, the authenticity of the story is thrown into question by its reliance on the narrator's reconstruction of events for which he has little firsthand evidence; his knowledge is hearsay, acquired as a boy. As the forester remarks at the end, the narrator's supposed reminiscences are in fact "poetry," contrived by the powers of his creative imagination.

But narrative structure plays the most crucial role in Storm's oeuvre in his historical or chronicle novellas. As in *In the Great Hall* and

Immensee, in these works a concrete object—a picture, pieces of a building—from the present serves as the point of departure for recounting past events. And as in Storm's early novellas the fact that such objects, themselves crumbling with age, are the only tangible remnants of lost experience stands as a reminder of the transience of all things. These historical novellas take place in the distant past, and the central object often leads to the discovery of a manuscript or chronicle containing the story itself. This device is intended to lend to these works a greater degree of credibility and reality, augmented by the use of archaic expressions and elements of local color from the period described. Despite their historical character these novellas treat many of the same themes as Storm's works with contemporary settings. For instance *Eekenhof* (1879) and *Zur Chronik von Grieshuus (A Chapter in the History of Grieshuus,* 1884), both set for the most part in the seventeenth century, explore the dark, fatalistic consequences of hereditary influences and familial conflicts (incest, enmity between father and son and between siblings); and *Ein Fest auf Haderslevhuus (A Festival at Haderslevhuus,* 1885) is a morbid tale of marital strife, adultery, and revenge in the Middle Ages.

Storm treats the joint themes of transience and paternal guilt most effectively in his first chronicle novella, *Aquis submersus* (1876). A fairly detailed plot outline will indicate the complicated narrative structures he uses in these later novellas. Here the objects that set the narrative in motion are two fading portraits discovered by the narrator in a village church in what is clearly Storm's native region: one of a dead boy and another of an intimidating-looking man in a priest's collar, said to be the boy's father. The narrator's curiosity is particularly piqued by the letters "C.P.A.S.," which he notices in the corner of the boy's picture. Years later he happens on another painting of the boy in a house in town and, on asking the residents of the house about it, is given an old chronicle manuscript

by their seventeenth-century ancestor Johannes, the painter of the picture. The text of the manuscript, written in seventeenth-century language, makes up the bulk of the novella and holds the key to the mystery of the paintings. It unfolds the story of Johannes' childhood love for Katharina, the daughter of his noble patron in Holstein, and of their eventual separation when Johannes leaves to undertake an apprenticeship in Amsterdam. On returning years afterward, he learns that Katharina's brother is urging her to marry a brutish but wealthy baron against her will—a plot situation reminiscent of *Immensee.* Johannes and Katharina share one night before he is wounded by her brother for daring, as a commoner, to ask for her hand. By the time he recovers from his wound she has disappeared. He locates her again by chance some five years later in a North Sea town, and during their passionate reunion her son—their son—drowns in a nearby pond. The curse on their lives is fulfilled. Johannes is forced by the man who had married the pregnant Katharina, the intimidating priest of the portrait in the church, to paint the dead boy's picture as a moral warning. Thus the narrative circle is closed, the significance of the letters beneath the boy's portrait revealed—"*Culpa Patris Aquis Submersus*"—"Vanished beneath the waters through the guilt of the father."

As in *Immensee, In the Sunlight, Hans und Heinz Kirch, A Chapter in the History of Grieshuus,* and other works by Storm, in this novella the idyllic moment of young love is ultimately overthrown by considerations of class or professional position. And, as in those works, Storm's social criticism is complemented by a more general sense of the inherently tragic nature of human life in the face of mortality, by the awareness that even works of art, which seem to offer a means of preserving past experience, will also eventually "vanish beneath the waters" of time. Indeed, the inscription that both the primary narrator of *Aquis submersus* and Johannes notice on the house containing the third portrait sums up one of the major messages of Storm's entire oeuvre: "Just as smoke and dust vanish, so does man."

The most intricate narrative situation in Storm's writings, and probably in the whole history of the German novella, is found in the work usually regarded as his masterpiece, *Der Schimmelreiter* (*The Rider on the White Horse*, 1888). Here the primary narrator recalls a magazine article he read some fifty years before in which a traveler related a story he had heard in the 1830's from a village schoolmaster in North Frisia. Nowhere in Storm's oeuvre is the North Sea landscape more vividly depicted than in the schoolmaster's tale of the rise and fall of Hauke Haien, who from boyhood is fascinated by the technology for constructing dikes. Through careful study Hauke becomes convinced that the traditional method is outdated, and after he realizes through marriage his long-standing ambition to become *dikegrave*, he sets out to have a new, more effective dike built to buttress the old one. Hauke increasingly alienates his workers through his imperiousness, his innovative thinking, and his opposition to their superstitious beliefs. He is isolated not only from the community but from his family as well; he becomes so obsessed by his work that he neglects his wife, and he feels estranged from the retarded child she bears at last because of the child's closeness to old Trin Jans, the chief representative of the superstitious attitudes he despises. His outsider status is dramatically shown in the image of his white horse, a proud, rebellious animal that will tolerate no other rider. Paradoxically, Hauke is ultimately defeated not by hubris but by weakness. Debilitated by a bout of malaria, against his better judgment he allows inadequate repairs to be made on the town's old dike. When it later bursts during a tidal wave, he plunges with his horse into the flood after seeing his wife and child washed away.

Although the village schoolmaster, like Hauke, is an enlightened champion of reason, his story includes bits and pieces of local lore, such as the suspicion that Hauke's horse was a supernatural creature. Moreover, his narration is triggered in the first place by the traveler's report that he has just passed a pale man with blazing eyes riding a white horse along the dike—according to superstition, the ghost of Hauke Haien. Unable to comprehend or reluctant to accept Hauke's distinctiveness and superiority, the townspeople have stylized him into a phantom in order to account for his special qualities. The triple-frame narrative, involving the primary narrator's recollection of the traveler's written version of the schoolmaster's oral story about a person he did not know, distances us as readers so effectively from the protagonist that we cannot penetrate him either. The polar opposites that propel the story—reason and superstition, individualism and conformity, progress and tradition, history and legend—are balanced so carefully that it is difficult to make final judgments about one side or the other. In this work Storm comes close to achieving perfect objectivity. The novella's ambiguity is heightened by its stylistic mixture of realistic and poetic or lyric features—its interweaving of true-to-life descriptions of North Frisian customs, carefully researched detail, and the vocabulary of dike technology, with gloomy, demonic depictions of the elemental forces of nature. The work's two-sidedness parallels its suggestion that even the heroic ethic of the imperialistic Bismarckian era, with its exaltation of the ambitious, hardworking, "monumental" individual, could ultimately prove hollow in the face of the contradictions of fate. *The Rider on the White Horse* is a fitting culmination of Storm's oeuvre. He died just a few months after completing it, in July 1888.

GOTTFRIED KELLER

Just as evocations of the North Sea landscape around Husum give much of Storm's poetry and prose its characteristic flavor, the topography and spirit of his native Switzerland are never absent from the works of Keller. The country still recognizes him as one of the greatest writers in its history, one especially successful at voicing Swiss concerns and at depicting the peculiarities of the Swiss temperament. Keller was born on 19 July 1819, two years after Storm, in Zurich. At the time Zurich was a small city still strongly medieval in appearance and provincial in mentality, little resembling the cosmopolitan metropolis it is today.

In childhood and adolescence Keller met with a number of misfortunes that are worth mentioning because of the mark they left on his work, particularly on the novel *Der grüne Heinrich* (*Green Henry;* first version 1854–1855, second version 1879–1880). The first of these was the sudden death of his father, a master lathe worker, when Keller was only five. He thus became acquainted very early with something he was to experience again several times, financial hardship. Although his mother remarried not long after her husband's death, she was soon divorced. The second major setback in Keller's life occurred in 1834, when he was expelled from school because of his participation in a minor student uprising. From then until he entered the University of Heidelberg in 1848 he was largely self-taught.

Not long after his expulsion Keller decided that his calling lay in the art of painting. This was, incidentally, an inclination shared by many nineteenth-century German-language writers, a fact not surprising in light of the descriptive, painterly quality of realist literature. After spending the next few years in rather unsystematic attempts to train himself as a landscape painter, Keller left home in 1840 for the Art Academy in Munich, long one of Germany's leading cultural and artistic centers (Munich's Schwabing, a kind of German Greenwich Village, still attracts many aspiring young artists today). But he encountered no one in Munich properly equipped to instruct him and was unable to develop the discipline or find the inspiration necessary to pursue his artistic tendencies. Following two years of unfocused bohemianism, he returned to Zurich depressed and penniless.

Where the painter failed, however, the poet took over. Stimulated by his reading of the German romantic novelist Jean Paul Richter in 1843, Keller moved away from painting and toward writing as a vocation. As with Storm, his first literary efforts were in poetry. His career as a poet received its decisive impetus from his contact in the 1840's with German writers who had emigrated to Zurich because their liberal political views met with resistance at home. Émigrés such as August Follen, Georg Herwegh, Ferdinand Freiligrath, and August Heinrich Hoffmann von Fallersleben encouraged Keller (either by giving advice or through their own examples), helped publish some of his early poems, and spurred his fervor for radical causes. Keller in fact emerges as the only poetic realist to have had strong liberal leanings throughout his life. He sided, for instance, with the Protestants against the Catholic rural cantons, which opposed the increased centralization sought by the Swiss liberals. With eager interest he watched the conflicts that culminated in the victory of the radicals in a short, almost bloodless civil war in 1847, its result being the transformation of the confederation into a federal union under a new constitution in 1848. He thus saw the Swiss achieve what the German liberals were fighting for so energetically and were not to attain until more than two decades later.

Keller's first collection of poetry, published in 1846, testifies to these political inclinations. Its most famous poem, "An das Vaterland" (To the Fatherland, 1843), was set to music by Wilhelm Baumgartner and later became the Swiss national anthem. Beginning with the lines "O mein Heimatland! O mein Vaterland! / Wie so innig, feurig lieb' ich dich!" (O my homeland! O my fatherland! How deeply, how ardently I love you!) and disparaging foreign monarchy in favor of Swiss democracy, it resembles a number of Storm's early poems, whose pro-German and antiaristocratic sentiments were inspired by Schleswig's war of independence in the late 1840's. Keller's volume of 1846 and subsequent collections from the early 1850's include poems on other than topical Swiss issues, but the best of Keller the poet is to be found in *Gesammelte Gedichte* (Collected Poems, 1883). Prepared by the writer himself, the volume contains poems treating the typically romantic themes of nature, love, and death, as well as political poems and pieces commemorating various events in nineteenth-century Swiss history. Keller was not so fine a lyric poet as Storm; for the most part he lacks the originality and songlike simplicity of Storm, and he is remembered primarily for his prose writings. Even so, Keller's "Abendlied" ("Evening Song," 1879) is among the best-known poems in the German tradition. A latter-day variation on the carpe diem motif, it balances melancholy in the face of death with joy in life on earth, thus embodying a contrast found in much of Keller's work in prose. Its last lines, "Trinkt, O Augen, was die Wimper hält, / Von dem goldnen Überfluss der Welt!" (Drink, O eyes, as much as your lashes can hold of the world's golden profusion!), epitomize the writer's lifelong passion for seeing and describing earthly things.

Keller's secularism stems to a significant degree from his encounter with the teachings of the atheistic philosopher Ludwig Feuerbach in Heidelberg, where Keller was a scholarship student from 1848 to 1850. For Feuerbach, what human beings call God is merely a projection of their own best qualities. Like Auguste Comte and other nineteenth-century positivist and materialist philosophers, he advocated improving life on earth rather than speculating about life after death, about which we can know nothing. Repeatedly denied a professorship at the university, Feuerbach lectured at the invitation of Heidelberg students in the city hall. Under his influence Keller, like Storm, came to reject Christian conceptions of God and immortality. The Heidelberg years thus represent a crucial turning point in

Keller's career. Much of his later writing is colored by the notion, expressed by the protagonist of *Green Henry*, that "God radiates earthliness" (2.11). Indeed, Keller's release from a preoccupation with life after death seems to have unleashed his literary powers, since his most productive period followed his departure from Heidelberg and move to Berlin in 1850; during his five years there he managed to finish *Green Henry* as well as parts of several other works. He accomplished all this despite periods of loneliness, homesickness, and extreme poverty, even hunger.

Many of Keller's difficulties in the first thirty-five years of his life are immortalized in *Green Henry*, the greatest novel of poetic realism. This massive autobiographical work stands firmly in the tradition of the German bildungsroman, or novel of development, the prototype of which is Goethe's *Wilhelm Meister* (*Wilhelm Meisters Lehrjahre* [*Wilhelm Meister's Apprenticeship*, 1795–1796] and *Wilhelm Meisters Wanderjahre* [*Wilhelm Meister's Travels*, 1821]). Like Wilhelm Meister, Keller's protagonist, Heinrich Lee, is a middle-class man of above-average sensibility and imagination who progresses from youthful innocence and idealism to resigned practicality and from artistically inclined egocentricity to involvement in the community. Along his path Heinrich encounters a variety of milieus, characters, professions, and artistic and philosophical systems and becomes emotionally entangled with a series of female figures. By ripening his mind and sensibility, these influences help him to discover and cultivate his natural tendencies, to find his true self and his role in society. The novel spans the period from childhood and adolescence in the canton of Zurich through the stay in Munich and the author's ultimate return home.

The primary tension in Heinrich's life is that between what can broadly be termed idealism and realism. Particularly in his younger years he shuns truth, nature, and the real world in favor of his fanciful conceptions of these things. This tendency manifests itself above all in his childhood, when his overactive imagination is given to conjuring up fantastic visions of God, interpreting natural scenes in a highly poeticized fashion, and fabricating lies. The same tendency characterizes his vacillation between the two major loves of his adolescence, Anna and Judith. Although powerfully attracted to the older Judith, who is sensual and down-to-earth, radiantly healthy, and an obvious personification of nature, he resists entering into a sexual relationship with her because of his platonic ties to the delicate, innocent Anna, who seems more an angelic spirit than a human being. After Anna grows ill and dies, Heinrich rejects Judith, and with her the chance for a genuine engagement with life, and remains solipsistically bound to his memory of the dead girl. His entrapment in a world of his own devising is also evident in his approach to landscape painting, his chosen vocation. His first important drawing of the Swiss countryside is a "monstrosity" (1.20), and even after he goes to Munich for professional training, he succeeds only in producing idealized paintings that little resemble actual landscapes. Disillusioned and poverty-stricken, he decides to return to Switzerland.

On the way home Heinrich stops at the castle of a count, whose beautiful and intelligent foster daughter, Dortchen Schönfund, incorporates a synthesis between the spiritual and the sensual elements that had been divided between Anna and Judith. Dortchen acquaints Heinrich with the writings of Feuerbach and in general attempts to direct him toward an immediate concern with the here and now. Although he loves her, with his characteristic passivity he fails to propose to her. In the novel's second version, he comes into unexpected money through the sale of his paintings and returns to Switzerland just in time to watch his widowed mother, whom he has long neglected to write to, die. Realizing that he should have worked to support her rather than waste his time with aimless artistic endeavors, he decides to take a job in the civil service. He is lifted out of his feelings of guilt and depression by the return of Judith. But despite their mutual love, at the suggestion of Judith, whom experience has made skeptical, they renounce marriage and spend the twenty years until her death as close platonic friends.

This conclusion is considerably brighter than the ending written in 1855, which Keller describes in his autobiography of 1876 as "cypress-dark." In the first version Heinrich returns home to find his mother already dead. Stricken by grief and guilt, he subsequently languishes and dies himself. Keller conceived the new conclusion after critics repeatedly observed that Heinrich's death was insufficiently accounted for. Other differences between the two versions are largely structural. On the advice of Storm, with whom he began corresponding in 1877, Keller organized the later version chronologically. And whereas the earlier version alternates between the first and the third person, the version of 1879–1880 is told entirely in the first person by the middle-aged Heinrich himself. Its narrative form has much in common with that of Dickens' *Great Expectations* (1860–1861), in which the adult Pip recollects the events of his childhood and youth with an insight that the child could not have had.

Heinrich takes increasing control of his own fate as the novel progresses. Whereas the character as a young man is content to let providence shape his course, by the time he returns home from Munich his skepticism toward traditional Christianity is such that he has come to rely on his own will. The gesture of renunciation with which *Green Henry* ends is reminiscent of a good deal of Biedermeier literature and of *Wilhelm Meister,* the second part of which is subtitled *Die Entsagenden (The Renunciants).* In fact renunciation is virtually built into the German bildungsroman, which in contrast to the *Künstlerroman* (novel about the artist) traces the movement of its hero away from a diverse, artistic way of life and toward a single social occupation. In its belief in the individual's successful integration into society, the nineteenth-century bildungsroman demonstrates an optimism that was to disappear from the genre in the twentieth century. In Mann's *Der Zauberg* (*The Magic Mountain*, 1924), for instance, Hans Castorp descends from his seven-year stay at the mountaintop sanitorium only to enter into battle in World War I. The fundamental optimism of *Green Henry* is evident even in its title. Heinrich is "green" not only because of his green clothing (the original source of his nickname) and because throughout most of the novel he is very much a greenhorn; he is repeatedly associated with images of hope, which is traditionally symbolized by green— the color of rejuvenation and new life. The association is appropriate to Heinrich; despite all his trials he never loses faith in humanity.

Although the German bildungsroman typically moves its young protagonist away from art as a profession, it carefully records the effects of works of art on his mental, ethical, and cultural development. Stifter's *Der Nachsommer* (Indian Summer, 1857) contains the most extensive examples of this kind of charting. In *Wilhelm Meister*, Wilhelm's production of *Hamlet* plays a decisive role in his growth. In Keller's novel as well, literature influences Heinrich's evolution. As a child he acts the part of a monkey in the witch's kitchen scene of Goethe's *Faust I* and becomes enamored of the "bright day" of the theater as opposed to the "sad confusion" of real life (1.11). The same attraction is evident in the appeal Jean Paul Richter's writings later have for him. A change occurs, however, when in a forty-day reading marathon Heinrich devours the collected works of Goethe, which awaken in him an appreciation for the coherence and depth of this world.

Green Henry is further typical of the German bildungsroman in that it does without a conventional, action-filled plot and contains numerous digressions on minor characters, art, religion, science, forms of work, and philosophy. This characteristic of the bildungsroman, stemming from its focus on the culti-

vation of the inner life of its protagonist, is one of the chief differences between the German novel of development and the European novel of social realism, which depicts individuals within the context of contemporary social and historical events.

On the other hand, *Green Henry* comments more on politics than do other nineteenth-century German novels of development; for although Keller views Swiss democracy favorably, he is by no means uncritical of it, and the narrow philistinism of his countrymen comes in for a good deal of censure. His novel is full of vivid characters, details of Swiss rural customs, unforgettable depictions of the Swiss countryside, and remarkable insights into the way a child's mind works. But Keller's realism is infused throughout with a sensitivity and compassion that give the novel a subtly poetic stamp. It is above all the goal of Heinrich's self-cultivation that distinguishes this monument of poetic realism from other German novels of development: to realize the Goethean ideal of humanity within the limitations of everyday life, to discover, in other words, the poetry of a seemingly prosaic world.

At the same time, *Green Henry* is not free from moral didacticism. As Keller expressed it in a letter of 3 May 1850 to his publisher Vieweg: "He who is unsuccessful in managing his personal and family affairs is also incapable of occupying an effective and honorable position in society." This aspect of the novel anticipates much of Keller's later work, particularly his popular *Die Leute von Seldwyla* (*The People of Seldwyla*; vol. 1 1856, vol. 2 1873–1874). Seldwyla is an imaginary, rather frivolous Swiss town whose name derives from the Middle High German word *saelde*, meaning "blissful or sunny." The "blissfulness" of Seldwyla usually lies more in Keller's humorous treatment of its inhabitants than in their lives as such and it is in the novellas of this collection that Keller comes into his own as the master humorist among the poetic realists. Humor serves to temper his criticism of the folly of his countrymen and to underline his didactic intention, which assumes that people are capable of improvement.

A product of the culture that had given birth to such pedagogical figures as Jean Jacques Rousseau and Johann Heinrich Pestalozzi, Keller develops an instructive moral in each of the Seldwyla novellas, whose characters often undergo an education, notably in *Pankraz, der Schmoller (Pankraz, the Sulker)* and *Frau Regel Amrain und irh Jüngster (Regula Amrain and Her Youngest Son)*, both in volume 1. In the first of these, a mini-bildungsroman, Pankraz returns to Seldwyla to tell his mother and sister how he has been cured of sulking through an experience of unrequited love in British India and an extended staring contest with a lion in the far reaches of Africa. As is typical of the Seldwyla novellas, the humor of the situation is given an ironic edge. Having fallen asleep during his long narrative, Pankraz's mother and sister miss the story of his amorous experience abroad, exactly that part of his adventures which they had been intent on hearing, and he refuses ever to mention it again. The fact that Pankraz is in effect talking to himself and that his tale remains unshared within the novella serves to heighten the reader's sense of the man's isolation. The lighter aspects of the work are further counterbalanced by the character of the heartless and egocentric Lydia, the object of Pankraz's affections and the first in a series of cruel female figures in Keller's work. These character portraits undoubtedly owe much to experiences of the author, who suffered a number of unhappy love affairs and remained a bachelor all his life. A further autobiographical element in *Pankraz, der Schmoller*, as well as in *Green Henry* and *Regula Amrain*, is the situation of the fatherless household. *Regula Amrain* is virtually a fictionalized treatise on pedagogy, demonstrating through entertaining examples Frau Amrain's efforts to develop her youngest son into

a model of moderation and good sense with a commitment to his community at large. As such, he embodies a distinct contrast to his fellow Seldwylans.

The most satiric of the novellas in the first volume is *Die drei gerechten Kammacher (The Three Righteous Combmakers)*. As the narrator tells us at the outset, the moral of the tale is that while the Seldwylans have proved that a city full of unjust or frivolous people can coexist peaceably, three righteous men cannot live together for long under the same roof without getting into each other's hair. In fact the "righteousness" of the three journeymen consists in their obsession with work and their excessive thriftiness, qualities that spring from the desire of each to buy their master's combmaking business and win the wealthy old maid Züs Bünzlin.

This novella makes especially clear that Keller, in his pointed, humorous unmasking of middle-class ambition and hypocrisy, is closest, among the poetic realists, to the contemporaneous social realists in France, Russia, and England. His social criticism is sharper than Storm's, whose attention to social ills is almost overshadowed by existential concerns, such as the awareness of transience in all things or a sense of the inescapability of heredity. But Keller's fiction lacks the panoramic sweep of a Stendhal, a Tolstoy, or a Thackeray, whose characters take us through the battlefields and ballrooms of Europe. In his novellas Keller is more interested in what people eat and wear, where they live, and how they amuse themselves than in history-making events. Keller's realism is as provincial as Storm's; it reflects the fact that the German-speaking world had made less industrial and political progress than other parts of Europe. In *The Three Righteous Combmakers*, we even find remnants of the guild system, and the rivalry among the three journeymen is fueled by their differing regional origins. Yet with his painter's eye Keller is the equal of a Balzac or a Dickens in describing food, clothing, and

927

possessions, particularly small objects. One of the most memorable microrealistic "thing-portraits" is the list of the contents of Züs Bünzlin's lacquered chest, including a cherry pit with a minuscule set of bowling pins inside and a nut that contains a tiny image of the Virgin Mary behind glass.

Keller's humor moves into the realm of the grotesque in his account of the race the three journeymen run to determine which of them will continue to work for their master: the Saxon and the Bavarian become so preoccupied with holding each other back that they fail to notice they have passed their destination. There is something of a fairy-tale quality in the fact that the Swabian, the youngest and poorest of the three, wins the race, the business, and Züs Bünzlin. But as in *Pankraz, der Schmoller*, the levity turns harsh at the end. The Saxon hangs himself, the Bavarian becomes dissolute, and the Swabian spends the rest of his days under his wife's thumb.

The fairy-tale element reaches full expression in another Seldwyla novella from the first volume, *Spiegel, das Kätzchen (Mirror, the Cat)*. On the surface it shares many properties with the conventional fairy tale. It takes place "several hundred years ago" and features talking animals, a witch, and a sorcerer who needs cat fat for his wizardry. Furthermore, Mirror, a decidedly middle-class cat, incorporates in his down-to-earth wisdom an idealizing mirror of human virtue. Yet once again Keller fuses his poeticization of the world with nineteenth-century realism. In recounting how Mirror's good qualities decline as his hunger increases after the death of his mistress, so that he is finally forced to make a kind of feline Faust pact with Pineiss the sorcerer, the tale demonstrates the belief that material well-being is the prerequisite to morality. As in a true fairy tale, however, good wins out over evil, when Mirror not only uses his wits to escape death at the hand of Pineiss but also succeeds in binding the sorcerer for life to another of Keller's unforgettable harridans.

The darkness apparent on the horizon in most of the Seldwyla novellas moves to the foreground in what is probably the most famous of them all, *Romeo and Julia auf dem Dorfe (A Village Romeo and Juliet,* 1856). In Shakespeare the union of the "star-cross'd lovers" is prevented by a quarrel in existence long before the play begins; in Keller the corresponding feud is part of the present action. At the suggestion of a government official the farmers Manz and Marti both lay claim to the neglected strip of land between their two fields, their common greed and sense of "honor" generating the enmity that eventually ruins them and their children, Sali and Vrenchen.

In its depiction of a childhood love destroyed by money-grubbing, *A Village Romeo and Juliet* follows the pattern of the subversion of the idyllic moment found in Storm's *Immensee* and so many other products of poetic realism. Keller's aim here is to expose the vulnerability of social ideals such as honor and of the Christian teachings they are supposed to reinforce by calling attention to their relativity. For example, although Vrenchen outwardly accepts the Seldwylan equation of both honor and heaven with property, she privately defines heaven in terms of her love for Sali. Since in light of their fathers' feud Vrenchen feels that marriage with Sali would in fact bring her not prosperity but disgrace, her private definition of heaven directly opposes the public definition. This private heaven finds a public counterpart in the *Paradiesgärtlein* (Paradise Garden), the inn where Sali and Vrenchen spend a few frenzied hours dancing during their last day of happiness together. A haven for homeless wanderers, bohemian artists, unmarried lovers, and the poor, the Paradise Garden accommodates those barred from society's traditional heaven of respectability and material well-being. Notably, this inn is the habitat of the "black fiddler," the novella's clearest opponent of conventional social values.

Yet Sali and Vrenchen are unable to remain in the Paradise Garden, unable, that is, to overcome the desire for a traditional bourgeois marriage which the former honor of their fathers' houses instilled in them—the same sense of honor that now makes marriage impossible. In the face of this dilemma they act out in a double suicide the final rejection of Christianity's heaven for the sake of their private one, attainable only in childhood and death. Keller's bias in favor of the love between Sali and Vrenchen and against the forces hindering it is obvious; the narrator observes that "honor's shield can quickly become a tablet of disgrace." This comment is characteristic of the narrators of Keller's novellas, who are in general omniscient, often ironic third-person observers. Keller's narrative style contrasts sharply with Storm's, whose intricate framing structures lend his works a greater objectivity. The peasant milieu of *A Village Romeo and Juliet* distinguishes it from the other Seldwyla novellas and links it to the nineteenth-century German tradition of *Dorfliteratur* (village, or peasant, literature) represented by writers such as Karl Immermann, Jeremias Gotthelf, Berthold Auerbach, and Peter Rosegger. Unlike his compatriot Gotthelf, however, Keller does not reproduce the regional dialect of his characters, thus broadening the audience that can read his work with ease.

The condition of nineteenth-century Germany, where urbanization was less advanced than elsewhere and regional differences more pronounced, began to change with the establishment of a unified German nation under Bismarck in 1871, repercussions of which we encountered in Storm's treatment of monumental individualism and the clash between new technology and backward thinking in *The Rider on the White Horse*. Similarly, the novellas in the second part of *The People of Seldwyla* register Keller's reactions to the wave of speculation and business expansion that swept across Switzerland in the wake of the new empire. *Das verlorne Lachen (The Lost Smile)*, for instance, presents the confrontation between preindustrial values, defended

by Jukundus Meyenthal, and the capitalist system, fostered by the nouveau riche Glor family. After marrying Justine Glor, Jukundus decides to go into the lumber business—Seldwyla's rich forests being the town's only natural resource—but leaves it in disgust when profit-crazed lumber dealers endeavor to cut down even the giant oak tree that he reveres as a monument to old Germanic times. Though Justine becomes temporarily alienated from Jukundus because of his failure in the business world and her involvement with a religious sect, the two are eventually reconciled. In one of the most memorable idyllic scenes in Keller's works, they celebrate their reunion with a walk through the countryside on a beautiful summer morning, and the mutual smile that had disappeared during their separation returns to light up their faces. But this restored idyll—as is suggested by the clearing full of newly planted trees they encounter—rests on values of the past. Just as Storm looked back nostalgically to the rococo era in the face of the upheavals of his day, Keller briefly recaptures here a happier time about to be lost, like the smile in the title of the story. In its defense of marriage and its undercutting of religion *The Lost Smile* echoes Keller's *Sieben Legenden (Seven Legends, 1872)*, a collection of fanciful short tales in which even the Virgin Mary fights for the demands of a healthy married life in opposition to the asceticism of the church.

Keller had great difficulty finishing the *Seven Legends* and the second volume of the Seldwyla novellas because of his post as cantonal secretary of Zurich, which he assumed in 1861. After resigning in 1876 he was able to complete the *Züricher Novellen (Novellas of Zurich, 1876–1877)*, a cycle of five tales, the first three of which are told in the 1820's to a young Zurich resident by his godfather as pedagogical examples of true originality; the frame is abandoned in the last two. In these five stories, based on moments in Zurich's history from the Middle Ages to the mid-nineteenth century, Keller deliberately presents a more cheerful picture of Swiss life than in *The People of Seldwyla. Hadlaub,* for instance, ends with the marriage of the title character, the peasant scribe of the famous Manesse manuscript of medieval love poetry, to the aristocratic Fides. And *Das Fähnlein der sieben Aufrechten (The Banner of the Upright Seven)* is a tribute to the reassertion of Swiss democracy in the new constitution of 1848. But Keller's oeuvre ends on a note of disillusionment. Like *The Lost Smile,* his late novel *Martin Salander* (1885–1886) looks to the family as the last bastion of stability in an era of social decay. Twice driven bankrupt by the machinations of the unscrupulous businessman Louis Wohlwend, Salander is sustained only by the loyalty of his wife and son. Lacking both the compassion of *Green Henry* and the humor of the novellas, *Martin Salander* reflects the unhappiness of Keller's last years, which he spent living with his sister Regula until her death in 1888. He died in 1890, a lonely and disheartened man, but one much mourned by the country whose soul his works had never ceased to explore.

CONRAD FERDINAND MEYER

Although C. F. Meyer lived for most of his first twenty years in his native Zurich, his childhood and adolescence were very different from Keller's. Born on 11 October 1825, he was the son of a well-to-do politician and historian who imbued in him at an early age cultural and historical interests that transcended the limits of his provincial environment. Unlike both Storm and Keller, Meyer never experienced financial difficulties. But he had other problems. He inherited the delicate physical and psychic constitutions of his parents and was strongly influenced as a child by the religious beliefs of his mother, who attempted to counteract her tendency to nervousness and depression by a fervent pietism. Throughout much of his youth Meyer alter-

nated between states of lethargy and extreme irritability, and his disturbed behavior was exacerbated by the death of his father when he was fifteen. Bilingual in German and French, he spent a year at the age of eighteen in Lausanne, Switzerland, where he began the acquaintance with French literature that was to figure prominently in his intellectual development. At his mother's urging Meyer began studying law at the University of Zurich in 1844, but he gave it up before long in favor of a lonely period of reading, writing, and drawing. In addition to German writers such as Novalis, Ludwig Tieck, and Friedrich von Schlegel he read history, thus laying the foundation for his later historical novellas. In contrast to Storm and Keller, he seems to have been scarcely moved by the turbulent political events of the 1840's and did not respond to them in his poetry.

For several years Meyer's only confidante was his younger sister Betsy, who remained close to him all his life. During this period of introversion a number of things served to unsettle his already precarious mental state. Relations with his neurotic and overbearing mother were strained. Like Keller, he soon realized he did not have the talent to become a painter. More upsetting was the unfavorable estimate of his early poetry in 1844 by a Swabian writer whose opinion his mother had sought. In 1850 he read a critical work by the theologian and professor of German literature and aesthetics Friedrich Theodor Vischer, *Kritische Gänge* (Critical Paths, 1844), that made a strong impression on him. It advocated literary realism and attacked the belated romanticism of recent German art. Vischer thus challenged Meyer's highly aestheticized way of life and his conception of literature as a means of transcending reality. Increasingly withdrawn, spending days behind closed shutters and going out only at night, Meyer was in so aggravated a neurotic state by 1852 that he had to be admitted to the clinic at Préfargier near Neuchâtel. As would often happen again, his condition improved with the change of scene, and he left after only a few months.

Meyer's self-confidence received a boost during a stay in 1853 in Lausanne, where he renewed his acquaintances of ten years before and became an adept conversationalist in French-Swiss society. He spent the next few years immersing himself in French literature and translating French historical works into German. But his cosmopolitan inclinations were given freest reign when the inheritance he received after the suicide of his mother in 1856 enabled him to begin traveling extensively. Whereas the limited means of both Storm and Keller forced them to work in the civil service and prevented them from ever going beyond the confines of the German-speaking world, Meyer's financial independence made it possible for him to travel to Paris (1857), Rome, Florence, and Siena (1858), Verona and Venice (1871–1872), and Corsica and southern France (1875–1876), as well as throughout Switzerland and to Munich. His travels left their mark not only on his historical novellas of the 1870's and 1880's but on his poetry, which began appearing in the 1860's. Many of his poems, such as "In der Sistina" ("In the Sistina," 1891), were inspired by the paintings and sculptures he had seen abroad. With his tendency to stylization and his frequent use of works of art as subjects, he anticipates much of the later aestheticist poetry of Hugo von Hofmannsthal, Stefan George, and Rainer Maria Rilke. His first published collection, *Zwanzig Balladen von einem Schweizer* (Twenty Ballads by a Swiss, 1864), greatly enriched the tradition of the German ballad, which had enjoyed its first flowering in the late eighteenth century with the work of Gottfried August Bürger, Goethe, and Schiller. Many of Meyer's ballads deal with historical figures from the same periods as his novellas—the sixteenth and seventeenth centuries. For example "Die Füsse im Feuer" ("The Feet in the Fire," orig-

inally entitled "Der Hugenott" [The Huguenot]), his most popular ballad, tells the story of a royal courier's return to a castle where he had killed a woman three years before while pursuing Huguenots. The courier's memory of the murder is narrated only obliquely, through references to the image of the woman's feet twitching in the fire as he tries to make her reveal her husband's whereabouts. The drama and suspense of the poem are heightened by its abrupt alternations between present and past, its use of short, disjointed phrases, and its thematic repetitions. Other historical ballads explore the kinds of issues that were to interest Meyer in his novellas, such as the relationship between power and duty or between politics and justice.

Meyer is best known for his shorter lyric poetry, and it is there that he achieves the innovations that make him the most significant poet among the poetic realists. The numerous revisions he made in his poems over the years for their first collected publication in 1882 are legendary. Because Betsy preserved all her brother's manuscripts, it is possible to trace the changes away from romantic subjectivity and toward depersonalized objectivity that link Meyer's poetry to the French symbolist tradition, which culminated in Stéphane Mallarmé. The new impersonality of Meyer's poetry is most evident in his so-called *Dinggedichte* (thing-poems). In contrast to romantic poetry, which often demonstrates what John Ruskin called the "pathetic fallacy" of expressing human emotions by subjectively attributing them to inanimate phenomena, the thing-poem strives for an objective portrayal of the object in itself. Though the object may possess symbolic meaning, the emphasis is on its universal rather than its personal significance. The technique may be illustrated through reference to two of Meyer's best-known thing-poems, "Zwei Segel" ("Two Sails," 1870–1882) and "Der römische Brunnen" ("The Roman Fountain," 1860–1882). Like "Schwüle" (Sultry Day, 1869–1882),

931

"Eingelegte Ruder" ("Oars Pulled Up," 1869–1882), "Im Spätboot" (In the Night Boat, 1881–1882), and other of Meyer's poems, "Two Sails" has a lake setting, reflecting his attachment to his series of homes on Lake Zurich. Yet none of his own feelings is allowed direct expression in the poem. Throughout, the focus is on the two sails and the manner in which each imitates the action of the other. While the harmonious relation between the sails suggests that the poem is symbolically about love, its concentration on the external object and its total absence of the confessional mode distinguish it technically from romantic love poetry.

Similarly, in the famous "The Roman Fountain," inspired by a fountain in the gardens of the Villa Borghese in Rome, contemplation and description replace immediacy. A classic thing-poem, this much revised work is concise and straightforward, stripped of all references to a lyrical "I" who reacts to the fountain. Rather, the poem suggests an understanding of the inner principle of the fountain itself, the give-and-take among its three marble bowls, which symbolizes perhaps, on the broadest level of interpretation, the eternal flux of human existence. In its show of objectivity and impersonality Meyer's protosymbolist poetry represents a stylistic break with the tradition of *Erlebnisdichtung* (poetry of personal experience) predominant in German literature since the Storm and Stress period of the 1770's. The degree to which he was ahead of his time is evident in the perplexed reactions of his contemporaries. Storm, for example, was disturbed by the lack of direct emotional expression in Meyer's lyric poetry.

Meyer did not proceed directly from composing poetry to writing novellas but rather tried his hand first at a transitional genre, the verse narrative, notably in *Huttens letzte Tage* (Hutten's Last Days, 1871). The work reflects the abating of the writer's Francophile sentiments and his increasing commitment to the German cause in the face of the Franco-Prus-

sian War, which ended with Bismarck's victory in 1871. Sharing the interest of his contemporaries in great individuals and especially captivated by the Renaissance because of his reading of Jakob Burckhardt, Meyer viewed Bismarck as a kind of modern Renaissance man. Yet unlike Keller and Storm in the majority of their works, he chose to deal not with the present but with historical subjects, partly in order to mask himself and to place the reader at a greater distance. As he expressed it in a letter of 19 May 1887 to the minor writer Louise von François, the present was "too crude and too close" for him.

In many ways Meyer's depiction of the German Renaissance humanist Ulrich von Hutten parallels and illuminates his own situation at the time he was composing the work. Just as Hutten's writings, which attacked Roman Catholicism and expressed his loyalty to the German people, not only drew inspiration from the Protestant Reformation but furthered its cause, Meyer's treatment of Hutten was both motivated by the Franco-Prussian War and enthusiastically received in the wake of Bismarck's victory. *Huttens letzte Tage* was especially popular during the 1870's and the decade before World War I. Meyer himself saw it as a work of patriotism: he had his publisher donate the royalties to a fund for German soldiers wounded in the Franco-Prussian War.

In spite of all this, *Huttens letzte Tage* is not the product of a one-sided "conversion" of the Swiss Meyer to the Prussian cause. Just as he shows Hutten to be torn between his debt to Renaissance classical humanism and his commitment to the Reformation ("a human being with his contradictions": poem 26), Meyer continued to be shaped by French cultural influences even after he became caught up in German nationalism. Similarly, Meyer's depiction of the exiled Hutten dying on an island evokes the isolated, alienated, and politically ineffective artist-figure so prominent in German literature during the previous hundred years. Yet Meyer's portrayal of the soldier-poet meditating on his past suggests the new role of politically engaged citizen that the founding of the German nation could offer the writer—a role Meyer himself adopts in composing *Huttens letzte Tage.*

Meyer's eleven novellas, published between 1873 and 1891, also look back to the past. They treat periods extending from the age of Charlemagne through the seventeenth century and are set in locales in Italy, France, England, and Sweden as well as Meyer's native Switzerland. The cosmopolitan quality of these works, reflecting the broad cultural education of their author, contrasts sharply with the parochial character of most products of poetic realism. Although Meyer's novellas deal with actual historical figures, he occasionally alters the facts in order to highlight particular personal traits. And as in *Huttens letzte Tage,* the historical situations allow him to veil experiences of his own that he is reluctant to write about directly.

The most moving example of this technique is *Das Leiden eines Knaben* (*A Boy Suffers,* 1883), which takes place in the France of King Louis XIV. Its depiction of the sensitive, mentally slow Julian Boufflers, who is tortured to death by his Jesuit schoolmasters because his father has brought to light the order's unethical money-lending practices, doubtless owes much to Meyer's memories of his own unhappy, isolated youth and to his sense that his parents had made no effort to discover his true aptitudes and wishes. Rather than treating this theme in an openly autobiographical fashion, Meyer places it in the context of historical power struggles. Similarly, his relationship to his sister Betsy may have unconsciously influenced his portrayal of the passion between the supposed half-siblings Wulfrin and Palma in *Die Richterin* (*The Judge,* 1885), set in ninth-century Graubünden in Switzerland. This was at any rate the opinion of Freud, who was so captivated by the novella that he chose it for his first psychoanalytic interpretation of a literary text. In a letter of 20 June 1898 to his close friend Dr. Wilhelm Fliess of Berlin, Freud construes *The Judge* as Meyer's defense against his memory of an affair with his sister, insofar as the novella's end reveals that Wulfrin and Palma are in fact not related but that Palma's mother, Stemma, the judge of the region, had poisoned her husband (Wulfrin's father) after conceiving Palma by another man. No evidence exists that Meyer and Betsy were ever physically intimate, as Freud assumes, but there is no doubt that they were very close and that Meyer's work as a writer was of foremost importance to his sister. Her unswerving dedication probably also colors his treatment (in *Angela Borgia,* 1891) of Lucrezia Borgia's fierce loyalty to her brother Cesare, a devotion that surpasses even her commitment to her husband.

Meyer's use of historical material sometimes disguises critical comments on the society of his day. *Die Versuchung des Pescara* (*Pescara's Temptation,* 1887), in which the sixteenth-century Italian general Pescara is offered the crown of Naples in return for betraying the Spanish emperor Charles V and joining the league to free Italy from Spanish rule, can be read as a comment on questionable aspects of the drive for independence and national unity in nineteenth-century Germany. The same is true of the depiction of the title character in *Jürg Jenatsch* (1874), whose boundless patriotism compels him to stop at nothing in his campaign to liberate his homeland of Graubünden from foreign rule during the Thirty Years' War. Meyer's use of history for indirection is well illustrated through a contrast between this novella and Keller's *A Village Romeo and Juliet.* There, in protecting Vrenchen from her father's brutality, Sali gives him a blow that leaves him an imbecile, just as in *Jürg Jenatsch* the love between Jenatsch and Lucretia is definitively barred from fulfillment by his murder of her father, Pompejus Planta, his political and religious enemy. Again, in a scene reminiscent of the Paradise Garden sequence in Keller's novella,

Lucretia and Jenatsch enjoy an idyllic interlude together in the mountains before parting. But where Keller's lovers are separated by their fathers' feud over a small piece of land, reflecting the author's unmasked criticism of contemporary provincial Swiss society, in Meyer's novella the idyllic moment is sacrificed to historical religious and political differences that split Europe for two centuries. Interestingly, it was Keller's reading of *Jürg Jenatsch* that prompted his first letter to Meyer, thus beginning a correspondence that was to continue intermittently until Keller's death. In this letter, dated 3 October 1876, Keller expresses admiration for all but the end of the novella, where Lucretia delivers the deathblow to Jenatsch with the same ax with which he had killed her father. Keller and Meyer came to know each other personally, but their relations were never warm, a fact not surprising in light of their very different backgrounds and outlooks on life.

Meyer's distancing technique is also apparent in *Gustav Adolfs Page* (*Gustav Adolf's Page*, 1882) in the figure of August Leubelfing, who allows his female cousin, disguised as a page, to enter the king's service, because he is afraid to go off to the battlefield himself. In the portrayal of this cowardly merchant whose main objection to the Thirty Years' War is that it might cost him money, the reader detects an indirect comment on the business-oriented bourgeoisie of nineteenth-century Switzerland. Swiss middle-class morality is satirized in a lighter vein in *Der Schuss von der Kanzel* (*The Shot from the Pulpit*, 1878). Because of his low birth and lack of property, the young pastor Pfannenstiel has little hope of marrying Rahel, the daughter of Wilpert Wertmüller, pastor of Mythikon (a fictitious city in the vicinity of Zurich). But Wilpert's cousin, General Rudolf Wertmüller, who had fought with Jenatsch years before, arranges things for the couple by means of an elaborately contrived scheme. Playing on Wilpert's passion for firearms, Rudolf shows him a pistol with a broken trigger and then secretly substitutes for it a properly functioning gun that looks exactly the same. The "shot from the pulpit" occurs when Wilpert is unable to resist handling the pistol during his sermon, and it shocks the congregation into a frenzy. Rudolf placates his fellow townspeople by bequeathing to them a piece of his wooded property that they have long coveted and by designating Wilpert to be overseer of his estate after his death, on the condition that he give up his job as pastor to Pfannenstiel—who is, Rudolf stipulates, to marry Rahel.

The farcical plot of *The Shot from the Pulpit* is unusual for Meyer. Its lightheartedness probably owes a good deal to the new peace of mind gained from his marriage in 1875 to Luise Ziegler, the daughter of a former president of Zurich. But ordinarily Meyer, like Storm, felt that the comic mode did not suit him. Except for *Angela Borgia*, an atypical work in which a number of depraved characters undergo transformations, the only novella besides *The Shot from the Pulpit* in which the protagonist does not die is *Plautus im Nonnenkloster* (*Plautus in the Convent*, 1881). Here too historical treatment veils Meyer's criticism of contemporary institutions, in this case the church. Like Storm and Keller, Meyer questions traditional religion, his skepticism being nourished by his memories of the unhealthy atmosphere of exaggerated devoutness in which his mother had reared him. *Plautus in the Convent* offers a comment on church hypocrisy. Here the fifteenth-century Florentine humanist Poggio tells how in tracking down a Plautus manuscript in a Swiss convent he saved a young peasant girl from taking the veil and united her with her beloved by unmasking the "miracle of the cross" that novitiates there were required to perform. The miracle in fact depends on the substitution of a lightweight cross for the inordinately heavy one that the novices supposedly lift up with divine assistance on the day of their initiation into the convent. In its satiric portrayal of Christian conventions and its upholding of marriage in preference to a life of religious celibacy, *Plautus in the Convent* is strongly reminiscent of Keller's *Seven Legends.*

Meyer projects the matter of his tales not only through historical invention but also through the narrative structures he creates. Unlike Keller and many nineteenth-century novelists, whose omniscient, authorial narrators are in evidence and do not hesitate to give us their opinions about what they are narrating, Meyer, like Storm in his later work, often uses a frame within which the authorial voice recedes behind a second narrator. The bulk of *Das Amulett* (*The Amulet*, 1873) consists of the Swiss Protestant Hans Schadau's first-person recollections of his youth, culminating in his story of the Saint Bartholomew's Day massacre of the Huguenots by the Catholics in Paris in 1572. Schadau is inspired to set down his reminiscences by a visit in 1611 to the father of the Swiss Catholic Wilhelm Boccard, a friend who had lost his life protecting Schadau during the massacre. Schadau's brief account of the visit is itself framed by the authorial narrator's statement that what follows is his contemporary translation of yellowed documents from the early seventeenth century. Meyer thus seems to remain clinically detached, his stance neutral. He sums up his attitude in a letter of 12 November 1884 to Paul Heyse: "My inclination for the frame technique is totally instinctive. I like to keep the object of my tale at a distance from myself or, more precisely, as far as possible from my eye." He does not judge the characters in *The Amulet*, and since Schadau is telling the story, we are able to form judgments about him only by observing the inconsistencies between his professed opinions and his behavior. The most striking of these is that while as a Protestant he scoffs at Boccard's steadfast belief in the miraculous power of his holy medallion—his amulet—Schadau is finally compelled to call on it himself in attempting to save his wife.

Meyer's desire to keep the object "as far as possible from [the] eye" creates ambiguity about what is being narrated, making it impossible for the reader to know exactly what has happened. This aspect of his work reflects the intellectual climate of his times, which were increasingly dominated by positivism. Positivistic thinking favors the acquisition of "positive" knowledge that can be verified by the five senses rather than speculation about metaphysical questions that cannot be empirically resolved. Anticipating the work of later writers such as Arthur Schnitzler in Austria and Henry James, Virginia Woolf, and James Joyce in the English tradition, Meyer's narrative situations implicitly call attention to the impossibility of omniscience, to the fact that our knowledge of the world is limited to our own perceptions of it. One of the best manifestations of this awareness is *Der Heilige* (*The Saint*, 1879–1880). In this novella the story of the events leading up to the murder in 1170 of Thomas à Becket by the knights of Henry II of England is told some twenty years later by Hans the bowman, who as the king's personal servant had witnessed many dramatic scenes between Henry and his talented chancellor Becket. Because Hans's knowledge of Becket's motives is limited, it is left up to the reader to determine whether Becket's conversion from the worldly, almost dandified chancellor to the ascetic archbishop of Canterbury rests on genuine religious devotion or whether it has been carefully planned as a means for Becket to thwart the king's policies, in revenge for Henry's seduction of Becket's beautiful young daughter Grace. The ambiguity of the bowman's narration is heightened by interruptions from his listener that challenge the accuracy of certain details. A comment Hans makes in defending his account could serve as a motto for much of Meyer's work: "Sir, in making judgments, as in shooting, everything depends on one's point of view." Similarly, the reader cannot know to what degree the story of Julian Boufflers' suffering in *A Boy Suffers* is colored by the grudge that the tale's narrator Fagon, Louis XIV's personal physician, bears against the Jesuits. And even

Fagon is unable to know what goes on inside the mind of the introverted boy, who in his impenetrable isolation stands as a poignant reminder of the extent to which we are incapable of truly knowing other human beings.

The same thinking underlies the novella with the most elaborate narrative situation in all of Meyer's works, *Die Hochzeit des Mönchs* (*The Marriage of the Monk*, 1883–1884). To entertain his Veronese patron, Can Grande, and members of his court on a long, cold evening, Dante is asked, like a character in the *Decameron*, to make up a tale based on the theme of sudden change in one's profession. He tells the story of a monk who promises his father on his deathbed to marry a woman he does not love, Diana, so that his father's line will be continued and his fortune kept within the family. Having strayed thus far from his holy calling, the monk Astorre takes an even greater leap by immediately throwing over his new wife Diana for Antiope, a girl who had attracted him years earlier. As in Shakespearean tragedy, the tale ends with a ghastly heap of corpses: Diana murders Antiope, and Astorre and Diana's brother kill each other in hand-to-hand combat. These events, which sound straightforward, are in fact cloaked in ambiguity. Dante's listeners repeatedly interrupt him to call his facts into question. Moreover, Meyer adds a manneristic twist to the novella by having Dante borrow the names and external characteristics of his listeners for the figures in his tale, thus intertwining the work's primary and secondary narrations. Most significantly, Dante refrains from any attempt to explain Astorre's behavior, since, as he emphasizes to his audience, it is impossible to read the "inner natures" of others. The narration suggests that Astorre may have been in love with Antiope for years and that this attachment may have unconsciously prompted him to renounce his monastic vows, but Dante says nothing explicitly, nor does he assign guilt to Astorre, Antiope, or Diana. Like Meyer himself, the Italian poet-storyteller strives for the look of objective reality.

The ambiguity created by Meyer's narrative method parallels the pervasive relativism of his works, born of a world where traditional systems were being overturned. The loss in the nineteenth century of a general belief in divine authority led to the need for a "revaluation of all values," in Friedrich Nietzsche's famous phrase; as individuals were thrown back on their own judgments, absolute positions gave way to relative perspectives. Just as Meyer's novellas repeatedly call attention to the difficulty of truly knowing others, they demonstrate that absolute value judgments are illusory and even dangerous, since every position has validity from someone's viewpoint. In *The Amulet,* for instance, neither Schadau's Protestantism nor Boccard's Catholicism is clearly condemned or favored, and in *Jürg Jenatsch* the motives of the title character, his rival Planta, and the honorable duke whom Jenatsch ultimately betrays are all presented as justified to a certain degree. Even the heavy satire of the church in *Plautus in the Convent* is counterbalanced by a slight irony toward Poggio, an aesthete who delights in his literary discoveries with the zeal of a lover rejoicing in his beloved.

Meyer's skepticism about absolute evaluative hierarchies based on title or position is evident in his portrayal of political and military leaders. Just as the great writer Hutten is inwardly split by his commitment to both the German Protestant Reformation and classical humanism, Meyer's kings and generals are often not what their titles would lead us to expect. In *The Amulet* the French king Charles IX is weak, volatile, and immature; Henry II is dominated by his sensual desires in *The Saint;* it is intimated in *A Boy Suffers* that Louis XIV has covered up the Jesuits' shady business dealings; in *The Marriage of the Monk* the ruler Ezzelino inadvertently brings about the deaths of Diana's first husband and his brothers and condones Astorre's bigamous marriage to Antiope; and the renowned general Pescara is shown to be distinctly inconsistent in his attitude toward Christianity. Meyer's realism precludes the black-and-white method of characterization typical of much inferior romantic literature. As Fagon observes to Louis XIV in *A Boy Suffers,* we all "have a bit of the Jesuit in us."

Meyer's awareness that things are not always what they seem is evident even in the titles of his novellas. Boccard's "amulet" twice helps out the Protestant Schadau, who does not believe in its powers, but it is ultimately ineffective in saving the life of its Catholic owner; the motives and authenticity of Becket's "saintliness" are highly questionable; the judge Stemma turns out to be a murderess herself; and Pescara cannot in fact be "tempted" at all by the offer of the crown of Naples, since he has received a wound he knows is fatal. Similarly, the titles *The Shot from the Pulpit, Plautus in the Convent,* and *The Marriage of the Monk* all juxtapose concepts one would not expect to find together, and *Angela Borgia* is oxymoronic, linking an allusion to angelic innocence with the connotations of unspeakable evil evoked by the Borgia name. Pointing to the ironies and contradictions that emerge from beneath the surface of appearances, Meyer's paradoxical titles urge us to reexamine our conventional ways of perceiving and judging.

With Meyer, as with Storm and Keller, traces of the poet are visible in the novellas. The condensation characteristic of Meyer's poetry is apparent in the plot structure of his prose works, which typically skip over periods of time and focus on a few key events in quasi-montage fashion. Like Keller, Meyer unsuccessfully tried his hand at the drama, but the powers that could never quite succeed in that genre flourish in his novellas. Nowhere is Storm's comparison of the novella to the drama more graphically illustrated than in Meyer's fiction, which is rich in stark contrasts, rapid shifts of locale, and highly dramatic scenes, such as Schadau's escape from the king's marauding soldiers in *The Amulet* or Hans's attempt to steal Becket's daughter away to safety in *The Saint.* Paralleling the ob-

jectivity of Meyer's poetry and of the narrative method in his novellas, the emotional states of his characters are often conveyed indirectly, through descriptions of facial expressions, gestures, or even landscape, rather than through direct narration. The prose works are "objective" also in that there, as in the poetry, objects play an important role. In addition to the amulet, the two pistols in *The Shot from the Pulpit,* the two crosses in *Plautus in the Convent,* and other such things, drawings and paintings are of special symbolic significance, frequently serving to echo or foreshadow the action. The best examples of this device are found in *Pescara's Temptation,* one of whose symbolic paintings depicts Christ being pierced by the lance of a mercenary who is modeled on the Swiss soldier who gives Pescara his fatal wound. The importance of paintings complements the prevalence of works of art and artists themselves, particularly writers. Besides Dante in *The Marriage of the Monk,* we find Montaigne in *The Amulet* attempting to take the Huguenot Chatillon away to the security of his palace to read Horace before the massacre; and Ludovico Ariosto in *Angela Borgia* composing his *Orlando furioso,* which brings the only comfort to Giulio d'Este after his brother Ippolito has him blinded because his beautiful eyes are attractive to Angela. Like so many turn-of-the-century aestheticist writers after him, Meyer seems to be defending the unique value of art.

Even art could not sustain Meyer through the difficulties of his final years, however. From the end of 1887 until the fall of 1888 he was incapacitated by illness and depression. Although his oeuvre is filled with violence and betrayal, the exaggerated and nearly gratuitous cruelties abounding in *Angela Borgia,* his last novella, represent a turning point and reflect the diminution of his creative abilities. When his nervous strain was compounded in 1892 by delusions, he was admitted to a mental institution at Königsfelden, where he exhibited symptoms of acute psychosis. Though he returned home to his estate at Kilchberg near Lake Zurich in 1893, his literary powers were gone. His condition was not helped by the growing tensions between his sister and his wife, Luise, who resented Betsy's attempts to oversee the editing of his works and who finally succeeded in alienating the then malleable writer from his lifelong soul mate. After several years of semivegetation, Meyer died in 1898, on the threshold of the century to which his work looks ahead. For although the subject matter of his novellas is drawn from ages long past, in their attention to the relative nature of experience they anticipate the literature of the future.

Selected Bibliography

Theodor Storm

EDITIONS

INDIVIDUAL WORKS

POETRY

Gedichte. Kiel, 1852, 1856, 1859; Berlin, 1864, 1875, 1880, 1885. Each edition expanded.

NOVELLAS

Marthe und ihre Uhr. Volksbuch auf das Jahr 1848 für die Herzogthümer Schleswig, Holstein und Lauenburg.

Im Saal. Volksbuch auf das Jahr 1849 für die Herzogthümer Schleswig, Holstein und Lauenburg.

Immensee. Volksbuch auf das Jahr 1850 für die Herzogthümer Schleswig, Holstein und Lauenburg.

Im Sonnenschein. In *Drei Sommergeschichten* (with *Marthe und ihre Uhr* and *Im Saal*). Berlin, 1854.

Späte Rosen. Argo: Album für Kunst und Dichtung. Berlin, 1860.

Viola tricolor. Westermanns Illustrierte Deutsche Monatshefte 35 (1874).

Pole Poppenspäler. Deutsche Jugend 4 (1874).

Ein stiller Musikant. Westermanns Illustrierte Deutsche Monatshefte 38 (1875).

Aquis submersus. Deutsche Rundschau 9 (1876).

Carsten Curator. Westermanns Illustrierte Deutsche Monatshefte 44 (1878).

Eekenhof. Deutsche Rundschau 21 (1879).

Hans und Heinz Kirch. Westermanns Illustrierte Deutsche Monatshefte 53 (1882).

Zur Chronik von Grieshuus. Westermanns Illustrierte Deutsche Monatshefte 57 (1884).

Ein Fest auf Haderslevhuus. Westermanns Illustrierte Deutsche Monatshefte 59 (1885).

Ein Doppelgänger. Deutsche Dichtung 1 (1886).

Der Schimmelreiter. Deutsche Rundschau 55 (1888).

COLLECTED WORKS AND LETTERS

Sämtliche Schriften: Erste Gesamtausgabe. 6 vols. Braunschweig, 1868. Continued under the title *Gesammelte Schriften.* 19 vols. Braunschweig, 1877–1889.

Sämtliche Werke. Edited by Albert Köster. 8 vols. Leipzig, 1919–1920. The standard edition.

Sämtliche Werke. Edited by Peter Goldammer. 4 vols. 3rd ed. Berlin, 1972.

Briefe. Edited by Peter Goldammer. 2 vols. Berlin, 1972.

TRANSLATIONS

Aquis submersus. Translated by James Millar. London, 1910.

A Chapter in the History of Grieshuus. Translated by James Millar. London, 1908.

Eekenhof. Translated by James Millar. London, 1980.

A Festival at Haderslevhuus. Translated by James Millar. London, 1909.

Immensee. Translated by Ronald Taylor. In *Three German Classics.* London, 1966. Reprinted New York, 1980.

Renate. Translated by James Millar. London, 1909.

The Rider on the White Horse, and Selected Stories (also contains *In the Great Hall, In the Sunlight,* et al.). Translated by James Wright. New York, 1964.

The Senator's Sons. Translated by J. M. South. In *German Narrative Prose,* vol. 1, edited by Eva Engel. London, 1965.

Viola Tricolor: The Little Stepmother. Translated by Bayard Q. Morgan. New York, 1956. Also contains *Curator Carsten,* translated by Frieda M. Voigt.

BIOGRAPHICAL AND CRITICAL STUDIES

Alt, A. Tilo. *Theodor Storm.* New York, 1973.

Artiss, David. *Theodor Storm: Studies in Ambivalence.* Amsterdam, 1978.

Bernd, Clifford A. *Theodor Storm's Craft of Fiction: The Torment of a Narrator.* 2nd ed. Chapel Hill, N.C., 1966.

Goldammer, Peter. *Theodor Storm: Eine Einführung in Leben und Werk.* 2nd ed. Leipzig, 1974.

McCormick, E. Allen. *Theodor Storm's Novellen: Essays on Literary Technique.* Chapel Hill, N.C., 1964.

Müller, Harro. *Theodor Storms Lyrik.* Bonn, 1975.

Rogers, Terence J. *Techniques of Solipsism: A Study of Theodor Storm's Narrative Fiction.* Cambridge, 1970.

Schriften der Theodor-Storm-Gesellschaft. Heide in Holstein, 1952–

Schuster, Ingrid. *Theodor Storm: Die Zeitkritische Dimension seiner Novellen.* Bonn, 1971.

Stuckert, Franz. *Theodor Storm: Sein Leben und seine Welt.* Bremen, 1955.

Wedberg, Lloyd W. *The Theme of Loneliness in Theodor Storm's Novellen.* The Hague, 1964.

Wooley, Elmer O. *Studies in Theodor Storm.* Bloomington, Ind., 1943.

Vinçon, Hartmut. *Theodor Storm.* Stuttgart, 1973.

BIBLIOGRAPHIES

Teitge, Hans-Erich. *Theodor Storm Bibliographie.* Berlin, 1967.

Gottfried Keller

EDITIONS

INDIVIDUAL WORKS

POETRY
Gedichte. Heidelberg, 1846.

Neuere Gedichte. Braunschweig, 1851. 2nd ed., 1854.

Gesammelte Gedichte. Berlin, 1883.

NOVELS
Der grüne Heinrich. Braunschweig, 1854–1855. Second version, Stuttgart, 1879–1880.

Martin Salander. Deutsche Rundschau 46–48 (1886).

NOVELLAS
Die Leute von Seldwyla. Vol. 1, Braunschweig, 1856. Vol. 2, Stuttgart, 1873–1874.

Sieben Legenden. Stuttgart, 1872.

Züricher Novellen. Deutsche Rundschau 9–11 (1876–1877).

Das Sinngedicht. Deutsche Rundschau 26–27 (1881).

COLLECTED WORKS AND LETTERS

Gesammelte Werke. 10 vols. Berlin, 1889.

Sämtliche Werke. Edited by Jonas Fränkel and Carl Helbling. 24 vols. Vols. 3–8 and 16–19, Erlenbach-Zurich; all other vols., Bern, 1926–1949. The standard edition.

Sämtliche Werke und ausgewählte Briefe. Edited by Clemens Heselhaus. 3 vols. Munich, 1956–1958.

Gesammelte Briefe. Edited by Carl Helbling. 4 vols. Bern, 1950–1954.

TRANSLATIONS

The Banner of the Upright Seven and Ursula. Translated by Bayard Q. Morgan. New York, 1974.

Clothes Make the Man. In *Twelve German Novellas.* Translated and edited by Harry Steinhauer. Berkeley, Calif., 1977.

The Governor of Greifensee. Translated by Paul B. Thomas. *The German Classics,* vol. 14, edited by Kuno Francke. New York, 1914.

Green Henry. Translated by A. M. Holt. New York, 1960.

Martin Salander. Translated by Kenneth Halwas. London, 1963.

The Misused Love Letters and Regula Amrain and Her Youngest Son. Translated by Michael Bullock and Anne Fremantle. New York, 1974.

The People of Seldwyla and Seven Legends. Translated by M. D. Hottinger. London, 1931. Reprinted Freeport, N.Y., 1970.

Stories. Edited by Frank G. Ryder. New York, 1982. Includes selections from *The People of Seldwyla, Seven Legends,* and *Novellas of Zurich.*

A Village Romeo and Juliet. Translated by Paul B. Thomas and Bayard Q. Morgan. New York, 1955.

BIOGRAPHICAL AND CRITICAL STUDIES

Boeschenstein, Hermann. *Gottfried Keller.* 2nd ed. Stuttgart, 1977.

Ermatinger, Emil. *Gottfried Kellers Leben.* 8th ed. Zurich, 1950.

Hauch, Edward F. *Gottfried Keller as a Democratic Idealist.* New York, 1916.

Kaiser, Gerhard. *Gottfried Keller: Das gedichtete Leben.* Frankfurt, 1981.

Kaiser, Michael. *Literatursoziologische Studien zu Gottfried Kellers Dichtung.* Bonn, 1965.

Lindsay, J. M. *Gottfried Keller: Life and Works.* London, 1968.

Lukács, Georg. *Gottfried Keller.* 2nd ed. Berlin, 1947.

Muschg, Adolf. *Gottfried Keller.* 2nd ed. Munich, 1977.

Meier, Hans. *Gottfried Kellers ''Grüne Heinrich'': Betrachtungen zum Roman des poetischen Realismus.* Zurich, 1977.

Pascal, Roy. *The German Novel.* Toronto, 1956. Pp. 30–51.

von Passavant, Rudolf. *Zeitdarstellung und Zeitkritik in Gottfried Kellers ''Martin Salander.''* Bern, 1978.

Preisendanz, Wolfgang. *Humor als dichterische Einbildungskraft: Studien zur Erzählkunst des poetischen Realismus.* 2nd ed. Munich, 1976. Pp. 143–213.

Reichert, Herbert W. *Basic Concepts in the Philosophy of Gottfried Keller.* Chapel Hill, N.C., 1949.

Richter, Hans. *Gottfried Kellers frühe Novellen.* Berlin, 1960.

Schumacher, Hans. *Ein Gang durch den Grünen Heinrich.* Kilchberg, 1974.

Swales, Martin. *The German Bildungsroman from Wieland to Hesse.* Princeton, N.J., 1978. Pp. 86–104.

BIBLIOGRAPHIES

Preisendanz, Wolfgang. ''Die Keller-Forschung der Jahre 1939–1957.'' *Germanisch-Romanische Monatsschrift* 39:144–178 (1958).

Zippermann, Charles. *Gottfried Keller Bibliographie 1844–1934.* Zurich, 1935.

Conrad Ferdinand Meyer

EDITIONS

INDIVIDUAL WORKS

POETRY
Zwanzig Balladen von einem Schweizer. Stuttgart, 1864.

Romanzen und Bilder. Leipzig, 1870.

Huttens letzte Tage. Leipzig, 1871.

Engelberg. Leipzig, 1872.

Gedichte. Leipzig, 1882, 1883, 1887, 1891, 1892. Each edition expanded.

NOVELLAS
Das Amulett. Leipzig, 1873.

Jürg Jenatsch: Eine Geschichte aus der Zeit des dreissigjährigen Krieges. Die Literatur 2 (1874).

Der Schuss von der Kanzel. Züricher Taschenbuch auf das Jahr 1878.

Der Heilige. Deutsche Rundschau 21–22 (1879–1880).

Das Brigittchen von Trogen (later retitled *Plautus im Nonnenkloster*). *Deutsche Rundschau* 29 (1881).

Gustav Adolfs Page. Deutsche Rundschau 33 (1882).

Julian Boufflers: Das Leiden eines Knaben. Schorers Familienblatt 4 (1883).

Die Hochzeit des Mönchs. Deutsche Rundschau 37–38 (1883–1884).

Die Richterin. Deutsche Rundschau 45 (1885).

Die Versuchung des Pescara. Deutsche Rundschau 53 (1887).

Angela Borgia. Deutsche Rundschau 69 (1891).

COLLECTED WORKS AND LETTERS

Novellen. 2 vols. Leipzig, 1885.

Briefe Conrad Ferdinand Meyers nebst seinen Rezensionen und Aufsätzen. Edited by Adolf Frey. 2 vols. Leipzig, 1980.

Sämtliche Werke. Edited by Hans Zeller, Alfred Zäch, and Rätus Luck. 15 vols. Bern, 1958–. Vols. 5–7 and 15 still unpublished. The standard critical edition.

Samtliche Werke. 2 vols. Darmstadt, 1978.

TRANSLATIONS

The Complete Narrative Prose of Conrad Ferdinand Meyer. Translated by George F. Folkers, David B. Dickens, and Marion W. Sonnenfeld. 2 vols. Lewisburg, N.Y., 1976.

BIOGRAPHICAL AND CRITICAL STUDIES

Brunet, Georges. *C. F. Meyer et la nouvelle.* Paris, 1967.

Burkhard, Arthur. *Conrad Ferdinand Meyer: The Style and the Man.* Cambridge, Mass., 1932.

Burkhard, Marianne. *C. F. Meyer und die antike Mythologie.* Zurich, 1966.

————. *Conrad Ferdinand Meyer.* Boston, 1978.

Dahme, Lena. *Women in the Life and Art of Conrad Ferdinand Meyer.* New York, 1936.

Evans, Tamara S. *Formen der Ironie in Conrad Ferdinand Meyers Novellen.* Bern, 1980.

Fehr, Karl. *Conrad Ferdinand Meyer.* 2nd ed. Stuttgart, 1980.

Henel, Heinrich, ed. *Gedichte Conrad Ferdinand Meyers: Wege ihrer Vollendung.* Tübingen, 1962. Poems with commentary.

————. *The Poetry of Conrad Ferdinand Meyer.* Madison, Wis., 1954.

Hertling, Gunter H. *Conrad Ferdinand Meyers Epik: Traumbeseelung, Traumbessinnung und Traumbesitz.* Bern, 1973.

Isaak, Gudrun. *Der Fall C. F. Meyer: Ausserliterarische Faktoren bei der Rezeption und Bewertung eines Autors.* Frankfurt, 1980.

Meyer, Betsy. *Conrad Ferdinand Meyer in der Erinnerung seiner Schwester.* Berlin, 1903.

Mussberger, Max. *Conrad Ferdinand Meyer: Leben und Werke.* Frauenfeld, 1919.

Williams, William D. *The Stories of C. F. Meyer.* Oxford, 1962.

Zäch, Alfred. *Conrad Ferdinand Meyer: Dichtkunst als Befreiung aus Lebenshemmnissen.* Frauenfeld, 1973.

BIBLIOGRAPHIES

Du Preez, Hélène. *The Poetry of Conrad Ferdinand Meyer.* Johannesburg, 1974.

Konrad, Gustav. "C. F. Meyer: Ein Forschungsbericht." *Der Deutschunterricht* 3:72–81 (1951).

Oberle, Werner. "Conrad Ferdinand Meyer: Ein Forschungsbericht." *Germanisch-Romanische Monatsschrift* 6:231–252 (1956).

General Works

TRANSLATIONS OF POETRY

Anthology of German Poetry Through the Nineteenth Century. Edited by Alexander Gode and Frederick Ungar. New York, 1964.

The German Classics. Vol. 11 for Theodor Storm. Vol. 14 for Gottfried Keller and Conrad Ferdinand Meyer. Edited by Kuno Francke. New York, 1964.

German Verse from the Twelve to the Twentieth Century in English Translation. Edited by John W. Thomas. Chapel Hill, N.C., 1963.

The Penguin Book of German Verse. Edited and translated by Leonard Forster. Harmondsworth, 1957.

Twenty German Poets: A Bilingual Collection. Edited and translated by Walter Kaufmann. New York, 1962. Includes poetry by Conrad Ferdinand Meyer.

STUDIES ON POETIC REALISM AND THE GERMAN NOVELLA

Aust, Hugo. *Literatur des Realismus.* 2nd ed. Stuttgart, 1981.

Bennett, E. K. *A History of the German Novelle.* 2nd ed., revised by H. M. Maidson. Cambridge, 1961.

Bernd, Clifford A. *German Poetic Realism.* Boston, 1981.

Boeschenstein, Hermann. *German Literature of the Nineteenth Century.* New York, 1969.

Brinkmann, Richard, ed. *Begriffsbestimmung des literarischen Realismus.* Darmstadt, 1969.

————. *Wirklichkeit und Illusion: Studien über Gehalt und Grenzen des Begriffs Realismus für die erzählende Dichtung des neunzehnten Jahrhunderts.* 3rd ed. Tübingen, 1977.

Bucher, Max, et al., eds. *Realismus und Gründerzeit: Manifeste und Dokumente zur deutschen Literatur 1848–1880.* 2 vols. Stuttgart, 1975–1976.

Ellis, John. *Narration in the German Novelle: Theory and Interpretation.* Cambridge, 1974.

Fehr, Karl. *Der Realismus in der schweizerischen Literatur.* Bern, 1965.

Fuerst, Norbert. *The Victorian Age of German Literature.* University Park, Pa., 1966.

Himmel, Hellmuth. *Geschichte der deutschen Novelle.* Bern, 1963.

Kinder, Hermann. *Poesie als Synthese: Ausbreitung eines deutschen Realismus-Verständnisses in der Mitte des 19. Jahrhunderts.* Frankfurt, 1973.

Klein, Johannes. *Geschichte der deutschen Novelle von Goethe bis zur Gegenwart.* 4th ed. Wiesbaden, 1960.

Kunz, Josef. *Die deutsche Novelle im 19 Jahrhundert.* Berlin, 1970.

————, ed. *Novelle.* 2nd ed. Darmstadt, 1973.

Lockemann, Fritz. *Gestalt und Wandlungen der deutschen Novelle.* Munich, 1957.

Löwith, Karl. *From Hegel to Nietzsche: The Revolution in Nineteenth-Century Thought.* Translated by David E. Green. New York, 1964.

Martini, Fritz. *Deutsche Literatur im bürgerlichen Realismus, 1848–1898.* 4th ed. Stuttgart, 1981.

Preisendanz, Wolfgang. *Wege des Realismus: Zur Poetik und Erzählkunst im 19. Jahrhundert.* Munich, 1977.

Sagarra, Eda. *Tradition and Revolution: German Literature and Society 1830–1890.* London, 1971.

Silz, Walter. *Realism and Reality: Studies in the German Novelle of Poetic Realism.* Chapel Hill, N.C., 1954. Reprinted New York, 1979.

Stern, Joseph P. *Idylls and Realities: Studies in Nineteenth-Century German Literature.* London, 1971.

Swales, Martin. *The German Novelle.* Princeton, N.J., 1977.

Widhammer, Helmuth. *Die Literaturtheorie des deutschen Realismus (1848–1860).* Stuttgart, 1977.

von Wiese, Benno. *Novelle.* 6th ed. Stuttgart, 1975.

————, ed. *Deutsche Dichter des 19. Jahrhunderts: Ihr Leben und Werk.* 2nd ed. Berlin, 1979.

————. *Die deutsche Novelle von Goethe bis Kafka: Interpretationen.* 2 vols. Düsseldorf, 1968–1971.

GAIL FINNEY

GÉRARD DE NERVAL

(1808-1855)

GÉRARD DE NERVAL is known as the author of some of the most difficult and memorable sonnets in the French language, and of a number of lucid and delicate prose pieces. Marcel Proust said he was "assuredly one of the three or four greatest writers of the nineteenth century."

In his lifetime Nerval was seen chiefly as a charming madman, a golden youth who had lost his way and kept breaking down and needing care in mental hospitals—a sort of combination of Scott Fitzgerald and his wife, Zelda. He acquired a measure of fame in this respect. A brief biography appeared the year before he died—exaggerated, full of mistakes, Nerval said—and he twice had to resurrect himself in the face of well-meaning attempts to bury him. "Those who have known him," an article by Jules Janin began in 1841, "could bear witness to the grace and innocence of this noble spirit. . . . He was barely thirty years old. . . . He lived from day to day. . . . He had been rich at one point." Janin was referring to Nerval's first major attack of insanity—Nerval himself called it a simple nervous crisis—but the poet had recovered and was far from dead; except that people now thought he was, or knew he was crazy and looked at him with eyes full of crushing pity. "So that, my dear Janin," he wrote in response to the article, "I am the living tomb of the Gérard de Nerval whom you have loved."

Some twelve years later, when Alexandre Dumas *père* wrote what Nerval called the epitaph of his mind, seeming to consign him terminally to madness and irresponsibility, the latter replied with an alarmingly sensible letter, published as a preface to *Les filles du feu* (*Daughters of Fire,* 1854), in which he explained that he was a writer who was rather more carried away than others by the figures of his imagination. "Now . . . I am no longer riding the hippogriff," he wrote, "and . . . to mortal eyes I have recovered what is vulgarly called the use of reason." "The last madness that will probably remain to me," he ended, "will be to believe I am a poet."

It is hard not to see the pain hiding in these mild-seeming ironies. But then we have the benefit of more than a hundred years of hindsight. We know how justified, how sane, Nerval's belief in his vocation was, and we know, as Nerval's friends could not, that on the freezing night of 25–26 January 1855 he would hang himself from a railing in the rue de la Vieille Lanterne in Paris. He was forty-six, and he departed so discreetly, Charles Baudelaire said, that his discretion resembled contempt.

What is striking about this life is the contrast between the courtesy of its conduct and the violence of its end—or perhaps more generally between Nerval's well-attested gentleness and the rough quarrels he got into in his bouts of frenzy, from which occasionally he emerged in a straitjacket. He was a precursor

943

of Robert Louis Stevenson's Dr. Jekyll; he thought frequently about the claim of Goethe's Faust that two souls dwelled in his single breast. But we should not rush to find simple schemes for this doubleness of being: good and bad, let us say, man and beast, or respectability and its repressions. It will be enough for the moment to suggest that Nerval covered the darkest of preoccupations with the lightest of manners, and that this is precisely the effect his writings create. He has the air and often the topics of a minor talent: fragile verse mourning the passing of time, casual memoirs recounting voyages and encounters, prose poems serenading an inaccessible love. And for much of the time the talent, although fluent and unmistakable, *is* minor. But in certain works the same soft style allows an extraordinary urgency to peep through, an anguish made more eloquent by the poet's tendency to look away from it. In the sonnets called *Les chimères* (*Chimeras*, 1854), for example, an unusual directness of address, recalling Robert Herrick or Pierre de Ronsard, is combined with a density of reference of the kind found in John Milton or T. S. Eliot. And behind the references, to Greek, Egyptian, Christian, and other mythologies, and to elusive moments in the poet's life or contemporary history, stalk the nightmares the exotic or cryptic names are meant to embody and hold at bay: "Je ressème à ses pieds les dents du vieux dragon" (I sow again at her feet the teeth of the old dragon). "Je sais pourquoi là-bas le volcan s'est rouvert" (I know why the volcano there has opened again). "Et j'ai deux fois vainqueur traversé l'Achéron" (And I have twice crossed the Acheron as a victor). The allusions are to the story of Cadmus, a recent eruption of Vesuvius, and a river in hell; the tone suggests a certainty, a confident relation to monsters and turbulence and death that the poet cannot have felt in life. The result is heroic pathos, the courage of despair caught in a language neither hermetic nor straightforward but haunted. "When we read *Les chimères*," Norma Rinsler has remarked,

"we are aware of great areas of meaning pressing behind the printed words." It is a language that looks ahead to that of Stéphane Mallarmé ("to paint not the thing but the effect it produces") and of William Butler Yeats ("All, all are in my thoughts tonight being dead"). Albert Béguin, one of the very first critics to set in motion this century's revaluation of Nerval, has written that the speech of a poet is always a scandal in the eyes of the world. "The greatness of Nerval," he added, "is that he never made this scandal into a scandal."

Nerval—he later borrowed the name from a family property in the country not far from Paris—was born Gérard Labrunie on 22 May 1808. His father was a doctor in Napoleon's army, and his mother, accompanying her husband, died during the brutal campaign of 1810 and was buried in Poland. She caught a fever, Nerval wrote, crossing a bridge loaded with corpses. "My father, forced to rejoin the army at Moscow, later lost her letters and her jewels in the waters of the Berezina." Nerval dreams of the mother he never knew, but also recalls this impression of his father:

> I was seven, and I was happily playing in the doorway of my uncle's house, when three officers appeared, the blackened gold of their uniforms scarcely shining beneath their soldiers' cloaks. The first one embraced me so effusively that I cried out, "Father, you're hurting me."
>
> (*Promencier et souvenirs*, 4)

There is an element of mythology here, of course, the grim old family romance: hard father; young, ethereal mother. But Nerval was determined to live out his myth—indeed this became an aspect of his madness—and Doctor Labrunie seems to have done his bit too. Late in life the poet records a visit to his father, who was out of humor and would not let his son help him take in some wood. This is too small an incident to build much of an interpretation on, but Nerval, in his laconic way, plainly means it to stand for a good deal that is left unsaid, and his poems too are full of harsh or absent fathers. "We are all orphans," Christ exclaims in a text by the German poet Jean-Paul Richter, and Nerval turned this into a sequence of five sonnets, "We Are Without a Father": "Le dieu manque à l'autel où je suis la victime" (There is no god of the altar at which I am a victim), Nerval's Christ says. This was the theme of a whole romantic generation, in France and England and Germany, echoing in Lord Byron and Alfred de Vigny and Goethe. Its heroes were Cain and Jesus abandoned by God. But in Nerval's case the theme had a peculiarly literal force. Far from inflating his private concerns into cosmic proportions, he colored these great dramas with a marked personal touch, giving God's silence the intimacy and familiarity of Doctor Labrunie's disapproval. "My chief torment in all my moments of solitude," Nerval wrote to his doctor, "has always been the thought of my father."

But the mother plays an even larger part in the myth. She figures, explicitly or implicitly, in almost everything Nerval wrote. She is *la morte* (the dead one), but also *la mort* ([a welcoming] death). She is a version of the goddess Nerval usually calls Isis but who represents an astonishing amalgam of humanity's most mysterious and enduring consolations, all comforts with a feminine face. "I am the same as Mary," the goddess says in one of Nerval's dreams, "the same as your mother, the same person, too, whom in different forms you have always loved. At each of your trials, I have removed one of the masks with which I veil my features, and soon you will see me as I am." This is a promise, however, not a revelation, and a recurring image in Nerval's work is that of the goddess fleeing or fading, taken from sight just as her presence seems most certain: "La déesse avait fui sur sa conque dorée" (The goddess had fled on her golden shell). In one of the visions of *Aurélia*, "A divinity, always the same, threw off smiling the furtive masks of her diverse incarnations, and took refuge at last, unreachable, in the mystic splendors of the Asian sky."

This vision, maternal and receding, plainly represents more than a missed mother. She is the emblem of Nerval's constricted desire, of a love that can be saved from the profanation of its object only by a renewed loss. And if she has her origin and continuing authority in Madame Labrunie, she has another important human avatar in the actress Jenny Colon, whom Nerval met in 1834, and who died in 1842. Much has been written about this relationship, virtually all of it guesswork. Was the attachment purely platonic, did something specific go wrong, was Nerval impotent? Nerval speaks repeatedly of a fault committed against Jenny, of the need for pardon, but we are in Franz Kafka's world here: it may be a need for guilt that produces the crime, if indeed there is one, rather than the other way around. All we really need to know is that Jenny focused and dominated Nerval's dreams from the time he met her until his death; she became the summary and delegate of all women for him, the Beatrice who would lead him through purgatory and initiate him into a new life. Nerval was fond of these Dantean allusions, conscious of borrowing patterns of pilgrimage from the *Commedia* (*Divine Comedy, ca.* 1300) and the *Vitanuova* (*New Life, ca.* 1281), much as he borrowed the struggle against damnation from Goethe's *Faust* (1808, 1832). But like the allusions to Christ, they have an oddly personal, literal resonance. He actually idolized Jenny, made her an icon, as Beatrice was not, and it was important that she should be an actress, a creature in her element on the other side of footlights, cut off from the spectator by the apparatus of illusion. "Nothing is more dangerous," Nerval wrote, "than a serious love for a person in the theater." Nothing was more appealing either, and painful as all this was, Nerval could see the humor in the paradox. "It is an image I pursue, nothing more." "Seen close up, a real woman upset our ingenuity," he wrote of himself and his generation; "she had to be a queen or a goddess, and above all, we were not to get near her."

But the dilemma was no less deep because Nerval could see its foolish structure. He could love Jenny, or any other woman, only by neglecting or transforming her—this is the story in the novella *Sylvie* (1853); and the prose narrative *Aurélia* (1854) records not only Nerval's two descents into madness but also the memory of a love lost and found and lost, Orpheus empty-handed again. "Eurydice! Eurydice!" Nerval cries, "Lost for a second time!" The distressing thing here is that the despair, however authentic and however much it makes Nerval suffer, is obviously something he needs. Happiness would be unthinkable, even more intolerable. As Rinsler says, the choice is not, as it seems to be, between the ideal woman and a modest or complicated living person. Nerval has already chosen the ideal because she is easier to lose.

In the absence of his parents the young Nerval was brought up by a maternal great-uncle at Mortefontaine in the Valois, a region of lakes and forests between Paris and Compiègne. It was an area where old French songs and tales were still to be heard, and Nerval later collected some of them. Jean Jacques Rousseau's tomb was nearby at Ermenonville. Nerval's uncle, a farmer, was a kindly man and an amateur archaeologist who found Roman and Celtic remains in recently ploughed fields. He lived like a Christian, Nerval says, but was full of the ideas of the Enlightenment. When the boy asked him what God was, he said, "God is the sun." It is not farfetched to see the uncle's influence in Nerval's lifelong interest in comparative religion. He wanted to believe that all faiths contain a portion of the truth, and thought that the death of religions was more frightening than the fall of empires. In his bad moments he felt this very openness to possibilities was a form of heresy and said, "When one believes in everything, one believes in nothing." He explained several times why he held off from orthodox Christianity ("Ignorance can't be learned," he noted sharply), but he was also afraid of God's vengeance and feared a terrible punishment for his skepticism.

The young Nerval went to school in Paris, at the Collège Charlemagne, and lived with his father. Théophile Gautier was one of his companions. At thirteen and a half he wrote a nostalgic poem entitled "L'Enfance" (Childhood) about the vanished joys of childhood:

> *Qu'ils étaient doux ces jours de mon enfance*
> *Où toujours gai, sans souci, sans chagrin,*
> *Je coulai ma douce existence.*

How sweet they were, those days of my childhood / When always happy, without a care or sorrow,/ I let my sweet existence slip away.

This is pure rhetoric, and it would be some time before this facile regret would acquire an all too urgent accent. He published patriotic poems about Napoleon and glory, full of lyres and lutes and laurels and abysses—again a diction Nerval would later redeem from its tepid modishness. Before he was twenty he had completed a translation of the first part of Goethe's *Faust*, much admired by Goethe himself. "This translation is a prodigy of style," Goethe said. "Its author will become one of the purest and most elegant writers of France." Nerval went on to translate a selection of poems by German romantics and preromantics, Friedrich Klopstock, Gottfried Bürger, Friedrich von Schiller, and more Goethe; and he also, some years after, translated Heinrich Heine, who was to become a close friend. He joined the skirmishes of the French romantic movement, attending the famous first night of Victor Hugo's *Hernani* in 1830. Romanticism in France was radical in aesthetics—Hugo boasted of having put the French Revolution's red cap on the old dictionary—but on the whole royalist in politics, much in love with ancient and aristocratic grandeurs. It was at this time that Nerval took his pseudonym, adding the noble-sounding *de*, and began to fabricate a genealogy that had him descended from a distinguished but impoverished knightly family in the Périgord.

But Nerval, although well acquainted with all the young romantics and an admirer of Hugo, was a classicist at heart. He did not want to revolutionize the dictionary; he wanted to restore its archaic simplicity. And he went back to Joachim Du Bellay and Ronsard to look for models. A poem he wrote in this period, "Fantaisie" ("Fantasy"), now frequently anthologized, manages to reconstruct not only the vision but also the voice and freshness of an earlier time. The combination of music and memory, of music mentioned and also the light music of the poem itself, the memory both lovingly restored and rather fragile, is characteristic of Nerval's best work.

Il est un air pour qui je donnerais
Tout Rossini, tout Mozart et tout Weber,
Un air très vieux, languissant et funèbre,
Qui pour moi seul a des charmes secrets!

Or, chaque fois que je viens à l'entendre,
De deux cents ans mon âme rajeunit . . .
C'est sous Louis treize; et je crois voir s'étendre
Un coteau vert, que le couchant jaunit,

Puis un château de brique à coins de pierre,
Aux vitraux teints de rougeâtres couleurs,
Ceint de grands parcs, avec une rivière
Baignant ses pieds, qui coule entre des fleurs;

Puis une dame, à sa haute fenêtre,
Blonde aux yeux noirs, en ses habits anciens,
Que, dans une autre existence peut-être,
J'ai déjà vue . . . et dont je me souviens!

There is a tune for which I would give/All Rossini, all Mozart, and all Weber,/ A very old tune, languishing and sad,/Which has secret charms for me alone!

Now each time I come to hear it,/I grow younger by two hundred years . . . /It is the time of Louis XIII, and I think I can see/A green slope spreading, and yellowed by the sunset,

Then a brick-built château with corners of stone,/With windows dipped in reddish colors,/

Surrounded by great parks, with a river/Bathing its feet, flowing among the flowers;

Then a lady, at her high window,/Blond with black eyes, in her old-fashioned clothes,/Whom, in another existence perhaps,/I have already seen . . . and whom I remember!

These were the years of Nerval's reckless bohemian life, a Bohème to be celebrated by Henri Murger and Giacomo Puccini, and of which Nerval himself has left an amusing record. There were suppers, parties, women, rambles through nocturnal Paris, occasional escapades and arrests for disturbing the peace. Nerval had two very brief spells in the Sainte-Pélagie prison, one of them because he had been mistaken for a political conspirator. This was the age of Louis-Philippe, the citizen-king, and in 1831 Nerval was already mourning "our political dreams, our unthroned future." For two years, following his father's wishes, Nerval studied medicine at the Faculty in Paris, and in 1832 he visited a large number of cholera victims. Compassion seems to have been an instinct with him, encouraged rather than blurred by his own mental troubles. "When one feels unhappy," he wrote, "one thinks of the unhappiness of others." Many would say just the opposite.

At this time Nerval began a novel, Le prince des sots (The Prince of Fools), and wrote plays and operettas, both alone and in collaboration with Alexandre Dumas père. Their Piquillo was produced in 1837; their Alchimiste (Alchemist) in 1839. Nerval's own Léo Burckart, accepted earlier, was also staged in 1839. It is a substantial romantic drama, one of the best of the period, set in Germany in the years immediately after the fall of Napoleon. A liberal thinker who is threatened with jail and then made a minister by the prince of a small state discovers the murky realities of rule, the need for police spies and repression. He is caught between those representing the forces of reaction, who wish to co-opt him, and the young revolutionaries, who have sworn to kill him. But he escapes with his life and dignity, if not his ideals, intact, and the play ends with the suicide of the muddled would-be assassin. Nerval found the premise for his play in the 1819 killing of Otto von Kotzebue, thought to be a Russian spy, by the young German student Carl Sand.

Meanwhile Nerval had met Jenny Colon, had come into some money, and had founded a review, *Le monde dramatique*. He was a deft and conscientious journalist who always had difficulty in shifting to what he saw as the more durable key of poems, theater, the study of poetics, and the like. Generally he was inclined to use old material whenever he could, so that several of his books are rather heterogeneous compilations, and his texts are generally an editor's headache. He even followed this procedure for poems, which were not journalism in the first place. Seven of the twelve *Chimères,* for example, were published in *Petits châteaux de Bohème* (Little Castles in Bohemia, 1853) before appearing in *Daughters of Fire;* and these seven had already appeared in magazines eight and nine years earlier. Of the remaining five poems, two were certainly written shortly before their publication in 1854, but the others are probably much older. The same story holds for most of Nerval's books. It is not a matter that needs going into here, but the point requires mention.

Nerval traveled in Belgium and Austria in these years, and translated the second part of *Faust,* which appeared in a version of the full text, with a suggestive preface by Nerval, in 1840. "It would be consoling to think," he writes there, "that nothing dies if it has once struck the intelligence." With a slight change of emphasis, the thought was to become a major thread of *Aurélia:* "I believe the human imagination has invented nothing that is not true, in this world or in the others." The idea was to find its fortune with Proust, who demonstrated more thoroughly than Nerval that the imagination always tells the truth, even in this world, although it often resorts to what look like the untruths of metaphor.

In 1841 Nerval had his first complete breakdown—hours of exaltation and incoherence followed by catalepsy—and was hospitalized for several months. On his recovery he took a year-long journey to the Middle East, visiting Malta, Egypt, Lebanon, Cyprus, Rhodes, Smyrna, and Constantinople, and collecting stories and impressions that he published in newspapers and then gathered into his *Voyage en Orient (Journey to the Orient,* 1851), one of the most charming and relaxed travel books ever written, in which, as Edward Said says, myths of the mysterious East are displaced by characteristic Nervalian myths of irretrievable absence.

Nerval wrote theater criticism and supplied the words for Hector Berlioz's *Damnation de Faust (Damnation of Faust,* 1846). But treatment for nervous disturbances became more frequent, and from 1851 onward he was in and out of hospitals, alternately lucid, frantic, and depressed. He managed to bring together various writings in a book he called *Les illuminés* (The Enlightened, 1852), a study, he said, of "certain eccentrics of philosophy" who were also "precursors of socialism." They were remote, not always plausible precursors: a seventeenth-century madman who looked like King Henry II; a seventeenth-century priest; the novelist Restif de la Bretonne; Jacques Cazotte, the author of *Le diable amoureux (The Devil in Love,* 1772), who was executed on the orders of a revolutionary tribunal; Cagliostro, an eighteenth-century magus; and Quintus Aucler, the proponent of a spiritualist and astrological alternative to Christianity. "Can we extract something reasonable even from folly?" Nerval asked, and it is clear that he identified closely with these ill-assorted, out-of-step figures. It is in this book that he writes of "the most terrible danger of the literary life, that of taking one's own inventions seriously."

Nerval became increasingly anxious about his work—the day before his death he confided to his friend the short-story writer Charles Asselineau that he felt unable to write a line and was afraid he might never produce anything again—and furiously began to collect his scattered pieces. But he was also, at least until very shortly before the end, writing a lot and well; and his best work—*Sylvie, Aurélia*, the most outstanding of the *chimères*—was all done in the last year of his life. It is terror, alas, that makes him a major writer, or rather terror confronted by a gift of lucidity and the prodigies of style Goethe spoke of. But the victories in prose and verse were not enough to keep off the final defeat in the one material life Nerval had. "And I have twice crossed the Acheron as a victor." Twice, but not a third time. The great poems of *Les chimères* are glossed by a grimly frivolous epitaph that Nerval wrote for himself—"a stupid sonnet," he called it:

> *Et quand vint le moment où, las de cette vie,*
> *Un soir d'hiver, enfin l'âme lui fut ravie,*
> *Il s'en alla disant: "Pourquoi suis-je venu?"*
> ("Épitaph," 12–14)

And when the moment came in which he was tired of life,/One winter evening, and his soul at last was taken away,/He went off saying, "I wonder why I came?"

and by another last poem, where the mixture of misery and wit is even more extraordinary:

> *Sans feu dans mon taudis, sans carreaux aux*
> *fenêtres,*
> *Je vais trouver le* joint *du ciel ou de l'enfer,*
> *Et j'ai pour l'autre monde enfin bouclé mes*
> *guêtres.*

No fire in my hovel, no panes in the windows,/I am going to find the *juncture* of heaven or of hell,/And I have fastened on my gaiters for the other world.

LES CHIMÈRES

A *chimère* is a chimera, a monster from Greek mythology that has a lion's head, a goat's body, and a serpent's tail. The word also means more generally a thing of hybrid character or a fanciful conception. But it is far more frequently used in French than in English, and in that language it has the quite familiar sense of dream or illusion, a product of the imagination unsupported by reality. It is employed in this way in Rousseau's *Confessions* (1782), for example, and often found in Nerval's early verse: "Votre amour n'est qu'une chimère" (Your love is only an illusion). "Ah! préférons cette chimère / À leur froide moralité" (Ah, let us prefer this illusion / To their cold morality). "O chimère de l'homme! o songe de la vie! / O vaine illusion, d'illusions suivie!" (Oh delusion of man, oh dream of life! / Oh vain illusion, by illusions pursued!). "Such are the dreams" ("Telles sont les chimères"), Nerval says at the end of *Sylvie*, "that occupy us early in life."

Since Nerval came to believe that the imagination was always right on one plane or another, the word *chimère*, almost mockingly applied to his late poems, takes on a flavor of intricately mingled irony and diffidence. These works may seem strange to you, we may hear him saying to Dumas and others, mere madman's fancies; and they have seemed so to me at times. But I am convinced they are not. The title is thus both a modest defense and a quiet act of defiance. Nerval knew that the poems he was calling *chimères* were difficult, different from almost anything that had been written before. But he also knew that their difficulty and difference were not mistakes or misfortunes. The poems were not more incomprehensible than G. W. F. Hegel or Emanuel Swedenborg, he humorously wrote to Dumas, "and to explain them, if explanation were possible, would be to rob them of all their charm."

"If explanation were possible." The phrase has been taken as a "no trespassing" sign, disarming all criticism; and as a challenge, inviting endless investigation. We must be careful not to underestimate Nerval's wit, the poise it permits him. We have to dispel some of the mystery of these poems in order to read them, and their charm certainly survives considerable inquiry. We have to respect the mystery of the poems if we are not to treat their language simply as a code to be cracked, a tricky translation of something that can adequately be put in other terms. This principle may well hold for all poetry, but that of Nerval makes our need for it exceptionally evident.

Twelve years, twelve sonnets, Jeannine Moulin has remarked of the poems Nerval wrote from 1843 to 1854 and brought together as *Les chimères* in the volume *Daughters of Fire.* Eight other sonnets have since been discovered in manuscript, and are usually published as *autres chimères* (more chimeras). Strictly, only four of the eight are different poems. Three are alternative versions of poems included in the original twelve, and one actually conflates two of the twelve, joining the quatrains of one to the tercets of the other. I shall come back to the implications of this odd interchangeability.

Occult and other significances have been found for the sequence in which Nerval finally presented these poems, and certainly the pattern looks intentional, leading us from the desolation of "El Desdichado" (The Unfortunate One, 1853) through various clashing religions and the agony of Christ to the timidly optimistic pantheism of "Vers dorés" ("Golden Verses"). But the poems are both unequal and markedly distinct from each other, and I would suggest that their particularity is more important than anything that can be found by running them together. I shall look at them separately, in their probable order of composition, combining them only where the combination seems irresistible. I do not mean to imply that the time of writing matters more than the poet's last view of where he wished his poems to be placed, only to recommend a measure of skepticism about all meanings generated by moving poems about, whether the mover is the poet or the critic.

However, the earliest of these poems is a set of poems, "Le Christ aux oliviers" ("Christ on the Mount of Olives"), five sonnets based on the speech of Jean Paul's orphaned Jesus. The disciples sleep in Gethsemane and do not hear Christ's news: "Dieu n'est pas! Dieu n'est plus!" (God does not exist, God no longer exists). Christ describes his journey through the "immensities" of space, with its "worlds" and "milky ways," and his finding only a "dark well" where he sought the eye of God. He addresses the power behind all this as Destiny, Necessity, Chance, Father, wondering whether an "immortal breath" is still communicated from world to world, or whether the universe is dying by degrees. Has God Himself been vanquished by the dark angel? Christ is the "eternal victim": "Hélas, et si je meurs, c'est que tout va mourir" (Alas, and if I die, then everything will die). Judas and Pilate then do their work, and Christ is swept up into classical mythology in the fifth sonnet, which associates his voyage and death with the failed flights of Icarus and Phaeton, and with the murder of Attis. Olympus itself shakes at the hour of the crucifixion, but all oracles are silent, no questions are answered, and the poem returns to the notion of an "original power" that "gave a soul to the children of the mire," to the begetting father who is now obstinately dead or turned away from his family.

The work is, as I have suggested elsewhere, close to Vigny's "Mont des Oliviers," but also to poems by Hugo and Leconte de Lisle, even to portions of Tennyson's *In Memoriam* (1850). It is one of the mid-century's many poems of doubt, remarkable only for its resolute syncretism, its sense of the Christian story as a version of a myth that has many forms; and for its anxious suggestion that Christ's death, which must follow from the absence or demise of God, a crucifixion with no resurrection to come, would break a larger chain of generation:

Es-tu sûr de transmettre une haleine
  immortelle,

Entre un monde qui meurt et l'autre renaissant?

(35–36)

Are you sure of communicating an immortal breath/Between a dying world and another being born?

This is cosmic catastrophe: the universe itself halts, but its collapse is movingly presented as something like a possible technical slip, a spark that fails to ignite, the world ending neither with a bang nor with a whimper but with a fizzle. I have already mentioned the biographical undertow that gives this talk of a silent father a covert, but clearly perceptible, urgency.

"Antéros" is a poem not of doubt but of rebellion, a rather belated Byronic shaking of the fists at a tyrannical heaven. Anteros was the brother of Eros, and the avenger of offended love. Nerval associates him with the giant Antaeus, who renewed his strength by touching the earth, and with Dagon and Baal, the Old Testament rivals of Jehovah. The bombast of the poem is not persuasive: "Oui, je suis de ceux-là qu'inspire le Vengeur" (Yes, I am among those inspired by the Avenger). But a certain interest arises from a curious, almost buried, hesitancy in the rebellion. The poem begins:

Tu demandes pourquoi j'ai tant de rage au coeur
Et sur un col flexible une tête indomptée;

You ask me why I have so much rage in my heart /And bear an indomitable head on flexible shoulders. . . .

Here are rage and an indomitable head, but the rage is in the heart, a smoldering emotion rather than a source of action, and the shoulders are flexible. This double feeling, the rebel's defeat both acknowledged and denied, finds its perfect expression in the poem's most memorable lines:

Sous la pâleur d'Abel, hélas! ensanglantée,
J'ai parfois de Caïn l'implacable rougeur!

Beneath the bleeding pallor of Abel,/My color is at times the implacable red of Cain.

"At times" is a desperate confession of weakness, and Nerval mingles here not different religions, but different figures within a single myth. To be both Cain and Abel or, more precisely, to be Abel and wish you could be Cain more often, is a more complex and more human posture than the poem in general seems to propose. "Antéros" offers an image of bravery diluted by debility, but then insists a little too much on the no longer quite credible heroic stance—or on a heroism that sounds like bluff and bravado rather than the achieved thing.

"Golden Verses" is, as Jean Richer has said, a "theoretical text," a profession of faith in the multifarious life of nature. Its epigraph comes from Pythagoras ("Everything has feeling"), and it mocks the complacency of man, who believes he is the only thinking creature in the universe. There are spirits in beasts, souls in flowers; there is "a mystery of love" in metal, and "a hidden God often inhabits an obscure being." The poem impressively condenses difficult ideas into brief lines, but would be rather banal in its comfortable pantheism were it not for its disturbing and characteristically Nervalian flavor of what we can hardly refuse to call paranoia. Spirits, souls, mysteries, and a hidden God sound reasonably encouraging, but "Crains dans le mur aveugle un regard qui t'épie" (Fear the spying eye in the blind wall) is a good deal less so. The poem is close in thought and feeling to Baudelaire's "Correspondances" ("La Nature est un temple . . . ; L'homme y passe à travers des forêts de symboles / Qui l'observent avec des regards familiers" [Nature is a temple . . . ; Man walks there through forests of symbols / That watch him with familiar eyes.]). Nerval lacks Baudelaire's authority but introduces his own disquieting note into the subject all the same: those eyes that are no longer familiar but hidden and to be feared.

We come now to the sonnets with inter-

951

changeable parts, "Delfica" and "Myrtho." They are not easy of access, but they are major poems, and Nerval's reputation must rest substantially on them, taken together with "El Desdichado" and "Artémis." "Delfica" was published in 1845; "Myrtho" was probably written at the same time, but it was not published until 1854. Two of the *autres chimères* offer versions of the closing lines of "Delfica," and one, as I have indicated, replaces the tercets of "Delfica" with those of "Myrtho." I shall look at "Delfica" in detail, and then ask what happens when we conflate the poem with "Myrtho."

La connais-tu, DAFNÉ, cette ancienne romance,
Au pied du sycomore, ou sous les lauriers blancs,
Sous l'olivier, le myrte, ou les saules tremblants,
Cette chanson d'amour . . . qui toujours
    recommence? . . .

Reconnais-tu le TEMPLE au péristyle immense,
Et les citrons amers où s'imprimaient tes dents,
Et la grotte, fatale aux hôtes imprudents,
Où du dragon vaincu dort l'antique semence? . . .

Ils reviendront, ces Dieux que tu pleures toujours!
Le temps va ramener l'ordre des anciens jours;
La terre a tressailli d'un souffle prophétique . . .

Cependant la sybille au visage latin
Est endormie encor sous l'arc de Constantin
—Et rien n'a dérangé le sévère portique.

Daphne, do you know that old ballad,/At the foot of the sycamore, or beneath the white laurels,/Beneath the olive tree, the myrtle, or the trembling willows,/That song of love . . . always beginning again?

Do you recognize the temple with its immense peristyle,/And the bitter lemons where your teeth left their mark,/And the cave, fatal for its incautious guests,/Where the ancient seed of the defeated dragon sleeps?

They will return, those Gods you weep for still!/Time will bring back the order of the older days;/The earth has quivered with a prophetic breath . . .

And yet the sybil with the Latin face/Still sleeps beneath the arch of Constantine/—And nothing has disturbed that severe gate.

The poem is addressed to a young woman, Daphne (a maiden of that name is transformed into a laurel tree in Ovid), who is both a generalized figure of pastoral and one of the "daughters of fire," in whom Nerval sought the incarnation (or perhaps the disincarnation) of the feminine. Its accent and imagery recall a famous poem by Goethe ("Knowst thou the land where the lemon trees blossom . . . ?"), although Nerval gives the lemons those wonderfully immediate teeth marks, and Goethe's land has become, characteristically, Nerval's song. It is an *old* song, a ballad, and hints of the past are strewn about the poem: *ancienne, antique, anciens;* knowledge becomes memory, *connais-tu* turning to *reconnais-tu.* A classical temple is associated with a cave where the seed of a dragon sleeps and therefore may be awakened. The poem makes the young woman a promise about the return of the gods, and the prophetess seems about to speak—when it first appeared the sonnet had an epigraph from Vergil referring to the Sybil of Cumae, the sybil with the Latin face. But she does not speak. The old gods, like Nerval's mother goddess, are just off the horizon, and what dominates the perspective is a modern, Christian calm, represented by Constantine's arch, emblem of a victory over paganism. The sybil, the voice of that vanquished world, is asleep—like the dragon's seed.

The balance of this poem, caught between past and future, between actuality and promise, between antiquity and Christianity, is remarkable. The song begins again, the temple is recognized, but only in questions to which we do not hear the young woman's answer. The gods return, but only in a future tense that is less certain than it sounds. The finality of the seen fact, the Christian victory—"And nothing has disturbed that severe gate"—is opposed to the hopes and fears associated with the young woman mourning her conquered faith. The hesitations that complicate "Antéros" without deepening it here become the poem's theme, a dream of the deposition of the single, authoritarian God that seems both improbable and indispensable, the replacement of severity by a tolerant, plural world of olives and laurels and lemons and daughters of fire. The dragon's seed reminds us that the old gods are not simply a sentimental fantasy.

If we now, as Nerval experimentally did, substitute for the tercets of "Delfica"—concerning the old order, the breath of prophecy, the sybil, and Constantine's arch—those of "Myrtho," the poem will end in this way:

Je sais pourquoi là-bas le volcan s'est rouvert . . .
C'est qu'hier tu l'avais touché d'un pied agile,
Et de cendres soudain l'horizon s'est couvert.

Depuis qu'un duc normand brisa tes dieux
*   d'argile,*
Toujours, sous les rameaux du laurier de Virgile,
Le pâle Hortensia s'unit au Myrte vert!

(9–14)

I know why the volcano has opened there again . . . / It is because yesterday you touched it with an agile foot, / And the horizon was suddenly covered with ashes.

Since a Norman duke broke your gods of clay,/ Forever now beneath the branches of Vergil's laurel,/The pale hydrangea mingles with the green myrtle.

The "prophetic breath" of "Delfica" becomes an eruption of Vesuvius—the earlier lines of "Myrtho" clearly set the Italian scene—and the young woman, mythologized, has caused this threatening motion of the lower powers, a version of the dragon's seed being awakened. But then once again the calm returns, and it is greeted with that curious Nervalian note both of relief and of despair. The line about the Norman duke is extremely cryptic, but probably refers to the conquest and consequent Christianization of Naples by

a Norman in the twelfth century. The last line looks obscure too, but the myrtle is a familiar classical tree, and the hydrangea is a plant not known before the eighteenth century. It seems reasonable, then, to see here the suggestion of a union between ancient and modern times beneath the patronage of Vergil—the Vergil who made the sybil speak, of course, but also the Vergil of the *Eclogues* (A.D. 37–42), who was popularly seen as announcing the birth of Christ; and even the Vergil of Dante, who led the pilgrim to the borders of a territory he himself could not enter.

The poem becomes more conciliatory with this ending—flowers entwine in the place of the severely looming arch. But then the volcano has been more violent than a sleeping dragon seed, and we may note that the myrtle is green while the hydrangea is pale, suggesting a freshness in the old order that the new order lacks. One thinks of Algernon Charles Swinburne's "pale Galilean," and indeed of the pallor of Nerval's own Abel. If Abel had killed the implacable Cain, would that have been another form of the survival of the fittest? That, apparently, is what Nerval sees in Christianity, or Christianity-as-modernity: the visible hegemony of a faith that is in many ways inferior to the faiths it has conquered.

If we return the tercets to "Myrtho" we meet the young woman again, under another name; and in the place of Delfica's teeth marks in the bitter lemons we see Myrtho's golden hair decorated with black grapes:

Je pense à toi, Myrtho, divine enchanteresse,
Au Pausilippe altier, de mille feux brillant,
A ton front inondé des clartés d'Orient,
Aux raisins noirs mêlés avec l'or de ta tresse.

C'est dans ta coupe aussi que j'avais bu l'ivresse,
Et dans l'éclair furtif de ton oeil souriant,
Quand aux pieds d'Iacchus on me voyait priant,
Car la Muse m'a fait l'un des fils de la Grèce.

Je sais pourquoi. . . .

I think of you, Myrtho, divine enchantress,/Of proud Posilipo, lit by a thousand fires,/Of your

953

face flooded with the brightness of the East,/Of the black grapes mixed with the gold of your hair.

I sipped my drunkenness in your cup too,/And in the furtive flash of your smiling eye,/When I was found praying at Bacchus' feet,/For the Muse has made me a son of Greece.

I know why. . . .

I shall not pursue this poem, or these poems, through the other versions, except to mention an interesting Indian alternative to the glitter of Italy and Greece—"If you see Benares," instead of Delphi or Posilipo—and one wonderful line, which does to geography what Nerval so often does to religion, recombining its elements into a vision where the impossible becomes almost palpable, where difference is both asserted and repealed. "La neige du Cathay," the line runs, "tombe sur l'Atlantique" (The snows of Cathay fall on the Atlantic): a chimera of the atlas.

"Horus" transposes a number of Nerval's themes into an Egyptian key, although there are echoes of Greece and, perhaps, in the image, already mentioned, of the goddess fleeing on her golden shell, a memory of Sandro Botticelli's Venus. But it also seriously shifts in emphasis. The earth shakes not because the old gods are returning but because an old god is dying, and the death is fiercely welcomed. The new god, the "new spirit," is not the tyrannical Jehovah or the warlike Christ who suppressed paganism, but Horus, the son of Isis and Osiris, spiritual son of Hermes and god of the rising sun—a prefiguration of Christ in a kinder, more open mood, the child born in a manger and kin to a host of Middle Eastern deities. The rebellion of "Antéros" is here not crushed but about to be accomplished, and an earlier version of the poem takes this political (and psychological) line a stage further. The new spirit is identified as Napoleon, and the dying god is called "the old father." The poem has one marvelous line evoking the hoarfrost issuing from the old

god's mouth, but it is worth quoting in full for the contrast it offers with "Delfica": the new order blessed rather than the old order mourned. We should not try to make Nerval mean one proposition rather than the other, or to move from an earlier to a later position, seeing, for example, a decline from youthful optimism if we take "Horus" as the earlier of the two, or an encouraging change of heart if it is later. The date of composition of "Horus" is not known, but it is likely to have been written at much the same time as "Delfica." Both arguments about dying and conquering gods are possible, and the possible, as Baudelaire said, is one of the provinces of truth. It was, in a sense, the only province of truth for Nerval, and a corollary of the imagination's always being right is that a thought once entertained cannot simply be canceled. The new order is welcomed, a rescue from tyranny; the new order *is* the tyranny. Both propositions cannot be true at the same time, but both are plausible and will apply to all kinds of realities, domestic and public. Both are true of moments in Napoleon's career, for instance. As we shall see in *Aurélia*, Nerval's besetting difficulty was his crippling faith in *all* the readings he made of his experience. "Horus" is not an answer to "Delfica" but a sort of twin, less impressive as a poem but valuable for its registering of the reverse vision. We may note too that the promise of the newborn child is followed by the disappearance of the goddess, leaving only her adored image, the sparkling rainbow sky:

Le dieu Kneph en tremblant ébranlait l'univers:
Isis, la mère, alors se leva sur sa couche,
Fit un geste de haine à son époux farouche,
Et l'ardeur d'autrefois brilla dans ses yeux verts.

"Le voyez-vous, dit-elle, il meurt, ce vieux
    pervers,
Tous les frimas du monde ont passé par sa
    bouche,
Attachez son pied tors, éteignez son oeil louche,
C'est le dieu des volcans et le roi des hivers!

"L'aigle a déjà passé, l'esprit nouveau m'appelle,
J'ai revêtu pour lui la robe de Cybèle . . .
C'est l'enfant bien-aimé d'Hermès et d'Osiris!"

La déese avait fui sur sa conque dorée,
La mer nous renvoyait son image adorée,
Et les cieux rayonnaient sous l'écharpe d'Iris.

The god Kneph shook the universe as he trembled:/Isis, the mother, then raised herself on her couch,/Made a gesture of hatred to her fierce husband,/And her old ardor gleamed in her green eyes.

"Do you see him," she said, "he is dying, this perverse old creature,/All the hoarfrosts of the world have passed through his mouth,/Bind his twisted foot, put out his squinting eye,/He is the god of volcanoes and the king of winter.

"The eagle has passed, the new spirit calls me,/ I am wearing for him the robe of Cybele . . ./He is the well-beloved child of Hermes and Osiris."

The goddess had fled on her golden shell,/The sea returned to us her adored image,/And the skies sparkled beneath the sash of Iris.

We come now to the two late sonnets "El Desdichado" and "Artémis," both written in 1853, less then eighteen months before Nerval's death. We might call "El Desdichado" Nerval's most famous poem if it were not his only truly well-known one. Its second line finds its way into Eliot's *Waste Land* (1922), and indeed its use of the tarot pack as a discreet structuring principle may have prompted Eliot to look in the same direction. ("I am not familiar with the exact constitution of the Tarot," Eliot wrote; but he was familiar with Nerval.) The poem has been commented on more than almost any other poem in French, read in terms of astrology and alchemy, and repeatedly seen as holding the secret of Nerval's disturbed life and abrupt end. For a start, though, it will be as well to listen to its music, to allow a sense of its charm to precede the unraveling of its meanings:

Je suis le Ténébreux,—le Veuf,—l'Inconsolé,
Le Prince d'Aquitaine à la Tour abolie:

Ma seule Étoile est morte,—et mon luth constellé
Porte le Soleil noir de la Mélancolie.

Dans la nuit du Tombeau, Toi qui m'as consolé,
Rends-moi le Pausilippe et la mer d'Italie,
La fleur qui plaisait tant à mon coeur désolé,
Et la treille où le Pampre à la Rose s'allie.

Suis-je Amour ou Phoebus? . . . Lusignan ou Biron?
Mon front est rouge encor du baiser de la Reine;
J'ai rêvé dans la grotte où nage la Syrène . . .

Et j'ai deux fois vainqueur traversé l'Achéron:
Modulant tour à tour sur la lyre d'Orphée
Les soupirs de la Sainte et les cris de la Fée.

I am the Dark One, the Widower, the Unconsoled,
The Aquitaine prince of the tumbled Tower.
My only *Star* is dead, and my spangled lute
Bears the black *Sun* of *Melancholy.*

You who consoled me in the night of the Tomb,
Give me back Posilipo, and the Italian sea,
The flower that so pleased my sorry heart,
And the trellis where the Vine and the Rose are joined.

Am I Eros or Phoebus? Lusignan or Biron?
My face is still flushed from the queen's kiss.
I have dreamed in the grotto where the siren swims . . .

And I have twice crossed the Acheron as a victor:
Modulating in turn on Orpheus' lyre
The sighs of the Saint and the Witch's screams.

The last line literally reads "The sighs of the saint and the cries of the fairy," and I have departed here from the literal translation I have used everywhere else. Sound is always important in Nerval (as in any poet), but in this case it seems that to lose the sound, or some sort of equivalent for it, is to lose everything. The poet is claiming to have returned from the underworld, like Orpheus, and to have done so twice, with two Eurydices—or rather to have turned the voices of two women, or aspects of woman, the saint and the fairy, into a single song. The saint is all sibilants ("soupirs de la sainte") and the fairy all tight, squeezed vowels ("cris de la fée"). The opposition in sound, the squealing last words—it would have been different if the poem had ended with the sighs of the saint—may suggest that the victory is not as complete as it appears, that the modulation makes up not a single, harmonious tune but a painful oscillation between two melodies. I think it is also true that a fairy in English represents rather minor magic, and is no rival for a saint. Nerval's *fée* is more like a witch (benign or otherwise), and his manuscript note on the poem mentions Melusine, a lady who took the form of a snake on certain days and was surprised by her lover in this incarnation. The place where this incident occurred was the château of Lusignan, the family name that comes up earlier in the poem.

This is a sonnet more than usually full of allusions, and tends to send critics scampering to biography and mythology. The title comes from Sir Walter Scott's *Ivanhoe* (1820), although it means in Spanish not "the disinherited," as the knight there is called, but "the unfortunate one." We can find the prince of darkness, the tumbled tower, and the star, respectively, in the tarot picture cards numbered fifteen, sixteen, and seventeen, so perhaps Nerval is following the sequence of a particular telling of fortune, or has taken the order of cards in the pack as a form of destiny. The figure of melancholy appears in an engraving by Albrecht Dürer; the phrase "Dans la nuit du tombeau" occurs several times in Jean Racine. Biron was a nobleman who served Henry IV of France, and who is remembered in one of the Valois folk songs Nerval collected. Italy and the grotto come from an episode in Nerval's life recounted in the story "Octavie" (1853), and the queen's kiss appears in a children's game in *Sylvie.*

We can fill out the poem with all this, and much more, and all clues and hints are to be welcomed. But we must be careful not to assume that we have understood the poem when we have merely found a handful of its sources. Even so astute an interpreter as Moulin can slip into this way of thinking at times. The crossings of the Acheron, she writes, are the two attacks of madness in 1841 and in August 1853. The attacks are plainly what Nerval is chiefly referring to, but he is *calling* them escapes from the underworld. This is an active revision of his experience, which is now associated with all kinds of other crossings, ancient and modern, fantastic and metaphorical, of the deathly river. He is not simply evoking his madness by another, evasive, or "poetic" name, and if he had wanted only to mention his madness, he did not need the Acheron at all.

The strength of "El Desdichado" lies within it. In fact, the density of this poem, as of the other *chimères,* arises less from the often cryptic allusions than from the curious architecture of the work. As is suggested by Nerval's shuffling of octaves and sestets in "Delfica" and "Myrtho," the poems are composed essentially of loose blocks of thought rather than lines or phrases or images or sequences. The blocks are coherent in themselves, syntactically and semantically complete, but they are merely placed next to each other, not joined by an articulating logic. This is poetry singularly lacking in words such as *and, but, for, because,* and *therefore,* or rather, the words are sometimes there but are singularly weakened. "El Desdichado" uses *and* six times, for example, but merely to introduce items in a list. It has *or* twice, but the options each *or* introduces seem uncertain, perhaps unreal. The most striking conjunctions, like *since* ("Myrtho") or *and yet* ("Delfica"), read like riddles, since we cannot find in the sentence the argument they seem to announce. There is a song (in "Delfica"), a classical temple, a promise that the gods will return, a glimpse of a sleeping prophetess. A god shivers (in "Horus"), Isis speaks, the goddess escapes across the sea. We can combine these elements in various ways, make "stories" out of them (in the sense of newspaper stories), and some of these combinations will be plausible, one or two perhaps indispensable. But they are not given by the poem. The effect is that of a surrealist collage or the later parts of *The Waste Land*, except that there is nothing random or disheveled about Nerval's arrangements. He is not raiding his dreams for their chaos—he once wrote that he wished to direct his everlasting dream instead of submitting to it, which is the reverse of a surrealist ambition—and he is not exactly shoring fragments against his ruin. He is holding his fragments up to the light, wondering about their possible places in several brilliant puzzles.

This procedure is very clear in "El Desdichado." The first stanza *asserts*, tells us what the poet is: desolate, abandoned, haunted. There is a flicker of irony here that is part of the poem's beauty: Nerval knows that to call himself *le ténébreux* (the dark one) is to romanticize a despair that is all too real. The next stanza *appeals* to the person who could perhaps (or could she? is this only a helpless, rhetorical plea?) restore the floral, sunny world of an earlier time. The rhyming of *inconsolé* with *consolé* courts a flagrant contradiction, then resolves it: he was consoled once, is unconsoled now. The absence of logical linking here is quite glaring. The *because* we wish to supply between the stanzas—because you consoled me once, you can do it again; it is because I am in my present plight that I need to conjure up former consolations—is carefully omitted by Nerval. Of course a good deal of modern poetry works in just this way, and we are more familiar with such elliptical structures than Nerval's contemporaries were. Even so, we still often understand a work without recognizing the full extent of our collaboration in the creation of its order.

The third stanza begins by *questioning*. It is, as I have suggested, hard to see the force of these alternatives, what difference it would make if the poet were Eros rather than Phoebus, Lusignan rather than Biron. I think we should probably take the line as evoking a general panic of identity, a profusion of tempting roles, all imaginary, none stable or satis-

factory. In this case the line would be another assertion, despair becoming frantic, agitated. In any event the last five lines of the poem do return to *assertion*, although the claims are braver and brighter now. The darkened lute becomes a tuneful lyre, and the dead star is rescued from hell, although her sighs and cries, as I said earlier, and her divided nature may temper the triumph a little. What the poet has achieved, we feel, is a genuine but precarious moment of credible confidence, a posture that is not a pose but that requires all the courage and faith he can muster, and that appears marvelously to be *found* in the course of the poem, between assertion and assertion. We have shared the poet's work but that means we share his apparent surprise too: we do not quite know how we got from the darkness to the half-light, or how long the half-light will last.

It does not last in "Artémis," and it is hard not to see in this remarkable poem, as most critics have, the beautifully composed trace of a terrible relapse. The saint and the fairy have now become twin saints, divine and infernal. The poet longs for the former, addresses to her desolate, unanswerable questions, and chooses the second. I think of Nerval's suicide not as the meaning of this poem but almost as the consequence he drew from it. Giving up on heaven, he crossed into the underworld for good.

La Treizième revient. . . . C'est encor la première;
Et c'est toujours la Seule,—ou c'est le seul
  moment;
Car es-tu Reine, ô Toi! la première ou dernière?
Es-tu Roi, toi le Seul ou le dernier amant? . . .

Aimez qui vous aima du berceau dans la bière;
Celle que j'aimai seul m'aime encore tendrement:
C'est la Mort—ou la Morte. . . . O délice! Ô
  tourment!
La rose qu'elle tient, c'est la Rose trémière.

Sainte napolitaine aux mains pleines de feux,
Rose au coeur violet, fleur de Sainte Gudule:
As-tu trouvé ta Croix dans le désert des Cieux?

Roses blanches, tombez! vous insultez nos Dieux,
Tombez, fantômes blancs, de votre ciel qui brûle:
—La Sainte de l'Abîme est plus sainte à mes yeux.

The Thirteenth returns. . . . She is the first again;/And she is always the Only One,—or it is the only moment;/For are you the Queen, the first or the last one?/Are you the King, the last or the Only lover? . . .

Love the one who loved you from the cradle to the grave;/The one I alone loved still loves me tenderly:/It is Death—or the Dead Woman. . . . O delight, O torture!/The rose she bears is the rose-like hollyhock.

Neapolitan saint with hands full of fire,/Violet-hearted rose, Saint Gudula's flower:/Have you found your Cross in the desert of Heaven?

White roses, fall, you insult our gods,/Fall, white phantoms, from your burning sky:/—The Saint of the Abyss is more saintly in my eyes.

This is an extremely difficult poem, but I think a good deal of its incantatory power can be felt at once. The thirteenth suggests superstition, and the king and queen perhaps a deck of cards. We are in a world of good and bad fortunes, and of time, since the thirteenth hour is also the first. We can probably arrive at this reading on our own, but a manuscript note of Nerval's specifies "the thirteenth hour (pivotal)," and an alternative title for the sonnet was "Ballet des heures" (Ballet of the Hours). Nerval's play *L'Imagier de Harlem* (*The Image Maker of Harlem*, 1851) has a song of that name, which associates flowers with hours and speaks of retaining the passing instant. An hour that returns, like a playing card coming up again, is the same and not the same, both repetitive and unique. The genders of the French language permit Nerval an elaborate balance of persons and personifications: not only king/queen but also moment/hour and lover/mistress, a sort of ballet of the sexes, an alternating dance like that of one of those clocks where tiny figures of men and women come wobbling out and in. The stanza hovers between the security of return and the

always imminent departure, but the very return seems to destroy a privilege or an identity. Nerval here seems to be questioning the solace of sameness, one of his most cherished consolations: "I am the same as Mary, the same as your mother." If the goddess is all these women, perhaps this means she is no one, not a queen at all but just a passing and returning hour. "It is scarcely possible to admit," Nerval says of Restif de la Bretonne in *Les illuminés*, "that he ever loved only one woman . . . in three persons." And if the goddess is not a queen, then her consort is not a king, but only a circling moment. The Artemis of the title of the poem is a virgin deity whose emblem is the moon, another image of revolving time and unappeased love.

In the face of this distress the second stanza finds its apparently simple instruction: "Love the one who loved you." Or rather, since "Artémis," like the other sonnets of *Les chimères*, is made up of disjunct blocks of mood and meaning, this is the bridge I propose between the first two blocks. It is worth noting that the first stanza is unusually full of conjunctions—*and, or, for, or, or*—and yet far from organizing a proposition, they contribute to a sense of rising panic. The woman who loved us from the cradle to the grave can only be a goddess or a mother. The temptation to dip into Nerval's biography here only brings us back to the density of the poem. If the dead woman is in part Jenny Colon, she is merged with Madame Labrunie. Aurélia, Nerval's otherworldly revision of the earthly Jenny, appears holding a stem of hollyhock, and it is, I take it, the sheer undeniable *presence* of the figure that amazes the poet and is evoked in the poem. The dead woman, the very sign of absence, is *there*.

But then the dream (or the reality) is invaded by doubt, an almost theoretical skepticism centered on Saint Rosalie, whose statue Nerval saw in Naples, and Saint Gudula, for whom a church in Brussels is named. The conventional symbol of the cross here takes on an ambiguity—it means both salvation and suffering—worthy of George Herbert, and a heaven that is a desert is perhaps a sufficient answer to the poet's question. The rain of roses is borrowed from the second part of *Faust,* and the burning sky suggests torture rather than redemption. Once again, as in "Delfica" and "Myrtho," the Christian order appears to have prevailed over "our gods," but it is again a hollow, even vicious victory. The pale hydrangea is bleached now to an empty, scorching desert, and the poet proclaims his allegiance to the depths of paganism and hell and despair.

But what has happened to the poet's instruction, where are the safety of love and comfort of death, or the dead woman? It is as if Orpheus, before his journey to the underworld, were to expect to find Eurydice in heaven and then to discover, with terror and surprise, that she was beckoning quite another way. The pattern and context of Nerval's feelings become clearer when we read *Aurélia,* but the poem itself is expressive enough. In a characteristic Nervalian movement a solace turns to nightmare, and the nightmare is embraced. Nerval chose what he saw as certain damnation, betrothed himself to the dark saint, the "more saintly" lady of the abyss, when he could no longer live with the uncertainties of his flickering hope.

For "Artémis," even more than for other poems by Nerval, we must heed his hint to Dumas about explanation. It is not that the sonnet loses its charm if we explore it, and in fact *charm* is not the word for its uncanny power, the impression it gives of a deft but nervous magician juggling life and death and time. *Charm* was one of Nerval's favorite words, one of his means of making large achievements look modest (merely "charming"), and of keeping his wilder fears and ambitions from his friends. "Artémis" will take all the scrutiny we care to give it, but we must be prepared to allow it a sort of permanent resistance to interpretation, a reluctance to confess all. I am not recommending obscurity for its own sake but suggesting that this poem is both precise and secretive; that like an oracle,

it measures out assertion and elision in its own unique dosage, asks us to live with doubts we should require other poems to resolve. "The Thirteenth returns. . . ." The thirteenth what? Well, woman, or hour. But the poem does not *mention* either, and its reticence is part of its meaning. The importance of "Artémis," and of the other *chimères,* is that they begin to alter the boundaries of comprehension, to show us that we know things we thought were beyond us and misunderstand much that seems simple and close at hand. The equation between death and a loved one, for example, which sounds so mystical, seems easier to grasp than the daily return of the hours. Same time, same place, we say, knowing all the while that places and times cannot be stepped into twice.

Formally the *chimères* are Petrarchan sonnets, using various rhyme schemes (abba, abba, ccd, eed; abab, abab, cdd, cee), but always employing only two rhymes for the first eight lines. The octave of the sonnet is thus firmly separated from the sestet, which may be tightly knit in its rhymes, as in "Myrtho" (cdc, ddc) or "Artémis" (cdc, cdc), or slightly freer, as in "Delfica" (ccd, eed) or "El Desdichado" (cdd, cee). The tact and reticence I have just described are echoed in Nerval's technique. The manuscript of "El Desdichado" shows, for example, that he had thought of introducing the word *ancolie,* which is the name of a flower representing sadness and insanity. It is also, as André Rousseaux has pointed out, the richest rhyme imaginable for *melancolie,* and Nerval seems to have rejected it for this very reason. On the other hand, this same poem has several delicate internal rhymes (*morte/porte, fleur/coeur, lyre/soupirs*) that are very much part of its music.

The diction and grammar of the poems are formal, even stately. Carefully balanced cadences contain decorous terms and discreet inversions: "Et de cendres soudain l'horizon s'est couvert." Recurring words suggest spells, a certain innocence or superstition in the midst of sophistication. Thus, as Richer has said, in "Artémis" Nerval uses five forms of the verb *aimer (amant, aimez, aima, aimai, aime)*, and seeks out assonances for these words or echoes of their central consonant *(moment, première, m'aime, Mort, Morte, tremière, mains)*. And as I have suggested earlier, the poems often achieve a startling directness: "Ils reviendront," "Aimez qui vous aima." Indeed, if we reflect on the force (and the vulnerability) of these phrases, we glimpse something like the inner motion of most of the sonnets. They travel from assertion to assertion, as I have said, using questions and instructions as their signposts and instances: "Je suis le ténébreux" becomes "Et j'ai deux fois vainqueur traversé l'Acheron"; "La Treizième revient" leads to "La Sainte de l'Abîme est plus sainte à mes yeux." But at the center of each poem is a claim of revelation, the announcement of an assurance that will still the poet's or his interlocutor's distress. These are Nerval's direct, disturbingly simple phrases: they tell us that the gods will come back, that the poet knows why volcanoes erupt, that love is an uncomplicated imperative. And then these claims, in every poem, are replaced by an ambiguous but always slightly sinister or depressed vision: the pale hydrangea, the sleeping sybil, the saint of the abyss. The claim to certainty is not denied— the absence of connections between stanzas means the poems offer guesses and hunches rather than arguments—but it is somehow met and foiled by these images. They drain away the poet's conviction. It is true that in "Artémis" this loss produces a new conviction, a preference for the saint of hell, and that in "El Desdichado" the claimed revelation comes at the end of the poem, and is only faintly modified by the fading *cris de la fée*. But I think the pattern is worth noting. Nerval, a man hounded not only by doubts but also by possibilities, dramatized in his best poems not the cure for his ills or the failure of his cures, but the terrible proximity of a faith that eluded him, that seemed to promise in-

fallible truth before settling into the shape of an enigma. As the work of Kafka suggests, both belief and disbelief are comfortable conditions when compared with the state of someone whose skepticism is harrowed by occasional miracles.

SYLVIE

Nerval's prose is considerable in its volume and in its attractions. I have already mentioned his plays, journalism, *Journey to the Orient,* and *Les illuminés.* But his lasting fame as a prose writer rests on *Sylvie,* a light confessional short story where the word *charm* for once does not seem misplaced or unduly oblique, and *Aurélia,* the lucid, desperate memoir of Nerval's madness. Both of these works, like "El Desdichado" and "Artémis," center on a woman found and lost, although the story is now complicated by other, more worldly or more pathological concerns.

Sylvie first appeared in the *Revue des deux mondes* in 1853, but was then collected in *Daughters of Fire* the following year. This volume contained the twelve *chimères;* an essay, full of examples, on Valois folk songs and legends; and five pieces with the names of women for their titles: "Angélique," "Sylvie," "Octavie," "Isis," "Corilla." "Angélique" is a rambling non-novel ostensibly about a quest for a rare book, but really a framework for historical anecdote of the kind found in *Les illuminés* and an introduction to some of Nerval's favorite land- and townscapes: Senlis, Chaalis, Ermenonville. "Corilla" is an elegant little play set in Naples and originally published in 1839. An actress gives a rendezvous to two suitors at the same time, and finds one of them too mundane and the other too poetic—to the second she says, as Jenny Colon must have said to Nerval, that he perhaps loves only the actress in her. The play ends amicably and humorously, with all three figures having supper together. "Octavie" was published in three different versions before arriving in *Daughters of Fire*. It recounts the Neapolitan adventure that haunts several of the *chimères*. The writer meets a woman who does gold embroidery for church ornaments. Her room is full of magical-seeming objects: a black madonna, old paintings of the four elements, a statue of Saint Rosalie. During the night a minor eruption of Vesuvius covers the town in a hot, sulphurous dust, and the poet is tempted by suicide, imagines Death as waiting for him with a smile, "after the happiness, after the intoxication," and saying, "I am not beautiful, but I am kind and helpful, and I do not give pleasure but eternal calm." He is saved from these "fatal thoughts" by the memory of the meeting he has arranged for the following day with a young Englishwoman. The person who consoles the poet of "El Desdichado" "in the night of the tomb" may thus be either the woman he spent the night with or the woman he remembered in the morning—or, more eerily and characteristically, a conflation of both. "Isis" describes a visit to the temple of the goddess at Pompeii, culminating in an evocation of the divinity herself, paraphrased from Apuleius' *Golden Ass* (2nd century A.D.). Cybele, Minerva, Venus, Diana, Proserpine, Ceres, Juno, Bellona, Hecate, Nemesis—all are names for Isis, "mother of nature, mistress of the elements." Anticipating Friedrich Nietzsche's *Die Geburt der Tragödie* (*Birth of Tragedy*, 1872), Sir James Frazer's *Golden Bough* (1890), and Robert Graves's *White Goddess* (1947), Nerval finds patterns and parallels in a variety of cults. Above all, as the poems make clear, he perceived in Christianity a proliferating oriental religion that finally overcame the gods of Greece and their heirs. And yet this new/old fable is itself a promise of another victory. A murdered son is mourned by his mother; the enemy has won, but the son will come again. At the climax of "Isis" he asks:

"Why is the one they seek and weep for called Osiris in one place, Adonis in another, Atys in still another? and why does a different clamor coming from the depths of Asia also seek in mysterious grottoes the remains of a sacrificed god?—A divine woman, mother, wife, or mistress bathes with her tears this bloody and disfigured body, victim of a hostile principle that triumphs on his death but that will be conquered one day.

The "different clamor" is Christianity; and the "divine woman" is Mary as well as Isis.

Before looking more closely at *Sylvie* it will be useful to pause briefly over a piece Nerval published a little less than a year earlier, in 1852. In *Les nuits d'octobre* (October Nights) we can see him finding and beginning to perfect a very personal fictional form: the mock travel tale that is really a mixture of essay and short story. Effectively, this is the form both of *Sylvie* and of *Aurélia*, different as those works are in tone and implications. The man who had journeyed in the East now journeys in his mind, finding in Paris and its environs a map for far more secret and frightening voyages.

Les nuits d'octobre opens as if by accident. Nerval is a master of this careful effect, a great imitator of chance. He describes himself as wandering about Paris, planning a trip to Meaux. He meets a friend, chats, misses his coach, and has dinner in a restaurant where he reads a few newspapers and magazines. He comes across a translation of an article by Charles Dickens on London at night. "The realistic intelligence of our neighbors," he exclaims, "is satisfied with the absolutely true," whereas an equivalent piece in a Paris paper would be full of anecdotes and sentimental adornments. "In fact," Nerval adds, "can a novel ever catch the strange combinations of life? You invent man, because you don't know how to observe him." Nerval and his friend ramble about Paris until dawn, visiting cafés, dubious clubs, run-down districts. Then Nerval takes his coach for Meaux.

The apparent aside on Dickens is the thread of the story. Playfully taking up what he sees as a challenge, Nerval is out to test Paris against London for night life, and to show that a Frenchman can be as much a realist as the next writer. There is a nice irony here, since realism, in the nineteenth-century sense, in painting and literature, was essentially a French invention and fashionable at the time Nerval was writing. He meant, as we shall see, to show both the advantages and the limits of the doctrine as his contemporaries understood it.

Nerval's stance is to offer, straight-faced, a seemingly random, factual account of his wanderings, what he calls a daguerreotype of truth. But his narrative, even so, takes on a more and more phantasmagoric quality. In Meaux he finds a traveling sideshow that includes a handsome woman who has the dark fleece of a merino sheep growing in place of her hair. She has, an advertisement proclaims, already excited the wonder of Queen Victoria. Nerval sees this marvelous creature, has terrible dreams the following night, although not about her, pursues his travels in the region of Meaux, and is put in prison for not carrying the proper identifying papers with him. In prison he has another dream, in which a fierce tribunal accuses him of being a fantasist, a realist, and an essayist—all of which, of course, he is. Part of the charge ingeniously insists that "from realism to crime is but a step; for crime is essentially realist." Nerval concludes his apparently haphazard tale with the words "And that is a faithful account of three October nights that have taught me a lesson about the excesses of too absolute a realism; at least I hope they have."

A sly passage late in this amusing book gives us the clue to the whole enterprise. Realism is hard work, Nerval complains, and in any case art is not interested in this petty, daily sort of truth. What could be more false than the *Iliad*, or Torquato Tasso's *Gerusalemme liberata* (*Jerusalem Delivered*, 1881): "What's true is what's false, at least in art and poetry." This phrase is often taken to signify Nerval's rejection of the realism he has been dabbling in. After all, the implicit argument goes, the author of the hermetic *chimères*

could not be a serious realist. But Nerval's meditation here is subtle and balanced. Art alters truth, he is saying, and who is to quarrel? But noble art misses things like women with fleece instead of hair. Or again, dreams are nightly facts: we really do dream, even if the contents of the dreams are illusions, and this too is an opportunity for realism. Absolute realism is a myth, Nerval suggests, a form of foolishness or gossip, and his own narrative mimes the directionless effect the mode often encourages. But the intuition of the realists is right: reality is full of quirks and colors that shame our often meager inventions. Nerval knew, as the surrealists were to urge, that realism can be the fastest road to the fantastic.

This is the form of realism Nerval practices in *Sylvie*. The truth of life includes its subject's troubled perceptions of it. *Sylvie* is much closer to autobiography than it is to fiction, but it acknowledges the fictions that wind among the hardest or the least arranged of facts. Again Nerval takes a journey, although he is now far more consciously seeking the past.

The narrative opens with the poet platonically in love with an actress. He has not attempted to get close to her as a person, he says, because he is afraid of disturbing "the magic mirror" in which he sees her reflection. A friend points out a man who is the actress' lover, but the poet is unconcerned. "It is an image I pursue," he says, "nothing more." However, a sudden upheaval on the stock market makes the poet rich overnight, and a romantic affair begins to seem a practical possibility after all. Was it lack of funds that made him hold back before? Not exactly, and he sees that the very thought of buying the actress' favors belongs to an older, more freely philandering time. Still, the money gives him a new card to play, and later in the story he plays it. For the moment, his eye runs over the newspaper that has informed him of his fortune and catches sight of the announcement of a traditional rural ceremony in his home province, a "druidic" rite that has survived passing monarchies and religions. That night he cannot sleep and revisits in thought his country childhood, particularly a dance on the lawn of a sixteenth-century château where his companion was the dark-eyed Sylvie, a village girl, and the queen of the ball was the blond Adrienne, daughter of a local aristocratic family. Adrienne later became a nun. "Everything was explained to me," Nerval now affirms, "by this half-dreamt memory." The child Adrienne was the first avatar and model of the actress he loves at such a careful distance: "To love a nun in the shape of an actress . . . and what if they were the same person! It is enough to drive a man mad!"

The irony is especially delicate here. Nerval had already been literally, violently, desperately mad, and yet he is still able to use this bland cliché with apparent ease. He was always aware that madness, the painful phenomenon, cannot really be represented in words; that when we imagine we are talking about it we are usually talking about something else, something milder, more orderly, more manageable. In *Les nuits d'octobre* he quotes Pascal and La Rochefoucauld on the subject: "Men are mad, necessarily so mad that it would be another sort of madness not to be mad." "It is a great madness to wish to be sane all on one's own." Nerval's laconic comment speaks volumes about the gap between such fine pronouncements and the life of the asylum. "Such maxims," he calmly says, "are consoling."

Nerval did seem at times to deny his madness. His attacks were just an amusing dream, he said in a letter, and he had to be labeled as crazy because "there are doctors and deputies here who see that the fields of poetry do not encroach on the public highway." Partly he is claiming the protection of the romantic equation between madness and poetry, partly insisting on the real truths revealed in his insanity, insights that are not simply to be consigned to insignificance by what we sometimes complacently call reason. But Nerval never denied the terror of his madness, only

insisted that there were precious things entangled in the nightmare. When he said it was not a nightmare, he was being polite, like those people who always say they are well when they are not, who will not bore others with the tale of their ills.

The poet in *Sylvie* is obviously even less able to sleep once he has come across the dizzying chance that the actress and the nun may be the same. He hurries mentally back to what he calls "the real" Sylvie, the beautiful country girl who is neither a great lady nor a nun nor a stage illusion. It is three years since he has seen her, and even now she must be at the ball following the ceremony announced in the paper. It is one o'clock in the morning. By five, the poet reckons, he could be at Loisy, the scene of the festivities. He boards a coach and embarks on the major flashback of the work, its central panel.

The place is the same—Loisy, in the heart of Nerval's loved Valois—and again a traditional festival is in progress. But the atmosphere is now that of the eighteenth century, with a ruined neoclassical temple set in a rustic landscape, and the flavor of a painting by Jean-Antoine Watteau—Nerval mentions the *Voyage à Cythère* (*The Embarkation for Cythera*, 1717). Several years have passed; Sylvie is even more beautiful than she was at the dance on the château lawn; the poet has become a student in Paris. The two are happy to meet again and talk (already) of their memories of childhood. The poet escorts Sylvie home and spends the warm night on a heath near the forest of Ermenonville. His mind is full of Sylvie, he says, and yet the walls of a nearby convent remind him of Adrienne and her vocation. The next day Sylvie and the poet visit Sylvie's aunt in a neighboring village, and a scene of remarkable grace and appeal follows. An ancient portrait of the aunt when young is effectively brought to life when Sylvie finds the old lady's wedding clothes in an attic and puts them on. The poet dresses up as the groom; time is halted or even canceled. Sylvie is "the image of [the aunt's] youth," and the young couple are married not so much symbolically as in a solemn game, a rite of great beauty but of no consequence in the continuing world. "We were husband and wife for a whole fine summer morning," Nerval writes, looking forward to a prose poem by Arthur Rimbaud in which a couple make themselves king and queen by the sheer force of their wishing: The man cries, "I want her to be queen"; the woman says, "I want to be queen." "And indeed," the poem goes on, "they were king and queen for a whole morning . . . and afternoon" ("Royauté").

The flashback ends here, and we return to the night coach from Paris. But the poet has one more memory to evoke (or to allay). Another party is taking place, but a private one this time, in the ruins of the abbey of Chaalis. The girls from a convent close by are putting on a mystery play: the world has been destroyed, and a spirit rises from the abyss inviting the angels to admire Christ in his glory. The part of this spirit is taken by Adrienne— the nun is now literally the actress. This memory is so haunting and so eerily appropriate that the poet himself wonders whether he is actually remembering it at all: "Perhaps this memory is an obsession." Perhaps he has read the actress back into a dreamed Adrienne, placed an imagined girl in the real ruins.

With this the poet arrives at Loisy, finds Sylvie at the dance, and confesses all to her. He falls at her feet, weeping, tells her about the "fatal specter" of the actress/nun, and begs her to "save" him. The scene is interrupted by the arrival of others, but Sylvie's looks are tender—merely kind, no doubt, but the poet (and we) are inclined to see promises in them. Again, in the present as in the past, the poet wanders alone in the landscape, returns to his uncle's old house, finding there a stuffed dog he had known when it was alive, and visits Rousseau's tomb. Other things have changed and died as well as the dog. Sylvie, as the poet discovers when he sees her the next day, has become cultured, sings opera instead of country tunes, has herself read Rousseau, and compares a local scene to a passage in Scott. Far from applauding these improvements, the poet can see only loss in them, a sense confirmed by the fact that the old aunt is dead. He asks about Adrienne, and Sylvie is mildly irritated: "How you go on about your nun." He begins to think again of his actress too, wonders what role she is playing that evening. A little later he learns that Sylvie is engaged to be married, to the son of his own wet nurse. He departs discreetly, back to Paris and the theater, and the world of images.

The rest is epilogue, or rather a double epilogue. The poet sends flowers to his actress and leaves for Germany, where he writes a play designed for her. On his return, she accepts the principal role and becomes his mistress. Touring the provinces with her and her company, the poet returns to the château where he first saw Adrienne. He tells the actress his story (as he told Sylvie about Adrienne and the actress), and is firmly rebuffed for his pains. "You do not love me," the actress says. "You want me to say: the actress is the same as the nun; you are looking for a play, that is all, and the resolution escapes you." She rapidly transfers her affections elsewhere.

The second epilogue involves a visit to the now married Sylvie, whom the poet, with lamentable fidelity to his fixation, takes to see his former mistress in a local theater. Doesn't the actress resemble someone they know? he asks. Sylvie wonders who. "Do you remember Adrienne?" And Sylvie, in what is at once the most refreshing and the most heartrending moment in the work, bursts out laughing. "What an idea," she says. She adds that Adrienne died some years ago in her convent.

Certain details of *Sylvie* bring us very close to the world of *Les chimères*, and especially of "El Desdichado." Sylvie's window is said to be surrounded by tangled vines and roses, as is the window of the hotel room where the poet stays when he is in the provinces, recalling the "trellis where the vine and the rose are joined." Sylvie and Adrienne together, the poet suggests, make up a single star, "alternately blue and pink like the deceptive light of Aldebaran." In this context, "my only star is dead" points to both the death of Adrienne and the loss of Sylvie. But to read *Sylvie* as a key to the poem, as many commentators do, is to miss the real differences between the works and to assume that prose is likely to tell the plain truth, which poetry distorts or elides. In some ways *Sylvie* is more complex than "El Desdichado." The poem is obscure, oblique, powerful, but its distress is *given:* the woman is gone, the poet has only his pleas and his questions, and his brave claims of victory. In the prose work the distress is incurred and diagnosed. And implicitly we get the diagnosis of the diagnosis.

Like an analyst who is his own patient, the poet decides that the memory of the spiritual, otherworldly Adrienne has created his love for the actress, a dream distanced by footlights, the connection seemingly authenticated by being discovered in a state of half-sleep. The actress herself accepts this interpretation without question and without sympathy. Sylvie, on the other hand, and in this view, is the here and now, the present and the possible, forfeited by relentless flights into fantasy. Adrienne and Sylvie, Nerval says after his remark about Aldebaran, "were the two halves of a single love. One was the sublime ideal, the other sweet reality."

But this, as our suspicions and Sylvie's laughter strongly suggest, is to mythologize and mystify a more fundamental problem. The poet asks Sylvie to save him from thoughts of the actress, but he seems also to have been using thoughts of the actress and Adrienne to save him from the accessible Sylvie. As Jean-Pierre Richard has commented, the poet wants Sylvie "both to destroy and to justify his obsession." The obsession, that is, even as it is denounced, will make reality seem poor, the tame currency of the merely available. And yet of course the reality in this case is as much an invention as the ideal. Sylvie herself, we may

say, is more tangible and appealing than the remote Adrienne or the avoided actress, and this no doubt is why the work is named after her. But her role in the poet's mental drama is no less phantasmagoric. She is "sweet reality," a sort of emanation of pastoral. "If I were to write a novel," Nerval says, "I should never be able to make acceptable the story of a heart caught up in two simultaneous loves." The implication is that he has made the story acceptable by writing a non-novel. In fact he has drawn a picture of something far more desolate and disturbing: a heart that has split its love in two parts *in order* to be crucified by the impossibility of having either. This sounds pathological, and *Sylvie* would be a clinical document—writers do take it this way—if it were not narrated with such extraordinary poise. The health of the language continually implies what Nerval must have grasped in his best moments: that there is no resemblance between Adrienne and the actress, that we cannot console ourselves by tracing current panics to long-lost fantasies; that the warmest appreciation of Sylvie would be not to call her "reality" but to see what she sees. In such moments, Nerval knew how impossible the impossible was, and counted the cost of continuing to long for it. He saw, if only intermittently, that the poet's explanation of his case was but a further symptom of it.

Nerval gives a historical flavor to his case by suggesting that the state of mind he presents is characteristic of a certain type of period: the aftermath of a revolution or the fall of a great regime. This is a period neither of vice nor of gallantry, neither of skepticism nor of orgies, but one that offers "a mixture of activity, hesitation and laziness, brilliant utopias, philosophical and religious aspirations, vague enthusiasms." Nerval's age was one both of world-weariness and of rather disorganized promise; the age of Alfred de Musset and Alphonse de Lamartine but also the age of Charles Fourier and the rise of socialism. It is for this reason that Rousseau is so important in *Sylvie*, something like its secular patron

965

saint. The poet not only visits the famous tomb, he talks to people who knew the philosopher, and in a crucial conversation Rousseau's vision of innocence is challenged. An old man remarks that Rousseau was right to rail against urban life: "Man is corrupted in the poisonous air of cities." We must remember that the whole movement of *Sylvie* rests on the plausibility of this claim: from Paris to Loisy, from present to past, from actress to village girl, the story travels toward Rousseau. But when it arrives, it discovers the sort of truth that journeys often deliver. The poet answers the old man sadly, saying, "You know all too well that man is corrupted everywhere." With this, the countryside itself becomes another "chimera," the dream of disappointed city folks. Sylvie is what she is: neither corrupt because she has changed nor pure because she has not. She is Sylvie, not the sentimentalized reality that will save a man but the living reality that eludes him and that eluded, Nerval suggests, a whole postrevolutionary generation, adrift in a world become unrecognizable.

AURÉLIA

Aurélia, a prose text of about a hundred pages, began to appear in the *Revue de Paris* a little less than a month before Nerval died. It is a work of great pathos and beauty, but not because, as many have thought, it is the true diary of a madman or because, as Nerval hoped, it penetrates the secrets of dreams and the spirit world and certifies the immortality of the soul. It offers a literally incomparable picture of a man doing battle with his demons, struggling to make sense of a life that keeps skidding away from him. It is the struggle that is memorable, success or failure in it being subordinate to the precision and the intimacy of the record.

"Dreams," the book begins, "are a second life," a region where "the self, in another form, continues the work of existence." Nerval thinks of Dante, Apuleius, Swedenborg, all travelers in unknown worlds, and decides to follow their example by "transcribing my impressions of a long malady that occurred entirely among the mysteries of my mind." This will be, he says, his *Vita nuova*. Later he calls it a descent into Hades, and this conflation of the pilgrim Dante and the poet Orpheus may be said to define the reach of the work. It gives the pagan Orpheus something of Dante's Christian hope, but it also robs Dante of Beatrice, who is lost because of some unspecified equivalent of looking back when one was told not to: "Everyone can seek among his memories for the most distressing emotion, the most terrible blow struck by fate." This, Nerval says, will give us an idea of how he felt when he forfeited the love of Aurélia—which is the name he gives to his Beatrice/Eurydice—through his own fault.

The possibility of a reconciliation with her produces an excitement that edges him toward madness. He sees a house number that coincides with the number of years of his life and thinks that either his or Aurélia's death is announced in this sign. He dreams of corridors and galleries and a spectacular fallen angel who resembles Dürer's Melancholy. His conversations with friends become more and more agitated; he quarrels with a companion in the street, takes off his clothes, and is arrested. In the police station he sees his friends arrive to collect him, only to go off with an imposter who looks just like him: his double. "There is a mistake," he cries. "They came for me, and it is someone else who is leaving." Later his friends arrive in reality and take him away. He is relatively calm the following day, but at night he collapses completely and is taken to a private hospital. It is with this episode, Nerval says, that "the spilling of dreams into real life" begins; and his account corresponds closely with his actual experiences of 1841.

He now recounts several dreams he had at this time, visitations during his hospital life. In one of them he meets various ancestors and dead relatives, and is assured of their and his immortality; he arrives in a sort of city paradise inhabited by a race that is highly civilized yet "loving and just." In another dream he enters a garden where a woman carrying a long stem of hollyhock grows and grows, like Lewis Carroll's Alice later, until she becomes one with the landscape. "Don't leave," Nerval cries in anguish, "for nature dies with you." The garden turns into a cemetery and voices are heard saying, "The universe is in darkness." The meaning of this second dream, Nerval says, he discovered only later: Aurélia is dead. In effect, if we are keeping biographical track of things, we may note that Jenny Colon died in 1842.

Nerval, still in the hospital, mixes dreams and waking fantasies into a mythical history of the world, in which a group of powerful necromancers corrupts the work of creation and tortures "the eternal Mother": "on a mountain swept by water, an abandoned woman who cries, her hair disheveled, wrestling with death."

"Little by little," Nerval writes, "calm returned to my mind," and his narrative leaps over a number of quieter years to the next relapse—in 1851, in historical reality. He begins to be seriously disturbed by the double he had glimpsed, the other self whom he now sees clearly as a usurper. A mystical marriage is being arranged with the immortal Aurélia, and "the other one" is the bridegroom: "an evil genius had taken my place in the world of souls." In a dream he disrupts the wedding, and feels immediately that he has committed a grievous fault. Later he will feel that the "other" is not his enemy but his brother, Christ or a good angel, now mortally, irreparably offended. For the moment he perceives only his disarray and, in language that recalls that of Vergil in its mournful authority, describes the dream's end: "The irritated shades fled away crying and tracing fatal circles in the air, like birds at the approach of a storm."

In a manner familiar to anyone who has seen compulsions at work, Nerval exacerbates his illness by interrogating it, convincing himself of the truths to be found in the depths of illusion. His reading and his travels have helped, of course. A proliferating Orient and a mass of cabalistic writings live in his mind—"the tower of Babel in two hundred volumes," as he deprecatingly says. With the graceful irony that can so suddenly illuminate even the most strangling of his obsessions, Nerval returns to the jovial cliché I have already discussed in connection with Sylvie: "There was enough to make a wise man mad; let's see if there is enough to make a madman sane."

He wishes to visit Aurélia's grave but cannot find it. He leaves Paris for the missed adventure recounted in Sylvie. Guilt rises: he has failed to heed the warnings that God, or the gods, have given him. He visits his father, thinks of confessing to a Catholic priest, is distraught by the conviction that the Virgin Mary, like Aurélia, is dead and cannot be prayed to. His visions run to apocalypse—he sees a black sun in the empty sky, a globe of blood above the Tuileries, several moons speeding by: "I thought the earth had left its orbit and was wandering in the firmament like a mastless ship." His friends take him to a hospital.

Here he has more comforting dreams, including one in which a goddess appears, saying to him the words quoted earlier: "I am the same as Mary, the same as your mother, the same person too whom in different forms you have always loved." But then his idea that the spirit world is intelligible to us turns to nightmare and anxiety. If we can grasp it, so can they, the torturers of Isis, butchers of the eternal mother.

At this point Nerval introduces—or planned to introduce; later editors actually did it for him—a series of old letters to Aurélia, possibly sent by Nerval to Jenny or intended for her. They plead and pose, rejoice and tremble, and are generally less attractive than the rest of the work leads us to expect. Their self-deception is a little too watertight and is cast in rather stilted terms. The note of irony is (understandably enough, if they are real letters) missing.

Nerval dreams again of the agonizing goddess, sees a vast mural full of the figures of mutilated women, from queens and empresses to peasant girls: "It was the history of all crime." But he dreams also of pardon, and ends with his apparent cure. "I was able," he says, "to judge more sanely the world of illusions in which I lived for some time. However, I am happy with the convictions I have acquired." In the last phrase we hear both the brave voice of a man who will not give up what is valuable to him and the doomed murmur of his persisting madness, which will not give him up either. "Despair and suicide," he says at one point, "are the result of certain situations that are fatal for those who do not have faith in immortality." Did he lose his fragile faith that cold day in January 1855, or are there other situations that lead to the same freezing end?

A close interpretation of this remarkable work would take many pages, but the pattern it makes can be fairly quickly described. To a large extent it is the pattern of *Les chimères*, a diagram of perpetual, lacerating uncertainty. The poet cannot be forgiven; may be forgiven. His double is a usurper and an evil omen; he is a friend and savior. We die once and for all; we are immortal and paradise is our waiting home. The goddess is tortured and killed; she is eternally alive and our unfailing comfort. But where the poems portray the riddle of these contradictions, the terrible logical cage of the perfect enigma, *Aurélia* allows us to follow the movement of Nerval's mind among alternatives, to share the sheer pain of the oscillation. It is not that he is caught between competing possibilities, and cannot choose. He chooses *both*, passionately, frantically, one after the other and backward and forward. This is the danger of taking dreams for testimony. They are uncontrollable, cannot be compared, verified, confirmed. They offer only *certainties*, so to speak. If the goddess promises consolation, that is *the* truth. If she dies

before your eyes, that is the truth too. Nerval's phrase "When one believes in everything, one believes in nothing" takes on an extra desperperate dimension in this context. He is torn to pieces not by doubt but by conflicting, exclusive beliefs.

Beneath the patent psychological content of these visions and dilemmas—the haunting mother dismembered by the dream-deputies of the father, the son terrified of repeating the father's murderous act—we can see one of the great dramas of the orphaned nineteenth century, cut off from the old sureties. The need to believe is so imperious that it creates the object of faith. Since the object is humanly created, it turns out to inspire only the ghost of faith, to collect tokens of the faith one wishes one had. But then a lapse into doubt revives the need in all its force, and the cycle, or the zigzag, starts again. In *Aurélia* as in *Sylvie*, Nerval gives a historical point to this condition. The French Revolution laid open more than the Bastille, inaugurated a world where, as Nerval says, "all beliefs are broken." It is because they are broken that they rise again in the mind, like the old never-slain Nordic snake, also mentioned in *Aurélia*, or the pieces of the body whose literal resurrection is promised to Christians. It is because they were more broken than the century knew that their resurrection was sought mainly in dreams. Aurélia is the name not only of a loved and deified woman but also of a scene from the last days of God. Nerval's allegiance to the goddess expresses a form of revolt against the angry and unyielding Jehovah, but the revolt itself takes place within the confines of a general and undiminished religious need. Nothing has replaced the broken beliefs, and no one has learned how to live without them.

Nerval does not figure seriously in literary histories until well into this century. The 1950 edition of Gustave Lanson and Paul Tuffrau's much-used history of French literature, for example, picks him up in a footnote. But if at first he seemed to have little posterity, he gradually acquired at least three different ones. As Rinsler has suggested, his translations of German poets introduced a new mode, both casual and philosophical, into French verse; and Nerval's influence can be found in Paul Verlaine, Jules Laforgue, and later writers. *Sylvie* became a favorite text of French nationalists, who saw it as celebrating, in limpid prose, the sweet, simple traditions of old France. To Arthur Symons and others, *Les chimères* came to seem a symbolist work before its time, a contemporary rather than an antecedent to the poems of Paul Valéry and W. B. Yeats. But as Proust saw, there is a falseness in these separations. The author of *Sylvie* is the author of *Les chimères* and the translations: we cannot divide a simple from a complicated Nerval. Our pleasure in *Sylvie*, Proust said, responding to the view of Maurice Barrès and the nationalists, is composed of trouble. The very grace of Nerval's writing ends in madness. Conversely, the most hermetic poems retain something of the freshness of a folk song.

Nerval's principal legacy is to be found in two books: Alain-Fournier's *Le Grand Meaulnes* (*The Wanderer*, 1913) and Proust's *À la recherche du temps perdu* (*Remembrance of Things Past*, 1913–1927), both explorations of vanishing countries, realms where Aurélia is queen, paradises that are true, as Proust was to say, because they are lost. But we may also hear Nerval's accents in Joseph Conrad's *Lord Jim* (1900) and a range of other works in which the modern mind dips toward privacy and the claims of the unattainable ideal. "A man who is born falls into a dream"—Nerval is one of the first and one of the best of our guides to the zone where dreams leak into life, and life becomes the dreamlike element in which we swim. "The Muse entered my heart," he wrote, "like a goddess with golden words; she escaped from it like a pythoness howling with pain." He did indeed journey in his brief career from lightness of heart to acute despair, but he brought beauty out of anguish, modulating sighs and screams and far less describable sounds into enduring Orphic music.

Selected Bibliography

FIRST EDITIONS

Elégies nationales. Paris, 1826, 1827.
Faust. Paris, 1828. A translation from Goethe.
Poésies allemandes. Paris, 1830. A translation.
Piquillo. Paris, 1837. In collaboration with Alexandre Dumas *père.*
Léo Burckart. Paris, 1839.
Faust I et II. Paris, 1840. A translation from Goethe.
L'Imagier de Harlem. Paris, 1851.
Voyage en Orient. 2 vols. Paris, 1851.
Les nuits d'octobre. Paris, 1852.
Les illuminés. Paris, 1852.
Petits châteaux de Bohème. Paris, 1853.
Sylvie. Paris, 1853.
Les filles du feu. Paris, 1854. Includes *Les chimères.*
Aurélia. Paris, 1854.

MODERN EDITIONS

INDIVIDUAL WORKS
Many editions of individual or selected works are readily available. The following are of exceptional interest.
Les chimères. Edited by J. Moulin. Geneva and Lille, 1949.
————. Edited by J. Guillaume. Brussels, 1966.
————. Edited by N. Rinsler. London, 1973.
Nerval par lui-même. Edited by J. Richer. Paris, 1964.
Sylvie. Edited by A. Clouard. Monaco, 1946. Includes *Léo Burckart* and *Aurélia.*

COLLECTED WORKS
Oeuvres. 2 vols. Edited by A. Béguin and J. Richer. Paris, 1952, 1956.
————. 2 vols. Edited by H. Lemaître. Paris, 1958.
Oeuvres complémentaires. 6 vols. Edited by J. Richer. Paris, 1959–1967.

TRANSLATIONS

Aurelia. Translated by R. Aldington. London, 1932. Includes *Sylvie* and selections.

Chimeras. Translated by A. Hoyem. San Francisco, 1966.

Les Chimères. Translated by R. Blaser. San Francisco, 1965.

Fortune's Fool. Translated by B. Hill. London, 1959. Thirty-five poems.

Journey to the Orient. Translated by N. Glass. New York, 1972.

Selected Writings. Translated by G. Wagner. New York, 1957.

BIOGRAPHICAL AND CRITICAL STUDIES

Béguin, Albert. *L'Âme romantique et le rêve; Essai sur le romantisme allemand et la poésie française.* Paris, 1939.

————. *Gérard de Nerval.* Paris, 1945.

Cellier, Léon. *Gérard de Nerval: L'Homme et l'oeuvre.* Paris, 1956.

Fairlie, A. "An Approach to Nerval." In *Studies in Modern French Literature.* Manchester, 1961.

Gascar, Pierre. *Gérard de Nerval et son temps.* Paris, 1981.

Geninasca, Jacques. *Analyse structurale des "Chimères" de Nerval.* Neuchâtel, 1971.

Jeanneret, M. *La lettre perdue.* Paris, 1978.

Jones, Robert Emmet. *Gérard de Nerval.* New York, 1975.

Kofman, Sarah. *Nerval: Le charme de la répétition. Lecture de "Sylvie."* Lausanne, 1979.

Marie, Aristide. *Gérard de Nerval: Le poète et l'homme.* Paris, 1914. Reprinted 1955.

Poulet, Georges. *Trois essais de mythologie romantique.* Paris, 1966.

Proust, Marcel. *Contre Sainte-Beuve.* Paris, 1954.

Richard, Jean-Pierre. *Poésie et profondeur.* Paris, 1955.

Richer, Jean. *Nerval: Expérience et création.* Paris, 1963.

————. *Nerval par les témoins de sa vie.* Paris, 1970.

Rinsler, Norma. *Gérard de Nerval.* London, 1973.

Rousseaux, A. "Sur trois manuscrits de G. de Nerval." In *Domaine français.* Geneva, 1943.

Said, Edward W. *Orientalism.* New York, 1978.

Sowerby, Benn. *The Disinherited.* London, 1973.

MICHAEL WOOD

NIKOLAY VASILIEVICH GOGOL

(1809–1852)

I

NIKOLAY VASILIEVICH GOGOL, one of the world's funniest and most profound writers, was born, appropriately enough, on April Fool's day in 1809, to a modest landowning family in the Ukraine. His grandfather had obtained patents of nobility in 1772, probably on the basis of a forged document because his ancestors had belonged primarily to the minor clergy. He did so to meet the stipulations of a much more distinguished family, with whose daughter he had eloped. Gogol's father, Vasily, claimed to have had two mystical visions: in one the Virgin pointed out his future wife in the shape of an infant; in the other, thirteen years later, she revealed the young woman whom the infant had grown to be. His imagination was active in more conventional ways as well: he wrote several comedies in Ukrainian (Gogol later drew on them for epigraphs and some situations) and managed the large private theater of a neighboring grandee.

Shortly after Gogol's birth, his father retired to his estate; its natural abundance would be celebrated by the writer in his earliest works as typical of the Ukraine. Although all of Gogol's writings and letters are in Russian, the language spoken at home, Ukrainian left some mark on his prose. So, too, did the Ukrainian puppet plays and the amateur theatricals his father mounted at home and elsewhere. These are important sources of his work, even though his most characteristic material deals with the petty tribulations of minor officials living in Saint Petersburg and provincial towns where the setting is not only not charming, but drab and unattractive, if not downright sordid.

Gogol was a sickly infant who was not expected to live, and throughout his life he was plagued by real and imaginary illnesses. Like Albert Einstein, he apparently did not speak until the age of three. At five, according to his own report, he drowned a cat that had terrified him as the incarnation of evil. Little is known of his early life except through the reminiscences of his doting mother (who credited him with, among other things, the invention of railroads), but he seems to have been an inward child. When he attended high school at Nezhin, he distinguished himself by slovenliness and poor conduct as well as an extraordinary acting ability, most strikingly displayed in the roles of old women. And something inexplicable in his character struck his fellow students, who labeled him "the mysterious dwarf."

Upon graduation in 1828 Gogol went to Saint Petersburg. At first he shied away from assuming a post in the civil service, intending evidently to make his mark in literature. The following year he published at his own expense his first book, *Hans Küchelgarten,* a long, derivative verse idyll that already presents a characteristic duality in Gogol: on the one hand, the depiction of a bourgeois existence; on the other, a protagonist given to meditations, visions, and dreams. It was mercilessly panned in the two short reviews it received. Gogol frantically bought up all the available copies and burned them. He then left on a brief and shadowy trip to Germany. He appropriated money his mother had forwarded for his mortgage payments and left by ship on August 3, at first informing her, in a transparently false letter full of rhetorical pathos, that he was so tormented by love for an exalted being that, unless he escaped, his life would disintegrate. Then, when he changed his mind about proceeding further, he wrote in another letter that he had made the trip on a doctor's recommendation to seek treatment of a rash on his hands and face. When he returned six weeks later, he found to his horror that his mother had concluded that he had a venereal disease. He vehemently protested his innocence, purity, and moral probity. This incident abounds in precisely the sort of grotesquerie and misapprehension that inform his art.

In 1830 Gogol assumed the first of several minor posts in the civil service, began to study art, and continued writing. He asked his mother to send him material on Ukrainian folklore and customs—such things were in great vogue then—and began to publish stories set in the Ukraine that were collected a year later as *Evenings on a Farm near Dikanka.* In 1831 he also met his idol, the great Russian poet Alexander Pushkin, whom he saw occasionally thereafter. Pushkin, in reviewing Gogol's book of stories, related that when Gogol walked into the printing plant where his book was being set, he found the printers chuckling and spluttering with mirth. The foreman explained their hilarity by informing the author that they were splitting their sides with laughter while setting his book. Gogol's fantastically imaginative mind is obvious in his work, but it was also frequently employed in inventions about his own life. The story is likely a fabrication of Gogol's, and Pushkin's source was likely Gogol himself. The book was a great success, and more stories appeared a year later, in 1832, as part 2 of *Evenings on a Farm near Dikanka.* Exploiting his growing reputation, Gogol published a volume of related stories, *Mirgorod* (the name of a Ukrainian town), in 1835.

In the meantime, bored by the senseless routine of his civil service post, Gogol wangled an appointment as a teacher of history in a distinguished institution for daughters of the nobility. This post gave him more time for literary pursuits and fed his innate desire to instruct others. Setting his sights on greater prestige and a wider audience, he sought an appointment as a professor of history at the University of Kiev; when this failed, he accepted a lectureship on world history at the University of Saint Petersburg, in 1834. He went to great trouble to prepare his first lecture, which was rhetorically striking if meager in content, and had ambitious plans for writing either a ten-volume history of the world or an eight-volume history of the Ukraine. But his qualifications for the post were inadequate, and, in any case, his talent lay elsewhere. Soon he stopped preparing for class altogether, with results that were recalled years later by Ivan Turgenev in *Literary Reminiscences* (1868):

I was one of his students in 1835 when he lectured(!) on history to us at St. Petersburg University. His lecturing, to tell the truth, was highly original. In the first place, Gogol usually missed two lectures out of three; second, even when he appeared in the lecture hall, he did not so much speak as whisper something incoherently and showed us small engravings of views of Palestine and other Eastern countries, looking terribly embarrassed all the time. We were all convinced that he knew nothing of history (and we were hardly wrong) and that Mr. Gogol-Janovsky, our professor (that's the way he appeared in the catalogue) had nothing in common with the writer Gogol, already familiar to us as the author of *Evenings on a Farm Near Dikanka.* At the final examination on his subject he sat with his face tied up in a handkerchief, as though suffering from a toothache, looking terribly depressed, and—never opened his mouth. Professor J. P. Shulgin put the questions to the students for him. I can still see as though it were before me today, his thin, long-nosed face with the two ends of the black silk handkerchief sticking out like two huge ears. No doubt he recognized very clearly how utterly comic and awkward his position was: he sent in his resignation that very year. That, however, did not prevent him from exclaiming: "unrecognized I mounted the rostrum and unrecognized I descend from it." He was born to be the instructor of all his contemporaries, but not from a university chair.

In 1835 Gogol published a number of articles and the three important stories that begin his "Petersburg" tales in a volume entitled *Arabesques;* he also wrote two plays: *Marriage,* a farce about courtship, and *The Government Inspector,* the greatest Russian comedy; and he began his great novel, *Dead Souls.* It is extraordinary that in three years he completed or began almost his entire oeuvre and that he so quickly moved from his early efforts directly into his mature style. When *The Government Inspector* was performed at the czar's initiative and in his presence in 1836, it was a public and critical failure. Following the controversy of its reception, Gogol left Russia and lived abroad for a dozen years, primarily in Rome, only rarely visiting his native land. In Europe he completed *Dead Souls,* which was published in 1842 and showed his towering stature as a writer. That same year he published "The Overcoat," the most brilliant and profound, and the most wildly misinterpreted, of his short stories. For the rest of his life he worked at the continuation of *Dead Souls,* which he came to consider a sort of modern *Divine Comedy* in which the protagonist, after passing through hell, moves to a purgatory where he repents and changes his ways, and finally succeeds if not to an earthly paradise, then at least to a meaningful, productive, and moral existence. The work went slowly and was beset by difficulties. Gogol increasingly felt that he had a messianic mission as the instructor of mankind.

A turning point in Gogol's life came around 1840. His health deteriorated dangerously from symptoms that seem to have originated in psychological stress. When he was convinced he was dying he had a mystical vision whose nature he never disclosed to others. Like his father, he accepted the putative import of his vision unquestioningly. He turned to a mystical faith in Russian Orthodoxy and was seized by the conviction that he was destined to instruct mankind in Truth. This new attitude is reflected in revisions of his earlier work (particularly "The Portrait" [1835], which deals with the nature of art and religious inspiration); in post hoc explanations of the spiritual significance of *The Government Inspector;* and most obviously in a work he conceived after he recovered from another serious illness, in 1845, and published two years later, *Selected Passages from Correspondence with Friends.*

Selected Passages is a carefully structured work consisting of thirty-two letters: many actually written to friends, but with eventual publication also in mind, and others specifically intended to be published, including four devoted to *Dead Souls.* The letters exhibit a consistent mystical religiosity applied to all aspects of behavior and art, expressed in a style skillfully adapted to the matter, though vastly different from Gogol's creative writing. The book called down on him the wrath of the overwhelming majority of the Russian reading public and many of his friends, who objected to its ultraconservative views of life, morality, serfdom, and monarchy, and the author's unctuous tone—in Sergei Aksakov's words, "fierce pride beneath a mask of humility." They found it a betrayal of his former art— which Gogol renounced as pointless and harmful—the tasteless preaching of distasteful ideas. These ideas advance the cause of a Christian (Orthodox) social structure with art in its service. Gogol's critics objected to his apostasy from "enlightened liberal views" and to repellent sermonizing, such as his advice to a landowner to burn a pile of money before his gathered peasants to show them that he is concerned with the soul, not with material possessions; or his advice to a housewife to budget her money in seven envelopes, each with its appointed purpose. According to Gogol, although art affects the heart and transforms life, and although man can be improved and virtue taught (because sin is caused by ignorance), education and literacy are of doubtful benefit to the "low" people, or serfs (he wholeheartedly approved of the institution of serfdom). Few critics had good words for this message, although Apollon Grigoriev recognized at once that its underlying point was that "one must treat words honorably."

The *Correspondence* elicited from the fiery critic Vissarion Belinsky (1811–1848) a rebuttal famous in Russian literature, the "Letter to Gogol," in which he calls him "an apostle of the knout, of obscurantism, of mystical demagoguery." Belinsky's view of what was required for Russia's regeneration is as questionable as Gogol's, but the letter is the finest expression of his liberal creed. It was widely circulated, but publication during Czar Nicholas' reign was out of the question. Mere possession of it was punishable by exile. This happened to Feodor Dostoevsky, who had read it aloud at a meeting of a radical group.

The blow dealt to Gogol by the negative reception of the book ushered in the final phase of his troubled existence. He went on a brief and rather desultory pilgrimage to Jerusalem and on his return came increasingly under the influence of a certain Father Matthew, an ignorant and fanatical priest who tried to convince Gogol that literature was the devil's work and that he should destroy all his writing. Gogol was obviously torn between a sense of the justness of his religious views and mission, and his love for literary creation. He was in a state of complete physical and mental exhaustion when on 12 February 1852, at three in the morning, he made a fire, carried in a bundle of papers, lit them, and sat down to wait for them to be consumed. Afterward he crossed himself, returned to his room, lay

down, and burst into tears. He had burned the second part of *Dead Souls,* which was almost finished. The following day he maintained that he had burned it by mistake (although he had burned an earlier version several years before), but the circumstances make that seem unlikely. With the end of *Dead Souls* his own death was near. In an excess of lenten zeal he literally starved himself to death. After harrowing torments by friends who tried to keep him alive by force-feeding, immersion into freezing baths or hot broth, and application of leeches to his very large nose, he died on 4 March 1852. Supposedly his last words were "a ladder, quick, a ladder."

Gogol's personality remains a puzzle and a mass of contradictions. His unctuous, groveling letters to his mother and others coexist with peremptory instructions to relatives and friends; his deep religiosity and terror of eternal damnation coexist with an extraordinary emphasis on triviality and an almost manic gaiety; abstemiousness with gluttony, concentrated work and a sedentary life with aimlessness and a compulsion to constant motion and travel, explosions of literary creativity with periods of total barrenness, dithyrambs and paeans in praise of women and womanhood with no demonstrable physical relations with and little interest in women, great seriousness and probity with blatant lies and outrageous impositions on others, humility and self-effacement with overbearing pride and self-service, proclamations of service to others with total self-centeredness. The story of his life suggests a bizarre character whose nature one cannot quite grasp. It is reflected in his work, which also eludes final critical analysis.

II

While Gogol's work is startlingly idiosyncratic and original, it has roots in a number of identifiable literary modes and traditions. His first collection, *Evenings on a Farm near Di-*

kanka, parts 1 and 2, is a series of oral tales told by several different narrators that combines the disparate worlds of witches, devils, charms, and transformations—the world of German romantic demonology and fairy tales that he had encountered in the works of E. T. A. Hoffmann and Ludwig Tieck—with the coarser world of the Ukrainian folk tale. In addition, there are Western influences of sentimentalism, with its emphasis on feeling and rhetoric, and the Gothic horror tale. From native sources there is the all important Ukrainian puppet theater, from which Gogol derived two vital notions: first, that beneath the quaint and joyous surface of a life where lusty swains court beautiful maids, there is a serious, even gloomy, moral and metaphysical world; and second, that in the struggle between good and evil, God and the devil, it is frequently the dark forces that triumph. This duality permeates Gogol's work from first to last: surface and depth, humor and seriousness, manic verbal exuberance and gloomy moral strictures. His means for conveying his vision became increasingly more masterly and complex.

"Sorochinsky Fair," the story that opens the collection, introduces many other aspects of Gogol's art. It begins with a renowned description of a summer day in the Ukraine ("How intoxicating, how splendid, is . . . "), the first of Gogol's purple passages and lyric digressions. This paean catalogs bounties of nature that can only coexist rhetorically: gray haystacks and golden sheaves of wheat, cherry and apple trees, gulls and quail. At first glance it seems convincing because it accumulates so many objects and colors, in cadenced prose inflated with pathos and hyperbole ("cloud-touching oaks"). But on reflection it has nothing to do with reality. It is an overture. It establishes a narrative style, one that is undercut in subsequent pages. The figures in the story also have the deceptive appearances of living, if highly traditional, characters. Only at the end of the story, at the wedding celebration, does Gogol show human beings behaving mechanically, as if controlled and manipulated by a puppeteer, for they lack anima:

A strange, ineffable feeling would have overcome anyone who saw the whole crowd transformed into a scene of unity and harmony at one stroke of the bow of the fiddler, who had long twisted moustaches and wore a homespun jacket. Men whose sullen faces seemed never to have known the gleam of a smile were tapping with their feet and wriggling their shoulders; everyone was whirling and dancing. But an even stranger and more unaccountable feeling would have been stirred in the heart at the sight of old women, whose ancient faces breathed the indifference of the tomb, pushing their way among the young, laughing, living human beings. Nothing but drink, like a puppeteer manipulating lifeless automatons, made them perform actions that seemed human; caring for nothing, without the joy of youth, without a spark of sympathy, they slowly wagged their drunken heads, dancing after the rejoicing crowd, without so much as glancing at the young couple.

It is the first suggestion in Gogol of the soullessness, the void in human beings. The story concludes with the counterpart of the joyous opening description. A moral stated in sentimental rhetoric restates Gogol's view: "Is it not thus that joy, that beautiful but fleeting guest, flies from us and in vain a last solitary note tries to express gaiety. . . . Sad is the lot of one left behind! Heavy and sorrowful is his heart and nothing can help him!" It is among the more blatant of Gogol's endings, and unusual in its seriousness. Thus from the beginning it is possible to see seriousness lurking beneath the quaint surface and gaudy prose.

Much has been made of the cadenced prose, the inflated rhetoric, the cossack and medieval background of "The Terrible Vengeance," a horror tale of incest, murder, and revenge that posits the proliferation of evil. But many critics dismiss the folksy tomfoolery, courtship, and magic that dominate Gogol's first collection in such stories as "Saint John's Eve," "May Night," "Christmas Eve," "The Enchanted Spot," and "The Lost Letter." One story, however, "Ivan Shponka and His Aunt," stands apart. It is the only one presented as a "written" work rather than a transcription of an oral tale. Hence its style and devices are quite different, startlingly anticipating the mature artist. It sounds a major theme in Gogol: boorishness and the emphasis on physical existence, with no interest in or comprehension of spiritual or other values. It is characteristic in other ways, too: in its depiction of smug complacency, self-satisfied mediocrity, shoddiness (what the Russians call *poshlost,* a term that conveys much more than its literal translation, "vulgarity," and Gogol is the great master at conveying it in all phases of existence); in its rural setting that becomes an emblem for human provinciality; in its making trivia and even nothingness so amusing that one momentarily forgets the intellectual and moral void they imply; and in its attitude toward the erotic. There is in Gogol a fear of women (except elderly aunts and mothers) and of sexuality that is quite pathological. There is no room for courtship, except in the stilted and stylized folk tales of the early collections, or in verbal nonsense that turns courtship into a parody of love interest, as in the plays.

In the story, Ivan Shponka (the name means button) is ordered by his aunt to get married. His courtship, consisting of two labored platitudes on the weather, is harrowing enough to provoke in him the surrealistic nightmare on wives that terminates the story (as in many of Gogol's works, one cannot speak of an "ending," for even if there is a formal conclusion, it may directly contradict ostensible and/or covert meaning in the work). Part of the humor in the story lies in presenting Ivan as an obedient, shy, rather bumbling little boy, although he is a lieutenant close to forty, a man who rarely has a thought or a desire to do anything. He has remained at the threshold of emotional and intellectual development. In his aunt, a woman of gigantic stature, "nature seemed to have made an unpar-

donable mistake in condemning her to wear a brown gown with flounces . . . though a dragoon's mustache and high boots would have suited her best." She remains unmarried, declaring that "she valued her maiden state above everything." Men seem very timorous in her presence.

Gogol's next collection, *Mirgorod,* deepens the implications of these themes and extends the provincial setting in the opening and closing stories. The first, "Old World Landowners," apparently expresses nostalgic affection for an old couple living idly off the superabundance of their estate, spending their days and nights exclusively in filling their stomachs with an amazing array of tempting food, to the exclusion of everything else except sleep. The story abounds in iterative and imperfective verbs and repeats words such as "usually," "always," "frequently," implying continuity, repetition, even unchangeability, and emphasizing the vacuity and absolute inaneness of the couple. This second-rate paradise disintegrates after the death of the wife (significantly they have no children). The plundering of the carelessly run estate by servants increases, and after the husband's death the heirs complete the destruction. They use the proceeds merely to satisfy equally empty passions, such as collecting or trading.

The narrator's nostalgic affection is qualified immediately. His description of the house and its noises suggests the rumblings of the digestive tract; abundance mocks real and figurative sterility. The main event of the story is the enticement of the pet cat by a band of roving toms. The cat's subsequent preference for "a life of passion and poverty" over indolent comfort is taken by the wife as the harbinger of her death. A lengthy digression on the wild despair and attempts at suicide by a young man in reaction to his wife's death and his subsequent remarriage and bliss suggests that habit is a vital ingredient of behavior: it is stronger than passion. The contrast between the outside world and the enclosed idyll, between the wild bounty of nature and the hot-house comforts of the landowners, between indulgence and deprivation, ultimately make the couple far less attractive than they first seem. What begins as a nostalgic commemoration becomes richly ironic as the context of the story unfolds.

The last story in the volume, "The Story of the Quarrel of Ivan Ivanovich with Ivan Nikivorovich," presents two devoted friends who quarrel over a trifle, sever relations, and spend the rest of their lives in litigation and vain efforts to even the score. A splendid mock eulogy begins the story. The apparently sympathetic narrator, while comparing and praising his protagonists, manages to degrade them and make them ridiculous through a series of non sequiturs: the two are indistinguishable except that one looks like a radish with its root up, the other with it down; one is fearful, the other wears pants; the first is a fine man, the second a fine man, too—his favorite food is melons. The reader finds the Ivans and their lives so innocuous that one comes to feel that the houses and yards and, especially, the puddles of Mirgorod are more interesting and have a more vivid existence than its human inhabitants. This may be the underlying reason for the mistaken interpretation that celebrates Gogol as an observer of reality—he has so far reduced the function of man that objects perforce stand out with unusual sharpness. One Ivan likes to lie immersed in a bath in a camera obscura that reflects the outside world, and to drink tea there. The other Ivan, more active, likes to survey his yard and all his possessions. Just when he has congratulated himself on all he owns, his glance strays into the other Ivan's yard, where he spies a rusty old rifle, incongruously hung out to air with other things on a clothesline. He covets it, and the attempt to obtain it eventually leads to the collapse of the devoted friendship.

So long as the scene had been bathed in the atmosphere of hot Ukrainian summers, the narrator was able to maintain his enthusiasm, however ironic, for the inhabitants. But years later he visits the town again in the gray, drizzly, muddy autumn. He finds the world transformed, the two Ivans grotesquely wasted, each monomaniacally convinced of imminent victory over the other. As the narrator leaves the town, he notes "again the same fields, furrowed in some places, black, in some places green, with soggy jackdaws and crows, monotonous rain, a tearful sky without a bright spot." Gogol breaks off and ends the volume with the now famous sentence: "It is dreary in this world, gentlemen." It may well be dreary if life is no more than the pettiness Gogol has so entertainingly shown.

Between these two stories there are two others. The first is a historical romance of cossacks and love in the seventeenth century, "Taras Bulba." Gogol used some of the material he gathered for his projected history of the Ukraine to lend a sort of epic quality to his portrayal of military valor. Its more interesting pages deal with the boisterous aspects of cossack life and war, and the striking if rather wooden figure of Taras (his last name means potato in Ukrainian). His son betrays the cossacks because he has fallen in love with a Polish lady during one of the forays, and eventually he is killed by his father. Gogol attempts to endow the cossacks with a nobility they do not have, to convey the horrors of siege and starvation, as well as torture, by recourse to a rhetoric that strikes the reader as hollow. Yet the work retains a kind of popularity with adolescents and fans of rousing yarns.

The second story, "The Viy," one of Gogol's most imaginative tales, is a weird blend of fantasy and reality, with an undercurrent of relentless doom. It involves a divinity student, Thomas Brutus, who, for getting the better of a witch in a sublimated erotic way, is made to read prayers over her corpse on three successive nights. If he lasts out the ordeal, he will be forgiven. He manages the first two nights, though his hair turns white and he fails in his attempts to escape. On the last night the witch returns from the dead with allies, and he is literally frightened to death by the viy, a terrible gnomelike monster with an iron face and eyelids of lead that reach to the ground and cover a deadly gaze. Thomas is punished for his amatory transgressions but also because he consistently refuses to see, to understand, to reach moral judgment. Blindness and insight are symbolically contained in the viy, who, despite the author's introductory footnote claiming that he is a Ukrainian myth figure, is entirely a figment of Gogol's brilliant imagination. The story blends the humorous with the horrible, the actual with its wildest possible distortions. At the end, as Thomas falls dead, the hobgoblins in the church rush out helter-skelter to escape before the third crowing of the cock, but not all of them make it. Some get stuck in the windows and doors:

> The entering priest stopped at the sight of such desecration of a church and did not dare to celebrate mass in such a place. So the church remained for a long time, with monsters fixed in the doors and windows, was overgrown by a forest, roots, high grass, and thorn bushes, and no one can find the way to it now.

The duality of life; the existence of evil, vulgarity, smugness; the incredible indifference to anything other than physical comfort may be seen more fully and in a more ominous way in the city than in the more or less gay world of Gogol's Ukraine. A series of stories published in *Arabesques* in 1835 and in the journal *The Contemporary* in 1836 have a different kind of unity, a deeper significance. First, there is a unity of place: they are preeminently "Tales of Saint Petersburg" (as they were entitled in subsequent collections), beginning with "Nevsky Avenue"—the main street of that city—and reaching beyond its brilliant facade in "The Portrait," "Notes of a Madman," and "The Nose." The gentle Ukraine now cedes to the grim life of the city. Second, themes that were previously in the background now come clearly to the fore and are elaborately developed, making them in a philosophical and programmatic fashion tales of good and evil. Finally, the humor, the sty-

listic skill, the sparkling verbal surface become more polished and subtle, the humor rising practically in inverse proportion to the deepening of the themes.

All this is implied, indeed stated, as a kind of overture, in the long description of Nevsky Avenue that begins the story of that name and sets the tone for the following works. While the basic purpose of the street is to be an artery of communication, Gogol presents it as the stage setting for a parade of man's follies and strange pursuits. As in "Old World Landowners" and the "Quarrel of the Two Ivans," the narrator's opening apostrophe—"There is nothing finer than the Nevsky, not, at any rate, in Saint Petersburg"—is immediately undercut. Gogol calls it a phantasmagoria (a shifting succession of things seen or evoked in the imagination), and describes it at different times of the day, populated by a wide range of humanity, from beggars and hardworking shopmen to the cream of elegant society. The action of the story begins at dusk, when less decorous objects and people make their appearance. Gogol presents two friends, an artist, Piskarev, and a lieutenant, Pirogov, each of whom pursues a female passerby. The artist is an idealist who worships beauty, and he thinks of his lady as a beauty in a Perugino painting. She is merely a tart who lures him to the brothel, where she lives. He flees in horror, then thinks of rescuing and marrying her, but she scorns the notion of working at embroidery or housekeeping. She likes her mode of life. Piskarev commits suicide, unable to stand the corruption of beauty by something evil.

Crassness is further shown in Lieutenant Pirogov, who follows a woman he thinks is a tart, but turns out to be the stupid but incorruptible wife of a German artisan. One day during Pirogov's courtship the husband returns home and gives Pirogov a thrashing. Pirogov is in high dudgeon, but he calms himself with a couple of cakes (in Russian, *pirogi*—he has had them in his name all the time) and returns to the pursuit of his habitual pleasures. Pirogov's episode is a mirror image of Piskarev's, one in which only the physical exists. The story has bifurcated from the Nevsky and returns there for a summary. Gogol points out again that appearances are everywhere deceptive. The Nevsky is all frustrated expectation, physical and spiritual, but it is especially so "when the demon himself lights all the streetlamps to show everything in anything but its true colors."

The duality of this story is emphasized by Gogol's presenting a tragic and a comic view of what is essentially the same situation. Those two views are now treated in greater detail and more unified form in "The Portrait" and "Notes of a Madman," both of which develop notions associated with the artist Piskarev. In 1836, the following year, in two of Gogol's most comic stories, "The Nose" and "The Carriage," the amusing representation of vulgarity and moral shabbiness in the smug and self-satisfied Lieutenant Pirogov was greatly extended. It is important to remember that all but the last two stories appeared in *Arabesques* (1835), which also contained other works. These include Gogol's introductory lecture to his course on history and two rhapsodic pieces that present some of Gogol's notions more directly than their fictional embodiments. The first, entitled "Woman," is a blend of Platonic and romantic philosophy and posits aesthetic idealism, which holds that beauty will regenerate the world. Woman is the vessel of spiritual beauty, inspiring the artist to create and man to perform worthy deeds. Physical passion, however, leads to the destruction of the ideal and to chaos. The second essay, "Sculpture, Painting, and Music," posits a hierarchy of the arts, opposes Christian art to the pagan, and again uses the notion that art, the beautiful, leads man away from commonplace concerns to an intimation of the divine. As Gogol had shown in "Nevsky Avenue," physical beauty is not equivalent to spiritual beauty; the discrepancy may be shattering for the idealist. Nor can physical beauty lead a petty, shallow, and self-centered man

like Lieutenant Pirogov to a higher spiritual state.

In "The Portrait," a struggling artist buys for a pittance the portrait of a man whose eyes fascinate him and exert a strange power on him. The subject turns out to be a doomed soul who can avoid hell as long as his portrait remains on earth. This spirit promises success for the artist if he will work for money and worldly fame. The artist, Chertkov (the name variously suggests "devil," "trait," "line," and "to draw"), succumbs to temptation, achieving great success at the expense of his talent. It is surely significant that the painting that launches his career, a socialite's portrait, begins as a study of Psyche, the soul. Later, in despair at his loss of talent, he frantically buys up and destroys all the art he can. He is finally found dead, presumably after great torments; and it is implied that perhaps the devil has carried off his soul.

At first glance this appears to be a horror tale, like those of Edgar Allan Poe or E. T. A. Hoffmann, or a Gothic scenario in which portraits exert evil influences because they contain the soul of the devil. Gogol greatly extends the scope of such tales by the breadth of his treatment of artistic problems. The eyes in the portrait appear "alive"—they are real, but they are no longer art. A line has been crossed. While art can reveal the divine, it can also disclose what Gogol called "the black dregs in man's soul." The second part of the story traces the portrait's origin and shows how the artist may atone for perverting the high function of art. The original painter retires to a monastery and then the wilderness until he is purified by repentance and may again work on the holy picture he found impossible to continue. Gogol splendidly conveys the power and influence of art and its irrationality, but he is far less convincing when he tries to foist religious meaning on art with high-flown rhetoric. This is particularly true in the revised version of 1842, when Gogol's sense of religious mission had assumed major proportions. Yet the ending there is artistically more satisfying. In the first version the power of the devil was to end after a specific term, and indeed the portrait fades away and is replaced by a landscape. But in the second version, when the listeners turn to look at it, the portrait has disappeared. Apparently evil will once again tempt mankind.

The protagonist of "Notes of a Madman" was originally conceived as a musician, but Gogol decided to substitute for a man with expressive means and imagination a poor, dull, insignificant civil servant whose madness is precipitated by a thwarted passion for the beautiful daughter of his chief. Part of the humor lies in the jarring conflict of his bureaucratic mind with his amorous disposition, of his grandiose plans with his pitiful resources. It is precisely because he can neither formulate his plight nor improve his lot—while feeling its increasing burden—that his mind gives way. The process is already quite advanced when the story opens: the madman reports a conversation between his idol's lapdog and another dog. Later he confiscates their correspondence. Because the story is a first-person narration, the reader must try to account for the psychology, the process that leads to the distortions of a reality behind the hallucinations. In some way the protagonist is aware of the ridiculous figure he cuts. The dogs' letters express it, yet he refuses to acknowledge it. When his idol is engaged to be married, his mind gives way. He has always been incapable of understanding the world in terms other than hierarchy ("her handkerchief has the smell of a general's rank"). Now he has lost all sense of his place in that hierarchy. When he reads that the Spanish throne is vacant, he solves his own problem and that of Spain by becoming king himself. He fashions his uniform into a royal cloak and "walks along the Nevsky incognito." The dates of his entries mark the breakdown of his sanity ("2000 A.D., April 43") and become increasingly distorted. Eventually he is removed to an asylum, where he undergoes terrible torments. Gogol attenuates the horror with a pas-

sage of great pathos and a final note of humor that ends the story.

"Notes of a Madman" is the first important statement in Russian literature of the theme of the poor and oppressed civil servant, the first story to deal with the seamier side of life in Saint Petersburg, and the first to broach the crucial existential problems that permeate Russian literature. For Gogol questions the place of man in a world without values, portraying the lack of aspirations at all levels, even those the madman aspires to.

The two humorous tales "The Nose" and "The Carriage" develop without tragic overtones the satiric comedy in vulgar careerism. "The Nose" is the story of the disappearance one morning of the nose of Collegiate Assessor Kovalyov, his attempts to recapture it, and its final reappearance on his face. Many modern commentators, noting the exceptional prominence of Gogol's own nose and the peculiar absence of women in both his life and his works, have seen this story as a humorous yet terrifying projection of a castration complex. But there are literary antecedents and traditions of noses and other parts of the body that assume a life of their own, scabrous and otherwise, that Gogol weaves together in this fantasy. The story was originally entitled "A Dream" (in Russian *son;* nose, *nos),* and the dates given at the beginning and end are from the Julian and Orthodox calendars, so that actually only one night passes.

Kovalyov is one of those splendidly vacuous creations through whom Gogol communicates stupidity, vulgarity, and lack of moral sense. Kovalyov has two major concerns: his recently acquired rank and his attraction to pretty women. He is described entirely in terms of his starched white collars and his whiskers (others in the story, a doctor and a policeman, are also described only in terms of their whiskers). He is in Saint Petersburg to find "a post befitting his rank" or to get married to a wife with an adequate dowry. The unexpected loss of his nose, which he suspects is in some way connected with a female acquaintance whose daughter he seems to have misled, naturally thwarts his plans. He has recourse to the police, to newspapers, to individuals, none of whom will help although all seem to recognize his plight. A newspaper clerk refuses his advertisement for the return of the nose, suspecting it contains a hidden message, and without thinking offers him snuff. A doctor suggests he display the nose as a curio and charge admission. Even the barber who finds the nose inside his breakfast roll as the story opens merely tries to get rid of it, for his wife curtly says, "Get it out of here." Once the nose reappears on Kovalyov's face, he resumes his former ways, which have now been revealed to the reader as empty. Gogol's looking-glass world shifts all values. Kovalyov is unharmed, but the barber is in difficulties with the police: he has been apprehended by a myopic policeman in the attempt to throw the nose into the river.

Perhaps no work shows Gogol's essence more clearly than "The Nose." It begins with an impossibility (one thinks of Kafka's "Gregor Samsa awoke one morning to find he had been changed into an enormous vermin") that is then exaggerated through the wildest improbabilities. Alogical reasoning dominates the events of the story as it does its stylistic leaps. The nose assumes a life of its own, with a rank much higher than Kovalyov's. When they meet, it even rebuffs him as being far beneath it. The nose prays in church, travels in carriages, and is finally apprehended trying to escape to Riga. It may do so because Kovalyov has no identity of his own. Gogol purposely fails to motivate events and desires. He destroys the nominal connections between the subject and the object of his observations. Ultimately he himself pretends to be unable to account for these strange events, ending only with the assurance that "such things happen rarely, but they do happen."

In the amusing story "The Carriage," a landowner far gone in drink invites some officers to dine with him the next day and inspect his supposedly remarkable carriage. But when he arrives home he is too drunk to inform his wife of the invitation, and when he wakes up to discover the entire contingent descending on his estate he flees and hides in the carriage rather than face them. The bewildered officers, whose bumbling pretensions have been detailed during dinner the preceding night, decide to look around and inspect the carriage. They find it quite ordinary. When they open its door they find their host huddling there in his bathrobe. One of the amazed officers exclaims, "Ah, there you are!" slams the door shut, and they all leave. It has been suggested that the story tracks evil to its lair. Evil in Gogol is almost always pictured in trivial guise, since man is petty, lacking higher aspirations. The anticlimax of the ending is striking: Chertokutsky (his name suggests a dock-tailed devil) is merely exposed, not punished. But who could judge him? The officers are of the same ilk.

The greatest of Gogol's stories, the most famous and influential of all Russian stories, is "The Overcoat" of 1842. Akaky Akakievich is a lowly civil servant whose life is exclusively devoted to copying documents. One day he finds that his tattered coat is beyond repair. By dint of hardship and deprivation he accumulates the necessary money and buys a new coat. Returning from a party thrown by his colleagues to celebrate the purchase of the coat—the only outing of his life—he is robbed of it. He tries to get official redress but cannot. Eventually he takes a decisive step and brings his complaint to "an important personage," a highly placed official, who dismisses him with a lecture. He dies and is replaced in his job. Shortly after his death someone begins to filch coats from passersby, until one day this "corpse" takes "the important personage's" own coat. Thereafter the thefts stop.

Early in the story, after a hilarious account of how Akaky received his name and the depiction of his total indifference to every manifestation of life, the clerk, pushed beyond endurance by the baiting of his fellow workers, exclaims: "Leave me alone, why do you torment me?" In this, one of his co-workers seems to hear the words "I am a fellow human being," a statement that profoundly affects him. Critics have taken this episode, in conjunction with the portrayal of Akaky's abject poverty and miserable existence, as a humanitarian plea. This is the sort of sentimental interpretation that was greatly favored by the "civic minded" criticism of the mid-nineteenth century. It should be remembered, however, that the co-worker's statement is only one of many assertions in the story, and can only be taken as a partial view presented in a highly complex narrative structure. More recent critics have shown that Akaky is barely presented as a human being at all. He exists at the lowest level of human intelligence and feeling. He rejects a promotion because he is incapable of changing the wording in the documents he copies from the first person to the third. His interests are entirely mechanical: the process of copying, not the contents, attracts him; he eats without noticing the food, and only stops when his stomach feels full; he never goes out; his speech consists of interjections, prepositions, and the like, with no connection. So his squalor should not strike the reader as an injustice.

Through the tailor's insistence that a new coat be made, Akaky's life begins to assume a minimal purpose and meaning. Though he must skimp on the barest necessities, he has "spiritual nourishment . . . a fuller existence . . . as though he were no longer alone . . . but had an agreeable life companion." His indecisiveness and vagueness vanish. He has "the most audacious ideas: why not have a real marten collar?" Once he almost makes a mistake while copying. On the day the coat is finished he basks in its warmth, he enjoys his food, he goes to a party for the first time in his life, he even takes a few steps in pursuit of a woman on the Nevsky. When this new object in his life is taken from him (the Russian *shinel*, overcoat, is feminine, unlike the masculine "nose"), when all hope for its return is lost, he dies. The fantastic ending, with its Akaky-like "corpse" stealing coats from others, has similarly been interpreted in a romantic vein to mean Akaky's taking his revenge, exacting rights that were denied to him during his life. Complaints multiply, orders are issued to "catch the corpse, dead or alive, regardless of trouble and expense." After the depredations stop, Akaky's "corpse" no longer appears. At the end an "apparition" does, but it does not resemble Akaky in the least. It has a fist resembling that of Akaky's assailant. It "vanishes into the darkness of the night." It may simply be that thieves take advantage of the rumors to strip expensive coats from others. The richness of meanings and the complexity of narrative and verbal art make this most analyzed of Gogol's stories inexhaustible. No simple notion of compassion, of punishment and reward, is adequate.

In a more profound way the story concerns itself with the place of man in the universe, with his significance and meaning. The overcoat has been seen as a symbol for something covering a spiritual void. Psychologically, it suggests an awakening to life and love, but, as characteristic in Gogol, drastic consequences and retribution follow. The loss of the coat and the vain protest to higher authority has also been seen as suggesting man's isolation in a world indifferent to his plight. Within the story, the impossible becomes a reality: Akaky obtains his new coat and for a moment achieves fulfillment. But the story is also literally a travesty: Akaky is replaced by the coat, which is honored by the party. Ultimately, this brilliantly comic story of Akaky's life (and transfiguration) is a tragic conception: it returns man to the nakedness in which he is born.

III

Gogol had a lifelong interest in the theater. His father was an amateur dramatist, and Gogol grew up in the midst of theatricals.

Playacting, in the literal and figurative senses, was a staple of his life. He was a consummate actor and reader of his work—both on stage and off—though he failed in an attempt to become a professional actor. Throughout his life he wrote on the shortcomings of Russian repertory, staging, and acting, as well as on more theoretical elements of the drama.

Two aspects of his art, at first glance contradictory, are connected with his comedies. The first is his tendency to present matter through dramatic scenes. Extensive dialogue and scenic representation occur in all the stories. The second is his tendency to communicate through first-person narration, by monologue. But Gogol's narrative tone (or tones) is enormously effective in approximating oral discourse. He is a master of what Russian scholars call the *skaz* technique (from the root "to speak," "to tell"), the creating of a character through the expedient of his verbal peculiarities, his repetitions, vocabulary, etc., so that he exists primarily because of the way he speaks rather than through what his explicit meaning may be. This technique is essentially dramatic in nature. Gogol was able to catch the idiosyncrasies and intonations of his narrators so well that they appear to be substantial beings. Only naive or untrained readers could accept narrators' comments at face value as Gogol's own. Gogol himself clearly distinguished narrative and dramatic uses. He also repeatedly stated that drama takes place in the theater, when it is acted, not when it is on paper.

Gogol's mature dramatic works date from 1832 to 1836. In 1832 he had started *The Suitors*, which was to be revised and published in 1842 as *Marriage*, and *The Vladimir Medal, Third Class*, of which only four scenes survive. It shares with "Notes of a Madman" the idea of a civil servant losing his mind because his desires are thwarted. He also worked on a historical drama, *Alfred*, left in fragments, and a short play about cardsharpers and double dealings entitled *The Gamblers*, published in 1842. The single play on which his reputation as a dramatist ultimately rests is *The Government Inspector* (1836), based on an anecdote by Pushkin about mistaken identity, and it is Russia's greatest comedy. As in the case of "The Overcoat," it has given rise to gross misinterpretation, not the least by Gogol himself, who wrote two short dramatic works to explain it.

The first sketch, *After the Play*, outlined shortly after the failure of the premiere in 1836, analyzes the responses of viewers and critics and claims that laughter is the single positive character in the play. Laughter for Gogol is not merely an effect of amusement but has a moral and educational function. It discloses man's emptiness and insignificance to him, instructing those capable of learning and shaming those not so capable. The second critique, *The Government Inspector Unraveled* (1846), expanded the following year, claims that the play is an allegory. The city is our spiritual city, the officials are passions, and the bogus inspector, Khlestakov, is a light-minded worldly conscience. Gogol returned to the subject yet again in the *Author's Confession* (1847), where he claimed that in the play he lumped together all that was bad in Russia, the better to laugh at it, and from that time forth he recognized his mission as a writer. A writer's achievement and his desire to explain it for mankind's instruction has rarely been so divergent as in Gogol's case.

The play begins with an announcement by the mayor of a small town to the officials he has summoned that an inspector is coming. As measures are taken to clean up the town and hoodwink the inspector, the corruption of the officials and their extraordinary foibles, petty interests, and characters are revealed. A flighty young man staying at a local inn, who has been fleeced in a card game and cannot pay his bill, is mistaken for the inspector, because fear has addled the mayor and his colleagues. Khlestakov, the young man, is feted and pampered by the officials, each of whom plies him with a "loan"—a bribe—and after a whirlwind courtship of the mayor's insipid daughter (and of his wife) he leaves, promising to return for the marriage, but interested only in recouping his gambling losses. The last act is a reversal of the first, as the officials realize that they have been duped and start blaming each other. At the height of recriminations a messenger announces that the inspector has arrived and is waiting for them at the inn. After a minute's silence and a dumb show of petrifaction, the curtain descends.

No wonder the characters are even more astounded and horrified by the closing than by the opening announcement. At first they cannot grasp why an inspection should take place at all, though such inspections in fact had once been routine; but there has not been one in thirty years, and the town is so obscure that "you could gallop for three years in any direction without reaching a border." They try to account for the inspection by improbable conjectures—war against Turkey, sedition—but refuse to face the chief reason for their fear, the exposure of corruption and abuse of power (though the mayor suspects that there may have been a denunciation). Extortion, bribe-taking, incompetence, indifference, and stupidity are shown by Gogol devastatingly. There is, however, no warrant for regarding the play as a document of Russian life. The characters are exaggerated. Gogol depicts social evils, but the emphasis is on perennial human folly. Beneath the riotously funny presentation there is always a recognizable source of pollution. When in act 1 the mayor talks of the town as "filthy—as soon as you put up a monument or even a fence, people drag rubbish of all sorts there [forty truckloads of it]. . . . I don't know where they get it from," he of course points to moral corruption as well. Gogol makes the narrow and futile lives led by his characters enormously entertaining. It is a measure of his theatrical genius that even the punishment that surely seems forthcoming from the real inspector may be illusory: Why should he not be hoodwinked and bribed, as the first one was?

Most of the effects of the comedy lie in its verbal play, the brilliant surface that unfortunately is untranslatable. There is much arrant nonsense (like Khlestakov's invitation to the mayor's wife to come with him "beneath the shade of a babbling brook" and the mayor's apothegm "You're not taking bribes according to your rank!") that has, like the characters' names, become proverbial in Russian. The characters have no essence—they are all surface. Their definition and self-sufficiency is verbal, not realistic or psychological. That makes it enormously difficult to stage the play successfully: it cannot be presented as a realistic play, nor purely as a grotesque or as an expressionist play. Nevertheless, its popularity, at least in Russia, remains undiminished.

Gogol brilliantly adapted theatrical conventions to his own genius. The play at first seems to be a traditional one of mistaken identity; vice disclosed, unmasked, and castigated; a marriage between the young hero and the innocent daughter of the villain projected as a comedy of manners. But none of this takes place. Khlestakov leaves with the "loans" he has amassed before he can be apprehended (indeed, he has not done anything wrong; he barely seems to understand what is going on, though his down-to-earth servant does). The courtship of the daughter is a farce: Khlestakov's improvisations in love are like his great lying monologues—they have no substance, no reality, no object; and he indifferently courts the daughter, then the mother, then the daughter again (Gogol said, "Khlestakov gets carried away, he lies with feeling, with pleasure"). No one is punished, at least within the play, and the comedy of manners turns into an extraordinary gallery of eccentrics and grotesques, what Dostoevsky called "a demonic vaudeville."

Gogol's other major play, *Marriage: A Completely Improbable Event in Two Acts*, deals with the courtship of an obtuse but rich merchant's daughter by four suitors, each of whom has an ulterior motive. The main character, Podkolyosin (Mr. Underwheel), is goaded to get married by his friend Kochkaryov, perhaps in revenge for having gotten married himself. At the last moment Podkolyosin, a passive and timorous man, would rather face the ignominy of jumping out of the window and running away than to commit himself to be married.

The types Gogol introduces are extraordinary: a Mr. Friedeggs, who checks the inventory of all the property that comes with the bride; a former naval officer, Mr. Chewer, who has been rejected seventeen times, and whose generalized admiration of women (they are all "little roses") yields only to his pleasant memories of a French-speaking Sicily he mistakes for Venice; Anuchkin, who looks for a wife who knows French because his father was too ignorant to teach it to him; and Agatha, the object of courtship herself, who cannot choose among them without recourse to throwing lots. The play gives the illusion of representing for the first time the benighted Russian mercantile class, a whole realm of dull-mindedness, outmoded traditions, and meaningless forms, which was to be developed by the realistic dramatist A. N. Ostrovsky, who dominates mid-nineteenth century drama. Though it lacks the verve of *The Government Inspector*, it may be as original in conception. No one before Gogol had presented courtship in a way so bereft of amatory interest and by such unprepossessing characters. The play opens new avenues for considering impulses and motivations. The conflict between the desire for marriage and fear of it is the basis of the play. Desire, or lack of it, is treated without spiritual and with few physical components. The frock coat Podkolyosin has made so that he can get married is more significant to him than his prospective bride. Kochkaryov seems disappointed in his expectations of marital bliss, but even the distinct prospect of it is more than Podkolyosin can commit himself to. The brilliant inanities of the play make it comic: but ultimately it points to aspects of life and behavior more disturbing than amusing.

IV

Gogol started *Dead Souls* in 1835, after Pushkin urged him to write something more substantial than stories, giving Cervantes as an example of a writer who would not have come down to posterity merely on the basis of his novellas. He confided to Gogol an idea that he had planned to use himself (later he complained, "You have to watch that Ukrainian, he steals your ideas from you").

Until the abolition of serfdom in 1861, serfs (called "souls") were an indicator of their owner's wealth, which would be given not in terms of money or land, but of a certain number of souls. A poor landowner might have fifty; a moderately comfortable one, five hundred. Gogol's father owned 130. In Aleksei Pisemsky's best-known novel, *A Thousand Souls* (1858), the hero's goal becomes the acquisition of wealth and position in that form. Turgenev, who was a wealthy man, shared in an estate of three thousand souls. Grigori Potemkin, Catherine II's favorite, who practically ruled Russia, was given fifty thousand souls by her—an astounding gift the Romanovs could easily afford, for they owned a quarter of Russia's serfs. Serfs not only provided labor, but they could be used as collateral for a mortgage with the state bank, which eventually wound up with an enormous number of unredeemed serfs. The male serfs, or souls, were taxable, and if they died their owners had to continue paying the head tax until they were struck from the rolls at the next census. If one had a turn for business and a fraudulent mind, the system could be used to advantage. There are several recorded instances of landowners' trying to mortgage dead souls, and even of some trying a scheme like the protagonist of Gogol's novel: buying dead souls for exactly that purpose; one such person was rather close to Gogol's family. Gogol was not so much interested in the scheme as in its implications and the possibility it provided for a rambling novel that would permit him to introduce all sorts of characters, places, and adventures.

Again there are identifiable traditions: the adventure based on a journey with a higher end in mind, as in Miguel de Cervantes' *Don Quixote* (1605–1615); the picaresque novel (a rogues to riches story) that exposes the society the picaro preys on, as in *Lazarillo de Tormes*; the sentimental journey, as in Laurence Sterne's *Tristram Shandy* (1760), in which time is suspended in order to introduce whatever interruptions, lengthy digressions and judgments, whatever random seeming material the author considers worth including; and the humor apparent in perambulatory novels like Charles Dickens' *Pickwick Papers* (1836–1837), which utilizes travels to encompass an ever larger range of society.

The point is worth making because Gogol himself came to refer to *Dead Souls* as a *poema*, and that word is the largest and most striking on the cover Gogol designed for the first edition. At the time the Russian word designated a long heroic or epic (or mock-epic) verse narrative. Gogol might have wished to point to his conception as a grandly conceived work connected with the epic mode. There are certainly epic qualities about it—in the Homeric plenty and the Homeric similes, in the catalogs, in the attempt to present a full view—though in the main the spotlight is turned on very un-epic things, on the mock epic. Gogol later distinguished between the novel, which "though in prose can be a lofty poetic creation" but requires plot and a significant event in a single life; and the tale, "which may be called a *poema*," that is, used to depict the characteristic features of a particular time, place, or way of life. But, he explains, a "lesser form of the epic" had come into existence, and he proceeds to a further definition really formulated on the basis of *Dead Souls*:

In modern times there came into being a kind of narrative work that constitutes a sort of a mean between the novel and the epic, whose hero, though a private and unremarkable character, is nonetheless in many ways significant for the observer of the human soul. The author traces his life through a series of adventures and changes, in order at the same time to . . . present a faithful picture of everything that is significant in the traits and mores of the time in question. . . . Many [such works] although written in prose, may nonetheless be classified as poetic creations.

(from *Selected Passages from Correspondences with Friends*)

Later writers, like Dostoevsky in *The Double* (1846) or Ivan Bunin in *The Village* (1910) and "Sukhodol" ("Dry Valley," 1911), gladly availed themselves of the subtitle "Poema" to designate a prose work in the grand Gogolian tradition.

The question of genre is an interesting one. Pushkin challenged classical forms by subtitling *Eugene Onegin* (1832) "A Novel in Verse" (novels were written in prose), and Boris Pasternak was to reverse the process by subtitling *Dr. Zhivago* (1957) "A Novel in Prose." Mikhail Lermontov subtitles his *Hero of Our Times* (1839) "A Composition" or "A Work" (*sochinenie*); Turgenev and Dostoevsky (like Gogol before them) have in their titles "notes" (*zapiski*). In some unused prefatory remarks to *War and Peace* (1866), Tolstoy, facing comparable formal problems of genre, points out that these works and other Russian masterpieces created new and unique forms. For Gogol's masterpiece the issue is of the essence: the work will question all norms and forms and will take final refuge in the word itself, will let words assume such life that they vivify the most commonplace object, transform it at will into something else, and determine the subject. Words, not context, create meaning in Gogol. Or perhaps words determine the context, not vice versa. The reader must be aware that the ostensibly superficial humorous surface of the work, with all its variety, has vital implications and that the tension between surface and context provides the only adequate approach for considering the plot and characters, the possible moral, sociological, or other significance of the novel.

This may be illustrated in the construction of the novel's opening sentence and paragraph, where the verbal picture dislodges our perceptions: "Into the gates of the inn of a certain provincial capital entered a rather handsome small carriage on springs, of the kind used by bachelors, retired lieutenant-colonels, second captains, landowners possessing a hundred souls or so of peasants—in a word, all those who are called the fair-to-middling sort." It conveys motion but nothing animate—a gate, an inn, a town, a carriage (supposedly favored by a certain average type, but its exemplars show little in common except Gogol's yoking them together). As yet there is no occupant for the carriage. When that occupant appears in the next sentence, he is deprived of distinguishing features (he was neither this, nor that) and is reduced to something different from the fair-to-middling sort his carriage identifies him as being: a person without qualities. The next sentence, when the reader expects something more about the occupant or about the significance of the entry of the carriage into the yard of the inn, begins with a total denial of the importance of what has just been presented: "His arrival produced absolutely no stir of any kind in the town and was not accompanied by any remarkable event" (why then bother with it?). Only "two Russian muzhiks" ponder the merits and capacity of one of its wheels (not of the whole carriage) and decide that the wheel will make it as far as Moscow, but not as far as Kazan. "And with that the conversation ended." A passing figure, whose dress is described in minute detail, observes this entrance but never reappears in the book. These four sentences are unlike anything that has opened a novel before. They take commonplaces and turn them into something different

and unexpected. They propel the reader into a world where people are secondary to things, where unwarranted assumptions and opinions are given as fact, where comic but potentially weighty discussions are indulged in by inappropriate people who have no reason to raise the questions, where peripheral figures impress themselves indelibly on the mind and then disappear. In short, the reader finds himself in a world of inanimates and busybodies where much is unmotivated, where a great deal of nonsense and absurdity is presented with the same gravity as quite ordinary, "real" things, where alogical reasoning reigns.

So, for example, in the next paragraph, Chichikov (as yet unnamed) is shown his hotel room, "the usual room . . . where for two rubles a day travelers get a restful room with [the reader expects "breakfast"] cockroaches peeking out of every corner like so many black plums." The room, the inn, the parlor are like all other rooms, inns, and parlors. The word "the same" anaphorically begins most clauses. The grimy setting is presented in great detail, which is, however, very selective and moves at will to the most fanciful remarks and most exotic lands:

> The same pictures [as in all inns], covering the entire wall and painted in oil—in a word, everything the same as you would find everywhere; the only difference was that one picture depicted a nymph with such enormous breasts as the reader, in all probability, has never beheld. Such freaks of nature, however, are to be met with in various historical pictures which were brought to Russia, although no one knows by whom, when, or from where, but now and then perhaps by our grandees, amateurs of art, who must have bought them in Italy on the advice of the guides that took them around.
>
> (ch. 1)

The procession of Chichikov's belongings is described as it comes into the room. The last item, after a trunk, a box, and shoe trees, is "wrapped up in blue paper [what could it be?], a roasted chicken." On his walk through town Chichikov sees a sign: "Vasily Feodorov, Foreigner." When Chichikov returns, his servant, Petrushka, is lying on his cot practicing spitting at the ceiling, "and quite successfully, too" (idiomatically the phrase means "idling away time"). Everything breeds something else, some new anomaly, whether by verbal placement, by logical displacement, or by incredibly inventive leaps.

The verbal surface in Russian contains other comparable delights, which are the translator's despair. At every point there are astonishing juxtapositions of disparate stylistic levels, of totally unexpected turns, of striking sound patterns, of verbal inventions. The words themselves generate a world of their own, as, in a lesser way, may be seen in Petrushka's reading:

> He even had a noble impulse toward enlightenment—i.e., the reading of books, the contents of which presented no difficulty whatsoever to him: it was all one to him if the book dealt with the adventures of an enamored hero or whether it was simply a dictionary or a prayer book—he read everything with the same attentiveness. . . . It wasn't what he read that pleased him, but rather the reading itself or, to put it better, the very process of reading—lo and behold, some word or other inevitably cropped up from out of the welter of letters, even though, at times, the Devil only knew what that word might mean.
>
> (ch. 1)

The ultimate extension of words begetting worlds of their own occurs in chapter 10, in the hilarious and gruesome inset story "The Tale of Captain Kopeikin." It is a kind of miniature of the methods of the novel, where the verbal surface so brilliantly subsumes that which it relates that it almost eliminates it. Gogol again demonstrates his mastery of *skaz*, the illusion of oral recitation highly colored by the personality and idiosyncratic speech of the narrator, in this case the postmaster of the

town Chichikov has visited. Earlier, Gogol had signaled the postmaster's speech as "garnished by sundry tag-ends and oddments of phrases such as 'my dear sir,' 'thus and so,' 'you know,' 'you understand,' 'relatively speaking,' 'you can just imagine,' 'so to say,' 'in a sort of a way,' and other such verbal small change." These are the terms that dominate this comic tale. Ostensibly the postmaster tells this story to explain who Chichikov really is, when the townspeople try to ascertain his purposes. He begins by informing his listeners that "during the campaign of 1812 . . . whether it was at Krasnoe or at Leipzig, the fact remains, can you just imagine, that he had an arm and a leg blown off," and rushes on with his tale of the captain's seeking a pension so that he can live ("I've, so to speak, shed my blood for the Fatherland; I have, in a way, lost an arm and a leg, don't you know"). Many pages later the postmaster is interrupted with the comment that Chichikov has all his arms and legs, which might have been done right away. But that is merely the starting point: the verbal improvisation determines its own course.

This kind of verbal pullulation is a reflection of the universe Gogol depicts, where one thing begets another because there is no basis or meaning to anything, and everything may be stretched beyond limit because no limits exist. This is perhaps best illustrated when Nozdrev shows Chichikov his estate and leads him to its boundary:

> "There's the boundary!" said Nozdrev. "Everything that you see on this side is all of it mine, and even on the other side, that whole forest that shows so blue over there is mine, as well as everything beyond the forest—it's all mine too."
>
> (ch. 5)

The energy, the exuberance, the humor of Gogol's progressions constantly demonstrate that literary art alone, artistic transformation, gives substance to the materials of life, not some assertion about their intrinsic worth. Questions of meanings—reality, psychology, ideas, aspirations—can only rise in that context. Gogol appears to present things with great detail and exactitude, but at the same time to be evasive, to tergiversate, to deny specific characteristics, frequently to pretend to be incapable of defining or understanding. It is up to the reader to ferret out the relation of presentation to meaning and to the void Gogol suggests exists behind the appearance.

Two major stylistic devices, simile and hyperbole, support such an approach. The first compares one thing to something else; the second exaggerates a thing beyond belief and thereby destroys its reality. A combination of the two appears early, when the "host of teacups perched on the waiter's tray was as great as the birds you might find on the shore." The technique recurs in other forms and shapes throughout. The noise of the writing quills in the registry office of chapter 7 "resembled the sound of several carts laden with brushwood driving through a forest piled high with dead leaves." It hovers toward metaphor in the conversation between the two ladies of chapter 9, one of whom says the governor's daughter is "a statue, pale as death," while the other claims that "she puts on rouge in a godless manner." The first insists, "She is chalk, pure chalk," the second, "She puts on rouge as thick as your finger and it even breaks off in pieces, like plaster" (what then is her complexion "really," and does it matter?). Apart from the humor and ridicule, Gogol also uses the procedure to demean a character or subject—his similes and descriptions tend to magnify or diminish—to mirror the mind of the speaker, and to emphasize the senselessness of direct statement.

An intriguing feature of the simile in *Dead Souls* and elsewhere in Gogol is that there is frequently no nominal connection between the object and the thing to which it is compared. Indeed, Gogol dislodges the function of connectives like "and," "but," "with," and especially the alogical "even": Chichikov can speak of "virtue even with tears in his eyes," the governor "was good-hearted and even occasionally embroidered fancywork on tulle with his own hands,"—almost always "even" signals some anomaly. But in the similes something special happens. One sentence has been frequently cited because while Gogol takes special pains to emphasize the grayness of life, the flatness of existence, to lament the lack of vibrant colors and distinguishing traits, he finds unique ways to make the dull and average interesting:

> Even the weather had obligingly accommodated itself to the setting: the day was neither bright nor gloomy but of a kind of blueish-gray shade like that only found on the worn uniforms of soldiers in a garrison, who otherwise are a peaceful class of warriors, except for being somewhat unsober on Sundays.
>
> (ch. 1)

A special case is the epic or Homeric simile, the lengthy and vividly developed comparison that assumes a life of its own before returning to that which it is supposed to illustrate. In Gogol it is in the comic mode of course, where frequently it loses sight of its purpose. There are several famous passages in *Dead Souls:* one compares the men in dress coats at the governor's ball to flies disporting themselves around a sugarloaf; another compares the chorus of barking dogs as Chichikov enters Korobochka's domain to the timbre of voices in a chorus when a concert is in full swing.

Hyperbole is not necessarily grotesque, but in Gogol the two frequently merge as another phase of his distorting art. The result is a world of monsters, of gargoyles, of "rips in the fabric of humanity," the memorable phrase applied to Plyushkin:

> Really, what extraordinary faces there are in the world. In one the role of commandant is played by the nose, in another by the lips, in a third by

the cheeks, which have pushed themselves into the foreground at the expense of the lips and even of the nose, so that the latter is no bigger than a waistcoat button; one man has a chin so long that he must cover it with a handkerchief in order not to spit on it. Another . . .

(from a draft of ch. 6)

Characters are seen only externally, frequently metonymically as whiskers, beards, or some other feature, even an article of apparel. Events can similarly be made grotesque: the chiming of Korobochka's clock (the hissing of an uncoiling dragon), the description of her coach, numerous other instances that jar our sense of reality.

Gogol also makes striking use of mere repetition. At several points he resorts to multiple repetitions of the same phrase or motion as if to emphasize the senselessness of an action or its superficiality or lack of meaning. Thus in giving directions to reach Manilov's estate, which Chichikov mistakenly calls "Zamanilovka," "one of the peasants who had more sense and a wedge-shaped beard" repeats four times in ten lines that there is a Manilovka but not a Zamanilovka. When Chichikov arrives, there is a quadruple repetition of exchanges on who shall go through the door first; a triple repetition of identical line marks Chichikov and Nozdrev's first three moves at checkers.

That Chichikov should have made a mistake in a place name is also significant, for the error of adding the prefix *za* emphasizes the dreamy attraction that Manilovka already suggests in Russian. Almost every proper name in Gogol suggests something: They are more Pecksniffian than Dickens': Nozdrev, a nostril; Sobakevich, a dog; Plyushkin, ivy; and Korobochka, a little box. When Chichikov (a sneeze?) reads a playbill, we find the names Poplyovin (Spitter) and Miss Zyablov (Frostbitten), "while the others were even less outstanding." The scores of names that proliferate in the book do their share in adding to the nonsensicality and humor of Gogol's world: dead souls like Neuvazhai-Koryto (Disrespect-Trough); Manilov's son, Themistoclius (a romanized Greek); Sysoi Macdonaldich (a Scotsman?) and Macdonald Sysoich (his son?).

There are many other stylistic levels; lyrical digressions; reflections on youth, city, ardor, travel; authorial asides on what might properly constitute material for a novel; observations on what might be made of more promising material. These are a constant reminder that what goes into *Dead Souls* and how it is presented are primary themes of the novel. Only in that light is "content" properly approached.

IV

In translation the reality of life and human behavior that underlie the brilliant surface is more readily apparent than technique. After making allowances for Russian customs and places, we recognize a physical setting not so different from others of the period elsewhere. Gogol is at pains to tell the reader that certain things are specifically Russian—inns, service, deference and servility, climate, scenery, and many more—when in fact they are universal. Contemporaries even claimed that Gogol did not know Russian customs and he himself asked for reports on Russia when he was writing the second part of *Dead Souls*. His characters, who for Russians have come to designate types, are recognizable distortions or hyperbolized personifications of individual vices or failings: Manilov, the mawkish sentimentalist; Korobochka, the grasping widow; Nozdrev, the liar and braggart; Plyushkin, the miser; Sobakevich, the physical stalwart bereft of a soul—it is as memorable a gallery of types made into original characters as any in literature.

The prime and central representative of this world is Chichikov, the incarnation of the commonplace, tawdry, and vulgar, of the Russian *poshlost*—trivial vulgarity in taste, intellect, interests—the depiction of which is one of Gogol's greatest talents. Chichikov has no distinguishing characteristics other than his trumpeting nose. He is neither this nor that, precisely average, therefore typical. We soon see that he is the most adaptable of creatures, chameleonlike, suiting himself to his surroundings and his interlocutors. Everything with him is surface—his cleanliness, his rotundity, his agreeable manners. A hint about his interests and drives emerges from the description of his many-tiered box with successive layers of toiletries, business forms and utensils, mementos, and a secret compartment—the very center of his life and the sanctuary where he keeps money. Throughout the chapter in which Chichikov is introduced Gogol emphasizes that the setting and the character's behavior are typical of a way of life. Everything points to falseness: the scrawny trees are reported in the local paper as "cooling shade trees," the rutted earthen streets as "infinitely broad boulevards." Everything is accepted without question or discussion by all the characters.

After Chichikov becomes acquainted with the officials of the town and gathers the data he needs, he embarks on his travels, to attempt to purchase dead souls. It is clear that the five visits Chichikov makes are procedurally handled the same way. In each case there is first a description of the estate he approaches. The general appearance of the property always gives a clue about the owner, for it reflects his salient trait—carelessness, solidity, or the like. Then there are the amenities of greetings, a preliminary broaching of the topic, then a repast, after which negotiations begin. Through these Gogol communicates the essence of the type with whom Chichikov comes in contact. On Manilov's property the unfinished cottages, the green slime on the pond in the midst of an "English garden" with a "Temple of Solitary Meditation," the incomplete furnishings of the house reflect Manilov's inconsequentiality. He is incomplete, unthinking; he accepts everything around him with saccharine sentimentality, is unable or incapable of confronting reality, cannot complete a thought any more than he can complete his furnishings. Chichikov, after all, raises a point that puzzles Manilov: Is such a sale legitimate (in other terms: Is the law a fraud, or is fraud the law)? All he can do is puff away on his pipe, until his doubts are resolved when Chichikov points out that the state will benefit from the transaction because it will collect transfer fees. Manilov is then happy and content. He refuses to charge his new friend for the souls and daydreams a whole scenario of his future friendship with Chichikov as the latter leaves. Nothing in his life makes sense: there is merely indiscriminate acceptance. At the end even the document containing his list of dead souls is senselessly and uselessly prettified with curlicues and tied with a pretty bow.

Nowhere does Chichikov seem quite so oozily vulgar as here. For if his great skill lies in adapting himself to the personality of his interlocutor, he has nothing to adapt to here. Gogol specifically states that there are no distinguishing traits to Manilov, that he has not so much as a hobby, and Chichikov can only duplicate his mawkishness, which the reader already feels is in stark contrast to his peculiar and perhaps sinister undertaking.

The obvious contrast to Manilov is Sobakevich, the ponderous rough-hewn churl concerned only with his physical self. Manilov's courteous formulas are replaced by Sobakevich's gruffness, his delicate care for his visitor's comfort by Sobakevich's clumsiness. When Chichikov repeats Manilov's praises of the town's officials as charming, endearing men, Sobakevich replies that they are all scoundrels. The whole town, he says, is nothing but a robbers' den. So long as his personal comfort is not disturbed he does not care. Since Chichikov wants to buy dead souls, he must have a use for them, so Sobakevich drives a hard bargain. Eventually he even cheats Chichikov by introducing a female serf (therefore not mortgageable) into the list. Everything on his estate and in his house is solid, substantial, unwieldy: the peasants' huts outside, the furniture inside, the pictures of warriors with enormous thighs and mustaches—and resonant Greek names—even the starling in its cage—everything seems to cry out, "I am a Sobakevich, too." His dead peasants have the same solidity, it turns out, for in addition to listing them Sobakevich enumerates their skills and physical attributes. But it is all external: there seems to be no soul in him at all.

In one sense each of the characters is an aspect or reflection of Chichikov—his unthinking existence, his physical comforts, his grasping, his lying, his shrewdness in business, his lack of judgment. It must be sheer folly to broach such a proposal to someone like Nozdrev, who is a dangerous bully and braggart, or Korobochka, who is a suspicious gossip, for either might divulge Chichikov's doings and thereby ruin his scheme. But when he reaches Plyushkin, Gogol moves to less superficial aspects of human behavior, perhaps even to something potentially tragic, and he heralds it by a change in method. The chapter begins with a lyrical digression on general disenchantment with life, the passing from youth to age, lamenting lost freshness and cheer. It sets a different mood. In contrast to the absence of soul we see something like the emergence of human emotion for a moment, and we are given the first excursion into the past in the story of Plyushkin's life. There is something even more striking, a splendid lengthy description of Plyushkin's overgrown garden, with its mixture of wild nature and art, of beauty and ugliness, a symbolic representation of the world of *Dead Souls* and of Plyushkin himself. A ray of sunlight suddenly appears in the garden, transforming everything it illuminates into beauty. It suggests at least a possibility for escape from the world Gogol has depicted.

But human impulses in Plyushkin are checked by the habits of miserliness, the deliberate shutting out of the ray of light. For that reason the portrait of the miser is all the more horrifying, and more disturbing than that of the other characters. Chichikov is again seen in a particularly bad light, for he ignores all the implications of his visit in his satisfaction at the large number of souls he has gotten. Gogol frames the experience with a disillusioning picture of the town as Chichikov returns: the seamier side of life appears and destroys the idealistic illusion of youth. None of this has any meaning for Chichikov, who calmly drops off to sleep.

The adventure novel shares with pornography one major difficulty: How can one sustain interest when repeatedly describing the same thing? To avoid this difficulty Gogol now moves into another realm, into another circle of hell. In chapter 7 the souls are registered in an elaborate parody of both pagan underworld and Christian hell, presided over by an office chief who can shorten or extend office hours the way Homer's Zeus regulates daylight. The chapter provides a transition to the social life of a provincial town, those things included in Gogol's conception of a *poema*. At a ball in chapter 8 Chichikov pays excessive attention to the governor's daughter and thereby offends the ladies of the town. To his consternation, Nozdrev, in drunken exuberance, loudly chatters about Chichikov's purchase of dead souls from him. Extremely troubled, Chichikov leaves the ball. While he stays in his room for two or three days nursing a cold, we are introduced to a whole slew of new characters, not necessarily by name or civic function but as general types: two women, indistinguishable—one called "the lady pleasant in all respects," the other merely "the pleasant lady"—and others who populate a world of gossip, superstition and corruption. These busybodies assess the merits of Chichikov's purchases and supposed resettlement of souls, as in the opening page the two peasants had speculated on the limits of travel for one wheel. They debate the safety of the move, the docility of the souls, the suitability of terrain and climate. They elaborate preposterous motives for Chichikov's purchase: the ladies are certain he intends to elope with the governor's daughter; the men reject that notion but are apprehensive about "dead souls" since this term may refer to recent shady doings in town. They conclude after some wildly amusing conjectures that the "dead souls" are merely a cover and that Chichikov is a brigand or a counterfeiter. Both sexes fail to recognize the obvious fact of the fraud itself. They cannot figure Chichikov out because to recognize what he is and what he is doing implies recognizing what they themselves are: he is, after all, exactly like them. Gogol's inventive genius makes it possible for Chichikov to disappear from the narrative for a long period. He is not missed because he is not noticeably different from those presented in the meantime.

It should be noted that Chichikov does not fall into disrepute because his scheme is exposed. Rather, by unwittingly slighting the ladies he offends the sensibilities and code of the town and becomes prey to gossip and social ostracism. He leaves in bad odor, but for the wrong reasons. His quest has ended successfully. He leaves bearing the deeds to his dead souls and (in another reading) the signatures of those who have damned themselves to hell.

In the last chapter we finally get a full explanation of the inception of Chichikov's scheme and the story of his early life. Many critics have objected to it as an incongruous afterthought, as inferior to the inventions of the rest of the novel, as traditional and unjustifiable methodologically, as perhaps preparing the reader for a continuation by rounding out a character who will reappear in a sequel. Yet the biography is more than a belated attempt to expand the character: it is a catalog of significant modes of vulgarity, a demonstration of how one can, through meekness, cunning, industry, diligence, falseness, and illegality—through denial of nonmaterial values—move ahead in the world. Just in case the reader missed the implications, Gogol preaches a sermon at the end: "It is not that readers are dissatisfied with my hero that worries me. What worries me is that within my soul there is the deep conviction that readers may have been pleased with that very hero, with that same Chichikov." But the real end is the famous passage in which Chichikov's carriage is likened to the troika rushing Russia along the road "with other peoples and nations standing aside and giving it the right of way"—an inspired bit of lyricism similar to others in the novel but gaining particular importance from its placement. It is a rhetorical assertion that there is something worthwhile, even something magnificent, about Russia and Russians—an assertion completely unjustified by anything in the book. It is effective, however, not only rhetorically, but because it supplants the rider with the vehicle, the vulgarian with the communal potential, ending the book with a real flight into the open from the circumscribed world Gogol has presented.

The spectacle of that world is not edifying, though it is terribly amusing. It forces the reader to consider who and what the dead souls are. The question had come up several times as Chichikov made his requests. Gogol also asked, in presenting Sobakevich, whether there was a soul in him at all. Near the end, when one of the leading officials, the procurator, is literally scared to death by the fuss and implications aroused by Chichikov's purchases, doctors are summoned, but "it became apparent that he was a soulless corpse. Only then was it learned with regret that the deceased had had a soul, which out of modesty he had never shown." Chichikov's various prospects are puzzled by his offer to buy "dead souls" (the locution before the novel was "deceased souls": *ubyvshie dushi;* afterward it became "dead souls": *myortvie dushi*). What is a dead soul worth? "You hold the soul as cheap as a turnip," says Sobakevich in his bargaining. And indeed the censor objected not only to the price Chichikov paid for these souls but also to the title. For how can the soul, the immortal part of man, be dead, he asked. So the book first appeared as *Chichikov's Adventures, or Dead Souls.* There must be a peculiarly Gogolian touch in that solution to the censor's objection: Why is a subtitle different from a title? But the reader knows in any case who the dead souls are, for they populate the whole book.

V

Lev Arnoldi, who was present at Gogol's reading of part 2, chapter 1, of *Dead Souls* in July 1849, reported that Gogol began despondently:

> Why describe poverty and more poverty and the imperfection of our life, digging up people from the back woods and distant corners of the empire? What is one to do if the author is of such a nature and, infected by his own imperfection, can describe nothing else but poverty and more poverty and the imperfection of our life, digging up people from the back woods and distant corners of the empire? And now we have landed again in the back woods, again chanced upon an out of the way spot.

Then he looked up, and triumphantly, resonantly, continued: "But then, what a back woods and what an out of the way spot!" Arnoldi reports details of the plot and is one of several witnesses who commented on the splendor of the novel's continuation.

Gogol probably began to work on part 2 in 1840, and he had written a great deal when he burned the manuscript in 1845. He returned to it in 1848, and those who heard the final version, including the writer Sergei Aksakov, insist that it was in no way inferior to part 1 and mention glowingly several passages that no longer exist, as well as details of the plot

between the end of chapter 4 and the later fragments. The work that remains is from an earlier version, probably between 1843 and 1845, which Gogol had neglected to burn, and the rough draft, with numerous corrections and variants, of the final chapter. Gogol's method consisted of constant revision and refinement. Drafts of other works show that what seems in the printed work to be spontaneous, obvious, and fitting, is arrived at only after painstaking work over many years. To judge even the first four chapters in anything but a tentative way would be similar to discussing Igor Stravinsky's *Petrushka* or Richard Wagner's *Götterdämmerung* on the basis of a piano score. Yet certain things stand out. In his first published letter on *Dead Souls* Gogol noted that many readers had been struck to the quick (*zadet za zhivoe*) by the "comicality, truth, and caricature," but that part 2 was to be "a true mirror, not a caricature," and that its psychology would be different. In 1847 he wrote to a correspondent that he wished to portray more important characters, "to penetrate deeper into the lofty meaning of life, which we have made so spiritually shallow, and not to show the Russian man merely from any *one side alone.*"

It is not only a matter of introducing "positive" characters, like the idealized landowner Konstanzhoglo or the incorruptible official Murazov, but also presenting foibles of mankind that are less trivial than those of part 1, showing that the disintegration of personality is the result of good impulses thwarted or gone astray and is not always irremediable. Thus we have the memorable portrait of the sluggard Tentetnikov, who, after youthful enthusiasm and the desire to work for the welfare of mankind, returns to his estate and gives way to lethargy: all his plans are overwhelmed by a useless existence; or the portrait of Platonov, a former dandy who is disillusioned in love and succumbs to hopeless boredom; of Khlobuyev, kindhearted and pious but irresolute, lacking the will to do anything constructive;

even of the patriotic and simpleminded General Betrishchev. These lives are potentially recoverable. There are, however, also memorable "caricatures" like those in part 1: the glutton Petukh, whose entire life and conversation are given to food, in incredible and mouth-watering detail; Koshkarev, the colonel who organizes his estate on a military and bureaucratic pattern that makes it impossible to perform the simplest task without burdensome formal procedures and an enormous amount of paperwork; or the overzealous governor-general who speaks only in superlatives. But even these have an enthusiasm for their monomania that is a far cry from Sobakevich, Plyushkin, or Korobochka.

After many obscure adventures and again a great deal of moralizing, this narrative ends like part 1, with Chichikov's departure:

> It was not the old Chichikov. It was a ruin of the old Chichikov. One would compare the inner state of his soul to a building broken down into its component parts; this building was knocked down with the intention of constructing a new one out of it; but the new one had not yet been begun because the architect had not yet sent the final plan and the workers stood there perplexed.

Some characters are redeemed and resume a meaningful existence, even in part 2. Others—Chichikov, Khlobuyev, even Plyushkin—were to undergo a further purgatory of part 3. Gogol enigmatically said of the others that they too might be reborn, "if they wished." Yet that is idle speculation. The most probable suggestion is that the analogy to Dante's *Divine Comedy* is tenuous: description of Paradise is difficult to conceive in terms of the realistic psychological novel into which Gogol's *poema* turned, just as the description of the Inferno was possible only in the former hyperbolic mode, which Gogol had renounced.

We perhaps do best to ignore Gogol's intentions and the extant chapters of part 2. Its purvey and methods seem to differ noticeably from those of part 1, as do those of the second part of *Don Quixote* from the first. But in Gogol, part 1 is self-contained, complete. Part 1 has many subjects, but strictly speaking they are all created by its methods. It is the most brilliant, variegated, entertaining, and immediately apprehensible portrait in literature of life bereft of content and meaning in a unique form that suggests the different ways this life might be presented in art. Therein lies its extraordinary modernity, its greatness, its endless fascination.

VI

Astounding as it may seem, much of Gogol was misread in the nineteenth century, and is still misread by most Soviet critics, as a realistic portrayal of Russia, despite the patent absurdity of this view. The reasons for such misinterpretations are complex. Historically, Gogol was writing at a time when interest in local color led to a new form of short story that was canonized in the next decade as the sketch *(ocherk)*, the presentation of new literary subjects and types. Consequently, there was also an increasing interest in deglamorized, even ugly, descriptions of humble abodes; unexotic cityscapes; quaint, picturesque, or gloomy and unattractive corners of the city and the suburban fringe; and of the lower classes—people who had not figured previously as literary subjects: merchants, students, civil servants, ecclesiastics, and the like—in short, a move toward lower subjects and realia. It was also the beginning of an era of general philanthropism or sentimental humanitarianism, as in certain works by Victor Hugo, George Sand, and Charles Dickens; of the desire to commiserate with, if not to ameliorate, the lot of the poor and the oppressed and the deprived. The two notions—reality and sympathy—and the increasing demand that literature have a "social purpose"—since political expression was suppressed by Czar Nicholas I's censorship—led to a misguided emphasis on Gogol's "content" and the failure to see that Gogol's humorous presentation greatly affects this apparent content.

Russia's leading literary critic, Vissarion Belinsky, wrote two important articles that fixed this dominant approach to Gogol in the nineteenth century. The first, *On Gogol's Stories* (1835), points to the indigenous, genuinely Russian folk matter in the stories and praises their "fidelity to life" and their "natural" character. Fidelity to life for Belinsky is essentially what he meant by "realism." The term "natural" indicated the lack of the fantastical and imaginary, with an emphasis on depicting poverty and physical details of everyday life, but eventually it became a shorthand way to refer to those elements of Gogol's art that Belinsky emphasized. The designation "Natural School" was coined, in a pejorative sense, by the critic Faddei Bulgarin in 1846 (and was soon prohibited by the censorship) to designate this aspect of Gogol and his followers—followers at least in so far as they shared general themes and subjects and, occasionally, emulated his style.

Belinsky's second article, on *Dead Souls*, extends the critic's notion of the reality contained in Gogol's satire to emphasize its function as a criticism of that reality. Clearly there is some recognizable real world that underlies Gogol's fiction. But it is difficult to see how such extraordinary grotesques as Gogol's characters and events, or such extravagant lyric apostrophes and purple passages as those that appear throughout Gogol's work, could be construed as any kind of reality other than the reality of literary form and practice, though of necessity this art raises a host of questions about morality, psychology, religion, and the like. Belinsky, unlike some of his followers, at least recognized Gogol's artistry, his ability to present "low" material in artistic form, and called him "the poet of real life."

Subsequent criticism until the end of the century elaborated the realism, satire, and social ideas of Gogol and ignored his means of expression and artistic modes. Perhaps only the critic Apollon Grigorev demonstrated a concern with Gogol's verbal distortions; and his view may have affected Dostoevsky's disciple, the outstanding essayist and innovative prose writer V. V. Rozanov, who as early as 1893 elaborated Grigorev's view of the hyperbolic element in Gogol. More important, Rozanov expanded Gogol's statement that he had merely created puppets, figments of his imagination, in order to rid himself of his own tormenting shortcomings. Rozanov pointed out that readers and critics were so impressed by the surface detail of Gogol's characters that they never realized there was nothing beyond the surface—that there was a physical, psychological, and moral void behind the facade. He thereby overthrew the "realistic" approach and opened a modern era of interpretation. The symbolist poet Valery Bryussov gave his epoch-making lecture "Burnt to Ashes" ("Is-pepelenny") in 1909, stressing Gogol's exaggeration and hyperbole as the core of his art, and pointing out that Gogol's hyperboles preclude realism. The spate of stylistic and other studies that followed in Russia and more recently outside it have opened new vistas on Gogol's work. There are even attempts to catalog and explain Gogol's humor—by and large a stodgy and thankless undertaking. Does it really help to explain the following example: "His father was captured by the Turks . . . but disguising himself as a eunuch, he managed to escape"? What modern critics have demonstrated is that Gogol has a much broader range and far deeper implications on all levels—artistic, moral, psychological, philosophical, religious—than his early critics discovered. They have made more accessible what many readers have sensed: that while Gogol is among the most entertaining writers he is also one of the most profound, modern, and challenging; and that his grotesquely distorted universe makes us look in new ways at the world in which we live.

Selected Bibliography

EDITIONS

INDIVIDUAL WORKS

Evenings on a Farm near Dikanka. 2 vols. St. Petersburg, 1831–1832. Contains "Sorochinsky Fair," "St. John's Eve," "May Night," "The Lost Letter," "Christmas Eve," "The Terrible Vengeance," "Ivan Shponka and His Aunt," "The Enchanted Spot."

Mirgorod. St. Petersburg, 1835. Contains "Old World Landowners," "The Viy," "Taras Bulba," "The Story of the Quarrel of Ivan Ivanovich with Ivan Nikivorovich."

Arabesques. St. Petersburg, 1835. Contains "The Portrait," "Nevsky Avenue," "Notes of a Madman," and essays.

The Government Inspector. St. Petersburg, 1836.

The Nose. St. Petersburg, 1836.

The Carriage. St. Petersburg, 1836.

Dead Souls. Moscow, 1842.

The Overcoat. Moscow, 1842.

Marriage. Moscow, 1842.

Selected Passages from Correspondence with Friends. Moscow, 1847.

COLLECTED WORKS

Polnoe sobranie sochinenii i pisem. 14 vols. Moscow, 1937–1952.

TRANSLATIONS

Arabesques. Translated by A. Tulloch. Ann Arbor, Mich., 1982.

Collected Tales and Plays. Translated by C. Garnett. Edited by L. J. Kent. New York, 1964.

Dead Souls. Translated by B. G. Guerney. New York, 1942.

The Government Inspector and Other Plays. Translated by C. Garnett. New York, 1927.

Hanz Küchelgarten, Leaving the Theatre, and Other Works. Translated and edited by R. Meyer. Ann Arbor, Mich., 1983.

Marriage: A Completely Improbable Event in Two Acts. Translated by Bella Costello. New York and London, 1969.

Selected Passages from Correspondences with Friends. Translated by J. Zeldin. Nashville, Tenn., 1969.

The Theatre of Nikolay Gogol. Translated by M. Ehre and F. Gottschalk. Chicago, 1980.

BIOGRAPHICAL AND CRITICAL WORKS

Bely, A. *Gogol's Mastery.* Moscow, 1934. Translated by Robert Maguire. Ann Arbor, Mich., 1981.

Belinsky, V. G. "Letter to N. V. Gogol." In *Belinsky, Chernyshevsky, and Dobrolyubov.* Translated and edited by R. E. Matlaw. New York, 1962.

Driessen, F. *Gogol as a Short Story Writer.* The Hague, 1965.

Erlich, V. *Gogol.* New Haven, Conn., 1969.

Fanger, D. *The Creation of Nikolai Gogol.* Cambridge, Mass., 1977.

Gippius, V. V. *Gogol.* Moscow, 1924. Translated by Robert Maguire. Ann Arbor, Mich., 1981.

Karlinsky, S. *Gogol's Sexual Labyrinth.* Cambridge, Mass., 1977.

Maguire, R., ed. *Gogol from the Twentieth Century.* Princeton, N.J., 1974. Contains the most important essays written on Gogol in the twentieth century.

Nabokov, V. *Nikolai Gogol.* Norfolk, Conn., 1944.

Peace, R. A. *The Enigma of Gogol.* Cambridge, 1981.

Rancour-Laferriere, D. *Out from Under Gogol's Overcoat. A Psychoanalytic Study.* Ann Arbor, Mich., 1982.

Rowe, W. W. *Through Gogol's Looking Glass.* New York, 1976.

Setchkarev, V. *Gogol: His Life and Work.* New York, 1965.

Trahan, E., ed. *Gogol's "Overcoat"; An Anthology of Critical Essays.* Ann Arbor, Mich., 1982.

Woodward, J. B. *Gogol's Dead Souls.* Princeton, N.J., 1978.

BIBLIOGRAPHIES

Frantz, P. *Gogol: A Bibliography.* Ann Arbor, Mich., 1983.

RALPH E. MATLAW

ALFRED DE MUSSET

(1810–1857)

ALFRED DE MUSSET is one of that company of French authors, along with Racine, La Fontaine, Marivaux, and Verlaine, whose genius seems so intricately tied to the nature of their language as to render them inaccessible to foreign readers. Translations of such authors are scarce and unsatisfactory; manuals of world literature treat them as exotic flora whose enduring appeal to native readers is an inexplicable, even quaint, ethnological phenomenon.

Under the dictates of the French literary-historical establishment, these writers have been given their proper places in the Gallic pantheon. In the wake of Hippolyte Taine and Gustave Lanson, all the greater and lesser lights of French literature, from François Villon to Paul Valéry, have been assigned their positions of relative significance, influence, and importance, which literary fashion is unlikely to change. The self-reference and self-containment of this most institutionalized of all national literary traditions may have made it difficult to situate many French writers in the larger context of European and world literature, since their significance has been defined in terms of their own historical lineage.

This problem is complicated, in Musset's case, by the fluctuating and ambiguous fortunes of his work within the French establishment. During his lifetime—not as short as the precocious date of his greatest works tends to make one think (he was almost as young as Arthur Rimbaud when he wrote them, but ten years older at his death)—his reputation varied considerably, starting with the succès de scandale of his first volume of ultra- or pseudo-romantic poetry, the *Contes d'Espagne et d'Italie (Tales of Spain and Italy,* 1829), when he was only nineteen; through the dismal fiasco of his first produced play, *La nuit vénitienne (The Venetian Night),* the following year; the relative critical and popular success of the first volume of *Un spectacle dans un fauteuil (Armchair Theater)* in 1832; followed in 1834 by the almost total silence that greeted the more important second volume, which contained Musset's four best plays, today considered the backbone of nineteenth-century French repertory theater. Once Musset parted company with his friends and colleagues in the romantic movement—Victor Hugo, Charles Augustin Sainte-Beuve, Alphonse de Lamartine—who suspected him of satirizing them in the *Tales* and were dismayed by his independent pronouncements in subsequent poems and essays, his poetry was attacked and he was damned as a renegade by both classicists and romantics. His one completed novel, *La confession d'un enfant du siècle (Confessions of a Child of the Century,* 1836), was written as an act of self-accusation, and of altruistic justification of his mistress, George Sand, after their notorious adventure in Venice (the subject of further dispute in such works as George Sand's *Elle et lui* [*She and He,* 1859], his brother Paul's *Lui et elle* [*He and She,* 1859], and Charles Maurras's *Les amants de Venise* [*The Lovers of Venice,* 1902]). Its introductory chapter, which seeks to generalize Musset's personal amorous misfortunes on the level of zeitgeist, helped to turn the novel into a credo for a generation of young Frenchmen; but Musset came to regret the success of the work, which was in a genre for which he had little sympathy, and which perpetuated the legend of an era of his life that he would have gladly forgotten.

The series of major poems, written between 1835 and 1837 and dominated by the four well known in *Nuits (Nights),* achieved success with readers. It did not, however, establish him as a major poet in the eyes of contemporary literary arbiters like Sainte-Beuve, who in 1842 still relegated him to the second rank among his generation. His intensive and varied output during the 1830's included a dozen plays, a novel, seven or eight major poems, a large body of occasional verse, and newspaper articles and essays on a variety of subjects, including art and drama criticism. But all this work did not prevent contemporaries, perhaps deceived by his elegant and aristocratic mien, from thinking of Musset as a dilettante, despite his solid culture and his lofty definition of the poet's art; so that it seemed only natural to speak of his "paresse" (idleness) during the 1840's, when Musset's declining physical and mental health, compounded by self-censorship and a growing dependence on alcohol, led to a radical decrease in his literary production. His major source of literary revenue during this period, two series of short stories entitled *Nouvelles (Short Stories;* anthologized in 1848) and *Contes (Tales,* 1854), were undertaken strictly as cash propositions, to be cut off as soon as contractual obligations were fulfilled. Belated recognition of his talents as a dramatist came with the staging of his brilliant but minor comedy, *Un caprice (Caprice),* at the Comédie Française in 1847; but success centered on his lesser theater works at the expense of his more serious and original crea-

tions, thus consolidating his reputation as a miniaturist. Even consecration as an "Immortal" by the Académie Française in 1852 came only after a series of humiliating defeats, at a time when the poet's almost definitive creative silence made the honor sadly ironic.

After Musset's death in 1857, the remarkable year that saw publication of Gustave Flaubert's *Madame Bovary* and Charles Baudelaire's *Les fleurs du mal (Flowers of Evil),* his fortunes with the critical establishment continued to seesaw. His reputation as a lyric poet prospered well into the first quarter of the twentieth century; then it began a relative decline, which has continued into the present. Whereas he was once considered one of the pillars of the romantic lyric, along with Lamartine, Hugo, and Alfred de Vigny, the eclipse of that movement by the symbolists and their successors led to depreciation of his qualities of spontaneity and eloquence. His lone novel, the *Confessions,* lost out to the major currents of realism and naturalism, eventually reaching the status of a literary-historical curiosity. His art and literary criticism could not bear comparison with the weightier and more influential writings of a Baudelaire. Only his theatrical works began, from the time of his death, a gradual rise that has led to his instatement as the major French dramatist of the nineteenth century.

The overall curve of Alfred de Musset's creative life, as well as some of the extravagant or glamorous vicissitudes of his personal story, led to his becoming one of the great literary myths of his time. Like Lord Byron, Rimbaud, and Georg Büchner (or Wolfgang Amadeus Mozart, Franz Schubert, and Frédéric Chopin), he provided his century with a specific model of precocious, self-destructive genius: in Musset's case, that of the elegant and beautiful poet who survived his own creative "death" at the age of thirty, living on as a pathetic shadow vainly attempting through dandyism to maintain his dignity against the inroads of illness and alcohol. The nineteenth-century cult of genius and the individual did much to enshrine and perpetuate that image. Indeed many of Musset's early works show a remarkable prescience, evoking heroes who commit deliberate or involuntary suicide out of disappointed idealism, or survive disillusion as empty shells of their younger selves. That, perhaps, is why the Musset myth had a particular appeal to the youth of his and succeeding generations: more than those who died young, at the prime of their creative genius, the poet seemed to represent the common fate of youthful passion in a world where banal survival was more to be feared than death.

Few authors, even in that romantic generation, conceived of more varied forms in more diversified literary genres for the mythologizing of self. The historical personae into which Musset projected himself range the centuries and nations, with a special bias toward the Italian Renaissance. His alter egos are to be found in the heroes of novels, short stories, dramas, and narrative poems, and in the dialogic voice of lyrics: as dandies and debauchees; as dual personalities, failed painters, and an illustrious regicide; as a Bavarian court jester; as a romantic poet arguing, not always successfully, with a passionate, very feminine muse.

Yet unlike Byron, who furnished one of his earliest literary models, or Alexander Pushkin, that other provider of magnificent personal myths, Musset did not live a life marked by extensive travel, multiple passions, and generous commitment to political causes. Indeed, the passage in which he formulates the most objectified and generalized of his personal myths—the first chapter of the *Confessions*—delineates his protagonist in the context of a generation that was born too late for heroics, following the disintegration of the Napoleonic dream: or in the words of an earlier narrative poem, "Rolla" (1833), "Je suis venu trop tard dans un monde trop vieux" (I came too late into a world too old). Certainly the opportunities for Mesolóngions and duels of honor (Musset had only negligible experi-

ence of the latter) were far from absent. But either the spirit of the age or, more likely, the character of the poet was likely to drain such gestures of conviction. Even the mock-heroics of the romantics' "battle" for possession of the Comédie Française, immortalized in Théophile Gautier's account of the 1830 premiere of Hugo's *Hernani*, found the young Musset a somewhat skeptical observer, despite his recent ties to the Cénacle coterie, which led the fight to establish the supremacy of romantic drama over the reigning neoclassicists.

The one exceptional circumstance of Musset's life, uniting as it did travel, passion, adventure, and even, to an extent, political commitment, marked Musset's character and work once and for all. It also made a profound impression on his public, critics, and biographers. The period of approximately twenty-one months, from the summer of 1833 to the spring of 1835, during which the poet and his mistress, George Sand, carried on their tumultuous, complex, and, finally, rather perplexing love affair, represents a brief passage in Musset's life, for all its intensity. The actual "drame de Venise" itself, although it concentrated considerable passion and suffering on both sides, lasted less than four months; from 12 December 1833 (the date of their joint departure from Paris) to 29 March 1834 (Musset's departure from Venice). Even if it had a deeper and more enduring impact on the poet's life than on George Sand's, which was longer, more continuously productive, and more eventful, the "drama" should not be endowed with more significance than it can bear in the otherwise circumscribed life of an aristocratic Parisian bachelor. If that life included the prescribed number and variety of love affairs, the vicissitudes of rising and descending fortunes, the love or friendship of some celebrated and interesting contemporary figures, and two or three moments of unalloyed glory, it was due primarily to his great personal attractiveness and charm, the noble origins and manners that opened many doors, and above all the remarkable creative endowment he fulfilled at certain stages of his life. What is most striking is the degree to which Musset's life and career were set in salon interiors, the occasional country house, and the poet's own apartments—especially when we compare him with the restless sightseers of his time: Chateaubriand, Stendhal, Mérimée, Nerval, Gautier, Baudelaire, even Flaubert, the "hermit of Croisset." Events, for the most part, were private, internal, psychological—and Parisian, in a socially quite limiting sense.

Musset was born in Paris on 11 December 1810. On his father's side he belonged to an old, though not particularly important, noble house from the region of Vendôme. There were family connections with Pierre de Ronsard and Joachim du Bellay, the principal poets of the sixteenth-century *Pléiade*. More recently, Musset's father had published a monumental study and edition of the works of Jean Jacques Rousseau. His mother's family, the Guyot-Desherbiers, were bourgeois magistrates: they too claimed literary connections and modest eighteenth-century poetic and dramatic talents. Young Alfred, endowed by nature with beauty, wit, and charm, albeit with a certain weakness of the nerves, seems to have become the focus of his family's adoration. His older brother, Paul, would later carry fraternal veneration to the point of marrying one of Alfred's most devoted mistresses, Aimée d'Alton, after the poet's death, so that they might consecrate themselves to fostering his literary reputation. From 1819 to 1827, Musset pursued highly successful classical studies at the Lycée Henri IV, which culminated in the second prize for Latin philosophical dissertation in the national examination.

Like so many other literary and artistic figures of nineteenth-century France, where paternal expectations often reflected bourgeois pragmatism, the aristocratic Musset had to undertake studies with a view toward a "serious" career: first law, then medicine, both soon abandoned for the more attractive pursuit of music, painting, and literature. In 1828, at the age of eighteen, he achieved his first literary success with a rather free translation of Thomas de Quincey's *Confessions of an English Opium-Eater*, which had appeared in England seven years earlier; Musset's interpolations into the English text include some personal recollections of the dissections that helped to turn him definitively away from the medical profession. Through his friend and classmate Paul Foucher, the brother-in-law of Victor Hugo, the young poet published his first poem, "Un rêve" ("A Dream"), in a Dijon periodical that same year. More significantly, Foucher introduced him to the Cénacle, the romantic literary salon that met at the house of Charles Nodier, librarian of the Arsenal, and that came to be increasingly dominated by Hugo.

This post-baccalaureate year, so important in Musset's literary development, also saw the formative stages of two decisive aspects of his life: his association with the elegant and wealthy *viveur* Alfred Tattet, whose friendship lasted through wild parties and post-sentimental depressions, until Tattet's marriage and "retirement" some fifteen years later; and Musset's first, somewhat mysterious love affairs. The identity of the women in question is still not entirely clear, but some experience of betrayal seems to have left a deep imprint in the heart of the impressionable young man attempting to play the role of precocious roué and debauchee. The theme of that disillusionment would reappear throughout the poet's productive years, most pathetically and directly in the "Nuit d'octobre" ("October Night," 1837): "Honte à toi qui la première/ M'a appris la trahison" (Shame on you who first/ Taught me betrayal).

Musset's relationship with the Cénacle was a shifting and ambivalent one. The eighteen-year-old Alfred was at first only too happy to be allowed to dance, play cards, flirt, and listen to the conversation of such leading romantic figures as Nodier, Hugo, Vigny, Émile and Antony Deschamps, and Lamartine. He seems to have impressed the others as a remarkably handsome and graceful young man: Lamartine spoke later of his "dreamy eyes, two stars rather than two flames. Resplendent in his youthful grace, his strong Byronic chin, his broad forehead molded by genius, and his head of blond hair giving him the appearance of a young god." But despite occasional readings of his verse or dramatic scenes, little seems to have prepared the Cénacle regulars for the shock created by Musset's first published volume, the *Tales of Spain and Italy.*

This collection of dramatic, narrative, and lyric verse, which appeared at the end of 1829, could be taken either as a brilliant application of some of the romantics' most daring innovations, or a reductio ad absurdum of them. The one-act verse drama "Les marrons du feu" (the first example of Musset's penchant for proverbial titles; it translates as "Irons from the Fire") features a lecherous Italian priest who murders the hero, his noble rival (himself an offhand killer), at the behest of the hero's jealous dancer-mistress, la Camargo, only to be frustrated at the end by the latter's capricious refusal to be the priest's mistress. In keeping with proclaimed romantic prosodic doctrine, alexandrine verse lines are rhythmically dislocated and fragmented (once into as many as five dialogue exchanges); the vocabulary encompasses such uncommon expressions as "sow" and "club-foot" (in rhyme position), "belly-bearer," "snore," and a dancer's "beautiful breasts that wander about deliriously"; the lesson of the play is stated at the end with a cynical pirouette by the clerical voluptuary: "I've killed my friend, I've earned hell-fire, I've gotten stains on my doublet, and I've been dismissed. That's the moral of this comedy."

The remainder of the volume demonstrated equal bravura and mastery of fashionable poetic modes. "Don Paez" mingles narrative and dramatic verse in a story of betrayal and bloody revenge following a violent love scene in an exotic Spanish setting. Perhaps the greatest scandal greeted Musset's "Ballade à la lune" ("Ballad to the Moon"), a brilliant pastiche of the revolutionary verse forms pioneered by Hugo in his own "medieval" *Odes et Ballades* (1826; 1828). Readers were taken aback by flippant references to the moon, traditionally a chaste and cold goddess, as "the dot of an i over the yellow steeple," as a worm-eaten crescent, and as a one-eyed peeping tom watching a newly married couple racketing through their conjugal duties. A long, loose-jointed narrative poem, "Mardoche," which Musset added at the end of the volume at the request of his publisher to fill it out, mingles a story of urban adultery with relaxed, Byronic reflections on any number of more or less related topics drawn from Parisian life of the 1820's. Typically, it was not clear whether the nineteen-year-old poet intended more insult to the classical traditionalists, by the liberties taken with form, content, and morality; or his romantic comrades, by the strong hints of parody and mockery of their aesthetics and ethics on nearly every page of the volume. And this ambiguity was to persist and grow more acute in the subsequent works of Musset, turning him into a problematic literary quantity.

Otherwise it is difficult to view the *Tales of Spain and Italy* as more than an earnest of future accomplishment. More blatantly "romantic" in form and content (in the quasi-political sense the term connoted) than anything Musset would produce in his maturity, its subjects were more exotic, more objective, and less related to his deepest moral and personal preoccupations. The volume served to single him out among his contemporaries, for better or for worse; it created expectations that in some ways his subsequent evolution as a writer was bound to disappoint. But even if Musset had produced nothing else afterward, the *Tales* would have sufficed to mark him as one of the extraordinary phenomena of a highly eventful period in the arts.

It is perhaps not surprising if the years from 1830 to 1832 were ones of relative silence for Musset, just turned twenty. Indeed after his succès de scandale it was probably important to the development of his talent for him not to continue on the showy path he had initiated.

On the one hand, the decided bent for dramatic organization that several of the *Tales* had evidenced needed further nurturing, even though the romantic theater of the time, under Hugo's leadership, was heading toward even greater doses of an exoticism and melodrama it was just as well for Musset to avoid. On the other hand, the poet's talent for pastiche gave proof of his mastery of language and form, but further intellectual and emotional growth was needed for Musset to establish himself as an original writer.

In verse, this period of reflection was marked most significantly by two medium-length poems (120 to 140 lines each), which Musset published in the recently founded *Revue de Paris* where, along with the later *Revue des deux mondes,* a great deal of his production was henceforth to appear. The fragment "Les secrètes pensées de Rafael, gentilhomme francais" ("The Secret Thoughts of Rafael, a French Gentleman") appeared on 4 July 1830. It was a declaration of artistic independence, addressed to the critics who had misread the *Tales of Spain and Italy,* the "authorized chemists of good taste, sublime distillers" who had taken his "Ballade à la lune" seriously. He sent ironic greetings to both sides of the literary battlefield: the "young champions of a somewhat elderly cause,/ Close-shaved classicists, with your cherry-red faces,/ Bearded Romantics, with your pallid countenances." But personally he preferred to withdraw from the fray: "A veteran, I sit down on my punctured drum./ Racine, encountering Shakespeare on my table,/ Falls asleep beside Boileau, who has forgiven them both." This truce between the French and English dramatists who had lent their names to the opposing literary camps under the aegis of Nicolas Boileau, the seventeenth-century arbiter of neoclassical taste, affirmed Musset's refusal henceforth to be counted among the ranks of the Cénacle. The rest of the poem confirmed the poet's adherence to a social and cultural elite: a curiously prescient, though defiant affirmation, just weeks prior to the revolutionary "trois glorieuses" of July 1830, which ended the Restoration and put the "bourgeois" king Louis Philippe on the throne of a constitutional monarchy, thus redefining the status quo and consolidating power in the hands of the wealthy few.

"Les voeux stériles" (Sterile Vows), published three and a half months later in October, reflects both the intervening political turmoil and a maturation of the poet's artistic and moral personality. It is a bitter meditation on the role of the poet in times of social and political upheaval, torn between the temptation to action and the demands of personal integrity. The poet evokes the prostitution inherent in the poetic métier, "Since it is your business to make a prostitute/ Of your soul, and since everything, joy or sorrow,/ Ceaselessly demands release from your heart." All that he can offer to a crass and unfeeling world is his own self: "There exists one sole being/ That I can know in its entirety and constantly,/ About which my judgment can at least bear witness,/ Only one! . . . I despise it.—And that being is me." But if the artist is a "merchant" and art a "business," it is also a destiny incurred by genius. Though the poet may feel himself to be an exile from the Golden Age, when art and society were one— from a legendary Greece or Renaissance Italy where creation was not prostitution—he will drink the bitter cup, like Vigny's romantic Christ, and follow his Calvary to the fatal end: "Mais si loin que la haine/ De cette destinée aveugle et sans pudeur/ Ira, j'y veux aller.— J'aurai du moins le coeur/ De la mener si bas que la honte l'en prenne." (But however far my hatred/ Of that blind and shameless destiny/ May go, I will go, too.—I will at least have the courage/ To take it so far down that it will blush for shame.)

Here, for the first time, Musset confronts the conflict between artistic and ethical idealism, and political action; like all of the romantic generation, he was to face this conflict increasingly after the 1830 revolution, up to the greater upheavals of 1848. Many of his contemporaries, like Hugo and Lamartine, would be drawn further into the political arena, identifying themselves with militant republicanism and socialism. Others, like our poet and his friend Vigny, would find themselves more and more dismayed at the price in truth and purity exacted by political commitment: that, indeed, was soon to become a major theme of Musset's monumental historical drama, *Lorenzaccio* (1834).

The evolution of Musset's dramatic imagination during this period was marked by few public manifestations, though one of them was sufficiently "scandalous" to become a significant part of the poet's myth. It was not surprising, following the critics' recognition of the dramatic flair evident in the *Tales of Spain and Italy*, that Musset was approached by theatrical producers for scripts. One of these, not published and discovered only about a century later by Maurice Allem, is of minimal interest: a sort of Gothic melodrama entitled *La quittance du diable* (The Devil's Due), based on Sir Walter Scott's *Redgauntlet* (1824); for some reason, although it was accepted early in 1830 by the Théâtre des Nouveautés, it was never actually performed.

Another play, however, *La nuit vénitienne, ou les noces de Laurette (The Venetian Night, or the Marriage of Lauretta)*, received a few performances, starting 1 December 1830, at Paris' "second theater," the Odéon. The fiasco that then took place is part of French theater legend, as well as Musset's own. Even today the real causes of the play's failure are not entirely clear. The traditional explanation—that the leading actress backed into a freshly painted green trellis with her white dress on opening night, inciting a riot of laughter and catcalls that drowned out the rest of the performance—seems more folklore than fact, and scarcely explains the magnitude and duration of the public's displeasure. A more likely reason was the recent publication of Musset's two poetic declarations of independence from the romantics, coupled with the fact that one of the play's protagonists, Ra-

zetta, was an obvious comic parody of the romantic hero typified by Hugo's Hernani: the "fatal," obsessed, violent outcast. Worse still, in Musset's play Razetta is jilted by Lauretta, despite dire threats of vengeance, in favor of the sensible princely fiancé her family has found for her, and Razetta ends up consoling himself with wine and other women, moralizing inconsequentially, "May all the follies of lovers end as joyously as mine."

It seems certain, therefore, that it was political enmity rather than the faults of the work or its production that incited a fiasco. The play itself is rather charming, opposing two sorts of lovers around its heroine, with a kind of idealized, playful, and sentimental salon dialogue, in the Marivaux tradition, which Musset was to perfect in his later comedies. Both in the parodic romantic hero and in the heroine's uncle and guardian, it anticipates the comical grotesque characters who would enliven some of his best future plays. Musset thought enough of it, despite the catastrophe of its performance, to publish it in the second volume of his *Armchair Theater*.

The principal effect of this experience was to turn Musset away from any thought of stage production until much later. Not until 1847 would another of his plays be performed on the Paris stage, initiating a belated and only partial success of his works for the theater. Meanwhile, however, he did not lose interest in drama as a literary genre. There followed a series of inconclusive experiments with dramatic verse: the Byronic drama *La coupe et les lèvres (The Cup and the Lip)* and the delightful if lightweight comedy *A quoi rêvent les jeunes filles (What Young Girls Dream About)*, which constituted the dramatic content of the first volume of *Armchair Theater*, published in 1832 (as in the case of the *Tales*, Musset was obliged to pad the slim volume with a narrative poem, "Namouna"). Musset also attempted a historical drama in prose, *André del Sarto*, whose artist-hero and themes of amorous betrayal and moral disillusionment clearly foreshadow the works to come, which he was to create within a period of months: the four great prose dramas that constitute his unique contribution to French theatrical history. But their quality is due in great part to his isolation from the imperatives and limitations inherent in the professional theater of his time, which left him able to conceive of his dramas in the freedom of his imagination and sentiment, without reference to staging necessities and conventions.

FOUR GREAT PLAYS

The suddenness with which Musset arrived at artistic maturity during his twenty-third year is one of those events from which literary legend is made. It is rendered more difficult to fathom by the uncertainties surrounding the poet's development as a man and as an intellect during the period of incubation from 1830 to 1832, coupled with the degree of his personal reserve, which made the pathetic and public events of the "drame de Venise" all the more striking. Two events in his life that had great immediate effect and far-reaching consequences certainly must have contributed powerfully to his rapid evolution: the death from cholera of his father in April 1832 (this event had both a deep emotional and, at least for a while, a financial impact on the poet's life); and especially the beginnings of his love affair with George Sand in the summer of 1833, which brought his emotions and his talent into intimate contact with a very different creative spirit, dominated by ethical commitments of a sort the poet had hitherto tended either to ignore or to treat with ironic disdain.

The sequence of events constituting the "drame de Venise" (which was only the central act of a drama extending several months before and more than a year after) can be best appreciated in the numerous biographical studies devoted to it, notably Pierre Gastinel's monumental *Le romantisme d'Alfred de Musset*, published for its centennial. It interests us for the moment mainly as the biographical matrix in which the four great dramas came into being, although the precise circumstances of their creation remain somewhat clouded compared with the details of the poet's emotional life. Only as recently as 1957 has an article by Jean Pommier securely established Musset's drafting of *Lorenzaccio* as prior (rather than subsequent) to the lovers' voyage to Italy. Exactly when work on *On ne badine pas avec l'amour (You Can't Trifle with Love)* was suspended before the trip, and then taken up again for completion following Musset's return to Paris, is matter for conjecture based primarily on the internal evidence of the text. Only *Les caprices de Marianne (The Whims of Marianne)* and *Fantasio*, published in the *Revue des deux mondes* at dates placing their composition just before and in the early stages of Musset's romance with George Sand, have spared literary historians the sort of detective work that has surrounded the other two plays. Not surprisingly, the influence of George Sand is principally evident in the two later works, both in their treatment of theme and character and in textual and structural details: *You Can't Trifle with Love* contains passages quoted almost verbatim from the novelist's letters, and *Lorenzaccio* was based originally on the elements of a dramatic sketch George Sand had made with her previous lover Jules Sandeau under the title "Une conspiration en 1537" ("A Conspiracy in 1537").

Each of these four plays is a masterpiece; but their weight and importance vary considerably, ranging from the bittersweet two-act "bluette," or sketch, *Fantasio*, to the more intense two-act comedy (with a tragic ending), *The Whims of Marianne*; the melodramatic, increasingly serious pastoral comedy (again finally tragic), *You Can't Trifle with Love*, to the monumental historical tragedy in five acts, *Lorenzaccio*.

The Whims of Marianne, set in a Neapolitan carnival atmosphere of uncertain era, tells of the attempt of Coelio, a dreamy, idealistic lover, to win the heart of Marianne, a young woman who is married to a grotesque elderly judge, Claudio. Since his efforts to speak to Marianne have failed, he enlists the aid of his friend Octave, a carefree young frequenter of wine shops and brothels who is a distant cousin of the lady and who, unlike Coelio, is never at a loss for words. As might be expected, Marianne, during a series of encounters with the go-between, ends up falling in love with Octave's easy charm and magnetism. To spite her husband who, in defense of his judicial dignity, has forbidden her to speak with the young rake, Marianne invites Octave to a rendezvous; he loyally passes the invitation on to his timid friend Coelio, and the latter is killed in an ambush arranged by the jealous Claudio with the aid of his servant, Tibia. Coelio goes voluntarily to his death believing he has been betrayed by his friend, since he hears Marianne warn the supposed Octave in the darkness to beware of her husband's trap. The final scene, by Coelio's grave, shows a bitter, empty Octave rejecting the still amorous Marianne: it was only the idealistic Coelio who could really have loved her.

The play is brilliant in its apparently free alternation of comic and passionate scenes; in its absurdly comic (and increasingly sinister) exchanges between Claudio and Tibia; in the elegant symmetry of its mirror-image presentation of the two male protagonists, Coelio and Octave, who are (as we can read in the letters of Musset and George Sand) the conflicting faces of the author's own dual personality; and in the passionate male-female confrontation between Octave and Marianne, which reaches its remarkable climax in the heated exchange of act 2, scene 1, where each is given a moment of triumphant, irrefutable logic in a verbal battle of the sexes that states the dilemma of nineteenth-century man and woman in their parallel, conflicting search for emotional fulfillment. Here it is couched in the metaphorical terms of inebriation that run through the play:

Marianne: I thought it was the same with wine as with women. Isn't a woman also a precious vessel, sealed like this crystal flagon? Doesn't she contain a gross or divine intoxication, according to her strength and her worth? And isn't there among them the wine of the common people and the tears of Christ [Octave is drinking lachryma cristi]? What a miserable heart yours must be, for your lips to teach it a lesson! You wouldn't drink the wine that common people drink; you love the women they love; the generous and poetic spirits of this golden flagon, these wonderful juices that Vesuvius' lava has fermented under its burning sun will carry you stumbling weakly into the arms of a whore. . . .

Octave: . . . How long do you think one has to court this bottle you see here to enjoy her favors? As you say, she is chock full of heavenly spirits, and the common people's wine is no more like it than a peasant is like his lord. Still, look how she surrenders herself!—I don't suppose she has received any education, she has no morals; see what a sweet girl she is! One word was enough to make her leave her convent; still covered with dust, she ran away to give me a half hour of oblivion, and to die.

The poet's mastery of dramatic form and language in a completely personal formulation of traditional materials—commedia dell'arte, Shakespeare, Marivaux, and other sources come to mind—is startling when compared with the generally derivative, fashionable, or trivial theatrical creations that preceded this work such a short time before. Those who have seen *The Whims of Marianne* in the Théâtre National Populaire productions of the 1950's by Jean Vilar, with Gérard Philipe and Geneviève Page, know how powerful and effective a stage work it can be.

Fantasio is a very different sort of play, lacking a serious love story; it is a "fantasy," as its title suggests. Based in part on the recent politically motivated marriage of Louis Philippe's daughter, Princess Louise, to King Leopold I of Belgium, the comedy is a sort of ideal revenge on reasons of state and all other serious concerns by its hero, Fantasio, a young burgher of Munich. In order to flee from his creditors, and from the tedium and banality of middle-class German life, he disguises himself as a court jester to the king of Bavaria. In this costume and free-associating persona, Fantasio succeeds in upsetting the plans to marry off the king's daughter, Elsbeth, to the stupid prince of Mantua, who, in a grotesque parody of Molière, Marivaux, and Hugo, has changed places with his own aide de camp, Marinoni, in order to win the princess' love without benefit of his rank. In the process of doing so (and indeed persuading the princess that the pretended aide de camp is ill or deranged), the prince gives a fine demented imitation of a romantic hero (again Hernani is the principle model). Fantasio completes his rout of the grotesque suitor and wins freedom for both the forlorn princess and himself by lifting the prince's wig from his head—actually Marinoni's, but princely dignity has been symbolically compromised—with a fish hook and line as the royal party passes through the castle gate. Elsbeth promises Fantasio that he can return at will to her garden when debts and ennui beset him, but only under the deforming guise of the jester.

With its evident German romantic influences (Jean Paul Richter's is particularly notable), its playfully melancholy view of life as subject to a suffocating blanket of bourgeois tedium and as random—Fantasio says to Elsbeth: "Je parle beaucoup au hasard: c'est mon plus cher confident" (I often talk with inconsequence: he's my dearest confidant)—*Fantasio* has been seen by critics like Jean Starobinski as one of the prime French examples of romantic irony. Despite its airy disdain for the serious, its apparently improvisational plot, its refusal to commit its protagonists to any such stable human institutions as marriage, statecraft, or career, the play leaves us with an overall impression of gentle sadness, expressed poetically in Fantasio's well-known exclamation: "Quelles solitudes que tous ces corps humains!" (What solitudes all these human bodies are!).

If we treat *You Can't Trifle with Love*—and it is usually so anthologized—as the third of the great quartet, it is not because of its chronological relation to *Lorenzaccio*. Though it was evidently begun at some point in the Musset-Sand affair prior to the "drame de Venise," it was the last of the four plays to be completed following Musset's return to Paris, and it was not published until July 1834, in the *Revue des deux mondes*. Critics generally agree that the first act, and the first four scenes of the second, were written before the couple's departure in December 1833: there is a verse treatment of uncertain date of the opening scene, evidently the earliest text of the play, which harks back to Musset's first dramatic experiments. But the final scene of act 2, which contains an almost textual quotation from George Sand's letter to Musset of 12 May 1834, and the entire third act were written after the traumatic Italian adventure. This genesis in two stages is apparent to any careful reader of the play, which undergoes a remarkable "sea change" at the point of its belated continuation. What had started out as an agreeably stylized pastoral in a marked eighteenth-century vein (the echoes of Musset's father's hero, Rousseau, are stronger here than in any of his other major works) turns into an ardent, darkly romantic struggle for dominance between the two main characters, leaving the others around them as bewildered as the play's readers.

The work opens with a symmetrical series of announcements to a peasant chorus by the hero's epicurean tutor, Maître Blazius, and the heroine's puritanical chaperon, Dame Pluche, of their charges' imminent return to their childhood home, a provincial French castle, after completion of their education: he, Perdican, at the University of Paris; she, Camille, in a convent. In the couple's first scene together in the salon of the baron, Perdican's father and Camille's uncle, it becomes evident that their tutors are caricatures of what the young people's education has sought to make them. The baron, with a typical Musset grotesque's love of order and symmetry, sees them as a perfect match. But Camille's convent-bred prudery does not lean her toward emotional fulfillment. As for Perdican, he is as willing to marry his childhood companion as he is to flirt with the pretty young peasant Rosette: what he has come home to seek, after his brilliant quadruple doctorate ("literature, botany, Roman law, canon law," as Blazius proudly explains to the baron), is that sweetest of all sciences, "l'oubli de ce qu'on sait" (forgetting what one knows). The baron's plans go awry; the grotesques (including the baron's confessor, Maître Bridaine) carry on a comically contrapuntal series of skirmishes parallel with the protagonists' amatory jousting.

With the final scene of act 2, however, the game and its stakes are transformed. Camille explains to Perdican that the example of a convent sister's unhappy love affair has led her to take a vow of chastity. Perdican, whose opinion she still values for some reason, professes his unwillingness to accept the justification of a life of abnegation based on vicarious experience and pride. The scene rises to an agitated climax, ending with Perdican's quotation of George Sand's words to Musset:

Farewell, Camille, go back to your convent, and when they tell you those hideous tales that have poisoned your mind, answer them this way: "All men are liars, unfaithful, false, prattling, hypocritical, proud and cowardly, despicable and sensuous; all women are treacherous, guileful, vain, indiscreet, and depraved; the world is just a bottomless sewer, in which the most formless monsters crawl and writhe on mountains of slime; but there is one holy and sublime thing in the world, the union of two of these imperfect, horrid creatures. We are often deceived in love, often wounded, and often unhappy; but we love, and when we are on the edge of our grave, we turn around to look back, and say to ourselves—I have often suffered, I was wrong at times, but I have loved. It is I who have lived, and not an artificial being created by my pride and my ennui."

From this point on, the final act is a duel between Camille and Perdican, with Rosette as unwilling pawn to their pride. Perdican intercepts a letter from Camille to her convent friend, boasting of driving him to despair. To prove his indifference, he woos the bewildered Rosette, seasoning his professions of love with high-flown eighteenth-century phrases. Camille traps Perdican into admitting his love for her, then derisively shows him the unconscious Rosette, who has fainted on overhearing them. In a spiteful reaction, Perdican vows to marry the peasant. All this turmoil and confusion has thrown the four grotesques, as well as the peasant chorus, into consternation: their remarks provide an absurd, ironic commentary on the highly charged play of the protagonists. Finally, Perdican and Camille, meeting by chance in the castle chapel where the young woman has been praying for guidance, confess their mutual love to each other. But at the moment of their union, a cry is heard from the next room: it is Rosette, for whom this second disappointment has proven fatal. Camille's closing words are: "She is dead. Farewell, Perdican!"

This metamorphosis of a wry, bucolic comedy into the most melodramatic of tragedies is probably unique in the history of the theater, and provides testimony to the effect that Musset's adventure with George Sand had on his creative processes, as well as on his emotional life. But it did not prevent the work from achieving great success—perhaps the greatest of all Musset's major dramas—on the French repertory stage, from its first performance in 1861, four years after Musset's death, until the present. Marie Bell and Pierre Fresnay were particularly admired protagonists during the 1930's; and Gérard Philipe, acting with Suzanne Flon under Jean Vilar's direction at the Théâtre National Populaire, set his inimitable mark on the character of Perdican during the 1950's. In its peculiar mixture of tragedy and comedy, exalted rhetoric and farcical puppet babbling, complex psychological analysis and caricature, fatal modern protagonists and rustic antique chorus, lovers and automatons, elegy and melodrama, it is in some ways the most perfect realization of the ideas Hugo propounded in his romantic manifesto, the preface to *Cromwell* (1827), lacking only verse and a historical subject to complete it. That is paradoxical considering Musset's estrangement from the main line of romantic dogma and his intense desire for independence from what was happening on the Parisian stage. But it was precisely his independence that allowed him to take the liberties permissible in ''armchair theater'' that were unavailable to those writing for production under existing stage conditions: proof of this lies in the fact that when Musset prepared some of these plays for later production, he deliberately set about ''regularizing'' and bowdlerizing them.

These qualities of freedom and originality are even more apparent in the last of the quartet, *Lorenzaccio*. This is a play that was so far beyond the capacities of the mid-century French (or any contemporary) stage that it only reached production—in a gravely mutilated and simplified form—in 1896, more than sixty years after its publication and forty years after the author's death. Even that production came about only through one of Sarah Bernhardt's peculiar whims: she wanted to add Lorenzo to her gallery of male roles, which included Hamlet. This had the unforeseeable further effect of marking it thenceforth a transvestite role, a tradition that (fostered by the hero's apparent sexual ambiguity) continued on the Paris stage through 1945, when Marguerite Jamois played it in Gaston Baty's production. Only in 1948, with Pierre Vaneck as Lorenzo, was a new tradition started. But once again, it was Gérard Philipe who defined the role anew; he played it under Jean Vilar at the Théâtre National Populaire in a 1952 production that brought the entire

original text to the stage for the first time and initiated a series of revivals that have made the play a mainstay of the European repertory theater.

There is little in Musset's previous dramatic writing to prepare us for the dimensions and complexity of *Lorenzaccio*: five acts, thirty-eight tableaux with constant change of scenery, scenes ranging from monologues to large crowd ensembles, twenty-six characters, and dozens of extras. The action carries the shifting and fragmentation of the three other plays to a new extreme (Shakespearean in inspiration, it can be seen as a possible model for Büchner's *Danton's Death* [1835], as *You Can't Trifle with Love* was for his *Leonce and Lena* [1850]). It consists of three separate, converging plots, all tied to one greater dominant theme: the conspiracy to overthrow Alexander de' Medici's tyranny over Florence in 1536. More than any other work of Musset's, *Lorenzaccio* is imbued with the political ferment of the author's times, so that we constantly feel, behind the historical setting the author drew from George Sand's sketch and Benedetto Varchi's *Storia Fiorentina* (1527–1538; published 1721), the insistent analogical presence of current events: particularly the 1830 revolution.

The central action of the play is the attempt of the protagonist, Lorenzo de' Medici (''Lorenzaccio'': the suffix is pejorative) to foment a revolution that will reestablish the Florentine republic and liberate it from its foreign dominators by killing his cousin, Duke Alexander. In order to win the latter's confidence while awaiting the best time for the deed, Lorenzo has become Alexander's companion in debauchery, his pimp, and, it is suggested strongly, his paramour. To throw everyone off his scent, he feigns weakness and cowardice: a striking early scene shows him fainting at the sight of a sword when challenged to a duel by a man whom he has insulted. Furthermore, to strengthen his intimacy with Alexander, Lorenzo has informed on some of those same libertarian plotters whose aid he will need in order to reinstitute the republic once Alexander has been killed; a powerful scene shows republican exiles leaving Florence, cursing the city and Lorenzo. Thus when at the climax of the fourth act Lorenzo finally murders his cousin, the brief moment of sensual exaltation he experiences (he calls it his "wedding day") soon gives way to disillusion, since none of the influential people of Florence are willing to follow his initiative. The play ends with Lorenzo's sordid murder in Venice by men anxious to claim the price on his head, and with the ubiquitous, cynical Cardinal Cibo having the new duke of Florence, a self-effacing "bourgeois" ruler reminiscent of France's Louis Philippe, swear renewed obedience to the pope and to Emperor Charles V.

There are two major subplots; one centers on the marquise Cibo (the cardinal's sister-in-law), whose attempt to transform the brutal Alexander into an enlightened prince through an adulterous love affair ends in his boredom at her tedious sermons and her tawdry reconciliation with a complaisant husband who prefers to ignore conjugal dishonor. The other follows the idealistic, scholarly Philippe Strozzi, who refuses, once he has encountered personal tragedy when his beloved daughter is poisoned, to take responsibility for leadership of the principal families' conspiracy against Alexander, thus dooming the attempt to reestablish the old oligarchy to failure.

In the central scene of the drama (act 3, scene 3), Lorenzo unmasks himself for the first time to his friend, Philippe, and to the audience; and in doing so, he delineates the moral problems inherent in the play—and indeed in all Musset's dramatic works of this period. Lorenzo, as a young man fresh from his classical studies, has resolved one night in the Roman colosseum that he would be a new Brutus and rid his country of one of its tyrants. But having chosen Alexander and finding himself under the obligation to embrace his life-style, he has gradually been himself transformed into a pleasure-loving, vice-ridden creature. In addition, Lorenzo's activities as

procurer and go-between have shown him the fawning, passively vile faces of his victims, who are unwilling or unable to find the courage to resist, and thus led him to disillusionment as to the potential beneficiaries of his act. Finally, the "mask of vice," as he terms it, in sticking to him and gradually becoming his real face, has made it impossible for any potential allies in moral revolt to recognize him as one of them. Thus has the need to adapt the ideal of a Brutus to the reality of a new Caesar (or Tarquin, since both Brutuses are evoked) led to corruption and the impossibility of any effective action.

There is a current of disillusion and moral bankruptcy running through the play at all levels of its complex structure. A pair of merchants comment recurrently on the events taking place among the aristocracy, but their complaints and analyses remain merely "bavardage," the willingness to talk without doing anything that Lorenzo sees as the core of human nature. Lorenzo himself corrupts those around him, sardonically making two "liberal" manufacturers accept favors from the duke, whom they have just been attacking verbally. A pair of scholarly poets speak pompously of their sonnets, which after celebrating first Alexander and then the incipient republic end up singing the praises of the new duke. An idealistic young artist, whom Lorenzo engages to paint Alexander's portrait stripped to the waist so that he can steal the duke's chain-mesh undergarment prior to stabbing him, forgets his patriotic love of his "mother" Florence and takes fright at the cynical, violent talk among Alexander and his henchmen. Philippe Strozzi's son, Pierre, abandons the Florentine cause, out of spite at the refusal of the others to follow him instead of his father, and goes to join a traditional enemy of Florence, the king of France. With all its prescient evocation of foreign domination, internecine strife and intrigue, cynicism and moral deliquescence, it is not surprising that *Lorenzaccio* suddenly took on a new relevance in 1945 after the Nazi occupation of Paris, when Gaston Baty's production achieved the first total success for the play; nor that a remarkable Czech production, which Otomar Krejca directed in Prague shortly after the Russian occupation in 1968, attempted to point up the play's relevance and yet attenuate some of its universal pessimism by strengthening the will to action and resistance of some of the minor figures, such as the artist. Coincidentally, that Czech production involved a most innovative and imaginative solution of the monumental problem of the transformation scenes by using portable, semi-abstract properties, shifted by the members of the large cast in rapidly choreographed movements.

These four plays, forming the core of the second volume of *Armchair Theater* brought out in August 1834, attracted less attention than did Musset's previously published books. Only a very few sympathetic readers, like Gautier and Hippolyte Fortoul, appreciated the originality of these works (Gautier called *Lorenzaccio* ''an admirable dramatic study which no master would disavow, a magnificent philosophical study, of a terrible and harrowing comic character''). More than any of Musset's preceding or subsequent works, they expressed his psychological and ethical preoccupations: the difficulty of love and the insurmountable barriers between men, and between men and women; the conflict of thought and action and of art and life; the inevitable corruption of the ideal, the tedium of existence in a bourgeois world, and the struggle of the artist's imagination to survive; friendship and betrayal, the conflict between youth and age, and the inexorable destruction of beauty and hope by time. If Musset's later dramatic works no longer so deeply reflected his troubled, inquiring mind and feelings, that was no doubt due in part to the lack of response to his worthiest efforts in the genre, adding to the bitterness of his one experience in the theater. The aftershocks of the ''drame de Venise,'' extending over the next several years, tended to impel him toward a more intimate genre,

the lyric, as well as to the peculiar apologetics of his lone autobiographical novel, *Confessions of a Child of the Century*. For whatever reason, when he returned to dramatic writing, as early as mid-1835 (with the minor romantic comedy *La quenouille de Barberine* [*Barberine's Distaff*]), it was with a different, more superficial commitment to the genre; and from that point until he wrote his last stage work, *Carmosine*, in 1850, although several of his comedies from the period have remained highly stageworthy and viable, he produced nothing comparable to his masterpieces.

These later plays include, principally: *Barberine's Distaff*, based on a tale of Matteo Bandello, which extolls the virtues of common sense and marital fidelity in a medieval Bohemian setting; *Le chandelier (The Candle-Bearer)*, written in late 1835, in which the young hero, Fortunio, a law clerk, after unwittingly playing the role of screen for the amatory affairs of his elderly master's young wife, ends up by replacing her soldier-lover in her affections; *Il ne faut jurer de rien (Never Say Never)*, written in mid-1836, which pits Valentin, a worldly-wise young man bent on saving his bachelorhood, against both a rich uncle who is determined to see him married and a guileless young girl, Cécile, whose innocent good sense sees through his attempts to prove that she can be seduced like any other woman: the ''rake'' ends up gladly surrendering his freedom to his ''victim''; *Caprice*, from mid-1837, a one-act comedy in which a wandering husband is brought back to his loving, devoted wife by the wiles of the shrewd, good-humored woman he has flirted with; *Il faut qu'une porte soit ouverte ou fermée (You Can't Have It Both Ways* or, literally, a Door Must Be Either Open or Shut), written in late 1845, which involves a count and a marquise, alone together in the latter's empty salon on a rainy day, who finally come to an understanding about the man's intentions after a good deal of charming idle chatter and misunderstanding: it is marriage that he seeks and she requires;

and *Carmosine,* a sentimental fairy tale commissioned in 1850 by a newspaper editor, more or less as a gesture of charity to the financially hard-pressed, increasingly idle poet: based on a tale from Boccaccio's *Decameron* (1348–1353), it tells of a young girl's hopeless love for King Pedro of Aragon and of Queen Constance's restoration of the girl to her true lover, and to health. It can be seen, even from these brief synopses, that the thematics of these "mature" plays have a marked discontinuity from the four masterpieces, tending toward a reconciliation with the world and with middle-class virtues that is reflected in their uniformly happy endings. It is no accident if these plays, with their brilliant sense of salon dialogue, their appeal to generally approved sentiments (even *The Candle-Bearer* shows the triumph of youthful ardor over military arrogance—and the husband *is* old), and their reassuring world view, were the first of Musset's dramas to achieve success in the theater, displacing the major works there until after the poet's death.

THE "DRAME DE VENISE" AND THE CONFESSIONS

The period from 1834 to 1836, following the "drame de Venise," was certainly the most emotionally turbulent for Musset, and biographically vexing for scholars, of the writer's entire life. After a series of catastrophic events, of which the accounts are confusing or contradictory owing to the conflicting viewpoints and interests of the witnesses—principally Musset, George Sand, and their respective friends—Musset, upon his return to Paris and a restorative cure in Baden-Baden, sought to recover the relative moral and psychological equilibrium he had known prior to his adventure with the novelist. Both the peculiarly exalted, febrile quality of the poet's letters to his former mistress (with whom he was to go through several stormy periods of reconciliation before their final, painful split) and the

diary George Sand herself kept during this time testify to the extraordinary effect of the experience on both of them. In the long run, it was the older, emotionally more stable, strong-willed, and industrious Sand who recovered more lastingly and completely from their debilitating relationship. Musset, although he went on to other adventures, seems either to have lost some quality essential to his balance and self-esteem or discovered a serious flaw in his psychological makeup, a flaw that contributed to what was clearly, by 1840, a decline in his personal and creative capacities. Between 1834 and that time, however, the spiritual fever and restlessness that immediately followed the "drame de Venise" resulted in the production of some of Musset's most remarkable work: the part of his oeuvre in fact that, until the establishment of his drama as the core of his enduring reputation, was most widely read and perhaps most influential. These were the autobiographical novel *Confessions of a Child of the Century,* and the series of four lyric poems known as the *Nights.*

The project of writing the *Confessions* dates from very shortly after Musset's return to Paris from Venice (he spoke of it in a letter dated 30 April 1834 to George Sand, who was still there), although most of the writing seems to have been done during the spring and summer of 1835. From the beginning, the aim of the project was clearly more apologetic than literary: Musset wanted to give an "official" version of the events and the emotions surrounding the "drame de Venise" in response to some of the rumors and slanders that had already started to circulate before his return. Most particularly, and surprisingly in view of the later tensions between the two lovers and their respective camps, Musset sought to "raise an altar" to his former (and at various occasions during the novel's genesis, reinstated) mistress, to exculpate her from accusations of betrayal, and to take the burden of responsibility for their painful separation on himself. It was only this "altruistic" project that seems to have permitted him to persevere in the completion of a novel he was to regret undertaking; whereas his two other attempts in this alien genre (a *Roman par lettres,* or "Epistolary Novel," and *Le poète déchu,* "The Fallen Poet") were abandoned well before his literary decline.

Since the autobiographical element in Musset's nonlyric work, although insistent and important, is generally transformed by a process of historical disguise, stylization, or fragmentation (and even in the *Nights* we must not undervalue the depersonalization wrought by the poet's dramatic mise-en-scène), we must not look in the *Confessions* for a literal account of his love affair with the novelist. Though it was clear to all his readers just who the main characters of the novel represented, names, places, events, occupations, and nationalities were modified almost beyond recognition; and, given the poet's aim of praising George Sand if need be at his own expense, so were important aspects of the two leading characters and those surrounding them. A modern reader, without the key that biographical exegesis gives, could be excused for failing to notice that the *Confessions* really has to do with the poet's love for a female novelist, their ill-fated voyage to Italy, some turbulent goings-on in Venice, and the poet's return to France and to a sporadically interrupted recovery.

It is therefore advisable to outline here the biographical events from which the novel took its rise. Musset and George Sand met at a literary dinner in June 1833, became lovers toward the end of July, went on a first excursion together in mid-August to the forest of Fontainebleau, where the poet underwent some troubling hallucinations while walking in the gorge of Franchard, and left for Italy on 9 December, after Sand had won his mother's reluctant consent by promising to take care of her son. They traveled a part of the way with Stendhal, who was heading for his consulate at Civitavecchia; they stopped at Genoa and Florence, and they arrived in Venice on 30 January 1834. Although George Sand had suffered more than her lover from the usual travelers' complaints along the way and upon their arrival in Venice, leaving Musset to carry on the sightseeing and a certain amount of carousing by himself, it was Musset who soon became seriously ill with what has been diagnosed as a form of typhoid fever with nervous complications. The poet had alternating periods of violent delirium and complete exhaustion that required constant surveillance. Fearing for his life, his mistress called in a young Venetian doctor, Pietro Pagello: it was thanks to his ministrations and to George Sand's tireless devotion that Musset was able to pull through, but it was several weeks before the fever was conquered, and weeks more before the poet was strong enough to depart alone for Paris, on 29 March. Meanwhile, there had occurred some now famous incidents: the teacup from which both George Sand and Pagello had drunk, espied by Musset in one of his early moments of lucidity; a letter that the poet surprised his mistress writing, and that she threw out the window to keep him from reading; Musset's morbid fear of being committed for insanity by his mistress and the doctor; and the parting blessing the poet gave George Sand and Pagello, convinced by them that their nascent love had remained platonic. This was the basic material on which Musset's analysis of his affair and a good part of the plot of the novel were to be based, conceived as the latter was during the period between Musset's return to Paris and his discovery in November 1834, thanks to Pagello's confession to Tattet of the facts of George Sand's amorous relationship with the doctor in Venice during Musset's convalescence. Elements of the couple's subsequent reconciliations and breakups were to complicate further the seething brew of emotional material, but the major creative impulse came from the events preceding Musset's return from Venice and his desire to cast them in a light favorable to George Sand.

How strong that desire was can be judged by

the overwrought style and tone of his letter to her of August 1834:

> I will not die without writing my book, about me and you (you, especially); no, my beautiful, holy fiancée, you will not lie down in the cold earth without its knowing whom it has borne [the robust George Sand outlived her young lover by twenty years]. No, no, I swear by my youth and my genius, nothing will grow from your grave but spotless lilies. I will affix on it, with these very hands, your epitaph in a marble purer than the statues of our ephemeral glories. Posterity will repeat our names like those of the immortal lovers who have but one [name] between them, Romeo and Juliet, Héloïse and Abelard.

What is remarkable is that the project defined here, still in the feverish aftermath of the "drame," with its adolescent exaltation of the other and its self-abasement, was carried through basically unchanged following the revelations, deceptions, and final separations of late 1834 and early 1835. It may be that once the personal motivations that first pressed for the novel's creation ceased to exert their original force, more strictly literary ones took over, pushing Musset's imagination in the same generous, self-negating direction. Certainly the line of "confessional" novels stemming from Goethe's *Werther* (1774) and Rousseau's *Julie, ou la nouvelle Héloïse* (1761), which in Musset's day had come to include Chateaubriand's *René* (1802), Étienne Senancour's *Obermann* (1804), Benjamin Constant's *Adolphe* (1816), and Sainte-Beuve's *Volupté* (1834)—curiously, all these works tended to be their authors' primary venture in the genre—was illuminated by a similar quasi-masochistic light reflected backward from some sort of final conversion.

The hero of the *Confessions*, an idle young dilettante named Octave (like the hero of the *The Whims of Marianne*) who, like Musset, has abandoned legal and medical studies, discovers one evening that his mistress and a close friend are lovers. (Musset uses the circumstances of his own similar discovery at an earlier age: bending down at table to pick up a fork, he espies his beloved's leg entwined with his friend's.) Octave brutally casts off his mistress, fights a duel with his friend, and tries to drown his dejection in drink. But despite the worldly-wise sermons of his comrade-in-pleasure Desgenais (modeled after Tattet), he is unable to forget this betrayal of love and friendship, to take life's joys as they offer themselves. Desgenais takes charge of him, leading him into places where facile pleasure can be found or bought. But this life of debauchery succeeds only in draining and depressing Octave. The women he encounters inspire momentary desire and then pity or disgust. In the midst of frenetically animated company, he feels nothing but solitude.

One day, informed of his father's ill health, Octave goes to join him in the country, only to find his father has already died. This shock has a profound effect on the young man, who decides to spend the summer at his country home communing with nature and his father's memory. For the first time in his life, he begins to feel virtuous and contented.

During an evening walk, he encounters Brigitte Pierson, a young widow several years older than himself, taking care of a dying peasant woman in a humble cottage. She is known to the country folk as Brigitte la Rose, for her good works. Octave goes from admiration to love of the young woman. She resists his growing passion, first leaving on a short trip, then asking him to undertake a longer one. But on his return, Brigitte becomes Octave's mistress. At first their mutual love is a source of intense satisfaction and well-being. Gradually, however, with the intervention of bystanders like a jealous, hypocritical priest, Mercanson, Octave begins to have doubts about Brigitte's past and her other male friends. Musset portrays the young man as poisoned by his earlier disillusion, tortured by doubt, and driven to analyze, to seek hidden answers, to question all that his mistress says and does. He abuses her, driven by a demon he cannot escape. Brigitte tries to hide her suffering, which is increased by the gossip and slander of the local gentry. Octave tries to leave her for her own good, but Brigitte clings to him, and they depart together for Paris, planning to undertake a long voyage as a cure for Octave's spiritual illness.

Somehow the couple cannot go beyond the planning stages for their trip. They remain in Paris, suffering but unable to change their lives. Little by little, the young man begins to suspect a repressed love between his mistress and Smith, an upright, levelheaded friend of Brigitte's family. Octave's "strange curiosity" compels him to put the two young people into dangerous situations. One day he thinks that they have drunk out of the same teacup, which for him is a sign of guilty intimacy. Finally, when the tension between Octave and Brigitte has reached its paroxysm, they decide that they must leave at once on their long deferred voyage. But before leaving, Octave insists on knowing whether Brigitte is in love with Smith. She denies having ever loved anyone but him, accusing him of destroying all sentiment by his doubts. Octave, horrified by what he has done to their relationship, is tempted to kill himself. After a sleepless night, however, he discovers an unsent letter of farewell from Brigitte to Smith, confessing her love but saying she is obliged to sacrifice herself to save Octave from himself.

Shaken, Octave decides to depart alone. After a final day with Brigitte, he leaves her with the "good, kind, and honest" Smith, generously blessing their union, and sets out on his travels alone.

The transformation of Musset, the poet, into Octave T., the dilettante and debauchee; of George Sand, the liberated, trousers-wearing, cigar-smoking novelist, into Brigitte Pierson, the provincial widow and angel of mercy; of the Venetian doctor and Don Juan, Pagello, into the discreet, upright merchant Smith; of Paris into the countryside and Venice into Paris; of George Sand's Parisian friends into the jealous small-town gossips—all of these

obvious but superficial changes are merely symptomatic of the deeper change, from what we know of the psychology, motivation, and actions of the participants in the "drame de Venise." All tend to accentuate the version of the story that Musset's partisans—including his most important modern biographer, Pierre Gastinel—saw as a plot on the part of George Sand, with the complicity of Pagello, to persuade an unstable, debilitated Musset, already prone to the illusion that he was a precocious victim of his own debauchery, that the events in Venice were his fault rather than his mistress'. Playing on his fear of insanity (already aroused by the hallucination in the gorge of Franchard), his earlier disillusionment, his weakness for pleasure and drink, and his penchant for self-irony, George Sand was said to have done all in her power to build up in Musset's mind the structure that informs his roman à clef. Even when Pagello's confessions to Tattet and other revelations accompanying the couple's stormy reconciliations had made it clear that this version could not stand up as a valid explanation of their "drama," Musset stuck to it for the plot of his novel, written after their final separation. Moreover, he allowed it to shape his future development as a man and as a writer in subtle and pervasive ways, so that the myth of the incorrigible debauchee, doubter, and dilettante became a self-fulfilling prophecy.

Musset's sole completed novel, which had considerable success in its time and is one of the major French romantic works in its genre, is difficult to evaluate today. Unlike the great literary couples whom Musset evoked in his letter to George Sand, Octave and Brigitte—or rather Musset and George Sand—have become part of socioliterary history, symptomatic of their own time and ethos. That is due in great part to the style and composition of Musset's first-person narrative, dominated by lengthy soliloquies, rhetorical questions, apostrophes, vague, lyric meditations on nature, confessions addressed to the reader—in short, that hyper-romantic style Musset himself defined as the "abuse of adjectives" in his satirical "Letters of Dupuis and Cotonet" (1836–1837).

As if to attenuate the uneasy adaptation of an essentially lyrical voice and perspective to the novel, Musset appended an introductory chapter that sought to place the personal events recounted in a larger vision of history. Adopting an apocalyptic, allegorical style, he blamed his era's disillusion and loss of faith on an "illness of the century," a new manifestation of the post-revolutionary ennui and loss of faith that Chateaubriand had written of in *René.* Here it is the fall of the empire, the descent from an active military generation to one of idle sons, victims of destructive new ideas coming from abroad, that brings about the disillusionment:

> When the English and German ideas passed thus over our heads, it was as a baleful and silent disgust, followed by a terrible convulsion. For to formulate general ideas is to change saltpeter into gunpowder, and the Homeric brain of the great Goethe had sucked out, like a still, all the liquor of the forbidden fruit. Those who did not then read his works thought they knew nothing of him. Poor creatures! The explosion carried them off like grains of dust into the abyss of universal doubt.
>
> (*Confessions* 1.2)

Octave thus was meant to represent one of a lost generation, an individual example of the larger illness that characterized the youth of his time. This introduction, which was the most influential and widely anthologized part of the novel, had little organic connection with what followed. But it constituted by itself one of the clearest and most characteristic myths of the era in France. Musset was thus able to depersonalize, to objectify and to enlarge, at least to some extent, the novel's limited, sentimental, biographical import, and to give it some claim to a place alongside his more enduring works: the four major dramas that preceded it and the series of lyric poems that, following close on the novel, complete the relatively brief cycle of Musset's great creative period.

"ROLLA" AND THE NIGHTS

Musset's lasting place as a lyric poet, alongside contemporary figures like Lamartine, Vigny, and Hugo, is defined primarily by five major poems: "Rolla," dating from the middle of 1833, which looks backward and provides a lyric summation of the pre-George Sand period in Musset's artistic and emotional life; and the four *Nights,* the May, December, August, and October "Nights," dating from June 1835 to October 1837, which trace the poet's evolution during the troubled but productive period following the "drame de Venise" and the lovers' final separation. Although the two groups of poems seem thus to belong to discreet moments of the poet's creative evolution, they are related by their mature mastery, the number of inspired, memorable verses they contain, and that combination of personal confession (veiled and objectified in "Rolla") and didacticism that characterizes their specific rhetoric and voice.

As early as 1830, in the uncompleted fragments of a long narrative poem, "Le saule" (the "willow" that was to be planted by admirers on the poet's grave), Musset had begun to redefine his poetics. He breaks away from the formally innovative, lexically rich, exotic and precise, prosodically sophisticated verse advocated by Hugo and the Cénacle group, returning to a preromantic mode in the tradition of André Chénier (as continued by Lamartine), in which spontaneous, harmonious expression of sentiment takes precedence over form and technique. Musset's elegiac evocation there of the singing of a young American expatriate, Georgina Smolen, becomes a hymn of praise to the power of music and, by extension, of all art, especially poetry, to translate directly the movements of the heart:

> Fille de la douleur! harmonie! harmonie!
> Langue que pour l'amour inventa le génie! . . .
> Douce langue du coeur, la seule où la pensée,
> Cette vierge craintive et d'une ombre offensée,
> Passe en gardant son voile, et sans craindre
>   les yeux!

> Daughter of sorrow! harmony! harmony!
> Language that genius invented for love! . . .
> Sweet language of the heart, the only one
>   through which thought,
> That timorous maiden offended by a shadow,
> Passes with her veil intact, and without fearing
>   others' eyes!

The identification of emotion with creation—of "heart" with "genius"—is to be found in a short poem dedicated to Musset's former classmate, Edouard Bocher, in lines that have become far more familiar than the text containing them (which, significantly, puts them in the context of a reading of Lamartine, the founder and guiding spirit of French romantic poetry): "Ah! frappe-toi le coeur, c'est là qu'est le génie./ C'est là qu'est la pitié, la souffrance et l'amour." (Oh, strike your heart, that is where genius is./ That is where pity, suffering and love are). It is the heart that is the source of Lamartine's genius, and of true poetry.

Similarly, in the dedicatory poem of the first volume of his *Armchair Theater*, Musset exalts emotional spontaneity and expansion over form:

> L'amour est tout,—l'amour et la vie au soleil.
> Aimer est le grand point, qu'importe la maîtresse?
> Qu'importe le flacon, pourvu qu'on ait
>   l'ivresse? . . .
> Un artiste est un homme,—il écrit pour des
>   hommes.
> Pour prêtresse du temple, il a la liberté;
> Pour trépied, l'univers; pour éléments, la vie;
> Pour encens, la douleur, l'amour et l'harmonie;
> Pour victime, son coeur;—pour dieu, la vérité.

> Love is all,—love and life in the sun.
> To love is the main point, what matters which
>   mistress?
> What matters the flagon, as long as we have the
>   intoxication? . . .
> An artist is a man,—he writes for men.
> As priestess of his temple, he has freedom;
> As tripod, the universe; as elements, life;
> As incense, sorrow, love and harmony;
> As victim, his heart;—as god, truth.

In reply to critical accusations based on the fashionable derivativeness of his previous poetry—his echoes of Byron, particularly—the author made a declaration of independence that was also an affirmation of the self and gave further praise to "intoxication" as the source of poetic creation: "Mon verre n'est pas grand, mais je bois dans mon verre" (My glass is not large, but it is mine that I drink from). Henceforth his poetry was to be original, spontaneous, personal, harmonious, expressive of the experienced passions. Although these qualities cannot be said to constitute anything approaching a poetics, it is certainly as good a characterization of the five major poems that followed as one can find.

"Rolla," which was published in the *Revue des deux mondes* in August 1833, is the account of the last night on earth of the eponymous hero, a twenty-year-old debauchee; it is also a meditation on the historical causes of the *maladie du siècle* (illness of the century) that would later be developed in the *Confessions*. The only one of Musset's major mature lyrics to make use of a hero-persona to represent the author's moral vision, it looks back to his earlier poems; while the sententious voice of the narrator, with its striking rhetorical formulas, looks forward to the later poems, although without their direct, dialogic, dramatic quality.

The poem opens with an elegiac "regret" for the moral and sensual clarity of primitive, classic times:

> Regrettez-vous le temps où le ciel sur la terre
> Marchait et respirait dans un peuple de dieux . . .

Où, du nord au midi, sur la création
Hercule promenait l'éternelle justice . . .

Do you long for the time when heaven on earth
Walked and breathed in a population of gods . . .
When, from north to south, over creation
Hercules carried eternal justice . . .

and then for the now-ended Christian era:

Regrettez-vous le temps où d'un siècle barbare
Naquit un siècle d'or, plus fertile et plus
    beau? . . .
Où, sous la main du Christ, tout venait de
    renaître?

Do you long for the time when, from a barbarous
    age
Was born an age of gold, more fertile and more
    beautiful? . . .
When, in the hand of Christ, all had just been
    reborn?

The narrator places himself in a post-Christian generation, which has lost its faith and its hope:

O Christ! je ne suis pas de ceux que la prière
Dans tes temples muets amène à pas
    tremblants . . .
Je ne crois pas, ô Christ! à ta parole sainte:
Je suis venu trop tard dans un monde trop vieux.
D'un siècle sans espoir naît un siècle sans
    crainte.

O Christ! I am not one of those whom prayer
Brings with trembling step into your silent tem-
    ples . . .
I do not believe, O Christ! in your holy word:
I came too late into a world too old.
From a century without hope is born a century
    without fear.

The "century without hope," as we learn from a digression later in the poem, is the eighteenth century, the age of the materialist philosophes, the century of Voltaire, whose "hideous smile" destroyed the religious and political structures on which human stability was built.

The protagonist of this narrative, Jacques Rolla, is a young man who has squandered his fortune in the space of three years, and who has come to spend his last gold pieces, and his last night, in the arms of a fifteen-year-old prostitute, Marion. This image of Musset's generation, throwing away its heritage, profaning the ideal of love, and soiling the innocence and purity of youth, evokes pity and indignation from the narrator, who combines chastisement of Voltaire with a sensual evocation of the young people's loveless coupling during the course of their night together. In the morning, Rolla meditates on his coming death as he watches the sleeping Marion, taking pity on her precocious, involuntary corruption. When she awakens, she tells him of a dream in which they were both lying on tombs in a graveyard. Upon learning that Rolla intends to kill himself now that his fortune is spent, she offers to pawn her jewelry. But he takes poison and dies, after a last kiss in which, "for a moment, both of them had loved."

The poem is too long and occasionally overwrought, in the manner of its times. But it has memorable moments. Its principal characters achieve something approaching mythic stature (the Marion is a sentimental forerunner of the figure depicted in Édouard Manet's *Olympia* [1863], and Musset here develops several of those extended animal metaphors of his personal bestiary that illuminate his *Nights*—the image of a wild mare dying of thirst in the desert, not knowing that water may be had by following the caravans to the city; a fledgling eaglet taking flight for the first time, learning he is an eagle by performing the act that distinguishes him from baser creatures.

The cycle of four *Nights,* although they mark four separate points in two and a half years of Musset's life (from mid-1835 to late 1837), and although they refer to psychological events connected with at least three different love affairs, have traditionally been viewed as reflecting the gradually dying resonances of his liaison with George Sand. There is no doubt some truth in the tradition, since that traumatic experience did condition the artistic and emotional life of the poet both consciously and unconsciously until the end of his career—certainly it transformed his own estimation of himself in radical ways. But it is a simplification to read the individual works and to judge them as a cycle according to that grid. As a series of dialogues, for the most part between the artist and his muse (the "Nuit de décembre" ["December Night"] is almost a monologue, with a brief reply by the poet's "vision" at the end), the *Nights* form a statement—or rather a dramatization—of the author's idea of poetry in a crucial, turbulent period of his career; they are also the most brilliant and moving realization of that idea that his talent ever produced. The cycle opens with the muse's passionate exhortation to the poet to begin singing once again, following the distressing, destructive affair that has silenced him. After a series of encounters and discussions in a variety of contexts, it closes with the poet finally determined to forget past disillusions and betrayals, and to consecrate himself henceforth to love of the muse.

The "Nuit de mai" ("May Night"), which opens the series, was first published in the *Revue des deux mondes* in June 1835. It consists of ten stanzas of unequal length, in which the muse, who speaks in alexandrine verse, has a far larger part than the reticent poet, who replies in briefer, more prosaic octosyllables. In the first series of exchanges, the muse gives an increasingly pressing, ardent, and circumstantially detailed sequence of exhortations, all prefaced by the ambiguous invitation, "Poète, prends ton luth et me donne un baiser" (Poet, take up your lute and give me a kiss). The inspiration to creation that she proffers is initially quite insistently sensual, as if to arouse the poet at the level of animal passion, with spring's revival of nature:

I   *Le printemps naît ce soir; les vents vont*
     s'embraser;

Et la bergeronnette, en attendant l'aurore,
Aux premiers buissons verts commence à se
   poser.

Springtime is born this evening; the winds are
   catching fire;
And the wagtail, waiting for dawn to come,
Is starting to alight on the first green bushes.

III *La rose, vierge encore, se referme jalouse*
    Sur le frelon nacré qu'elle enivre en
      mourant . . .
    Ce soir, tout va fleurir: l'immortelle
     nature
    Se remplit de parfums, d'amour et de
     murmure,
    Comme le lit joyeux de deux jeunes
     époux.

The rose, still virginal, closes jealously
Around the pearly hornet which she intoxicates
   as it dies . . .
This evening, all will bloom; immortal nature
Is filled with fragrance, love, and murmurs,
Like the joyous bed of a young couple.

V . . . *le vin de la jeunesse*
    Fermente cette nuit dans les veines de Dieu.
    Mon sein est inquiet; la volupté l'oppresse,
    Et les vents altérés m'ont mis la lèvre en
     feu . . .

. . . the wine of youth
Is fermenting tonight in the veins of God.
My bosom is restless; desire weighs upon it,
And the hot, dry winds have set my lips aflame.

The poet replies, uncertain at first as to the source of a voice he hears only dimly, as if it were a hallucination induced by his vigil; at last he recognizes it as that of his "poor muse," the only "modest and faithful being," his "mistress" and his "sister." There is a fine imitation of an excited heartbeat in the rhythm of his second reply: "Pourquoi mon coeur bat-il si vite? . . . / Ne frappe-t-on pas à ma porte?" (Why is my heart beating so fast? . . . / Did somebody knock at the door?).

After this dramatic introduction, with its gradual adjustment of "wavelengths" of communication between the poet and his inspiration, the muse evokes a long travelogue to tempt the poet's imagination: romantic evocations of Scotland, Italy, and in especially lengthy detail, Greece; dreams of battle, love, and sainthood, of medieval France or Napoleon's empire—all the more seductive in contrast to satires on present-day corruption. Her tone becomes increasingly impassioned, but the poet sadly resists her blandishments. His sorrow is too great, and in these circumstances "La bouche garde le silence/ Pour écouter parler le coeur" (The mouth keeps still/ To hear the heart speaking).

At this point the muse responds with the most familiar and celebrated of all Musset's verses, a praise of sorrow as the source of poetic creation. After exhorting him to exploit the "wound" that experience has opened in his heart—"Laisse-la s'élargir, cette sainte blessure/ Que les noir séraphins t'ont faite au fond du coeur" (Let it open wider, that sacred wound/ That the black seraphim have made in the depths of your heart)—the muse tells him that suffering is the stuff from which great poetry is made: "Les plus désespérés sont les chants les plus beaux,/ Et j'en sais d'immortels qui sont de purs sanglots" (The songs of deepest despair are the most beautiful ones,/ And I know immortal ones that are pure sobs). And then, in illustration of her thesis, the muse evokes the extended image, which Musset drew from medieval bestiary allegories of Christ, of the pelican that, returning empty-handed (if the expression may be used) to its hungry progeny, tears open its breast and feeds them with its own blood. Thus the poet offers nourishment to other men, his spiritual wards, from the wellsprings of his own passion and suffering. Continuing the metaphor of the wound, she states: "Leurs déclamations sont comme des épées:/ Elles tracent dans l'air un cercle éblouissant,/ Mais il y pend toujours quelque goutte de sang" (Their declamations are like swords:/ They trace a dazzling circle in the air,/ But there is always some blood dripping from them). The

poet closes, however, echoing Wordsworth's "emotion recollected in tranquillity," that "Man writes nothing in the sand/ While the north wind's tempest blows," and if he were to try to sing now, the slightest expression of his grief would "break [his] lyre like a reed."

The inconclusive ending of the poem, along with its disproportion between the expansive, voluble muse and the terse, reticent poet, leaves the reader with a clear sense that this work is part of a larger structure, awaiting its synthesis at another time and level. Of course the poet's "refusal" to sing is belied both by the muse's inspiration, so eloquently realized in his verses, and by the poetically effective and expressive contrast created by the poem's dramatic structure. It thus becomes one of the first in that remarkable series of nineteenth-century French lyrics singing brilliantly of the problem of creation and sterility—although in a very different mode from those of Baudelaire or Stéphane Mallarmé. But that was in keeping with the dramatic, dialogic character of Musset's imagination. It is worth recalling the description of his writing of the "May Night" contained in his brother Paul's still useful, though often suspect and controversial, biography:

> In the evening, he returned to work as if to a lovers' rendezvous. He had a light supper served in his room. He would readily have asked for two places to be set, so that the Muse could have her cover laid as well. All our candlesticks were put to use; he lighted twelve candles. The servants, seeing that illumination, must have thought he was giving a ball.
>
> (*Biography of Alfred de Musset*, ch. 9)

Musset's taste for self-dramatization was among his brother's earliest childhood memories, and it continued to be associated with the act of creation as long as the poet's productive powers lasted.

"December Night," the next poem in the cycle, was published in the *Revue des deux mondes* in December of the same year. It is the only one of the series not to bring the poet's muse on stage; instead, it is a long monologue of the poet (eighteen octosyllabic six-line stanzas, and ten nine-line stanzas of mixed octosyllabic and decasyllabic verse), followed by the three brief six-line octosyllabic stanzas of his "Vision." It has been pointed out that Musset's evocation of this specter is related to the hallucination the poet had experienced with George Sand in the gorge of Franchard: he seems to have been subject to pathological attacks of what is rather loosely called "autoscopy," a personal variant of the doppelgänger phenomenon prevalent in his European generation (echoes of it are to be found in *Lorenzaccio* and *The Whims of Marianne*). Biographers also point out that this poem is as much related to Musset's rift with a more recent mistress, Madame Jaubert, as it is to the "drame de Venise" and its sequels.

The opening of the poem is structured on a series of five parallel evocations in two stanzas of the poet's encounter with a vision at successive stages of his life: as a schoolboy, an adolescent, a young lover, a libertine, and on the death of his father. In each of these, the vision is dressed in black and resembles the poet "like a brother." It is silent and responds to the poet's questions with a gesture or a sign of understanding. The eight remaining six-line stanzas evoke all the places in the poet's travels where he has encountered his somber double.

With the expansion into nine-line stanzas, the poet shifts to an interrogation of his vision—"Who are you then? . . . You are not my guardian angel,/ You never come to warn me"—and an anguished lament over a recent, unhappy love affair evoked by the "letters of the day before, locks of hair, debris of love . . . / Those ruins of happy days" that the poet is storing away when the specter once again reappears. (This "keepsake" meditation, typical of the romantic generation, is the one Baudelaire treated with bitter irony in the second "Spleen" poem of his *Flowers of Evil* and Flaubert satirized in the clutter of Rodolphe's

desk in *Madame Bovary*.) The vision replies at the end that it is indeed the poet's "brother," that heaven has given it custody of his heart, and that it will always be with him in his hours of grief. "Mais je ne puis toucher ta main,/ Ami, je suis la Solitude" (But I cannot touch your hand,/ Friend, I am Loneliness).

This poem, which marks the psychological low-water mark in the cycle, is also the one that, thanks to the absence of the muse and to the self-reflexive nature of its central dramatic metaphor, seems to have the least to say about the act of poetic creation. But if we see this wintry "Solitude" figure, the poet's vision, in the larger context as an avatar of the muse, an altered perspective on inspiration—Narcissus clothed in black and adapted to romantic vision—it can be taken as a significant stage in the author's representation of his poetics, indeed the least "dramatized" and thus the most personal, even essential, of his four texts. The more univocal form of the poem tends to substantiate that view.

The return of the muse in the "Nuit d'août" ("August Night"), published in the *Revue des deux mondes* in August 1836 (the poet's brother insists that Musset received "her" with a joyous fête like that of "May Night"), also marks the return to a more evident centrality of the theme of artistic creation. Here the argument focuses on that conflict between art and life, between poetic creation and love, that was later to become the theme of Musset's best and most personal short story, "Le fils du Titien" ("Titian's Son," 1838). But whereas that work's praise of love at the expense of art would be inspired by the aristocratic Aimée d'Alton, "August Night" reflects Musset's brief, happy affair with a young shopgirl neighbor, Louise Lebrun (who also became the heroine of the more somber short story Frédéric et Bernerette" ["Frederick and Bernerette," 1838]).

The human, dramatic quality present in "May Night," which cast the muse in the role of ardent mistress and the poet as her hesitant lover, here transforms the muse into a jealous woman chastising her poet/lover for his frequent absences from their rendezvous. The central notion, of course, is the intermittence of the poet's creativity, reflecting the long interval (eight months) since his last poem in the cycle. But the half-stated allusion here, which adds piquancy and some degree of retrospective sadness to our reading of the poem, is the more sentimental reflection of the fickle Musset's habitual cycles of love and indifference during this period: it adds a touch of bittersweet domestic comedy to the drama of the poem.

In answer to the muse's tender recriminations and her warnings that the poet's repeated experiments with the hopes and disillusions of love will kill his creative powers, he replies with bantering affection that, like the wild rose's blossoms, men's loves are always most beautiful when most fresh; and like the bird that has just lost its young, he always sings with renewed hope. But the muse, in a lengthy sermon, warns him of the cumulative effect of these experiences, reminding the poet of his more single-minded pursuit of her when they both were younger and fresher: "Ainsi que ta beauté, tu perdras ta vertu" (Along with your beauty, you will lose your power).

At this point the poet, for the first time in the cycle using his own voice in regular, full stanzas of alexandrine verse, gives his final and serious reply. It begins with an expansive three-stanza sequence whose clauses are introduced with rising frequency and insistence by the unifying conjunction "puisque" (since), repeated eight times and climaxing:

Puisque, jusqu'aux rochers, tout se change en
    poussière;
Puisque tout meurt ce soir pour revivre demain;
Puisque c'est un engrais que le meurtre et la
    guerre;
Puisque sur une tombe on voit sortir de la terre
Le brin d'herbe sacré qui nous donne le pain. . . .

Since everything, even the rocks, changes into
    dust;
Since everything dies this evening to live again
    tomorrow;
Since murder and war are fertilizers to life;
Since we see on a grave rise up from the earth
The blade of sacred grass that gives us
    bread . . .

The poet will and must continue to love, reliving the cycle of all nature:

J'aime, et je veux pâlir; j'aime et je veux
    souffrir;
J'aime, et pour un baiser je donne mon
    génie . . .
Et je veux raconter et répéter sans cesse
Qu'après avoir juré de vivre sans maîtresse,
J'ai fait serment de vivre et de mourir
    d'amour . . .
Après avoir souffert, il faut souffrir encore:
Il faut aimer sans cesse, après avoir aimé.

I love, and I will grow pale; I love and I will
    suffer;
I love, and for a kiss I would give up my
    genius . . .
And I will recount and repeat incessantly
That after swearing to live without a mistress,
I have made an oath to live and die for love . . .
After suffering, one must suffer again;
One must love incessantly, after one has loved.

The mastery of rhetorical devices like repetition and chiasmus, and the long, arching grammatical periods of this suddenly expansive reply in which the poet takes on the muse's eloquence after the laconic playfulness of his previous interventions, make this conclusion the emotional high point of the cycle; it acts as a third-act climax that fits into the traditional curve of drama prior to the fourth-act denouement of the "Nuit d'octobre" ("October Night"). Here, the apparent resolution of the conflict between art and life in favor of a reiterated plunge into life (which includes in its cycle the necessary forces of death and change) still leaves a sense of unresolved tension insinuated by the unanswered questions of the muse: What must happen to the poet's creative powers as a result of his emotional excesses? The insistent repetition of "puisque" by the poet, instead of persuading our minds of the logic of his reply, suggests a powerful, visceral necessity, the claim of the life force on the poet's senses, impelling him to that blind sacrifice and death he sees as characteristic of the procreative activity of nature.

"Le mal dont j'ai souffert s'est enfui comme un rêve" (The illness from which I suffered has vanished like a dream), says the poet at the opening of the concluding poem of the cycle, "October Night," published in the *Revue des deux mondes* in October 1837. If this claim seems not entirely true at the inception of the poem, it is at least the intent of the process of catharsis that informs this final lyric inspired by the George Sand adventure. (There is a belated postscript, "Souvenir" ["Remembrance"], in 1841.) Here the dialogue between muse and poet becomes a kind of therapy session in which the erstwhile mistress and arouser of the poet's blunted senses strikes us as remarkably moralistic and reasonable, and the poet himself as passionate and irrational. The form of the poem contributes to this sense of dialectic and discussion. At the start, the exchanges are relatively brief and frequent; the two interlocutors have exchanged meters from "May Night," with the poet speaking in alexandrines and the muse responding in octosyllables. It is clear that Musset intended, in closing the cycle, to evoke resonances of the opening poem and to resolve some of the psychological and moral tensions it had left hanging. Indeed, the poet's brother saw "October Night" as "the necessary sequel to "May Night," the final word of a great sorrow and the most legitimate as well as the most overwhelming of revenges, forgiveness." But he tended to view much of the poet's work in this period as part of the ongoing proceedings between Musset and George Sand. The fact is that the strong emotions evoked in this poem reflect a number of love affairs, recent and remote; the most insistent echo present in "October Night" is that of the poet's first,

treacherous mistress—even though she takes on a physical air strongly reminiscent of George Sand.

After eight stanzas of this introduction, in which it is the poet who tries to arouse the muse to activity and the muse who hesitates to commit herself to belief in her lover's recovery, the poet begins to sing, in a single stanza of alternating decasyllables and octosyllables, railing bitterly against the treachery of a woman and the vindictiveness of fortune. In reply to the muse's gentle reproaches, the poet recounts, in a long sequence of alexandrines, the story of his first betrayal by a woman. Striking in this account is the sense of fatal necessity, of "nagging portent," which announces betrayal to him even as he awaits the hour of his rendezvous: self-fulfilling prophecy is the most obsessive theme of Musset's life and works. The increasingly agitated voice of the poet belies the declaration of healing that opens the poem, and the muse intervenes to calm him before his "wound" reopens. In an unusual incantatory series of heptasyllables, structured on the words "honte à toi" (shame on you), the poet inveighs against the woman "who first taught [him] betrayal" (but she is also the "somber-eyed woman" we can identify with the descriptions and iconography of Sand), who took advantage of his innocence, who was "mother of [his] first sorrows" and opened the wellspring of his tears.

The muse, taking over his alexandrines, gives the poet a lengthy lesson on the benefit of tears. Sorrow is the great teacher:

L'homme est un apprenti, la douleur est son
  maître,
Et nul ne se connait tant qu'il n'a pas souffert . . .
Aimerais-tu les fleurs, les prés et la verdure,
Les sonnets de Pétrarque et le chant des oiseaux,
Michel-Ange et les arts, Shakspeare et la nature,
Si tu n'y retrouvais quelques anciens sanglots?

  Man is an apprentice, sorrow is his master,
  And none may know himself as long as he has
    not suffered . . .

Would you love the flowers, the meadows and
the trees,
The sonnets of Petrarch and the song of the
birds,
Michelangelo and the arts, Shakespeare and
nature,
If you did not find in them some of your former
tears?

Indeed, she suggests to him that the treacherous woman was perhaps only fulfilling her—and his—destiny, in order that he might become a poet.

The poem closes with the poet's octosyllabic last word: in a long rhetorical period, a vow structured on the repetition of the preposition "par" (by), the poet swears "by that brilliant sparkle/ That bears the name of Venus," "by the grandeur of nature, by the goodness of the Creator . . . by the power of life, by the vigor of the universe, to banish from [his] memory the remains of an insane love." With his final lines, he invites the muse to renewed transports of love, as nature reawakens with dawn: "Nous allons renaître avec elle/ Au premier rayon du soleil!" (We will be reborn with her/ In the first rays of the sun!).

And so the cycle ends with a reaffirmation of the creative urge, based on the forgetting of past pain and sorrow—or, if we are to take the muse's reasoning as valid, the sublimation of it into a new, enhanced perception that is at the basis of art. The cycle of life, death, and rebirth basic to nature myths is here identified with the poet's love life, metaphorically assimilated—both through emotional experience and through the inspiring muse—to the process of poetic creation. It is hard to judge how conscious was the poet's irony in thus singing of renewed love and creativity with a muse self-proclaimed older and more tired. Given Musset's habitual lucidity, it is difficult not to see the closing of the *Nights* cycle at least in part as a prophetic vision of that conflict between will (always the poet's weakest suit) and habit, between intelligence and pas-

sion, between the critical sense and the creative urge, that was soon to evolve into the celebrated idleness and lengthy silence of his last fifteen years.

Musset by no means ceased writing poetry, even good poetry, at the conclusion of the *Nights* in 1837. The poem of 1841, "Remembrance," with its last thoughts on the Sand adventure, is a much anthologized work often compared with Lamartine's "Le lac" (1840; written in the same meter) and Hugo's "Tristesse d'Olympio" (1840), other well-known treatments of the theme of memory as poetry's raison d'être. Musset had already dealt with it in 1836 in his "Lettre à Lamartine" ("Letter to Lamartine"), where he wrote: "Qu'est-ce donc qu'oublier, si ce n'est pas mourir? . . . / Ton âme est immortelle, et va s'en souvenir" (What is forgetting, then, if not dying? . . . / Your soul is immortal, and will remember). In "Remembrance," Musset tells of a heartrending return to the forest of Fontainebleau, and of an encounter with George Sand, who greeted him with cool indifference. He judges the forgetfulness of the latter (whom he calls a "whited sepulchre") far more terrible than the wounds reopened by the scene of the earlier incident, concluding with the affecting lines, reminiscent of those he had borrowed from George Sand herself in *You Can't Trifle with Love*:

Je me dis seulement: "A cette heure, en ce
lieu,
Un jour, je fus aimé, j'aimais, elle était belle.
J'enfouis ce trésor dans mon âme immortelle,
Et je l'emporte à Dieu!"

I only tell myself: "At that time, in that place,
One day, I was loved, I loved, she was beautiful.
I bury that treasure in my immortal soul,
And I bear it off to God!"

Several of Musset's better poems from the post-*Nights* period have to do with experiences in the musical or legitimate theater, praising singers, actresses, or works. The best of these is "Une soirée perdue," ("A Wasted

Evening,'' 1840) satirically recounting a ''wasted evening'' at an almost empty Comédie Française, where the author was ''only Molière'': the criticism of contemporary theatrical taste is concluded with a gently self-mocking snap at the author's own distracted sensuality. Of another sort is the famous sonnet ''Tristesse'' (''Sadness'') of 1840, marking the poet's thirtieth year, which begins ''J'ai perdu ma force et ma vie/ Et mes amis et ma gaieté'' and concludes ''Le seul bien qui me reste au monde/ Est d'avoir quelquefois pleuré'' (I have lost my strength and my life/ And my friends and my gaiety . . . The only possession that remains to me in the world/ Is to have sometimes wept). Indeed the sonnet form became increasingly the poet's most effective vehicle—particularly those dedicated to Tattet and Hugo, and the two sonnets inserted in ''Titian's Son.'' But they tend to have a commemorative ring and to be closely tied to the circumstances of their writing; it cannot be said that they place Musset among the important nineteenth-century masters of the form such as Baudelaire and Mallarmé.

THE SHORT STORIES: ''TITIAN'S SON''

During two periods of his later life—and both times for pecuniary reasons—Musset transformed himself temporarily from a poet/dramatist into a short-story writer. It is not the least characteristic irony of his artistic life that his short stories (written from 1837 to 1839 and collected in 1848) and his tales (written mainly between 1842 and 1845 and collected in 1854) should have been among his most widely read and lucrative works, along with the *Confessions:* his is truly the story of the ''Fallen Poet,'' as he entitled an unfinished novel dating from the period in which he was writing the *Short Stories.*

It is easy to understand the popular success of these works, written in an elegant, conversational style that came naturally to Musset. They deal—particularly the later *Tales*—with social or psychological situations having only a superficial connection with the author's obsessive personal themes. Indeed, only one story among the *Tales,* ''Histoire d'un merle blanc'' (''The Story of a White Blackbird'') of 1842, a rather leaden satirical fable alluding to the George Sand affair, has any real connection with the mainstream of Musset's life; the rest are extended, graceful anecdotes, often in a worldly or historical setting, that occasionally attain a moderate degree of pathos. The earlier *Short Stories* are more personal in material (thus illustrating the progression toward disengagement characteristic of Musset's later career): all but two are literary transpositions of episodes in the poet's love life. ''Les deux maîtresses'' (''The Two Mistresses'') recounts an amatory dilemma in which he found himself torn between a poor woman and a wealthy one, and is thus at least reminiscent of the pervasive duality noted in the plays; ''Emmeline'' retraces an early stage in his relationship with Madame Jaubert; ''Frederick and Bernerette'' transports us into a different world, the poet's proletarian affair with a neighboring *midinette* (shopgirl). But in all these stories, the emotional problem is the only vector of relationship with Musset's dominant themes, unlike his major works, in which the structure interweaves the ''love story'' (or its equivalent) with ethical, psychological, or artistic problems, endowing them with enhanced resonance and depth compared to the generally unidimensional, anecdotal *Short Stories.*

One of the latter, however, stands out from the rest and thus merits extended attention, both as a literary creation and as an element of the poet's biographical mythos: ''Titian's Son,'' which first appeared in the *Revue des deux mondes* in May 1838. The bedraggled but jaunty figure of Pomponio Filippo (''Pippo'') Vecellio described at its opening is strongly reminiscent of another young man whom we can imagine at dawn on the same locale in Venice, 250 years later: Musset himself. The central event of the tale, the gift of a purse by the artist's unknown admirer, who hoped to inspire prudence and foresight, was transcribed from Musset's recent experience with Aimée d'Alton. This story thus poses problems concerning the relationship between life and art in its genesis, as it does, although in different terms, in its central theme.

Of course it is not surprising to find biographical echoes in the work of a romantic. But it is precisely because Musset considered himself essentially a poet and felt personal statements to be the eminent domain of the lyric that we are justified in wondering why this short story should contain conspicuous elements of the poet's private experience. The problem is complicated by our awareness that the *Short Stories* were undertaken as a financial expedient. Indeed, the project was so alien to Musset that he is said by his brother to have brought the last of them, "Croisilles" (1839), to an abrupt close because he had reached the required minimum of pages for the *Revue*. A letter to Aimée d'Alton confirms the involuntary nature of this undertaking: "I am chained down and forced to write shoddy goods against my will."

But we must keep in mind also that Musset often needed such pretexts for neglecting the women he loved. The poet's brother relates the enthusiasm with which Musset undertook certain of his "little novels"—specifically "Titian's Son." The subject of the story had roots not only in the poet's experience but in literary projects going back five or more years in time. The drama *André del Sarto,* which dates from 1833, treated the theme of the diminished artist, torn between the demands of art and love for his faithless wife, who resolves the dilemma by suicide. By 1838 Musset no longer conceived this problem in such melodramatic terms. But the conflict between love and art remained a constant preoccupation throughout his creative and emotional life.

The theme of artistic inactivity, which links *André del Sarto* with this story, was to pursue its course as a dominant motif in the poet's future work: his 1842 poem, "Sur la paresse ("On Idleness"), for example. Though in the year he wrote "Titian's Son" Musset was still in his most productive phase, he was already on the downward curve of his creative cycle. In the words of Paul, "The year 1838 was one of hopes." But frequently an author's works, seen in retrospect, reveal a premonitory pattern that emerges from the creative subconscious. In Musset's case, this took the shape of an insistent threat of failure, most often as a pathetic survival in diminished form, as we have seen.

In "Titian's Son" we find the pattern in curious and revealing counterpoint with the theme of redemptive love inspired (in reality) by Aimée d'Alton. The details of the latter affair bear a close if not exact resemblance to the plot of the story. Aimée d'Alton, like Beatrice Loredano, aroused her lover's curiosity with the anonymous gift of a purse. Two sonnets addressed by the artist-hero to Beatrice were actually sent by Musset to his mistress some time before the composition of the story; Beatrice's early-morning entry into Pippo's apartment parallels Aimée's first rendezvous with the poet; like Beatrice, Aimée hoped through her affection to encourage the poet in his work. Indeed the two love stories are so strikingly similar that Musset evidently intended "Titian's Son," like Pippo's portrait of Beatrice, as a gift in tribute to his mistress' grace and charm. The essential difference is that, unlike the love of Pippo for Beatrice, Musset's love for Aimée d'Alton soon faded, and although she remained so devoted as to marry his brother after Alfred's death in order to dedicate herself to the publication of his works, there was on his part no voluntary abandonment of art for love. This thematic idealization is no doubt the essential tribute intended in Musset's literary offering. It adds a further, biographical element to the dominant themes of gift and self-sacrifice that inform the story.

Musset's transformation of autobiographical material is paralleled by his free treatment of the historical material on which his story is based. Musset (quite certainly deliberately) confuses the hero of his tale, Pomponio, second son of Tiziano Vecellio (Titian), with his older brother, Orazio. The latter did indeed die in the same epidemic that claimed his father, but it was he who inherited his father's talent and whose painting was destroyed by fire in the doge's palace in 1577. Pomponio, Musset's hero, is recorded only as having inherited a considerable fortune and squandered it; there is no mention of his being an artist. Furthermore, the name Tizianello, which Musset bestowed on him, designated a cousin whose work Pippo derides in the story rather than either of Titian's sons. The author thus modified history freely in order to align it with the thematic and plot requirements of his tale.

The major reason for these modifications seems to be Musset's desire to tighten the links between the false Tizianello and himself. He too was a younger son whose father (the author of minor literary works) had died a few years earlier of cholera. He was thus able to have his hero combine both family status and artistic talent in such a way as to provide a persona through which to represent his own character and situation, to create by analogy a romantic historical myth-figure reminiscent of Vigny's Moses and Samson, or Nerval's Christ. The difference lies mainly in the intensity of the figure's personal relevance, for Musset, in keeping with the short story's limited seriousness as a genre for him, takes an offhand and humorous attitude toward his persona.

Even more important than this apologetic aim is the thematic importance, for Musset, of his Tizianello as a mythic figure of survival in decadence, a kind of living elegy. Pomponio lives out his life in a dream of requited love with Beatrice; but he is reminiscent of a group of more pathetic heroes in the poet's work: Andrea del Sarto, the last, impotent representative of an age of great painters; Lorenzaccio, who outlives the meaningfulness of his long meditated political assassination; Octave, in the *Confessions,* who represents a generation born too late for heroism. Pippo's love flourishes at the expense of his talent, and it is sterile, producing neither works nor progeny. The idea of time as a degenerative force is all-pervading and is symptomatic of a pattern of destructive value reversals that causes Pippo's veneration of art to be transformed into sterility: he seems incapable of completing the portrait of his mistress, and when he is on the point of finishing it he erases the essential part, its expression. When at length the portrait is done, it bears in epigraph the self-canceling message of his sonnet, which disclaims ultimate value for the painting, "since, beautiful as it is, this portrait is not worth/ (You can take my word for it) one kiss from its model." This depreciation of art was foreshadowed by Pippo's earlier idea of an allegorical painting that would represent the artist Raphael's self-immolation by love. The process of destruction is completed by the final sentence of the story: "It is to be regretted that the pride of the Loredanos, wounded by this notorious affair, destroyed the portrait of Beatrice, as chance had destroyed Tizianello's first painting." The cyclical pattern takes us back to the first page of the story, where Pippo contemplated a burning building in which his painting was destroyed, uniting the theme of artistic sterility and destruction with the love plot: the protagonist's love, like his art, has been swallowed up in the whirlpool of time, chance, and human malice. "Titian's Son" thus stands as a small-scale but perfectly realized idealization of the penultimate stage in Musset's myth of the artist-genius as failure.

MUSSET AS ESSAYIST

There remains one area of Musset's literary activity that, although it reveals a certain amount about his creative and intellectual evolution, is harder to assess in the broader context of his times: his essays on art, music, theater, and literature. A good part of his work on the first of these, as we have seen, was contained in the plots, characterization, and dialogue of his creative works, particularly the dramas and short stories. Most of the rest is to be found in the occasional review articles he did on expositions or salons, for *Le temps* in 1830–1831 and for the *Revue des deux mondes* in 1833 and 1836. There he showed himself to be a knowledgeable and sensitive amateur, particularly strong in the Italian Renaissance yet open to the new currents and capable of appreciating rising modern artists like Eugène Delacroix and Jean Corot. But through all his writings on art, which are never less than intelligent and informed, there runs a common thread that marks them as essentially dilettantish. It is formulated most clearly in the article "Un mot sur l'art moderne" ("A Word on Modern Art"), published in the *Revue des deux mondes* in September 1833:

> There is no art, there are only men. Do you call art the craft of the painter, the poet, or the musician, insofar as it consists of scraping canvas or paper? Then there is art as long as there are people scraping paper or canvas. But if you understand thereby what governs the material labor, what results from that labor; if, in pronouncing the word *art,* you want to give a name to that being which has a thousand: inspiration, meditation, respect for the rules, the cult of beauty, reverie, and realization; if you baptize thus some abstract idea or other, in that case, what you call art is man.

This tendency to see through the transparency of the medium, to eliminate the technical and structural considerations that distinguish the graphic arts from other forms—and artists from each other—in fine; this tendency to see the artist qua painter as a metaphor for the Artist (and we should read, Poet), although it echoes back to Denis Diderot's criticism and looks forward to Baudelaire's, does not permit Musset to deal meaningfully with art as a genre in itself. It shares the weakness of Musset's writings on literary criticism or theory, which are among the sketchiest and least satisfactory of any major author of his period. Unlike such figures as George Sand, Flaubert, and Rimbaud, whose correspondence provides rich sources of insight into their authors' creative processes, Musset's published correspondence sheds light primarily on his emotional life; and unlike those of Hugo, Vigny, and many others of their generation, Musset's prefaces are deliberately, indeed provocatively, flippant and sketchy, refusing to make the sort of bold aesthetic statement one can often find in the body of his creative works. Similar conclusions can be drawn about the author's writings on music, which, outside of the context of his poetry and stories, are limited to occasional pieces like the delightful tongue-in-cheek paean to the galop in Daniel Auber's comic opera *Gustave III* (1833; the libretto later inspired Giuseppe Verdi's *Un ballo in maschera* [1859]).

The well-known series of four satirical "Letters of Dupuis and Cotonet," published in the *Revue des deux mondes* in 1836 and 1837, might seem to form an exception to this generally unimportant critical writing. They are often anthologized or excerpted in literary histories as a major piece of evidence for any case study of the romantic phenomenon in France. In them, two alleged provincial subscribers to the *Revue*, writing from La Ferté-sous-Jouarre (the French "heartland"), vainly struggle to penetrate the arcana of the romantic movement. Their celebrated conclusion—that romanticism is essentially the abuse of adjectives—makes abundantly clear what was announced by their initial exhortative greeting: "May the immortal gods assist you and preserve you from the new novels!" Musset, in the throes of that final rejection of the romantic aesthetic that had once held some charm for him, was increasingly identifying himself with the "classical" reaction, at least in public utterances like his newspaper essays and reviews.

This was especially true of his drama criticism during this time, which, between the period of his greatest creative activity and his belated public recognition as a dramatist, saw a spate of such writing. Of particular interest are two articles, "De la tragédie" (On Tragedy) and "Reprise de *Bajazet* au Théâtre-Français" (Revival of [Racine's] *Bajazet* at the Comédie Française), published in the *Revue des deux mondes* in November and December 1838. These articles no doubt reflected a renewed public interest in the classic French tragedy, which culminated in 1843 in the coincident failure of Hugo's romantic drama *Les Burgraves* and the triumph of François Ponsard's new classical tragedy *Lucrèce*, events traditionally cited as signifying the "fall" of romanticism in France. But they also permitted Musset to express some typically ambivalent ideas concerning the conflict between the two literary schools; while admitting the right to existence of the romantic aesthetic, he congratulated the older tradition on remaining very much alive for the Parisian theater public. In his opinion it was still a valid system, respecting its unities, prosody, and linguistic purity, for writing new works in the genre. If anything—and this is perhaps where Musset paradoxically shows his cryptoromantic colors—the author proposes a return to an earlier classical tradition, to Sophocles rather than Jean Racine and Pierre Corneille.

But we note, as did Musset's contemporaries, that these articles were above all a panegyric to the young tragedienne Rachel, who had recently made her spectacular debut at the age of seventeen. Rather than enunciate a literary doctrine, they communicate Musset's intense admiration for the actress, whose success was to be as bright as her life was brief (she died a year after Musset, at the age of thirty-eight), and whose talent was a prime mover in the classical revival. The poet's interest soon became more than professional, and his plans for writing dramatic works for her (principally a never finished historical tragedy, "La servante du roi" [The King's Serving-Maid]) paralleled the steep upward and downward trends of their intermittent love affair. Rachel is supposed to have said punningly of Musset: "He makes scenes, but he won't make a role for me to play." The author subsequently had affairs with several other actresses and did write roles for a few of them, but never with the success that finally came to his earlier works. Only one of his actress friends was connected with these: Madame Allan-Despréaux, who "discovered" the one-act *Caprice* while on tour in Russia and initiated the series of Musset's theatrical successes in 1847 when she performed it at the Comédie Française. But never again did these amatory flashes produce any significant critical or theoretical writing, as in the case of Rachel. Musset by that time was beyond the period of his active intellectual and creative involvement in the artistic currents of his time.

From 1843 on—the last fifteen years or final third of his life—the story of Musset is a paradigm of psychological and physical decline. The consequences of the spiritual and constitutional shocks of Venice, compounded by the poet's high-strung and delicate nervous system, began to show increasingly in the bouts of "pulmonary congestion" to which he fell subject, as well as the "aortic insufficiency" whose visible symptom, a nervous nodding of the head, became known as the "signe de Musset" in French medical language. More extensive and frequent sieges of depression or "lassitude" overcame him, affecting his writing and his personal relationships; alternating fits of jealousy and suspicion of those closest to him did nothing to improve the latter. Add to this Musset's growing addiction to drink, particularly a peculiar combination of absinthe and beer for which he became noted, and one has a "portrait of the artist as a prematurely old man," a portrait made more poignant by the visible reminders of youthful beauty he carried into his decline. All his contemporaries were struck by the contrast. Heinrich Heine made one of his barbed puns at Musset's expense, calling him "un jeune homme de beaucoup de passé" ("a young man with a great past before him," playing untranslatably on the expression "un jeune homme de beaucoup d'avenir," "a young man of great promise"). Flaubert, in a letter to Louise Colet—as she was the mistress of both writers, the novelist was not entirely without malice—said of him: "Musset seems to have been a charming young fellow, and then an old man." Even the vestiges of his youthfulness appeared to play cruel, ironic tricks on him. Lamartine characterized him in verse during this period as an "enfant aux blonds cheveux, jeune homme au coeur de cire,/ Poétique jouet de molle poésie . . . / Qui prend pour passion ta vague fantaisie" (Blond-haired child, waxen-hearted young man,/ Poetic plaything of soft poetry . . . / Who takes your vague fancies for passion), as if he were the imitative adolescent beginner of ten years before. And the Académie Française, at a time when his financial need was great, could find nothing better to award him than a prize for "promising young poets," which Musset's stubborn pride made him turn over to a war relief fund. It is fitting to note that August Vacquerie, of Hugo's literary circle, wrote a premature epitaph of the poet in one of his reviews: "Ah! cet homme qui était un poète et qui n'est plus qu'un tombeau!" (Oh! this man who was once a poet and is now nothing but a tombstone!). The Académie Française's election of Musset to its ranks in 1852, after two humiliating defeats by distinctly minor literary talents, was a fitting anticlimax to his career: everyone knew it came too late, when the poet was only a shell of his former self. Yet the reception speech by Désiré Nisard (a long-forgotten apologist for classicism) had oddly patronizing echoes of the tendency to treat Musset as someone who had not yet quite fulfilled his first promise.

Still, by any normal standard of measurement except the strange personal myth that he lived out until his death, we can see Musset today as a decidedly major literary figure of nineteenth-century French and European letters, one who had a significant influence on writers as diverse as Paul Verlaine, Jean Giraudoux, and Jean Anouilh in France; Büchner and Arthur Schnitzler in Germany; Algernon Charles Swinburne and Oscar Wilde in England. His collected works, published in 1852 and 1854, continued to appear at regular intervals throughout the century and up to the present time; in France, many of them are found in popular editions at bookstores, newsstands, and those temples of consumer taste, the supermarkets. In the year 1957, the centenary of his death, there was a flowering of critical studies worldwide. His major plays have kept a tenacious hold on the repertory stage, not only at the Comédie Française but also in regional and community theaters throughout France, as well as in other European countries. The attraction of his myth may have played a promotional role in all this, but it is not sufficient explanation for the affection and admiration Musset continues to elicit from successive generations of readers and playgoers.

It seems reasonably safe to conclude that the *Confessions of a Child of the Century* will continue to be read, not only as an affecting document of the highly charged historical era from which it stems, but also as an effectively objectified novelistic rendering of a personal drama whose power depends as much on the universal emotions it evokes—the mixture of generosity and destructiveness that characterizes the crisis of post-adolescent passions—as on the glamor of the celebrated "drama" it masks. Lovers of poetry, particularly in the earlier stages of discovery that feed on enthusiasm and passionate emotion, will continue to find inspiration and satisfaction in the lyrics of the *Nights,* with their special combination of drama, rhetoric, eloquence, and music, reinforced by the biographical echoes that lend them a larger, mythic dimension. And, most particularly, both theatergoers and amateurs of "armchair theater" will continue to savor, in Musset's four great plays as well as in the less exalted comedies that follow them, the unique theatrical voice that, through the most innovative and original dramatic imagination of its period, expresses so poignantly the dominant themes of Musset's life and work: the conflict of the real with the ideal, the psychological inroads and ravages of time and experience, the passions of youth and the abdications of maturity, the barriers to understanding between lovers—in short, what the Musset scholar Bernard Masson has called "la difficulté d'être" (the problem of being) so powerfully felt in that time of passage known as adolescence and young manhood.

Selected Bibliography

EDITIONS

INDIVIDUAL WORKS
Contes d'Espagne et d'Italie. Paris, 1830.
Un spectacle dans un fauteuil. Paris, 1832. First printing.
————. 2 vols. Paris, 1834. Second printing with added volume.
La confession d'un enfant du siècle. 2 vols. Paris, 1836.
Comédies et proverbes. 2 vols. Paris, 1840.
Poésies nouvelles. Paris, 1840.
Nouvelles. Paris, 1848.
Contes. Paris, 1854.

COLLECTED WORKS
Poésies complètes. Paris, 1854.
Oeuvres complètes d'Alfred de Musset. Edited by Paul de Musset. Paris, 1877.
Oeuvres complètes d'Alfred de Musset. Comédies et Proverbes. 4 vols. Paris, 1952.
Poésies complètes. Edited by Maurice Allem. Paris, 1957. Pléiade edition.
Théâtre complet. Edited by Maurice Allem. Paris, 1958. Pléiade edition.
Oeuvres complètes en prose. Edited by Maurice Allem and Paul Courant. Paris, 1960. Pléiade edition.
Oeuvres complètes. Paris, 1963.

CORRESPONDENCE

Correspondance (1827–1857). Collected and edited by Léon Séché. Paris, 1907.
Lettres d'amour à Aimée d'Alton. Paris, 1910.
George Sand et Alfred de Musset. Correspondance, journal intime de George Sand. Monaco, 1956.

TRANSLATIONS

A Comedy and Two Proverbs. Translated by George Gravely. London, 1957. Contains *Caprice, A Door Should Be Either Open or Shut, It's Impossible to Think of Everything.*
The Complete Writings. Translated by various hands. 10 vols. New York, 1905.
Confessions of a Child of the Century. Translated by Robert Arnot. New York, 1927.
Fantasio. Translated by Jacques Barzun. In Eric Bentley, ed., From the Modern Repertoire, series 1. Denver, 1949.
Seven Plays. Translated by Peter Meyer. New York, 1962.

BIOGRAPHICAL AND CRITICAL STUDIES

Gastinel, Pierre. *Le romantisme d'Alfred de Musset.* Paris, 1933.
Haldane, Charlotte. *The Passionate Life of Alfred de Musset.* New York, 1961.
Lafoscade. *Le Théâtre d'Alfred de Musset.* Paris, 1901. Reprinted 1966.
Masson, Bernard. *Musset et le théâtre intérieur.* Paris, 1974.
Musset, Paul de. *Biographie d'Alfred de Musset.* Paris, 1877.
Rees, Margaret A. *Alfred de Musset.* New York, 1971.
Sices, David. *Theater of Solitude. The Drama of Alfred de Musset.* Hanover, N.H., 1974.
Tieghem, Philippe van. *Musset, l'homme et l'oeuvre.* Paris, 1957.

DAVID SICES

THÉOPHILE GAUTIER

(1811–1872)

IN THE LAST chapter of "Une nuit de Cléopâtre" ("One of Cleopatra's Nights," 1845), Théophile Gautier as narrator suddenly breaks off to complain that the French language is "so chaste, so icily prudish" that it cannot possibly describe the orgy that is to come at the climax of the tale. "Really, Théo," the reader is tempted to ask, "you are not serious, are you? 'Chaste' you call the language of François Rabelais, Nicolas Restif de le Bretonne, the comte de Mirabeau, the marquis de Sade, and so many more?"

Yet beneath the exaggeration there lies a truth that accounts for Gautier's frustration. The French literary language, especially of the seventeenth and eighteenth centuries, tends to prefer the abstract to the concrete, the generic to the particular. A sense of propriety, a kind of aloofness, seems almost built into the language. John Cleland's *Fanny Hill* (1748–1750) was translated as *Les mémoires de Françoise de la Colline*. Anglo-Saxon bawdiness takes on a certain Gallic elegance as it crosses the English Channel.

Moreover, as a Romance language the French of the classical period was noted for its etymological unity, which became equated, as an aesthetic, with purity. The mixture of Anglo-Saxon and Anglo-Norman that one finds in Shakespeare would have struck the French ear as a cacophonous hodgepodge. Why instead of saying "This goodly frame the earth" could not Hamlet have said "This admirable edifice . . ."? And as for the generic versus the particular, is not the word *fleur* (flower) preferable to the 500-odd flowers and plants that Shakespeare calls by name?

With Shakespeare and Jean Racine, the greatest of the classical French poets, in mind, the contemporary poet Yves Bonnefoy differentiates between the realism of English, stressing as it does the tangible aspect of things—a "mirror" Bonnefoy calls it—and the idealism of French, which tends to turn in upon itself, "like a sphere." English is an "opening," French a "closing up."

Thanks to such an aesthetic Racine was able to compose his flawless masterpieces in which the rhymed alexandrine couplets produce subtle and haunting effects. Racine's imitators of the eighteenth and early nineteenth centuries did not fare so well, however, and by 1830 the French poetic language had become so anemic, in the eyes of poets, anyhow, that some sort of transfusion was bound to take place. The instrument was Victor Hugo's play *Hernani* (1830), during the first performance of which classicists and romanticists literally came to blows. From that moment, those who had rallied around Hugo were committed to the "illustration" of the French language, to use the term of Joachim du Bellay, who with Pierre de Ronsard and the other poets of the Pléiade had sought three centuries earlier to implement their program of linguistic enrichment.

Gautier, at nineteen, fought in the "Battle of *Hernani*," wearing his famous *gilet rouge*, which has been variously translated as "rose-colored waistcoat," "cerise doublet," "shocking-pink-purple waistcoat," "rose-colored satin doublet." In his nostalgic *Histoire du romantisme* (*A History of Romanticism*, 1874), written shortly before his death in 1872, Gautier gives a detailed description of the garment and predicts that it will remain for posterity as his principal claim to fame.

This last remark is typical of Gautier's modesty. One of his most endearing traits was his diffidence, a kind of self-deprecatory attitude that was richly nourished by the humiliations he suffered from publishers in nineteenth-century Paris.

Gautier was himself a Parisian through and through. Born in Tarbes, in the Pyrenees, on 30 August 1811, he was brought to Paris at the age of three; there he remained, except when traveling, until his death in 1872. Hearing in Geneva of the siege of Paris in 1870, he is said to have exclaimed: "I've got to get back. They're beating Mama!"

Gautier attended the Collège Louis-le-Grand, then the Collège Charlemagne, where he became a close friend of Gérard de Nerval, three years his senior. In 1829 the Gautier family, which now included two young sisters, Émilie and Zoé, moved to 8 place Royale (today the place des Vosges), the early seventeenth-century architecture of which was to make a deep impression on the lad. A year later Victor Hugo moved to number 6. It was largely thanks to his admiration for the leader of romanticism that Gautier, who had been attending the academy of the painter Rioult during his last year at the college, decided to become a poet rather than a painter. Shortly after the "Battle of *Hernani*" he published his first volume of verse, called simply *Poésies*. Unfortunately its publication date (28 July 1830) coincided exactly with the "trois glorieuses" (July 27, 28, 29), the three days of street fighting of the Revolution of 1830, and the book was totally ignored.

This coincidence may have contributed to Gautier's growing distaste for political involvement. In 1831 he joined the group of younger romanticists known as "Le Petit Cénacle" (Nerval, Petrus Borel, Auguste Maquet, Philothée O'Neddy, and others), which met in the studio of Jehan Duseigneur on the rue de Vaugirard. It was there in an effort to keep the romantic movement uncontaminated by notions of "useful art" that the credo known as "l'art pour l'art," eventually to become the "art for art's sake" movement in England toward the end of the century, took hold. One can follow its evolution in the prefaces that Gautier wrote for his poem *Albertus* (1833), his collection of short stories in *Les Jeunes-France* (1833), and the novel *Mademoiselle de Maupin* (1835–1836), leading eventually to the volume of poems that is usually considered his masterpiece, *Émaux et camées* (*Enamels and Cameos*), the first edition of which appeared in 1852.

The publication of *Mademoiselle de Maupin* brought Gautier to the attention of Honoré de Balzac, who invited him to *La chronique de Paris* as a contributor. But it was mainly with *La presse*, directed by Émile de Girardin, that Gautier, beginning in 1836 and continuing for almost two decades, established his reputation as a drama critic, art critic, literary critic, and feuilletonist. Gautier thus became the first major French writer to depend entirely on journalism ("journalistic martyrdom," writes one biographer) for his livelihood. In 1855 he left *La presse* for *Le moniteur universel*, the official paper of the Second Empire. Under the protection of the Princess Mathilde, Gautier remained faithful to the regime until its fall in 1870. He apparently felt no qualms about supporting an authoritarian government. "All his life," claimed his friend Maxime Du Camp, "he called for the reign of a Medici or a Francis I."

The routine of weekly deadlines for copy was broken periodically by trips outside Paris that, incidentally, Gautier had to arrange for himself; he was not a "roving reporter" in the usual sense. His main purpose for each trip was artistic, and his most successful—those to Spain, Italy, Russia, and the Middle East—made of him one of the outstanding travel writers of his day.

Gautier was never married. Of his numerous liaisons the most lasting were those with Eugénie Fort and the singer Ernesta Grisi. As for Ernesta's sister, Carlotta Grisi, the dancer, Gautier's "strange and impossible" love for her—a bit like Nerval's for Jenny Colon—inspired the work for which he is best remembered, the story of *Giselle* (1841), "the apotheosis of the romantic ballet," according to the choreographer and ballet master Serge Lifar.

Gautier spent most of his last years still meeting deadlines but living quite comfortably in Neuilly, outside Paris, with his sisters and cats, and receiving such guests as Charles Baudelaire, the Goncourts, Eugène Delacroix, Alexandre Dumas *père,* and Gustave Doré. His last work to be published was the definitive edition of *Enamels and Cameos* (1872). He died on 23 October 1872 and was given a state funeral.

Returning to the *gilet rouge,* we see it mainly as a symbol of Gautier's determination to put color back into what he calls the "Racinian dialect." In an essay on Baudelaire he speaks for himself as much as for the younger poet when he writes: "One can well imagine that the fourteen-hundred words of the Racinian dialect hardly suffice for an author who has taken on the difficult task of rendering modern ideas and things in their infinite complexity and their multiple coloration." Baudelaire in turn relates that on his first visit to Gautier the latter asked him somewhat suspiciously if he liked to read dictionaries. "Fortunately I had had a bad case of lexicomania since childhood, and I saw that with my reply I rose in his esteem."

It is clear that for the romanticists linguistic reform meant vocabulary building. Victor Hugo claimed that he had put the Phrygian rebel's cap on the old dictionary, meaning that

the French equivalent of a spade was henceforth to be called a spade. As for syntax, however, "leave that alone," admonished Hugo. Gautier among others followed this advice, and his sentences have a simplicity of structure that follows faithfully the comte de Rivarol's eighteenth-century dictum: "Ce qui n'est pas clair n'est pas français" (If it isn't clear, it isn't French).

In richness of vocabulary, Gautier vied with, some say even surpassed, Hugo and Balzac. Gautier had an incredibly retentive memory. He is said to have recited all the 158 lines of Hugo's "Les lions" the very day it came out. It was this capacity that led him to lodge an encyclopedia in his brain. Henry James compared him to Rabelais: "an immeasurably lighter-handed Rabelais," who "had an almost Rabelaisian relish for enumerations, lists and catalogs—a sort of grotesque delight in quantity."

Indeed Gautier's productivity was vast. He estimated shortly before his death that if all his writings were published in book form they would amount to some 300 volumes. This may seem somewhat exaggerated, but one must recall that journalism was his bread and butter. Art critic, drama critic, music critic, roving reporter, feuilletoniste, he was all of these. The only translation into English of his so-called complete works is a not-so-complete twelve-volume publication that appeared in various editions, limited and otherwise, at the turn of the century. The translator was an English-born Harvard professor named Frederick-Caesar de Sumichrast. Despite a touch of quaintness in expression, his translations, which date from 1900 to 1903, are still quite readable today. They include an introduction in which the professor expresses his rather singular views of "the Romanticist school." The short novel *Fortunio* (1838), today considered one of Gautier's more original works, is condemned as "gross," "coarse," and "repellent." (According to *Who's Who in America* for 1910 Professor de Sumichrast was president of the Victorian Club of Boston. One would like to know why he chose Gautier in the first place.)

The vastness of Gautier's erudition and of his literary output attest to his hope of becoming a new Adam, "the great nomenclator." If we recall Bonnefoy's metaphors, Gautier was trying to flatten the sphere of the French language if not actually transform it into a mirror. Gautier would have loved to "Anglo-Saxonize" his language not only literally—he introduces words into French like "splash" and "sneer," which announce the onomatopoetic words that Mallarmé noted later in *Les mots anglais* (1877)—but also figuratively, because of his belief that words should designate tangibly the things of the world. "I am a man for whom the external world exists," he once said to the Goncourt brothers. He saw art, it would seem, in terms of mimesis. Purely descriptive passages fill a very large number of pages in his fiction. And it is to the visible world that Gautier, a painter manqué, was by far the most sensitive. Like Stendhal he proceeded by "little details."

Gautier loved the outside world with childlike enthusiasm. One reads in his *Voyage en Russie* (*Travels in Russia*, 1867) how he awoke to find snow falling in Saint Petersburg. "I dressed as fast as I could." This understatement conveys the joie de vivre that fills the travel books and much of the fiction. Again Henry James:

> Descriptive writing, to our English tastes, suggests nothing very enticing—a respectable sort of padding, at best, but a few degrees removed in ponderosity from downright moralizing. . . . But there is no better proof of Gautier's talent than that he should have triumphantly reformed this venerable abuse, and in the best sense, made one of the heaviest kinds of writing one of the lightest.
>
> ("Théophile Gautier," in *French Poets and Novelists*)

One wonders how much of a left-handed compliment this may be but, English or not, each reader must decide for himself whether to read or skip. For the hasty ones Gautier often facilitates matters by making each salient feature the subject of the sentence or clause. One has only to run the eye down a page such as this one, which contains a description of a Hindu maiden, Priyamvada, in the novel *Partie carrée* (Change Your Partners, 1851): "A girl of incredible beauty. . . . Her complexion. . . . Her almond-shaped eyes. . . . The nose. . . ." And so forth for four pages, when the narration resumes. But what a pity to miss the sumptuousness of the uncut passage, which must be savored at one's leisure. Here, for example, is the nose:

> The nose, thin and delicately formed, with rosy nostrils, was slightly tattooed at the root, with tincture of gorothchana; and from the nostrils hung a gold ring, studded with diamonds, through the circle of which shone purest pearls set in a smile as golden as the fruit of the jujube tree.

Gautier was criticized for excessive detail. The comte de Gobineau, apparently with his own "superior individualism" of *Les pléiades* (1874) in mind, wrote bitingly of *Fortunio*:

> The purpose of this book seems to be to render as exactly as possible the cut of a gown, the shape of an armchair, the wallpaper design of a bedroom; it would seem that all the superior beings gathered there have reduced the notion of happiness to a knowledge of fabrics.
>
> ("Théophile Gautier," in *Études critiques* [Paris, 1844–1848])

Gautier once defended such "microscopic amplification," as one critic called it, by claiming that he wrote for posterity. Without him there would be no record of many endangered objects—indeed this is quite true of some of his art criticism. But this in turn makes Gautier, like Balzac, "a secretary of society," which as the original partisan of "l'art pour l'art" he had no intention of becoming. Let us simply say that he relished detail; without it, he once said, there would be no story. For the reader the weightiness of the detail depends largely on the pace of the story. We are all the more inclined to delight in the features of Priyamvada because of the respite they offer from the breakneck pace of the novel.

Implicit in Gautier's descriptive writing is the notion that the language he uses, indeed that language itself, is above all an instrument for depicting reality, but that the depiction can never attain the beauty or the intensity of the original—"the sublime poetry of reality," as he says in *Mademoiselle de Maupin*. But Gautier believed with equal fervor in the self-sufficiency of language. "For the poet words have within themselves and beyond the meaning they express a beauty, a value of their own." And he saw nothing contradictory in this dual function of language. Take, for example, his piece on Nijni-Novgorod in *Travels in Russia*:

> Nijni-Novgorod had long cast that irresistible spell upon me. No melody sounded so delightfully in my ears as its dim, distant name; I repeated it unconsciously like a litany, with a feeling of individual pleasure; its configuration took my fancy as if it were an arabesque of curious shape.

Lured by the name, Gautier visits the place. One expects him to indulge in the usual romantic disenchantment. Not at all. The reality is not exactly "sublime," but it has none of the barrenness that Nerval and Baudelaire found on Cythera, for instance. The great disappointment for Gautier would have been rather to discover that in 1932 the name Nijni-Novgorod was replaced by Gorki.

On the whole Gautier was able to accommodate himself cheerfully to the coexistence of a nonverbal and a verbal reality. The former, the "external world," finds its truest expression in the straightforward prose of the descriptive writing, stripped of tropes, rhetorical devices, euphemisms, or "fig leaves," as Gautier calls them, where precision and accuracy count above all, as in this description of the approaches to Paris, worthy of the realism of Émile Zola or Guy de Maupassant:

> There surely cannot be anything meaner than the houses, the sides of which have been laid bare by the demolition of their neighbors', and which still preserve the blackened imprint of the chimney flues, rags of wall paper and traces of half-effaced paint; the waste ground intersected by pools of water and flecked with hillocks of refuse.
>
> (*Travels in Russia*)

The prose writing can be equally unadorned in the recording of an object of beauty, a landscape or seascape, such as this view of the Cyclades from the island of Syros, where only the phrase "wildly romantic" and the allusion to painting at the end mar the simple objectivity of the description:

> Behind us rose the crest of the mountain upon which Syros is built; on the right, looking seaward, fell away an immense ravine broken and torn in the most wildly romantic fashion; at our feet sank in successive terraces the white houses of upper and lower Syros; farther in the distance shone the sea with its luminous gleam, and the circle of Delos, Mykonos, Tinos and Andros, which the setting sun bathed in rose and changing tints, which, if they were represented in painting, would be declared impossible.
>
> (*Constantinople*, 1853)

But along with these direct, ground-floor pictures of reality there are, with Gautier as with every poet, the transformations wrought by the language of the imagination. Three factors in particular, either separately or by their convergence, make for the distinctiveness of Gautier's style in both his prose and his verse: his self-consciousness as an author, his addiction to allusiveness, and the plethora of his "transpositions d'art." Let us examine each of these.

Gautier's preoccupation with his role as author goes considerably beyond that of the usual romantic in France, for whom *le moi* (the ego, or self) as lover or martyr overlaps *le moi* as writer. For such writers, who wanted their "woe to show," the presence and the identity of the reader were secondary matters. Gautier, on the other hand, enjoyed talking directly to the reader either as friend or foe. He gave such familiar phrases as "dear reader" and "our hero" fresh applications. His first prose work, the collection of short stories called *Les Jeunes-France*, contains a preface on the subject of—prefaces. He chides the readers who are fatuous enough to skip over them, for, says he, the preface, along with the table of contents, contains the choicest bits of the book. Like the "P.S." of a woman's letter, it expresses the book's most precious thoughts. "You need not read the rest."

Gautier's irony is presumably directed here against those who do not "read the rest," the so-called progressive readers of the period for whom literature had a strictly utilitarian function, readers whom Gautier attacked more violently two years later in the name of art for art's sake in his famous preface to *Mademoiselle de Maupin*. He proclaims there that all that is useful is ugly.

It is mainly in his fiction that Gautier takes the reader into his confidence, making him an accomplice, almost a fellow craftsman. Of a simile that is, he confesses, a bit farfetched he writes: "Never mind, we'll keep it, out of pure orientalism" *(Mademoiselle de Maupin)*. When he writes: "We forgot to say that the Marquis de Bruyères was married" *(Le Capitaine Fracasse)*; or "I have invented so perfect a hero that I am afraid to make use of him" *(Fortunio)*; or when, after relating an episode, he announces that he will delete it because it is too hackneyed *(Fortunio)*, Gautier is not only winking at the reader but also giving him glimpses of the creative process.

One is tempted to draw from such examples an image of Gautier as a precursor of modernism, with its shift in emphasis from the notion of the work of art as a faithful copy of nature

to the notion of the work as an expression of the creative process. But Gautier did not have the theoretical bent to formulate aesthetic doctrines, modernist or otherwise. His preface to *Mademoiselle de Maupin* is a sparkling polemic and historically important; but except for the claim that beauty must be "useless," it is rather weak in theoretical formulations. Baudelaire's arguments for the autonomy of art were considerably more cogent.

It is more likely, then, that when he intrudes on the narrative with a phrase like "I shall be obliged to kill her on p. 127" *(Fortunio)*, he is simply being playful. When he writes a preface about prefaces is he being any more modernist than Shakespeare, who wrote an epilogue about epilogues in *As You Like It* (1623)?

Gautier's playfulness occasionally leads him to trick the reader. In one of his later novels, *Spirite* (*Stronger than Death; or Spirite*, 1866), there is an eloquent defense of realism, with its goal of a completely objective rendering of the material world. We assume that Gautier is expressing his own views until we suddenly recall that the speaker is a disembodied spirit. Presumably this is Gautier's way of conveying his ambivalent feelings about the spiritual and the material worlds.

To sum up, the reader who lets himself get caught up in a narration may be quite disconcerted when the author intrudes. But the intrusion itself is a reminder that writer and reader are together in a world of discourse. An irate husband rushing around the bedroom in search of a dagger, a knife, anything to stab his unfaithful bride, mutters: "This is all very Shakespearean" *(Partie carrée)*. This is all very self-conscious, too, and the reader is wise to accept it as such.

The mention of Shakespeare brings us to the second distinctive trait in Gautier, the richness of literary allusion. Of course there is hardly a writer in the Western tradition who has not reached into the grab bag of Greek and Roman mythology, biblical lore, medieval romance, hagiography, and so forth. What distinguishes Gautier is not merely the breadth of erudition underlying his references and the mixture of the classical and modern but above all the fusion, in so much of his work, of painting and sculpture with the literary. Jacques Barzun has spoken of the "extraordinary resonance of remembered art" in Gautier. There is hardly a page that does not evoke directly or indirectly an earlier creation from Homer on, or, as Gautier himself puts it, "from Orpheus to Lamartine," and we could add "from Apelles to Delacroix."

Let us look first at the literary allusions. The great majority come from what looks like a Great Books syllabus: Homer, the Greek tragedians, Vergil, Ovid, Dante, Rabelais, Shakespeare; and among the moderns: Goethe, Hugo, Lord Byron, Heinrich Heine, Nerval. Of the French classical writers Gautier makes short shrift; and when he alludes to Don Juan, as he often does, we know from the cast of characters that it is Mozart's, not Molière's.

The allusions serve a variety of functions. As one arm or another of a comparison, they intensify the metaphorical effect. Mademoiselle de Maupin, wanting to stress her masculinity, compares herself to Achilles disguised as a maiden among maidens; like him "I would willingly leave the mirror for the sword." The analogy may seem quite obvious, but it very aptly succeeds in enhancing the ambiguity of Mademoiselle de Maupin's sex, for she becomes at one and the same time one of the maidens and the most virile of heroes.

. Gautier on occasion combines the familiar and the less familiar allusion to produce a cumulative effect. In *Le Capitaine Fracasse* (*Captain Fracasse*, 1863), the protagonist, Sigognac, who comes from the provinces, is warned about the perils of sailing in the "sea" that is Paris. Not content to speak metaphorically of the "reefs" and "shoals" together with the inevitable Scyllas and Charibdes, the author adds the unexpected Euripos, which probably sends many a reader scurrying to the

encyclopedia. This strait, which separates Euboea from the mainland of Greece, is noted for its rough crosscurrents. It is precisely this navigational danger that Gautier wants to stress, whereas a later poet, Guillaume Apollinaire, will underline the agitation itself: "La vie est variable aussi bien que l'Euripe" (*Alcools;* Life is as uncertain as the Euripos).

Gautier has no qualms about mixing races and religions so long as the mixture seasons a text. In *Captain Fracasse* the duke of Vallombreuse proclaims his misogyny in no uncertain terms. Henceforth he will be as frigid as Hippolytus and as contemptuous as Joseph. Does the duke know that both young men were punished for their temerity by the women they had spurned? In any case the double nature of the allusion, drawn from Greek myth and the Bible, respectively, underscores the duke's determination.

Certain names turn up like recurrent images. Dante's Ugolino elicits varying degrees of pathos each time he appears, and on one occasion, at least, a bit of black humor, not unusual in Gautier. In *Voyage en Espagne* (*Travels in Spain*, 1843), he relates how once in Andalusia he suffered from hunger for the first time in his life. "Ugolino in his tower was not more famished than I, and I did not have, like him, four sons to eat."

By their repetition certain allusions take on an obsessive quality that the author would be the first to admit to. The references to Ovid's Samalcis, the nymph who became united in body with Hermaphroditus, reveal a fascination with the theme of androgyny that finds its fullest expression in *Mademoiselle de Maupin*.

This brings us back to Shakespeare, since chapter 11, the central chapter of this novel, contains a performance of *As You Like It*. In other works allusions abound also, mainly to *Hamlet* (1603) and the festive comedies. It is almost as though Gautier had learned to speak Shakespearean. He often adapts the quotations, especially the more familiar ones, to his own purposes, for instance to check the flow of excessive sentimentality over the death of the actor Matamore in *Captain Fracasse,* when another actor, known as the Pedant, exclaims: "Alas, poor Matamore . . ." and the author breaks in with the comment: "Little did the good Pedant know that he was repeating the exact words of Hamlet, Prince of Denmark, skull in hand of Yorick, the late king's jester, as it transpires in the Tragedy of Master W. Shakespeare, distinguished poet of England under the protection of Her Majesty the Queen Elizabeth." The author's affected verbosity—let us call *him* the Pedant—is no doubt a disguise to make the identification of Hamlet more palatable without insulting the reader's intelligence.

Gautier's allusions to painting, sculpture, and architecture are particularly evident in the poetry. In *España,* a volume of verse inspired by the trip to Spain, the allusiveness extends from mere passing references (Prometheus, Venus, Le Cid, Moses, Behemoth, Balthazar, Titan, Hercules) to entire poems, with titles such as "Sur le Prométhée du musée de Madrid" (On the Prometheus in the Museum at Madrid), "Ribeira" (Ribera), "L'Escurial," "La vierge de Tolède" (The Virgin of Toledo), "Deux tableaux de Valdès Léal" (Two Pictures by Valdès Léal), "A Zurbarán," and so on. These latter are usually designated as "transpositions d'art," a genre that is the third distinctive feature of Gautier's work. For the moment let us examine some of his "remembered art" allusions, especially in painting and sculpture.

If there is one constant in Gautier it is the evocation of feminine beauty. Like Priyamvada in *Partie carrée,* each heroine is of surpassing beauty. Detailing the features in much the same way and usually in the same sequence (hair, eyes, nose, mouth), Gautier introduces nonetheless, as in the medieval *blasons,* a wide variety of descriptions, as diverse as the names of the beauties who decorate the pages of his prose fiction; this is only a partial list: Angela, Takoser, Spirite, Giselle, Arria Marcella, Nyssia, Cleopatra, Edith and Ana-bel, Omphale, Clarimonde, Katy (who is merely "pretty"), Prascovie Labinska, Alicia Ward, Ra'hel, Musidora, Madeleine, Rosette, Isabelle, Zerbine.

Such a concentration on beauty accounts in large measure for Gautier's preferred artists, whose names are scattered through his work: Phidias, Praxiteles, Leonardo, Raphael, Titian, Rubens, Watteau, Boucher, Canova, Ingres, Chassériau. For the reader who knows their paintings and sculptures, such names, together with the details of verbal description, serve to characterize a particular type of beauty. ("She is a perfect Rubens.") Sensuality predominates; as one of his own characters says, Gautier replaces "le beau idéal" with "le beau matériel," or the ideal with the materially beautiful. Female phantoms have rarely been evoked so sensuously as those in his *Récits fantastiques* (Tales of the Fantastic). Nudes that are not looked upon as particularly erotic become so under his pen. Of the Venus de Milo he writes: "The arms have gone, but it seems as though, if they were found, they would spoil the delight of the eye by preventing one from seeing that superb bosom and those wonderful breasts" (*Guide de l'amateur au Musée de Louvre* [*The Louvre,* 1882]).

Aesthetic pleasure, however, is not all that attracts Gautier. His preference for a fusion of mystery and beauty explains, no doubt, why he alludes so often to Leonardo da Vinci. Gautier could be speaking of his own ideal when he writes: "He [Leonardo] is at once truthful and fantastic, accurate and visionary; he mingles reality and dream in surprising proportions." The "Mona Lisa" (1503) inspires an extended metaphor that takes us from Don Giovanni to Icarus and Albrecht Dürer. If the Don had met the Mona Lisa there would have been no need for the catalog of 1,003 women (the *mille e tre* of Leporello's list): "He would have written but one name, for the wings of his desire would have refused to bear him farther; they would have melted and fallen in the black sunshine of those eyes." Incidentally, the image of the black sun of melancholy, most familiar as a line from Nerval's sonnet "El desdichado" (1854), was first penned by Gautier under the influence of Dürer's engraving "Melancholia" and became a recurrent image throughout his work.

Somewhat less complex but more bizarre is the reference in the same "guide" to Leonardo's "Saint John the Baptist" (*ca.* 1515) with its "troubling slyness" and "diabolical smile," like "another portrait of the Mona Lisa, more ideal, mysterious and strange." Having just read that the angel in "the Virgin of the Rocks" is a "celestial hermaphrodite," one is prepared for the suggestion of sexual ambiguity that relates this study of Leonardo to the theme of androgyny in *Mademoiselle de Maupin.*

Gautier's writings on Leonardo bring us to the question of the "transposition d'art" as a genre. Gautier is responsible for the term and has contributed some of the finest examples in prose and verse. In an apostrophe to Titian about his "Venus," Gautier writes:

> *Pour rendre sa beauté complète*
> *Laisse-moi faire, grand vieillard,*
> *Changeant mon luth pour ta palette,*
> *Une transposition d'art.*
>
> ("Musée secret")

To render her beauty complete let me, O grand old man, changing my luth for your palette, make a transposition of art.

The stanza suggests that unless an exchange, a "transposition," is made between painting and poetry, the portrayal of beauty will be incomplete. Gautier has spoken elsewhere of "tableaux à la plume," or written paintings, and he once confessed how much he enjoyed placing next to a canvas a page on which the theme of the painter is taken up by the writer. The term is sometimes confused with synaesthesia, as in Gautier's "Symphonie en blanc majeur" (Symphony in White Major), but this poem cannot really be called a "transposition d'art" merely because color (white) and sound (symphony) are fused in the title. The simplest definition is probably the best: a poem about a painting (or a painter), it being understood that "poem" includes "prose poem" and that "painting" can be replaced by other works of art (sculpture, architecture, and the like).

Transpositions in the reverse sense have long been traditional. Renaissance and neoclassical painting and sculpture are based on poetry, drama, and legend. Gautier concludes his description of Nyssia, the wife of King Candaulus, with: "There are things that can be written only in marble" ("Le roi Candaule," ["King Candaulus," 1844]). James Pradier, a prominent sculptor of the day, took up the challenge, and when Gautier, as art critic, saw Pradier's "Nyssia" at the Salon of 1848 he wrote with emotion: "I could never have aspired to such an honor."

Gautier was himself an accomplished artist. The technical mastery of some of his self-portraits, for instance, shows that he profited from the months at the Rioult atelier in his late teens. And it was mainly with a painter's eye that he viewed the world. But once he had decided that his true vocation was literature, he never abandoned the written word. For him the "transposition" went only one way.

The volume of verse *La comédie de la mort* (Death's Comedy, 1838) has an assortment of transpositions under such titles as "Rocaille," "Pastel," "Watteau," "Melancholia," "Niobe," "Les Cariatides," "Le Sphinx," "Versailles," and "Terza-rima." "Watteau" is remarkable for its compactness. Its four decasyllabic quatrains relate a lonely walk in a landscape desolate except for an enclosed park in the manner of Antoine Watteau. The poet looks at it through the iron grillwork and walks away both dejected and delighted, for he has realized

> *Que j'étais près du rêve de ma vie*
> *Que mon bonheur était enfermé là.*

That I was near the dream of my life, that my happiness was there enclosed.

Despite certain details that, as Maxine Cutler has pointed out, evoke rather a seventeenth-century garden in the manner of André Le Nôtre, most readers will probably recall the landscape of Watteau's "L'Embarquement pour l'île de Cythère" ("The Embarkation for Cythera"), and will feel the same nostalgia for an enchanted land that is evoked by the painting. To the extent that poem and painting contribute to the same effect, Gautier's "Watteau" can be considered an authentic "transposition." There is a fine description of the "Embarkation" in the Louvre, including such details as the lady catching the train of her dress. "Only Watteau could catch these feminine gestures."

There are three Spanish painters whose art Gautier transposed into alexandrines in *España:* Francisco de Zurbarán, Jusepe Ribera, and Juan de Valdès Léal. Why did Gautier, the lover of classic beauty, choose these three, who are about as far removed from Praxiteles as the mummies of Bordeaux (see *Travels in Spain*, ch. 1)?

The answer lies partly in the poems themselves. In "A Zurbarán," the poet addresses the monks who were painted by this seventeenth-century religious artist—he was, by the way, a contemporary of Rubens—and asks them why they mortify the flesh. The body is beautiful. It was in the human body that Jesus became incarnate; they have no right to revile it. In "Ribeira" the poet speaks directly to the artist, again asking: Why all this "triste amour du laid"? Why this obsession with the hideous? In the "Deux tableaux de Valdès Léal" the poet is torn between impatience at the artist's nightmarish allegories of death—as if to say: "Why repeat what we all know?"—and admiration for the plethora of lurid details, which the poet in turn puts into a "cascade" of words, concluding with the powerful alexandrine couplet addressed to death:

> Et vous nous promettez, pour consolation,
> La triste égalité de la corruption.

And you promise us for consolation the sad equality of decay.

It would seem that if Gautier chose those three, there lies beneath the ostensible reason—the obligation in the name of beauty to refute their morbidity, their vicarious cruelty, their self-imposed suffering—a kind of voluptuousness that Gautier himself shared and that it was his pleasure to transpose into words, as he did with such relish for Goya. We shall see in fact that in some of his fiction he sought to fuse beauty and death. In the collection *La comédie de la mort* it is to Death that he addresses the line: "Je te consacrerai mes chansons les plus belles" (I shall devote to Thee my most beautiful songs). And in a number of the "transpositions d'art" of that volume this is what he does.

At times Gautier's prose writings on art reach a greater degree of intensity than his verse. Such is the case with his work on Francisco de Goya. Gautier was largely responsible for acquainting the French public with this name, thanks to an essay published in his *Travels in Spain.* Largely biographical and critical, it contains certain portions that can stand on their own as poetic evocations. In order to stress what he views as the "grotesquely horrible" aspects of Goya's caricatures in *Los caprichos*, Gautier overwhelms the reader with the sheer quantity of his horrendous details: nightmares, witches' sabbaths, old hags, demons, spiders, toads' bellies. Gautier compares Goya's dreams with the "songes drolatiques" (spicy dreams) of Rabelais. Apparently he also had Rabelais, the inexhaustible enumerator, in mind as he piled one aberration on another.

Other prose passages, properly abridged, may well qualify as "transpositions d'art." In the second chapter of *Mademoiselle de Maupin* one finds a eulogy of Peter Paul Rubens. Gautier was obsessed by the Flemish master's sensuality and had indeed wandered all over Belgium with Gérard de Nerval in search of an actual embodiment of the Rubens type. In this passage the tone is rhetorical, the description directly physical: "ces bras potelés, ces dos charnus et polis" (those chubby arms, those fleshy, polished backs). Baudelaire in a quatrain on Rubens in the poem "Les Phares" (The Beacons) in *Les fleurs du mal* (*The Flowers of Evil,* 1857) uses metaphors in apposition—"Rubens . . . oreiller de chair fraiche" (Rubens . . . pillow of cool flesh)—in order to intensify the sensuality, but at the same time making it so cool that any kind of deep love is precluded. We may infer from Gautier's omission of any suggestion of coolness that the presence of love was a foregone conclusion.

It is tempting to compare Gautier's transpositions with those of Baudelaire in "Les phares." Rubens, Leonardo, Rembrandt, Michelangelo, Watteau, Goya, Delacroix—these are among the European masters both poets admired. "Les phares" is made up of alexandrine quatrains that evoke the style of each artist, leading the reader to the concluding stanzas, which affirm the power of art as the means for overcoming our mortal condition; it is, as André Malraux was to put it, an "antidestin." This belief Gautier most certainly shared.

Despite the temptation it would be unfair to set up the highly chiseled lines of Baudelaire's poem against the scattered transpositions of the older poet. Much of the pleasure of reading Gautier on art is that of discovering hidden gems. When he wished, Gautier could create a lapidary style as fine as that of any of his contemporaries. Witness the final poem "L'Art" in *Enamels and Cameos.*

As a genre the "transposition d'art," inaugurated by Gautier, perfected by Baudelaire, was to flourish in twentieth-century France with such poets as Apollinaire, Pierre Reverdy, Paul Éluard, and René Char.

An art form that every reader of Gautier comes to know sooner or later is the tapestry. There is hardly a wall in all his works that is without "une tapisserie de haute lisse" (a tapestry of high warp) or of some other sort. The most noteworthy come down from, if not Penelope, at least Queen Nyssia ("King Candaulus") and figure in such disparate works as *Mademoiselle de Maupin,* the short story "Omphale" (1834), and *Captain Fracasse.* It is not surprising that the greatest number (including some frescoes) represent scenes from classical mythology. The reader is thus enticed into seizing the connection between the wall scene and the situation it is witness to; a series on Jason and Medea, for example, sinister in its bloody violence and, in the same room, lying beneath, the inanimate body of the duke of Vallombreuse, perhaps done in like one of Jason's Argonauts by the hero of Gautier's most popular story, *Captain Fracasse.*

In Gautier's fantastic world it is only one step from the tapestry figures as witness to those who participate in the action. Hercules remains immobile on the wall while his coquettish wife, Omphale (in the story of the same name), steps down to seduce the handsome Cherubino who is the narrator. The style of the tapestry is very "Pompadour," as Gautier himself calls it, even down to the artificial beauty mark (in French, the *assassin*) just beneath Omphale's eye, and the special way in which Hercules raises his little finger as if to take a pinch of snuff.

Charming as it may be, this story hardly constitutes a "transposition d'art." The only tapestry text that would seem to qualify is a paragraph from *Mademoiselle de Maupin* in which Mademoiselle, after speaking of her strange preoccupation with the fantastic world created by the tapestry weavers, continues:

I love passionately that imaginary vegetation, those flowers and plants that don't exist in reality, those forests of unknown trees where unicorns are wandering, and caprimules and snow-colored deer, with golden crucifixes among their antlers, forever pursued by red-bearded hunters in Saracen habits.

(ch. 12)

The accumulation of details builds up a composite picture of tapestries in general, especially medieval ones, and evokes the ambiance of the fantastic more effectively than the description of distinct mythological scenes.

Apparently speaking for the author, Mademoiselle de Maupin goes on to say that when she was a child she could never enter a tapestried room without feeling a kind of shudder. "But," asks the reader, "why shouldn't a painting, or a fresco for that matter, produce the same effect?" Gautier replies that it is the undulation of the fabric and the play of light that help create the impression of the fantastic for the child. Of course there are other factors, such as the very size of the tapestry and the sumptuousness with which it covers the walls. There seems to be no doubt that Gautier's own recurrent use of this decorative art form stems from that "shudder," a mixture of terror and fascination, that he felt as a child whenever he saw a tapestry.

Gautier was on the whole less drawn to architecture than to painting and sculpture as an inspiration for "transpositions d'art." Poems such as "Versailles" (*La comédie de la mort*) and "L'Escurial" (*España*) express rather an active dislike for certain styles. The Escurial is a "debauch of granite," and Versailles is not even ancient; it is merely "superannuated." If Gautier shares with other romantics a special affection among architects for Giovanni Piranesi, it is mainly because of the "architectures effondrées," the "poetry of ruins," that Piranesi's engravings express. In *Enamels and Cameos*, Gautier describes an old castle:

> Aux vastes salles délabrées,
> Aux couloirs livrant leur secret,
> Architectures effondrées
> Où Piranèse se perdrait.
> ("Inès de la Sierras," 11. 9–12)

with vast dilapidated rooms, with halls yielding up their secrets, crumbling architectures in which Piranesi would get lost.

Yet two architectural motifs carry special connotations in Gautier's work. One is the Henri IV–Louis XIII style of mansion, the most recognizable feature of which is the red brick wall with interlocking white stone corners. In *Captain Fracasse*, this is the style of the Château de Bruyères, where our hero, the baron de Sigognac, had an idyllic stay with his troupe of traveling players. Gautier informs us that the style of the château recalls that of the townhouses in the place Royale in Paris. He does not tell us that his family lived on this square when he was in his teens and that although he is no longer a child it remains a place of enchantment for him.

When d'Albert, the protagonist of *Mademoiselle de Maupin*, imagines the ideal spot where he will one day meet his elusive soulmate, he visualizes the window of an Henri IV château from which she will be gazing "mélancoliquement appuyée sur le balcon" (leaning on the balcony with an air of melancholy). This is chapter 1. By chapter 9, Madeleine de Maupin, alias Théodore, has entered the story. The scene is repeated: again it is an Henri IV château, again the beloved is at the window "accoudé [leaning] mélancoliquement." But the feminine ending of "accoudé" is missing. D'Albert puts it succinctly: "il n'y manquait rien, seulement la dame est un homme" (nothing was missing; only the lady is a man). Gautier lets the reader react as he will, but there is no indication that the château in the style of Henri IV–Louis XIII has lost any of its magic. It was left to Gautier's friend Nerval to make the most haunting transposition of this particular form of architecture in his poem "Fantaisie" (*Odelettes*, 1853).

A second recurrent motif in Gautier is the city skyline. Customarily a silhouette that emerges from a combination of different architectural styles and shapes, it gives the author an opportunity to vary his enumerations while following the same method. The opening chapter of Le roman de la momie (The Romance of a Mummy, 1858) lists a series of vertical structures that adorn the ancient city of Thebes: obelisks, pylons, the entablatures of temples and palaces, capitals with lotus flower decorations, all of which break the horizontal lines of the roofs of the private houses. Similar cutouts appear, usually at sunset, in any number of cities. Gautier seems less concerned on the whole with their symbolic value than with their beauty as such. When, however, he compares each structure of the Paris skyline to the black teeth of a shark biting the horizon with his immense jaws ("Le sommet de la tour" in La comédie de la mort) it is fairly obvious that the beautiful gives way to the monstrous.

Somewhat subtler is the analogy in the following passage, which would make a good candidate for a "transposition d'art." It describes the harbor of Bordeaux (Travels in Spain, ch. 1):

> The harbor is filled with vessels from every country and of every tonnage; in the twilight mist they resemble a multitude of cathedrals adrift, for nothing is more similar to a church than a ship with its masts soaring up like spires and the entangled lines of its rigging.

This excerpt could well serve as an "intertext" for the passage in Marcel Proust's Remembrance of Things Past (1913–1927) in which the painter Elstir, looking at the port of Carquethuit, sees steeples as masts and masts as steeples, and goes on to discuss metaphors of plasticity with the narrator. Gautier is quite content to mention in passing the analogy between churches and ships and let it go at that. More a poet than a novelist in this respect, he rarely subjects his metaphors to the exhaustive analysis they receive in Proust.

Looking back for a moment at Gautier's three distinctive stylistic features (the self-conscious author, the prevalence of literary and art allusions, the creation of "transpositions d'art"), we realize that what they have in common is their degree of "distancing" from nonverbal reality. In the first case, the author creates the illusion of reality only to break through and dance a kind of chassé with the reader. In the second case, the reference is to the imaginative work of other writers and artists. And in the third case, a substitution in the medium allows an imitation of reality twice removed.

This filtering of reality reaches its extreme in the dream states that Gautier describes. In the works published in a modern edition as Récits fantastiques, and in certain poems and travel writings, the word rêve (dream) becomes synonymous with a fanciful vision that is based less on fragments of observed reality than on "art remembered," literary or pictorial. As he is about to cross the border into Spain (Travels in Spain, ch. 2), Gautier becomes fearful lest "the Spain of my dreams" fly away, the Spain, he goes on to say, of the romancero, of the ballades of Victor Hugo, the stories of Prosper Mérimée, and the tales of Alfred de Musset. And he quotes a comment made to him by Heine: "How will you manage to speak of Spain after you have been there?"

The ingredients that make up a city like the Venice of his dreams are somewhat more varied: "stories, engravings, the view of a map, the euphony or the peculiarity of a name, a tale read as a child" (Voyage en Italie, [Travels in Italy], 1852, ch. 7). These are the foundations of what Gautier calls "la ville intuitive" (the intuited city), apparently using the adjective intuitive because the vision is direct and immediate. As with Nijni-Novgorod, the real city does not necessarily obliterate the fanciful one. On the contrary the city of his intuition may persist as the stronger, the more solid of the two.

In order to convey the solidity, the tangibility, not only of this sort of inner experience but of dream states in general, including visions, nightmares, chimeras, hallucinations, the world of the occult and the supernatural where the dead and the living mingle, one would expect Gautier to apply the same method of minute description, of "microscopic amplification," that he uses for the external world. And in fact he does, up to a point; but here too the characteristic stylistic devices come into play, as in the following literary allusion: "Octavien, all pale and petrified with horror, tried to speak; but his voice remained stuck in his throat, if we may use a line from Vergil" ("Arria Marcella," 1852). The reader, prepared to become petrified like Octavien, is suddenly reminded, thanks to the intrusion of Vergil, that he is in a world of language. The moment of horror, having been intellectualized, melts away.

Allusion is thus the main instrument for bringing to the surface the riches of art and literature of the past. Gautier seems to have been more aware than most of his fellow romantics that a literary text or a painting is often an ensemble of eclectic elements "from Orpheus to Lamartine," and that one cannot truly appreciate the work without an awareness of them. The title of the poem "In deserto" in *España,* for example, means merely "in the desert" until the reader on a second or third perusal (and with the help of Michael Riffaterre's *The Semiotics of Poetry*) is able to supply the allusion to Saint John the Baptist's reply: "Vox clamantis in deserto," thus throwing a whole new light on the poem.

Gautier had a sense of the continuity of language and the possibility of revitalizing titles, phrases, refrains by their use in new contexts. The epigraphs for his early poetry include quotations not only from such French poets as Chartier, Théophile de Viau, Marot, DeBaïf, Desportes, Ronsard, Du Bellay, Saint Amant, and Villon but also classical poets (Callimachus, Catullus, Vergil), English poets (Shakespeare, of course, Byron, Wordsworth), and many others. It was Gautier who resuscitated the fame of François Villon by an article written in his early twenties. It seems incredible that the refrain "Où sont les neiges d'antan?"

(Where are the snows of yesteryear?) was unknown to Ronsard, Racine, Molière, and Voltaire, but we must suppose it to have been so.

In a word, Gautier's erudition in literature and the fine arts, the retentiveness of his memory, and the energy of his mind joined together to create the festival of allusiveness that we have noted. "Superabundance" d'Albert calls it in *Mademoiselle de Maupin,* and whereas in his case it paralyzed ("I am unable to produce anything, not from sterility but from superabundance," ch. 11), with Gautier it definitely created—about 300 volumes.

Before we turn to some of these works for comment, we must ask how Gautier composed. He put it very simply: "I never think about what I am going to write; I take up my pen and I write." Add to this the importance he attaches to chance and the unexpected and we are remarkably close to the method of the surrealists. Gautier himself seemed surprised that his sentences were syntactically correct. "I throw my sentences up in the air; I am sure that like cats they will land on their paws." What is more, there are very few erasures or corrections in his manuscripts. Gautier is at the other extreme from the "blank paper" school of poets.

But this impression of facility leads to a contradiction we must resolve. For Gautier has also spoken of "the fatigue of rolling the rock of a sentence, heavier than that of Sisyphus." If we distinguish between the spontaneity of his journalism at one end and the laboriously chiseled verse at the other, the so-called Parnassian lines that make up *Enamels and Cameos,* the volume that is traditionally looked on as his masterpiece, we can imagine the degrees that fall between. It would be impossible to set up an accurate sequence of works along this linear scale other than the distinction between verse and prose; but as we examine them according to the principal genres we shall keep this spectrum in mind. It may turn out that some of the prose that lands upright is more in tune with twentieth-century taste than the rhymed alexandrine couplets or the octosyllabic lines in the *Poésies*.

Gautier did not have a very high opinion of journalists or their readers: "Newspaper reading prevents the creation of true scholars, true artists; it is like a daily debauch that brings you all enervated and exhausted to the bed of the Muses, those harsh, demanding maidens who want young vigorous lovers" (preface to *Mademoiselle de Maupin*). And yet Gautier lived from his feuilletons, and although he may have been a martyr to them, as Gustave Flaubert and many other contemporaries claimed, they nonetheless contain some of his best writing, not merely in criticism and travel literature but in fiction as well.

CRITICISM

Gautier's first critical enterprise was a series of feuilletons: *Exhumations littéraires* (*Literary Exhumations*, 1834–1836), later published under the title *Les grotesques* (1844) and including essays on Villon, Théophile de Viau, Marc-Antoine de Saint-Amant, Cyrano de Bergerac, Madeleine de Scudéry, and Jean Chapelain, all relatively unknown at the time and recognized today as major figures of the baroque period. Their rich and often earthy vocabulary suited Gautier's program of enrichment of the French language. As portraits these essays resemble a later series on Gautier's contemporaries: Hugo, Balzac, Baudelaire, Nerval, Heine, et al. Gautier had a rare capacity for admiration. He once wrote: "What distinguishes Satan is that he can neither admire nor love." His generosity of spirit may have affected his critical judgment on occasion. His very moving essay on Nerval, written after his friend's suicide, has been criticized for failing to grasp the connection between Nerval's madness and the power of his fiction, especially "Sylvie" (1854). Be that as it may, his laudatory style, free of pettiness,

has a contagious quality about it even though he may have taken too much to heart the admonition of Jean-Baptiste-Siméon Chardin to the critics at the Salon of 1765: "Gentlemen, gentlemen, be kind!"

In 1859 appeared the sixth and final volume of the collected drama criticism, consisting mainly of the weekly reviews that had been appearing for twenty-five years. Gautier's final critical work, *Histoire du romantisme* (*A History of Romanticism*, published posthumously in 1874) has the authentic ring of an author who was a participant; it remains today one of the instructive and readable accounts of the romantic movement in France.

Gautier's art criticism is scattered and voluminous. Like Denis Diderot before and Baudelaire and Apollinaire after, he covered the annual Salon and numerous exhibits. Furthermore he used every occasion, whatever genre he was practicing, to introduce his favorite works of art. He has been criticized for excessive attention to detail in contrast to Baudelaire, who stressed rather the effect of a painting on the viewer. But is not descriptive richness, along with allusiveness, the distinctive trait of Gautier's style in general, accounting for the beauty of many of his "transpositions d'art," as we have seen? Gautier is probably at his best when characterizing the style of a work, literary or artistic, by a fusion of descriptive detail and metaphorical language. One might ask whether the following passage on Nerval is a critical text or a prose poem; the line of demarcation is very thin. Gautier is speaking of some particularly hermetic sonnets

> *dont l'obscurité s'illumine de soudains éclairs comme une idole constellée d'escarboucles et de rubis dans l'ombre d'une crypte. . . . On dirait les oracles d'un dieu inconnu.*

the obscurity of which is suddenly illuminated by lightning flashes, like an idol studded with garnets and rubies in the shadow of a crypt. . . . One might say the oracles of an unknown god.

THÉOPHILE GAUTIER

TRAVEL WRITINGS

The travel literature includes three major works: *Travels in Spain,* based on a trip made in the summer of 1840; the feuilleton *Italia* (1852), published posthumously as *Travels in Italy;* and *Travels in Russia,* based on two trips between 1858 and 1861.

The most popular of the three is the first. According to Apollinaire, Gautier's writings are in themselves an "homage to youth," and there is zest in all he writes about Spain. He seems predisposed to love it. The very inadequacy of his Spanish he puts to good use: it makes the stories he hears about bandits, which he only partially understands, all the more terrifying. (This, incidentally, suggests a method for distorting reality that it is surprising the surrealists did not adopt: stories only half understood because they are told in a foreign tongue.) It is with great relish that, having piled horror on horror in the text on Goya, Gautier stops halfway through to say: "Well, that takes care of the factual side." And indeed he goes on to praise what he calls Goya's "demonographic verve" in the portrayal of monstrous beings.

Throughout *Travels in Spain* one senses in the author an unaffected candor. He enjoys being called by his first name, Don Teofilo, and attending *tertulias,* which he describes in detail. He swears to the reader ("je vous le jure!") that the resemblance between the Scheldt in Flanders and the Guadalquivir is real. There is only one sight in Spain that depresses him, it seems: the Escurial, boring and *maussade* (sullen). Gautier crisscrossed the country from the Bidassoa to the Guadalquivir, returning by way of Valencia and Barcelona. The trip lasted from May through September and the account of it has all the warmth and airiness of the summer season.

Travels in Italy is based on a trip Gautier made ten years after the one to Spain. It comprised visits to Florence, Rome, Naples, and Venice. In Madrid, he had written that chance is the best tourist guide and that one must be on the lookout for the unexpected. Nonetheless, his preparations for Italy were quite careful and methodical; he wanted to make certain he knew the masterpieces he was going to inspect. And whereas the pages on El Greco and Goya reveal the joy of discovery, those on the Italian paintings and monuments, especially in Venice, read more like a confirmation.

Still, the imaginary city, "la ville intuitive," the one created by the poet before leaving Paris, may persist, crowding out the real. In that case, the poet turns his visionary eye on the city and "surrealizes" it, as Professor Riffaterre has shown in a study on *Travels in Italy.*

The depiction of San Marco at sunset ranks among the more remarkable "transpositions d'art" in Gautier.

> At certain hours of the day, when the darkness deepens and the sun sheds but a faint light under the vaulting, the poet and the seer behold strange effects. Tawny gleams suddenly flash from the golden background, the small crystal tubes sparkle in spots like the sea in the sunshine, the contours of the figures tremble in the glimmering network, the silhouettes, clearly marked just now, become fainter, and the stiff folds of the dalmatics seem to soften and wave; a mysterious life revives the motionless figures; the staring eyes live, the arms, with their Egyptian gestures, move . . . the characters in the mosaics become processions of phantoms which ascend and descend along the walls, move along the galleries, and pass before you in the waving gold of their glory. You are dazzled, bewildered; you are under the spell of a hallucination. The real meaning of the cathedral, its deep, mysterious, solemn meaning, seems then to become plain. It appears to be the temple of a Christianity anterior to Christ, a church built before religion was. The centuries are lost in infinite perspective. . . . Is it Horus or Krishna whom the Virgin holds in her lap? Is it Isis or Parvati?
>
> ("San Marco")

The syncretic notions that Gautier shared with Nerval combine here with the undulation of the Byzantine mosaics to produce rhetorical questions about the beliefs of mankind.

Gautier made his two trips to Russia in order to gather material for a work never completed on the artistic treasures of that country. He resided mainly in Moscow and Saint Petersburg and followed the Volga to Nijni-Novgorod. He was considerably less preoccupied with the dream world here than in Italy. In fact *Travels in Russia* would justify the conventional view of Gautier as a writer blind to all but the visible world. He describes the luxury of the upper class in Saint Petersburg and notes their carriages: coupés, berlins, landaus. The following passage, translated by Sumichrast, on the troika is a fine example of precise description for its own sake. There is no hidden symbolism, no magic attached to the number three, no Platonistic allusiveness. The troika is simply a troika, its description an exacting exercise in language.

> But the finest thing in this way is the troïka, a peculiarly Russian vehicle, full of local colour, and exceedingly picturesque. It is a large sleigh holding four people seated opposite each other, besides the coachman, and drawn by three horses. The centre horse, placed between the shafts, has a collar, and curved douga above the withers; the two others are harnessed to the sleigh by an outer trace only, and a loose strap fastens them to the collar of the shaft horse; four reins are sufficient to drive the three animals, for the two outer horses are driven each with a single outside rein. It is a beautiful thing to see a troïka fly along the Nevsky Prospect or Admiralty Square at the hour for the promenade. The shaft horse trots, stepping straight ahead; the two other horses gallop, spreading out like a fan; one of them must seem fiery, spirited, untameable, must throw up its head, pretend to shy and to kick,—that is the furious one; the other must shake its mane, bringing its head to its breast, curvet, prance, touch its knees with its nose, rear prettily, spring to right or left according as its high spirits and its caprices impel it,— that is the coquettish one. These three noble steeds, with their cheek-straps, metal chains, their harness as light as ribbons, on which spar-
kle here and there, like spangles, delicate gold ornaments,—recall those equipages of antiquity that draw upon triumphal arches bronze cars to which they are not fastened. They seem to play and gambol in front of the troïka, moved merely by their own desire. The middle horse alone seems somewhat serious, like a quiet friend between two lively companions. Of course it is not easy to maintain this apparent disorder, when the speed is great, and when each animal has its own gait:—sometimes the furious one plays its part in real earnest, and the coquettish one rolls in the snow, so that it takes a consummately skilful coachman to drive a troïka. It is exciting sport, and I am surprised that no gentleman rider in London or Paris has thought of copying it.

("Winter—The Neva")

SHORT STORIES AND NOVELLAS

Gautier wrote some twenty-five works of fiction, variously called *contes, nouvelles, récits, romans,* with no clear line of demarcation among them. Although for the sake of the narration in his short stories Gautier reduces considerably the amount of descriptive detail, he nonetheless retains enough to situate the action in a sharply defined milieu. Into this realistic decor he then introduces elements of the dream world and the fantastic. The reader is transported by these juxtapositions, or would be were it not for Gautier's playful interpolations, which often break the spell. This suggestion of conspiring with the reader is what distinguishes Gautier from most romantic short-story writers. Another characteristic feature is the word play, bilingual tricks that are often basic to the unfolding of the story.

In "La cafetière" ("The Coffee Pot," 1831), the earliest of the *Récits fantastiques,* published when Gautier was nineteen, we find what the French call the *poncifs,* or stereotypes, of the literature of the fantastic during the period of romanticism, borrowed mainly in this case from the tales of E. T. A. Hoffmann: portraits and tapestries that come to life, the witching hour of midnight, the frenetic dance, the lark that sings at dawn, and at the center the beautiful damsel in distress, or, more precisely, the double metamorphosis from chinaware coffeepot into the angelic Angela and back to coffeepot, this time broken into bits. Gautier's particular brand of humor shines through. The narrator finds a group of family portraits so bizarre that "in spite of my terror I could not help laughing": the patriarch, who looks like Falstaff, has a hard time getting his belly out of the frame, and so forth.

Gautier candidly admits his debt to Hoffmann in his next story, "Onuphrius" (published in *Les Jeunes-France*), which carries the subtitle: "ou les Vexations fantastiques d'un admirateur d'Hoffmann." One of our writer's more endearing traits is his willingness to reveal his sources. Among the more Hoffmannesque characteristics of "Onuphrius" is the sense of horror engendered by the "vexations" of the young artist and poet, who is being pursued by the devil. He suffers from a gruesome nightmare in which he sees himself buried alive; his soul wanders free, simultaneously aware and unaware of its identity.

The narration of the nightmare fills almost a third of the story, and when Onuphrius awakens it is only to enter a hallucinatory state more terrifying than the dream itself. The reader is never quite sure which is which. At one point, the soul of Onuphrius flies into the Louvre, where he sees one of his own paintings exhibited alongside the work of Delacroix and Ingres—but the signature is not his. At the Porte Saint-Martin, where one of his plays is being performed, a different author is acclaimed. Assuming that the "I'm being buried alive!" theme is borrowed from Hoffmann and the "I've been plagiarized!" is pure Gautier, who can say which of the authors is more aware of the fantastic?

We have already had a glimpse at "Omphale." Its original subtitle, "La tapisserie amoureuse" (The Tapestry in Love), suggests the similar "La morte amoureuse" (The Dead Woman in Love) of the story that followed in 1836. In each case a beautiful woman comes back to life and is in love with the narrator, but there the similarity stops. Where the marquise de T, alias Omphale, is a delightful coquette full of charm and flippancy, Clarimonde oppresses us with her conventional alabaster complexion and her morbid orgies. In the one story, the lover-narrator is a perky Cherubino; in the other, a humorless priest who is so victimized by his passion that when he discovers that Clarimonde is a vampire and that it is his blood she wants to suck, he feels no disgust at all. Clearly Gautier's sympathies go to the marquise. Could it be because, unlike Clarimonde, she is a work of art—she has emerged from a tapestry? Gautier always feels more at home with reality that has been distilled into art.

"La pipe d'opium" (1838, translated in *My Fantoms* as "The Opium Smoker") and "Le club des hachichins" ("The Hashish Club," 1846) are not, strictly speaking, works of fiction. The first is an opium dream narrative, similar to those written by the surrealists, in which author and narrator fuse. The second describes a hashish seance, modeled on one in which Gautier participated at the Hôtel Lauzun on the Ile Saint-Louis. In both accounts the description of the hallucinations is remarkable for its vividness and precision.

These are apparently Gautier's only texts on the effects of narcotics. In his essay on Baudelaire he mentions the experiments with hashish, but goes on to say that they gave them up because "the true writer needs only his natural dreams and does not want his thought subjected to the influence of any outside agent."

In the two short stories "Le chevalier double" ("The Twin Knight," 1840) and "Deux acteurs pour un rôle" (translated as "The Actor," 1841), there are two scenes that resemble each other so closely as to justify comparison. In the former, Count Oluf, a knight in arms, encounters his mirror image. The only difference is in the color of the plume each wears: Oluf's is green, his adversary's red. In the duel that ensues "le vainqueur souffrait autant que le vaincu" (the winner suffered as much as the loser), for Oluf, the good knight, is fighting his doppelgänger.

In "The Actor," Heinrich, a young actor who plays the role of Mephistopheles, stands, just before the curtain goes up, face to face with the real Mephistopheles. Another mirror image? Not quite, for they would resemble each other were it not for the hellish laughter of the archdemon, which Heinrich can never hope to imitate.

One can read into these stories whatever symbolism or moral one wishes, but Gautier's linguistic proclivities tempt us to view them also as verbal constructs. The one is based on two forms, active and passive, of the same verb: *vaincre, vaincu* (vanquish, vanquished); the other on the idiom: *jouer le rôle du diable* (play the role of the devil). In any case they are stories that, with a little help from Hoffmann and Goethe, exist for the sheer pleasure of experiencing the fantastic.

In somewhat the same vein, "Le pied de momie" (The Mummy's Foot, 1840) is built around a transfer from the figurative to the literal meaning of the formula: "to ask for one's hand in marriage." Our narrator, having acquired the detached foot of a mummy in a Paris bric-à-brac shop, sees in a dream the beautiful but crippled Egyptian princess Hermonthis and graciously restores the foot. To the query from the grateful father, the pharaoh: "What can I offer you?" the narrator tells us: "Je lui demandai la main d'Hermonthis: la main pour le pied me paraissait une récompense antithétique d'assez bon goût" (I asked him for the hand of Hermonthis: a hand for a foot seemed to me an antithetical reward rather in good taste). The story is written throughout with a kind of mock pomposity that exactly fits the style of this denouement. Like Zeuxis, the ancient Greek painter who is said to have created his ideal woman, Helen, from a half-dozen models each of whom excelled in a particular part of the anatomy—

arm, breast, neck, torso—Gautier customarily created his beauties by an amalgam, an *ars combinatoria* of fragments.

Occasionally, however, Gautier focuses on a particular fragment: the hands in "Études de mains" (*Enamels and Cameos*), or a mummy's foot, as we have just seen. The problem in such cases is to reconstruct the whole from the part, as in an archaeological find. Octavien, the young French tourist in Gautier's "Arria Marcella," had tried and failed to recreate the form of an ancient Roman woman from the hair that remained in her tomb. Now at the Studii Museum in Naples he has just seen the shape, preserved by lava, of a woman's breast—all that remains of this victim of the destruction of Pompeii. Octavien conceives for this object a wild passion that the reader finds rather difficult to share; for despite the "charming contour" and "noble form," it is after all a "black coagulated cinder." Can one really fall in love with a fragment? The author apparently senses this contradiction and obliges both Octavien and the reader by taking us back to the reign of Titus, just before the volcanic eruption. In an erotic encounter, Octavien sees the fragment of the breast, or at least the contour of it, united with the rest of the body of the lovely Marcella, who thereupon disintegrates into a pinch of ashes mixed with calcined bones.

At the end of the novella *Avatar* (1857), one of the characters wonders whether our souls in paradise will still speak a human language. (The phenomenon of language preoccupies Gautier in a number of works.) Unlike many writers whose characters of different lands communicate in a kind of neutral tongue, as though the Tower of Babel had never been built, Gautier is careful to make the means of communication explicit, especially in the tales of the fantastic, where the details of verisimilitude must be exact to make the situation acceptable. In "Le pied de momie," Princess Hermonthis carries on the dialogue with her foot in an ancient Coptic tongue that "fortunately," says the narrator, "I knew to perfection that night." Somewhat more plausible is Octavien's dialogue in Latin in a street of Pompeii. Octavien, it seems, had won Latin prizes in the "concours général" at school, though he still had a strong Parisian accent.

In *Avatar* the spoken language becomes the crux of the matter. At his own request, Octave de Saville undergoes a soul transplant in order to bring himself closer to the lovely Countess Prascovie Labinska, whom he adores. The body that his soul now inhabits is none other than that of her husband, Count Olaf Labinski, whose soul has in turn been transposed, by trickery, to the body of Octave.

Unfortunately, Octave has ignored the language question. What is the native tongue of the count and the countess, the intimate language they speak to each other? Prascovie, alone with the new, would-be husband, "pronounces in a tender, harmonious voice full of chaste caresses a phrase in Polish!!!" (The three exclamation marks are Gautier's.) Octave's complete befuddlement opens the way to the denouement, sad for Octave, happy for the ever-loving Labinskis.

In *Jettatura* (1857), Gautier gives a new turn to the proverb: "Vedi Napoli e poi muori" (See Naples and die), changing it from its usual connotation as an expression of admiration to one of horror. Paul d'Aspremont gradually becomes aware in Naples that he has the evil eye *(la jettatura)* and that among his potential victims is his own fiancée, Alicia Ward, who seems to be wasting away. The Neapolitan Count Altavilla, also in love with Alicia, tries to fight off the fatal influence of Paul, only to succumb in a freakish duel that the rivals fight blindfolded. Paul, shocked by the monstrosity of his power as a "jettatore," gouges out his eyes, hoping thus to save Alicia. But it is too late. She too succumbs, and Paul throws himself into the Bay of Naples.

Jettatura is beyond a doubt the most grotesque of all Gautier's stories. What saves it is the ironical twist of the proverb. Before blinding himself Paul takes one last look at Naples and its bay. There follows a detailed descrip-

tion of this famous sight. Paul commands his eyes to intoxicate themselves with that "splendid spectacle of creation." The reader, recalling the proverb from the introduction to the story, repeats it now at the end, with the three victims in mind and with the stress on the verbs as imperatives: "*See* Naples and *die!*"

Most of Gautier's stories are laid in the contemporary world, but his love of the exotic and his bent for archaeological reconstruction, including Egyptology, combined to produce, in addition to "Arria Marcella," the ever-popular "One of Cleopatra's Nights," "King Candaulus," and the novel *The Romance of a Mummy*.

The plot of "One of Cleopatra's Nights" is simple. A young commoner, Meïamoun, dares to penetrate the baths of Cleopatra; instead of having him executed immediately the queen agrees to an exchange: "ta vie pour une nuit" (your life for one night). This allows the author to indulge in a profusion of exotic detail, a kind of verbal orgy that equals in intensity the one actually going on, including a digression on the sumptuousness of the fabulous East.

The story of King Candaulus of Lydia was first related by Herodotus. Gautier's version makes the king an ardent Hellenophile, a collector and something of an artist himself. He admires the beauty of his foreign wife, Nyssia, so much that he feels he must show her off. Gygès, the head of the royal guard, is coerced into becoming a voyeur. Nyssia spots the burning eyeballs, understands the complicity, orders Gygès: "Meurs ou tue!" (Die or kill). Gygès kills the guilty aesthete Candaulus, marries Nyssia, and launches a new dynasty.

Gautier's conclusion is very simple. If only Candaulus had married a Greek instead of a barbarian, the daughter of a satrap, he could have had her pose for the best painters and sculptors of the land, like Campaspe, the mistress of Alexander the Great, who posed in the nude for Apelles. Between Greek freedom on the one hand and barbarian (or Christian) prudishness on the other, the choice is clear.

THÉOPHILE GAUTIER

NOVELS

The Romance of a Mummy is a novel within a novel. Three archaeologists, veritable caricatures—Lord Evandale, Dr. Rumphius, and Mr. Argyropoulos—discover the mummy of Queen Tahoser in Egypt. Next to her lies a papyrus roll that Dr. Rumphius will spend three years deciphering and rendering into Latin. The French translation that we are about to read is entitled *Le roman de la momie,* and as the narrative proceeds, we realize we are following the story of the exodus, based of course on the Book of Exodus but related from a completely new perspective, that of our Egyptian heroine, who has become the wife of Pharaoh but is still in love with Poëri, a young Israelite. Her attempts to intercede on behalf of Poëri's people are of no avail. Pharaoh pursues them vengefully, following them even into the Sea of Algae, as Gautier calls it. Our last view shows Pharaoh, more than half engulfed, hurling his javelin at the unknown God: "qu'il bravait encore du fond de l'abîme" (whom he was still defying from the depth of the abyss)—a line that, if one ignores the mute *e* of *encore*, makes for a most eloquent decasyllabic finale. Gautier is careful to keep the Egyptian perspective throughout, even in the spelling of the Hebrew names, which the French reader does not immediately recognize: Ra'hel, Mosché, Aharon. Only one minor lapse has been found: "the Egyptians like to eat outdoors." Would an Egyptian author, writing for an Egyptian audience, have made such an unnecessary observation?

Gautier wrote five other novels: *Fortunio, Partie carrée, Spirite, Mademoiselle de Maupin,* and *Captain Fracasse. Fortunio,* which like Musset's *Fantasio* (1834) has a Shakespearean ring, is the name of a Parisian dandy who has a white cat ("Imagine a great puff with a pair of eyes in it") and a mistress named Musidora, and who, by the end of the story, has set up for himself a luxurious oriental oasis in the heart of Paris.

It is in *Fortunio,* more perhaps than in any other single work, that the self-conscious author weaves his way between verbal and nonverbal reality ("I shall be compelled to kill her on p. 127" or "Never mind, we'll keep [the simile].") Implicit in this game is a sensitivity to language that pervades the book. In *Fortunio* Gautier tells the story of a gambler who, having lost his entire fortune, is on the point of committing suicide when he realizes with horror that he lacks an epitaph. He tries one in rhymed alexandrines only to discover—and it is true—that there is no rhyme for *triomphe.* Fortunately, the arrival of a friend who has just recouped his fortune saves him. Absurd? Perhaps, but the problems of language raised by this little anecdote—the peculiarity of a word that has no rhyme (and Gautier must have consulted a rhyming dictionary); the contrast between the meaning of the word as victory and its suggestion, in the context, of defeat; the frustration of the attempt to complete the text of the epitaph because of the shortcomings of language; the very necessity of an epitaph—all these become more significant than the suicide attempt as such. And the reader who is sensitive to these problems is ready to accept the exotic estate of Fortunio for what it is, a linguistic structure.

We mentioned earlier the rapid pace of *Partie carrée.* It begins with the kidnapping of Benedict Arundel at the entrance to the London church of Saint Margaret's, where his wedding with Annabel Vyvian was to be celebrated. A second wedding in the same church the same day is followed by the mysterious disappearance of the bride, Edith Harley, and the groom, the count of Volmerange—the same count, incidentally, who keeps muttering "This is all very Shakespearean" as he runs around searching for a blade with which to murder his bride after he hears her confess to being unfaithful. Edith escapes, jumps into the Thames, and is picked out of the water by the crew of the *Belle-Jenny,* under the command of Sir Arthur Stanley, who is the kidnapper of Benedict.

We soon realize that this is no ordinary kidnapping. Benedict belongs to a secret society of Byronic heroes, headed by Sir Arthur and determined to change, by their noble exploits, some of the great events of history. Members of this brotherhood have, for example, fought in the Greek revolution against the Turks. The two weddings at Saint Margaret's would have signaled a refusal to heed Sir Arthur's call; for Volmerange, too, is a member of the brotherhood; and while he, thinking his bride dead, is now free to set off to liberate India, Benedict has no other recourse but to follow Sir Arthur as the *Belle-Jenny* sails out of the Thames toward the South Atlantic with the crew and Edith aboard. Its mission: to liberate the lone captive of Saint Helena! The plan would have worked but for one unforeseen circumstance: Napoleon's death on the eve of the rescue. Sir Arthur decides that the great ideas embodied in his exploits had best remain in the world of ideas. "Love someone," he says to Edith, "a man, a child, a dog, a flower, but never an idea—that is dangerous."

Partie carrée is translated by Sumichrast as *Quartette.* A more exact rendering would be "Change Your Partners." Both couples switch their loves in what Gautier calls a "bizarre symmetry." Unlike Volmerange and Annabel, who end their days tragically, Edith and Benedict, apparently taking Sir Arthur's advice, spend their old age peacefully as Mr. and Mrs. Smith on the island of Rhodes. There has been no recent edition of *Partie carrée* (also called *Belle-Jenny*). It is a pity since this is one of the more enjoyable of Gautier's works. It is a fine adventure story that would make a film full of suspense.

In *Spirite,* the protagonist, Guy de Malivert, succeeds in communicating with the disembodied soul of Lavinia d'Aufideni, now called Spirite, whose body is buried in the Père-Lachaise cemetery. The dialogue not only recounts the spiritual fusion that the couple seek to attain ("We shall be unity in duality, the ego in the nonego, motion in rest, desire in fulfillment") but also actually heightens the intensity of the language. Despite the author's exasperation with its inadequacies—he has Spirite allude to a paradise "of which no words in our poor, scanty, heavy, imperfect speech can suggest even the remotest idea"—there are moments when Gautier's own language becomes white-hot, as in this description of the verses that Guy wrote under the inspiration of Spirite: "The old forms, the worn out moulds burst asunder, and sometimes the molten phrase broke forth and overflowed in splendid splashes like rays of broken stars." This could almost be a description of the "bursting asunder" of the prose poems that were to form Arthur Rimbaud's *Illuminations* (published 1886). It is in *Spirite,* perhaps as much as in any other work of Gautier, including his verse, that language tends to become ritualistic; that, in Baudelaire's phrase, it becomes a kind of "evocative sorcery."

Gautier's bookishness, if we may call it that—some call it his preciosity, his mania for the literary or artistic backdrop—produced its finest exemplar in his first novel, *Mademoiselle de Maupin,* with its "intertext," Shakespeare's *As You Like It.* Madeleine de Maupin, who actually existed as a dashing young seventeenth-century amazon embroiled in numerous "skirt and dagger" intrigues, becomes, in the Gautier novel, under the alias of Théodore de Sérannes, the pivotal figure of a love triangle. Her Shakespearean counterpart is Rosalind. The hero of the novel, a young nobleman named d'Albert, cherishes his mistress, Rosette, until the moment Théodore comes along. We have already witnessed his perplexity in the Henri IV balcony scene. As with Orlando in the play it is love at first sight. D'Albert is not willing to admit to anything more, however, than "a strong attraction" for Théodore. As for Rosette, who becomes completely infatuated with Théodore, the hopelessness of her love recalls that of Phebe.

It may be that Gautier used a Shakespeare comedy to give a certain fanciful tone to a theme of confused erotic identity that was considered quite scandalous in 1835. But there is no doubt about the enrichment that derives from the parallels. They are set forth in chapter 11 in the form of a letter from d'Albert to his friend Silvio. The chapter begins with a defense of the "fantastic" theater, which leads to a colorful eulogy of Shakespearean comedy, a eulogy that can stand alone as a prose poem. D'Albert goes on to describe a performance of *As You Like It,* which he is staging, in French of course, with his friends. Naturally he stresses those scenes that place him as Orlando opposite Théodore as Rosalind. The characters thus act out the text as well as their own intimate situation, making for what Gautier calls "a play within a play"—and he might have added "within a novel."

For instance, when Théodore-Rosalind first appears, disguised for act 1 as a woman (which "he" is), d'Albert-Orlando is as overwhelmed by her beauty (now convinced that it is she, not he, whom he loves) as he is relieved that the attraction is not "monstrous." Sure of his love for her, he wonders if she will respond. Thus when Rosalind disguised as Ganymede tells him (Orlando) his love will be cured if he will only call her "Rosalind," she speaks with such a visible intention, writes d'Albert, looking at him in such a strange way, that he cannot help but believe she is expressing her true sentiments.

Emboldened by this hope, d'Albert after the performance writes to Théodore, whom he calls Rosalind, the declaration of love that leads to the denouement. The performance of *As You Like It* has not only given a new depth to the characters of the novel but has also played an integral part in the progress of the plot. Furthermore, Gautier's Forest of Arden (described in chapter 11) is even more "educated" than Shakespeare's: every rock becomes a desk for the writing of songs, sonnets, *concetti* (conceits), epistles. Gautier's characters are in fact forever writing letters; most of the novel is in epistolary form.

The Forest of Arden blends with the forests and parks of French châteaux in the style of Henri IV–Louis XIII. The characters of *As You Like It* emerge from the text as from a tapestry to fuse with their French doubles. All in *Mademoiselle de Maupin* tends toward a fusion, which Gautier himself calls the "hermaphroditic" ideal.

We have saved *Captain Fracasse* for last because its creation covers almost the entire span from *Mademoiselle de Maupin* to *Spirite,* some thirty years. The miracle is that Gautier finished it at all in view of the journalistic obligations that always took priority. In the preface of 1863, Gautier writes:

> You will find no political, moral or religious thesis here. No great problem is debated. We plead for no one. The author never expresses an opinion. It is a purely picturesque work—objective, as the Germans would say.

If purity is the absence of impure alloys, *Captain Fracasse,* with all these negatives, stands as one of the purest of novels, approaching those of Alexandre Dumas *père.*

The novel relates the adventures of a troupe of itinerant players during Gautier's favorite period, the early seventeenth century. An indigent young nobleman, the baron de Sigognac, joins the troupe, takes the stage name of Captain Fracasse, falls in love with the beautiful actress Isabelle, and saves her from his archrival, the villainous duke of Vallombreuse, who turns out to be Isabelle's brother and who from evil changes to good as easily—presto—as Oliver, the wicked brother in *As You Like It.*

But Gautier could never have been content with pure adventure, and among the "impurities" of the novel are the ideas it expresses on the theater and the performing arts—a *théâtre en liberté* already suggested in *Mademoiselle de Maupin,* drawing its strength from popular sources and introducing the spectator to a world of fantasy and magic. Gautier wrote a half-dozen plays in this vein, collected in the volume *Théâtre de poche* (1855). It was undoubtedly this aesthetic as much as his love for a ballerina that led Gautier to the ballet where, along with those of *La péri* (1843) and *Sacountalá* (1858), he wrote the story of the work for which he is best known, *Giselle.* After Gautier's funeral, Edmond de Goncourt wrote in his journal: "The most touching voices of the Opéra sang the requiem of the author of *Giselle.*"

POETRY

Gautier's poetry extends from the 1830 volume *Poésies* through the definitive edition of *Enamels and Cameos* the year of his death. Other volumes include *Albertus,* a long poem inspired by the satanism of the time; *La comédie de la mort,* which reveals Gautier's obsession with death; and *España,* based on the trip to Spain. Most of the poems are one or two pages long, in regular (eight-, ten-, or twelve-syllable) meter. The octosyllabic quatrain seems to have been his favorite form, with the *abab* (feminine-masculine feminine-masculine) rhyme scheme. This at any rate is the form of almost all of the fifty-seven poems of *Enamels and Cameos.* It produces a terse, compact effect, owing in part to the concluding masculine rhyme. When this rhyming syllable is liquid, as in the *-our* rhyme below, a particularly resonant sound is obtained:

> Au tombeau-sofa des marquises
> Qui reposent, lasses d'amour,
> En des attitudes exquises,
> Dans les chapelles Pompadour.
> ("Buchers et tombeaux," 11. 88–92)

To the tomb-sofas of the marquises who recline, tired of love, in exquisite postures in Pompadour-style chapels.

As the title *Enamels and Cameos* suggests, Gautier preferred (as he said) to treat "tiny subjects in a severely formal way." He liked to evoke visible things: the curve of a woman's hand, the folds of a pink dress, the shape of two spit curls, the trace of a tear on a sheet of paper, the flight of swallows, the view from a mansard window.

In a number of pieces, using each quatrain and the concrete object or objects it names as a kind of building block, Gautier constructs the poem from the piling up of stanzas as they relate to a unifying theme. Thus in "Symphonie en blanc majeur" the succession of things white—swan, snow, glacier, bosom, marble, ermine—as attributes of an unnamed woman from the north leads line by line to the poet's final burst of impatience before the implacability of the whiteness.

Enjambment from one quatrain to another is rare in Gautier's verse; each "block" thus retains its syntactical independence and on occasion may be excerpted to serve various purposes. Biographers of Gautier isolate stanza 11 of the "Symphonie en blanc majeur"—

> L'ivoire, où ses mains ont des ailes,
> Et, comme des papillons blancs,
> Sur la pointe des notes frêles
> suspendent leurs baisers tremblants;
> (11.41–44)

The ivory where her hands have wings, and, like white butterflies, on the tip of the frail notes suspend their trembling kisses;

as evidence of the rich juncture of music, painting, and poetry as, one evening in Frédéric Chopin's apartment, the icily beautiful Marie Kalergis, the Polish wife of the Greek ambassador, played the piano while Delacroix drew her portrait in sepia and Gautier conceived his "Symphonie."

Because of its close association with music and dance, the actual text of another poem has suffered somewhat. I am thinking of "Le spectre de la rose," one of six pieces from *La comédie de la mort* set to music by Berlioz under the collective title "Les nuits d'été" (Summer Nights). In our century the same poem has inspired the Jean-Louis Vaudoyer ballet, first performed by the Ballets Russes in Monte Carlo in May 1911. Thanks to these two "transpositions" away from Gautier, the title "Le spectre de la rose" has become considerably more familiar than the poem that it introduces. Yet it deserves to be studied on its own merits. It typifies the way Gautier can attenuate the fear of death through the subtle mixture of sensuality and preciosity, leaving at the same time a most disturbing aftertaste:

Soulève ta paupière close
Qu'effleure un songe virginal;
Je suis le spectre d'une rose
Que tu portais hier au bal.
Tu me pris encore emperlée
Des pleurs d'argent de l'arrosoir,
Et parmi la fête etoilée
Tu me promenas tout le soir.

O toi qui de ma mort fus cause,
Sans que tu puisses le chasser
Toute la nuit mon spectre rose
A ton chevet viendra danser.
Mais ne crains rien, je ne réclame
Ni messe ni De profundis;
Ce léger parfum est mon âme,
Et j'arrive du paradis.

Mon destin fut digne d'envie:
Pour avoir un trépas si beau,
Plus d'un aurait donné sa vie,
Car j'ai ta gorge pour tombeau,
Et sur l'albâtre où je repose
Un poète avec un baiser
Ecrivit: Ci gît une rose
Que tous les rois vout jalouser.

Open up your sleeping eyelid that is touched by a virginal dream; I am the specter of the rose that you wore yesterday eve to the ball. You plucked me still bepearled with the silver tears of the sprinkler and through the starlit fête you bore me all evening long.

O you who caused my death, at your bedside my rose-colored specter will dance all night without your chasing it away. But fear not, I request neither a mass nor a De profundis; this light perfume is my soul, and I come straight from heaven.

My destiny was worthy of envy: To have such a beautiful death, many would have given their lives; for your bosom is my tomb, and on the alabaster where I lie, a poet wrote with a kiss: Here lies a rose that every king will envy.

Gautier combines two literary stereotypes here: the rose as symbol of love and a short life and the ghost as symbol of a living presence after death. It is in the fusion of these two as announced in the title that the originality of the poem lies. Furthermore the reader, accustomed to imagining a ghost in more or less human shape—certainly not as a plant—willingly accepts the attributes that apply to one or the other, flower or phantom. As a rose it can be covered with pearly drops; it can give forth a light fragrance; it can be worn as a corsage. As a phantom it can dance and speak; the whole poem is indeed a monologue.

But what reveals this work most tellingly as coming from Gautier is the sexual ambiguity, already implicit in the title, where we find a masculine article le for spectre and a feminine article la for rose. In dying, the rose, traditionally feminine like its gender, takes on male traits so that it may address the young woman of the poem as a lover. The fusion announced in the title persists throughout the three stanzas, with male or female traits dominating depending on the context.

As if to confirm the androgynous nature of the poem we note that in Berlioz's song the specter's monologue is sung by a soprano, whereas in the ballet the same role, that of the specter, is played by a male dancer. (It was Vaslav Nijinsky at the premiere.)

What on a first reading then strikes us as a charming bit of gallantry radiating from the central conceit—"Car j'ai ta gorge pour tombeau" (for your bosom is my tomb)—emerges on further readings as a disquieting relationship rendered all the more complex if we perceive each one of the expressions—poem, song, ballet—through either of the other two.

If "Le spectre de la rose" is the most familiar title in Gautier, certainly the most quoted quatrain is the ninth stanza of "L'Art," the concluding poem of *Enamels and Cameos.*

> Tout passe.—L'art robuste
> Seul a l'éternité:
> Le buste
> Survit à la cité.
> ("L'Art," 11.41–44)

Here the eight- are replaced by six-syllable verses, with a two-syllable line in the middle to produce an effect of even greater concision.

The British Parnassian Austin Dobson has given a rather free rendering under the title "Ars Victrix" (1895):

> All passes. ART alone
> Enduring stays to us;
> The Bust out-lasts the throne—
> The Coin, Tiberius.

Curtis Page, in the epigraph to *Songs and Sonnets of Ronsard* (1924), has made a more faithful translation:

> All passes, Art alone
> Out-lasteth all;
> The carven stone
> Survives the city's fall.

The terseness of Gautier's rhyming quatrains spoke directly to Ezra Pound and T. S. Eliot, especially in their reaction against the Anglo-American craze for vers libre around 1920. René Taupin has given convincing evidence of a conscious imitation of Gautier by each poet. With Eliot it is not only the well-known "Hippopotamus" (to be compared with "L'Hippopotame" in *La comédie de la mort*), but this quatrain from "Whispers of Immortality" (1920):

> Grishkin is nice: her Russian eye
> Is underlined for emphasis;
> Uncorseted, her friendly bust
> Gives promise of pneumatic bliss.

to be read alongside the opening stanza of "Carmen" (*Enamels and Cameos*):

> Carmen est maigre,—un trait de bistre
> Cerne son oeil de gitana;
> Ses cheveux sont d'un noir sinistre;
> Sa peau, le diable la tanna.

Carmen is skinny—a brownish shadow underlines her gypsy eye. Her hair is black and sinister. Her skin was tanned by the devil.

With Pound the resemblances are somewhat subtler. Note these lines from *Mauberley* (1920):

> "His true Penelope
> Was Flaubert"
> And his tool
> The engraver's.
>
> Firmness
> Not the full smile
> His art, but an art
> in profile;

Compare the style of "L'Art," especially with its Flaubertian mots justes and the allusion to the engraver's tool. Pound's second stanza recalls specifically stanza 7 from "L'Art":

> D'une main délicate
> Poursuis dans un filon
> D'agate
> Le profil d'Apollon.

With a delicate hand pursue in a vein of agate the profile of Apollo.

If the two disciples outdistanced their French master it may have been that Gautier himself suffered from the strict rules of French prosody, with their stress on even-numbered syllables and rich rhyme. He could not have excluded himself entirely when he wrote of those poets "who consider in the world only the ending of words and never go back further than the penult." One senses a certain constraint in the *Poésies* that must derive from the author's obsession with the lapidary style. The Parnassian is trying to take over from the romantic, the partisan of Order (to use Apollinaire's terminology) from the partisan of Adventure.

The distinctive traits that we have examined, the self-consciousness, the allusiveness, the art transpositions, are at their most sparkling in the prose passages. One has only to recall the characterization of the poetry of Nerval, and of Guy de Malivert in *Spirite;* the evocation of Goya's *Los caprichos,* the description of San Marco at sunset; the masterly chapter on Shakespeare's comedy in *Mademoiselle de Maupin.* Gautier, like Jean Cocteau, could have classified his work under the rubric *Poetry: Critical Poetry, Travel Poetry, Poetry of the Novel,* and so on. Here perhaps, more than in the verse of *Enamels and Cameos,* Gautier lives up to the name of poet and appeals to today's reader.

And what of Cleopatra's orgy? Gautier succeeded also in making the French language considerably less "chaste" and "prudish" (if it ever was). He and his fellow romantics managed to flatten the Racinian sphere. But French, with its Platonistic core, is a stubborn instrument. Twentieth-century poets, such as Reverdy and Éluard, the Racine of surrealism, have preferred the abstract and the generic. A recent Saul Steinberg cartoon shows a rugged, earthbound capital E on the landscape and above it in a "bubble" its dream of its idealized self, refined, svelte, and topped by a grave accent—obviously a French È. And any number of Gautiers will not burst this bubble.

Beyond the French language, however, Gautier had certain notions about language itself, what the French call *le langage,* not always distinctly or consistently formulated but foreshadowing nonetheless some of our contemporary theories: the belief in a verbal reality, a world of discourse; the self-sufficiency of language; its generative force (Mallarmé's "leave the initiative to the words"); the interdependence of literary texts ("from Orpheus to Lamartine" and beyond) on a kind of upper floor, higher than language as mere mimesis of external reality. These notions, perhaps only intuitively perceived, produced nevertheless a plethora of lively texts—call them "self-referential structures" or simply "l'art pour l'art"—that delight today's reader as much as they did the author. For both, "le bon Théo" and his "cher lecteur," have enjoyed the sight of those agile sentences landing squarely on their paws.

Selected Bibliography

WORKS

FIRST EDITIONS

Poésies. Paris, 1830.

Albertus ou l'âme et le péché. Paris, 1833.

Les Jeunes-France, romans goguenards. Paris, 1833.

Mademoiselle de Maupin. Paris, 1835–1836.

Fortunio. Paris, 1838.

La comédie de la mort. Brussels, 1838.

Une larme du diable. Paris, 1839. Includes "Une nuit de Cléopâtre," "Omphale," and "La morte amoureuse."

Voyage en Espagne. Paris, 1843.

Les grotesques. 2 vols. in 1. Paris, 1844. Originally published as a series of articles entitled *Exhumations littéraires* (1834–1836).

Nouvelles. Paris, 1845.

Partie carrée. Paris, 1851. Published as *La Belle-Jenny,* Paris, 1865.

Italia [*Voyage en Italie*]. Paris, 1852.

Émaux et camées. Paris, 1852. Enlarged ed., Paris, 1872.

Constantinople. Paris, 1853.

Théâtre de poche. Paris, 1855.

Les beaux-arts en Europe—1855. Paris, 1855–1856.

L'Art moderne. Paris, 1856.

Jettatura. Brussels, 1857.

Avatar. Paris, 1857.

Le roman de la momie. Paris, 1858.

Histoire de l'art dramatique en France depuis vingt-cinq ans. 6 vols. Paris, 1858–1859.

Romans et contes. Paris, 1863.

Le Capitaine Fracasse. Paris, 1863.

Spirite. Paris, 1866.

Voyage en Russie. Paris, 1867.

Histoire du romantisme. Paris, 1872. Enlarged ed., Paris, 1874.

Théâtre: Mystères, comédies et ballets. Paris, 1872.

Portraits contemporains. Paris, 1874.

Portraits et souvenirs littéraires. Paris, 1875.

Guide de l'amateur au Musée du Louvre. Paris, 1882.

MODERN EDITIONS

Le Capitaine Fracasse. Preface by Antoine Adam. Paris, 1972.

Émaux et camées. Commentary by Madeleine Cottin. Paris, 1968.

Émaux et camées. Albertus. Edited by Claudine Gothot-Mersch. Paris, 1981.

Fortunio et autres nouvelles. Introduction and notes by Anne Bouchard. Lausanne, 1977.

Mademoiselle de Maupin. Edited and annotated by Michel Crouzet. Paris, 1973.

Poésies (1830). Edited by Harry Cockerham. London, 1973. French text with English introduction and notes.

Récits fantastiques. Chronology, introduction, and notes by Marc Eigeldinger. Paris, 1981. Includes "La cafetière," "Onuphrius," "Omphale," "La morte amoureuse," "La pipe d'opium," "Le chevalier double," "Le pied de momie," "Deux acteurs pour un rôle," "Le club des hachichins," "Arria Marcella," *Avatar, Jettatura.*

Le roman de la momie. Edited with an introduction by Adolphe Boschot. Paris, 1963. Also includes "Une nuit de Cléopâtre," "Le roi Candaule," and "Arria Marcella."

Spirite, nouvelle fantastique. Introduction by Marc Eigeldinger. Paris, 1970.

Voyage en Espagne. Edited by Jean-Claude Berchet. Paris, 1981.

COLLECTED WORKS

Oeuvres complètes. 26 vols. Paris, 1880–1903.

Poésies complètes. 3 vols. Edited by René Jasinski. New edition, revised and augmented. Paris, 1970.

TRANSLATIONS

Complete Works. 12 vols. Translated and edited by F. C. de Sumichrast. London and New York, 1900–1903.

My Fantoms. Short Stories. Selected, translated, and with a postscript by Richard Holmes. London, 1976.

BIOGRAPHICAL AND CRITICAL STUDIES

Barzun, Jacques. *Introduction to Mademoiselle de Maupin.* New York, 1944.

Binney, Edwin, 3rd. *Les ballets de Théophile Gautier.* Paris, 1965.

Book-Senninger, Claude. *Théophile Gautier, auteur dramatique.* Paris, 1972.

Cutler, Maxine. *Evocations of the Eighteenth Century in French Poetry, 1800–1869.* Geneva, 1970.

Delvaille, Bernard. *Théophile Gautier.* Paris, 1968.

Fauchereau, Serge. *Théophile Gautier.* Paris, 1972.

Grant, Richard B. *Théophile Gautier.* New York, 1975.

James, Henry. "Théophile Gautier." In *French Poets and Novelists.* London, 1878.

Richardson, Joanna. *Théophile Gautier, His Life and Times.* London, 1958.

Riffaterre, Hermine. *The Occult in Language and Literature.* New York, 1980. Pp. 65–74.

Riffaterre, Michael. "Rêve et réalité dans *L'Italia* de Théophile Gautier." *L'Esprit créateur* 3:18–25 (Spring 1963).

————. *The Semiotics of Poetry.* Bloomington, Ind., 1978.

Smith, Albert B. *Ideal and Reality in the Fictional Narratives of Théophile Gautier.* Gainesville, Fla., 1969. University of Florida Monographs, Humanities Series 30.

Spencer, M. C. *The Art Criticism of Théophile Gautier.* Geneva, 1969.

Taupin, René. *L'Influence du symbolisme français sur la poésie américaine (de 1910–1920).* Bibliothèque de la revue de littérature comparée, vol. 62. Paris, 1929.

Tennant, P. E. *Théophile Gautier.* London, 1975. Athlone French Poets Series.

Warren, Rosanna. "The Last Madness of Gérard de Nerval." *Georgia Review* (Spring 1983).

LEROY C. BREUNIG

IVAN GONCHAROV
(1812–1891)

OUTSIDE RUSSIA, GONCHAROV'S *Oblomov* has gradually won a measure of fame, if only as a curio. We know it as the novel about a man who will not get out of bed (though for much of the book Oblomov is very much on his feet). For Russians *Oblomov* is a central work of their tradition and Ivan Goncharov one of their major novelists. He wrote relatively little—three novels, a volume of travel sketches, and a handful of short stories, sketches, reminiscences, and literary criticism. His first novel, *Obyknovennaya istoriya* (*A Common Story*, 1847), was instrumental in the birth of Russian realism. Upon its appearance the champion of the new movement and the most influential critic of Russian literary history, Vissarion Belinsky, hailed it as an important blow in the battle of the young generation of the 1840's against the excesses of romanticism. Goncharov's third novel, *Obryv* (*The Precipice*, 1869), met a hostile reception from the reviewers but long enjoyed popularity among the reading public. The account of his voyage to Japan, *Fregat "Pallada"* (*The Frigate Pallas*, 1855–1857), continues to charm numerous readers.

Oblomov (1859) has had a profound impact on the Russian imagination. It is one of those exceptional works of literature—Leo Tolstoy's *War and Peace* is another—that have crossed the usual limits of literature to become part of the fabric of national consciousness. It is a fact of culture, an expression of the way Russians have seen themselves and their society. "Oblomovism," the term Goncharov coined for the psychological malaise of his eponymous hero, is now a word in the Russian language, describing "inertness, moral apathy, spiritual indolence"—all of which various Russians at various times have bewailed as conditions of the "Russian soul." In his writings and speeches, V. I. Lenin frequently exhorted his fellow Russians to stamp out "Oblomovism." For non-Russian readers the novel has acquired a distinctively modern complexion. Like many of the remarkable achievements of nineteenth-century Russian literature, it is rooted in the particulars of time and place and yet transcends them to present an image of the problematic character of modern man and the human condition.

In his life Goncharov went through a process of acculturation traversed by many Russians since the age of Peter the Great (1682–1725) and common in underdeveloped countries today. His passage from childhood to maturity was simultaneously a journey from the backward provinces of Russia to the urbane and cosmopolitan society of its cultural elite. He was born in 1812 into a family of grain merchants in the middle Volga town of Simbirsk (now Ulyanovsk). His paternal grandfather had through military service earned membership in the hereditary gentry. Nominally "gentlemen," successful in business, Goncharov's grandfather and father had not achieved a level of culture significantly above that of their merchant milieu or even the mass of illiterate peasants surrounding them. In a semi-feudal society like Russia, the merchant class more closely resembled a medieval guild than a modern middle class. Its depiction in the plays of Alexander Ostrovsky as insular, tyrannical, and superstition-ridden earned the critic Nikolay Dobrolyubov's epithet "dark kingdom"—a name that has stuck. Like many merchants, the Goncharovs may have been Old Believers, the most tradition-bound of Russian Christians. Ivan's mother also came from a family of merchants, but her position as a woman responsible for the management of a large household of servants and children (four of six survived) prevented her from attaining even the modicum of knowledge of the affairs of the world that the Goncharov men had acquired. From all accounts the family was characterized by a mixture of narrow traditionalism, religious formalism, and the practical shrewdness of businessmen.

It was also a home marked by "suspiciousness," as the novelist later described it. The suspiciousness of the Goncharovs seems to have been more far-reaching than usual provincial mistrust of the outside world or the habitual caution of merchants. For Goncharov it was the "innate and inherited illness" of his family. His father, who was fifty when he took a bride of nineteen, was a melancholic though extremely pious man. Goncharov adored his mother. He respected her talent for maintaining an orderly home. He also remembered her as severe, strict, and mistrustful. The sudden death of his father when Ivan was only seven surely heightened the insecurity of a child growing up in a troubled and repressive household. Separated in age by almost six decades from an otherwise self-absorbed father, he was now irrevocably separated from him by the fact of death. Understandably he put all his hopes in his mother. If she was cold, the child could still see a sign of caring in her diligent housekeeping, a token of love in her dispensing of food, strength and control in her

severity. Fathers are as absent from Goncharov's fiction as mothers (or maternal figures) are omnipresent. His novels convey an aching nostalgia, often viewed ironically, for the protective maternal world of early childhood.

The Goncharovs were the kind of family a child, if he does not submit to it, seeks to escape. He may escape into dreams that soften the reality, as Goncharov sometimes did, or try to make himself over into something different. A glimpse of the possibility of another way of life appeared to the young Ivan in the form of the man who stepped into the breach caused by his father's death. Nikolay Tregubov, a boarder in the family home and the godfather of the now fatherless children, assumed responsibility for their upbringing. Tregubov was everything the Goncharovs were not—an aristocrat not only by birth but in manner and culture. The man Goncharov called his substitute father possessed considerable wealth, formal education, and, as a naval officer, experience of the larger world beyond Simbirsk. He was one of a small circle of local aristocrats who were typical figures of the age of Catherine the Great (1762–1796) and Alexander I (1801–1825)—cosmopolitan in outlook, liberal in politics, ardent disciples of the French Enlightenment. Several, including Tregubov, had contacts with the Decembrists, a progressive segment of the aristocracy who attempted a coup d'etat in 1825 to install a constitutional monarchy (some even wanted a republic). Their liberalism proved futile in the wave of reaction that followed on the heels of that abortive rebellion. Aristocrats in a despotic, bureaucratic state, they were denied the possibility of real political influence. Russia offered relatively few opportunities for professional careers, and their aristocratic mentality made them averse to pursue even these. As a result they turned into what Russian literature has dubbed "superfluous men"—men whose education and values set them apart from Russian society (including the great majority of their own class) but who in the absence of realizable goals sank into abstract dilettantism.

It was among such men that the young Goncharov first encountered liberal, humanistic ideas and a more subtle and varied way of life than that of a narrow, tradition-rooted merchant family.

Goncharov never fully reconciled the two aspects of his upbringing. On the surface he made himself into a gentleman in the Tregubov mold. He received the sort of humanistic education given to the gentry, assimilated ideals of enlightenment and reason, learned to speak French fluently and to write a Russian that is a model of smoothness and polish. As a famous writer he hobnobbed with assorted aristocrats and high officials in the czarist government. At the same time he always remained a bit of an outsider in the society of the Russian aristocracy, painfully conscious of his different origins. He was not above resentment toward those who, like his rival Ivan Turgenev, had the good fortune to have been born into wealth and high social standing. Though Goncharov could not shake off the melancholy image of "the narrowness and suffocating atmosphere" of his youth, its "lack of freedom, of fresh air, of a purer and more decent society, of human beings, ideas, feelings," he also, perhaps unaware, continued to measure the world by his family's values. The Goncharovs' business sense left a deep mark. In his reminiscences he fondly recalled Tregubov as exerting a softening influence on the harsh authoritarianism of his family, nurturing "tender feelings in the hearts of the children." Yet this genteel softness is also the butt of his irony. Ultimately Tregubov and his friends are seen as congenial and charming eccentrics, men whose intelligence, culture, and generosity of spirit are wasted. They have failed to translate fine sentiments into constructive action. For this son of merchants compelled to fend for themselves by cunning and frugality, Tregubov and his class were impractical dreamers—"superfluous men," victims of "Oblomovism."

A measure of alienation, though painful in life, can be an advantage for an artist. Goncharov's situation—close enough to feel sympathy for the ideals and values of the Russian gentry and yet distant enough to cultivate critical detachment—enabled him to become one of the great chroniclers of that class. Attracted by the refinement, urbanity, and idealism of the more enlightened segment of the gentry, which despite its small numbers set the tone of Russian culture, he continually measured its worth against standards of practical efficacy and constructive achievement.

Ivan and his brother Nikolay were the first of the Goncharovs to receive a formal education. At the age of eight Ivan was enrolled in a local boarding school for children of the gentry, where he began his study of French and German. Two years later his mother packed him off to the Moscow Commercial School, presumably to prepare for a career in business. The Commercial School offered an extensive curriculum in the liberal arts and the sciences. Though the curriculum differed little from schools for the gentry, the teachers were inferior and the treatment of students harsh. Goncharov remembered the place with special bitterness. Perhaps because the family business had run into difficulties, he left the Commercial School without taking his degree and in 1831 entered Moscow University. A degree from the university traditionally led to a career in the civil service, offering young men of the lower and middle social strata (excluding serfs) one of the few opportunities existing in Russia to rise in status.

Goncharov unwittingly came to Moscow University at an exciting time in the life of that institution and a fateful moment in Russian intellectual history. Though the government envisaged it as a kind of prep school for aspiring bureaucrats, after the debacle of the 1825 revolt intellectually curious sons of the aristocracy began to turn to the university in a search for alternative values to those of official institutions. Professors educated in the great German universities and teachers under the sway of German philosophy had been added to the faculty to satisfy the needs of a more serious generation of students. Those students were the glory of the institution. Among Goncharov's classmates were, besides the poet Mikhail Lermontov, several remarkable young men who were to shape the thought of their age: the future dean of Russian radical criticism, Vissarion Belinsky; Alexander Herzen, a leading figure of the Russian revolutionary movement and the father of Russian socialist thought; the prominent Slavophile Konstantin Aksakov; and the influential philosopher Nikolay Stankevich. In the 1840's, when these precocious young men came to prominence—they are called "the men of the forties"—they split into rival groups of Westernizers and Slavophiles. In their student days the shared style of thought was heavily romantic.

The sources of Russian romanticism were largely German, though Herzen and his circle were also drawn to French utopian socialism. The German idealist philosophers—Friedrich Schelling in the 1830's, G. W. F. Hegel in the 1840's—were the rage. Schelling's assertion of the value of the self and his exaltation of art struck a chord in the sensibilities of young men mired in a society in which the individual was little valued and in which art provided an exceptional outlet for creative expression and personal ambition. The idealized heroes and heroines of Friedrich von Schiller's plays, who proclaim the absolute worth of personality, friendship, and love in the face of cynical power and crass philistinism, furnished a literary counterpart to the yearnings of philosophical idealism. Paradoxically—and the paradox is at the heart of romantic thought—the extreme individualism of this generation, its urgent demand for complete self-expression and self-realization, coexisted with a longing to identify with embracing totalities, whether the world-mind, the organic oneness of nature, or the more durable collectivities of nation, people, and the march of history.

Goncharov, as was to become his habit, stayed aloof from the famous intellectual circles of his student days (later, in 1846, he did participate in discussions at Belinsky's Saint Petersburg home). By nature he was wary of unfamiliar ideas and extreme enthusiasms. Undoubtedly his middle-class upbringing contributed much to his sober, often conventional attitudes. He remained throughout his life a firm believer in the "bourgeois" virtues of hard work, good sense, moderation, and gradual social and material progress. As a young man he was attracted to more restrained and balanced figures than the prevailing romantic culture heroes. His favorite writers were Alexander Pushkin; the art historian Johann Winckelmann, whose aestheticism appealed to the young Goncharov; and especially Nikolay Karamzin, the leading exponent of Russian sentimentalism. Though sometimes called the Russian Rousseau, Karamzin was basically a conservative thinker. For all his talk of feelings and "the heart," his close ties were to the eighteenth-century age of enlightenment and reason.

Few men remain completely untouched by the climate of their times, however, and there is evidence that Goncharov passed through a romantic phase. The experience told in an abiding faith in the autonomy and supreme dignity of art, the unconscious provenance of its products, and a lifelong sense, often at odds with his ironic skepticism, that men require an ideal, even if unattainable, of the beautiful and the perfect. His literary corpus may be viewed as an ongoing dialectic with the romantic temper, parodying its excesses while simultaneously affirming some of its values, particularly the primacy of art and the creative imagination.

In 1835, a year after graduating from Moscow University, Goncharov accepted a position as a translator in the ministry of finance. He did not retire from government service until 1867, two years before publication of his last novel. Throughout his active life he was a full-time bureaucrat and part-time writer, working at literature during summer vacations and moments snatched from his official duties. Famous as a writer, he was also successful as a bureaucrat. He rose through the ranks of the official hierarchy, eventually becoming an Actual Councillor of State, the fourth-highest rank of fourteen, which entitled him to be called "Your Excellency."

In the late 1830's Goncharov became a habitué of the Maykov salon in Saint Petersburg. The Maykovs were an old aristocratic family who had long distinguished themselves in Russian cultural life. In their circle Goncharov, who was shy and reclusive, found a congenial environment and formed a few lifelong friendships. The Maykovs encouraged his first literary efforts—a few poems and stories that were never published in his lifetime. The poems are stilted exercises in a fashionable melancholy; the stories are told in a tone of light banter (or "romantic irony") that resists taking either character or situation seriously. Both manners are typical of the artistic atmosphere of the Maykov salon and symptomatic of a romanticism already on the wane. The inflated and stereotyped language of the poems—what Turgenev dubbed the "pseudo-sublime" style of the 1830's—became a continuing object of Goncharov's parody (they are put into the mouth of the hero of his first novel). The stories, though told in a subjective manner Goncharov was to abandon, show instances of the parodic method he cultivated in his novels.

Russia in the 1840's witnessed a general revolt against romanticism. The scene was dominated by the so-called Natural School. Though elements of romanticism survived in the frequent melodramatics and grotesquerie of the Natural School writers (Nikolay Gogol was the overriding influence), their interest in the documentary rendering of ordinary life formed a bridge to the realism that dominated Russian literature until the 1880's.

Goncharov's entire trilogy was to some degree a product of the 1840's. His three novels, though written over a twenty-five-year span, were begun or conceived from 1844 to 1847. They all evidence the manner of the Natural School in their leisurely and highly detailed depictions of everyday life. Also, though the three novels sometimes respond to contemporary issues, many of their concerns stem from the earlier period of Goncharov's life. His fiction is very much rooted in his personal history. The novels tell the stories of three young men—Alexander Aduev, Ilya Oblomov, and Boris Raysky—whose journey through life is similar to that of their creator: childhood in the remote provinces, a move to the city, study at the university, a career in the government service. Two of his heroes see themselves as writers and artists, and one, Oblomov, has the imagination, though not the vocation, of a poet. Goncharov was in his midthirties when he planned his trilogy, and each novel describes a crisis of identity and a disillusionment with life that have run their course by the time the hero is in *his* midthirties.

Was there some catastrophe that struck Goncharov in the middle of life's journey and that he felt impelled to translate into art? We do not know, but from what we do know it is likely that he despaired—a despair that grew more intense with the years—because *nothing* had happened. He had come to that difficult time in life, the passage from youth to middle age, when the routines of existence have become firmly established and one looks forward to more of the same and back on the yet unrealized dreams of youth as perhaps unrealizable. Goncharov's dissatisfaction with his occupation as a bureaucrat and his failure to marry, though he very much longed for a family, certainly contributed to his malaise. Art was a means of escape but also a way of self-discovery.

A Common Story has been called Russia's first truly realistic novel. Earlier works that might make such a claim are neither entirely novels nor entirely realistic in the narrow literary usage of that term. Pushkin's brilliant *Eugene Onegin* (1823–1831) is in verse; and, though its good sense and beautifully portrayed characters made a deep impression on many Russian writers, including Goncharov, its lyricism and digressive manner place it outside the central realistic tradition. Nikolay Gogol dealt the death blow to a protracted Russian neoclassicism by, among other things, opening literature to vulgar detail, but his masterpiece, *Dead Souls* (1842), is again extremely lyrical (it is subtitled "a poem") and its characters are comic grotesques. Lermontov in *A Hero of Our Times* (1840) achieved a remarkably spare, virile prose, but the work is essentially a string of stories and more atmospheric in tone than most realistic novels. *A Common Story* was the first Russian novel of any importance written consistently in a plain, unadorned style—emotionally neutral and transparent. The narration is in the "objective" third person; the characters are all ordinary men and women. They are unmarked by the special fatality of an Onegin or a Pechorin (of *A Hero of Our Times*), or the grotesque exaggerations of Gogol's comic manner. As was characteristic of realism, especially in its early stages, the novel spends much of its energies debunking romanticism. For a sentimental view of experience it substitutes an attitude that is totally ironic.

A Common Story tells of the education into the ways of the world of its hero, Alexander Aduev. It follows his transplantation from the country to the city, which is also a process of systematic disillusionment. The pattern is central to the Western realistic novel, though less frequent among the Russians; *A Common Story* has often been compared to Honoré de Balzac's *Les illusions perdues*, which may have inspired it. Our young provincial, who is an aspiring writer, arrives in Saint Petersburg full of high hopes for love and glory. He stays with his Uncle Peter, a dry bureaucrat and industrial entrepreneur who serves as his foil. Alexander is sentimental, sensitive, and dreamy; experience has made Peter suspicious of feelings and skeptical of imagination. He has turned himself into a paragon of practical efficiency, a walking machine. Aghast at his nephew's provincial naiveté, he undertakes the task of educating him in the realities of urban society and modern life. A running dialogue between the two dominates the novel. Alexander makes a failed attempt at a writing career and becomes infatuated with several young women, but these experiences are merely occasions for uncle and nephew to resume their debate. Their argument, which in simplified form confronts romanticism with realism, grows out of the intellectual climate of Russia in the late 1840's. This was a time when thinking Russians sought to discredit romantic speculations and attitudes and to turn their reader's attention to the dismal actualities of contemporary life.

For the literary imagination, pedagogical issues may be concentrated in the problem of mastering a style. Though Peter instructs his provincial nephew about the various civilities and stratagems of urban life—from correct dress and table manners to the quickest road to career and fortune—he spends the larger part of his educative energies on Alexander's speech. For Peter, "le style c'est l'homme." His instructional method follows the traditional procedure of writers who are trying to wean themselves or their audiences from atrophied literary conventions—parody. The parody results from placing Alexander's affected, self-consciously literary language alongside the uncle's colloquial speech:

> [Alexander:] My uncle . . . is very prosaic . . . It is as if his spirit were chained to the earth and never rose to a pure reflection, insulated from earthly squabbles, of the phenomena of the spiritual nature of man. For him heaven is inseparably bound to the earth, and he and I, it seems, will never merge our souls completely.

> [Peter:] He's a quiet fellow. He has his odd points—he throws himself upon me to kiss me, speaks like a seminary student—well, he'll soon get over it, and it's a good thing he isn't hanging on my neck.

> (*Sobranie sochinenii*, 1955 ed., 1.2)

More frequently, Peter parodies Alexander's style by the simple substitution of a prosaic and concrete term for the other's abstract rhetoric:

> [Alexander:] Life is like a lake. . . . It is full of something mysterious, alluring, concealing in itself so much. . . .
>
> [Peter:] Slime, my good fellow.
>
> (1.2)

Though many romantic writers—Lord Byron, Heinrich Heine, Nikolay Gogol—play with a mixture of the vulgar and lofty, this procedure of systematic deflation to the prosaic, as if only the concrete were real, lies at the heart of literary realism. It is not unlike Prince Andrew's redefinition in Leo Tolstoy's *War and Peace* of glory as our desire for the love of strangers when we ought to seek the love of those we know. Underlying realism's parodic impulse is the suspicion that abstractions lie. Words ought to be true to things as they are:

> [Alexander:] And I imagined you were bidding farewell . . . to your true friends, whom you sincerely love, with whom you would recall for the last time your gay youth, and perhaps, on parting, would press fast to your heart.
>
> [Peter:] Come now! In those several words of yours there is everything that does not and should not exist in life. . . . Really! You say "true friends" when there are just friends, and "goblet" when people drink out of wineglasses or ordinary glasses, and embraces "on parting" when there is no question of parting. Oh, Alexander!
>
> (1.3)

A Common Story is very much a programatic novel—both an exploration of and a statement about how novels should be written. In finally abandoning his inflated diction for "the poetry of a gray sky, a rickety fence, a wicket gate, and a muddy pond" (Goncharov's paraphrase of Pushkin), Alexander rejects romantic emotionalism to assert an aesthetic whereby language will be true to things. The things celebrated are from ordinary life.

"Common" forms part of the novel's title, and the argument directed against Alexander's view of art (and of self, for they are intimately entwined) reduces the artificial to the natural, the exceptional to the ordinary, the "uncommon to the common." Alexander's reading—works by Byron and Schiller and French romances—and his own writing are about exceptional individuals in extraordinary circumstances. Literature, he believes, should concern itself only with exalted heroes—"a corsair, a great poet, an artist." Peter as usual converts the extravagant to the habitual. Dissuading his impassioned nephew from taking vengeance on a rival in love (the tales Alexander reads are also about bloody acts of revenge), he points out that Saint Petersburg is not the Kirgiz steppes and that a duel in "our age" is conducted not with swords but with wit and cunning, whose purpose is "to present the rival in a common aspect, to show that the new hero is 'so-so'" (1.6). When Alexander notes the editorial comments "excessive ardor," "unnaturalness," "there are no such people" on one of his rejected manuscripts, he asks himself, "Can I be expected to portray these vulgar heroes one meets at every step, who think and feel like the crowd, who do what everyone else does—these pitiful characters of everyday petty tragedies and comedies, who are not marked by a special seal?" (1.5). The question might very well be asked by the protagonists of Goncharov's other novels, who also feel their uniqueness threatened by the claims of routine life. The novel itself provides an answer to Alexander's rhetorical question, for *A Common Story* is Alexander's "common story," the story of how he gives up his dreams of an exceptional fate and extraordinary personality to become ordinary, "common," like "everyone else."

That story is told in a manner analogous to the parodic dialogue of uncle and nephew. Practically every chapter (there are twelve and an epilogue) follows a deflationary course from high expectations to a comic pratfall. Repetitive action belongs to the comic design of the novel, but it also results in a somewhat mechanical symmetry. In a typical chapter, Alexander falls rapturously in love with a fairly ordinary girl named Nadenka. He hires a boat to take him across the Neva River for a rendezvous. Shortly after wishing he were able to hasten his journey by walking on the water, he slips into the river. Blind to Nadenka's conventional character, he conceives of his love as the attainment of an idyllic happiness of the kind he has read about in pastoral romances: "We shall always be alone: we shall withdraw far from others; . . . rumors of sorrow and misfortune will not disturb us, just as now, here in the garden, no sound disturbs this solemn silence" (1.4). No sooner are the words uttered than a voice (Nadenka's mother's) interrupts to inform the starry-eyed lover that his yogurt is on the table. Alexander ruminates: "A moment of inexpressible bliss— and suddenly yogurt! . . . Can all life be like that?" (1.4). In Goncharov's world it is. Each of his fictional heroes dreams of an idyllic state removed from the humdrum world of the "others," only to have the bubbles of his fantasies burst by the intrusion of ordinary reality. Goncharov's fiction is always alert to human attempts to poeticize reality, to see life as more than it is.

One can also see it as less than it is. Though most of the novel is devoted to exploding Alexander's illusions, it simultaneously, almost surreptitiously, undermines his uncle's narrow practicality. It does so, appropriately for a work in which speech is character, by a manipulation of language. Throughout the book repeated phrases and gestures serve as comic signatures of character. Alexander compulsively parrots expressions like "sweet bliss," "sincere effusions," "colossal passion," while dismissing the money his uncle offers him as "filthy lucre." The uncle, who until the end of the novel denies that this overwrought provincial can truly be an Aduev, habitually responds to his outpourings with prosy quips, exclamations of exasperation ("Oh, Alexander!"), a nonchalant puff on a cigar, a well-timed dodge of a fervent embrace, or by forgetting the names of Alexander's romantic attachments (Nadenka becomes succesively Marya, Anyuta, Sofya, Katenka, Yuliya, Varenka, Verochka). He does not take Alexander seriously. "Career and fortune," another repetition, is what the conflict is ostensibly about. Alexander's infatuations block his path to career and fortune; his uncle will not recognize him as his nephew until he has them.

But one of these reiterated items is misplaced. An image connected with the world of sentiment, which should properly belong to Alexander, turns out to belong to his uncle. Yellow flowers grow along the bank of a lake on Alexander's ancestral estate. They become a symbol of the powers of poetry, love, and friendship, which Alexander so heatedly espouses, and also of the old easy ways of the rural gentry. Yellow flowers stand for what has been left behind—the intimacies of life lived in a familial setting close to nature, before people moved to the impersonal, competitive city. Though Peter attempts to project the associations tied to yellow flowers onto his nephew, they, as Alexander discovers, refer instead to what the uncle has left behind. Peter also once knew a life of sentiment not unlike that of his nephew, a life that he has denied for worldly success. *A Common Story* is only apparently the story of two characters diametrically opposed to each other. Actually, it is a novel in which one character recapitulates the history of the other, in which each moves from youthful enthusiasm to cold sobriety. The uncle's "common story" has taken place before the novel begins.

As one strand of the novel reaches into the past to reveal the uncle's secret romantic life, another leads beyond its formal conclusion into the future. That conclusion exhibits a tidy symmetry, characteristic of *A Common Story* and reminiscent of neoclassical comedy—a tradition that may have influenced this first Russian realistic novel. The denouement is marked by a juncture of the governing images and set phrases of the novel in what is apparently an achievement of total harmony. Alexander, worn out by his posturing, surrenders his "colossal passion" and "sincere effusions" and accepts his uncle's "filthy lucre." In turn, his uncle, seeing that Alexander has employed his capital to advantage, accepts him: "And a career, and a fortune! . . . And what a fortune! And all of a sudden! . . . Alexander, . . . you are of my blood. You are an Aduev! All right, embrace me!" But as the differences that separated them are illusory, so is their final reconciliation ephemeral. Peter at the end of the book has declined both physically and morally. His deterioration has been hinted at earlier by a chronic backache—one of the finer comic touches in the novel—which comes to represent his emotionally sterile life. At the conclusion a graying, stooped, and unsteady Peter confronts a fat, rosy, balding but successful Alexander. However, Alexander has already begun to slide downward. His uncle's fate awaits him: "You resemble me completely. Only the backache is missing." Alexander replies: "I already have a stitch there sometimes." Uncle and nephew enjoy the triumph of a brief instant of accord on the descending slope of their lives. Behind the flush of success lies the inevitability of decay. "Finally! For the first time," Peter declares in the epilogue, bestowing upon his nephew the long awaited embrace. "And the last, Uncle. This is an uncommon incident."

Uncle and nephew have pursued the same course—from a sentimental view of the world to disillusionment, from success in business to a decline, or, in Alexander's case, incipient decline, which is the price of that success. The novel, seemingly presenting two views of existence irreconcilably at odds, actually tells the story of two identical careers spread over different periods, each commenting ironically on the other. We observe Alexander's romantic infatuations from the standpoint of his uncle's more worldly understanding of life, Alexander's success with the knowledge of what that sort of success has cost Peter. Likewise,

Peter's self-assured and mocking denial of the claims of feelings is undermined by our knowledge of his secret affinity with his nephew—his past of "yellow flowers." Neither sentiment nor practicality is affirmed as an absolute value. *A Common Story* instead resolves itself in an ironic deadlock in which both Alexander's way and Peter's way—the way of poetic imagination and sensibility and that of practical activity—are delimited to partial and hence insufficient responses to the problem of living.

The stalemate that is at the heart of the novel, however, is anything but grim. *A Common Story* is a playful work, somewhat thin, at times repetitive, but amusing. Goncharov's first novel, though important in his development and the history of Russian literature, is still tied too closely to the light anecdotal stories he wrote in the Maykov salon. Its farcical tone and elaborate plot also echo the vaudevilles so popular in his day. *A Common Story* is essentially an entertainment. Goncharov keeps a severe distance from his characters and holds them firmly in rein. We seldom see their pain. They stand halfway between fully realized fictional characters and the generalized types of traditional comedy. Alexander and Peter, though skillfully drawn, always stand on the edge of slipping into the abstract roles of "romantic dreamer" and "practical man." They exist in good measure for the plot that controls them—the ironic twist that reveals uncle and nephew to be carbon copies of each other. The telling of the same story twice encloses the novel in the kind of excessively tidy symmetry that marks its separate chapters. It also serves to dampen whatever interest we may have in the characters as individuals. Instead they become types caught in an eternal comedy of coming of age, loss of illusions, and the compromises of maturity. The novel's subject is comedy's "way of the world," its "common story."

In 1852 Goncharov embarked on an exceptional adventure in his otherwise cautious and sedentary life. Bogged down in his work on *Oblomov*, bored by his bureaucratic duties, he accepted a post as secretary to an admiral on an official expedition to inspect Russian possessions in North America, which the expedition never reached, and to negotiate a commercial treaty with the Japanese. Goncharov lived in continual fear that his creative energies might dry up. It was his hope that the trip would stimulate him to write an easier sort of book than a novel, a volume of travel sketches in which he might simply jot down what he saw "without any literary pretension." His journey took him first to England, then around the Cape of Good Hope and through the Indian Ocean to China and Japan. The outbreak of the Crimean War made further travel by ship dangerous, since the British controlled the seas, and he returned to Saint Petersburg through Siberia. His account, entitled *The Frigate Pallas* after the ship on which he spent almost two years of his life, may very well be his second-best book.

The Frigate Pallas is something more than a volume of travel sketches, but even as an account of a cultivated Russian's impressions of England, Africa, Java, the Philippines, China, Japan, and Siberia, it holds our interest despite some overlong sections. Goncharov was an intelligent, sometimes acute observer. His smooth, lightly ironic prose was ideal for a travel book. The sections on Japan, which were originally published as a separate volume and may still be read as such, have a special charm. The refinement and dignified bearing of the Japanese officials strongly attracted him; their elaborate ceremoniousness proved irresistible to a writer always on the watch for the comic possibilities of the curious and eccentric. The blend of warm sympathy and ironic playfulness that fills the pages on the Japanese are surpassed in Goncharov's writings only by *Oblomov*.

Under the guise of a travel book, however, Goncharov wrote a highly self-conscious literary work that in some ways resembles his novels. Like them it is built on principles that are essentially parodic. The European image of the Orient in the nineteenth century was of places exotic, mysterious, sensual, primeval, and pristine—in a word, "romantic." Goncharov commences his journey with just such an image in mind, though he is quite aware of its literary sources. The book is organized so as to deflate it. It consistently moves from heightened expectations of enchanting scenes, idyllic landscapes, wild and stormy seas (also a favorite image of the romantics) to an actuality of squalid ports, shabby hotels, sullen natives, a sea that is mostly boring.

Everywhere the ordinary, the mundane, the "common" lie in wait for this most unlikely of world travelers, as they did his fictional hero Alexander Aduev before him. Goncharov comes ashore on his first tropical island, one of the Cape Verde group, off the west coast of equatorial Africa, only to discover the natives lying on the sand playing a local variant of a card game popular in Russia. Souvenirs of his stay on the Cape of Good Hope turn out to be imports from England. Manila promises "something flowering . . . luxury, poetry" (*The Frigate Pallas* 2.5) but initially offers only foul smells. The Chinese are disappointing—they all look monotonously alike. Too much of what Goncharov sees is merely a second-hand Europe. What is unmistakably indigenous is often dull: "You see one or two [Korean] villages, one or two groups [of natives], and you've seen them all" (2.6). At the end of his trip, when he finds himself on a surprisingly well-traveled and fairly safe Siberian trail that fails to substantiate "dark legends [of Siberia] as a land of brigandage, extortion, and unpunished crimes," he can only exclaim somewhat wistfully: "Alas! Where is romanticism?"

On one occasion Goncharov thinks he has found what he is ostensibly seeking—an idyllic land of "eternal summer," "bright temples" of nature in which creation has assumed a "finished" form. The account of his journey to this land of "the golden age"—an island of the Ryukyu chain, south of Japan—reflects in miniature the pattern of the book. The traveler initially views the island through a prism of art and literature: its ordered and decorative landscapes resemble a painting by Jean Antoine Watteau; playful silvery streams and clamorous cascades seem "theatrical," forests and ravines "picturesque"; friendly shepherds recall the Chloe and Daphnis of Theocritus and Salomon Gessner; life here is as the Bible and the *Odyssey* of Homer describe it.

Another view of this idyllic land follows, and it is sinister. According to a local missionary, the several seemingly friendly natives who follow the Russian visitors about the island are actually spies; the local inhabitants are courteous only because they are afraid; the "innocent" shepherds are prone to drunkenness, gambling, and violence. Goncharov is at first skeptical, but he has also become skeptical of his literary sources. When he later encounters the local chief, a gray-haired old man with all the signs of "a great lack of continence"—misshapen features, blue and reddish veins around a red nose—Goncharov is forced to exclaim in familiar accents of disillusionment, "Alas, farewell idyll!"

Since the world offers little excitement for the traveler, Goncharov puts himself—or, rather, masks of himself—at the center of his book. Setting out on his journey, he wonders how he can reconcile the two images, in his words "the two lives," fate has thrust upon him—that of "a modest bureaucrat in an official frock coat quailing before his superior's glance, fearing colds," and the image of "the new Argonaut in a straw hat . . . hurtling over the deeps in search of the Golden Fleece" (1.1). He solves his dilemma as he solved it in his novels, by playing off one against the other. Once again a prosaic self is set against a poetic self. *The Frigate Pallas* is, besides a travel book and a parody of romantic travel literature, another comedy in Goncharov's unfolding series of comic perceptions of himself in the world.

Both images, the expectant Argonaut and the dull bureaucrat—the Alexander and Peter Aduev of this book—are viewed ironically. As distant lands never coincide with the illusions of the adventurer, the bureaucrat never proves to be quite up to the adventures of the world he has reluctantly set out to explore. Goncharov continually highlights the incongruity of his own position—the timid Saint Petersburg official cast upon the great seas, the landlubber who insists on calling the deck "a street" among men for whom the sea is home, the world traveler plagued by rheumatism, weariness, boredom, and homesickness. The "Argonaut" had embarked on a quest for those idyllic lands of "eternal summer"; the bureaucrat's voyage turns into a quest for a moment of comfort on inhospitable oceans, a brief period of respite from incessant motion. If the scenery of a place attracts him he remains painfully conscious that reaching it over muddy potholed roads can be "true torture in spite of picturesque ravines and hills" (1.4). At times a dull indifference, an obtuseness that is perhaps as much an ironic pose as it is a reflection of his weariness, overtakes him. At such moments he stays on board and lets the sights go unseen: "So what," he exclaims in a not uncharacteristic fashion when urged by his excited shipmates to come and inspect a crocodile. "I'll see it at Zam's [zoo] when I return to Petersburg; they have a small one there; it will have grown up by that time" (1.5).

Travel, however, has its consolations. For one thing, there is good food and good company. Much of the work has the character of a dinner menu, as Goncharov describes with relish innumerable meals, from English roast beef to subtle Chinese dishes, that send him into raptures of praise. Another means of consolation is to see the strange in familiar terms. If exotic places turn out to be ordinary, it is, one feels, because Goncharov very much wants it that way. As a writer his eye is not on the spectacular but on the usual, upon those homely habits of everyday life that people hold in common. No matter how wild the place, he manages to find something comparable to a Russian estate, a street in Saint Petersburg, or, at the very least, middle-class England. Even when what he sees is authentically different, he strives to project on it qualities of the familiar—if only in his imagination. In a revealing passage the traveler, gazing at the charming and picturesque scene of Nagasaki and its environs, tells us that

> in my thoughts I covered all these hillocks and groves with temples, cottages, pavilions and statues, and the waters of the harbor with steamships and thickets of masts; I populated the shores with Europeans; I already saw paths of a park, galloping horsewomen, and closer to the city I envisioned Russian, American and English factories.
>
> (2.3)

Raw nature was for Goncharov a vacuum he abhorred and felt compelled to fill.

His distaste for the uncultivated and love of the familiar and comfortable provoked him to insert an essay into *The Frigate Pallas* that is the fullest statement of his social views. They are unashamedly "bourgeois." Two trying years at sea had confirmed Goncharov's confidence in the virtues of soft easy chairs, clean linen, fine cuisine, and all the trappings of a well-furnished middle-class home, and he would have the rest of the still-benighted world share the blessings he has known. He compares the concepts of luxury and comfort—all to the advantage of the latter. Luxury is aristocratic; its pleasures can be enjoyed only by a privileged few, as in the despotic Orient and Renaissance Venice and Spain (or, he might have added, in contemporary Russia). Comfort, on the other hand, is rational and democratic. It is but the fulfillment of "the reasonable needs of the majority." The manifest destiny of Europeans is to carry to less fortunate peoples "the banner of security, abundance, peace, and that well-being which [the traveler] enjoys at home." This heroic undertaking of European society has already begun to bear fruit, so that "what was inaccessible luxury for the few is, thanks to civiliza-

tion, becoming accessible to all: in the north a pineapple costs 5 or 10 rubles; here—a half-kopeck. The task of civilization is to transport it quickly to the north and drive the price down to 5 kopecks, so that you and I may enjoy it" (1.6).

Prosy attitudes like these earned the scorn of many of Goncharov's contemporaries. Nevertheless, there is vision at work here. Having derided one version of the golden age—the idyll of the "natural"—Goncharov postulates another quite different idyllic condition. His vision is of a world that has become perfectly domesticated, where all the wildernesses and deserts are covered with tidy farms, comfortable homes, clean hotels, and well-provisioned restaurants, presumably moderately priced; where roads are paved and seas offer few hazards to swift steamships; where strange peoples with difficult-to-pronounce names have turned into courteous and respectable burghers barely distinguishable from their European models. Despite its homely, middle-class air, it is a prophetic vision foreseeing the shape of the modern world, with its increasing uniformity and universal demand for the comforts that were once the luxuries of a few. It is also unquestionably utopian, brimful of a cheerful and naive optimism that the tortured history of our century has made difficult to maintain.

What appeared to Goncharov's fellow Russians as smug complacency was a reflection of psychological needs of which they were not aware. The writer who, when invited by his excited shipmates to admire a lightning-spangled southern sky, could only exclaim "Deformity, disorder!" was of course a parodist countering conventional responses of literature—here the lyrical reflex to nature—with a prosaic demurral. He was also a man with a compulsive urge toward "form" and "order." Face to face with untamed nature, Goncharov felt profoundly uneasy. In *The Frigate Pallas* he expresses his hope of seeing a world where everything is familiar and safe.

Goncharov was aware of some of the limitations of his utopia. In a world become totally rationalized, human spontaneity would be lost. Throughout his travels he keeps coming across a frock-coated Englishman, umbrella in hand, in the most remote places. His Englishman is a comic embodiment of the predictable sameness of the world, as England is the pattern of the future. At one point he compares him to a Russian squire. Where the Englishman is energetic, punctilious, and mechanical, the Russian is indolent, disorderly, and yet blessed with the gift of spontaneity. The opposition echoes that of Alexander and Peter Aduev and anticipates the confrontation of Oblomov and Stolz. Goncharov had already published his second novel's famous chapter, "Son Oblomova" (Oblomov's Dream), and at the outset of his journey he assures his readers that no matter how far or long he travels he will carry with him the soil of native Oblomovka—an image of Russia that for all its lazy backwardness has preserved a naturalness lost in the modern world. This ambiguous attitude toward Europe, admiring of its material progress and suspicious of its evolving social order, was nearly universal among Russians of the nineteenth century. While in his conscious mind Goncharov looked to the future and admired those rationalistic, mechanical men who served as its emblems, nostalgia continually drew him back to his native Oblomovka.

In the fall of 1855, shortly after his return to Saint Petersburg, Goncharov, now a bachelor of forty-three, fell in love. The object of his affections, Elizaveta Tolstaya, was fifteen to seventeen years younger and strikingly beautiful. Goncharov enjoyed the company of women but feared intimacy with them. No doubt Elizaveta detected his ambivalence. She turned him down and married someone else. Rejection caused him much torment. It may have been the first and was certainly the last time he was seriously and romantically involved. He quickly overcame his pain by cloaking himself in his habitual irony.

Elizaveta failed to rescue him from his solitary life, but she may have had considerable impact on his creative activity. By 1855 Goncharov had not gotten beyond the static comic play and the famous dream sequence in part 1 of *Oblomov*. What he needed was a plot or action that would allow his hero to unfold and achieve complexity. In the finished novel the love story of Oblomov and Olga serves this purpose. Goncharov seems to have had a vague idea of it well before 1855, but his encounter with Elizaveta may have given him an incentive to work through his sufferings in art, as well as a fund of personal experience to draw on.

In the summer of 1857 Goncharov, on vacation in Marienbad, completed in six weeks the novel he had brooded over for a decade. The Marienbad summer of furious creative activity remained for him the great and singular moment of his life. He explained his feat by referring to his belief in the unconscious provenance of art and its slow organic maturation:

How did it happen that I, a dead man, weary, indifferent to everything, even to my own success, suddenly undertook a task about which I had begun to despair? And how I undertook it! . . . I barely contained my excitement; my head pounded; Luisa [a servant] found me in tears; I paced my room like a madman, ran along hills and through forests, not feeling the earth beneath me. . . . It will seem strange that almost the entire novel could be written in a month— not only strange, even impossible. But it is necessary to remember that it ripened in my head over the course of many years and almost all that remained was for me to write it down. . . . If there had not been years, nothing would have been written in a month. The fact is that the entire novel had matured up to the smallest scenes and all that remained was to write it down. I wrote as if by dictation. And truly, much appeared unconsciously; someone invisible sat next to me and told me what to write.
(From letters of 29 July and 2 August 1857 [old style]. *Sobranie sochinenii*, 1955 ed., 8.285, 291–292.)

The slow ripening of the novel is reflected in its final form. *Oblomov* is narrated at a leisurely, unhurried pace. Goncharov shuns sharp dramatic edges and also the contrived symmetries and mechanical plot of the kind he superimposed on his first novel. He lets his hero take over. The novel is very much Oblomov's—a watchful account of every motion of his mind. Experience, no longer narrowed to the purposes of the anecdotal, is allowed to evolve freely and determine the shape of the book. The extended period of writing also resulted in shifting tones—now comical, now lyrical and pathetic.

Part 1, written in the 1840's, is most closely tied to the manner of the Natural School and its interest in the rendering of the details of daily life. Static and plotless, it depicts with playful humor a typical day in the life of its colossally indolent hero—his enormous efforts to raise himself out of bed, to place his feet in his slippers, to get his equally indolent servant, Zakhar, to tidy up. Zakhar is well-meaning but inept, a Chaplinesque figure whose futile attempts to balance a tray of sliding dishes or navigate a doorway are sheer slapstick. Oblomov and Zakhar, like their probable prototypes, Don Quixote and Sancho Panza, are comic eccentrics isolated from the bustling world of activity. Time itself seems to have come to a standstill in their dingy Saint Petersburg flat. Dust blankets the windows, so that Oblomov relies on occasional visitors to ascertain even the season of the year. It has coated scattered newspapers bearing the dates of other years, and the yellowed pages of books left open at that point in the past when reading stopped. Cut off from a larger world of action and purpose, Oblomov and Zakhar, master and serf, have only each other. Circumstances have joined them in a curious ménage, a kind of marriage, in which they whine, fuss, and quarrel, fully aware that they are inseparable.

Equally passive, Oblomov and Zakhar are yet different enough to establish the major comic pattern of the novel. Oblomov, like Alexander Aduev, lives in words; Zakhar amid things. Zakhar may not be able to handle things, but they circumscribe his reality. He opens each of his comic encounters with his master by reminding him of some concrete circumstance that is pressing in on them from the world beyond the dusty windows—bills to be paid, a landlord eager to evict them—to which his master responds with bursts of grand but misplaced rhetorical indignation. Zakhar perceives that Oblomov's authority as a master has become purely verbal: "You are a master only at speaking odd and pathetic words." And indeed Oblomov regards words as the equivalent of acts. Enraged by Zakhar's suggestion that "other people" would find no difficulty in handling their most recent crisis—the impending eviction—Oblomov retorts that he has a plan to restore their failing ancestral estate of Oblomovka. For Oblomov, to have made a plan, a verbal construct, is already to have acted:

> How did your tongue manage that? . . . And in my plan I had already assigned you a separate house and a kitchen garden, a regular measure of grain, and I had fixed a salary! You are my steward and major-domo and my special assistant! Peasants bow to you from the waist. Everyone calls you Zakhar Trofimych, yes Zakhar Trofimych! And he's still not content, compares me to "the others!" That's my reward! A fine way to honor his master!
>
> (1.8)

Pressed by necessity, Oblomov finally does attempt to act, but he characteristically gets caught up in side issues. Faced with the threat of a double dispossession—from his Saint Petersburg apartment and his foundering estate—he exhausts his energies trying to locate paper and ink and settle on a proper style to address his landlord. Setting his world straight becomes a question of getting his relative pronouns right.

As one focus of the novel reduces Oblomov to a contest with trivia, another enlarges him to gigantic proportions. Experience is viewed as if through both ends of a telescope. Oblomov is a dreamer, and his dreams, like his rhetorical flights, are grandiose:

> He sometimes loved to imagine himself as some invincible commander before whom not only Napoleon but even Eruslan Lazarevich [the hero of a Russian fairy tale] meant nothing; he invented a war and a cause for it: for instance, he had the people of Africa pouring into Europe, or he organized new crusades, decided the fate of nations, ravaged cities, showed mercy, wreaked vengeance, performed deeds of virtue and magnanimity. Or he chose the part of a thinker or a great artist: everyone paid homage to him: he gathered laurels; crowds pursued him, exclaiming, "Look, look, there goes Oblomov, our renowned Ilya Ilyich."
>
> (1.6)

As *A Common Story* juxtaposes poetic and prosaic views of reality, *Oblomov* plays off two heroisms: Oblomov's mock-heroic efforts to cope with the slightest obstacles of everyday life, and his dreams of heroic glory. The Russian gentry, like other aristocracies, was originally a military class; and throughout the novel Oblomov's fallen state is parodically contrasted to older, more legitimate versions of heroism, whether from Russia's legendary past, Western chivalric traditions, or romantic literature. Unlike his ancestors—both historical and literary—who were knights "without fear and reproach," Oblomov is "a knight with both fear and reproach." Like Don Quixote, he finds himself in a world where he can be a hero only in dreams or in words. His nobility has become the mark of his alienation: "Who am I? What am I? . . . I am a master, and I don't know how to do anything" (3.9). *Oblomov* has been called the great swan song of the Russian gentry. It is a "song" that is conceived comically, not sentimentally.

Though *Oblomov* follows the deflationary parodic scheme of *A Common Story*, its realization is much fuller. Alexander Aduev is all postures and poses; Oblomov is serious. His aborted attempts at action are often ludicrous, but they win our sympathy. We slowly become aware that for Oblomov, if not for "the others," writing a letter, moving to a new apartment, and (later) marriage are truly heroic undertakings. His dreams, again humorous, serve to soften and humanize him. In his dreams he not only reveals his own secret life but manages to touch the secret parts of all of us—here, in part 1, our childish fantasies of glory and fame. In *Oblomov* Goncharov discovered ways to flesh out the mechanical patterns of his earlier fiction with the stuff of real life.

Also, whereas Alexander Aduev is pressed into the services of a preordained plot, Oblomov's dreaming mind gives shape to his novel. The book falls into a rhythmic pattern, as Oblomov regularly moves from passivity to action, or, more usually, to the mere thought of action, only to fall back into reverie and dream:

> . . . and thoughts would suddenly flare up in him rushing through his head like waves of the sea. Then they would grow into intentions, set all his blood on fire; his muscles would begin to twitch, his veins tighten; intentions would be transformed into strivings. Moved by a moral force, he would rapidly change his position two or three times in one minute; with shining eyes he would half sit up in his bed, stretch out a hand and gaze about inspiredly—a moment and the striving would be realized—and then, O Lord! . . .
>
> But the morning would flash by, the day wane toward evening, and with it Oblomov's exhausted powers would decline to rest. . . . Silently, thoughtfully, Oblomov would turn over on his back, and, fixing his sad gaze on the window and toward the sky, his eyes would mournfully follow the sun setting magnificently behind a four-story house.
>
> (1.6)

The total pattern follows a curve similar to Oblomov's smaller movements; for as Oblomov turns from dream and reflection to aborted action to a decline back into dream, his book proceeds from the famous chapter entitled "Oblomov's Dream," to a failed attempt to retrieve the dream in reality through his love of Olga Ilinskaya, to a final decline into dream and death.

The rhythms of experience are paralleled by the rhythms of nature, further enhancing the novel's quality of "felt life." In the above passage Oblomov's decline into reflection is accompanied by the slow setting of the sun. Part 1, except for "Oblomov's Dream," follows the motion of a day, from morning to the descent of dusk. Oblomov's love of Olga is the love of a summer. It fades in autumn with the annual death of the green world. Winter is the scene of its final extinction, as falling snow buries Oblomov's hopes. As Oblomov's thought fades from the possibility of action to reverie, as his love fades from hope to futility, the natural world turns from bright summer, through gray autumn, to the lifeless landscapes of winter. The plot of *Oblomov* is the imitation of a life, the life of a mind seen with such concentrated inwardness that the patterns of its thought become projected on all nature. By symbolizing the movement of Oblomov's life in the cycles of the natural world Goncharov also confers upon it a sense of inevitability. Oblomov's is a failed life, a story of opportunities missed, but like all our lives, it moves irrevocably to extinction.

"Oblomov's Dream," first published in 1849—ten years before the rest of the novel—and often anthologized, is frequently read as a portrait of rural life in Old Russia. Despite its surface ironies, it is the great lyrical moment in Goncharov's prosy world. A dreamlike atmosphere of mystery saturates its pages. Undercurrents of fairy tale and legend run through it like the murmur of a stream.

It is a dream of paradise. Oblomov's dreaming mind transforms his ancestral estate of Oblomovka into a homely Russian arcadia, an Eden of ramshackle barns, busy kitchens, cackling geese and bleating sheep, indolent masters and their indolent serfs. True to his parodic method, Goncharov sets the flat landscapes of Oblomovka (or Russia) against the dramatic configurations of romantic nature, but the urge here, though not unmixed with irony, is celebrative. He sings the praises of an absence—of what Oblomovka is not. Like the narrator of *The Frigate Pallas*, the dreamer reduces inhospitable and indifferent nature to a human scale and fills it with human presences. The hills of Oblomovka are "only models of those terrible faraway mountains that terrify the imagination." The boundless, anonymous sea turns into a river that "runs gaily, playing and romping." The sky that elsewhere is distant and cold here "presses closer to the earth . . . in order to embrace it firmly and with love." Oblomovka is a land of "joyful, smiling *paysages*," of seasons that follow each other "correctly, . . . in a prescribed . . . order." Nature is so predictable that storms come only at their "appointed time." Winters do not freeze, nor do summers scorch. The world is joined in perfect harmony, as "the sun once again with its clear smile of love scans . . . the fields and hillocks, and the earth again smiles in happiness in response to the sun."

The perfection of Oblomovian life is preserved by keeping the uncertainties of passionate life and historical change at bay. The Oblomovians regard work as punishment, never torment themselves with intellectual or moral questions, and scrupulously shun all forms of passion, whose place is the stormy sea and menacing mountains, not the flat, orderly terrain of Oblomovka. They inhabit a timeless universe, captured by a narration that revolves around typical occasions, eternal cycles of nature and custom, whereby experience continually returns to the same "inevitable rooted occurrences." Nothing has changed in Oblomovka "from time immemorial." If its inhabitants are dimly aware of historical time—time as a progression from a past through a present to a future, each in some way different from the other—it is a knowledge they obstinately resist with the prayer that "every day be like yesterday, every yesterday like tomorrow." They even turn their backs on that surest token of the finality of things, the fact of death, which in Oblomovka is viewed as an "extraordinary occurrence." The central images of this land of perfect peace and repose are the loving benevolent sun and the calm, immutable river of life: "They need nothing: life, like a river, flows by them; their lot is only to sit on the shore and observe the inevitable phenomena which, in turn, without invitation, appear before each one of them."

And as in mythological Edens, the peace of Oblomovka comes at the price of strict observance of taboos. A host of prohibitions circumscribes the activities of Oblomov as a child: he must not stray far from the house nor play in the sun; he must not approach the barnyard animals; in the forest, wood-goblins, demons, and ghosts lie in wait for disobedient children. Most of all, he must never go near the ravine, which becomes a symbol of the forbidden, for the smell of death is there.

The child has not yet sunk into the inert passivity of the man. Ilyusha is a frisky boy, a bit of a rebel. He chooses life over peace. Unobserved, he rushes out into the sun, to the forbidden places; eats wild roots, which he prefers to his mother's jam and apples; even ventures to the dread ravine. Returned to his mother's side, he is drawn away by the fragrance of lilacs, as later he will be drawn to the lilacs surrounding the image of Olga Ilinskaya. Toward the end of the "Dream," he makes a last desperate attempt to escape Oblomovka's encircling ring. He finds himself with the peasant children ("the others"), throwing snowballs, the wind rushing in his face, "his breast seized with joy." It is not for long. Parental authority quickly reasserts itself: "They took possession of the young master, wrapped him up in a sheepskin coat . . ., then in two blankets, and triumphantly carried him home in their arms." The "Dream" ends in defeat. When we next encounter Oblomov, he tells us that "as my life began, it was extinguished."

The images of "Oblomov's Dream" are the controlling images of the novel. The sun that "with its clear smile of love" protects Oblomovka, the "bright days" that bless its summers also watch over Oblomov's summer love of Olga and return for a last moment to brighten the darkness of his demise. The image of life as a peaceful, immutable flow, like that of a river, recurs, curiously, for his friend and foil, the resolute Andrey Stolz, as well as Oblomov. There are prohibitive lines throughout the novel: the line Oblomov perceives as separating life from knowledge, himself from society or "the others"; and, finally, the boundary formed by the Neva River, for he will be on one side, Olga on the other, and the river will prove uncrossable. The novel moves from light to dark, from summer to winter, a pattern presaged by the "Dream," as a typical day in the life of Oblomovka is traced from sunrise to dusk and the entire dream sequence turns from midsummer to winter.

Finally, the child's story presages the story of the man. The child tries and fails to break through Oblomovka's enclosing ring, and the man tries and fails to escape his isolation and join "the others." The "Dream" ends in winter with a symbolic death of the spirit—the sheepskin coat thrown in triumph over the mutinous child. At the climax of the novel Zakhar throws Oblomov's fateful dressing gown—the mark of his indolence and passivity—over the defeated man, as the snows of another winter cover the earth like "a death shroud." In *Oblomov* paradise is the persistent object of human desire. It is also a dream tainted with death and defeat. Human life—a life of active self-assertion, creativity, love, and suffering—lies this side of Eden.

Compared to the animated comedy enacted by Oblomov and Zakhar in part 1 or the poetic richness of "Oblomov's Dream," the romance between Olga and Oblomov in parts 2 and 3 is pale. Its tone is sometimes precious, its heroine too good to be true. Written much later than part 1 (in 1857), it smacks of the manner of Ivan Turgenev, the most elegant of Russian novelists, whose work was enormously popular in the late 1850's.

Yet the romance is of central importance in the development of the novel. For all the creative energies that went into part 1, it was not on the way to becoming a novel. Goncharov was still too closely joined to the Natural School and its predilection for typical moments and characters, often rendered with grotesque humor in imitation of Gogol. In the early sections of the novel Oblomov is something of a caricature—larger than life in his dreams, smaller in his bumbling ineptness. He is imaginative but odd. What Goncharov needed was a story to bring Oblomov to a human level. In recounting his desperate attempt to escape his isolation and reach another human being, Goncharov informs Oblomov's life with pathos and dignity. No longer a comic curio, he is now a man like other men, struggling against his fate.

Oblomov, like Alexander Aduev before him, though more poignantly, envelops his love in a poetic haze. Olga for him is the lilac of spring, the radiance of the summer sun, and a song—"Casta diva" from Vincenzo Bellini's *Norma.* She is Nature and Art: "the flower of life," the light of redemption, the music of transcendence. Oblomov seeks to recapture through her Oblomovka's benevolent sun and its peaceful river. During his romance "hot summer reigns" and "feeling flows smoothly like a river." The light Olga radiates is "smooth, peaceful." Living with her "he would feel life, its quiet flow, its sweet streams." Her touch makes him dream of "flowering valleys."

Above all, the romance is another attempt to stop time. "Oblomov's Dream" evokes a timeless condition of eternal returns to the same "rooted occurrences." His romance, by dwelling on the images of light, lilac, and music, attempts to concentrate time into a single poetic moment: "Their meetings, their conversations were all a single song, a single sound, a single light which burned brightly" (2.9).

If much of this seems too rarefied, too self-consciously poetic for modern tastes, Goncharov knew that something was wrong, and his lovers soon discover it. The ironic conception of experience so characteristic of his art—its setting of a hero's private imaginings against the imperatives of society and history—holds even in Oblomov's romance. Love changes, from poetic idealization to human actuality. Olga turns out to be a woman after all, and makes demands on Oblomov, including sexual demands. Oblomov crumbles. Passion, along with time, is what his "Dream" sought to escape. Passion belongs to the mountains, the sea, and the forests encircling Oblomovka, not its peaceful river and nurturing sun. Passion disrupts the analogous "magic circle of love," the poetic aura in which the lovers have enveloped themselves. Out in the world, exposed to the vicissitudes of passion and the claims of responsibility, Oblomov is consumed by terror and guilt. Paradise is the dream of childhood. Attempting to break through its magic circle and discover his manhood, Oblomov strays into the forbidden terrain of his dreams: "He found himself in a forest at night, where in every bush and tree there seems to be a robber, a corpse, a wild beast" (3.8).

Passion explodes his idyllic romance, and so does the intrusion of time. Poetic love, which Oblomov took for the whole, turns out to be only a part, a lyrical but irretrievable moment in the course of human love: "The poem passes and stern history commences" (3.2). Sunny skies darken, bright summer changes to somber autumn, lilacs fade. Oblomov discovers that nothing lasts. History and time "never take a rest"; the "bright days" for which men struggle and suffer "run on and all life only flows and flows, and everything crumbles and shatters" (1.6). The knowledge fills him with anguish:

And love also? But I thought it would hang over lovers like a hot noon and nothing would move or breathe in its atmosphere. But there is no

IVAN GONCHAROV

peace in love either; it too constantly keeps moving forward. . . . And there has not yet been born the Joshua who would command it, "Stand still and do not move!"

(2.10)

Stolz is Oblomov's friend. Like Olga, he is conceived allegorically. Stolz is half-German, and he embodies all the bourgeois virtues—practicality, diligence, machinelike efficiency—so lacking in Oblomov and, implicitly, in the Russian gentry. Through Stolz and Oblomov Western purposiveness confronts Russian inertia. Men like Stolz, it is implied, are Russia's hope.

But Stolz is more complicated than he appears at first glance. He is also half-Russian—his mother's half. His militantly purposive character has been achieved through the denial of values that the novel perceives as Russian, aristocratic, and maternal. Learning lessons of diligence and self-denial from his bourgeois father, he has turned his back on his mother's "Russian" sensibility—her "tender image," her sensitivity to art and music, her love of things Russian.

Stolz, for all his allegorical rigidity, also has a story. It is the reverse side of Oblomov's. The two friends grew up together. Stolz's birthplace was once part of Oblomovka. In the distant past there existed a wholeness that has been lost. Separated by "that line where tenderness and grace lose their rights and the realm of manhood begins" (3.7), Stolz and Oblomov look achingly to each other for the missing parts of their selves, the lost "half of life" as Goncharov phrases it. Oblomov turns to Stolz for those qualities of manliness he has not yet achieved, Stolz to him for the "tender image" he has left behind. When Olga leaves Oblomov for Stolz, he feels no rancor. Instead he takes consolation in the fact that he has played a role in their happiness. Stolz sees Olga's greater maturity, her womanliness, as the outgrowth of her relationship with Oblomov. What Oblomov passes on to the lovers is never made explicit, but he can give only what he

has: his tenderness and his visions of the fullness of being. "Tender, tender tender," Olga sighs ruefully, though not without irony, when Oblomov fails her. Stolz's life, which is all striving, resembles "a broad, loudly rushing river with seething waves"; in marriage "the rushing subsides" and "both their lives, hers and Andrey's, flow together in one riverbed . . . ; everything was peace and harmony, . . . even as Oblomov had dreamed."

History passes Oblomov by. He is an aristocrat who cannot adjust to the evolving modern world, a child who will not grow up. But Goncharov, like Shakespeare in *A Midsummer Night's Dream*, sees life with a "parted eye, when everything seems double." Oblomov's fatality is also his power. Aristocratic culture is doomed because it cannot cope with the demands of an industrial, bureaucratic order; but at its best, in Goncharov's view, it cultivates virtues of courtesy, delicacy, and, above all, sensitivity to the values of art that must find a place in modern bourgeois culture. The child cannot remain a child, but he is blessed with a sense of the wholeness of being whose loss is a deprivation. Oblomov's complaint against modern society is that it fragments man by identifying his nature with his occupational functions: "Man, give me man!" he cries in anguish. Oblomov, round and corpulent where Stolz is "all bone, muscles, and nerves," asserts a completeness of self and oneness with nature that he can locate only in his paradisical memories of childhood. For Goncharov paradise is a maternal garden of warmth and tenderness, perfect and whole, that must be surrendered and yet whose memory informs and enriches adult life. In turning to Oblomov, Stolz turns back to his own childhood and his mother's "tender image." Drawn to his friend's "bright, childlike soul," he finds momentary respite from life's incessant bustle. A calm and peace descend on him, as if he had returned "to the birch grove where he roamed when still a child."

Stolz, however, looks backward for only a moment. Ultimately he rejects Oblomov. Ob-

1079

lomov attracts him, but he also makes him anxious, for his aimless life puts a question to Stolz's fervid purposiveness. Stolz, we are told, "feared imagination above all," and Oblomov, the only imaginative character in the novel, projects the timeless gardens of childhood into the future, so that his beginnings become his desired end. "Doesn't everyone strive for the very same things I dream of?" he asks Stolz. "Isn't the goal of all your running about, your passions, of wars, trade, politics . . . this ideal of a lost paradise?" (2.4). It is a question that the novel puts to modern bourgeois culture: Does perpetual striving make sense or have value if there is no end to strive for? In the happiness of his marriage to Olga, Stolz again confronts the paradox implicit in his own purposefulness—the goal achieved, should not striving stop? Bourgeois to the bone, he responds by asserting purposefulness without purpose, work "for the sake of work and not for anything else." If the question of an ultimate meaning to life continues to gnaw at the soul, he recommends stoicism. As paradise possesses Oblomov's imagination, Stolz's mind is circumscribed by images of the Fall: "This is the price for Prometheus' fire! . . . This is the sorrow of all mankind" (4.8). Drawn to each other by an intuition of their own incompleteness, Oblomov and Stolz yet remain opposites. Where one would seduce us into dreaming passively of final ends, the other would limit us to a stoical and unquestioning suffering of the passing minutes of daily existence.

The novel concludes with a double marriage. Stolz's practical talents are wedded to Olga's spiritual grace (enhanced by Oblomov's tenderness) in an ideal union. Oblomov marries his housekeeper, the matronly Agafya Matveevna, has a son, and sinks back into a vegetable existence. His last days are dragged out in a world of mute things—cupboards crammed with food, the assorted bric-a-brac of ordinary domesticity. The didacticism of the parallel is clear but unconvincing. From the date of the novel's appearance many readers have found Stolz's success suspect, and have detected a secret sympathy on Goncharov's part for Oblomov. Much of the ambivalence arises from the manner of presentation, though it may also be that the novel as a genre is inhospitable to representations of perfection. Stolz's success in overcoming Oblomovian inertia is told in summary fashion, as if the novelist cannot wait to get his paragon, once his perfection is announced, offstage. Oblomov's descent into the rituals of domestic habit is shown in loving detail. Part 4, the final section of the novel and the scene of Oblomov's putative defeat, returns to the style of "Oblomov's Dream." "Enter Agafya's courtyard and you are enveloped by a living idyll" (4.9), the narrator exclaims. Interminable catalogs of casseroles, pots and pans, jugs brimming with butter and cream, pantries stuffed with hams, cheeses, smoked fish, sacks of mushrooms function as lyrical appreciations, a kind of poetry of things. The narration returns, as in the "Dream," to the circular rhythms of domestic life, moving leisurely from mealtime to mealtime, holiday to holiday, season to season. While Stolz's story summarizes and conceptualizes, Oblomov's renders mimetically the aimless flow of life as it is being lived.

A manner of narration at cross-purposes with its didactic intent may be perplexing. It is, however, consistent with the imaginative energies that animate the novel. *Oblomov* is a book of enormous nostalgia. Its characters—even Stolz—come alive when they open themselves to the pleasures, fears, and wishes of childhood. The rich feeling for the rhythms and things of domesticity found in Agafya's modest home is, like much of the richness of the novel, a product of things remembered. In coming to Agafya, Oblomov has come home. He recovers for a fleeting moment the benevolent nurturing sun of Oblomovka. In one of the many ironies of the novel, his homely and simple-minded housekeeper, not the spiritual

Olga, turns out to be the enchanted beauty of Russian folklore, Militrisa Kirbitevna, promised to him as a child in Oblomovka:

> Indolently, absentmindedly, as if unconscious, he gazed into the housekeeper's face and a familiar image he had seen somewhere emerged from the depths of his memories. . . . And there appeared before him the large, dark drawing-room lit by a tallow candle in the home of his parents; his dead mother and her guests were sitting at the round table sewing; they sewed in silence; his father paced in silence. Past and present had merged and intermingled.
>
> He was dreaming that he had reached that promised land where rivers of milk and honey flow, where people eat bread they have not labored for and go clothed in gold and silver.
>
> He listened to the tales of his dreams, their tokens, the rattle of plates and the clatter of knives; he pressed close to his nurse, listened attentively to her ancient quavering voice: "Militrisa Kirbitevna!" she said, pointing to the image of the housekeeper.
>
> (4.9)

The novel has inscribed a circle from dream to dream, from idyll to idyll, from childhood lost to childhood regained. But Goncharov's vision of childhood remains as ambiguous as ever, and if the ending is inconclusive he may have wanted it that way. Childhood in *Oblomov* is concurrently a standard of all value and the arena of defeat, a realm of absolute freedom and a confinement of the spirit, a condition one longs for and seeks to escape. This double vision is analogous to modern psychoanalytic theory, whose "wisdom," according to Norman O. Brown (in *Life Against Death: The Psychoanalytical Meaning of History*, 1959), "directs us to childhood—not only to the immoral wishes of childhood for the substance of things hoped for, but also to the failure of childhood for the cause of our disease."

If Goncharov is tentative about choosing between Stolz's way and Oblomov's way, he is certain about one thing—the force of history. Time may be his true subject. The progress of time makes eternal childhood impossible; history is destroying Oblomov's class. His dreams are a grandiose attempt to stop history, to scream Joshua's command: "Stand still and do not move!" While Oblomov combats time by retreating to the rhythms of nature and the rituals of custom, to a cyclical time that eternally returns to the same, Stolz empties time of substance. By depriving action of ends, Stolz's time becomes a mere succession of moments, pointless and without shape. Oblomovian time, the time of primitive man and agricultural societies (like Old Russia), though it went no place, had meaningful content. It revolved about the fundamental experiences of human life—birth, marriage, death, the returning seasons upon which people pattern their labors. Stolz's time is perhaps the distinctive time of modern life, a time in which people continually strive for a future without definition, where, as a result, they are reduced to working "for the sake of work and not for anything else."

To these conflicting conceptions of time Goncharov in part 4 opposes a third: "geological time."

> Life did not stand still. Its phenomena were constantly changing, but they were changing as gradually and as slowly as the geological transformations of our planet: here a mountain was slowly crumbling away; there the sea was running up onto the shore or receding as it had for centuries and was forming new land. . . . The gradual raising or settling of the bottom of the sea and the crumbling away of mountains took place everywhere.
>
> (4.1)

Time in this new conception is neither merely preservative, as is Oblomov's time, nor merely sequence, as is Stolz's. It admits history—extinction and renewal, death and birth, destruction and creation. Mountains crumble away, but new land is formed out of the sea. Social systems like those of Oblomovka (or Old Russia) decay, but men and women proceed to create others. Oblomov dies, but his son by Agafya takes his place. Life does not stand still; the shape of things is "constantly changing." Yet a world survives as an arena for human action and possibility. Despite their radical differences as writers, Goncharov's sense of life in *Oblomov* is close to that of Tolstoy in *War and Peace.* For all the sadness and futility of Oblomov's life, his novel moves, as does *War and Peace,* to acceptance of the nature of things.

So does Oblomov. In the final pages he returns to his dream of Oblomovka. He has failed to join "the others"—the adults busy in their occupations and families. A changing world passes him by. Oblomov is a man doomed by his unbending allegiance to a dream. His novel traces the severe limitations of a life lived almost totally in imagination. But it also bestows on the imagination a power to bring coherence to life and even to transform it. Oblomov at the end is no longer the comically anxious recluse of the opening. In connecting past and present—Oblomovka's drawing room and Agafya's kitchen—his dreaming mind recognizes the inevitability of his life. By turning Agafya's modest home into a simulacrum of the paradise he has always sought, he converts his necessary end into his desired end. Unable to escape his fate, he learns to live with it and even like it. His moments of peace cannot last—life does not stand still; the mountains keep crumbling—but he resigns himself to the world's inevitable flow.

Oblomov does not conclude with Oblomov's death. Just as alluvial silt is washed away from one shore only to form new land on another, the novel ends with an intimation of a new regenerative cycle that is continuous with the dying phase. Oblomov's son, though raised by Stolz and Olga, is an image of his father's delicacy. It is Goncharov's hope that the aristocratic virtues of the father, tempered in the son by Olga's and Stolz's strength, will survive in the coldness of the modern world. His mourners—Olga and Stolz among their objets d'art, Agafya in the midst of her kitchen utensils—remember him. Oblomov's power of memory passes on to them. The memory of Oblomov's "tender image" softens the harsh rigors of Stolz's life. The gift of memory turns Agafya from a dull domestic drudge into a woman conscious of a past, as it allows her to preserve "the soft light of seven years, which had flown by like a single moment, . . . for a lifetime" (4.10). As time in *Oblomov* reduces experience to a fleeting moment, memory retains what has been lost and grants man a permanence of the unforgetful imagination—the only kind of permanence the novel allows.

Goncharov was never a stable man. With the passage of the years his neurotic difficulties worsened. They became acute at about the time *Oblomov* appeared in print. Perhaps success and fame were more than he could bear; certainly the writer's block that kept him from completing his final novel, *The Precipice,* was a source of intense frustration. In 1859 Goncharov accused Turgenev of plagiarism. Though Turgenev had been his friend, he envied his rival's aristocratic background, his social grace and popularity, and the facility with which he regularly produced novels and stories. A group of writers, convened as an impartial panel, judged that there was no basis in fact to the accusation. Goncharov continued to nurse his grievances in private. A manuscript entitled *An Uncommon Story,* which Goncharov worked on from 1875 to 1878 but did not publish in his lifetime, revealed that his suspicions had assumed the proportions of paranoia. Turgenev, he claimed, had stolen all his ideas and projects and had used them himself or passed them on to his French friends, who turned them into the foundation of an entire literary movement. The theft of Goncharov's thoughts, he felt, had caused both the failure of *The Precipice* and his inhibitions about writing. The scandal that followed Goncharov's public accusation of Turgenev was a major reason for the self-imposed seclusion of his later years.

From December 1855 until his retirement from government service in 1867, Goncharov was an official of Russian censorship. His tenure coincided with far-reaching reforms in Russian society, the most significant of which was the emancipation of the serfs in 1861. It was also a time of intensified political polarization. The left wing moved to hardened revolutionary positions, while most of the artists and intellectuals of Goncharov's generation recoiled from the intransigence of the young "nihilists," as the radicals were called. The men of the 1840's, mostly of the gentry, had been brought up in a period of philosophic idealism; the radicals of the 1860's, many of whom were from the middle stratum between gentry and serfs, were captivated by the positivistic and materialistic theories popular at mid-century. Since the radicals exerted on the educated public and the press an influence disproportionate to their numbers, writers like Goncharov felt themselves isolated. It seemed to him that, almost overnight, he had lost his audience. Writers were being judged on the basis of their immediate political relevance and utility to the cause of social progress. Goncharov's position as a censor of the czarist regime, though not uncommon for Russian writers, exposed him to savage attacks and ridicule. His reaction was to withdraw further into himself.

Goncharov's censorship activity was generally tolerant. Not a political animal, he was in the Russian context a liberal. He believed in a free exchange of ideas as long as criticism did not touch fundamental institutions, a position that was more or less the government's in these years of reform. In practice he tended to identify the fundamental Russian institutions with the family. In a backward and repressive country like Russia political and economic issues seemed remote, and men of Goncharov's class tended to personalize them. Also, as a lonely bachelor he idealized what he

did not have. In his censorship reports his severest strictures are directed not against the political or economic theories of the radicals but against their disregard for the autonomy of art and their denigration of the family.

Goncharov's religious convictions were as lukewarm as his politics. Nominally an Orthodox Christian, he ceased observing the rites of his church or attending services until his last years. His religious faith, such as it was, brought him little consolation in his sufferings. The great and perhaps only passion of his life was for art.

The Precipice was one of many political novels of the 1860's and 1870's directed against the nihilists—Feodor Dostoevsky's *The Devils* (1871–1872), also translated as *The Possessed,* is another (there were also works of distinction sympathetic to the revolutionary movement). The Russian novel of that period is not only more overtly political than its forerunners, it is also more dramatic. Russian prose fiction had moved from the detailed sketches of everyday life of the 1840's, to biographical novels in the 1850's (*Oblomov* is the story of a life), to more tensely dramatic forms in the 1860's, as writers confronted conflict—between classes, between the revolutionary movement and the state, between the individual and society. The novel also became more decentralized, shifting its focus from the biography of a single person to the life of society as a whole. In moving from *Oblomov* to *The Precipice* Goncharov was accommodating his art to new trends in Russian literature.

He held, however, to some of his old preoccupations. Once again a manorial estate of the gentry—here called Malinovka—is taken as a microcosm of traditional Russia. Once again the estate is the locus of an idyllic life, surrounded by an area of taboo. The precipice of the title, reminiscent of the ravine of Oblomovka, is a forbidden terrain. Its associations are explicitly sexual. It is a place where good girls are not supposed to go. The plot centers on the competition of three men for the love of the darkly mysterious Vera: the vacillating artist Boris Raysky, the reliable and practical Ivan Tushin (the Peter Aduev or Stolz of this novel), and the villainous nihilist Mark Volokhov. Volokhov, whose nihilism does not go further than parroting Proudhon's statement "Property is theft" and espousing free love, seduces Vera at the bottom of the precipice. The community of Malinovka (Russia) draws together to condemn him and exclude him from its beneficences. Tatyana Markovna, the matriarch of Malinovka, forgives her greatniece. Vera no doubt will marry the solidly reliable Tushin. Tushin is seen as an authentic Russian, Volokhov as something alien. Russia triumphs. All except the irresolute and self-pitying Raysky (in many ways a self-portrait of Goncharov) seem destined to live happily ever after.

The Precipice is an inferior novel. In his earlier fiction Goncharov had introduced characters with idealized views of life—Alexander Aduev, who tries to live in poetry; Oblomov, who tries to live in dreams—so as to make comedy out of their confrontations with actuality. Yet, through their hopes and dreams, however misplaced, his comically obstinate heroes, especially Oblomov, had called into question the nature of the social world in which they found themselves. *The Precipice* shows little such uncertainty. Malinovka is good; Volokhov is a scoundrel. *The Precipice* is melodrama not only in its unequivocal distinctions between virtue and vice, but also in the almost unalleviated bombast and affected urgencies of its language. The only relief from its incessant moralizing and melodramatics are the occasional sketches of the rounds of daily life at Malinovka—the kind of genre painting at which Goncharov remained a master to the end.

The novel's politics, however, are not as retrograde as a plot summary may make them seem. They seek a middle ground between reactionary traditionalism and revolutionary radicalism. Tushin, the positive hero of the novel, is a firm believer in progress, educa-

tion, and social and economic amelioration. He has even been touched by socialist ideas. Taking his inspiration from Robert Owen, also a source for the radicals of the 1860's, he has established a forestry commune and regards the peasants as his fellow workers. Ready, perhaps eager, to accommodate the young generation on political and economic issues, which little interested him, Goncharov drew the line at personal behavior that affronted custom and decorum. At times the novel makes Russian radicalism seem to be merely a case of bad manners. Volokhov cleans his ears with the pages of Raysky's rare books and casually puts his feet up on the table "in the American fashion." As an artist and as a man, Goncharov was always wary of sexual passion. He condemns Volokhov's sexual licentiousness and affirms the traditional Russian family as a bulwark against moral laxity. Sex is the issue that divides the generations in *The Precipice*. A century of revolutionary change had made men of Goncharov's class and generation nervous. The family appeared as a singular point of stability in a rapidly changing world. It and art are the only two institutions that the novel opposes to "nihilism."

Why did Goncharov's art turn sour with *The Precipice*? No doubt his psychological difficulties were a hindrance. Like his heroes, he had come to confuse private imaginings with reality and had lost the ironic perspective that had previously kept the two apart. Also, his talent was not easily adaptable to dramatic forms. His style, at its best, is leisurely, reflective, slyly ironical, humorous, at times softly lyrical. Lacking verve or dramatic power, it was yet the perfect vehicle for his sole masterpiece. *Oblomov* is a meditation on a life. Other characters are brought in for contrast (Stolz) or to pose a test (Olga). Goncharov's fiction is to a large extent about himself. Biographical in form, *Oblomov* is not, however, mere confessional outpouring. The self is placed at a distance, incarnated in a fictional character who is to be examined and understood, pitied, laughed at, and loved. Goncharov was perhaps too little interested in other people to realize convincingly the broad social canvas he outlined in *The Precipice.*

Before he decided to update his novel by making it politically relevant and dramatically intense, he may have had in mind a biographical novel not too dissimilar from his other fiction. From its conception in 1849 until at least the winter of 1857–1858 the manuscript bore the title *Raysky, the Artist,* or simply *The Artist,* and Goncharov declared his intention to show "the heart of an artist and the backstages of art" (from a letter of 9 August 1860 [old style]; *Sobranie sochinenii* 8.350). As Alexander Aduev and Oblomov try to impose their imaginings on life, Raysky sees life through the prism of art. However, Raysky's imagination is obsessed by sex. Instead of pursuing the implications of his hero's confusion of art with life, which is at the same time a confusion of aesthetic feeling with sexual impulse, Goncharov, one feels, got cold feet. He lived and wrote in a very prudish age that offered no models for the kind of investigation he seems to have had in mind. Instead of pursuing his original subject, he resorted to the simplifications of melodrama. He projected sexual appetite upon an operatic villain (Volokhov), manufactured yet another passionless strong man (Tushin) to wed yet another feminine icon (Vera), and effectively closed the doors of his idyllic estate to any emotion more intense than familial affection. Once Volokhov has been gotten rid of, an image familiar to us from *Oblomov* returns, as "peace hung over Malinovka [and] life, held back by catastrophe, once again, like a river, . . . flowed on more smoothly" (5.11). In *Oblomov,* however, this sort of peace—the peace of the manorial estate, of a child's Arcadia— has to share the stage with history and the claims of human responsibility. *Oblomov* is a comedy about the irreconcilable conflict in a man torn between nostalgia for nurture and comfort and a longing for fulfillment. In *The Precipice* the resolution is unequivocal and the peace complete, but it is only escapism.

After the hostile critical reception of *The Precipice,* Goncharov virtually retired from writing. The scattered efforts of his last years are largely an old man's exercises in nostalgia—reminiscences of childhood, of Moscow University and Belinsky, and, the best of his late works, "Slugi starogo veka" ("Servants of Old Times," 1888), a fond account of the several servants who had attended him through his lonely bachelor's existence. He became increasingly reclusive and restricted his social contacts to a few old friends. His housekeeper, Alexandra Treigut, cared for him in his declining years. He grew close to this woman "of the people"—as Russians used to refer to their lower classes—and extremely fond of her children. He had finally found a family and, like Oblomov perhaps, his Agafya Matveevna. In 1890 he suffered a mild stroke and died a year later. In his will he ignored his surviving relatives and left the bulk of his estate to his housekeeper and her children.

Selected Bibliography

EDITIONS

INDIVIDUAL WORKS
Obyknovennaya istoriya. Saint Petersburg, 1848. First appeared in *Sovremennik* nos. 3–4 (1847).
Fregat "Pallada": Ocherki puteshestviya. 2 vols. Saint Petersburg, 1858. Individual sketches appeared in various journals, 1855–1857.
Oblomov. Saint Petersburg, 1859. First appeared in *Otechestvennye zapiski* nos. 1–4 (1859). "Son Oblomova" ("Oblomov's Dream") first published in *Literaturnyi sbornik s illyustratsiyami.* Saint Petersburg, 1849.
Obryv. Saint Petersburg, 1876. First appeared in *Vestnik Evropy* nos. 1–5 (1869).

COLLECTED WORKS
Polnoe sobranie sochinenii. 8 vols. Saint Petersburg, 1884. A ninth volume was added in 1889. The 3rd ed., published in 1896, includes all nine volumes.
Sobranie sochinenii. 8 vols. Moscow, 1952.
————. 8 vols. Moscow, 1952–1955.

IVAN GONCHAROV

TRANSLATIONS

A Common Story. Translated by Constance Garnett. New York and London, 1894.

Oblomov. Translated by Natalie Duddington. New York and London, 1929.

————. Translated by Ann Dunnigan. New York, 1963.

————. Translated by David Magarshack. Harmondsworth, 1954.

The Precipice. Translated by M. Bryant. New York, 1916. Abridged beyond recognition.

The Same Old Story. Translated by Ivy Litvinov. Moscow, 1957.

The Voyage of the Frigate Pallada. Edited and translated by N. W. Wilson. London, 1965. Abridged.

BIOGRAPHICAL AND CRITICAL STUDIES

Annensky, I. "Goncharov i ego Oblomov." *Russkaya shkola* 4:71–95 (April 1892). A sensitive essay by an outstanding Russian poet.

Belinsky, V. G. "Vzglyad na russkuyu literaturu 1847 goda." *Sovremennik* 3:13–32 (1848). English translation in Matlaw, below.

Chizhevsky, Dmitry. *History of Nineteenth-Century Russian Literature.* Vol. 2: *The Realistic Period,* edited by Serge A. Zenkovsky and translated by Richard Neal Porter. Nashville, Tenn., 1974. A solid scholarly history.

Dobrolyubov, N. A. "Chto takoe oblomovshchina?" *Sovremennik* 5:59–98 (1859). English translation in Matlaw, below. An enormously influential essay coloring views of Goncharov and nineteenth-century Russian literature until today, especially in the Soviet Union.

Ehre, Milton. *Oblomov and His Creator: The Life and Art of Ivan Goncharov.* Princeton, N.J., 1973.

Freeborn, Richard. *The Rise of the Russian Novel: Studies in the Russian Novel from "Eugene Onegin" to "War and Peace."* Cambridge, 1973.

Ganchikov, Leonida. "Il tema di 'Oblomovismo.'" *Richerche slavistiche* 4:169–175 (1955–1956).

Gifford, Henry. *The Novel in Russia: From Pushkin to Pasternak.* New York, 1965.

Grigorev, Apollon. "Russkaya literatura v 1851 godu." *Moskvitianin* 1:65–66 (1852).

————. "Turgenev i ego deyatelnost." *Russkoe slovo* 8:4–14; 39–40 (1859). Also in Grigorev's *Sochinenii.* Saint Petersburg, 1876. This and the above article are readings of *A Common Story* and *Oblomov* by an intelligent, conservative critic. May be instructively compared to the better-known interpretations of the famous radical critics Belinsky and Dobrolyubov.

Harrison, Jane Ellen. *Aspects, Aorists and the Classical Tripos.* Cambridge, 1919. Includes an interesting discussion of time in the Russian novel and in *Oblomov.*

Krasnoshchekova, E. *"Oblomov" I. A. Goncharova.* Moscow, 1970. A sensitive study.

Lavrin, Janko. *Goncharov.* New Haven, Conn., 1954.

Louria, Yvette, and Morton I. Seiden. "Ivan Goncharov's Oblomov: The Anti-Faust as Christian Hero." *Canadian Slavic Studies* 3:39–68 (Spring 1969).

Lyngstad, Alexandra, and Sverre Lyngstad. *Ivan Goncharov.* New York, 1971.

Macauley, Robie. "The Superfluous Man." *Partisan Review* 19:169–182 (March–April 1952). One of the best essays on Goncharov in English.

Manning, Clarence A. "Ivan Aleksandrovich Goncharov." *South Atlantic Quarterly* 26:63–75 (1927).

Matlaw, Ralph E., ed. *Belinsky, Chernyshevsky, and Dobrolyubov: Selected Criticism.* New York, 1962. Locates *A Common Story* in the context of Russian realism at the inception of that movement.

Mays, Milton A. "Oblomov as Anti-Faust." *Western Humanities Review* 21:141–152 (Spring 1967).

Mazon, André. *Ivan Gontcharov: Un maître du roman russe.* Paris, 1914. Still the most comprehensive biography, though much new material has since come to light. As literary criticism, it is old-fashioned.

Merezhkovsky, D. S. *Polnoe sobranie sochinenii.* Vol. 18: *Vechnye sputniki.* Moscow, 1914. Includes an essay on Goncharov.

Mirsky, D. S. *A History of Russian Literature: From Its Beginnings to 1900.* New York, 1949. Rev. ed. by Francis J. Whitfield. The best history of Russian literature, even when it is wrong. Continually stimulating.

Pereverzev, V. P. "K voprosu o monisticheskom ponimanii tvorchestva Goncharova." In *Literaturovedenie,* edited by V. F. Pereverzev. Moscow, 1929. Pp. 201–229. A sample of articles on Goncharov by an independent and interesting Marxist critic.

Poggioli, Renato. "On Goncharov and His *Oblomov.*" In *The Phoenix and the Spider.* Cambridge, Mass., 1957. A first-rate essay by an outstanding scholar of Russian and comparative literature.

Polyakov, M. Ya., ed. *I. A. Goncharov v russkoi kritike: Sbornik statei.* Moscow, 1958. A sampling of Goncharov criticism, mostly from the radical tradition. Includes the essays by Belinsky (abridged) and Dobrolyubov cited above.

Pritchett, V. S. *The Living Novel.* London, 1946. Charming and urbane essays on Goncharov and other Russian and non-Russian novelists.

Prutskov, N. I. *Masterstvo Goncharova-romanista.* Moscow and Leningrad, 1962. A competent and often original work by a prominent Soviet scholar.

Rapp, Helen. "The Art of Ivan Goncharov." *Slavonic and East European Review* 36:370–395 (1957–1958).

Reeve, F. D. "Oblomovka Revisited." *American Slavic and East European Review* 15:112–118 (1956).

Setchkarev, Vsevolod. *Ivan Goncharov: His Life and His Works.* Würzburg, 1974.

Stender-Petersen, Adolf. *Geschichte der russischen Literatur.* Munich, 1957.

Stilman, Leon. "Oblomovka Revisited." *American Slavic and East European Review* 7:45–77 (1948).

Superansky, M. "Vospitanie I. A. Goncharova." *Russkaya shkola* 5–6:1–19 (May–June 1912).

Tseitlin, A. G. *I. A. Goncharov.* Moscow, 1956. A mine of information, intelligent though orthodox in its interpretations.

BIBLIOGRAPHIES

Alekseev, A. D. *Bibliografiya I. A. Goncharova: 1832–1964.* Leningrad, 1968.

——————. *Letopis zhizni i tvorchestva I. A. Goncharova.* Moscow and Leningrad, 1960. Gives a day-by-day account of Goncharov's life and work, with sources. Invaluable.

MILTON EHRE

FRIEDRICH HEBBEL

(1813–1863)

TO THIS DAY Hebbel's work has been the object of much controversy. While his position as an important figure in the history of German literature is secure, his significance as a dramatist in the context of pre- and post-revolutionary Germany and Austria is still being debated. Likewise, his stylistic and period classification are by no means definitive. Nevertheless, his work is a part of the literary canon. Along with his contemporary Franz Grillparzer, Hebbel is considered the most significant playwright to follow J. W. von Goethe and Friedrich von Schiller.

Hebbel, although he knew he could not be the great innovator he would have liked to have been, had the ambition to write the best play on any given subject, as, for example, his *Demetrius* (1864) fragment (the same subject had been treated by Schiller) or his *Nibelungs* (1862).

Hebbel had to overcome formidable odds in his personal life as well as in the attitudes of his age to achieve greatness. It was his good fortune to be imbued with the talent of a great artist and possessed of the indomitable will to "reach for the stars." Not only did he have a most difficult start in life but also he lived at a time when greatness was considered "dangerous" and when artists felt isolated and even threatened by the dawning of the age of materialism and technology. Although he lived to be only fifty, his life spanned the defeat of Napoleon; the flowering and waning of the romantic and idealistic periods; the dominance of G. W. F. Hegel's philosophy; the Vienna Congress of 1815 (which resulted in the restoration of monarchic rule and repression in Western Europe, Britain, and Russia under Prince Metternich); the rise and fall of the pre-realistic, rhetorical, and reactionary Biedermeier period; the abortive revolutions of 1848; the rise of nationalism in Europe; and the emergence of realism in the arts. Hebbel was a part of all that, however strenuously he may have denied it and however much he may have struggled against the artistic styles and sociopolitical trends of his day.

I

Christian Friedrich Hebbel was born on 18 March 1813, in Wesselburen, a small village near the North Sea in the region of Dithmarschen in Holstein. He was proud of his descent from the fiercely independent Dithmarschers. Dithmarschen had once been a minuscule peasant republic. In 1559, after the battle of Hemmingstedt, it fell to the duchy of Holstein, which, at the time of his birth, belonged to Denmark. Like his fellow countryman and poet Theodor Storm, Hebbel was therefore a Danish subject by birth. Aside from his parents' influence, Hebbel attributes his virtues and faults to the influence of the Dithmarschers, a tribe that never lost pride in its heritage of personal and political independence.

His father, Claus Friedrich, was a bricklayer and very poor. What we know about the playwright's youth we know from his own accounts. "Aus meiner Jugend" ("Recollections of my Childhood"), a first installment of which Hebbel published in 1854 in Karl Gutzkow's *Unterhaltungen am häuslichen Herd* as part of his autobiography—a project he abandoned shortly thereafter—is the main source. Since he had tried deliberately to model his account on Goethe's autobiography, *Dichtung und Wahrheit* (*Fact and Fiction*, 1811–1833), Hebbel had these memoirs published together with tales and novellas in 1855, rather than (as he had set out to do the previous year) separately as an essay or factual account. His autobiographical account deliberately passes over the unhappy moments of his youth in favor of those experiences that had a positive effect on him and that might even inspire others in a similar positive way. Thus he writes in his "Recollections,"

> The main attraction of one's childhood consists of the friendliness and benevolence shown one by everybody, down to the domestic animals and pets; for from this springs the feeling of security that leaves the child with the first step he takes into the hostile world and thereafter is lost forever. This experience is especially true of the lower classes. . . . This benevolence was shown my brother and myself in great abundance, especially by the tenants of our cottage.
>
> (*Sämtliche Werke*, R. M. Werner ed., *Werke* 3.84)

Hebbel's father owned a small house that was subdivided into three apartments to help make ends meet. The Hebbels occupied one of these apartments. Attached to the house was a garden with some fruit trees. What status the young Hebbel enjoyed among his peers derived from this petty-bourgeois background. Every summer he would barter some of the fruit from his father's garden for toys and other objects he desired. (To be sure, the Hebbels hovered between petty-bourgeois and proletarian existence. Marxist critics have tended to emphasize the proletarian side, in spite of the property Hebbel's father owned, however marginal.) It was therefore not only a serious blow to his parents and brother, but also to the six-year-old boy, when his father had to give up the small house he had inherited from his parents. Hebbel's grandfather had been talked into co-signing a loan shortly after his marriage. The friend for whom he had done the favor defaulted. But for the fact that the creditor had been jailed for arson, the Hebbels would have had to relinquish their house even sooner. In a strained sense, Hebbel was now a "deposed aristocrat," and his loss of status among his peers contributed in no small measure to his later resolve to gain status and acceptance in life.

We know from the poet's diaries that his father was a moody, ill-tempered man who felt trapped by his marriage and economic circumstances. His two sons he called "the wolves," because they were two hungry mouths to feed in a household where there was never enough to eat, especially in the winter when work was scarce. In his autobiography, however, Hebbel describes his father as merely serious at home, being lively and talkative outside of it. He could not brook laughter and enjoyed singing church hymns. Hebbel's mother, Antje Margarete Schubert, worked as a domestic to supplement the family's income. It was his mother who defended her son's inclinations to listen to stories and dream when her husband insisted the boy follow in his footsteps and work to become a bricklayer. He had the boy go with him to his jobs and fetch and carry for him. Hebbel's mother put a stop to that. Nevertheless, Hebbel insisted that his father had been a good man, and that poverty had overshadowed his father's soul. Hebbel said that although his mother was unselfish and gentle, she too was quick-tempered. She forgave and forgot, however, just as easily. These traits, which were part of Hebbel's own make-up, he later traced to his mother's influence.

At the age of four Hebbel entered the nursery school of a pipe-smoking spinster called Susanna. He writes:

> Susanna's table, laden with school books, stood in the middle of the room and she herself, her white clay pipe in her mouth and a cup of tea in front of her, sat behind it in an awe-inspiring antique armchair. In front of her lay a long ruler . . . which was used to punish us . . . and next to it was a bag of raisins intended to reward virtuous behavior. The swats and raps, however, were more frequent than the raisins . . . [and in spite of her efforts to dole them out sparingly] the bag, at times, was completely empty; we thus learned about Kant's "categorical imperative" early on.

> (*Werke* 8.89)

At Christmastime the children of the affluent families were given more than those of the poor, and Hebbel's status placed him somewhere in the middle of that hierarchy. In any case, the poet insists that one of the earliest lessons he learned in Susanna's school was that life is unfair.

When he transferred to the village elementary school at the age of six, he had already learned to read and write. The head of the school, Franz Christian Dethlefsen, had taken a liking to Friedrich and helped his intellectual development greatly. By permitting him the use of his library, by helping him with the expenses toward buying candles so the boy could read nights, and finally by recommending him to the parish magistrate as an assistant, Dethlefsen earned Hebbel's lifelong gratitude.

In 1827, at the age of thirty-seven, Hebbel's father died. Friedrich and his brother, Johann, were now their mother's exclusive charge and burden. On the recommendation of Dethlefsen, Friedrich, now fourteen years old, became errand boy and clerk to J. J. Mohr, the magistrate of the parish of Wesselburen. Accounts vary, but it is certain that without this considerable stroke of good fortune Hebbel would not have had the opportunity and the requisite time to continue his education. When in later years he complained bitterly that Mohr had treated him like a servant (he had to share a bed under the stairs with Mohr's coachman, even when the latter was sick, and he had to take his meals with the servants), it should be remembered that Hebbel's duties were light and that Mohr permitted him the use of his library, where the boy spent the greater part of the day. Among Hebbel's duties were the issuing of visas, the keeping of the police blotter, and the serving of court papers. In all respects he proved a quick learner and very reliable, so that Mohr gave him an excellent reference later on. Wesselburen's isolation made it very difficult for Hebbel to pursue studies of any kind. Hebbel's interest in the arts and in letters could only be furthered by self-education. His employer had no interest in literature and the arts, although his library contained books by Schiller, Heinrich von Kleist, F. G. Klopstock, and E. T. A. Hoffmann, as well as poems by Ludwig Uhland. The Uhland poems were especially important to Hebbel. His early attempts at writing poetry had been entirely in the manner of Schiller's reflective or intellectual lyrics; Uhland's natural simplicity struck him as a revelation, and he came under the spell and influence of this famous though mediocre poet. In fact, as late as 1857, on the occasion of the first edition of his collected poems, Hebbel made his dedication to Uhland, "premier poet of the present." When Uhland died in 1862, however, Hebbel entered in his journal the following critical comments:

> [Our] literature loses nothing; he only had one spring, no summer, and no autumn; for I used to overestimate his dramas, and concerning all else he did, he could have been replaced by the most mediocre specialist . . . no other poet affected me in my youth in quite the same way as he; yet this

would have been the case to a lesser degree if I had been familiar with Goethe.

(*Sämtliche Werke*, R. M. Werner ed.,
Tagebücher 4.5983)

His extensive, though entirely eclectic, reading soon prompted Hebbel to try his hand at writing. He had some stories and poems printed in a regional newspaper published in nearby Friedrichstadt. His subjects were romantic: dreams, pain, compassion, darkness, night, and the uncanny. At this time he also became acquainted with some philosophical ideas drawn notably from Immanuel Kant's *Kritik der praktischen Vernunft* (*Critique of Practical Reason*, 1781; a treatise on ethics), Hegel's dialectics, and Ludwig Feuerbach's materialism. These ideas came to him indirectly through the study of a popular didactic poem (in six cantos) by Christoph A. Tiedge entitled "Urania" (1801) and subtitled "Of God, Immortality, and Freedom"; Gotthilf Heinrich Schubert's *Symbolik des Traumes* (Dream-Symbolism, 1814) and *Ansichten von der Nachtseite der Naturwissenschaften* (Views on the Dark Side of Natural Science, 1808); and Ludwig Feuerbach's *Gedanken über Tod and Unsterblichkeit* (Reflections On Death and Immortality, 1830). These texts were kept closely guarded secrets by Hebbel; they did not come to light as sources of his philosophical ideas until nearly a century later. They are especially revealing with respect to Hegel's dialectics of history and aesthetic ideas, and they figure prominently in some of Hebbel's dramas. Throughout his productive career, however, Hebbel persistently denied any Hegelian influence. We know that as a student in Heidelberg and Munich he had studied Hegel's aesthetics, but he could never penetrate Hegel's philosophical system in its entirety. His poetic or creative nature prompted him to extract from the ideas of others what seemed important to him, rather than to study them systematically and critically and, as behooves the scholar, to credit his sources in the process.

Hebbel was also the director of an amateur theater in Wesselburen and the intellectual leader of a small band of young followers, not unlike the young admirers who gathered round him in his mature and successful years in Vienna. His early poems already contain the notions of existential guilt—a result of the individual's separation from his divine origin, which constitutes the dualism of the universe—that later form the basis of Hebbel's tragedies. At this stage Hebbel viewed the poet as the creator of the unity of God and his world, an idea reminiscent of the romantic conception of the poet–priest.

After some futile attempts to break out of his confining circumstances in Wesselburen, Hebbel mailed some poems and stories to the *Pariser Modeblätter*, a journal published in Hamburg and edited by Amalia Schoppe, a writer of popular but trivial novels. One of these poems, "Die Schlacht bei Hemmingstedt" (The Battle at Hemmingstedt, 1833), thus came to the attention of Frau Schoppe. It was a patriotic poem that Hebbel thought timely, because the 1830's was a period of political unrest in the duchies, turbulent in the wake of the uprisings in Poland and France. The German populace in the Danish controlled portions of Schleswig-Holstein were politically a functional minority. This poem, an exception for the otherwise apolitical Hebbel in those years, met with an enthusiastic response by Frau Schoppe. One of her ambitions was to discover artistic talent and to help foster it. She had many young protégés whom she advised and otherwise sought to advance. In February 1835, after two years of correspondence, Amalia Schoppe arranged for Hebbel to move to Hamburg. She had collected money from friends to enable him to study Latin and thus prepare himself for admission to a university. This assistance included promises of free meals at the homes of some of her friends. And so, at the age of twenty-two, Hebbel set out for Hamburg, leaving behind him years of growth, sorrow, and frustration.

His arrival in Hamburg not only marked an important turning point in his life but also signified an extraordinary event in the annals of German literature. On 23 March 1835 Hebbel began the first entry into a journal that he vowed to keep until his death. His journals, which indeed he kept until a few days before his death, on 13 December 1863, are an invaluable source of information for the historian and biographer. They must be taken with a grain of salt as far as the accuracy of certain events in the poet's life are concerned; but they do represent an extraordinary record of the artist and the man. The four volumes represent an important part of Hebbel's work, on a par with his dramas and poems. With self-mockery yet great confidence in his destiny, he begins his journal as follows:

First Journal. Reflections on World, Life, and Books, mainly, however, on myself in the manner of a diary, by K. F. Hebbel. Begun on 23 March 1835.

I begin this journal not merely as a favor to my future biographer, although, given my prospects for immortality, I can be certain to get one. It is to be a musical score of my heart, and it is to preserve faithfully, and for my future edification, those notes that my heart sounds. Man is different from a musical instrument that repeats all notes in a perpetual cycle, albeit in the most remarkable combinations; the sensation that dies in his breast, dies forever; the same ray of sunlight never produces the same flowers in the psychic as it does in the physical world. Thus every hour becomes a world unto itself which has its grand or small beginning, its boring middle and its longed-for or feared end. And who can be an indifferent witness to the fall of so many thousands of worlds within oneself and not have the desire at least to preserve the divine [spark], be it pleasure or pain, which permeated them? Therefore, I may be forgiven, if I devote a few minutes of each day to this journal.

(*Tagebücher* 1.1)

A year later, he notes another reason for keeping a diary:

I consider it the greatest obligation of a human being who is a writer that he furnish the material for his biography . . . his errors are as important to his fellow man as the profoundest truths of a great man. Therefore, I shall from now on use this book as a gauge for the current seasonal changes of my soul, and I shall at the same time turn my glances backwards to see if here and there I am able to discover an intellectual turning point.

(*Tagebücher* 1.136)

Above all, his diaries are the record of his ceaseless struggles to overcome the obstacles circumstances had placed in his path. For example, throughout his life he lamented that he was self-educated and lacking in the knowledge and graces that would have been his had he come from at least the middle of the middle classes. The journals also reveal his profound insights, his great talent, and the raw materials for his dramas. He never wavered in his resolve to commit his feelings and thoughts to paper, and it is fair to say that, psychologically, the diaries (as well as his poems) helped him to clarify his thoughts and to articulate his difficulties in order to overcome them.

Hebbel had free room and board at the house of the stepfather of Elise Lensing, a seamstress. Nine years his senior, she showered him with love and devotion which, although they became lovers, he never fully returned. Her sympathy and modest financial support helped sustain him. Among his problems was the realization that he was too old to acquire the requisite background for admission to a university. His Latin studies were a failure, and his dependency on Amalia's generosity and friends gnawed on his sense of pride. He persuaded his benefactress to give him the money set aside for his education and allow him to depart for Heidelberg, where he intended to attend lectures at the university without benefit of matriculation. Frau Schoppe's watchfulness and constant interference in his personal affairs had strained their relationship—not least because of his liaison with Elise, of which she disapproved; Hebbel and Amalia henceforth continued on a much more perfunctory footing. In 1851 she moved to the United States; Hebbel exchanged only two letters with her during an absence of seven years. Upon her death in 1858, he composed a distich in her memory; it is inscribed on her gravestone in the Vale Cemetery in Schenectady, New York.

Hebbel stayed in Heidelberg from April until September 1836. He kept up a lively correspondence with Elise. The most memorable event of his stay at the university was the close friendship he entered into with Emil Rousseau, a fellow student. Rousseau was the son of a judge from Ansbach who, like Hebbel, sought a humanistic education, although his course of study was the law. Hebbel's detailed descriptions of the town and its natural surroundings in his letters to Elise were as much a preliminary exercise for his journalistic ambitions as they were intended to entertain Elise. His journalistic ambitions had, of course, a practical reason, and indeed Hebbel engaged in a lifelong activity as reporter, critic, and journalist to supplement his income. The reports and reviews Hebbel produced in the years after his arrival in Heidelberg are a record of ceaseless industry, wide reading, and constant attempts to broaden his intellectual horizons. He would complain on numerous occasions, of course, that his journalistic endeavors kept him from devoting sufficient time to his more important work.

In September 1836 Hebbel traveled to Munich on foot. He did so ostensibly to continue his studies; in reality, however, he intended to establish contacts on the way with Hermann Hauff, the editor of a Stuttgart newspaper called *Morgenblatt für gebildete Leser.* Hauff had already printed some of Hebbel's poems and proved willing to accept his services as a correspondent in Munich. Hebbel also visited Uhland, his revered poetic mentor. He was disappointed in what he regarded as Uhland's banal nature. Emil Rousseau had followed him to Munich, and his friend's companionship was one of the highlights of Hebbel's sojourn. In Munich, Hebbel stayed at the house of a joiner named Schwarz, and entered into an affair with his daughter, Josepha (Beppi); Beppi and her father were to figure prominently in his middle-class tragedy, *Maria Magdalena* (1844). In 1838 Hebbel's mother died; he wrote in his diary: "She was a good woman whose positive and less positive sides seem inextricably intertwined with my own nature. I share with her my bad temper and no less the ability to forgive and forget everything quickly and without further ado" (*Tagebücher* 1.1295). In October that year his friend Emil died of typhoid fever; it would seem that Hebbel regarded him as the only true friend he ever had. Only Emil's family, especially his sister Charlotte, with whom he kept up a correspondence for many years, and Beppi's love and care kept him from becoming despondent. His financial resources exhausted, Hebbel returned to Hamburg in March 1839. Hungry and unable to afford transportation, he again journeyed on foot. In Hamburg, he returned to Elise and accepted a position as correspondent for Karl Gutzkow's *Telegraph für Deutschland.* Gutzkow, a leading member of the group known as "Young Germany," was to become one of Hebbel's more prominent enemies in his later years as a playwright. The Young Germans, with their tendentious writings and plays, dominated the theater of Germany and Austria; and many an intrigue and argument with Heinrich Laube, Gutzkow, and even Franz von Dingelstedt, Hebbel's apparent friend and mentor, caused him much anxiety and often prevented his plays from receiving the attention they deserved. As the directors of three of Germany's and Austria's important stages, these men had the power and influence to play a critical role in the staging of Hebbel's dramas.

At the end of 1839 Hebbel began writing his first drama, *Judith* (1840). We know that he took the material from the apocrypha rather than from literary models, which existed in plenty. Hebbel's private studies in Munich, especially of Greek tragedy, Hegel's aesthetic writings, and Kant's second critique, as well as the Schelling lectures he attended, all came together in this quickly written masterpiece of German dramatic literature. Napoleon, still an overwhelming personality whose career reverberated in Germany twenty-five years after his defeat, figures in the drama in the guise of the general Holofernes, Judith's antagonist. Through the good offices of Auguste Stich-Crelinger, an actress at the court theater in Berlin, Hebbel's play was staged on 6 July 1840 and proved a great success. Hoffmann and Campe in Hamburg published the play in July 1841, after it had also been performed in Hamburg in December of the previous year. Shortly thereafter, Hebbel's many thoughts and ideas concerning the drama, which he recorded in his journal, were summarized in an essay entitled *Mein Wort über das Drama* (*My View on the Drama*, 1843). This as well as the preface to *Maria Magdalena* (1844), contain his dramatic theories. Shortly after this burst of productivity, he completed another drama, *Genoveva* (1843). In the meantime Hebbel had had a love affair with Emma Schröder, the daughter of a Hamburg senator whom he had met at a social gathering in the summer of 1840. The affair did not last long but left its traces in the diaries and his relationship with Elise. Elise, who by now was expecting a child by Hebbel, knew of the affair. He was beset by feelings of guilt and remorse, and the figure of Golo in *Genoveva* reflects these feelings.

On 5 November 1840 Elise gave birth to a son, who was named Max. Hebbel's financial situation was desperate, despite the royalties from *Judith*. His publisher, Julius Campe, did not suspect the author's dire need, nor his very immediate need for a sponsor merely so he could borrow books from the Hamburg public library. In this situation Hebbel decided to apply for a professorship in aesthetics at the University of Kiel. The Danish royal family, especially King Christian VIII, were well known for their support of the arts; and Hebbel, as a Danish subject, decided to petition the king for a professorship at Kiel or some other position. In the winter of 1842 he journeyed to Copenhagen. The well-known Danish poet Adam Oehlenschläger became Hebbel's advocate and supporter at court. During the winter months, while Hebbel was waiting for an audience with the king, he and Oehlenschläger discussed German literature and visited the great sculptor Albert Bertel Thorvaldsen. A year later, after Thorvaldsen's death, Hebbel memoralized him in a poem. Finally in the spring of 1843 Hebbel, with the support of Oehlenschläger, had obtained from the king a two-year travel grant of twelve hundred thalers, a stipend that was larger than customary and certainly more advantageous than any position he might have obtained, because it permitted him to pursue his studies and education without any obligation on his part.

He returned to Hamburg and left Elise half of the grant to help support herself and their child. The primary purpose of the grant was to enable young artists to travel freely in order to further their education and knowledge of the arts. Hebbel decided to go to Paris and Rome. On 9 September 1843 he set out for Paris. His knowledge of French was poor, and he came to depend greatly on the services and subsequent friendship of Felix Bamberg, the Prussian consul in Paris. Bamberg was the first critic to publish an essay on Hebbel as a dramatist, and he was also the initiator of scholarly interest in the playwright after his death, when he edited and published Hebbel's diaries and correspondence. Another memorable encounter in Paris was with the poet Heinrich Heine, who was also from Hamburg and already knew of Hebbel through his poems and plays. Hebbel's journal and his letters to Elise testify to the ups and downs of his sojourn in Paris. He felt inadequate for the familiar reasons, that is, his lack of social graces and his poverty, all of which he never forgot to mention as the legacy of his family background. He lived frugally. Through Heine, Hebbel also met the young Hegelian, philosopher, and socialist Arnold Ruge, who together with Karl Marx edited the *Deutsch-Französische Jahrbücher* (Franco-German Annuals).

His enjoyment of Paris ended abruptly when Hebbel learned that his son had died, on 2 October 1843. Elise's despondency was evident in her letters to him. At the time she was expecting their second child, and Hebbel feared for her life. It is here, too, that he recognized the gulf between the sexes that plays such an important role in his plays. He despaired over the apparent inability of men and women to comprehend one another when, after eight months, Elise was still unable to put the pain and anguish of her loss behind her. For Hebbel, pain caused by the state of the world (a part of his "pan-tragic" world view) outweighs pain suffered at the loss of an individual. To him the death of the individual is necessary for the preservation and progress of humanity as a whole. He wrote that he envied her and her sisters their imperviousness to such considerations. At one point, however, he was so gripped by remorse and guilt that he offered to marry Elise and share the rest of his stipend with her. It was Felix Bamberg who prevented him from taking such a drastic step by repeatedly reminding him of his poetic mission.

In September 1844 Hebbel left Paris for Rome and like so many who had preceded him, found it difficult to leave this "beautiful, magnificent, and hospitable city." His stay in Rome and later in Naples yielded little except some poems, epigrams, and the plot for his tragicomedy *Ein Trauerspiel in Sizilien* (Sicilian Tragedy, 1847). In Rome he met the German painter Louis Gurlitt and the literary historian Hermann Hettner, subsequently the friend of Gottfried Keller. Hebbel's friendship with Gurlitt was to last over many years.

In May 1844, before Hebbel left Paris, Elise had given birth to another son, Ernst. Despite this new tie, Hebbel broke with Elise in harsh and uncompromising letters from Rome. To

be sure, she knew that Hebbel's feelings for her were less than passionate, and she had always assured him that he was free to do as he wished, that she had no claim to his fidelity. Still, she had hoped that he would succeed in obtaining a doctorate, which would provide them with the financial security to live together. Hebbel had intended to submit his theoretical treatise *My View on the Drama: A Reply to Professor Heiberg in Copenhagen* to the University of Erlangen in lieu of a doctoral thesis. Because Denmark's leading literary critic, Johan Ludvig Heiberg, had attacked Hebbel's views (which he had published a few months earlier under a different title), Hebbel felt obliged to elaborate his original ideas and in the process to clarify them considerably. For a long time, however, he could not afford the required fee for the degree. He finally received his doctorate in 1846, after Emil Rousseau's father had advanced the money for the fee and submitted the treatise to the University of Erlangen. Because of his pride and sensitivity about his lack of a formal education, Hebbel felt he had earned a doctorate long before it was officially awarded, and as early as 1840 he had on occasion signed his formal correspondence "Friedrich Hebbel, Ph.D." As he once put it in a letter to Charlotte Rousseau, society had already awarded him the title, because no one in the tea rooms of Hamburg could imagine that a man of his ability lacked a doctorate.

In October 1845 Hebbel left Italy, intending to return to Hamburg. In early November he arrived in Vienna. Now the author of three plays (*Judith*, *Genoveva*, and most recently *Maria Magdalena*), he was no longer unknown, and the papers in Vienna announced his arrival. Two Galician noblemen, the wealthy brothers Julius and Wilhelm Zerboni, admirers of Hebbel's work, organized a grand party in his honor and showered him with attention and presents. Book dealers began to order his works, and the leading actress at the Vienna Burgtheater let it be known that she was interested in playing the roles of Judith and Klara in two of his dramas. This actress, Christine Enghaus, like Hebbel himself, hailed from northern Germany and was the parent of an illegitimate child. In May 1846, barely six months after his arrival, she and Hebbel were married. Thus, almost overnight, as in a fairy tale, Hebbel's fortunes had vastly improved. Vienna, which was to have been no more than a waystation on his return to Hamburg and an uncertain future, had suddenly become his new home.

From the point of view of middle-class values and morals, the social status of an actress and a starving poet and playwright was marginal at best and even more so in this instance because of the personal circumstances of both partners. Given their roles as single parents, their marriage was therefore above all a very practical step. Moreover, Christine's relative financial security enabled Hebbel to concentrate entirely on his creative and journalistic efforts. Beyond that, however, it was also a very happy marriage, as Hebbel's diaries and his letters to and from Christine attest. Thanks to Christine's generosity, he was able to resolve his relationship with Elise Lensing in an amicable, if highly unconventional, manner. The young couple decided to invite Elise to visit them in Vienna. Hebbel's marriage had caused Elise much bitterness at first, and the death of Ernst, their second son, on 12 May 1847 was the immediate reason for the invitation. Elise's good nature prevailed over her rancor; she accepted the invitation and stayed with the Hebbels for over a year in a kind of innocent ménage à trois. Christine's illegitimate son, Carl, whom Hebbel had adopted but whom he had come to resent, was placed in Elise's care to raise as her own as a substitute for Ernst. Moreover, Christine and Hebbel's first child had just been born. Emil, called "Ariel" in jest, died a few months later. Elise and Christine kept up a correspondence until Elise's death in 1854, although Hebbel no longer did so himself. On Christmas Eve 1847 a second child, Christine (Titi), was born, his only child to grow to adulthood.

Hebbel spent the rest of his life in the Austrian capital. The decade after the revolution of 1848 was his most productive and successful. With increasing though moderate fame he acquired a measure of financial independence, permitting him to purchase a modest summer home on the Traunsee in Gmunden, near Vienna, in 1855. Hebbel's dramas, and his columns and reviews in Austria's and Germany's best papers and journals, had brought him into contact with the aristocracy of his day. The king of Bavaria and the grand duke of Saxe-Weimar especially took an interest in him. The Munich and Weimar courts had artistic pretensions that went beyond the tradition of royal patronage of the arts. Maximilian II awarded him a high decoration for his dramas, as did the grand duke. His plays were staged at the court theaters in Munich and Weimar. On his fiftieth birthday Hebbel was awarded the honorary title of private librarian to the duke of Weimar.

In addition to royal patronage Hebbel enjoyed friendship and collaboration with the leading intellectuals of Vienna, mostly liberal Jewish literati and journalists. However, his relations with the great artists of his day were fraught with hostility and mutual lack of understanding. At the head of the list were Adalbert Stifter, Grillparzer, Johann Nestroy, and Richard Wagner. Notable exceptions were Ludwig Tieck, Eduard Mörike, and the composer Robert Schumann, all of whom, however, lived in Germany in contrast to the first group whose members, with the exception of Wagner, were Austrian. (Wagner and Hebbel had met in Vienna, however.) In April and May 1857 Hebbel traveled to Hamburg, Frankfurt, Weimar, and Stuttgart. In Frankfurt he met Artur Schopenhauer, who did not reciprocate the enthusiasm with which Hebbel greeted the philosopher. In December he received the Tiedge Prize for his epic poem *Mutter und Kind* (*Mother and Child*, 1859). In 1858 he traveled with Emil Kuh, his friend and later his biographer, to Cracow, where he hoped to gather Slavic material for his *Deme-*

trius project (which, however, like Schiller's play, was to remain a fragment). In January 1861 Hebbel went to Weimar, where the first two parts of his most ambitious dramatic project to date, *The Nibelungs,* were performed. His wife, Christine, played Brunhild on the first evening and Kriemhild on the second. The plans for the drama date back to 1855. More than any other work this German heroic epic, in new and typically Hebbelean dramatic guise, helped establish his fame among the educated throughout Germany. It received public acclaim, coming at a time of rising nationalism; but Hebbel was still a Danish subject and wished to remain so. After the complete tragedy had been published by Campe in Hamburg (March 1862), *The Nibelungs* was staged in Vienna (February 1863). In June Hebbel journeyed to Paris and to the World Fair in London, in the company of John Marshall, secretary to the grand duchess Sophie of Weimar, and Siegmund Engländer, a critic and correspondent for a Viennese journal.

In March 1863 Hebbel became ill. He suffered from what was diagnosed as rheumatism, although he had been a lifelong swimmer and exercise enthusiast. His real ailment, it turned out, was a progressive weakening of the bones, possibly bone cancer or at least osteoporosis. In the end he could neither walk nor even hold his head erect. Shortly before his death, one more honor was bestowed on him. On 7 November the king of Prussia awarded him the Schiller Prize for his *Nibelungs.* Later that month his illness was complicated by pneumonia, and on 13 December he succumbed. He was buried in Vienna's protestant cemetery at Matzleinsdorf.

II

Hebbel's first biographer, Emil Kuh, hoped to publicize his friend's work by bringing out a collected edition shortly after his death in 1863. Over a decade later, in 1877, Kuh published Hebbel's biography in two volumes.

Neither effort produced the desired result. No real interest in Hebbel's works developed. It was not to gather momentum until Felix Bamberg, Hebbel's friend and admirer from his Paris days, edited the letters and diaries between 1885 and 1890. Bamberg's commentaries, his article "Hebbel" in *Allgemeine Deutsche Bibliographie* (vol. 11, 1880—the standard German biographical reference work), and the correspondence between Theodor Rötscher, a Hegel disciple, and Friedrich Hebbel alerted academicians to the fact that here was a man of both artistic and philosophical significance. Finally, after the completion of Werner's critical edition of Hebbel's works, the poet gained admission to the pantheon of German literature. He was now a "classic," a part of the curriculum of schools and universities, and of the repertory of the most important theaters in the land.

To this day the playwright's works have been discussed from various points of view, all of which, or at least the most important of which, demonstrate Hebbel's thematic and philosophical orientation: the *dualism* or *pantragedy* thesis, whereby Hebbel is seen as the metaphysician of the dialectic between "idea" and "individuation," as the poet or minstrel of a divided divinity; the *evolution* thesis, whereby Hebbel appears as a practitioner of Hegel's dialectic of history; the *nihilism* thesis, which views the dramatist as representing the ideological crisis of the nineteenth century between theodicy and nihilism, acceptance or rejection of the divine origin and order of the world; the *idealism* thesis, which sees Hebbel as an ethically normative poet who represents the new humanism of existence as ethical challenge; the *sex* thesis, whereby Hebbel's dramas represent the permanent struggle between the sexes and the question of the emancipation of women; and finally, the *Marxist* perspective from which Hebbel is viewed as a bourgeois reactionary who sought to overcome the disadvantages of his lowly origins by catering to the ruling classes to whose favorable attitudes he owed his economic existence. Instead of being on the side of class struggle and human progress, Hebbel retreats into a pseudo reality of abstract conflicts that have to justify the existence of his neoclassical and middle-class dramas.

Whatever one's theories about Hebbel's dramas and other works, it is logical and reasonable to view them first and foremost in the context of his time, against the political and cultural history of which the poet and dramatist was a part, and to refer to his own ideas and theories about his works. As Hebbel himself saw it, and as a matter of historical fact, his dramatic works represent the "present" of his own day and "history" in the sense of historical fact as well as in the sense of a form of "optimum historical writing." Simply put, the comedy *Der Diamant* (1847), the tragedies *Maria Magdalena, Ein Trauerspiel in Sizilien, Julia,* and the epic poem *Mutter und Kind,* represent the "present" and all others are "historical" works. Hebbel expressed his intentions in a letter to Campe as follows:

I intend to accomplish no less than to portray the entire condition of the world as it has developed in the course of history and as it has escalated toward a catastrophe (for we are undeniably faced with such a catastrophe concerning the state, the church, and the arts and sciences) in a series of life-portraits which correspond with one another. Whether or not I shall attain this goal or whether I shall have to leave part of the work for some successor I have no way of knowing; but I do know this: dramatic art must address this challenge and anyone who does not follow this path will be counted among the dead and the ghosts. The principle has been established; the only question remaining is my personal attitude toward this principle. I shall attempt to deal with the challenge through a sequence of plays all of which are to form an unbroken chain. The past [will be portrayed] in Judith (Judaism and paganism), Genoveva (Christianity), Maria Magdalena (morality, ethics, honor, family), Moloch (positive religion), Christus (mystery). The present [is to be

represented] in Fiat iustitia et pereat mundus; Genie und Welt [Genius and World]; der Diamant; the future, in Zu irgend einer Zeit [At Some Time in the Future]. In between will be merely some connecting links.

(2 June 1844)

Only half of the dramas mentioned were completed. The Latin title refers to a motto attributed to Emperor Ferdinand I—Let justice be done, though the world may perish—which later figured in Hebbel's skepticism about the events of 1848. Aside from the imagined or real need to "sell" this idea to his publisher, Hebbel had indeed intended to produce a kind of dramatic (and tragic) counterpart to Honoré de Balzac's "human comedy." The Moloch play remained a fragment, the comedy *Der Diamant* was to be the only play dealing with "the present," and the plays devoted to "the future" were never begun.

In addition Hebbel had some ideas regarding the implicit historical nature of the drama, a fact that may or may not be seen as being in conflict with his stated plans for a series of dramas dealing with the "present condition of the world":

I am convinced . . . that the true historical character of the drama does not rest with the facts themselves. Rather, a pure invention, such as a love-story, can be quite historical provided it is filled with a breath of life, and provided it is created for posterity which does not care to know how we viewed our grandfathers but which cares to know about us. . . . For the poet, history is a vehicle for the embodiment of his views and ideas rather than the poet being the angel of the resurrection of history.

(*My View on the Drama, Werke* 11.9)

Either way, Hebbel stipulates the authenticity of his dramas as applied to the present— even when the subject matter is historical. Was Hebbel primarily an ideologue or was his ideology merely incidental to his artistic calling?

The answer to this question depends in

1099

large measure on the weight one is willing to give to the evidence of Hebbel's dependence on Hegelian philosophy, especially Hegel's aesthetic notions. In spite of Wolfgang Liepe's groundbreaking studies in 1952, in which he establishes the early sources for Hebbel's aesthetic ideas and denies any direct influence of Hegel on Hebbel—in keeping with the playwright's own assertions—we incline toward the strong though indirect evidence in favor of Hebbel's assimilation and deliberate application of Hegel's aesthetic ideas. In his theoretical writings, mainly *My View on the Drama* and the preface to *Maria Magdalena,* Hebbel developed dramatic theses whose resemblance to those of Hegel is too striking to be merely accidental. These two tracts date from 1843 and 1844, respectively, and they express ideas that Hebbel, with some variations, was to adhere to for the rest of his life.

Regarding Hebbel's dramatic production, two factors are important: his idealistic concept of the hierarchy of genres and his conception of history. With Hegel, Hebbel accepts the notion of the need to "regenerate" Western tragedy as the highest form of poetic expression and as the vehicle for establishing a divine presence in the world, the original raison d'être of tragedy according to both thinkers. In his views on history, Hebbel was in opposition to the Biedermeier zeitgeist, which viewed history as an objective phenomenon, the study and knowledge of which would lead to ever greater self-consciousness and insight into the world and humanity. For Hebbel and Hegel too, history has a religious source whose manifestation in the world is through ethical values. Thus Hebbel's historical dramas have a "higher" purpose than the historical tragedies of his day, which served only narrow nationalistic interests, according to him. In *My View on the Drama* he writes: "This type of drama [Hebbel's new historical drama] could become universal, since subject matter and plot should be of equal concern and interest to all peoples of the world; and to contemplate such a play at a time when na-

tional differences are waning may not be too daring" (*Werke* 11.35). Aside from the strikingly modern view of "waning national differences" at a time of rising nationalism in Europe, Hebbel clearly seeks to establish a synthesis of the cultural achievements of the West in a symbolic and universal way. It is part of what has been known as Hebbel's concept of pan-tragedy.

In his concept of tragic guilt, life creates guilt not merely by accident but of necessity, because life exists only individually and as such is incapable of moderation. Since the drama, in Hebbel's idealistic view, is the highest form among the three classical genres, it has the task of representing individual life in continuously emerging historical contexts. These different historical contexts, or dramatic subjects, show the nature of man to be immutable, no matter how much change occurs around him. In all of this, Hebbel stresses that "dramatic guilt does not stem from the idea of free will as does Christian original sin, but directly from volition itself, from the rigid, autonomous expansion of the self . . . therefore, it is dramatically inconsequential whether the hero fails because of a positive or a negative deed." The problem of free will derives from the paradox of the incomprehensible freedom of the individual, who remains a part of the whole even after the completion of the process of individuation. Through separation from the original nexus with the "whole," that is, his individuation, the individual incurs guilt (dualism theory as one of several approaches to Hebbel's dramatic and poetic works).

Finally, Hebbel's idealistic notion of the challenge of the dramatic arts consists in the representation of the universal historical process of the humanization of all power structures, secular and spiritual. The playwright's task is to assist in this. Hebbel, like all first-rate artists since the eighteenth century, felt very strongly the process of alienation that has characterized the relationship of the individual to society and of the artist to society. In a sense all of his works are about this alienation, or the conflict between the rights of the individual and an insensitive world encroaching upon them—the emerging metropolis, the abstraction of the state, and natural relationships in general. All of that began to emerge during Hebbel's lifetime and has become even more apparent since then. In a letter to Gustav zu Putlitz in 1857, Hebbel puts it in personal terms: "We too [he and his wife] find our greatest happiness in the home and leave only rarely and reluctantly the small circle to which we belong and which at most may accommodate a fourth or fifth member. A sea shell in the ocean! has always been a motto for myself and my wife."

Hebbel's first play, *Judith*, is undoubtedly one of his better plays, although he was only twenty-seven years old when he wrote it. During his lifetime it was performed more than twenty times, and it remains one of his more frequently staged plays. Although it was well-known that bedroom affairs—and certainly a biblical one—would be considered "tactless" if not tasteless by the directors of the court theaters at the time, Hebbel was too naive to realize it. Only after the revolution of 1848, when certain Biedermeier sensibilities, especially in sexual matters, had been overcome, did *Judith* have a chance on the stage. The drama is about the emancipation of women, but in a very idealistic way. To Hebbel, the nature of women is to love rather than to hate. Thus when Judith is driven to kill Holofernes, the enemy of her people, she is acting against her nature. Moreover she does so for personal reasons and thus incurs tragic guilt. All of this Hebbel makes plausible with great psychological insight into his characters, anticipating the naturalists and even more modern playwrights.

While working on the drama, Hebbel noted in his diary: "The biblical Judith is of no use to me . . . a widow who traps Holofernes through trickery and cunning; she is glad when she has his head in the bag, and she sings and rejoices with all of Israel for three months. That is vulgar; such a person is not worthy of her success" (*Tagebücher* 2.1872). Hebbel's purpose, as he saw it, is clearly defined in the instructions he gave Madame Stich-Crelinger (a student of August Iffland), the first actress to portray Judith:

The entire tragedy is based on the fact that extraordinary situations on a global scale call forth a direct intervention of the Deity that results in extraordinary human deeds beyond all normal bounds. Such an unusual situation existed when the mighty Holofernes threatened to crush the people of the covenant from whom the redemption of all mankind was to flow. The most extreme emergency occurred, when the spirit entered Judith to place the right idea in her soul. She does not dare adopt it until it has been ignored or rejected by all the men around her. This idea, of course, is no longer the pure product of divine inspiration but, in keeping with flawed human nature, it is the product of vanity as well. She meets Holofernes, "the first and last man on earth"; she feels, although subconsciously, that he is the only one whom she could love, she shudders when he stands before her in all his imposing physical splendor, and to gain his respect she reveals her secret to him, but she merely succeeds in being humiliated; Holofernes mocks all her motives and finally considers her his booty [he rapes her] and peacefully falls asleep. Now she commits her act [she stabs and kills him], carried out as a divine commandment, although she is aware only of her personal motives; like the prophets by Samaya, she is humiliated by her maid [Samaya, a citizen of Bethulia, tries to discredit two prophets in their midst: Daniel, the mute, through whom the Lord suddenly speaks, bidding him to have his brother Assad stoned to death; and Judith through whom the Lord intends to liberate Bethulia from Holofernes' threat]; she trembles when her maid reminds her that she may be with child [the result of a crucial change from the apocryphal account, whereby Judith is a seventeen-year-old virgin widow of a brief and unconsummated marriage; Hebbel's logic being that only a technical virgin (as opposed to a pure one, whose sole concern would be the protection of her virginity), could be counted on to do God's bidding, because as a virgin *widow* she longs for the encounter with

Holofernes, regardless of the consequences]. But already in Bethulia, Judith has the right idea: if her deed was divinely inspired, then God will also protect her from the consequences and prevent her pregnancy; if she gives birth, then she must die, lest her son commit matricide; she must be killed by her own people since she sacrificed herself for them. Only her doubts and vacillation after the deed is done make her a tragic heroine.

(Letter to Stich-Crelinger, 23 April 1840, *Briefe*, 2.35)

The question is whether God is an aesthetic symbol or a reality. Hebbel justified the appearance of a prophet (Judith) by stating that "created life" (history) had not yet been set free to the extent that divine intervention could be dispensed with. In other words, is history, as the will of the highest power, capable of being enacted by the individual in 1840 without divine intervention? In any case, the similarities between Holofernes and Napoleon on the one hand, and Judith and Joan of Arc on the other, are unmistakable, as is Judith's function as a necessarily guilty tool of history that affirms the greatness of Holofernes and produces his downfall in order to ensure human progress by way of a new historical reality or synthesis. As Judith herself states: "Der Weg zu meiner That geht durch die Sünde!" (The pathway to my deed is through sin!).

Hebbel's important plays dramatize major turning points in the history of the religions of the world in accordance with Hegel's concept of history. Hebbel experienced his own time as one of religious crisis, and he deliberately located his dramas at certain caesuras in history in order to anticipate the future by pointing to crucial transitions in the past: thus *Judith* portrays the confrontation of Judaism with paganism. In addition, there are points of contact between Hebbel and Marx and Schopenhauer, in that he sympathizes with the individual sacrificed by history for the sake of progress toward the ultimate Idea (*Weltgeist*).

Hebbel's best-known and most frequently staged drama to date is *Maria Magdalena*. The play belongs in the German tradition of the "bürgerliche Trauerspiel" (middle-class tragedy) dating from Gotthold Ephraim Lessing's *Emilia Galotti* from the latter half of the eighteenth century. As always, Hebbel intended to write a better drama of the type than anyone else before him. The combination of pantragic idealism and realistic psychological detail make this an extraordinary play indeed, and Hebbel, in the spring of 1843, after he had completed the first act, was rightfully convinced of its devasting power.

In many ways this tragedy is Hebbel's most personal work. It depicts the misery of the individual in confining circumstances such as those that characterized Hebbel's own family in his youth and the Schwarzes, the joiner's family with whom Hebbel stayed when he was a student.

The action takes place in a small German town in the first half of the nineteenth century. The key figures are Meister Anton, a master joiner; his wife; his daughter Klara; his son Karl; Friedrich the Secretary; Leonhard; and the merchant Wolfram. There are three acts. The parents are concerned about their children. Karl, spoiled by his mother, is dissatisfied with the confining circumstances of his family's life and with their narrow-minded views; Klara is worried because her relationship with Leonhard, an official in the town government, is based on fear and resentment. Klara's first and true love appears to have abandoned her when he left for college, and Klara has followed her mother's advice and accepted Leonhard as her future husband. During a dance Leonhard forces his fiancée to submit to him, because he is afraid that Klara's feeling for her erstwhile sweetheart, Friedrich the Secretary, may be rekindled. In order to disprove Leonhard's accusations of infidelity Klara submits to him, but as Leonhard says, "she was as cold as death."

Leonhard's character is revealed through his cynical report of how he came to be the

town treasurer. He had made sure his compet-
itor would show up drunk for the interview
and had also tried to court the mayor's hunch-
backed niece. Klara exlaims, "Oh my God, I
am tied to such a man." Rapidly the drama assumes tragic proportions. Karl is suspected of
having committed a jewelry theft in the house
of the merchant Wolfram, and he is arrested.
The shock of this news literally kills his
mother. Leonhard welcomes the opportunity
to renounce his engagement to a member of
the now disreputable joiner's family. Moreover, Leonhard has already been told by Meister Anton that he cannot count on any dowry
worth mentioning. Anton, who becomes suspicious because of certain dark hints by Klara
that she may be pregnant, makes her swear at
her mother's funeral that she is still a virgin.
She avoids answering him directly by vowing
that she will never bring shame on him. Meister Anton is an honest man who has carried
the burdens of a hard life for thirty years; despite his son's arrest, he is determined to face
all obstacles. Only one thing, he says to Klara,
could destroy him—that people might point
their fingers at Klara too. In that case he would
kill himself with his razor. This terrbile
pledge drives Klara into a conflict beyond resolution. In a retarding moment, we learn that
Karl is innocent, the merchant's deranged
wife having taken the jewels, and that the Secretary has returned and renewed his courtship. When Klara tells him about her liaison
with Leonhard and the reason for her despair,
he utters the devastating words: "no man can
forget something like that." Klara now begs
Leonhard to marry her in order to restore
her honor: "My father will cut his throat, if
I. . . ." Leonhard remains hard-hearted. Klara
now resolves to die. The Secretary, however,
seeks to avenge Leonhard's callous behavior
and challenges him to a duel. Leonhard is
killed and the Secretary badly wounded; he
barely manages to reach the joiner's house.
Karl has meanwhile been released from prison
and wants to become a seaman. First, however, he seeks revenge on the bailiff who had

carried a grudge against the family and who
had arrested him. Klara leaps into a well, hoping her death will be thought an accident; but
her maid has seen her jump. The dying Secretary tells Meister Anton that the fault for
Klara's suicide lies with himself and Anton,
because they both had valued the opinion of
other people above Klara's misery. Meister
Anton remains unmoved and merely says,
"Ich verstehe die Welt nicht mehr." (I no
longer understand the world.)

The tension of this tragedy does not arise
from conflict between two social classes but
from conflicts within the same class. In Hegelian terms, the destruction of the family is
the result of the unintentional hardness of
Meister Anton; his narrow-mindedness hin-
ders the development of more humane conditions and conceptions. The *Weltgeist* (World
Process, or Idea) thus leads to a higher historical form of social life. The static position of
Meister Anton, however morally strong and
subjectively justified, prevents the World Process from moving toward a synthesis; he thus
becomes the unwilling instrument of that historical process. Klara is its willing instrument,
although her actions are determined by the
same rigidity that characterizes her father's.

Hebbel himself was deeply moved by
Klara's fate and by the way in which she was
forced to leave this world. He wrote the play
in Copenhagen (hence the dedication to
Christian VIII in gratitude for the stipend),
Hamburg, and Paris. It was conceived in Munich when he was staying at the Schwarzes'.
At that point he called the play "Klara." It is
a further sign of his deep involvement and
sympathy with his subject that he finally
changed the title to *Maria Magdalena*, recalling the archetypal sinner of the biblical story.

This tragedy was first staged in Königsberg
in March 1846, and subsequently in Leipzig
and Berlin. During the revolutionary period of
1848, it was produced at the Hofburg Theater
in Vienna nine times, and two more times the
following year. At the end of the nineteenth
century the literary critic Franz Mehring al-

ready considered Klara's problem antiquated. Nevertheless, *Maria Magdalena* continued to be performed in Germany with greater frequency than any other play by Hebbel. After World War II, between 1955 and 1980, the play was staged more than one hundred times. Although pregnancy out of wedlock would no longer explain a woman's suicide to a modern audience, her destruction by a world of men, including those as likable as the Secretary and her brother, would carry more conviction for a contemporary audience than for the theatergoer in Hebbel's day. Not only do the men in Klara's environment fail to understand her but, in the last analysis, Klara agrees with their assessment of her situation; above all, she concurs in her father's judgment because she has internalized the values of this patriarchal world. In addition, even though the middle class is under current attack and not least by the women's movement, it is still sufficiently intact for its problems to interest the modern theatergoer. Aside from these social factors, however, there are structural features that have tended to make this tragedy as well as Hebbel's others appear quite modern. It is the author's interest in character and environment, his keen psychological insight, that make *Maria Magdalena* an unusual middle-class tragedy. Traditionally the situation alone and the opposition between one class and another provided the conflict. Hebbel, with his new approach, anticipated the later naturalists. Here the milieu itself constitutes the tragic necessity governing the actions of the dramatis personae. The rigid moral standards of his class make the master joiner a tyrant, although he loves his children and is loved by them. A dramatic technique that Hebbel employed with great success and that had been used by others before him (Lessing, Schiller, Kleist) is that of analytic exposition. With Hebbel, however, this analytic exposition, or handling of the plot by opening the drama not long before the castastrophe and showing the previous history in past perspective, is tied to the development of the characters conditioned by circumstances.

Hebbel's plays are tightly organized. He usually adheres to the classical five-act division or once, as in *Maria Magdalena,* to a traditional (classical) three-act division. By and large he avoids the retardation of the fourth act in favor of a clear idea of the outcome in the fifth:

> The idea [of a tragedy] must appear in the first act as a flashing light, in the second as a star that is struggling with mists, in the third as a dawning moon, in the fourth as a radiant sun which no one can deny any longer, and in the fifth as a consuming and destructive comet.
> (*Tagebücher* 3.2897)

The tragic necessity must become more and more visible with every passing scene, according to Hebbel: "first stage of artistic effect: it may be this way! second stage . . . : that is the way it is! third stage . . . : that is the way it must be!" (*Tagebücher* 3.4791). Edna Purdie, in her biography on Hebbel, points to the opening acts of her subject's tragedies as proof of his method.

> The main facts of the situation emerge clearly from the opening act in Hebbel's dramas, preparing the mind for a decision or event essential to the tragic sequence. "Dein Hochzeits-Kleid?" (Your wedding-dress?) are Klara's first words to her mother in *Maria Magdalena,* dimly foreshadowing the tragic theme, and through this . . . the situation rapidly develops, till the mother's wedding-dress becomes her shroud and Klara's own marriage fatally impossible.
> (p. 236)

Interestingly, despite Hebbel's adherence to the traditional structure of the classical Western tragedy, there are signs of the non-hierarchical or open-ended form, especially in *Maria Magdalena.* The individual scenes do not relate to one another hierarchically but with sequential equality. The language of the drama is heterogeneous (it is a prose play), and the metaphors are mostly biblical or theological fragments. The antagonist is the world of the middle class, represented by Meister Anton, rather than a powerful or villainous individual. Even Leonhard is a tool rather than the personification of evil. Klara's downfall is caused by an inhumane code of honor inextricably linked with the teachings of the church. The opponent is almost invisible, and the protagonists are confused, a situation typical of the modern open-ended drama. The sixth scene of the third act, the confrontation scene between the Secretary and Leonhard, reflects this confusion; the Secretary has just challenged Leonhard to a duel and the Secretary says to him sarcastically: "Courage, my boy, perhaps everything is going to come out alright; God and the Devil constantly seem to fight over the world; who knows who is in charge at any moment" (he grabs him by the arm and they go out). To be sure, these are implicit, not explicit, innovations. Hebbel did not depart as radically from the hierarchical structure of traditional drama as some of his predecessors (J. M. R. Lenz and Georg Büchner) or successors (Bertolt Brecht and his followers).

Because he was afraid he had represented the everyday milieu of a contemporary small town family all too graphically, Hebbel felt constrained to tack on to the play his famous preface to *Maria Magdelena*. In it he assured the world of his noble intentions and great regard for the drama as the highest possible form of artistic expression. The Greeks had as their purpose the representation of fate, and Shakespeare showed the destruction of the individual through his inherently demonic nature; while the drama of Hebbel's own time was to make visible the struggle between the extraordinary individual with the "will of the world" (God or history). Drama to Hebbel is only worthy of the name if it serves the highest and truest interests of its time, even if the fable or plot is taken from legend or myth.

Still, Hebbel came to regret the fact that Felix Bamberg in Paris, with whom he had had long discussions about Hegel's aesthetics, had urged him to add the preface after the completion of the tragedy, because it was received like a commentary on his play and was frequently used to attack him by pointing to seeming contradictions between his idealistic goals and naturalistic results.

After the completion of two relatively minor plays, the tragi-comedy *Ein Trauerspiel in Sizilien* and the tragedy *Julia*, which Hebbel called the sequel to *Maria Magdalena* (a daughter is rejected by a tyrannical father) in 1846 and 1847, Hebbel turned to a new and major tragic theme, the story of Herod and Mariamne. His source was a German translation of Flavius Josephus' *History of the Jewish People and Its Capital Jersualem* (*ca.* 65 A. D.). The account deals with the marriage of Herod, an Edomite and forced Jewish convert, to Mariamne, a descendant of the royal house of the Maccabees. With the help of the Romans, Herod had become king of Judea. Josephus reports that Herod's love for Mariamne was directly proportionate to her hatred for him. At this juncture Hebbel departs from his source, while in all other respects he follows it closely. In Hebbel's tragedy, Mariamne loves Herod as passionately as he loves her.

Hebbel knew nothing of the previous dramatic treatment of the theme by both major and minor playwrights, such as Hans Sachs (1552), Pedro Calderón de la Barca (1637), Voltaire (1730), Friedrich Rückert (1842), and Grillparzer's sketches (*The Last Kings of the Jews*, 1819–1822). There was also a German adaptation of an English treatment of the Herod theme by Johann Ludwig von Deinhardstein (*Ludovico*, 1849), which Hebbel had reviewed. (The English source was Philip Massinger's *The Duke of Milan* [1623], which transplants the Herod theme to Renaissance Italy.) In his review Hebbel summarizes the Josephus tale and thus gives us his own conception of the tragedy. Just as *Judith* represents an important turning point in history when Judaism triumphs over paganism and the synthesis of a more humane religion emerges, so *Herodes und Mariamne* (*Herod and Mariamne*, 1850), dramatizes an important turning point that signals the emergence of Christianity, a point emphasized in the last scene of the play, the so-called scene of the three kings.

Hebbel wrote the tragedy during the upheavals of 1848 in Vienna, since as a foreigner he could not join the national guard. Especially during the month of October, when Vienna was bombarded by troops loyal to the emperor under Windischgrätz, Hebbel made great progress; he finished the tragedy, whose beginnings date back to 1846, on 14 November 1848. He wrote to Gustav Kühne:

> During the worst days of the bombardment and the taking of the city I concluded the fifth act of a great historical tragedy, at which I had worked for two years. Not at home, in my room; I never work there. But in the street, as I always do, and the main scene during the last barrage, which, by the way, was executed with exceptional virtuosity [the fifth act, presumably]. Do not view this as egotism. No one is safe at such a moment; there are no more assured places of safety in a besieged city than on a sinking ship. I had to fear for my home and possessions like everybody else, even for the manuscript of the tragedy. . . . It was a simple stratagem of my nature to free itself from the pressure of the elemental.
>
> (21 November 1848)

The depiction of the struggles for the fortress of Zion is said to reflect some of the turmoil surrounding the writing of the last act.

Above all this tragedy represents another variant of Hebbel's representation of the battle between the sexes. The reduction of a human being (Mariamne) to the status of an object is a cardinal sin, and a world that permits that to happen is doomed. A higher regard and respect for the image of the individual (as a likeness of God's image) will be the commandment of a new era, the Christian.

That is the promise contained in Mariamne's tragedy in the scene with the three kings (or Magi). Love and compassion are to take the place of selfish megalomania.

In keeping with the grand perspective of its subject, the five-act tragedy is written in (blank) verse. It takes place in Jerusalem at the time of the birth of Christ. The main characters are Herod, King of Judea; Mariamne, his consort; Alexandra, his mother-in-law; Salome, his sister; Josephus, his brother-in-law; Soemus, his trusted friend; and Sameas, the Pharisee.

Herod's political power as king of the Jews rests on the good will of his Roman masters and on a claim of legitimacy stemming from his marriage to Mariamne, the last surviving member of the Maccabees. His power is threatened, however, by the machinations of Alexandra, Mariamne's mother, and by Sameas, the Pharisee. Alexandra lusts for power and has her eighteen-year-old son Aristobolus installed as high priest, an office equal to that of the king. Herod, who correctly perceives Aristobolus as a potential threat to his power, has him killed, disguising the murder as an accident. Sameas tries to stir the people of Judea to rebellion for religious reasons.

Alexandra now has the added motive of seeking to avenge her son's death, and she seeks to sow mistrust between Herod and the Romans by accusing her son-in-law of Aristobolus' murder; also, by hinting broadly at Mariamne's beauty, she hopes to appeal to the Roman triumvir Antonius' baser instincts, namely that after Herod's death, Mariamne would be a highly desirable widow. Herod is summoned before the triumvir. In his blind passion for Mariamne, and believing he cannot trust in her faithfulness after his death, Herod secretly orders Mariamne's death in the event of his own, i.e., his possible execution for the murder of the youth. His brother-in-law Josephus is given the order to kill her. Mariamne, however, remains loyal to her husband, in spite of the murder of her brother, Aristobolus, and in spite of a popular upheaval against Herod, instigated by Alexandra during his absence. When Mariamne learns from Josephus, however, that he has orders to execute her, she exclaims, "Das ist ein Frevel, wie's noch keinen gab" (That is a crime without precedent). Herod's sudden return—he had been amicably received by Antonius—leads to a confrontation between the couple.

When Herod discovers that Josephus has given away his secret he has him executed. He seeks in vain to justify his deed to Mariamne. Her humanity has been violated, and she says to Herod "Keiner will das Leben sich nehmen lassen als von Gott allein, der es gegeben hat" (No one wants to have his life taken except by God who gave it to him). Beyond that, doubt has been cast on Mariamne's honor as a wife and a woman. When Herod has to leave Jerusalem again, Mariamne wonders whether the previous insult had been inspired by "the fears of passion" in him or if his act was a revelation of his "innermost nature." Again, Herod places Mariamne "under the sword." This time it is his friend and confidant Soemus, governor of Galilee, who is to carry out the order. Soemus agrees to it merely in order to protect Mariamne more effectively. He does not intend to be used as Herod's tool, and like Mariamne, his "most sacred" feelings have been violated. This time Mariamne resolves to break with Herod, and she prepares a feast in order to do so in public. Upon his triumphant return—he is now king of Judaea and regent of Egypt—Herod is convinced of Mariamne's treason (his sister, Salome, accuses her of having prepared a feast to celebrate Herod's death) and her infidelity with the Roman captain Titus. Herod orders a trial. Mariamne refuses to defend herself; she has resolved to die. The judges try to save the last of the Maccabees. Before her death, Mariamne confides in Titus ("because you glimpsed a bit of our hell with equanimity") and makes him promise not to reveal anything until after her death. Herod is to be her executioner; that is why she gave the feast. If Herod had managed to control the demon in his soul, she would have for-

given him. "One human being may cause the death of another, but not even the most powerful can force the weakest among men to go on living." Titus would like to help, but he is bound by his word not to reveal her intentions. Only after Mariamne's execution does he tell Herod the true nature of Mariamne's behavior. Herod is a broken man. When the three wise men (kings) from the Orient arrive to announce the birth of a new "king of kings," Herod orders the death of all male infants in Bethlehem.

In keeping with Hegel's dialectics of history and aesthetics, the play ends on a conciliatory note. The arrival of the three wise men heralds the dawning of a new and more humane age that will synthesize the antithetical positions inherent in paganism and Judaism. Hebbel's adherence to Hegelian dialectics in locating the tragedy at a crisis point in the cultural history of the Occident does not signify his preference for Christianity as opposed to some other religion. He regarded its humanism as the touchstone of worth for any historical drama; and aware that he was competing with the famous Rückert, whose *Herod the Great* (1842) focused directly on the tragic aspects of the plot, he purposely sought to make his play more significant by emphasizing the overriding cultural aspects of the tragedy. The waning period of ancient Judaism and of Hellenism depicted in the tragedy has been and should be likened to the decline of our own cultural epoch. At the same time, the Roman republic is replaced by the Augustan empire, a fact that signals the arrival of the more stable order established by the emperor. In addition, the new order represents a transition to the Christianization of Rome that took place much later. The symbolic significance of the Roman captain Titus is precisely the greater stability represented by imperial Rome; it is he who catches the collapsing Herod after Herod has issued his infamous order to kill all the male infants of Bethlehem. With this symbolic gesture the tragedy ends.

Hebbel seeks to show how the religious and

political laws that govern the world also influence the private sphere of marriage. The rigidity of the Mosaic laws prevents Herod and Mariamne from relying on their love as a stable reality in their lives. "The Lord and the prophets are silent," say Mariamne; "we no longer know the way." Thus the declining Judaic order and Herod's dependence on his Roman masters cause both partners to be rigid in their attitudes, although Herod's share in the guilt for the tragic events may be greater than Mariamne's. Still, both are excessively proud and unyielding, and neither is controlled by social or political considerations that might have tempered their behavior. They are sitting on a volcano, as Hebbel put it.

If the tragedy as a genre was to be preserved, Hebbel felt he had to subordinate any realistic and psychological details (such as those in *Maria Magdalena*) to this abstract view of history; against this view as a backdrop the spectator was to ponder the subordination of the individual to the general (tragic) order of the universe. The open-ended, relativistic tragedy of the realists and naturalists no longer admitted of any such cosmic and grand vistas, because its underlying assumptions were based on the essentially materialistic nature of the universe and society. It was Hebbel's ambition to renew the ancient tradition of the Attic tragedy. The price he paid for his untimely ambition was the slight theatrical success of the play. *Herod and Mariamne* premiered in April 1849 at the Burgtheater in Vienna. Hebbel's wife, Christine, played Mariamne, a role he had intended for her when he created the character. Despite a stellar performance by Christine, the play did not meet with a warm reception, and to this day *Herod and Mariamne* lags far behind *Maria Magdalena* as a stage success.

Still in line with his theories on drama was Hebbel's next major effort, *Agnes Bernauer* (1852). It too is a religious drama, in keeping with Hegel's dictum that the basis of any tragedy must be metaphysical. This time however Hebbel wrote an "impure" historical drama, in that he had recourse to positive or material historical events rather than universal history as a reflection of the World Process. We know from his correspondence and his diaries that he hoped to gain access to the circle of literary neoclassicists around King Maximilian II of Bavaria and the rapidly rising court theater in Munich under the direction of Dingelstedt. To the same end he hoped to persuade Christine to resign from the Vienna theater and accept a position at the much less prestigious Munich stage. According to the playwright, this rapidly written prose play was to be "a modern Antigone." It is about the Wittelsbach dynasty and the marriage of the son of Duke Ernst to a commoner, Agnes Bernauer. As Friedrich Sengle in his recent Hebbel essay points out, Hebbel clearly sought to overwhelm the king and his coterie with a tragedy that was to demonstrate his sympathy with the restoration of aristocratic rule, albeit in the sense of medieval feudalism. But he was naive if he thought that Munich was the residence of a feudal lord rather than of an enlightened, constitutional monarch. In addition, he sought to rival Emanuel Geibel, the literary star of the neoclassical movement in Munich.

Agnes Bernauer, the beautiful daughter of a barber–surgeon in medieval Augsburg, is killed by Duke Ernst for reasons of state—that is, in order to prevent a civil war. Neither Herzog Ernst nor his son Albrecht (Agnes' husband), nor Agnes herself is intended to be a villain or legally and morally guilty. Agnes simply stands in the way of the World Process, which demands that the ruler fulfill his duties to the state. Since Agnes' beauty, innocence, and rightful claim to the rights and privileges of the wife of the heir to the ruler of Bavaria threaten to drive a wedge between the people and the dynasty (Albrecht was to marry a princess from Brunswick), and armed conflict threatens, the duke signs a death warrant: "In the name of the widows and orphans that would be created by war, in the name of the cities and towns that would be reduced to ashes, Agnes Bernauer be hanged!" After she is killed, Albrecht learns of this "legal" murder and is so outraged that he goes to war against his father. They meet on the battlefield. The duke now offers to acknowledge the dead Agnes as his son's legitimate wife and to celebrate a requiem mass for her "in order that the memory of the purest sacrifice ever made for the sake of necessity in the course of all ages may never die!" By making his son the judge of his actions and by abdicating the throne and retiring to a monastery, the father is reconciled with his son.

King Ludwig I of Bavaria, forced to abdicate himself amidst a scandal arising from his liaison with Lola Montez, whom he had tried to have elevated to the peerage, granted Hebbel an audience. Ironically, the former king was horror-struck by the cruelty of his medieval ancestor and told the playwright that he could never have contemplated the "legal" murder of another human being. Hebbel wrote to his wife that he replied, "but Your Majesty would have had to if You had been in power!" The Munich audience responded favorably to the play, partly because of the historical pomp and colorful setting provided by Dingelstedt.

To emphasize Hebbel's purpose once more: Agnes is guilty, not in a legal or moral sense but in a metaphysical sense. Her mere existence (her extraordinary beauty, which keeps Albrecht from his duties) disrupts the divine order of things. Agnes is compared to a perfect jewel that everyone wants to possess but that incites the worst passions in man and creates chaos. Her guilt is her existence. The world is imperfect and perfection cannot endure or be. Individual hubris (well-intentioned or evil) must not be tolerated in the scheme of things, because it brings forth its opposite. Hebbel wrote in his diary late in 1851: "I have wanted to portray the inevitable yet inadvertent demise of beauty from a tragic perspective for a long time, and Agnes Bernauer seemed ready-made for the purpose" (*Tagebücher*, 3.4941). Hebbel's sources were Konrad Mannert's *Geschichte Bayerns* (The History of Bavaria, 1826) and a dramatized ballad by Count von Törring-Cronsfeld, "Agnes Bernauerin" (1780). Neither source (nor the 1946 opera libretto by Carl Orff) condones or justifies the murder of Agnes, a solution that seems justifiable only in the context of Hegel's philosophy, whereby the state is entitled to demand the ultimate sacrifice. Thus Hebbel said that through this drama he wanted to "put up a cross for our old empire, slain in 1804 and buried in 1848" (letter to Franz Dingelstedt, 12 December 1851).

Following the performance of his play, Hebbel and his wife traveled to Venice and Milan. Earlier in 1851, before Hebbel had begun writing the Bernauer drama, he had been busy editing the complete works of the well-known physician, lyrical poet, and essayist Ernst Freiherr von Feuchtersleben (1806–1849). Hebbel's seven-volume edition was published in 1853. After his return from a trip to Hamburg and Helgoland later that same year Hebbel steeped himself in Goethe's classical dramas, especially *Iphigenia* (1787). At that point his attention was directed toward the legend of Gyges and Kandaules. His intention was to revive the tradition of the French theater in Germany, and he decided to base the idea for his latest tragedy on the accounts of Herodotus and Plato. From Herodotus he extracted the story; the ring episode was taken from Plato's *Republic* (ca. 410 B.C.); and Gyges and Rhodope were endowed with Oriental traits, for which the source was a book on Indian legends Hebbel had reviewed in 1848.

Although the drama is modeled on those of Jean Racine, the similarities between *Gyges and His Ring* (1854–1856) and Racine's plays are more superficial than profound. In a note appended to the list of characters—"the plot is pre-historic and mythical; it takes place within a period of two times twenty-four hours"—Hebbel makes an obvious reference to one of Aristotle's unities, practiced by Racine and the French classical theater. Again, however, it was Hebbel's ambition to prove that, like Schiller and Goethe, he could produce a synthesis of antiquity and modernity on the basis of what is applicable to all human beings. The conflict that could arise only at that point in history was to be solved in a generally human way, accessible to any and all times, according to the dramatist.

Written in blank verse, this five-act tragedy again dramatizes the conflict between the sexes, but this time on the basis of religion and custom. There are only three main characters: Kandaules, king of Lydia; Rhodope, his wife; and Gyges, a Greek. The young Gyges is the friend and guest of Kandaules. He wishes to participate in the impending cultic games of the Lydians; and as a sign of gratitude he offers Kandaules a precious ring, which has the magic power to make the wearer invisible. Kandaules and Rhodope are very different personalities. He is flexible, innovative, and a reformer; she hails from a place where "Indian and Greek customs" blend and where women—on pain of death—must not be seen except by their fathers and husbands. Rhodope is afraid of the ring and asks her husband to discard it or to give it to her. He is willing to accede to her wishes if she agrees to show herself in public on the occasion of the games. She refuses. When Gyges has won all the prizes, Kandaules notices his interest in Lesbia, a beautiful slave girl. He boasts to Gyges that he is in possession of an even more beautiful woman, namely his wife. His motive is to have the truth of this statement confirmed by someone else. The ring is to be used to accomplish this dangerous plan. When Gyges, himself invisible, glimpses the queen in her chambers, he is overwhelmed by her beauty and instantly falls in love with her. He deliberately makes himself visible for an instant, and the next day Rhodope is not sure what she has seen and heard but knows that something is wrong. She then resolves not to rest until she has found out what happened the previous night. Unlike Klara or Agnes, but like Mariamne, she has turned from a docile, passive figure into an avenging angel. She sends for Gyges. He indirectly confesses his love for her. She insists he must die. Kandaules enters at that moment. He will not accept Gyges' self-sacrifice. Rhodope changes her mind. She feels that Gyges has assumed the conjugal rights that her husband surrendered when he sent Gyges to her chambers. She demands Kandaules' death by Gyges' hand. They agree to a duel, although their friendship remains unimpaired. She will await the outcome at the altar of Hestia: if Kandaules wins she will kill herself; if Gyges returns she will marry him. Gyges prevails and returns to the altar, where Rhodope pledges herself to be Gyges' consort. Then she demands the "ring of death" from Gyges, who replies that it is still on the dead king's finger:

> Dann hat er schon den Platz, der ihm gebührt.
> Nun tritt zurück und halte Dein Gelübde,
> Wie ich das meinige! Ich bin entsühnt,
> Denn Keiner sah mich mehr, als dem es ziemte,
> Jetzt aber scheide ich mich so von Dir!

In that case it has found its proper place. Step back now and keep your vow as I am keeping mine! I have been cleansed, for no one has seen me except the one who had a right to, but now I am leaving you, thus!

she says, and stabs herself.

The conflict between husband and wife centers on Rhodope's strongly felt (or existential) adherence to custom and tradition and Kandaules' merely half-hearted acceptance of its meaning for her. The ring is the symbol of this fateful conflict and a gift of the gods. While Kandaules is only a half-hearted reformer, he nevertheless struggles with his guilt and finally acknowledges it. He realizes he challenged awesome forces when he used the ring for personal ends.

According to Hebbel, the central idea of the play is the violation or desecration of a time-honored custom. Kandaules, like Hebbel, and like other men in his dramas (Herod or Leonhard), is guilty of the sin of his sex, a failure to defend woman against defilement by men. Only in his defeat is Kandaules reconciled with the World Process, or Idea, because he has gained an understanding of his relationship to that Idea. This Idea implies pan-tragic (or existential) guilt through the inevitable separation of the individual from the whole, and therein lies the tragedy and "guilt" of Rhodope as well as of the others, brought on by their failure to grasp the workings of the World Process. At the core of the Idea, however, lies what Kandaules in his soliloquy toward the end of the fifth act calls "the sleep of the world." Having ignored what custom and tradition demand of Rhodope and attempted to be "modern" before the time is ripe, Kandaules has violated this "sleep." To effect radical change, as Heracles had done before him, he would have had to be much stronger. He should have recognized his weakness and hence he says: "and much too weak to equal him [Heracles], I weakened the foundations on which I stand and which now threaten vengefully to tear me down"; and that is as it should be "because the world needs its sleep like you [Gyges] and me," to recover from and to consolidate changes that took place at an earlier time. From this it is not difficult to understand Hebbel's attitude toward revolutionary change.

For example, he did not think that the revolutions of 1848 should have resulted in more than constitutional monarchy. He felt that the radical change demanded by the communists and socialists was premature. (Hebbel was a member of the delegation of Viennese writers dispatched to Innsbruck, where the royal family had fled, to persuade Archduke Johann of Hapsburg to accept the office of constitutional monarch.) Only if the new is stronger than the old does it have a right to supplant the old. He regarded the radical among the revolutionaries as sufficiently tainted and impure in the means to their ends to conclude that necessity demanded (as always) to submit to the will of the World Process (or God); and that meant only a small step forward: from absolutism to constitutionalism, preserving, though limiting, the rights of the ruling classes.

In much the same way, Hebbel restores the old order in the drama by making Gyges the instrument of the World Process through which it triumphs. This makes Gyges as tragic a figure as Rhodope, because he is the victim of what Hegel called "die List der Vernunft" (the cunning of reason) by which strategem universal history (the original Idea) works its way. Perhaps Rhodope is even less of a tragic figure than Gyges, because she adds a measure of personal guilt to her original sin of existence when she experiences feelings of love and affection for the man whose gaze has defiled her. In that sense—and given her background and extreme sensibilities—she has even broken faith with her husband. For to Rhodope, the basis of all morality, to which custom (*Sitte*) is tied, is religious; the enormity of Kandaules' and Gyges' deed becomes evident when one realizes that she feels the order of the world, as willed by the Gods, has been violated when her personal honor is desecrated.

Even Kandaules senses that Rhodope's demand for atonement is justified, because in the process she is never in doubt about her course of action. Kandaules now knows that he has no new and better values with which to replace the old. For Hebbel, the key word here is *Pietät* (reverence). He comments in his diary on pious respect for traditional values as follows:

When the ancients recognized that the orbit of tradition was not fully encompassed by positive laws and that an uncharted region remained, they invented the word "Pietät." This reverence is, like sleep, the main anchor of man as a moral being and can no more be replaced by laws than the latter can by food and drink.

(*Tagebücher* 3.4888)

The victory of the Idea in *Gyges and His Ring*, however, is achieved in a more realistic sense than is ordinarily the case with tragedy of the idealistic type. Hebbel points the way to a new age by devoting more attention to human psychology than to general cosmology. Psychologically, the character of Gyges is carefully developed—and Hebbel implies that universal change will come from a heightened consciousness (or rationality) and hence a more profound humanity. In that sense, he adhered to an idea dear to the realists of his day (to whom he was opposed in theory), namely the need for a more humane civilization. One way to reach this goal was to gain a deeper understanding of human psychology, of human motives and needs.

Gyges and His Ring could not be performed in the age of realism. Given his differences with the Young Germans in general—and one of their exponents, Heinrich Laube, the director of the Vienna Burgtheater, in particular—the playwright had to be content with the public reading of the drama in April 1855, which he undertook himself. The play did not premier until 1889, long after the death of its author.

Hebbel's most impressive work is his dramatic version of the most German of all legends, the heroic epic *The Lay of the Nibelungs.* His interest in the material dated from 1847, when he saw his wife in the role of Kriemhild in Ernst Raupach's dramatization of the epic. He began working on his own version in earnest in October 1855 and with many interruptions completed the drama at the end of 1860. Although there had been treatments of Germany's national epic before him by such notables as Raupach, Geibel, Friedrich Fouqué, and Wagner (portions of the *Ring*), Hebbel's *Die Nibelungen* was not only a great success on the stages of Weimar and Vienna, but the trilogy also helped establish Hebbel's national fame, albeit a somewhat fleeting fame that did not become an enduring one until this century. The staging of the drama at Vienna in 1863 was due to the great success of the Weimar performance, which helped thaw the icy atmosphere at the Burgtheater. The subtitle of the trilogy ("A German Tragedy in Three Parts") was aimed at the rising nationalism in all German-speaking countries, and his success with it as well as the unbroken popularity of the national myth from the time of Wagner to official Nazidom's enthusiasm for Wagner's *Der Ring des Nibelungen* confirm Hebbel's instincts in the matter. In post-war Germany *Die Nibelungen* has very rarely been staged. It finally received an avant garde and "de-nationalized" treatment in 1973, when the trilogy was staged in Cologne under the direction of Hansgünther Heyme.

Hebbel based his version on the Middle High German text of the *Nibelungenlied* as well as on the "Edda." He rejected the then popular theory of Karl Lachmann, according to which the epic consisted of multiple "songs" by several authors—"To trace the Nibelungs to many poets means to claim that an apple is not the product of a tree but of a forest" (*Tagebücher* 4.5582), wrote Hebbel. Concerning his own role, he compared himself to a watch repairman who cleans and adjusts a timepiece to ensure that it runs well and who therefore should not be confused with its maker; he is merely its caretaker.

Hebbel's absolute or metaphysical concept of guilt is also evident in this "eleven-act monster," as he called it. Moreover, and again in keeping with his Hegelian view of history, it brings into relief a point of crisis in the history of religion and culture when barbaric Germanic paganism yields to the considerably more civilized, monotheistic Christian view of the world. Again, as in *Gyges*, Hebbel sought—and, he felt, achieved—the creation of an entirely human and natural tragedy on the foundation of a purely mythical subject. Again, in Hegelian dialectic terms, the worlds of primitive Germanic myth (thesis) and Christianity (antithesis) are coequal in their right to exist (thesis and antitheses are necessarily parts of the truth, which is emergent, because "the whole truth" is not known, though the world is continuously evolving or moving toward it); and the clash of the two opposites produces a new and higher reality (synthesis). Together, they create a new world, as Hebbel wrote to Marie Sayn-Wittgenstein on 24 August 1858. The worlds represented in the Nibelungen myth are those of the primitive Norse gods and Siegfried, Brunhild, and Frigga, all of whom stand at the dawning of history; and of the heathen characters, the Burgundians, the Huns, and Kriemhild, whose lives are governed by loyalty, bravery, and revenge, the last of which necessarily brings about their downfall. Rüdeger, Dietrich von Bern, and the chaplain represent the emerging norms of Christianity: self-control, compassion, and forgiveness.

Hebbel's tragedy is in three parts. The first part, or prologue, entitled *Der gehörnte Siegfried* (*The Invulnerable Siegfried*) consists of one act. It is an example of Hebbel's familiar technique of analytical exposition combined here with action that anticipates further developments of the plot. Time and place are the sixth century A.D. at the court of King Gunther in Worms on the Rhine. The main characters are Gunther, king of the Burgundians; Hagen, the king's vassal; Dankwart, Hagen's brother; Volker, the minstrel; Giselher and Gerenot, Gunther's brothers and fellow kings; Siegfried; Ute, the Queen Mother; and Kriemhild, Gunther's sister (Ute's daughter).

Volker, the minstrel, tells the tale of Siegfried, the dragon slayer, who became invulnerable by bathing in the dragon's blood, and the tale of Brunhild, who lives "in the dark and distant north, where night never ends." "He who courts her, courts death." She lives protected by a sea of flames and any suitor is challenged to engage in deadly combat with the superhuman maiden. She has never been defeated in combat. Hearing about this invincible lady, Gunther resolves to make her his. As this point, Siegfried, "the hero of the Netherlands," arrives at the head of twelve armed men. After Siegfried, Gunther, his brothers, and Hagen have engaged each other in a contest to test their strength, with Siegfried emerging as the winner, Gunther persuades Siegfried to help him subdue Brunhild, so that she may become his betrothed. In return, Siegfried is allowed to marry Kriemhild, whose beauty has impressed the young hero and whose sentiments are returned by her, when she watches the contest from her window. Siegfried warns Gunther of the dangers of the undertaking, and he tells him about a previous encounter with Brunhild, whose beauty, to be sure, had left him unmoved; yet he also knows that of all men only he can conquer her. He is the possessor of Balmung, the magic sword that can extinguish the flames engulfing her castle, and he also possesses Alberich's cap of invisibility that can afford him entry without being seen. Finally, he possesses the treasure of the Nibelungs, making him very wealthy. The men enter into a secret pact, and Hagen reminds Gunther and Siegfried that death is the fourth and silent partner, because its secret must never be revealed.

The second part, *Siegfrieds Tod* (*Siegfried's Death*), is in five acts and takes place shortly after the time of the prologue in Isenland (Brunhild's abode), the Odenwald forest, and in the city of Worms. Frigga, Brunhild's nursemaid, reveals to her mistress what had hitherto been unknown to her, namely that Brunhild is descended from Norns (the goddesses of fate) and Valkyries and that she should be on her guard, because she senses great danger lying ahead. Brunhild, however, believes in a revelation according to which she will be "without fate, yet knowing about fate" and immune from death. But Brunhild is proven wrong. The Burgundians arrive with Siegfried being introduced to her as Gunther's vassal. The men succeed with their plan and Brunhild is taken to Worms. In order to subdue Brunhild for Gunther on their wedding night, Siegfried's help has to be enlisted again. In the course of their struggle, Siegfried wrests a belt from Brunhild and tucks it away in his shirt. Kriemhild, who became his wife after Siegfried's return from Isenland, discovers the belt and demands to known how it has come into his possession. Almost absentmindedly, he reveals the secret. Kriemhild's jealousy is aroused, and she cannot keep the secret either. In a public confrontation with Brunhild in front of the steps of the cathedral, Kriemhild calls her her husband's mistress. Brunhild, who has lost her superhuman powers, believes Gunther to be the strongest man on earth. Realizing that she has been deceived, Brunhild seeks revenge, "because I was not good enough to be Siegfried's wife, merely good enough to be the penny that bought him one." Hagen, as Gunther's loyal follower and also envious of Siegfried's power, agrees that the terms of the pact have been violated and that he will be Siegfried's executioner. Pretending to be concerned about her husband's safety, Hagen contrives to have Kriemhild reveal to him her husband's vulnerable spot, left when a leaf from a linden tree dropped on his back while bathing in the blood of the slain dragon. On a hunt in the Odenwald, Hagen thrusts his lance in Siegfried's back. When Siegfried's body lies in state in the cathedral, his wound begins to bleed when Hagen passes by the bier. Kriemhild accuses him of the murder of her husband. Hagen, unconcerned about the accusation, removes Balmung, the sword, from Siegfried's body. Kriemhild is outraged by this added insult and vows to avenge her husband's murder even if it means dragging down the house of Burgundy with her.

The third part, *Kriemhilds Rache* (*Kriemhild's Revenge*) also is in five acts. It takes place a few years later in the city of Worms, on the banks of the Danube, and at King Etzel's court. Etzel, king of the Huns, sends an emissary to Worms, Margrave Rüdeger, to ask for Kriemhild's hand in marriage. At first, she refuses. However, upon learning that Hagen also had advised against this marriage, she changes her mind. After an unsuccessful attempt to persuade her brother, the king, to bring Hagen to trial for Siegfried's murder, she agrees to the marriage with Etzel on one condition. She extracts a promise of unconditional loyalty from Rüdeger and, through him, from Etzel as well. Rüdeger agrees. Kriemhild's brothers do not accompany her to Etz-

el's castle. Seven years later, however, the Burgundians set out to visit Kriemhild. After a sojourn at Bechlaren on the Danube, Rüdeger's castle, where Giselher is married to Gudrun, Rüdeger's daughter, and where Hagen has a vision of the impending doom of the Burgundians, Gunther and his retinue arrive at Etzel's court in Vienna. Since Kriemhild has borne Etzel a son and heir, the king of the Huns is willing to give her wish for revenge free rein, although he would have preferred to meet the Burgundians in open combat. But Kriemhild demands "a murder for a murder," and is especially intent on having Hagen killed. A terrible blood bath ensues in the course of which even Otnit, Kriemhild's and Etzel's young son, is beheaded by Hagen. Gunther's vassal is captured and brought before Kriemhild. She demands to know where the Nibelung treasure is buried. He replies that as long as one of the Burgundian kings is still alive, he will not reveal the secret. Kriemhild has her last surviving brother, Gunther, killed. Hagen now rejoices in the knowledge that only he and God share in the secret of the hidden treasure, whereupon Kriemhild kills him with Balmung, Siegfried's magic sword. The ancient Hildebrant, loyal follower to Dietrich von Bern, now has had enough and kills Kriemhild on the spot. Shaken to his depths, Etzel hands the reins of government to Dietrich von Bern, who in turn assents "in the name of Him who died on the cross."

Hebbel's major change from the epic has once again to do with conflict between the sexes. This time, he illuminates the mythical through the legendary and human spheres. Brunhild and Siegfried belong to the mythical realm. Hebbel neither could nor would invest the characters of the ancient lay with psychological realism, but he tried to show a connection between human reason and conscience and the ultimate reason for all things (God). Siegfried and Brunhild are thus tied together. After her betrothal to Gunther, she returns from the world of man to the mythical realm when she ponders why Siegfried took Kriemhild rather than her, when, according to a prophecy, he had always been destined to be hers. Siegfried explains to the kings of Burgundy that when he first saw Brunhild in her castle on Isenland he was unmoved by her beauty; and he felt that he must not court whom he could not love. In the world of human conventions, Siegfried's attitude is praiseworthy, but in the mythical sphere (or irrational, primordial religious sphere) he has committed a grave sin. In the latter respect the two figures belong together, and he should have recognized Brunhild as preordained for him and loved her as such.

Moreover, he compounds his sin of omission by one of commission: he uses his mysterious powers to subdue Brunhild for Gunther in order that she may serve as the pathway to the possession of Kriemhild. Again, the cardinal sin of the male, of Siegfried, Holofernes, Herod, Kandaules, or even of Hebbel himself against Elise Lensing, is to have misjudged the nature of woman and to have degraded her by reducing her to the status of object. It has its ultimate foundation in the realm of primordial myth, the prehistoric time of the beginning of the separation of the world from its origin. Thus the guilt incurred by Siegfried and Gunther is metaphysical or absolute. Only through the promise of a more humane state of the world, figured in the abdication of Etzel, is the endless chain of bloody revenge broken and does the guilt of Siegfried assume another dimension: the world has now progressed toward a state where reverence for life and respect for mutual humanity will prevent the sexes from misapprehending each other's natures.

Perhaps the greatest compliment paid Hebbel's *Nibelungs* in recent times is Friedrich Sengle's statement that this dramatic work signifies a historic moment at which the German nation was just as strong by virtue of its moderation as by virtue of its power. It represented not only a moment of national maturity but also a personal triumph for the playwright, who was always riven by internal conflict. Even his arch literary rival, the cofounder of "programmatic realism," Julian Schmidt, conceded Hebbel's greatness after he had read the tragedy. Hebbel's artistic mastery had finally been acknowledged by friend and foe alike, contributing much to his satisfaction and inner peace.

Much of what Hebbel wrote apart from his poems and major dramas, such as his two mediocre comedies (*Der Rubin* [1849] and *Der Diamant* [1847]), his critical essays and literary reviews, various dramatic fragments, and one opera libretto, are of interest only to the specialist, although his entire literary production reflects his humanism, his desire to further a more humane world in his own time in any and all ways open to him.

As to his prose fiction, short stories all, it must be said that they cannot compete with the short fiction of Hebbel's major contemporaries. Even "Anna" (1847) and "Die Kuh" ("The Cow" [1849]) do not compare favorably with other Gothic literature of the time. Within Hebbel's oeuvre as a whole, his short fiction may at best be regarded as experimental. As a prose piece his autobiographical sketch, "Recollections of My Childhood," is certainly superior to his prose fiction, which is lacking in atmosphere and immediacy. In fact the writer himself regarded his autobioical fragment as the best piece of writing he had ever done.

III

While Hebbel was occupied with his Nibelungen drama, he sporadically worked on a epic poem, *Mutter und Kind (Mother and Child)*, whose beginnings date from 1847, the first year of his marriage. He took up work on the verse tale in 1856 and finished it in March the following year. It was not published until the end of 1858, shortly after the publication of his collected poems. This epic, written in hexameters and modeled on Goethe's famous idyl *Hermann und Dorothea* (1797), was awarded the Tiedge Prize as the best of its kind in the Goethe tradition. This poem, as well as some of his plays, brought him to the attention of the grand duke Alexander of Weimar and his circle, in particular Princess Caroline Sayn-Wittgenstein and her daughter Marie. Marie and the playwright became lasting friends and entered into a correspondence that dealt primarily with Hebbel's works but also with discussions of literature in general. He relied on her criticism a great deal, and she was the first to receive the unpublished Nibelungen manuscript. The grand duke too held Hebbel in high esteem; he thought his *Nibelungs* the equal of the works of Schiller and Goethe.

Long before Hebbel, the son of a lowly bricklayer, had reached such dizzying social heights and artistic recognition, he had been a writer of poems, of which *Mother and Child* was to be the last, if one disregards the many intensely lyrical passages of his last verse drama, *The Nibelungs. Mother and Child* is set in Hebbel's native region, mostly Hamburg. It is the tale of a wealthy merchant and his wife who more than anything else in the world want to have a child. When they hear of Christian and Magdalena, who are unable to marry for lack of money, they agree to set up the younger couple on a farm in return for their first-born baby. When the baby is born, however, the young mother cannot give it up. Christian and Magdalena return the farm to the merchant and attempt to leave for America. When the merchant and his wife hear about the young couple's plight, they send word through former acquaintances that they no longer lay claim to the child. When the couples meet again Christian and Magdalena are no longer bound by any contract regarding the child, but they also have ownership of the farm restored to them. The merchant's wife is cured of her excessive desire for a child, and she and her husband exert their energies helping the poor instead. The poem was undoubtedly inspired by Hebbel's love for Christine,

his own youth, and his classicist ambitions, which included the artistic expression of his sense of humanity. The positive, noble, and idealistic characters did not fail to impress his readers, and the poem was hailed by critics and the reading public alike.

Hebbel's first collection of lyrics appeared in 1842, followed by *Neue Gedichte* (New Poems) in 1847; his own rearrangement of all his poetry into cycles was published in 1857. In a sense, Hebbel's poetic production was a part of his entire life, covering his youth to the year of his death. The critical evaluation of his poetry has by and large focused on a comparison with the lyrical tradition begun by Goethe (the lyric of the private experience) and the realism period at mid-century, exemplified above all by Theodor Storm. In such comparisons Hebbel's poetry must of necessity appear flawed. On the other hand, Friedrich Hebbel's and Eduard Mörike's epigrams represent the culmination of didactic poetry in the German literature of the century. A lyrical canon for his shorter verse has evolved over the decades; it reflects a romantic and Goethean orientation. The early Hebbel was undoubtedly influenced by the romantics and some of the poems in the canon, such as "Herbstbild" ("Autumn Picture," 1852), "Sommerbild" ("Summer Picture," 1844), "Nachtlied" ("Night Song," 1836), and "Sie sehn sich nicht wider" ("The Swans," 1841), reflect this influence. The range of Hebbel's poems is indeed remarkable. He experimented with many sounds and rhythms; his emotional palette ranged from happy and serene to sad and sarcastic tones, from the pure lyric in the folksong tradition to the intellectual and reflective poem. As a dramatist—and like Grillparzer—his dialectical bent found its expression in epigrammatic statements as well as in the sudden appearance of reflection in the midst of an idyllic or otherwise sense-oriented poem. Metrically, trochees and dactyls (as "classical" and relatively somber and stately measures) predominate, and among the strophic forms there are more sonnets than any other; with the epigrams, the distich is the dominant form.

It is hardly surprising that Hebbel's ideological or profoundly metaphysical inclinations should be reflected in his lyrics. His tendency toward symbolism and abstraction is in fact an anticipation of a trend at the end of the nineteenth century, exemplified by such symbolist poets as Stefan George, Rainer Maria Rilke, and Hugo von Hofmannsthal.

It has been pointed out that Hebbel also shows a preference for the lyrical address in the manner of an ode. A well-known epigram is his "An den Tragiker" (To the Tragedian, 1858), which, not surprisingly, is frequently quoted. Its distichs, with occasional rhymes at the caesura, are the stately habit for this poem about the highest calling in the poet's (and Hegel's) view:

Packe den Menschen, Tragöde, in jener erhabenen
    Stunde,
Wo ihn die Erde entläßt, weil er den Sternen
    verfällt,
Wo das Gesetz, das ihn selbst erhält, nach
    gewaltigem Kampfe
Endlich den höheren weicht, welches die Welten
    regiert,
Aber ergreife den Punct, wo beide noch streiten
    und hadern,
Daß er dem Schmetterling gleicht, wie er der
    Puppe entschwebt

> Grip, tragedian, your fellow man, in that solemn hour/ when the earth lets go of him, because he is struck by the stars,/ where the law that sustains him—after a mighty struggle—finally yields to something higher that governs the worlds,/ but seize the point where both still struggle and fight/ that he resemble the butterfly as it drifts off from its cocoon.

Some of his epigrams are satirical and center on the subject of literature. As a group they represent some of his aesthetic views, as for example, "Bilderpoesie" (Image or Genre Poesy, reflecting his rejection of this literary trend of his day as a fragmented view of reality); "Die Secundairen" (1857, the critics are second to the artists); or "Meister und Pfuscher" (Masters and Quacks, reflecting his intolerance of mediocrity in literature).

Among his ballads, "Schön Hedwig" (Beautiful Hedwig, 1839) has long been accepted as one of his better ones, as well as "Der Bramine" (The Brahman, 1863), which dates from the last year of his life. It has been noted of his ballads in particular that they are of biographical interest because of their confessional character: from the angst of his early years expressed in "Der Heideknabe" (The Boy of the Moor, 1844; set to music by Robert Schumann) to the confident and serene acceptance of the world seen in "Der Bramine," and "Gmunden, in schweren Leiden, 22. Juli. 1863" (Gmunden, Severely Stricken, 22 July 1863). It should not be overlooked, of course, that "Der Heideknabe" is also a ballad indebted to romantic gothicism and Uhland.

As an example of Hebbel's intellectual lyric, the sonnet "Welt und Ich" (The World and I, 1841), which is included in the canon, should be cited. The strophic form of the sonnet, with its inherent antithetical structure, is well suited to its philosophical metaphors:

Im ungeheuren Ozeane
Willst du, der Tropfe, dich in dich verschließen?
So wirst du nie zur Perl' zusammenschießen,
Wie dich auch Fluten schütteln und Orkane!

Nein! öffne deine innersten Organe
Und mische dich in Leiden und Genießen
Mit allen Strömen, die vorüberfließen;
Dann dienst du dir und dienst dem höchsten
    Plane.

Und fürchte nicht, so in die Welt versunken,
Dich selbst und Dein Ur-Eignes zu verlieren:
Der Weg zu dir führt eben durch das Ganze!

Erst wenn du kühn von jedem Wein getrunken,
Wirst du die Kraft in tiefsten Innern spüren,
Die jedem Sturm zu stehn vermag im Tanze!

In the immense ocean/ you, the drop, desire to be enclosed within yourself?/ Thus you will never be a pearl/ No matter how much shaken by floods and hurricanes!/ No! you must open up all your senses/ and mingle in sorrow and joy with all the streams which pass./ Then, you will serve yourself and the ultimate purpose./ And thus immersed in the world, do not fear/ to lose yourself and what is uniquely yours:/ The pathway to yourself must lead through the Whole!/ Only when you have partaken of every wine,/ Will you sense the power deep down,/ which is able to endure any raging storm!

The playwright's penchant for dialogue and abstract argument is evident in the rhetorical questions and in the metaphysical basis of this poem, which lies in the separation between the whole and the individual, a dualism that underlines his concept of tragedy.

A similar idea is expressed much more lyrically in the short iambic verses "Ich und Du" (I and Thou, 1843; dedicated to "the noble Oehlenschläger in veneration and friendship"), combining the lyrical song of experience (relatively rare with the poet, but a part of the canon) with the reflective depth of the intellecutal lyric:

> Wir träumten voneinander
> Und sind davon erwacht,
> Wir leben, um uns zu lieben,
> Und sinken zurück in die Nacht.
>
> Du tratst aus meinem Traume,
> Aus deinem trat ich hervor,
> Wir sterben, wenn sich eines
> Im andern ganz verlor.
>
> Auf einer Lilie zittern
> Zwei Tropfen, rein und rund,
> Zerfliessen in eins und rollen
> Hinab in des Kelches Grund.

We dreamed of one another/ And it awakened us/ We live to love each other/ And fall back into the night./ You stepped from my dream/ And I from yours/ We die once one is lost completely within the other./ Upon a lily quiver/ two droplets, pure and round/ they merge and roll off/ into the bottom of its cup.

The allegorical conclusion—the transformation of the two selves into droplets—is typical of Hebbel and the Biedermeier period. The metaphor is even more pronounced in the following, often quoted, hymnlike free verse poem, "Gebet" (Prayer, 1843):

> Die du über die Sterne weg
> Mit der geleerten Schale
> Aufschwebst, um sie am ewigen Born
> Eilig wieder zu füllen:
> Einmal schwenke sie noch, O Glück,
> Einmal, lächelnde Göttin!
> Sieh, ein einziger Tropfen hängt
> Noch verloren am Rande,
> Und der einzige Tropfen genügt,
> Eine himmlische Seele,
> Die hier unten in Schmerz erstarrt,
> Wieder in Wonne zu lösen.
> Ach, sie weint dir süsseren Dank,
> Als die anderen alle,
> Die du glücklich und reich gemacht;
> Laß ihn fallen, den Tropfen!

You who ascend beyond the stars
With the empty cup
To replenish it hurriedly
from the eternal source:
Tip it one more time, oh fortune.
One time, smiling Goddess!
Behold, a single drop is clinging
Forlorn to the rim,
And this single drop suffices
To free blissfully
A heavenly soul
That is frozen in pain here below.
Alas, it will weep for you in sweeter gratitude
Than all the others,
Whom you have made happy and rich;
Let it fall, your drop!

These verses in the form of the customary Biedermeier prayer—a substitute for the ode and hymn of earlier periods and of antiquity—despite the free verse form, have a classical ring, perhaps in the manner of Schiller and the early Goethe. This classical quality is not only a function of subject matter and a solemn, declamatory style, but also of the weighty trochees interspersed with dactyls in each line, a hallmark of Hebbel. The allegorical significance of these verses with their apostrophe to Fortuna instead of God is contained with typical Biedermeier moderation in the image of the drop (no mortal should wish for more than that, because he does not need more than a drop from the cup of good fortune). The allegory of the goddess of fortune is within the rhetorical tradition of the seventeenth century, which still reverberates in the poetic imagery of the prerealistic mid-nineteenth century. Thus the appearance of a pagan goddess was not felt to be in conflict with the Christian tenets of the period, quite apart from the fact that Hebbel was not a practicing Christian but had a more abstract (Hegelian) concept of the Divinity. Indeed, there are signs that Hebbel, who was strongly influenced by Feuerbach's materialism in his youth, did not feel it to be contradictory to take a biological and generally Darwinian view of material reality. Hence it would have been out of character for him to address a prayer (even an allegorical one) to "his" God. This "Gebet," then, is an example of the Biedermeier tradition of the allegorical apostrophe, which Hebbel would have denied being a part of because he rejected the genre as narrow and insignificant. The poem was composed in 1843 and sent to Elise Lensing with the remark that he had thought of her when he wrote it because "du bist so leicht zufrieden gestellt" (you are so easily satisfied). "Auch ich bin genügsam, Gott ist mein Zeuge" (I too am frugal as God is my witness), he hastens to add (*Werke* 7.297).

We conclude with an even earlier poem, dating from the end of 1836, that seems to summarize Hebbel's humanism and that typifies his thoughts and feelings. He calls it "Höchstes Gebot" (Ultimate Commandment). It is an exhortation to all men and especially to himself. He was twenty-three when he wrote it.

Hab' Achtung vor dem Menschenbild,
Und denke, daß, wie auch verborgen,
Darin für irgendeinen Morgen
Der Keim zu allem Höchsten schwillt!

Hab' Achtung vor dem Menschenbild
Und denke, daß, wie tief er stecke,
Ein Hauch des Lebens, der ihn wecke,
Vielleicht aus deiner Seele quillt!

Hab' Achtung vor dem Menschenbild!
Die Ewigkeit hat eine Stunde,
Wo jegliches dir eine Wunde
Und, wenn nicht die, ein Sehnen stillt!

Respect the image of man!/ And consider that no matter how concealed/ in it for some tomorrow/ a germ of the highest promise is growing./ Respect the image of man/ And consider, that no matter how deeply concealed/ a breath of life that may awaken it/ May come from your soul!/ Respect the image of man!/ Eternity has an hour/ When everything may heal a wound/ And if not that/ may satisfy a longing!

Hebbel wrote:

This poem, composed on New Year's Eve, I am setting down in my journal, because for me it is ethically an epoch. It is the standard by which I shall live. But what good is it to call oneself a sinner if one doesn't stop sinning, and that is the case with me. Nothing assails the inviolability of a person more than my shabby sensitivity which oversteps all bounds, because he can neither protect nor defend himself against it, since he thinks he has to be considerate toward an illness or a neurosis.

(*Tagebücher* 1.576)

A year later, in February 1838, he wrote to Elise Lensing: "Only when the individual embraces all mankind as he normally would a chosen individual, has he completed the circle that was prescribed for him. All that is in my poem: Höchstes Gebot" (*Werke* 7.287–288). Hebbel's remorse, but also his high ambition to develop into a truly civilized man, are evident from these lines. The combination of a practical and idealistic humanism (the poem and his commentary) is characteristic of the poet's code of ethics, which he wished to govern his own behavior, both public and private, and which provided the basis for the conflict in his major tragedies, from *Judith* to *The Nibelungs.*

Selected Bibliography

EDITIONS

INDIVIDUAL WORKS

Geschichte des dreizigjährigen Kriegs. Hamburg, 1840.

Geschichte des Jungfrau von Orleans. Hamburg, 1840.

Judith. Eine Tragödie in fünf Acten. Hamburg, 1841.

Genoveva. Eine Tragödie in fünf Acten. Hamburg, 1843.

Mein Wort über das Drama. Eine Erwiderung an Professor Heiberg in Kopenhagen. Hamburg, 1843.

Maria Magdalene. Ein bürgerliches Trauerspiel in drei Acten. Hamburg, 1844.

Maria Magdalene. Ein burgerliches Trauerspiel in drei Akten. Nebts einem Vorwort, betreffend das Verhältnis der dramatischen Kunst sur Zeit und verwandte Punkte von Friedrich Hebbel. Hamburg, 1844.

Der Diamant. Eine Kömedie in fünf Acten. Hamburg, 1847.

"Über den Styl des Dramas." In H. Th. Rötscher, ed., *Jahrbücher für dramatische Kunst und Literatur* 1:35–40 (1847).

"Wie verhalten sich im Dichter Kraft und Erkenntnis zu einander?" In H. Th. Rötscher, ed., *Jahrbücher für dramatische Kunst und Literatur* 1:310–313 (1847).

Herodes und Mariamne. Eine Tragödie in fünf Acten. Vienna, 1850.

Julia. Ein Trauerspiel in drei Acten. Vienna, 1851.

"Abfertigung eines ästhetischen Kannegießers." *Julia.* Leipzig, 1851.

Michel Angelo. Ein Drama in zwei Acten. (Manuscript für Bühnen.) Leipzig, 1851.

Der Rubin. Ein Märchen-Lustspiel in drei Acten. Leipzig, 1851.

"Aus meiner Jugend." *Unterhaltungen am häuslichen Herd* 2.40:625–626 (1854).

Agnes Bernauer. Ein deutsches Trauerspiel in fünf Aufzugen. Vienna, 1855.

Erzählungen und Novellen. Pest, 1855. Stories and novellas collected from various journals, where they had first appeared between 1841 and 1849.

Gyges und sein Ring. Eine Tragödie in fünf Acten. Vienna, 1856.

Gedichte. Gesammt-Ausgabe, stark verbesseret und vermehrt. Stuttgart and Augsburg, 1857. Dedicated to "dem ersten Dichter der Gegenwart: Ludwig Uhland."

Mutter und Kind. Ein Gedicht in sieben Gesägen. Hamburg, 1859.

Die Nibelungen. Ein deutsches Trauerspiel in drei Abteilungen. Parts 1 and 2: *Der gehörnte Siegfried* and *Siegfrieds Tod.* Hamburg, 1862. Part 3: *Kriemhilds Rache.* Vienna, 1862.

Demetrius. Eine Tragödie. Hamburg, 1864.

Tagebücher. Edited by Felix Bamberg. 2 vols. Berlin, 1885–1887.

Briefwechsel mit Freunden und berühmten Zeitgenossen. Edited by Felix Bamberg. 2 vols. Berlin, 1890–1892.

Hebbel-Dokumente. Edited by Rudolf Kardel. Heide, 1931.

Briefe an Friedrich Hebbel. I: 1840–1860; II: 1861–1863. Edited by Moriz Enzinger and Elisabeth Bruck. Vienna, 1973–1975.

Friedrich Hebbel: Briefe. Edited by Henry Gerlach. Heidelberg, 1975.

Briefe von und an Friedrich Hebbel. Edited by Henry Gerlach. Heidelberg, 1978.

COLLECTED WORKS

Sämtliche Werke. Historisch-Kritische Ausgabe. Edited by Richard Maria Werner. 24 vols. Berlin, 1901–1907. Vols. 1–12: *Werke;* Vols. 13–15: *Tagebücher;* Vols. 17–24: *Briefe.* Reprinted Bern, 1968–.

Werke. Edited by Gerhard Fricke, Werner Keller, and Karl Pörnbacher. 5 vols. Munich, 1963–1967.

TRANSLATIONS

Agnes Bernauer. A German Tragedy in Five Acts. Translated by Bayard Q. Morgan. New York, 1958. Typescript on microfilm at Columbia University.

"Anna." Translated by Frances H. King. In *The German Classics of the Nineteenth and Twentieth Centuries: Masterpieces of German Literature Translated into English.* Edited by Kuno Francke and William Howard. 20 vols. New York, 1914. Reprinted New York, 1969. Vol. 9, pp. 166–173.

"Aphorisms on Art and Aphorisms on the Drama." Translated by Ludwig Lewisohn. In his *A Modern Book of Criticism.* New York, 1919. Pp. 41–44.

"Autumn Picture." Translated by Alma Hoernecke. *Poet Lore* 52:352 (1946).

"Extracts from the Journal of Friedrich Hebbel." Translated by Frances H. King. In *German Classics . . .*, above. Vol. 9, pp. 255–267.

German Lyrics and Ballads Done into English Verse. Edited by Daisy Broicher. London, 1912. Pp. 50–59. Contains eight poems by Hebbel: "The Swans," "Picture of Summer," "Picture from Reichenau," "The Blessed Hour," "Proverbs and Parables," "Enlightenment," "Requiem," and "The Last Tree."

The Genius of the German Theater. Edited by Martin Esslin. New York, 1968. Contains extracts from essays by Hebbel.

Herod and Mariamne. Translated by Paul H. Curts. Chapel Hill, N.C., 1950.

Judith. A Tragedy in Five Acts. Translated by Carl Van Doren. Boston, 1914.

"Ludolf Wienbarg's 'The Dramatists of the Present Day.'" Translated by Frances H. King. In *The German Classics . . .*, above. Vol. 9, pp. 200–208.

Maria Magdalena. Translated by Carl R. Mueller. San Francisco, 1962.

"My View on the Drama." Translated by Moody Campbell. In *Hebbel, Ibsen and the Analytic Exposition.* Edited by Thomas M. Campbell. Heidelberg, 1922. Pp. 78–85.

The Nibelungs. A Tragedy in Three Parts. Translated by Bayard Q. Morgan. New York, 1958. Typescript on microfilm at Columbia University.

"On Theodor Korner and Heinrich von Kleist." Translated by Frances H. King. In *The German Classics . . .*, above. Vol. 9, pp. 174–199.

Poems. Edited by Henry Losch. Philadelphia, 1913. P. 176. A poem by Hebbel, "Man."

"The Prince of Homburg, or the Battle of Fehrbellin." Translated by Frances H. King. In *The German Classics . . .*, above. Vol. 9, pp. 174–199.

"Preface to *Maria Magdelene.*" Translated by M. Campbell. In *Hebbel, Ibsen and the Analytic Exposition*, above. Pp. 78–85. Abridged.

"Recollections of My Childhood." Translated by Frances H. King. In *The German Classics . . .*, above. Vol. 9, pp. 221–254.

Three Plays. Translated by L. H. Allen (*Gyges and His Ring, Herod and Mariamne*) and Barker Fairley (*Maria Magdalena*). New York, 1914. Everyman's Library.

Three Plays by Hebbel. Translated by Marion W. Sonnenfeld. Lewisburg, Pa., 1974. Contains *Judith, Herod and Mariamne, Gyges and His Ring,* excerpts from "My View on the Drama," and introductions to translations.

BIOGRAPHICAL AND CRITICAL STUDIES

Alt, Arthur Tilo. "Die kritische Rezeption Friedrich Hebbels in den USA." In *Hebbel Jahrbuch 1978*: 163–180.

Bornstein, Paul. *Friedrich Hebbels Persönlichkeit.* 2 vols. Berlin, 1924.

Campbell, Thomas. *The Life and Works of Friedrich Hebbel.* Boston, 1919.

Flygt, Sten. *Friedrich Hebbel.* New York, 1968. Twayne World Authors Series, 56.

Graham, Paul. *The Relation of Drama to History in the Works of Friedrich Hebbel. Smith College Studies in Modern Languages* 15 (1933–1934).

————. "The Principle of Necessity in Hebbel's Theory of Tragedy." *Germanic Review* 15:258–262 (1940).

————. "Hebbel's Study of *King Lear.*" *Essays Contributed in Honor of President William Allan Neilson. Smith College Studies in Modern Languages* 21: 81–90 (1939–1940).

Hewett-Thayer, Harvey. "Ludwig Tieck and Hebbel's Tragedy of Beauty." *Germanic Review* 2:16–25 (1927).

Issacs, Edith. "Concerning the Author of *Herod and Mariamne.*" *Theatre Arts Monthly* 22:886–890 (1938).

Kreuzer, Helmut, ed. *Hebbel in neuer Sicht.* Stuttgart, 1963.

Kuh, Emil. *Biographie Friedrich Hebbels.* 2 vols. Vienna and Leipzig, 1877. 3rd ed., 1912.

Liepe, Wolfgang. "Ideology Underlying the Writings of Friedrich Hebbel." *American Philosophical Society Year Book 1953.* Philadelphia, 1954. Pp. 221–225.

Lütkehaus, Ludger. "Hebbel in historischer Sicht. Zum gegenwärtigen Stand der Hebbel-Forschung." In Hilmar Grundmann, ed., *Friedrich Hebbel. Neue studien zu Werk und Wirkung.* Heide, 1982. Pp. 13–29.

Meetz, Anni. *Friedrich Hebbel.* Stuttgart, 1962. 2nd ed., 1965.

Müller, Joachim. *Das Weltbild Friedrich Hebbels.* Halle, 1955.

Purdie, Edna. *Friedrich Hebbel: A Study of His Life and Work.* London, 1932.

Sengle, Friedrich. *Biedermeierzeit.* Vol. 3: *Die Dichter.* Stuttgart, 1980. Pp. 332–414.

Wiese, Benno von. *Die deutsche Tragödie von Lessing bis Hebbel.* 2 vols. Hamburg, 1948. Vol. 2, pp. 334–461.

Wright, James. "Hebbel's Klara: The Victim of a Division in Allegiance and Purpose." *Monatshefte* 38:304–316 (1946).

BIBLIOGRAPHIES

Gerlach, Henry. "Hebbel-Bibliographie 1970–1980." *Hebbel Jahrbuch 1983.* Pp. 157–189.

Hebbel-Bibliographie. Ein Versuch. Edited by Hans Wütschke. Berlin, 1910.

Hebbel-Bibliographie 1910–1970. Edited by Henry Gerlach. Heidelberg, 1973.

ARTHUR TILO ALT

SØREN KIERKEGAARD

(1813–1855)

KIERKEGAARD'S THREE CHIEF BODIES OF LITERATURE

MOST OF SØREN Kierkegaard's best-known books were published in Danish during a three-year period at an astonishing rate, beginning with the two large volumes entitled *Either/Or*, published in February 1843, and ending with his most important philosophical work, the massive *Concluding Unscientific Postscript*, which appeared in February 1846. The other well-known works published during this period were *Fear and Trembling* and *Repetition* (1843), *Philosophical Fragments* and *The Concept of Anxiety* (1844), and *Stages on Life's Way* (1845). Kierkegaard published other works in these years, but this group of seven books makes up a distinct body of work, which Kierkegaard called his "authorship." Rather than publishing them under his own name, Kierkegaard supplied whimsical pseudonyms for each. For example, one Vigilius Haufniensis is listed as the author of *The Concept of Anxiety*, while the author of *Repetition* is named, repetitiously enough, Constantin Constantius. Each of the three parts of *Stages on Life's Way* has its own pseudonymous author, while the whole work is edited by a certain Hilarius Bookbinder. Kierkegaard's name does not appear at all on the title pages of most of these works, but the two explicitly philosophical works, *Philosophical Fragments* and *Conclud-*ing Unscientific Postscript*, both attributed to Johannes Climacus, list S. Kierkegaard as "responsible for publication." Some of the works are novelistic in form, others more discursive; but there is a continuity of theme among them, and a pronounced psychological interest.

While Kierkegaard was composing this substantial pseudonymous authorship, he began producing a "second literature," very different in tone and intent, which he called "upbuilding" (*opbyggelig*, sometimes translated "edifying"). At first he published small volumes containing from two to five brief "Upbuilding Discourses," often on the same date as one of the pseudonymous works. The themes of the upbuilding literature are ethical and religious. The discourses resemble sermons, not only in their use of biblical texts, but also in their homiletic style, directly addressing the reader in the second person. They differ from sermons, however, in being addressed to readers rather than to listeners, to the individual rather than to a congregation. That is a point of some importance to Kierkegaard. Morally and spiritually decisive steps, he thought, can only be taken by persons singled out in their individuality, who take personal responsibility for these steps. He, for his part, took personal responsibility for the discourses by signing his own name to them.

As the pseudonymous authorship drew to a close, the upbuilding literature increased. It also grew more and more transparently Christian in its assumptions. Besides further collections of short discourses, Kierkegaard began publishing substantial books in the upbuilding mode: *Upbuilding Discourses in Various Spirits*, including *Purity of Heart Is to Will One Thing* and *The Gospel of Suffering* (1847); *Works of Love* (1847); *Christian Discourses* (1848); *The Sickness unto Death* (1849); *Training in Christianity* (1850); *For Self-Examination* (1851). *Judge for Yourselves!*, written in 1851–1852, was published posthumously. In these works Kierkegaard challenged "the individual" with the claim of a radical Christianity more and more explicitly at odds with what was commonly preached in the churches. For two of these books, *The Sickness unto Death: A Christian Psychological Exposition for Upbuilding and Awakening* and *Training in Christianity*, he invented a new pseudonym, Anti-Climacus, because they demand an intensity of Christian commitment that Kierkegaard felt was still personally beyond him. Kierkegaard's policy as an author was to attach his name only to ideas that he was embodying in his own life.

Besides these two published literatures, the pseudonymous and the upbuilding, Kierkegaard produced a vast private literature, his journals and papers. These writings are extremely varied in character and importance. The most interesting have the character of entries in a personal diary; but there are also extended notes on his reading, copies of letters, prayers, random thoughts, and sketches for possible works, the sort of thing one would expect to find in a writer's notebooks. These diverse *Papier* have been collected in twenty-two large volumes in the modern Danish edition. The most extensive English translation is a selection in six hefty volumes, edited and translated by Howard V. Hong and Edna H. Hong, entitled *Søren Kierkegaard's Journals and Papers* ("autobiographical" entries are collected in volumes 5 and 6). Some of the entries date from childhood, but Kierkegaard had no particular design for these private jottings

until, at the age of twenty-four, he made a formal decision to keep a journal. Like every important subsequent event in his life, we can date this decision exactly, because it is duly recorded in his journal: "Resolution of July 13, 1837, made in our study at six o'clock in the evening." Typically, in fact, we can even follow the train of thought that led to this resolution, for Kierkegaard then began conducting much of his thinking pen in hand. He reflected that writers he admired, such as E. T. A. Hoffmann and Georg Christoph Lichtenberg, kept journals and recommended the practice. But he himself had always found the idea distasteful, because such writing seemed to entail the possibility of publication, so that he would feel bound to work his ideas out with a care that would make the practice burdensome and might smother the spontaneity of his thinking.

> I think, instead, that it would be good, through frequent note-writing, to let the thoughts come forth with the umbilical cord of the original mood, and to forget as much as possible all regard for their possible use . . . ; rather, by expectorating myself as in a letter to an intimate friend, I gain the possibility of self-knowledge and, in addition, fluency in writing, the same articulateness in written expression which I have to some extent in speaking, the knowledge of many little traits to which I have given no more than a quick glance, and finally, the advantage, if what Hamann says is true in another sense, that there are ideas which a man gets only once in his life.
>
> (*Journals and Papers*, vol. 5, p. 103)

So the journal was to contain his thoughts just as they came to him. In the margin of this particular entry Kierkegaard added another consideration: the "wealth of fancies and ideas" that come to him can create a psychic unease "similar to that which a cow suffers when it is not milked at the proper time . . . Therefore one's best method, if external conditions are of no help, is, like the cow, to milk oneself."

If ever a young man suffered such a burden of intellectual hyperactivity, it was Kierkegaard. In an entry dated 9 February 1838 he says that at times the "commotion in my head . . . is as if goblins had hoisted up a mountain a bit and are now having a hilarious ball in there." He needed the journal not only to relieve the pressure, like the cow, but to exorcize the goblins. In a Latin tag from Horace, Kierkegaard seemed to provide himself a motto for his resolution to keep a journal: *Nulla dies sine linea* (Not a day without a line). In fact, for the rest of his life few days were to pass without many lines.

Fifteen years and many thousands of pages later, he again exposed the nerve of his literary productivity: "A deep depression has been kept down by writing." That note of melancholy sounds through all the wit, insight, piety, petulance, and self-analysis that fill these pages. In 1840, during a trip to the Danish mainland, he reflected wryly on the motto with which he had provided his journals: "Just as it is customary to say: *nulla dies sine linea,* so can I say of this journey: *nulla dies sine lacryma*" (Not a day without a tear). This entry is headed by the sign of the cross. The tears, the lines, and the cross reappear in constant counterpoint in these journals, together with more lighthearted material.

In one respect Kierkegaard gradually altered his original resolution in keeping the journal. He began writing it for other eyes than his own, for the eyes not of his contemporaries but of posterity. He expected that it would be published some time after his death. For such a secretive man as Kierkegaard such a deliberate self-exposure is extraordinary, even if projected into the distant future. In reading his diary, we are observing the very moments and hours of this man's life, a life lived to a large extent at the writing desk. That impression can be seriously misleading, for this apparent self-disclosure is, of course, also a self-interpretation, much of it conscious and some of it very sly, laying many traps for the unwary, like any autobiography. Still, for a pa-tient reader, able to salt sympathy with more than a grain of skepticism, this sophisticated process of self-presentation extending over the last eighteen years of Kierkegaard's life is itself a virtuoso performance and among his supreme literary achievements.

Besides the three formidable bodies of literature we have discussed, Kierkegaard wrote many other published and unpublished works. Some precede the authorship proper, including a published work on his Danish contemporary, Hans Christian Andersen, *From the Papers of One Still Living* (1838), and his academic dissertation, *The Concept of Irony: With Constant Reference to Socrates* (1841). There are also many newspaper articles and polemic pieces, and a small book, *Two Ages: The Age of Revolution and the Present Age* (1846), which uses a contemporary novel as point of departure for some acerbic social criticism. A major theological study is addressed to books by A. P. Adler, which Adler claimed were based on private religious revelations; though Kierkegaard prepared his manuscript for publication, he decided out of consideration for Adler not to publish it, and it was never published in Danish except in the *Papirer.* Usually called The Book on Adler, this work was published in English under the title *On Authority and Revelation.* Finally, in the last year of his life, Kierkegaard published a number of polemic articles and leaflets directed against the Danish church. They were collected and translated into English under the title *Attack upon "Christendom"* and will be discussed below.

LIFE

Kierkegaard's life is a study in Scandinavian gothic. Not its least uncanny feature is that so much of it was spent writing. His prodigious outpouring of words, particularly during the 1840's, has scant precedent. The desk on which most of his books and journals were written was a handsome one with a slanting top and tall legs, so that he could write standing up. Standing, and also pacing, circling around his study, he formed his sentences aloud until they were ready to be set down with pen and ink. His frequent carriage rides in the country, his daily walks through the streets of Copenhagen, the pacing in his study, were so many concentric circles around that high writing desk. This centripetal pattern of his adult life reflected that of his thoughts, restlessly circling around a few basic themes closely related to the crises and tensions in his own life. He can be said to have lived his adult life in his writing, and it is thus possible to *read* Kierkegaard's life, not merely to read *about* it. He did not earn a living, did not raise a family, did not serve in the military or go to meetings or carry on love affairs and flirtations, did not take up hobbies. He wrote. On a typical day he would rise early, say his prayers, and write until breakfast. After breakfast he wrote; dined; took his daily stroll, chatting with shopkeepers, servants, workers, and any acquaintances who happened to fall in with him for a few blocks; then went back to the study to write. He supped, wrote, said his evening prayers, and went to bed. With most writers it is possible to distinguish between the life and the work. It is not so with Kierkegaard. Nothing bulks so large in his biography as the single-mindedness with which he devoted himself to putting words on paper. All his effective energies were put into the current book, the discourse, the daily entries in the journal. His contemporaries were amazed and appalled at how prolific he was, without being aware that his published work was only the tip of the iceberg. Since he commonly put his published works through several drafts, he was incensed when critics charged him with producing in haste. They could point to no evidence for this alleged carelessness, but if he were not careless, how could he write so many big books?

There was nothing careless about his productivity, but it was obsessive, bound up with

suffering in a way that defies analysis. Consider a journal entry of 1848:

> How often this same thing has happened to me that now has happened to me again! I am submerged in the deepest suffering of despondency, so tied up in mental knots that I cannot get free, and since it is all connected with my personal life I suffer indescribably. And then after a short time, like an abscess it comes to a head and breaks—and inside is the loveliest and richest creativity—and the very thing I must use at the moment.
>
> (*Journals and Papers*, vol. 6, p. 41)

Any effort to tell the story of Kierkegaard's life must place at the center this wracking symbiosis between his pain and his work. That is not to say that there is any very convincing biographical explanation of his work, though his life is so well documented, thanks to his journals, that the effort to concoct a biographical or psychopathological explanation has tempted many scholars.

Kierkegaard came under the yoke of this prodigious literary discipline in his twenties. But even before he took on the gothic image of the demon-ridden author, the picture is gothic enough. Søren Aabye Kierkegaard was born in Copenhagen on 5 May 1813, the seventh child of Michael Pedersen Kierkegaard and Ane Sørensdatter Lund Kierkegaard. His father was fifty-six and his mother forty-five years old when he was born. Ane had been the maid of Michael Pedersen's first wife, Kirstine, who had died in 1796 after two years of marriage. Ane stayed on as a servant in the house, and Michael Pedersen married her after she became pregnant with his first child. His sense of guilt for this sin of the flesh did not prevent him from siring six more children with Ane, but it was painful enough to cast a pall over the entire household for the rest of his life. It seems simply to have deepened a shadow that had hung over Michael Pedersen since his early childhood, when as a desperately poor peasant boy suffering from hunger and cold while tending sheep on a Jutland heath, he had cursed God. He and his family were convinced that this curse had recoiled on him and the entire household.

Yet in a worldly sense Michael Pedersen's career had been an extraordinary success. He was still a boy when he came to Copenhagen to work for his uncle, a hosier, and he went into that line of trade himself. For a time he peddled his wares through the countryside, until he had earned enough to buy into a partnership in a shop in the city. From that time on, his prosperity grew steadily, through fortunate investments as well as trade, in good times and bad. At the age of forty, not long before he married Ane, he was in a position to retire from business, and for the rest of his long life he devoted himself to his family and to the books that poverty had denied him when he was young. Though he had little education, Michael Pedersen possessed a keen mind and a vivid imagination, qualities his youngest son inherited along with his dark forebodings. If there is any truth to the claim that traditional Protestants tend to regard worldly prosperity as a sign of divine favor, Michael Pedersen was a conspicuous exception. A man of bleak but intense piety, whose reading included a heavy measure of devotional literature, he was convinced that all his success was only a way of lifting him up in order to dash him down in some dreadful calamity. Finally his children began to die, and the thought seized him that his curse would be to outlive his children, like Job. Four of the seven were dead by 1834, when Ane died, and by the end of the year his youngest daughter had died after childbirth. Only Søren and his brother Peter Christian were left. Even after their father died in 1838, Søren continued to be oppressed by a sense of family doom. A few weeks after his father's death, his critical study of Hans Christian Andersen's novels was published under the title *From the Papers of One Still Living, Published Against his Will by S. Kierkegaard.*

He had been a spindly and ungainly boy, always in frail health. His intellectual precocity and sharp wit compensated for his physical weakness, but he never felt that he was a whole human being. He seemed to himself to have been born old, the extended shadow of the elderly father to whom he was devoted. In a journal entry of 1844 entitled "Quiet Despair—a Narrative," he very likely was describing his father and himself:

> There were a father and a son. Both were highly endowed intellectually and both were witty, especially the father. Everyone who knew their home was certain to find a visit very entertaining. Usually they discussed only between themselves and entertained each other as two good minds without the distinction between father and son. On one rare occasion when the father looked at the son and saw that he was very troubled, he stood quietly before him and said: Poor child, you live in quiet despair. But he never questioned him more closely—alas, he could not, for he, too, lived in quiet despair. Beyond this not a word was exchanged on the subject. But the father and the son were perhaps two of the most melancholy human beings who ever lived in the memory of man.
>
> (*Journals and Papers*, vol. 1, pp. 345–346)

Kierkegaard also received from his father a stark but powerful impression of Christianity as a world-rejecting faith in a savior whom the world had tortured to death on a cross. Josiah Thompson, a recent biographer, writes:

> Kierkegaard's lifelong ambivalence toward Christianity cannot be disentangled from his ambivalence toward his father. He hated this old man who had so branded and crippled him: "As a child I was strictly brought up in Christianity; humanly speaking, crazily brought up. A child travestied as a melancholy old man. Terrible!" He also loved the father "who made me unhappy, but out of the best of convictions." . . . He

complains: "Merciful God, how terribly unjust to me was my father in his melancholy—an old man who put the whole weight of his melancholy upon a poor child," and then in the next line he exclaims: "And yet for all that, he was the best of fathers." For although the old man was solemn and strict, he opened himself and his world to the child. He was (as Søren later pointed out) the boy's sole playmate.

(*Kierkegaard*, pp. 37–38)

Certainly playmates among his peers were few. Aloof and dressed in somber clothes, sharp-tongued and unathletic, he struck them as strange.

At least outwardly, Kierkegaard seemed to blossom when he entered the university. He bowed to his father's desire that he study theology, like his brother Peter; but unlike Peter, who had excelled and was clearly bound for an outstanding career as a churchman, Søren proved an indifferent student in this field. He seemed to have found livelier things with which to occupy himself. Literature, music, and theater were his loves; he affected a dandified style of dress and began enjoying the free-spending ways of a rich man's son.

> He smoked four cigars a day, attended lectures irregularly, read only what he pleased, and could usually be found in the Student Union, in a cafe, or walking around town in animated conversation with one of his acquaintances. He showed up at home only for meals, and if his tea shop bills are any indication, even this was not too often. . . . By 1837 he had run up tailor bills of 492 rd. (about $3,400), and in June 1835 he described himself as a "man in modern dress, glasses on his nose and a cigar in his mouth."
>
> (Thompson, *Kierkegaard*, p. 47)

He wrote articles, mostly on literary topics, for fashionable local journals, and he joined in student political debates, though his speeches tended to be in an acerbic and ironic mode that implicitly poked fun at the people who were taking the debates seriously. He entered society where his budding literary reputation and his lively conversation opened the doors of the more fashionable salons to him. But with Kierkegaard appearances are almost always deceiving. While he cultivated a public image of himself as a bright but rather frivolous young man-about-town, long extracts and summaries in his journals testify to heavy reading in philosophy and even in theology, and also register the deep strain of melancholia that marked him as the son of Michael Pedersen. Leading a double life appealed to a love of ironic mystification that Kierkegaard never abandoned. He liked being hidden away from the world, but hidden in plain view, in a public persona that gave no hint of his inner life. In the spring of 1836 he was, for instance, a regular guest at Copenhagen's most brilliant literary salon, presided over by J. L. Heiberg, a successful playwright and savant, and his wife, Johanne Luise, the leading lady of the Danish Royal Theater. That same spring Kierkegaard published three articles in a journal edited by Heiberg and joined the Heibergs' inner circle. "On June 4," according to Thompson, "he attended a special soiree," to which they had invited many of Copenhagen's literary luminaries.

> The wine flowed, witty conversation bubbled from every corner, and at the center of the merriment was Kierkegaard—sparkling, acerbic, enormously witty. After the party he returned to the Nytorv town house, where he was still living, climbed the darkened steps to his room, and wrote in his journal:
>
> I have just now come from a party where I was its life and soul; witticisms streamed from my lips, everyone laughed and admired me, but I went away—yes, the dash should be as long as the radius of the earth's orbit————
>
> ————————————and wanted to shoot myself.
>
> (*Kierkegaard*, p. 74; see also *Journals and Papers*, vol. 5, p. 69)

This often quoted journal entry offers a good example of Kierkegaard's sense that he is going about in disguise. The entry implies that the convivial young litterateur at the party is mere appearance, while the solitary figure contemplating suicide is the reality. Indeed, the contrast between appearance and reality is so melodramatic in this entry that it may also illustrate a recurrent tendency of the journal to present the author in a suspiciously poetic posture. The gifted young man flirting with suicide was after all a common figure in romantic fiction. There is no reason to think that Kierkegaard is misrepresenting his experience, but where art and life are so evidently fused, the line separating reality from appearance can be elusive.

The year 1840 seemed to mark another important turning point. First, he finally settled down to studying for his theological degree. In a journal entry dated 20 December 1839 he took whimsical leave of the thoughts he used to let "go strolling in the cool of the evening," but he promised to return. This decision was in good part an act of filial piety toward his dead father, who had so earnestly wished for his son to take his theological degree and whose patience had been so sorely tried. He applied himself diligently for six months, complaining all the while, until he completed the examination, magna cum laude, on 3 July. He underwent practical pastoral training the following winter, and in the summer of 1841 he presented his substantial dissertation, *The Concept of Irony: With Constant Reference to Socrates*, for his magister's degree. So he ended the pleasantly aimless years of his student life with a sudden burst of purposefulness.

Meanwhile he had fallen in love. Regine Olsen was only fourteen years old when he met her in 1837. He first mentions her name in a journal entry dated 2 February 1839, where he calls her "Sovereign queen of my heart, . . . hidden in the deepest secrecy of my breast." He preserved this secrecy so well that she herself seems to have been taken quite by surprise on 8 September 1840 by his sudden, impassioned proposal of marriage. Regine was then seventeen years old, intelligent and attractive, and of a prominent upper-bourgeois family. Kierkegaard was twenty-seven, in possession of a considerable patrimony; he had recently passed his university examinations and was a man of obvious promise. Regine's father found the match satisfactory; she herself found Kierkegaard acceptable, if a bit bewildering; two days later she accepted. In a long account of the engagement, written in his journal ten years later, he claims he realized the very next day that he "had made a mistake. Penitent that I was, my *vita ante acta*, my melancholy—that was sufficient. I suffered indescribably during that time." Nevertheless, the couple was initiated into the extremely elaborate social rituals that an engagement called for in that era, place, and social class, and there can be no doubt that Kierkegaard seriously courted Regine after they were engaged and that she responded.

An engagement was understood to entail the same social and spiritual commitments as marriage. So when Kierkegaard broke the engagement thirteen months later the breach created a major scandal. Yet he continued to be deeply in love with Regine for the rest of his life. The journals are filled with expressions of his longing for her. It is clear that both before the break and after, he equated marriage to Regine with his only hope of human happiness; when he renounced the one he renounced the other. Why did he do it? The many dreary pages written by him and his biographers in an effort to answer the question only deepen the mystery: the Kierkegaard family curse; some nameless sin of his youth; his melancholia; his fear of destroying Regine's happiness; some physical disability; a spiritual or emotional inability to enter into a genuine human relationship; his extreme introversion, the *indesluttethed* (literally "shut-in-ness") that was a major theme of some of his later works; a sense of religious vocation entailing celibacy. Perhaps all of these factors were at work, or none of them. In fact no one really knows why Kierkegaard broke his engagement to Regine. He often spoke of it as his secret and took considerable pains to prevent anyone from uncovering it (though it is not certain that he himself really understood his own motivation).

Whatever may have caused the break, it had three important effects in Kierkegaard's sense of his life and vocation. First, his renunciation of Regine led him to abandon all hope of earthly happiness. Second, it decisively committed him to a spiritual path. Finally, it made him a writer. His former fiancée became the muse to whom he attributed all his literary achievements. The life revolving steadfastly around his writing desk was his eternal fidelity to Regine.

Two weeks after breaking the engagement in October 1841, Kierkegaard fled to Berlin. There he seems to have lived in almost total seclusion, broken only by solitary visits to lecture halls, theaters, and restaurants. The plan for the authorship began to take form. He returned to Copenhagen in March, and after one false start (the unfinished *Johannes Climacus; or, De Omnibus Dubitandum Est*), he brought the two large volumes of *Either/Or* to publication on 20 February 1843.

BROKEN ENGAGEMENT AS A LITERARY THEME

Either/Or, a masterpiece within the Kierkegaardian corpus, was published before he had turned thirty years old. It laid the foundation for the entire pseudonymous authorship and introduced most of its characteristic themes. One of these themes, the relation of art to life, is addressed at the beginning of the first volume:

What is a poet? An unhappy man who in his heart harbors a deep anguish, but whose lips are so fashioned that the moans and cries which pass over them are transformed into ravishing music. His fate is like that of the unfortunate victims whom the tyrant Phalaris imprisoned in a brazen bull, and slowly tortured over a steady fire; their cries could not reach the tyrant's ears so as to strike terror into his heart; when they reached his ears they sounded like sweet music. And men crowd around the poet and say to him, "Sing for us soon again"—which is as much as to say, "May new sufferings torment your soul, but may your lips be fashioned as before; for the cries would only distress us, but the music, the music, is delightful."

(*Either/Or*, vol. 1, p. 19)

Kierkegaard's continued suffering over his break with Regine Olsen was certainly his own experience of Phalaris' bull. It made him, he said, a poet, and as a poet he turned three times to the situation of broken engagement as a subject for narrative treatment. What is striking about these three stories is that the outward circumstances are virtually the same in each case, and they just happen to resemble the circumstances of Kierkegaard's own break with Regine. The difference is in the character of the male protagonists in the three stories, especially in their motives for breaking the engagement. The experience of the young women appears roughly the same in the three stories, but since in each case the story is told from the man's point of view, the reader can see that the subjective motivations of the three narrators are radically different. The surface similarity in their comportment is deceptive. Outward circumstance gives no clue to inner reality. The "sweet music" of poetry is also quite different in tone, tempo, and texture among the three pieces.

The first of these stories, entitled "Diary of the Seducer," concludes volume 1 of *Either/Or*. Volume 1 consists of a series of eight loosely related pieces, beginning with a series of aphorisms, many of them gleaned from Kierkegaard's journals, entitled "Diapsalmata." We have quoted the first of these, presenting Phalaris' bull as a metaphor for the suffering of the poet. Most of the pieces that follow the Diapsalmata are aesthetic studies of various literary and theatrical works, in which the theme of betrayed love figures prominently. "Shadowgraphs," for instance, features three seduced and abandoned heroines, Marie Beaumarchais and Gretchen in Goethe's *Clavigo* and *Faustus,* respectively, and Donna Elvira in Mozart's *Don Giovanni.* Each tries and fails to come to terms with her betrayal. Such studies prepare the ground for Johannes the Seducer, whose lengthy "Diary" concludes the volume.

Johannes is no vulgar skirt-chaser, taking his women any way he can. He is a poet of seduction, pursuing his little projects as a series of aesthetic experiments, each conducted differently. Who would want to write the same poem twice? Some episodes are minor; in one case it suffices to win a deep curtsy from a girl on the street. "All I want is this greeting, nothing more, even if she were willing to give [more]." But one experiment described in the "Diary" is major. A chance encounter on the street with a young woman in a green coat so engages Johannes that he goes out stalking her day and night for weeks without a glimpse. At last he sees her again, learns that her name is Cordelia, begins spying on her, staking out her daily routine, and finally lets himself be noticed by her in carefully arranged circumstances that will seem to her like chance encounters. Slowly and patiently, savoring every move in his master plan, he maneuvers into an innocuous position in her circle of acquaintances; becomes adviser to her hapless young suitor; and wins the confidence of her aunt, who is her guardian, by showing a keen interest in agricultural pursuits. At last he makes his move. Taking Cordelia totally by surprise, but with scarcely any show of passion, he proposes to her.

The aunt gives her consent, about that I never had the slightest doubt. Cordelia accepts her advice. As regards my engagement, I do not boast that it is poetic, it is in every way philistine and bourgeois. The girl doesn't know whether to say yes or no; the aunt says yes, the girl also says yes, I take the girl, she takes me—and now the story begins.

(*Either/Or*, vol. 1, p. 371)

The story unfolds in Johannes' diary, told not only with careful attention to detail but with rich poetic commentary. In fact the literary replication of the affair in the diary is from Johannes' point of view integral to the whole affair, which consists precisely in the transmutation of life into poetry. Through Johannes' unobtrusive manipulation, Cordelia herself undergoes a process of steady etherealization, inwardly detaching herself from the concrete details of family life and social routine, dwelling more and more transparently in a region of romantic ideality. The social rituals of engagement are presented to the reader, and to Cordelia herself, as ridiculously banal, comic, but contrived to be so offensive to the romantically developing girl that she is spiritually repelled out of everyday life altogether. Meanwhile Johannes finds ways to communicate an entirely different possibility to his young fiancée, a magical eroticism that will transport her beyond that repellent reality. He chooses, for instance, strategic moments to send her poetically inspired love letters that strikingly resemble those Søren Kierkegaard had sent Regine Olsen during the year of their engagement. Though she sees Johannes every day, her inner development seems to be progressing quite independently of his mundane presence. Yet he is present to her in a different way that she scarcely suspects. He has become her daimon, steadily possessing her spirit.

So now the first war with Cordelia begins, in which I flee, and thereby teach her to triumph in pursuing me. I constantly retreat before her, and in this retreat, I teach her through myself to know all the power of love, its unquiet thoughts, its passion, what longing is, and hope, and impatient expectation. As I thus set all this before her in my own person, the same power develops correspondingly in her. . . . With every movement of mine, she becomes stronger and stronger; love is awakening in her soul, she is becoming initiated into her significance as a woman. Hitherto I have not set her free in the ordinary meaning of the word. I do it now, I set her free, for only thus will I love her. She must never suspect that she owes this freedom to me, for that would destroy her self-confidence. When she at last feels free, so free that she is almost tempted to break with me, then the second war begins. Now she has power and passion, and the struggle becomes worthwhile to me. . . . That the engagement should bind her is foolishness; I will have her only in her freedom. Let her forsake me, the second war is just beginning, and in this second war I shall be the victor, just as certainly as it was an illusion that she was the victor in the first. The more abundant strength she has, the more interesting for me. The first war was a war of liberation, it was only a game; the second is a war of conquest, it is for life and death.

(*Either/Or*, vol. 1, pp. 379–380)

It is in fact Cordelia who breaks the engagement; what are mundane social arrangements to her? For "in her bold flight she loses sight of marriage, and of the mainland of reality in general . . . for Cordelia's way of life is already so ethereal and light that reality is to a large degree lost sight of. Besides I am always on board, and can always break out the sails." She is ready to put out to sea with her daimon, far beyond ordinary human habitation. Only now is she his entirely. "Light have I made her, light as a thought, and why should not this, my thought, belong to me!" A tryst is arranged, a convenient coach ride away from the city; there is a night of love, after which Johannes breaks all contact, leaving her poignant letters unanswered.

The affair has soared above mundane time in quite a different way than Cordelia had expected. She takes her place in the gallery of betrayed literary heroines presented in "Shadowgraphs," and for Johannes the affair is consummated poetically in his "Diary." The affair and the diary converge in their conclusion. Cordelia has become a figure of poetry.

Many details of the affair resemble the course of Kierkegaard's engagement with Regine Olsen, but Kierkegaard is no Johannes the Seducer. Johannes is one of his pseudonyms, the fictive author of the "Diary." The diary is discovered by a young man identified only as "A," the pseudonymous editor of the first volume, whose papers, together with those of "B," are discovered in a most unlikely way and prepared for publication by one Victor Eremita (Victor the Hermit), who remarks that "one author seems to be enclosed in another, like the parts in a Chinese puzzle box." Kierkegaard's name does not appear at all, so that he seems to be removed from the story by the work of three pseudonymous writers. The sufferer in Phalaris' bull has been made to sing a song as dissociated from his own screams and moans as possible.

Repetition, a novella published in 1843, only a few months after *Either/Or*, again features a broken engagement. Subtitled *An Essay in Experimental Psychology*, it is attributed to a rather cynical middle-aged bachelor and amateur psychologist named Constantin Constantius. Constantin interests himself in the case of a nameless "young man" who is passionately in love, but possessed of such prodigious imagination that he has already transfigured his sweetheart into a figure of poetic ideality. That is in fact the essential conflict of the work. Unlike Johannes the Seducer, the young man does not want to compose a poem but to love a real woman, and regards his transmutation of her into a poetic figure as a faithless betrayal of the real woman he loves. The desired "repetition" is to become a man and a lover again, but his romantic fantasy stands in the way. He disappears, leaving his sweetheart to come to her own conclusions, and he addresses a series of letters, without return address, to Constantin. He meditates on the Book of Job, hoping that like Job he may get back what he has lost. Meanwhile, like Regine Olsen at the time this book was being written, his beloved sensibly marries another man. He achieves repetition in the unexpected sense that he accepts his vocation as a poet, with a certain tendency toward religion. This bare plot summary does scant justice to the whimsy and pathos of Kierkegaard's most strictly literary work, and to the important category of "repetition" elusively introduced in this novella.

Even more difficult to summarize is the third treatment of the theme of broken engagement, which makes up part 3 of *Stages on Life's Way*, one of Kierkegaard's longest books. This concluding part, more than twice as long as parts 1 and 2 together, is entitled "'Guilty?'/'Not Guilty?' A Passion Narrative" and subtitled "A Psychological Experiment," by Frater Taciturnus. The taciturn brother contributes an introductory "Advertisement" and a lengthy concluding commentary on the main text, which is again a diary, this one attributed to one Quidam (Latin for "a certain person"). Quidam's diary is undoubtedly Kierkegaard's most autobiographical work, borrowing heavily from the mass of journal entries bearing on his own unhappy love affair, some of which are reproduced verbatim. For instance, the entry entitled "Quiet Despair" appears under the same title in Quidam's diary. Yet it would be incautious to leap to the conclusion that Quidam *is* Søren.

Quidam's diary runs from 3 January through 7 July, with no year given. Each entry reports on the events of exactly a year earlier, the period of Quidam's love affair, and meditates on its meaning in light of its unhappy ending. The author seems doomed to repeat this process indefinitely. Freed from his diary after 7 July, he will resume it when 3 January comes around again. For half a year he lived and loved. Now he seems left with nothing but the task of perpetual commentary. The last entry, dated "July 7, Midnight," begins:

Lo, now I leave off for this time. My dormant period of repose with reference to her now begins. I have my discharge. The third of January the

disquietude begins again. When one is discharged the command is: right face—left about—march! That is a bit satirical, for my misfortune is that I cannot do either right face, left about, or march.

The period of disquietude is the half year, which returns again and again until I become free.

(*Stages*, p. 361)

Liberation would presumably consist in resolution of the fundamental conflict: guilty/not guilty. In the eyes of the world, in her eyes, and from the point of view of ethical responsibility, he is guilty of blackest betrayal. An honorable woman accepted his proposal of marriage in good faith and gave him her love. Without explanation he abandoned her. If he protests that his love is true in spite of everything:

. . . against me I have language, have her, have the human race against me, I have nothing I can appeal to, nothing to support me. Do I not love her? "Is that love," retorts she and language and the race, "when one deserts her?"

(*Stages*, p. 319)

Guilty then. Yet he has an intimation of a divine calling, still uncertain and ambiguous but linked to his present melancholy unease with the world, that is incompatible with marriage. The passion of his faith cannot resolve the uncertainty, because uncertainty is the precondition of his faith. Such a special calling has no secure models.

Placed as I am in the religious catastrophe, I grasp after the paradigm. But, behold, I am not able to understand the paradigm, even though I venerate it with a childlike piety which will not let it go. One paradigm appeals to visions, another to revelations, a third to dreams.

(*Stages*, p. 242)

But in his case there are no such signs, no secure guidance, no explanation. It is in just this ambiguity that he is singled out as an individual. "I have never been able to understand it in any other way but that every man is essentially thrown back upon himself," he says, and Frater Taciturnus echoes this conclusion: "the only thing remaining is the individual himself, the single individual, placed in his God-relationship under the rubric: Guilty? Not guilty?"

"Diary of the Seducer," *Repetition*, and Quidam's diary treat the same situation, so far as external circumstances are concerned, but the three protagonists from whose point of view the story is told could scarcely differ more among themselves in their inner motivation or what Kierkegaard called their "life-view" *(livs-anskuelse)*. Many autobiographical details are scattered through all three treatments, yet none of these writings is basically autobiographical. For this unhappy lover is first and last a writer, whose personal experience has been transmuted to serve the purposes of a literary-philosophical project quite detached from his private life. If it has anything to do with him personally, he insists that it has only the same relation that it could have to any reader of these works.

THE "STAGES" IN THE PSEUDONYMOUS AUTHORSHIP

There is a theatrical method in Kierkegaard's pseudonymous authorship. Kierkegaard was a lover of the theater who often wrote about plays and operas, and his most fully developed pseudonymous characters are allowed to speak for themselves, in their own distinctive voices, like characters in drama. That was his greatest poetic achievement. The individuality of each is realized in the style and intonation with which he expresses himself, as different from the others as, say, Iago and young Prince Hal. Each expresses a distinct "life-view," a way of situating himself in his world of experience. He does not simply represent a philosophical position allegori-

cally, but presents it to the reader embodied in a unique style.

Kierkegaard sometimes uses the term "stages" for these life views or ways of life. The term is misleading in some respects. Kierkegaard does not think that human beings can be sorted out into general types in some sort of ascending scale. If he did think that, he could have spared himself the trouble of creating such fully realized pseudonymous voices. What the term "stages" does suggest is the possibility of movement, within an individual life, from one existential position to another. The authorship is designed to present that possibility to the reader: not that he is to become like one or another of the pseudonymous characters, none of whom is paradigmatic, but that these figures embody such existential choices and clarify their dynamics.

Kierkegaard's authorship is usually identified with three general stages, the aesthetic, the ethical, and the religious. But only in *Stages on Life's Way* do we find something like those three categories presented as such, in the three parts of the book. Even there, our sketch of Quidam's predicament ought to be sufficient warning against treating him as a paradigm of the general category "religion." If he could have found paradigms at hand there would have been no predicament. More typically, each text treats only two concrete but conflicting life possibilities, with a protagonist poised between. "Either/Or" might be the general title of the entire pseudonymous authorship.

In the text that actually bears that title, the first volume presents various forms of purely aesthetic life possibility. Kierkegaard, an avid student of classical languages and literature, uses the word "aesthetic" in a way that carries the force of its Greek cognate, αἰσθάνομαι, a verb meaning "to understand," "to sense," or "to perceive"; "to experience" might be the most adequate English translation. Works of art, for instance, are artifacts presented to us as rich objects of experience to be heard, viewed, read. Of course, our experience goes far beyond works of art; on Kierkegaard's terms, one of the two primary ways in which we relate to the world is aesthetically. The other way is through our own action upon the world. Now an aesthetic way of life is one in which a person lives in and for experience, without making more active commitments. Everyone, to be sure, must do many things, but there are kinds of doing that are performed purely for the sake of the experience they will bring. Johannes the Seducer, for instance, who represents an extreme form of the aesthetic way of life, downright diabolical in fact, is admittedly a very busy man. But all his activity is directed to arranging for himself exquisite experiences that can finally be transmuted into the poetry of his diary.

The pseudonymous writer designated simply "A," who is responsible for the other pieces in the first volume of *Either/Or,* is also an aesthete, though not nearly so far gone as Johannes. His little introduction to "Diary of the Seducer," which he claims to have purloined from Johannes' desk drawer, expresses both horror and fascination. Johannes' life, he says, "had been an attempt to realize the task of living poetically. With a keenly developed talent for discovering the interesting in life, he had known how to find it, and after finding it, he constantly reproduced the experience more or less poetically." At the same time, in "his infinite self-reflection" Johannes seems to him in a manner to evaporate, making no impression on the real world, "for his feet were so formed that he left no footprints." "A" is especially struck by the fact that entries in the diary begin with definite dates, but as the text progresses the dates are more often omitted; as the story "comes nearer to being idea . . . the time designations become a matter of indifference." For "A" himself is much preoccupied with time, or more precisely with strategies for liberation from time. In one of the Diapsalmata, he speaks of the dangers, but also the satisfactions, of remembering: "The

life that is lived wholly in memory is the most perfect conceivable. . . . A remembered life relation has already passed into eternity, and has no more temporal interest." His fascination with works of art, expressed in a number of essays on art criticism in the volume, is inspired by the fact that an aesthetic object, complete and whole in itself, achieves a timeless quality. Such timelessness can be achieved reflectively, in poetry for instance, or in Johannes' project of poetic-reflective seduction. Or it can be achieved through the opposite strategy: a concentration in the instantaneous present so intense that it holds the past and future at bay. This immediacy he finds, for instance, in Mozart's musical rendering of Don Juan. In a magnificent essay on the opera, he says that Don Juan's life

> is the whole power of sensuousness, which is born in dread, . . . but this dread is precisely the daemonic joy of life. When Mozart has thus brought Don Juan into existence, then his life is developed for us in the dancing tones of the violin in which he lightly, casually hastens forward over the abyss. When one skims a stone over the surface of the water, it skips lightly for a time, but as soon as it ceases to skip, it instantly sinks down into the depths; so Don Juan dances over the abyss, jubilant in his brief respite.
>
> (*Either/Or,* vol. 1, pp. 128–129)

Don Juan represents erotic immediacy, Johannes the Seducer the other pole of the aesthetic, erotic reflection; the first can only be perfectly expressed in music, the other in language.

"A"'s interest in art and in aesthetic theory is not what makes him an embodiment of the aesthetic way of life. An ethical or a religious person, for instance, could equally well be an artist, and plenty of aesthetes are indifferent to the arts. He is an aesthete, however, to the extent that he attempts to organize his way of life according to categories that are appropriate for a work of art. He seeks to overcome the tyranny of time either through the intensity of momentary experience or through reflection. He seeks what is interesting, avoids the boring. In a whimsical essay (in *Either/Or*) entitled "The Rotation Method," he declares that "boredom is the root of all evil." A love affair is an interesting experience in the immediate mode. Philosophizing is interesting, in the reflective mode. But marriage as a constancy in time is the epitome of everything boring and should at all cost be avoided.

The second volume of *Either/Or* consists largely of two long treatises written in defense of marriage by a married man. These two treatises are written in the form of letters to the author of the first volume. Their style is prosaic and often hortatory. The author, "B," is also identified as a judge named William, who composes his epistles on legal-size sheets of paper. He speaks for an ethical way of life, involving friendship, the duties of good citizenship, the responsibility to earn a living, and above all the commitment of marriage, which is emblematic of the ethical life. Though he finds the ethical life interesting, he does not defend it on that ground. For the distinction between the interesting and the boring is aesthetic, whereas the ethical man contends with good and evil. Again, he does not defend the ethical life because it offers a richer experience (though he is convinced that it does), but because it is the life of committed action. Only an active person, who makes the weight of his existence felt in the real world, can become a completely human self. In Judge William's second epistolary treatise, "Equilibrium Between the Aesthetical and the Ethical in the Composition of Personality," he argues that only the ethical person, in the courage of his choices, can lead a full life of experience and find existence beautiful. The aesthetic way of life is self-defeating: the person who lives only for his own entertainment will in the end find life turning to ashes in his mouth. So he exhorts his young friend to choose, to choose first of all actively to choose. An aesthetic life is not necessarily evil, but it is empty, because

the very distinction between good and evil does not exist for the aesthete.

> What is it, then, that I distinguish in my either/or? Is it good and evil? No, I would only bring you up to the point where the choice between the evil and the good acquires significance for you. Everything hinges upon this . . . yea, no young girl can be so happy with the choice of her heart as is a man who knows how to choose. So then, one either has to live aesthetically or one has to live ethically. In this alternative, as I have said, there is not yet in the strictest sense any question of a choice; for he who lives aesthetically does not choose. . . .
>
> (*Either/Or*, vol. 2, p. 172)

In choosing one does not escape from time, but takes command of time, wills the way he will live his moments and days and years. The ethical man has time on his side. When he falls in love with a woman he proposes marriage, because only in the strength of the marriage vow can the lovers achieve what the aesthetic immediacy of their love demands: that they shall belong to one another and never part.

We have described the style of these epistles as prosaic, and yet there is a quiet ardor in them. The style lacks the brilliance and wit but is also free of the undertone of melancholy that suffuses the pieces in the first volume. The judge stands before us in his business suit, cheerful, stable, thoughtful, his feet firmly planted on the ground. A nighttime atmosphere pervades the papers of "A," many of them said to be delivered as lectures before a ghostly society known as the *Symparanekromenoi*, a fellowship of the dead. The judge, on the other hand, belongs to the daylight and the everydayness of ordinary life. Yet his magisterial treatises introduce many of the characteristic themes of Kierkegaard's authorship—choice, anxiety, despair, time and the primacy of the future, radical freedom, and the active achievement of self.

These are Kierkegaard's most influential themes. Not that he had much influence during his own century. But Kierkegaard, who never wanted to be the father of anything or anybody, became known in the twentieth century as the father of a loosely identified school of thought labeled "existentialism," and such themes, introduced by the stolid Judge William and developed in further writings, were primary sources for this school.

Within the framework of *Either/Or*, in which Kierkegaard presents only these two basic types of life possibility, the existential moves are necessarily assigned to the ethical life. Here we are shown the basic conflict between a self that lives as the subject of experience and a self that is the agent of resolute action: between the observing self and the committed self, between the denial of lived temporality and its ardent embrace. There is in principle no end to the proliferation of Kierkegaardian stages. Judge William, for instance, enumerates four states in the aesthetic life in his polemic against it. Yet the stark dyad, the aesthetic vs. the existential, is basic to the entire pseudonymous authorship. The energy of ethical choice is the gateway to all the existential possibilities.

For Judge William himself, of course, it is much more than a gateway. He claims the entire existential field for his vision of the ethical life, including a religious piety of a sort designed to support the pursuit of the ethical path. The hint of a more radical religiosity does appear at the conclusion of the work, in a sermon by a country pastor in Jutland. The very title of this sermon—"The Edification Implied in the Thought That as Against God We Are Always Wrong,"—seems at least a challenge to ethical assumptions, though Judge William seems unaware of any conflict. He sends it along to his young friend, the aesthete, with a brief note commending it to his attention. It reads like something out of Kierkegaard's upbuilding literature, and ends by sweeping aside all reflection that is not directed to the "building up" of a serious spirituality in the life of the individual: "for only the truth which edifies [*opbygger*—builds up] is truth for you."

If the claim of religious transcendence is only this small cloud on the horizon of *Either/Or*, it becomes a storm in *Fear and Trembling* by Johannes de Silentio, which was published a few months later on the same date as *Repetition* by Constantin Constantius and *Three Edifying Discourses* by S. Kierkegaard. *Fear and Trembling* is in some respects Kierkegaard's literary masterpiece. His peculiar genius had two sides, poetic and dialectical, both present in varying degrees in all his work. In some books, such as *Repetition*, the poetic, novelistic side predominates, with some pregnant philosophical asides. Others, for instance the expressly philosophical Climacus literature, are primarily discursive, enlivened by occasional narrative passages or flights of lyricism. In *Fear and Trembling*, subtitled *A Dialectical Lyric*, these two sides are in the most perfect balance Kierkegaard ever achieved, poetry and dialectic woven together as warp and woof.

All the more disturbing, therefore, is the theme of this remarkable work: the harmony of religious faith with ethical norms breaks into open conflict. The subject is the biblical story of Abraham on Mount Moriah, prepared to sacrifice his only son, Isaac, at the inexplicable command of God. It is important to emphasize that this work presupposes the validity of ethical norms. Otherwise there would be no fear and trembling. Johannes de Silentio does not see in Abraham's act the institution of a new ethic, according to which a parent's murder of a child becomes a generally permissible sacrifice. He constantly emphasizes that Abraham is bound to Isaac not only by the deepest ties of human affection but by the highest ethical norms, according to which it is a parent's duty to nurture and protect a child. To de Silentio, Abraham's willingness to obey this horrendous command is as inexplicable as the command itself. Yet in this very act Abraham becomes the biblical father of faith.

De Silentio is himself a man of religious piety, but a piety that stops short of any such transcendent faith. He calls himself a knight of infinite resignation, implying among other things a readiness for personal sacrifice on his own part, in the best ethico-religious tradition. But Abraham is not only willing to sacrifice his son: he is confident, at the same time, that he will somehow receive Isaac back again, directly from the hand of God. This "double movement" de Silentio cannot understand at all. Yet he recognizes that it is the epitome of faith. A "knight of faith" gives up all claim to the finite things he loves, yet he does not cease to love them. He takes refuge in the infinite God, in full expectation that in some manner he will be given those finite objects of his love as divine gift. Such a faith exists, as de Silentio repeatedly testifies, "in virtue of"—or in the power of—"the absurd."

He never tries to explain Abraham, except negatively, by bringing forth one example after another of situations that seem to resemble Abraham's, and showing in each how the resemblance breaks down. Agamemnon, for instance, is presented as an ethical hero for whom two contrary ethical claims come into conflict: his duty as a father to his daughter Iphigenia and his duty as a king to his army. That he resolves this dilemma by sacrificing his daughter is tragic, yet understandable on the basis of commonly recognized ethical norms. Not so Abraham. Abraham never speaks for himself, except in the few laconic utterances attributed to him in Genesis; according to de Silentio he cannot speak for himself because there is nothing in common language that could explain his deed. We see him purely through de Silentio's eyes, see him disappear from the region of common understanding across "the borders of the marvelous."

The "young man" of Repetition is no Abraham, and he does speak for himself in his letters to Constantin Constantius. Yet again, as in Fear and Trembling, we see this real protagonist of the work from the point of view of the pseudonymous author, who espouses an essentially different life-view from that of the protagonist. In both cases the conflict is expressed by letting the protagonist move outside the framework established by the point of view of the pseudonymous narrator.

A similar dialectical strategy is at work in the next pair of pseudonymous works, also virtually simultaneous in their publication. But in Philosophical Fragments by Johannes Climacus, published 13 June 1844, and in The Concept of Anxiety by Vigilius Haufniensis, published four days later, the more discursive side of Kierkegaard's literary gift predominates. Ideas are discussed abstractly, without narrative. The pseudonymous author expresses a secure philosophical position, but he conceives a set of ideas that he cannot accommodate on the basis of his position. These paradoxical ideas are not represented by a concrete protagonist, such as Abraham or the "young man" of Repetition, but a tension arises in purely dialectical fashion between the philosophical ground occupied by the narrator and the paradox he conceives. He can describe the paradox but cannot explain it.

Climacus is a disciple of Socrates, at least in the broad terms in which the entire Western tradition of philosophical idealism can be said to have unfolded under Socratic inspiration. He offers a warm description of the Socratic teacher as an intellectual midwife who helps the learner bring to birth the truth that is in him, under the assumption that any rational being has the capacity for true knowledge and moral insight. Climacus not only describes this teaching method, but exemplifies it in relation to the reader. Yet the "thought experiment" he proposes is to conceive of a kind of truth that is beyond human capacities, into which the learner has no natural insight. This truth is inherently paradoxical, and therefore cannot be evoked through the Socratic method. It soon becomes apparent that what is being proposed in this thought experiment is in fact the Christian gospel. It is never identified as such, except by the humorous device of having an indignant objector spring to his feet at the end of each chapter and accuse the author of plagiarism. Each philosophical term in its Socratic framework is strained to accommodate this "new" paradoxical content until it finally breaks down altogether, and the vocabulary of faith is cryptically introduced in its place. In place of a general truth that can be conceptually grasped, for instance, we are confronted with an incarnate God. But with this collapse of philosophical terms, understanding breaks down as well. If a new, Christian "stage" can be said to make its appearance in this elusive fashion, it is left entirely to the reader to come to terms with it. Climacus tells us in the preface that it is none of our business what he himself thinks of it; each individual must decide for himself. Faith is not the conclusion of an argument, but a "leap" of passion. *Philosophical Fragments* can only confront us with the starkness of the choice: Socrates or Christ—either/or.

In *The Concept of Anxiety*, as in the second volume of *Either/Or*, Kierkegaard presents some of his most original ideas in the least engaging style he can summon. If Judge William is prosaic, Vigilius Haufniensis is downright pedantic. The work is psychological, so Haufniensis introduces it with a disquisition on the relation of psychology to other intellectual disciplines, ethics and dogmatics in particular, in the course of which he denounces Hegel for the confusion he has sown among the disciplines. Yet in a parody of Hegel's philosophical style, *The Concept of Anxiety* reads like a systematic textbook. But as with *Philosophical Fragments*, there is a dissonance between form and content, for the book's most pregnant concepts fall between the disciplines that have been so carefully discriminated: anxiety, inwardness, seriousness,

possibility, freedom, temporality, guilt, sin, spirit, the leap. "Anxiety" (*angest,* earlier and perhaps better translated "dread"), for instance, can be described psychologically, but not finally explained. Unlike fear, anxiety has no distinct object. The anxious person is not afraid of anything in particular that might threaten him. His anxiety is inwardly generated, and there is as much fascination in it as there is terror. A simple example may bring out this difference between fear and anxiety. If a person is walking along a cliff and worries that his foot may slip or the ledge may give way, he experiences fear, and takes precautions. But if it should occur to him that he might take it into his head to fling himself off the cliff, he will be gripped by anxiety. Anxiety is the premonition of freedom that a person has as a spiritual, self-determining being, even before he is aware that he is a spiritual being. What is he afraid of? Nothing. Spirit is concealed even as it expresses itself: it "tempts its possibility but disappears as soon as it seeks to grasp for it, and it is a nothing that can only bring anxiety . . . anxiety is freedom's actuality as the possibility of possibility." Haufniensis, however, is concerned about quite a different sort of fall than a leap from a cliff. His treatise presents the state of anxiety as the premonition of a distinctively spiritual self-destructiveness, the leap into sin, which is complicated by membership in a sinful race. Anxiety does not cause sin. Sin is not caused at all and cannot be explained psychologically. Dogmatics can describe it after it has occurred but is equally powerless to explain its occurrence. "How sin came into the world, each man understands solely by himself. If he would learn it from another, he would *eo ipso* misunderstand it." As with faith, we have a "leap" that no words in a book can account for. We must be prepared for paradoxes in dealing with Kierkegaard. The supreme paradox in this particular text is that this darkest of anxiety-producing possibilities is the disclosure to the individual that he is a spiritual being, in league with transcendence, indeed a self-transcending being capable of salvation.

Aside from the great religious interest of this text, its notion of anxiety as freedom's possibility has made it a fountainhead of twentieth-century existential philosophy, even among thinkers such as Jean-Paul Sartre who totally reject its religious point of view. Its central themes reverberate through such major works as Martin Heidegger's *Being and Time* (1927) and Sartre's *Being and Nothingness* (1943). Of special importance in this connection is Haufniensis' treatment, in the third chapter, of the peculiar temporality created by this disclosure of possibility.

The last two works of Kierkegaard's pseudonymous authorship are both massive books, and each of them appears superficially to be a reprise of an earlier work. *Stages on Life's Way*, edited by Hilarius Bookbinder (1845), is reminiscent of *Either/Or*, and the full title of the last work is *Concluding Unscientific Postscript to the Philosophical Fragments* (1846), by Kierkegaard's philosophical spokesman, Johannes Climacus; in this thick *Postscript* to the slender *Fragments* S. Kierkegaard is again listed as "responsible for publication."

Stages on Life's Way presents three treatments of the great theme of erotic love. The first, "*In vino veritas*," by William Afham, reports on a lavish banquet, reminiscent of Plato's *Symposium*, which brings together a merry band of aesthetes who offer postprandial speeches on love. Among the speakers, all well lubricated with excellent wine, are the well-known authors Victor Eremita, Constantin Constantius, and Johannes the Seducer. Johannes, who speaks last, is in particularly fine form. Woman was created by the gods, he says, because they became fearful that their most magnificent creation, man, would reach such lofty heights as to eclipse the gods themselves. In order to tame and domesticate him, "the enchantress was fashioned; the very instant she had enchanted men she transformed

herself and held him captive in all the prolixities of finiteness." Most men went for the bait and were hooked forever. But a certain select group, the seducers, while no less attracted, saw through the plot and knew how to avoid the hook:

> . . . they dine upon the most seductive fancy which issued from the most artful thought of the gods, they dine constantly upon bait. Oh, luxury beyond compare! Oh, blissful mode of living! They dine constantly upon bait—and are never caught.
>
> (*Stages*, p. 84)

The evening, which is full of such tributes to women, at last turns gray with dawn. Since the aesthetes live for the moment, they have arranged for a wrecking crew to appear at the end of the speeches and demolish all vestiges of the feast, while the revelers flee before them like wraiths at cockcrow. As they are making their way home in the first morning light, they happen to come upon a little country house in the arbor of which they find none other than Judge William and his lovely wife enjoying their morning tea. In contrast to the revelers, who spy on them, the judge and his lady belong to the light of day. When the couple retires to the house after this charming domestic scene, the revelers discover that the judge has left behind a manuscript, which Victor steals, containing yet another epistolary treatise entitled "Various Observations About Marriage in Reply to Objections," which makes up the second part of *Stages*.

In the judge's hands this favorite theme again proves inexhaustibly rich, with sharp polemics against precisely the purely aesthetic views of love that have been advanced in the speeches at the banquet. Thus far, *Stages* may seem a recapitulation of *Either/Or*. But now the judge has got to defend marriage on another front as well: against the possibility that someone might reject marriage on religious rather than aesthetic grounds. In general the judge rejects this possibility, because marriage is an ethical bond and he holds that any authentic religion can only reinforce ethics. He cannot imagine anything more sacred than the marriage vows, which are exchanged, after all, before the altar. Yet at the conclusion of his treatise he does acknowledge that there might be a religious "exception" to the norm of marriage. But Judge William specifies several stringent conditions a person would have to meet in order to be justified in claiming that he is such an exception: he must, for instance, really be in love, and he must already be married, at least in the sense that he has taken on the ethico-religious commitments of marriage; even after he has renounced it he must "love life," in particular must appreciate the beauty of married life even more than those who remain in it. He is not entitled to renounce marriage out of mere inexperience, or because he has soured on it. Finally, the judge makes the keen dialectical point that a justified exception can never be certain that he really *is* a justified exception! In laying down the law for the would-be exception by specifying these strict conditions, the judge has set the scene for part 3: in Quidam's diary, as we have seen, there is the self-portrait of a man who has met all these conditions, remaining in excruciating uncertainty whether God has required this renunciation at all.

Earlier works have presented two positions or "stages" in conflict, though these dyads have differed from one book to another. But here, at last, we do seem to have three "stages on life's way"—the aesthetic, the ethical, and in a torment of uncertainty, the religious. But part 3 does not merely add a third stage to the aesthetic vs. ethical scheme of *Either/Or*. Quidam's diary and Frater Taciturnus' commentary on it so call into question the certainties of the ethical life that the judge's pugnacious defense of it appears, in hindsight, to be a work of desperation. The ground on which the

judge seems to stand so firmly is in fact shaking under his feet. Such, at least, is the opinion of Frater Taciturnus: " . . . for poetry is glorious, religion still more glorious, but what lies between them is prattle, no matter what talent is wasted upon it." Frater Taciturnus regards the ethical stage as merely transitional, an impossible demand culminating in repentance.

> The aesthetic sphere is that of immediacy, the ethical is that of requirement (and this requirement is so infinite that the individual goes bankrupt), the religious sphere is that of fulfillment, but note, not such a fulfillment as when one fills a cane or a bag with gold, for repentance has made infinite room, and hence the religious contradiction: at the same time to lie upon seventy thousand fathoms of water and yet be joyful.
>
> (*Stages*, p. 430)

Of course this is simply the view of the taciturn brother. The design of the pseudonymous authorship is such that each text, each pseudonymous author, comments on the stages from a different point of view.

Climacus, in *Concluding Unscientific Postscript*, presents us with four stages—aesthetic, ethical, and two carefully discriminated religious stages, Religion A oriented to divine immanence, and Religion B oriented to transcendence. He also delineates the two intermediate stages of irony and humor (irony at the boundary between the aesthetic and the ethical, humor between the ethical and the religious), and in a footnote offers a significantly different sevenfold scheme. But Kierkegaard's philosophical spokesman has more important things on his mind than the mere enumeration of stages. *Postscript* launches a major polemic against the Hegelian premises predominating in Danish thought at the time, in particular the Hegelian subsumption of Christianity into philosophical idealism. On its more constructive side, the work offers a "phenomenology of spirit" the direct opposite of that offered by Hegel in his masterpiece bearing that title. Hegel's phenomenology culminates in a corporate identity that he designates as "absolute knowledge," to be articulated in a philosophical system. Climacus denies that such knowledge is available to the "existing individual" and also denies that the system can comprehend this individual. For him the phenomenological movement consists in the more and more radical singling out of the individual before God.

This "unscientific" (antisystematic) postscript, another major contribution to twentieth-century existential philosophy, "concludes" Kierkegaard's pseudonymous authorship. It includes some forty pages devoted to "A Glance at a Contemporary Effort in Danish Literature," in which Climacus reviews all the preceding pseudonymous works. "S. Kierkegaard," furthermore, adds "A First and Last Declaration" in which he acknowledges that he has written them. At the same time, insisting on the integrity and independence of each work as the reflection of the life-view of its particular author, he insists that "in the pseudonymous works there is not a single word which is mine, I have no opinion about these works except as a third person, no knowledge of their meaning except as a reader, not the remotest private relation to them." It is very clear how this particular "reader" understood these works. In a little book entitled *The Point of View for My Work as an Author,* written in 1848 and published after his death, Kierkegaard declares that he has been a religious writer throughout, in aesthetic disguise. The problem of the entire authorship, he says, is "how to become a Christian." But this is a judgment of hindsight, written in the throes of a religious crisis in Kierkegaard's own life. The disclaimer enunciated in the "First and Last Declaration," in which he puts himself in the position of any other reader, is truer to the design of the authorship, from which it is possible to reach quite different conclusions.

TWO PUBLIC CRISES AND KIERKEGAARD'S "SECOND" LITERATURE

The religious crisis of 1848 was private, involving among other things a crisis of vocation. Kierkegaard took certain experiences as signs that he was perhaps being called to a different religious task from that of an author, though in the end the crisis confirmed him in that vocation. The issue had already been raised two years earlier, shortly before the publication of the *Postscript* with which he had intended to "conclude" his literary work. At that time Kierkegaard had precipitated a public crisis by publishing a newspaper article, on 27 December 1845, denouncing a satirical journal called *Corsaren* (The Corsair), which had had the temerity to praise some of the pseudonymous works: he wanted no praise from a scandal sheet! The journal picked up the gauntlet, launching a steady campaign of ridicule against Kierkegaard, whose personal eccentricities made him only too apt a target. Articles and cartoons depicting the addled author with uneven pant legs created a popular image that Kierkegaard never lived down. People made fun of him in the streets, children shouting "Either/Or!" at him. He finally had to give up his walks, and became more isolated than ever. A strange consequence, however, was that the episode helped him decide what to do after he had "concluded" the pseudonymous authorship. The possibility of becoming a clergyman, which he had often considered, was now out of the question. Furthermore, an obstacle to the further development of his "edifying" literature had been the worry that by communicating directly with his readers in his own name he might be asserting too much personal authority over them; for it had been a cardinal principle of all his work to assign the reader ultimate responsibility for his own decisions. He always stressed in prefaces to the edifying works that they were written "without authority." But now that he had been popularly pilloried as an eccentric fool he felt he need no longer have any concern on that score! So this public crisis had the unexpected effect of launching him, with redoubled energy, on the major works of the edifying literature, which became more and more outspokenly Christian in viewpoint. That decision was confirmed in the "private" crisis of 1848.

As was indicated, all of these works were written in his own name except two attributed to "Anti-Climacus." Anti-Climacus was the counterpart of the "philosophical" Climacus, addressing some of the same issues from a forthrightly Christian viewpoint. *The Sickness unto Death: A Christian Psychological Exposition for Upbuilding and Awakening* (1849) not only treats some of the themes of the Climacus literature in this new way, but also furnishes a sequel to the other "psychological" work, *The Concept of Anxiety.* But now the psychological theme is despair, of which the work supplies a systematic taxonomy, in far more brilliant style, presenting faith as the only antidote. *Training in Christianity* (1850), also by Anti-Climacus, is a masterpiece in the genre of devotional literature, holding up the most rigorous standards of the Christian life. This work also shows an unmistakable polemic tendency, directed against the more socially acceptable version of Christianity being preached in the established church. The strategy was to confront this bogus version with the genuine article.

This polemic against the Christianity of "Christendom," and the Danish state church in particular, became an underlying motif of all Kierkegaard's later Christian writings. It was muted by a certain tact, motivated by Kierkegaard's filial respect for the man who had been his father's pastor and confidant and was now Bishop Primate of Denmark, Jacob Mynster. Kierkegaard was himself on close personal terms with Mynster, and it has been frequently noted that his edifying discourses owe something to the style of Mynster's sermons. Nevertheless, Kierkegaard had become convinced that this venerable figure was an epitome of the cultural-religious confusion of "Christendom," in which the radical claims of the gospel had become domesticated.

Mynster died in January 1854 and was duly eulogized by Hans Martensen, who had been Kierkegaard's theological tutor and was soon to be appointed Mynster's successor.

"From the man whose precious memory fills your hearts," Martensen had intoned, "your thought is led back to that long line of witnesses to the truth, which like a holy chain stretches through time from the Apostles up to our own day." What fired Kierkegaard's anger was Martensen's use of the term "witness to the truth" (sandhedsvidne), which at that time could be found in no Danish dictionary for the simple reason that it was a recent Kierkegaardian coinage. Kierkegaard had invented it to characterize those martyrs and apostles who, in their suffering, "witnessed" the truth of Christianity. He had used it in *Works of Love* (1847), *Christian Discourses* (1848), *Two Minor Ethico-Religious Treatises* (1849), *Training in Christianity* (1850), and *For Self-Examination* (1851). And now Hans Martensen . . . had stolen his coinage to eulogize a churchman who stood for everything Kierkegaard opposed in contemporary Christendom.

(Thompson, *Kierkegaard,* p. 219)

It was too much. Kierkegaard bided his time until Martensen was safely installed as bishop, but on 18 December he published in a newspaper the passionate attack he had written shortly after the funeral, entitled "Was Bishop Mynster a 'Witness to the Truth,' One of 'the Genuine Witnesses to the Truth'—Is This the Truth?" This article was the first of twenty-one published in *Faedrelandet* (The Fatherland), and the newspaper attack was followed by thirteen issues of a pamphlet he called *The Instant.* In these articles and pamphlets, written for the general public in a popular, even violent style different from that of any of his other works, he denounced the established church and all its works, and declared that the Christianity of Christendom was a lie, "especially in Protestantism, especially in Denmark"—a kind of refrain attached to many of his denunciations. He demanded of the church the common human honesty of admitting that it had nothing to do with the Christianity of the New Testament.

The attack created a scandal and made Kierkegaard, for the second time, a notorious figure throughout Scandinavia. Long after his other works were forgotten, this passionate Christian was remembered popularly as "that shockingly anti-Christian writer." Otherwise he was virtually unknown during the nineteenth century. Only as his writings began to be translated into German and other major European languages, early in the twentieth century, did he become a major influence.

As his attack on the church continued into the autumn of 1855, Kierkegaard's health began to fail. At an evening party in late September, as another guest recalled:

> He was sitting on the sofa and had been so gay, amusing, and charming, when he fell to the floor; we helped him up: "Oh, leave—it—'til the maid—clears it away—in the morning," he stammered, exhausted.
>
> (Quoted in Thompson, *Kierkegaard*, p. 230)

He had a number of such spells, finally collapsing in the street. Before being admitted to the hospital, he sent all that remained of his money to a friend to cover his hospital and funeral expenses. He died on 11 November at the age of forty-two.

Selected Bibliography

EDITIONS

COLLECTED WORKS

Samlede Vaerker. Edited by A. B. Drachmann and J. L. Heiberg. 14 vols. Copenhagen, 1901–1906.

————. Edited by A. B. Drachmann, J. L. Heiberg, and H. O. Lange. 15 vols. Copenhagen, 1920–1931. Second edition, includes index.

————. Edited by Peter P. Rohde. 20 vols. Copenhagen, 1962–1964. Third edition, updated from the second.

Søren Kierkegaards Papirer. Edited by P. A. Heiberg, V. Kuhr, and E. Torsting. 13 vols. Copenhagen, 1909–1948. Published in 18 fascicles.

————. Edited by N. Thulstrup. Copenhagen, 1969–1970. Reprint with three additional volumes of papers and indices.

TRANSLATIONS

Note: A new collected edition of *Kierkegaard's Writings* translated into English under the direction of Howard V. Hong is in process of publication. Twenty-five volumes are projected, with a twenty-sixth as cumulative index, of which several volumes have already appeared as of this writing. The published volumes of this edition are listed below.

Attack upon "Christendom." Translated by Walter Lowrie. Princeton, 1955.

Christian Discourses. Translated by Walter Lowrie. New York and London, 1940.

The Concept of Irony: With Constant Reference to Socrates. Translated by Lee M. Capel. New York, 1965.

Concluding Unscientific Postscript. Translated by David F. Swenson and Walter Lowrie. Princeton, 1941.

Crisis in the Life of an Actress and Other Essays on Drama. Translated by Stephen Crites. New York and London, 1967.

Edifying Discourses. Translated by David F. and Lillian M. Swenson. 4 vols. Minneapolis, 1943.

Either/Or, Vol. 1. Translated by David F. and Lillian M. Swenson with revisions and a foreword by Howard A. Johnson. Princeton, 1959.

Either/Or, Vol. 2. Translated by Walter Lowrie with revisions and a foreword by Howard A. Johnson. Princeton, 1959.

For Self-Examination and *Judge for Yourselves!* Translated by Walter Lowrie. Princeton and London, 1944.

The Gospel of Suffering and *The Lilies of the Field.* Translated by David F. and Lillian M. Swenson. Minneapolis, 1948.

SØREN KIERKEGAARD

Johannes Climacus; or, De Omnibus Dubitandum Est, and a Sermon. Translated by T. H. Croxall. Stanford, Calif., 1958.

Kierkegaard's Writings. Edited by Howard V. Hong. Princeton, 1978–.

Vol. 6: *Fear and Trembling; Repetition.* Translated with intro. and notes by Howard V. and Edna H. Hong. 1983.

Vol. 8: *The Concept of Anxiety.* Translated with intro. and notes by Reidar Thomte in collaboration with Albert B. Anderson. 1980.

Vol. 13: *The Corsair Affair.* Translated with intro. and notes by Howard V. and Edna H. Hong. 1982.

Vol. 14: *Two Ages: The Age of Revolution and the Present Age. A Literary Review.* Translated with intro. and notes by Howard V. and Edna H. Hong. 1978.

Vol. 19: *Sickness unto Death: A Christian Psychological Exposition for Upbuilding and Awakening.* Translated with intro. and notes by Howard V. and Edna H. Hong. 1980.

Vol. 25: *Letters and Documents.* Translated with intro. and notes by Henrik Rosenmeier. 1978.

Forthcoming volumes are as follows:

Vol. 1: *Early Polemical Writings: From the Papers of One Still Living; Articles from Student Days; The Battle Between the Old and the New Soap-Cellars.*

Vol. 2: *The Concept of Irony: Schelling Lecture Notes.*

Vol. 3: *Either/Or, I.*

Vol. 4: *Either/Or, II.*

Vol. 5: *Eighteen Upbuilding Discourses.*

Vol. 7: *Philosophical Fragments; Johannes Climacus; or, De Omnibus Dubitandum Est.*

Vol. 9: *Prefaces; Articles Related to the Writings.*

Vol. 10: *Three Discourses on Imagined Occasions.*

Vol. 11: *Stages on Life's Way.*

Vol. 12: *Concluding Unscientific Postscript.*

Vol. 15: *Upbuilding Discourses in Various Spirits.*

Vol. 16: *Works of Love.*

Vol. 17: *Christian Discourses* and *The Crisis and a Crisis in the Life of an Actress.*

Vol. 18: *Without Authority: The Lily of the Field and the Bird of the Air; Two Ethical-Religious Essays; Three Discourses at the Communion on Fridays; An Upbuilding Discourse; Two Discourses at the Communion on Fridays.*

Vol. 20: *Practice in Christianity.*

Vol. 21: *For Self-Examination* and *Judge for Yourselves.*

Vol. 22: *The Point of View: The Point of View for My Work as an Author; Armed Neutrality; On My Work as an Author.*

Vol. 23: *The Moment* and *Late Writings.*

Vol. 24: *The Book on Adler.*

On Authority and Revelation. Translated by Walter Lowrie. Princeton, 1955.

Philosophical Fragments. Translated by David F. Swenson. Revised by Howard V. Hong. Princeton, 1962.

The Point of View. Translated by Walter Lowrie. New York, London, and Toronto, 1939.

Purity of Heart Is to Will One Thing. Translated by Douglas V. Steere. New York, 1948.

Søren Kierkegaard's Journals and Papers. Edited and translated by Howard V. and Edna H. Hong, assisted by Gregor Malantschuk. 7 vols. Bloomington, Ind., and London, 1967–1978.

Stages on Life's Way. Translated by Walter Lowrie. Princeton, 1945.

Thoughts on Crucial Situations in Human Life: Three Discourses on Imagined Occasions. Translated by David F. Swenson. Minneapolis, 1941.

Training in Christianity. Translated by Walter Lowrie. Princeton, 1947.

Works of Love. Translated by Howard V. and Edna H. Hong. New York, 1964.

BIOGRAPHICAL AND CRITICAL STUDIES

Collins, James. *The Mind of Kierkegaard.* 2nd edition. Princeton, 1983.

Crites, Stephen. *In the Twilight of Christendom: Hegel vs. Kierkegaard on Faith and History.* Chambersburg, Pa., 1972.

Croxall, T. H. *Kierkegaard Commentary.* New York, 1956.

Diem, Hermann. *Kierkegaard's Dialectic of Existence.* Edinburgh, 1956.

Johnson, Howard A., and Niels Thulstrup, eds. *A Kierkegaard Critique.* New York, 1962.

Mackey, Louis. *Kierkegaard: A Kind of Poet.* Philadelphia, 1971.

Malantschuk, Gregor. *Kierkegaard's Thought.* Princeton, 1971.

———. *Kierkegaard's Way to the Truth.* Minneapolis, 1963.

Nordentoft, Kresten. *Kierkegaard's Psychology.* Pittsburgh, 1978.

Scmuëli, Adi. *Kierkegaard and Consciousness.* Princeton, 1971.

Swenson, David F. *Something About Kierkegaard.* Minneapolis, 1941.

Taylor, Mark C. *Kierkegaard's Pseudonymous Authorship: A Study of Time and the Self.* Princeton, 1975.

————. *Journeys to Selfhood: Hegel and Kierkegaard.* Berkeley, Los Angeles, and London, 1980.

Thompson, Josiah. *The Lonely Labyrinth: Kierkegaard's Pseudonymous Works.* Carbondale, Ill., 1967.

————. *Kierkegaard.* New York, 1973.

————, ed. *Kierkegaard: A Collection of Critical Essays.* Garden City, N.Y., 1972.

STEPHEN CRITES

RICHARD WAGNER

(1813–1883)

FRIEDRICH NIETZSCHE WROTE in *Toward a Genealogy of Morals* that the artist is, "after all, only the presupposition of his work, the womb, the soil, at times the dung and manure on which and out of which it grows—and accordingly, in most cases, something one must forget if the work itself is to be enjoyed." Richard Wagner engrossed Nietzsche's thoughts as he wrote this passage.

To an extraordinary extent Wagner's operas—so abundant in tonal beauties—are sublimations of ignoble ideas and instincts, sublimations of that ruthlessness and fanaticism many of his admirers put out of mind when under the spell of his compelling, captivating, powerful music. Finding his ideology troubling, indeed, embarrassing, they either ignore or deny it. To shut one's eyes to his ideology is, perhaps, consoling to those without intellectual curiosity and thus without interest in the cultural meaning of his whole achievement; but denial is utterly in vain: the monumental record of Wagnerian thought survives in his own hand—the prose works, so fascinatingly rich in mental perversities.

I

During the great decades of Wagnerism (1880–1920), Wagner's essays were considered prodigious in style and profound in substance, their significance attested by both the few devotees who had read them and the many who had not. The composer's followers celebrated him as a philosopher of commanding literary power in the tradition of Friedrich Hegel, Ludwig Feuerbach, and Arthur Schopenhauer—indeed, as a master who had put such predecessors quite in the shade. It was the supposed universality of his genius that captured the imagination and made him appear matchless, his adherents hailing his impostrous role of commentator, critic, aesthetician, and social, political, and racial theorist no less fulsomely than his musical genius. For the most part, in matters Wagnerian his disciples stripped themselves of reason, discrimination, and judgment.

Political and racial elements buttressed German Wagnerism. However, for the French symbolists and those in the related English aesthetic movement, Wagner's clamorous nationalism, vulgar anti-Semitism, and ritual vegetarianism had less attraction. Rather, his theories of art stirred in them intimations of the ineffable, of secret and marvelous things. For a variety of reasons, in which the magic of his music played the most consistent part, men of talent the world over entangled themselves to varying degrees in Wagnerism, among them the junior Rossettis, Algernon Charles Swinburne, John Galsworthy, Aubrey Beardsley, George Bernard Shaw, Alphonse

Daudet, D. H. Lawrence, Paul Verlaine, Stéphane Mallarmé, Charles Baudelaire, Paul Valéry, Camille Saint-Saëns, César Franck, Henri Duparc, Ernest Chausson, Vincent d'Indy, Gabriele D'Annunzio, and Walt Whitman.

Societies of Wagnerism, enlisting the talented, the amateur, and the philistine, proliferated. One of the century's most complicated and fascinating movements, it proved especially attractive to the young, many of whom became cultists obediently manifesting an understandable idolatry of Wagner's music, a no less ardent (if less comprehensible) admiration of his poetry and prose, an inflexible antagonism toward the Jews, and a scornful contempt for any contemporary composer save their master.

Among the few consolations of Hugo Wolf's tragic life were his pilgrimages to Bayreuth, the very heart of the cult, the site of Wagner's theater (the *Festspielhaus*), and of his press. Wolf embraced Wagner's vegetarianism and particular loathing of Johannes Brahms and attempted—happily, rather unsuccessfully— a stern anti-Semitism. For his part, young Gustav Mahler was less doctrinaire: born of Jews, he made no effort to repudiate them; nor could he summon up anything but respect for Brahms; but he did follow the teaching of his revered Wagner by renouncing animal flesh, an act he believed would speed the arrival of the cleansed and regenerated Wagnerian world promised by Bayreuth.

Of course, for such sensitive and gifted young men, Wagner's music counted above all else. It stirred them to the depths and cast the spell that entangled them in the rest of his work. After a performance of *Parsifal* at Bayreuth, Wolf threw his head into his hands and sobbed. Franck's pupil, the young Guillaume Lekeu, fainted and had to be carried from the *Festspielhaus* as the prelude to *Tristan* unfolded; Emanuel Chabrier, no longer a youth—he was close to fifty—reportedly shed tears during the same performance. Two generations of Wagnerites surrendered themselves to the monumental pathos, to the overwhelming presence of the Wagnerian drama. At twenty-five, Richard Strauss still trembled merely thinking about the sound of Wagner's orchestra.

The eventual downfall of Wagnerism was hastened by the plethora of nonsense published by its leading journals: in Germany Wagner's own *Bayreuther Blätter;* in France the *Revue wagnérienne;* in England *The Meister.* The less sense Wagnerians made the more they understood one another: both the fallaciousness of Wagnerian theory, so carefully wrapped in pseudoprofundities, and the foolishness of Wagner's prose stood forth—unwittingly laid bare by his own devotees.

From the time Wagner's comprehensive essays began to circulate, many had questioned the quality of Wagnerian thought. In the 1890's the Viennese critic Eduard Hanslick, one of the most distinguished and persistent opponents of Wagnerism, predicted that within a short time "the writings of the Wagnerites will be looked upon in amazement as the relics of an intellectual plague." During the preceding decade, Nietzsche, once a Wagnerite, wondered how he had been capable of taking Wagnerism seriously; he too had come to recognize it as a malady: "Is Wagner a man at all?" he asked. "Is he not rather a disease?" Some twenty years Hanslick's junior, Nietzsche realized how enduring the infection would prove; he sensed the terrible future. The new generation of Wagnerites would include Houston Stewart Chamberlain, Alfred Rosenberg, and Adolf Hitler, all of whom found refreshment and inspiration not only in the master's scores but in his prose. Many of its motifs were to reappear in the design of the disasters Nazism visited upon the world. Bizarrely compelling in their earnestness and with a weird, sinister logic of their own, Wagner's writings set in motion vibrations dangerous to culture itself; and no simplification, however consoling, can mask the fact that the ethical problems they pose implicate Wagner's music dramas as well.

II

Wagner (born on 22 May 1813) looked upon his operas as projections into art of all he wished to accomplish as a social and political reformer, his aesthetic theories and stage works being, in his eyes, but implements of this higher purpose. The lion's share of his prose writings elaborate this social/political/aesthetic composite that, over the years, he untiringly reiterated and amplified. He would certainly knit his brows at attempts to separate his art from the ideas from which it grew. He was proud of his didactic program meant to restructure the Germanic world, and he ceaselessly lamented the failure of most of his contemporaries—especially those in power—to pay attention to his teachings. (One suspects that in his subconscious Wagner appreciated his true purpose and concern—the creation of great music—which, in his prose, he so often confused with his message.) He laboriously raised a strange house few desired to enter apart from a small group of faithful commentators whose murky writings then worked on the nervous systems of a later and troubled generation; his theoretical ramblings—especially his racial theories—became a legacy to be exploited and carried to its logical and appalling conclusions in the century following his own. Wagner left the "solution" to those more reckless than he.

His earliest serious interests were literary. While a student at Dresden's Kreuz School he enjoyed a reputation as a poet and began a giant, demoniacal tragedy, *Leubald*, awkwardly pieced together from elements taken from Shakespeare, Goethe, and Heinrich von Kleist—from the beginning his way with words was ungracious. A performance of Goethe's *Egmont* with Beethoven's incidental music brought him revelation: *Leubald*, too, required music to achieve its full effect; he immediately sought instruction in composition. He had moved from word to tone but would soon reverse the procedure. His next adolescent attempt for the stage was a pastoral play modeled on Goethe's *Laune des Verliebten* (The Lover's Whim) and with music suggested by Beethoven's Sixth Symphony. Wagner later recalled: "While I wrote the score on one page, I had as yet not even considered a text for the following."

His verse became an extension of his musical inspiration. Indeed, he came to speak of setting his librettos to music as a process of recollection, an exercise in remembering—or sometimes tortuously struggling to remember—that first musical impulse. Too often composing became for him, in his own words, a question of: "'How did it go?' instead of 'How is it?'; not 'How is it to be?' but 'How was it?' and then having to search about until one finds it again." "It is not my way," he explained (in a letter to Karl Gaillard on 30 January 1844) quite early in his career,

to select any pleasing material, put it into verse, and then ponder how to add suitable music to it. Were I to proceed in this way, I would expose myself to the inconvenience of having to inspire myself twice, which is impossible. My way of creating is quite different: to begin with, only that material can appeal to me which displays to me not only poetical but also, and at the same time, musical significance. Before starting to write a verse or even to sketch a scene, I am already intoxicated by the musical aroma [*Duft*] of my creation; I have all the tones, all the characteristic motives in my head so that when the verses are finished and the scenes put in order, the opera proper is also finished for me, the detailed musical treatment being rather a calm and considered afterwork that the moment of real creation has preceded.

(*Richard Wagner Briefe*, p. 154)

The poetic idea of the unfolding dramatic situation incited a tonal correlative, which in turn called forth the almost simultaneously fitted text in a seemingly fated fusion of tone and word.[1]

His prose, alas, had no such intoxicating origins. Yet the effort to traverse it should be made. One suffers the infelicitous poetry of his librettos for the rewards of their musical investiture; his tangled prose also offers recompense: an understanding of Wagner's purpose in constructing the giant machine of his so-called *Gesamtkunstwerk* (the all-embracing work of art) and a recognition of the forces that forged this purpose. The essays lay open the thinking that engendered the initial "intoxication" and with it Wagner's first apprehension of the music; they convey whatever may be known of the origins themselves.

III

Except for his autobiography, Wagner's prose is rarely read. Stretching in time from an aspiring young composer laboring in Paris at his first consistent literary attempts to the disordered scribblings of a celebrated master dying in Venice, it includes journalistic articles and reviews, polemic essays, and ambitious speculative treatises. Of the influences that helped form this almost half-century of writing, among the first was Heinrich Heine. A fellow student in Leipzig, one Schröter, introduced Wagner to works—probably the *Reisebilder* (1826–1831)—of the Rhenish poet, whose light and elegant manner of expression

the young Wagner would all too briefly attempt to imitate during his first stay in Paris. Another source was E. T. A. Hoffmann, especially his *Fantasiestücke in Callots Manier* (1814–1815). In *My Life* Wagner recalls this youthful enthusiasm: "I really lived and moved amid Hoffmann's artistic, ghostly apparitions." More lasting impressions derived from two of his mentors: the convoluted syntax of both his uncle, Adolf Wagner, a scholar, literary critic, and translator resident in Leipzig, and a young teacher at the university, Christian Hermann Weisse—already a respected Hegelian—the obscurity of whose lectures on aesthetics set the young man aflame. For a while Wagner's diction became so complicated that he could not be understood, and his elder brother Albert grew concerned at his mental state. Abstruseness was to remain an essential of the Wagnerian literary manner.

As a prose writer Wagner's earliest attempts are uncharacteristic of his more mature work. Having written his first opera, *Die Feen* (The Fairies), during 1833, in the German romantic idiom of Felix Mendelssohn, Carl Maria von Weber, and Heinrich Marschner—a complicated, haunted northern world of chivalry and supernatural forces—he suddenly and unexpectedly trumpeted forth a newfound admiration of the simplicity and warmth of the Mediterranean temperament. Prompted by the novelist Heinrich Laube, a leader of progressive German youth, the young composer took Vincenzo Bellini as his new idol and Italian sensualism as his new ideal, tendencies characterizing his second opera, *Das Liebesverbot* (The Ban on Love), and discussed in two of (his earliest) articles of 1834. The first, "Die deutsche Oper" ("On German Opera"), appeared in Laube's *Zeitung für die elegante Welt;* the other, "Pasticcio," in the *Neue Zeitschrift für Musik,* Robert Schumann's new periodical. For the moment Wagner saw the Latin spirit as a symbol of freedom, the Teutonic temper as the essence of puritanical narrowness. His articles con-

---

[1]Wagner's purely literary works are for the most part of a disagreeableness painful to comtemplate—his play, *Eine Kapitulation: Lustspiel in antiker Manier* (*A Capitulation,* 1870), for example. The mass of his music composed without connection with words—marches, salon pieces—has a similar distinction. Exceptions are his splendid libretto for *Die Sarazenen* (*The Saracen Woman,* 1841–1842) and his sketch of a drama called *Die Sieger* (*The Victors,* 1856). But since both came into being without initial musical stimulus, he could not find suitable ways of providing them with scores. At best they served to contribute literary elements to later works, the first to *Tannhäuser* and *Die Walküre* (*The Valkyrie*), the second to *Parsifal.*

demned the Germans as too intellectual, too learned to create warm, human figures on the stage. Mozart, he admitted, had succeeded, but only with the aid of Italian song—erudition being the source of every German ill. Through Bellini he sought simple, noble beauty in song and with it the operatic image of true life.

A third article concentrated its fire on German operatic music. Its delight in the orchestral, Wagner insisted, created a tawdry scene of boundless disorder, a patched and doctored jumble in which countless pedantic commentaries from the orchestra fought for attention and distracted the mind; in contrast, the Italians, especially Bellini, could apprehend a dramatic situation vocally with clear and firm melodic strokes. This paean to the enrapturing qualities of Bellinian song appeared anonymously in the Riga *Zuschauer* in December 1837. Wagner had been gaining experience as a conductor in the grubby theaters of one provincial German town after the other: Würzburg, Magdeburg, Königsberg, and then Riga. By the time he quit the Livonian capital, he had again changed his artistic course by his new predilection for grand opera, the pompous genre recently fabricated by Gasparo Spontini and Giacomo Meyerbeer; with them as his models, he began the composition of his mammoth *Rienzi.*

Wagner's way of quitting a job usually took the form of flight from his creditors. His exit from Riga was particularly undignified, for he also had to evade the police. By way of Prussia and then England he eventually made his way to Paris in 1839. There he had no success and sustained himself by fresh borrowing, by working as a musical hack, and by turning out a series of stories and articles for the *Gazette musicale*, a magazine owned by the German publisher Moritz Schlesinger. Writing in German—which the *Gazette* put into French—Wagner adopted a light, readable style, a watered mixture combining the weirdness of E. T. A. Hoffmann and the sparkle of Heine. Some of the tales are not without fine effect,

especially two interrelated narratives: "An End in Paris," whose autobiographical burden is the unhappy lot of an impecunious German musician in the glittering capital, and the moving "Pilgrimage to Beethoven," a fictional account of the same artist's visit to the master. Here Wagner provided a startling adumbration of his future mode of expression relative to his music dramas. He has Beethoven declare that were he to write an opera after *Fidelio*, he would abandon the "number" opera—"no arias, duets, trios, none of the stuff with which they patch together operas today"—and instead create true musical drama by opposing "the wild, unfettered elemental feelings, represented by the instruments, to the clear, definite emotion of the human heart as represented by the human voice." The "Pilgrimage" was a first step toward the essays of Wagner's Swiss period, that climacteric in his development as a theorist.

In Paris he also became correspondent for a Dresden newspaper, the *Abendzeitung*, dispatching to it the German originals of some of his *Gazette* articles and additional observations on the local musical life. To August Lewald's journal, *Europa* (Stuttgart), he sent a pair of witty pieces (1841): "Parisian Amusements" and "Parisian Fatalities for the Germans," the latter ending with a prayer for the redemption of the thirty thousand Germans living in the French capital. He was striving to keep his name alive in his homeland and to demonstrate his attachment to it.

"On German Music" (1840), his first contribution to the *Gazette*, had revealed the depth of his enthusiasm for grand opera as offered at the great Paris Opéra, an especially magniloquent and calculated kind of historical pageant accompanied by music, an ingenious genre brought to its ultimate point by a German, Giacomo Meyerbeer, in *The Huguenots.* Wagner had fully done with his Italian flirtation and his concomitant contempt for the operatic ability of his countrymen. The article hailed the particular and historic gift of the Germans to "denationalize" themselves in the realm of opera:

> The universal tendency of which the German spirit is capable made it easy for the German artist to naturalize himself on foreign terrain. German genius appears to be almost destined to seek out among its neighbors what is not native to its motherland, to lift this above its narrow boundaries and thereby create something universal for the entire world.

"On German Music" was not only a tribute to Meyerbeer's methods but also an avant-courrier for *Rienzi*, that Brobdingnagian grand opera, which, Wagner hoped, might outdo Meyerbeer and topple him from his throne.

The longer he lingered in Paris the more Wagner prized things German. As German history, medieval German literature, and Teutonic myth increasingly commanded his interest, his Meyerbeer fever subsided: *The Huguenots* now seemed to him too contrived, its composer an artful charlatan. Wagner's failure to make an impression on Paris made him resent Meyerbeer's extraordinary success all the more; resentment turned to anger, anger to hatred. Moreover, Meyerbeer was a German and a Jew, two words Wagner had come to regard as mutually exclusive: he no longer looked upon Meyerbeer as a representative of the German spirit. Henceforth, an almost pathological anti-Semitism would play its baleful part in the development of Wagnerian theory, which—ironically—availed itself boldly and unashamedly of constituents of Meyerbeer's art while characterizing them as newly born and of immaculate Aryan strain.

With the completion of *Rienzi*, set under the brilliant sun of Rome, Wagner began work on a new opera, *Der Fliegende Holländer (The Flying Dutchman)*, which unfolds amid the mists and wild cliffs of the Scandinavian fjords. Both works received their premieres soon after Wagner's return to Dresden (1842), where he had quickly been named *Kapellmeis-*

ter of the Royal Theater. The triumphs that had eluded him in Paris he finally met on his native soil.

By the end of his seven-year tenure of the Dresden podium, Wagner had added *Tannhäuser* and *Lohengrin* to his creations and become a famous if increasingly difficult man, with a tendency to inflate his domestic, personal, and professional problems into transcendant political, moral, and artistic issues. Moreover, he had grown to see himself and his art as *the* quintessential expressions of the German spirit. Most of his major essays—tracts might be a more accurate word—would take the form of attempts to substantiate this extraordinary claim, a bizarre manifestation of an ego that astounded even Bismarck.

Despite outward success, Wagner realized that audiences remained indifferent to the national elements coloring his work since the *Dutchman.* They looked upon *Tannhäuser* as they did upon *Rienzi* or *Huguenots*—that is, as splendid grand opera—and showed little interest in his crescent, ponderous Germanism. In *Lohengrin*—it would not be staged until after his departure from Dresden—he had made the affairs of the Reich the very fulcrum of the action: the hero, just before his embarkation, is favored with a vision of an invincible Germany. Wagner faced the fact that he commanded a vogue based on a misconception of his aims, an acknowledgment that determined his new course: to bestir himself to help bring about those immediate political changes that would pull the mask of complacency from the eyes of the German public and thus begin its transformation into a knowledgeable assembly dedicated to his true meaning. The route to the permanent revitalizing of German politics and culture lay—he was certain—in a complete reform of Germany's operatic tradition. With the ambitious intention of creating a new kind of Teutonic music drama, he devoured the *Volsunga Saga*, the *Nibelungenlied*, the Eddic poems, the writings of the brothers Grimm, and other works on the

Nordic tales. He put on paper "Der Nibelun-gen-Mythus als Entwurf zu einem Drama" ("The Nibelungen Myth as Scheme for a Drama")—it contains the essence of the later *Ring*—and from it derived a dramatic poem, *Siegfrieds Tod* (*Siegfried's Death;* later titled *Götterdämmerung,* or *The Twilight of the Gods*). When provided with its musical score, it was to stand forth—so he imagined—as the first of his major instruments of German rebirth. But they could come into being only when he had cleared his way of two stumbling blocks: German officialdom (had not Saxon courtiers ignored his "Draft for the Organization of a German National Theater . . . "?) and the Jews. He extolled revolution and anti-Semitism: "The real artwork cannot be created now but only prepared for, yes, by revolutionary means, by destroying and beating down all that deserves to be destroyed and beaten down."

During several days of civil war in Dresden, Wagner was in the center of revolutionary activity. The rising failed, and by a providential escape he eluded indictment for treason and a possible death sentence. He sought refuge in Switzerland, awaiting there the pan-European conflagration he felt certain to be in preparation and devoting his time to writing: "I myself must come, and those who are interested in my artistic being must come with me, to a clear understanding." He determined to make his position and purpose unmistakable in a series of treatises: "It is most essential that I accomplish this work and send it into the world before going on with my immediate artistic production."

Wagner had anticipated something of the ambitious polemic of his Swiss period in *The Wibelungs,* written shortly before his Nibelung scenario. In that essay he attempted to sort out and codify his reading and thinking on the Rhenish myths of Siegfried and the Nibelung Hoard and their relation to German history. By the time he arrived in Switzerland, he was ready to offer the world a master plan

and the rationale of his future activities. He intended it to bestow critical legitimacy on his coming Nibelung music drama whose purpose, in turn, was to lead the Germans back to the essential greatness and profundity of their national spirit, to redeem a nation degraded and led astray by the seductions of Parisian and Jewish pseudoart.

Four tracts completed in Switzerland represent the very heart of Wagnerian thought: *Die Kunst und die Revolution* (*Art and Revolution,* 1849), *Die Kunstwerk der Zukunft* (*Artwork of the Future,* 1849), *Das Judentum in der Musik* (*Jewry in Music,* 1850), and *Oper und Drama* (*Opera and Drama,* 1851). They set forth a bizarre and complicated dialectic of dramatic and musical art.

The first discussed Athenian drama, which had brought together the arts of poetry, music, dance, and design in a profound civic and religious expression; only revolution, Wagner maintained, could free the Germans from a materialism hindering the emergence of a similar and equally great communal utterance in their midst. If the Greek artwork, as he recognized, could not be reborn, its spirit could be born anew in Germany.

The second essay described both Wagner's conception of the Folk (the epitome of all who feel a *gemeinschaftliche Noth,* a common and collective want) and his special perception of the fate of the Greek dramatic synthesis: after its decline and disintegration, he asserted, the individual arts had gone their egoistic, separate ways; having in the present time reached the limits of these divided routes, they now longed to reunite, languishing for absorption, dissolution, and redemption in a new Germanic universal artwork. Its creator could be only that unique poet through whom the unconscious, unfettered genius of the Folk might rise to consciousness.

Jewry in Music arraigned the Jew as the materialist hindering the pure instincts of the German Folk from realizing the artwork of the future through its own Teutonic Aeschylus.

The Jew, Wagner reasoned, must therefore be eliminated from German life.

The final link in this speculative tetralogy, having sweepingly surveyed operatic and dramatic history, proceeded to describe—or, as will be seen, purported to describe—the philosophy and technique of Wagner's coming composite artwork, with its close relation between word and music and its expanded orchestral eloquence that would utter the unspeakable. *Opera and Drama* postulated a compound of verse and its parallel vocal melody. The poet's part, presenting the conceptual elements, would beget the musician's vocal line. The latter was to interpret the text through artfully calculated juxtapositions of rhythm, accent, pitch, and key relationships. The resulting congruity of verse and musical phrase was to be further confirmed both by an orchestra providing harmonic modulations and instrumental color appropriate to the stage situation and by dramatically compatible contributions on the part of singing actors. The orchestra with its many tongues would take over the operatic tasks traditionally assigned to the chorus. The artwork was to be unified by a system of motifs, reiterating and stressing the conditioning forces of the drama. Toward this end, certain musical phrases were to be extracted from their positions under their correlative verses and repeated by voice or orchestra in later dramatic situations whenever ideas associated with the original words had particular pertinence. As well as recalling the emotional content of past thoughts, the motif could also awaken foreboding. Accordingly, through a subtle integration of word and tone, the conceptual was to be conveyed in terms of the musical.

To summarize this quartet of treatises: revolution was to provide the political atmosphere in which the *Gesamtkunstwerk* might flourish; the German Folk, itself, would bring it into being by inspiring the national poet; those not truly of the Folk and thus inimical to its need for the *Gesamtkunstwerk* were to be weeded out; the poetic/literary elements in the *Gesamtkunstwerk* would form the fecundating element and affect as offspring the music and other participating arts.

Tortuous in style, speciously reasoned, and often historically inaccurate, the Swiss essays became the peculiar rock upon which Wagner built his church; and this despite the fact that in *Opera and Drama* he described a creative process the very opposite of his own. Eager to present the German-speaking world with music dramas that would establish him as the new national poet, yet at the same time acutely aware of the limited intellectual respectability enjoyed by most musicians, he thought it politic to claim to be first of all a poet. In *Opera and Drama* he pretended that his music flowed from his verse; that, notwithstanding the powerful floods of music engulfing his so-called poetry, the word had the superior power and functioned as the dominating, regulating element of his music dramas. From this false assertion there grew with the years a maze of amorphous explanations, desperate defenses, and perplexing contradictions, a labyrinth through which many of his succeeding articles would wind. He never contrived publicly to extricate himself from this dilemma of his own creation, though to his second wife, Cosima, he later confided the depth of his embarrassment concerning *Opera and Drama:* "I know what Nietzsche didn't like in it—it is the same thing . . . that set Schopenhauer against me: what I said about words. At the same time I didn't dare say that it was music that produced drama, although inside myself I knew it."

Uneasiness about the paramount role assigned to the word in *Opera and Drama* had inspired Wagner to cite the finale of Beethoven's Ninth Symphony as rendering the *Gesamtkunstwerk* historically legitimate. In the *Artwork of the Future* he maintained that in this movement Beethoven had become a musical Columbus: exploring the seemingly shoreless sea of absolute music, he had caught sight of the undreamed-of coast of the Wagnerian music drama, this great climax of the

Ninth, in which a symphonic web discoursed upon sung poetry, anticipating the Wagnerian synthesis. (In the famous recitative for low strings Wagner claimed to sense the point of decision on Beethoven's part: his instruments, pressing toward articulateness, could of necessity but call to their aid the human voice and thus prepare for the Wagnerian music drama.) *Opera and Drama* in turn espoused Germanic myth as the worthiest subject for such discourse but held that it must proceed one voice at a time, ensembles (duets, trios, and so forth) being censured, along with formal arias, as Italianate and hence un-German.

In *Opera and Drama*, Wagner also pondered the language of his projected national drama. Writing librettos had always set him on thorns.[2] Despite his youthful belletristic pretensions, both the verse and plan of *Die Feen* had been foolish and shamelessly slipshod. The remarkable improvement evident in the literary quality of *Das Liebesverbot* must be credited to Shakespeare, whose *Measure for Measure* here provided both model and inspiration; lacking these, the verse of *Rienzi* returned to the deplorable level of *Die Feen's*. Though by the time of Wagner's Paris–Dresden period he had taken Eugène Scribe as exemplar, the books of the *Dutchman*, *Tannhäuser*, and *Lohengrin*, their fine poetic moments notwithstanding, revealed a hand incapable of mastering the mechanism of the well-made play. Yet by this time the shortcoming was made good by music, much of it so magical and imposing that it transformed the faulty librettos, rendering them convincing and covering their frequent solecisms and awkwardness. Only the increasingly long narratives, designed to explain what more skillful dramatists would have woven into the body of the plot, defied the metamorphosing powers of

Wagner's music; it is a problem he never overcame.

Opera and Drama also outlined a course by which Wagner hoped to find a permanent solution for his difficulties with texts, at least in respect to diction: his Nibelung tragedy would put to use the old alliterative verse called *Stabreim*. Forsaking formal metrical patterns and terminal rhyme, he would instead rely on pithy accented first syllables and explosive consonants, vigorous devices in which he believed to have glimpsed the deepest roots of the German language. Moreover, the dense and concise configurations into which *Stabreim* could be hammered offered Wagner a compensatory opportunity for musical expansiveness.

Wagner's Nibelung drama grew to gigantic proportions as, adding to the material already in his Nibelung scenario, he developed it into theatrical form and penned three expository dramas elucidating the series of mythic, cosmic events leading to the catastrophe, the death of Siegfried. Wagner ended (1852) with a cycle of poetic dramas called *Der Ring des Nibelungen (The Nibelung's Ring)*, a trilogy preceded by a prologue—and thus often termed a tetralogy—consisting of *The Rhinegold*, *The Valkyrie*, *The Young Siegfried* (later simply *Siegfried*), and *The Twilight of the Gods*. The titles of the *Ring* operas as we know them today were fixed by the summer of 1856.

Thus the *Ring* grew from the piling up of antecedent dramas designed to elucidate those that followed. At the same time, Wagner retained tracts of repetitive narrative in all of the units in order to permit them independent lives on the stage. From these circumstances—in addition to his frequent need, even in the ordinary course of events, to turn to narrative when his dramatic craft failed—were born the celebrated longueurs of the *Ring*. Thus Wagner brought into being a bizarre genre, not without elements of precedent in the dramas of Germany's greatest poet, Goethe: a series of expanded narrative and reflective monologues masquerading as drama,

[2]Today only the most believing Wagnerian disciples maintain the claim that Wagner's librettos are self-sufficient works of art or that he was as great a poet and playwright as a musician. It is the marvelous music that carries the *Gesamtkunstwerk*.

a masquerade made convincing by great music. In general, the *Ring* dramas are inert and passive, Wagner's characters either chronicling past events or expressing their reactions to the woeful situations in which they, for the most part, find themselves. They narrate, argue, meditate, or lament, but rarely act. Though in the *Ring* (and in *Tristan* and *Parsifal*), a bit of stage action often has the force of an event, Wagner's supreme artistic moments remain these subjective deliberations, for they provide opportunities for a kind of music that turns seemingly unhistrionic cogitations into powerful drama.

IV

Even before completing the four dramatic *Ring* poems—which he himself hailed as the greatest ever written—he had turned to the German-speaking world and, in a largely autobiographical pamphlet, *Eine Mitteilung an meine Freunde* (*A Communication to My Friends,* 1851), appealed for financial help to bring about the poetic and musical realization of the *Ring* and its mounting at a specially appointed festival. (The *Communication* remained the richest source of biographical facts concerning Wagner until the appearance of *My Life.*)

Banned from returning to German lands after his revolutionary escapade, he sought to guide from a distance the increasing number of Wagnerian productions in his homeland. He wrote *Über die Aufführung des Tannhäuser* (*On Performing Tannhäuser*) in August 1852 and at the end of the year issued a similar pamphlet on the mounting of *Dutchman;* these instructions were forwarded to theaters evincing an interest in these operas. By this time he had renounced the unrealistic idea of making tiny Zurich the center of Wagnerian activities, evidently his hope while putting together his article "Ein Theater in Zurich" ("A Theater in Zurich," 1851).

His prolonged involvement with prose works did not really steal for literature energies better devoted to music: as a composer he had found himself in a virtually complete musical paralysis since the completion of the prelude to *Lohengrin* in August 1847. Though the music of the *Ring* was shaping itself in his inner ear, he remained unable to gather his musical strength, impotent to dredge the notes from the depths and put them on paper. It is doubtful that any other major composer ever suffered so long a musical drought.

Not until September 1853 did the hour come and the music of the *Ring*'s opening scene begin to rise to the surface of his consciousness. He proceeded to compose the score of *Rhinegold*, that of *Valkryie*, and the first two acts of *Siegfried* over a period of almost four years, completing the orchestral sketch of the latter on 30 July 1857. But at the point when Siegfried was approaching the fire-enclosed Valkyrie rock to awaken Brynhild from her magic slumber, Wagner suddenly put aside all work on the *Ring;* he had thrown himself into the affairs of a quite different kind of hero. By 20 August he had begun to sketch the libretto of *Tristan.*

Since his Dresden days he had known the story of Tristan, but only after the poet Georg Herwegh (also a German exile in Switzerland) introduced him to the philosophy of Arthur Schopenhauer did Wagner awaken to the musical and dramatic possibilities of the tale. He now interpreted Tristan's character in terms of Schopenhauerean disaffirmation and negation. Wagner had borrowed many ideas from Goethe: not only the disaffected hero and the mother goddess or "Eternal Feminine" as his savioress, but also the concept of a transfiguring renunciation. But studying Schopenhauer made Wagner apprehend this motif—in Goethe one of quiet withdrawal—in terms of violent annulment; he came to see in the figure of Tristan the very essence of this annihilative spirit. Wagner now identified himself not with the mythological, heroic Siegfried exalting action and victory but with a medieval knight preaching self-extinction and oblivion. In short, Wagner was no longer attuned to the *Ring:* as the Tristan theme increasingly took possession of him, it drove from his mind the robust and at times boisterous music of *Siegfried* and replaced it with intimations of those chromatic harmonies of passion and sorrow now inseparable from the very idea of Tristan and his beloved Isolde. Wagner's creative energies first reawakened in *Rhinegold,* fully flowing in *Valkyrie,* and then blocked in *Siegfried,* had found a new channel. He finished the score of *Tristan* in Lucerne on 6 August 1859.

His journey from the joyous Siegfried to the melancholy Tristan had been prepared by two disappointments: the collapse of his marriage (long foundering) and the failure of the revolutionary movement. In the great capitals of Europe uprisings had come and gone, leaving matters much as before. In particular, Louis Napoleon's coup—the preparation for the second French empire—had made Wagner despair of Europe's artistic and political future. Ironically, it was this new emperor who indirectly helped restore him to his homeland. Napoleon III had commanded a production of *Tannhäuser* at the Paris Opéra, for which occasion Wagner rewrote and expanded whole sections of the work. Armed with whistles and flageolets, a group of socialites, eager to embarrass Napoleon and to show disapproval of Wagner in particular and of Germans in general, turned the performances (March 1861) to shambles. News of the shameful demonstrations made Germans close ranks behind a composer whom foreigners had come to regard as a symbol of the nation. At home complete amnesty was but a matter of time. By March 1862 the last barrier had fallen: his native land of Saxony lay open to him.

With the completion of *Tristan,* Wagner was still unready to resume work on the *Ring.* Instead, he returned to a plan conceived as early as 1845: to write a light comedy about

Hans Sachs and the Meistersinger as a kind of satyr play following the tragedy of Tannhäuser, a comic, Aristophanic complement to the heavier work. (The rewriting of *Tannhäuser* in Paris had evidently rekindled the project.) Moreover, comedy was the genre most likely to open the doors of German theaters. Wagner had not had a premiere since that of *Lohengrin* in 1850. The unfinished *Ring* was locked in his desk, and the enormous difficulties in the orchestral and vocal parts of *Tristan* for the moment precluded its performance. Somehow he had to start a flow of new royalties: Hans Sachs was needed to open the sluice.

The language of *Tristan und Isolde,* with its extravagant, often grotesque, alliterations, repetitions, and forced rhyme, is so overwrought and at times so private that phrases frequently yield more mood and effect than sense. Indeed, without the help of the poem's prose draft many turns of the plot would remain incomprehensible. In its own way no less heavily mannered—though it often descends to doggerel—the poem of *Die Meistersinger von Nürnberg* is at the same time buoyed up by the charming and quaint folk vocabulary coloring many of its pages, terminology Wagner borrowed from Johann Christoph Wagenseil's famous study of the Meistersinger and their customs. In its attempt to succeed as a well-made play, *Meistersinger* does not carry the day as felicitously as the earlier *Liebesverbot,* the device of the exchanged clothes and identities in the second act, for example, completely missing the mark. With such details Wagner was utterly helpless. In any case, *Meistersinger* emerged as a traditional historic grand opera and announced Wagner's return to this Parisian genre, to the line of *Rienzi* and the middle acts of *Tannhäuser* and *Lohengrin.* Fittingly, he wrote and completed the poem in the French capital (December 1861–January 1862). Retreating from the scenic complexities, the transformations and magic, of the *Ring*—even if finished, it appeared doomed to remain a silent score—he had come back to a more practical, yet no less impressive, kind of theater. Moreover, his mood had changed: he no longer identified himself with Tristan's longing for self-dissolution; though relinquishing his beloved Eva, Hans Sachs remains very much of the world. In its earliest stages of creation, *Meistersinger* seemed to pour from the composer, who found himself writing down the music as he simultaneously framed the libretto. Such had not been the case since the pastoral drama of his youth. He was to finish this masterly score years later and under extraordinary patronage.

V

In 1864 the young king of Bavaria, Ludwig II, summoned Wagner to Munich, there to live under royal protection and, free from material care, to devote himself to completing the *Ring.* Ludwig determined to give his capital a monumental theater in which model performances of Wagner's works might be given, and the composer began to organize his thoughts about a complementary conservatory in which to train singers, instrumentalists, and conductors in his style. The result was his "Bericht an Seine Majestät der König Ludwig II von Bayern über eine in München zu errichtende deutsche Musikschule" ("Report to His Majesty Ludwig II, King of Bavaria, Concerning a German Music School To Be Erected in Munich," March 1865), the kind of work in which Wagner showed himself at his best: his discussion of the state of music education in Germany reveals the astute professional who had built his career on the podiums of the nation's provincial theaters; for whole stretches his writing is incisive, businesslike, and without the more usual flow of nonsense on racial, social, and political matters. In much the same spirit he had, a year and a half before, written *Das Wiener Hof-Operntheater* (*The Vienna Opera House*), a pamphlet urging that the great theater rising on the newly created *Ringstrasse* adopt the organizational proce-

dures of the Paris Opéra, whose methods he so admired. For a while he had imagined that Vienna would be his final home, the scene of his crowning endeavors.

In Munich Wagner's major error was to assume that his operatic projects would become one with Bavaria's governmental policies and that the concept of artistic and political rejuvenation through his music dramas would spread from this new center to all of greater Germany. He was perhaps surprised by the long memory of the Bavarian court, which looked on him with deep suspicion because of his involvement in the Dresden insurrection. To allay this animosity, Ludwig asked him soon after his arrival to define his political thinking of the moment. From this request had grown the essay "Über Staat und Religion" ("On State and Religion") of July 1864. It maintained that he had "never descended to the province of politics proper." Limited creatures like police officials—those who judge only from outward appearances—had accused him of being a revolutionary; a sensitive statesman like Ludwig, Wagner declared, could never make such a mistake. This defense was completely mendacious: he had been over his head in political intrigue. But in truth Wagner was no longer the firebrand of Dresden. The revolutionary, having experienced a period of resignation and apathy nourished by Schopenhauer, had returned to honor the authoritarianism and monarchism so dear to him since youth. "On State and Religion" celebrated the king as a kind of superman. The *Ring,* born of the revolutionary spirit, now tortured its creator with seemingly insoluble problems of adjustment and revision: during his Munich days he had no clear idea of how to end it, much less how to explain it.

During the autumn of 1865, for the king's instruction, Wagner had begun a political journal. (It appeared later in revised form under the title "Was ist deutsche?" ["What is German?"].) Here he scorned the revolutionary disturbances of the late 1840's as "un-German," the very concept of democracy, in fact, being un-German, "a completely translated thing," a French concept foisted on the nation by its Jewish press. He condemned not only the Jews—"the completely alien element" corrupting the German Spirit—but also the Prussians: "The German . . . sees himself . . . squeezed between Junker and Jew." Redemption for Germany, that is, salvation from contaminating Franco/Judaic/Hohenzollern influences, could come only from that prince who had made the Wagnerian music drama the very center of his thought and endeavor. Such observations lay bare how few ideas really make up Wagnerian "thought": his so-called metaphysics and politics, hailed as revelation by his disciples, boil down to a few preposterous ideas, repeated, expanded, and only slightly varied through the decades.

The brilliant premiere of *Tristan und Isolde* (*Tristan and Isolde;* Munich, 10 June 1865) demonstrated that Wagner's presumed unsingable and unplayable operas were, indeed, singable and playable. He now appeared unassailably entrenched in Bavaria. But it was not long before his arrogance, as formidable as his musical genius, led him to a fatal blunder: he sent to a local newspaper an article—under the shield of anonymity, so he thought—that painted the monarch as more faithful to Wagnerian interests than to those advocated by his cabinet. Wagner had done the unthinkable in terms of etiquette by exploiting his friendship with the king in print. Court and public were coming to look on him as a danger to the state. A royal request bade him leave the kingdom, and on 10 December 1865 he once again departed for exile in Switzerland.

VI

Whatever his disappointment in respect to Wagner's character and judgment, Ludwig persisted in his idealism concerning Wagnerian opera. He continued his lavish support of the composer, who settled on a splendid estate near Lucerne and returned to the score of *Meistersinger.* Coincident with work on its final act, he began (September 1867) a long essay, "Deutsche Kunst und deutsche Politik" ("German Art and German Politics"). He had resumed his self-imposed role of mentor to the nation.

The passing months, the preoccupation of the press with the conflict between Austria and Prussia (in which, to its cost, Bavaria took the Hapsburgs' part), and Wagner's residence in Switzerland had helped cool Munich's hostility toward him. Ludwig could now anticipate visits from his friend, whom he expected personally to supervise the premiere of *Meistersinger* at the Royal Theater. Tensions had relaxed to such a point that Wagner found himself encouraged to dispatch to Munich on a regular basis contributions to the *Süddeutsche Presse*, a new government newspaper sustained by both treasury funds and the king's personal benefactions. Wagner was expected to concern himself only with material appropriate to the section on the arts. The very title of his first contribution, "German Art and German Politics," should have put the editor, the famous Julius Fröbel, on guard; he must have known that Wagner saw the two as one.

"German Art and German Politics" (which was to appear in fifteen installments) is essentially an expansion of Hans Sachs's final address to the German Folk in the third act of *Meistersinger*, a famous tirade disparaging French, and extolling German, art. The series, which, alas, lacks the antidote of the tirade's magnificent music, appeared anonymously; but as usual the idiosyncratic style betrayed the author from the first. Unashamedly, he served up his usual terrine of clichés, hardly bothering even to freshen them. Once again he expected the public to digest such stale nuggets as the degeneracy of the French, the shallowness of their art, the contrasting vigor of the German Folk destined through the instrumentality of the *Gesamtkunstwerk* to civilize the globe, and so forth. Most shocking to contemporary readers was Wagner's panegyric (in the ninth installment) on the young assa-

1159

sin who in 1819 had struck down the celebrated Weimar-born playwright, August von Kotzebue, distinguished for having brought a particularly Parisian flair and facility to his dramas. Germans sympathetic to things French were, according to Wagner, seducers of German youth, betrayers of the German Folk; the only truly German response to those like Kotzebue—Wagner implied—was the dagger.

The astounding inappropriateness of such material to an official Bavarian publication makes one wonder why the government permitted the articles to continue beyond the first few. Perhaps Ludwig held back from one issue to the next in the hope that Wagner's arguments might take a happier turn. But by the thirteenth installment both palace and cabinet realized that matters had reached an intolerable pitch, Wagner's anti-French and anti-Prussian bias threatening to disturb Bavarian foreign policy. A sudden royal order required whatever remained of the type to be broken up: "German Art and German Politics" vanished from the pages of the *Süddeutsche Presse.* A period of estrangement between Wagner and Ludwig ensued. It ended when the triumphant premiere of *Meistersinger* (Munich, 21 June 1868) rekindled their dedication to what originally had been the main and mutual goal of their friendship: the completion of the *Ring.*

Since those parts of the cycle already in score still remained unperformed, few realized that, though *Rhinegold* and the first two acts of *Valkyrie* to a limited extent followed the spirit of the Swiss essays, its concluding act revealed a thickening orchestral fabric betokening a dramatic change in Wagner's apprehension of the relation between the word and its accompanying music. Yet, if the Nibelung scores remained a sealed book to Wagnerites, many of those who had heard *Tristan and Isolde* must have recognized it as violating almost every prescription of *Opera and Drama:* the composer, it appeared, had drawn the pen through the Wagnerian commandments. How could he maintain his pretense that the word remained the regulating and dominating element in his works? *Tristan* showed itself not an opera or music drama (the term Wagner preferred) but a symphonic poem with auxiliary vocal parts. In measure after measure sweeping musical tides washed the libretto, drenching the knotty text in orchestral sound, reducing it to an overall incomprehensibility from which there fitfully emerged those repeated words and phrases Italian librettists call *parole sceniche.* Moreover, the lovers, ignoring the injunction of *Opera and Drama* to sing alternately, joined their voices at the climax of their great duet.

In *Meistersinger* Wagner departed even further from his own orthodoxy; in fact, he now threw all of it to the winds: putting aside his declaration that myth alone provided themes worthy of the German stage, he here offered a historical grand opera in the manner of Meyerbeer. The closed Italian forms he had once denounced in Switzerland reappeared: arias, marches, ensembles (including a quintet), elaborate massed choruses, a ballet, and a rousing crescendo finale. Only initiates knew that in the opening act of *Siegfried* Wagner had provided the hero with two swaggering arias. Yet even at this point Wagner, ever wishing to present himself as primarily the poet, refused publicly to deny the validity of his Swiss pronouncements; almost to the end of his life he attempted, through reinterpretation, to harness them anew, to bring them into harmony with a view utterly denying their very basis: as early as 1857 in his open letter to Princess Marie Wittgenstein (published as "Über Franz Liszts symphonische Dichtungen" ["On Franz Liszt's Symphonic Poems"]), he had accepted Schopenhauer's estimate of music as the highest art.

During the years following the completion of *Tristan and Isolde,* Wagner had begun the attempt to resolve this aesthetic predicament. A sheaf of essays bears witness to his continuing struggle to force his mind along paths essentially alien to his temperament—he rarely found himself at home in the realm of abstract thought—and to persuade his followers (and himself) that his principles and his practice could yet be reconciled, that his open endorsement of music's superiority over the other arts did not contradict his Swiss pronouncements concerning reciprocal relationships within the *Gesamtkunstwerk*, that the author of *Opera and Drama* could lie at Schopenhauer's side in peace.

He found himself turning back to attitudes enunciated in his pre-Swiss writings. Two of his articles for the *Gazette musicale* ("Über deutsches Musikwesen" ["On German Music"], 1840; and "'La Reine de Chypre' von Halévy" ["Halévy and the Queen of Cyprus"], 1842) had extolled music as the superior component in opera. His "Zukunftsmusik" ("Music of the Future"), written in September 1860, acknowledged music as the more powerful agent in its union with poetic drama, the latter now being described as playing a mediating role between Schopenhauer's metaphysical, ideal world of music and the conceptual, material world of the listener: the libretto was the "plastic expression" meant to clarify music's abstract language of feeling, while poetry had as its ultimate goal the longing "to ascend" to music. Nevertheless, poetry, for its part, did provide an essential lack in music: the capacity to reply to the question, "Why?" Only when poetic drama joined music and related it to phenomena could this disturbing but indispensable question be answered. Yet, ironically, these arts, when united, had the power to transport auditors into an ecstatic state in which no inquiries were made and all answers given—a superb evocation of the intoxicating effect of the *Tristan* score. The poet was to be measured by what he left unsaid; the musician, echoing the poet's silence, was to speak the unutterable.

Ingenious as this mystification was, it did not disguise the fact that things had indeed changed: no longer, as in *Opera and Drama*, did Wagner describe music as a parallel and derivative expression of the words. Though he persuaded himself that "Music of the Future" pictured a *Gesamtkunst* structure in which the planes of music and dramatic poetry mutually penetrated and supported one another, the essay really described a fabric held aloft mainly by the musician.

With his return to grand opera and the creation of *Meistersinger*, Wagner made even more determined efforts to deck out his works with an elaborate theoretical apparatus, to bestow Germanic philosophic status on a genre that was, in reality, a somewhat sybaritic product of the Parisian boulevards. The imposing final act of *Meistersinger* is permeated with the concept of life and art as mutually reflecting dream mirrors. "On State and Religion" of 1864 had touched upon the concept of the theater as a series of ideal dream images (*Wahngebilde*). The idea owed much to Schopenhauer's *Parerga and Paralipomena*. Using it as his point of departure, Wagner began mythologizing his music dramas as emanations of the Metaphysical Will, which, he indicated, informed his genius through the allegory of dreams and visions (or apparitions), music paralleling the former, drama the later. By the time of his essay *Beethoven* (1870), he was postulating the additional concept of telepathic aural expressions paralleling the ocular, all of these experiences occurring simultaneously in the case of his brain, which thus received nothing less than composite communications from the Metaphysical Will. He had traveled light-years from the phenomenal correlatives of the Swiss essays by means of this highly idiosyncratic adaptation of Schopenhauerean theory.

The improved literary style, ingenious dialectic, and poetic insights of Wagner's *Beethoven* owe not a small debt to his discussions with a new young friend, Friedrich Nietzsche, who was at this very time writing his first large-scale work, *The Birth of Tragedy from the Spirit of Music*. Though still a devoted

Wagnerite and no doubt flattered to catch echoes of his own voice in Wagner's essay, Nietzsche was not slow to recognize that, despite great adroitness, it represented a hopeless attempt to reconcile the irreconcilable: Wagner continued to build a theory of opera on Schopenhauerean principles—principles that really denied the genre.

In *Beethoven,* however, Wagner discarded nearly all pretense concerning *Opera and Drama. Beethoven* hailed music as the towering component in the *Gesamtkunstwerk—* drama (with its stage action) being music's visible but subordinate complement, verse the element of least significance. At most, Wagner now maintained, poetry evoked the mood that evoked the music—the last really a plaintive plea that the reader recognize at least some thread of continuity in Wagnerian theory.

Über die Bestimmung der Oper (The Destiny of Opera), an address Wagner delivered to the Berlin Academy in 1871, continued the course set in *Beethoven,* the *Gesamtkunstwerk* here emerging as essentially a synthesis of music—the principal element—and mimetic action. Since the margin of improvisation open to actors of the spoken word shrank on the operatic stage because of the musical score's restricting demands, Wagner saw the composer's role as that of a ventriloquist speaking through the singers and the orchestra and thereby bestowing on the whole the necessary spirit of the extempore. Though in his article "Über die Benennung 'Musikdrama'" ("The Name 'Music Drama'") of 1872, he continued to exalt the transfiguring role of music in the *Gesamtkunstwerk—*here he spoke of music's "ancient dignity as the very womb of drama"—Wagner could never free himself of the ambivalence that had prompted him in the preface to *The Destiny of Opera* to declare it to be in complete agreement with *Opera and Drama,* which he had in fact reissued in a new edition in 1868. He continued to insist that though everything was different, nothing had changed.

VII

When the scandal attendant on his love affair with Cosima von Bülow—a daughter of Franz Liszt and the wife of Wagner's disciple Hans von Bülow—reawakened the old antagonisms in Munich, Wagner recognized that the premiere of the completed *Ring* could never be realized there. Abandoning his ties to Bavaria and King Ludwig, he turned for patronage to Prussia and the house of Hohenzollern, a move to the side of power: Prussia's minister-president Bismarck, having prevailed in greater Germany by both arms and diplomacy, had herded the German states he permitted to survive (excepting defeated Austria) into a reborn German empire with Berlin as its capital and with its king as emperor; with the defeat of the army of Napolean III at Sedan (1870), the Prussians had become suzerains of the Second Reich. During this period Wagner began to yearn for a theater of his own in some small German city—he eventually chose the Franconian town of Bayreuth— where he might bring the entire *Ring* to performance. The court at Berlin, so he believed, would help him achieve this end. The Prussians whom, for Ludwig's sake, he had formerly denounced as enemies on a par with the French and the Jews, now received his fulsome praise. By the end of the Franco-Prussian War he had determined to complete the *Ring* as a tribute to Prussia's new and ascendant position in Europe.

Wagner did not grow mellow. Quite early he had admitted to Liszt that hatred of the Jews had become as necessary to his nature "as gall is to the blood," and with the passing years this motif possessed him more and more, tenaciously invading his conversations, letters, and articles. On this subject he was to end not far from mad. In addition, the Franco-Prussian War drew the worst from him, his undying hatred of the French producing the jingoistic poem "An das deutsche Heer vor Paris" ("To the German Army Before Paris," dispatched via Lothar Bucher to Bismarck himself) and the tasteless farce *Eine Kapitulation (A Capitulation)*, which ridiculed the sufferings of the population during the siege of Paris.

Bismarck and the Prussian royal family remained aloof: they looked on Wagner as the adornment of King Ludwig's cultural preserve and did not want to appear to be poaching on Bavarian terrain. Though Wagner had yoked his *Ring* to the Prussian chariot by turning the Bayreuth project into a pan-German venture centered in Berlin—he first called the Bayreuth Theater the "National Theater"—his hopes of luring substantial sums from the Hohenzollern proved illusory. Moreover, the public sale of certificates in the Bayreuth enterprise continued to be embarrassingly light, despite his tours through the Reich during which he conducted concerts and attended endless banquets, fund-raising efforts that drained his strength. He had yet to complete *The Twilight of the Gods;* he struggled to find the time and energy.

His travels did permit him to take stock of singers and personnel in Germany's opera houses in his search for the artists to bring the *Ring* to life on the Bayreuth stage. He recorded his impressions in an article, "Ein Einblick in das heutige deutsche Opernwesen" ("A Glance at the Condition of Contemporary German Opera," 1873). A happy return to the finest period of his prose, Wagner here recapturing the roguish spirit of many of his pieces for the *Gazette musicale* as he discoursed on what he knew best: professional music-making. His witty, biting descriptions spared neither fools nor incompetents, especially in his hilarious accounts of productions of his *Dutchman, Tannhäuser,* and *Lohengrin.* Articles of this type—workaday, light, instructive but eschewing the philosophic—found Wagner at his most readable; one thinks, for example, of his brisk and entertaining "Erinnerungen an Auber" ("Reminiscences of Auber") of 1871.

Not only Berlin's reticence in respect to Bayreuth but the Reichstag's bestowal of equality of citizenship on the Jews made him veer from Prussia in outrage and disgust. He turned back to King Ludwig and wooed him again. In the end the king provided the capital needed to turn Bayreuth into a Wagnerian principality: he built and equipped the theater (or *Festspielhaus*) and constructed and furnished a palatial residence for the composer—*Haus Wahnfried.* Wagner took possession of it on 28 April 1874 to begin a reign that ended with his death (13 February 1883), a period during which Wagnerism—in which his prose works played no small part—took institutional shape.

VIII

The first Bayreuth Festival, consisting of the three premiere performances of the complete *Ring,* unfolded during August 1876. By the following autumn Wagner had begun to express the hope that the existence of the *Festspielhaus* would make Bayreuth *the* educational center of German national art: in this unique theater a new generation might be trained to take part in model performances of the masterpieces of the German lyric stage with the focus of attention on his own works from *Dutchman* to *Parsifal.* The latter was already taking form on paper; suffering from a serious heart complaint, Wagner recognized in *Parsifal* his final opera.

The plan for this Bayreuth academy collapsed, but out of his didactic mood came the founding of the official journal of Wagnerism, the *Bayreuther Blätter (Bayreuth Leaves),* originally intended as the Wagnerian academy's literary organ. Its main purpose was to give the aging and increasingly weary master a forum from which to address Wagnerites the world over—Wagner Societies had come into being not only on the Continent but in England and America too—though its pages were open to other writers as well. Initially, Wagner had looked forward to appointing

Nietzsche its editor, but the philosopher's turning into the leading apostate from Wagnerism made him choose instead the wealthy young Prussian and fanatical Wagnerite Hans von Wolzogen. Under his aegis—more correctly, under that of Cosima Wagner, whose instrument he became—the journal's maiden issue appeared early in 1878.

The completion of *Parsifal* became a race with death; Wagner tired easily, and there were periods during which memory refused his summons, a frightening state of affairs for a master accustomed to describe composing in terms of recollection. Amid these frustrations—and thus parallel with his intermittent exertions on the score of *Parsifal*—he ground out a group of articles of a bizarre cast of thought for the *Bayreuther Blätter:* "Religion und Kunst" ("Religion and Art," 1880) and its three supplements entitled "Was nützt diese Erkenntniss?" ("What Avails This Knowledge?" 1880), "Erkenne dich Selbst" ("Know Thyself," 1881), and "Heldentum und Christentum" ("Heroism and Christianity," 1881), the last greatly influenced by Arthur de Gobineau's *Essay on the Inequality of Races.* Since Wagner regarded the journal essentially as a means to apprise subscribers of "the obstacles to a noble development of the German artistic capacity . . . and the efforts necessary to conquer them," it is not surprising that these contributions were liberally laced with anti-Semitism. But it was but one of many—and often related—themes in this series of preposterous rambles that too often revealed the accelerating corruption of his faculties. One encounters such leitmotifs as the ethnologic superiority and innate nobility of the Teutonic Aryans, their godly descent and their destiny as world rulers, the inferiority of all other races, the crossing of races and the decline of racial pride, Germany's racial crisis, the possibility of the nation's racial regeneration—and with it the necessity that the Jews vanish—the Aryan as innate Schopenhauerean, the reestablishment of society and salvation through an Aryan Jesus. Most insistent in their return are irrational denunciations of vivisection and an equally irrational advocacy of vegetarianism, both positions resting on a grotesque perversion of Darwin's *Descent of Man:* it had made Wagner conclude that, since man descended from the beast, man and beast must share the same substance, the salvation of the Cross thus extending to beast as well as to man and to vegetation too—a blessed state of affairs Gurnemanz celebrates in his Good Friday discourse in *Parsifal.* Wagner presented these ideas most completely in "Offenes Schreiben an Herrn Ernst von Weber, Verfasser der Schrift: 'Die Folterkammern der Wissenschaft'" ("An Open Letter to Herr Ernst von Weber, Author of the Book: *The Torture-chambers of Science,"* 1879). In Weber, a former African explorer and diamond miner, Wagner found a fellow crusader against vivisection.

Wagner had in fact built the book of *Parsifal* from these shabby materials. Yet, despite much in it that is morally monstrous, the libretto proved to be Wagner's most ingeniously wrought; though the text suffers from passages of astounding turgidity (the "blood" arias of Amfortas, for example), there are nevertheless many moments of surpassing lyric expressiveness. For its part, the subtle music of *Parsifal* with its superb tone painting betrays nothing of the struggle that accompanied its realization. Nietzsche, who recognized *Parsifal* as "a work of malice, of vindictiveness, of poison secretly brewed to envenom the prerequisites of life, a *bad* work . . . an outrage on morality," also acknowledged the skillfulness of its literary construction and the overwhelming beauty of its music. In many ways Wagner's final opera was his most accomplished. Moreover, it epitomized the ambiguities of the *Gesamtkunstwerk;* to quote Nietzsche's magnificent summing-up: "As musician, Wagner belongs among the painters; as poet, among the musicians; as artist, really among the actors."

Sixteen performances of *Parsifal*—the premiere (26 July 1882) and fifteen repetitions—

made up the second Bayreuth Festival. Some two and a half years earlier, during a search for the health and calm needed to complete the opera, Wagner had vacationed in Naples and there devoted himself to the completion of what would become his most widely read literary work—his autobiography, *My Life,* which he had begun to dictate to Cosima in 1865. It was to appear in a private edition meant exclusively for the eyes of King Ludwig and a few intimates; only in some indefinite future, Wagner calculated, would it be used as the basis of an "official" biography.

In *My Life* Wagner concealed and misrepresented incidents in his past. The protégé of the Bavarian king, for example, found it politic to forget his active role in the Dresden revolution, just as the lover of Cosima thought it equally wise to describe the often affectionate years with his first wife, Minna, as utterly hateful, and his turbulent and celebrated affair with Mathilde Wesendonk as of little account. In general, his many post-factum manipulations and suppressions approached the scandalous as he attempted to edit a new Wagner into existence.

From the very start of his labors on the autobiography, Wagner had planned to stop when he reached May 1864, the month the royal summons had brought him to Munich. Immediately beyond this point lay the complications of his relationship with Cosima. The Wagner who first sat down to dictate *My Life* had but recently thrown himself into the unpredictable adventure of having a passionate affair with the person to whom he was dictating—the wife of his closest friend. With good reason the composer desired to defer to the remote future any official description of this period about which he was, at the moment, concocting various and often conflicting informal explanations: for the forseeable future, he realized, a persuasive authorized account lay beyond even his powers of invention. He therefore imposed on Cosima—almost a quarter of a century his junior—the duty of one day completing the story of his life

from the spring of 1864 to the day of his death. Toward this end she began a diary on 1 January 1869, soon after she had once and for all abandoned her husband to join Wagner. Yet she could never face up to the embarrassing gap between the end of *My Life* and the first page of her diary, a period during which she had passed back and forth between the two men. Eventually she left the literary solution to Carl Friedrich Glasenapp whom, after Wagner's death, she chose as his official biographer.

Thus, despite its imposing length, *My Life* is but a torso: it breaks off before the truly great triumphs of Wagner's career. The first three volumes of the private printing appeared between 1870 and 1875, the fourth and final part in 1880, the public edition of the whole reaching the press in 1911. The book varies in style. That Wagner often dictated it after concluding the main business of his day is too frequently reflected in sluggish paragraphs. Still they sometimes give way to sudden spurts of energy as he returns to the animated manner of his days at the *Gazette musicale.* He holds the reader most firmly when exercising that causticity renowned in his conversation. His descriptions, for example, of the premieres of *Liebesverbot,* of the Paris *Tannhäuser,* of Spontini and Karl Ritter as conductors, of the peculiarities of Liszt's personality, are extraordinarily incisive and witty too. Not surprisingly, part 4 finds Wagner at low ebb: it details his least interesting years (1861–1865), and there was little humor left in him by 1880.

Though the letters of Richard Wagner remain outside the compass of this essay, it should at least touch on them. This vast trove—approximately five thousand specimens survive—offers not only a broader and more complete picture of him and his artistic development than does *My Life,* but also a more accurate and spontaneous view. The letters show him marvelously varied: comradely and warm toward his boyhood chum Theodor Apel; moving and often full of love for his wife Minna; political and violent in mood and diction in his outbursts to his Dresden friend Theodor Uhlig; pretentious and schoolmasterish toward Mathilde Wesendonk; highly mannered—a nineteenth-century late baroque style unto itself—in dispatches to Ludwig of Bavaria; down-to-earth, a kind of prose he easily recaptured when writing to members of his family; Jovian, in communications to those concerned with the business of the Bayreuth Festival. An element in common binds these diverse approaches: through most of his letters run, like threads of scarlet, passages of romantic exaltation and lamentation, arias of love, woe, and hate in which he quits the world of the cogitative to wander in the realm of the impulsive and compulsive. Here is the intrinsic Wagner.

He arrayed instinct against reason[3]: to be a successful Wagnerite one had to deny the intellect—an injunction Nietzsche, for one, found unendurable. Wagner's magnification of instinct led him to the doctrine of the unerring impulses of the German Folk and into the dark waters of the collective right and freedom, in which individualism and dissimilitude are subdued in a mass destiny—only a short distance from the perilous concept of an infallible leader as symbolic extension of the Folk's wisdom. In some marvelous and poetic way Wagner saw himself—in his words, "the most German of Germans"—filling this role. Nevertheless, he shied from detailing the means by which his countrymen might achieve what he called the "great solution," a course of conduct in which, having "overcome all false shame," they would then "not shrink from ultimate knowledge" ("Know Thyself"). In an elaborate afterthought to *Jewry in Music*, published in 1869, he remarked: "Whether the deterioration of our culture can be arrested by a violent ejection of the malefic foreign element I have no capacity to judge, since that would require forces with whose existence I am unacquainted."

As a political and social thinker, Wagner was a major precursor of Adolf Hitler. The Führer revered Wagner's prose works, emulated their turgid style, enthroned him as artistic god of the Third Reich, and acted on many of the ideas in the essays, especially the late ones. Indirectly, Wagner played a devastating role in Europe's political history. From the pages of the *Bayreuther Blätter* grew a cult of militant Wagnerism. Encouraged by Cosima and given a sharper focus by Wagner's son-in-law, Houston Stewart Chamberlain, in his *Foundation of the Nineteenth Century*, this accumulating tradition provided Hitlerism—via Alfred Rosenberg—with many of its most virulent features. The mythology of Wagnerism became the mythology of Nazism; there are few of Wagner's prejudices that did not become part of Nazi culture.

With Hitler's arrival in power, it did appear that Wagner's art might be swallowed by its own hypotheses; many—especially those who read and pondered his prose works—turned from him in horror. Yet his art soars beyond concepts reconcilable with the figure and acts of this wicked and arrogant little man. For his music he could tap deep wells of spirit from which rose streams of compassion, the gigantic framework of his creations enclosing blooms as delicate, intimate, and moving as a Schumann song. Even his most bitter detractors have never been able to dismiss Wagner as he dismissed others. Both Nietzsche and Hanslick extolled his vital musical enchantment, that most precious of his gifts; it works the charm that renders his artistic synthesis—however bogus its theory—valid on its own extravagant terms.

[3]In his many essays the great composer rarely discussed technique. An anomaly, "Über die Anwendung der Musik auf das Drama" ("The Application of Music to Drama," 1879), touches on the methods he called into play to unify his operas, Wagner emphasizing the difference between the structural demands of opera and those of the symphony, especially in regard to tonality and motivic manipulation. A more typical Wagnerian quality dominates "Über das Dirigiren" ("On Conducting," 1869–1870)—essentially, a recommendation that in matters of tempo, phrasing, and tone color the opera house become the model for the concert hall, the ultimate end being the stirring impression. In any case, Wagner maintained, only the pure-bred German musician with his inherent spontaneity, certainly not the Jew with his pseudoculture, possessed the gift of finding the proper rendering.

Selected Bibliography

EDITIONS

The first two collections are the "classical" editions of Wagner's prose and poetry and are the ones most often found in European and American libraries.

Sämtliche Schriften und Dichtungen. 12 vols. 5th ed. Leipzig, 1911.

Gesammelte Schriften und Dichtungen in zehn Bänden (Goldene Klassiker-Bibliothek). 10 vols. Berlin, Leipzig, Vienna, and Stuttgart, n.d.

Richard Wagner Briefe. Edited by John N. Burk. Frankfurt, 1953.

TRANSLATIONS

Richard Wagner's Prose Works. Translated by William Ashton Ellis. 8 vols. New York, 1966. This is a photographic reprint of the K. Paul 1892–1899 London edition. Ellis succeeds in making Wagner's prose even more difficult to read in English than in German; moreover, the translation is often treacherously wrong. Still, it is the only rendering of the *Gesammelte Schriften* prose in English.

BIOGRAPHICAL AND CRITICAL STUDIES

Barzun, Jacques. *Darwin, Marx, Wagner.* 2nd rev. ed. Chicago, 1981.

Boucher, Maurice. *The Political Concepts of Richard Wagner.* Translated by Marcel Honoré. New York, 1950.

Donington, Robert. *Wagner's "Ring" and Its Symbols.* New York, 1963.

Gutman, Robert W. *Richard Wagner: The Man, His Mind, and His Music.* New York, 1968. This is the standard one-volume life of Wagner, which forms the basis of much of the material in this essay.

Hanslick, Eduard. *Vienna's Golden Years of Music, 1850–1900.* Translated and edited by Henry Pleasants III. New York, 1950.

Newman, Ernest. *The Life of Richard Wagner.* 4 vols. New York, 1933–1946. The grandest, most monumental life of Wagner in any language. The reader, however, must bear in mind that it was written before the opening in 1950 of the Burrell Collection with its hundreds of items of Wagneriana.

————. *The Wagner Operas.* New York, 1949.

Shaw, George Bernard. *The Perfect Wagnerite.* Chicago and New York, 1904.

Stein, Jack M. *Richard Wagner and the Synthesis of the Arts.* Detroit, 1960.

Stein, Leon. *The Racial Thinking of Richard Wagner.* New York, 1950.

Viereck, Peter. *Metapolitics: The Roots of the Nazi Mind.* New York, 1961.

Zuckerman, Elliott. *The First Hundred Years of Wagner's "Tristan."* New York and London, 1964.

ROBERT W. GUTMAN

GEORG BÜCHNER
(1813–1837)

GEORG BÜCHNER WAS born in a period when the shock waves of the French Revolution were still reverberating throughout Europe. The aftermath of the Revolution was felt with particular force in Germany, where, between Büchner's birth in 1813 and his death in 1837, the faces of the social, political, and artistic worlds were changed drastically. Since neither Büchner nor his work could escape the extraordinary pressures exerted by these events, we must look at this historical context in more detail before turning to the specifics of his life and literary activity.

The most important event, or rather series of events, to mark the intellectual and political climate of Europe after 1800 was the process that in France had led from the overthrow of the monarchy through the republic to Napoleon and the empire. Politically and spiritually, the overthrow of the aristocratic social order signaled as well the inevitable collapse of a system of beliefs that in one form or another had held sway in Europe for hundreds of years. It had been assumed that only the will of the king and the laws of the church, as representations of divine providence, could determine the fate of peoples and nations. The Revolution gave the lie to such notions and thereby released a chaos of alternative views, each with its own concept of society, each armed in the name of justice and tranquillity. Out of these conflicting positions, and in part as a response to them, arose a far more powerful imperative: Napoleon came to power and his armies began to march across Europe, expanding the conflict and sending thousands of men into a protracted military and ideological struggle. Napoleon, who had been hailed as a harbinger of liberty, fraternity, and equality, of the democratic principles proclaimed in the writings of Jean Jacques Rousseau, Thomas Paine, and other intellectuals, became for a time master of the continent, and the revolutionary ardor that had been unleashed by the overthrow of the French monarchy was slowly stifled under the weight of his dictatorship. In Germany many leading figures from the world of art and letters, including the philosophers Immanuel Kant, Friedrich von Schelling, and Johann Gottlieb Fichte, the poets Friedrich von Schiller and Johann Christian Friedrich Hölderlin, the musician and composer Beethoven, had at first welcomed the arrival of the French armies. But after 1804, when Napoleon had himself proclaimed emperor, the liberal intelligentsia began to realize that any hope of political change would now involve a struggle against the "liberators" as well as against local princely authority.

When Napoleon was at last defeated at Leipzig in 1813 and then crushed at Waterloo in 1815, the destruction of the empire brought not democracy but a harsh conservative reaction. At the Congress of Vienna (1814–1815), under the guiding hand of Clemenz Lothar von Metternich, the victorious monarchic powers redrew the borders of the German states and at the same time reestablished the prerevolutionary principle of dynastic rule. Liberal demands for political unity; for equality before the law; for freedom of speech, the press, and religion were sometimes paid lip service to by the newly restored governments, but by and large they were ignored. Though reduced from several hundred petty principalities to a mere thirty-five, the German states remained divided and subject to absolutist political structures. Despite these setbacks, the struggle for liberty continued, underground, during the ensuing years, the years of Büchner's childhood and early manhood.

In July 1830 the Bourbon king Charles X was overthrown in France and once again the disenfranchised of Europe took the event as a sign that their own revolutionary dreams might be realized. The renowned German poet Heinrich Heine expressed this hope when he wrote that the rights of the "people" had at last been secured. Unfortunately, reality fell somewhat short of the mark. Louis Philippe of Orleans was crowned king, and in combination with the old aristocracy a new financial elite took control of the state. Honoré de Balzac's novels chronicle the prelude to these developments—and record his distaste for the new upper class. Neither in France nor elsewhere did the hoped-for social and political changes emerge. Once again the liberal intellectuals of Europe experienced the bitter discrepancy between their political idealism and the concrete reality of their situation.

This was particularly true in Hesse, the duchy in which Büchner was born. After the restoration of its full powers in 1815, the Hessian government had been one of the most reactionary in all the Germanies. Wilhelm Grimm, whom we know best for his studies in folklore but who was also a political activist, wrote that in Hesse

> freedom had declined to the point that no one who had not already experienced it had any idea of its meaning. . . . The police, both regular and secret, under orders and voluntarily, examined everything and poisoned trust in social interaction. . . . Only one thing was certain: any opposition to the expressed will [of the head of state], whether direct or indirect, was a crime.
>
> (Johann Ernst, ed., *Georg Büchner: in Selbstzeungnissen und Bilddokumenten* [Hamburg, 1958], p. 61)

Thus, questions of individual liberty and political authority were more than simple topics of intellectual concern for the young Büchner. Indeed, within his own family the same issues were embodied in the conflict between his parents. Büchner's father, for all his liberality in religious matters, defended the absolute authority of the state. His mother, on the other hand, remained attached to the ideal of subjective and individual values as they were proposed by German romanticism. Even the day of Büchner's birth was experienced differently by each of his parents: 17 October 1813 brought a double occasion for joy to Büchner's mother: her first son was born, and Napoleon was defeated at Leipzig. Büchner's father, who had served as a doctor in the French armies and who idolized Napoleon, was considerably less happy. In any case politics had already entered Büchner's life.

We know very little about the ensuing twelve years of Büchner's childhood. He was at first educated at home by his mother and then entered high school in Darmstadt in 1825. There he pursued a curriculum that would prepare him to begin the study of medicine. It is at this time that the first signs of his philosophical, political, and literary inclinations appeared. In a school essay written in 1830 Büchner expresses his ideas about the relationship between the French Revolution and the Reformation in Germany. Borrowing much of his argument from Fichte, Büchner attempts to show that Martin Luther's Reformation represented a first step in the process of human liberation. The more earthly (as opposed to otherworldly) attitudes announced by the Reformation signaled for Büchner the advent of a new notion of human existence, one that allowed for a tremendous expansion of personal, intellectual, and creative freedom. The ideas of the French Revolution had in turn added the possibility of social and political freedom to the purely subjective and religious. In making this historical linkage, Büchner not only shows his interest in political theory—he also sets forth what was to become the central organizing principle of his social and aesthetic perspective: human life and human creation are valuable in and of themselves and should not be subject to religious, political, or economic restraint. Human activity should move toward the full liberation of the individual in society. All of Büchner's later work will attempt to deal in one way or another with the obstacles, public and private, political and intellectual, that block the development of a truly creative and egalitarian society.

However, another step had to be taken before Büchner actually began his public career. He needed to combine his youthful idealism with practical experience of the world. This process began in earnest when, after graduation from high school, he moved to Strasbourg to study medicine. He arrived in the city in early October 1831, at a time when Alsace was in political turmoil. The predominantly Protestant Alsatians were neither culturally nor financially supported by the new government that had been established in Paris after the July Revolution. Therefore, unlike the Parisian bourgeois elite, the Alsatian middle class felt deprived of the political and economic security created by the new regime. For this reason it sided with the lower classes against the central government. A number of political action groups sprang up, among them the Friends of the People and the Society for Human Rights. Büchner knew people in both these groups. Furthermore, he was a witness to the political turmoil, the strikes and the armed rebellions, that occurred as the Alsa-

tians tried to throw off the rule of the new, Parisian ''bourgeois aristocracy'' and reestablish their own economic stability.

The impact of these events is reflected in several letters Büchner wrote to his parents in 1833:

> This is my opinion: If there is anything that will help our era it is force. We know what we have to expect from our princes. Everything that they allow has to be wrung from them by necessity. And even that which is allowed is thrown to us like a blessing we have begged for, like a miserable child's toy intended to make the ever inquisitive *people* forget its overtight fetters. . . . Young people have been reproached for their violence. But are we not in an eternal state of violence? Because we are born and raised in prison we no longer notice that we are jailed, gagged and manacled hand and foot.
>
> (15 April 1833)

A few months later Büchner clearly identified the direction his political activity would take:

> I will, of course, always act in accord with my own principles, but in the recent past I have learned that only the real needs of the masses can produce changes. All individual activity and shouting is useless fool's work.
>
> (June 1833)

Büchner's recent experience and his revolutionary zeal had, at this point, led him to reject not only the monarchy, but also the new bourgeois society that, in his eyes, while promising equality really exploited the lower classes. He could not therefore side with the liberal middle class. Instead he longed for a truly popular reorganization of political, economic, and social structures; but he also knew that the time was not ripe for this brand of revolution. Nonetheless he immersed himself in the political debates that swirled around him.

The feverish excitement of Büchner's stay in Strasbourg came to an abrupt end in the summer of 1833 though. Hessian law, which allowed students to attend universities outside the duchy, stipulated that the last four semesters' study had to be spent at the state university. Thus in the late fall of that year Büchner found himself in Giessen. There he was once more to breathe the repressive atmosphere of his homeland. In upper Hesse there had been several rebellions brought on by restrictions imposed by the government, but these rebellions had been put down quickly. The rebel farmers and cottage laborers who had been driven to this violence by their poverty only found their situation worse. Giessen also lacked the climate of revolutionary thought that had been so stimulating to Büchner in Strasbourg. So we should not be surprised that the pain of leaving his Strasbourg friends and especially his fiancée, Wilhelmine (Minne) Jaegle, combined with the social and intellectual oppression he confronted, produced in him a phase of thoughtful and somewhat melancholy withdrawal. In a letter to his fiancée he expresses a sense of alienation that, he says, only she could help him overcome.

These same feelings seem to motivate another letter that he wrote in March 1834. He complains that he cannot bear the mediocrity he finds in Giessen. He then goes on to say:

> I have been studying the history of the [French] Revolution. I felt overwhelmed by the terrible fatalism of history. I find in human nature a shocking uniformity, in human relations an implacable force, granted to all and to none. The individual is only foam on the wave, greatness a mere accident, the mastery of genius a puppet play, a ridiculous struggle against a brazen law, to recognize which is the highest achievement, to overcome impossible.

This portion of Büchner's letter has frequently been cited as proof of a spiritual crisis that culminated in a break with his earlier belief in social and political change. Critics who take this position portray the later Büchner as a pessimist or even as the first modern existentialist or absurdist. His plays and prose are then interpreted from this position. These critics fail, however, to take full account of the rest of Büchner's letter or of the intellectual context within which it is framed. Büchner goes on to say he

> will no longer bow down before the parade horses and bystanders of history. I am used to the sight of blood. But I am no guillotine blade. The word *must* is one of the curses with which human beings are baptized. The proverb "offenses must come, but woe to him through whom they come" is terrifying. What is it in us that lies, murders, steals!

These closing words of the letter may at first glance also seem to be an abstract and "fatalistic" questioning of human nature. But although the tone is melancholy, we cannot overlook Büchner's insistence that he will no longer bow down before authority (two of the "parade horses" he refers to are probably Napoleon and Caesar, who, for Büchner, were archenemies of the people). Bloodshed, the inevitable upshot of revolution, is something he is already used to. In these lines we have the picture of a rebel, not a passive observer. And indeed in the very month he wrote this letter he was instrumental in founding a political action group called the Society for Human Rights, an organization modeled on those he had been acquainted with in Strasbourg. He also joined forces with the liberal publisher and activist Ludwig Weidig, of whom we will hear more later.

If we return to the "fatalism" letter itself, we note that Büchner says he had been studying the French Revolution. Once we know which sources he had been reading, we have a better grasp of what sort of "fatalism" it is that Büchner was thinking of. Adolphe Thiers and François Auguste Mignet, the French historians Büchner consulted, were known as the founders of the so-called *école fataliste* (fatalist school) of history. Their aim was to discard the traditional "great man" approach in favor of a new view of human experience in which the historical context determines much of what happens and what is possible in society. This point of view was itself revolutionary, since historiography up to this time had usually been based on the assumption that only the prince or great leader could hold power because only he had the god-given intellectual capacity and the personal will necessary to enact changes in government or social order. This position, which corresponded perfectly with the old feudal and monarchic political structures, was obviously useless as a means of accounting for the clash of beliefs and the massive popular uprisings that had occurred during the Revolution. Thiers and Mignet, in an effort to describe and explain these events, came to the only conclusion possible: there are multiple forces external to individual will (we might say ecological, social, and economic conditions) that produce change and that are often the hidden incitement to human action. Necessity, they saw, often binds people to actions they might not opt for if they were free to choose. This "fatalism" need not stand in the way of what would be considered positive social development, however. Indeed, from his French mentors Büchner clearly learned that social conditions are not fixed and that history is synonymous with the process of change. And as the letter cited above indicates, he also saw that the homage paid to the great men of the past made it impossible to see that they too were, on a certain level, merely "puppets," the agents of the working-out of that historical process. Furthermore, the older view prevented those not in power from taking up the roles that history offered them, and thus helped prevent change. Revolution and a new, truly democratic order were possibilities, then. The problem with the new history, the problem that Büchner broaches in his letter, is not that of pure determinism, but rather of personal, moral responsibility in a world thus defined. If we are forced to act at times, how are we responsible for those actions? How are we to measure the correctness

of our actions and the degree of our obligation to others? Büchner had as yet no answers for these questions. His anguish did not, however, lead him to withdraw from personal, intellectual confrontation or from the political struggle at large. As we shall see, both in his politics and in the play *Dantons Tod* (*Danton's Death*, 1834), his first major literary work, these questions were worked through and to a great extent resolved.

As mentioned earlier, the same month that he wrote to his fiancée about the "fatalism" of history, Büchner made contact with Ludwig Weidig, a leader of the Hessian opposition and publisher of an underground newspaper. This political alliance between the liberal Weidig and the popular revolutionary Büchner was from the beginning rather tenuous. But almost as a demonstration of the new view of history, their common opposition to corrupt and oppressive Hessian government drew them together. Weidig agreed to publish a tract that Büchner wished to write, a tract that would test the political spirit of the farmers and workers of Hesse. This was Büchner's first published work; his literary career begins therefore with a revolutionary call to arms in the tract "Der Hessische Landbote" ("The Hessian Courier," 1834).

Into this tract, which opens with "Freedom to the huts, war to the palaces," Büchner pours his recent personal experience and the knowledge gained from his study of the Revolution. It contains a systematic analysis of the manner in which Ludwig I and his government exploited the poor through exorbitant taxes and political despotism. Büchner does not limit his attack to the grand duke and his minions. His assault is aimed at all those individuals, aristocrats and bourgeois alike, who live by the sweat of the poor. Echoing his letter to Minne Jaegle, Büchner asserts that the duke and his followers are in fact puppets, both manipulators and manipulated.

In place of the present government, Büchner suggests that the people establish a constitution of their own making, for they as a

1173

group are the true basis of the law. Here he obviously draws on the French constitution of 1793. He proposes a popular republic. In this Büchner's idea of the "people" was more generous than Weidig's. The liberals expected only the established members of the middle class to vote and hold office. Büchner wants the government to be a direct expression of the will of the masses. In fact as far as Büchner is concerned, anyone who earns or possesses money beyond the value of his actual work is part of the "rich" and exploiting class.

As an example of a popular uprising Büchner naturally points to the French Revolution. But it is not the Revolution as a whole that interests him. Only the period from 1793 to 1794, when the new government, under Maximilien Robespierre, made its greatest concessions to the sansculottes—to the pressure of popular, antibourgeois demands—is of special relevance. As far as Büchner is concerned, this is the moment when the French began to acquire a semblance of freedom and self-representation. It is also the moment when they began to relinquish their freedom. According to Büchner, they sold it "for the glory that Napoleon offered them." By informing the people of Hesse of these events and of their own oppression, Büchner wished to create the kind of popular democracy that Jacques René Hébert and others in France had supported. He wanted to see if presenting the masses with the facts of their political and economic situation would precipitate a revolution. As an intellectual, he felt that his job was to inform the people so that they could act. As he wrote to Karl Gutzkow, "The relationship between the poor and the rich is the only revolutionary element in the world" (letter from Strasbourg, 1835).

Unfortunately, Büchner's text was never really put to the test. Weidig, who was both a supporter of the middle class and very religious, found his demands for socioeconomic as well as political change totally unacceptable. He preferred to look at the Hessian situation as a struggle between God and the devil,

between liberal middle-class ideals and feudal, aristocratic oppression. This difference in point of view led Weidig to rewrite Büchner's text. The "Courier" now had "aristocrat" where Büchner had written "rich." Weidig also eliminated the author's attacks on the liberal opposition and added a number of biblical references as well as a new closing section. These changes so outraged Büchner that he no longer wished to be associated with the tract. He had little time to argue the point, however. In August 1834, just as the printed tract was to be distributed, a member of Weidig's group informed the police about what was afoot. Shortly thereafter Weidig was arrested; and in March 1835, after being interrogated several times, Büchner fled to Strasbourg to avoid arrest himself.

In order to finance his flight Büchner wrote *Danton's Death,* the first and perhaps most famous of his plays. The play was written in just five weeks and then sent to Gutzkow, one of the leading liberal writers in Germany. It was published, thanks to Gutzkow's support, but not until it had been cleansed of what Gutzkow referred to as the "mercuric" flowers of [Büchner's] imagination and everything that makes one think of [certain] streets in Frankfurt and Berlin." Gutzkow's target was, of course, Büchner's sexually explicit language and humor. Once again Büchner fell prey to the censorship of those who preferred their own literary and social ideals to his uncompromising realism. Büchner attempted to clarify the literary and political differences between himself and Gutzkow in several letters he wrote later in 1835 and early in 1836. Since these statements have a bearing on our reading of *Danton's Death,* as well as on our general understanding of Büchner and his work, we will look at them in some detail.

After returning to Strasbourg, Büchner did not abandon his hopes of a complete transformation of society. That the revolution had not materialized in Hesse simply demonstrated that the time was not yet ripe. As he wrote to his brother in July 1835, "There is nothing one can do; anyone who sacrifices himself at this time is a fool carrying his own hide to market." Political action was out of the question then, but literary activity for the sake of political ends was not. And it was here that Büchner made a clear distinction between himself and other writers of the day. Even if Gutzkow had been persecuted for his liberal ideals, idealism was not enough. "I am in no way connected to the so-called Young Germans, Gutzkow's and [Heinrich] Heine's literary party. Only a complete misunderstanding of our social conditions could make people believe that a total transformation of our religious and social ideas could be brought about by today's literature" (1 January 1836). The postromantic, Young German literary movement, of which Gutzkow was thought to be the leader, had "not taken the best path. Reform through ideas, through the educated class? Impossible! Our age is purely materialistic" (letter to Gutzkow, 1836).

If Büchner thought that the literature of the day, with its intellectual idealism, failed to meet the needs of the "materialist" age, what led him to write *Danton's Death*? In what way did he understand his literary effort to be different from those of other postclassical, postromantic writers of the period? A long letter written to his parents in the summer of 1835, shortly after he had completed the play, gives us a detailed answer to these questions and presents us with a clear theory of the dramatist's role as he himself conceived it. In response to Gutzkow's criticism of the "immorality" of his play Büchner asserts:

The dramatic poet is, as I see it, nothing but a writer of history, but he is superior to the latter because he consciously recreates history and puts us in immediate contact with the life of an epoch instead of giving us a dry narrative; gives us characters instead of characteristics and [living] figures instead of descriptions. His highest responsibility is to come as close as possible to history as it really happened. His book must be no more or less moral than history itself; history is not created by the good Lord as reading matter for young ladies, and I will not take it badly if my play is equally unsuitable in that respect. I cannot make virtuous heroes out of Danton and the bandits of the revolution! If I wanted to show their decadence I had to let them be decadent; if I wanted to show their godlessness, I had to have them speak like atheists. If a few disreputable expressions are used in the play one should remember the well-known obscenity in the speech of the day. What my characters say is only a weak imitation. . . . The poet is no teacher of morals, he finds and creates figures, he revives the past, and people should *learn* as much from that as from the study of history or the observation of what happens in life. If one wishes it otherwise one should not study history, because it tells of a number of immoral things; one should cross the street blindfolded since otherwise one will see things that are indecent.

If we use this letter as an outline of his theory of theater, we can see that Büchner rejected the old formulaic notion of the drama just as he rejected the "dry narrative" of the old history. Both of them had the same drawback: they enclosed the manifold events of life in a rigid, causal-narrative pattern. Büchner, on the other hand, wanted a drama that inscribed the complex, living action of history, so that we could learn its lesson, the lesson of socio-historical reality. If we can see history enacted on stage, it is both alive and at a distance from us. We can therefore both observe and comprehend its movement; we can learn from history, but only if we are willing to face it directly. By reliving history in this way, we have the advantage of confronting historical figures in the emphatic context of particular events; we are not merely led off into the abstract byways of narrative recitation or moral demonstration. In this confrontation, we learn not only what has been done, but we are also given the opportunity to decide what else *might* have been done. We can learn about the possibilities for change and the historical limits placed on those possibilities; that man is both free to act and, as Büchner suggests in his "fatalism" letter, constrained by the very nature of things in terms of the number of choices he has. The lessons of this theater are, therefore, not lessons reducible to preexisting moral precepts, but lessons in human action and responsibility. As far as Büchner is concerned, the literature produced by his liberal friends had exactly the opposite effect:

> If someone tells me that the poet should present things as they ought to be rather than as they are I will reply that I do not want to make things better than God himself did. . . . As far as the so-called poets of the ideal are concerned, I find that for the most part they have just given us marionettes with sky blue noses and affected pathos, not human beings of flesh and blood, whose sufferings and joys I experience and whose actions repel or amaze me. In a word, I think a great deal of Goethe and Shakespeare but very little of Schiller.
>
> (letter to his parents, July 1835)

These lines complete Büchner's explanation of his literary-political position. He rejects the idealism of the Young Germans because it provides ready-made answers ("marionettes")—fictions in the place of reality. We can learn nothing of value, be it social or aesthetic, from such works. Thus, for all his linguistic and technical proficiency, for all his interest in history, Schiller is excluded from the list of Büchner's literary progenitors. By altering and idealizing certain aspects of history, Schiller, Büchner seems to be saying, prevents us from understanding reality and what can in fact be changed. The early Johann Wolfgang von Goethe and Shakespeare, on the other hand, provide us with pictures of the multiple and colliding forces that actually constitute the movement and process of history.

It is precisely this possibility of presenting a multiplicity of points of view, a multiplicity of times and places, that led Büchner to opt for an open, or fragmented, structure in *Danton's Death* and his other plays. He rejected the closed, linear form of the neoclassical drama for the same reason he rejected the closed con-

ceptual systems of the "idealists." These latter authors presented the historical world and the world of the intellect either as fixed or as unfolding in a single direction, within a single frame of reference. Only the openness of the Shakespearean form allowed Büchner the necessary space within which to juxtapose the figures and attitudes that constitute *Danton's Death*. This process of juxtaposition, which allows characters and actions to serve as commentary on or counterpoint to each other, provides the formal basis for the play as a whole. It also provides us with a means of reading the text on its own terms.

The play opens in the year 1794, the time of the constitution and the tension-filled cooperation between the middle-class Jacobins and the sansculottes—precisely the period to which Büchner referred in "The Hessian Courier." Here he attempts to bring this revolutionary moment to life. He wants his audience both to experience and to study these events so that it can learn why a "government and legislators elected by the people" ("The Hessian Courier") failed to produce the free society it had promised. Most of all, Büchner wants us to understand why this particular alliance between the people and the middle-class political leadership could not succeed. We can be confident that the play is an attempt to analyze the failure of the middle class and not an effort to describe the failure of popular political theory, since the work opens on the very day (24 March 1794) that Hébert and his followers, the leading advocates of a popular social revolution, were put to death. The political factions that remain, and which are examined in the play, are Robespierre's group, which claimed the support of the people, and Danton's party, which had, in part, withdrawn from the government because the government had moved too far "left." This is an essential point to remember: Danton was part of the middle-class opposition, not just to the "Terror," but also to the establishment of a social order based on the needs of the masses. If Büchner focuses on Danton, it is not to make him a heroic counterpoint to Robespierre—it is, rather, to show the consequences of the disjunction between the man's extraordinary potential as a revolutionary leader and his willingness to assume social and moral responsibility for his position—the very problem Büchner announced in the "fatalism" letter. If, in his confrontations with Robespierre, Danton sometimes appears to be the "better" man, this does not mean he is the "hero" of the play. It is rather that the contrast between the two figures allows each to expose the other's flaws. Danton's rhetoric is more appealing to us, but for all his ability to analyze and understand his situation intellectually, he too fails to respond to the social and economic needs of the people; and thus he too helps subvert the Revolution. Büchner expects us to remember that the result of the conflict between Danton and Robespierre was not more freedom, but the arrival of Napoleon.

From the very beginning of the play Büchner focuses on the difference between rhetoric and action. The first scene introduces us to Danton, his wife, Julie, Hérault-Séchelles, and several other members of Danton's faction. At the same time, it establishes the formal-analytical procedure that operates throughout the rest of the text.

> DANTON: Look at the charming lady over there; how cleverly she plays her cards. She really knows the game; they say she deals her husband hearts and the others a more interesting suit.—You women could make any man fall in love with a lie.
> JULIE: Do you believe in me?
> DANTON: How do I know? We know so little about each other. We are thick-skinned; we reach out to one another but in vain; we just rub a little leather off—we're very lonely.
> JULIE: But you know me, Danton.
> DANTON: Yes, it's called knowing. You have dark eyes and curly hair and lovely skin and always say "Georges, dear" to me. But (*he points to her forehead and eyes*) there, there, what goes on behind them? No, our senses are coarse. Know each other? First we would have to break open our skulls and tear each others thoughts out of the fibers of our brains . . .
> A LADY: (*to Hérault*) What are you doing with your fingers?
> HÉRAULT: Nothing.
> LADY: Don't twist your thumbs down like that, its unbearable.
> HÉRAULT: But look, the thing has a physiognomy all its own.
> DANTON: No Julie, I love you like the grave.
> JULIE: (*turning away*) Oh!
> DANTON: No, listen! They say that there is peace in the grave, that the grave and peace are one. If that's the case, when I lie in your lap, I'm already lying buried. You sweet grave, your lips are funeral bells, your voice is my death knell, your breasts my grave mound and your heart my coffin.
> LADY: You lose.
> HÉRAULT: That was an adventure in love; it costs money just as they all do.
> LADY: In that case, you made your declarations of love with your fingers, like a deaf-mute.
> HÉRAULT: And why not? Some say that the fingers are easiest to understand: I arranged a liaison with a queen; my fingers were princes turned to spiders; you, Madame, were the good fairy. But it didn't work. The queen was always with child, bearing a jack a minute. I wouldn't let my daughter play such games. The kings and queens fall on top of each other quite indecently and all the knaves come right behind.

Absent from these lines is any hint of the "classical" exposition one might expect in a play written at this time. We are not provided with narrative tidbits about the characters or the action to come. There is no clear indication of a perspective from which to observe and understand the rest of the play. Büchner has deliberately done away with these introductory devices so that his text does not turn into a "dry narrative," a fiction in which history seems to depend more on the will and point of view of the author than on the discordant tones of the events themselves. He wants figures "of flesh and blood" rather than the "marionettes" of the idealists. Therefore, in lieu of the traditional, linear presentation of plot and character, we have a series of fragmented scenes and passages of dialogue that cut across each other and establish a counterpoint.

The effect of this form (and here we are reminded of Gustave Flaubert's later use of this technique in the fair scene in *Madame Bovary*, 1857) is to call into question the validity of the assertions, however serious they seem, made by the characters. As Danton points to Julie's forehead and eyes, wondering "what goes on behind them," as he muses about human alienation, he is interrupted, and the play cuts to the otherwise unnamed Lady, who demands, "What are you doing with your fingers?" Hérault then repeats Danton's interest in physiognomy but at the level of his thumb's structure rather than in metaphysical terms. After Danton launches into the extended metaphor in which he equates his love for Julie with the grave, he is again interrupted by the Lady, who comments, "You lose!" Hérault finishes this sequence by creating an equally elaborate if somewhat coarser figuration of "love." The Lady, who does not appear again, seems to be introduced specifically to suggest a different voice, an alternative point of view, this one female, which challenges and subverts the high seriousness of Danton's observations. Hérault's lines provide an echo of Danton's that further reduces the status of his comments. And since Hérault's comic trope arises from a game of cards, we are reminded that such elaborate metaphors, for all their ostensible seriousness, are always a form of game or play.

The result of this ironic fragmentation is to open up a space for us between words and actions, between the surface level of Danton's comments and their potential meanings. We learn that we are entering a world that is not fixed by reference to a specific rhetoric or specific set of ideas embodied by one of the characters. We discover that figurative and symbolic expression, the formative stuff of much romantic literature, is exposed as linguistic play with little actual content. Indeed, as the play progresses we find romantic rhetoric one of the central problems affecting Danton and his friends—they expend themselves in verbiage, in the consoling sounds of their own rhetoric, instead of applying this energy to the needs of the Revolution: At the close of the first scene, after Hérault says that the "Revolution must end and the Republic begin," Camille Desmoulins responds with an apostrophe to the state as a "transparent vestment" that should reveal the body of the people—a body that he then transforms into a sinning, naked France. "We want naked gods," he says, "bacchantes, Olympic games, and from melodious lips a song of unrestricted wicked love." This is heady stuff, this "guillotine romanticism" (the expression is Camille's), and no doubt more appealing than the stern "Roman" rhetoric we will soon hear from Robespierre; but one is free to wonder if it will be of much use to the impoverished masses of revolutionary France.

We need not wonder for very long, however. In the next scene we are introduced to the poor citizens of Paris. Just as Danton's speeches found their counterpoint in the comments made by Hérault and the Lady, so too the playful but actionless rhetorical stances of Danton's faction are now contrasted with the language, gestures, and needs of the people. From the drunken Simon and his wife we learn that poverty has led the poor to prostitute themselves or their daughters to young men of wealth. We will see in a later scene (1.5) that the Dantonists are of this latter group. The new political leadership is little better than the old.

FIRST CITIZEN: . . . You have hunger pangs and they have heartburn. You have holes in your jackets and they have warm coats. You have calluses on your hands and theirs are smooth as silk. Ergo you work and they do nothing; ergo you have earned and they have stolen. . . .

THIRD CITIZEN: They told us: "Kill the aristocrats, they are wolves!" We hung the aristocrats from lampposts. . . . They said, "The Girondists are starving you." We guillotined the Girondists. But they stripped the bodies and we go naked and freezing. . . . Forward! Kill whoever has no holes in his coat!

FIRST CITIZEN: Kill anyone who can read and write. . . .

ALL: (screaming) Kill them! Kill them!

These speeches, which obviously echo Büchner's position in "The Hessian Courier," also show the violence of the populace—revolutionary energy run amok. But violence is not inherent in these people. Büchner shows it to be a result of the deceptions they have experienced. And lest we think they are incapable of better thoughts, Büchner continues the scene. He brings on a young, well-dressed man whom the people-turned-mob wants to hang from a lamppost. When he quips that hanging him like that will not light up their lives, they let him go—they understand and enjoy the point of his humor. These people have intelligence and wit. But they do not, as Danton does, have much opportunity to indulge it. Point and counterpoint.

As soon as the young man is freed, Robespierre appears on the scene: the third part in the revolutionary triangle (Danton, people, Robespierre) is presented to us. His first assertion is that people should act only in the name of the law—the statutory will of the people. But when a member of the crowd says that they *are* the people and therefore free to act as they please, we find that Robespierre has a different idea of who or what defines the French masses. He launches into an almost biblical tirade in which he insists that it is the Jacobin leadership that will "watch over" and guide them. His rhetoric promises freedom but actually exercises control. In these lines and those given to Robespierre and his followers in the third scene, we see the "virtuous" pose that masks the Jacobins in the manipulation of the populace. In scene 3, Robespierre addresses the members of the Jacobin Club in a lengthy harangue that mixes biblical language with references to the Roman republic, classical Latin authors, and eighteenth-cen-

tury notions of property rights. He idealizes and personalizes the Revolution as "Terror" and "Virtue." At moments he even sounds quite convincing, but Büchner has made sure we do not mistake Robespierre's words for true revolutionary sentiment. As early as the opening scene of the play, we are warned by Hérault and Camille about Robespierre's "Roman" rhetoric, and in the second scene we listen to poor, drunken Simon, who, berating his wife for his daughter's whoredom, also speaks in the tones of a virtuous Roman.

SIMON: Ancient Virginius, veil your hairless head—the raven of shame sits there and pecks at your eyes. Give me a knife, Romans. . . . Ha, Lucretia! A knife, give me a knife, Romans! Ha, Appius Claudius!

This display, which belongs more to the theater than to real life, as does Simon's later reference to Hamlet, draws attention to the socially false, that is, theatrical, nature of such speech, and functions in much the same way as Hérault's comments in the first scene. These reveal the distance between the speaker's reality and his "performance." And so we understand that Robespierre, too, is an actor who has assumed a role. He hides himself, the insecure, puritanical figure we see in scene 6, behind a verbal mask. Once again rhetoric replaces reality, and once again we see why the Revolution is doomed to failure: Robespierre is incapable of true sympathy for others. His actions are all attempts to overcome his personal fears and sense of alienation, both from himself and others. While extolling the "virtues" of the Revolution, he in fact seeks power and identity. As in the case of Danton's failed communication with Julie, a fiction, a private rhetoric, overturns the possibility of interpersonal contact. Language, the necessary tool for building mutual understanding and political unity, becomes a vehicle for self-indulgence.

At this point we grasp the full significance of Julie's initial questions. The tragedy of the play is built around a destruction of the linguistic bonds between the self and the other (be it Julie or the "masses") that renders valid social change impossible. Both Danton and Robespierre merely "play," while the Terror consumes Paris. Thus, when Danton and Robespierre express their sense of aloneness, we must not interpret these statements as a definition of the human condition. On the contrary, we are in a position to see them as signs of the revolutionary leadership's failure to come to terms with its responsibility toward the people it claims to represent.

In the last act, just before Danton and his friends are executed, Camille once more draws our attention to this failure. In response to the playful rhetoric that Danton uses to comment ironically on death, Hérault says, "That's just rhetoric for posterity, right, Danton? It really doesn't concern us." And Camille adds:

> From the face he's making it looks as if he would turn it to stone so that posterity could dig it up as a bit of classical antiquity. . . . We should take off the masks for once. . . . Sleeping, digesting, making children, we all do that; all other things are just variations on the same theme. And still we tiptoe about and make faces, we are embarrassed in front of each other! . . . Scream and whine with some spontaneity. Don't just make virtuous faces and such witty, heroic, genial grimaces! We *know each other,* save yourselves the trouble.
>
> (4.5, italics added)

Thus Camille offers an answer to the question Julie posed earlier. Danton and his friends do indeed know each other. They know that they have been playing political and intellectual games and that they have refused to show themselves unmasked. They have not been willing to accept their fundamental equality with others or their insignificance in the face of history; and, therefore, they not only die alone, they die for nothing. Their demise thus becomes the tragedy of the Revolution as a whole.

More than any of the other characters in the play, Danton is in a position to seek an alternative mode of action. In the second act he shows an awareness of the discrepancy between his language and his actions. He is troubled by not always having been as in control of events as he would wish:

> Offenses must come, but woe to him through whom they come! That "must" was this "must." Who is going to curse the hand upon which the curse of "must" has fallen? Who voiced this "must"? Who? What is it in us that lies, whores, steals, and murders?
>
> We are puppets, manipulated by unknown powers. We ourselves are nothing, nothing!
>
> (2.5)

Danton uses practically the same words Büchner did in the "fatalism" letter (Danton adds "whoring" to the list of immoral acts), but he does not speak for Büchner. On the contrary, in this new context, Danton's lines help Büchner resolve the problem invoked in the letter. We, unlike Danton, are in a position to see that his anxiety and existential doubt arise out of his failure to understand that the "puppets" of history are also part of history and can therefore take direct responsibility for their involvement with others. Danton refuses to take this step in self-recognition. Most of all, he wants to believe that he is somehow more important than other people, that his individual presence is necessary to the Revolution. About his possible arrest, he says to himself as he has said to his friends, "That's just meaningless noise, they want to frighten me. But they wouldn't dare" (2.4). He does not believe in the value of the other people's words any more than he values the willpower and intelligence of others. He suffers from the same egocentric view of life that had constituted providential history prior to the Revolution. To borrow a phrase from Büchner, Danton wishes to see himself as one of the "parade horses" of history. When he cannot, he simply blames "unknown powers" and thus refuses responsibility for his part in what has occurred. This faulty perception leads to his fear and inaction when confronted by the events that now overwhelm him. He can only identify with the notion of grand personal actions, not with being subject to history or a mere participant among many nameless others. He fails the people and therefore, true to the dialectical form of the play, the people arrive in the next scene to arrest him. At his trial he once more assumes the mask of the fiery revolutionary, but his rhetoric is ultimately as empty as that of his enemies.

Büchner does not end his play on this note, however. The world, which has been turned upside down by idealist rhetoric and its companion, egocentrism, is righted once more, albeit in ironic fashion. This work, interestingly enough, is left to a foreigner and two women. In the first scene of act 3, Thomas Paine (who in fact was jailed in Paris during the Revolution) attacks the abstract rhetoric and rationality of the French middle class while debating the existence of God. The butt of Paine's attack is the faulty connection these revolutionary intellectuals make between the self—one's personal egocentric desires—and the idea of a divine being who created the world as they might wish it.

> MERCIER: But a cause must exist.
> PAINE: Who denies that? But who says that this cause is the one that we think of as God, that is as perfection? Do you think the world is perfect?
> MERCIER: No.
> PAINE: How can you assume a perfect cause for an imperfect effect? Voltaire dared offend God as little as he dared offend kings, that's why *he* did it. Anyone who had nothing but his reason and then doesn't know how or doesn't dare to use even that consistently is an incompetent.
> MERCIER: Well, let me ask you this: can a perfect effect, that is, can something perfect create the imperfect? Isn't that impossible, since what is created can never have its essence in itself, which, however, as you said, is a property of perfection? . . .

> PAINE: You're right; but if God *must* create, and can create only the imperfect, He would be smart to pass up the occasion. Isn't it a weakness on our parts to think of God only as a Creator? Because *we* need to be movers and shakers in order to convince ourselves we exist, must we attribute this miserable need to God? . . . I act according to my nature, what is appropriate to it is good for me and I do it, what is contrary to it is bad for me and I don't do it and defend myself against it when it comes my way. You can, as one says, remain virtuous and defend yourself against so-called sins without despising your enemies.

(3.1)

Once again the word "must" appears, but here it is a "must" fabricated by shortsighted and self-indulgent individuals who, afraid for their own identities, attribute the need for creative action to God, in order to recapture a sense of their own being by emulating this active pattern. This gesture is at the heart of Danton and Robespierre's actions. It is the source of their rhetoric, their politics, and their alienation—an alienation created by metaphysical self-indulgence, not by simple human experience. Paine, on the other hand (and here his words are very close to Büchner's in the letter of June 1833), rejects the idea that individual action alone can produce change or meaning. Only when one operates with others and not self-indulgently can a balance be struck that will produce valid transformations in individual existence.

It is left to the wives of Danton and Camille to demonstrate on another level the generosity toward others of which Paine speaks. Julie dies by her own hand. Hers is a quiet, almost noble end. It requires none of the heroic apostrophe, none of the grandiloquent verbal play that Danton and his friends embolden themselves with in the face of death.

> JULIE: . . . (*She gives the Boy a lock of her hair*) There, bring that to him and say that he won't go alone—he will understand. And come back quickly, I want to read his look in your eyes.

(4.1)

1181

Julie has, from the beginning, known the answer to her question. She is willing to stake her life on it. And Danton *does* understand her gesture: "I won't go alone—thank you, Julie" (4.3). How different this statement is from the speeches that surround it. It shows a capacity for communion and understanding that he has made no attempt to develop. Julie's wish to see, to read in the Boy's eyes the reality of Danton's comprehension, is a further comment on his refusal to "see" or accept Julie's initial point of view. It is likewise a comment on his refusal to see the needs and reality of others in general.

Lucile, younger and less in control of herself than Julie, is driven mad by the loss of her beloved Camille. And in her madness she provides us with one of the most savage ironies of the play. Standing next to the guillotine where Camille has just been beheaded, she shouts out a determined "Long live the King!" (4.9). Her cry is aimed at the failed Revolution that has just murdered her husband; it is not meant as support of the old monarchy. In her world, a world of failed idealism and gross egocentrism, the meaning and value of language have been turned upside down. "Revolutionary" rhetoric has become antirevolutionary; it can produce no certain ends. Only the old terms are sure of success in this case—they guarantee one's death, a final escape from the catastrophe of language and gesture gone astray. With Lucile's death the Revolution will die too. What remains for the French is the coming of Napoleon. What remains for Büchner's audience depends on its response to the whole play, however. For it, there is still the hope of learning about the connections between language and politics, between the individual and society at large. This is the hope that Büchner carries through his next works and through the remaining three years of his life.

Since he had demonstrated his mastery of dramatic form in *Danton*, we might expect him to continue to mine this rich vein; but the protean nature of his genius and his varied in-

tellectual interests led him in quite other directions. Büchner soon began work on the novella "Lenz" and at the same time put the finishing touches on his doctoral dissertation, which examines the cranial nerve structure in fish. He did not abandon the drama altogether, however. Still in need of money to finance his enforced sojourn in Strasbourg, Büchner again turned to Gutzkow, despite the latter's participation in the censoring of *Danton's Death*. Büchner had little choice in the matter; without the means to remain where he was, he would be forced to return home, where he faced the certainty of arrest and imprisonment. Gutzkow agreed to publish "Lenz" in a new magazine of his. At the same time he commissioned Büchner to translate Victor Hugo's plays *Lucrèce Borgia* (1833) and *Marie Tudor* (1833) into German. Büchner completed these translations in the summer of 1835 and then proceeded with his investigations into the life and works of the man who was to be the subject of his first prose text: J. M. R. Lenz (1751–1792). Lenz was a contemporary of Goethe and Schiller's and a major figure in the Sturm und Drang movement that arose in Germany at the end of the eighteenth century.

Büchner's interest in Lenz was neither completely accidental nor surprising. Lenz's plays and their pronounced social and political views were well known in Germany. That Büchner was sympathetic to these views is obvious—he borrows frequently from Lenz, not only in the construction of plot but of character. Furthermore, *Woyzeck*, as we shall see, is in many ways a recasting of Lenz's *Die Soldaten* (*Soldiers*, 1776). There are other, nonliterary connections between the two men. Büchner, as part of his medical studies, had become interested in psychic disorders and found in the story of Lenz's descent into madness a topic of profound social and psychological interest. Although neither psychological nor literary interest would have necessarily come into play if Büchner had not been in Strasbourg. As it happened, Johann Jaegle, the father of Büchner's fiancée, had been an acquaintance of Johann Oberlin, a man with whom Lenz had lived and who kept the diary on which Büchner based his story. Pastor Jaegle was able to acquaint Büchner with details about Oberlin's life that became an essential part of the background to the novella. In addition, Oberlin's diary and some letters written by Lenz were in the hands of the Strober family, Strasbourg friends of Büchner's. August Strober had, in fact, published a series of essays on Lenz in 1831.

We need not spend much time on the details of these connections or on Oberlin's life. It is, however, important for us to know that Oberlin had established a model of social reform and civic improvement in Waldersbach, a town in Alsace, prior to the day in January 1778 when Lenz arrived at his doorstep. Oberlin had supervised the construction of schools, roads, and bridges; worked to improve agricultural output; and even founded a savings bank for the farmers and laborers of the region. These projects, plus the simple, productive life he fostered in the community, had gained him an international reputation—to the extent that a town and a college in Ohio had already been named for him before Büchner began work on ''Lenz.''

That Büchner knew of Oberlin's projects is certain. He even makes passing reference to them in the novella. We must therefore assume that this knowledge played a part in Büchner's decision to portray only that part of Lenz's life that unfolded in Waldersbach (called Waldbach in Büchner's story), while he was living with Oberlin. Indeed, the whole of the novella is a chronicle of the palliative effects Oberlin and his community have on a deeply disturbed Lenz. The narrative is more than a simple account of these effects or of Lenz's struggle with schizophrenia. It is also a critique of the world outside Waldersbach, the world in which Lenz first went mad. And it is an extended assault on romantic literary tropes and the literary idealism that Büchner had so often attacked before.

To understand how these social and aesthetic concerns of Büchner's are intertwined, we must turn to the text. The novella opens on 20 January 1778. We find Lenz high up in the mountains, surrounded by snow-covered slopes, boulders, and pine branches that hang down heavy and damp along his path. This is a typical scene from the literature of German romanticism: the lonely poet wanders through the mountains, far away from ''civilization,'' communing with nature. But Büchner does not complete the scene in the manner of the romantics. Lenz does not draw new energy or poetic strength from these surroundings; he is in fact indifferent to them. Like so many of his romantic counterparts, he searches for something as he walks, but unlike them he finds nothing. Nature does not speak to him: it gets in his way. At one moment he is irritated because he cannot walk on his head; at another because he cannot move across the distance between the mountain heights and the valley below in a few steps. When he pauses, wide-eyed, to observe and draw a passing storm into himself, to burrow into the universe, these desires, more psychic than physical, cause him momentary pain and then pass, forgotten. They are, of course, the wishes of a madman, as is his desire to walk on his head. But the romantic context and Lenz's grandiose fantasies make Büchner's critical intent obvious. Here we see that man and nature are not and cannot be one. Man is forever isolated from the power and the expanse of the purely physical world. By espousing a literary ideal that would join man to nature, the romantics, like Lenz, wish to alter their condition, to invert the relationship and control their interaction with the natural world. From Büchner's point of view, they, like Lenz, want to walk on their heads. Unlike Lenz they do not realize this is impossible. Their texts are therefore filled with fictions about man *in* nature and empty of valid consideration of man in the one realm that truly belongs to him—the social world, with all its constraints and interpersonal difficulties.

GEORG BÜCHNER

Lenz, like his romantic counterparts, has fled a society that has increased his sense of alienation and begun to drive him mad; but unlike them he finds no solace in nature:

> Toward evening he came to a high ridge in the mountains. . . . He sat down . . . as far as he could see, nothing but peaks . . . and everything so still and gray in the twilight. He suddenly felt terribly lonely; he was alone, completely alone.

This situation, this sense of aloneness, is in many ways parallel to the one that Danton experiences. But here it is a beginning condition, not a mistaken conclusion about life. Büchner places Lenz in this context not only to explore and expose certain romantic myths, but also so that he can introduce Lenz into a different social situation. On this level of the narrative, Lenz's trek through the mountains represents a movement from the problematic middle-class world in which he had lived to the new world he finds in Waldbach. As the story progresses, he descends from the alien heights of the mountains to the warm social atmosphere created by Oberlin and the people of the village. "He went through the village. Lights shone from the windows; he looked as he went by: children at the table, old women, girls, still, calm faces. It seemed to him that the light must come from them. He felt relieved." Once he settled in his room at Oberlin's his fear of being alone strikes him again, as it had on the mountain. But this crisis passes, and during the days that follow the sense of community produced by the people of the area has a powerful calming effect on him. They are "silent and serious as if they could not bring themselves to disturb the peace of the valley." At the same time, these people show themselves to be both lively and friendly when Lenz and Oberlin visit their homes. They are in fact the antithesis of the people Lenz had lived with earlier. (This becomes clear later in the narrative when Kaufmann enters the picture.) The villagers are also the opposite of those people Büchner had known in Hesse and elsewhere in Germany. In many ways the people of Waldbach resemble the Swiss citizens Büchner wrote of in a letter to his family.

> Switzerland is a republic, and since most people know no better than to assert that no such republic is possible, the good citizens of Germany constantly repeat tales of anarchy, murder, and assassination. You would be surprised if you visited me. Even on the way there are friendly villages everywhere with beautiful houses and then, the closer you come to Zurich and the lake, there is real prosperity; villages and towns have an aspect that is unknown to us. The streets are not full of soldiers and lazy bureaucrats; one does not risk being run over by an aristocrat's coach; instead one sees healthy, strong people everywhere and, at little cost, a simple, good, wholly republican government that maintains itself through taxes on one's total wealth, a form of taxation that, in Germany, would be cried down as the height of anarchy.
>
> (20 November 1836)

Büchner's feelings about governmental oppression, whether through military force or through unjust taxation, had clearly not changed since he wrote "The Hessian Courier." Furthermore, we see that he now has a concrete (if idealized) model with which to oppose the bureaucratic-aristocratic politics of his homeland. In this letter the Swiss people, like the people of Waldbach, are seen as capable of expressing their individuality in their daily work and in the process of creating their community. In "Lenz," Oberlin plays a central role in this process,

> laying roads, digging canals, visiting the school.
> Oberlin was untiring, now conversing, then taking care of business, then again absorbed in nature. It all had a beneficial and calming effect on [Lenz]. He often had to look Oberlin in the eyes, and the immense peace that comes over us in the deep woods, in the moonlight on a melting summer night when we sense nature at rest, seemed even nearer to him in these calm eyes, this worthy serious face.

Clearly this is the opposite of Danton's alienation and self-absorbtion. Oberlin is no more in control of the movement of history than Danton, but by choosing to express himself responsibly in relation to his fellowman, he has helped resolve some specific problems that impeded the social and economic growth of his community. For him language and gesture are one. This is why he has such a calming effect on Lenz, an effect that Büchner here ascribes to working with others and grants a greater restorative power than that promised by an idealized nature in romantic literature. Lenz's schizophrenia subsides into productive human activity: "He helped Oberlin, he drew, read the Bible, old hopes revived in him." In sensing the possibility of constructive contact with others, he begins to feel his own reality. The pain of his aloneness is thus translated into the creative pain of being alive—and with this change comes the possibility of rest and sleep.

We must not assume that Lenz is cured, however. Büchner is too much a realist, too aware of both social and psychic reality to permit such a simple solution. He uses Lenz's illness as a metaphor for the condition of the individual in society. He cannot be cured (as indeed Lenz was not), since society itself has not been made whole. The egotism and the political oppression that Büchner depicts in *Danton* can only produce greater isolation. In Büchner's novella, these forces appear only indirectly, in the form of a visitor from outside the valley. Kaufmann, a friend of Lenz's, comes to visit him at Oberlin's house. This visit provides the setting for two lengthy discourses by Lenz, both of which are central to the development of the text as a whole. The first discussion takes place at the dinner table. Kaufmann speaks in defense of the literature of German romantic idealism. Lenz's reply is a powerful and sensitive extension of the ideas Büchner himself had expressed earlier. Once again we hear that idealist authors, those who wish to "transfigure" reality, are not to be endured.

In all things I demand—life, the possibility of being . . . then we do not need to ask if it is beautiful or ugly. . . . We find it in Shakespeare, it resounds in folksongs, sometimes in Goethe; all the rest can be thrown in the fire. . . . They want ideal figures, but all that I have seen are wooden puppets. This idealism is a shameful mockery of human nature. They ought for once to try immersing themselves in the life of completely insignificant individuals, and reproduce it, its palpitations, its implications, and its whole, subtle, hardly perceived play of expression; he had tried to do that in *The Tutor* and *Soldiers*. Those are the most prosaic characters in the world, but the vein of sensitivity is the same in almost everyone, only the shell that we must break open is more or less thick. One only needs eyes and ears for that.

These lines not only recall Büchner's letter to his parents outlining his conception of drama, they also provide a basis for understanding much of *Danton's Death*. Once again we see the importance of ordinary people—the Simons of the world. And Lenz provides a counterstatement to Danton's belief in the impenetrability of other people's existence. Like Julie, Lenz contends that communication and understanding between individuals is possible. One can both see and know others; and such seeing and knowing, not the abstract or the ideal, is, according to Lenz (and Büchner), the source and subject of great art.

After Lenz discourses on literature and aesthetics, Kaufmann shifts to another subject, Lenz's failure to support his father, his willingness to throw his life away in Waldbach instead of setting goals for success in the world. These notions are the socioeconomic counterparts to the idealism Kaufmann had espoused earlier. For Kaufmann, obedience to middle-class rules determines the value of one's existence. Thus Lenz is supposed to work in order to earn enough to help his father and at the same time establish goals that will provide him both social and economic well-being. In Kaufmann's eyes, being is produced only in terms of the abstract values that lie behind these goals. Lenz totally rejects the ideology that gives rise to these ideas.

> Leave here, leave? Go home? Go mad there. You know I couldn't survive anywhere but here. . . . Leave me in peace! . . . Everyone needs something, when one can rest, what more can one have! To always climb, struggle, and thereby throw away forever what the moment can bring; always starve for the sake of something to be enjoyed later! Be thirsty while a bright spring gushes across your path!

Lenz does not want to give up the present in the name of the future. Kaufmann's teleology is part of the problem of life, not a solution. For Lenz, as for Büchner, life is its own goal and should be enjoyed as such, in all its fullness and immediacy. Büchner refuses to equate life, the time of human existence, with money—money to be stored away and later used as a sign of wealth and power; neither is work to be considered in terms of any end but itself. Life is to be used, shared with others, to produce individual peace and communal well-being—equality, not difference. The philosophical basis for this point of view is expressed directly in "On Cranial Nerves," Büchner's doctoral lecture, given in Zurich in 1836, the year after he wrote "Lenz":

> Nature does not operate according to goals, it does not unfold in terms of an endless series of goals, each of which determines the next. It is in all of its expressions immediately sufficient unto itself. Everything that is is there for its own sake.

Seen in this light, to impose an arbitrary, goal-oriented structure on individual activity is a perversion of life itself.

Lenz's original madness is a sign of this perversion, and we should not be surprised that it erupts again after Kaufmann brings these demands, this way of life, into the simple immediacy of Oberlin's valley. Lenz's schizophrenia, which embodies his struggle for being, is reawakened by contact with the oppressive world of his past. Only the pain he inflicts on himself reminds him now that he is alive; beyond this he ceases to be in contact with himself or others. Yet, strangely enough (here we have another example of Büchner's mordant irony), "he seemed completely rational, spoke with people. He did everything that others did; but then there was a terrible emptiness in him; he felt no more fear, no need, his existence was for him a necessary burden—so he lived on."

These closing lines of the novella (which omits Lenz's later bouts with insanity and his final death in the streets of Moscow) once again draw our attention to the connection between Lenz's illness and that of society at large. There is no longer any difference between the life of the madman and that of other, equally alienated individuals. Here, life becomes a state of suffering that, once accepted, produces a creature empty of feeling and incapable of human response. This is not man's fate, however. It is his condition only insofar as freedom, equality, self-expression, and communal productivity are suppressed.

What additions and changes Büchner might have made to revise his text had he lived to complete it are uncertain. As it stands, "Lenz" is nonetheless a masterpiece of literary creativity and metaphoric commentary. It is also a profoundly moving document about the schizophrenic deterioration of a sensitive and intelligent human being.

Büchner's next work uses the bright colors of comedy, but the cultural frame of reference remains the same. If in "Lenz" he chose to show what can happen to the individual overwhelmed by a socially induced sense of alienation, in *Leonce und Lena* (*Leonce and Lena*; completed in 1836, first published 1838) he gives us a comic rendition of the phantasms, boredom, and insensitivity that infected the ancien régime and that continued to infect the aristocracy of the postrestoration era. The attacks on the nobility found in "The Hessian Courier" are here turned into the stuff of parody and farce. Indeed, in this play Büchner anticipates the position Karl Marx and others took later. In 1843 Marx wrote that

> the modern ancien régime is merely the comedian of a world order, the real heroes of which are dead. History . . . passes through many phases as it carries an old order to the grave. The last phase of a world-historical formation is its comedy. . . . Why does history move in this fashion? So that mankind can joyfully part with its past.
>
> ("Zur Kritik der Hegelschen Rechtsphilosophie" in Karl Marx and Friedrich Engels, *Werke,* vol. 1 (1961), p. 382)

Like Marx, Büchner had begun to realize that the historical importance of the old order was on the decline. In "Lenz" it is middle-class ideology that has become the oppressor. Thus, while dealing with the questions of personal freedom and identity, Büchner is at liberty to give a lighthearted demonstration of the inadequacy of the aristocratic perspective in matters of constructive human existence.

The play's "hero," Leonce, might be an aristocratic Danton. He too is bored with life. But unlike Danton he has no access to history in action. He is totally engulfed by his own limited experience and by the rhetoric and practice of empty, aristocratic, court life. As the play opens he upbraids his tutor for expecting him to work on his lessons.

> What do you want from me, Sir? That I prepare for my profession? I already have my hands full, I don't know what to do with all the work I have. You see, first I have to spit on this stone three-hundred-and-sixty-five times in a row. Have you ever tried that? Do it—it gives a very special pleasure. . . . Oh, if only one could see the top of one's head. That's one of my ideals. . . . Am I an idler? Have I nothing to do?

All this labor and observation has made poor Leonce quite melancholy. He has come to the conclusion that all activity arises out of boredom. All effort stems from idleness. He is even too bored to become a "poor puppet" like his father, the king, and his courtiers. Despite his disclaimers, however, he has no intention of giving up his privileged position. The work he turns to has no connection with everyday labor or economic productivity. And when his servant, Valerio, announces his creed of idleness at the end of this scene, Leonce embraces him as one of those "godly beings" who pass through life unbesmirched by sweat and dust. In so doing Leonce reminds us of those individuals mentioned in "The Hessian Courier" for whom "life is a long Sunday," who "live in beautiful houses, wear elegant clothing, have fat faces, and speak their own language," while others work to provide food for their tables. Büchner leaves it to the reader to recognize the empty, exploitative nature of Leonce's life and his "ideals." He also leaves it up to the reader to notice that Leonce's and Valerio's lines are parodies of a trope popular in the upper-class literature of the late eighteenth and early nineteenth centuries. Goethe, for example, had written a poem in praise of "godly" boredom and Friedrich von Schlegel, in *Lucinde* (1799) wrote, "Why else are gods gods but that they consciously and deliberately do nothing?"

Once we have met Leonce, the scene shifts to his father's bedchamber. Here we meet King Peter and the courtly pattern of conduct against which Leonce has claimed to be rebelling. Büchner shows the king dressing for a day at court (1.1). At first he is almost naked. He calls for his "attributes, modifications, affectations, and accessories" in what amounts to a caricature of the actual court ritual of the king's toilette, or *levée du roi.* There is also a somewhat more serious connection between this scene and the analysis Büchner made in "The Hessian Courier":

> "In the name of the Grand Duke," they say, and the man they give this name becomes: inviolable, holy, sovereign, Royal Highness. But go up

GEORG BÜCHNER

to this child of man and look through his princely cloak. . . . Behold, he came naked and soft into the world like you and will be as hard and stiff when he is carried out, and yet his foot is on your necks, . . . he has power over your lives through laws he makes, he has ladies and gentlemen around him known as the court.

King Peter is such a man. We see him clothe his naked humanness in the robes of state, garments that signal the fetishized power of the king and his court. As he himself says, he is at first "the thing in itself"—an unmodified human being. As he dresses, and as Büchner continues his parody of rational idealism, King Peter acquires the "attributes, modifications, affectations, and accessories" that mask his original condition. By the time he is dressed, in lieu of personal action or opinion, King Peter is only capable of statements that consecrate his role.

One might compare this scene to the second scene in Bertolt Brecht's *Galileo* (1934), in which the pope gets dressed. Both playwrights show the individual becoming submerged in the forms (sartorial *and* rhetorical) that denote his status. Later, upon learning that Leonce and Lena, the princess to whom he has been engaged, have fled the country rather than marry, King Peter exclaims:

> Have I not resolved that my Royal Majesty would rejoice today and that a marriage would be celebrated? Was that not our solemn resolution? . . . And would I not compromise myself if I did not carry out my resolution. . . . Have I not given my royal word?—Well, I will carry out my resolution immediately, I will rejoice (*rubs hands together*). O, I am extraordinarily happy.
>
> (3.3)

Since King Peter's announced goal—his happiness—requires that a marriage be celebrated, and because the bride and groom have run away, he decides to celebrate the marriage in effigy. His fictions are thus on the verge of supplanting reality.

Although these scenes help us understand why Leonce might want to flee the court, we must also bear in mind that his attitudes are *not* superior to those of his father. In fact, the form of self-gratification he practices is, if anything, more virulent than his father's, since it toys with other people's emotions. Before he leaves home he decides to break off with his former love, Rosetta. He does this by informing her that he has loved her only out of boredom. If he has pretended to love her, the function of this "love" has simply been to cover the social and emotional void in his existence. Because he is unable to develop sincere feelings for another person, when Rosetta begins to cry he passes off her tears as "a fine epicureanism." He abstracts her suffering into an object of personal contemplation. As Leonce bids her good-bye he comments, "I shall love your corpse" (1.3). We in turn must remember that Danton made a similar connection between love and death. For Büchner this gesture is a sign of the speaker's incapacity to deal positively with life and the experience of the other. Only memory and the ideal, the totally private and subjective, remain available to Leonce. And of this, nothing lasting or worthwhile can be made. Indeed, when Valerio suggests that Leonce submit to his father's wish and become a "useful member of society," Leonce replies, "I'd rather resign from the human race" (1.3).

Instead of taking that rather difficult step, Leonce runs off to Italy. There, quite by chance, but as proper in a romantic parody, Leonce meets Lena, who has also run away from the marriage prepared for her. Büchner, here disguised as "fate," leads these two young people together—and, of course, they fall in love. The romantic motif, flight from a cruel world, and its sequel of pastoral love are presented with a grand flourish—and then demolished by the rest of Büchner's presentation. The encounter between Leonce and Lena does not produce an honest, direct emotional bond. In fact, they do not actually meet or speak to each other. Instead, each uses the words and the presence of the other to indulge in private romantic fantasies. These reveries are so extreme that Leonce, after a single kiss, decides to commit suicide, since he can imagine no greater pleasure. "My whole being was in that one moment. Now die. More is impossible" (2.4). But this grand gesture, which clearly mocks the tradition made popular by Goethe's *Werther* (1774), is interrupted by Valerio, who comments (as much to the audience as to Leonce), "Hasn't Your Highness outgrown that sort of lieutenant's romanticism yet?" To which Leonce replies, "Man, you just ruined a beautiful suicide for me." With that all-too-self-conscious judgment of his little drama, Leonce promptly settles down to sleep.

The next day, which also begins the final act of the play, Leonce announces that he intends to marry Lena, despite the fact that they know nothing about each other. In keeping with the romantic tradition, they do indeed return to King Peter's realm—just in time to stand in for the puppets King Peter had ordered be constructed for the wedding he insisted must take place. Leonce and Lena pretend to be mechanical figures, and after some further comical business that emphasizes the inhuman and mechanical nature of life as organized by these aristocrats, the play closes with their marriage and an absurdly happy conclusion. Peter makes Leonce king and in so doing turns the whole kingdom into a plaything for his son, who immediately proposes transforming the realm into a utopian world without clocks or calenders and without a winter season. Valerio concludes this picture, and Büchner's commentary, by declaring that "whoever gets calluses on his hands shall be placed in custody, and whoever works himself sick will be criminally prosecuted, [and] anyone who claims to eat his bread in the sweat of his brow will be declared insane and dangerous to society" (3.3). How this revision of Genesis (3:19) and transformation of the actual condition of the working class is to be brought about is not mentioned. As Büchner has shown before, the organizers of such ideal

worlds seldom wish to be bothered with the reality of history when escapist fictions are ready at hand.

Büchner himself did care, cared passionately, about the well-being of the lower classes, however; thus, his next play, *Woyzeck* (begun in 1836), can be understood in part as a plea for the rights of the poor. It is as serious about exploring the forces oppressing the people at the bottom of the social hierarchy as the characters in *Leonce and Lena* are frivolous and even cruel about such matters. Unfortunately, Büchner never completed this final work. He died of typhus on 19 February 1837, before final revisions and additions could be made. Thus the text remains a series of scenes reworked in part by Büchner but with many questions of plot and intention unanswered. Editors and translators have attempted to resolve these problems by organizing the extant scenes into a satisfactory whole. Unfortunately, these efforts have for the most part altered what appear to be some of Büchner's own preferences. Many editions, for example, place Woyzeck's scene with the Captain first, despite the fact that it appears as scene 5 in Büchner's late revision of the play. These alterations cannot be dealt with in detail here, but the reader must keep them in mind. Only an edition that compares the various manuscript versions can give a fair picture of the actual development of the play.

This said, we can turn to the content of the extant scenes. As in *Danton* and *Leonce and Lena*, the scenic structure is quite loose. The effect is again to break open the world of the play so we can examine individual actions or pieces of action. This allows us, Büchner's public, to come to some judgment about them. The traditional (neoclassical) dramatic form, with its demand for adherence to the unities of time, place, and action, did not allow for this kind of analysis. Therefore Büchner rejected it, much as in *Danton* he rejected the old closed, linear history.

Büchner was by no means the first to turn to the open dramatic form. Goethe, Schiller,

Lenz, and other playwrights of the Sturm und Drang period had already turned away from neoclassical form. Indeed the general structure of the plot and some of the material in *Woyzeck* (the illegitimate child, social oppression, a revenge murder) are found in Lenz's *Soldiers.* Given Büchner's interest in Lenz, one might even go so far as to say that Lenz's play is a partial model for *Woyzeck.* On the level of plot, what distinguishes Büchner from Lenz is his decision to shift the focus from a stuggle between the aristocracy and the middle class to an examination of the problem of how simple working people are exploited and oppressed by the emerging and supposedly enlightened bourgeoisie—a problem Büchner first defined in "The Hessian Courier."

The historical basis for this investigation is to be found in the case histories of three soldiers, each of whom murdered his mistress. Of these three, it was Johann Christian Woyzeck who gave his name to the play; the other two, Daniel Schmolling and Johann Diess, simply provided Büchner with further clinical material about the environment and psychology of such hapless individuals. In writing the play Büchner wished to take exception to the judgments handed down in these cases. All three individuals, though clearly disturbed, were summarily convicted of their crimes. No effort was made to understand their mental condition or their social situation. Schmolling and Diess were imprisoned and Woyzeck beheaded. With these judgments, "justice" was supposedly rendered. Büchner challenged this position. In *Woyzeck* he sketches a set of environmental factors that could drive a competent but simple person first to madness and then to murder. His aim is to put society on trial.

To accomplish this, Büchner took an enormous risk as a dramatist. Rather than showing us the process of Woyzeck's psychological disintegration, he opens the play with a scene which indicates that Woyzeck is already slightly deranged. He has begun to hallucinate, imagining a fire blazing over the nearby town and almost biblical trumpet blasts ringing out in the sky. Judgment day seems to be at hand in these delusions, and Büchner's public could easily have been alienated by them. But this risk had to be taken in order to concentrate on the events that put Woyzeck on an irreversible course toward murder.

Our initial impression of him is very cleverly modulated by his next scene (all references are to the scenic arrangement in Büchner's fourth and final draft of the play). He appears with Maria, the woman he loves, who has borne him a child. This family picture and Maria's comments about his current state of agitation give us to understand that he was once a different person. Indeed, their comments on their relationship and their child imply that there was, at some time in the past, the possibility of a "normal" union between these two impoverished but potentially happy individuals. What then, the play seems to ask, has led Woyzeck to this pass? Rather than providing us with an immediate answer, the next scene (3) shows Maria and Woyzeck in front of a booth at a carnival sideshow. The barker for this particular show extols the virtues of his educated horse, and while he does so we acquire a perspective from which to view the events yet to come in the play.

> BARKER: . . . Yes, that's no stupid brute of an individual, that's a person, a human being, a beastly human—and, still, an animal, a *bête* (*the horse behaves indecently*). So, you'd make the *société* here blush. You see, the beast is still nature, unideal nature. Learn from him! Ask the doctor, other ways are very unhealthy. The meaning is: Man, be natural! You are made of dust, sand, and filth. Do you want to be more than dust, sand, filth?— Look—what powers of reason. It can add, but can't count on its fingers. Why? Can't express itself, can't explain.

It is clear that Woyzeck is this animal. We will see him try to explain and defend his nature, but he will fail, not because he is an incompetent, but because bourgeois "*société*" and its spokesmen in this play impose a code of actions and attitudes that leaves no room for his self-expression. As the play proceeds he is slowly robbed of what little speech he has been given to organize his world.

As part of his duties as a common soldier Woyzeck serves as a barber, and in scene 5 we see him shaving the Captain. Büchner's portrait of the Captain is not elaborate. Though a representative of order and social discipline, he appears in fact to be frightened by the instability of the world in which he lives. As in *Leonce and Lena*, Büchner does not want us to focus on an individual so much as on the rhetoric and gestures that characterize him. Despite his rational stance, the Captain has no inner sense of security; he is afraid of time, of life's movement toward death, a movement that none of his middle-class values can stave off. In order to compensate for this fear, this loss of identity in the face of the relentless movement of time, the Captain asserts his superiority over Woyzeck. By belittling his social inferior he shores up his own shaky existence.

> CAPTAIN: Woyzeck, you always look so stirred up. A good man isn't like that, a good man with a good conscience. . . . Oh, you're stupid, terribly stupid . . . Woyzeck, you have no morality. Morality, that means being moral, understand. It's a good word. You have a child without the blessings of the church, as our garrison chaplin says,—without the blessings of the church.

Woyzeck tries to defend himself; but his response, drawn from the Bible and Jesus' defense of little children, only leads to another attack by the Captain. "Woyzeck, you have no virtue. You're no virtuous person." Once again, Woyzeck tries to defend himself: "Yes Captain, virtue—I haven't figured it out yet. You see, us common people, we don't have any virtue, but if I were a gentleman and had a hat and a watch and a coat and I could speak polite, then I would be virtuous." Like the impoverished citizens of Paris in *Danton's Death*, Woyzeck has the ability to grasp his situation and the distinctions imposed by a class

society, but also like them his social condition is such that he is psychologically unable to stand up against the continued onslaught of the middle-class rhetoric that seeks to define and control him.

Woyzeck's agitation is further clarified through his visit to the Doctor in scene 8. The Doctor, who embodies science devoid of humanity, has put Woyzeck on a strict diet of peas in order to measure the physiological and psychological effects of such a regimen. He too belittles Woyzeck, first for urinating in public (like the horse in the sideshow scene) and then for "philosophizing." Woyzeck is not granted the right to think for himself, but neither is he allowed to be a simple, "natural" creature. He garners praise from the Doctor only when he develops symptoms of madness. "Woyzeck, you have a beautiful *Aberratio mentalis partialis*. Woyzeck, you're getting a raise."

We must remember that Büchner himself was a doctor of medicine and deeply concerned with the psychic as well as the social well-being of the masses. Here he takes aim at all medical investigation that uses human beings as guinea pigs in order to resolve abstract scientific questions rather than concentrating on the alleviation of human suffering. Neither the science nor the morality of the middle class is responsive to this suffering, according to Büchner. The Captain and the Doctor instead reiterate the language and confirm the structure of an authority that, though it promises a better world, leaves no place in that world for the poor and the disenfranchized. And so Woyzeck, without the wherewithal to stabilize his existence, slips ever deeper into emotional confusion.

As Woyzeck grows more disoriented, Marie is tempted by the gifts and the apparent strength (physical and emotional) of a drum major. She too wants a bit of pleasure from life, but in order to have it she must betray Woyzeck, the man she has loved, the man whose child she has borne. And because of this, she, like Woyzeck, feels the weight of moral judgment descend on her. "I'm an evil person! I could stab myself—oh what a world! Everything goes to the devil, man, and woman alike" (4: "Marie's Room").

Her infidelity, understandable though it may be, is the final blow to Woyzeck's already fragile psyche. When the Doctor and the Captain taunt him with it (9), Woyzeck finally loses control and turns on Marie as the incarnation of the evil that has been tormenting him. He murders her and thus completes the ironic movement of Büchner's analysis: Woyzeck has destroyed the one person he truly loves. Deprived as he is of the tools of self-expression and social analysis, he is unable to confront the real forces of oppression that surround him. This murder becomes a blind and pointless cry of rage—a cry of existential madness.

Since Büchner did not complete the final draft of the play, we can only speculate as to the closing scenes—the scenes after Woyzeck's arrest. The meaning is clear, however. The murders for which such men are condemned are in fact only the end result of the slow psychic murder perpetrated against such people in the name of middle-class values.

Although there is no hope for Woyzeck at the end of the play, the work itself is not without hope. We must remember Büchner's theory of the drama. It remains for the audience to learn from this history and, by learning, discover the ways in which it can transform social inequality into equality, and oppression into democracy and self-expression. This is the modern legacy of Büchner's brief but extraordinary career.

Selected Bibliography

EDITIONS

INDIVIDUAL WORKS

Dantons Tod. Dramatische Bilder aus Frankreichs Schreckenherrschaft. Frankfurt, 1834.
Der Hessische Landbote. Offenbach, 1834. 2nd rev. (unauthorized) ed. Marburg, 1834.
Leonce und Lena. In *Telegraph für Deutschland* vol. 1 (1838).
"Lenz. Eine Reliquie von Georg Büchner." In *Telegraph für Deutschland* vol. 2 (1839).
Lenz, Leonce und Lena. In *Mosaik, Novellen und Skizzen,* edited by Karl Gutzkow. Leipzig, 1842.

COLLECTED WORKS

Georg Büchner: Nachgelassene Schriften. Edited by L. Büchner. Frankfurt, 1850.
Sämtliche Werke und handschriftlicher Nachlass. Erste Kritische Gesamt-Ausgabe. Edited by E. Franzos. Frankfurt, 1879.
Werke und Briefe. Gesamtausgabe. Edited by Fritz Bergman. Rev. ed. Wiesbaden, 1958.
Georg Büchner und Ludwig Weidig: Der Hessische Landbote. Texte, Briefe, Prozessakten. Frankfurt, 1965. Commentary by H. M. Enzensberger.
Sämtliche Werke und Briefe. Historische-Kritische Ausgabe, mit Kommentar. Edited by W. R. Lehmann. 4 vols. Hamburg, 1967. Only vols. 1 and 2 have been published. Supplemented by Lehmann's *Textkritische Noten, Prolegomena zur Hamburger Büchner,* Hamburg, 1967.

TRANSLATIONS

INDIVIDUAL WORKS

Danton's Death. Translated by J. Maxwell. Introduction by M. Esslin. Rev. ed. London, 1979.
Danton's Death and Woyzeck. Introduction by M. Jacobs. 3rd rev. ed. Manchester, 1971.
Leonce and Lena. Lenz. Woyzeck. Translated by M. Hamburger. Chicago, 1972.
A Play in Four Acts: Danton's Death. Translated by S. Spender and G. Rees. London, 1939.
Woyzeck and Leonce and Lena. Translated by C. R. Mueller. Introduction by L. Baxandall. San Francisco, 1962.

COLLECTED WORKS

Georg Büchner. Complete Plays and Prose. Translated by C. R. Mueller. New York, 1963.
Georg Büchner: The Complete Collected Works. Translated by H. J. Schmidt. New York, 1977. This volume is the best critical edition available in English.

GEORG BÜCHNER

BIOGRAPHICAL AND CRITICAL STUDIES

Armstrong, William Bruce. "'Arbeit' und 'Musse' in den Werken Georg Büchners." *Text und Kritik* (Büchner Issue 1981), pp. 63–98.

Arnold, Heinz Ludwig, ed. "Georg Büchner I/II." *Text und Kritik* (Special Issue 1979). See especially articles by Reinhold Grimm and Thomas Michael Mayer.

Benn, Maurice B. *The Drama of Revolt: A Critical Study of Georg Büchner.* London, 1976.

Böchenstein, Bernard. "Büchners Jean-Paul Rezeption." *Jarhbuch für Internationale Germanistik* 2:67–73 (1976).

Duvignaud, Jean. *Georg Büchner, Dramaturge.* Paris, 1954.

Ebner, Fritz. *Georg Büchner ein Genius der Jugend.* Darmstadt, 1964.

Ernst, Johann, ed. *Georg Büchner in Selbstzeungnissen und Bilddokumenten.* Hamburg, 1958.

Helbig, Louis F. *Das Geschichtsdrama Georg Büchners: Zitatprobleme und historische Warheit in "Dantons Tod."* Bern, 1973.

Hauser, Ronald. *Georg Büchner.* New York, 1974.

Hinck, Walter. "Büchner und Brecht." *Text und Kritik* (Büchner Issue 1981), pp. 236–246.

Jansen, Peter K. "The Structural Function of *Kunstgespräch* in Büchner's *Lenz.*" *Monatshefte* 67:145–156 (1975).

Knight, Arthur H. J. *Georg Büchner.* Oxford, 1951. New York and London, 1974.

Lukens, Nancy. *Büchner's Valerio and the Theatrical Fool Tradition.* Stuttgart, 1977.

Mayer, Hans. *Georg Büchner und sein Zeit.* Rev. ed. Frankfurt, 1972.

McCarthy, John A. "Some Aspects of Imagery in Büchner's *Woyzeck.*" *Modern Language Notes* 91:543–551 (1976).

McColgan, M. "The True Dialectic of *Dantons Tod.*" *New German Studies* 6:151–174 (1978).

Michelsen, Peter. "Die Präsenz des Endes: Georg Büchners *Dantons Tod.*" *Deutsches Vierteljahresschrift für Literaturwissenschaft und Geistesgeschichte* 52:476–495 (1978).

Mischke, Joachim. *Die Spaltung der Person in Georg Büchners "Dantons Tod."* Ph.D. diss. Marburg, 1970.

Moser, Samuel. "Robespierre, die Augsgeburt eines Kantianers: Immanuel Kants Philosophie als Schlüssel zum Verständnis der Robespierre-Figur in Georg Büchners Drama *Dantons Tod.*"

Text und Kritik (Büchner Issue 1981), pp. 131–149.

Mosler, Peter. *Georg Büchners "Leonce und Lena": Langeweile als gesellschaftliche Bewusstseinsform.* Bonn, 1974.

Pascal, Roy. "Büchner's 'Lenz': Style and Message." *Oxford German Studies* 9:68–83 (1978).

Patterson, Michael. "Contradictions Concerning Time in Büchner's *Woyzeck.*" *German Life and Letters* 32:115–121 (1979).

Reddik, John. "Mosaic and Flux: Georg Büchner and the Marion Episode in *Dantons Tod.*" *Oxford German Studies* 11:40–67 (1980).

Reeve, William C. *Georg Büchner.* New York, 1979.

Regina, Mario. *Struttura e significato del Woyzeck di Georg Büchner.* Bari, 1976.

Schmidt, Henry J. *Satire, Caricature and Perspectivism in the Works of Georg Büchner.* The Hague, 1970.

Seis, Jürgen. *Zitat und Kontext bei Georg Büchner. Eine Studie zu den Dramen "Dantons Tod" und "Leonce und Lena."* Göppingen, 1975.

Schröder, Jürgen. *Georg Büchners "Leonce und Lena": Eine verkherte Komödie.* Munich, 1966.

Solomon, Janis L. "Büchner's *Dantons Tod:* History as Theatre." *Germanic Review* 54:9–19 (1979).

Squadrani, Enrico Luigi. "Georg Büchner: Politica e commedia." *Cristallo* 20:55–66 (1978).

Swales, Martin. "Ontology, Politics, Sexuality: A Note on Georg Büchner's *Dantons Tod.*" *New German Studies* 3:109–125 (1976).

Treitler, Leo. "*Wozzeck* and the Apocalypse: An Essay in Historical Criticism." *Critical Inquiry* 3:251–270 (1976).

Turk, Horst. "Das politische Drama des *Danton:* Geschichte einer Rezeption." In *Literatur und Lesser: Theorien und Modelle zur Rezeption literarischer Werke,* edited by Gunther Grimm. Stuttgart, 1975. Pp. 208–222.

Ullman, Bo. *Die sozialkritische Thematik im Werke Georg Büchners.* Stockholm, 1972.

Wetzel, Heinz. "*Dantons Tod* und das Erwachen von Büchners sozialem Selbstverständnis." *Deutsche Vierteljahresschrift für Literaturwissenschaft und Geistesgeschichte* 50:434–448 (1976).

————. "Die Entwicklung Woyzecks in Büchners Entwürfen." *Euphorion* 74:375–396 (1980).

Wittkowski, Wolfgang. *Georg Büchner: Persönlichkeit, Weltbild, Werk.* Heidelberg, 1978.

GEORG BÜCHNER

INDEX

Rössing-Hager, Monika. *Wortindex zu Büchner, Dichtung und Übersetzungen.* Berlin, 1970.

BIBLIOGRAPHIES

Knapp, Gerhard P. *Georg Büchner: Eine kritische Einführung in die Forschung.* Frankfurt, 1975.

—————. "Kommentierte Bibliographie zu Georg Büchner." *Text und Kritik* (1979), pp. 426–455.

Schlick, Werner. *Das Georg Büchner-Schriftum bis 1965. Eine internationale Bibliographie.* Hildesheim, 1968.

MICHAEL HAYS

MIKHAIL YURIEVICH LERMONTOV

(1814–1841)

MIKHAIL YURIEVICH LERMONTOV retains his reputation as a poet second only to Pushkin and as the author of the first fully developed Russian novel of psychological realism. His mature work reveals him as Janus-faced: his poetry and prose embody features typical of Russian romanticism, but they also establish patterns that were to become canonical for Russian realism.

From birth he was destined to be at the center of controversy, whether of his own or others' making. A scarring custody battle involving his father and grandmother lasted from his infancy to his adolescence, at which time there began a constant struggle to assert his personal dignity in the face of a largely unsympathetic public and a hostile czar. In the era immediately following the debacle of the Decembrist uprising of 1825, when circles close to the court were guilty of sycophancy and contempt for ethical values, Lermontov openly used his art to indict his contemporaries for lack of civic courage and to express his personal opposition to the autocracy.

Lermontov was a difficult person—aloof, independent, fearless, and the possessor of a relentless satirical wit. He had only a handful of close male friends, mostly companions of his youth, and he never married, although his relationships with several women were intense and typically concluded with his sense of betrayal. But although some of his contemporaries may have had reason to complain of his treatment of them, subsequent generations can only be grateful for his legacy of poetry and prose.

Lermontov was a descendant of a Scottish mercenary, George Learmont, who had entered the service of the court of Muscovy in the early seventeenth century. Family legends spoke of kinship with the thirteenth-century Scottish bard Thomas the Rhymer, and also with the Spanish dukes of Lerma, stories that strongly affected the poet's imagination as a youth. The poet's father, Yuri Petrovich Lermontov, retired from the army in 1811 after a career that had gained him a captaincy but had been otherwise undistinguished. He was of modest means and had a reputation as a bon vivant, but he was handsome and attracted the interest of the seventeen-year-old Mariya Mikhailovna Arsenieva, the only daughter of Elizaveta Alekseevna Arsenieva, a propertied widow from the ancient and important Stolypin family. Objections to their union were raised by the mother's family, but the couple married (the date and place remain unknown, perhaps because they eloped) and settled in Moscow, which at that time was just beginning to be rebuilt after the invasion by Napoleon and the fire set by the inhabitants. There, on the night of 2–3 October 1814, a son was born, christened Mikhail and bearing the patronymic Yurievich. The family soon left Moscow for Tarkhany, the grandmother's estate in the government district of Penza, where the future poet was to pass his childhood and youth.

Lermontov's mother had musical talent, and the poet claimed to remember the songs she sang to him as an infant. But he may have remembered stories told him later, since she died before he was two-and-a-half years old. Mariya's death brought into the open a smoldering animosity between Yuri Petrovich and her mother, who was not fond of her son-in-law and who ascribed her daughter's poor health and premature death to anxiety caused by her husband's behavior. The grandmother insisted that only she could provide the proper education and environment for the young Mikhail, since the father was without means. Indeed there has been speculation that the father's desire to have custody of his son was a pretext to extract money from the grandmother. He did receive an unusually large loan from her, perhaps for agreeing to relinquish control until the boy reached legal majority at sixteen. For whatever reason, Yuri Petrovich did give the boy into Madame Arsenieva's care, an arrangement that she sought to guarantee by writing a will disinheriting her grandson in the event that his father or any relative on the paternal side took him away. Lermontov's father died in 1831, when his son was seventeen, thus ending a struggle that left deep emotional scars on the young man. As we shall see, themes of family discord play a dominant role in Lermontov's early dramatic works.

Yet life for young Lermontov had pleasant aspects as well. Tarkhany was a picturesque estate in the Russian heartland, with a pond and copses, pathways and an arbor, sweeping views of forests across rolling fields. So that her grandson would not be lonely, the grandmother arranged to have children of his own age live and study at her estate; at one time no less than ten boys were in residence. An intelligent woman, Madame Arsenieva engaged qualified tutors, not the usual peripatetic French hairdressers and retired German postilions who passed themselves off as professors to the ignorant provincial gentry. Jean Capet, a Frenchman who had remained in Russia following Napoleon's defeat, proved a good tutor and friend of the youth, teaching him mathematics, science, Greek, Latin, and modern languages. Lermontov's governess was a German, Christine Remer; thanks to her he mastered German while still a youth. He learned his Russian from the serfs at Tarkhany and from their children, who were often mobilized along with his companions from the gentry to play soldiers with him. The peasants' tales about the war against the French provided the color and colloquial language the poet later used in his famous poem "Borodino" (1836), which celebrates the heroism of the common Russian soldier. Some critics have seen in this poem the inspiration for Ley Tolstoy's *Voina i mir* (*War and Peace*, 1863–1869), which also stresses the quiet courage of the anonymous peasant troops.

As a child, Mikhail was often sick, and in 1818 and 1820 his grandmother took him to the northern Caucasus for his health. The spas there, especially those of Pyatigorsk (Five Peaks), were renowned for their curative mineral waters. When Madame Arsenieva took her grandson there for a third time in 1825, her entourage included the tutor, the governess, and a household physician, Anselm Levi. As Lermontov's later notes and poetry demonstrate, this trip created lasting impressions of awesome mountains, fascinating natives, and local legends. This was the land of Europe's highest mountain, Elbruz, and of the eternal snows of the sawtoothed Mount Kazbek, turbulent rivers, rebellious Circassian mountaineers, Asian culture, and eloquent folklore. The Caucasus imprinted permanent images upon the memory of the ten-year-old boy, who established a lifelong spiritual affinity for the region.

One of the most memorable experiences of Mikhail's third journey to the Caucasus was his visit to a fortified farm, Sheykozavodsko, where his grandmother's sister, Ekaterina Khostatova, lived in circumstances similar to those of American settlers, close to nature and subject to forays by hostile natives. There Mikhail experienced first love. He wrote about it in a notebook five years later:

> Who will believe that I had already experienced love at the age of ten years? We were a large family group at a Caucasian watering spot: grandmother, aunts, and cousins. To my cousins' came a woman with a 9-year-old daughter. . . . Once, I remember, I ran into a room. She was there playing dolls with a cousin. I began to have palpitations of the heart, I became weak in the knees. I don't remember anything more, but nevertheless it was passion, strong, although that of a child. This was sincere love.

In the spring of 1827 Madame Arsenieva moved from Tarkhany to Moscow, where her grandson was to prepare to enter the Gentry *Pension*, a secondary school attached to the University of Moscow. Details of that summer are unclear, but we know that Mikhail spent some time with his father on the latter's estate of Kropotovo, in the government district of Tula, prior to joining his grandmother in Moscow that fall. His tutor, Jean Capet, died shortly after the move and was succeeded by an émigré royalist, Jean-Pierre Gendreau, who himself died within a year. An Englishman, Winson or Winston, was engaged to teach Mikhail English, and he was also tutored at home by Aleksey Zinoviev, a teacher of classics and literature at the Gentry *Pension*, who prepared him to pass the entrance examinations.

The school was recognized for its academic excellence, sharing many of its faculty members with the university. Once in the school, Lermontov had a chance to see and meet leading figures from Moscow's literary circles, among them Semyon Raich, editor of the almanac *Galateya*; Mikhail Pogodin, editor of the periodical *Moskovskii vestnik (Moscow Herald)*; and Nikolay Nadezhdin, editor of *Teleskop (The Telescope)*, all of whom taught at the university. Professor Merzlyakov, noted classical scholar, translator, and poet, was employed by Madame Arsenieva to tutor Mikhail at home. He, Zinoviev, and Raich encouraged the youth's first serious poetic efforts, although their classical training inhibited them from sharing their pupil's enthusiasm for Alexander Pushkin and other contemporary romantic poets.

The school was recognized as a center of liberal thought, and in 1830 Count Benckendorff, chief of gendarmes, felt obliged to communicate his suspicions about the institution to Czar Nicholas I:

> Among the young people educated abroad or in Russia by foreigners, and also the students at the Lyceum [at Tsarskoe Selo] and the Moscow University *Pension* . . . are many who have been fed on liberal ideas, who dream of revolution and believe in the possibility of constitutional government in Russia.

If Lermontov had avoided exposure to liberal ideas at the school, which is unlikely, he might well have picked them up from Gendreau, who not only was one of those foreigners educating young people in Russia to whom Benckendorff alluded but also was under police surveillance at the time of his death. In March 1830, the czar paid an incognito visit to the school, where he was appalled and angered at the apparent lack of discipline. Orders were given for its reorganization. Meanwhile, in late May, Lermontov graduated with a certificate testifying that he had studied languages, arts, ethics, mathematics, and literature "with outstanding diligence, laudable behavior, and excellent achievement."

After he entered the University of Moscow in the fall of 1830, Lermontov seems to have withdrawn into a jealously guarded world of his own. An acquaintance noted that he used to sit alone in a corner of the main lecture hall reading some book in English and paying no attention to the lectures. When once the acquaintance just mentioned approached Lermontov to ask what he was reading, the poet rewarded him with an unfriendly glance and the remark that it was pointless to answer the question since his acquaintance was incapable of understanding the book.

Among Lermontov's fellow students were a number destined for fame in the literary world. Many belonged to clandestine circles engaged in discussing German philosophy, Russia's destiny, and, to judge by their later activities, constitutional democracy. Vissarion Belinsky, who became the dean of radical critics and a leader of the Westernizers in the 1840's, led a circle, as did Nikolay Stankevich, who popularized German idealistic philosophy. Alexander Herzen, subsequently editor of émigré publications, Nikolay Ogarev, who became a prominent poet, and the future novelists Ivan Goncharov and Konstantin Aksakov were also students at that time. Lermontov seems to have had little contact with any of them, preferring a small number of close friends from his social circle. The most intimate of these were his cousin Aleksey Stolypin and Nikolay Shenshin, Aleksey Lopukhin, and Nikolay Polivanov, with whose families Lermontov's grandmother had long been acquainted.

In 1830 Lermontov began reading Thomas Moore's *Letters and Journals of Lord Byron: With Notes of His Life* (1830) and became acquainted with Byron's work in the original. His notebooks of this period are filled with references to Byron, between whose life and his own he sought to draw similarities: "When I began to scribble verses in 1828 (in boarding school), as if instinctively I rewrote them and put them in order. I still have them. Now I read that Byron did the same thing. This similarity astounds me." Again, in an entry of 1830 he notes that an old woman in Scotland had prophesied to Byron's mother that her son would be a great man and marry twice; in the Caucasus a midwife had predicted the same thing to his grandmother: "God willing this should happen to me, even though I should be as unhappy as Byron." And the account of Lermontov's first love at age ten has a footnote: "It is said (Byron) that an early passion signifies a soul that will love the fine arts. I think there is a great deal of music in such a soul."

Although Byron did have a significant influence on the young poet, clearly the "Byronic" qualities in Lermontov's early poetry preceded his direct acquaintance with the English poet's works. Themes of alienation, love of nature, mistrust of others, and betrayal are all present before 1830. In Byron, Lermontov found a congenial spirit; hence the recurring references to Byron, the quotations from his works, and the translations of his poetry.

The reclusive student did exhibit solidarity with his classmates by taking part in the so-called Malov incident in the spring of 1832, when a group of taunting students drove their unpopular professor of criminal law from the classroom. The matter was hushed up by the university authorities, but they did not forget it. Lermontov, who was majoring in literature, was not tactful with his teachers, often letting them know that he was better informed than they about modern literature, which was doubtless true, owing to his acquaintance with contemporary French, English, German, and Russian writers. He further exasperated them by refusing to answer by rote at examinations, as was expected. Whether or not by mutual agreement, he decided to leave the University of Moscow at the end of the spring term in 1832 and transfer to the University of Saint Petersburg. His jaundiced appraisal of life at the University of Moscow appears later in the largely autobiographical and often irreverent narrative poem entitled *Sashka* (ca. 1835–1836):

A sacred place! Recall I as in dreams
Your lecterns, halls, and corridors,
Among your sons the haughty quarrels
On everlasting life, on God and morals,
And how to drink: rum with tea or straight.

. . .

Ah so it was, as soon as eight had struck
Along the sidewalk surged the learned crowds,
Some passed the night at work by lamp,
Some drunk with Bacchus in the mud and
  damp.
But, nonetheless, now silent, full of thought
They stream along, arrive, raise a commotion.

1198

MIKHAIL YURIEVICH LERMONTOV

A thin professor enters all for naught,
They make more noise, he leaves, truth to tell
The next is even worse. A real hell!
                (3.404–405,1294–1298,1301–1311)

The lyrics of Lermontov's Moscow period reflect an eclecticism remarkable for so young a poet. The critic Boris Eikhenbaum, whose formalistic study of Lermontov's art, published in 1924, is still valuable, sees this eclecticism as Lermontov's response to the very success of the previous generation of Russian poets, a number of whom were almost of Pushkin's caliber, but who were apparently unable to develop new forms and styles. Eikhenbaum notes that traditional genres were exhausted, and so Lermontov's task was to recombine them, to alter their expected elements, to experiment with new metrical combinations and poetic diction. He eagerly made use of foreign sources, not only Friedrich von Schiller and Byron, who were prominent favorites of the aspiring poet, but also Auguste Barbier, Victor Hugo, Alphonse de Lamartine, Sir Walter Scott, François de Chateaubriand, and Heinrich Heine—all of whom provided ideas, poetic forms, metaphors, and meters, some appropriated directly and others via Russian imitators and translators.

Lermontov's diminishing concern for genre distinctions took place simultaneously with experimentation with new meters to replace the outworn classic iambic tetrameter of Pushkin. In addition to iambs Lermontov used trochaic, dactylic, and amphibrachic feet, sometimes mixing these and varying the syllable count of lines, sometimes using all masculine rhymes. A characteristic feature of his poetry is a certain repetitiousness of locution or image, often borrowed. In fact, certain phrases from his own earliest verses recur in his mature works; sometimes even quite long passages are subjected to this sort of transplanting.

I have translated literally the first lyric of 1830, "Kavkaz" ("The Caucasus"), to give an idea of the tone, the clichés of diction, and the typical autobiographical emphasis. Each stanza has four lines of amphibrachic tetrameter followed by one of amphibrachic bimeter, with masculine rhymes throughout:

Although at the dawn of my days I was torn
By fate from you, O southern mountains,
There must be time to remember them always.
Like a sweet song of my homeland,
I love the Caucasus!

In years of infancy I lost my mother,
But I dreamed that in the hour of rosy evening,
The steppe repeated a voice I remembered.
For this I love the peaks of those cliffs,
I love the Caucasus!

I was happy with you, mountain gorges.
Five years have gone by, I'm still homesick for
   you,
There I saw a pair of divine eyes,
And the heart stammers remembering that gaze:
I love the Caucasus!
                                        (1.66)

While living in Moscow, Lermontov spent his summer vacations at Serednikovo, a park-like estate outside the city belonging to one of his grandmother's brothers. In the summer of 1830 he wrote a great deal of poetry, much of it expressing his typical self-centeredness. "1830. Maya, 16 chisla" ("1830. May 16") begins:

I fear not death, O no!
I fear complete extinction.
I want the world to see some time
My work of inspiration.
                                (1.121.1–4)

That same summer was a difficult one for Russia. The Poles were rebelling against Russian domination, and a cholera epidemic was causing riots at home. Echoes of these events find expression in Lermontov's lyrics, among them "Chuma v Saratove" ("Plague in Saratov"); the somber "Chuma" ("The Plague"); and "Predskazanie" ("A Prophecy"), which predicts "a black year for Russia," when the crown of czars will fall, plague will wander through starving villages, and a powerful avenger with forged sword will appear. More personal impressions connected with his amorous interests are reflected in "K S." ("To S."), addressed to Ekaterina Sushkova, who tormented her young adorer that summer at Serednikovo.

The story of the poet's involvement with Sushkova does neither of them credit. She was two years older than he, and apparently she deliberately played with his adolescent emotions when the two were together at Serednikovo. His poem to her, written on returning to Moscow, indicates a desire for her company but states, "I love you not, why hide it!" Four years later, however, as we shall see, he called her a "predatory bat" and deliberately compromised her in the eyes of Saint Petersburg society. He lamely rationalized his cruel plot by stating that "she had forced a child's heart to suffer, whereas I but tortured the vanity of an old coquette." Some time after Lermontov's death, Sushkova published her *Notes*, autobiographical reminiscences devoted mostly to her relationship with the poet, who is portrayed as both a devoted slave and a heartless scoundrel. As for herself, Sushkova insists on her role as his muse.

The summer of 1831 occasioned another visit to Serednikovo and another love affair, this time with Natalya Ivanova, who became the addressee of many verses professing adoration. Lermontov carried this flirtation back to Moscow, but by early the next year the poet was speaking of betrayal in poems linked to that second summer's infatuation.

Although there is little remarkable in most of the lyrics of the Moscow period other than technical competence, a few works merit attention. The first, "Net, ya ne Bayron, ya drugoy" ("No, I'm not Byron, I'm Another"), contains a poignant prophecy:

No. I'm not Byron, I'm another,
A chosen one, as yet unknown my role,
A wanderer like him, whom the world
Pursues. But with a Russian soul.
Earlier I began, and earlier shall I end. . . .
(1.350.1–5)

A second work, "Angel" ("An Angel"), is remarkable for its precocity and for qualities that have caused it to become a standard anthology piece. Owing to its otherworldliness, it was a favorite with the symbolists at the turn of the century. The translation is literal, the original being in amphibrachic tetrameter:

Through the midnight heaven flew an angel,
And it sang a quiet song;
The moon, the stars, the clouds all round,
Attended that sacred song.

It sang of the blessedness of sinless spirits,
Under plants in gardens of paradise;
It sang of great God,
And its praise was not false.

It carried a young soul in its embrace,
For the world of sorrow and tears;
And the sound of its song in that young soul
Remained—without words, but alive.

And for a long time that soul endured in the
    world,
But the boring songs of earth could not
Replace the sounds of heaven.
(1.228.1–16)

The Sushkova and Ivanova attachments suggest that Serednikovo inspired merely transitory summer sentiments. However, the attraction to Varvara Lopukhina, which began in the summer of 1832, was to endure for the rest of Lermontov's life. The young poet had known the Lopukhins as Penza neighbors, and Aleksey Lopukhin was one of his close Moscow friends. But Lermontov had not previously paid any attention to Aleksey's sister, Varvara. That summer she was sixteen, a blonde with dark eyes, a modest and educated provincial girl without the affectations typical of young ladies of Moscow society. Unexpectedly she and Lermontov found in each other engaging companionship and, ultimately, love. Lermontov's relationship with Varvara is not chronicled by any cycle of angry or despairing poems, and from the few poems to her that exist it appears that their friendship was one of quiet enjoyment of each other's company. But, as we shall see, separation intensified their mutual attraction.

Over fifty poems of 1829 have been preserved, and for the following two years there are over one hundred lyrics for each year. Lermontov's productivity drops by half in 1832, the post-Moscow lyrics of that year generally revealing more sophistication and higher poetic value. As he leaves Moscow, the youth declares pathetically in "Ya zhit khochu!" ("I Want to Live!"):

> What is the life of a poet without suffering?
> What is the ocean without storms?
>
> (1.361.7–8)

Although one may praise Lermontov as poet and novelist, it is difficult to find much that is original or particularly engaging in his efforts at drama. His plays are sometimes staged in the Soviet Union, principally because their negative depiction of the gentry supports official views of what life was like before the revolution of 1917. To us, their interest lies in what they reveal of the influences on him and of his reactions to his circumstances, especially the effects of the antagonism between his father and grandmother. We note also his sense of personal superiority and his obsession with betrayed love.

Ispantsy (The Spaniards), a five-act tragedy in unrhymed iambic pentameter, was begun toward the end of the summer of 1830. The setting is Castile, a location doubtless suggested by its author's putative Spanish heritage, if not also by Schiller's *Don Carlos* (1785; 1787). Lermontov's hero is Fernando, a proud and determined foundling driven to desperation by the refusal of his benefactor, the haughty Don Alvarado, to permit him to marry his daughter, Emilia. She falls into the clutches of the libidinous Father Sorrini, an agent of the Inquisition. Fernando is attacked by the priest's henchmen and left for dead, but he is found by a Jew, Moses, whose life he had recently saved. Fernando is nursed back to health by Moses' daughter, Naomi, who falls in love with him, only to discover that he is her brother, who had been abandoned years before on the steps of a church by his fleeing parents. Fernando then finds the abducted Emilia, but he is forced to kill her to save her honor. Seized by the Inquisition, the youth goes bravely to his death in the dread auto-da-fé.

The play reflects the acquaintance of its sixteen-year-old author with a wide variety of dramatic literature, including works by Gotthold Lessing, Schiller, and William Shakespeare. There is also evidence of the *école frénétique*, including necrophilia, incest, murder, and suicide.

Somewhat less violent, but certainly no better, is *Menschen und Leidenschaften* (Men and Passions, 1830). Notwithstanding the German title, the setting is contemporary Russia and the themes more directly autobiographical than those of *The Spaniards*, which Lermontov wrote concurrently. It reflects the conflict between the poet's grandmother and his father, and his own intense feeling of victimization by the discord. Interwoven is the theme of betrayal by friends both male and female, perhaps prompted by his summer affair with Sushkova. In the first act the hero, Yuri Volin, declares:

> I am not that Yuri whom you knew before, not that person who threw himself into everyone's embrace with childish simplicity and trust, not that person who was seized with a vague but beautiful dream of brotherhood of men on earth, whose heart would leap at the very mention of freedom, and whose cheeks would flush. O, my friend! That youth was buried long ago. The person before you is merely a shadow, a person half alive, almost without a present and without a future, with only a past, which no power can give to me.
>
> (4.130)

To fulfill his own prophecy, Yuri takes poison and dies melodramatically.

The last of the early dramas, *Stranny chelovek* (*Strange Fellow,* 1831), was initially completed in July 1831, but Lermontov continued to modify it throughout that fall. Its hero, the poet Vladimir Arbenin, again a projection of the author, dies at the end, but he was to be resurrected several years later as the hero of *Maskerad* (*The Masquerade,* 1842) and its variant, *Arbenin. Strange Fellow* is provided with an introductory statement:

> I decided to express in dramatic form a true occurrence, which for a long time has bothered me and perhaps will not cease to concern me for the rest of my life. The characters whom I have depicted are all taken from nature, and I should like them to be recognized, for then remorse will visit their souls. Let them not accuse me: I sought to, I had to exculpate the ghost of an unfortunate one! Have I described society correctly? I do not know! In any case it will always remain for me a collection of insensitive people, to the highest degree egotistical and full of envy for those in whose soul is preserved even the smallest spark of heavenly fire!

This protest concludes with a sacrificial gesture: "And to this society I give myself for judgment" (4.183).

Strange Fellow has two epigraphs from Byron's "The Dream," both of which refer to unrequited love and wisdom in madness. However, its strongest ties are to a Russian work, Alexander Griboedov's *Gore ot uma* (*Woe from Wit,* 1824), to whose misfit hero, Chatsky, Arbenin owes his character. The heavy social satire of *Strange Fellow* reiterates many themes found in Griboedov's trenchant criticism of Moscow society. Vladimir states, in fact:

> Yes, I am my own enemy, because I sell my soul for one caressing glance, for a single not too chilly word. My madness reaches the farthest limits, and with me woe is not from wit but rather from stupidity.

(4.195)

In *Strange Fellow* the hero is trapped emotionally between his stone-hearted father and his loving but sinful mother, who had deceived her husband years before and had been driven away when she begged for a reconciliation. She is dying and has returned to plead for forgiveness. Arbenin implores his father to receive the penitent woman, but in vain. His mother dies, and the woman he loves marries his best friend. The final curtain falls as news of Arbenin's death is received, his funeral scheduled for the same day as the wedding of his faithless friends.

Strange Fellow is sharply critical of the institution of serfdom. It contains, for example, a scene in which abused peasants beg to be purchased from a master who has tortured and mutilated them without fear of retribution. The presence of this kind of protest in a work occupied primarily with social satire and the exteriorization of personal feelings reflects its young author's political consciousness, a trait typical of students attending the University of Moscow. The play mentions student circles; and, interestingly enough, Belinsky, Lermontov's classmate, depicted mistreatment of serfs with very similar details in his own play of 1830. Belinsky came from Chembar, which was near Tarkhany, and it is likely that both aspiring playwrights were acquainted with the same local incident of brutality as a source for their scenes. Among the dramatis personae of Lermontov's drama there is even a character named Belinsky, but his role is that of Arbenin's lucky rival.

Lermontov's first known effort in narrative poetry is *Cherkesy* (*The Circassians*), begun in Chembar in the summer of 1828. It shows clearly the vivid impressions retained by its thirteen-year-old author from his sojourn in the Caucasus three summers earlier. This poem was followed by *Kavkazky plennik* (*The Prisoner of the Caucasus*), the inspiration and title, as well as some phrases, being taken from Pushkin, with a lesser debt to Ivan Kozlov's translation of Byron's *The Bride of Abydos* (1813). Both authors again influenced another work of that year, *Korsar (The Corsair)*—the title is also Byron's—in which we find typical themes of alienation, aloneness, and untimely death coupled with a strong expression of the love of nature.

After *The Corsair* there are no fewer than a dozen efforts in this genre before 1833, with little thematic originality. Unpublished, these poems are essentially exercises in composition, with lines and sections of earlier efforts transposed into later ones. Of some interest, however, is *Posledny syn volnosti (The Last Son of Freedom)*, featuring a legendary, pre-Christian hero of Novgorod, Vadim, who sought to preserve that traditionally free city-state from Varangian domination under Rurik. Here the historical element is secondary to clichéd situations involving unrequited love, betrayal, and revenge, topped by a lively conclusion featuring a single combat between Rurik and the hapless Vadim:

> And silently Vadim did fall
> To earth, not seeing, moaning not.
> He fell in blood, he fell alone,
> *The last free Slav*, his battle fought.
> (3.135.807–810)

Three narrative poems written in 1832–1833 have lavish Caucasian settings and share a host of common themes: *Izmail-Bey*, a work of over 2,000 lines and by far the longest of the group; *Aul Bastundzhi;* and *Hadji Abrek*. *Izmail-Bey*, whose two parts bear epigraphs from Byron's *Giaour* (1813) and Scott's *Marmion* (1808), was based on a tale Lermontov had heard from an aging Chechen while visiting the Caucasus in 1825. It concerns a Caucasian mountaineer who served the Russians, returned to his homeland, and joined the fight against the Russian invaders. The plot is complicated, with a surprise ending in which Izmail is found to be a secret Christian. In *Aul Bastundzhi*, Selim is unrequited in his love for his older brother's wife, Zara, who remains faithful to her husband, Akbulat. But her fi-

delity enrages the jealous Selim, who kills her. Akbulat then sets fire to the village.

Hadji Abrek is another bloody canvas of Caucasian lore. An old mountaineer asks help in recovering his last surviving daughter, Leila, who has been abducted by Bey-Bulat. Hadji promises to return the girl to her father and rides to Bey-Bulat's *aul* (village), where he finds Leila alone. She tells him that she is truly in love with her abductor, Bey-Bulat. Hadji then reveals that the Bey had killed his brother and that he, Hadji, had vowed a special revenge. Leila realizes he intends to kill her, and she pleads with him to spare her, but the unmoved Hadji beheads her. Hadji returns his daughter's head to the father and gallops off. A year later the corpse of Bey-Bulat is discovered, along with that of an unidentified antagonist.

The dating of this last poem is unclear, because according to one of Lermontov's messmates it was written after he left Moscow and was already a military cadet in Saint Petersburg. The composition of the work would thus be in late 1832 or 1833. However, clearly the work belongs to the cycle of poems composed in Moscow; it differs generically from the narrative poems we know Lermontov did write after he entered military school. *Hadji Abrek* was Lermontov's first major published work, appearing in *The Reader's Library* in 1835. A schoolmate who was eager to see his friend's work in print submitted it without Lermontov's permission. The author is reported to have been incensed.

Arriving in Saint Petersburg in early August 1832, Lermontov found the capital inhospitable, boring, and filled with self-centered and arrogant officials:

> Alas, this town is dull,
> With all its fog and water!
> And everywhere red collars [of officials]
> Stare at you with scorn.
> ("Accept this wondrous *message* . . ."
> ["Primite divnoe *poslane*," 1832]
> 1.374.5–8.)

The poet fails to be excited even by his first sight of the sea, his favorite metaphor for freedom, power, chaos:

> And finally I saw the sea,
> But who deceived the poet?
> From its expanse so charged with fate
> There came no thoughts whatever great.
>> (*ibid.* 1.374.17–20)

It is not clear why Lermontov did not correspond with Varvara Lopukhina once he had left Moscow. He seems to have relied on her older sister, Mariya, ten years his senior, to be his confidante and go-between. In a postscript to a letter of 2 September he wrote:

> I would very much like to ask you one question, but my pen refuses to write it. If you guess, then good, I will be happy. If not, that means that even if I had asked this question you would not know how to answer it.
>> (5.374)

In mid-October he received his answer:

> Believe me, I have not lost my ability to guess your thoughts, but what do you want me to say to you? She is healthy, apparently happy enough, in general her life is so monotonous that there is nothing to say about it—today is like yesterday. I imagine you will not be excessively angry to learn that she leads such a life, because it protects her from any temptation. But as for me, I would wish a little distraction for her, because what sort of a life is this for a young person, crawling from one room to another, and where does such a life lead? A person becomes nothing, that's it. Well? Did I guess what you wanted? Is this the pleasure you wanted from me?

Lermontov's plans to enter the University of Saint Petersburg were frustrated by that institution's refusal to grant him credit for his work at the University of Moscow. Against the general opposition of his family, he decided to enter the School of Cavalry Junkers and Ensigns of the Guard, a military academy for youth of the gentry. His decision may have been influenced by the fact that several of his Moscow friends, including Shenshin, Polivanov, and Stolypin, were also enrolling. He announced his decision to Mariya Lopukhina in October:

> Until now I had intended a literary career for myself and had brought a great many sacrifices to my ungrateful muse, and suddenly I have become a warrior. Possibly this is the shortest road, and if it does not lead me to my original goal, probably it will lead to the final goal of everyone. To die with a lead bullet in the heart is better than the slow agony of old age.
>> (5.376)

In November he was sworn in as a subaltern in the Life Guard Hussars.

The final lyrics of 1832 include four short ballads incorporating folklore motifs, and another often anthologized piece, "Parus" ("The Sail"). The opening line, taken directly from a narrative poem of Alexander Bestuzhev (whose pseudonym was Marlinsky), is a covert allusion to the exiled Decembrist poet and author, then serving in the Caucasus as a common soldier. Owing to the censorship, which forbade mention of Decembrists, poets and authors often made cryptic reference to their exiled compatriots:

> White shows the solitary sail
> Against the sea's blue fog!
> What seeks it on the distant strand?
> What did it leave in its homeland?
>
> . . .
>
> Beneath it streams of bright azure,
> Above it rays of golden sun.
> And it, rebellious, seeks the storm,
> As if in storms the battle's won!
>> (1.380.1–4, 8–12)

The would-be "warrior" later referred to his period at the guards school as "two terrible years." Emphasis was on drills, formations, and other training activities. Only limited instruction in liberal arts was provided, and most of the teachers were no more than competent. There was little, if anything, they could teach the young cadet about writing, and so his creative efforts continued to be self-directed. While his days were spent in monotonous drills, at night, in violation of regulations, he labored secretly over the composition of a historical novel.

The historical novel on the model of Scott became a literary rage in Russia in 1829 with the appearance of Mikhail Zagoskin's *Yury Miloslavsky, ili Russkie v 1612 godu (Yuri Miloslavsky; or, The Russians in 1612)*. In the next several years many authors essayed this genre, the most prominent among them Nikolay Gogol, with *Taras Bulba* (1832–1834, 1842), and Pushkin, with *Kapitanskaya dochka (The Captain's Daughter*, 1836). Lermontov's unfinished novel, perhaps begun while he was still seventeen, was untitled but traditionally bears the name of its protagonist, Vadim. It concerns the same historical event as Pushkin's work, the Pugachev uprising of 1773–1775, but precedes the latter's composition by several years.

It is difficult to say exactly when Lermontov began this work. In any case we presume he began it before entering the guards school, since a letter of 28 August 1832 to Mariya Lopukhina states:

> I am writing a little, I am reading less. My novel becomes a work of desperation. I rummaged in my soul to draw out everything capable of being changed into hatred, and I have poured it *pell-mell* onto paper. You would pity me when reading it.
>
> (5.370)

The important point here is that the work is derived from its author's personal emotional reminiscences, as was typical of so many of his earlier works. But the hero this time has a new image, for Vadim is a hunchback, a monster of enormous strength and magnetic eyes, an avenger capable of tender emotion and gruesome murders.

Growing up in Tarkhany, Lermontov was filled with tales of Pugachev's crimes, for when the rebel leader arrived in the Penza area in August 1774 his henchmen executed many gentry, among them relatives and neighbors of the Arsenievs. The rebellion functions in this novel only as a historical backdrop that permits intensification of the plot involving Vadim, who uses the rebels as pawns in a personal vendetta.

The work was never finished, probably because of internal contradictions. At the beginning, Vadim is justified in seeking to avenge his father, who had been deprived of his property and his life by a dishonest neighbor, Palitsyn. Concealing his identity, Vadim enters Palitsyn's service and gains his confidence, meanwhile trying to save his comely sister, Olga, who is Palitsyn's ward, from the old man's libidinous advances. However, when Yury, Palitsyn's handsome son, returns on leave from the army, a love affair begins between him and Olga; Vadim, who now has incestuous designs on Olga, becomes a maniacal avenger. He incites murders for no purpose and rapidly loses our sympathy. Ultimately the Palitsyns and Olga become fugitives from Vadim's wrath, and the story breaks off as the demonic avenger is about to discover their place of sanctuary.

Vadim reveals its author's close acquaintance with contemporary literature, not only with Scott and his many imitators but also with writers of France's most egregious type of fiction, that of the *école frénétique*. The godfather of this genre, which was also known as *Jeune France*, was the Irish author Charles Maturin. His *Melmoth the Wanderer* (1820) inspired a generation of French authors, including Charles Nodier, Victor Hugo, and Honoré de Balzac. Jules Janin's parody of the movement, *L'Ane mort et la femme guillotinée*, was taken seriously by many enthusiastic readers when it appeared in 1829.

Some general similarities may link *Vadim* to Balzac's *Les Chouans* (1829), which concerns civil war during the Consulate, or to Hugo's *Notre-Dame de Paris* (1831), whose beauty-and-the-beast theme finds its analogue in Olga and Vadim. A much closer similarity, though, is found with Victor Hugo's first novel, *Bug-Jargal* (1826), in which a demonic dwarf named Habibrah uses the uprising of the slaves in Santo Domingo in 1791 as a means to avenge his wounded pride. Habibrah's penchant for delivering impassioned creeds on the state of his psychic condition is paralleled by Vadim's, and they are twins in their degenerate lust for power and their delight in doing evil. One may also see shadows of Byron's mysterious avenger, Lara, who incites a peasant rebellion to further his personal vengeance, and perhaps also Byron's Arnold, the embittered cripple of *The Deformed Transformed* (1824; unfinished) who seeks help from the Devil in his nefarious plans.

Irrespective of the merits of *Vadim* as a novel, it represents an important first step toward Lermontov's ultimate vast contribution as the modernizer of the prose literary language. One should be aware that no wholly suitable prose language existed in Russia for literary purposes in the 1830's. As a literary form, prose had achieved respectability only at the end of the eighteenth century, when Karamzin had introduced Russian readers to sentimentalism, presented in his so-called salon style, a literary language heavily dependent on French diction and syntax and deliberately excluding Old Church Slavonic words and the language of the lower classes. Since French was the language of the gentry and was spoken in the beau monde, there often were no Russian equivalents for common locutions of conversational speech. Prose writers of the 1830's, including Pushkin, constantly complained about the difficulties they faced, and many simply continued to use the clichés perpetuated from the time of Nikolay Karamzin.

One of the most popular precursors of Lermontov was Alexander Bestuzhev-Marlinsky, an author of adventure stories and historical novelettes, whose style was heavily metaphorical, filled with elaborate and strained com-

parisons, and given to purple passages. Some critics have defined this style as a hybrid form linking the diction of poetry with that of prose. In composing *Vadim*, Lermontov allowed himself free access to the "Marlinisms" current in the contemporary prose tradition. We find constant examples of this throughout the novel, especially in passages dealing with Vadim's emotional state. Vadim reproaches Olga for her attachment to Yury:

> . . . you are beautiful, you are an angel. It is impossible not to love you, I know that. Oh, look at me. Is it possible that not one glance, not one smile is for me? All are for him! All are for him! Do you know that he should be content with one-tenth of your tenderness? Do you know that for one word from you he would not give up his entire future, as I would?
>
> (5.64)

The metaphorical density typical of romantic prose finds continual expression in the work:

> . . . each old and new cruelty of the master was inscribed by his slaves in the book of vengeance, and only their blood could wipe out these shameful chronicles. When the people suffer they are usually submissive, but if they once succeed in throwing off their burden, then the lamb is transformed into a tiger.
>
> (5.9)

Historical novelists contemporary with Lermontov, such as Zagoskin, Ivan Lazhechnikov, and Ivan Kalashnikov, typically introduced descriptive material and anthropological information in a straightforward manner. Such realistic local color had been traditional in the genre from its inception, and we find many examples of this in *Vadim*. Descriptive passages of a realistic-impressionistic quality also occur; those were to become very characteristic of Lermontov's later prose. The description of the environs of Palitsyn's estate provides an example:

> Boris Petrovich's house stood on the bank of the Sura on a high hill, which ended at the river in

a clayey-colored precipice. Around the courtyard and along the bank were smoky, black, toppling huts, which stretched in two rows along the sides of the road like beggars bowing to a passer-by. In the distance on the other side of the river one could see birch groves and, still further, forest-covered hills showing black with firs. To the left the low riverbank, strewn with coppices, stretched in a smooth expanse, and far, far away were blue hills like waves. The evening sun at times played on the roof and windows with golden rays. The carved and painted shutters, moved by the wind, knocked and squeaked as they swung on rusty hinges.

(5.9)

One notes here that Lermontov located very specifically all of the objects forming his picture, exactly as an artist would sketch the outline of his landscape. The sun is mentioned; there is liberal use of color; there are movement, personification, sound, and emotional intensification: "far, far away." This type of landscape description, though perhaps more technically perfect, is also found in Lermontov's *Geroy nashego vremeni* (*A Hero of Our Times*, 1836).

Although Lermontov failed in *Vadim* to produce an integrated work of particular merit, the novel is moderately entertaining. The real significance of *Vadim*, of course, is that it was the author's first exercise in prose, a rudimentary but necessary step leading to his famous novel *A Hero of Our Times*.

Conceptually and stylistically *Vadim* relates to the Moscow period, as does *Hadji Abrek*. More characteristic of the guards school period are four narrative poems, all quite short, that present individual and group sexual exploits of the military students in graphic, or pornographic, detail. Several of these poems, and perhaps others that have been lost, appeared in *Shkolnaya zarya (The School Dawn)*, a collective work of handwritten contributions circulated from time to time during 1834 among the students and their Saint Petersburg acquaintances. "Gospital'" ("The Hospital"), "Petergofsky prazdnik"

("A Peterhof Holiday"), and "Ulansha" ("The Uhlan's Wife") are satirical depictions of others' adventures, but the longest, "Mongo," is autobiographical. The title is the nickname given to Lermontov's cousin and brother-in-arms Aleksey Stolypin, but whether he had that name before the poem was written or acquired it because of the poem is not clear. The work celebrates an adventure of Mongo and his friend Mayeux, the latter a nickname given to Lermontov because of his general resemblance to the witty hunch-backed hero of the French satirical magazine *Charivari*. "Mongo" is more polished than its three companion pieces; the fun it pokes at the plight of the two cadets who during a clandestine visit to a ballerina are surprised by the appearance of her protector and forced to jump out a window, makes it more amusing than salacious. This poem circulated widely through Saint Petersburg in many copies and variations, a circumstance that created a notoriety for its author that he later had to overcome. Like most of Lermontov's works before 1837, the "Hussar cycle" did serve as an exercise leading to more mature works, and the atmosphere, the lightly cynical touch, and the ebullient verse of "Mongo" were to find later expression in "Tambovskaya kaznacheysha" ("The Tambov Cashier's Wife," 1838) and "Sashka."

To the surprise of those who had predicted that Lermontov would be reduced to the ranks for disobedience, in November 1834 he was commissioned a cornet (equivalent to second lieutenant) in the Life Guard Hussars. His regiment was stationed not far from Saint Petersburg, near the imperial summer palace at Tsarskoe Selo. There the young officer established his quarters, enjoying the services of a servant, two coachmen, and a cook. His duties were nominal, he had a decent salary that was supplemented by his grandmother, and much of his free time was spent in the revels typical of his calling, that is, escapades similar to those described in the salacious narrative poems. His behavior occasioned some stays in the guardhouse, where his friends visited him. Once he appeared on parade in front of the grand duke wearing a toy sword, an act for which he was arrested. Later he showed up wearing a huge sword and was again arrested.

Notwithstanding his grandmother's influence and wealth, Lermontov had neither the name nor the money to enjoy any special position in Saint Petersburg society. But he understood its values and its workings, so he deliberately set about creating a "pedestal," as he called it, on which to become more prominent. He determined to acquire a reputation as a Don Juan by compromising the faithless Ekaterina Sushkova, his summer tormentress of 1830. For the purposes of his plan, he behaved toward her as a serious suitor, and she, dreading spinsterhood, responded warmly. At the moment a proposal was expected, he wrote Ekaterina an anonymous letter that denounced Cornet Lermontov as a deceiver whose relationship with her had already been compromising. When her family learned of this, Lermontov was no longer admitted to their company. So low was the moral level of Saint Petersburg society that Lermontov partially achieved his desired recognition and approbation by means of this scheme, for Ekaterina was seen as the dupe of a clever Don Juan.

Lermontov's attitude toward society was ambivalent, for while he was seeking to construct his pedestal by means of the Ekaterina scheme, he was also caustically satirizing Saint Petersburg mores in yet another attempt at drama entitled *Maskerad* (*The Masquerade*, 1835). The central figure is again Arbenin, this time in the guise of a reformed professional gambler who has found unexpected happiness in marriage to a young and charming woman, Nina. Arbenin uses his skill at cards to save his friend Prince Zvezdich from bankruptcy after Zvezdich has lost everything gambling; the two then go to a masquerade ball at the Engelhardts'. Through a series of coincidences, the prince gains possession of a bracelet that Nina had lost at the ball, and Ar-

benin, like a latter-day Othello, is led to believe that his wife loves the prince. Overcome with hatred and the desire for revenge, he lures the prince into a card game, accuses him of cheating, and throws the cards in his face. He refuses the prince's challenge, leaving him unavenged and thus dishonored. Arbenin then poisons his wife.

The government censor was displeased with this work for several reasons. He was offended by the attack against masked balls at the Engelhardts' (the name of an actual family) and the throwing of cards into the face of a prince; he also suspected that the play was based on real events. The work was deemed unacceptable, as were several subsequent versions. In the spring of 1836 Lermontov recast the drama under the title *Arbenin*, shifting the focus from social satire to the hero's psychological state. The censor approved the elimination of the poisoning and other "nastiness," but again the work was prohibited by higher authority from being either published or staged.

In the spring of 1835 Lermontov's grandmother set off for her estate, leaving him apprehensive at being alone for the first time in his life. He wrote to his cousin Alexandra Vereshagina, "dans toute cette grand ville il ne restera pas un être qui s'intéresse véritablement à moi"(in this entire city there is not one being who is genuinely concerned about me: 5.386). In that same letter he informed her that he had learned that Varvara Lopukhina was to marry Nikolay Bakhmetev, and with considerable venom he added that he wished Varvara a life of conjugal peace until her golden wedding or beyond, if she did not become disgusted before then. That fall Lermontov himself, en route to Tarkhany, was in Moscow for a protracted period and he met the newly wedded Bakhmetevs. The poet seems to have felt that he had been betrayed by Varvara, who, he suspected, had been attracted by the prestige and wealth offered her by her much older husband. This idea is advanced in a play, *Dva brata (Two Brothers)*, started during or immediately following Lermontov's stay in Moscow. Melodramatic and clichéd, the work unsuccessfully seeks to interweave autobiographical circumstances into a pattern suggested by the conflict and personalities of Schiller's Franz and Karl von Moor, in *Die Räuber* (1781). This effort to exteriorize the complex emotional circumstances surrounding Lermontov's meeting with Varvara Lopukhina-Bakhmeteva was to find a more extensive and successful treatment in his next prose endeavor, *Knyaginya Ligovskaya* (*Princess Ligovskaya*, 1836).

Lermontov's artistic precociousness is nowhere better revealed than in the composition *Princess Ligovskaya,* written before he had reached twenty-three. For this work not only shows a significant improvement over *Vadim,* but also, as we shall see, represents stylistic developments necessary for the evolution of Russian romantic fiction in the direction of realism. *Princess Ligovskaya* is a so-called society tale, a short novel dealing primarily with the lives and loves of the haut monde. A taste in Russia for this type of story had been stimulated by French novels, especially those of Balzac, which provided intimate glimpses into the social and private activities of the aristocracy. A number of Russian authors essayed this genre, including Marlinsky, Orest Somov, Ivan Panaev, Vladimir Odoevsky, and Pushkin, whose only completed society tale, *Pikovaya dama* (*The Queen of Spades,* 1834), was a parody of both that genre and the tale of the supernatural. But none of these authors went so far as Lermontov did in developing the psychological portrait of his protagonist. It is precisely in this area of "psychologizing" that he reveals himself as the future author of the first novel of psychological realism, *A Hero of Our Times.*

There is evidence that *Princess Ligovskaya* was written in collaboration with his friend Svyatoslav Raevsky, a godson of his grandmother and a frequent visitor at her Saint Petersburg home. Raevsky, who was five years older than Lermontov, had studied literature at the University of Moscow, and, despite his occupation as a civil servant, he was close to Saint Petersburg literary circles. One must note, however, that there is no clear indication of dual authorship other than Lermontov's letter to Raevsky of 8 June 1838, in which he writes: "The novel that we began has become involved and is not likely to be finished" (5.397).

The triple plot centers around Grigory Pechorin, a studiedly blasé young officer who consciously manipulates others to satisfy the demands of his sensitive ego. Pechorin is a dynamic version of Pushkin's lethargic Eugene Onegin; as Belinsky noted, the Onega and the Pechora are both rivers, the first placid, the latter turbulent. The main intrigue derives from the same source as *Two Brothers,* that is, Lermontov's chagrin at the marriage of Varvara Lopukhina. Here again we have a princess, Vera Ligovskaya, married to a doltish but rich older husband; the emotional conflict involves the aggrieved Pechorin, who seeks to humiliate Vera for her supposed betrayal, and the offended but rueful young bride, who now regrets her marriage of convenience.

A second amorous intrigue concerns Pechorin and Elizaveta Negurova, a superficial but cunning woman who seeks to trap Pechorin into marriage but instead finds herself his victim. The intrigue here is based on Lermontov's success in compromising Ekaterina Sushkova. The third plot line concerns the antagonism between Pechorin and a proud but poor clerk named Krasinsky, a young man of aristocratic Polish heritage who has been forced by political and economic circumstances to eke out an existence in Saint Petersburg so that he can support his aged mother. Krasinsky protests Pechorin's calculated condescension after the officer's speeding carriage almost crushes him, but because he is the sole support of his mother he is powerless to protect his honor by challenging Pechorin to a duel. Later Pechorin, seeking to assist the clerk, introduces him to Prince Ligovskoy, who has need of some business assistance, and Krasinsky makes an excellent impression on Vera and her husband. Still later, however, the clerk is humiliated when they fail to recognize him on their way to a ball. This plot line is not further developed, but we may assume that Krasinsky would not have remained indifferent to the captivating Princess Vera: a typical situation in the society tale was illicit love involving the titled heroine and an impoverished but sensitive and talented young man, most often an artist, a poet, or a musician. In this case Krasinsky's nobility of spirit and good looks would have qualified him for the role of the exceptional young lover.

The best society tales were satirical; they sought to expose the vanity, moral turpitude, and intellectual vacuity of high society. Despite Lermontov's opportunistic efforts to find his niche in this milieu, he was able to see objectively what Saint Petersburg high society represented; his tale exposes that society with vigor, wit, and often indignation. In this sense we see a maturation of Lermontov's perspective, for the author who once viewed the world exclusively as it affected himself now is able to look outward and see how the world affects others.

Princess Ligovskaya was a roman à clef, and as such it includes caricatures of people well known to Saint Petersburg society. The author's treatment of Varvara Lopukhina-Bakhmeteva in this work is much more positive than in *Two Brothers;* it is even sympathetic. Lermontov seems to have sublimated his chagrin, and now he sees Varvara more as a victim trapped in an intolerable and distressing situation. One might note, however, that Lermontov's attitude toward his lucky rival remains intensely negative, and doubtless he derived much satisfaction from depicting Prince Ligovskoy as peerlessly banal:

Having married a young woman, he tried to appear young, despite his false teeth and certain wrinkles. In the course of his entire youth this man had had no passion for anything, neither women, wine, cards, honors, but nonetheless to please his comrades and friends he very often got drunk, fell in love three times as a favor to the women who wanted to please him, lost thirty thousand when it was the fashion to lose, ruined his health in the service because this was gratifying to his superiors. Being an egoist to the highest degree, he nonetheless was known as a good fellow, ready for any good turn, and he had married because all his family had desired it.

(5.152)

Why Lermontov abandoned this work unfinished is not known, but one may speculate that compositional and personal reasons dictated this decision. The plot seems to present problems for further development; one finds it difficult, for instance, to project the Krasinsky-Ligovskoy relationship. Perhaps, however, Lermontov realized that the publication of this work would further humiliate Varvara and do no credit to himself, a realization that, if it *did* occur, would represent a sign of maturity on the part of the "betrayed" lover.

Much of the satirical material derives its pith from a method akin to the old comedy of humors. The description of the oddities assembled at a ball reveals Lermontov's perception of the ridiculous nature of much of society's behavior in formal circumstances:

Meanwhile, music already resounded in the hall, and the ball began to be animated. Here was everything that was the best of Saint Petersburg. Two ambassadors with their foreign retinues, composed of persons who spoke French well (which is, however, quite unsurprising) and because of this arousing a deep interest among our beauties, several generals and government people, an English lord who traveled to save money . . . , his spouse, a noble lady belonging to the bluestocking class and at one time a fearful persecutor of Byron. . . . Here were five or six of our homegrown diplomats, who had traveled at their own expense no further than Reval and who loudly asserted that Russia is a completely European state and that they know it from top to bottom because they have been several times to Tsarskoe Selo and even to Pargo-lovo. . . . Here military men with toupees, civil servants with hair *à la Russe* . . . who had recently been introduced into high society by some well-known relation. Not having succeeded in making the acquaintance of the greater part of the ladies and being afraid that if they invited one whom they didn't know for the quadrille or mazurka they'd meet one of those icy and terrible glances which make the heart turn inside out, as it does when a patient is confronted with a dark potion, they encircled the flashing quadrilles as a timid crowd of spectators and ate ices, they ate ices voraciously.

(vol. 5, pp. 166–167)

Lermontov's satire continuously exposes the rather amusing but harmless antics of the Saint Petersburg beau monde. However, at times he abandons his satirical approach and directly denounces the shortcomings of society. For example, the flawed system of values that determines public opinion is angrily excoriated:

The judgment of public opinion, everywhere fallacious, is grounded on completely different foundations in Russia than in the rest of Europe. In England, for example, bankruptcy is an indelible dishonor, sufficient cause for suicide. Dissolute frivolity in Germany closes forever the doors of good society. I will not speak about France: in Paris alone there are more varieties of public opinion than in the rest of the world. But with us Russians a known bribe-taker is received very well everywhere. He is justified with the phrase: "But who doesn't do that?" A coward is everywhere fawned upon—because he is a peaceful fellow. But one involved in an affair [euphemism for "duel"], oh, there's no mercy shown him. Mamas say, "God knows what sort a person he is," and papas add, "The scoundrel!"

(5.120)

Lermontov's most significant artistic achievement in this society tale was, however, not in the realm of satire but in that of realistic character delineation. One must realize that prior to the appearance of Pechorin in

Princess Ligovskaya, the number of realistically conceived and psychologically motivated characters in Russian literature was extremely limited. The most successful was Pushkin's Eugene Onegin, whose psychological portrait emerges in the course of the narrative poem that bears his name. In prose, however, there were simply no three-dimensional characters.

Because *Princess Ligovskaya* is an exteriorization of its author's relationships with Varvara Lopukhina-Bakhmeteva and Ekaterina Sushkova, its hero, not surprisingly, shows a marked resemblance to Lermontov himself:

. . . he was of short stature, broad at the shoulders, in general out of proportion; and he seemed of strong constitution, incapable of sensitivity and irritation. His gait was rather cautious for a cavalryman, his gestures were abrupt, although they often indicated laziness and careless indifference. . . . But through this cold shell the true nature of the man often broke out. It was evident that he didn't follow the general fashion but restrained his feelings and thoughts because of suspicion or pride . . . and in society it was asserted that his tongue was malicious and dangerous. . . . His face was swarthy, irregular, but full of expressiveness . . . and people said that there was something special in his smile and in his strangely shining eyes.

(5.111)

Notwithstanding the extent to which Lermontov patterned Pechorin on himself, he "constructed" him by utilizing metonymic devices. At the outset the reader is provided with a detailed description of Pechorin's study (doubtless suggested by Pushkin's description of Onegin's study), where the furnishings are revelatory: the desk heaped with pictures, books, papers, and trinkets shows broad but dilettantish interests; the Persian carpets and Chinese drapes suggest a sybarite; the busts of composers reflect musical tastes; and the portrait of Byron's Lara reveals admiration for the English author and possibly a romantic and rebellious nature as well.

Pechorin's behavior toward each of the individuals he encounters is different, a realistic touch. With his sister he plays the role of the supercilious older brother who cannot abide the immaturity of youth; with Krasinsky he is self-possessed but seeks to convey the impression of disinterestedness; with Negurova he adopts the pose of one overcome by weltschmerz; with Princess Ligovskaya he adopts a sarcastic tone, actually against his will, to cover his wounded vanity and emotional turmoil.

Further evidence that Lermontov was consciously occupied with matters of methodology in creating lifelike characters is seen in his provision of biographical detail for the three main figures, from which we learn of their youth, education, and family background; all of these affect their roles in the story. But of particular effectiveness in creating a realistic quality is the dialogue, especially in the encounters between Vera and Pechorin. Their first meeting is punctuated by embarrassing lapses in the conversation, the encouragement of silly tales by a third person to fill the constrained silence, stilted remarks, secret animosity, and feeble attempts at wit. There Lermontov shows keen insight into the most personal regions of human relationships, as well as considerable ability to convey the emotional atmosphere of such encounters.

Nonetheless, *Princess Ligovskaya* contains evident stylistic flaws. Although the dialogue is usually lifelike, we find, particularly in the speeches of the humiliated clerk Krasinsky, certain regressions to the timid harangues of Vadim. Lermontov reverts on occasion to the metaphorical elegance of the earlier novel, thus showing the lingering influence of Marlinsky. The expository passages lack stylistic consistency, ranging from the predominant matter-of-fact narration to addresses to the reader, aphoristic digressions, didactic comments, and other intrusions of the authorial personality. The author seems unable to define his perspective with respect to his narrative, at times being omniscient, then adopting the pose of a witness; at times having access to all facts, later confessing ignorance of similar information. This may reflect the dual authorship of Lermontov and Raevsky, but one cannot be sure.

Although *Princess Ligovskaya* gave promise of being an outstanding work within the limits of its genre, it remained unfinished and was not published until 1882. Thus, it made no contribution either to the society tale or to Russian literature. Its importance is that it served as a preliminary exercise for a much more significant work, *A Hero of Our Times.*

The recognition for which Lermontov thirsted came suddenly and unexpectedly. On 29 January 1837 Pushkin died of a bullet wound received in a duel with Baron Georges d'Anthès, a Frenchman serving in Czar Nicholas' guards. Lermontov was on sick leave at his grandmother's home in Saint Petersburg when news reached him of his literary idol's tragic death. Immediately he wrote a fifty-six-line elegy, "Smert poeta" ("The Death of the Poet"), expressing grief at Russia's loss and excoriating both Pushkin's murderer and those circles in society that he felt had goaded the jealous poet to a duel. The poem was instantly circulated around Saint Petersburg, copied and recopied, memorized and recited. Shortly, however, word reached Lermontov that some people were openly taking the side of d'Anthès and expressing satisfaction with the outcome of the duel. Lermontov then wrote a brief supplement to his elegy, putting the blame directly on the court:

You greedy crowd which hangs around the throne,
Hangmen of Freedom, Genius, and of Fame!
Behind the cover of the law you sneak,
Before you truth and justice cannot speak!
But there's a sacred justice, it awaits,
You cronies of debauchery, it's stern,
And by your jingling gold it can't be bought,
It knows yet in advance your deed and thought.
Then when in lies you seek to hide again,
This second time your hopes will be in vain,

And your black blood in all its fearful flood
Will not wash out the Poet's righteous blood!

(3.17)

Someone sent a copy of this poem to the czar with the notation, "A call to revolution." Lermontov was put under house arrest, and Raevsky, who had been instrumental in circulating the poem, was jailed. An investigation followed that resulted in Raevsky's exile to northern Russia under police surveillance. Lermontov was ordered to join the Nizhny Novgorod Dragoon Regiment, at that time on active duty in the Caucasus.

While under arrest in 1837 in the guardhouse, Lermontov resumed writing lyric poetry, an activity he had suspended almost totally after entering the guards school. Denied writing materials, he wrote on the paper in which his bread was wrapped, concocting an ink from wine and soot and writing with match-sticks. Among the four works written in this manner, "Uznik" ("The Prisoner") and "Sosed" ("Neighbor") refer to his captivity, while "Kogda volnuetsya zhelteyushchaya niva" ("When Billows the Yellowing Field") expresses a religious feeling that arises in the presence of nature. "Molitva" ("A Prayer") addresses the Virgin Mary with a request that she protect an innocent maiden, provide her with a bright youth and peaceful old age, and when death comes send the best angel to receive this beautiful soul. There is unconfirmed speculation that the poem alludes to Varvara.

At the time of Lermontov's exile, a Russian army under General Aleksey Veliaminov was seeking to establish a line of forts along the northern coast of the Black Sea to interdict supplies to the warring Caucasian tribesmen. Fighting was fierce and casualties heavy, with malaria a pervasive menace. Lermontov's regiment was in Anapa, and he intended to join it there; but on the road in early May he had a severe attack of rheumatism and ended his journey at a military hospital in Pyatigorsk.

He lingered in Pyatigorsk and its environs until September, enjoying an active social life, some aspects of which are echoed in "Princess Mary," one of the tales forming *A Hero of Our Times*. In September he set off for Anapa via Taman, where he had the almost fatal encounter with smugglers that formed the basis of another adventure story in his novel. Meanwhile, his regiment had been posted to Tiflis, so the poet's path led him across the Caucasus. Prior to Lermontov's arrival in Tiflis in November, the czar had arrived to inspect the troops and was favorably impressed. Count Benckendorff interceded with the czar for the exiled officer, whose absence was apparently overlooked, and achieved his transfer to the Grodno Hussars, a regiment stationed in Novgorod.

Writing to Raevsky after his arrival in Tiflis, Lermontov enthusiastically describes his travels:

Since I left Russia, would you believe that until now I have been constantly traveling by post and on horseback? I covered the entire military front from Kizlyar to Taman, crossed the mountains, was in Susha, Kuba, Shemakha, Kakhetin, dressed like a Circassian, with a rifle slung over my shoulder, spending nights in the open, falling asleep to the cries of jackals, eating *churek*, even drinking Kakhetin wine.

(5.393)

His ebullience is boundless as he recounts his adventures—his narrow escape from capture by a band of Lesgians; his climb to the summit of the snow-covered Mount of the Cross, whence he could see half of Georgia spread out below:

. . . and rightly I won't undertake to explain or describe this magnificent feeling: for me the mountain air is balsam, melancholy goes to the devil, the heart quickens, my breast heaves, and at that moment I have need of nothing. I could sit and gaze for my whole life.

(5.393)

He adds that he is studying the Tatar language, that he hopes to go to Mecca and Persia, and that he expects to take part in a military campaign to Khiva.

Leaving Tiflis in early December, he recrossed the Caucasus on the Georgian Military Highway; stopped over in Stavropol, where he met some of the exiled Decembrists; and by early January reached Moscow. He stayed there briefly and then traveled to Saint Petersburg, where he remained almost a month. There he met some of Pushkin's friends, among them the poets Vasily Zhukovsky and Prince Peter Vyazemsky, who accepted his narrative poem "Tamborskaya kaznacheysha" for *Sovremennik* (The Contemporary), a periodical that Pushkin had established shortly before his death.

This slightly salacious poem concerns a provincial paymaster whose obsessive gambling leads to the loss of his fortune, his house, and finally his wife, the lucky winner being an officer of hussars. The work is delightfully humorous, with sharply satirical treatment of the appearance, attitudes, and activities of provincial society. The ribald intent and jocular tone of this work link it to the earlier "Mongo" and the later "Sashka," an unfinished burlesque of the poet's own biography.

Lermontov's first work written during his Caucasian exile was "Pesnya pro tsarya Ivana Vasilevicha" ("The Song of Czar Ivan Vasilevich, the Young Oprichnik [Bodyguard], and the Bold Merchant Kalashnikov," 1837), later made an opera by Anton Rubinstein. This narrative poem is in the style of the Russian historical song, a folklore genre with complex metrical and stylistic formulas. Set in the time of Ivan the Terrible, it relates how the merchant Kalashnikov, whose wife had been dishonored by the czar's bodyguard, Kiribeevich, comes forth at a boxing match organized to amuse the czar, challenges Kiribeevich, and kills him with one mighty blow. The czar considers this an act of lese majesty and

sentences the merchant to die, at the same time promising to protect his family. Kalashnikov is buried in an unnamed grave.

From the moment of its appearance in print, the work aroused a great deal of curiosity on the part of biographers, literary historians, and critics. Belinsky saw it as evidence of Lermontov's desire to withdraw from an oppressive reality to a distant past; others have seen it as inspired by boxing matches that Lermontov organized at Tarkhany in the winter of 1836; some have considered it a polemical work demonstrating the poet's views regarding the proper way to adapt folklore for literary purposes. There is also speculation that the work derived from a scandal that took place in Moscow in 1831 involving a merchant whose wife had been kidnapped by an officer. Almost all scholars have been perplexed, though, at how the young poet could so quickly and apparently without study have assimilated the principal features of the genre of the historical song. The explanation is not complex: Lermontov was acquainted with the genre through existing examples such as those in the Kirsha Danilov collection, published in 1818; he seems instinctively to have assimilated the distinctive features. His work was composed rapidly as a clandestine act of revenge for his exile: it was his poetic Trojan horse, a covert treatment of Pushkin's conflict with d'Anthès.

When his publisher, Andrey Kraevsky, wrote to Lermontov that his "Song" had enraptured the public, he replied that he had sketched it out of boredom during an illness that did not permit him to leave his room. We know that in the first months of his exile he arrived in Pyatigorsk suffering from incapacitating rheumatism and confined to bed. During this illness he must certainly have contemplated avenging his unjustified punishment for writing the elegy on Pushkin. Open conflict was impossible, but poetic vengeance was within his means. In setting the work in the sixteenth century, the poet concealed the contemporary nature of the content, and the folklore form further screened the biographical details. Nonetheless the poem is filled with allusions to Pushkin's personal problems with the court and his wife's alleged infidelity with d'Anthès; the fistfight itself, in which the boxers each deliver but one blow, clearly represents a duel rather than a boxing match. Implanted in the work are intentional anachronisms as well as many other apparent mistakes that commentators have attributed to the poet's unfamiliarity with the genre, his ignorance of sixteenth-century history, and the haste with which he wrote the work. These "mistakes," however, become completely understandable if we accept the poem's allegorical intention.

The "Song" was more than a gesture of defiance against those who had punished Lermontov for the accusations contained in "The Death of the Poet." It was also an act of poetic justice in which the dishonored husband was vindicated and the murderer punished. The miscarriage of justice that had occurred in reality would be corrected in a poetic world, and Kalashnikov, the Pushkin figure, would defeat the malefactor Kiribeevich, whose career so closely follows that of d'Anthès.

While in Transcaucasia, Lermontov visited the ancient Georgian capital of Mtskhet and there heard the story that provided a plot for one of his most romantic narrative poems, "Mtsyri" ("The Novice," 1839) also later adapted as an opera by Anton Rubenstein. Its poetic genealogy goes back to "Ispoved" ("A Confession," 1829–1830) and includes "Boyarin Orsha" ("Boyar Orsha," 1835–1836), a tale of the sixteenth century in which the dominant theme of a guilty but unrepentant youth is developed within a plot involving the illicit love of a foundling, Arseny, for the boyar's daughter. Discovered in her quarters, Arseny is imprisoned, awaiting execution. He defiantly admits his love to the old monk who hears his confession. Somehow Arseny escapes and later, having joined the Lithuani-

ans, meets Orsha on the battlefield. Mortally wounded, Orsha tells Arseny to hasten to his castle, where the daughter awaits him. Arseny breaks into her locked chamber:

> This is what his gaze disclosed,
> A yellow skull without its eyes,
> A silent and eternal smile,
> Amidst the bones in their white pile.
> (3.310.1009–10012)

In Lermontov's poem the love element plays no role, but much of Arseny's confession has been transposed verbatim.

"Mtsyri" presents the tale of an orphaned Caucasian youth raised by Russian monks and made a novice. Although Russified, he constantly pines for his family and homeland. He escapes from the monastery and for three days, despite privation and exhaustion, delights in his freedom. Finally, mortally wounded in a fight with a snow leopard, delirious from his injuries, he returns to the monastery. On his deathbed he makes his confession, or rather his profession of faith, in which he insists that he would exchange the Christian promise of paradise and eternity for several minutes among the cliffs where he had played as a child.

The poem provides the poet with almost unlimited range for his romantic fancies, since the themes are as rich and as abstract as the landscape against which they are developed. Alienation, desire for freedom, vague memories of infancy, the symbolism of storm and combat all find expression here. The novice recounts how he became friends with the storm, how he grasped lightning bolts in his hands, how he subdued the dread leopard; and all this seems plausible in the emotionally heightened context of the poem.

"Mtsyri" represents the final embodiment of an idea dating from early in the poet's career—the confession of an unrepentant youth in captivity. The same theme is evident in its companion piece, "Demon" ("The Demon,"

1839), also the source of an opera by Rubenstein. The theme of the love of a demon for a mortal comes from Western literature, most prominently from Alfred de Vigny's *Eloa, ou la soeur des anges* (1824), and Lermontov played with the theme from 1829 until 1841, during which period "The Demon" underwent eight major revisions. In the final version the mortal is Princess Tamara, whose fiancé is destroyed by the jealous Demon, doomed to an eternity without love. Tamara's pity makes her the Demon's victim, but she is saved from perdition by her vigilant angel.

The verse is rich and sonorous, full of the poet's favorite imagery and typical romantic vagueness and ambiguity. A good example is the opening line, "Sad Demon, spirit of exile," in which one has no way of knowing whether the Demon is a spirit exiled or an exiling spirit. Lermontov gave higher priority to poeticality than to semantics, and this line remained unchanged through all the variants.

Both "Mtsyri" and "The Demon" are favorite recitation pieces even today. A brief quotation may convey some of the "The Demon's" rhetorical richness. The Demon declares to Tamara:

> Of earthly slaves I am the scourge,
> Of knowledge and of freedom the czar,
> I am the foe of heaven, nature's evil,
> But I am at your feet, you see!
> In tenderness I brought to you
> A quiet prayer of love,
> An earthly torment that's my first
> And tears which are my first.
>
> (3.473.600–607)

Lermontov joined the Grodno Hussars in Novgorod in late February 1838, but thanks to further intercession by Count Benckendorff he was back in Tsarskoe Selo, with his old regiment of Life Guard Hussars, by the middle of May. Military life stifled him, but numerous requests for leave were denied. The doors of Saint Petersburg society were now open, but life in the beau monde, once such a desirable goal, no longer appealed to him. At the end of the year he wrote to his confidante Mariya Lopukhina:

> For a whole month I have been in fashion . . . All this society, which I have insulted in my verse, joyfully surrounds me with flattery. The most beautiful women ask for my verses and boast of them as of the greatest triumph. Nonetheless, I am bored. I have asked for duty in the Caucasus—refused. . . . There was a time when I sought to be accepted by this society . . . I failed. And now I am in this same society not as a suppliant but as a person who has earned his right . . . I am a *lion*, yes, I, your Michel, a decent chap . . . Little by little I feel this is intolerable. Without question, there is no place so base and ridiculous.
>
> (5.399)

The poet's feelings of dissatisfaction with his surroundings and his personal situation are contained in two deeply pessimistic poems of 1838, "Glyazhu na budushchnost s boyaznyu" ("With Fear I Gaze upon the Future") and "Duma" ("Meditation"). The former expresses Lermontov's desire to know the purpose of life's joys and passions and the destiny that God intended for him. It concludes with one of his recurring metaphors, one that likens his "weary soul" to a "premature fruit, desiccated, withered by the storms of fate under the sultry sun of existence."

"Meditation" is the reflection of a mentality profoundly disturbed by its observations of contemporary society. Lermontov came of age in the period immediately following the unsuccessful attempt of December 1825 to overthrow the czar, and he was acutely aware of the hypocrisy that permeated the gentry following the suppression of the uprising. There was hardly a gentry family in Russia that was not touched by the event, and the convicted officers who were sentenced to penal servitude and exile had family connections throughout the empire. In court circles the uprising was a proscribed subject; in order to maintain favor at court, even those whose closest relatives had been sent to Siberia pretended that nothing had happened. Lermontov saw this behavior as craven toadyism, and he said so:

> Sadly I look upon our generation,
> Its future is either empty or dark. . . .
> To good and evil shamefully indifferent,
> At the outset we wilt without a struggle;
> Before danger shamefully fainthearted,
> And before power—despicable slaves.
>
> (2.39)

The poem continues with charges of apathy, indifference, fear of involvement in life. The conclusion contains a prediction:

> As a gloomy and soon forgotten crowd
> We pass across the earth without a sound or trace,
> For future centuries sowing neither fertile thought
> Nor works begun with genius.
> And our descendants, with the severity of judge
>   and citizen,
> Will insult our ashes with contemptuous verse:
> The betrayed son's bitter mockery
> Of his prodigal father.
>
> (2.40)

In the March 1839 issue of *Otechestvennye zapiski* (*Notes of the Fatherland*) appeared the suspenseful adventure tale "Bela", the first of five stories subsequently combined to form *A Hero of Our Times.* In November the episode that was to conclude the novel, "Fatalist" ("The Fatalist"), was published in the same periodical, which in its February 1840 issue contained yet another story by Lermontov, "Taman." Meanwhile he composed and published "Pamyati A. I. Odoevskogo" ("Memories of A. I. Odoevsky," 1839), a warm tribute to the exiled Decembrist ånd fellow poet whom Lermontov had met while himself a Caucasian exile.

In the course of 1839 the poet became increasingly involved in Saint Petersburg literary salons such as that of Madame Ekaterina Karamzina, widow of Karamzin, the famous writer, reformer of the literary language, and historian of the Russian state. There he met Pushkin's close friends Zhukovsky, Prince Vyazemsky, A. I. Turgenev, and other so-called mandarins. At the end of the year he met Ivan Turgenev, as yet unknown as a writer, who left a description of the poet that repeats many of the details of the appearance of Grigory Pechorin in *Princess Ligovskaya.* Lermontov also participated actively in an informal group that called itself "The Sixteen," doubtless in imitation of Balzac's dauntless avengers, *les treize.* They met nightly after the theater, balls, or soirees to discuss all manner of things, including politics, confident that any criticism of the regime would remain unrepeated.

At a ball at Countess Laval's on the night of 21 December, Lermontov was sardonically regarding the scene when he was approached by two masked figures, one of whom remarked that perhaps Monsieur Lermontov's pensive silence was owing to his thoughts about Circassian women. He replied that were *they* Circassian women he would know what to do with them. As Lermontov was aware, they were the daughters of Czar Nicholas, and they reported the insult to their father, who was not amused. The episode is alluded to in the poet's first poem of 1840, dated 1 January, which begins, "How often, by the motley crowd surrounded," and speaks disdainfully of the "flitting images of soulless people, masks convened by social habit"; when such people destroy his idyllic reverie of childhood, the poet longs "to throw an iron verse into their faces."

The czar bided his time, and within weeks an incident occurred providing a convenient pretext for the poet's second exile. Ernest de Barante, son of the French ambassador, apparently perceived an insult to himself or his countrymen in Lermontov's elegy "The Death of the Poet," in which he spoke of Pushkin's murderer, a Frenchman, as "like hundreds of other fugitives seeking fortune and rank, cast upon us by the will of fate." A quarrel developed; de Barante issued a challenge; on 18 February the duel took place. The authorities learned of the conflict in early March, and, since dueling was prohibited, Lermontov was ordered to provide a statement. He obliged with one that is notable for its jejune objectivity:

> Since Mr. Barante felt himself the injured party, I offered him the choice of weapons. He chose swords, but we also had pistols with us. We had hardly succeeded in crossing swords when the end of mine broke, and he lightly scratched my chest. We then took pistols. We were to fire together, but somehow I was late. He missed, and I fired aside. After that he shook my hand and we parted.

Lermontov was arrested and confined while a military court considered his case. After a month's incarceration, he was sentenced to be reduced to the ranks, but the punishment was mitigated when reviewed by higher authorities. The czar himself rendered the final decision: "Transfer Lieutenant Lermontov to the Tengin Infantry Regiment at his present rank. . . . Execute this order today."

Lermontov's confinement was not particularly onerous, and he was permitted some visitors, among them Belinsky, on whom he had made a poor impression when they had first met in Pyatigorsk in 1837. However, Belinsky came away from their later meeting with a completely altered impression, having found the poet an engaging conversationalist with thoughtful ideas about Russian and foreign writers. Whether this visit preceded or followed the appearance of the first editon of *A Hero of Our Times*, which occurred while Lermontov was under arrest, is not certain; but in any case they also discussed that novel, which Belinsky subsequently lauded in his critical articles.

A Hero of Our Times, Russia's first fully developed novel of psychological realism, is crafted from several well-established shorter genres, such as travel notes, the intensified anecdote of suspense, the supernatural tale, the society tale, and the physiological sketch,

which are combined and shaped to provide the reader with an increasingly intimate acquaintance with the protagonist.

The first story, "Bela," is an adventure anecdote framed by travel notes. While crossing the Caucasus on the Georgian Military Highway, a traveling author, otherwise unidentified, encounters an old Caucasian veteran, Junior Captain Maksim Maksimych. When bad weather interrupts their journey, the author encourages the captain to relate an adventure from his years in the service. Maksim Maksimych relates an event that occurred five years previously, when a young officer, Grigory Pechorin, had been posted to his remote fortress. While there Pechorin schemed to have Bela, the daughter of a local chieftan, kidnapped and brought to the fortress, where she became his mistress. Their affair ended tragically, with Pechorin's loss of interest in her ultimately contributing to her violent death.

This exciting tale, full of exotic Caucasian local color, violent deeds, an enigmatic hero, a Chechen princess, and native cutthroats, obviously belongs to the romantic tradition, but Lermontov took what was a clichéd situation, the love of a giaour for a simple native girl, and revitalized it by transposing it into the colorful idiom of the Caucasian veteran and framing it with the traveling author's descriptions of the awesomely beautiful Caucasian landscape:

> A wonderful place is this valley! On all sides are inaccessible mountains, reddish cliffs hung with green ivy and crowned with clusters of plane trees, yellow precipices lined by torrents, and there, high, high above, is a golden fringe of snow, and below the Aragva river, having embraced another nameless stream that breaks noisily out of a mist-filled gorge, stretches in a silver thread, and glistens like the scales on a snake.
>
> (5.187)

These nature descriptions have an emotional content; they are filled with color and detail, sound and movement; their foreground and background give the impression of verbal oil paintings. It should be noted that Lermontov was a talented painter whose oils, watercolors, and sketches of Caucasian and Georgian scenes, natives, horses, skirmishes, and battles capture the flavor and detail of these regions.

The physiological sketch, which derived from Étienne Jouy's depictions of typical Parisian tradesmen or bourgeoisie, was widely imitated in Russia and provided a pattern for delineating the representative features of Maksim Maksimych as a Caucasian veteran. Later in 1841 Lermontov too composed a "pure" physiological sketch entitled "Kavkazetz" ("The Caucasian Veteran"), which reiterates many of the features found in Maksim Maksimych's characterization:

> The Caucasian veteran is a being half Russian and half Asiatic. An inclination for Eastern customs is prevalent, but he is ashamed of this in the presence of outsiders, that is, travelers from Russia. For the most part, he is thirty to forty-five years old; his face is sunburnt and somewhat pockmarked. If he is not a junior captain, then surely he is a major. The real Caucasian veterans are found on the Line [active front].
>
> (5.322)

The initial description of Maksim Maksimych provides details of his appearance:

> Behind it [the cart] walked its master, smoking a small Kabardinian pipe inlaid with silver. He was wearing an officer's coat without epaulettes and a shaggy Circassian hat. He appeared to be about fifty. The swarthy hue of his face revealed a long acquaintance with the Transcaucasian sun, and his prematurely grayed moustache did not harmonize with his firm gait and vigorous appearance.
>
> (5.187)

These physical details are later supplemented by self-revelation in Maksim Maksimych's own tale of Pechorin and Bela. Lermontov pays particular attention to the unliterary and pithy language of Maksim, a language revealing his forthright, opinionated, childlike personality. Pechorin is an attractive but completely enigmatic individual, in the old veteran's estimation.

The second story, "Maksim Maksimych," is a pendant to "Bela." In it the traveling author recounts a subsequent meeting with the old veteran at Vladikavkaz, on the Georgian Military Highway. Pechorin himself unexpectedly arrives while they are there. This episode provides the traveling author with an opportunity to describe Pechorin and to speculate on his character as reflected by his appearance, something that Maksim Maksimych could not logically have done. The reunion of Pechorin and the old veteran betrays the latter's anticipation, for Pechorin affects indifference; will not discuss what happened five years earlier at the fortress, especially the subject of Bela; and refuses to delay his departure to reminisce with his old friend. Maksim Maksimych is devastated and petulantly throws from his trunk Pechorin's notebooks, which he had been carrying around since their days together at the fortress. The traveling author takes them, and the two part for good.

The traveling author then provides a "Zhurnal Pechorina predislovie" ("Introduction to Pechorin's Journal"), in which he justifies publication of the officer's private notes on the ground that he has received word of Pechorin's death in Persia. At this point we have moved from a twice-removed perspective on Pechorin—that is, from the hearsay report of Maksim Maksimych conveyed by the traveling author to the firsthand account provided by the traveler. And now we are ready to move within the protagonist's own mind by means of his journal.

"Taman" is Pechorin's account of an almost fatal encounter with a band of demonic smugglers when he was forced to lay over in that "most wretched of Russia's maritime towns" while traveling on military business. Irritated comments about Taman and his misadventure provide a realistic frame, but the bulk of the story is pure romanticism, with an enigmatic and catlike girl who almost drowns Pechorin, a blind boy who robs him, a witch-like deaf old woman whose house is both ''uncanny'' and ''dirty,'' and a Tatar boatman of incredible courage and prowess. Interwoven are hints of some demonic presence of which the narrator, Pechorin, is unaware. This tale reinforces our earlier understanding of the hero as a fearless seeker of adventure but also a person heedless in his quest for emotional stimulation and arrogant in his conviction of his ability to dominate people and situations.

''Knyazhna Meri'' (''Princess Mary''), a society tale presented in journal form, takes us deep into Pechorin's psyche. As he relates his amorous adventures in Pyatigorsk and the conflicts that they create, he also comments upon his motivation, provides a self-appraisal, and rationalizes his attitudes toward others. At times these confessional passages border on interior monologue; the critic Nikolay Chernyshevsky saw this work as the origin of that device, subsequently refined by Tolstoy. The story develops the line of intrigue involving Pechorin and Vera earlier sketched in Lermontov's unfinished society tale, ''Princess Ligovskaya,'' but it also incorporates a new element of plot in which Pechorin competes with another officer, the immature poseur Grushnitsky, for the affections of Princess Mary, a competition that proves disastrous for Mary and fatal for Grushnitsky.

All of these stories, which lead us further and further toward an intimate knowledge of Pechorin's psychology, essentially tell us *what* sort of person he is, but they do not explain *why* he behaves as he does. The final tale, ''The Fatalist,'' provides the solution. Pechorin is an egomaniac with an almost pathological desire to dominate. Possessed of the attributes for success—wealth, good looks, superior mind, strong constitution, and natural charm—he easily assumes control of people and situations. Such control provides satisfaction for his ego, but when events take an unexpected turn or his victims prove uncoop-

erative and tragic results ensue, he refuses responsibility and puts the blame on fate. Having no religion to provide ethical constraints, and neither believing nor disbelieving in fate, he wanders through life capriciously exercising his power but eschewing moral responsibility for his acts.

As its title underscores, the last tale has as its core the theme of fate. The matter of fate versus free will is pointedly discussed (but not by Pechorin) as an introduction to two extreme experiments with fate or predestination. In the first a certain Vulich tempts fate by pulling the trigger of a loaded pistol pointed at his temple; he escapes death but later that night is murdered by a drunken Cossack. Pechorin himself tests fate when he disarms the murderer under circumstances of utmost danger. But following the success of his ''experiment,'' he remains uncertain as to his attitude toward fate. Lermontov's point is that Pechorin's destructive life is the result of absence of conviction coupled with self-assertiveness: When things go well, Pechorin prides himself on being his own master and master of others, but when they turn out badly, he blames fate and insists that he bears no responsibility. This is the ''hero of our times,'' the same ''hero'' castigated so vehemently in ''Meditation,'' a poem whose litany of charges against the contemporary generation all apply to Pechorin, with the one exception of cowardice.

A Hero of Our Times has many connections with Western European literature, especially French and English. The form of ''Bela'' and ''Maksim Maksimych,'' with a veteran military officer's anecdote presented in the frame of travel notes, is similar to Alfred de Vigny's ''Lurette, ou le cachet rouge'' in *Servitude et grandeur militaires* (1835), and some minor incidents in ''Princess Mary'' seem to echo Charles de Bernard's *Gerfaut* (1838). Pechorin's literary genealogy is particularly rich; among his direct ancestors are Samuel Richardson's Lovelace, François de Chateaubriand's René, Étienne de Senancour's Obermann, Benjamin Constant's Adolphe, and the Byronic hero in general. Alfred de Musset's *La confession d'un enfant du siècle* (1836), an analytical novel concerned with the moral deterioration of contemporary youth, was probably Lermontov's closest model, as its title suggests.

The poet left Saint Petersburg in early May for Moscow, where he spent the better part of the month. Visits to literary friends, such as A. I. Turgenev and Prince Vyazemsky, occurred frequently, and he was present at a gala name-day party given for Gogol by the publisher and author Mikhail Pogodin, an event attended by Moscow's literary and intellectual elite. Leaving Moscow in late May, he arrived on June 10 in Stavropol, where his orders to the Tengin Regiment were countermanded and he was sent to Fort Grozny, on the left flank of the Russian front in Chechnya. At that time the Islamic prophet Shamil had united the mountain tribesmen in a holy war to drive out the invaders, and the fighting was constant and bloody. Lermontov was immediately in action, and in early July he distinguished himself in battle at the Valerik River, an engagement involving two thousand Russians and seven thousand tribesmen. In that battle thirty Russian officers and three hundred troops were killed, while Shamil's forces lost six hundred. The official report reads:

> Lieutenant Lermontov of the Tengin Infantry Regiment had the duty of observing the actions of the leading attack column during the storming of enemy fortifications at the Valerik River and of informing the head of the detachment of its success, which exposed him to great danger from the enemy, who were hidden in the forest behind trees and bushes. But this officer, disregarding all danger, fulfilled his duty with notable valor and coolness and fought his way into the enemy fortifications along with the first ranks of the bravest soldiers.

On this and other occasions Lermontov was recommended for awards for bravery, but ultimately they were all denied by the czar.

The poet's personal involvement in the battle did not lead to chauvinistic attitudes or prevent him for seeing the wrongness of war. In "Ya k vam pishu" ("I Am Writing to You," 1840), also known as "Valerik," a long poem (261 lines) addressed to someone he "loved, so long, so long," he describes in realistic detail the hand-to-hand combat that turned the river tepid with blood, a description that leads to a philosophical reflection:

> Now all grew still. The bodies of the dead
> Were dragged into a heap. Blood streamed,
> Its vapors hanging heavy on the air,
> As down around the rocks it streamed.
> On a drum our general sat in shade
> And listened to reports the soldiers made.
> The forest there around as in a cloud
> Was blue with smoke from all the powder burned.
> But there eternally serene and proud,
> Far away and roughly in a row,
> The mountains stretched—and Mount Kazbek
> Glistened with its sawtoothed peak.
> With sorrow that was heartfelt but unseen
> I thought: What does man seek?
> Pathetic man. The sky is clear,
> There's room for everyone beneath that sky.
> But constantly and pointlessly it seems
> He alone is hostile—tell me why?
>
> (2.95)

From time to time Lermontov was in Pyatigorsk on leave, returning to Fort Grozny in October to take command of a guerrilla force of Cossacks and volunteers previously commanded by Rufin Dorokhov, who had been wounded (Dorokhov was apparently the model for Tolstoy's Dolokhov in *War and Peace*). For the rest of the autumn he was constantly in action, a conspicuous figure on his white charger, audaciously attacking superior numbers of the enemy and the first to break through enemy lines. His active service continued until the middle of January 1841, when he was given two months' leave. He reached Saint Petersburg in early February, when carnival was at its height, and the day after his arrival he was again in trouble with the authorities for daring to appear at a ball given by Countess Vorontsova-Dashkova prior to reporting his arrival to his superiors.

The poet's sojourn lasted two months, and it was filled with activity. Writing, visits with old friends, social events, and literary evenings occupied his days and nights. The publication of a second edition of *A Hero of Our Times* was negotiated, and he engaged in discussions about a future devoted exclusively to literature. These were happy and hopeful months in which the poet received his due attention, at least outside official circles, as an artist and military hero. His mood is reflected by an elaborate practical joke he played on his friends. According to Countess Evdokiya Rostopchina, a writer of romantic society tales with whom he established a close friendship at this time, he invited some thirty acquaintances to the reading of a new novel, which was to occupy four hours, insisting that they arrive on time and that the doors be locked against latecomers. He appeared with a bulky manuscript and began to read, but within minutes he abruptly concluded at a climactic moment. Apparently the unfinished story had been written specifically as a prop for his hoax.

The work is untitled, but it has since become known as "Shtoss," a triple play on words that involves a proper name mentioned in the story, the name of a card game, and the homophone for "What, sir?" (*Shto-s*). An artist, Lugin, who suffers from hallucinations (people seem to have lemons instead of heads) follows a mysterious inner voice that tells him to find the house of a certain Shtoss. He finds the house, rents an apartment there, and is shortly visited by a specter in robe and slippers who bears a resemblance to a lifelike portrait in the apartment. Lugin gambles at *shtoss* with the specter, whose name he understands to be Shtoss, betting his money against an indistinct white figure that accompanies the ghost. Subsequently, the transparent figure materializes into an incomparably beautiful woman, and Lugin determines to gamble until he wins her. After a month of losing he is bankrupt and makes a decision. The story ends. Some critics have chosen to ignore the whimsical origins of the work and have evaluated it as an unsuccessful attempt at a supernatural tale recounted in the florid prose typical of Bestuzhev-Marlinsky and his imitators of the early 1830's. However, it is inconceivable that an author who had already completed a sophisticated psychological novel could have regressed to a style already abandoned, or that he would have undertaken to combine in a serious work outmoded genres like the supernatural tale and the *Kunstlernovella* (tale about artists). Rather, "Shtoss" is a parody of these genres and their typical stylistic features, particularly as exemplified by E. T. A. Hoffmann and his sometime disciple Gogol. As such, "Shtoss" continues an antiromantic polemic initiated by Pushkin's *The Queen of Spades*, a polemic with which Lermontov as the author of *Vadim* would not have agreed but as the author of *A Hero of Our Times* could only have strongly supported.

In early April Lermontov was summarily ordered to report for duty with the Tengin Regiment, and within a week he departed for Moscow. There he remained five days, meeting, among others, the German poet and translator Friedrich Bodenstedt. In Tula he overtook his cousin "Mongo" Stolypin, who was en route to Tiflis, and together they traveled to Stavropol. An indication of the poet's mood is found in his farewell, "Proshchay, nemytaya Rossiya" (Goodbye, unwashed Russia):

> Goodbye, unwashed Russia,
> Land of slaves, land of lords,
> And you, blue uniforms,
> And you, submissive hordes.
>
> Perhaps beyond Caucasian peaks
> I'll find a peace from fears,
> From czars' all-seeing eyes,
> From their all-hearing ears.
>
> (2.88)

MIKHAIL YURIEVICH LERMONTOV

Lermontov was understandably irritated by his treatment by the authorities, and he decided to go to Pyatigorsk rather than directly to his regiment. "Mongo" was opposed, but they tossed a coin and Lermontov won. In Pyatigorsk they easily obtained papers authorizing a stay for medical treatment and rented a small house in town, where they were immediately involved in an active social life. Included in the circle of their friends was N. S. Martynov, a classmate from guards school days. Martynov was retired as a major, and like many Russian officers he affected Caucasian ethnic dress. Lermontov dubbed him *"Monsieur le Poignard"* because he embellished his costume with a large sword, and caricatured Martynov, as well as himself, in the albums of the local young ladies. On several occasions Martynov asked Lermontov to desist from his joking, but Lermontov did not take his annoyance seriously.

Meanwhile, some conservative members of Pyatigorsk society objected to what they considered the poet's indecorous behavior. He was particularly criticized for organizing an elaborate outdoor ball at the Grotto of Diana, an affair that lasted until dawn. On 13 July Lermontov and Martynov were together at an evening party, and Martynov, taking umbrage at some jest of the poet, challenged him to a duel. Fellow officers sought a reconciliation, but since dueling was an accepted sport in Caucasian military circles, no one, including Lermontov, was particularly concerned. On 15 July he dined with friends until late afternoon and then proceeded to the dueling site, outside Pyatigorsk, at the foot of Mount Mashuk. "Mongo" Stolypin was his second; apparently there were others as well, because four officers, in addition to the principals, were named in the official investigation. The barrier beyond which the duelists were not to advance was set at ten paces, and they were to begin ten paces further back. At the command "Approach" they moved forward. Martynov fired and killed Lermontov on the spot.

Lermontov was buried in Pyatigorsk, but in 1842 his remains were taken to Tarkhany. His grandmother had suffered a fatal stroke when the news of his death reached her. Martynov was subjected to nominal punishment. Subsequent rumors that he had been a tool of the government are not credible, nor are any of the theories of conspiracy. A number of people were not unhappy with the outcome of the duel: Czar Nicholas, on hearing of Lermontov's death, is reported to have commented, "A dog's death to a dog."

Thoughts of death had been very much on the poet's mind when he began his third exile, as a number of his friends later noted and as his poetry itself testifies. Only weeks before his fatal duel he had composed the prophetic "Son" ("A Dream"):

In the vale of Dagestan in midday heat
Motionless I lay, a bullet in my breast.
And from the wound so deep still rose the steam
As drop by drop my blood did stream.

There on the vale's sand I lay alone
Around me pressed the fundaments of cliffs,
Their golden crests burned by the sun's hot
    breath,
And I, too, burned by it—I slept the sleep of
    death.

I saw then in a dream with brilliant lights
An evening feast there in my native land.
Among young wives with flowers wreathed who
    sat,
About myself occurred a pleasant chat.

Not entering into that pleasant chat,
Sat one there deeply sunk in thought,
Her youthful soul into a gloomy dream
Was plunged by that which God alone had seen.

She saw in dream the vale of Dagestan,
She knew the corpse that lay there in that vale,
The steaming wound a crimson color showed
As from the breast the chilling stream still
    flowed.

(2.127)

Lermontov's lasting contributions to Russian literature have been mentioned earlier, but several final generalizations are appropriate. After 1830 poetry gave way to prose as Russia's so-called golden age of poetry was reaching its conclusion. Pushkin's death in 1837 would have signaled its end had it not been for Lermontov, whose unusual talent and innovations added almost five more years to the period. At the same time, he accomplished for Russian prose what no one had yet done: he provided the first developed novel of psychological realism, and he set an example for the prose literary language that endured past the end of his century. Tolstoy adapted Lermontov's interior monologue, and some believe that *War and Peace* had its origin in the poet's tribute to the common soldier, "Borodino," written in 1836. Turgenev's first fictional characters emerged from the complex personality of Pechorin, who also fascinated Feodor Dostoevsky. Anton Chekhov proclaimed "Taman" the best short story in the Russian language, a conviction he shared with Tolstoy. Lermontov's early and pointless death was a tragic loss for literature, but literature gained enormously from even that brief life.

Selected Bibliography

EDITIONS

M. Yu. Lermontov (1814–1841). Polnoe sobranie sochinenii v pyati tomakh. Redaktsiya teksta i kommentarii B. M. Eikhenbauma. Moscow and Leningrad, 1936–1937.

TRANSLATIONS

The Demon and Other Poems by Mikhail Lermontov. Translated by Eugene M. Kayden. Introduction by Sir Maurice Bowra. Yellow Springs, Ohio, 1965.

A Hero of Our Own Times. Translated by Eden and Cedar Paul. Introduction by Sir Maurice Bowra. New York and London, 1958.

A Hero of Our Time. Translated by Vladimir Nabokov. Garden City, N.Y., 1958.

A Lermontov Reader. Edited, translated, and with an introduction by Guy Daniels. New York, 1965.

BIOGRAPHICAL AND CRITICAL STUDIES

L'Ami, C. E., and Alexander Welikotny. *Michael Lermontov: Biography and Translation.* Winnipeg, 1967.

Eikhenbaum, B. M. *Lermontov.* Translated by Ray Parrott and Harry Weber. Ann Arbor, Mich., 1981.

Garrard, John, *Mikhail Lermontov.* Boston, 1982.

Kelly, Laurence. *Lermontov: Tragedy in the Caucasus.* New York, 1978.

Lavrin, Janko. *Lermontov.* New York and London, 1959.

Mersereau, John, Jr. *Mikhail Lermontov.* Carbondale, Ill., 1962.

Troyat, Henri. *L'Étrange destin de Lermontov.* Paris, 1952.

JOHN MERSEREAU, JR.

JACOB BURCKHARDT
(1818–1897)

JACOB BURCKHARDT WAS one of the profoundest of nineteenth-century historians, indeed perhaps of the entire modern age. His view of history was very different from that of his historian contemporaries, which is remarkable, for it was during Burckhardt's lifetime that modern professional historiography came into its own. The merit and enduring value of Burckhardt's work have been proved by the fact that during the last hundred years his achievement has been generally recognized and respected. There has been hardly any wavering in his reputation, even though his unique historical philosophy and method have had few emulators and though he has not been widely read. His vision remains as fruitful and timely as ever. In sum, Burckhardt, like all great writers and seers, transcends his time.

During his lifetime his reputation rose slowly; he did not seek the approbation of his fellow professionals and moved in their circles not at all. The German historian Friedrich Gundolf was the first who called him "the sage among historians" and the most imaginative among them. "My starting point is a vision," Burckhardt wrote, "otherwise I cannot do anything." This was very different from the nineteenth-century ideal of scientific and professional objectivity. In the introduction to *Reflections on History* Burckhardt writes:

The word amateur owes its evil reputation to the arts. An artist must be a master or nothing. . . .

In learning, on the other hand, a man can be a master in only one particular field, namely as a specialist, and in some field he *should* be a specialist. But if he is not to forfeit his capacity for taking general views or even his respect for general views, he should be an amateur at as many points as possible. . . . Otherwise he will remain ignorant in any field lying outside his own specialty and perhaps, as a man, a barbarian.

Burckhardt's main contribution to the writing of history was his creation of art history and cultural history. There his methods justify a recent comment by Gottfried Dietze: "Although a conservative, Burckhardt was nevertheless an innovator of the first rank." At least as important as this achievement are his philosophical reflections on history, delivered orally to small classes of university students and small audiences in his native city of Basel. Immediately after his death some of these texts were collected and published by his pupils, relatives, and friends, with the result that Burckhardt's reputation in his native country and within the German-speaking world suffered no lapse. At least in the German language, most of his lectures (many of them equal to the contents of finished books) and most of his correspondence have become available during the twentieth century. His admiring students and successors have published the body of Burckhardt's work, in addition to a massive six-volume biography by Werner Kaegi, the foremost Burckhardt scholar of this century.

JACOB BURCKHARDT

A principal reason for Burckhardt's renown is the excellence of his prose. Unlike many other German writers and historians, Burckhardt's sentences are short and direct; the character of the knowledge he wants to convey is such that he has no need of the many qualifying clauses on which most German writers depend. He is admirably clear, a master of the *mot juste* even in complex and recondite matters of philosophy or aesthetic judgment. Burckhardt's intellectual penchant for the Latin world, as well as his extraordinary comprehension of the classics, may have contributed to his literary gifts. His faultless knowledge of French and Italian, too, was the result not only of linguistic ability but also of the fortunate condition of his being Swiss, a son of a nation speaking the three principal languages of the Continent. Like the great Dutch historian Johan Huizinga, whose view of history was similar to Burckhardt's, he benefited from belonging to a small western European country closely acquainted with and deeply sensitive to the culture of the larger nations bordering its own. Still it was only gradually that the cosmopolitan—or more precisely the supranational—genius of Burckhardt emerged from his originally strong attachment to German thought.

I

Jacob Burckhardt was born in 1818 in the ancient town of Basel, in that historic triangle where three frontiers of Switzerland, France, and Germany meet. His ancestors were Baslers *(Bâlois)*, many of them pastors and teachers; his father was a minister in the cathedral of Basel, founded in the eleventh century; his mother's family had settled in Basel in the fifteenth century. We must be careful not to draw an idealized picture from these conditions. As Burckhardt's biographer Kaegi writes, the society of Basel before Burckhardt's time was "hardly more human than the Athens of Socrates." The social standards and the intellectual climate were cramped and philistine, fearful of the new winds that wafted across Switzerland from revolutionary France. Even later, when Burckhardt's fame had been solidly established, there were patricians and bourgeois among the Basel families who muttered that this Burckhardt had a touch of the charlatan. However, the young Burckhardt was blessed with the spiritual and mental security offered by his bourgeois family, and especially by the serene integrity of his mother who, as Burckhardt states in one of his letters, "lived and died a saint." She died when Burckhardt was twelve years old. Several years before, she had begun a letter to Jacob's eldest sister, which was also meant for her son who, she feared, might one day grow skeptical of his father's simple and stern religious beliefs: "O, do not let yourself be cheated of your childlike faith; they will give you nothing, absolutely nothing, in return." Jacob Burckhardt was deeply moved by this admonition.

At first he was an indifferent student in the gymnasium. Then the romantic—or rather, sentimental—Sturm und Drang idealism of the Young Germans took hold of his spirit. He depended on the close companionship of friends, to whom he wrote long letters:

> If only you could have gazed . . . into my storm-swept mind, so much in need of affection! . . . I would exchange my life, at any moment, in favor of never having been born, and, were it possible, return to the womb—although I am not guilty of any crime and grew up in favored circumstances. . . . Poetry means more to me than ever, and I have never before felt its beneficent powers so active within me. But I have quite given up any idea of literary fame.

Thus he wrote at the age of twenty. He had just returned from his first journey to Italy. Violent and contradictory emotions surged within him. In Florence "the whole sky was deep blue; the Apennines were violet in the evening light; the Arno flowed at my feet, and I could have cried like a child." A few days later, still in Florence: "I felt utterly alone and realized how little the outer world counts if the inner world is not in harmony. That is the point where resignation is most painful: to do without the company of someone who loves us." And he quoted the German idealist poet Count August von Platen: "What heart is that which is untorn by pain?"

This was typical of the early, "Germanic" Burckhardt. He thought—with every reason—that the intellectual and political atmosphere of Switzerland was too cramped, insufficient for a healthy intellectual existence. He went to Germany to study in quest of a wider and clearer mental climate. From Frankfurt, at the age of twenty-one, he wrote his sister:

> I am like Saul, the son of Kis, who went out to look for lost asses, and found a king's crown. I often want to kneel down before the sacred soil of Germany and thank God that my mother-tongue is German! I have Germany to thank for everything! . . . I shall always draw my best powers from this land. What a people! What wonderful young people! What a land—a paradise!
>
> (*Letters*, p. 61)

In another letter he wrote as if Germany were a holy land: "the debt I owe to Germany lies more heavily than ever on my soul." He was thinking of devoting himself to writing a history of the Counter-Reformation in Switzerland:

> But first and last I shall say to my countrymen: remember that you are Germans! Only a definite—though not political—union with Germany can save Switzerland. I am not disloyal, dear Louise, when I say this, for only someone who tries to further the interests of German culture can be of any use in Switzerland; there is only *one* remedy against the threatening decline of a people, and this is: to renew its links with the origins. . . . I will make it my life's purpose to show the Swiss that they are Germans.
>
> (*Letters*, p. 63)

Within a few weeks of his arrival in Berlin he wrote:

> My eyes were wide with astonishment at the first lectures I heard by Ranke, Droysen, and Böckh. I realized that the same thing had befallen me as befell the knight in *Don Quixote:* I had loved this science of mine on hearsay, and suddenly here it was appearing before me in gigantic proportions—and I had to lower my eyes. Now I really am firmly determined to devote my life to it, perhaps at the cost of a happy home life; from now on no further hesitation shall disturb my resolve. . . . I have found my main subject, *history.*
>
> (*Letters*, p. 49)

He was as good as his word. Yet the crystallization of his unique view of history, something that soon would be very different from his professors', had already begun. Within a few months he grew disillusioned with the atmosphere of Berlin: "Berlin qua Berlin is a preposterous abode." His initial admiration for his instructors, especially for Leopold von Ranke, was disappearing fast. Even before his recognition of the insufficiency of the professional and academic and scientific method, he was aware that one cannot separate history from the historian, that the ideal of scientific objectivity could be a self-serving professional illusion, and that—this was his most important realization—history was more than an academic discipline: it was a form of thought. Burckhardt was not yet twenty-two when he wrote to his friend Friedrich von Tschudi:

> My poetry, for which you prophesied fair weather, is in great danger of being sent packing now that I have found the height of poetry in history itself. There was a time when I looked upon the play of fantasy as the highest requirement of poetry; but since I must esteem the development of spiritual states, or quite simply, inner states as such, higher still, I now find my satisfaction in history itself, which exhibits this development in two distinct phases running parallel, crossing and intermingling, and indeed identical: I refer to the development of the individual

and the development of the whole; add to that the brilliant *outward* events of history—the gorgeous motley dress of the world's progress, and I find myself back at the old and much misunderstood saying that the Lord is the supreme poet. . . .

At twenty-four, Burckhardt's self-imposed task was clear to him. In June 1842 he wrote to another friend:

Although you are a philosopher, you must allow me the truth of the following: A man like me, who is altogether incapable of speculation, and who does not apply himself to abstract thought for a single minute in the whole year . . . my surrogate is *contemplation*, daily clearer and directed more and more upon essentials. I cling by nature to the concrete, to visible nature, and to history. But as a result of drawing ceaseless analogies between *facta* (which comes naturally to me) I have succeeded in abstracting much that is universal. Above this manifold universal there hovers, I know, a still higher universal, and perhaps I shall be able to mount that step too one day. You would not believe how, little by little, as a result of this possibly one-sided effort, the *facta* of history, works of art, the monuments of all ages gradually acquire significance as witnesses to a past stage in the development of the spirit. Believe me, when I see the present lying quite clearly in the past, I feel moved by a shudder of profound respect. . . . To me history is poetry on the grandest scale; don't misunderstand me, I do not regard it romantically or fantastically, all of which is quite worthless, but as a wonderful process of chrysalis-like transformations, of ever new disclosures and revelations of the spirit.

"Genius," José Ortega y Gasset wrote, "is the ability to invent one's own occupation." This apothegm clearly applies to the young Burckhardt.

His life in Berlin ("a sandy desert") was not difficult. He had many friends; he earned money as tutor in the house of a former ambassador from Holland. After less than three years in Berlin he returned to Basel. The town was in the midst of agitation: the political struggle between conservatives and liberals was rising in intensity during the 1840's. "I had the courage to be conservative and not to give in," Burckhardt writes. "The easiest thing of all is to be a liberal." But he was not interested in politics: "I am obliged to keep myself to myself, as I despise all parties: I know them all and belong to none." There was also a personal crisis about which even Kaegi's detailed biography tells us very little: Burckhardt offered marriage to a young woman; the offer was gently refused. In 1845 he took up the job of writing articles for the *Basler Zeitung*. Conditions in Switzerland, he writes to his friends, were disgusting and barbarous; they "have spoiled everything for me, and I shall expatriate myself as soon as I can . . . God willing, in the summer of 1846." This expatriation led to results very different from what he had imagined.

In April 1846 Burckhardt indeed left for Italy: but his journey, which lasted five months, was soon aglow with an inspiration that he had not foreseen. If it was an escape, it was an escape forward; everything about the journey was exhilarating. There is a nervous, rapid quality in Burckhardt's letters of that time; the effusions of his Sturm und Drang period have evaporated. Art, and the history of art, have become the focus of his eye and mind. His political worries and disappointments about his native city and country lessen; and his enthusiasm for German civilization is being replaced subtly by something else, an enthusiasm for the reconstruction of the historic past of Europe: "We may all perish; but at least I want to discover the interest for which I am to perish, namely the old culture of Europe." He has now abandoned the idea of writing about the Counter-Reformation in Switzerland; newer plans—writing either about the declining centuries of the Roman Empire or about the Italian Renaissance—replace it. Eventually he would do both of these.

In September 1846 he goes again to Berlin via Basel, and after two months writes that his efforts are:

> now all concentrated on saving enough money to be able to go south once more; *then*, when once I am there, I shall not be got out so easily again. I hope to be able to get to the point of solemnly turning my back on the wretched and meretricious life here, its literature and politics. . . . In (present) Germany no man can develop harmoniously.

He writes two months later:

> My "fancy" is beauty, and it stirs me profoundly in all its forms more and more. I can do nothing about it. Italy opened my eyes, and since then my whole being is consumed by a great longing for the golden age, for the harmony of things, and the *soi-disant* "battles" of the present seem to me pretty comic.

Thus Burckhardt's short journey of 1846 to Italy was the turning point of his career. He had emerged from despair and saw the purpose of his life clearly. He returned to his native town, settling down to an outwardly dull but inwardly exciting existence as a writer and teacher, a pattern of life that, except for occasional travel, was not to be altered for the rest of his life, that is, for nearly fifty years. Burckhardt wrote three great books in less than eleven years: *Die Zeit Konstantins des Grossen* (*The Age of Constantine the Great*, 1853), the *Cicerone* (1855), and *Die Kultur der Renaissance in Italien* (*The Civilization of the Renaissance in Italy*, 1860). As a teacher Burckhardt devoted the rest of his life to his students. But what a teacher he was! Burckhardt, says Kaegi, was "not a specialist of the Renaissance but a historian of Europe"; to which we may properly add that he was *the* magisterial teacher of European civilization. He taught and wrote concurrently. He never missed a class in more than four decades of teaching. The purposes of his teaching and his writing were fused. The evidence is in Burckhardt's vast literary legacy, in the completeness of the texts and notes that he left behind. They could be and were published posthumously, some immediately after his death: *Errinerungen aus Rubens* (*Recollections of Rubens*, 1898), *Der Griechische Kulturgeschichte* (*History of Greek Culture*, 1898–1902), *Die Weltgeschichtliche Betrachtungen* (*Reflections on History*, 1905).

Burckhardt's conversion of 1846 reconciled him not only to returning to Basel but also to entering the teaching profession. The University of Basel, though ancient and respectable, was somnolent; when Burckhardt first went to Berlin, Basel had fewer than three dozen regular students. After receiving his doctorate (from Basel) Burckhardt taught for a time in a gymnasium, as Swiss university teachers were required to do; he earned money by contributing articles to the great German *Brockhaus* encyclopedia. In the mid-1850's he moved to Zurich for a few years to teach in the new polytechnic. In 1857 he returned to Basel, never to leave it again. Already his close-cropped hair and moustache had turned entirely white. Ten years later Friedrich Nietzsche became first one of Burckhardt's students and then one of his younger colleagues. Their association and friendship lasted only a few years, but Nietzsche's respect for Burckhardt remained deep and strong: he said that every cultured citizen of Basel reflects the fact of having been born in the city of Jacob Burckhardt. Burckhardt's former student Albert Gessler writes that "for those who knew Burckhardt he was an 'educator,' a mentor [*ein Erzieher*], in the highest, most spiritual sense of that word."

By 1860, at forty-two, he had renounced, as he himself said, all scholarly ambition. He published nothing more during his lifetime. Invitations to German universities, including one in 1874 to occupy the chair of Ranke at Berlin, he rejected without hesitation: "In Basel I can teach what I like." In 1860 the old town of Basel leveled its remaining medieval walls; and Burckhardt wrote to a friend that "in the crisis of the declining nineteenth century things can only be changed by ascetics, men who are independent of the enormously expensive life of the great cities." He was himself such an ascetic in the original Greek meaning of the word, self-disciplined and austere, but he was neither a hermit nor a recluse. He liked food and wine; he loved music (he composed songs on occasion); he traveled to Italy again and again, and on occasion as far as London, Vienna, and Prague. He disliked professors, and was happy when he was not taken for one—except of course in Basel. There, he carried his large portfolio of photographs of art and architecture to class every day: the scene with "this old man with a portfolio" was captured in a charming photograph that survives. He prepared his lectures with the greatest care; but he did not bring notes to class.

The extraordinary range of his lecturing may be seen from this list for one semester in 1860 alone: 1) the history of painting; 2) tapestries; 3) Calderón; 4) Byron; 5) La Rochefoucauld; 6) Manzoni; 7) Rabelais; 8) Gothic monasteries; 9) the Corpus Christi festival in Viterbo (1462); 10) the beginnings of landscape painting; 11) Greek sculpture in the British Museum.

Seven years later, after he had completed the section on architecture for his study of Italian Renaissance art, Burckhardt's interests moved toward the even larger sphere of the history of history and the relation of perennial forces to and within the history of civilizations. Between 1867 and 1872 he gave the series "Introduction to the Study of History" at the university and another series at the Museum of Basel for the Basel public. These lectures were not collected or published until many years after his death, when they appeared as *Reflections on History* and *Historische Fragmente* (*Judgments on History and Historians*, 1929). These two volumes have acquired a fame during the twentieth century equal to that of the works published in his lifetime. They expound Burckhardt's historical philosophy—something very different from a "philosophy of history." As Alexander Dru puts it, "In conformity with the requirements of a small university, he regarded his task as Professor of History as consisting less in the communication of special knowledge than in generally encouraging an historical outlook."

We do not know whether Burckhardt ever faced those hardly avoidable attacks of doubt that beset teachers when they face an audience of unimaginative students; what we know is that he enjoyed his teaching until the end of his life. He himself declares:

> In my experience, learned authorship is one of the most unhealthy, and mere teaching (however troublesome it may be, and however circumstantial the studies and preparations need to be) one of the healthiest *métiers* in the world. To be always standing, walking and talking, and to go for a good hike once a week, whatever the weather, now and then a bottle of the best, no overheated rooms in the winter, and an open collar, that is good for one.
>
> (*Letters*, p. 161)

He gave up his professorship of history in 1885 but kept his chair in the history of art until 1893, his seventy-fifth year. He enjoyed the company of students, who would visit him in the evening in his little rooms overlooking a river. His conversation was sparkling and light, like the northern Italian wines he preferred.

Burckhardt always found his trips to Italy invigorating. "I am in excellent health in spite of running to and fro," he writes from Rome in 1875; "among other things, I am enjoying not having to know ex officio who painted the reredos in the X chapel of St. Thingumbob." When he visited London in 1879 he was full of excitement and wrote long letters to friends nearly every day. He muses: "Are the few drops of Italian blood that have come to me through several marriages since the sixteenth century still flowing in my veins?" The Italian people were good, their physical beauty had not declined, "although peasant coloring is becoming rarer. On the other hand, foreign tourists are much worse than they used to be, and the sight of the Piazza di Spagna, as it is now, makes me despair. I can stand the English, but a certain other nation somewhat less." He meant the Germans. He regarded "leisure as the mother of contemplation and of the inspiration that springs from it." This too was the very opposite of Ranke, who, upon being ennobled by the German emperor, chose the motto *Labor ipse voluptas* (Work itself is pleasure).

Leisure, compounded with the self-discipline of his tasks, remained the practical ideal of Burckhardt's life. He enjoyed his daily siesta, rereading the Greek tragedies as he lay on his sofa, as well as the conversations with his friends, and his correspondence. He was much more cheerful at sixty than at thirty. "One begins to feel as though one were going to evening service on a rainy Sunday," but the wisest thing is to be "as cheerful as possible, and not behave as though there were bad omens in the sky." He was witty and sociable till the end, a kind uncle and granduncle, a sage without being in the least oracular, cynical, or bitter. He was consistent in refusing to have his papers and lectures published, even though during his last years he agreed that his nephew Jacob Oeri might edit some for eventual publication. He often said of his lectures and notes that they would look "like carpets the wrong side up." They were, in reality, tapestries of unexpected magnificence of design.

II

Burckhardt was not yet twenty-two when he wrote that "the history of art will always draw me like a magnet." Note that he wrote of the history of art, not of art alone. He was interested in the relation of art to life—more precisely, in its relation to historical life: that is, the ways in which the vision and work of artists reflect changing views of life itself. As early as *The Age of Constantine the Great,* his first published work and one that does not deal with the history of art, we find a passage that sums up Burckhardt's purpose:

It is a fact that from approximately the middle of the second century the active production of works of art, which had hitherto flourished, ceases and degenerates to mere repetition, and that henceforward internal impoverishment and apparent overelaboration of forms go hand in hand. The deepest causes of this phenomenon can probably never be plumbed or comprehended in words. If the developed Greek system of forms could maintain itself for six centuries under all the vicissitudes of history and always throw out new shoots, why should it lose its power and its creative energy precisely from the age of the Antonines downwards? Why could it not have lasted into the fourth century? Perhaps an a priori answer may emerge from a general philosophic consideration of the period, but it is more prudent not to seek to determine the lifespan of a spiritual force of such magnitude.

(pp. 214–215)

Three years later Burckhardt published the *Cicerone.* This extraordinary book, the first of Burckhardt's works translated into English, bears the modest English subtitle: "An Art Guide to Painting in Italy for the Use of Travellers and Students." The original German subtitle is even more telling: "An Introduction to the *Enjoyment* [the italics are mine] of the Art Treasures of Italy." Of course the *Cicerone* is more than a guide. It describes all of the valuable paintings in Italy, including those in the remotest corners of abandoned churches, and it is equipped with a splendidly practical index of painters and places, from which the reader can instantly see *where* this or that picture by, say, Bellini is to be found; or again, it tells us *what* is worth seeing in, say, Bergamo. Yet the *Cicerone* is essentially historical. Burckhardt begins with painting in the early Middle Ages and goes to the middle of the seventeenth century. The work is encyclopedic in its scope; yet unlike a guide, it can (and ought to) be read with profit from beginning to end. It is not only a splendid walk with the best guide (*cicerone* means "guide" in Italian) through the vast sunlit museum that Italy is, but also a splendid walk through Italian history over a span of nearly 1,500 years.

Burckhardt does not hesitate to give summary judgments: "In emotional scenes Mantegna is sometimes coarse and unbeautiful." Sandro Botticelli "often painted with a great deal of haste." Burckhardt's best passages reveal the relation between forms of art and forms of life and thought. In a mosaic,

> the artist no longer invents; he has only to reproduce. . . . The repetition of something learned by heart is the essential characteristic of what we call the Byzantine style. . . . It is astonishing to observe this complete dying out of individual character, which is gradually supplanted by a uniform type, similar in every detail. . . . The expression of holiness always takes the shape of moroseness, since art was not permitted to arouse the thought of the supernatural by producing forms that were free as well as grand. Even the Madonna becomes sulky, though the small lips and thin nose seem to make a certain attempt at loveliness; in male heads there is often a repulsive indignant expression.

Or consider this summary reflection upon the difference in spirit between the Italian Renaissance and the Flemish Renaissance, as exemplified by a work of art:

> Another "Deposition" in the *Uffizi*, No. 795, ascribed to Roger van den Weyden, raises the question how it could be possible that the old Netherlanders should observe the details of reality with so sharp an eye, and copy it with such a

sure and unwearied hand, and yet misconceive life and action as a whole.

The chapter on the Renaissance begins with a sublime introduction, "The Character of the Renaissance":

> In the beginning of the fifteenth century a new spirit entered into the painting of the West. Though still employed in the service of the church, its principles were henceforward developed without reference to merely ecclesiastical purposes. A work of art now gives more than the church requires; over and above religious associations, it presents a copy of the real world; the artist is absorbed in the examination and the representation of the outward appearance of things, and by degrees learns to express all the various manifestations of the human form as well as of its surroundings. Instead of general types of face, we have individuals; the traditional system of expression, of gestures and draperies, is replaced by the endless variety of real life, which has a special expression for each occasion. Simple beauty, which hitherto has been sought for and often found as the highest attribute of the saints, now gives place to the distinctness and fulness in detail which is the principal idea of modern art.
>
> (p. 57)

Burckhardt's introductory summaries about the great masters indicate the breadth and sureness of his powers of description. Michelangelo was an architect and sculptor,

> but for the expression of that ideal world which he carried within himself, painting afforded materials so much more various that he could not do without it. . . . It was against his nature to enter into any traditional feeling of devotion, any received ecclesiastical type, the tone of feeling of any other man, or to consider himself as bound thereby. . . . He creates man anew with grand physical power, which in itself appears Titanic, and produces out of these forms a fresh earthly and Olympian world. They move and have their being like a race apart from all earlier

generations. What in painters of the fifteenth century is called characteristic finds no place here, because they come forth as a complete race—a people; but where personality is required, it is one ideally formed, a superhuman power.

(pp. 122–123)

Titian "either adopted, or himself created, or gave the original idea to the younger generation of all that Venice was capable of in painting. There is no intellectual element in the school that he does not somewhere exemplify in perfection; he certainly also represents its limitations." Burckhardt continues:

With *Caravaggio* and the Neapolitans drawing and modeling are altogether considerably inferior, and they think they may rely on quite other means for effect. Commonplace as their forms are . . . in their vulgarity they are only too often vague as well. . . . From *Luca Giordano* downwards the drawing of the Neapolitan school falls into the most careless extemporization.

Burckhardt's *Recollections of Rubens* were not published until 1898, a year after his death. As early as 1842 Burckhardt said that Peter Paul Rubens had been "in general unreasonably criticized." The Rubens book is a perfect piece of work. Its synopsis, compiled and arranged by Burckhardt, is so detailed and comprehensive that we wonder not only at the scope of Burckhardt's knowledge and interests but also at his capacity to compress all of this in a relatively short space. Among his surviving manuscripts this was the easiest one to present to the printer because of its perfection. The book begins with a sublime consideration of Rubens' character:

It is an exhilarating task to evoke the life and personality of Rubens; good fortune and kindliness abound in him as in hardly any other great master, and he is well enough known for us to feel sure of our judgment of him. In the consciousness of his own noble nature and great

powers he must have been one of the most privileged of mortals. No life is perfect, and trials came to him too, but the sum of his life so illuminates all its details that, looked at as a whole, it seems exemplary. It did not come to a premature end, like that of Masaccio, Giorgione, and Raphael, while on the other hand he was spared the weakness of age, and it was in his last years that he created some of his grandest work.

(p. 5)

It was "extraordinarily fortunate for the Catholicism of the entire north to find so great, so willing, and so happy an interpreter, who was himself fired by enthusiasm for the life of all the great religious figures." Yet Burckhardt finds Rubens inadequate in his madonnas, "not within the limits of the style we have once accepted as his, but in relation to the imaginative implications of the problem and to the rest of great art":

At the risk of appearing most one-sided and unscholarly, and of judging a master by a standard that was not his, we must admit as witnesses against him not only Titian's "Transfigured Madonna" and Raphael's "Sistine Madonna" but even Guido Reni's Munich "Assunta" and his altarpieces of the "Holy Conception." And it is not the spirituality of the features in these pictures that we should have the right to feel the lack of in Rubens; it is the spirituality of the expression. . . . Her head shows that rich, matronly, unreligious modeling of Rubens's other Madonnas, and it is only in the Antwerp picture that she takes on a greater sweetness.

(p. 94)

These passages indicate the extraordinary quality of Burckhardt's art criticism. There is in his writing a constant concern with the relation of art to history—not in the sense of chronological placing or even in the recognition of important correspondences of place and of time, but in the connection of a particular work of art with the culture of Europe in general. Burckhardt's description of Rubens'

"Lesser Last Judgment" and of his "Fall of the Damned into Hell" (where "Rubens' mastery of space finds its ultimate expression") would alone qualify Burckhardt as one of the greatest analysts of art of all times ("the incredible spatiality is brought out by a powerful light falling from the sky onto every ghastly group"). But he wishes to remind us of something else, a corresponding verity on yet another level:

> If we survey the art and poetry of all times for a comparable imaginative power, we shall most probably recognize it in its exact opposite, namely, in a horrible description of nonspace. But the speaker is Mephistopheles in the second part of *Faust,* and he is giving Faust instructions for his journey to the "Mothers." Thus by entirely different roads, men like Rubens and Goethe arrive at the same goal—the stirring within us of profoundest mythological feelings.

Burckhardt was not only one of the founding fathers of art history but also one of the original creators of cultural history. Yet his astonishing knowledge and insight were balanced by a modesty that was private rather than social, since it sprang from his demanding more effort and work from himself:

> There is nothing more precarious than the life of works dealing with art history. All things considered, I wish a better man than I had written a *Cicerone* (according to the plan I had before me)—but *what* was there excepting Murray, in 1853, by way of guide to art that made any attempt to take in the whole of Italy and all the forms of art?
>
> (*Letters,* p. 134)

We must not think that Burckhardt *advanced* from the history of art to the history of culture: many of the foregoing extracts reflect his inclination to see the history of an age in its syncretic wholeness. Remember what he wrote even in the Sturm und Drang phase of his youth: "I will at least seek out the interest

for which I am to perish, namely the culture of Old Europe."

III

Jacob Burckhardt was the first master of cultural history—or of what may perhaps be more precisely called the history of a culture. This means that he visualized and attempted to describe the spirit and the forms of expression of a certain age, a certain people, a certain place. It does not mean that because of his fineness of perception Burckhardt regarded the high culture of a certain period as the most important element in its history. Although he was one of the first historians to lift his sights above the nineteenth-century notion that "history is past politics and politics current history," and although his concentration on the spirit of a certain age was very different from the Hegelian conception of zeitgeist, what moved Burckhardt were the richness and variety of significant evidence—significant where it reflected what people thought and believed at a certain time. This was something quite different from intellectual history or the history of ideas.

This resolve to describe the ideals and realities of an entire age—Burckhardt being aware of the fact that idealism and realism complement one another, the true antitheses being idealism and materialism—is evident in *The Age of Constantine the Great.* Dealing principally with the reigns of Diocletian and Constantine, the book begins somewhat slowly, but the author's purpose soon becomes apparent; then it develops with a verve peculiarly his own, especially in the later chapters, where Burckhardt moves further and further from matters of politics and imperial administration and closer to matters of culture and belief. Chapter 7, "Senescence of Ancient Life and Its Culture," is as masterly a chapter as Burckhardt would ever write; it is there that his conception of cultural history is set forth, in the superb wording previously cited. As Burckhardt says in a preface to the second edition of *Constantine* in 1880:

> When the material for this book was assembled, nearly three decades ago, and its writing was taken in hand, the objective in the mind of the author was not so much a complete historical account as an integrated description, from the viewpoint of cultural history, of the important period named in the title.

After *Constantine* Burckhardt wrote the *Cicerone*, and then began the most important, eventually the most famous, of his works, *The Civilization of the Renaissance in Italy*, published in 1860. Compared to *Constantine*, the *Renaissance* sold very poorly during his lifetime: during the first two years of its publication no more than 200 copies were sold. Then in the late 1870's Burckhardt's international reputation began to emerge; the first English translation of the *Renaissance* appeared in 1878.

That the *Renaissance* is cultural history rather than art history appears clearly from the order of its six major parts: the state as a work of art; the development of the individual; the revival of antiquity; the discovery of the world and of man; society and festivals; and morality and religion. This order—starting with politics and concluding with morality and religion—reflects Burckhardt's view of the hierarchy of historical factors, though he is never didactic about these levels of influence. Like a great painter who is not too conscious of his methods, Burckhardt is not concerned to explain his technique.

He begins this great work with a modest proposition: "This work bears the title of an essay in the strictest sense of the word." In this "essay" Burckhardt on occasion expresses the scope of his work as a matter of fact:

> Here, as in other things in Italy, culture—to which poetry belongs—precedes the visual arts and, in fact, gives them their chief impulse.

More than a century elapsed before the spiritual element in painting and sculpture attained a power of expression in any way analogous to that of the *Divine Comedy*. How far the same rule holds true for the artistic development of other nations, and of what importance the whole question may be, does not concern us here. For Italian civilization it is of decisive weight.

(p. 189)

Here is an example of Burckhardt's questions:

> Why did the Italians of the Renaissance do nothing above the second rank in tragedy? That was the field in which to display human character, intellect, and passion, in the thousand forms of their growth, their strength, their struggles, and their decline. In other words: why did Italy produce no Shakespeare?

(p. 201)

His ability to find the right kind of evidence for his kind of history is manifest throughout the book. In the chapter dealing with the revival of antiquity he directs our attention to an episode in 1485 when the rumor was current that the corpse of a beautiful young lady of ancient Rome, "Julia, daughter of Claudius," had been found, wonderfully preserved: "The touching point in the story is not the fact itself, but the firm belief that an ancient body, which was not thought to be at least really before men's eyes, must of necessity be far more beautiful than anything of modern date"(p. 112).

What was changing during the Renaissance was a state of mind, the way in which people were looking at things as well as at themselves. For example:

> Differences of birth were losing their significance in Italy. . . . Much of this was doubtless owing to the fact that men and mankind were here first thoroughly and profoundly understood. This one single result of the Renaissance is enough to fill us with everlasting thankfulness. The logical notion of humanity was old enough—but here the notion became a fact.

(p. 215)

This is not a simple summation of Renaissance humanism. Burckhardt now draws our attention to the distinction between the desire for honor and the desire for fame:

> Let us begin by saying a few words about that moral force which was then the strongest bulwark against evil. The highly gifted man of the day thought to find in it the sentiment of honor. . . . This sense of honor is compatibile with much selfishness and great vices, and may be the victim of astonishing illusions; yet nevertheless, all the noble elements that are left in the wreck of a character may gather around it, and from this fountain may draw new strength. . . . It lies without the limits of our task to show how the men of antiquity also experienced this feeling in a peculiar form, and how, afterwards, in the Middle Ages, a special sense of honor became the mark of a particular class. . . . It is certainly not always easy, in treating of the Italian of this period, to distinguish this sense of honor from the passion of fame, into which, indeed, it easily passes. Yet the two sentiments are essentially different.
>
> (p. 321)

At the same time Burckhardt warns us against categorical statements. In his chapter on morality he says that these matters "may be investigated up to a certain point, but can never be compared to one another with absolute strictness and certainty. The more plainly our evidence seems to speak in these matters, the more carefully we must refrain from unqualified assumptions and rash generalizations." Again, he states:

> It is the most serious difficulty of the history of civilization that a great intellectual process must be broken up into single, and often into what seem arbitrary, categories in order to be in any way intelligible. It was formerly our intention to fill up the gaps in this book by a special work on the "Art of the Renaissance," an intention, however, which we have been able to fulfill only in part.
>
> (p. 3)

Burckhardt's reference is to his *History of Architecture and Decoration of the Italian Renaissance,* published in 1867. It is a continuation of the *Cicerone* rather than a complement to the *Renaissance.* His *Notes on Renaissance Sculpture* were published posthumously. Of his intended *History of Renaissance Painting* (a work distinct from the *Cicerone*) the three completed chapters were published in 1898.

In cultural history Burckhardt's second great achievement was his *History of Greek Culture,* of which an abbreviated English edition exists. The original edition in German was published in four volumes from 1898 to 1902 and republished twice after that time. This monumental work is composed of his lectures. When one of his friends urged him to publish it, Burckhardt answered in a letter:

> No, my dear sir, such a poor outsider who does not belong to the guild should not attempt such a thing: I am a heretic and an ignoramus and my particular views will only arouse the anger of the Learned Savants. Yes, yes, believe me. I know these people. I need peace in my old days.

Nonetheless the *History of Greek Culture* is a complete, near-encyclopedic work. Again its contents tell us something about the character of Burckhardt's cultural history. From the Greek conception of state and nation he moves on to the fine arts, poetry, music, philosophy, science, and rhetoric. In his introduction he tells his students:

> What we are attempting is to make the history of Greek culture into the subject of a . . . course; but we admit in the beginning that this course is an experiment and will remain so; that the teacher is, and will remain, a colleague among his students; and he also wishes to remark that he is not a philologist.
>
> (1.3)

Then Burckhardt warms to his task:

> The events are those that are easiest to learn from other books; we, on the other hand, must

construct *perspectives* for the events. When we, during less than sixty hours, wish to communicate the really worthwhile things about Greek antiquity (indeed, also for nonphilologists) we can hardly proceed otherwise than through the history of culture.

Our task, as we conceive it, is this: to give *the history of the Greek way of thought and of the Greek way of seeing;* and to strive to grasp some understanding of the living *forces,* the constructive as well as the destructive ones, that were at work in Greek life. . . . It is *upon this,* upon the history of the Greek mind and spirit [*Geist*] that the study will concentrate.

(1.4–5)

In this introduction, written and delivered in 1867, Burckhardt says that although the study of history is undergoing a crisis throughout the West, the history of culture is less dependent on changing circumstances and standards of academic practice, for its sources are definite and obvious. The history of culture attempts to reconstruct, to recapture something of the inner life of past humanity; it tries to find out how people looked and acted, what they wanted, what they thought, what they saw and attempted *(was er war, wollte, dachte, schaute und vermochte).* To his friend and correspondent Friedrich von Preen, Burckhardt confessed a few years later:

To me, as a teacher of history, a very curious phenomenon has become clear: the sudden devaluation of all mere "events" in the past. From now on in my lectures I shall only emphasize cultural history, and retain nothing but the quite indispensable external scaffolding. Just think of all the defunct battles in the notebooks of all the Learned Savants in their professorial chairs!

IV

Having considered Burckhardt the historian of art and Burckhardt the historian of culture, we must now direct our attention to Burckhardt the historical philosopher. This was Burckhardt the unwilling philosopher and the unwitting prophet whose ideas struck a surprising variety of readers, especially in German-speaking Europe, with the shock of recognition. That shock occurred first thirty years and then again fifty years after his death. Burckhardt was indifferent to his reputation, although he thought that some of his most polished lectures (on Rubens, for example) might be published posthumously. But he would have been greatly surprised at his own posthumous fame. Eight years after his death, his nephew Jacob Oeri printed *Reflections on History,* but not until 1929 did *Judgments on History and Historians* appear, in the first edition of the *Collected Works.* During the deepening crisis of Weimar Germany in 1929–1933 some of the best German thinkers and historians became aware of Burckhardt's prophetic historical views. After Adolf Hitler's assumption of power this feverish interest in Burckhardt died out, at least in public.

Again in 1947–1949 Burckhardt's vision of history struck certain Germans as astonishingly relevant to the crisis of their nation and of European civilization after World War II. In those three years four separate editions of *Reflections on History* appeared in Germany. It was in 1948 that Friedrich Meinecke, the last great surviving German historian from the "classic" period, reflected on the differences between Ranke and Burckhardt in a lecture with that title, suggesting the temporal shortcomings of the former's and the enduring validity of the latter's view of history, and their respective relevance to German life. (See *The German Catastrophe,* Meinecke's last book, 1947.)

There were two reasons for these developments. One was Burckhardt's serene morality, which, unlike the avowed principles of many professional historians and philosophers of history, shone untarnished after the catastrophic experiences of dictatorships and two world wars; the other was his forewarning of the dangers of demagoguery in the rising age of the masses. Burckhardt was not only skeptical of the liberal and radical ideas of progress; his conservatism, too, differed profoundly from the nationalist conservatism that was to dominate German and central European historical thinking until at least 1945.

Reflections on History has three parts: the text of Burckhardt's university course "Introduction to the Study of History," given in 1868–1869 and again in 1870–1871; his three lectures entitled "The Great Men in History," given at the Basel Museum in 1870; and the lecture "On Fortune and Misfortune in History," given at the museum in 1871. Burckhardt's *Judgments on History and Historians* was compiled by Emil Duerr from the lectures Burckhardt gave between 1865 and 1885. These are meditations on the history of the world; in other words, what the history of antiquity and modern Europe signified for Burckhardt about the relation of historical forces. The lectures differ radically from what is known as philosophy of history and are as different from Oswald Spengler as they are from Arnold Toynbee. Burckhardt would have rejected the biological determinism of the former and the systematic categorizing of the latter. It might be argued that the *Reflections on History* is more philosophical and *Judgments on History and Historians* more historical: but such impressions arise only because the former is more general and the latter more chronological. The major part of *Reflections on History* deals with the relationships of state, religion, and culture, which to some extent indicates the evolution of Burckhardt's interests from art through culture to historical philosophy on the grand scale.

Just as Burckhardt the historian of art and of culture is unique, so is Burckhardt the historical philosopher. Instead of seeking a pattern for history, he was fascinated by the very opposite: by the historicity of our existence in all of its protean forms. "The philosophy of history," he writes, "is a centaur, a contradiction in terms, for history coordinates, and hence is unphilosophical, while philosophy subordinates, and hence is unhistorical." Instead of looking for a system that would eventually lead to the abstract knowability of all history, he was interested in the concrete historicity of knowledge, of consciousness, of thought. Nor was Burckhardt influenced by Darwinism or the consequent extension of historical studies to "prehistory." He told students that he wished to begin with the Greeks, and that he had relatively little to tell them about the Babylonians or Assyrians. For him, "the Hellenes embodied free will and hence have become the standard of excellence for ages to come."

Burckhardt also decries all kinds of prophecy: "To know the future is not more desirable in the life of mankind than in the life of the individual. And our astrological impatience for such knowledge is sheer folly. . . . A future known in advance is an absurdity." Burckhardt did not believe in the cyclical theory or any other kind of determinism, whether biological, geographical, psychological, or Hegelian-idealist. If Burckhardt had a forerunner at all, it was Giovanni Battista Vico, who also proceeded from the assumption that man's knowledge of man is not only more important but also prior to man's knowledge of nature. (But we have no evidence that Burckhardt had read Vico.)

History, says Burckhardt, differs from natural science; it is "the breach with nature caused by the awakening of consciousness":

Every species in nature possesses complete what it needs for its life; if this were not so, the species could not go on living and reproducing itself. Every people is incomplete and strives for completion, and the higher it stands, the more it strives.

In nature, individuals, particularly among the highest species of animals, mean nothing to other individuals except perhaps as stronger enemies or friends. The world of man is constantly acted upon by exceptional individuals.

In nature, the species remains relatively constant: hybrids die or are sterile from the outset.

JACOB BURCKHARDT

Historical life teems with hybrids. It is as if they were an essential element of fecundation for great mental processes. The essence of history is change.

At times a single sentence in the *Reflections* illuminates a large subject: "During the great migrations we encounter first the remarkable attempt to elude a sharing of power with the priests by the adoption of Arianism." "Byzantinism developed analogously with Islam and frequently interacted with it." "The schools in the Catholic and Protestant countries oscillate between state and church control." In Athens "there was no exaggeration of music, for us the cloak that covers a multitude of incongruities; nor was there any false prudery concerning a mean and secret malevolence." "Originality must be *possessed,* not striven for." Such summations usually come either in the beginning or at the end of his remarkable short paragraphs. These summations were a stylistic habit of his. In *Constantine* we find the characteristic clarity of expression that strikes us with all the force of lightning: "A state is as able to survive nationality as a nationality a state."

Judgments on History and Historians is still more epigrammatic. "Aristocracies will abdicate but do not flee as princes do." Mohammed was "a trivial demagogue" and Islam "the triumph of triviality . . . but the great majority of people *are* trivial." "Mohammed is personally very fanatical; that is his basic strength. His fanaticism is that of a radical simplifier and to that extent is quite genuine. It is of the toughest variety, namely, doctrinaire passion, and his victory is one of the greatest victories of fanaticism and triviality." Cola di Rienzo (whom Richard Wagner and Hitler admired) was "no better than a poor deluded fool." Richard III of England "was no monster, but a terrorist. He did not commit a pointless crime; later he was fair to his victims. He acted in a spirit of 'expediency.'" "Calvinism . . . became the Reformation of those countries that did not like the Ger-

mans." Cardinal Richelieu "is the greatest accelerator of France's later political development, for good as well as for evil. Alone with his idea of the state, which he completely identifies with his person, he confronts a world of selfishness." After the execution of Louis XVI "the spiritual survival of the monarchy is comparable to sensation in an amputated limb." Napoleon Bonaparte "had a sixth sense in all military matters and a seventh for everything relating to power. His deadly enemy, like that of all such people, was impatience; it brought his later career to disaster." "He believed that he had all the princes in his net, because they were afraid of the *democratic inclinations of their peoples* (which was the case in Austria); but he would not hear the peoples' despair and anger that were directed against *him* and that *must* in the end sweep along the princes, according to circumstance."

These epigrammatic passages give us a taste of Burckhardt's thought. What is important, too, is that the book is not disjointed, though *Judgments on History and Historians* is a series of lecture notes. True, its full savoring requires some knowledge of the history of Western civilization. Whether even a century ago readers other than Burckhardt's best students possessed this kind of knowledge we cannot tell. What we can tell is that here as always Burckhardt is the historical thinker par excellence: a prophet of the past. And so we face what at first sight may seem a paradox: this prophet of the past was also a prophet of the future.

The quality and intensity of Burckhardt's vision was such that the light he poured on the past illuminated the then present and its sequel. He was telling people things about the darkened landscape that lay behind them, of what they and their ancestors had left behind; but the luminosity of his words would bathe, if only for moments, the mountainous route ahead. Indeed often the first thing that strikes people in reading Burckhardt is this vision of the future. The reason is Burckhardt's comprehension of the human condition, together with his comprehension of its historicity. He does not think that human nature essentially changes, although this does not mean that history ever repeats itself. Certain historical conditions may indeed recur; but the sources of this recurrence lie in human nature itself. Often one of Burckhardt's statements about a monarch, an institution, a crisis of many centuries ago strikes us with a sudden sense of its pertinence to the present. We are surprised because Burckhardt is seldom, if ever, didactic; his purpose is not to demonstrate historical parallels.

We have seen how Burckhardt, in his early maturity, turned away resolutely from speculations about the troubles of the present and its politics, devoting himself only to "Old Europe." Twenty years later the pessimism of that resolution had given way to a more stoical and less bitter concern with the present. Thus both *Reflections on History* and *Judgments on History and Historians* contain brief, but remarkably significant, statements about nineteenth-century Europe. He saw very clearly what the monstrous ascendancy of the modern state meant. He had no sympathy for G. W. F. Hegel, and especially not for Hegel's idealization of the state. Burckhardt respected Otto von Bismarck, but he also saw in the unification of the German states a great danger. He recognized the demonic element in Wagner. After a few years of friendship Burckhardt turned away from his admirer Nietzsche. (Their relationship had certain similarities with that of Alexis de Tocqueville and Joseph, comte de Gobineau).

Like Nietzsche, Burckhardt foresaw the degeneration of parliamentary democracy and the coming of the "terrible simplifiers," whom the emancipated and semieducated masses would naturally follow. But Burckhardt had no sympathy for Nietzsche's passionate attack on tradition as well as hypocrisy. Unlike Nietzsche, Burckhardt saw that the waning of the power of the churches was a complex and unpredictable phenomenon, not necessarily identical with the dying out of religious belief. Burckhardt abandoned many of his earlier prejudices against Catholicism; now he saw the weakening of liberal Protestantism and foresaw that the resistance to tyranny would, perhaps surprisingly, come from traditional beliefs and conservative churches: "In fact, we have not yet experienced the full impact of the masses, of numbers, on religion, but it may yet come." He had no respect for capitalists because of their often thoughtless materialism; but socialists too, he writes, are dangerous because of their ignorance, "their narrow optimism and their wide-open mouths." Capitalists as well as socialists will have little to do with a development he discusses in his letters to von Preen: "You may be surprised . . . but I fear that the military state will become industrialist." In the *Reflections* he says that by 1789 rulers had learned that

> opinion makes and changes the world—as the traditional authorities had become too feeble to put obstacles in its way, and as they themselves had begun trafficking with some of its features. . . . But today the success of the press lies more in the general leveling of views than in its direct function . . . often the press shrieks so loud *because* people no longer listen.

Statements such as this may explain the relative neglect of Burckhardt the philosophical historian (as distinct from Burckhardt the art historian) in the English-speaking world. They stand in contrast to the Anglo-American liberal and progressive intellectual tradition. Unlike Tocqueville, Burckhardt was indifferent to the United States and often sharply critical of modern democracy. Yet, latest of all his successes, after World War II Burckhardt gained the recognition due him among historians and thinkers of the English-speaking world, in part because of his achievements in cultural history, in part because of the obvious truth of many of his views. The contemporary historian Hugh Trevor-Roper writes that while "the 'scientific,' 'factual' history of Ranke has now run nearly dry . . . the unscientific 'cultural' history of Burckhardt still excites us."

In 1871, at the end of his *Reflections on History*, Burckhardt had said that the danger was now that everything has become possible, "mainly because there are everywhere good, splendid, liberal people who do not quite know the boundaries of right and wrong, and it is there that the duty of resistance and defense begins; it is *these* men who open the doors and level the paths for the terrible masses everywhere." Still, Burckhardt would not take refuge in an aristocratic kind of despair. Was the present tendency of Europe, he asked, "a rising or falling one? That can never be determined by mere calculation. The peoples of Europe are still exhausted physically, and in the intellectual and moral sphere one *must,* in order to think correctly, *reckon* with *invisible forces, with miracles.*" As he wrote at the end of his subchapter on "Morality and Judgment" in the *Renaissance*:

> What eye can pierce the depths in which the character and fate of nations are determined?—in which that which is inborn and that which has been experienced combine to form a new whole and a fresh nature?—in which even those intellectual capacities which at first sight we should take to be most original are in fact evolved late and slowly? Who can tell if the Italian before the thirteenth century possessed that flexible activity and certainty in his whole being—that play of power in shaping whatever subject he dealt with in word or in form, which was peculiar to him later? A tribunal there is for each one of us, whose voice is our conscience; but let us have done with these generalities about nations. For the people that seems to be most sick the cure may be at hand; and one that appears to be healthy may bear within it the ripening germs of death, which the hour of danger will bring forth from their hiding place.

V

This essay is about Burckhardt the writer, rather than about Burckhardt the philosopher, inseparable though the two actually are. And the reason is clear: it is not only Burckhardt's practice in historiography but also Burckhardt's idea of the historian—of the duties and purposes of writing history—that is important to us. We have seen that Burckhardt's artistic inclinations were apparent from his formative years; even at the time when his interest in history had crystallized he was already dissatisfied with the established standards of "scientific" history. He was appalled by the pettiness, vanity, and opportunism of some of the most reputable professionals then at the pinnacle of their fame. "You can have no idea," he wrote a few months after he had arrived in Berlin, "of the envy and vanity of the greatest scholars here! Unfortunately, as everyone knows, Ranke, though very pleasant to meet, is lacking in character; you can see that in black and white in . . . his writings." Burckhardt was shocked when he found that at a reception Ranke professed opinions and preferences that were the very opposite of what he had enunciated earlier that day. To his sister Burckhardt wrote: "If only all the professors were not archenemies! But what is the use of complaining when Ranke and Raumer always lecture at the same time (12 to 1) out of sheer spite?" Ranke

> learned a lot from the French, only he won't admit it. People are always talking about the art of writing history, and many of them think they have done enough when they replace [Schlözer's] labyrinthine sentences by the dry narration of facts. No, no, my dear chap, what's needed is to sift the facts, to select what can interest *man.*
>
> (*Letters*, p. 158)

From this early emphasis on the necessity for an authentic human interest in history Burckhardt never departed.

At fifty-five Burckhardt summed up his philosophy of teaching in a letter to Nietzsche:

> I have done everything I possibly could to lead them on to acquire personal possession of the past—in whatever shape or form. . . . I wanted them to be capable of picking the fruits for themselves; I never dreamed of training scholars and disciples in the narrower sense, but only wanted to make every member of the audience feel and know that everyone may and must appropriate those aspects of the past that appeal to him personally, and that there can be happiness in so doing. I know perfectly well that such an aim may be criticized as fostering amateurism, but that does not trouble me.
>
> (*Letters*, p. 158)

We must, however, go beyond Burckhardt's modest self-assertion, which might naturally lead to the conclusion that among the great historians of the nineteenth century Ranke was the prototype of the "professional" and Burckhardt of the "amateur." It would leave the impression that Burckhardt, for all his talents and the respect he inspires, belongs to a much earlier age, when history was regarded as a branch of literature. The opposite is true. Burckhardt was no amateur with a touch of genius, but an innovator whose view of a hierarchy of historical forces ran counter to the then professional concentration on the primacy of politics. His work also stands up against the dominant social-scientific tendency of twentieth-century intellectuality (including historiography) to seek (and then pretend to find) the motive power of human history in categories of material "factors." Burckhardt was convinced—and has convinced many of his readers—that the most important "force" is what people think, believe, and take for granted. At the end of his lectures on Greek civilization (as indeed at the beginning of the *Renaissance*) he repeats somewhat ironically his creed of "amateurism": "We are 'unscientific' (*unwissenschaft-*

lich) and have no particular method, at least not the one professed by others."

What was his actual method? It was very simple but at the same time complex. The student of history, Burckhardt says, "must *want* to seek and find; and *bisogna saper leggere*" (must know how to read). His interest in history must be authentic, not merely professional or bureaucratic; he must know how to read between the lines. This authentic interest must be personal. Burckhardt was profoundly aware of the inevitable relation between the observer and the observed. In this respect he was one of the earliest thinkers in the West who, without philosophizing about it, began to transcend the Cartesian division of the cosmos into "object" and "subject." For Burckhardt historical knowledge was neither objective nor subjective but participatory. He used to admonish his students so as to make them grasp the distinction between *Parteilichkeit*—partisanship—and *Vorliebe*—elective affection: the first the serious student of history must eschew; the second is his own privilege and possession. We find an elaboration of this point in his *History of Greek Culture*:

> Furthermore we must understand that when we try to immerse ourselves wholly in the reading of a classic, only *we alone* can find what is important *for us*. No reference work in the world with its quotes can replace that chemical bonding that mysteriously occurs when a phrase found by ourselves illuminates something in our mind, crystallizing itself into a real piece of spiritual property that is ours.

This conception is something very different from amateurism, as well as from subjectivism. Burckhardt wanted students and others to read certain works or passages several times, to find in them essences and ideas that might escape the mind on the first reading: "There are authors, such as Hesiod, whose each rereading opens new questions and new perspectives. Aeschylus' *Prometheus* reveals to us new characteristics upon every new perusal." The work of the historian, Burckhardt adds, is never finished. To him, of course, history was the constant rethinking of the past; the past ("not the reading of the newspapers") must be the source of our spirituality. Seeing the present with the eyes of the past and the past with the eyes of the present is a state of mind we must be constantly aware of: we may find in Thucydides something of the greatest present importance but "which may not be seen to be such until a hundred years from now."

Unlike many of the pessimist and fatalist thinkers of the twentieth century, Burckhardt, for all of his conservative inclinations and for all of his stoic comprehension of the world, maintained his high faith in the potentiality of the human spirit: "The spearhead of all culture is a miracle of mind—namely, speech, whose source, independently of the particular people and particular language, is in the soul; otherwise no deaf mute could be taught to speak and to understand speech. Such teaching is explicable only if there is in the soul an intimate and responsive urge to clothe thought in words." In keeping with this fundamental belief in the participant relation of people to the universe, Burckhardt was fond of quoting Goethe's great maxim "Unser Auge ist sonnenhaft, sonst sähe es die Sonne nicht" (Were our eye not like the sun, the sun it could not see).

Burckhardt distinguished between true and false skepticism: the latter was senseless and destructive, proceeding as it did from the false assumption that what human beings could not conceive could not exist. A historical skepticism, however, "has its indisputable place in a world where beginnings and end are all unknown, and the middle in constant flux . . . though the consolation offered by religion is here beyond our scope."

We live, Burckhardt said, not for ourselves alone but for the past and future as well. As James Hastings Nichols wrote, "He was thus more profoundly Christian than the good churchmen Hegel and Ranke." And he was no less a historian than the most accomplished of his fellow professionals.

For a long time Burckhardt was neglected. Upon the publication of the *History of Greek Culture* immediately after his death, the great classicist Uhlrich von Wilamowitz-Möllendorf attacked it. Two of Wilamowitz's students continued the denigration. After a time these attacks ceased; and the work came to be treated by the greatest German scholars with more than respect, indeed, with awe.

Like all works, even those of the greatest masters in art and letters, Burckhardt's were not without faults. In *Constantine* Burckhardt's chronological attribution of an important source has since been revised. In the *Cicerone* there are a few—in retrospect, astonishingly few—mistaken attributions of paintings. There is some evidence that in his *History of Greek Culture* Burckhardt may have been influenced by Fustel de Coulanges, whose *Cité antique* was published in 1864, though Burckhardt made no reference to Fustel. Burckhardt was certainly impressed (though not uncritically) by some of the writings of another contemporary, the Munich historian Ernst von Lasaulx. Burckhardt's intellectual relation to Tocqueville still awaits a monograph by a patient and perceptive historian. Burckhardt and Tocqueville differed greatly in background, personality, and character; but their historical philosophy had much in common and so had their historical interests. As Kaegi points out, Burckhardt began to write about the age of revolutions "almost in the same moment when Tocqueville had laid down his pen"—in 1859. Burckhardt wrote in his mature years:

I like themes that straddle the frontier between the Middle Ages and modern times, because of their many different forms and vitality. And long before the dustmen have got their refuse carts moving and shout disagreeable things after us, we are already over the hills and far away.

(*Letters*, p. 136)

Burckhardt lived what he preached. What he wrote about history being a participant's knowledge was integral to his own thinking self. Yet he was not thinking of himself when he wrote that "character is much more decisive for man than richness of intellect . . . personality is the highest thing there is," a statement applicable to him. Like Tocqueville, he was a great correspondent. A very important part of Burckhardt's legacy are his letters in nine volumes. They show his multifarious interests and the attractive facets of his versatile personality; they contain some of his deepest thoughts. Unlike Tocqueville, he was blessed with a devoted circle of students, some of whom were his relatives. It was they who after his death began the resurrection and the reconstruction of his immense legacy. In the hurried, troubled, at times catastrophic world of twentieth-century Europe, these modest scholars performed a feat comparable in kind, though not in extent, to the painstaking work of the monks copying and preserving the classics during the Dark Ages; they deserve our abiding thanks.

Selected Bibliography

EDITIONS

Briefe. 9 vols. Basel and Stuttgart, 1949–1980. Contains 1,300 of Burckhardt's letters.
Gesammelte Werke. 10 vols. Basel and Stuttgart, 1955–1959.

TRANSLATIONS

The Age of Constantine the Great. Translated and with an introduction by Moses Hadas. New York, 1949. Paperback ed. 1956.
Cicerone: An Art Guide to Painting in Italy. Translated by Mrs. A. H. Clough. London, 1873. Reprinted New York, 1979.
The Civilization of the Renaissance in Italy. Translated by S. G. C. Middlemore. New York, 1954. Includes an introduction by Hajo Holborn; other editions published in 1958 and later.
Force and Freedom: Reflections on History. Edited by J. H. Nichols. New York, 1943.
History of Greek Culture. Translated by Palmer Hilty. New York, 1963. From an abridged ed. of *Griechische Kulturgeschichte.* The 1977 paperback edition contains an excellent and detailed introduction by Werner Kaegi.
Judgments on History and Historians. Translated by Harry Zohn with an introduction by H. R. Trevor-Roper. New York, 1958. Paperback ed. 1965.
The Letters of Jacob Burckhardt. Edited and translated by Alexander Dru. London, 1955. An excellent selection of Burckhardt's letters.
Recollections of Rubens. Edited by H. Gerson. New York, 1950.
Reflections on History. Introduction by Gottfried Dietze. Indianapolis, Ind., 1979.

BIOGRAPHICAL AND CRITICAL STUDIES

Däuble, Richard. *Die politische Natur Jacob Burckhardts als Element seiner Geschichtsschreibung.* Heidelberg, 1929.
Gass, A. L. *Die Dichtung im Leben und Werk Jacob Burckhardts.* Berne, 1967.
Kaegi, Werner. *Jacob Burckhardt: Eine Biographie.* 7 vols. Basel and Stuttgart, 1947–1977. The standard biography.
Löwith, Karl. *Jacob Burckhardt: Der Mensch inmitten der Geschichte.* Stuttgart, 1966.
Martin, A. W. O. von. *Nietzsche und Burckhardt: Zwei geistige Welten im Dialog.* Basel, 1947.
————. *Die Religion Jacob Burckhardts.* Munich, 1947.
Salin, Edgar. *Jacob Burckhardt und Nietzsche.* Basel, 1938.
Schneider, M. F. *Die Musik bei Jacob Burckhardt: Eine zeitgemässe Betrachtung.* Basel, 1946.

JOHN LUKACS

CHARLES MARIE LECONTE DE LISLE
(1818–1894)

LECONTE DE LISLE is something of a paradox in the history of French literature. His work is scarcely known outside France and little read today even in France, yet he impressed his mark on French nineteenth-century poetry to an extent that would make a valid account of it impossible without recognizing his contribution. Part of the disfavor in which his work is held may doubtless be attributed to unfamiliarity with his poetry as well as a certain snobbery on the part of many who don't really know it, both of which feed on each other. Another reason is that Leconte de Lisle is so quintessentially a product of his time. He belongs to the generation of Charles Baudelaire, but where Baudelaire is a unique genius, eternally modern, Leconte de Lisle represents the highest poetic expression of the characteristic concerns of the Second Empire. This was the period of Joseph Renan and Hippolyte Taine, of Charles Darwin and Gustave Flaubert—in other words, of an obsession with research and erudition such as France had not experienced since the Renaissance. Leconte de Lisle was saturated with the spirit of his time, and it is quite impossible to fathom the meaning of a major part of his writing without reference to contemporary intellectual currents.

Does this mean that he is a simple reflection of the forms and thought of a realistic age? Clearly not. In 1856 he emphasized the idea that a poet must reproduce what he sees "in all the poetry of its reality," but he "remains *himself* before the multiplicity of diverse forms; his substance, his manner of being . . . does not change"—a view to which Flaubert would have subscribed. Thus it is that Leconte de Lisle has created something original in French poetry, something entirely his own, so that we may now say, "This is the manner of Leconte de Lisle," as we may also say, "This is clearly the manner of Baudelaire or Victor Hugo or Stéphane Mallarmé." Still, the need for substantial background knowledge to appreciate much of his work has put readers off.

Concepts of poetry have changed radically since the mid-nineteenth century. A certain exclusivist view of poetry today will no longer allow that philosophizing, or the re-creation of fundamental ideas of humanity at different periods of its development, or the painting of pictures of exotic civilizations, no matter how brilliantly and faithfully, is admissible in poetry. What is called for today is a more intimate rendering of experience, an esoteric alchemy of thought and feeling, a linguistic transfiguration of impressions, none of which can be accommodated by the majestic splendor of Leconte de Lisle's monumental poetry. How many poets of the past have escaped the onus of this exclusivism? One may well ask how widely such poets as Alphonse de Lamartine or Alfred de Musset or Alfred de Vigny are read today outside the schools. How much of their work, beyond a few poems in anthologies, is well known? Are these writers not simply consigned each to his own niche in critical thought—Lamartine as limp and sentimental, Musset as maudlin and chaotic, Vigny as ponderously thoughtful and pedestrian in technique? Such prejudice seems to impoverish a poetic heritage to which each of the masters has contributed his unmistakable accent. So it is with Leconte de Lisle, whose poetry appears to have held up at least as well as that of most of the romantics. As with the romantics, a goodly portion of his creation is considered aesthetically inert today, but there is more than enough to make of him one of the masters of his century. Had he been willing to make his own anthology, had his production been as limited as that of, say, Baudelaire or Mallarmé, the present judgment of criticism might well have been different. Be that as it may, he had the most profound influence on an entire generation of poets—greater than that of any other writer—and his work stands to this day, for those who are familiar with it, as a unique monument.

PREPARATION

Charles Marie René Leconte de Lisle's origins gave little hint of his future career. He was born in 1818 thousands of miles from France, on the little island of Bourbon (today called Réunion) off the coast of southeast Africa, at a time when it took three months to sail from that colony to France. There is a lamentable paucity of firm information concerning his childhood and early youth; biographically, Leconte de Lisle is the least well known of the major French poets of the nineteenth century. It is worth noting, however, that, like his contemporary Flaubert, he came of a scientific background, his great grandfather and father having been doctors, his grandfather a pharmacist. Following the final fall from power of Napoleon, his father emigrated to Bourbon, where he married a native of the island and settled down to become a planter and slave-owner.

Leconte de Lisle spent his early childhood in this lush, semitropical island covered by heavily forested mountains and slashed by huge gorges and magnificent waterfalls. In this brilliantly illuminated setting, he acquired his love of unequivocal coloration, so markedly different from the misty uncertainty of Lamartinian atmosphere or the symbolists' tremulous suggestiveness. In a note to his biographer, he later attributed the origin of his vocation "first of all to the good fortune of being born in a marvelously beautiful, semi-savage land, rich in strange vegetation, under a dazzling sky." The inspiration of his native island was to endure into his advanced years, producing ever more intense expressions of nostalgia, such as "La ravine Saint-Gilles," "Le bernica," and "Le manchy" (The Palanquin), which are among the most finely chiseled jewels of descriptive poetry in French.

After spending three years in his birthplace, he went with his family to France, where he remained until 1832, after which he returned to Bourbon to spend his adolescence. From that point we begin to follow the genesis of the poet through early correspondence, verses, and stories with the island as setting. Unlike any of the major French poets of his century, Leconte de Lisle had to come from very far behind. He had little support for his poetic leanings; the literary and intellectual atmosphere of the island was nil. His education was desultory, a remarkable circumstance for a man who was to become the accredited champion of erudite—even pedantic—poetry and a translator of Greek classics. He lived among the islanders but was not one of them. "His very physical personality gives the lie to the usual idea we have of Creoles," wrote Baudelaire, alluding to the presumed apathy of Creoles. He was essentially a creature of feeling and longed for sensitive companions to whom to communicate his lyrical impulses. Not finding them, he withdrew into solitude and cold reserve. Later he would write: "The solitude of a youth deprived of intellectual sympathies, . . . the dreams of a heart swollen with tenderness, necessarily suppressed, gave the impression for a long time that I was indifferent and even foreign to emotions more or less felt by everybody, when I was really choking with the need to pour out my passionate tears." Such pronouncements are significant first because they give a clue to the strong romantic substratum of his later work, carefully channeled, disciplined, or disguised, though never smothered; and second because they alert us to the fallacy of the stubborn myth of "impassivity" that hounded him all his life.

Serious, indeed almost humorless ("I challenge that fellow to make me laugh," Flaubert would later write), idealistic, and sensitive, he looked about him and condemned his contemporaries not because they were slave-owners but because of their aesthetic and moral insensitivity. "Is there any more flagrant immorality," he asks, "than indifference to and scorn of beauty?" He began to read poets at random, particularly Victor Hugo's *Les orientales* (1829), which "was like an immense and sudden flash of light illuminating the sea, mountains, woods, and nature of my land." He remained bored, maladjusted, and solitary; and fashioned verses that are little more than lymphatic laments. Already he vaguely sensed the identity of life with suffering, regarded time as the great corroder, turned back nostalgically to the past, and looked forward with foreboding to the future.

In such circumstances he was bound to feel alienated and long for escape. The opportunity came in 1837 when he was sent back to France to prepare for a legal career; he remained in Brittany for the next six years. Compared with that of other poets, Leconte de Lisle's work at nineteen (an age at which Hugo and Musset were finishing important initial collections of poetry) was quite unremarkable. His entry on the literary scene was not to be a precocious leap forward but a prolonged process of self-examination and self-

formation, which helps explain the principled and carefully crafted nature of his mature work. Few poets have shown such conscious attention to the nature of their art or such unrelenting effort to perfect their technique.

In Brittany, Leconte de Lisle suffered a difficult initiation into society while becoming increasingly aware of new metaphysical concerns and experimenting with literary form. His unsocial behavior of Bourbon rapidly developed into distinctly antisocial attitudes. His uncle wrote testily back to Bourbon about the young man's vanity, intransigence, cold and aloof nature, and open defiance of authority and tradition. In a thoroughly reactionary atmosphere, he flaunted republican opinions and judged the church severely. His letters reveal a habitual tendency to criticize, condemn, or sneer; a ready attraction to the weak, stupid, cruel, or ludicrous side of people; and a corresponding unwillingness or inability to adapt. This friction, this intractability and uncompromising manner of judging that refused to allow for human fallibility, was fertile soil for a work that would be virtually devoid of compassion, although obsessed with man's inhumanity to man. His romantic desire to share intimacies was no less strong than in Bourbon, but his critical asperity destroyed all possibility of such closeness. In his maturity he remained tender to a very few and savage to many. Even his admirers approached him with trepidation, while for Léon Daudet he was "an executioner on vacation who had forgotten his blade, though its glint still flashed from his eyes!"

Like a good romantic of the thirties, he found his moral solitude growing apace with the conviction of his superiority: "I like the city of Rennes very much," he wrote; "nothing is missing—the library, the theater, a quiet, comfortable room, and no friends!!! What more could I ask for?" He did not communicate with his family, who longed for news from him; he felt increasingly estranged from everyone. We see germinating not only the spirit of revolt that inspired one of his most famous poems, "Qaïn" (Cain), and many of the unyielding heroic dissenters of his epic compositions, but also the need to withdraw, which infuses many other pieces, particularly "Midi" (Noon).

These circumstances could have made Leconte de Lisle only a misanthrope, but spiritual interests were developing another dimension in him. He was fascinated by the vague religiosity of George Sand and the democratic Christianity of Lamennais; he discussed theology with a friend; and he became interested in a new book by a rabbi denying Christ. From these early days on he revealed a restlessness of spirit and, in the midst of a traditional Catholic environment, a spiritual cosmopolitanism that impelled him to seek new solutions to fundamental problems. For a time Christianity gave form to his idealism. His verses from this period are replete with words such as God, angel, prayer, faith, divine hope, and immortal soul. He longed for union with the godhead. His lofty sweeps of diffuse lyricism translated no clear religious notions; but a need for spiritual elevation, a dissatisfaction with reality, and a yearning for the absolute that liberates from despised contingencies are evident. Without realizing it, he was preparing himself for that desperate odyssey through the many religious symbols of humanity that constitute a major portion of his work. His adolescent metaphysics and abrasive personality are correlative aspects of the same temper.

With such a temper and such aspirations, needless to say, Leconte de Lisle's legal career went begging. The law was "a vile mess that makes me vomit!" It was only with the greatest difficulty and after long months that he made minimal progress toward his professional goal. In 1840, he helped found a journal, *La variété,* and soon became its chief editor, contributing poems and critical prose. He tried his hand at religious verse, love lyrics (wholly hypothetical), elegies, political statements, philosophical meditation, even satirical verse. The problems of form never left his consciousness; he was utterly engrossed in literature to the virtual exclusion of all else. His uncle in France and family in Bourbon grew worried and cut off his allowance. He appeared to submit, but did not change course. Finally, in 1843, he was summoned back to Bourbon, a failure for all practical purposes in the eyes of his family, but a poet in every fiber of his being.

His reaction to his last sojourn in Bourbon (1843–1845) was now wholly predictable. In his youth on the island he had longed to escape. In Brittany one of his poetic themes was his intense nostalgia for his beloved island. But a month after returning he wrote: "I am in one of my black days and suffering miserably." Various reasons can be offered as possible explanations, but actually there was nothing new or specific. Leconte de Lisle was innately unhappy. In January 1845 he fumed: "I've been in Bourbon fourteen months: 420 days of constant agony, 10,080 hours of moral misery, 604,800 minutes of hell." Neither the presence of family nor the absence of friends made any difference; he seemed to welcome his solitary suffering: "I've lived alone in Bourbon with my books, my heart, and my head; they are, after all, better companions than the vast majority of my contemporaries with their guilty indifference and their blasphemous negations of truth."

What else he did on the island is a mystery, but from a comparison of his Breton poetry with what he would soon publish in France we may be certain that he never ceased honing his technique and meditating new themes. "My form is clearer, more severe and richer," he commented quite accurately. But beyond this he announced a critical personal development in 1845: "I observe with a kind of terror that I am in the process of detaching myself from individuals in order to live in thought solely with the mass. I am eliminating myself, synthesizing myself!" This sounds like the grandiloquent trumpet call of a young man, but there is no doubt that it characterized the beginning of a wholly new orientation in his work. At precisely the time when romanticism was visibly fading in France, Leconte de Lisle was detaching himself from romantic aesthetics and themes and turning increasingly to more impersonal concerns. He already sensed what his later work would represent: a brilliant crystallization of the vast forms of collective life.

At this time Leconte de Lisle received and accepted an invitation from the review *La phalange* and the newspaper *La démocratie pacifique* to come to Paris and contribute poems and articles. Both were organs of a group whose purpose was to propagate the socialist ideas of Charles Fourier. There is no evidence that he was at all familiar with this sentimental, incoherent, and bizarre doctrine. He had previously expressed republican sympathies and hostility to the church, but essentially he was only peripherally concerned with political or social matters. What really concerned him were metaphysical and moral problems and, above all, literary matters. Furthermore, he had grown increasingly pessimistic over the years, and lost little love on other human beings. In a sense, then, he was entering a period of paradox: an artist, idealist, and misanthrope became associated with a highly sanguine and pedestrian, albeit utopian, school of social reform.

The importance of this final formative and productive period (1845–1848) can hardly be overemphasized. Some 2,500 lines of poetry were published in *La phalange.* Of these almost half, dealing generally with social questions, were discarded in the *Poèmes antiques* of 1852. Those retained are mostly of Hellenic inspiration, showing far greater mastery of technique than the "social" pieces; they are calmer, clearer, more unified compositions, some of which—"Hypatie" and "La fontaine aux lianes," for example—are even today among his most admired works. But the social pieces are more immediate and emotional, showing a pressing crisis in the poet, and therefore throw a brighter light on his confused state of mind. They reveal mismatched elements dwelling together in an uneasy alliance. The new social message in his work is so surprising that the true nature of these poems has usually been misconstrued.

The poems of 1845 all have a social message, but a close examination makes them puzzling. The first, "Hélène," reveals the artificial duality of all the social pieces. Threefourths of the poem dwells lovingly on a fond dream of returning to ancient Greece and is infused by a horror of the present. This is followed by a spuriously attached conclusion urging hope for the future. "Architecture" again illustrates this inner conflict. A long (150-line) indictment of contemporary artistic degeneracy is resolutely negated at the end by a brief (20-line), vague, and self-conscious message of hope. In both thought and imagery, the poem anticipates Leconte de Lisle's famous denunciations of the modern era, "Les montreurs," and "Aux modernes." (Similarly, "Tantale" (Tantalus, 1846) reviles the masses, depicting them as a stupid and derisive, not a tragic, Tantalus.) "Les épis" (The Ears of Grain) is a parable of the struggle between good and evil. First the poet describes a scene of devastation, then a joyous harvest that is ruthlessly destroyed; finally he provides a hopeful conclusion. But it is the scenes of devastation that remain vivid throughout the poet's work, as in the poems "L'Astre rouge" and "Le dernier dieu" (published in *Poèmes tragiques,* 1884), "Paysage polaire," and particularly "Solvet seclum," which concludes *Poèmes barbares* (1862) with a gleeful vision of total destruction.

The year 1846 was pivotal in Leconte de Lisle's life. In addition to prose and poetry appearing elsewhere, he published nine substantial poems in *La phalange,* of which five were of purely Hellenic inspiration. This was a time when France was experiencing a revived interest in Greek civilization, begun by François René de Chateaubriand and André de Chénier and nourished by sympathy for the cause of Greek independence, recent archaeological discoveries, accounts of travelers, and works of philologists and aestheticians. In Leconte de Lisle's new "Greek" poems, picturesque qualities, local color, and historical precision become increasingly important, gradually eclipsing social issues. But his veneration for the art of ancient Greece fails to ameliorate his growing sense of metaphysical frustration. "Les sandales d'Empédocle" (The Sandals of Empedocles) portrays a solitary, disenchanted hero longing for death and uttering lines ("Deliver me from time and from number and space") that were transferred almost intact to the famous concluding litany of *Poèms antiques*, "Dies irae" (1852), where Empedocles becomes "the human Spirit," pleading for release from life—a strange message from a supposed Fourierist.

This emerging despair is further evidenced in a trilogy of very lengthy and highly significant poems: "La recherche de Dieu" (The Search for God), "Le voile d'Isis" (The Veil of Isis), and "Les ascètes" (The Hermits). The poet, increasingly tormented by doubt, turned increasingly to religion. "La recherche de Dieu" is an anguished pilgrimage (Christianity, German romantic virtues, Epicureanism) in quest of the ideal and of a justification for life. The poem is clearly symptomatic of the analogous concerns of some of Leconte de Lisle's contemporaries; for example, Edgar Quinet (*Prométhée*, 1838) and Louis Ménard ("Prométhée délivré," 1843), who had similarly painted pictures of mankind in search of the absolute and obliged to explore various religions through which the truth is gradually revealed. Leconte de Lisle again appended a hopeful Fourierist sermon about justice, but the poet's real concern was with a humanity plunged into the night of cosmic ignorance and doubt.

This concern reappears in "Le voile d'Isis," an impassioned dialogue between the pharaoh and the high priest of ancient Egypt. The final, obligatory Fourierist message about the triumph of "love and knowledge" displaces the pharaoh's real problem: "Speak! Who am I? Where am I going?" he demands, a question that was later repeated in a Hindu setting in

"La vision de Brahma." The ontological problem also reappears in "Les ascètes," but since the poem was not published in any Fourierist publication, the ringing final optimism is quite missing. Indeed, the poet was deeply sympathetic to the Christian martyrs of the past who, like himself, lived in a wretched age and sought spiritual refuge in austere or masochistic devotions. They, too, aspired to a divine absolute. Plainly the Fourierist solutions had resolved nothing for Leconte de Lisle, and the poems of 1846 show this clearly enough in the implications of the Greek poems, the lassitude of Empedocles, the derision of Tantalus, and above all the three "religious" pieces. After eighteen months in France, Leconte de Lisle was clearly becoming both a more accomplished craftsman and a more serious, though disturbed, thinker.

The five poems published in 1847 are among the most significant of the period. Leconte de Lisle continued to perfect his technique—some of the pieces were retained with little change in *Poèmes antiques*—and he nourished his growing interest in comparative religion, increasingly neglecting and finally ignoring completely his Fourierist notions. It is worth noting that of the poems from 1845 only one out of four was published in 1852; of the poems from 1846, six out of ten were included; and of the poems from 1847 all appeared. As the months went by, Leconte de Lisle's verbosity and declamation gradually disappeared—his writing grew increasingly sober, concise, and clear; the emotion more intense and hopeless; and the themes more in keeping with the poet's character. And it is on a note of deep personal despair, "La fontaine aux lianes," that the prerevolutionary poems end.

The explosive revolutionary events of 1848 provided the backdrop for the final year of Leconte de Lisle's formation. The duality of his thought was apparent in the poems of 1845–1847, but he was still at that time a Fourierist. One side of him, the social creature, trivial by comparison with the artist and thinker, was caught up in the feverish activity and rhetoric of utopian socialism. Indeed, in the very year that he published his poems of religious anguish, he grew increasingly incendiary politically. In a month's time, between October and November 1846, he discharged three violent articles in *La démocratie pacifique,* in which he was swept away by a whirlwind of passion for social justice and reveled in an orgy of eloquence. Mere platitudes are couched in a profusion of rhetorical exclamation and dire threats about oppression and injustice. It is as though there were two distinct Leconte de Lisles with virtually no relationship. His correspondence is no less inflammatory: "With what joy I will come down from my calm contemplation of things to take part in the struggle and discover the color of the blood of cowards and brutes!" But Leconte de Lisle was not cut out to be a man of action and could never match his behavior to his furious rhetoric.

As the historical crisis grew, so did his vehemence, and when the Revolution finally erupted, he was not thinking of the absent God or the vile masses or inevitable evil or even art. He joined a revolutionary club and was sent to Brittany to propagandize the masses. The attempt was a total failure. There was nothing unusual about this; all over France missionaries of the Revolution were encountering setbacks. The situation was disappointing but hardly disastrous. What is astonishing, therefore, is the lightning-quick reversal in the letters of Leconte de Lisle—astonishing, that is, if one ignores the steady evolution of his interests and attitudes from his early youth. In reality he was struck by no pessimistic thunderbolt in 1848, as is still, apparently, the widespread notion. The Revolution was no more than a catalyst precipitating an inevitable reaction.

A letter several weeks after his arrival in Brittany reveals the disgust and dismay that underlay his impulsive political violence. "May the devils of hell destroy these filthy provincial populations," he fulminates, and then adds: "Let them die of hunger and cold;

it is not for them that we will be fighting but for our sacred ideal." The remark is significant because the bulk of his work will indeed show little interest in people as human beings; instead he will be concerned with their representative value. He at last recognized the dichotomy of the previous years: "There is a great tumult in the depths of my brain," he wrote, "but the higher part knows nothing of contingencies." He sought eternal truth and beauty, while his contemporaries subordinated principles to men and ideas to facts. The mask that fit him imperfectly dropped away, leaving him face to face with his desolate vision of the universe. This despair is evident in *Poèmes antiques.*

The revolutionary episode brought to an end what may be considered the exciting part of Leconte de Lisle's life. The rest of his career—and he was only thirty—was devoted almost exclusively to his work. One looks in vain for anything resembling the remarkable incidents in the lives of his romantic predecessors. There were no sensational love affairs; though he did have some relationships, they have left only minor traces in his poetry. He was perhaps the most impecunious of all the major poets of the nineteenth century, keeping body and soul together with petty grants, prizes, lessons, articles, translations, a secret pension from Napoleon III (which became a major scandal for the old republican in 1870), and finally a sinecure as librarian of the Senate. Critics recognized his work slowly but progressively; and he became, in the sixties and seventies, the unchallenged leader of the Parnassian school, a heterogeneous group generally rejecting the aesthetics of the romantics. He was finally elected to the French Academy, after an unconscionable delay, due to personal and political animosities, in 1886, to fill the seat left vacant by Hugo. His final years were spent in relative equanimity, though he was embittered to see the younger generation slipping away from his principles and gravitating to the new ideas of the symbolists. When he died in 1894, his work, his aesthetic, his concept of poetry, and the concerns of his generation were already in many ways a thing of the past.

WORK

The chronology of Leconte de Lisle's collections of poetry is quite simple. In 1852 he published *Poèmes antiques;* in 1855, *Poèmes et poésies;* in 1862, *Poésies barbares,* whose title was later changed to *Poèmes barbares.* The poems of *Poèmes et poésies* were then distributed between the next editions of *Poèmes barbares* (1872) and *Poèmes antiques* (1874), leaving only two volumes. *Poèmes tragiques* was published in 1884. Finally, *Derniers poèmes,* an assemblage of miscellaneous poetic works, prefaces to earlier collections, critical articles, and his inaugural discourse at the French Academy (1887), was published posthumously by the poet's friends in 1895. In his lifetime there were five editions of *Poèmes antiques* (1852, 1874, 1880, 1886, 1891), five of *Poèmes barbares* (1862, 1872, 1878, 1881, 1889), and two of *poèmes tragiques* (1884, 1886).

No purpose would be served by attempting an analysis of Leconte's work collection by collection. There are certain general differences. *Poèmes antiques* is almost entirely composed of poems of Hellenic subjects, though it begins with a series of Indian poems of generally Buddhist or Hindu inspiration and ends with some miscellaneous compositions. *Poèmes barbares* introduces poems concerning the myths, legends, or history of various "barbarian" peoples; that is, all those aside from the Greeks and Indians (the Scandinavians, Finns, Celts, Egyptians, Arabians, Polynesians, and even biblical Israelites), but there are also animal, nature, and personal poems. In these works Leconte de Lisle creates poetry expressing the quintessential qualities of past civilizations. But all his volumes are, in fact, composite, since he often let practical considerations control his publication and therefore mingled different types of poetry, new themes with old. One cannot easily discuss any of his volumes without reference to the others. It would be possible to talk of the "architecture" of his collections (as has been done for Baudelaire's poetry) only in the most general sense. Nor is there any need to explore the poet's sources or attempt an assessment of the historical accuracy of the poems (a work that has been accomplished with scholarly precision by Joseph Vianey and Alison Fairlie, who concluded that, in relation to the erudition of his day, Leconte de Lisle was remarkably well informed, though he altered his material frequently either for poetic effect or to reflect his own outlook). More useful for the general reader is an analysis organized around Leconte de Lisle's approach to three fundamental areas of experience: divinity, humanity or the nature of life, and society.

Divinity

One strong indication that these erudite reconstructions of myths, symbols, theogonies, and cosmologies were founded in more than a simple taste for the picturesque or the unusual, a new romanticism, or a bizarre obsession with archaeology is Leconte de Lisle's instinctive gravitation toward similar situations in very different settings. In reality, these elaborately represented cultures had a very personal significance for the poet. He insisted on precision of detail, even in the use of proper names (for example, refusing to assimilate Greek divinities with their Roman counterparts, as was so often done at this time), sometimes using peculiar spellings and even translating wholly foreign expressions into French at the risk of bewildering his readers, who knew little of Nordic legends and even less of Hindu mysticism.

Underlying all of Leconte de Lisle's work is an intense strain of idealism, and this early took the form of religious aspiration. From his youthful verses to the end he would continue to use religious terminology, whether to characterize death or describe nature or affirm his concept of art. Indeed, his contemporaries described his very dress, speech, and manner as hieratic. In Brittany, as a youth, he had been influenced rather easily by the pious atmosphere, and had fashioned abundant verses in the purest Lamartinian vein: God, heaven, the hereafter, the angels were liberally represented; and however conventional their manner, they gave particular form to his idealism. Lamartine's *La chute d'un ange* (The Fall of an Angel) had appeared in 1838, soon after Leconte de Lisle's arrival in Brittany, and a close examination reveals marked similarities between Lamartine's and Leconte de Lisle's spiritual aspirations, even in the latter's mature work. Lamartine longs to divest himself of his flesh and rise to spiritual heights ("Dieu," "Le Chrétien mourant"); so, too, does Leconte de Lisle: "Spirit! rise in your turn to the only light. . . . Rise to where the fiery Source burns and springs forth whole" ("In excelsis," 1872). In the 1830's this represented a diffuse romantic longing shared even by nonreligious poets such as Théophile Gautier, but for Leconte de Lisle it was clearly religious. Just the same, his religion was actually no more than religiosity; he was already hostile to the church (although the Christian substratum of his verse is plain). Everywhere the dualism is apparent: on the one hand, the material world, old, limited, and unsatisfying, and on the other, the ideal world, infinite and providing spiritual joy. The aspiration toward the ideal was a nebulous but fundamental impulse, recalling Madame de Staël's well-known concept of the "sorrowful feeling of the incompleteness of destiny," rather than specific worship. In various early poems heaven is envisaged as the source and natural abode of all that is good: love, happiness, harmony, beauty—even sleep! As a youth Leconte de Lisle thirsted for the absolute and readily turned to religion to slake this thirst. Back in Bourbon he wrote to a friend: "False joys are in vulgar life, true joys are in God." His religious inclinations, as we have seen, did not

endure, yet the impulse to soar aloft to purer realms never left Leconte de Lisle. In his memoirs Ernest Renan wrote: "I feel that my life is still controlled by a faith I no longer have. Faith is peculiar in that it continues to act even after it is gone." So it was with Leconte de Lisle. In a Hindu poem ("La mort de Valmiki") he writes: "The Spirit, impatient with human bonds,/Longs to flee beyond appearances." In a Greek poem ("Khirôn"): "Avid for light . . . the earth is always black, the skies always low." And in the biblical "Qaïn": "The immortal dream in the nothingness of the moment."

This strong, enduring idealism would in itself be sufficient indication, even if other elements did not add abundant substantiation, to demonstrate that Leconte de Lisle's work is more than an artist's or archaeologist's impassive curiosity about the kaleidoscopic variety of man's civilizations. Had it been possible to satisfy this idealism, he might never have made his anguished pilgrimage through the numerous theogonies and mythologies of the world. Besides the Greek, Indian, and ancient civilizations, he was also attracted to the Middle Ages, despite his revulsion for its barbaric cruelty. He empathizes with the monks of "La mort du moine," ending the poem in an ecstasy of religious passion, even though its subject is one of the very butchers he abhors. Jules Barbey d'Aurevilly once offered Baudelaire the choice of conversion or suicide. For Leconte de Lisle, too, these choices were the only alternatives to despair. The voluptuous mirages of Chateaubriand, the flaccid religiosity of Lamartine, the robust confidence of Hugo were no longer possible in the scientific 1850's and 1860's. But ritualized Christianity was even less acceptable to Leconte de Lisle's rebellious and freedom-loving spirit. Thus, when the tenuous bonds holding him to his God snapped, he was left with an overflowing of spiritual energy and no spiritual object to absorb it.

An entire generation of writers and thinkers suffered the same sort of crisis. To some extent the natural sciences played their role in this tragedy by refusing man a privileged place in the universe, by explaining him as a natural phenomenon governed by the same laws as those governing animals, and by denying or ignoring all supernatural design in human affairs. "For Catholic nations," wrote Taine, "the discord, instead of weakening, grows worse; the two pictures, the one painted by faith, the other by science, are growing increasingly disparate, each developing in an opposite manner."

But the dominant factor underlying the collapse of faith in the Second Empire was the development of the critical and historical approach to the study of religion. The flippant political sneering of Voltaire and other eighteenth-century philosophers was resolutely dismissed as frivolous. "Voltaire, so weak as a scholar, Voltaire, who seems to us so lacking in the feeling for antiquity, to us who are initiated to a better method"—so Renan described him. Christianity was no longer a target; scholars went beyond Christianity to study all the forms assumed by the numerous religions, and beyond the forms themselves to the circumstances governing their origin, growth, decline, and disappearance. Politics and polemics were discarded by these scholars, who sought neither to define nor attack but simply to understand and explain. Scientific objectivity was both the goal and the method; personal faith or incredulity were irrelevant.

Even more than archaeology, ethnography, and geology, which Leconte de Lisle mentions in his preface to *Poèmes antiques,* the instruments used to analyze religion were history and philology, as scholars set about studying ancient and Oriental languages, establishing accurate texts of the sacred writings, and dissecting, comparing, and interpreting their messages. Not just the Hebrew, Greek, and Latin sources were analyzed but also the popular myths and legends of the Germanic and Scandinavian peoples, while a vast Indian literature opened a new world in the 1840's. The

scholarly movement that had begun in Germany with Friedrich Creuzer and O. Muller quickly spread to France, where its principal representative was Renan.

Briefly, what these scholars hypothesized was that the fundamental base common to all faiths is the feeling of the infinite. Beyond that, however, the religious forms and numerous gods and myths vary with the peoples who create them, who in turn vary with the geographical, geological, historical, astronomical, and climatic conditions. The gods, therefore, depend on purely human phenomena and change and evolve with the men who fashion them in their own image. Far from having any factual reality, myths and symbols are allegories under whose surface is layer upon layer of the fears, hopes, observations, and beliefs of the different races. From the most primitive tribes to the most advanced and sophisticated modern groups, gods and religious myths are a response to man's curiosity and fears and are created as explanations of the mysterious universe. They are, furthermore, the most important element of any civilization since out of its religion come, of necessity, its political institutions, arts, poetry, philosophy, ethics, customs, and even, to an extent, its history. In a word, religions could be judged by the society they created. Thus, when Leconte de Lisle lauded Greek polytheism, he would use as an argument the glories of Greek civilization—in "Hypatie," in "Hypatie et Cyrille," in his preface to *Poèmes et poésies,* and elsewhere. All these myths were directly comprehensible to the ancient races; today they have become enigmas, whose true sense can be rediscovered—however imperfectly—only by the most careful scholarship and technical precision.

All at once religion had become equated with history and philosophy. It was doubtless the most vital element in the history of any people, but was envisaged in a purely secular light and in relation to other secular phenomena. The divine had gone out of it. Revelation, supernatural communion, the miracle, all fell in a dry heap. Religion became a strictly human creation and a relative matter, a question of taste, an opinion, a fiction. Some incorporated the new religious relativism into the more general philosophical relativism of Hegel; the absolute had vanished. From Hegel, too, came the idea of "becoming" as distinguished from "being," all phenomena being subject to transformation through inner contradictions and eventual extinction. The application of this concept to the history of religions was inevitable, and Leconte de Lisle and his contemporaries had but to observe the endless procession of faiths arising, being absorbed or conquered by others, and dying, to conclude that every vision of truth is doomed to failure and man condemned to eternal doubt, ignorance, and solitude. One of the most disturbing factors for traditional religion in this vast movement was the fact that the new scholars—Quinet, Jules Michelet, Taine, Renan, Émile Littré—were lay saints in their daily lives, neither fools nor scoundrels, writing not only with the scrupulous objectivity of the dispassionate scientist but usually with manifest sympathy for the religious forms they studied, the human necessity of which they gladly recognized. Never again could critics of religion be dismissed as easily as Voltaire.

The most intense poetic expression of this fundamental religious crisis of the nineteenth century was to be created in France by Leconte de Lisle. His idealism aspiring to the absolute collided head on with the philosophical relativism that undermined it. The impact shows itself from the very first months of his return to France in 1845 through the *Phalange* poems of 1846. His initial reaction was to reach out and sympathetically embrace other faiths. From the prevailing intellectual atmosphere he absorbs the idea that each religion reveals, if not the entire truth, at least some segment of it, and is therefore deserving of reverence and love for having formulated the aspirations of a particular people. It was an idea that endured until the end of his life; in his Academy discourse he still talked of the "truth" of all religions, "since they were the ideal forms of [man's] dreams and hopes." In 1847 he turned his attention to pre-Christian and even preclassical faiths, and soon afterward to the Hindu metaphysic.

It was no accident that Leconte de Lisle returned so often in his poems to the same type of situation. Both his aesthetic and his moral instincts were ineluctably drawn to the critical moment when one faith is being supplanted by another, partly because of the pathetic beauty of the crisis but also because this moment best embodied his moral position. He glorifies each ideal, not because it fulfills his particular spiritual needs but precisely because it *is* an ideal. There is thus no incongruity in "Chant alterné" (1846–1852) in mourning both Greek paganism and the Christianity that destroyed it. In 1847 ("Hypatie") he poured out his compassion for the famous Alexandrian philosopher, Hypatia, martyred by fanatical Christians. Heroically and hopelessly she resists, remaining faithful to her ideal. What her contemporaries frantically seek she already possesses in her gods: a metaphysical justification, a natural explanation, and a moral guide. What a tragedy, then, to destroy her! Her death is the death of an ideal. The poem is a passionate defense of all ideals fighting for their lives, and Leconte de Lisle, despite his professions of impersonality, salutes her in the first person.

Yet, in the same year, the poem "Niobé" appeared—a hymn of intense admiration for the last defender of the prehistoric religion of Greece. Niobe's guides are the Titans, who are dethroned by the very gods exalted by Leconte de Lisle in "Hypatie," and these gods are here furiously denounced by Niobe. The poet reveres Niobe exactly as he reveres Hypatia and for the same reason. He returned to the subject in 1858 with "Hypatie et Cyrille," a dramatic confrontation between Hypatia and Cyril. The sublime woman recognizes the value of all religions, and insists that the truth of her gods is exemplified by the superior civilization they created. Leconte de Lisle admired Greek polytheism more than any other religion for its diversity, its dignity, its ideals of beauty, strength, joy, and harmony; and, despite much authentic detail in the Greek poems, he deliberately idealizes Greek civilization, consciously deleting the violent, mean, immoral, or coarse aspects of Hellenism. The ferocious Christian zealot Cyril, on the other hand, will admit the validity of no god but his own, and solves the whole problem by simply murdering Hypatia. But she goes to her death confidently—"I shall be immortal"—which is Leconte de Lisle's manner of saying that all ideals represent truths that cannot die. "Religion will not die," wrote Renan. "It will forever be the protest of the spirit against the inferior region of vulgar life." Renan's prose frequently seems a running commentary on Leconte de Lisle's poetry (and the poet seemed to recognize this in his original dedication to Renan of "La vigne de Naboth"). His description of heroic last defenders was continued in "Le barde de Temrah," whose hero champions his druidic faith against St. Patrick; in "Le massacre de Mona," in which the Cymric gods go down to a glorious death under the barbaric onslaught of the Christians; and in "Le runoïa," where the Finnish deity, whose naturalistic cult is being annihilated, cries out to Christ: "You too will die!" But Christ, too, is celebrated as an eternal ideal, along with his equals, in "Le Nazaréen."

This universal tolerance entailed a double problem for Leconte de Lisle. On the one hand, an all-embracing sympathy inhibited in him, as in so many of his contemporaries, the acceptance of any one religion. "Oh, I would give considerable money to be either an atheist or a mystic, but something complete and whole," lamented Flaubert in 1839. So, too, Leconte de Lisle was caught midway between the need to believe and the incapacity to do so, and the result was despair. With his dogmatic and idealistic temper he would have had to forget erudition and allow himself to be borne aloft to the divine on the wings of any faith.

But instead he was convinced that each faith was only one among many. Analysis intervened to impede the soul's impulse; the absolute was devitalized by the relative, while the need for the absolute remained potent to the end. Leconte de Lisle could have served as an object lesson for those scholastics of the Middle Ages who preached distrust of the intellect; "for in much wisdom is much grief," warns Ecclesiastes, "and he that increaseth knowledge increaseth sorrow." Leconte de Lisle did not possess the sinuous moral nature of the relativist philosopher, which would have permitted him to adjust to such a dilemma; he was an idealistic poet who needed to believe with all his heart and soul—and he could not.

On the other hand, the erudition on which his poems are based revealed to him the fallibility of all faiths. In "Khirôn" the centaur is disturbed by the constant fighting of the Greek gods, and in "La vision de Brahma" it is the suffering of the supreme Hâri that disturbs Brahma. "Qaïn" is a savage denunciation of the biblical god for his arbitrary injustice. All the gods reveal their weakness; they are all products of man's creation, and time therefore becomes a function of the life and death of all religions, as it is of all other phenomena. Christianity itself is on the brink of death.

Thus Leconte de Lisle could not settle on any one religion because all are equally *true*. And he could not believe in any of them because all are fallible and ephemeral and therefore *false*.

Still, this universal relativism and the void it produced would not have had such serious consequences had Leconte de Lisle been able to come to terms with the most immediate spiritual problem of the Western world, Christianity, if not as a divine faith, then at least as a program of action or an ethical system or an aesthetic haven. Even Renan, who did more than anyone else in France to drain faith of its vitality, recognized the necessity of the religious fiction represented by the church. But of all the religions considered by Leconte de

CHARLES MARIE LECONTE DE LISLE

Lisle the one he loathed most—indeed, the only one he really loathed—was Christianity. He had not placed the naive trust of his youth in other religions as he had in Christianity, and when it collapsed as a spiritual support, the ardor of his contempt and fury went beyond that of his former hope.

It would require an extended analysis to do justice to the poet's view of Christianity. Only a brief summary is possible here. Leconte de Lisle scrupulously separates Christ from Christianity, the primary religious symbol from the depraved institution. In various poems Christ is depicted as a child; a noble youth; a tragic figure meditating in despair on the night of his betrayal, nailed to the cross, and then dying; and even returning in spirit, inspired with sadness. Almost everywhere he is depicted as tender and compassionate. Few antireligious poets have written of Christ with such reverence as Leconte de Lisle in certain lines of "Le corbeau" (The Raven) or particularly "Le Nazaréen."

But Christ is a god of the past and another part of the world. The church is an artificial and pernicious institutionalization of what was once a natural ideal, and it is endlessly flayed by the poet for its betrayal of Christ's spirit. Christianity is a religion of sadness; unlike Greek polytheism, it impedes the free development of man's natural faculties ("Le runoïa")—not only joy, but thought, will, knowledge. It exalts suffering in the name of God and makes of it a virtue. Hypocritically it sacrifices the only existence we know to one it claims is far superior, but of which it really knows nothing—and which does not exist. The promise of immortal beatitude held out as bait merely exploits man's egoism; the faithful practice virtue not for its own sake but for eternal reward ("Hiéronymus," "La bête écarlate" [The Scarlet Beast]), and even rejoice in the damnation of their less fortunate brothers. Leconte de Lisle converts the most orthodox Christians into monsters who hoard their happiness while others suffer.

If the bright side of the Christian afterlife draws sardonic scorn, the dark side provokes the most profound horror and loathing. The idea of eternal retribution for the misdeeds of a fleeting existence is not merely a degradation of humane standards of behavior but of Christ's spirit of forgiveness ("La vision de Snorr"). It is arbitrary and mechanical, condemning even virtuous pagans, unbaptized children, and unintentional transgressors. The God in whose name this monstrous system has been constructed is the antithesis of the Greek gods; they showed human traits, and man felt close to them; while the Christian god is a remote, forbidding, and cruel despot ("Qaïn"). Small wonder, then, that his influence for improving man's nature has been nil. Worse, his religion has degraded man, and made worship consist of blind, abject submission. Where polytheism ennobled man, Christianity destroys human dignity and freedom, perpetually using as its principal instrument the threat of hell ("La vision de Snorr"). One of the most striking poems of this cycle is "Les raisons du Saint-Père," directly inspired by Dostoevsky's The Brothers Karamazov (1879–1880), where Christ confronts a dogmatic and belligerent pope and is obliged to retire in defeat.

As the years went by in the 1860's, Leconte de Lisle belabored with increasing frequency and emotion the cruelty of Christianity throughout its history. It became an obsession. In such poems as "Les paraboles de dom Guy," "La bête écarlate," "Les siècles maudits" (The Cursed Centuries), and "L'Holocauste," he concentrated with demonic delight on the crimes of the church. There is an extraordinary proliferation of harsh qualifiers and expletives; invective and vituperation are everywhere, making these poems not merely horrible but monotonous. In "La mort du moine" a monk rails at his audience, calling it "scum of the earth, dregs of infection, hideous breed, infamous plague." He, in turn, is excoriated with terms like "enraged beast, monstrous bastard, impure carnal offspring." "Cozza et Borgia" presents a seven-line sequence with nothing but loathsome epithets, beginning with "heretic, crook, murderer, excrement," and ending with "vomit of the Devil." Leconte de Lisle here finally leaves the realm of art and wallows in blatant rhymed polemics. The aesthetic balance and restraint of the previous religious poems have been lost.

Such endless fury with the bestiality of the church can be explained, I believe, only by the repressive, reactionary, clerical atmosphere of the Second Empire, when power, wealth, and hypocrisy went hand in hand with aggressive bigotry and persecution. Most important writers and thinkers of the time were anticlericals, and Leconte de Lisle is merely their most raucous voice. I think it fair to say that an intolerable stimulus had finally produced a reaction essentially false to Leconte de Lisle's own religious attitudes. But he was a poet, not a historian or a philosopher. As he grew older and more embittered, he looked for the worst in man, and found it in the Christian Middle Ages. He turned aside from his customary concern with eternals to engage in a specialized dispute. It is not to these poems that we turn for his finest religious attitudes but to such noble poems as "Le Nazaréen," where he acknowledges that, if the gods of Olympus were created for the free and happy man, Christ will endure eternally to console a suffering humanity: "You will not have lied so long as the human race/ Continues to weep in time and eternity."

The tension between his thirst for the absolute and his critical faculties forged in the crucible of an erudition that devitalized all religions and saw a horror in Christianity made of Leconte de Lisle a desperate poet, quite possibly the most desperate poet in the French language. He is unquestionably in this respect the spokesman for his time. Thus, Renan wrote in his *Souvenirs* (1883), "I was terribly disoriented. The universe seemed to me a dry and cold wilderness. Once Christianity ceased to be the truth, all the rest seemed to me indifferent, hardly worthy of interest." In no period of French literature do we find so many poets haunted by the collapse of faith. René Sully Prudhomme, Léon Dierx, Jean Lahor, Louise Ackermann—all are tormented by a corrosive and uncontrollable faculty for analysis. They *know* the reasons for their despair. All are blood brothers of Renan and Taine. Leconte de Lisle's distinction is his transfiguration of philosophical problems into splendid images, powerful sonorities, and intense emotion. The "eyes of a poet opened on the hypotheses of science"—this is how Paul Bourget characterized Leconte de Lisle. And Sully Prudhomme wrote too: "Cold and self-assured science facing a religious specter which refuses to give in—this is the tragedy of modern human thought."

Like Leconte de Lisle, the entire generation faced the same fundamental impasse: the need for illusion coupled with the incapacity to believe, a compelling need for truth side by side with horror about its consequences. It is because of this religious crisis that the despair expressed by Leconte de Lisle could have emerged *only* in his age and not, for example, in that of Lucretius or François de La Rochefoucauld or Lord Byron. His contemporaries sought for and sometimes found substitutes—stoicism, for example, or honor or duty or altruism or heroic action or positivism. But Leconte de Lisle never found a general consolation—apart from art itself. Neither Hindu ideas of vanity, nor the fascination of death, nor the glory of a dead Hellas could give his life affirmative meaning. His religious attitudes oscillated violently from passionate regret to inflamed revolt, from hatred to despair. Only six years before his death he again reviews all the gods, dead for all time, "but who will haunt you till your last day" ("La paix des dieux"). No one illustrates better than Leconte de Lisle Blaise Pascal's description of the godless man: "He is visibly lost, fallen from his proper place and unable to find it again." Neither relativism nor Pyrrhonism could satisfy him as they satisfied, at least partly, Michel de Montaigne or Anatole

France. Nor could absolute negation set his mind at rest. So cosmic solitude remained to the end an acute source of suffering. This part of his work remains as a solid literary monument because it is the only truly poetic formulation of the religious crisis of the Second Empire. But if today faith still struggles with the demoralizing effects of scientific progress, if the weakening of Christianity and of religion in general continues to darken man's horizons, then Leconte de Lisle's religious poems—apart from their specialized aspects of Hellenism, Hinduism, and the like—are surely no less relevant today than they were to the generation of Renan. In this sense he wrote not just for his time but also for ours.

Humanity

In its approach to the fundamental experiences of life, apart from the religious, Leconte de Lisle's poetry is far more accessible to a wide public; his most impressive compositions are not the vast epic reconstructions but the shorter poems. One may discern a certain analogy with the religious poems; just as they represent a long pilgrimage from the most primitive cults to the most advanced systems, ending in defeat, so the poems concerning the nature of life trace man's existence from youth to the grave, and end in similar defeat. There is a similar devitalization of the absolute, a similar general absence of the good reinforced by the horror of aggressive evil, and a similar resignation to ultimate death.

Leconte de Lisle begins his metaphysical experience with fervent faith, and his journey through life with avid fascination. His initial reaction is ecstatic. "I instinctively loved everything I saw," he wrote in 1840, "the sky, the earth, the sea, mankind." Just as his metaphysical despair is the more intense because of his initial hope in God, so his disappointment with life is keener because of his deep need for beauty, love, strength, freedom, courage, justice, and joy. He describes his youthful ecstasy in some of his most striking poems,

"Ultra coelos" (Beyond the Stars), and "Mille ans après" (A Thousand Years Later); and it is transmitted to his Greek poems, such as "Khirôn," in which the centaur says: "I embraced the Universe in my sinewy arms" or "Glaucé" ("I would like to seize the world and embrace it"), and to the Hindu poems, such as "La mort de Valmiki." Selections from the purely rhapsodic poems would astonish readers acquainted only with the epic or anthology pieces. "Be blessed Forever!" exclaims the poet, "I love, I can die,/ For I've lived the best and the loveliest of dreams" ("You by Whom I Have Felt"). The intense love depicted in the Hindu poem "Çunacépa," the joyful remembrances of the old poet in "La mort de Valmiki" ("Dazzling laughter illuminated the world"), or the ecstasy of the nature paintings and personal love poems reveal Leconte de Lisle as a lyric poet passionately drawn to life, a romantic who feels and loves rather than a thinker who dissects and denies. Being an uncompromising absolutist, he even fixes an imperious condition for these joys of life; they must be everlasting. Permanence in earthly phenomena is to him the counterpart for the absolute in religion. It is obviously an ominous condition to attach to life. Along with this goes a genuine dread of death: "This sudden decomposition of our poor organization is such a terrible mystery," he exclaimed with a shudder in his youth. Thus, his first collection, *Poèmes antiques*, opens with a vigorous and hopeful Vedic hymn to the rising sun and joy of life, "Sûryâ," immediately followed by a hymn expressing fear of death, "Prière védique pour les morts."

In a very real sense, it was the instinctive attempt to escape the ineluctable disappointment engendered by such intense lyrical impulses that led Leconte de Lisle to his espousal of the cult of youth and the past. Had he been a consistent philosopher of despair, there would have been little point to the attempt to redeem the present in the image of the past, for youth could be no more satisfying than old age. Thus, in "The Almanach Vendor" (*Operette morali*, 1827), Giacomo Leopardi cannot think of a single year in the past he would like the coming year to resemble; and Flaubert once wrote to a friend: "I envy you for regretting anything in your past." Yet poets are often paradoxes, and Leopardi, in his poem "The Solitary Life" (1821), does not hesitate to qualify his youth as "my barren life's one solitary bloom."

Few poets, however, have longed for their youth with such persistent fervor as Leconte de Lisle. The theme may be traced without interruption from the earliest extant verses to his posthumous collection. It is his way of recapturing lost joy, prolonging existence through imagination, and accentuating by contrast the misery of present reality. The happiness he longs for does exist, but virtually always in the past. In the Greek poems ("Hélène," "Khirôn"), in the barbarian cycle ("Le massacre de Mona," "Le dernier des Maourys"), or the personal pieces ("Dies irae," "L'Illusion suprême"), his instinctive reaction to sorrow is to leap backward to the joy of youth. "Flesh about to vanish, evaporating soul,/Are filled with visions which haunted the cradle" ("L'Illusion suprême"). It is in youth alone that man is able to feel himself destined for eternity. And precisely the same instinct inspires the poet's nostalgia for the youth of the world, since the past was a time not only of faith later lost but of vigor and beauty, innocence and purity, spontaneity and freedom. It is a picture to soothe his sensibilities. We have observed how he deliberately idealized Greek civilizations of the past; in the same manner, his depiction of the barbarian races emphasized their nobility, dignity, virility, and high morality to the virtual exclusion of the naive, materialistic, immoral, or comical traits in his sources; in the Latin imitations he suppressed all brutal or familiar realism. In an essay on Vigny, he outlined this manner of reliving the past as a theoretical justification of his concept of art, and his theory is happily wedded to his lyrical impulse, for his work is a long paean of glory to the past.

Yet this is but the surface level of the poet's consciousness, though critics have usually been content merely to note this fascination for youth. Under this level is the antithesis. "What splendid morning has ever had eternal moments?" asks a character in one of the Hindu poems ("Djihan-Arâ"). What is more ephemeral than youth, and how can one possibly recapture it? The idealized image Leconte de Lisle paints is not that of a young man. He sees youth through disenchanted eyes and the bitterness of long experience. Everywhere the figures who look back at the lost paradise are old men who have suffered long and look forward to nothing but grief and death. There is the poet Valmiki, the aged centaur Khirôn, the bard of Temrah, and the last survivor of the Maoris. It is the same in the more personal "Requies" and in "L'Illusion suprême." Some of his purest poetic expressions picture a desolate humanity yearning for the past.

> Bent beneath the burden of the multiple years,
> The human Spirit stops, and, gripped by
>   weariness,
> Pensively turns back to forgotten days.
>
> ("Dies irae")

The paradise of the past only serves to exacerbate the infernal nature of existence. Leconte de Lisle vividly illustrates Dante's famous lines from *The Divine Comedy:* "Nessun maggior dolore che ricordarsi del tempo felice nella miseria" (There is no greater sorrow than to remember happy times when one is wretched). There is a profusion of expressions of heaviness, slowness, frigidity, exhaustion, and sterility with which the poet paints his inner landscape. The dream world of Leconte de Lisle may be young and dazzling, but his real world is decrepit. Nor can the past be held up to the present as a model for the future, since we can never go back. As in religion, so in life the reality can never be joined with the dream. This is why he envies the girl who died young. "The years have not weighed on your immortal grace" ("L'Illusion suprême"). Leconte de Lisle continued the secular theme he inherited from Sophocles, Menander, and Cicero: that it were better never to be born, but once having seen the light of day it were best for man to die young.

In this desolate landscape love appears as a refreshing oasis. While his poetic adoration of youth was darkened by reflection, his reaction to love remained youthfully romantic. There are, to be sure, poems describing the doleful effects of love, cries of agony, or melancholy plaints. They are emotional compositions, as far from a calm philosophical judgment of love as those of Musset, and almost as personal. "La vipère" (Poèmes antiques) is explosively passionate: "Tear out of your breast the mortal viper,/ Or be still, coward, and die, die for having loved too well!" The poem was later removed to Poèmes barbares, where it is today in the company of other frank love poems, such as "Le dernier souvenir" ("Someone has devoured my heart. I remember."). Love is portrayed as an acute pain, the sting of a wasp, etc. What is notable for this "impersonal" poet is that these pieces are undisguised expressions of personal grief. Some appeared in 1855, immediately after his most violent disappointment in love, an affair with the wife of a friend. In "Les oiseaux de proie" he denounces love ("O Passions, black birds of prey, . . . I fall from heaven yet cannot perish); in "Les damnés" he bewails his fate ("And so I went,/ Mingling in the senseless frenzy/ With the lamentations of the damned in love"); and in "Le sacrifice" he does not recoil from the most melodramatic romanticism ("I would like, both victim and sacrificer,/ Spilling at your feet love, hatred and grief,/ To bathe with all my blood the altar where I worship you!"). To be sure, these pieces cannot be wholly identified with the love poems of the romantics; Leconte de Lisle does not evoke

dramatic incidents like Musset, or supply commentaries for the curious like Lamartine, or fling imprecations at his tormentors like Vigny. Still he writes emotionally about himself, and some of his lines ("Les spectres," 1864) sound strangely like the lymphatic laments of the moon-gapers earlier in the century. In "Ekhidna" love is portrayed as a monster with the head and bust of a woman enticing unwary lovers to their destruction in her grotto. And this attitude even infiltrates the Greek poems, where Hélène speaks for the poet: "I will flee the bitter joy of pleasure."

Despite all this, like Musset, Leconte de Lisle is irresistibly drawn back to the joy and intensity of the experience of love. Of all the Parnassians, he has written probably the most authentic love poetry. In the pieces that exalt love and even in those that decry it, he has not allowed analysis to undermine his feeling. Many readers will continue to prefer "Le manchy," for example, to his philosophical pieces. In quatrains, alternating alexandrines, and octosyllables that produce a light, graceful rhythm, the poet combines brilliant exotic details like rare jewels in a ring as he describes the young girl of his early dreams in Bourbon being borne to church by her slaves:

> With your bracelets on your wrists and your chain
> on your ankle,
> And your yellow kerchief coiled on your
> chignon,
> Two Telingas, your faithful companions,
> Carried your bed of manilla mats.

The poem ends with an exquisite wistful sigh for the girl who now lies buried in the strand among the cherished dead. Baudelaire eulogized the piece as an "incomparable masterpiece" in L'Art romantique, adding the incisive remark: "It is perhaps because this is his most natural manner that he has neglected it most." In certain of his poems, love almost replaces religion, since the intensity of the experience makes it a sacred moment of eternity

("Christine"), and it is described in religious terms:

> Love! You can die, O light of our souls,
> For your brief flash contains all eternity
> ("Soleils! Poussière d'or" [*Suns! Dust of Gold*])

What is remarkable is what Leconte de Lisle has *not* absorbed from his age. The independence of his inspiration is especially striking when we look around him. His contemporaries, poets and prose writers alike, were experiencing and loudly declaiming profound weariness, distrust, or cynicism in love. The whole generation, reacting against the romantics' unrestrained, maudlin sobs and cries of ecstasy, faced love with an oppressive feeling of satiety. Alexandre Dumas *fils* repeatedly returns in his plays to the theme of purely physical pleasure. Guy de Maupassant describes the desolation of surfeit. Out of this excess came not only lassitude but also an exacerbated, self-conscious search for refinement or the unusual or morbid in love (as with Baudelaire). In addition, this was an intellectual generation of writers, one that experienced an irresistible need to analyze and dissect every movement of the heart (as with Edmond and Jules de Goncourt). "If a man loves a woman, he dissects her like a corpse in the hospital," wrote Maupassant, and Dumas makes of woman his "incessant study." It is as though the importunate prying of Psyche had driven Cupid away with the drop of burning oil. Woman was also denounced as a downright evil; a strange, incomprehensible creature; or else stigmatized as the deadly enemy of the serious artist. Dumas foreshadows the savage indictment of women by August Strindberg. The concept of the separation of the sexes grew rapidly (Théophile Gautier, Baudelaire), eventually turning into a disguised but profound antagonism, the most sensational example of which is Vigny's "La colère de Samson" (1864). Most devastating of all, perhaps, was the Schopenhauerian view

of love as a purely physiological instrument used by nature to perpetuate the species. The tenderest of passions thus became a disguise for a Machiavellian design: "Love is a child which wants to be born" (Ménard); "love is posterity imposing itself" (Sully Prudhomme). The concept can be found also in the pages of Anatole France, Paul Bourget, Pierre Loti, Octave Mirbeau, Gabriele D'Annunzio, and Thomas Hardy. In fact, it seemed to be the exception not to express these attitudes.

Out of this morose background Leconte de Lisle emerges virtually untainted. Not once does he attempt to cultivate strangeness, morbidity, sordidness, or excessive sensuality. The idyllic love of "Çunacépa" appeared in the same year (1857) as Flaubert's *Madame Bovary* and Baudelaire's *Les fleurs du mal*. Where his contemporaries felt love to be old and worn out or abused, Leconte de Lisle never ceased seeing love as a youthful thing. When he was sixty-five, he still called out: "Oh! let your young love . . . come back to my heart" ("Les roses d'Ispahan"). Where the period emphasized the physiological, the poet maintained intact his virginal notions of modesty, reserve, and dignity ("Épiphanie"). He will not decompose and destroy; he insists on restoring to love the ardor his contemporaries are analyzing out of existence. He refuses to look on love from the biologist's or philosopher's point of view; love does not propagate but beautifies and ennobles. It was a deliberate rejection of his times, stemming from a native romanticism he never overcame. To the end he never abandoned his lyrical adoration of woman.

Sadly, despite the momentary impression of eternity, love, like youth, is ephemeral. Leconte de Lisle depicts love as a flash of lightning, its sensation of brilliance and swiftness accompanied by danger and destruction. It is associated, as in the work of so many other poets, with death, and Leconte de Lisle envies the lot of lovers who die before the extinction of their love ("Christine"). Thus he quickly leaves his oasis and returns to his moral wilderness. He seeks the external, but all is ephemeral.

Transcending all other experiences is the fragility of life itself. This is the counterpart of relativism in religion. As long as his early religiosity endured there was at least faith in an afterlife. But once that hope had crumbled, the narrowness of earthly limits (and even their existence) became a fundamental tragedy: "Then nothing! The earth opens, a bit of flesh falls" ("Le vent froid de la nuit" [The Cold Wind of the Night]). The shock of a materialistic concept of life for a fervent idealist is clear throughout his work, as he repeatedly returns to the tragedy of death ("L'Illusion suprême").

Many thinkers of the time laid emphasis on the theme of universal death. Flaubert's correspondence is full of it. Joseph de Gobineau meditated about "the word of the prophets on the instability of things [which] applies to civilizations as to peoples, to peoples as to States, to States as to individuals . . ." (*Essay on the Inequality of Races*, 1853–1855). Probably at no time since the fifteenth century had there been such a widespread obsession with death. With Gautier and Baudelaire, François Villon's consciousness of bodily death was reborn. So, for Leconte de Lisle, life itself is a necessary defeat since it is not an absolute; like religions it reduces itself to a series of contingent phenomena, a "prey to rapid time." The idea permeates his work. One can hardly read two or three poems without coming upon some martyr or victim, some figure close to death or meditating upon death. The titles themselves speak eloquently: "The Death of Valmiki," "The Death of Sigurd," "The Death of the Sun," "To the Dead," "Dead Dreams." Death is an integral part of his conception of love, religion, life: "The secret of life is in closed tombs" ("Le secret de la vie"). It is permanently present in his consciousness: "I hear the dead groaning under the crushed grass" ("Le vent froid de la nuit"). It filters into his imagery in the same poem as the snow becomes a winding sheet, and earth a shroud. He dwells with apparent satisfaction on the dead landscape of the moon ("Les hurleurs" [The Howlers]). Everywhere scientists were proposing theories about the end of the earth, the sun, the universe. The earth might freeze or be incinerated or collide with some spatial migrant. Second Empire poets were attracted to this theme, which satisfied both their taste for erudition and their hopeless outlook. In this regard, too, Leconte de Lisle is both the representative of his age and its highest poetic expression. He concludes *Poèmes barbares* with a savage description of the end of the world ("Solvet seclum") in which the grating vocabulary indicates with dramatic clarity the personal dilemma of this problem poet who longs for the infinite and is unable to grasp it:

Furious blasphemy driven by the winds, . . .
Frightful clamor of the eternal wreckage, . . .
Mind and flesh of man, one day you will vanish!

. . .

Sterile block torn from its immense orbit,
Stupid, blind, full of supreme howling,
The globe will dash its wretched old husk
Against some universe. . . .

Wherever Leconte de Lisle looks in life he finds death. It is inherent in all existence: man, nature, the universe. He cannot think of any phenomenon without conjuring up its negation. Spiritual idealism is doomed by materialism, youth is but the memory of old age, love inspires the death wish, and life is "a somber accident between two infinite sleeps." The single fundamental principle common to all things is their certainty of ultimate nonbeing. For Leconte de Lisle only that which is immutable has reality. Existence is ephemeral, only nonexistence permanent. The deep current of Leconte de Lisle's thought thus leads him irresistibly to a belief in the unreality of existence. Nonbeing is reality and being is a deception, an illusion. This seems to be the deepest meaning of "Le secret de la vie":

> And the ultimate nothingness of beings and
> things
> Is the sole reason for their reality.

The vanity of existence is hardly a new concept. But the nineteenth century found new reasons for believing in the nothingness of being: the unreality of the gods, various subjectivist philosophies widely debated in the Second Empire, the multiple explanations of the sciences concerning the unreliability of sensory testimony, the concept of endless "becoming," all contributed to this belief. For Leconte de Lisle doubtless the most basic argument for illusion was the impermanence of all phenomena ("Fiat nox," "L'Ecclésiaste," "À un poète mort"). It is hardly surprising that when the sacred Hindu texts were published in translation in France in the 1840's (first by Eugène Burnouf, followed by Simon Langlois and Hippolyte Fauche), Leconte de Lisle found himself powerfully attracted to this newly discovered ancient philosophy. He found a compelling ontology to which his own thoughts on the nature of life—even before the revelation of the Hindu texts—had drawn him instinctively. The fundamental idea of nothingness in his Hindu poems—such as "Bhagavat," "La vision de Brahma," and especially the striking piece "La Maya," which concludes *Poèmes tragiques* and is often anthologized—is intrinsic to his work. Through the ages and across the continents he had found his true brothers in the sages of the Ganges.

Nothing exists; all is illusion. Inevitably such nihilism, which was beyond doubt a deeply felt conviction in Leconte de Lisle, would provoke in critics of the time incredulous resistance or simply hilarity. Even more recently, various scholars have doubted the poet's sincerity. How could a Westerner, one who had, moreover, studied various philoso-

phies, accept such a conclusion? It is true, of course, that Leconte de Lisle was not destined to be a Hindu sage. He lacked the patience, resignation, and compassion for humanity preached by Buddha, and the willingness to immolate his own individuality, all so necessary for Hindu salvation. His furious denunciations ("Qaïn," "Les siècles maudits," "Aux modernes") are the antithesis of the ascetic Oriental attitude, and his concrete imagination doubtless prevented him from fully grasping the peculiar spirituality of Hindu concepts. Yet this idea of universal illusion appears over and over again, not just in Leconte de Lisle but in letters, personal journals, and published works of numerous writers of the period. Flaubert wrote: "Our joys, like our sorrows, are but optical illusions, mere effects of light and perspective"; or again, "I believe in the eternity of only one thing, namely Illusion, which is the real truth. All the others are but relative." The same idea occurs in various forms in Vigny, Ménard, Jean Lahor, Léon Dierx, Sully Prudhomme, and Louise Ackermann (who ends her *Thoughts* [1882] with: "I cannot believe in the reality of what surrounds me. It seems to me that I have loved and suffered and shall soon die in a dream. My last word will be: I have been dreaming!").

In addition, Leconte de Lisle's poetry is related to a philosophy dating back to the Greeks, which denied the reality of secondary phenomena (as size, shape, and color). The theory was represented by Democritus, Galileo, and Leibniz; and in the eighteenth century George Berkeley extended the idea from the secondary to the primary qualities, or matter itself, denying the existence of objects apart from perception. Later David Hume adopted Berkeley's phenomenalism, arguing that objects are nothing more than the sum of their qualities, which exist only in the mind; and the entire objective universe therefore exists only as a construction of the consciousness. He went further by denying even the existence of Berkeley's Self as being independent of the perceptions on which experience is based. Thus, when Leconte de Lisle wrote: "The mind which has dreamed you drags you down to oblivion" ("L'Illusion suprême"), he was, like Berkeley, denying the world as anything other than a configuration of the individual consciousness. But when in "La Maya" he adds: "But what is the heart of ephemeral man, O Maya! if not you, the immortal mirage?" he is, in effect, adopting Hume's thoroughgoing skepticism and denying the separate existence of the Self. The subject as well as the object ceases to have any ultimate substance, and the solid world dissolves, like a dream, into a kaleidoscopic unreality of perpetual change. It becomes clear, then, that under the archaic guise of Hindu exoticism, Leconte de Lisle's poetry has as an intellectual principle some of the more abstruse theories of his time.

Corresponding to Leconte de Lisle's aspiration for the divine is his lyrical love of life. Just as historical relativism drained that aspiration of its vitality, so impermanence and illusion devitalized his attraction to life. Finally, just as the absence of the metaphysical good was exacerbated by the aggressive evil of Christianity, so the absence of the good in life was complemented by a powerful awareness of life as a positive evil. Suffering is not an unfortunate circumstance, an accident of time and place, but the necessary and inherent condition of existence. Leconte de Lisle saw the fundamental and universal cause of suffering as "desire," a concept that came to him from Buddhism. The Oriental explanation to which he naturally gravitated was that all existence is suffering since being and action spring from desire, which in turn is engendered by the illusory phenomena of the universe. Once man recognizes the inanity of the goals of desire, he is in a position to negate it and, thus, by overcoming the necessity of endless reincarnation, to end all suffering.

In the early nineteenth century Schopenhauer had developed a system curiously similar to Buddhism. His fundamental principle explaining all existence from inanimate mat-

ter to man was "Will," a blind, unconscious, purposeless impulse urging being to "the greatest possible augmentation of life." The essence of Will is effort, which, implying an unfulfilled need or desire, is by nature painful; therefore existence is identical with suffering.

There is no evidence that Leconte de Lisle had any real knowledge of Schopenhauer; it was rather through Buddhism that he became conscious of the philosophical explanation of suffering several decades before Schopenhauer began exerting any clear influence in France. The poet's initial impulse denies Schopenhauer. Where the philosopher cannot admit the existence of joy other than as a negative interlude between periods of anguish, the poet conjures up a good and beautiful experience in his vision of youth. But he soon comes to recognize that desire spares no one. Youth is "happy" only because desire has not yet become an active force. Its privilege is that the basic vital drive is still latent ("Dies irae," "Djihan-Arâ"). But it would be as feasible to stifle desire even in youth as it would be to prevent the volcano from erupting. His picture of joyful youth is dictated by his lyric temper; reflection shows him that even youth is disturbed ("L'aigu bruissement"), and finally, as he looks back on the past, he is "seized by horror, trembling lest the past be reborn" ("La paix des dieux").

But once man has emerged from youth, as he must, then desire dominates all. Desire is all of man's needs and aspirations, his ambitions, joys, passions, regrets, hopes, fears, and anxieties. It contains all of life's physical and spiritual energies; or rather it is life itself, a ceaseless effort to reach out, related to the Hegelian idea of becoming in that it is a process eternally realizable yet never realized, or to Renan's concept of God: "The universal effort to be and be more and more." Desire for Leconte de Lisle is as inclusive as Buddhist desire or Schopenhauerian Will. It takes an infinite number of forms: insatiable lust for new conquests ("Le dernier des Maourys"), love, even the hunt for food. It is pointless to achieve any goal, since desire itself can never be eradicated; it is the "ardent attraction of a good impossible to grasp" ("Qaïn"). Its decoys are phantoms serving only to torture and exhaust.

The concept of suffering in Leconte de Lisle has thus gone far beyond the happenstance notion of it in the work of the romantics. Specific reasons for sorrow have little importance in themselves, and it is idle to evoke them in one's art. The poet does not hold himself up to the reader as an object of pity, nor does he have any personal nemesis stalking him, nor is there anything arbitrary in man's fate. Universal desire includes all, and Leconte de Lisle does not hesitate, at times, to write in the first person because he writes as a man among men. It is life itself that is the problem: "If you wish to suffer, then live," says the sage in "Çunacépa." The bitterest expression of desire (despite the customary interpretation among critics) is in "Ultra coelos," which shows man tragically destined to strive forever and to be forever unfulfilled. "It is the bitter chalice of desire that we need," the poet reflects bitterly. And he will never be able to root out this hateful instinct. Beyond man, Leconte de Lisle extends suffering to animals ("L'Oasis," "Les jungles," and especially the intense etching of the wild dogs on the African cape, desperately extending their snouts to the winds and waves and howling their savage grief in "Les hurleurs"). Even nature and the planets are caught up in this suffering, as Leconte de Lisle laments in one of his most moving passages:

Everything groans, the star weeps and the
    mountain laments,
A sorrowful sigh is exhaled from the forests. . . .
                                                ("Qaîn")

This Buddhist approach to the problem of evil, perceptible even in many non-Buddhist pieces, is the poet's reaction to the inner nature of being. But Leconte de Lisle was not a Parnassian, living in a period of literary real-ism, only to confine his vision to the abstraction of the will to live. His concrete poetic eye would inevitably supplement this view with the observation of relationships between phenomena, and he found confirmation of his bitter outlook in what may be called their Darwinian aspect—cruelty. His remarkable series of animal poems address this aspect. Leconte de Lisle is unquestionably the outstanding animal poet of the French language. No poet before or after him has been able to match his striking portraits of untamed beasts, whether they be quadrupeds, birds, reptiles, or fishes. Written around 1855, these poems depict a panorama of the animal kingdom—the black panther, tiger, elephant, lion, jaguar, python, condor, albatross, shark. They are not, as in Vigny's "La mort du loup" (1843) or Baudelaire's "L'Albatros" (1859), transparent symbols of a "message"; or, as in Jean de La Fontaine, disguises for human traits. Always Leconte de Lisle begins by setting them in their natural habitat, and then, with three or four brief strokes of his brush, he transcribes the savage nature of each animal:

His throat rattles with pleasure, he ruffles his
    plumes,
Extends his muscular, naked neck,
Rises up whipping the harsh snow of the Andes,
With a raucous scream he ascends where the
    wind cannot reach,
And there, far from the black globe, far from the
    living star,
Sleeps in the frozen air, his wings spread wide.
                                    ("The Condor's Sleep")

Just as he bends his efforts to put himself in the place of the barbarians he depicts, so he attempts to feel the instincts of the beasts. We recall that this is the period not only of Darwin but of the great French animal sculptors Antoine Barye and Emmanuel Frémiet.

Certain critics have attributed his desperate views to Darwinism. This is true but oversimplified. Charles Darwin himself and Thomas Huxley, after all, were highly sanguine in their outlook. Darwin, in *The Origin of Spe-*

cies (1859), stresses "the grandeur in this view of life . . . ; endless forms most beautiful and most wonderful have been and are being evolved." Applying Darwinian principles to the human mind and society, Herbert Spencer could write phrases like: "Progress is not an accident but a necessity," or "Evil tends perpetually to disappear." Thus even suffering was not to be deplored but accepted as a necessary agent in an endless ascent.

This is not the view of Leconte de Lisle. True to his somber nature, he was drawn not by the constructive talents of animals and even less by their evolution, but rather by their ferocity, fear, and especially hunger. He adopted the negative side of Darwinism. Everywhere the brutal struggle for existence reveals the total absence of direction and morality and nature's absolute indifference to any concept of justice. It is here that Leconte de Lisle comes closest to the impassivity for which he has so often been reproached. There is neither pity for the victim nor revulsion for the aggressor. "Sacred hunger is a long and legitimate murder," he wrote in his poem on the shark ("Sacra fames") in a rare lapse into preaching. In this panorama of universal evil without guilt there is no hint of a higher purpose served. As in his religious views, the idealistic poet accepted a materialist's view of life. Longing for love, he saw the universe through the eyes of the shark, with philosophical resignation. It is only when he found the principles of Darwinism operating in humanity that his bitterness surged forth and he lost his equanimity. Men kill less for necessary food than for patriotic dissensions ("Le soir d'une bataille"), religious creeds ("Le massacre de Mona"), love ("La mort de Sigurd"), power ("Nurmahal"), or material possessions ("Le lévrier de Magnus"). He compared men with wolves, dogs, pigs, horses, foxes, jackals, and vipers. Man is governed by the same appetites and passions as beasts. Indeed, in various execution scenes, he painted the positive delight of men seeing others agonize. And eventually he even decided to bridge the gap

directly by having his savages actually devour their human victims ("Le dernier des Maourys"). But this addition was not necessary; he had already made his meaning abundantly clear: "The tiger is better than man with his heart of iron" ("Çunacépa").

Suffering within and cruelty without—in both respects natural forces combine to produce the inevitable result of evil. In a sense, Leconte de Lisle modernized the ancient concept of Fate, and he used the word in both Greek and non-Greek pieces. It is not, to be sure, the Fate of the Greeks but the scientific and psychological phenomena that the nineteenth century saw as the root of all behavior. Being a concrete poet, Leconte de Lisle was strongly tempted to infuse the malevolent force of nature with a personality. He had lost his faith but not his religious feeling, and so identified destiny with divinity. In the presence of a cruel or incomprehensible deity one might either submit humbly, like Lamartine, or else revolt and blaspheme, like Byron. The proud, intransigent Parnassian chose the latter, and thus created one of his most dramatic and powerful masterpieces, the very long poem, "Qaïn."

Conceived in 1846, and heavily influenced by Byron's *Cain* (1821), various works by Lamartine and Proudhon, and Ludovic de Cailleaux's *Le monde antédiluvien* (1845), it was not published until 1869. It is a grandiose drama consisting of three parts: first, a description of the monstrous city of Hénokhia, which is a kind of immense tomb for Qaïn, and which the poet makes into one of the most splendidly barbaric descriptions of primitive times to be found in French literature; then, the brusque intrusion of a celestial horseman, followed by the awakening of the accursed rebel Qaïn, who launches into an impassioned diatribe denouncing God for cosmic evil; and finally, a vision of the great deluge, out of which emerges the ark destined to avenge suffering humanity—the three parts framed for the purposes of artistic unity in the dream of the seer Thogorma.

The poem seems a contradiction in the work of Leconte de Lisle. He did not, of course, think of God as some omnipotent autocrat, as did Vigny. Had he not seen the transitory nature of all gods and concluded that they were the creation of man? How, then, could he blame God for man's suffering? Actually, he was launching a vehement protest against the nature of being itself, the compelling source of suffering and crime. His protest is the same as that so simply expressed in Romans 7:19: "For the good that I would, I do not: but the evil which I would not, that I do." Qaïn remonstrates: "The thirst of justice . . . devours me." And the Angel replies: "Bow your head, slave, and submit to your fate." But "fate" for Leconte de Lisle is not a mysterious entity but rather the natural laws of the universe. "Qaïn" is thus the struggle of an ideal sense of justice against the facts of the real world. It is a protest against the iniquity of an order of existence for which man is in no way responsible. The same idea comes through in various other poems. "Surely, my punishment was an unjust thing, for I did not know, Master, and was obeying my nature" ("Le lévrier de Magnus"). So, too, in "Qaïn": "Was it I who commanded: 'Desire!' and then punished for obeying?" Interpreted in the light of the poet's general outlook, the composition is really not an enigma. God represents not a divine presence but the fate of man, not a mystical concept but a natural one. Analogous ideas are found in Renan's work: "God, that is, the reality of things," or "the will of the gods, that is, facts." The personification of fate in God fulfills an emotional and poetic need for Leconte de Lisle. He must blame someone for all this sorrow. Throughout his life he tried to find a scapegoat; who but God is worthy of his supreme wrath against life itself? Cursing nonexistent gods is undoubtedly irrational but conforms to what Leconte de Lisle calls "literary truth." Thus Prosper Mérimée quotes Stendhal as saying: "The only thing that excuses God is that he doesn't exist."

While there is nothing basically incongruous about the major part of "Qaïn," despite the melodramatic joust with God, what remains puzzling is the conclusion. Where Byron's *Cain* ends on a note of hopelessness, Leconte de Lisle's Qaïn ends by dethroning God and reconquering Eden. What can this mean? The literal meaning is an absurdity. Some have suggested a political meaning, relating it to the despotism of the Second Empire, but this is far too specific and limiting in the vast context of *Poèmes barbares.* Moreover, a letter the poet wrote in the very year he was finishing his work expressly disclaims any intention of ever going back to an active political life. Does he mean the essence of life can eventually be altered and evil suppressed? His entire work denies this. Does he mean man can reconquer his primal joy once he has destroyed the notion of divinity? This, too, is highly unlikely; in "Le runoïa" he describes man as utterly degenerate once he has suppressed all religion definitively.

What is most likely is that Leconte de Lisle allowed this poem to serve as a catharsis, satisfying his emotional needs and poetic talents far more than his intellect. This may be the reason for the quarter-century delay in publication; some contemporaries claimed he even intended to burn his poem. One understands why—the conclusion is shocking. Leconte de Lisle is everywhere the poet of the hero crushed by circumstances. His heroes remain proud and erect; their role, however, is not to prevail but to struggle, suffer, and die. Therefore Leconte de Lisle took good care to negate his own conclusion. Just as he opens *Poèmes antiques* with the hopeful hymn "Sûryâ" and closes with the despairing "Dies irae," he opens *Poèmes barbares* with the atypical "Qaïn" and ends the collection with "Solvet seclum," which uses identical images of fear, hatred, anger, crime, blasphemy, and shipwreck to proclaim vehemently that Eden will never be reconquered, that in the last scene earth will explode and vanish into oblivion! Until that day evil will reign supreme.

The ultimate solution for this desperate

outlook is death. Revolt is spurious since it is a manifestation of the vital instinct, only intensifying suffering. Furthermore, throughout his work and in his correspondence, Leconte de Lisle shows a clear predilection for inaction. Stillness rescues man from normal experience, suspends desire and struggle, and allows a kind of participation in the absolute. Along with the philosophical and sensuous attraction to stillness and silence there is an implied aesthetic principle; beauty is equated with calm. Some of his most striking pieces reflect this idea; "Midi" and "Le bernica" incorporate scenes of utter quiet, and "Les eléphants," very slow movement. Moreover, Leconte de Lisle saw death as a release, since he lacked a stoic nature. Throughout his life he oscillated between furious revolt and withdrawal from the source of pain. Escape is his most characteristic response: from the present to the past, from age to youth, from the earth to the stars, from man to nature, and from life to death. So longing for death is expressed constantly, and always it is enveloped in a mood of bitterness. It has nothing to do with nirvana, which is sometimes inaccurately identified by critics with death. And in the end even death is not a consolation, since consciousness, and therefore suffering, may survive ("L'Ecclésiaste").

Society

Leconte de Lisle, as we have seen, attaches importance only to what is permanent. After enumerating the presumed joys of life in "L'Illusion suprême," he adds what may be his most often quoted line: "But what is all that if it is not eternal?" As a consequence, his work is almost exclusively concerned with spiritual and aesthetic values and the enduring problems of the life process. Society as such had little interest for him, and he left virtually no place in his work for it. What he saw all around him was a nation engulfed in a tidal wave of materialism along with general indifference to the only values that mattered. Like

Renan, like Flaubert and Baudelaire, Leconte de Lisle found himself with a chosen few adrift in an ocean of vulgarity, charlatanism, and intrigue. His reaction is entirely predictable and hardly original. Where Renan analyzes dispassionately, where Flaubert vituperates vehemently, Leconte de Lisle, in the rare poems addressed to his own age ("Aux modernes," "L'Anathème") renders his contempt in images of sterility, impotence, and exhaustion. Or else he stigmatizes his age by disguising his own contemporaries as the degenerates of the past ("Le runoïa").

His reaction to the literature of his time is analogous. One of his most famous and striking poems, "Les montreurs" (The Showmen), a scathing sonnet that is also a kind of literary manifesto, denounces the "clowns and prostitutes" of contemporary literature. He develops these derogatory ideas mainly in the provocative prefaces of his 1852 and 1855 collections and in a series of essays on various French poets published in 1861 and 1864. He considers all modern literature (that is, since the Greeks) as decadent and barbaric. His own idea of great poetry is one that instinctively expresses the essence of a people, its characteristic traditions, historical destiny, and religious myths. Since modern man can no longer be spontaneous, he must turn back and reproduce these fundamentals through conscious erudition. He thus calls *Poèmes antiques* a "collection of studies." No one in modern times, he insists, achieves this type of typical universal poetry; even Dante, Milton, and Shakespeare have proved only their individual genius. He scornfully rejects the personal, sentimental, social, utilitarian, or moralistic tendencies of romantic poetry; his own poetry he intends to be impersonal, and much of it is, at least on the surface. As for the "realistic" poetry of his age, which glorifies modern technology, he shows nothing but contempt for it.

His contempt for society shows itself throughout his work. Often it is the familiar romantic feeling of the extraordinary suffering of the superior individual. Thus, even progress cannot be considered a consolation. From his youth to his death, Leconte de Lisle spoke in the name of the chosen and cursed. The pain of greatness is accepted as axiomatic, and in various poems we can even detect a grim delight in this type of pain. He thus extracts a kind of sinister compensation for his bitterness. His superior victims are characteristically portrayed as solitary victims of society. Martyrdom is glorified, particularly in the champions of dying faiths. But the feeling of loneliness is present also in his portraits of great birds, which are scornful, obstinate, and remote, like their creator ("Le sommeil du condor," "L'Albatros"). Some have interpreted his admiration for the noblest animals in a similar light. In short, Leconte de Lisle is too bitter about society to extend any pity to suffering humanity. It is only with difficulty that we may ferret out an example or two that may be interpreted as voicing pity—and here may be an additional reason for the coolness of his reception. In this respect he differs markedly from other despairing poets such as Vigny or Leopardi, who do show compassion. One reason for this, I think, is that he was more concerned with eternal ideals than with humanity as such; even his superior individuals are incarnations of some principle rather than creatures of flesh and blood. Nowhere, for example, do we find the tenderness toward contemporary individuals apparent in Baudelaire. It may be fairly said that Leconte de Lisle's poetry expresses an idea-centered rather than a man-centered universe. Perhaps the single remarkable exception is a twenty-one-line threnody in "Bhagavat," beginning: "A lament is deep in the murmur of the night" and ending: "O vanquished conqueror, who will not weep over thee." Rare as this is, it allows us a precious glimpse of a tenderness that the poet felt deep within himself, although it was thoroughly submerged by his misanthropy.

Leconte de Lisle turned readily to nature as a tentative refuge from society. A great deal has been written about his attitude toward na-

ture, but remarkably these discussions have centered on a single striking stanza of "La fontaine aux lianes" in which he says: "Nature is indifferent to human sufferings." Critics have compared the poem with Vigny's "La maison du berger," which concludes with a denunciation of nature, and drawn the conclusion that Leconte de Lisle was hostile to nature. One critic, Jules Lemaître, admits he is not really sure about this hostility but is influenced by the lugubrious atmosphere of the poetry as a whole.

But Leconte de Lisle was a poet, not a consistent philosopher, and contradictions abound in his work. The very number of his nature poems, some of which are among the most remarkable paintings in the language (particularly those of his native island), should give us a clue about the potent attraction of nature for the poet. Descriptions of luxuriant, sunlit scenery came easily and naturally to him, and he dwelt on them lovingly, unlike Vigny, whose descriptions are apt to be dry inventories, merely forming a framework or else serving as a source for images. Leconte de Lisle repeatedly expressed the consolation nature provided him (as in "Nox"). To be sure, he is not deluded by the pathetic fallacy and does not make of nature a personal confidante. The progress of the critical spirit, the weakening of religious faith, the advance of science had taken the beneficent soul out of nature. His whole generation—Flaubert, Baudelaire, Taine—had turned away from nature to the artificial, and some, like Vigny, even made an enemy of nature. Their irritation is really an inverted romanticism; while nature was no longer for them a maternal protector, they still felt the need of infusing it with a personality.

In this respect Leconte de Lisle stands apart. He, too, knew that nature is impassive and indifferent ("La ravine Saint-Gilles"), but he accepted this and did not find it offensive. On the contrary, he welcomed nature's impassivity as a boon in which he found repose from life's endless agitation, from the horrors of human passions, and from despised society ("Midi"). His landscapes are devoid of humanity. Nature became a kind of substitute for religion as he allowed himself to be absorbed in its universal beauty and lost his individuality ("Le bernica"). In this mood, he does not see the rapacious shark in the waters or the contemptuous eagle on the mountain. And, further, he embraces impassive nature because, as we have seen, calm is an element of his aesthetics.

But if nature is a refreshing oasis, its waters still reflect the surrounding desolation, since all nature implies death and consequently vanity. The ultimate unshakable stronghold to which this quintessential representative of Second Empire literature retires is art. Art grants what nothing else can, and in its own way it grants everything. It provides a superhuman existence that negates all negative phenomena and validates everything positive. It is the sole cure for the incurable. Nature is a tentative refuge subject to man's depredations; art, on the other hand, is beyond the reach of the destroyers. No one more than Leconte de Lisle is so imbued with this absolute faith. For Schopenhauer art was consoling but an essential illusion affording only fleeting respite from the goading of the Will. In Flaubert, too, doubt about art can be traced through numerous letters. His furious monomania often seems to himself a means of concealing the abyss. Such skepticism is hardly surprising in desperate men. But in the final analysis Leconte de Lisle is not a reasoner but a poet with a faith. All is illusion yet art is real. It is the true substitute for lost religion. Everywhere, in verse and prose, his references to art are couched in fervent religious terms. He describes art as the believer would describe God: "the supreme summit where the paths of the mind end, . . . an infinity having no possible contact with any other inferior concept." He refers to beauty as a burning flame, a shining light. Where in other experiences he was constantly tempted to flee, here he consented to sacrifice himself as a martyr.

Art became a code of ethics, involving renunciation, suffering, study, and heroism. There is the same exclusivism, the same fanaticism, indeed the same peremptory dogmatism as in the rites of ancient religions. Art overcomes the limitations of space and time and allows participation in the absolute. Since it is independent of life and exists as an absolute, it conquers death itself ("Hypatie"). A skeptic in all other experience, Leconte de Lisle resisted the pressure of doubt on his citadel of art. Art became his sole god, his faith, and his ideal. It was a leap beyond the ephemeral into the eternal and immutable. And it accorded him an incontrovertible assurance of aristocracy, while compensating for this solitude by providing a spiritual body into which he could incorporate himself. Here, at last, was the harmony between aspiration and reality he had so anxiously sought and could achieve in no other way.

Selected Bibliography

The section on Individual Works below gives only editions published during Leconte de Lisle's lifetime. A complete bibliography of Leconte de Lisle's works can be found in Edgard Pich, *Leconte de Lisle et sa création poétique*, Saint-Just-la-Pendue, 1975, which lists all editions of the separate collections of poetry, his prose works, his collections of correspondence, his translations, prefaces, articles, and interviews, as well as dates and periodicals where individual poems first appeared.

EDITIONS

INDIVIDUAL WORKS
Poèmes antiques. Paris, 1852, 1874, 1880, 1886, 1891.
Poèmes et poésies. Paris, 1855, 1857. Contains the poems that were later distributed between editions of *Poèmes antiques* and *Poèmes barbares.*
Poésies complètes. Paris, 1858. Contains *Poèmes antiques*, *Poèmes et poésies*, and *Poésies nouvelles.*

Poésies barbares. Paris, 1862. The title was changed in subsequent editions to *Poèmes barbares.*

Poèmes barbares. Paris, 1872, 1878, 1881, 1889.

Poèmes tragiques. Paris, 1884, 1886.

Derniers poèmes. Paris, 1895.

COLLECTED WORKS

La dernière illusion de Leconte de Lisle: Lettres inédites à Émilie Leforestière. Edited by Irving Putter. Geneva, Switzerland, and Berkeley, Calif., 1968. Contains letters from July 1885 to January 1890.

Leconte de Lisle, articles, préfaces, discours. Edited by Edgard Pich. Paris, 1971.

Oeuvres de Leconte de Lisle. Edited by Edgard Pich. 4 vols. Paris, 1977–1978.

Poésies complètes. Edited by Madeleine and Vallée. 4 vols. Paris, 1927.

Premières poésies et lettres intimes. Paris, 1902. Contains letters from January 1838 to October 1840.

SELECTED WORKS

Choix de poèmes. Edited by Pierre Gallissaires. Paris, 1969.

Choix de poésies. Paris, 1930.

Poèmes choisis. Edited by Edmund Eggli. Manchester, 1943.

BIOGRAPHICAL AND CRITICAL STUDIES

BOOKS

Badesco, Luc. *La génération poétique de 1860.* 2 vols. Paris, 1971.

Baillot, A. *L'Influence de Schopenhauer en France.* Paris, 1927.

Calmettes, Fernand. *Un demi-siècle littéraire, Leconte de Lisle et ses amis.* Paris, 1902.

Canat, René. *Le sentiment de la solitude morale chez les romantiques et les Parnassiens.* Paris, 1904.

———. *La renaissance de la Grèce antique (1820–1850).* Paris, 1911.

Cassagne, Albert. *La théorie de l'art pour l'art en France, chez les derniers romantiques et les premiers réalistes.* Paris, 1906.

Charlton, D. G. *Positivist Thought in France During the Second Empire (1852–1970).* Oxford, 1959.

di Orio, Dorothy M. *Leconte de Lisle: A Hundred and Twenty Years of Criticism (1850–1970).* University, Miss., 1972.

Dornis, Jean. *Essai sur Leconte de Lisle.* Paris, 1895.

———. *Leconte de Lisle intime.* Paris, 1895.

Ducros, Jean. *Le retour de la poésie française à l'antiquité grecque au milieu du XIXe siècle.* Paris, 1918.

Elsenberg, Henri. *Le sentiment religieux chez Leconte de Lisle.* Paris, 1909.

Estève, Edmond. *Leconte de Lisle, l'homme et l'oeuvre.* Paris, 1922.

Fairlie, Alison. *Leconte de Lisle's Poems on the Barbarian Races.* Cambridge, 1947.

Fath, Robert. *De l'influence de la science sur la littérature francaise dans la seconde moitié du XIXe siècle.* Lausanne, 1901.

Flottes, Pierre. *Leconte de Lisle, l'homme et l'oeuvre.* Paris, 1954.

———. *Le poète Leconte de Lisle.* Paris, 1929.

Fusil, C. A. *La poésie scientifique de 1750 à nos jours.* Paris, 1918.

Grant, Elliott Mansfield. *French Poetry and Modern Industry (1830–1870).* Cambridge, Mass., 1927.

Hunt, Herbert J. *Le socialisme et le romanticisme en France.* Oxford, 1935.

———. *The Epic in Nineteenth Century France.* Oxford, 1941.

Ibrovac, Miodrag. *José-Maria de Heredia.* Paris, 1923.

Leblond, Marius-Ary. *Leconte de Lisle.* Paris, 1906.

Mendès, Catulle. *La légende du Parnasse contemporain.* Brussels, 1884.

Petitbon, René. *L'Influence de la pensée religieuse indienne dans le romantisme et le Parnasse.* Paris, 1962.

Peyre, Henri. *Louis Ménard.* New Haven, Conn., 1932.

Putter, Irving. *Leconte de Lisle and His Contemporaries.* Berkeley, Calif., 1951.

———. *The Pessimism of Leconte de Lisle: Sources and Evolution.* Berkeley, Calif., 1954.

———. *The Pessimism of Leconte de Lisle: The Work and the Time.* Berkeley, Calif., 1961.

Revel, Émile. *Leconte de Lisle animalier et le goût de la zoologie au XIXe siècle.* Marseilles, 1942.

Schwab, Raymond. *La renaissance orientale.* Paris, 1950.

Souriau, Maurice. *Histoire du Parnasse.* Paris, 1929.

Vianey, Joseph. *Les poèmes barbares de Leconte de Lisle.* Paris, 1933.

————. *Les sources de Leconte de Lisle.* Paris, 1907.

Whiteley, John Harold. *Étude sur la langue et le style de Leconte de Lisle.* Oxford, 1910.

ARTICLES

Baudelaire, Charles. "Leconte de Lisle." *Revue fantaisiste* (15 August 1861).

Bernès, Henri. "Le 'Qaïn' de Leconte de Lisle et ses origines littéraires." *Revue d'histoire littéraire* (1911), pp. 485–502.

Carcassonne, E. "Notes sur l'indianisme de Leconte de Lisle." *Revue d'histoire littéraire* (1931), pp. 429–434.

————. "Leconte de Lisle et la philosophie indienne." *Revue de littérature comparée* (1931), pp. 618–646.

Charlton, D. G. "Positivism and Leconte de Lisle's Ideas on Poetry." *French Studies* (July 1957), pp. 246–259.

Chisholm, A. R. "The Tragedy of the Cosmic Will: A Study of Leconte de Lisle." *French Quarterly Review* (1931), pp. 69–97.

Estève, Edmond. "Byron en France après le romantisme et le byronisme de Leconte de Lisle." *Revue de littérature comparée* (1925), pp. 264–298.

Flottes, Pierre. "De l'obsession verbale chez Leconte de Lisle." *Revue d'histoire littéraire* (October–December 1952), pp. 469–482.

Putter, Irving. "Vers et prose de jeunesse de Leconte de Lisle." *Studi francesi* 31:64–75 (January–April 1967).

————. "Leconte de Lisle et l'hellénisme." *Cahiers de L'Association Internationale des Études Françaises* 9:174–199 (1958).

————. "Leconte de Lisle's Abortive Ambitions: Unpublished Correspondence." *Modern Language Quarterly* 19:255–261 (September 1958).

————. "Les idées littéraires de Leconte de Lisle d'après une correspondance inédite." *Revue d'histoire littéraire* 66:451–473 (July–September 1966).

————. "Lamartine and the Genesis of 'Qaïn.'" *Modern Language Quarterly* 21:356–364 (December 1960).

————. "Leconte de Lisle and the *Cathéchisme Populaire Républicain.*" *Romanic Review* 57:99–116 (April 1966).

————. "Leconte de Lisle and the French Academy: A Caveat." *Modern Language Quarterly* 27:418–430 (December 1966).

Zyromski, Ernest. "L'Inspiration fouriériste dans l'oeuvre de Leconte de Lisle." In *Mélanges offerts . . . à M. Gustave Lanson.* Paris, 1922. Pp. 456–476.

IRVING PUTTER

IVAN TURGENEV
(1818–1883)

MANY CRITICS NOW consider Ivan Turgenev the most dated of the great masters of the novel in nineteenth-century Russia. His exquisitely planned, finely wrought books are "faded," they say; the political issues that concerned him have long since lost their immediacy; his approach is sentimental, even mawkish; he supplies nourishment only to "those who find meat and drink in clouds and nymphs," in the words of an unkind contemporary scholar. So runs the standard list of complaints about the most civilized and cosmopolitan of Russian writers. And indeed there is some truth in them. Turgenev cannot boast the verbal exuberance and astounding inventiveness of a Nikolay Gogol; the profound energy and conviction of a Feodor Dostoevsky, wrestling with problems of a sort our age thinks very relevant; the epic sweep of description and inquiry to be found in Leo Tolstoy; the painstaking attention to detail and psychological analysis of an Ivan Goncharov. Yet despite all this, Turgenev displays strengths that led the American author and editor Albert Jay Nock to call him "incomparably the greatest of artists in fiction"—or Virginia Woolf to describe his books as "curiously of our own time, undecayed, and complete in themselves"—and which ensure that he will continue to be read both in his native country and in the West for as long as we can foresee. The intellectual fashions may be against him at the moment and may remain so

for some time, but Turgenev has never been totally eclipsed, and such a fate is scarcely likely to befall him in the near future.

Turgenev wrote primarily brief novels and short stories. He was a master of literary form and a superb stylist, with a command of the Russian language that was the envy of his contemporaries. His skill at painting with words, especially in his nature descriptions, has never been surpassed. Turgenev was a genuine literary professional. As he was independently wealthy, he had time to polish his efforts, for he did not depend on literature for his living (an economic reason for the inordinate length of many Russian novels is that Russian writers of the nineteenth century were paid according to the number of pages they produced). He watched the contemporary political scene closely, and any reader who wishes to obtain a detailed understanding of Russian intellectual and political life of the mid-nineteenth century is well advised to read Turgenev. He was a subtle student of human psychology, especially as it manifests itself in the relationships between men and women. He was concerned with the great questions of life and death, too, and although his responses to them were shallower than those of Dostoevsky or Tolstoy, much more akin to those of Mikhail Lermontov before him or Anton Chekhov after, it remains true that to study Turgenev carefully is to gain a fuller appreciation of life. Such strong points as these guarantee that, for all his weaknesses, Turgenev will continue to occupy a secure niche in the pantheon of his country's greatest authors.

Ivan Sergeevich Turgenev was born on 28 October 1818 in the town of Orel, located in the heartland of Russia. Orel was not far from the Turgenev family estate at Spasskoe, which later became the writer's principal Russian retreat. His mother, who evidently loved to dominate those under her authority, repelled the young Ivan by her cruelty to her serfs. His handsome father, who died in 1834, was content to let his wife manage the estate while he pursued local females more attractive to him than his spouse. After 1827, for the greater part of the year the family resided in Moscow, returning to Spasskoe only in the summer. Thus from childhood Turgenev was intimately acquainted with the life of a Russian country estate, that small fiefdom which could be culturally and economically almost independent, and which he made the setting for much of his later fiction.

Turgenev was first educated at Moscow boarding schools, then tutored at home, in the best tradition of the Russian gentry, for several years before he entered Moscow University in the fall of 1833. Moscow University was, intellectually speaking, the place to be at that juncture. An entire generation of talented men, including the poet Lermontov, the novelist Goncharov, the journalist and revolutionary Alexander Herzen, the radical poet Nikolay Ogarev, and the critic Vissarion Belinsky, found spiritual sustenance there—sometimes within the lecture halls, more often outside them, in student circles of their own. Moscow University nurtured the great intellectual generation of the 1840's in Russia, many of whose members had had their careers terminated or interrupted by 1850, though not before they had stamped their impress on Russian intellectual life. Despite this, Turgenev soon elected to desert Moscow for Saint Petersburg University, arriving just in time to attend lectures in world history given there by Gogol and graduating in 1837, at the age of eighteen.

Never again would Turgenev spend as many as eighteen years uninterruptedly in his homeland. In the spring of 1838, feeling that his undergraduate days had given him no more than the bare rudiments of an education, he set out for the source of European enlightenment, the University of Berlin. Thus began his lifelong odyssey through Europe. From September 1838 to September 1839, Turgenev spent most of his time in Berlin, following the latest developments in German philosophy and gaining entrance to the world of Teutonic culture. But it was also in Berlin that he met the semi-legendary embodiment of Russian culture of the time, Nikolay Stankevich. Stankevich, who has come down to us as the prototype of the pure, idealistic Russian intellectual of the 1830's, died an untimely death at twenty-seven in 1840, only a short while after he and Turgenev had met again, this time in Rome, and become close friends. Turgenev has left us a highly spiritualized portrait of him in the character of Pokorsky in the novel *Rudin* (1856). It was also in 1840, and again in Berlin, that Turgenev made the acquaintance of the famous anarchist Mikhail Bakunin. Their mutual interest in German philosophy created a tight though short-lived bond between them, and one that spawned embarrassing consequences when Turgenev visited Bakunin's multitudinous brothers and sisters for a few weeks at the end of 1841: a sister of Bakunin's fell extravagantly in love with him, and he extricated himself from the situation only with some difficulty. His reluctance to become involved with Bakunin's sister did not spring from any antipathy toward women: he had evidently been introduced to sex early on by a peasant woman, and just at the end of 1841 another peasant woman at Spasskoe was carrying his daughter, Pauline, born in the spring of 1842. Turgenev saw to her upbringing, and in the 1860's succeeded in marrying her off to a French businessman despite her illegitimate origins.

IVAN TURGENEV

Affairs of the heart did not overwhelm the life of the mind, however. Turgenev spent the academic year 1840–1841 at the University of Berlin, and in the spring of 1842 took his examinations for the degree of master of philosophy at Saint Petersburg University. From 1842 through 1847 he lived chiefly in Saint Petersburg, though he took several trips to Moscow, Spasskoe, and western Europe.

The year 1843 saw the initiation of two relationships that were perhaps the most fateful of Turgenev's life, with the critic Belinsky and the singer Pauline Viardot. Although he had known Belinsky's articles for some time, Turgenev first met the foremost Russian critic of the nineteenth century, that man "exceptionally dedicated to truth," as he put it in his reminiscences written twenty-five years later, in the summer of 1843. The two subsequently spent long hours in philosophical discussions of great intensity: Turgenev later recalled that when he once interrupted a conversation of theirs to wonder about dinner, Belinsky remonstrated with him quite seriously, "We haven't yet decided the question of God's existence, and you want to eat!" Just as he had done with Stankevich, Turgenev spent time with the mortally ill Belinsky, in Salzbrunn in 1847, less than a year before Belinsky died of tuberculosis in Saint Petersburg at the age of thirty-seven.

Turgenev's connection with Pauline Viardot, one of the most famous singers of her day, was of a different sort. In 1840 she had married Louis Viardot, an art historian and critic some twenty years her elder. She met Turgenev while on tour in Moscow in 1843, at which point there began one of the most extraordinary ménage à trois arrangements in the history of literature. From then until 1883, a span of forty years, Turgenev's thoughts were rarely far from her, and for long periods of time he lived near the Viardots. The three were almost inseparable, and Turgenev and Louis Viardot died within months of each other. Turgenev's attachment to Pauline Viardot (it may possibly have been platonic) pre-vented him from ever thinking seriously of marrying. In a way he possessed a complete family, but his "wife" was bound to another man and his daughter was the offspring of a woman he cared nothing for. The situation hardly seems to have been satisfactory.

In the Saint Petersburg period of his life, between 1842 and 1847, Turgenev did not keep at any very definite formal employment for long. Most of his energies were devoted to literature. His first, immature effort, the dramatic poem "Steno" (1834), had been composed in verse, the dominant genre of the 1830's. But his initial serious effort, the narrative poem "Parasha," dated from 1843 and was subtitled "A Short Story in Verse," in an obvious reference to the subtitle of Alexander Pushkin's *Eugene Onegin* (1824–1831), "A Novel in Verse." Belinsky dedicated a lengthy article to "Parasha," commending it warmly for being composed in "splendid poetic verse" and "imbued with a profound idea and completeness of inner content." For some time Turgenev continued to work the same vein, producing such narrative poems as "A Conversation" (1843) and "The Landowner" (1845), in addition to a quantity of lyric poems. Simultaneously, however, he tried his hand in other areas; for example, plays and some short stories in prose, especially "Andrey Kolosov" (1844), in which the narrator generously resolves to take up a young woman jilted by one of his best friends, only to discover that when she responds to his overtures he loses interest and shamefacedly drops her too. It is clear that in his earliest stories and poems Turgenev has already treated the chief themes of his career, most especially that of love gone awry. This fact has been obscured to some extent, however, by the fact that toward the end of the 1840's he made a slight but significant detour in his literary development. The first hint of this was the appearance in 1847 of the initial sketch of a group that eventually constituted *A Hunter's Notes* (1852).

This piece, "Khor and Kalinych," was subtitled "From a Hunter's Notes" by an editor and tucked away in the miscellaneous section of *The Contemporary*, the leading literary journal of the day. In it the author, with great richness of detail and psychological skill, delineates the distinct and contrasting personalities of two serfs. Each is shown as a full and interesting human being, and each is shown—so subtly as to make it seem almost incidentally—as weighted down by his servile status and unconvinced that his lot has genuinely improved of late. This story, along with a few others published by the end of 1847, caused Belinsky to conclude that Turgenev's future lay precisely along the lines of the hunting sketches, rather than those of his early poetry. If the critic was not wholly right in this estimate, he was entirely correct in remarking that a "chief characteristic" of Turgenev's talent was his inability "accurately to create a character whose like he had not encountered in reality"—that reality must always serve as Turgenev's touchstone.

Though the sketches in *A Hunter's Notes* have remained among Turgenev's highest achievements, they are not the most typical of his works, for later on he reverted to the type of story illustrated by "Andrey Kolosov." For the time being, however, he accepted Belinsky's prescription, publishing further peasant sketches individually and then collecting them under the general title *A Hunter's Notes* (a final three were added as late as 1874). In his last years Turgenev used to congratulate himself on the contribution his book had made to the emancipation of the serfs in 1861. And indeed his claim was probably substantial. The book made a solid political point while not ceasing to be art.

The chief thrust of *A Hunter's Notes* as a whole continued to be the characterization of peasants as human beings, but human beings diminished by an officially sanctioned system of enslavement. The peasant boys in "Bezhin Meadow" who sit about a fire of an evening telling one another frightening tales, Kasyan with his pungent personality in "Kasyan of Krasivaya Mecha," Khor and Kalinych—all

are unforgettable portraits. The reader also remembers the almost unconscious cruelty of the landowners who are accustomed to giving their serfs short shrift: "The way I see it, if you're a master then be a master; if you're a peasant then be a peasant," one of them says in "Two Landowners." However, it would be an error to think of the entire collection as structured around a contrast between admirable peasants and bestial landowners. Some landowners, though perhaps feckless, are depicted as genuinely interested in their peasants' welfare; and the serfs are often drawn as not particularly honest (Turgenev noted as one of their main characteristics a tendency to lie purely for the sake of lying) and occasionally downright repulsive, as in the scene of the drunken, swinish peasants at the conclusion of "The Singers." Moreover, the author is interested in a number of things with no direct bearing on social relationships: he transmits the folk beliefs of the common people, or investigates the manner in which individuals face the immediate prospect of death ("A Country Doctor" is a poignant story of a lonely, incompetent doctor who falls deeply in love with a dying young woman he cannot save). Turgenev is also concerned with aesthetic matters: he gives an extraordinarily detailed description of the singing competition in "The Singers," and what most readers remember from the welter of detail—the quantity of detail that makes it difficult to recall the outline of any particular story is perhaps the book's main weakness—is his magnificent nature descriptions. The final sketch, "Forest and Steppe," consists entirely of unsurpassed lyrical word-painting.

Turgenev's best-known single story dedicated to the unfortunate condition of the serfs is "Mumu" (1852), not included in *A Hunter's Notes.* Much anthologized in the Soviet Union today because of its relatively overt social criticism, the tale describes the hard lot of a deaf and dumb serf who for lack of any other object forms an attachment to a dog, but has even this small solace taken from him through the unheeding cruelty of his captious, elderly female owner. The hero, Gerasim, is drawn as a very positive character despite the physical affliction that makes him a trifle peculiar and for which no one can be held responsible; but few of those around him, including his fellow serfs, make any effort to ease his situation. His position would have been trying enough had he been a free man, but the far-reaching powers over him granted to his owner by the institution of serfdom certainly intensify his misfortunes. "Mumu" stands as Turgenev's most forthright indictment of the system of serfdom.

Over the years when the stories in *A Hunter's Notes* were appearing, Turgenev wrote other works as well. In 1849, while living abroad, he wrote a work of cardinal importance for all Russian literature, "Diary of a Superfluous Man," published in 1850. The phrase "superfluous man" has since become the mightiest cliché in the criticism of nineteenth-century Russian literature, utilized as it now is to link Pushkin's Onegin, Lermontov's Pechorin, Goncharov's Oblomov, and several other literary creations as essentially positive characters unjustly treated by contemporary society. But it was Turgenev who, through his story, gave the phrase its first wide currency, even though his hero, Chulkaturin, is more psychologically than socially or politically superfluous. The work is cast in the form of a diary kept by Chulkaturin in the last days before his death, which occurs on April Fools' Day, appropriately enough. Though the consciousness of his impending demise weighs on both Chulkaturin and the reader, Turgenev underlines the complete indifference of nature toward the fortunes of her creatures, of whom man is only one: there is a constant and jarring discord between the budding life of the incipient spring in which the narrative is set and Chulkaturin's morbid sickliness.

Chulkaturin is a sensitive though excessively self-conscious individual, capable of analyzing himself as well as others with im-

pressive penetration. This is especially the case now, when he is summing up his life; but at the same time he realizes that in the actual situations he looks back on, he either acted totally inappropriately or misinterpreted the deeds and attitudes of others. The most central of Chulkaturin's characteristics is his "superfluity," his quality of always being a "supernumerary." "Evidently nature had not counted on my putting in an appearance," he says, "and therefore treated me like an uninvited and unexpected guest. . . . All during the course of my life I constantly found my place already occupied, perhaps because I looked for that place where I should not have." The narrative illustrates this apparently almost fated trait of his life: he has hopes of winning the love of a young lady but is frustrated by the appearance of a dashing nobleman who wins her heart instead; when he attempts to defend her honor he merely earns her hatred; at the end he "magnanimously" resolves to cover for her sins, only to discover that yet another rival has preceded him. Nothing remains for him but to acquiesce first in his own humiliation, then in his own dissolution. Chulkaturin is an outstanding literary creation: he is both sufficiently individualized and sufficiently generalized to endure in the treasury of world literature.

Given Turgenev's general literary approach, one might expect him to be interested in writing for the stage, and indeed for a time it seemed he might leave a large body of dramatic writing. Beginning with a brief piece in a Spanish setting dating from 1843, Turgenev produced some ten plays of varying length before abandoning the genre permanently after 1852, largely for extraliterary reasons: the theatrical censorship at the time was unusually strict, so that he despaired of even getting his plays published, much less staged. And later on, when the situation improved, he somehow failed to try his hand at the drama again.

Turgenev's finest play—one that remains a staple of the Russian repertory to this day and is often presented on Western stages as well—is *A Month in the Country,* written in 1850. A play of Chekhovian mood created before Chekhov was born, it is based on a situation reminiscent of Turgenev's own relationship with the Viardot family. The hero, Rakitin, is a freeloader and a devotee of the lady of the house, whose husband is too preoccupied with managing the estate to pay her much heed. However, Rakitin is also an educated man with a morbid sensitivity to the beauties of nature. The world of the estate—outwardly idyllic but inwardly full of discontent and potential unhappiness—is disturbed by the arrival of a young tutor, whose unaffected naturalness and energy awaken the love of both the jaded mistress of the estate, Natalya Petrovna, and her seventeen-year-old ward, Vera. Rakitin follows the situation almost as an external observer and, though at first incredulous, soon realizes that the only solution is for both him and the tutor, Belyaev, to take their leave. Rakitin then departs for the future of a lonely bachelor; Belyaev leaves for the more important things he presumably has the capacity to achieve; Vera escapes what has become an intolerable situation at home by accepting the proposal of a kind but dull man thirty years her elder; and Natalya Petrovna subsides into the rut of existence on her husband's well-managed estate. Thus the tutor's brief stay on the estate precipitates a whole series of crises: the situation of the characters at the end is very different from what it was at the beginning, and the majority of them are worse off than before. The entire piece is imbued with an autumnal atmosphere: everyone's situation is somehow out of joint, and there are no real prospects for improvement. *A Month in the Country* encountered difficulties with censorship: it could be published only in modified form, with Natalya Petrovna a widow rather than a wife, in 1855, and not in its original version until 1869.

The period during which Turgenev established his literary reputation was not a propitious one for Russian literature: the years 1848 to 1855, from the European revolutions to the death of Czar Nicholas I, are now called the "epoch of censorship terror." Herzen, sensing what was below the horizon, left his homeland in 1847 never to return; Belinsky died an early death in 1848; Dostoevsky was exiled to Siberia for subversive activities in 1849. During this period Belinsky's name could not be mentioned in print, and any hint of disloyal intent was blue-penciled by the censors. At first Turgenev was not especially affected by these conditions. Between 1847 and 1850 he traveled extensively in western Europe, particularly France and Germany, and though he may have been regarded by some in the government as a carrier of the revolutionary virus, nothing untoward happened to him until 1852. Then, ironically enough, he suffered for writing an obituary extolling Gogol, politically the most conservative of the great Russian writers, whom Belinsky had attacked scathingly not long before his own death. But evidently the government did not care to see any writers praised, and Turgenev was jailed in Saint Petersburg for a month, though not under very arduous conditions, for his friends could visit him freely and his meals were brought to him from outside. Thereafter, from May 1852 to November 1853, he was exiled to Spasskoe, which he had inherited after his mother's death in 1850, returning to the capital only at the very end of 1853.

The year 1855 saw the opening of a new era in the history of nineteenth-century Russia. When the country was far along toward losing the Crimean War, Nicholas I, remembered as the greatest tyrant among the czars, was succeeded by Alexander II, the "czar-liberator," who decreed the emancipation of the serfs in 1861. The beginning of Alexander's reign was a period of high hopes: it saw the lightening of the censorship and a resultant quickening of intellectual life. In addition, the 1850's witnessed a transition from the philosophical idealism of the 1840's to the politically radical activism of the 1860's. If the first half of the decade was a period of stagnation, the second was a time of ideological reorientation. It was then that the consistent old-line liberal Turgenev noted the first hints of trouble from those to his political left. This occurred when *The Contemporary,* under the editorship of his old friend Nikolay Nekrasov, began a process of radicalization under the guidance of the radical critics Nikolay Chernyshevsky and Nikolay Dobrolyubov. Chernyshevsky and Dobrolyubov were impatient with Turgenev's absorption with what they considered trivial affairs of the heart at a time when all honorable people were expected to be worrying about political and social problems. Turgenev never denied the importance of social problems, but at the same time he defended the artist's independence and his right to deal with other subjects he felt were also significant. Chernyshevsky and Dobrolyubov gradually took Nekrasov along with them, and after they had insulted Turgenev irreparably, the latter broke with both *The Contemporary* and Nekrasov.

By the end of the 1850's Turgenev was famous as the "great poet of the doomed love affair," to use Alfred Kazin's phrase of a later date. "Faust" (1856), a "Short Story in Nine Letters," displays several major themes in Turgenev's writing: the potentially malign influence of artistic literature on the minds of people unprepared to cope with it; an awareness of the supernatural intervening in human life; the violent, sudden snatching of the fruits of love from between outstretched hands: "What there was between us flashed by instantaneously, like lightning, and like lightning bore death and destruction." Some years after their first acquaintance the hero of "Faust" meets the heroine, now married to a pedestrian husband. Though the heroine's late mother had strictly forbidden her ever to read fiction, the hero, who could never comprehend the reason for this prohibition, begins to visit her estate and recite Goethe's *Faust* to her. The poem wreaks such a change in her character that the relationship between hero and heroine develops to the stage where each avows love for the other. On her way to the assignation that would have led to the consummation of their passion, however, the heroine is stopped by her mother's apparition. She returns home with a mysterious ailment to which she succumbs in two weeks, leaving the hero to the standard lonely future.

Just as in "Faust," artistic literature, represented in this instance by Pushkin's foreboding lyric "The Upas-Tree" (1828), plays a crucial role in the story "A Quiet Spot" (1854). A brief work that took Turgenev six months to compose, it is not particularly successful, partly because of the excessive number of plot lines but primarily because the heroine's character is delineated so sketchily that her final decisive act of committing suicide seems insufficiently motivated. The reader may surmise, however, that she is designed as a deeply passionate though disciplined soul compelled to live among potential or actual philistines, and that the impression made on her mind, so unaccustomed to artistic literature, by her reading of Pushkin's poem triggers her fatal decision.

In his love stories of the 1850's Turgenev rings the changes on the basic theme of the abrupt denial of love's fruits. "Asya," for example, written in Rome at the end of 1857 after the author had weathered a spiritual crisis, and published in 1858, may be viewed as one of the most characteristic of Turgenev's love stories. The tale is set in Germany rather than on a Russian estate, but the foreign environment serves primarily to bring the Russian characters—the narrator, N.; Gagin; and the latter's illegitimate half-sister, Asya—closer together than they might have been in a native setting. A consuming love sweeps over the heroine, reducing her to a state of physical illness. But when she offers her love to N. during the climactic scene, and he must accept or reject her on the spot, he declines to do either but instead temporizes wordily. To be sure, he quickly realizes his error and within twelve hours is prepared to grasp the opportunity presented him, but he is too late:

the Gagins depart, and he is unable to trace them. At the time he consoles himself with the thought that other opportunities may present themselves, but he is wrong: "Condemned to the loneliness of an old bachelor, I live out my dull years, but I preserve as something sacred her little notes and a faded geranium, the same blossom she threw me from the window once upon a time."

"First Love," a long short story of 1860, is among the most autobiographical of Turgenev's writings, being based in large measure on the situation in his own family, with his philandering father married to an unattractive and older woman. As is the case with "Asya," the story is recalled through the prism of intervening years by a hero for whom the events described were crucial; the impressions are those of a youth of sixteen not fully cognizant of what is happening about him, as recalled and interpreted by an older man. The narrator describes his first passion for a beautiful but impoverished noblewoman, Zinaida, a capricious and independent young woman who completely dominates her suite of admirers but submits to the narrator's father, a man who values independence and freedom above all. The reader must take some pains to piece together the history of the love affair between Zinaida and the father, for the narrator himself perceived it only fragmentarily, being most concerned with his own emotions upon first falling in love. And certainly the story is a masterpiece of psychological analysis in its description of the reactions of a boy in this state who realizes that he faces a successful rival in his own father, whom he greatly admires. But even successful love engenders disaster: the father dies of a stroke soon after the affair is terminated, leaving as a legacy the words, "My son, fear woman's love; fear that happiness, that poison"; Zinaida, after bearing an illegitimate child, makes the best marriage she can but dies a mere four years later. In "First Love," as in many of Turgenev's other works, love is like a disease that can re-

sult only in damage: it ruins one's life if unrequited, it ruins one's life if requited. The temporary joys it brings must be paid for in excessive measure.

Turgenev is now remembered as a novelist, though, even more than as a short-story writer. Although he did not get around to separating his novels from his short stories until 1880, Turgenev wrote six of them: *Rudin A Nest of Gentlefolk* (1859), *On the Eve* (1860), *Fathers and Sons* (1862), *Smoke* (1867), and *Virgin Soil* (1877). His novels differ from his short stories in that the latter deal primarily with personal emotions and love conflicts, whereas the former also treat broader social questions. However, even in the novels Turgenev's interest remains focused on his heroes' distinct personalities. He once remarked that he always began from a personality rather than an abstract idea, and thus it is not surprising to find him supplying his heroes with detailed prehistories either in his notes for a novel or in the novel itself, and setting them very carefully in historical context. Another hallmark of Turgenev as literary artist was the externalizing of his characters' psychology. He rejected Tolstoy's method of analyzing his heroes' psychological motives directly and at length. The artist, he held, should be a "secret psychologist": Turgenev knows quite as well as Tolstoy how his heroes think and feel, but he causes them to express their internal experience through words and external actions, so that the reader must deduce their inner feelings from outward signs, just as in real life. To be sure, Turgenev's characters occasionally deliver themselves of monologues that are more closely allied to Tolstoy's approach, but on the whole the reader is presented with a substantial task of interpretation in dealing with Turgenev's writing.

A famous article of Turgenev's, published in 1859 under the title "Hamlet and Don Quixote," is worth considering briefly as a key to his view of life and literature. In this piece Turgenev postulates the Hamlet type and the

IVAN TURGENEV

Quixote type as polar opposites in human character. To Turgenev's mind, Don Quixote represents primarily "faith," "faith in truth located beyond the individual." Don Quixote dedicates his life to a cause outside himself. This makes him appear mad to some, and it indisputably bestows a considerable monotony upon his mind: "He knows little, but he does not have to know much." At the same time, he is "the most moral creature in the world," this insane knight. Hamlet is quite the opposite: he represents "analysis first of all, and egotism, and therefore lack of faith." Though an egotist, Hamlet is simultaneously too skeptical to believe in himself. Though intelligent, he finds his own internal resources insufficient. His weapon is irony, where Don Quixote's is enthusiasm. Don Quixote would not fear to seem foolish in the eyes of the world, whereas Hamlet thinks there is nothing worse than this. Hamlet despises this life and wishes he could end it, but he is still too much attached to it to make any serious attempt to do so. Turgenev does remind us, though, that Hamlet suffers much more intensely than Don Quixote: the latter undergoes only physical discomfort inflicted by others, whereas Hamlet tortures himself spiritually.

The first of Turgenev's novels, *Rudin*, contains a central hero constructed largely on the pattern of Hamlet. Composed in six or seven weeks during the summer of 1855 at Spasskoe, it was published early the following year in *The Contemporary* and in a separate edition a few months later. The setting for the story is yet another isolated Russian estate, where Rudin appears abruptly and unexpectedly. When he leaves a short time later, everything remains outwardly much as it was before, but inward tensions have been created that will markedly alter the fortunes of the individuals in the group Rudin finds there. This group includes Darya Mikhailovna, the imperious and vain mistress of the estate; her daughter, Natalya, the book's heroine; a neighboring land-

owner, Volyntsev, who at first refrains from making an open avowal of his love for Natalya but who eventually wins her as his wife; the sycophant and secret sensualist Pandalevsky; the embittered misogynist and poseur Pigasov; and the earnest tutor Basistov. All of these are affected in one way or another by Rudin, especially by his flair for rhetoric, the "music of his eloquence." Words are Rudin's stock in trade. "Some of his hearers very likely did not understand precisely what he was talking about," the author comments, "but his breast heaved, some sort of curtains were withdrawn before his eyes, and something radiant flared up before him." After listening to him for a time Darya Mikhailovna calls him a "poet," and Turgenev emphasizes the fact the Rudin is often carried away by the music of his own eloquence in what is indeed a rather poetic fashion.

Rudin almost desperately uses words as a cover for his lack of inner emotion. Toward the end of the novel one character remarks that "Rudin has the nature of a genius," only to be corrected by another: "There is a touch of genius in him, . . . but nature—that's the whole thing, he really has no nature." There lies within Rudin an emotional void he strives to fill with words and intellectual convictions, but cannot. He is a man lacking in passion who feels that he should be passionate. But his predilection for intellectual analysis and verbalization destroys any possibility of true emotional commitment. In his student days he wrecked a love affair in which one of his friends was involved by insisting on analyzing it and informing other people about it. In the novel he does the same thing to his own love affair: when Natalya offers herself to him without reservations, he knows he should respond but can feel nothing. He therefore attempts to counterfeit the appropriate emotions, but fails, and afterward loses Natalya because he cannot take positive action at the time required. He tries to justify his failure in a lengthy analytic letter written to her when he leaves, but words simply cannot compensate for his lack of substance. At the end of the novel as originally published, Rudin is depicted dejectedly and aimlessly wandering through Russia.

Apparently, though, Turgenev was uncomfortable about leaving his hero in such an existential limbo, for in 1860 he took the unusual step of adding to the novel an epilogue presenting him in a slightly more favorable light. Rudin himself tells of several projects that he had undertaken but that had all come to naught because of his inability to accomplish anything practical. At the same time, he is reconciled with an old university classmate, who had been very much against him during the body of the novel; and the author grants that the uttering of the right words at the right time may be a form of action. At the end, in a scene whose appropriateness is open to some question, Turgenev brings Rudin to the Parisian barricades of June 1848 and there has him perish, shot through the heart, after the Revolution has already been put down. Thus in the final accounting he does prove capable of action, though fate decrees that even this shall be abortive.

Turgenev had been planning his second novel, *A Nest of Gentlefolk*, as early as 1856, but circumstances prevented serious work on it before a sojourn at Spasskoe in 1858. The book was written in the latter half of that year and published in early 1859 (publication early in the year is a nearly constant pattern with Turgenev's novels). Though *A Nest of Gentlefolk* was received by his contemporaries with approbation, its popularity has not stood the test of time, and it is now among the least read of his novels.

In the years immediately following 1855 Turgenev was for some reason at his most Slavophile or Russophile. Toward the conclusion of *Rudin* he had caused a character for whom he obviously felt some sympathy to make a strong statement against cosmopolitanism and to define the source of Rudin's unhappiness as his ignorance of Russia. "Russia can

get along without us," he says, "but none of us can get along without her. Woe to him who thinks he can, and double woe to him who actually does!" In *A Nest of Gentlefolk* Turgenev continued to work along lines such as these. This should not be taken to mean that he abandoned his Western predilections, but he did at that time look most sympathetically on the Russian traits of his heroes and most unfavorably on certain aspects of Western culture. This is exemplified by the history of the father of the book's hero, Lavretsky. The father was a scatterbrained Anglophile who tried to bring Lavretsky up as a rootless European. However, not only does Lavretsky rediscover the positive values of his native land, but his father is transformed into a Russian in the bad sense when he suddenly goes blind, wanders across Russia seeking a cure, and dies a crotchety Russian landowner of the classical type. Aside from this, in *A Nest of Gentlefolk* Turgenev also devotes a great deal of attention to the problem of the family as the foundation-stone of any society. He provides Lavretsky with the most extensive family history of any of his major characters, tracing his ancestors back several centuries and dwelling in much more detail than is usual even for him on Lavretsky's immediate family. In like manner, the "nest" of the title is a family nest depicted in loving detail at the end of the book. Lavretsky has nothing to do with its existence, but he appreciates the principle of human continuity that it embodies.

Lavretsky himself is a likable man with scholarly inclinations who is trapped between two women representing the poles of womankind in Turgenev's fiction. His wife, Varvara Pavlovna, is unredeemable: she exploits her husband, is blithely unfaithful to him with insignificant men, makes demands on him when she has nowhere else to turn, and generally blights his life. She is one of several women in Turgenev who feed their egos by exercising power over men. For a time, misled by a false report of her death in Paris, where he has left her in order to return to Russia, Lavretsky is deceived into thinking he can find true happiness with the book's heroine, Liza, the most ethereal, most moral, and strongest-willed of Turgenev's women. Intensely religious, Liza is disturbed by the notion of loving a man promised to another woman, even if the latter be dead. In a brief scene of suppressed passion, the two seem on the verge of happiness until all is suddenly destroyed by the reappearance of Varvara Pavlovna. Liza interprets the return of Lavretsky's wife as divine punishment for her spiritual insolence and resolves to take up life as a nun in a distant convent. Lavretsky is soon abandoned by his wife once again. The novel ends with a vignette describing Lavretsky's visit years later to Liza's convent. As he watches her pass by a few feet from him, "only the lashes of the eye turned toward him trembled slightly, she merely bent her emaciated face lower—and the fingers of her clasped hands, intertwined with prayer beads, clenched more tightly." In these external signs may be read the extent of Liza's inner strength.

One of the most dynamic male characters Turgenev ever created was Insarov, the Bulgarian hero of his third novel, *On the Eve.* The author began the book in the summer of 1859 while taking the waters at Vichy, although he had been nurturing the idea for it since 1855, when a friend had given him a manuscript describing an unfortunate love between a Bulgarian man and a young Russian woman. Completed in the autumn at Spasskoe, it appeared in the January 1860 issue of the *Russian Herald,* the journal in which Turgenev would publish for some years following his break with *The Contemporary,* despite its conservative politics and his general dislike for its editor, Mikhail Katkov.

On the Eve sharply contrasts the Russian male—in the persons of Shubin, an artist of ability and intelligence but lacking in constancy, and Bersenev, a good man and a scholar who ends by producing articles on such trivial topics as "On Certain Peculiarities of Ancient German Law in the Matter of Judi-cial Punishments"—and the dedicated Russian female in the character of Elena Stakhova. The single-minded Insarov is the only one who can satisfy her aspirations and meet her standards. Having grown up an independent soul, Elena has reached just the right age for love when she first meets Insarov, at that time a student in Moscow, in the period preceding the outbreak of the Crimean War in 1853. Insarov is totally devoted to the goal of freeing his country from its Turkish occupiers, and it is this complete dedication that makes him one of the most Don Quixote–like characters in Turgenev's fiction. The analytical Shubin presents the major traits of Insarov's character admirably in two sculptures he does of him. The first is a realistic bust in which his features are "honorable, noble, and bold," but the second depicts him as a rearing ram in whose countenance are expressed "dull pomposity, fervor, stubbornness, clumsiness, and narrowness." But the first Insarov is the one who remains predominantly in the reader's mind and the one who inspired Dobrolyubov to write his famous article "When Will the Real Day Come?" in which he lauds Insarov while at the same time looking to the appearance of his Russian counterpart in the near future.

Once Insarov and Elena meet, the plot develops rapidly. Elena takes the initiative in pressing her love on him. Though he knows a revolutionary should have no family ties, he accepts her when she agrees to support his cause wholly and make no demands of her own on him. She thereupon abandons her family and Russia to go with her husband to Bulgaria to fight for liberation. Evidently, however, the pair have upset the balance of fate by their actions. Insarov contracts an illness while attempting to make arrangements for his wife to accompany him. He recovers, but falls ill again in Vienna and finally in Venice, where he dies before regaining his native soil. It is Insarov himself who raises the question of whether his illness is not punishment, and perhaps it is—a sign that personal happiness cannot be combined with dedication to a political cause. Then, too, Insarov is a prime example of his creator's belief that if a man of action appears on the scene before history is ripe for him (after all, the Crimean War ended in Russia's defeat and the continued enslavement of Bulgaria), some indefinable force will cut him down. The final pages of *On the Eve* contain lengthy though inconclusive ruminations on the meaning of a death that cuts short such a significant life, ruminations grounded in the tension between Turgenev's innate philosophical nihilism and the optimism of a man with a goal, like Insarov. Turgenev could not himself believe with such conviction; however, he admired those who could, even though he was persuaded they were doomed to failure.

Nihilism as a political rather than a philosophical phenomenon was central to Turgenev's next and finest novel, *Fathers and Sons* (more precisely, *Fathers and Children*). He later wrote that he had first conceived of the book upon meeting an unnamed provincial doctor who impressed him as representative of a particular social type, which he then embodied in the novel's hero, Bazarov. Commencing work on the manuscript in October of 1860, he completed the first version about a year later, then spent the last months of 1861 revising the text and agonizing over whether he ought to publish it at all in view of the widespread political unrest among the peasantry and students following the emancipation of the serfs in the spring. But the editor Katkov knew a good novel when he saw one—he published Tolstoy and Dostoevsky as well as Turgenev—and substantially decided the matter for him, bringing it out in the February 1862 issue of the *Russian Herald.* In the summer of that year it appeared in a separate edition, with the addition of a dedication to Belinsky.

Fathers and Sons was composed with at least two major ends in view: to contrast representatives of the best in the older and younger generations and to demonstrate that the idealistic theories of the young, however admirable in the abstract, could not withstand confrontation with the realities of life.

The ideological standard-bearer of the older generation is Pavel Petrovich Kirsanov. An Anglophile and a man of cultivation, he is also a bachelor embittered by a long-term enslavement of passion to a captious and mysterious noblewoman. In his mouth Turgenev placed the major tenets of his own generation: a belief in principles as a guide to action; admiration of civilization and its accomplishments coupled with a denial that anything essential can be accomplished by brute force; a conviction that an enlightened aristocracy is essential for the well-being of the nation; respect for the proprieties and customs of social intercourse. His opponent, Bazarov, the primary representative of the younger generation, resembles him in many facets of his emotional and psychological makeup but differs from him sharply in his philosophical approach to life. Bazarov is the great "negator," the quintessential "nihilist" (though Turgenev did not invent the word, he gave it popularity as a tag for the political radicals of the 1860's). He denies any validity to existing customs and social structures, insisting that they be swept away and space cleared for something better to be built; he refuses to recognize received authorities and even scoffs at medicine, though he is studying to be a doctor; he denies that human beings possess any individuality: for him they are simply "copies," constituent parts of a social collective; he tends to equate evil with illness, which can be eliminated by altering the social order; he lacks any appreciation of art and aesthetics generally. Philosophically he is a thorough materialist. The intellectual clashes between Pavel Petrovich and Bazarov, intensified by their instinctive personal dislike for each other, constitute an important part of the book. Essentially these are debates rather than discussions. Since neither is genuinely willing to listen to the other, no meeting of minds occurs, but Bazarov usually bests his opponent because he is quite willing to push his arguments to their logical extreme on provocation, whereupon Pavel Petrovich can only gape. Later on the enmity between them results in a duel, which Bazarov wins, physically and then also spiritually, by magnanimously binding his opponent's wounds.

But if Bazarov gains the philosophical battle with Pavel Petrovich, and through him with the older generation as a whole, he loses the struggle with life. The very duel with Pavel Petrovich supplies an example of this: though Bazarov in theory rejects the notion of honor and dueling as a social institution, when he is actually challenged his pride causes him to accept the duel. The clearest instance of the failure of his doctrines to bear up under the testing of real life is his love for Odintsova, the book's beautiful but cold heroine, who does not mind flirting with him so long as the involvement does not become serious and disrupt her placid routine. Bazarov thinks love solely a matter of physiology: if one cannot "achieve one's aim" with one woman, drop her and find another. And in fact it is Odintsova's physical beauty that first attracts him: a physical lust akin to malice drives him to make his confession of love to her. But when Odintsova refuses him, Bazarov to his own amazement discovers that he cannot put her out of his mind. He keeps coming back to her in the hope that she may relent, and at the end summons her to his deathbed to bid her farewell. In this and other ways Bazarov partially falls prey to the "romanticism" of which he is so contemptuous. His theory of sexual attraction turns out to be invalid.

After love, death is the final irrational factor Bazarov had not reckoned with. Like Insarov, he is felled before he actually accomplishes anything: while dissecting a corpse he cuts himself and falls ill because no disinfecting substance is immediately available. Before the conclusion he grasps more clearly the mysteries of existence. "Yes," says the great negator on his deathbed, "just try to negate death. It negates you instead, and that's all there is to it."

After *Fathers and Sons* appeared, the question of the author's intent in writing it was paramount in the minds of the radical literary critics who discussed it. Dmitry Pisarev and his journal *Russian Word* argued that Turgenev had simply tried to be objective in picturing the younger generation, and that a young person should be quite pleased with Bazarov's portrayal. To be sure, Turgenev had included the figures of Sitnikov and Kukshina, two intellectual and moral travesties of Bazarov, but it had to be admitted that such people as these actually existed in reality and did no credit to the radical movement. Pisarev thus felt that there was nothing intentionally "antinihilist," or deliberately directed against the young radicals, in the book. But the other and more influential segment of the radical intelligentsia, led by Chernyshevsky and Dobrolyubov's heir, Maksim Antonovich, assailed Turgenev vigorously for having slandered the younger generation, declaring that, since he stood revealed as a reactionary, all of his previous novels should be consigned to oblivion. When Turgenev visited Saint Petersburg in the spring of 1862, he found to his dismay that those he considered his enemies welcomed him, while those he would have liked to think were his allies scorned him. Some, he later recalled sadly, had informed him then that they had burned photographs of him "with a hawhaw of contempt." In April 1862 Turgenev wrote a lengthy letter to a group of Russian students at Heidelberg University, defending his creation of Bazarov, proclaiming in the standard political idiom that his entire work was directed "against the gentry as the dominant class," and throwing up his hands at the students' claim that the idiotic Kukshina was his most successful character. But such was the intellectual atmosphere in Russia at the time that all his protestations availed him little.

The decade of the 1860's was a sharp-edged but seminal one in Russian intellectual history. The hopes aroused by Alexander II's accession to power were crowned by the emancipation of the serfs in 1861 and lesser but still important reforms, as of the courts, in subsequent years. But Chernyshevsky, Dobrolyubov, Pisarev, and their allies, the descendants of the philosophical radicals of the 1840's, were not content with even these substantial changes: they went on to demand much more. The agitation for drastic change reached a crescendo in 1862, after the radicals had denounced the emancipation as a hoax, but it was quelled in that year through such actions as the suspension of *The Contemporary* and *Russian Word,* the imprisonment of Chernyshevsky and Pisarev, and most especially the outbreak of a rebellion in Poland in early 1863, which rallied public opinion to the government's side. Thereafter, deciding that the arson and university closing of 1861–1862 had served little purpose, those hard-core radicals who were prepared to give their lives for the cause embarked on a course of individual terrorism against high government officials. A deflected shot fired in April 1866 at Alexander II in the heart of Saint Petersburg inaugurated the era dominated by assassins and bomb throwers, an era that culminated in the successful assassination of Alexander fifteen years later but that continued sporadically into the twentieth century. It is these terrorists, most of whom paid with their lives for their deeds, who were called "nihilists" by western Europeans in the 1870's and 1880's.

The relations between the old-style liberals like Turgenev and the younger generation of the 1860's were delicate at best. Turgenev felt nearer to the radical than the conservative camp; he took pains to cultivate the young radicals, explain his attitudes to them, and reach some sort of understanding with them. But in the 1860's they for the most part would not have him, and he was compelled willy-nilly to ally himself with the more conservative elements of the Russian literary world, publishing in their chief organ, *Russian Herald,* during most of the decade. He could not condone the violence and terrorism perpetrated by the radicals, but at the same time he remained convinced that they were essentially correct in their outlook. Thus it was that many years later, in a brief prose poem, Turgenev wrote sadly of his attempts to tell the truth, only to be met with disdain from "honorable souls." All he could do, he felt, was continue on his path and hope that eventually he would be understood. "Pummel me, but be healthy and well-fed" was the slightly masochistic way he put it.

The unexpectedly violent reaction to *Fathers and Sons* gave Turgenev pause. Indeed, for about a year after its publication he wrote virtually nothing of consequence. Then he reappeared bearing an odd concoction, begun some years before, entitled "Phantoms." When he printed it at the beginning of 1864 in a new journal edited by Dostoevsky, he went to great lengths to emphasize its apolitical character, subtitling it "A Fantasy" and equipping it with a brief introduction in which he asked the reader to take it at face value and not read anything into it. "Phantoms" is a series of disjointed sketches with an anonymous narrator whisked about nocturnally by a supernatural being called Ellis. Ellis is able to transport him at will not only through space but also through time: for example, she shows him Julius Caesar's legions marching in the days of imperial Rome's glory. During one of these nightly episodes, however, Ellis is attacked by a mysterious creature the narrator recognizes as death. He recovers consciousness lying on the ground near a beautiful woman, who embraces him passionately and promptly vanishes.

One of the few minor items Turgenev wrote in the years following "Phantoms" was another series, this time of brief ruminations, entitled "Enough" (1865) and subtitled "Passages from a Dead Artist's Notes." "Enough" is Turgenev at his sentimental and self-pitying worst, consisting as it does of meditations on melancholy themes of lost happiness, the indifference of nature, the inevitability of destruction and the void, all done in a mood redolent of Arthur Schopenhauer. The work ends with a Shakespearean quotation in English: "The rest is silence."

Though this retreat from literature was only temporary (among his friends his repeated declarations of intent to abandon literature forever became something of a joke, and Dostoevsky used them to embarrassing effect in his nasty caricature of Turgenev as Karmazinov in *The Possessed* [1871–1872]), his experiences of 1862 did alter the "mix" of his writing significantly. To be sure, he wrote two more novels, but they now appeared at less frequent intervals—whereas he published four between 1855 and 1862, he put out only two from 1862 to 1877—and the relative importance of the "mysterious" or the "supernatural" in his fiction increased. Turgenev did not believe in God, and superficially it might seem he would be little interested in supernatural phenomena. Yet he was haunted by a suspicion that there was something more to life than meets the eye. In 1864 he composed a small story entitled "The Dog," in which he described something that may have been an apparition—but then may have had a natural explanation too. He ventured no answer to the question with which he begins and concludes the story: "But if we allow the possibility of the supernatural, the possibility of its intrusion into real life, . . . then what role is left for common sense?"

"Knock . . . Knock . . . Knock" (1870), set in the romantic 1830's, is written in a similar vein. Its hero, Lieutenant Teglev, appears to others to be a "fatal" type who bears the seal of a man of destiny (in speaking of him, the narrator makes the interesting comment that a belief in fate is equivalent to a belief in the "significance of life"). Each of the individual occurrences in the chain leading to Teglev's decision to take his own life has a completely natural explanation, but the way in which they combine is at the very least mysterious: the overall pattern seems "fated," although at one point Teglev must do some forcing to fit a major event into the pattern. Here, as in "The

Dog," Turgenev left himself a way out so that he would not have to commit himself irrevocably to the proposition that the supernatural does play a role in human life.

As the 1860's wore on, Turgenev renewed his interest in the political novel—his last two novels were even more political than the first four. He began writing *Smoke* around the end of 1865, dropped it for a time, then published it in early 1867 in the *Russian Herald*, despite some disagreements over it with Katkov. Curiously enough, this work is built around a love affair of a typically Turgenevian stripe, but one in which the man, Litvinov, is determinedly and avowedly apolitical. The author masterfully develops the love conflict around the question of whether Litvinov will succeed in wrenching his beloved, Irina, from the stifling world of Russian high society in which she is embedded in the German resort town of Baden-Baden, or whether she will enslave him with chains of passion and make of him a "kept man" to whom she can repair for surcease from the banality of the social circles in which she moves. In the end she proves too weak, too permeated by the poisons that have circulated about her for so many years, to leave her husband and his social milieu and follow Litvinov; and since Litvinov is exceptionally strong among Turgenev's heroes and demands all or nothing from her, the two part. At the novel's conclusion it is for once the woman who has missed her opportunity and become embittered, while Litvinov is able to renew his relationship with his former fiancée.

The political aspects of *Smoke* are treated in conjunction with Litvinov and his love affair, though he is more an observer of political discussion than a participant in it. Turgenev delineates with acid pen the generals, high bureaucrats, and stultified nobility who constitute Irina's circle and who are incapable of a single original or even intelligent thought. In many cases he denies them the dignity of full names, designating them by initials. Even the tolerant Litvinov can find no redeeming features in them. The opposite end of the political spectrum is represented by the members of the Gubarev circle, which Litvinov visits on occasion. Though they waste their time in pointless wrangling, and though many of them eventually return to Russia and become petty despots, Turgenev feels that they are not really bad people at heart, but simply misguided ones. The rightist and leftist groups resemble each other in a number of ways, but their creator is noticeably inclined toward the latter.

Turgenev advanced many of his own favorite notions through an admirable but weak character in *Smoke*, Potugin. Potugin is what Litvinov is in danger of becoming: a man so helplessly in love with Irina that he trails about after her to do her bidding. In lengthy conversations (or monologues, to put it more precisely) with Litvinov, Potugin sets forth his political and philosophical views, as, for instance, that Russia has contributed nothing to the progress of humankind and that Western civilization holds the only promise for Russia's future development. Potugin believes firmly in the West, but without rejecting his homeland even though he sees it in a jaundiced light.

In view of Turgenev's "plague on both your houses" political approach in *Smoke*, it is not astonishing that he was reviled from all sides for it. Members of the establishment resented being pictured as empty-headed reactionaries, and the radicals took offense at the depiction of the Gubarev circle, which was in fact one of Turgenev's most "antinihilist" creations. Pisarev, the chief radical critic still on the scene at the time, continued to display understanding for Turgenev, but even he criticized him for abandoning the line he had followed in creating Bazarov and turning instead to such a socially insignificant hero as Litvinov.

During the bulk of the 1860's, from 1864 to 1870, Turgenev resided near the Viardots in Baden-Baden. He made an average of one trip a year to Russia to keep abreast of developments, but fundamentally he was now living abroad and merely visiting his homeland. Toward the end of the decade the political situation in Russia eased noticeably, so at that time he published his reminiscences of Belinsky as well as a series of comments "On the Subject of *Fathers and Sons*," in which he fell victim to the compulsion felt by many of the "antinihilist" novelists to justify their books, so badly "misunderstood" by their readers. Ordinarily these efforts did their authors little good, and Turgenev's was no exception to the rule.

If Turgenev was at his most Slavophilic in the later 1850's, while writing *A Nest of Gentlefolk*, he was at his most Slavophobic at the conclusion of the 1860's. He was a European, he used to say then, and not particularly a Russian: "So bin Ich . . . ganz und gar Deutsch" (I am totally and completely German), he wrote to a correspondent in 1870. It is thus the more ironic that the conflict of that same year between France and Germany, two great bearers of Western civilization, drove him from his European nest: after the outbreak of hostilities the Viardots, being French citizens, had to leave Germany, and Turgenev followed them, first to London, then to France. And it was in France that the Russian-German lived from then on.

During the 1870's, while residing in France and continuing to pay occasional visits to Russia, Turgenev maintained relationships with certain of the greatest French writers of that day on a footing of at least equality, and sometimes superiority. He wrote and spoke French and German with native fluency and could handle English with some competence, a rare accomplishment for a nineteenth-century Russian. His vast correspondence, which has only recently been brought together in something resembling its entirety, was conducted in any one of four languages, and contains an immense mass of interesting commentary on contemporary literary and political events. Henry James, who first met Turgenev in 1875, declared him "the richest, the most delightful, of talkers," and found him and his work fascinating, although he was grieved that evidently Turgenev had no such high opinion of his, James's, writing. At the same time, as James emphasized in his memoirs of Turgenev, he was not at all gallicized: "No sojourner in Paris was less French than he," James recalled. And indeed the brothers Goncourt record in their journal not only samples of Turgenev's stimulating table talk, but also the fact that he discoursed mostly about Russia and things Russian. All of this speaks of the ambivalence of his character: in Russia he was a European, in Europe a Russian.

Turgenev's closest literary associates in Paris included Alphonse Daudet, Gustave Flaubert, and Émile Zola. Daudet recollected first meeting Turgenev at Flaubert's. Daudet being unusual among Frenchmen in that he was familiar with Turgenev's work, and Turgenev being unusual among authors in that he loved music, the two had much in common. Turgenev and Zola also got along well—Turgenev evidently had a hand in arranging for him to write a series of articles for the leading Russian liberal monthly, *Herald of Europe,* between 1875 and 1880—but there must have been some powerful temperamental differences between them. Thus the Goncourts record that once the two quarreled about love: Zola maintained that the only thing special about this emotional state was the prospect of copulation, while Turgenev argued that it was an extraordinary phenomenon distinct from its material and physiological aspects. Temperamentally Turgenev was probably closest to Flaubert in these years. He spent many evenings in conversation at his home, and their friends felt the two almost made a couple, with Turgenev playing the feminine role. Daudet commented that sometimes in nature "feminine souls are embodied in titanic forms" (Turgenev was a man of large build), and James remarked that Turgenev and Flaubert each "had a tender regard for the other," mixed with some compassion for Flaubert on Turgenev's part.

At the very time that Turgenev was living abroad and consorting so extensively with foreigners, however, in his writing he manifested a deep interest in peculiarly Russian themes. In "A Strange Story" (1869) he describes a mad wandering Holy Fool attended by a girl of good family who has found in him a leader before whom she can humiliate herself. Though he does not sympathize with the form it has taken, Turgenev cannot help admiring the strength of her devotion. "A King Lear of the Steppes," a long short story published in 1870 and since unduly neglected by students of Russian literature, is extraordinarily Russian in its execution despite the fact that it takes its title and plot idea from English literature. The hero of the story is a landowner named Kharlov, a man of immense build and of undisputed authority over his two daughters, their husbands, and his peasants. But when he sees in a dream a black foal, which he interprets as a symbol of impending death, he resolves to distribute his earthly goods to his heirs before his demise, confident that they will continue to revere him as before even without any material motive for doing so. Unhappily, he is mistaken, for once they obtain title to his property his heirs gradually deprive him of what little he has retained until finally they drive him from the estate altogether. Up to this point Kharlov's pride has kept him from complaining, but an almost chance remark kindles his rage: what he has created he can also destroy, he thinks to himself. In the concluding scene he mounts the roof of his former house and sets to wrecking it with his bare hands until he falls to the ground and injures himself so severely that he shortly dies. "A King Lear of the Steppes" is remarkable not only for the drama of its plot but also for its language, based on the colloquial style of the narrator and on peasant speech, and for its treatment of certain facets of the Russian character, not all of them positive.

Turgenev's interest in things Russian did not submerge his internationalist approach. "Torrents of Spring" (1872), his lengthiest work aside from his novels, presents a Russian hero involved with an Italian heroine in a German setting (Frankfurt and Wiesbaden) of thirty years before. Its plot is reminiscent of that of *Smoke,* although the hero, Sanin, is much weaker than Litvinov. It begins as something unusual for Turgenev, an account of love apparently fulfilled, with Sanin meeting a crucial test of resolution that enables him eventually to win a promise of marriage from the beautiful Gemma against substantial obstacles. But precisely when the reader has been lulled into the belief that Turgenev is after all capable of picturing successful love, the author abruptly drops his hero into the abyss of abject enslavement to the most predatory heroine he ever created, Polozova. Polozova, a wealthy woman of peasant origin, finds meaning in her life solely by enslaving men through the power of lust: at the moment of her triumph over Sanin, "her eyes, wide and so light they seemed white, expressed nothing but pitiless insensitivity and the satiety of victory." As a result of Polozova's intervention, Sanin loses his self-respect as well as his fiancée, and ends as one of the most embittered of Turgenev's numerous stand of lonely, middle-aged bachelors. Life, he muses to himself in the introduction, is not so much a stormy sea as a calm one with transparent waters. But beneath this superficially benign surface are many mysteries and many evils: on the "dark, slimy bottom" there are "hideous monsters," "all life's infirmities, sicknesses, griefs, insanity, poverty, blindness," any one of which may at any moment rise to the surface and capsize the boat in which the observer floats. The catastrophic shift in Sanin's fortunes illustrates this danger, and there is much in "Torrents of Spring" to justify Turgenev's referring to it as an "abortion" and remarking to a correspondent that he had conceived of it as full of blue sky and the song of larks, but it had turned out a poisonous toadstool: "I have never been so immoral," he added. The novelette, as it were, took on an evil life of its own under the author's pen.

Turgenev's sixth and last novel, *Virgin Soil,* appeared in early 1877 in the *Herald of Europe.* He worked over it for many years, composing thumbnail biographies of chief characters for his own use, but this did not guarantee the success of the final product, artistically the weakest of his novels. Evidently his prolonged residence in western Europe and his lack of contact with Russian reality sapped the vitality of an art that sought to deal with contemporary times. The critics condemned *Virgin Soil* roundly on its publication, and the verdict of later generations has not been appreciably more generous.

Virgin Soil is the most political of Turgenev's novels, being an attempt to trace the early history of the "movement to the people" that began about 1868. The "movement to the people" was based on the notion that radical students and intellectuals should conduct propaganda and agitation among the peasantry in order to make them a revolutionary force. But the ideas the young people preached were too foreign to the outlook of the peasantry, and the entire movement proved a fiasco. Turgenev wrote *Virgin Soil* largely to demonstrate how and why the radicals failed despite their good intentions.

The book's principal hero is Aleksey Nezhdanov, who comes from an established family: his father was a high-ranking officer, and he has been given a first-rate education by a strict Swiss schoolmaster. His very inner being is aristocratic, moreover: his fine facial features are an external reflection of his love of the beautiful and his sensitive intellect. One of his major weaknesses as a revolutionary is a tendency to write poetry, an inclination he carefully conceals after joining the radical movement. The novel's climax occurs when he sallies forth in peasant clothing to enlighten the common people, only to discover that he cannot "simplify" himself to the degree required, and that furthermore he cannot overcome his instinctive aversion to some nasty peasant traits. The conflict between his inborn instincts and his intellectual convictions leads to self-destruction, in one of the few instances where a Hamlet-like Turgenevian personage goes so far as to take his own life. In Nezhdanov's personality the ideal enters into an irreconcilable contradiction with the real.

There are those in *Virgin Soil* who remain faithful to the cause, however: the plain-looking Mashurina, who loves Nezhdanov with an unrequited love, and the energetic Markelov, who also discovers it is no simple matter to conduct agitation among the peasantry. A species of ideological barometer in the novel is Marianna Sinetskaya, who deserts her guardian's home to run away with Nezhdanov but refuses to marry him until he commits himself totally to her. This Nezhdanov cannot bring himself to do, but by means of a letter written before his suicide he joins her with the character offered as the book's positive hero, Solomin. Solomin, a practical man who operates along English lines, manages a factory on his estate. He springs from the common people and is not a great talker, but he displays "common sense" in his judgments. Turgenev clearly hoped the future would belong to him.

The radical critics violently disputed Turgenev's assessment of the class to which the future might belong, and he, as usual, attempted to mollify them by agreeing with them as far as he could. But they would not be placated, despite the novel's satirical thrusts against the aristocratic establishment. These were embodied especially in the person of Kollomeytsev, a pseudo-Westernizer who, though outwardly charming and graceful, is in fact a cruel exploiter of his peasants and a deep-dyed reactionary. Another despicable personage is Valentina Mikhailovna Sipyagina, reminiscent of such predatory Turgenevian females as Natalya Petrovna (*A Month in the Country*) in her rivalry with her ward, and of Polozova ("Torrents of Spring") in her desire to bind the naive Nezhdanov to herself by the bonds of love in order to inflate her own ego. Still, the erotic element, though important, is relatively less central in *Virgin Soil* than in any of the other novels.

Turgenev received honors as well as abuse in the latter half of the 1870's. In 1875 he settled for what remained of his life at Bougival near Paris, not far from the Viardots. He continued his excursions to Russia, as in the late summer of 1878, when he was reconciled with Tolstoy and visited the latter's estate at Yasnaya Polyana. But he made his most triumphal return to his homeland during a visit to Saint Petersburg and Moscow during the first months of 1879. At this time he was extensively feted by his fellow liberals in Russian society, and responded with pleasure to the evidences of his popularity among the reading public. Shortly thereafter, in June 1879, he journeyed to England to receive the honorary degree of doctor of civil law from Oxford University, a token of esteem from a nation he esteemed, and that he therefore cherished.

Almost exactly one year later, in June 1880, Turgenev participated in ceremonies connected with the unveiling of a monument to the great Russian poet Alexander Pushkin in Moscow. The festivities remain one of the outstanding public occasions in the history of Russian literature. Many leading writers were in attendance, and Dostoevsky in particular delivered the most famous speech of his career then. Turgenev chose to be cautious in defining Pushkin's place in Russian letters. He was ready to dub him the first "poet-artist" in Russian literature, he was willing to acknowledge him as the synthesizer of Russian literary language, but he would not crown him the "national poet" in the same sense in which Shakespeare and Goethe were considered the national poets of their respective homelands. Such ambiguity, however honest it may have been intellectually, did not suit the tenor of the occasion.

After the publication of *Virgin Soil* Turgenev's relatively sparse production was limited to short pieces. "A Desperate Character" (1881) presents an absorbing analysis of a certain type of personality that cannot stand the proprieties of staid bourgeois society and seems desperately bent on its own destruction. "The Song of Triumphant Love," also dating from 1881, is unusual in that it is set in sixteenth-century Ferrara instead of contemporary Russia or Russia of the recent past, and in that it deals with plainly supernatural occurrences, though in the form of a legend, connected with an unsuccessful love. A unique treatment of the theme of love and death is offered in "After Death" (later known as "Klara Milich"), written in 1882, the last full year of the author's life. The hero, a sensitive, lonely young man named Aratov, inspires love in a singer and actress, Klara Milich, though they have not met at the time. A strong-willed character who has promised to "take" the man she loves if she ever encounters him, she commits suicide onstage after an abortive attempt to bring Aratov to her feet during an interview in Moscow. Having failed to conquer him in this world, she returns to capture him in the next: Aratov falls in love with her after her death, sees her in dreams and visions, and ends by passing blissfully through the gate of death to join her. "Klara Milich" is one of Turgenev's most powerful statements on the exceptional nature of love, which can overcome the grave.

At the twilight of his writing career Turgenev effected something of a return to the poetic attempts of his first years in the *Poems in Prose,* brief lyrical vignettes on various subjects of usually not more than a page, and sometimes only a few lines. Written at different times between 1878 and 1882, each of them is carefully dated. Though frequently oversentimental, they treat many themes that had long been constants in Turgenev's work, and at the very least they are instructive as indices to his thinking in those years. Certain of them embody distillations of a philosophy of life derived from many years of observation of humankind's weaknesses and related to the capsule one-sentence aphorisms on human behavior with which he studded his novels and stories from the beginning, and some of which could be quite cynical. Philosophically speaking, however, the center of gravity of the

Poems in Prose lies not in such vignettes as these but in pieces on more serious, usually very pessimistic, subjects. One theme is the indifference of nature to human aspirations, which early received notable expression in the introduction to his "Excursion to the Woodlands" (1857): in the presence of the great forest, Turgenev wrote then, man "feels that the last of his brothers might vanish from the face of the earth, and not a single needle on these pine branches would twitch." Similarly, in "Conversation" the Jungfrau and the Finsteraarhorn look down distantly on the world below at intervals of thousands of years and express their satisfaction when the frenzied activities of antlike human beings in the lowlands cease and all is frozen and quiet. When the narrator inquires of personified nature in "Nature" what she is turning her attention to at that moment, she replies that she is strengthening the muscles of the flea so that he may more easily escape his enemies. To the narrator's protestations about human values, she remarks that she cherishes human beings no more and no less than any other of her creatures. One of the few prose poems with a religious coloration is "Christ," in which Jesus is perceived as a man with a face "like all other human faces" who by implication incorporates everything human within himself.

Two of the most famous sketches from the *Poems in Prose* deal with Russia and its domestic political situation. "The Threshold" points up both the dedication of the Russian revolutionaries and Turgenev's ambiguous attitude toward them. Questioned before being permitted to pass through a door, a girl says she is ready to die herself or commit a crime; she even realizes that she may one day lose faith in the cause to which she now dedicates herself. As she enters then, two voices accompany her, the first crying "Fool!" as the second responds "Saint!" In "The Russian Language," dated June 1882, Turgenev found moral sustenance in the tongue of which he was such a master: "In days of doubt, in days of gloomy meditation upon the fate of my homeland—you alone are my strength and support, oh great, mighty, honest, and free Russian language! Were it not for you how could we help despairing over everything done at home? But one must believe that such a language can have been given only to a great people!"

The most persistent theme in the prose poems, however, is that of death. It is central to the reminiscence of Turgenev's last meeting with Nekrasov. Its inevitability and unexpectedness are underlined in "The Old Woman" and "Tomorrow." It is treated allegorically in "The Insect," a tableau of a crowded hall into which flies a large and menacing insect. Everyone sees it and retreats from it in horror except its victim, who expires when it stings him on the forehead. The stolid resignation or deep despair of the common people when faced with the death of loved ones is the subject of two sketches. But in two others, both of them for some reason associated with sparrows, Turgenev sounds a note of hope or defiance: in "We Will Still Put Up a Fight" he draws inspiration from the cocky cheerfulness displayed by a family of sparrows while far above them circles the hawk who can destroy them any time he chooses; and in "The Sparrow" the mother bird's readiness to defend her young against an immense dog causes Turgenev to meditate: "Love, I thought, is stronger than death and the fear of death. Life maintains itself and develops only through that, through love."

Turgenev had long been preoccupied with death, of course. It had concerned him in some of his earliest works, and once in 1872, while discoursing at Flaubert's, he commented that he had always somehow been surrounded by "an odor of death, of nonbeing, of dissolution," a death that he defined as the inability to love. The predominance given the subject in the *Poems in Prose* became immediately relevant to his life when he fell ill with cancer in April 1883. From that time on the die was cast, though he experienced periods of temporary improvement. He continued his literary work when he could, publishing some new pieces and laboring over an edition of his collected writings, but death, however imagined—a black foal in "A King Lear of the Steppes," the more conventional skulls in one of the *Poems in Prose*, or a monkeylike creature huddled in a boat and holding a flask of dark liquid in a striking dream of Aratov's in "Klara Milich"—would not forever be denied. On 3 September 1883, Turgenev died at Bougival after an extremely painful illness. "His end," Henry James wrote, "was not serene and propitious, but dark and almost violent." This remark points to depths within Turgenev that he himself could not plumb, though he was aware of their existence.

At the end the expatriate was returned to Russia. In Paris, prominent Frenchmen paid tribute to his memory at the station from which he began his last journey, and in Saint Petersburg crowds gathered to escort his coffin to a niche in the Volkovo cemetery. There Turgenev lies in a section set aside for literary men, among those, like Dobrolyubov, who were his enemies in life, and those, like Belinsky, who were his friends. Death, as he had said of Nekrasov, reconciles all.

Selected Bibliography

EDITIONS

INDIVIDUAL WORKS

"Diary of a Superfluous Man." Moscow, 1850.
A Hunter's Notes. Moscow, 1852.
A Month in the Country. Moscow, 1855.
Rudin. Moscow, 1856.
A Nest of Gentlefolk. Moscow, 1859.
On the Eve. Moscow, 1860.
Fathers and Sons. Moscow, 1862.
Smoke. Moscow, 1867.
Torrents of Spring. Moscow, 1872.
Virgin Soil. Moscow, 1877.

COLLECTED WORKS

Turgenev's individual works were ordinarily published in contemporary journals, then shortly thereafter (in the case of novels particularly) in separate editions. His collected works were issued in multivolume editions several times during his lifetime (in 1860–1861, 1865, 1869–1871, and 1880, for example) and his complete works in 1883 and many times thereafter. During the Soviet period there have been several multivolume selected or complete editions of his works (in 1949, for example, and from 1953 to 1958). The edition upon which all scholarly work must now be based, however, is the *Polnoe sobranie sochinenii i pisem v dvadtsati vosmi tomakh* (Complete Works and Letters in 28 Volumes, Moscow and Leningrad, 1960–1968), which allots 15 volumes to his works and 13 to his extensive correspondence. This edition may be supplemented, but it is unlikely to be superseded for many years.

TRANSLATIONS

Constance Garnett long ago rendered the bulk of Turgenev's writing into English in *The Novels of Ivan Turgenev,* including his short stories (15 vols., London, 1894–1899). Translations of individual works in this century are almost too numerous to mention. A convenient selected edition, though poorly translated and not very extensive, is *The Vintage Turgenev* (2 vols., New York, 1960). The hundredth anniversary of Turgenev's death saw the publication of two excellent annotated editions of his letters: A. V. Knowles, editor and translator, *Turgenev's Letters* (New York, 1983); and David Lowe, editor and translator, *Turgenev: Letters* (2 vols., Ann Arbor, Mich., 1983).

BIOGRAPHICAL AND CRITICAL STUDIES

Brodianski, Nina. "Turgenev's Short Stories: A Revaluation." *Slavonic and East European Review* 32:70–91 (December 1953).

Carr, E. H. "Turgenev and Dostoevsky." *Slavonic Review* 8:156–163 (June 1929).

Chamberlin, William Henry. "Turgenev: The Eternal Romantic." *Russian Review* 5:10–23 (Spring 1946).

Folejewski, Zbigniew. "The Recent Storm Around Turgenev as a Point in Soviet Aesthetics." *Slavic and East European Journal* 6:21–27 (Spring 1962).

Freeborn, Richard. *Turgenev: The Novelist's Novelist.* New York, 1960.

Garnett, Edward. *Turgenev: A Study.* London, 1917.

Gettman, Royal. *Turgenev in England and America.* Urbana, Ill., 1941.

Howe, Irving. "Turgenev: The Politics of Hesitation." In *Politics and the Novel.* New York, 1957. Pp. 114–138.

Kagan-Kans, Eva. "Fate and Fantasy: A Study of Turgenev's Fantastic Stories." *Slavic Review* 18:543–560 (December 1969).

————. *Hamlet and Don Quixote: Turgenev's Ambivalent Vision.* The Hague and Paris, 1975.

Ledkovsky, Marina. *The Other Turgenev: From Romanticism to Symbolism.* Würzburg, 1973.

Lerner, Daniel. "The Influence of Turgenev on Henry James." *Slavonic and East European Review* 20:28–54 (December 1941).

Lloyd, John A. T. *Ivan Turgenev.* London, 1942.

Lowe, David, *Turgenev's "Fathers and Sons."* Ann Arbor, Mich., 1983.

Magarshack, David. *Turgenev: A Life.* London, 1954.

————, ed. and trans. *Ivan Turgenev: Literary Reminiscences and Autobiographical Fragments.* New York, 1958.

Mandel, Oscar. "Molière and Turgenev: The Literature of No-Judgment." *Comparative Literature* 11:233–249 (Summer 1959).

Matlaw, Ralph. "Turgenev's Art in *Spring Torrents.*" *Slavonic and East European Review* 35:157–171 (December 1956).

————. "Turgenev's Novels: Civic Responsibility and Literary Predilection." *Harvard Slavic Studies* 4:249–262 (1957).

Moser, Charles. "Turgenev: The Cosmopolitan Nationalist." *Review of National Literatures* 3(1):56–88 (Spring 1972).

Peterson, Dale. *The Clement Vision: Poetic Realism in Turgenev and James.* Port Washington, N.Y., 1975.

Pritchett, V. S. *The Gentle Barbarian: The Life and Work of Turgenev.* New York, 1977.

Ripp, Victor. *Turgenev's Russia: From "Notes of a Hunter" to "Fathers and Sons."* Ithaca, N.Y., and London, 1980.

Sayler, O. "Turgenieff as a Playwright." *North American Review* 214:393–400 (September 1921).

Schapiro, Leonard. *Turgenev: His Life and Times.* New York, 1978.

Sergievsky, Nicholas. "The Tragedy of a Great Love: Turgenev and Pauline Viardot." *American Slavic* and *East European Review* 5:55–71 (November 1946).

Waddington, Patrick. *Turgenev and England.* New York, 1981.

Wilson, Edmund. "Turgenev and the Life-Giving Drop." In *Ivan Turgenev: Literary Reminiscences and Autobiographical Fragments,* by David Magarshack, editor and translator. New York, 1958. Pp. 3–64.

Woodcock, George. "The Elusive Ideal: Notes on Turgenev." *Sewanee Review* 69:34–47 (January–March 1961).

Woolf, Virginia. "The Novels of Turgenev." *Yale Review* 23:276–283 (Winter 1934).

Yarmolinsky, Avrahm. *Turgenev: The Man, His Art and His Age.* New York, 1959.

BIBLIOGRAPHIES

Yachnin, Rissa, and David Stam. *Turgenev in English: A Checklist of Works By and About Him.* New York, 1962.

CHARLES A. MOSER

THEODOR FONTANE

(1819–1898)

INTRODUCTION

IN THE TWILIGHT of the nineteenth century two remarkably gifted but very different writers, both living in the burgeoning metropolis of Berlin, made an extraordinary impact on German letters. One was hitherto unknown, the youthful and impulsive dramatist Gerhart Hauptmann, who, with his naturalistic dramas of mimicry and milieu, singlehandedly shook the German stage out of the lethargy and mediocrity into which it had fallen half a century before. The other was Theodor Fontane, already highly respected as a poet and critic, who now, late in life, wrote an astonishing series of multifaceted novels that, in their rich social fabric and thematic depth, breathed new life into the traditional epic mode in Germany, transforming it into a form able to compete with the great social novel then dominating the literary scene in England, France, and Russia. Almost simultaneously, these two writers, each in his own distinct way, took up the slackened reins of leadership in German letters at a time when those who had previously held them, the poetic realists, were withdrawing from the scene. Deftly and surely, with a keen sense of purpose and a sparkling vitality, both men redrew the map of German literature.

At first, and for a long time afterward, Hauptmann's achievements overshadowed those of Fontane. Hauptmann's plays electrified audiences night after night, in theater after theater, city after city. The German stage attained more color and candor than it had exhibited in decades, and the playwright's success was instantaneous, indeed almost hypnotic. But the breathtaking impact of Hauptmann's career had another effect, which has not been clearly pointed out in literary scholarship: it clouded the public's view of Fontane's literary accomplishments. These, though far less spectacular by comparison, and certainly much less sensational, were no less original. Fontane had published most of his innovative novels during virtually the identical span of years in which Hauptmann's best plays were written, but for the public—as well as for critics in the final decade of the nineteenth century—it was Hauptmann rather than Fontane who stood out as the premier writer of the day. So entrenched was this opinion, in fact, that it lingered on far into the twentieth century.

The sobering effects of historical perspective, however, are now in the process of reversing this view. The further we have moved away from the nineteenth century, the more the image of Hauptmann has faded while that of Fontane has become brighter. If Hauptmann's fame was more immediate, Fontane's is proving to be more enduring. As the plays of Hauptmann have lost their urgency and become less and less a part of the German stage repertoire, the number of editions of Fontane's novels has soared. It would appear that an increasingly solid case is developing for a reassessment of the two commanding figures in German literature during the closing decade of the nineteenth century.

The opinions on this subject of a writer of Thomas Mann's stature are worth noting. As late as 1925 Mann still considered Hauptmann to be "the nation's king." But as the years passed the exalted pedestal on which Hauptmann had once stood seemed to crumble, and Mann eventually came to speak of the dramatist in a tone that was more flippant than respectful. In 1949, referring to Hauptmann in *Die Entstehung des "Doktor Faustus"* (*The Genesis of a Novel,* 1961), he wrote: "Undoubtedly there had been something sham, something decidedly empty, about that personality. . . . You could hang for hours on the lips of the man, strangely spellbound, as he talked on with many gestures, his snow-white hair flying, and yet from all the talk scarcely anything would 'come out.'"

How unwavering, by contrast, was the genuine esteem in which the novelist throughout his life held the aged Fontane. As early as 1910 Mann ranked him with those "classic old men" who are "ordained to show humanity the ideal qualities of that last stage of life: benignity, kindness, justice, humor, and shrewd wisdom—in short a recrudescence on a higher plane of childhood's artless restraint." A tribute of this sort constitutes high praise for Fontane; coming from an imaginative writer of the stature and sensibility of Thomas Mann, it is the highest praise possible. "The spectacle of the old Fontane," he said, had "hardly a counterpart in the history of the intellect." It showed "a phenomenon of old age returning artistically, intellectually, and morally to youth, a second and true youth and maturity, in advanced years."

Mann's voice, rather solitary at the time, has proved to be prophetic. Decades were to pass before others would notice what he had realized almost immediately. He never strayed from his conviction. Indeed it seems that he grew more and more indefatigable as the years went by in his public praise of Fontane's sudden but mature blossoming at the end of the nineteenth century. In 1919 he boldly appealed to German critics to accept Fontane's *Effi Briest* (1895) as one of the six best novels of world literature. In 1939 he lectured the students of Princeton University in an effort to win them over to Fontane's late novels, especially to his favorite, *Effi Briest.* Three years later he endeavored to persuade Agnes Meyer, the influential wife of the owner of the *Washington Post,* to read the novel, saying that the aged Fontane had there displayed "incredible charm" as a writer and "truly supreme grace." To the very end of his life Mann remained unshaken in his conviction that Fontane, in old age, had reached extraordinary artistic and intellectual heights. He made many statements reaffirming this position, but in none did he reveal his unflagging opinion more clearly than in a remark made in 1951 to the American Fontane scholar Henry H. H. Remak; at that time Mann stated that his original essay of 1910, in which he had first ascribed classic greatness to Fontane, seemed in retrospect to be the finest critical piece he had ever written.

When in that seminal essay Thomas Mann detected the lasting radiance that the aged Fontane had bequeathed to German literature, he also speculated that the first six decades of Fontane's life had been spent in almost deliberate preparation for the last two. Rarely had a man of letters taken so long to prepare himself for greatness. The result was that when Fontane finally sat down to write the deep, rich novels of his old age, he had already acquired a mastery almost unparalleled in the history of literature. This mastery, derived from a lifetime of experiences as diversified, broad, and intense as any writer ever brought to the craft of the novel, combined with a powerful and acute mind that could mobilize these vast resources in the interest of fiction. In what follows we shall try to show how Fontane's greatness came about.

THEODOR FONTANE

EARLY LIFE

Theodor Fontane was born on 30 December 1819 in the sleepy Prussian town of Neuruppin, where his father had acquired a local pharmacy. Despite his provincial birthplace, everything about Fontane was decidedly unparochial from the start. His parents prided themselves on their dual Franco-Prussian heritage. Both were descendants of French Huguenot émigrés who had married into native Prussian families. A rich admixture of French and German cultures resulted, manifesting itself in numerous transnational family customs, language habits, and religious practices. Such was the invigorating atmosphere in which Fontane grew up. Later his ties to this dual cultural heritage were to be strengthened when he married his childhood sweetheart, Emilie Rouanet-Kummer (1824–1902). She came from the identical mixed ethnic background. They were married in 1850 in a French Reformed Church in Berlin, and after a marriage of almost fifty years, with four children who survived infancy, both found their final resting places in the French cemetery of Berlin.

At a young age Fontane moved with his family to Swinemünde, a seaside resort on the Baltic, and this contributed to another broadening of his cosmopolitan outlook on life. The town had belonged to Sweden and various German states at different times in its history, and Swedish and German elements had generously intermingled in its development. Many foreigners had also settled there. Together with the transient population of sailors and merchants visiting from all over northern Europe, they had given the town a truly international character, which, as Fontane himself later recalled, had made the local society peculiarly free of those narrow philistine values so typical of the average inland provincial town in Prussia. The citizens of Swinemünde also took a more than usual interest in happenings in other parts of the world, the details of which were rapidly circulated by the many seafaring visitors on the streets. Fontane records how deeply moved he was by stories about the War for Greek Independence of 1821–1832, the Russo-Turkish War of 1828–1829, the July Revolution in Paris of 1830, the conquest of Algeria that began in 1830, the Belgian revolt against the Netherlands during the 1830's, and the Polish Insurrection of 1830–1831, all of which occurred during his boyhood in Swinemünde.

In contrast to these events of global magnitude, daily school life appeared to young Theodor to be insufferably dull, and as a consequence he went in for truancy on a grand scale. He transferred from school to school in various towns of Prussia and finally left for good. Then he shifted from one apprenticeship to another in his father's profession of pharmacist. Concomitantly he started to write poetry, and was fortunate in having some of it published in newspapers. Through this activity, he came into contact with publishers and with men of letters.

THE IMPACT OF FREDERICK WILLIAM IV'S ANGLOPHILIA

Still, for all his literary inclinations and connections, Fontane might never have nurtured the ambition of supporting himself by his pen had he not found an unexpected vocation in letters as a result of the unprecedented wave of anglophilia that swept across Prussia at the time. Never before had such a surge of foreign influence reached the shores of the German-speaking world; nor was it ever to return. It assumed its unusual proportions with the accession of Frederick William IV to the throne of Prussia in 1840, precisely when Fontane was in his most impressionable years. Strangely enough, though, little mention has been made in Fontane criticism of how decisively the anglophilic whims of this extraordinary monarch affected the career of his youthful subject.

Frederick William IV nourished the romantic dream of setting up an ecclesiastical alliance between Prussia and Great Britain, at that time the two strongest Protestant nations in the world. The alliance was to have as its keystone a joint Prusso-English ecumenical bishopric with its seat at Jerusalem. The incumbent was to alternate between appointees of the Prussian and English crowns, with the entire enterprise financially supported equally by Prussia and Britain. The common interests and Protestant-Germanic heritages of both nations were to unite in a centralized location comparable to and even more important than the rival centers of Catholicism at Rome and Eastern Orthodoxy at Constantinople. Frederick William IV used all the energy at his command to make the project a reality, which it became when the charter establishing the Evangelical-Anglican bishopric was drawn up in 1841. The newly realized Anglo-Prussian bond of fraternity was then further cemented when the king journeyed to England in 1842 in order to stand as godfather at the baptism of the prince of Wales (later King Edward VII). Numerous visits to England by members of the Prussian royal family followed, and these eventually culminated in the marriage of the English princess royal and the heir to the crown of Prussia (later Emperor Frederick III).

Prussian Protestants now began to rally ever-increasingly around Britain as a champion of Germanic-Protestant ideology. The entire Prussian nation felt drawn to English culture and manners, and British institutions were studied with an assiduity and warmth of admiration as never before. Frederick William IV's ambassador to the Court of Saint James for more than a decade, Baron Christian Karl von Bunsen, took an English wife and shared with her a love for England stronger than that for his own country. The official court-appointed historiographer of Prussia, Leopold von Ranke, likewise married an English-woman, and when he took up his influential pen to write his voluminous *Englische Geschichte* (*A History of England*, 1875), it seemed only natural that the work should be richly colored by his monarch's pro-English bias, and that the torch Ranke carried so authoritatively should further stoke the fires of anglophilia in Prussia.

Fontane felt the impact of all this and was deeply moved by it. Less than four years after his monarch had begun to press for the new Anglo-Prussian alliance, he seized an opportunity to visit London. He had barely started his obligatory year of military service when a friend offered to take him on holiday to England. Fontane asked for a furlough from his military duties. It has been said that this request for a leave of absence from the Prussian army in order to take a private trip abroad bordered on the incredible, and that the idea that permission could be granted was even more bizarre. But neither the plea nor the affirmative reply it received was at all preposterous. Frederick William IV's eager determination to promote close contact with England must have made the officials of the realm as eager to approve the request as the young subject had been to make it. The furlough was instantly granted, and Fontane, having shed his uniform for civilian clothes, departed for London with haste and undisguised joy.

The trip proved to be seminal for the start of his vocation in letters. Ingeniously deciding to take advantage of the Prussian public's craving for stories about Britain during the height of the sovereign's anglophilia, Fontane became a diligent reporter of Britain's assets and liabilities, virtues and foibles, for the Prussian press. No other important German writer before or since has acquired a deeper knowledge of the whole range of British life and letters than he did, and this immersion in a foreign culture singularly furthered the development of his critical prowess and writing skill.

What engaged him most in his reportage of British institutions was the drama of the individual will pitted against social forces. Again and again he notes how the individual Englishman constituted little more than an insignificant speck in a huge, impersonal crowd. Particularly in London, the largest city in the world at the time, he is aware of this at almost every turn. Traditional Fontane scholarship has passed rather lightly over this negative side of the author's reporting on Britain, but there can be no doubt that his protracted commentaries on England reveal a strong preoccupation with the loss of individuality resulting from a grinding conformity to established social mores. Fontane continuously observes how individual values are sacrificed to such conventions as the widespread desire to keep up with fashions, the relentless race for wealth, the anxious concern to maintain proper etiquette, the inherited inclinations of pride and prejudice, and, above all, the worship of stifling tradition.

Thus the individual social life of the average Englishman seemed to Fontane to be strangled by a constricting web of established customs. Englishmen are inwardly not as free as the Prussians, he writes to his friend Theodor Storm in 1853. English democracy he denounces as a farce, pointing out that the elected legislators did nothing but pliantly obey the bidding of a capitalistic oligarchy; and individual religious life in the established Church of England constituted for him nothing more than mechanical churchgoing. Curiously, or perhaps significantly, never in his English letters does Fontane mention the stirring piety of dissenting Methodism, a phenomenon he could not have failed to notice in London. Nor does he ever make the slightest reference to the fervor of the High Church revival, which he surely must have encountered in his study tour of Oxford and heard about through *The Times*, a paper he read faithfully. Instead, he chooses to focus on the embarrassing, the incongruous, the hypocritical in English religious life. He notes, for instance, that the members of the English episcopacy receive their appointments from the crown to ensure that the crown will be obeyed. The regulations governing the observance of the English Sunday, as he interprets them, serve only to legislate a further denial of personal freedom. The individual citizen, he comments, is required by law to maintain and respect an austere silence on the sabbath while at the same time the ornate carriage of the archbishop of Canterbury clatters noisily down London's streets and the bands strike up their lively airs in front of the windows of the queen. In all, Fontane found it impossible to echo his sovereign's unrestrained enthusiasm for England and the English.

THE PREFERENCE FOR SCOTTISH OVER ENGLISH SOCIETY

Inevitable comparisons of English with Scottish society hardened Fontane's disturbing observations. Very early, it seems, he had been conditioned in favor of the latter. In his boyhood he had been an avid reader and passionate disciple of Sir Walter Scott; the spell of Edinburgh's popular son hung over him almost from the start. Fontane's roots in Calvinism lent the Scottish-Presbyterian world still more appeal. Then, alone in London in 1852, he struck up a deep friendship with a young man from a Scottish family, James Morris. The two often sat up together late into the night engaged in intense and amicable discussion. It is not difficult to imagine, therefore, what strong sympathies were kindled in Fontane for the land of the thistle.

Scholarship has been rather chary in pointing out how sharply Fontane's impressions of England and Scotland diverge. Yet the reader of Fontane's multifarious essays on Britain cannot fail to be struck by the degree to which the images of these two societies clash. In the rivalry between the English and Scottish capitals, Edinburgh is clearly Fontane's favorite. If in England, and especially in the metropolis of London, the individual seems to Fontane to lose his identity in a mire of convention, the Scotsman, he observes, prides himself on his nonconformist attitudes, on his forthright individualism, on the courage of his independent convictions (as evidenced, for example, by the anomalous temperance preachers on Edinburgh's street corners), on the primitiveness of his classless society, and on the wildness of his native scenery. If Fontane discusses English institutions uncharitably, indeed on occasion sardonically, he exults when he talks about the Scots, and most especially so when he refers to those regions of Scotland, such as the Highlands, that seem to him to be least touched by English manners. Significantly, Fontane sedulously avoids describing the manufacturing areas of the Lowlands; there is no reference to the submission of the workers to the monotony of inexorable factory discipline in the textile mills of Paisley; no portrait of the overcrowded tenement districts adjacent to the Clyde shipyards; and no intimation of the horrible squalor surrounding the Lanarkshire coalfields. Altogether, Fontane speaks so affectionately of the Scots that the reader senses a writer utterly bent on dismissing their vices in order to extol their virtues all the more.

Fontane's early-felt Scottish bias naturally aroused in him a literary interest in the belles lettres of Scotland; and that meant, above all, an interest in Scottish balladry, for it is in that genre Scotland excelled. He was as drawn to the power of Scotland's narrative verse as he had been to the magic of everything else Scottish. He read, reread, and never ceased to extol the Scottish ballads collected in Thomas Percy's three volumes of *Reliques of Ancient English Poetry* (1765) and in Scott's *Minstrelsy of the Scottish Border* (1802), both of which were reprinted many times during the nineteenth century. The Scots' ballads, with their rugged freshness and simplicity of language, appealed to him as strongly as the mannered verses of the foremost English poet of the day, Alfred Lord Tennyson, repelled him. Tennyson's lyrics seemed to him to have been written too much in response to the demands of an overly polished, overly sophisticated taste; and so they lacked the ability to voice basic human feelings. This was an elitist poetry for the chosen few, he felt, in contrast to the Scottish ballads, with their primitive, wide-ranging appeal to the common people.

The impression that this cardinal attribute of the Scottish muse made on Fontane cannot be overestimated. If in his observations of London society he had been annoyed by the sight of the individual unable to free himself from the constraints of custom and tradition, he now took buoyant pleasure in observing, via the compelling poetic medium of the ballad, the individual's triumph in his struggle against external forces—and in truth, the Scottish ballad takes special delight in making heroes out of such individuals.

Fontane became so enraptured by this balladry that it seemed only normal, given his literary inclinations, for him to want to imitate those jubilant songs of personal ascendancy. The burning desire to glorify the individual in ballad form now became, side by side with his journalism, a major force in his literary development.

MEMBERSHIP IN THE TUNNEL ÜBER DER SPREE

Still, Fontane might not have developed into a successful balladeer had he not been, during the many years in which he was busy passing judgment on British institutions, a member of the Berlin writers' club *Tunnel über der Spree* (Tunnel over the Spree). Modern criticism tends to play down the importance of this club for Fontane's literary vocation, brushing aside his membership in it as incidental, irrelevant, indeed even detrimental to the author's literary development. In particular, Fontane's chief modern biographer, Hans-Heinrich Reuter, has disparaging things to say about this club. Its members, in his opinion, were aesthetic snobs governed by rigid rules similar to those used in the sterile musical contests satirized in Richard Wagner's opera *Die Meistersinger* (1862–1867). Such a downgrading of the club is most unfortunate, and this negative opinion stands in need of correction. For it must be recognized that in his affiliation with this group Fontane reaped the benefit of a singularly valuable literary apprenticeship. Nowhere in the world at the time could the excellence of the literary schooling of the *Tunnel über der Spree* be matched, except perhaps in the congregation of remarkable literati gathered around Hans Christian Andersen in Copenhagen.

The *Tunnel über der Spree* took the first word of its name from the famous tunnel under the Thames completed in 1843, at the height of the raging anglophilia in Prussia; the last word substituted the name of the main river flowing through Berlin for its counterpart in London. The name itself signified an attempt to transplant a venerable institution from the Thames to the Spree, for the club was patently similar to "The Club" of Samuel Johnson a century earlier in London. In each instance the membership comprised an association of highly civilized men, some of the best minds in the city. Dr. Johnson's club included such notables as James Boswell, Oliver Goldsmith, Edmund Burke, David Garrick, and Sir Joshua Reynolds. Among those in the Berlin group were Franz Kugler, Adolf von Menzel, Emanuel Geibel, Paul Heyse, and Theodor Storm. Each group met regularly once a week for several hours in the smoke-filled room of a local tavern in order to apply its collective intelligence to the practical criticism of literature. Regardless of whether a club's member were giving or receiving criticism within such an intimate circle of fastidious minds, each session offered an occasion for thorough schooling in literary technique. In the constant crucible of rebuttal, amendment, and refinement one could temper and sharpen one's aesthetic judgment and develop felicity of expression.

In the Berlin club Fontane was thus able to present his ballad specimens to a company of congenial men thoroughly conversant with good literature; he could observe them taking pleasure in his successes or shaking their heads in dismay over his blunders. On other occasions he could listen to a fellow author reading from recent work, could take part in the heated but incisive give-and-take of subsequent debate, and—after replenishing his glass with cooling beer—could calmly cast his free, unhampered vote of acceptance or rejection concerning what his rival had produced. Here Fontane learned to orchestrate words, manipulate plots, switch details, regulate the overall balance, and avoid irrelevant sallies, all the while adding concreteness and credibility to what he said. Best of all, he learned to time the delivery of the punchline—in other words, to enlist even the most discriminating of audiences in his favor. It was Fontane's membership in the *Tunnel* that provided him with that combination of fellowship and discerning criticism that every writer secretly covets but few succeed in obtaining.

THE BALLADEER

Fontane now combined this exemplary schooling with his eager wish to imitate the balladry that was so fashionable in Scotland. He worked hard. As a result, he came to march, as Thomas Mann tells us, "at the head of the procession" of balladeers in Germany. He became the most eminent representative in his time of a long line of German ballad writers, some of them the most illustrious names in German literary history—Johann Wolfgang von Goethe, Friedrich von Schiller, Clemens Brentano, Joseph von Eichendorff, Annette von Droste-Hülshoff, Eduard Mörike, and Heinrich Heine.

Of all the ballads forged by Fontane in the purgatorial fires of criticism during sessions of the *Tunnel über der Spree*, none has endeared itself more to the hearts of readers and listeners than *Archibald Douglas*, which Fontane recited before a spellbound *Tunnel* audience on the evening of 3 December 1854. The reception accorded this particular ballad in the more than one hundred and twenty-five years since its birth has been extraordinary.

Few anthologies of German verse have failed to include it. Indeed, no other ballad written by Fontane either before or after has established itself in the anthologies with anywhere near as much persistence.

In *Archibald Douglas* Fontane produced a ballad of equal rank with the very best world literature has to offer in the genre. Similar in theme to Rudyard Kipling's immortal lyric "The Ballad of East and West" (1889), Fontane's poem tells the moving story of a Scottish king and a member of a dissenting clan who become brothers in peace and love after having opposed each other in strife and hatred. The starkly delineated story of these two characters is also a ballad about an individual at odds with his clan and a clan opposing its sovereign. Two heroes emerge: the one a mighty king who humbles himself in order to bring to a halt a destructive feud, the other a lonely subject whose abiding love gives him the superhuman strength to stem the tide of his sovereign's anger. On reflection, the reader wonders which of these two individuals represents the greater hero, the stubborn king whose stony heart melts in compassion or the simple clansman whose pure and indomitable love subdues his monarch's enmity. In the final analysis, however, we are given to understand that it is the individual subject who gains the ultimate victory, and so it is for him that Fontane has reserved the most distinctive laurels.

Despite the remarkable lucidity and simple urgency with which the story unfolds, the ballad exhibits an astonishingly high degree of artistic complexity. An abundance of clever structural devices continuously reflect the conflict between the two contrasting atmospheres, mirroring the characters. Narrative is interwoven with direct discourse, epic composure with dramatic action; past is juxtaposed with present, childhood with old age, strength with weakness, movement with rest, and constrained inertia with vibrant propulsion. The striking imagery contributes as much to the effect as does the paucity of inci-

dent; the imbroglios of real life seem to be as important to it as is the quaintness of remote legend. Fact and myth compete for our attention no less than the interchanging tetrameter and trimetric stress patterns, the alternating *abab* rhyme scheme, the opposing incantations of iambic and anapestic meter.

Later in his life, Fontane occasionally returned to the ballad form when a sudden inspiration compelled it—as, for instance, when he composed such isolated masterworks as *Gorm Grymme* (King Gorm of Denmark, 1865), *Die Brück am Tay* (*The Bridge on the Tay,* 1880), *John Maynard* (1886), and *Herr von Ribbeck auf Ribbeck im Havelland* (*Squire Ribbeck at Ribbeck in Havelland,* 1889). But his most intensive period of ballad writing came to a halt after his stunning success with *Archibald Douglas.* For the dire political and economic conditions at the time in Prussia convinced him that the ballad's presentation of heroic deeds contradicted the reality of the world closest to him. The concise form of the ballad, with its concentration on a hero-figure, created an image of the individual towering above, and even entirely removed from, society as a whole. Current events in Prussia belied such an assumption.

THE EXPERIENCE OF 1848 AND ITS AFTERMATH

In March 1848 a rebellion had erupted on the streets of Berlin; the citizens demanded universal suffrage and an end to absolutist rule. Frederick William IV, fearful that his throne might topple, reluctantly announced his readiness to make concessions. For some unexplained reason, though, shots rang out from somewhere among the insurgents. Royalist troops responded with a volley of gunfire. Soon revolution was in full swing; in response, the now totally intimidated sovereign quickly capitulated to the revolutionaries on all scores, readily granting a constitutional government.

For the populace, however, there was no real victory. The uprising had taken a terrible toll in suffering, injury, and death, and the economy lay in tatters: food became scarce and prices kept rising, as did unemployment. At the same time, the destruction wrought by the revolution had to be paid for; taxes became oppressive and bankruptcies were an everyday occurrence. The economic blight was exacerbated by incessant wrangling among the newly elected legislators over the best means to cope with it; this in turn doomed true parliamentary government to failure and returned power to the king, although in a weakened form. All of this naturally produced a political instability that served only to aggravate an already bad situation.

As a shroud of misery descended on the hapless nation, huge segments of the population began to emigrate. Year after year the number of emigrants seeking political freedom and relief from poverty abroad increased. The year 1854, when Fontane completed *Archibald Douglas*, proved to be the sorriest of all. In that year more citizens than ever left their homeland, hoping to escape the burden of the times. Fontane had been a daily eyewitness to all this turmoil. The grim state of affairs made him increasingly aware of how inextricably trapped all individuals, king and citizen alike, became in the shifting vicissitudes of political and economic imponderables. Against this background the jubilant ballads that glorified solitary feats of heroism seemed cruelly deceptive, and thus Fontane felt compelled to abandon the ballad as his principal form of literary expression.

THE WAR CORRESPONDENT

Turning now to prose, Fontane embarked upon the ambitious undertaking of chronicling the social and political events of the world as he saw them at close hand. For many years he wrote for a great variety of German newspapers and journals, and regularly during this period he modified his articles into book form. Between 1854 and 1889 sixteen volumes of his refurbished journalism were published. The earliest of these offers commentaries culled from his observations of England and Scotland. Other volumes consist of essays on the social and historical life of the countryside surrounding Berlin.

The bulk of Fontane's journalistic effort, however, and by far its most exciting part, comprises his war correspondence from the battlefields of the three major armed conflicts that led to Germany's unification under Prussian leadership: the Dano-German War of 1864, the Austro-Prussian War of 1866, and the Franco-Prussian War of 1870–1871. It is surprising that there has been so little investigation of these war chronicles. Fontane scholars have tended to dismiss this huge productivity as meaningless dabbling. Only a solitary historian, Gordon Craig, has taken any of these war books seriously, and very rightly so; for in these accounts Fontane reveals himself, no less than anywhere else in his writings, to be a ubiquitous witness of human life. For twelve long years, as he said in a letter to his old aristocratic friend Mathilde von Rohr in 1876, he had worked day and night on these accounts. The enormous amount of time and effort put into them should alone constitute sufficient warrant for emphasizing them in any survey of Fontane's life and work. But the war books also deserve to be read for their brilliance. The author reanimates for his readers the vast panoramas of the war theaters he saw; he allows his audience to eavesdrop in the tents where strategy was being made; and he passes judgment on the personages involved with an always convincing candor and assurance. Most impressive of all is the way he succeeds in enlisting our sympathies for genuine war heroes; and these are by no means limited to the Prussians. In the Prussian-Hanoverian conflict, for instance, Fontane clearly switches sides and tells us that it is the Hanoverians for whom he feels the warmth of affection. They fought gloriously, and they died gloriously; in defeat, he says, they were the true victors. The reader feels the same way.

Fontane is at his best in these war chronicles when great events are set in motion and great men people the stage. Whether referring to friend or foe, his accounts flare into life when they touch on great personalities. There is a flavor of the ballad-hero in all this, but now the central characters emerge as truly outstanding only when they are seen interlocked in a complex set of historical circumstances. The literary form of war correspondence thus offered Fontane the ideal medium to portray what he could not in the ballad: with the descriptions of colorful battle arenas and bewildering numbers of military participants, he could show how a multitude of factors play as large a role in life as do the calculations of prominent individuals. The accounts have as their backbone, therefore, narratives depicting an astonishing number of marching armies, involving vast resources of manpower and supplies as they move across wide stretches of Europe's terrain. The theaters of war become as momentous as individual acts of military heroism, to such an extent that the reader is sometimes kept guessing whether Fontane wishes to focus more attention on the multifarious scenes of battle or on the brilliant officers who, either in the triumph of victory or in the desolation of defeat, left their indelible mark on the history of their time. In the last analysis, however, neither the one nor the other but the incessant dialogue between these two forces, the individual and the external event, carries the heaviest accent in these accounts. Characteristically, grandiose battle scenes are interlaced again and again with extensive biographical vignettes of military strategists. Fontane develops a real passion for this interlacing technique; indeed, it constitutes perhaps his special literary achievement as a war correspondent, an achievement that becomes quite apparent, for instance, when his war chronicles are compared with those of that other master war correspondent who was to follow him a few decades later, Winston Churchill.

THE CHRONICLER OF THE PRUSSIAN COUNTRYSIDE

Fontane's coverage of the three major Prussian wars in his lifetime is so imposing in its sheer massiveness, so tumultuous and clamorous, so rich in colorful adventure and eventful episode, that one might reasonably expect it to distract attention from his less bulky and less exciting set of essays depicting the social and historical life of the quiet countryside surrounding Berlin. Like the war correspondence, though, these discourses, published in four volumes over a period of many years and known collectively as the *Wanderungen durch die Mark Brandenburg* (Travels Through the March of Brandenburg), are also notable for their penetration into both the general nature of social conditions and the peculiar nature of outstanding individuals.

The provincial life of a specific geographical area, both contemporary and historic, passes here before our eyes in a slowly shifting focus. In these pages Fontane depicts his travels up and down the countryside, mostly on foot, moving from town to town, from village to village; crossing featureless tracts of land as well as more noteworthy terrain; inspecting ancient castles, churches, and graveyards; gazing upon monuments and objects of art; visiting magnificent baronial estates, humble farmhouses, and wayside taverns. His readers may eavesdrop on conversations with local residents from every possible walk of life and learn with Fontane about matters of historic interest gleaned from all sorts of dusty papers and documents. The wealth of minute detail contributing to this panorama of the Brandenburgian landscape is truly impressive.

Yet at no time, it is important to note, does this scene-painting ever grow monotonous, for Fontane punctuates his travelogue with captivating biographical asides. These inject vigor into the geographical and historical descriptions and prevent the account from becoming a mere Baedeker of scenic points. As on a checkerboard, biographical vignettes alternate with descriptions of the countryside. We see, for instance, how noble squires from centuries-old aristocratic families guard and shape the landscape's destiny, just as we observe how the landscape conditions its gentry. Each holds the other in an eternal process. *"Vivat et crescat gens Knesebeckiana in aeternum"* (May the Knesebeck family live and increase forever), we read in reference to a noble family, whose various members in different generations loom prominently in the annals of the province. Brandenburg's horizon, as Fontane paints it, would be unthinkable without the quiet, unpretentious heroes of its landed gentry; they in turn would be unthinkable without the provincial soil and heritage that nurture them. Fontane goes to infinite pains in his chronicle to rescue an unusually large number of such parochial individuals from oblivion. He shows what eminent service they rendered to their community. The vicissitudes of fortune they endured in solemn loyalty to their native land make each of them a hero in his own right, give each a claim to fame. Throughout, this crisscross of biographical asides and environmental description in the tightly knit fabric of the *Wanderungen* parallels the interlocking of sharply drawn military heroes and panoramic battle scenes that gives Fontane's war correspondence its characteristic quality.

By early 1876 fifteen volumes of Fontane's reorganized journalistic correspondence had been published. Writing them had amounted to an exhaustive and exhausting undertaking, and had consumed a good part of his energy for more than twenty years. The final volume alone contains more than a thousand pages of print. In all these many volumes, in all the many years spent working on this correspondence, Fontane focused his attention almost incessantly, it seems, on the constant interplay of outstanding, heroic individuals with the forces of political, geographical, and environmental circumstance. Milieu had become for him as important as the solitary feats of heroism he had once glorified in the ballad; both, he now realized, were locked in a neverending contest.

THE LESSON OF THE KULTURKAMPF

Fontane's urgency to investigate further the relationship between the individual and his environment was quickened immeasurably as a result of employment he obtained in the 1870's with the *Vossische Zeitung,* the most outstanding newspaper at the time in the German-speaking world. He went to work as a theater critic, but the position he occupied is not in itself as important as Fontane scholars like to think, for the German stage in the 1870's suffered from an almost unbelievable mediocrity, and in light of the sterile nature of German drama at the time, Fontane's caustic reviews, however lively their manner, hardly constitute brilliant or noteworthy pieces of writing. It did not, after all, take too much ingenuity to find fault with plays that were full of faults.

What made employment with the *Vossische Zeitung* important for Fontane's development as a writer was rather that this new affiliation carried with it an attendant interest in the paper's reporting of the daily vicissitudes of German politics in the 1870's, and that meant, above all, an interest in the paper's coverage of the *Kulturkampf,* the German government's "battle for civilization" against the Catholic Church, which was undeniably the dominant political issue of the decade. As an employee of the *Vossische Zeitung,* Fontane was necessarily familiar with the paper's excellent reportage of the acrimonious debates in the national assembly, or *Reichstag,* the only forum in Germany where grievances against the policies of the imperial government could be freely aired without fear of governmental censure or suppression; and of all the debates in the *Reichstag* that inflamed the tempers of legislators in the 1870's, none raged more furiously than those accompanying the imperial government's *Kulturkampf.*

When the German nation became officially unified in 1871, the new imperial government immediately took steps to complete the process of unification by eliminating as much as possible all remaining vestiges of national diversity and parochialism, and by creating new institutions aimed at a more homogeneous and efficient nation. One of the most far-reaching laws to be enacted gave the centralized state complete authority over matters of schooling. The freedom of parents to make decisions at the local level about the education of their children was henceforth severely curtailed, if not altogether restricted. The Catholic church, seeing in this policy an infringement on the prerogative of parents to allow their children a religious education, protested violently. In reaction, the government enacted laws to deprive the church of its right to dissent. Clerics and others sympathetic to their cause who continued to protest, either from the pulpit or at large, were imprisoned or forced into exile. This left only the Catholic legislators in the *Reichstag*, the Center party, in a position to carry on the battle. Only they, speaking on the floor of the *Reichstag*, possessed the legal immunity necessary to protest; and protest they certainly did, with a vigor and a vehemence unparalleled in German history. The result was that in election after election during the 1870's their ranks swelled, and their verbal resistance to state supremacy in matters affecting religious liberty and the individual conscience grew ever more formidable.

Fontane must have taken a more than ordinary interest in the paper's comprehensive coverage of this legislative tug-of-war, for during precisely the same years he carried on a correspondence with the Roman Catholic cardinal-archbishop of Besançon, a correspondence that often touched on the controversies of the *Kulturkampf.* Naturally, Fontane's intimate exposure to this battle of wits and cudgels proved fruitfully suggestive for him. More than anything else, it triggered his ultimate debut as a novelist. Not that the religious question gave him the itch to write; for Fontane saw beyond the immediate church-state issue and observed in the struggle the more fundamental contest with which, in different shadings, he had long been familiar—the contest between the individual and the external forces of society. But now this contest appeared to him in a far more compelling light than ever before, for this time the two sides were embroiled in a "battle for civilization"; the struggle was adversely affecting the lives of millions of people in Germany, and it shocked and horrified many others outside of Germany.

VOR DEM STURM

By the end of the 1870's, then, the groundwork was fully prepared for Fontane's belated vocation as a writer of social novels having as their great concern the interrelation of the individual with the combined forces of society. Rarely had an author taken so long to embark on a career as a novelist. He was almost sixty when, in 1878, his fledgling novel, *Vor dem Sturm* (Before the Storm), appeared.

For a long time Fontane criticism has looked askance at this novel and sought to bury it under an ever-growing mountain of disparaging comment. The novel's diffuse style, in particular, has been criticized ad nauseam—quite unjustly, however, for Fontane is never a dull or second-rate writer, not even in his most loosely woven works.

The work offers a vast panoramic portrait of the finest period in Prussian history, the winter of 1812–1813. Only a few years earlier the nation had collapsed in the face of Napoleon's seemingly invincible army. On 27 October 1806 the French emperor had made his state entry into Berlin. When the victory monument on the top of the Brandenburg Gate was dismantled and sent to Paris, it appeared that Prussia had sunk forever into the slough of abysmal defeat. Indeed, Napoleon had so completely overrun and so thoroughly crushed the once grand nation of Frederick the Great that when the peace treaty was finally signed at Tilsit on 9 July 1807, only a sudden stroke of benevolent generosity prevented him from persisting in his plan to wipe Prussia off the map of Europe entirely. In the following years Prussia had no choice but to become the submissive vassal of the French dictator and to continue to struggle under a yoke of unprecedented servitude. A great reversal, however, occurred on 14 December 1812, when the defeated remnants of Napoleon's army, demoralized by the failure of the French campaign in Russia, recrossed the Prussian frontier in headlong flight back to France. That signaled a new dawn for Prussia. A rebirth of the nation's inner strength began, and hope overcame despair in its citizenry. *Vor dem Sturm* describes at great length the early weeks of this new awakening and gives us an intimate as well as substantial picture of Prussia's landscape, its life, tensions, and anxieties in this new period of growing national confidence.

In *Vor dem Sturm* we have, then, a novel that is closely synchronized with the political and sociological happenings of a very important moment in Prussian history. What makes this "history" particularly readable is the juxtaposition it establishes between the momentous event on the one hand and the commonplace on the other. The ordinary affairs of personal life, in particular the details of three interrelated love affairs—between Lewin and Kathinka, Tubal and Renate, Lewin and Marie—tend to obscure the portrait of Prussia's great moment; they convey the impression that the novelist is trying to relegate to the background the preparations for the revolt against Napoleon's sovereignty—about which, after all, the novel is ostensibly con-

cerned. Conversely, the stirring issue of the national awakening appears so overriding at other times that the manifold descriptions of individual citizens, especially when we are allowed to look into their love lives, never seem to be as exciting or full of passion as we should like them to be; it is as if the novelist were trying hard to make sure we would not tarry too long to listen to the characters' heartbeats for fear that we might lose sight of the national issue. The general political narrative and the tales of individual lives thus seem to mix in the novel as little as water and oil. The two strands remain as distinct and counterpointed as the monarchists and republicans in the Prussian nation, as the Germans and Poles living side by side, or as the Wends and Teutons of old, about all of whom we hear so much. And yet, curiously enough, both strands are inseparably woven together in the web of the fictional enterprise. We have before us therefore once more Fontane's well-known contest, but now in the new dress of the novel.

SCHACH VON WUTHENOW

If *Vor dem Sturm* was a work displaying the broad sweep so characteristic of the weighty German historical novels of Fontane's time, his next efforts in prose fiction are notable for a much tighter construction. Taking as his literary models the tersely composed novellas of the leading poetic realists of his day, Gottfried Keller, Conrad Ferdinand Meyer, and Theodor Storm, Fontane published, in initial serial form, such shorter pieces of prose fiction as *Grete Minde* (1879), *L'Adultera* (*The Woman Taken in Adultery*, 1880), *Ellernklipp* (1881), *Schach von Wuthenow* (*A Man of Honor*, 1882), *Graf Petöfy* (Count Petöfy, 1884), *Unterm Birnbaum* (Under the Pear Tree, 1885), and *Cécile* (1886). In their relative conciseness these works show evidence of Fontane's striving for a new artistic discipline. But the novella form was really not the appropriate vehicle for Fontane's expansive gifts. In accepting the conventions of the short novel—many of these works have alternatively been designated "novellas" and "short novels"—he was trying to compete with the popular novella-writers of poetic realism and, in the last analysis, attempting to be someone other than he was. In those works of his that we have come to admire most, Fontane was to color his canvases with much more environmental description than the shorter forms of fiction could accommodate. Yet he did achieve a certain measure of success with these novellas. Perhaps the clearest evidence of that success is to be found in *Schach von Wuthenow,* a work whose power results largely from its concise, economical handling of the thematic concerns already explored in *Vor dem Sturm.*

The scene of the story is Prussia, 1806, when the nation was being overwhelmed by Napoleon. A dashing officer, Schach von Wuthenow, is caught in a romantic triangle between a widow and her daughter. Circumstances of custom and age dictate that he concentrate his affections on the younger woman, but his independent mind tells him that her facial disfigurement, a result of smallpox, would undermine his peace of mind if he were to marry her; and so he postpones a choice by moving between her and her still attractive mother. The tightrope on which he performs his capers collapses abruptly, however, when in a moment of passion he compromises the daughter in such a way that the mother must demand that he legitimize his suit. He hesitates, fearing that marriage to the disfigured young woman will make him an object of ridicule to his regimental comrades and therefore alienate him from the Prussian military caste; not acquiescing to the marriage, on the other hand, would bring to light the scandal, which would make his resignation as an officer mandatory. The decision is forced by royal intervention compelling him to act in accordance with the prevailing code of honor in the officers' corps, which means marriage to the daughter. Bowing to the dictates of Prussian

convention, he marries the young woman he did not want as his bride and then shoots himself the night after the wedding.

At the end, the clash between personal disposition and the historic codes of the Prussian military establishment resounds once more—this time like a triumphant chorus—in the figure of the maltreated heroine, who in Rome, in voluntary reclusion from her native land, finds comfort in a solitary individualism perfumed by the incense of her newly found Catholic religion. If, with the death of the hero, the individual has succumbed to traditional Prussian institutions, with the heroine's new dawn of faith in the citadel of Roman Catholicism, and with Prussia's exhaustion at the hands of Napoleon (the unseen presence of the French dictator is in the background all the time), the situation is reversed, and the victory of the individual over the Prussian establishment dominates. Napoleon in his battle against the armies of Prussia proclaimed *victoire* (victory); the story's lonely heroine, illuminated by a religious rebirth as Prussia writhes in defeat, bears the name "Victoire." And Victoire has the final word.

Schach von Wuthenow is an intense and exciting novella; its action appears to move as fast as Napoleon's army rolling across the territory of Prussia. Not once does the reader's interest flag. The most exemplary writer of novellas in the German language, the stalwart Prussian aristocrat Heinrich von Kleist, would probably never have been an avid reader of Fontane; but he surely would have nodded in hearty assent to this dramatic tale of seduction, suicide, and personal triumph during one of the most critical moments in Prussian history.

IRRUNGEN, WIRRUNGEN

As fascinating as is the appeal of *Schach von Wuthenow,* the finest fruit of Fontane's sustained effort to produce a concentrated narrative turned out to be *Irrungen, Wirrungen (A Suitable Match)*, which appeared in serialized form in the columns of the *Vossische Zeitung* during the summer of 1887. This uncommonly forceful novel, possessing, in comparison with *Vor dem Sturm*, an increased precision of description and portraiture, and yet having a greater wealth of environmental detail than the pithy form of the novella could allow, treats an age-old theme: the hopeless love of a son of the aristocracy for a daughter of the lower classes. The hero, Botho von Rienäcker, vacillates between two irreconcilable worlds, the one filled with the enchantment of a secret, deeply felt love for a woman below him in social standing, the other majestically presided over by his mother and demanding his unwavering conformity to the conventions of the aristocratic society into which he is born. The two worlds alternate with a frequency almost as regular as the rapidly changing scenes of the short individual chapters, and they are separated again by the neat division of the novel into two halves of almost equal length, the first taken up primarily by Botho's illicit liaison, the second dominated by the consequences of his sober decision to settle into marriage and a comfortable life in conformity with his mother's desire and the prescriptions of family tradition.

Early in the novel, Botho is brought by chance into contact with the story's heroine, a poor embroideress by the name of Lene Nimptsch. Recognizing as he does the irreconcilable differences between their social stations, Botho never takes the trouble to introduce Lene to his austere mother. But when the hero falls deeply in love with her, he is placed in the position of having to choose between the two women and their spheres, and our perception of how closely the two worlds meet in the person of Botho is sharpened. He visits Lene again and again. With her, her foster-mother, and their unpretentious neighbors, he sloughs off the artificialities of his aristocratic

upbringing and shares the homely pleasures of the artisan class, delighting immeasurably in their good-hearted humor and finding himself fascinated by the maturity of their natural wisdom. He becomes so entranced by Lene that he plans a secret weekend rendezvous with her in a wooded retreat far removed, he thinks, from the social ambience in which he normally moves. He consummates his love for her, but then, to both his and her sorrow, he bids her farewell forever in order to return to the fold of social stability from which he emerged. There he enters into a loveless but financially rewarding marriage arranged by his mother. Although he forgoes his right to self-expression and individual happiness, he takes comfort in upholding the values and traditions of the fashionable milieu he belongs to.

Still, Fontane's story does not end on this note of aristocratic triumph. The author does not allow the reader to take leave of the novel in the belief that the established social order has prevailed over the wishes of the individual. Another totally different marriage takes place in the last chapter of the novel, and this marriage is juxtaposed to the socially convenient alliance of Botho and the bride of his mother's choosing. The novel's final wedding unites Lene with her subsequent suitor, Gideon Franke, in a dingy church located in a tenement district of downtown Berlin. It is a marriage spiting social convention, arranged by no one except the partners contracting it, and without regard to any family considerations. Lene, following her involuntary separation from Botho and the death of her foster-mother, has now become a lone individual, answering only to herself. Her groom likewise is without family or other ties; he remains a man marked by rugged nonconformity to any established social order. Answering exclusively to the dictates of his own uncompromising conscience, he exists almost in diametric contrast to the submissive Botho. His given name, Gideon, is reminiscent of the stubborn individual in the

Old Testament who single-handedly chases the oppressing Midianites out of Israel; and his utter opposition to the tyranny of conformity and tradition shows up again and again in Fontane's portrayal of his character.

Gideon is a native of the "free city" of Bremen. Very early in life, we learn, he freed himself of the constraints of society by emigrating to America, where he drifted from job to job, finally becoming an itinerant doctor, practicing the art of healing in one place after another, outside the legally recognized realm of medicine. In America he turned to divination as well, becoming a self-appointed interpreter of holy writ and a soap-box preacher of a morality and theology that had no counterparts in the tenets of any established religion. Indeed, after taking up the cause of one dissenting sect after another, he ultimately dissented even from the dissenters in order to found his own church. His odd dress, curious speech habits, and thoroughly asocial behavior further set him apart.

Of her own free will Lene marries this extremely unconventional if not eccentric individual. Their union signifies a triumph of individualism over the restrictive customs of the established order as much as the wedding of the nobleman Botho and his bride of high social standing represents a victory of conventionally sanctioned standards of behavior over the demands of one's own heart. The novel concludes with these two marriages poised in disturbing counterpoint, suggesting not only that the two worlds they represent can never converge in any abiding relation, but that when they do on occasion meet—as in the quiet intimacies of Lene and Botho—the consequences will be disheartening for both sides.

UNWIEDERBRINGLICH

With *Irrungen, Wirrungen*, written when its author was close to seventy, Fontane had set the standard for the social novels that were to follow in the final decade of his life. One of those possessing particular appeal is *Unwiederbringlich* (*Beyond Recall*), which Fontane started to write while the *Vossische Zeitung* was still in the midst of printing the various serialized installments of *Irrungen, Wirrungen*. He completed a draft of the new novel before the year 1887 came to a close but was not completely satisfied with it and revised it considerably. The final product was submitted to the prestigious literary monthly *Deutsche Rundschau* in December 1890 and published in serial form beginning with the January 1891 issue.

The novel is longer than *Irrungen, Wirrungen*, giving the author a broader canvas to work on. If the plot of the earlier novel had been somewhat slender, that of this new novel was rich and complex. The novelist created more room in which to play off tensions; the social pattern in which the individual characters are embedded is denser. In *Irrungen, Wirrungen* the reader senses the outcome of the central love affair almost from the very first. The lean plot leaves little place for doubt as to the direction it will take; everything falls neatly into place. Not so with *Unwiederbringlich*. Here the author extricates himself from that insulated social perspective characteristic of *Irrungen, Wirrungen*. The Prussian social scene is now replaced by a diverse European setting, providing the novel with a complex international political context.

The novel begins in the Dano-German duchy of Schleswig, then moves on to Denmark proper, where life in cosmopolitan Copenhagen and the Danish countryside is described with considerable effect; the same may be said when later the scene shifts to London, where we are given an entertaining glimpse of English metropolitan life in the Victorian era. In the concluding pages we return to Dano-German Schleswig. Further complicating the web of historical, political, and geographical forces are abundant references to the maze of court intrigues attending Denmark's reigning sovereign at the time, the amorous, much-married, much-divorced, and gluttonous Frederick VII. This notorious ruler, one of the most colorful monarchs in modern European history, was an object of ongoing fascination to his contemporaries. Never before in the long history of Denmark had there been a reigning sovereign whose pronouncements provoked such heated discussions in the official governmental circles of so many European nations.

The story unfolds against this wide-ranging background of European sociopolitical entanglements. These entanglements are as crucial to an understanding of the novel as is the date the author chooses for the opening of his narrative: the end of September 1859. In that month the duchy of Schleswig came nearer to tying itself legally and administratively to Denmark than at any other time in its history. The common constitution of Denmark and the twin duchies of Schleswig and Holstein had just been amended in order to give German-speaking Holstein an independent political existence. As a result, Holstein's historic ties to Schleswig were loosened, and Schleswig was drawn into a closer political union with Denmark. During the final week of September 1859 King Frederick VII briefly but ostentatiously moved his court from Copenhagen to Glücksburg in Schleswig in order to point up this new, closer union.

For the hero of the novel, Count Holk, these politico-historical events of September 1859 mark the beginning of a new era in his life. He is a member of Schleswig's landed aristocracy and therefore automatically a leader within the duchy's ruling caste; with the closer administrative union of Schleswig and Denmark, official duties take him more frequently to the capital city of Copenhagen. He spends prolonged periods of time away from home and is increasingly drawn into a myriad of bizarre allurements characteristic of life in the capital, much to the detriment of his marriage. His wife, Christine, cannot easily accompany him to Copenhagen. In his absence she has to watch over the day-to-day manage-

ment of the family estate, and more important, she needs to be near her German-speaking teenage children, for whom a transfer to Danish schools in Copenhagen is hardly feasible.

More and more, the marital partners become prisoners of the new circumstances intruding into their family life. The lax moral atmosphere of the court in Copenhagen quickly proves to be irresistible to the lonely Holk. The decadent environment into which he is plunged makes it easy for him to succumb to the temptations of other women, and these extramarital affairs estrange him from his wife to such an extent that divorce becomes inevitable.

But the vice-laden conventions of Copenhagen's court, encouraged and promoted by the king's erstwhile mistress and morganatic wife, the voluptuous and glittering actress Countess Danner, also drive the women of Holk's new love life into relationships with other men. As a result, the disenchanted and depressed Holk yearns to return to his former wife; but in vain, for the pressure of intervening circumstances in Christine's life has also alienated her from him. Scandalized by her husband's adulteries, she has retreated into a religious solipsism, finding doleful comfort in a preoccupation with the prospect of eternal life beyond the grave. Even while Holk was losing himself to exotic pleasures in the "Paris of the north," she had sealed him off from herself and her dream world. Her shipwrecked marriage has led to such a secure haven in the monastic confinement of her faith that she has no desire to resume the responsibilities of married life when her husband returns from his amorous intrigues and hopes to renew their relation. But the pressure of social conventions in provincial Schleswig—sustained by the local company of family, friends, and clergy—demands a reconciliation of the estranged couple. She yields, and the two remarry in the family's parish with all the traditional blessings of church and community. The marriage ceremony, however, proves to be hollow. The second wedding is based not on Christine's personal will, but on social necessity and custom; her religious integrity cannot remain compromised for long by such an arduous deception: she commits suicide.

In the background of this novel, serving as a majestic frame to all its scenes, stands the sovereign of both Denmark and Schleswig, Frederick VII. His hovering presence within the fictional structure has never been fully acknowledged by Fontane critics; nevertheless, he is never far from the scene of the action. His role in the novel is not unlike that of Napoleon in *Schach von Wuthenow*. Whether holding court at his castle in Glücksburg (one scant mile from the Holk family estate) or residing at his Copenhagen palace as Holk attends court there, or sleeping in Fredericksborg's castle on precisely the same night in which Holk, in another wing, succumbs to the passionate blandishments of one of the court's ladies-in-waiting, the monarch is always in evidence behind the scenes. And for good reason: his crown symbolizes the impossibility of harmonizing internal and external forces.

Fontane is here bringing to bear on his story a set of historical circumstances that function by means of analogy to deepen the significance of the main plot. Throughout his reign the real Frederick VII was caught up in an impossible political situation. Danish public opinion never ceased to urge him to incorporate the duchy of Schleswig into Denmark proper through outright annexation. The concert of European nations, on the other hand, steadfastly made clear to him that such a unilateral political action on Denmark's part would not be tolerated. What choices lay open to him? To which influence should he yield, the internal insistence of his subjects or the external pressure of foreign powers? Each alternative spelled disaster. To go against the obvious will of the majority of Danes would put his throne in jeopardy. Conversely, to ignore the grave warnings of the great powers of Europe would risk a European war, with certain defeat for Denmark. Frederick VII sedulously avoided giving his kingly assent to either alternative. He chose, instead, a route of cowardly indifference. Fleeing from the acceptance of political reality and from his royal prerogative to initiate diplomatic negotiations on the issue, he elected to take as little interest as possible in vital matters of state, leaving them to unreliable subordinates who shuttled in and out of office. As compensation for his inertia in mediating a settlement between the will of his nation and the concerted will of the European nations at large, he sought comfort in his infatuation for the adulterous Countess Danner. This adjustment naturally turned the court of Denmark into one in which affairs of the bedchamber took precedence over affairs of state and in which the distractions of scandal reigned supreme.

Such, then, is the political context surrounding the tragic collapse of the marriage of Holk and Christine. The recurring presence of Frederick VII behind the scenes is as integral a part of the novel's compositional principle as are the Holks and the host of subsidiary characters. The royal frame and the inner story complement one another in stressing that the two opposing worlds of the individual and the forces that surround him cannot converge, except in disaster.

EFFI BRIEST

With *Unwiederbringlich* still fresh in his mind, Fontane began to mull over another novel. In fact, he had already completed its first draft when *Unwiederbringlich* came off the press in 1891. Work on the revisions continued for years, and not until October 1895 did the new novel, entitled *Effi Briest*, appear in final form.

In this novel, which was to become his most renowned, Fontane varied a compositional principle he had already used with considerable effect in *Unwiederbringlich:* the in-

THEODOR FONTANE

A Suitable Match (*Irrungen, Wirrungen*). Translated by S. Morris. London and Glasgow, 1968.

Theodor Fontane. Short Novels and Other Writings. Edited by P. Demetz. New York, 1982. Contains *The Eighteenth of March* (*Der achtzehnte März*, a chapter in *Von Zwanzig bis Dreissig*), translated by K. Winston; *Jenny Treibel*, translated by U. Zimmermann; *A Man of Honor*, translated by E. M. Valk.

The Woman Taken in Adultery and The Poggenpuhl Family (*L'Adultera* and *Die Poggenpuhls*). Translated by G. Annan. Chicago, 1979.

BIOGRAPHICAL AND CRITICAL STUDIES

Attwood, Kenneth. *Fontane und das Preussentum.* Berlin, 1970.

Aust, Hugo, ed. *Fontane aus heutiger Sicht.* Munich, 1980.

————. *Theodor Fontane: "Verklärung." Eine Untersuchung zum Ideengehalt seiner Werke.* Bonn, 1974.

Bance, Alan. *Theodor Fontane: The Major Novels.* Cambridge, 1982.

Barlow, Derrick. "Fontane and the Aristocracy." *German Life and Letters* 8:182–191 (1955).

————. "Fontane's English Journeys." *German Life and Letters* 6:169–173 (1953).

Betz, Frederick. "Fontane Scholarship, Literary Sociology, and 'Trivialliteraturforschung.'" *Internationales Archiv für Sozialgeschichte der deutschen Literatur* 8:200–220 (1983).

Blessin, Stefan. "*Unwiederbringlich*—Ein historisch-politischer Roman? Bemerkungen zu Fontanes Symbolkunst." *Deutsche Vierteljahrsschrift für Literaturwissenschaft und Geistesgeschichte* 48:672–703 (1974).

Böckmann, Paul. "Der Zeitroman Fontanes." *Der Deutschunterricht* 11:59–81 (1959).

Brinkmann, Richard. *Theodor Fontane: Über die Verbindlichkeit des Unverbindlichen.* 2nd ed. Tübingen, 1977.

Demetz, Peter. *Formen des Realismus: Theodor Fontane. Kritische Untersuchungen.* 2nd ed. Frankfurt, 1973. A seminal study.

Field, George W. "Theodor Fontane and the Social Novel." In his *A Literary History of Germany: The Nineteenth Century, 1830–1890.* London, New York, and Toronto, 1975.

Fuerst, Norbert. "The Berlin Bourgeois" and "Fontane's Entanglements." In his *The Victorian Age in German Literature.* University Park, Pa., 1966.

Furst, Lilian R. "The Autobiography of an Extrovert: Fontane's *Von Zwanzig bis Dreissig.*" *German Life and Letters* 12:287–294 (1959).

Garland, Henry Burnand. *The Berlin Novels of Theodor Fontane.* Oxford, 1980.

Gilbert, Anna Marie. "A New Look at *Effie Briest:* Genesis and Interpretation." *Deutsche Vierteljahrsschrift für Literaturwissenschaft und Geistesgeschichte* 53:96–114 (1979).

Glaser, Horst Albert. "Theodor Fontane: *Effi Briest* (1894). Im Hinblick auf Emma Bovary und andere." In *Romane und Erzählungen des bürgerlichen Realismus: Neue Interpretationen,* edited by H. Denkler. Stuttgart, 1980. Pp. 362–377.

Guthke, Karl S. "Fontane's 'Finessen': 'Kunst' oder 'Künstelei'?" *Jahrbuch der deutschen Schillergesellschaft* 26:235–261 (1982).

Hatfield, Henry C. "The Renovation of the German Novel: Theodor Fontane." In his *Crisis and Continuity in Modern German Fiction: Ten Essays.* Ithaca, N.Y., 1969.

Hayens, Kenneth. *Theodor Fontane: A Critical Study.* London, 1920.

Hewett-Thayer, Harvey W. "Theodor Fontane the Realist." In his *The Modern German Novel.* Boston, 1924.

Jolles, Charlotte. *Theodor Fontane.* 3rd ed. Stuttgart, 1983. An indispensable reference work.

Jørgensen, Sven-Aage. "Dekadenz oder Fortschritt? Zum Dänemarkbild in Fontanes Roman *Unwiederbringlich.*" *Text und Kontext* 2:28–49 (1974).

Lohmeier, Dieter. "Vor dem Niedergang: Dänemark in Fontanes Roman *Unwiederbringlich.*" *Skandinavistik* 2:27–53 (1972).

Mann, Thomas. "Der alte Fontane." In his *Adel des Geistes.* Stockholm, 1945. Translated by H. T. Lowe-Porter as "The Old Fontane." In *Thomas Mann: Essays of Three Decades.* New York, 1947.

Martini, Fritz. "Theodor Fontane." In his *Deutsche Literatur im bürgerlichen Realismus, 1848–1898.* 4th ed. Stuttgart, 1981.

McHaffie, M. A. "Fontane's *Irrungen, Wirrungen* and the Novel of Realism." In *Periods in German Literature,* edited by J. M. Ritchie. Vol. 2. London, 1969. Pp. 167–189.

Mommsen, Katharina. *Gesellschaftskritik bei Fontane und Thomas Mann.* Heidelberg, 1973.

Müller-Seidel, Walter. *Theodor Fontane: Soziale Ro-*

mankunst in Deutschland. 2nd ed. Stuttgart, 1980. The most comprehensive study of Fontane's novels.

Nürnberger, Helmuth. Der frühe Fontane. Munich, 1971.

Pascal, Roy. "Theodor Fontane." In his The German Novel. Manchester, 1956.

Paulsen, Wolfgang. "Zum Stand der heutigen Fontane-Forschung." Jahrbuch der deutschen Schillergesellschaft 25:474–508 (1981).

Preisendanz, Wolfgang, ed. Theodor Fontane. Darmstadt, 1973. A collection of brilliant essays.

Remak, Henry H. H. Der Weg zur Weltliteratur: Fontanes Bret-Harte-Entwurf. Potsdam, 1980.

Remak, Joachim. The Gentle Critic: Theodor Fontane and German Politics, 1848–1898. Syracuse, N.Y., 1964.

Reuter, Hans-Heinrich. Fontane. 2 vols. Munich, 1968. The best biography of Fontane.

Ritchie, J. M. "Fontane." In The Age of Realism, edited by F. W. J. Hemmings. Harmondsworth and Baltimore, 1974.

Robinson, A. R. Theodor Fontane: An Introduction to the Man and His Work. Cardiff, 1976.

Rodger, Gillian. "Fontane's Conception of the Folk-Ballad." Modern Language Review 53:44–58 (1958).

Rowley, Brian A. "Theodor Fontane: A German Novelist in the European Tradition?" German Life and Letters 15:71–88 (1961).

Rychner, Max. "Fontane's Unwiederbringlich." In his Aufsätze zur Literatur. Zurich, 1966.

Sagarra, Eda. "Two Novelists of the Empire: Fontane and Raabe." In her Tradition and Revolution: German Literature and Society, 1830–1890. London, 1971.

Sakrawa, Gertrud. "Scharmanter Egoismus: Theodor Fontanes Unwiederbringlich." Monatshefte 61:15–29 (1969).

Schillemeit, Jost. Theodor Fontane: Geist und Kunst seines Alterswerks. Zurich, 1961.

Schmidt-Brümmer, Horst. Formen des perspektivischen Erzählens: Fontane's "Irrungen, Wirrungen." Munich, 1971.

Stern, J. P. "Realism and Tolerance: Theodor Fontane." In his Re-interpretations: Seven Studies in Nineteenth-Century German Literature. New York, 1964.

————. "Theodor Fontane: The Realism of Assessment." In his Idylls and Realities: Studies in Nineteenth-Century German Literature. London, 1971.

Subiotto, Frances M. "The Function of Letters in Fontane's Unwiederbringlich." Modern Language Review 65:306–318 (1970).

Teitge, H.-E., and J. Schobess, eds. Fontanes Realismus: Wissenschaftliche Konferenz zum 150. Geburtstag Theodor Fontanes in Potsdam. Berlin, 1972.

Wandrey, Conrad. Theodor Fontane. Munich, 1919.

Williams, W. D. "Theodor Fontane: Archibald Douglas." In Wege zum Gedicht, edited by R. Hirschenauer and A. Weber. Vol. 2. Munich, 1964.

CLIFFORD ALBRECHT BERND